Contemporary Authors ®

Explore your options!

Gale databases are offered in a variety of formats

GALE

The information in this Gale publication is also available in some or all of the formats described here. Your Gale Representative will be happy to fill you in. Call toll-free 1-800-877-GALE.

GaleNet SM
your information community

GaleNet

A number of Gale databases are now available on GaleNet, our new online information resource accessible through the Internet. GaleNet features an easy-to-use end-user interface, the powerful search capabilities of BRS/SEARCH retrieval software and ease of access through the World Wide Web.

Diskette/Magnetic Tape

Many Gale databases are available on diskette or magnetic tape, allowing systemwide access to your most-used information sources through existing computer systems. Data can be delivered on a variety of mediums (DOS-formatted diskettes, 9-track tape, 8mm data tape) and in industry-standard formats (comma-delimited, tagged, fixed-field).

CD-ROM

A variety of Gale titles are available on CD-ROM, offering maximum flexibility and powerful search software.

Online

For your convenience, many Gale databases are available through popular online services, including DIALOG, NEXIS, DataStar, ORBIT, OCLC, Thomson Financial Network's I/Plus Direct, HRIN, Prodigy, Sandpoint's HOOVER, the Library Corporation's NLightN and Telebase Systems.

ISSN 0010-7468

Contemporary
Authors®

**A Bio-Bibliographical Guide to
Current Writers in Fiction, General Nonfiction,
Poetry, Journalism, Drama, Motion Pictures,
Television, and Other Fields**

TERRIE M. ROONEY,
Editor

volume 154

GALE

DETROIT · NEW YORK · TORONTO · LONDON

STAFF

Terrie M. Rooney, *Editor, Original Volumes*

Kathleen J. Edgar, *Contributing Senior Editor*

David M. Galens, Jennifer Gariepy, Lynn M. Spampinato,
and Brandon Trenz, *Contributing Editors*

Christine M. Bichler and Stacy A. McConnell, *Associate Editors*

Carol A. Brennan, Richard Cohen, Jay Daniel, Laurie DiMauro, Nancy Edgar, Mary Gillis, Nancy Godinez,
Marian Gonsoir, Terry Kosdrosky, Jeanne M. Lesinski, Michelle M. Motowski, Nancy Rampson, Susan Reicha,
Sue Salter, Paula Pyzik Scott, Pamela Shelton, Ken Shepherd, Les Stone, Deborah Straub, Michaela A. Swart,
Arlene True, and Elizabeth Wenning, *Sketchwriters*

Pamela Willwerth Aue, *Managing Editor*

Victoria Cariappa, *Research Manager*

Andrew Guy Malonis, Barbara McNeil, Gary J. Oudersluys,
and Maureen Richards, *Research Specialists*

Laura C. Bissey, Julia C. Daniel, Michele LaMeau, Tamara C. Nott, Norma Sawaya,
Sean R. Smith, and Cheryl L. Warnock, *Research Associates*

Alfred A. Gardner I, *Research Assistant*

⊗™ This book is printed on acid-free paper that meets the minimum requirements
of American National Standard for Information Sciences-
Permanence Paper for Printed Library Materials, ANSI Z39.48-1984.

Library of Congress Catalog Card Number 62-52046
ISBN 0-7876-0131-4
ISSN 0010-7468

Printed in the United States of America

10 9 8 7 6 5 4 3 2 1

Contents

Indexing note: All *Contemporary Authors* entries are indexed in the *Contemporary Authors* cumulative index, which is published separately and distributed with even-numbered *Contemporary Authors* original volumes and odd-numbered *Contemporary Authors New Revision Series* volumes.

As always, the most recent *Contemporary Authors* cumulative index continues to be the user's guide to the location of an individual author's listing.

Contemporary Authors
was named an
*"Outstanding
Reference Source" by
the American Library
Association Reference
and Adult Services
Division after its 1962
inception.
In 1985 it was listed by
the same organization
as one of the
twenty-five most
distinguished reference
titles published in the
past twenty-five years.*

Preface

Contemporary Authors (*CA*) provides information on approximately 100,000 writers in a wide range of media, including:

- Current writers of fiction, nonfiction, poetry, and drama whose works have been issued by commercial publishers, risk publishers, or university presses (authors whose books have been published only by known vanity or author-subsidized firms are ordinarily not included)

- Prominent print and broadcast journalists, editors, photojournalists, syndicated cartoonists, graphic novelists, screenwriters, television scriptwriters, and other media people

- Authors who write in languages other than English, provided their works have been published in the United States or translated into English

- Literary greats of the early twentieth century whose works are popular in today's high school and college curriculums and continue to elicit critical attention

A *CA* listing entails no charge or obligation. Authors are included on the basis of the above criteria and their interest to *CA* users. Sources of potential listees include trade periodicals, publishers' catalogs, librarians, and other users.

How to Get the Most out of *CA:* Use the Index

The key to locating an author's most recent entry is the *CA* cumulative index, which is published separately and distributed with even-numbered original volumes and odd-numbered revision volumes. It provides access to *all* entries in *CA* and *Contemporary Authors New Revision Series* (*CANR*). Always consult the latest index to find an author's most recent entry.

For the convenience of users, the *CA* cumulative index also includes references to all entries in these Gale literary series: *Authors and Artists for Young Adults, Authors in the News, Bestsellers, Black Literature Criticism, Black Writers, Children's Literature Review, Concise Dictionary of American Literary Biography, Concise Dictionary of British Literary Biography, Contemporary Authors Autobiography Series, Contemporary Authors Bibliographical Series, Contemporary Literary Criticism, Dictionary of Literary Biography, Dictionary of Literary Biography Documentary Series, Dictionary of Literary Biography Yearbook, DISCovering Authors, DISCovering Authors: British, DISCovering Authors: Canadian, DISCovering Authors: Modules* (including modules for Dramatists, Most-Studied Authors, Multicultural Authors, Novelists, Poets, and Popular/Genre Authors), *Drama Criticism, Hispanic Literature Criticism, Hispanic Writers, Junior DISCovering Authors, Major Authors and Illustrators for Children and Young Adults, Major 20th-Century Writers, Native North American Literature, Poetry Criticism, Short Story Criticism, Something about the Author, Something about the Author Autobiography Series, Twentieth-Century Literary Criticism, World Literature Criticism,* and *Yesterday's Authors of Books for Children.*

A Sample Index Entry:

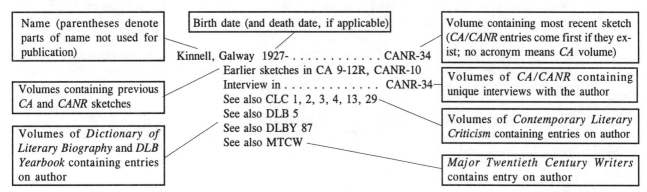

vii

How Are Entries Compiled?

The editors make every effort to secure new information directly from the authors; listees' responses to our questionnaires and query letters provide most of the information featured in *CA*. For deceased writers, or those who fail to reply to requests for data, we consult other reliable biographical sources, such as those indexed in Gale's *Biography and Genealogy Master Index,* and bibliographical sources, including *National Union Catalog, LC MARC,* and *British National Bibliography*. Further details come from published interviews, feature stories, and book reviews, as well as information supplied by the authors' publishers and agents.

An asterisk (∗) at the end of a sketch indicates that the listing has been compiled from secondary sources believed to be reliable but has not been personally verified for this edition by the author sketched.

What Kinds of Information Does an Entry Provide?

Sketches in *CA* contain the following biographical and bibliographical information:

- **Entry heading:** the most complete form of author's name, plus any pseudonyms or name variations used for writing

- **Personal information:** author's date and place of birth, family data, ethnicity, educational background, political and religious affiliations, and hobbies and leisure interests

- **Addresses:** author's home, office, or agent's addresses, plus e-mail and fax numbers, as available

- **Career summary:** name of employer, position, and dates held for each career post; resume of other vocational achievements; military service

- **Membership information:** professional, civic, and other association memberships and any official posts held

- **Awards and honors:** military and civic citations, major prizes and nominations, fellowships, grants, and honorary degrees

- **Writings:** a comprehensive, chronological list of titles, publishers, dates of original publication and revised editions, and production information for plays, television scripts, and screenplays

- **Adaptations:** a list of films, plays, and other media which have been adapted from the author's work

- **Work in progress:** current or planned projects, with dates of completion and/or publication, and expected publisher, when known

- **Sidelights:** a biographical portrait of the author's development; information about the critical reception of the author's works; revealing comments, often by the author, on personal interests, aspirations, motivations, and thoughts on writing

- **Biographical and critical sources:** a list of books and periodicals in which additional information on an author's life and/or writings appears

Obituary Notices in *CA* provide date and place of birth as well as death information about authors whose full-length sketches appeared in the series before their deaths. These entries also summarize the authors' careers and writings and list other sources of biographical and death information.

Related Titles in the *CA* Series

Contemporary Authors Autobiography Series complements *CA* original and revised volumes with specially commissioned autobiographical essays by important current authors, illustrated with personal photographs they provide. Common topics include their motivations for writing, the people and experiences that shaped their careers, the rewards they derive from their work, and their impressions of the current literary scene.

Contemporary Authors Bibliographical Series surveys writings by and about important American authors since World War II. Each volume concentrates on a specific genre and features approximately ten writers; entries list works written by and about the author and contain a bibliographical essay discussing the merits and deficiencies of major critical and scholarly studies in detail.

Available in Electronic Formats

CD-ROM. Full-text bio-bibliographic entries from the entire *CA* series, covering approximately 100,000 writers, are available on CD-ROM through lease and purchase plans. The disc combines entries from the *CA, CANR,* and *Contemporary Authors Permanent Series* (*CAP*) print series to provide the most recent author listing. It can be searched by name, title, subject/genre, nationality/ethnicity, personal data, and as well as advanced searching using boolean logic. The disc is updated every six months. For more information, call 1-800-877-GALE.

Online. The *Contemporary Authors* database is made available online to libraries and their patrons through online public access catalog (OPAC) vendors. Currently, *CA* is offered through Ameritech Library Services' Vista Online (formerly Dynix), and is expected to become available through CARL Systems and The Library Corporation. More OPAC vendor offerings will soon follow.

GaleNet. *CA* is available on a subscription basis through GaleNet, a new online information resource that features an easy-to-use end-user interface, the powerful search capabilities of the BRS/Search retrieval software, and ease of access through the World Wide Web. For more information, call 1-800-877-GALE.

Magnetic Tape. *CA* is available for licensing on magnetic tape in a fielded format. Either the complete database or a custom selection of entries may be ordered. The database is available for internal data processing and nonpublishing purposes only. For more information, call 1-800-877-GALE.

Suggestions Are Welcome

The editors welcome comments and suggestions from users on any aspects of the *CA* series. If readers would like to recommend authors for inclusion in future volumes of the series, they are cordially invited to write: The Editors, *Contemporary Authors,* 835 Penobscot Bldg., 645 Griswold St., Detroit, MI 48226-4094; call toll-free at 1-800-347-GALE; or fax at 1-313-961-6599.

CA **Numbering System and Volume Update Chart**

Occasionally questions arise about the *CA* numbering system and which volumes, if any, can be discarded. Despite numbers like "29-32R," "97-100" and "154," the entire *CA* print series consists of only 136 physical volumes with the publication of *CA* Volume 154. The following charts note changes in the numbering system and cover design, and indicate which volumes are essential for the most complete, up-to-date coverage.

CA **First Revision**
- 1-4R through 41-44R (11 books)
  Cover: Brown with black and gold trim.
  There will be no further First Revision volumes because revised entries are now being handled exclusively through the more efficient *New Revision Series* mentioned below.

CA **Original Volumes**
- 45-48 through 97-100 (14 books)
  Cover: Brown with black and gold trim.
- 101 through 154 (54 books)
  Cover: Blue and black with orange bands.
  The same as previous *CA* original volumes but with a new, simplified numbering system and new cover design.

CA **Permanent Series**
- *CAP*-1 and *CAP*-2 (2 books)
  Cover: Brown with red and gold trim.
  There will be no further *Permanent Series* volumes because revised entries are now being handled exclusively through the more efficient *New Revision Series* mentioned below.

CA **New Revision Series**
- *CANR*-1 through *CANR*-55 (55 books)
  Cover: Blue and black with green bands.
  Includes only sketches requiring significant changes; **sketches are taken from any previously published *CA, CAP,* or *CANR* volume**.

If You Have:	You May Discard:
CA First Revision Volumes 1-4R through 41-44R **and** *CA Permanent Series* Volumes 1 and 2	*CA* Original Volumes 1, 2, 3, 4 Volumes 5-6 through 41-44
CA Original Volumes 45-48 through 97-100 **and** 101 through 154	**NONE:** These volumes will not be superseded by corresponding revised volumes. Individual entries from these and all other volumes appearing in the left column of this chart may be revised and included in the various volumes of the *New Revision Series*.
CA New Revision Series Volumes *CANR*-1 through *CANR*-55	**NONE:** The *New Revision Series* does not replace any single volume of *CA*. Instead, volumes of *CANR* include entries from many previous *CA* series volumes. All *New Revision Series* volumes must be retained for full coverage.

A Sampling of Authors and Media People
Featured in This Volume

Mumia Abu-Jamal
Abu-Jamal is an award-winning journalist convicted of killing a police officer; he faces a death sentence, despite evidence that he is innocent. He relates his controversial story in *Live from Death Row*.

Chris Columbus
Columbus is the director of such popular films as *Home Alone* and *Mrs. Doubtfire*. He is also an accomplished screenwriter, with the films *Gremlins* and *Young Sherlock Holmes* to his credit.

Andre de Toth
A noted director of motion pictures in both America and his native Hungary, de Toth was at the helm on such films as the horror classic *House of Wax*. His memoir, *Fragments: Portraits from the Inside*, details his life and art.

Michael D'Orso
D'Orso is an established journalist and the author of a number of award-winning books. Among his better known works is *Like Judgment Day: The Ruin and Redemption of a Town Called Rosewood*.

Salvador Espriu
Twice nominated for the Nobel Prize in literature, Espriu is considered one of the finest Spanish writers of the twentieth century. His works include the biblical collection *Israel: Esbozos biblicos* and the dramatic monologue *El Dr. Rip*.

Lowell Ganz
Ganz began as a writer on such television series as *Happy Days* and *Laverne and Shirley*. With his partner Babaloo Mandel, he has made a successful career as the screenwriter of films like *Splash, Parenthood,* and *City Slickers*.

Bill Gates
As the founder and chair of software giant Microsoft, Gates has built a computer empire that has made him the richest man in the world. His book, *The Road Ahead,* outlines his vision of the world's technological future.

Temple Grandin
Born with autism, Grandin is an inventor who has made significant advances in animal handling and slaughter. She is also a notable author on the subject of autism and works to foster greater understanding of the affliction.

Laura Kasischke
An award-winning poet, Kasischke broke into fiction with her novel *Suspicious River*. The book elicited praise from literary critics and readers alike for its horrific imagery of small-town life.

Caroline Knapp
As an editor for the *Boston Phoenix,* Knapp wrote a humorous advice column under the pseudonym Alice K. In 1996, she adopted a more a serious tone in her autobiographical work, *Drinking: A Love Story*.

Babaloo Mandel
An Academy Award-nominated screenwriter and producer, Mandel is best known for his collaborations with fellow comedy writer Lowell Ganz. The duo gained notoriety with their work on such films as *Night Shift* and *Parenthood*.

Jane Mendelsohn
Mendelsohn's novel, *I Was Amelia Earhart,* made an impressive debut, selling over 150,000 copies within months of its release. The novel is a story of what could have happened had Earhart survived the ill-fated plane crash.

David J. Remnick
Remnick, a former foreign correspondent for the *Washington Post,* received the Pulitzer Prize for non-fiction in 1993, for *Lenin's Tomb*. In the book Remnick details the fall of the Soviet Union from 1991-93.

Henry Rollins
Rollins, a writer and musician, has drawn attention as the lead singer for the bands Black Flag and the Rollins Band. In his book, *Get In the Van: On the Road with Black Flag,* he chronicles his experiences from 1981-86.

Wislawa Szymborska
Polish-born poet and critic Szymborska received international attention in 1996 after winning the Nobel Prize for Literature. Her poetry brought attention to Poland's unrecognized, diverse poetic modes.

Emma Thompson
Thompson's screenplay adaptation of the Jane Austen novel *Sense and Sensibility* earned her an Academy Award in 1996. The screenplay was published along with journal entries from Thompson's film diaries.

A

ABAS, Syed Jan 1936-

PERSONAL: Born August 18, 1936, in Allahabad, India; naturalized citizen of the United Kingdom; son of Syed Mushtaq Bilgirami (a railway official) and Amna Khatoon; married first wife, Rosemary, July 6, 1957 (divorced June 4, 1993); married second wife, Janet (a teacher), August 25, 1995; children: Melanie Broadhead, Shamin Di Pilla, Madleine, Robin, Zara. *Education:* London University, B.S., 1963, Ph.D., 1967. *Politics:* "I fly no flags." *Religion:* "Neurobics." *Avocational interests:* Islamic geometric art, Neurobics.

ADDRESSES: Home—150 Penrhos Rd., Bangor, Gwynedd LL57 2BX, United Kingdom. *Office*—School of Mathematics, University of Wales, Bangor, Gwynedd LL57 IUT, United Kingdom. *E-mail*—S.J.Abas@bangor.ac.uk.

CAREER: University of Wales, Bangor, Wales, lecturer in maths and information technology, 1966—. Manchester University Computer Graphics Unit, research fellow; Journal of Speculations in Science and Technology, member of editorial board.

WRITINGS:

Computers in Health and Fitness, Charwell-Bratt (London), 1988.
(With J. R. Mondrayon) *Pascal: An Interactive Text* (textbook), Adam Hilyer (Bristol), 1990.
Rapid Turbo Pascal Graphics Tutor (textbook), IOP Publishers (Bristol), 1992.
(With A. S. Salman) *Symmetries of Islamic Geometrical Patterns,* World Scientific, 1995.

WORK IN PROGRESS: Neurobics: An Entirely Fresh Approach for Shattering the Age Barrier, The Grace of Islamic Patterns, The Beauty and Symmetry of Polyhedra; researching Islamic patterns on polyhedral surfaces.

SIDELIGHTS: Syed Jan Abas told *CA:* "I seem to have inherited writing in my genes. I am told that one of my great-grandfathers was the first person to start a daily newspaper. Several of my ancestors have been authors. One was a famous poet known as Akbar Allahabadi. Two of my sisters are published poets. My first book was written to explain to non-scientists how computers work and their relevance in a matter that concerns everyone—health and fitness. The next two books are university texts and came as a result of teaching innovation in computer programming and computer graphics. My latest book on Islamic patterns results from my love of Islamic geometrical art, which allows me to experience science and art in unity. The kind of book I would most like to write is one like *Supernature* by Lyall Watson. It employs science to point to the mystery of existence."

*   *   *

ab HUGH, Dafydd 1960-

PERSONAL: Legally adopted name; born in 1960. *Education:* University of California, Los Angeles and Santa Cruz, M.A. (mathematics).

ADDRESSES: Agent—c/o Pocket Books, Simon & Schuster Bldg., Avenue of the Americas, New York, NY 10020.

CAREER: Writer.

WRITINGS:

FANTASY NOVELS

Heroing, Baen (New York), 1987.
Warriorwards, Baen, 1990.

OTHER

Arthur War Lord (novel), AvoNova (New York), 1994.
Fallen Heroes (novel), Pocket Books (New York), 1994.
Balance of Power (novel), Pocket Books, 1994.

WORK IN PROGRESS: A sequel to *Warriorwards,* continuing the series.

SIDELIGHTS: Dafydd ab Hugh clearly writes in the sword-and-sorcery sub-genre, and his first two books, *Heroing* and *Warriorwards,* have as the heroine Jiana Analena, a swordswoman with strong magical powers. The first book, *Heroing,* takes the apparent form of a quest novel. Jiana seeks to join the party of Prince Alanai of Bay Bay in his quest for a magical artefact with the power to grant one wish, even if that wish means remaking the world. Jiana is turned down because she is a woman, with instructions to go home to her husband or father. But she is determined to join the quest in search of "foreverness," in search of a name. As she says: "I've fought creatures that would make Alanai's hair straighten! And I've won and lost enough treasure to buy a ladyship and a nice manor house on the coast somewhere. But who the hell's ever heard of *me?* When I'm dead, who's going to remember my name? I want to live forever—on tongues, if not in time! I want immortality."

Jiana begins following Prince Alanai's party, hoping to do some grand deed that will compel the Prince to allow her to join him. She eventually redefines her quest's purpose after seeing the destruction left by the "heros." Her altered quest is to stop Prince Alanai from attaining the magical artefact and remaking the world. She does succeed in sneaking it out from under his nose, but then is uncertain what to do with it; she has learned not to trust the desire for power, not to try to remake the world because of her fear of unintended consequences.

Along the way she has attracted an admirer and apprentice: the innocent farm-boy Dida; she learns the consequences of taking responsibility for someone. Already unhappy at his love being spurned, Dida is captured by Prince Alanai's forces. The next time they meet, Dida has willingly joined with the Prince on his quest. At the end of the quest, as soldiers filled with the rage of battle destroy the ancient city where the magical artefact has been hidden, Dida rapes a young girl and is driven to near madness with self-loathing. Jiana finds him and, when Dida expresses his inability to live with what he's done, gives him a knife. Somewhat to her surprise, he kills himself. Full of grief, rage, and guilt, blaming herself for having caused Dida to go wrong, Jiana uses the magical artefact to bring him back to life.

Prince Alanai is, naturally, enraged at this "waste." "WE COULD HAVE BEEN GODS!" he screams at her. To which she replies, "I know I'm a true warrior. I held the world in my palm—literally!—and I put it down again. Can you say the same?" The Prince, defeated, leaves, Jiana makes plans to go off with Dida, and the book is over with this apparently happy ending.

It is not long into *Warriorwards* before we learn that things did not turn out well and we see the long-term results of Jiana's heroism. Four years later, Dida has become an arrogant member of the ruling house's soldiery. Jiana has her name and the fame she desired, yet she feels like a failure, primarily because of how Dida turned out. Inspired by a vision given to her by a seer, she determines to take another apprentice, but to do it right this time. Her choice, or rather her destiny, is a girl with a crippled arm named Radience, a slave in the caravan of a Caliph of Tool. Jiana has herself sold into slavery among the Toolians. The rest of *Warriorwards* is devoted, as one might guess from the title, to Radience's training as a warrior. Jiana acts as a classic drill sergeant, teaching Radience not just technique, but to think and act as a warrior. Radience eventually betrays Jiana, but Jiana is able to escape. A third book was promised at the end of *Warriorwards.*

BIOGRAPHICAL/CRITICAL SOURCES:

BOOKS

Heroing, Baen, 1987.

ABU-JAMAL, Mumia   1954(?)-
     (Wesley Cook)

PERSONAL: Born Wesley Cook, c. 1954; raised in Philadelphia, PA; children: one daughter. *Ethnicity:* African American. *Education:* Attended Goddard College, 1972.

ADDRESSES: Home—Mumia Abu-Jamal #AM-8335, SCI Greene, 1040 East Roy Furman Highway, Waynesburg, PA 15370.

CAREER: Activist, 1968—; former print and radio essayist and journalist in Philadelphia, PA; has worked as a cab driver; currently in prison; writer.

MEMBER: Association of Black Journalists (Philadelphia chapter; past president).

AWARDS, HONORS: Peabody Award for a radio essay.

WRITINGS:

Live from Death Row, Addison-Wesley (Reading, MA), 1995.

Has continued to write from prison about racial inequality and the criminal justice system. Contributor to periodicals, including *Nation* and *Yale Law Journal.* Some writings have appeared under the name Wesley Cook.

ADAPTATIONS: HBO released a documentary, *Mumia Abu-Jamal: A Case for Reasonable Doubt,* based on the case, and Court-TV, in collaboration with HBO, staged a panel discussion, both 1996.

SIDELIGHTS: Mumia Abu-Jamal, an award-winning journalist and radio essayist, was arrested in 1981 for allegedly killing Philadelphia Police Officer Daniel Faulkner. Abu-Jamal has vigorously denied the charge, but on July 3, 1982, he was convicted of murder in the first degree and sentenced to death. Ever since his conviction, Abu-Jamal has been writing essays and commentaries about his observations on race, prison, and punishment from his prison cell.

In 1994, Abu-Jamal's observations were scheduled to air on a National Public Radio (NPR) program. Philadelphia police organizations launched a very visible protest, and members of Congress threatened to cut funding to NPR if they aired the controversial convict's essays. NPR withdrew the programming, but the commentaries and other writings by Abu-Jamal were published in his 1995 book *Live from Death Row.*

The publication of *Live from Death Row* incited more discord, and many literary personalities lined up on both sides of the debate: Should a man convicted of murdering a police officer be allowed to publish a book? Before the work was released, Faulkner's widow had launched a campaign to keep Abu-Jamal's book from being published, and after her attempt failed, she tried to prevent Abu-Jamal from making any money on the project.

The counterpoint to these debates was the plight of the man who had written the book. Shortly after the book's publication, Pennsylvania Governor Tom Ridge signed a warrant scheduling Abu-Jamal's execution for August 17, 1995. Abu-Jamal had been fighting for a second trial, given serious problems with the first trial—including allegations of suppressed evidence. Adding interest to his quest for a new trial is the fact that Abu-Jamal was a well-known radical, a former Black Panther who had spent much of his pre-arrest career criticizing the Philadelphia police department for poor race relations.

Critical response to Abu-Jamal's *Live from Death Row* was mixed. Michael Anderson, writing in the *New York Times Book Review,* asserted that Abu-Jamal's book does little to persuade people who may disagree with him, claiming that after reading the book "skeptics are likely to remain so." A critic in *Publishers Weekly* commented that *Live from Death Row* "presents a bracing challenge to complacent views about crime, race and incarceration." *Nation* contributor Patricia J. Williams defended Abu-Jamal's right to express himself while incarcerated claiming that "when we engage in the public pretense that there are no voices in the bonfires on the other side of prison walls, we conspire only in the ultimate loss of our own."

BIOGRAPHICAL/CRITICAL SOURCES:

BOOKS

Anderson, S.E., and Tony Medina, editors, *In Defense of Mumia,* Writers and Readers Pub., 1996.
Weinglass, Leonard, and the defense team of Daniel Williams, *Race for Justice: Mumia Abu-Jamal's Fight against the Death Penalty,* Common Courage Press, 1995.

PERIODICALS

Emerge, November, 1995, p. 46.
Entertainment Weekly, August 11, 1995, p. 55.
Library Journal, May 1, 1995, p. 116.
Monthly Review, April, 1996, p. 42.
Nation, July 10, 1995, pp. 59-64.
New Republic, September 4, 1995, p. 9.
New Yorker, August 14, 1995, p. 26.
New York Times, July 14, 1995; May 23, 1996, p. A10.
New York Times Book Review, August 13, 1995, p. 16.
Philadelphia Magazine, December, 1993, p. 53.
Progressive, May, 1995, p. 18; October, 1995, p. 18; May, 1996, p. 34.
Publishers Weekly, April 10, 1995, p. 49; May 1, 1995, p. 11; July 10, 1995, p. 16; November 13, 1995, p. 21.*

*   *   *

ADAMS, Abby 1939-

PERSONAL: Born March 11, 1939, in New York, NY; daughter of Hendrik Willem and Persis (Washburn) Cramer; married Junius Adams (divorced, 1979); married Donald E. Westlake (a novelist and screenwriter), 1979; children: (first marriage) Adrienne, Patrick, Katharine; (second marriage; stepchildren) Sean, Steven, Tod, Paul. *Ethnicity:* "English-Dutch." *Education:* Attended Queens College (now of the City University of New York), 1955-57. *Politics:* Liberal Democrat. *Religion:* "Agnostic Episcopalian." *Avocational interests:* Painting and drawing, gardening, books, travel, food.

ADDRESSES: Home—Ancram, NY. *Agent*—Knox Burger, Knox Burger Associates Ltd., 39-1/2 Washington Sq. S., New York, NY 10012.

CAREER: Writer.

WRITINGS:

An Uncommon Scold, Simon & Schuster (New York City), 1989.
A Gardener's Gripe Book, Workman Publishing (New York City), 1996.

WORK IN PROGRESS: The Unfinished Room, a memoir.

SIDELIGHTS: Abby Adams told *CA:* "Each of my books has been entirely different from its predecessors. A book can spring to life from a random thought—and then require many months of hard work before it is fully formed."

*   *   *

ADAMS, Roy J(oseph) 1940-

PERSONAL: Born June 28, 1940, in Philadelphia, PA; son of Robert and Marie (maiden name, Gaughran; present surname, Gibbs) Adams; married Marilyn Whitaker, January 5, 1964; children: Jennifer Beth, Emily Maude. *Education:* Pennsylvania State University, B.A. (summa cum laude), 1967; University of Wisconsin—Madison, M.A., 1970, Ph.D., 1973. *Avocational interests:* Hiking, scuba diving.

ADDRESSES: Home—50 Whitton Rd., Hamilton, Ontario L8S 4C7, Canada. *Office*—Michael G. DeGroote School of Business, DeGroote Building, McMaster University, 1280 Main St. West, Hamilton, Ontario L8S 4M4, Canada; fax 905-521-8995. *E-mail*—adamsr@mcmaster.ca.

CAREER: Chase Manhattan Bank, New York City, industrial relations specialist, 1967-68; McMaster University, Hamilton, Ontario, assistant professor, 1973-78, associate professor, 1978-83, professor of industrial relations, 1984—, head of Human Resources and Labour Relations Area, 1976-78, associate member of Labour Studies Programme, 1994—, acting director, Theme School on International Justice and Human Rights, 1996—; Antioch University, Washington, DC, adjunct professor, 1994—. Visiting professor at Rutgers University, 1980, Institute for International Studies and Training, Fujinomiya, Japan, 1985, Beijing University of Iron and Steel Technology, 1985, and European Institute of Business Administration, 1987; International Institute of Labour Studies, Geneva, Switzerland, visiting scholar, 1988; Case-Western Reserve University, Dallas M. Young Distinguished Lecturer, 1989; University of Science and Technology, Beijing, China, visiting professor, 1989; University of Toronto, Canadian Pacific Distinguished Visiting Professor, 1990; Institute for Labour Research, Budapest, Hungary, visiting professor, 1991; International Labour Office, Geneva, visiting scholar, 1991; Victoria University of Wellington, visiting fellow at Industrial

Relations Centre, 1992; University of Bologna, visiting professor, 1994; University of Western Australia, distinguished visitor, 1996; guest lecturer at colleges and universities throughout the world. Ontario Education Relations Commission, fact finder and mediator, 1975-76; Commission on Educational Leave and Productivity, chairperson and executive director, 1978-79; Employment and Immigration Canada, member of Expert Group to Evaluate the Impact of Worksharing, 1992; consultant to Ontario Law Reform Commission, Japanese National Institute for Employment and Vocational Research, and Ontario Ministry of Citizenship and Culture. *Military service:* U.S. Army, Airborne, 1961-64; served in Korea.

MEMBER: International Industrial Relations Association (co-chairperson of Study Group on Industrial Relations as a Field and Industrial Relations Theory, 1989-93; founder and senior listmaster of International Employee Relations Network, 1994—), International Sociological Association, International Political Science Association, International Employment Relations Association, Canadian Industrial Relations Association (member of executive board, 1978-83; president, 1981-82), Canadian Association of University Teachers, Canadian Labour Education and Research Association, Industrial Relations Research Association (co-chairperson of Committee on Computer Communication, 1994-95; president of International Section, 1996), University and College Labor Education Association, Society for the Advancement of Socio-Economics, Academy of Management, American Federation of Teachers, Comparative Industrial Relations Research and Teaching Society (co-chairperson), McMaster Faculty Associates.

WRITINGS:

White Collar Union Growth in Britain and Sweden, International Relations Research Institute, University of Wisconsin—Madison, 1975.
(Editor) *Comparative Industrial Relations: Contemporary Research and Theory,* Unwin-Hyman (London, England), 1991.
(Editor with Noah M. Meltz, and contributor) *Industrial Relations Theory: Its Nature, Scope, and Pedagogy,* Scarecrow (Metuchen, NJ), 1993.
Industrial Relations under Liberal Democracy: North America in Comparative Perspective, University of South Carolina Press (Columbia, SC), 1995.
(With Gordon Betcherman and Beth Bilson) *Good Jobs, Bad Jobs, No Jobs: Tough Choices for Canadian Labour Law,* C. D. Howe Institute (Toronto, Ontario), 1995.

Co-founder and co-editor of the book series "Studies in Industrial Relations," University of South Carolina Press, 1985—. Contributor to books, including *The Future of Industrial Relations in a Changing World,* edited by John Niland, Raymond Lansbury, and Chrissie Verevis, Sage Publications (Newbury Park, CA), 1994; *Union-Management Relations in Canada,* 3rd edition, edited by M. Gunderson and A. Ponak, Addison-Wesley (Don Mills, Ontario), 1995; and *Theories, Research, and Teaching in International Industrial Relations,* edited by Meltz and Jack Barbash, Centre for Industrial Relations Research and Teaching, University of Sydney (Sydney, Australia), 1996. Contributor of more than sixty articles and reviews to professional journals, popular magazines, and newspapers, including *Labour Relations News, Work Times,* and *Literacy.* Founder and editor, *Comparative Industrial Relations Newsletter,* 1990—; member of editorial board, *International Journal of Comparative Labour Law and Industrial Relations,* 1989-95, *Employee Relations, International Journal of Human Resources Management, Employee Rights and Responsibilities Journal, Journal of Individual Employment Rights, International Journal of Employment Studies, Canadian Labour and Employment Law Journal, Diritto delle Relazioni Industriali,* and *Yearbook of Polish Labour Law and Social Policy.*

WORK IN PROGRESS: Research on the development of labor relations in the Commonwealth Caribbean; research on the social dimension of freer trade and the link between trade and labor standards.

*   *   *

ADEPOJU, Aderanti   1945-

PERSONAL: Born July 17, 1945, in Oyan, Nigeria; son of Oba Afolabi (a traditional ruler) and Ester (a trader; maiden name, Oladunni) Adepoju; married, November 25, 1972; wife's name, Adinda (a consultant); children: Abiola, Adegboyega, Aboyepe, Adegoke. *Ethnicity:* "Yoruba." *Education:* University of Ife, B.Sc. (with honors), 1969; London School of Economics and Political Science, M.Sc., 1970, Ph.D., 1973. *Religion:* Christian. *Avocational interests:* Squash, music.

ADDRESSES: Home—Rue du 18 Juin, Dakar, Senegal. *Office*—UNFPA Project, IDEP, B.P. 3186, Dakar, Senegal; fax 221-23-64-41.

CAREER: University of Ife, Ile-Ife, Nigeria, began as lecturer, became professor, 1969-84; University of Lagos, Lagos, Nigeria, professor and dean, 1984-90; African Institute for Economic Development and Planning (IDEP), Dakar, Senegal, training coordinator for United Nations Fund for Population Activities (UNFPA), 1988—.

MEMBER: Union for African Population Studies (president, 1991-95), International Union for the Scientific Study of Population (IUSSP), UAPS, PAN, World Social Prospects Association.

WRITINGS:

(With James Currey) *The Impact of Structural Adjustment on the Population of Africa,* United Nations Fund for Population Activities, 1993.

(Editor with Currey) *Gender, Work, and Population in Sub-Saharan Africa,* International Labor Office (Washington, DC), 1994.

The African Family in the Development Process, Zed Press, 1996.

WORK IN PROGRESS: Research on population policies in Africa, their problems and prospects; research on emigration dynamics in sub-Saharan Africa.

SIDELIGHTS: Aderanti Adepoju told *CA:* "Writing is primarily a logical continuum in my research work. It enables me to present the results of my research to a wide audience. I have always been inspired to respond to critical topical issues in Africa: structural adjustment issues and the effect of this adjustment on the population, gender, and poverty, and the centrality of the African family in development. I find it enriching to collaborate with colleagues to share opinions and present analysis in a multi-dimensional manner."

*   *   *

ADNAN, ETEL 1925-

PERSONAL: Born February 25, 1925, in Beirut, Republic of Lebanon; naturalized U.S. citizen, 1986; daughter of a military commander of the Ottoman Empire. *Education:* Attended French convent schools in Beirut; attended L'Ecole Superieure des Lettres de Beyrouth; Sorbonne, Diplome d'Etudes Superieures de Philosophie, 1950; postgraduate studies at University of California, Berkeley, 1955-57, and Harvard University, 1957-58.

ADDRESSES: Home—35 Marie Street, Sausalito, CA 94965; 29 Rue Madame, Paris, 75006 France.

CAREER: Writer and artist. Worked for the Bureau de la Presse, Beirut, Lebanon, 1941-45; Al-Ahliya School for Girls, Beirut, teacher of French literature, 1947-49; Dominican College, San Rafael, CA, professor of philosophy, 1958-72; literary editor, *al-SAFA* and *L'Orient-Le Jour* (French-language newspapers), Beirut, 1972-75. Paintings exhibited in museums, including Tunis Modern Art Museum, Royal Jordanian Museum, British Museum, Musee de L'Institut du Monde Arabe (Paris), and National Museum of Women in the Arts (Washington, DC).

WRITINGS:

POETRY

Moonshots, [Beirut], 1966.

Five Senses for One Death, The Smith (New York), 1971.

"Jebu" [and] *"L'Express Beyrouth—Enfer",* P. J. Oswald (Paris), 1973.

(And illustrator) *L' Apocalypse Arabe,* Editions Papyrus (Paris), 1980.

From A to Z, Post-Apollo Press (Sausalito, CA), 1982.

Pablo Neruda Is a Banana Tree, Da Almeida (Lisbon), 1982.

The Indian Never Had a Horse, and Other Poems, Post-Apollo Press, 1985.

(And illustrator and translator) *The Arab Apocalypse,* Post-Apollo Press, 1989.

The Spring Flowers Own & The Manifestations of the Voyage, Post-Apollo Press, 1990.

Kitab Al Bahr (title means "The Book of the Sea"), [Beirut], 1994.

There (prose poem), Post-Apollo Press, 1996.

OTHER

Sitt Marie Rose (novel), Editions des femmes (Paris), 1978, translation by Georgina Kleege, Post-Apollo-Press, 1982.

(And illustrator) *Journey to Mt. Tamalpais* (essay), Post-Apollo Press, 1986.

Paris, When It's Naked (essay collection), Post-Apollo Press, 1993.

Of Cities and Women (Letters to Fawwaz), Post-Apollo Press, 1993.

Al Confini Della Luna (short stories translated into Italian), [Rome], 1995.

Contributor of poetry, short fiction, and essays to anthologies, including *Women of the Fertile Crescent,* edited by Kamal Boullata, Three Continents Press (Washington, DC), 1978; *Opening the Gates,* edited by Margot Badran and Miriam Cooke, Indiana University Press (Indianapolis), 1990; and *2000 and What?,* edited by Karl Roeseler and David Gilbert, Trip Street (San Francisco), 1996.

Author of television documentaries on the war in Lebanon, 1976; co-author, with Robert Wilson, of *Civil warS* (multi-language opera), 1984; co-author, with Delphine Seyrig, of screenplay based on the life of Calamity Jane, 1985-90.

ADAPTATIONS: A poem by Adnan was set to music by Tania Leon and produced in New York City, 1990; *The Adnan Songbook* (eight poems set to music by Gavin Bryars), broadcast on BBC-Radio, 1995.

SIDELIGHTS: Acclaimed both for her poetry and her painting, Etel Adnan is an Arab who writes in both French and English. Espousing a feminist viewpoint, her works contain strong political and philosophic undercurrents. Sometimes marrying her prose works with her own visual creations, Adnan has published in a variety of genres, including the novel *Sitt Marie Rose,* several volumes of poetry, screenplays and television scripts, and *Of Cities and Women (Letters to Fawwaz),* a collection letters written to a friend while their author was traveling through the cities of Europe and the Middle East between 1990 and 1992.

Born in 1925, in Beirut, Republic of Lebanon, Adnan was the daughter of a Syrian staff officer and commander of the Ottoman Empire who had served in World War I before marrying his second wife, a Greek. Adnan would grow up in a multilingual household where both Greek and Turkish were spoken; French would later be added to her store of languages when she attended a French-run Catholic school. In addition to her experience with many languages, Adnan was exposed to a diversity of religious thought as well: Her mother was a Christian and her father was Muslim. After the outbreak of the Lebanese civil war in 1978, Adnan would move to France for two years before establishing a permanent home in Sausalito, California. She now maintains dual residences in both the United States and France, reflective, perhaps, of the dualities experienced early in her life.

Adnan's first written work would be in the French language of the classroom; her first major poem, "The Book of the Sea," was completed when she was twenty-two. While many of her works would be translated into other languages by others, Adnan began to write in English after she became involved in the U.S. anti-war movement during the 1970s. The violence of war is a common thread in much of Adnan's work; a witness to much of the violence between Palestinians, Syrians, Shiite Muslims, and Israelis that has occurred within the city of Beirut in this century, she perceived that such attempts to solve cultural and religious conflicts through violence could only end in the total destruction of the planet. Poems such as "Jebu" and "L'Express Beyrouth—Enfer," as well as the longer *L'Apocalypse Arabe,* published in 1980, each explore the dilemma of Palestinians living in Lebanon during that period. In 1978's *Sitt Marie Rose,* an anti-war novel set in war-torn Beirut during the mid-1970s, Adnan compares such conflict with primitive tribal warfare.

While *Sitt Marie Rose* features the dramatic plight of women against the backdrop of war, Adnan's poetry contains imagery that is far less harsh. The lyrical verses collected in 1985's *The Indian Never Had a Horse, and Other Poems* focus on subjects of universal concern, such as the search for peace and the preservation of the planet. Exemplifying Adnan's broad-ranging experience of cultures and people, "Spreading Clouds. . ." compares the plight of the Native American people with the cultural and religious conflicts in Lebanon.

The examination of the position of women within diverse politics and cultures is characteristic of almost all of Adnan's writing. Her overtly feminist *Of Cities and Women (Letters to Fawwaz)* describes her travels through eight cities—Amsterdam, Aix-en-Provence, Beirut, Barcelona, Berlin, and Paris among them—and her perceptions of the lives of women living within the political culture of each. "In Barcelona," she writes, "the women, when in the street, don't seem to consciously play a role, or live an exception: they are part of humanity, of a place, of a climate, of a country." Similarly, Adnan's essay collection *Paris, When It's Naked* is imbued with a unique sense of place, time, and culture. "These books add up to more than the sum of their parts," Diana Abu-Jaber comments of both *Of Cities and Women* and *Paris, When It's Naked* in *Middle East Journal.* "The joy of reading both volumes derives from the great perceptions of Etel Adnan's eyes and the generosity of her heart. It is the joy of reading the work of a great soul."

BIOGRAPHICAL/CRITICAL SOURCES:

BOOKS

Adnan, Etel, *The Indian Never Had a Horse, and Other Poems,* Post-Apollo Press, 1985.
Adnan, Etel, interview with Hilary Kilpatrick in *Unheard Words,* edited by Mineke Schipper, Allison & Busby (New York), 1985.
Adnan, Etel, *Of Cities and Women (Letters to Fawwaz),* Post-Apollo Press, 1993.
Boullata, Kamal, editor, *Women of the Fertile Crescent,* Three Continents Press, 1978.
Feminist Writers, St. James Press (Detroit), 1996.

PERIODICALS

Los Angeles Times Book Review, August 15, 1993, p. 7; September 5, 1993, p. 11.
Middle East Journal, autumn, 1995, p. 686.
Nation, March 7, 1994.
PMLA, January, 1995.
Poetry Flash, November, 1987.
Publishers Weekly, July 12, 1994, p. 76.*

*   *   *

AKE, Claude   1939-1996

OBITUARY NOTICE—See index for *CA* sketch: Surname pronounced "AH-kay"; born February 18, 1939, in Omoku, Nigeria; died in a plane crash, November 7, 1996, northeast of Lagos, Nigeria. Political scientist, educator, activist, author. Ake was an authority on African economics and politics. He was the founder and director of Nigeria's Center for Advanced Social Science, which was devoted to the study of environmental and social issues. Ake began his career as an educator at Columbia University in New York in 1966, and later taught at Carleton University in Ottawa, Ontario, Canada. He served as dean of the faculty of social sciences at the University of Port Harcourt in Nigeria during parts of the 1970s and 1980s. He also was a professor of political economy at the school. He worked at various universities as a visiting professor, including the University of Nairobi and the University of Dar-Es-Salaam in Tanzania. He was a visiting professor at Yale University at the time of his death. Ake, who was outspoken about corrupt government practices, was an activist who was often critical about the Nigerian Government. He also worked with petroleum companies, such as Royal Dutch and Shell, to look into environmental issues. He resigned as an adviser to oil companies in 1995 in protest over the execution of Ken Saro-Wiwa, a human rights activist. Ake also worked for the *Journal of Political Economy* and authored books such as *A Theory of Political Integration, Revolutionary Pressures in Africa, A Political Economy of Africa,* and *Democracy and Development in Africa.*

OBITUARIES AND OTHER SOURCES:

PERIODICALS

New York Times, November 9, 1996, p. D25.
Washington Post, November 21, 1996, p. B6.

*   *   *

AKUTAGAWA, Ryunosuke   1892-1927

PERSONAL: Born Niihara Ryunosuke, March 1, 1892, in Tokyo, Japan; died of suicide by drug overdose, July 24, 1927; married Tsukamoto Fumi, 1918; children: three sons. *Education:* Tokyo Imperial University, degree in English, 1916.

CAREER: Short story writer. *Schinschicho* (New Thought) literary magazine, staff member, 1914; Naval Engineering College, Yokosuka, Japan, English teacher, 1916-17; *Osaka Mainichi,* literary staff member, 1919; fulltime writer, 1919-27.

WRITINGS:

Chuto, Iwanami Shoten, 1928.
Shuju no kotoba, Iwanami Shoten, 1932.
Shunpuku, Shinchosha, 1952.
Konan no ogi, Shinchosha, 1952.
TuTsz-Chun, translated by Dorothy Britton, Japan Publications Trading Co., 1965.
Japanese Short Stories, translated by Takashi Kojima, illustrated by Masakazu Kuwata, Liveright (New York), 1970.
Kappa, translated by Seiichi Shiojiri, Greenwood Press, 1970, translated by Geoffrey Bownas, Owen, 1970, C. E. Tuttle, 1971.
Hell Screen and Other Stories, translated by W. H. H. Norman, Greenwood Press, 1971.

Exotic Japanese Stories, translated by Takashi Kojimi and John McVittie, edited by McVittie and Arthur Pell, Liveright, 1972.

Hell Screen, Cogwheels, and A Fool's Life, foreword by Jorge Luis Borges, Eridanos Press, 1987.

Also author of several volumes of short stories published in Japan. Stories include "Rashomon," "Niwa," and "In His Grove."

ADAPTATIONS: "Rashomon" and "In His Grove" were adapted into the film *Rashomon* by Akira Kurosawa.

SIDELIGHTS: Ryunosuke Akutagawa was known for his haunting short stories; his accomplishments in the form have made him a mainstay of Japanese short story writing, despite his relatively short life and suicide. Richard P. Benton, writing in *Reference Guide to Short Fiction,* states that Akutagawa "brought the Japanese short story to maturity by his intelligence, imagination, and close attention to style and form. Indeed, his accomplishment made the short story recognized as an important part of Japanese literature."

Akutagawa had a literary interest both in ancient Japanese writing and in English and European works. While at the Imperial University of Tokyo, he majored in English and studied the works of William Morris, Edgar Allen Poe, and Jonathan Swift, among others. Akutagawa's themes arose as a combination of traditional Japanese and modern English-language literary concerns. In the early phase of Akutagawa's writing career, he published several important short stories, including "Rashomon." In this work, a poor Japanese servant finds an old woman stripping dead corpses of their hair. At first, he is angry at her, but when she explains that she does it in order to make wigs and therefore feed herself, he relents. Not, however, before he makes off with the woman's clothing himself. "Rashomon," according to Benton, "suggests that people have the morality they can afford." This story has become one of Akutagawa's more famous works in part because of Akira Kurosawa's film version, which used Akutagawa's concept of morality to tell a different tale. Other stories of this period explore horrifying aspects of the battle between good and evil.

By the year 1920, Akutagawa's writing began to change, as he explored his feelings about the importance of art and life. In "Niwa" ("The Garden"), he wrote about a family's beautiful formal garden and how it had gone to waste over the years as the family dissipated. The second son finds that he must return to his family home after becoming weakened by tuberculosis. His life work then changes as he tries to return the garden to its previous splendor, which he does shortly before he dies.

As Akutagawa's writing progressed, he found it more and more difficult to remain detached from his writing. That fact, coupled with his emotional problems, his withdrawn mother, his physical deterioration, and his addiction to drugs pushed him to suicide. His works during this period (1925 to 1927) echo his demise, as they increasingly focus on a narrator who is self-absorbed and obsessed with his sanity. Akutagawa himself became distressed with his literary output and considered his later works an artistic failure. In 1927, after several months of contemplation and planning, Akutagawa committed suicide by taking an overdose of drugs.

Hell Screen, Cogwheels, and A Fool's Life, published in 1987, introduced many English-speaking readers to Akutagawa's written work for the first time. The volume contains three of Akutagawa's most impressive and disturbing works. "Hell Screen" chronicles an artist named Yoshihide who has good feelings towards no one, except for his daughter, whom he adores. His feudal lord commissions him to paint a screen of the Buddhist hell, and Yoshihide launches into the project with furor, making his assistant submit to acts of torture so the artist can faithfully capture it. With only one element remaining, Yoshihide asks his lord to dress up a beautiful lady, put her in a cart, and set it on fire so he can paint it. The lord agrees, but puts Yoshihide's daughter in the cart. The artist is at first horrified, but then his artistic feelings overcome him and he finishes the painting while his daughter burns.

In "Cogwheels" and "A Fool's Life," Akutagawa ruminates on the struggle between staying sane in an insane world—a struggle with autobiographical overtones to it. In "Cogwheels," the narrator describes a hallucinatory experience of seeing cogwheels turning, and his inability to get rid of the image. Walter Nash wrote in the *London Review of Books* that "what is touching and terrible is the writer's awareness of madness coming on—as the cogwheels begin to turn—and his fight against it."

"A Fool's Life" is a collection of fifty-one entries that recount an artist and his descent into insanity, based closely on Akutagawa's last months of life.

"Akutagawa's minute description of his mental anguish, leading up to his suicide, is a moving document," noted Ian Buruma in the *New York Review of Books.* "You sense the life being drained from the man, leaving nothing but intellect, icily, horribly lucid, when not fading in and out of hallucinations."

BIOGRAPHICAL/CRITICAL SOURCES:

BOOKS

Akutagawa and Dazai: Instances of Literary Adaptation, translation and introduction by James O'Brien, Arizona State University, 1988.
Akutagawa Ryunosuke, Shinchosa, 1983.
Hiraoka, Toshio, *Remarks on Akutagawa's Works: With American Students' Opinions,* Seirosha, 1990.
Katsukura, Toshikazu, *Akutagawa Ryunosuke no rekishi shosetsu,* Kyoiku Shuppan Senta, 1983.
Takeuchi, Hiroshi, *Akutagawa Ryunosuke no keiei goroku,* PHP Kenkyujo, 1983.
Watson, Noelle, editor, *Reference Guide to Short Fiction,* St. James Press, 1994, pp. 21-2.
Yu, Beongcheon, *Akutagawa: An Introduction,* Wayne State University Press, 1972.

PERIODICALS

London Review of Books, May 19, 1988, p. 24.
New York Review of Books, December 22, 1988, p. 54.
Publishers Weekly, January 29, 1988, p. 414.
Times Literary Supplement, April 28, 1989, pp. 466-67.*

*   *   *

ALBERTS, Robert C(arman)   1907-1996

OBITUARY NOTICE—See index for *CA* sketch: Born July 15, 1907, in Pittsburgh, PA; died October 8, 1996, in Pittsburgh, PA. Salesperson, journalist, author. Alberts was a historian who recorded events and the details of people's lives in numerous books. He began his career as a sales manager with the Pittsburgh Coal Company in 1930. Eight years later he changed careers, joining the editorial staff of the *Pittsburgh Bulletin-Index Magazine.* He served as editor of the *Magazine* from 1940 until 1942, before beginning work as an account executive at the Ketchum, MacLeod and Grove, Inc., advertising

agency. He rounded out his duties at the firm as a vice president from 1956 until 1969. From 1970 until 1977 he served as a contributing editor to *American Heritage* magazine. Alberts was also an established author, penning his first book, *The Most Extraordinary Adventures of Major Robert Stobo,* in 1965. He wrote biographies of other historical figures, including William Bingham, H. J. Heinz, and George Rogers Clark. Among his other books are *Mount Washington Tavern: The Story of a Famous Inn, a Great Road, and the People Who Used Them,* the Christophers Award-winning *Benjamin West: A Biography, Pitt: The Story of the University of Pittsburgh, 1787-1987,* and *The Shaping of the Point: A History of the Pittsburgh Renaissance.* He was also editor of *Records of North American Big Game.* He won awards, including Letterman of Distinction from the University of Pittsburgh and the award of merit from the American Association of State and Local History.

OBITUARIES AND OTHER SOURCES:

BOOKS

Who's Who, 148th edition, St. Martin's, 1996.

PERIODICALS

New York Times, October 14, 1996, p. A15.

*   *   *

ALEXANDER, Ruth M.   1954-

PERSONAL: Born March 23, 1954, in New York, NY; daughter of Charles K. (an actor, playwright, and director) and Margaret (a psychiatric social worker; maiden name, Kachur) Alexander. *Education:* City College of the City University of New York, B.A. (cum laude), 1976; University of California, Santa Barbara, M.A., 1983; Cornell University, Ph.D., 1990; Colorado State University, postdoctoral study, 1994, 1995.

ADDRESSES: Home—Fort Collins, CO. *Office*—Department of History, Colorado State University, Fort Collins, CO 80523. *E-mail*—ralexander@vines.colostate.edu.

CAREER: Colorado State University, Fort Collins, assistant professor, 1988-93, associate professor of history, 1993—, acting director of American Studies

Program, 1993-94. University Press of Colorado, member of board of directors, 1996—.

MEMBER: American Historical Association, Organization of American Historians, American Studies Association, Berkshire Conference of Women Historians, Western Association of Women Historians.

AWARDS, HONORS: Judith Lee Ridge Article Prize, Western Association of Women Historians, 1989, for "'We Are Engaged as a Band of Sisters': Class and Domesticity in the Washingtonian Temperance Movement, 1840-50"; named Outstanding Professor of the Year, Mortar Board, 1995; Schlesinger Library grant, Radcliffe College, 1995-96; *The "Girl Problem"* was named an outstanding academic book for 1996 by *Choice.*

WRITINGS:

The "Girl Problem": Female Sexual Delinquency in New York, 1900-1930, Cornell University Press (Ithaca, NY), 1995.
(Editor with Mary Beth Norton) *Major Problems in American Women's History,* 2nd edition, Heath (Lexington, MA), 1996.

Contributor to books, including *Small Worlds: Children and Adolescents in America,* edited by Elliott West and Paula Petrik, University Press of Kansas (Lawrence, KS), 1992; and *Encyclopedia of American Social History,* Scribner (New York City), 1993. Contributor of articles and reviews to periodicals, including *Journal of Adolescent Research* and *Journal of American History.* Author of article "'We Are Engaged as a Band of Sisters': Class and Domesticity in the Washingtonian Temperance Movement, 1840-50," c. 1989.

WORK IN PROGRESS: A book on American women reformers and internationalism, 1900-1960.

*   *   *

ALLMAND, C. T.
(Christopher Allmand)

PERSONAL: Education: Attended Oxford University.

ADDRESSES: Office—University of Liverpool, Department of History, POB 147, Liverpool L69 3BX, England.

CAREER: Liverpool University, Liverpool, England, professor of medieval history.

WRITINGS:

Henry V (pamphlet), London Historical Association (London), 1968.
(Editor and compiler) *Society at War: The Experience of England and France during the Hundred Years War,* Barnes and Noble (New York), 1973.
(Editor) *War, Literature, and Politics in the Late Middle Ages: Essays in Honour of G. W. Coopland,* Liverpool University Press (Liverpool), 1976.
(Editor, with C. A. J. Armstrong) *English Suits before the "Parlement" of Paris 1420-1436,* Boydell Press for the Royal Historical Society, 1982.
Lancastrian Normandy, 1415-1450: The History of a Medieval Occupation, Clarendon Press/Oxford University Press (New York), 1983.
(As Christopher Allmand) *The Hundred Years War: England and France at War, c. 1300-c. 1450,* Cambridge University Press (Cambridge, England), 1988.
(As Christopher Allmand) *Henry V,* University of California Press (Berkeley and Los Angeles), 1992.

SIDELIGHTS: C. T. Allmand is a highly regarded historian who specializes in the late medieval period of English history. Considered an authority on Lancastrian Normandy, the period during the Hundred Years War when England ruled much of France, and on Henry V, the king who presided over England and its French colonies during the early part of the fifteenth century, Allmand has published several works that are deemed important contributions to the history of warfare and conquest and the social, political, moral, and psychological impact of warfare on both the conquerors and the conquered. His works are routinely praised for their readability, relevance to both students and scholars, and thorough grounding in contemporary documents as well as modern scholarship.

In 1968, at the beginning of his career, Allmand published a pamphlet entitled *Henry V* that offers a brief review of the career of one of England's most celebrated kings. Allmand's portrait revises the traditional heroic image of Henry V, which is based on Shakespeare's plays, and discusses the man's early influences, motivations, and accomplishments. A reviewer for the *Times Literary Supplement* dubbed Henry "unrelenting and apparently humourless" based on his reading of Allmand's first *Henry V*. More than twenty years later, in 1992, Allmand published a second, book-length work, also entitled *Henry V*. This treatment of an intensely studied subject brought the following accolade from Paul E. Kopperman in the *Journal of Military History:* "Quite possibly no contemporary scholar is better equipped to write a biography of Henry V than is Christopher Allmand, who has written extensively and well on a variety of topics related to the period of the Hundred Years' War."

During the two-plus decades that separate Allmand's two treatises on Henry V, the author built a reputation as a scrupulous and judicious scholar of the late medieval period. One of his earliest works was 1973's *Society at War: The Experience of England and France during the Hundred Years War,* a compilation of excerpts from a wide variety of documents, both famous and obscure, that illuminate the late medieval view of the social, moral, and economic impact of war and peace. Allmand translates all documents except those in Middle English, and glosses difficult terms in that language. These efforts prompted M. G. A. Vale, a reviewer for the *English Historical Review,* to lament the decline in educational standards, which places texts in Latin and medieval French out of reach for even serious undergraduate students of medieval history. Nevertheless, other reviewers found Allmand's translations accurate and his commentary both useful and enlightening. A *Choice* contributor characterized *Society at War* as "as good a source book in medieval history as has recently appeared."

Allmand's next project, the 1976 volume *War, Literature, and Politics in the Late Middle Ages,* approaches the same subject—the conduct and impact of war during the medieval era—from the perspective of modern scholarship rather than contemporary documents. This volume collects essays characterized by M. R. Powicke in the *American Historical Review* as "practical studies of warfare on the one hand and literary and legal studies on the other." In addition to editing the volume, Allmand coauthored an essay on fourteenth-century spies that Powicke asserted "break[s] new ground," concluding that "our knowledge of the importance of war in the later medieval society is significantly advanced" by the essays in this work.

Allmand's 1982 publication, *English Suits before the "Parlement" of Paris 1420-1436,* is an anthology of legal cases from the Hundred Years War gathered in collaboration with C. A. J. Armstrong. Together the two scholars offer original court documents pertaining to suits brought before the court (*parlement*) of Paris resulting from the exchange of large tracts of land between French and English hands during the course of the long war. The documents are printed in their original medieval French, summarized in English, and definitions of legal terminology are provided.

In *Lancastrian Normandy, 1415-1450: The History of a Medieval Occupation,* published in 1983, Allmand examines the fifteenth-century phase of the Hundred Years War, during which the king of England, a member of the house of Lancaster, by dint of conquest achieved sovereignty over the Normandy region of France, and encouraged English settlement there. English soldiers, administrators, and church officials prospered for a short time in what is known as Lancastrian Normandy, and Henry V established a university in Caen. Reviewers emphasized the diplomacy of Allmand's approach to the historically delicate subject of conquest; his reliance on both French and English documents of the time is praised. Allmand's synthesis of earlier scholarship on institutional and military aspects of the occupation is noted while his own contributions, emphasizing social and political impacts, are considered authoritative. *English Historical Review* contributor Michael Jones concluded: "this is a soundly conceived and generally well-executed book . . . which brings together a wealth of material for which all students of the period will be grateful."

Allmand's full-length biography, *Henry V,* was greeted with high praise by the critics, who, while noting the abundance of material already available on the subject, commented on the author's particular ability to place this figure in his proper historical context. D'A. J. D. Boulton, in a review in *American Historical Review,* remarked: "While Allmand's new biography . . . inevitably reiterates a good deal of information found in earlier works, it is nevertheless to be welcomed, both as the most thorough account of Henry's reign to appear since . . . [1929], and as an original contribution to the subject by a distinguished historian with particular expertise in the background history." In a review that appeared in *History Today,* Michael Jones declared: "The sense of balance that characterised the 1968 essay, as it steered between such unexpected extremes of adulation and the more critical, even cynical, views other modern commentators have expressed on the king's ambitions and achievement, is once again eminently sustained throughout this generously proportioned study."

Allmand's 1992 *Henry V* is divided into three parts, concerning the monarch's youthful exploits—during which he learned lessons important to his future roles as both military and political leader—his military campaigns during his reign as king, and his governance of Normandy. *Henry V* "contains well-informed, well-written chapters from which strong indications emerge of the quality of Henry's rule and the effectiveness of his government," according to G. L. Harriss in *English Historical Review*. Although Paul E. Kopperman makes a case in his review in the *Journal of Military History* that at times Allmand's claims for the historical importance of Henry V outweigh the evidence, he concedes that "undoubtedly, this is because that evidence is often rather slim, and Allmand is too good a scholar to do it regularly." Other critics noted that while it has become popular to judge Allmand's subject harshly, based on twentieth-century notions of justice, colonialism, and warfare, "Allmand's opinion of Henry both as king and man is clearly positive," observed Boulton, "and this in itself is rather refreshing."

BIOGRAPHICAL/CRITICAL SOURCES:

PERIODICALS

American Historical Review, June, 1977, p. 618; December, 1984, pp. 1324-25; June, 1994, pp. 888-89.
British Book News, October, 1982, p. 648.
Choice, April, 1974, p. 313.
English Historical Review, July, 1975, p. 635; January, 1978, pp. 170-71; April, 1986, p. 485; July, 1993, pp. 677-79.
Historian, November, 1985, pp. 98-99; autumn, 1993, pp. 105-6.
History Today, January, 1994, pp. 57-58.
Journal of Economic Literature, December, 1974, p. 1437.
Journal of Military History, July, 1994, pp. 520-21.
Speculum, October, 1985, pp. 939-41.
Times Literary Supplement, September 5, 1968, p. 954; March 2, 1984, p. 229.*

*   *   *

ALLMAND, Christopher
   See ALLMAND, C.T.

AMES, Louise Bates   1908-1996

OBITUARY NOTICE—See index for *CA* sketch: Born October 29, 1908, in Portland, ME; died of cancer, October 31, 1996, in Cincinnati, OH. Psychologist, educator, columnist, author. Ames was a psychologist who made significant contributions to the study of children, theorizing that a child's development occurs in various, definable stages. She worked with Arnold Gesell and Frances L. Ilg, helping to make parents aware of child development stages such as the "terrible 2's." Ames began her career at the Yale Clinic of Child Development in 1933, first as a research assistant. When she left the clinic in 1950, she had attained the rank of assistant professor. That year she helped found the Gesell Institute of Child Development and served as its research director until 1965. She was named director and president of the Institute in 1977. Other career accomplishments included work as the curator of Yale Films of Child Development from 1944 to 1950 and as a lecturer at the Child Study Center at Yale, beginning in 1991. She became emeritus assistant professor in 1993. Ames also wrote a syndicated column called "Parents Ask" and she was frequently seen on television. She drew attention in the 1980s when she advised parents against allowing preschoolers to see the movie *Bambi*. She cautioned parents because the title character's mother is killed by hunters, which could cause anxiety for young children. She was the author of more than thirty-five books, including *Child Care and Development*. She penned numerous volumes with Frances L. Ilg, such as *Child Behavior, Parents Ask, School Readiness,* and *Your Two Year Old*.

OBITUARIES AND OTHER SOURCES:

BOOKS

Who's Who in America, 52nd edition, Marquis, 1997.

PERIODICALS

New York Times, November 7, 1996, p. D27.

*   *   *

AMSTERDAM, Morey   1914(?)-1996

OBITUARY NOTICE—See index for *CA* sketch: Born December 14, c. 1914, in Chicago, IL (some sources say San Francisco, CA); died from a heart attack,

October 28, 1996, in Los Angeles, CA. Comedian, actor, and writer. His father, a concert violinist, wanted him to become a musician, but the wisecracking Amsterdam only used his cello as a prop in his comedy acts. Best known for his role as television comedy writer Buddy Sorrell on *The Dick Van Dyke Show* (1961-66), Amsterdam excelled at comedy in any medium—Vaudeville, radio, television, stage and writing. He started as a teenager, playing the straight man for his brother, and went on to write jokes for Will Rogers and Fanny Brice. After Al Capone raved about Amsterdam's stage act during a Chicago performance, the comedian had no problem getting booked. The brash wisecracks that earned Amsterdam the title of "Human Joke Machine" also landed him on radio shows in the 1940s, although he sometimes angered sponsors because he couldn't resist taking shots at their advertisements. Amsterdam made the move to television in 1948 on the variety show *Stop Me If You've Heard This One* and hosted his own show in 1950. From 1957 to 1959, Amsterdam starred on the program *Keep Talking* before landing his big role on the hit *The Dick Van Dyke Show*. He appeared on *Hollywood Squares* in the 1970s and did stand-up in Las Vegas and Atlantic City. He wrote the screenplay *Ghost and the Guest* (1943), and coauthored *Kid Dynamite* (1943) and *Don't Worry, We'll Think of a Title* (1966). Amsterdam also wrote material for Presidents Franklin D. Roosevelt, Lyndon Johnson and Ronald Reagan. He was the author several books, including *Keep Laughing* and *Betty Cooker Crock Book for Drunks*.

OBITUARIES AND OTHER SOURCES:

PERIODICALS

Chicago Tribune, November 11, 1996, Sec. 4, p. 8.
Los Angeles Times, October 29, 1996, p. A20; November 1, 1996, p. A34.
New York Times, October 30, 1996, p. D22.

*   *   *

ANDERSON, Trevor A(ndrew)   1959-

PERSONAL: Born November 17, 1959, in Adelaide, Australia; married; children: two. *Education:* Australian National University, B.Sc. (with honors), 1981; University of Sydney, Ph.D., 1988.

*ADDRESSES: Office—*School of Biological Sciences, James Cook University of North Queensland, Townsville, Queensland 4811, Australia; fax 61-077-251570. *E-mail*—Trevor.Anderson@jcu.edu.au.

CAREER: University of Newcastle, Newcastle, Australia, research assistant in medicine, 1981; New South Wales Institute of Technology, tutor in physiology, 1985; Nepean College, tutor in physiology, 1986-87; Department of Primary Industries and Energy, Canberra, Australia, scientist with Bureau of Rural Research, 1988; Deakin University, senior tutor, 1988-90, lecturer in aquaculture, 1990-93; James Cook University of North Queensland, Townsville, Australia, senior lecturer in aquaculture, 1994—.

MEMBER: World Aquaculture Society, European Society for Comparative Physiology and Biochemistry, Asia and Oceanic Society for Comparative Endocrinology, Australian Institute of Biology, Australian Marine Sciences Association, Australian Society for Fish Biology, Australian Mariculture Association, Asian Fisheries Society.

WRITINGS:

(With S. S. De Silva) *Fish Nutrition in Aquaculture,* Chapman & Hall (New York City), 1995.

Contributor of more than twenty articles and reviews to scientific journals.

*   *   *

ANDES, Karen   1956-

PERSONAL: Born March 27, 1956, in Philadelphia, PA; daughter of Charles (a marketing executive) and Garretta (maiden name, Roach; present surname, Long) Andes; married Martine Carcamo (a technician and builder), November 27, 1991. *Education:* Vassar College, B.A., 1978. *Politics:* "Open-handed." *Religion:* "Dogma, no; spirit, yes!" *Avocational interests:* Dance.

*ADDRESSES: Home and office—*Andes Productions, 1826 Fifth Ave., San Rafael, CA 94901; fax 415-459-5052. *E-mail*—http://www.imu.com/kandes/strongwomen.htm. *Agent*—Julie Herberg, Round Table Press, 805 Fifth Ave., New York, NY 10011.

CAREER: Andes Productions, San Rafael, CA, owner and producer of written, audio, and visual materials, 1988—. Has worked variously as a personal trainer, dance-movement teacher, and fitness consultant.

MEMBER: International Association of Fitness Professionals, American Council on Exercise.

AWARDS, HONORS: Scholar, Bread Loaf Writers' Conference, 1980, 1981, 1982; grants from New York State Creative Arts Public Service and New York State Council for the Arts, 1981, 1982.

WRITINGS:

A Woman's Book of Strength, Perigee Books (New York), 1995.
A Woman's Book of Power: Dancing the Divine Feminine, Perigee Books, 1997.

WORK IN PROGRESS: House of Bones, on home remodeling without contractors, completion expected in 1998.

SIDELIGHTS: Karen Andes told *CA:* "I've discovered that I can't just write books. I have to *live* them. It isn't enough to theorize. I am a dancer and athlete, after all. I have to experience these books through my cells, bones, and flesh before even I know what I am searching for or talking about. This is somewhat exhausting, but that is the only way I know that works.

"I started as a fledgling novelist, but my awful and mercifully unpublished two novels came out of my head and a need for approval. When I learned to sink deeper, first into my heart and then into my hips, new forms of writing began to spring forth. I am currently in mid-gush. I hope it lasts.

"My writing is not easy to categorize. In book stores I'm logged under Fitness, Dance, Women's Studies, Spirituality, and soon Home Improvement. I probably have the only book on weight training with poetry in it. My book on sacred dance blends history, mythology, religion, spirituality, fitness, sex, and the two hemispheres of the brain—and a dance form based on belly dance, tai chi, ballet, body building, and sacred geometry. I guess you could say I'm eclectic. My book on the house my husband and I built in Marin County, California, combines the how-to's of construction, storytelling, and insights into one highly tested marriage. One thread that runs throughout my writing is finding the sacred in everyday events. I am

also very much a feminist, not just in the modern sense, but in the archetypal sense. I believe in a female sacred force, and I wrote a book about it. I write to inspire myself and other women to bring this out.

"I'm not sure where my writing 'comes from.' I am convinced there is a much smarter writer than me tapping the keys. My job is to go to the keyboard and collaborate. I don't write books for specific markets. I write them for me and try to make them readable. Every word that goes out of my office has to pass the 'read-aloud test.' My first drafts are messy and explosive. I like to break rules, but I also like structure. Writing teachers to whom I am indebted include the late John Gardner and Stanley Elkin, also John Irving and Tim O'Brien—all teachers, supporters, friends from the Bread Loaf Writers' Conference."

*   *   *

ANNIKOVA, Galina
  See DUTKINA, Galina (Borisovna)

*   *   *

ARAX, Mark 1956-

PERSONAL: Born in 1956; father's name, Ara (a bar owner).

ADDRESSES: Office—Los Angeles Times, Times Mirror Co., Times Mirror Sq., Los Angeles, CA 90028.

CAREER: Writer. Has worked as a reporter for the *Baltimore Evening Sun* and the *Los Angeles Times.*

WRITINGS:

In My Father's Name: A Family, a Town, a Murder, Simon & Schuster (New York), 1996.

SIDELIGHTS: "On a cold January night in Fresno in 1972," journalist Mark Arax writes in his book *In My Father's Name: A Family, a Town, a Murder,* "when the tangerine tree in our backyard was pure sugar and the air smelled smoky and was full of fog, two white men in their early twenties walked into my father's nightclub wearing gloves. . . . They ordered two draft beers, played a game of eight-ball that took them past the open door of his office, left, returned 10 minutes later and, without provocation or a demand for money, shot him to death." Arax's book has attracted critical attention for its depiction of his investigation of the murder of his father Ara and of his coming to terms with his own feelings. The crime—committed when Arax was only 15—had never been officially solved, but Arax managed to pin down the murderers and discovered that they had links to local organized crime figures. "This narrative of his father's life and death (and his own pervasive sorrow and longing)," declares Kathleen Hughes in *Booklist,* "is both electrifying in its intensity and heartbreaking in its raw emotion."

One of the most intriguing factors in Arax's narrative is his rediscovery of his father. "Through high school and college and a career in journalism at the *Baltimore Evening Sun* and the *Los Angeles Times,* I never stopped fantasizing about revenge, even as the questions became more tangled," he writes in *In My Father's Name.* "How could my father move so easily between worlds, the Little League diamond by day and the bar and its underworld figures by night? What side was he on and what did I, his oldest child, owe him?" The journalist learns in the process of his investigation that his father—although weak in some ways and forceful in others—was at heart a good man who spoke out against corruption, drug dealing, and prostitution in Fresno. "He confirmed that his father was a good man," declared *Library Journal* contributor Sandra K. Lindheimer, "and he forced his uncle Navo to acknowledge that some of his closest friends were responsible for Ara's death."

Arax also finds links between the Armenian American community in California and the history of the Armenian American immigrant community. Many Armenians moved to the United States in the early twentieth century in order to escape Turkish or Russian persecution. In the U.S., they met with strong anti-Armenian feelings that left them isolated and encouraged the growth of criminal networks along with immigrants of Italian, Mexican and German descent. They also brought with them their family feuds. "There had already been . . . three complexly motivated murders in the Arax family before Ara's," explained Rosellen Brown in the *New York Times Book Review,* "two of them in the old country." The sense of lawlessness fostered by the lawlessness of the Fresno area—combined with the laxity of the local police force—helped create an atmosphere in which Ara's attempts to clean up illegal activities in his town were doomed to failure.

Critics praised Mark Arax's book for its depiction not only of his father and the circumstances surrounding his murder, but also for its relentlessly honest description of how the crime affected his own life. "What finally makes *In My Fathers Name* so compelling (and exhausting)," Brown declared, "is the spectacle, both courageous and off-putting, of a young man eaten alive by his ignorance and others' indifference. He lets no one off the hook, allows no silences; he pursues and provokes; for all his bravery, he admits that he must have been an obnoxious presence for many years." Throughout the book, Brown maintained, "Arax has learned at least as much about himself, both good and bad, as he has about his father."

BIOGRAPHICAL/CRITICAL SOURCES:

BOOKS

Arax, Mark, *In My Father's Name: A Family, a Town, a Murder,* Simon & Schuster, 1996.

PERIODICALS

Booklist, February 1, 1996, p. 900.
Library Journal, January, 1996, p. 118.
Los Angeles Times, February 4, 1996.
New York Times Book Review, March 17, 1996, p. 9.
Publishers Weekly, December 4, 1995, p. 48.*

*   *   *

ARCHBOLD, Rick   1950-

PERSONAL: Born in 1950.

ADDRESSES: Agent—c/o Warner Books, Inc., Time & Life Bldg., 9th Floor, 1271 Avenue of the Americas, New York, NY 10020.

CAREER: Journalist.

WRITINGS:

(With Eugene Whelan) *Whelan: The Man in the Green Stetson,* Irwin Publishing (Toronto), 1986.
(With Robert D. Ballard) *The Discovery of the Titanic,* introduction by Walter Lord, illustrations by Ken Marschall, Warner Books (New York, NY), 1987.

(With Richard Earle and David Imre) *Your Vitality Quotient: The Clinically Proven Program that Can Reduce Your Body Age—and Increase Your Zest for Life,* Warner Books, 1989.

Robert Bateman: An Artist in Nature, Random House (New York, NY), 1990.

(With Audrey McLaughlin) *A Woman's Place: My Life and Politics,* Macfarlane Walter & Ross (Toronto), 1992.

(With Ballard) *Lost Ships of Guadalcanal,* Warner Books, 1993.

JUVENILE

(With Ballard) *The Discovery of the Bismarck,* introduction by Ludovic Kennedy, illustrations by Ken Marschall, Warner Books (New York, NY), 1990.

(With Ballard) *The Lost Wreck of the Isis,* Scholastic/Madison Press (New York, NY), 1990.

(With Ballard) *Exploring the Bismarck,* Scholastic (New York, NY), 1991.

SIDELIGHTS: Canadian journalist Rick Archbold established his career in the 1980s and 1990s as author and coauthor of nonfiction books on subjects ranging from Canadian politics to the search for sunken ships. His first achievement, 1986's *Whelan: The Man in the Green Stetson,* is the autobiography of the Canadian politician Eugene Whelen. The book was rendered from tape recordings, and according to Oliver Bertin of Toronto's *Globe and Mail,* Archbold wrote the text while giving "full rein to Whelan's personality." Whelan was a colorful and controversial figure in Canadian politics, known for wearing a green Stetson hat and adopting a rustic manner, which served him well as Member of Parliament for a rural constituency. A member of the Liberal Party, he became Minister of Agriculture in 1972 and then launched an unsuccessful bid for party leadership. Later in his career, and after his resignation, he became keenly interested in trying to solve problems of Third World agriculture.

In 1987, Archbold began a long-lasting collaboration with marine geologist Robert D. Ballard with the book *The Discovery of the Titanic.* Ballard was the man who found the legendary sunken ocean liner on September 1, 1985, after repeated attempts beginning in 1977. Exploring the wreck, he formed a theory about the cause of the sinking. The collision with the iceberg, in the words of *Washington Post Book World* reviewer Duncan Spencer, "popped a series of rivets between the iron plates that formed the skin of these prewelding ships. A long seam only three-quarters of an inch wide allowed the water to pour in so that the 'watertight' bulkheads were soon overtopped." Spencer adds that while the captain of the *Titanic*'s motives for steering into an icefield remain unknown, the book "has given us roundness and an end to one of the world's unforgettable soap operas."

Archbold teamed with specialists in a different field, that of medicine, to produce the 1989 *Your Vitality Quotient: The Clinically Proven Program that Can Reduce Your Body Age—and Increase Your Zest for Life.* His coauthors were Dr. Richard Earle, cofounder of the Canadian Institute of Stress, and Dr. David Imre, a back specialist. The authors' thesis, as recounted by Judith Viorst in the *New York Times Book Review,* is that "prolonged periods of high stress can weaken our immune system, that without a strong immune system aging is accelerated and that therefore the way we handle stress determines just how rapidly we age." In this book stress victims are classified into six types: Speed Freak; Basket Case; Cliff Walker; Drifter; Worry Wart; Loner. The volume also discusses five "Vital Life Skills," which are aimed at coping with stress: Values/Goal Clarification; High-Performance Nutrition; Effective Relaxation; Self-Affirming Communication; Essential Exercise. Expressing some doubts about the new-age style in which this and similar books make their claims, Viorst nevertheless admitted, "there's a lot in them that makes sense from even the most conservative point of view."

Archbold's later coauthorships have further explored familiar subject areas. With Ballard, he has written more about sunken ships in *Lost Ships of Guadalcanal,* and for the juvenile audience *The Discovery of the Bismarck, The Lost Wreck of the Isis* and *Exploring the Bismarck.* In 1990 Archbold solely produced the biography *Robert Bateman: An Artist in Nature.* And in 1992 Archbold helped another Canadian politician, Audrey McLaughlin, the New Democratic Party member of the House of Commons, to write an autobiography titled *A Woman's Place: My Life and Politics.*

BIOGRAPHICAL/CRITICAL SOURCES:

PERIODICALS

Globe and Mail (Toronto), October 18, 1986.
New York Times Book Review, December 27, 1987, p. 19; April 9, 1989, pp. 30-31.
Washington Post Book World, November 6, 1987.*

ARCHER, Nathan 1958-

PERSONAL: Born July 25, 1958, in New York, NY; son of Samuel S. and Mary (Humphrey) Archer. *Education:* Princeton University, A.B., 1979. *Politics:* "Vague." *Religion:* "Even vaguer." *Avocational interests:* "Guns, cars, women."

ADDRESSES: Home—North Reading, MA; fax 301-990-9395. *E-mail*—N.Archer@ssf.net. *Agent*—Russell Galen, Scovil Chichak Galen, 381 Park Ave. S., New York, NY 10036.

CAREER: U.S. Government, Chicago, IL, intelligence analyst, 1979-92; writer, 1992—.

WRITINGS:

Star Trek: Voyager; Ragnarok, Pocket Books (New York City), 1995.
Star Trek: Deep Space Nine, Valhalla, Pocket Books, 1995.
Predator: Concrete Jungle, Bantam (New York City), 1995.
Mars Attacks: Martian Deathtrap, Del Rey (New York City), 1996.
Predator: Cold War, Bantam, 1997.

SIDELIGHTS: Nathan Archer told *CA:* "I always thought, when I was a kid, that writing science fiction looked like about the most fun in the world. When I grew up, I did the normal thing and got a real job instead. A writing career just didn't look practical. When I got laid off, I figured it couldn't hurt to try writing. A college classmate was a writer. I asked him for help, and he put me in touch with a couple of editors. I submitted the material and, hey, it worked. I doubt I'll ever get rich, but writing sure is fun! I never got to shoot anyone or blow anything up in my old job, and now I do it on paper all the time!"

*   *   *

ARNOLD, Edwin L(ester Linden) 1857-1935

PERSONAL: Born in May 14, 1857, in Swanscombe, Kent, England; died March 1, 1935; son of Sir Edwin Arnold (a writer); married Constance Boyce (marriage ended); married Jessie Brighton, 1919; children: (first marriage) one daughter. *Education:* Attended Cheltenham College.

CAREER: Writer. Cattle breeder in Scotland, then worked in forestry in Travancore, India in late 1870s; *Daily Telegraph,* London, staff member, until 1908.

WRITINGS:

FANTASY NOVELS

The Wonderful Adventures of Phra the Phoenician, 3 vols., Chatto and Windus (London), 1890, published in the United States, 1 vol., Harper (New York), 1890.
Lepidus the Centurion: A Roman of To-day, Cassell (London), 1901, Crowell (New York), 1902.
Lieut. Gullivar Jones: His Vacation, Brown Langham (London), 1905, Arno Press (New York), 1975, originally published in the United States as *Gulliver of Mars,* Ace (New York), 1964.

SHORT STORIES

The Story of Ulla and Other Tales, Longman (London and New York), 1895.

NOVEL

The Constable of St. Nicholas, Chatto and Windus, 1894.

OTHER

A Summer Holiday in Scandinavia, Sampson Low (London), 1877.
On the Indian Hills; or, Coffee-Planting in Southern India, 2 vols., Sampson Low, 1881.
Editor, *The Opium Question Solved, by Anglo-Indian,* Partridge (London), 1882.
Coffee: Its Cultivation and Profit, Whittingham (London), 1886.
Bird Life in England, Chatto and Windus, 1887.
England as She Seems, Being Selections from the Notes of an Arab Hadji, Warne (London), 1888.
The Soul of the Beast, P.R. Macmillan (London), 1960.

Contributor to periodicals, including the *Idler.*

SIDELIGHTS: From his father, who made an extensive study of Eastern religion and culture, Edwin L. Arnold obtained a strong interest in the idea of reincarnation and the notion of karma (the doctrine that every living being is heir to the accumulated effects of the soul's actions during previous incarnations). Arnold's first karmic romance was *The Wonderful*

Adventures of Phra the Phoenician, whose eponymous hero recalls a series of past "awakenings" in different eras of British history. His memories of youth are vague but he remembers having come to Britain as a merchant-adventurer, having bought a native bride named Blodwen from pirates. He is subsequently offered as a human sacrifice by Druids when the Romans invade, but a magical tattoo given to him by his witch-wife enables him to return periodically to serve as a soldier of fortune in various defenses of right and the realm. He witnesses the ultimate withdrawal of the Romans, is involved in opposition to the Norman invasion of 1066, fights at the Battle of Crecy and befriends an Elizabethan scientist who is trying to build a steam engine.

In the course of these various reincarnations Phra meets several women highly reminiscent of his beloved, her spirit seemingly being inextricably linked to his. As the novel ends he is attempting to secure a more permanent reunion with her beyond the earth. The florid mock-archaic style in which the story is told has relegated the novel to the status of a period-piece, but it was widely read and enjoyed in its own day, when its central motif enjoyed considerable fashionability.

Lepidus the Centurion: A Roman of To-day is the story of a young Englishman who discovers a Roman tomb in which Lepidus, a nephew of the emperor Vespasian, has long lain in suspended animation. The story has comic elements concerned with the virile Romans adaptation to Victorian life, but it is primarily a psychological melodrama. The two main characters are fragmentary aspects of a single soul, which come into conflict over the love of a woman. Like Phra, Lepidus commits suicide when he seems to have lost the prize, but his death somehow allows the hero to become complete for the first time, much as Rutherford becomes complete following the dream-revelation that he was descended from the true heir to his fortune as well as the false claimant.

Arnold's final fantasy novel, *Lieut. Gullivar Jones: His Vacation,* has attracted a good deal of interest from some modern readers by virtue of its intriguing similarities to the Martian fantasies of Edgar Rice Burroughs. In Arnold's swashbuckling traveller's tale, Gullivar Jones—an American naval officer temporarily frustrated in his desire to marry by virtue of his lack of means—is whisked away to Mars by magic carpet and sides with the decadent inheritors of an ancient civilization, who are trying to defend the remnants of their culture against marauding barbar-

ians. He saves the life of a princess of their race and then embarks on a quest to rescue her when she is given as a tribute to the barbarian king. He encounters many natural marvels before rescuing the princess, but his eventual success in this mission is inadequate to turn the tide of Martian history. The implacability of this fate is revealed in a final unfortunate confrontation with the prophetic globe of destiny, whose judgment is sufficiently dire to force Jones's return to earth, where he is reunited with his prosaic fiancee.*

* * *

ASH, Constance (Lee) 1950-

PERSONAL: Born in 1950; married to Ned Sublette (a musician).

ADDRESSES: Agent—c/o Publicity Director, Ace Publishing, 200 Madison Ave., New York, NY 10016.

CAREER: Writer.

WRITINGS:

FANTASY NOVELS

The Horsegirl, Ace (New York), 1988.
The Stalking Horse, Ace, 1990.
The Stallion Queen, Ace, 1992.

SIDELIGHTS: According to the many-worlds theory of Quantum Physics, there are numerous parallel dimensions surrounding us in every direction. Each choice we make in life, every time we go one way rather than another, a dimension is created in which an alternate self chose the other path. In her fantasy novels about Glennys the Stallion Queen, Constance Ash has created a dimension fairly close to ours, but far enough away to make it a little peculiar to our sensibilities. In volume one, *The Horsegirl,* Glennys is a child of eleven, living in a community of farmers who vaguely resemble a cross between the Amish, Mormons and Islamites. The religion of her world is divided; the wealthy and sophisticated worship Eve, the First Mother, the Mother of Creation, who found her first baby in the wilderness with the assistance of a horse. Glennys's people, The Alaminites, worship Alam, the first man.

Glennys is doomed from the beginning not to fit into this world. Though she doesn't know this, she is really the bastard of the local Baron, who apprentices her to his stablemaster when his son discovers her "horse sense," a power some women possess to communicate psychically with horses. This is a civilization that loves horses immensely, except for the Alaminites, who believe horses are ministers of evil. From the time Glennys leaves her farm for a better life in the Baron's house, her own people hate her. They hate the Baron and anyone who doesn't follow their own beliefs, and before the book finishes they manage to murder him. His plantation is destroyed, and Glennys goes to the city of St. Lucien to make her way on her own. Her mother wants her to return to the farm, but Glennys knows she can never live within the twisted community of her birth.

In volume two, *The Stalking Horse,* Glennys starts a new life in St. Lucien, where she is training to be a ballet dancer. Glennys is hired by the Queen's Theatre to train horses for the ballet, and she is joined in St. Lucien by another Alaminite girl, Thea, who is a healer. In the course of the book Glennys falls in love with Jonathan, a court musician, and becomes embroiled in a war between the King of Nolan and some nobles who want his throne for his inept brother. They finally kill the king, and the Alaminites go to war against the nobles, led by a truly crazy "Messiah" figure named Hans, who wants to marry Thea. She keeps running from him, and fortunately he never gets her.

Glennys puts herself under the protection of one of the nobles who is not involved in the conspiracy, Duke Albany. He buys her a lot of land out in the Saquave desert, where the horses are bred. By the end of the book the kingdom is in such chaos that Glennys, Thea, her half-brother Hengst, her mother Stella, two sisters and a large group of followers head into the desert to found Albany City.

By the opening of volume three, *The Stallion Queen,* twenty years have passed. Albany City (also known as Hometown to the residents) is a thriving if poor settlement, and Glennys, the acknowledged Stallion Queen, has made an alliance with most of the desert tribes. The kingdom is in chaos under the rule of the useless King Roald, and one day the real king, Leon II, now a man, shows up in Albany looking for refuge. Glennys takes him in, but the Hometowners are confronted with a terrible evil lurking near them in the mountains: the Alaminites following Hans have built a town called Silver City, surrounded by stone

walls, and they are systematically decimating the soil through mining and strip-logging, stealing women from Hometown and the tribes, and attempting to destroy the whole desert.

When Glennys's adopted daughter Cameron is kidnapped and given to two Alaminite brothers as a wife, it triggers a war for control of the desert and, ultimately, all of the kingdom. Right triumphs but not until after much bloodshed and destruction, caused by the Alaminites and the nobles who don't want Leon on the throne.*

*   *   *

ASIMOW, Michael 1939-

PERSONAL: Surname is pronounced "A-za-moe"; born July 22, 1939, in Los Angeles, CA; son of William (a certified public accountant) and Frieda (Miller) Asimow; married, December 18, 1983; wife's name, Barbara (a fundraiser); children: Daniel, Ian Lennard, Paul, Hillary Lennard, Courtney Lennard. *Ethnicity:* Caucasian. *Education:* University of California, Los Angeles, B.S., 1961; University of California, Berkeley, J.D., 1964. *Politics:* Democrat. *Religion:* Jewish. *Avocational interests:* Tennis, old movies, gardening.

ADDRESSES: Home—1330 Longworth Dr., Los Angeles, CA 90049. *Office*—Law School, University of California, Los Angeles, CA 90095-1476; fax 310-825-6023. *E-mail*—Asimow@law.ucla.edu. *Agent*—Angela Rinaldi, 2965 Motor Ave., Los Angeles, CA 90064.

CAREER: Irell & Manella, Los Angeles, CA, associate, 1964-66; University of California, Los Angeles, professor of law, 1967—, associate dean of Law School, 1992-93. Visiting professor at Stanford University, 1972, University of Michigan, 1984, Duke University, 1992, and University of the Witwatersrand, 1995. Loeb & Loeb, counsel, 1986-91; Bet Tzedek Legal Services, volunteer attorney, 1993—; AME Church-Temple Isaiah, founder of Public Counsel Legal Service Program, 1993, supervising attorney, 1993—. Insurance Commissioner's Task Force on Unfair Insurance Industry Practices, chairperson, 1991-93; Legislative Advisory Committee to Revise Procedures of the California Public Utility Commission, member, 1994. Jewish Community Foundation, member of board of trustees, 1989-93.

MEMBER: American Bar Association (member of council, Administrative Law and Regulatory Practice Section, 1990-95), Amnesty International (chairperson of Lawyers' Adoption Group, 1980-82), Common Cause (member of national governing board, 1985-91), California Common Cause (chairperson, 1983-85).

AWARDS, HONORS: Jeremiah Award, Los Angeles Jewish Federation, 1996, for creating a legal service clinic in south central Los Angeles.

WRITINGS:

Advice to the Public from Federal Administrative Agencies, Matthew Bender (New York), 1973.
(With Arthur Bonfield) *State and Federal Administrative Law,* West Publishing (St. Paul, MN), 1989, supplements, 1993, 1997.
(With Paul Bergman) *Reel Justice: The Courtroom Goes to the Movies,* Andrews & McMeel (Kansas City, MO), 1996.

Contributor to books, including *Federal Taxation of Income, Estates, and Gifts,* four volumes, Warren, Gorham & Lamont (Boston, MA), 1983; *California Practice Guide: Family Law,* Rutter Group, 1985, with annual supplements; and *Purchase and Sale of Real Property,* Rutter Group, 1995. Contributor to law journals, including *Tax Lawyer, Law and Contemporary Problems, Administrative Law Review,* and *Tax Law Review.*

WORK IN PROGRESS: Research for a new edition of *Reel Justice.*

SIDELIGHTS: Michael Asimow told *CA:* "Although I have written many books and articles intended for lawyers or law students, *Reel Justice: The Courtroom Goes to the Movies* is the first book I have written for the general public. Paul Bergman and I wrote it when we discovered that there were no guidebooks to the wonderful world of courtroom movies. Filmmakers have made trial stories since the dawn of motion pictures, and the genre is as popular today as ever.

"Our purpose in writing this book was largely to have fun, although we hope that it will be successful in the market. Both of us love the law and the movies, especially the old ones. Having the opportunity to watch well over a hundred trial films, research them,

and write about them was one of the most enjoyable professional experiences I've ever had.

"Our goal was to rank the movies (on our one-to-four gavel scale) to help readers select the best ones. Then we tried to answer all the questions a viewer would ask. What is circumstantial evidence, and what is wrong with it? When should the defendant take the stand, as unfortunately happened in *The Paradine Case* or *Knock on Any Door?* When can you put animals on trial, as in *The Advocate?* What is an irresistible impulse or a war crime (*Anatomy of a Murder* or *Judgment at Nuremberg*)? Did the lawyers in *Class Action* or *The Verdict* act unethically? If the movie is based on a real trial, like *Inherit the Wind* or *In the Name of the Father,* how closely did the filmmakers stick to the truth?

"We hope the readers will enjoy our book, be informed by it, have a few laughs, and find some wonderful trial films to rent next Friday night when they have the yen for a tasty cross-examination along with their microwave popcorn."

*   *   *

AWWAD, Tawfiq Yusuf 1911-1988

PERSONAL: Born November 28, 1911, in Bhirsaf, Lebanon; killed during the Lebanese Civil War, 1988. *Ethnicity:* Lebanese. *Education:* Studied at St. Joseph's University (Beirut), c. 1923.

CAREER: Writer and diplomat. Worked as a journalist until 1946; Lebanese Government, consul to Argentina, 1946-75.

AWARDS, HONORS: Best play, Society's Book's Friends (Lebanon), for *Al-sa'ih wa-al-turjuman;* honored as a leading figure in world literature by the United Nations Educational, Scientific, and Cultural Organization (UNESCO), 1974.

WRITINGS:

Al-sabi al-a'raj (short stories; title means "The Lame Boy"), [Lebanon], 1936.
Qamis al-suf, [Lebanon], 1937.
Al-raghif (novel; title means "A Loaf of Bread"), [Lebanon], 1939.
Al-'adhara, [Lebanon], 1944.

Al-sa'ih wa-al-turjuman (play; title means "The Tourist and the Interpreter"), [Lebanon], 1962.

Fursan al-kalam, [Lebanon], 1963, Maktabat Lubnan (Beirut), 1980.

Ghubar al-ayyam, [Lebanon], 1963.

Tawahin Bayrut (novel; title means "Treadmills of Beirut"), [Lebanon], 1972, translation by Leslie McLoughlin published as *Death in Beirut: A Novel,* Heinemann Educational (London), 1976.

Qawafil al-zaman (poems; title means "Caravans of Time"), [Lebanon], 1973.

Matar al-saqi' wa-qisas ukhra, Maktabat Lubnan, 1981.

Hasad al-'umr, Maktabat Lubnan, 1984.

Mansiyyat (prose poem; title means "Forgotten Pieces"), [Lebanon], 1985.

SIDELIGHTS: Although his appointment as a Lebanese diplomat in his thirties prompted him to refrain from publishing the majority of his writings for many years, Tawfiq Yusuf Awwad is considered to be perhaps the most important modern Lebanese writer. His works have been heralded for both their social and literary import; they address significant issues of social reform and have established new narrative techniques within the framework of Arab literature. While Awwad's publications are relatively few in number, they include poetry, drama, short fiction, and novels.

Educated at St. Joseph's University in Beirut, Awwad spent his early years working as a journalist. He was also active on the literary scene; his early literary efforts included a collection of short stories, *Al-sabi al-a'raj* (1936), and the novel *Al-raghif,* published in 1939. These works established Awwad's characteristic focus on themes of corruption and exploitation, emerging modern values, the status of women in Arab society, and Arab nationalism. While also translating two French novels into Arabic, Awwad would decline to put more than his initials on a product that was not completely his own.

When Awwad was named Lebanese consul to Argentina in 1946, he gave up publishing for a period of eighteen years. However, he did not stop writing and,

after working as diplomat in Lebanon for many years, he published the play *Al-sa'ih wa-al-turjuman* in 1962. Awwad's later work, the novel *Tawahin Bayrut,* would prove to be one of the author's most widely read works. Translated into German and English (under the title *Death in Beirut: A Novel*), it has been called "probably the most accomplished product of modern Lebanese literature" by Ernst Rose in *World Literature Today.* The story of Tamima Nassour, a young female student living in Beirut, *Death in Beirut* deftly deals with the personal struggles of the protagonist as well as the larger political and cultural upheaval that followed the Six-Day War of 1967. 'Abd al-Jabbar 'Abbas remarks in a review for *Al Adab* that the book "is both original and masterful. It combines two elements in one work: the novel as a stimulating work of creative imagination and a faithful historical document supported by citations that summarize the most significant features of modern Lebanese thought." *Death in Beirut* would take on added significance in 1975, when the social unrest it depicted accelerated into civil war in Lebanon. Awwad retired from the diplomatic service in 1975 and produced a handful of new works, including the experimental prose poem *Mansiyyat* in 1985. He died in 1988, a casualty of the last years of the fifteen-year-long Lebanese Civil War.

BIOGRAPHICAL/CRITICAL SOURCES:

BOOKS

Allen, Roger, *The Arabic Novel: An Historical and Critical Approach,* Syracuse University Press, 1982, pp. 52-55.

Allen, Roger, editor, *Modern Arabic Literature,* Ungar (New York City), 1987, pp. 61-65.

PERIODICALS

Al-Adab, February, 1957, pp. 13-15; March, 1973, p. 41.

Journal of Arabic Literature, Volume 14, 1983, pp. 81-82.

World Literature Today, autumn, 1977, p. 675; spring, 1984, p. 321.*

B

BACA, Murtha

PERSONAL: Education: University of California, Los Angeles, B.A. (summa cum laude), 1973, M.A., 1975, Ph.D., 1978.

ADDRESSES: Home—6932 Cantaloupe Ave., Van Nuys, CA 91405. *Office*—Getty Information Institute, 401 Wilshire Blvd., Suite 1100, Santa Monica, CA 90401; fax 310-451-5570. *E-mail*—mbaca@getty.edu.

CAREER: University of California, Los Angeles, lecturer in Italian, 1978-79; freelance editor and translator, 1979—; University of Southern California, Los Angeles, visiting assistant professor of Italian, 1984-85; University of California, Los Angeles, assistant director of Armand Hammer Center for Leonardo Studies, 1986-87; Getty Information Institute, Santa Monica, CA, assistant archivist for Provenance Index, Getty Art History Information Program, 1988, name authority editor, Vocabulary Coordination Group, 1988-90, senior editor, Standards and Research Projects, 1988—.

MEMBER: College Art Association of America, Visual Resources Association, Art Libraries Society/North America.

AWARDS, HONORS: ARLIS Award of Merit, Art Libraries Society, 1996.

WRITINGS:

(Editor with James M. Bower) *Union List of Artist Names,* G. K. Hall (New York), 1994.

Guest editor, *Visual Resources,* 1996.

TRANSLATOR

T. Pignatti, *Canaletto,* Barron's (Woodbury, NY), 1979.

P. Bianconi, *Breughel,* Barron's, 1979.

U. Ruggeri, *Duerer,* Barron's, 1979.

A. Chatelet, *Van Eyck,* Barron's, 1980.

R. Dalisi, *Gaudi: Furniture and Objects,* Barron's, 1980.

Janus, *Man Ray: The Photographic Image,* Barron's, 1980.

C. Pedretti, A. Vezzosi, and others, *The Leonardo Collection of the Countess of Behague at Vinci Castle,* Johnson Reprint (New York), 1982.

Leonardo da Vinci, *Codex on the Flight of Birds,* edited by A. Marinoni, Johnson Reprint, 1982.

da Vinci, *Codex Trivulzianus,* edited by A. M. Brizio, Johnson Reprint, 1983.

da Vinci, *Manuscript C, Manuscript H, Manuscript M, Manuscript I, Manuscript L,* edited by Marinoni, Giunti-Barbera (Florence, Italy), 1987-89.

Gastronomical Guide to Italy, Le Guide dell'Espresso (Rome, Italy), 1989, 3rd edition, 1992.

Lauro Martines, editor, *An Italian Renaissance Sextet: Six Tales in Historical Context,* Marsilio (New York), 1994.

Contributor to periodicals. Translator of the journal, *Academia Leonardo da Vinci,* 1988.

*   *   *

BAILEY, Robin W(ayne) 1952-

PERSONAL: Born August 2, 1952, in Kansas City, MO; married Diana Jean Piper, 1974. *Education:*

Northwest Missouri State University, B.S. (English), 1974, M.A. 1976.

ADDRESSES: Agent—Richard Curtis, 171 East 74th Street, New York, NY 10021.

CAREER: Writer.

WRITINGS:

FANTASY NOVELS

Frost, Pocket (New York), 1983.
Skull Gate (Frost series), Tor (New York), 1985.
Bloodsongs (Frost series), Tor, 1986.
Enchanter, Avon (New York), 1989.
The Lake of Fire, Bantam (New York), 1989.
Nightwatch, TSR (Lake Geneva, WI), 1990.
The Lost City of Zork, Avon, 1991.
Brothers of the Dragon, NEL (London), 1992, Roc (New York), 1993.
Straight on Till Mourning, NEL, 1993, published in the United States as *Flames of the Dragon,* Roc, 1994.
Triumph of the Dragon, Roc, 1994.

SIDELIGHTS: Robin W. Bailey's work is firmly in the tradition of quest fantasy. His first book, *Frost,* and its sequels follow the adventures of the eponymous heroine, a woman warrior who has lost her magical powers and been exiled because of a curse. The plot is enlivened by Frost's feisty personality, and by more moral ambiguity than might be expected from a story which revolves around a war between light and darkness.

Bailey's more recent books, *Brothers of the Dragon* and *Straight on Till Mourning,* are the first two parts of a new quest fantasy series. The action concerns the attempts of two brothers from this world, Eric and Robert Podlowsky, to defend Palenoc—an alternate, magical kingdom—from the ravages of both Shandal Karg, the Queen of the Dark Lands, and Keris Chaterit, the Lord of the Kingdoms of Night. The quest which faces Robert and Eric, however, is much less direct. The brothers are both martial-arts experts, though Scott is also a successful horror novelist, while Eric is an alcoholic mailman who considers himself a failure. Initially, they stumble into Palenoc, apparently by accident. Then it seems that Robert's friend Scott is somehow involved, even though Robert saw him die in New York. This involvement is kept pretty much in the background. Robert's main aim in Palenoc is to find Scott, whom he is convinced is still alive and in the power of Shandal Karg.

Brothers of the Dragon is mostly concerned with setting up the situation. It soon becomes clear that Robert looks like the Shaealuth, the incarnation of Or-dhamu—the organizing principle of the universe—that the people of Palenoc are expecting to redeem them. It is also clear to the reader, though never explicitly stated, that Scott would also fit this description. At the end of the novel one of their new allies kills Keris Chaterit. Robert returns to this world while Eric stays in Palenoc.

In *Straight on Till Mourning,* Robert has been accused of Eric's murder. The problem is swiftly dealt with, however, once he sends an old girlfriend, Katy, to retrieve Eric. Katy also elects to stay in Palenoc. The protagonists go off to plant a gem in a plain in the center of Chol-Hecate, one of the Dark Lands. They succeed, but only just, and at the end of the novel they have been split up, with each fearing the others dead.*

*   *   *

BARATTA, Joseph Preston   1943-

PERSONAL: Born June 24, 1943, in Manhattan, KS; son of Joseph John (an army officer) and Beatrice Wood (a homemaker; maiden name, Preston) Baratta; married Gay Diane Singer (divorced, 1974); married Virginia Mary Swain, January 1, 1995. *Ethnicity:* "Italian and English." *Education:* St. John's College, B.A., 1969; Boston University, M.A., Ph.D., 1982. *Politics:* Democrat. *Religion:* Society of Friends (Quakers). *Avocational interests:* Bicycling, hiking, city government, the peace movement.

ADDRESSES: Home and office—218 Thorndike St., No. 102, Cambridge, MA 02141-1508; fax 617-225-2253.

CAREER: Center for Global Community and World Law, Cambridge, MA, co-director, 1994—. Boston College, instructor in international organization, 1994-95. Coalition for a Strong United Nations, founding member and chair of executive committee, 1994—; East Cambridge Planning Team, member; Cambridge Bicycle Committee, member. *Military service:* U.S. Marine Corps, 1962-65.

MEMBER: Society for the Study of Internationalism (director, 1989-94), American Historical Association, St. John's College Alumni Association.

AWARDS, HONORS: Grant from U.S. Institute of Peace, 1989.

WRITINGS:

The World Federalist Movement: A Collection of Mainstream Journals, Norman Ross Publishing (New York), 1989.
Human Rights: Improving U.N. Mechanisms for Compliance, U.S. Institute of Peace, 1990.
The United Nations System: Meeting the World Constitutional Crisis, Transaction Publishers (New Brunswick, NJ), 1995.

Contributor to books.

WORK IN PROGRESS: Report to Madison, Wilson, and Kennedy: A History of the Ideal of World Federal Government; research on international cooperation through the United Nations.

SIDELIGHTS: Joseph Preston Baratta told *CA:* "I became a historian of international diplomacy and organization, first, because I wished to understand why the United States, which was founded as a popular, self-governing republic devoted to protecting the liberty of its citizens, had become, by the latter half of the twentieth century, a world military power. Secondly, I hoped, if possible, to make an intellectual contribution, within the scope of my own personal power, to showing the way by which the United States (my country) could take the lead toward establishing a world at peace.

"I find that, in writing history, I must often change my mind; indeed, this is one of the delights of history. By analogy, I imagine that one of the occasions when others change their convictions is in the privacy of their own minds as they are reading a fair account of the past or of some contemporary issue. In an age of telecommunications, I still think books provide the best reasoning on any subject. Moreover, they lie there on the shelf, patiently waiting until the reader is curious enough to take them up. My motivation is to create a learning experience in any reader who truly wishes to know.

"I served a tour of duty in the U.S. Marine Corps. Although I was fortunate to escape the worst of war, I saw enough never to forget the horror and absurdity

of this continuing institution in human life. I cannot get it out of my head. At the height of the Vietnam war, I came across a slim book from Robert M. Hutchins's Center for the Study of Democratic Institutions: *A Constitution for the World.* Reading this book, I immediately understood that the reason wars continue is that we the people of the world have no constitution and no world laws to abolish war. I then undertook to write, not a theoretical work, but a history of practical efforts to establish wider unions to create peace. The European Community (now the European Union) is the best contemporary example. But someday humanity will have to summon the intelligence and the will to establish something like a constitutionally limited, democratic, world federal government. I think about this project and record my thoughts.

"Like any historian, most of my work is to find and gather the sources and then to reflect broadly upon them in order to write a coherent, engaging, and yet reasonably brief account. I need perfect quiet in order to write, and often I write the first draft in longhand, with a fountain pen. I almost touch the imagined reader with my hand. The rest is a very self-critical, almost ruthless process of revisions, deletions, and corrections. History is a professional activity, and it must meet the standard of objectivity. My ideal is truth."

* * *

BARBUSSE, Henri 1873-1935

PERSONAL: Born May 17, 1873, in Asnieres, France; died of pneumonia, August 30, 1935, in Moscow, U.S.S.R. (now Russia); son of Adrien (a journalist and playwright) and Annie (Benson) Barbusse; married the daughter of poet Catulle Mendes. *Education:* Graduated from the College Rollin, 1893. *Politics:* Communist.

CAREER: Worked at civil service jobs after college; journalist, editor, and author. Founder of Clarte, a passivist/communist organization; formed the Republican Association of Ex-Service Men in France; founder and editor of *Monde,* a left-wing newspaper, 1928-35. *Military service:* Served in the French military, 1893-94; served in the infantry of the French Army during World War I; mentioned in despatches and received the Croix de Guerre.

MEMBER: Revue de la Paix, Paix par le Droit, Clarte, Republican Association of Ex-Service Men in France.

AWARDS, HONORS: Won literary prizes in college; Prix Goncourt from the Academie Goncourt of France, 1916, for *Under Fire: The Story of a Squad.*

WRITINGS:

Pleureuses (poetry; title means "Hired Mourners"), Charpentier (Paris, France), 1895.

Les Suppliants (novel; title means "The Supplicants"), Charpentier, 1903.

L'Enfer (novel), Librairie Mondiale (Paris, France), 1908; translated by Edward O'Brien as *The Inferno,* Boni & Liveright (New York, NY), 1913; translated by John Rodker, Joiner & Steele (London, England), 1932.

Meissonier, Lafitte (Paris, France), 1911; translated by Frederick Taber Cooper, Stokes (New York, NY), 1912.

Nous autres (short stories), Charpentier, 1913; translated by Fitzwater Wray as *We Others,* Dutton (New York, NY), 1918.

Le Feu: Journal d'une escouade (novel), Flammarion (Paris, France), 1916; translated by Wray as *Under Fire: The Story of a Squad,* Dutton, 1917.

Clarte (novel), Flammarion, 1919; translated by Wray as *Light,* Dutton, 1919.

L'Illusion, Flammarion, 1919.

La Lueur dans l'abime (essays; title means, "The Light in the Abyss"), Editions Clarte (Paris, France), 1920.

Le Couteau entre les dents (essays; title means, "The Knife between the Teeth"), Editions Clarte, 1921.

Paroles d'un combattant: Articles et discours (1917-1920) (essays; title means "A Fighter's Words: Articles and Speeches [1917-1920]), Flammarion, 1921.

Quelques Coins du coeur, Editions Coins du Sablier (Geneva, Switzerland), 1921.

L'Etrangere, Flammarion, 1922.

Les Enchainements (short stories), Flammarion, 1925; translated by Stephen Haden Guest as *Chains* (two volumes), International Publishing (New York, NY), 1925.

Trois Films: Force—L'Au-dela—Le Crieur, Flammarion, 1926.

Les Bourreaux, Flammarion, 1926.

Jesus (nonfiction), Flammarion, 1927; translated by Solon Librescot, Macaulay (New York, NY), 1927.

Les Judas de Jesus (nonfiction), Flammarion, 1927.

Manifeste aux intellectuels, Les Ecrivains Reunis (Paris, France), 1927.

Faits divers, Flammarion, 1928; translated by Brian Rhys as *And I Saw It Myself,* Dutton, 1928; translation also published as *Thus and Thus,* Dent (London, England), 1929.

Voici ce qu'on fait de la Georgie (nonfiction), Flammarion, 1929.

Ce qui fut sera, Flammarion, 1930.

Elevation, Flammarion, 1930.

Russie, Flammarion, 1930; translated by Warre B. Wells as *One Looks at Russia,* Dent, 1931.

J'accuse, Bureau d'Editions (Paris, France), 1932.

Zola (biography), Gallimard (Paris, France), 1932; translated by Mary Balairdie Green and Frederick C. Green, Dent, 1932, Dutton, 1933.

Staline: Un Monde nouveau vu a travers l'homme (biography), Flammarion, 1935; translated by Vyvyan Holland as *Stalin: A New World as Seen Through One Man,* Macmillan (New York, NY), 1935.

Le Feu, journal d'une escouade, suivi du Carnet de guerre (novel and journal), edited by Pierre Paraf, Flammarion, 1965.

SIDELIGHTS: French journalist and author Henri Barbusse is remembered both for some of his literary efforts and his political commitment to the causes of pacifism and communism. His most famous work is probably his 1916 novel *Under Fire: The Story of a Squad,* which was inspired by his experiences in the French Infantry during World War I. A scathing indictment of the horror and senselessness of war, it garnered him France's prestigious Prix Goncourt in the year it was published. Barbusse devoted the rest of his career to advocating an end to war and better conditions for the working class. He formed pacifist organizations such as Clarte and the Republican Association of Ex-Service Men in France, and founded and edited the leftist newspaper *Monde.* Other literary efforts by Barbusse that have been translated into English include the novels *The Inferno* and *Light,* as well as the short fiction collection *We Others.* He also penned a work of biography and literary criticism about fellow French author and creative influence Emile Zola, and two books—*Jesus* and *Les Judas de Jesus*—which put forth his theory that the historical Jesus was really a political activist concerned with the condition of the common people.

Barbusse was born in 1873, in Asnieres, France. His mother was an Englishwoman; his father, a French journalist and playwright. During his years at the College Rollin in Paris, Barbusse performed extremely well and was deemed "brilliant," according to J. E. Flower in the *Dictionary of Literary Biography*. He won prizes for his literary and dramatic efforts during his schooling, and became a protege of the French symbolist poet Catulle Mendes, whose daughter he married. Barbusse's first published work, in fact, was an 1895 collection of symbolist-influenced poetry with the title *Pleureuses,* which name Flower translated as "the hired mourners." He followed *Pleureuses* with his first novel, *Les Suppliants,* which was somewhat autobiographical and still influenced by symbolist poetry.

The novel, however, which began to make Barbusse's literary name in France—and which was the first of his works to be translated into English—was his 1908 effort, *The Inferno.* This book's protagonist, a depressed, inhibited, but sex-obsessed man, discovers a hole in his hotel room wall, from which he spies on succeeding occupants of the adjoining chamber. Sights described include a woman undressing, lesbian sex, and a man dying of cancer. Lola Ridge, reviewing *The Inferno* in the *New Republic,* compared Barbusse to author Frank Swinnerton, and observed that "the Frenchman's creations are like naked spirits—spirits seen through the pale luminosity of that *I* that enfolds them like an aura." Martin Shuttleworth, discussing in *Punch* a much later English-language printing of the book, judged that Barbusse's pages assert that, "men are lonely and lost, but also that man is magnificent; that he carries his remedy within him." John Daniel in the *Spectator,* by contrast, thought the novel had not stood up well to time, lamenting that "what were breathtaking assertions against patriotism and Catholicism have gathered dust."

We Others, a collection of short fiction, saw print in France at about the same time that World War I began, but was not translated into English until after the war's end. John Manning Booker, critiquing the stories in the *New Republic,* mentioned a difference between French and English readers' sensibilities, and offered his opinion that the latter reader "meets in Barbusse a kind of pity that for him is even more of a depressant than a purgative, and therefore, distasteful. He turns away from it with the feeling that these stories of pity do not match experience."

Barbusse's *Under Fire,* however, was a story of pity which apparently did match experience. Though the author had already served in the French military during the 1890s, and though he was already quite strong in his pacifist convictions, he volunteered to serve in the infantry during World War I. During his time in combat and as a stretcher-bearer, he kept a journal, and wrote letters home to his wife. At first, Barbusse was hopeful, believing—like many others— that this was the war to end all wars. It was not long, however, before the filthy conditions and harrowing battles both darkened his attitude toward the war at hand, and deepened his belief that humanity must come together to put an end to all war. While still in the military, the novel Barbusse based on his more immediate writings about the war saw print. As the subtitle indicates, *Under Fire* tells of the various experiences of members of a French fighting squadron. The book met with almost immediate critical and popular success. "How far [his] interpretation of the common soldier's mind will be accepted by those for whom M. Barbusse speaks, I cannot say," pondered Stephen Gwynn in the monthly periodical, the *Nineteenth-Century.* "But this I do know . . . he does not and cannot . . . overstate the greatness and the obscurity of their sacrifice." Francis Hackett in the *New Republic* hailed *Under Fire* as "invincibly complete," and "great because it is able to encompass everything, even the necessity of living by dying." Robert Herrick in the *Dial* lauded it as "the most searching, the most revealing statement of what modern war means both morally and physically." As for later estimations of the novel, Guessler Normand in the *Kentucky Romance Quarterly* referred to it as Barbusse's "masterpiece," further explaining that the author "was the first . . . to do what others were not sufficiently gifted to do, or who were too uncertain, fearful, or weak to express." Frank Field, in his *Three French Writers and the Great War: Studies in the Rise of Communism and Facism,* conversely labeled *Under Fire* "not the kind of book that can greatly impress the present-day reader." He did concede, however, "the visionary power that the novel still retains." Flower summed up *Under Fire* as "the best known and most influential French antiwar novel written during World War I."

Barbusse attempted to follow his success with *Under Fire* with another anti-war novel, *Light,* in 1919. Though *Light* was also partially set during World War I, the author was now more concerned with the ideologies of pacifism and communism than with realistically depicting war as he had done in his previous creation. Field assessed that the protagonist of *Light,* Simon Paulin, "is caught up on the First World War and although he is at first appalled by the brutality that he witnesses he eventually comes to realise that his experience has been a blessing in disguise." It teaches Paulin, according to Field, that "by uniting with his fellow soldiers in the struggle against militarism he can at last experience that sense of human brotherhood that had eluded him in the past." Jonathan King, in his piece for *The First World War in Fiction: A Collection of Critical Essays,* offered the point of view that in *Light,* "Barbusse allows [his] apocalyptic tone to get quite out of hand, merging it with a grandiose imagery and a religiosity which are no longer controlled by a firm documentary purpose. . . . The commitment to realism surrenders almost totally to prophetic pretensions." Flower concluded of *Light* that "the object of the book is to preach. As a result, the symbolism is too often naive . . . and Barbusse's authorial interference too obvious."

Barbusse worked predominantly on nonfiction after the publication of *Light.* He more openly advocated communism, and penned books about the Soviet Union and one of its dictators, Josef Stalin. Barbusse was on a visit to Moscow, in what was then the Soviet Union, when he came down with pneumonia and died in 1935.

BIOGRAPHICAL/CRITICAL SOURCES:

BOOKS

Dictionary of Literary Biography, Volume 65: *French Novelists, 1900-1930,* Gale, 1988.
Field, Frank, *Three French Writers and the Great War: Studies in the Rise of Communism and Fascism,* Cambridge University Press, 1975.
Klein, Holger, editor, *The First World War in Fiction: A Collection of Critical Essays,* Macmillan, 1976.

PERIODICALS

Dial, February 14, 1918, pp. 133-134.
Kentucky Romance Quarterly, Volume xxiv, number 4, 1977, pp. 449-459.
New Republic, October 27, 1917, pp. 358-359; September 28, 1918, pp. 262-263; September 3, 1919, pp. 146-148.
Ninteenth-Century, October, 1917, pp. 803-817.
Punch, July 27, 1966, p. 162.
Spectator, August 12, 1966, p. 210.*

—Sketch by Elizabeth Wenning

BARK, William (Carroll) 1908-1996

OBITUARY NOTICE—See index for *CA* sketch: Born December 10, 1908, in Tacoma, WA; died October 11, 1996, in Palo Alto, CA. Educator and author. Bark, a graduate of Stanford University, devoted much of his career to educating students at his alma mater. He began nearly four decades of teaching at Stanford, first as an instructor in history in 1936. After stints at Lawrence College and the University of Chicago, Bark returned to Stanford as an associate professor of history in 1947 and became a full professor ten years later. In 1974, he became a professor emeritus. His teaching career also included work as a member of the Carnegie Commission of Educational Inquiry and as senior research fellow at the Hoover Institute. His writings include *Origins of the Medieval World.* He was at work on a book at the time of his death entitled *Dionysius Exiguus and the Founding of the Middle Ages.*

OBITUARIES AND OTHER SOURCES:

BOOKS

Directory of American Scholars, Volume 1: *History,* 8th edition, R. R. Bowker (New York), 1982.

PERIODICALS

New York Times, October 27, 1996, sec. 1, p. 41.

*   *   *

BARLOW, Connie 1952-

PERSONAL: Born Constance C. Barlow in 1952, in Detroit, MI; daughter of Frederick and Helen (Chesley) Barlow. *Ethnicity:* "American." *Education:* Michigan State University, B.S. (zoology), 1974. *Religion:* "Religious naturalism." *Avocational interests:* "Restoration ecology and wilderness recovery."

ADDRESSES: Home—New York, NY. *Agent*—c/o MIT Press, 55 Haward St., Cambridge, MA 02142.

CAREER: Science writer.

MEMBER: Institute on Religion in an Age of Science (IRAS), Cenozoic Society, American Teilhard Association, International Society for the History, Philosophy, and Social Studies of Biology (ISHPSSB).

WRITINGS:

(Editor) *From Gaia to Selfish Genes: Selected Writings in the Life Sciences,* MIT Press (Cambridge, MA), 1991.

(Editor) *Evolution Extended: Biological Debates on the Meaning of Life,* MIT Press, 1994.

Contributor of essays to periodicals, including *Wild Earth* magazine.

WORK IN PROGRESS: Green Space, Green Time: The Way of Science, for Copernicus Books.

SIDELIGHTS: Connie Barlow has admitted to a childhood interest in science that was ultimately quashed by the reek of formaldehyde emanating from the dissection tray in biology class. However, as an adult, she returned to her love of biology after hearing a lecture by the scientist James Lovelock. With a new fervor for the topic, she set out to compile the thoughts of some of the greatest biologists of our time.

From Gaia to Selfish Genes: Selected Writings in the Life Sciences chronicles many divergent theories of life from the views of sociobiologist E. O. Wilson to Richard Dawkins' theory that "selfish" genes guide our actions. Stephen Young commented in *New Scientist* that "This is . . . a book with a number of different messages. Yet those messages are often so powerful—and the writing so persuasive—that somehow you long for them all to be true."

Barlow followed this volume with *Evolution Extended: Biological Debates on the Meaning of Life,* a sampling of famous scientists' thoughts on the theory of evolution. "In this compendium she traces their attempts to wrestle with the ineffable in order to find a larger meaning in their work," wrote Christopher Wills in *Nature.* "The ineffable wins, two falls out of three, but in general the evolutionists put up a brave battle." Mark Ridley, writing in *New Scientist,* concluded that "Barlow's selection is broad-ranging and well-balanced."

BIOGRAPHICAL/CRITICAL SOURCES:

PERIODICALS

Nature, June 6, 1991, p. 449; October 27, 1994.
New Scientist, September 14, 1991, p. 53; July 2, 1994, p. 38.
Times Educational Supplement, December 6, 1991.

BARNE, Kitty
See BARNE, Marion Catherine

* * *

BARNE, Marion Catherine   1883-1957
  (Kitty Barne)

PERSONAL: Born in 1883; died in 1957; married Eric Streatfeild. *Education:* Royal College of Music, London, England. *Avocational interests:* Musical activities for Girl Guides' Association.

CAREER: Writer of novels, nonfiction books, and plays, primarily for children. Also composed music. Worked in a hostel as a young adult. *Wartime service:* Women's Voluntary Service during World War II: assisted in the reception of juvenile evacuees from London to Sussex.

AWARDS, HONORS: Library Association (United Kingdom) Carnegie Medal, 1940, for *Visitors from London.*

WRITINGS:

FICTION FOR CHILDREN

Tomorrow, illustrated by Ethel King-Martyn, Hodder and Stoughton (London), 1912.
The Easter Holidays, illustrated by Joan Kiddell-Monroe, Heinemann (London), 1935; as *Secret of the Sandhills,* Dodd Mead (New York), 1949, Nelson (London), 1955.
Young Adventurers, illustrated by Ruth Gervis, Nelson, 1936.
She Shall Have Music, illustrated by Gervis, Dent (London), 1938, Dodd Mead, 1939.
Family Footlights, illustrated by Gervis, Dent, 1939, Dodd Mead, 1939.
Visitors from London, illustrated by Gervis, Dent, 1940, Dodd Mead, 1940.
May I Keep Dogs?, illustrated by Arnrid Johnston, Hamish Hamilton (London), 1941, Dodd Mead, 1942; as *Bracken My Dog,* Dent, 1949.
We'll Meet in England, illustrated by Steven Spurrier, Hamish Hamilton, 1942, Dodd Mead, 1943.
Three and a Pigeon, illustrated by Spurrier, Hamish Hamilton and Dodd Mead, 1944.
In the Same Boat, illustrated by Gervis, Dent, 1945, Dodd Mead, 1945.

Musical Honours, illustrated by Gervis, Dent, 1947, Dodd Mead, 1947.

Dusty's Windmill, illustrated by Marcia Lane Foster, Dent, 1949; as *The Windmill Mystery,* Dodd Mead, 1950.

Roly's Dogs, illustrated by Alice Molony, Dent, 1950; as *Dog Stars,* Dodd Mead, 1951.

Barbie, illustrated by Foster, Dent, 1952, Little Brown (Boston), 1969.

Admiral's Walk, illustrated by Mary Gurnat, Dent, 1953.

Rosina Copper, the Mystery Mare, illustrated by Alfons Purtscher, Evans (London), 1954, Dutton (New York), 1956, White Lion Publishers (London), 1976.

Cousin Beatie Learns the Fiddle, Blackwell (Oxford, England), 1955.

Tann's Boarders, illustrated by Jill Crockford, Dent, 1955.

Rosina and Son, illustrated by Foster, Dent, 1976, White Lion Publishers, 1976.

PLAYS

(With D. W. Wheeler) *Tomorrow,* Curwen (London), 1910.

(With Wheeler) *Winds,* music by Kitty Barne, illustrated by Lucy Barne, Curwen, 1912.

(With Wheeler) *Timothy's Garden,* illustrated by Lucy Barne, Curwen, 1912.

(With Wheeler) *Celandine's Secret,* illustrated by J. M. Saunders, Curwen, 1914.

Peter and the Clock, Curwen, 1919.

Susie Pays a Visit, Curwen, 1921.

The Amber Gate: A Pageant Play, Curwen, 1925.

Philemon and Baucis, Gowans and Gray (London) and Baker (Boston), 1926.

Madge: A Camp-Fire Play, Novello (London), 1928.

Adventurers: A Pageant Play, Deane (London), 1931, Baker, 1936.

(Adaptor) *The Grand Party,* based on the novel *Holiday House,* by Catherine Sinclair, in *The Theatre Window: Plays for Schools,* edited by W.T. Cunningham, Arnold (London), 1933.

Two More Mimes from Folk Songs: The Wraggle, Taggle Gipsies, O!; Robin-a-Thrush, Curwen, 1936.

They Made the Royal Arms, Baker, 1937.

Shilling Teas, Deane, 1938, Baker, 1938.

Days of Glory: A Pageant Play, Deane, 1946.

The "Local Ass": A Documentary Pageant Play for Girl Guides, Girl Guides' Association, 1947.

Also author of *The Lost Birthday,* Curwen.

FICTION AND MISCELLANEOUS

The Amber Gate, illustrated by Gervis, Nelson (London and New York), 1933.

Elizabeth Fry: A Story Biography, illustrated by Gervis, Methuen (London), 1933, Penguin (London), 1950.

Songs and Stories for Acting, illustrated by Gervis, Brown and Ferguson (Glasgow, Scotland), 1939.

Listening to the Orchestra, Dent, 1941, revised edition, 1946, Bobbs Merrill (Indianapolis), 1946.

Here Come the Girl Guides, Girl Guides' Association, 1947.

Introducing Handel, illustrated by Crockford, Dent, 1955, Roy (New York), 1957.

Introducing Mozart, illustrated by Crockford, Dent, 1955, Roy, 1957.

Introducing Schubert, illustrated by Crockford, Dent, 1957, Roy, 1957.

NOVELS FOR ADULTS

Mother at Large, Chapman and Hall (London), 1938.

While the Music Lasted, Chapman and Hall, 1943.

Enter Two Musicians, Chapman and Hall, 1944.

Duet for Sisters, Chapman and Hall, 1947.

Vespa, Chapman and Hall, 1950.

Music Perhaps, Chapman and Hall, 1957.

Many of Barne's writings for both children and adults have appeared under the name Kitty Barne.

SIDELIGHTS: A versatile writer for children and adults, Marion Catherine Barne enjoyed a prolific career that was unified by the subject of music, and secondarily by such subjects as animals and traditional English life. Her renown was at its height during World War II and the years surrounding it, when she was known as something of a pioneer in bringing realism to children's literature, a field which, to that point, had been largely the province of escapist adventure, romance, and mystery. Though Barne retained those nonrealistic elements in her work, she often presented them within realistic settings such as England during the blitz or Norway under Nazi occupation. The conflicts in her works, too, tended to be ones that many young readers might identify with, such as the question of whether or not to risk following an artistic career; and her treatment of adult characters, such as the father in her 1947 novel, *Musical Honours,* was notable for its mixing of positive and negative elements within a personality.

Having studied music as a child and having written and produced original dramas as early as elementary school, Barne undoubtedly had a sense of her calling from a very young age. Even so, however, she experienced a kind of struggle that many aspiring artists are familiar with: her early plays, though published, brought her little fame. It was when she turned to children's fiction in the late 1930's, perhaps at the urging of her husband's cousin, the popular children's writer Noel Streatfeild, that Barne's career took a marked upturn. Among the first of her novels for children was the 1935 volume *The Easter Holidays,* a mystery set in the Bristol countryside. On its republication in 1949 as *Secret of the Sandhills,* the *Saturday Review of Literature* commented that Barne's "skill in writing and her well-drawn characters lift what might have been just another mystery story out of the ordinary." *New York Times* reviewer Ellen Lewis Buell, on a similar note, said that "[a]s is not always the case in mystery stories, the characterization is incisively and amusingly drawn, and the background . . . is charming."

On first publication, however, it was the 1938 *She Shall Have Music* that won Barne her reputation. The story concerns the struggle of a young Irish girl, Karen, to follow her musical calling despite her family's lack of resources. Several reviewers at the time found the family "amusing and likable," to use the words of a reviewer in the *New York Times.* M. L. Becker, in *Books,* pointed out that the tale could be used as "a touchstone" by young readers who felt artistic callings themselves. Writing from the vantage point of later decades, however, Gary D. Schmidt, in the *Dictionary of Literary Biography,* commented with disfavor on the "fanciful" degree to which Karen's aspirations are gratified.

Barne's high point of official recognition came for the 1940 novel *Visitors from London,* the second in a series of books about a family named Farrar living on a Sussex farm named Steadings. The first volume in the series, the 1939 *Family Footlights,* had won praise for its "lightness of touch" from a critic in the *Times Literary Supplement,* and from Buell in the *New York Times* for the author's "faculty of writing about large families so that every member has a distinct and interesting personality" and of "assuming intelligence and humor" on the part of young readers. *Visitors from London* surpassed that volume both critically and commercially, in large part because of its gripping and realistic subject, the settlement of bombed-out London families in rural Britain during World War II. *Books's* Becker wrote that adults as well as children would enjoy the book; *Library Journal's* Marian Herr even worried that the book might be too mature for children; however, a reviewer in the *New Yorker* called it "perfect for family reading aloud," and Buell, in the *New York Times,* presented the novel as a children's equivalent of such adult-oriented home-front novels as *Mrs. Miniver.* The novel won the Carnegie Medal in 1940. Judging it retrospectively in 1989, in an article for *School Library Journal* on children's books about the World War II evacuations, Louise L. Sherman was less sanguine, finding stock characters who were drawn for purposes of humor rather than sympathy. In contrast, Schmidt wrote, "This novel represents Kitty Barne at her best. Her characters are vividly drawn and realistic to the experiences of any child living in Britain during the war," and called *Visitors from London* "a celebration of British life, particularly country life."

Another Barne novel set during World War II was *We'll Meet in England* (1942), in which two Norwegian children escape their nation's occupation by sailing to England in an Englishman's boat, rescuing a downed R.A.F. pilot along the way. Reviewers at the time and since, noting that this book was more of an escapist adventure than *Visitors from England,* have nevertheless found it an enjoyable yarn for children that conveyed a patriotic excitement appropriate under the circumstances. It was shortly after the war, when its effects on later civilian life could be measured, that Barne produced what may be her most memorable work, *Musical Honours.* This 1947 novel deals with the return of a father to his family after having been a prisoner of war for several years. The father, Charley Redland, was formerly a musician, a vocation his children have wished to follow; but on his return, he decides that music is too unstable an occupation, and tries to steer the children into white-collar fields. Reviewer H. F. Griswold, in the *Christian Science Monitor,* called *Musical Honours* "an entrancing story about life in England today during rationing and reconstruction." Schmidt, from the standpoint of 1996, commends the achievement up to a point: "All this is realistic: the uneasy return of the father into the family and the frustration of being told what one is to become when one is already embarked on a vocation." But he finds that Barne's resolution of such conflicts was not as realistic as her presentation of them: as in *She Shall Have Music,* success comes too easily for all the Redlands. Nevertheless, he finds, "Barne's reputation as a pioneer in realistic fiction for children—insofar as such a reputation exists—rests on such a novel as *Musical Honours.*"

Barne described her own work as realistic in an autobiographical entry for *The Junior Book of Authors,* which Schmidt quoted in the *Dictionary of Literary Biography.* Explaining her intentions, she wrote, "I knew they [children] were sensible, critical, and not at all romantic about their own affairs. . . . Whether the heroes and heroines of my books are running a dogs' motel, escaping from the Gestapo in Norway, getting up a play, helping a Polish girl find her feet in an English school, or persuading a returned POW father to change his mind about their future careers, they are all independent, energetic people, making up their minds about what they want to do with their lives and going all out to do it." Though Schmidt believed that Barne had not completely fulfilled her intentions, he commented favorably, if somewhat ironically, on Barne's "ability to take the most dreadful, calamitous atmospheres and pit against them the secure, safe worlds of loving families and music and tea by the fire in cozy chairs."

Barne's nonfiction books included biographies of composers such as Handel, Mozart, and Schubert, and a 1941 opus, *Listening to the Orchestra.* Written during a period of wartime crisis, this popular book, in Schmidt's eyes, carried on Barne's personal tradition—which is also a very British tradition—of finding cause for bravery in the preservation of civilization and its comforts. Barne herself, in eloquent words quoted by Schmidt, saw herself as affirming life: "the music-lover looks for the expression of the eternal truths above the din and smoke of the martyred earth."

BIOGRAPHICAL/CRITICAL SOURCES:

BOOKS

Dictionary of Literary Biography, Volume 160: *British Children's Writers, 1914-1960,* Gale, 1996, pp. 30-35.
Twentieth-Century Children's Writers, fourth edition, St. James Press, 1995, pp. 64-65.
The Who's Who of Children's Literature, compiled and edited by Brian Doyle, Schocken Books, 1968, pp. 19-20.

PERIODICALS

Books, March 19, 1939, p. 8; April 20, 1941, p. 8.
Christian Science Monitor, December 18, 1947, p. 16.
Library Journal, October 15, 1957, p. 152.
New Yorker, May 24, 1941.

New York Times, June 4, 1939, p. 10; January 21, 1940, p. 11; March 2, 1941, p. 10; March 6, 1949, p. 32.
Saturday Review of Literature, July 9, 1949.
School Library Journal, April, 1989, p. 42.
Times Literary Supplement, October 7, 1939, p. 578.*

*   *   *

BARNES, Jay 1958-

PERSONAL: Born June 28, 1958, in Southport, NC; married, June 1, 1991; wife's name, Robin; children: Heather, Lindsey. *Education:* Attended North Carolina State University, 1980; Syracuse University, M.F.A., 1988.

ADDRESSES: Office—North Carolina Aquarium, Pine Knoll Shores, NC 28512; fax 919-247-0663.

CAREER: North Carolina Aquarium, Pine Knoll Shores, exhibits curator, 1980-89, director, 1989—. Carteret sports leadership mentor.

MEMBER: American Zoological and Aquarium Association, Carteret Writers, Bogue Banks Lions Club (president, 1994-95).

AWARDS, HONORS: ASTC Design Award, 1984; Frisbee Nationals Design Award, 1986; shared book award, North Carolina Society of Historians, 1995.

WRITINGS:

North Carolina's Hurricane History, University of North Carolina Press (Chapel Hill, NC), 1995.
Florida's Hurricane History, University of North Carolina Press, 1997.

SIDELIGHTS: Jay Barnes told *CA:* "My interests in writing have revolved around the historical aspects of tropical hurricanes in the United States, with emphasis on the impact of these storms on people of the coastal region. My interests are beyond the meteorological details, dealing more with the tragedies and unusual events that often follow great storms. I have also compiled an extensive collection of historical photographs that add to our understanding of hurricanes. With a better understanding of our hurricane past, we all can know more of what to expect when the next great storm strikes our coast."

BARRETT, David M(arshall) 1951-

PERSONAL: Born December 7, 1951, in Alexandria, LA; son of Edward J. and Frances S. Barrett. *Education:* University of Notre Dame, B.A., 1973, Ph.D., 1990; University of Essex, M.A., 1985.

ADDRESSES: Home—P.O. Box 291, Villanova, PA 19085. *Office*—Department of Political Science, Villanova University, 262 St. Augustine Center, Villanova, PA 19085.

CAREER: WLOI-Radio, La Porte, IN, news director, 1974; WNIT Public Television, South Bend, IN, public affairs director, 1975-84; University of Wisconsin—Milwaukee, visiting assistant professor of political science, 1989-90; Villanova University, Villanova, PA, assistant professor of political science, 1990—. Democratic primary candidate for U.S. House of Representatives from Indiana's 3rd District, 1984.

MEMBER: American Political Science Association.

AWARDS, HONORS: Zahm travel grant from University of Notre Dame, 1989; Moody grant, Lyndon Johnson Foundation, 1991; grant from American Political Science Association, 1994; Dirksen Congressional Research Center, 1994.

WRITINGS:

Uncertain Warriors: Lyndon Johnson and His Vietnam Advisers, University Press of Kansas, 1993.
Lyndon Johnson's Vietnam Papers: A Documentary Collection, Texas A & M University Press (College Station, TX), 1997.

Work represented in anthologies, including *The Making of United States Foreign Policy,* edited by John Dumbrell, St. Martin's, 1990; and *The Executive Office of the President: A Reference History,* edited by Harold Relyea, Greenwood Press, 1994. Contributor articles and reviews to political science journals.

SIDELIGHTS: David M. Barrett told *CA:* "After two years as a radio news director, I was the public affairs director for WNIT Public Television for eight years. In that capacity, I produced documentaries, moderated political debates, and (for six years) hosted and produced a nightly interview program. I occasionally contributed background information for use by *The MacNeil-Lehrer News Hour* and appeared as a guest interviewer on William F. Buckley's *Firing Line* in January, 1984. I conducted occasional interviews for two syndicated television series produced by Oblate Media, Golden Dome Productions, and the University of Notre Dame's Institute for International Peace Studies from 1988 to 1991. These were shown on the Vision cable television network.

"My chief research interests are the American presidency and American foreign policy. American government was my first field of concentration during graduate studies, and I have taught courses on the presidency, introductory American politics, the civil rights movement, and southern politics. Due to my interest in the domestic sources of American foreign policy, I also was trained in the field of international relations, and I have taught courses on U.S. defense and foreign policy, congressional oversight of intelligence agencies, and problems of post-Cold War international politics.

"My recent book *Uncertain Warriors* presents a revisionist analysis of change over time in Vietnam War advisory interactions in the Johnson administration. It is based, in large part, on research conducted at a number of presidential and other archives, and on supplementary interviews with former administration officials. The analysis finds that there were significant changes in the range of advice and advisers surrounding President Johnson during the course of the war. In contrast to prevailing views of Johnson as a president largely closed off from dissenting anti-war views, it finds that distinctly diverse points of view were usually sought and listened to by Johnson. The analysis pays close attention to unofficial, but influential, advisers to the president.

"My latest book, *Lyndon Johnson's Vietnam Papers,* brings together many of the most interesting and important documents relating the conversations and debates that went on in the White House among Johnson and his advisers. Most of these documents were formerly classified as 'top secret' and have only become available in recent years. They include transcripts of White House telephone conversations and notes of many meetings, plus diary entries and memoranda to and from the President.

"My current research looks into congressional oversight of the CIA in the early decades of the Cold War era. Especially, I am researching the interactions of Senator Richard Russell (D-Georgia), who was virtually a one-person overseer of the CIA in the 1950s and 1960s, and Central Intelligence Agency leaders.

I hope that this research will lead to published articles and a book."

*   *   *

BARTKY, Sandra Lee 1935-

PERSONAL: Born May 5, 1935, in Evanston, IL. *Education:* University of Illinois, Urbana, B.A., 1955, M.A., 1959, Ph.D., 1963.

ADDRESSES: Office—Department of Philosophy, University of Illinois at Chicago, 601 South Morgan St., Chicago, IL 60607-7100.

CAREER: Writer and educator. University of Illinois at Chicago, associate professor of philosophy, 1970—, and chair of women's studies program.

AWARDS, HONORS: National Endowment for the Humanities fellow, 1968-69.

MEMBER: American Philosophy Association, Society for Women in Philosophy.

WRITINGS:

Philosophy and Feminism, Littlefield (Totowa, NJ), 1977, published as *Philosophy and Women,* Wadsworth (Belmont, CA), 1979.
Femininity and Domination: Studies in the Phenomenology of Oppression, Routledge (New York City), 1990.
(Editor, with Nancy Fraser) *Revaluing French Feminism: Critical Essays on Difference, Agency, and Culture,* Indiana University Press (Bloomington), 1992.

Contributor of essays to journals, including *British Journal of Aesthetics, Inquiry, Philosophic and Phenomenologic Research,* and *Social Theory and Practice.*

SIDELIGHTS: Sandra Lee Bartky is considered a pivotal figure in the development of modern feminist philosophy. Basing her line of thought on both Marxist ideology and phenomenology—the relationship between the viewer and the object viewed—she has been energetic in her support of the study of the basis of gender-based oppression. Using not only Marxism but the works of phenomenologist Martin Heidegger, Bartky has derived an explicitly feminist approach to

philosophy, which she outlines in a series of essays published in 1990 as *Femininity and Domination: Studies in the Phenomenology of Oppression.*

Bartky's ideas were first published in "Toward a Phenomenology of Feminist Consciousness," an essay written in 1973 and later reprinted in *Femininity and Domination.* In this work, Bartky states that she was motivated in her work "not only in order to make sense of what was happening in my own life but because of practical urgency"—the importance of ending the oppression of women. This early essay provided Bartky with both a forum through which to make a case for the need for a feminist philosophy and an opportunity to set forth her unique feminist theories.

While many feminist colleagues had traditionally cited gender or class as the root of female oppression in Western society, Bartky would broaden the source of that oppression to include age, race, and sexual orientation. Her views opened the way for the study of oppression to include women's experiences beyond an upper-middle class, white, college-educated perspective. Bartky uses a Marxist approach to analyze women's primary role as emotional care-giver, comparing it to the role fulfilled by the proletariat dominated within a capitalist society. She also draws on the work of French theorist Michel Foucault in such essays as "Femininity, and the Politics of Personal Transformation" and "Foucault, Femininity, and the Modernization of Patriarchal Power," all included in *Femininity and Domination.* In this essay, she uses Foucault's theory of "docile bodies" to show how such things as dieting, proper postures, and women's cult of personal hygiene and beauty produce a constant state of inferiority, causing women to ultimately fall into what she calls "relentless self-surveillance."

Bartky's work sparked such reaction from the academic community that the American Philosophical Association held a symposium in honor of her contribution to the advancement of feminist philosophy in 1991, the year following the publication of *Femininity and Domination.* As Douglas Kellner would comment in a paper later published in *Hypatia,* "It is the merit of [Bartky's work] that it provides indispensable aspects of a theory of oppression that challenges us to produce equally compelling theories and practices of resistance." Bartky remains active in philosophy, both as an educator, essayist, and theoretician. *Revaluing French Feminism: Critical Essays on Difference, Agency, and Culture,* which she co-edited, was published in 1992.

BIOGRAPHICAL/CRITICAL SOURCES:

BOOKS

Bartky, Sandra Lee, *Femininity and Domination: Studies in the Phenomenology of Oppression,* Routledge (New York City), 1990.

PERIODICALS

Hypatia, winter, 1993, pp. 145-99.
Publishers Weekly, November 2, 1990, p. 68.
Times Literary Supplement, June 7, 1991, p. 8.
Women's Review of Books, March, 1991, pp. 20-21.*

*   *   *

BAUDINO, Gael 1955(?)-

PERSONAL: Born in c. 1955; raised in Los Angeles, CA.

ADDRESSES: Home—Denver, CO.

CAREER: Writer.

WRITINGS:

FANTASY NOVELS

Dragonsword (Dragonsword series), Lynx Omega (New York), 1988.
Strands of Starlight (Starlight series), Signet (New York), 1989.
Gossamer Axe, Roc (New York), 1990.
Duel of Dragons (Dragonsword series), Roc, 1991.
Dragon Death (Dragonsword series), Roc, 1992.
Maze of Moonlight (Starlight series), Roc, 1993.
Shroud of Shadow (Starlight series), Roc, 1993.

WORK IN PROGRESS: Another novel in the Starlight series, *Strands of Sunlight.*

SIDELIGHTS: Gael Baudino writes fantasy novels where issues of sex and gender are central themes. Other important themes in her work are the necessity of change, even when not all the changes are positive, and the healing power of love. *Dragonsword,* Baudino's first volume of the Dragonsword series, establishes Suzanne Helling as the heroine in the fantasy world of Gryylth. She is a swordswoman who is reluctant to kill, though she gradually overcomes her pacifism.

Gossamer Axe brings together two worlds that might seem to have little in common: Celtic fantasy and heavy-metal music. Christa is a harper who was born in sixth-century Ireland and captured by the Sidh. She escaped with the help of a magical Sidh harp and has been trying for centuries to free her lover Judith, but has been unable to best the Sidh musician Orfide. In 1980s Denver she discovers the key: "the violence and passion of heavy metal" will break down the walls between the worlds and defeat Orfide. The newness and difference of rock and roll is one of Christa's weapons. Central to the book is the idea of music as magic. It has power to kill or to heal in the right hands, and one needn't be Sidh to wield it.

The series beginning with *Strands of Starlight* is set in an imaginary country, Adria, in the real medieval Europe, and tells the story of the decline and, in the forthcoming *Strands of Sunlight,* rebirth of the Elves. These Elves, though immortal, are not like the Sidh of *Gossamer Axe:* they feel, they grow, they make mistakes. They are like humans but better, wanting only to help and heal. It seems that they die out, not because humans don't need them any more, but because humans are not worthy of them.

BIOGRAPHICAL/CRITICAL SOURCES:

BOOKS

Gossamer Axe, Roc (New York), 1990.*

*   *   *

BAUMGARTNER, Frederick Milton 1910-

PERSONAL: Born June 5, 1910, in Richmond, Indiana; son of Milton Daniel (a professor) and Sarah Hill (a professor) Baumgartner; married A. Marguerite Heydweiller (a teacher), June 15, 1936; children: Theodore, William, Karl, Barbara. *Education:* Attended Butler University, 1927-31; University of Kansas, 1931-35; Cornell University, 1933-1936. *Politics:* Republican. *Religion:* Unitarian. *Avocational interests:* Life-long interest in birds, including bird counts at college and for Audubon Society.

ADDRESSES: Home—185 Witherspoon Road, Athens, GA 30706.

CAREER: Writer.

WRITINGS:

(With Marguerite Baumgartner) *Oklahoma Bird Life,*
    University of Oklahoma Press (Norman, OK),
    1992.

*   *   *

BAZZONI, Jana O'Keefe   1941-

PERSONAL: Born October 15, 1941, in Boston, MA;
daughter of Christopher T. (a newspaper proofreader)
and Mary (a teacher; maiden name, Cole) O'Keefe;
married Enrico A. Bazzoni (an executive chef), June
28, 1969; children: Christopher, Nicholas, Alexander. *Ethnicity:* "Irish, German." *Education:* St.
Mary of the Woods College, B.A., 1963; Hunter
College of the City University of New York, M.A.,
1974; City University of New York, Ph.D., 1983.
Religion: Roman Catholic.

ADDRESSES: Home—126 Second Pl., Brooklyn, NY
11231. *Office*—Department of Speech, Bernard M.
Baruch College of the City University of New York,
17 Lexington Ave., Box G1326, New York, NY
10010; fax 212-387-1655. *E-mail*—jobbb@cunyvm
.cuny.edu.

CAREER: United Service Organizations, performer
and choreographer for a tour of *Seventeen,* 1963; J.
Walter Thompson, casting associate, 1964-65; Doyle,
Dane, Bernbach, casting director, 1965-67; Guinness-
Harp Corp., administrative assistant for advertising
and public relations, 1969-72, office manager for
Wine Division, 1972-73; Italian Theatre Festival,
administrative manager, 1974; Images Unlimited
(casting consultants), founding partner, 1975-77;
Elizabeth Seton College, Yonkers, NY, instructor in
language and literature, 1975-86, academic adviser,
1981-87; lecturer at Drew University, Madison, NJ,
York College of the City University of New York,
Jamaica, NY, and Hunter College of the City University of New York, New York City, 1976-81; Bernard
M. Baruch College of the City University of New
York, New York City, adjunct assistant professor,
1980-85, assistant professor, 1985-94, associate professor of speech, 1995—. Producer and director of
plays produced off-off-Broadway, 1974-86; City University of New York Readers Theatre, founding
member, producer, writer, and performer, 1979-90.

Carroll Gardens Neighborhood Women, member of
board of directors; Adult Learning Center, member.

MEMBER: Modern Language Association of
America, Association for Theatre in Higher Educa-
tion, American Association of Teachers of Italian,
Association for Business Communication, Speech
Communication Association, Pirandello Society of
America.

AWARDS, HONORS: Grant from National Endowment for the Humanities, 1990.

WRITINGS:

(With Nina DaVinci Nichols) *Pirandello and Film,*
    University of Nebraska Press (Lincoln, NE),
    1995.

Contributor to books, including *The Luigi Pirandello
Companion,* edited by John L. DiGaetani, Greenwood
Press (Westport, CT), 1991. Contributor of articles,
translations, and reviews to periodicals, including
*American Theatre, Western European Stages, Modern
Drama, Review of National Literatures, Italica,* and
Offstage Perspective.

WORK IN PROGRESS: A book on national and international productions of Luigi Pirandello's *Six Characters in Search of an Author;* research on futurist theater, computer assisted learning, and internship management.

*   *   *

BEATTY, Paul

PERSONAL: Born in Los Angeles, CA.

ADDRESSES: Agent—c/o Houghton Mifflin, 222 Berkeley St., Boston, MA 02116.

CAREER: Performance artist; poet and writer, c.
1991—.

WRITINGS:

Big Bank Take Little Bank (poetry), Nuyorican Poets
    Cafe (New York, NY), 1991.
Joker, Joker, Deuce (poetry), Penguin (New York,
    NY), 1994.
The White Boy Shuffle (novel), Houghton Mifflin
    (Boston, MA), 1996.

Contributor to *Slam Poetry: Heftige Dichtung aus Amerika,* Galrev (Berlin, Germany), 1994.

SIDELIGHTS: The work of performance artist, poet, and novelist Paul Beatty is influenced by hip-hop music and reflects many aspects of contemporary African American street culture. His first volume of poetry, *Big Bank Take Little Bank,* was published by a small press in 1991. It drew enough favorable attention that Beatty's next collection, *Joker, Joker, Deuce,* was published by Penguin in 1994.

Joker, Joker, Deuce received good critical notice. Terese Svoboda in the *Kenyon Review,* discussing Beatty's reputation as a performance artist, asked the question: "Can the guy survive on the page?" and answered herself, "Yes. Invoke [Walt] Whitman, sixties' revolutionary rap, call and response, the 'Beats,' jazz, and stir in uncannily woven rhyme and rhythm, and Beatty explodes the page." A *Publishers Weekly* reviewer had high praise for *Joker, Joker, Deuce* as well, observing that "the writing is so lyrical that readers don't feel shouted at or wrongfully accused," even when Beatty writes of the racial prejudice facing African Americans. The poems in the volume include "Big Bowls of Cereal," which concerns—among other things—Beatty's grandmother's tastes in music; and "Verbal Mugging," which discusses the author's feelings about performance art.

Beatty's first novel, *The White Boy Shuffle,* became available to readers in 1996. Its protagonist, an African American boy named Gunnar Kaufman, comes from a long line of accommodating black people. One ancestor, Gunnar tells readers, bought his freedom from slavery by charging people "to rub me head for good luck." Another he describes as "exceedingly bootlicking even for a slave." Gunnar's own father serves with the Los Angeles Police Department and has a reputation for laughing heartily at racist jokes made by white fellow officers. Gunnar himself has spent most of his life in predominantly white Santa Monica, California, but must make huge adjustments after his parents divorce and his mother moves him to one of the tougher sections of Los Angeles. He is at first troubled by his inability to fit in, but is befriended by another young man to whom hip-hop culture is second nature. Eventually Gunnar overcomes, becoming not only a basketball star but an acclaimed poet.

The White Boy Shuffle, according to Richard Bernstein, writing in the *New York Times,* "is a blast of satirical heat from the talented heart of black American life." Bernstein went on to note that the novel "is saturated with the acerbity of [Beatty's] poetry" and that "what he makes us see is often startling, funny and full of the precision that the prism of mockery can provide." A *Publishers Weekly* contributor also applauded *The White Boy Shuffle,* judging that the author's "language and outlandish characters combine to produce an extravagantly comic vision of the American cultural moment." Bernstein concluded that "Beatty is a fertile and original writer, one to watch."

BIOGRAPHICAL/CRITICAL SOURCES:

BOOKS

Beatty, Paul, *The White Boy Shuffle,* Houghton Mifflin, 1996.

PERIODICALS

Kenyon Review, spring, 1995, pp. 155-57.
Newsweek, July 15, 1996, p. 56.
New York Times, May 31, 1996, p. C25.
Publishers Weekly, February 21, 1994, pp. 247-48; May 6, 1996, pp. 69-70.*

*   *   *

BECKER, Juergen 1932-

PERSONAL: Born July 10, 1932, in Cologne, Germany; son of Robert and Else (Schuchardt) Becker; married first wife, Marie, 1954 (divorced, 1965); married Rango Bohne, 1965; children: (first marriage) one son; (second marriage) one stepson, one stepdaughter. *Ethnicity:* German. *Education:* Attended University of Cologne, 1953-54.

ADDRESSES: Home—Am Klausenberg 84, 51109 Koeln-Brueck, Germany.

CAREER: Westdeutscher Rundfunk (radio), writer, 1959-64; Rowohlt Verlag, reader, 1964-65; writer, 1965—. Suhrkamp-Theaterverlag, director, 1974. Deutschlandfunk Koeln, head of drama department. Warwick University, writer in residence, 1988.

MEMBER: PEN, Deutsche Akademie fuer Sprache und Dichtung Darmstadt, Akademie der Kuenste Berlin.

AWARDS, HONORS: Foerderpreis from Landes Niedersachsen, 1964; stipendium from Deutsche Akademie, 1965 and 1966; prize from Group 47, 1967; Literature Prize from City of Cologne, 1968; Literature Prize from Bavarian Academy of Arts, 1980; Critics' Prize, 1981; Bremer Literature Prize, 1986; Heinrich-Boell Prize, 1995.

WRITINGS:

(With Wolf Vostell) *Phasen,* Galerie der Spiegel (Cologne), 1960.

Felder (short stories; title means "Fields"), Suhrkamp (Frankfurt am Main), 1964.

Raender (short stories), Suhrkamp, 1968, excerpted translation by A. Leslie Wilson published as "Margins" in *Dimension,* Volume 1, number 2, 1968.

Umgebungen (short stories; title means "Surroundings"), Suhrkamp, 1970.

Erzaehlen bis Ostende (short stories; title means "Narration until Ostende"), Suhrkamp, 1981.

Die Tuere zum Meer (title means "The Door to the Sea"), Suhrkamp, 1983.

Frauen mit dem Ruecken zum Betrachter, [Germany], 1989.

POETRY

Schnee: Gedichte, Literarisches Colloquium (Berlin), 1971.

Das Ende der Landschaftsmalerei: Gedichte, Suhrkamp, 1974.

Erzaehl mir nichts vom Kreig: Gedichte, Suhrkamp, 1977.

In der verbleibenden Zeit: Gedichte, Suhrkamp, 1979.

Gedichte 1965-1980 (title means "Poems 1965-1980"), Suhrkamp, 1981.

Fenster und Stimmen: Gedichte, Suhrkamp, 1982.

Odenthals Kuenste, [Germany], 1986.

Das englische Fenster, Suhrkamp, 1990.

Foxtrott im Erfurter Stadion: Gedichte, Suhrkamp, 1993.

Also author of the poem *Das Gedicht von der Weider-Vereinigten Landschaft,* 1988.

EDITOR

(With Wolf Vostell) *Happenings; Fluxus; Pop Art; Nouveau Realisme: Eine Dokumentation,* Rowohlt (Reinbek), 1965.

Elisabeth Borchers, *Gedichte* (poetry), Suhrkamp, 1976.

OTHER

Bilder, Haeuser: Hausfreunde: Drei Hoerspiel (radio play), [Germany], 1969.

Eine Zeit ohne Woerter (photographs; title means "A Time without Words"), [Germany], 1971.

Die Zeit nach Harrimann: 29 Szenen fuer Nora, Helen, Jenny und den stummen Diener Moltke, Suhrkamp, 1971.

Die Abwesenden: Drei Hoerspiel (radio plays), Suhrkamp, 1983.

(With wife, Rango Bohne) *Frauen mit dem Rucken zum Betrachter,* Suhrkamp, 1989.

SIDELIGHTS: Juergen Becker is a German experimentalist who has distinguished himself in both prose and poetry. His early, particularly radical exercises in prose include *Felder,* a 1964 volume which is constructed as a montage of straightforward prose, manipulated punctuation and spelling, dialects, and other aspects of language and writing. Equally radical is *Raender,* which mixes autobiographical accounts (constructed as single sentences of five pages in length), fragmented prose, blank pages, and other experimental forms of expression. In another volume, *Umgebungen,* Becker uses his montage technique as a means of lamenting the dehumanizing nature of industrialization, consumerism, and urban life. Becker's emphasis on the inadequacy of language before such dehumanizing conditions led him to publish, in 1971, *Eine Zeit ohne Woerter,* a photography volume void of narrative text.

In the 1981 publication *Erzaehlen bis Ostende,* Becker practiced his radical technique in less imposing ways by presenting narrative fragments within the context of a traveler's train journey. But even in this volume he seems to exult the primacy of memory and subliminal associations over that of linguistic communication. Two years later, with the introspective, rather impressionistic *Die Tuere zum Meere,* Becker once again focussed on the failings of linguistic communication. Robert Acker, writing in the *Dictionary of Literary Biography,* noted as much when he wrote: "Becker seems to be saying that one can only exist, with the aid of memory and imagination, in a nonlinguistic world and that a more perfect control of language moves one farther away from contact with this world." In addition to writing experimental prose, Becker has produced several volumes of poetry. But his verse, while only loosely structured, is far less radical, though—like much of his prose—it expresses the tenuous nature of modern existence.

BIOGRAPHICAL/CRITICAL SOURCES:

BOOKS

Dictionary of Literary Biography, Volume 75: *Contemporary German Writers, Second Series,* Gale (Detroit, MI), 1988.

PERIODICALS

Christian Century, May 11, 1994, p. 504.
World Literature Today, autumn, 1987; summer, 1989; summer, 1991.*

*   *   *

BECKER, Jurgen
  See BECKER, Juergen

*   *   *

BEDFORD, Martyn   1959-

PERSONAL: Born October 10, 1959, in Croydon, England; son of Peter (a sheet metal worker) and Marjorie (a wages clerk; maiden name, Skinner) Bedford; married Damaris Croxall (a librarian), January 8, 1994. *Education:* University of East Anglia, M.A., 1994.

ADDRESSES: Agent—Jonny Geller, Curtis Brown, Haymarket House, 28-29 Haymarket, London SW1Y 4SP, England.

CAREER: South London Press, London, England, reporter and features writer, 1980-85; *South Wales Echo,* Cardiff, sports writer, 1985-87; *Citizen,* Gloucester, England, reporter, 1988; *Oxford Mail and Times,* Oxford, England, features writer and subeditor, 1988-93; *Bradford Telegraph and Argus,* Bradford, England, subeditor, 1994-95; free-lance writer, 1995—. Ilkley Literature Festival, member of management committee, 1996—.

WRITINGS:

(Editor and contributor) *Matrix,* University of East Anglia (Norwich, England), 1994.

Acts of Revision (novel), Bantam (New York City), 1996.
Exit, Orange and Red (novel), Bantam, in press.

Work represented in anthologies, including *Down the Middle,* New Fiction (England), 1993.

SIDELIGHTS: Martyn Bedford told *CA:* "*Acts of Revision* has been translated into seven languages: German, Italian, French, Dutch, Swedish, Portuguese (for Brazil), and Japanese. The novel has also been optioned by a British motion picture company.

"I was working part-time as a free-lance journalist in the spring of 1995, when the manuscript of *Acts of Revision* was rescued from the slush pile by a London literary agent. There followed an auction between two leading publishers that resulted in a substantial advance as part of a two-book deal. It was one of the most significant sums paid to a debut author in the United Kingdom."

*   *   *

BEERBOHM, (Henry) Max(imilian)   1872-1956

PERSONAL: Born August 24, 1872, in London, England; died May 20, 1956, in Rapallo, Italy; son of Julius Ewald (a corn merchant) and Elizabeth (Draper) Beerbohm; married Florence Kahn (an actress), 1910 (died, 1951); married Elisabeth Jungmann, May, 1956. *Education:* Attended Merton College, Oxford University, 1890-94. *Religion:* Jewish.

CAREER: Writer and caricaturist. *Saturday Review,* London, drama critic, 1898-1910; broadcasted a series of talks on BBC-Radio, 1936, 1938-40. Caricatures have been exhibited in museums throughout the United States and Europe.

AWARDS, HONORS: Honorary fellow, Merton College; received honorary degrees from Edinburgh University, Cambridge University, and Oxford University; knighted, 1939.

WRITINGS:

ESSAYS

The Works of Max Beerbohm, Scribners (New York), 1896.

More, Lane (New York), 1899.

Yet Again, Chapman & Hall (London), 1909.

And Even Now (essays), Heinemann (London), 1920, Dutton (New York), 1921.

A Survey, Doubleday, Page (New York), 1921.

A Defense of Cosmetics, Dodd, Mead (New York), 1922.

A Peep into the Past, privately printed (New York), 1923, edited and expanded by Rupert Hart-Davis as *A Peep into the Past and Other Prose Pieces,* Stephen Greene (Brattleboro, VT), 1972.

Around Theatres (reviews), two volumes, Heinemann, 1924, Knopf (New York), 1930.

The Guerdon, privately printed (New York), 1925.

Leaves from the Garland, privately printed (New York), 1926.

A Variety of Things, Knopf, 1928.

Works and More, Lane, 1930.

Selected Essays, edited by N. L. Clay, Heinemann, 1958.

More Theatres, 1893-1903 (reviews), compiled by Rupert Hart-Davis, Taplinger (New York), 1969.

Last Theatres, 1904-1910 (reviews; originally published in *Saturday Review*), Taplinger, 1970.

FICTION

The Happy Hypocrite: A Fairy Tale for Tired Men, Lane, 1897.

(And illustrator) *Zuleika Dobson; or, An Oxford Love Story* (novel), Heinemann, 1911, Lane, 1912.

(And illustrator) *A Christmas Garland,* Dutton, 1912.

Seven Men (short stories), Heinemann, 1919, Knopf, 1920, as *Seven Men and Two Others,* Heinemann, 1950.

The Dreadful Dragon of Hay Hill (short story), Heinemann, 1928.

CARICATURES

Caricatures of Twenty-Five Gentlemen, Smithers (London), 1896.

The Poets' Corner, Heinemann, 1904.

A Book of Caricatures, Methuen (London), 1907.

Cartoons: "The Second Childhood of John Bull," Swift (London), 1911.

Fifty Caricatures, Dutton, 1913.

Rossetti and His Circle, Heinemann, 1922, Yale University Press (New Haven, CT), 1987.

Things New and Old, Heinemann, 1923.

Observations, Heinemann, 1925.

Max's Nineties: Drawings 1892-1899, Lippincott (Philadelphia, PA), 1958.

A Catalogue of the Caricatures of Max Beerbohm, compiled by Hart-Davis, Macmillan (London), 1972.

Beerbohm's Literary Caricatures: From Homer to Huxley, edited by J. G. Riewald, Archon (Hamden, CT), 1977.

OTHER

(Editor) *Herbert Beerbohm Tree: Some Memories of Him and of His Art,* Dutton, 1920.

Lytton Strachey (Rede lecture, Cambridge University), Knopf, 1943.

Mainly on the Air (radio talks), Heinemann, 1946, Knopf, 1947.

The Incomparable Max, Dodd, Mead, 1962.

Max in Verse: Rhymes and Parodies, edited by Riewald, Stephen Greene, 1963.

Max Beerbohm's Letters to Reggie Turner, edited by Hart-Davis, Lippincott, 1965.

The Bodley Head Max Beerbohm, edited by David Cecil, Bodley Head (London), 1970, as *Selected Prose,* Little, Brown (Boston), 1971.

Max and Will: Max Beerbohm and William Rothenstein, Their Friendship and Letters, 1893-1945, edited by Mary M. Lago and Karl Beckson, Harvard University Press (Cambridge), 1975.

Letters of Max Beerbohm, 1892-1956, edited by Hart-Davis, Norton, 1989.

Collected Verse, edited by Riewald, Archon, 1994.

Contributor to periodicals, including *Listener, Strand,* and *Yellow Book.*

ADAPTATIONS: *The Incomparable Max,* stage play based on Beerbohm's life and works, written by Jerome Lawrence and Robert E. Lee, Hill & Wang (New York), 1972; *Zukelia Dobson* was dramatized on BBC-Television's *Third Programme,* c. 1953.

SIDELIGHTS: Blessed with what Oscar Wilde would term "the gift of perpetual old age," Max Beerbohm joined fellow "decadents" Aubrey Beardsley, Arthur Symons, Wilde, and W. B. Yeats in the aesthetic school that dominated British art and literature from the 1890s through the turn of the century. A contributor to the *Yellow Book,* a journalistic mouthpiece for these avant garde aesthetes, Beerbohm went on to work as a drama reviewer in London for almost a decade before retiring to Italy to devote himself to his writing. Revered by many of his contemporaries as both a witty perfectionist and a consummate and self-confessed dandy, Beerbohm is best remembered as the wit behind countless prose parodies and deftly drawn caricatures of notable Victorian personalities. While several of his longer works are still studied—his only novel, *Zuleika Dobson; or, An Oxford Love Story,* is considered by some to be a comic triumph—Beerbohm's continued fame rests on his perceptively rendered portrayal of Victorian England's cultural elite.

Born in London in 1872, Beerbohm led a protected childhood, excelling at the study of Latin at the Charterhouse School between 1885 and 1890. Moving to Merton College, Oxford, the young scholar, inspired by the aestheticism of don Walter Pater, enjoyed the company of such young aesthetes as Symons, Wilde, poet Reggie Turner, and painter Will Rothenstein before withdrawing from academic studies in 1894 and returning to his family home. Oxford would be one of several universities to later grant Beerbohm an honorary degree.

The essay collection *The Works of Max Beerbohm,* published two years later, reflected the influence of Wilde in its paradoxical and satiric commentary on the cultural and intellectual milieu of the 1880s. Beerbohm's first published book, *Works* would be followed by *More, Yet Again,* and *And Even Now,* the latter released in 1920. Indeed, his powers as an essayist were held in high regard by many critics; as Charles Lam Markmann later wrote in a review of *Selected Essays* in the *Nation:* "Beerbohm's was the spirit that might well have been claimed as an ancestor by *The New Yorker* when it was in its best years, before it lost—as Beerbohm never did—the capacity for self-satire." Despite their archness, Beerbohm has been considered a minor writer of the period, measured against the stature of contemporaries like Wilde and George Bernard Shaw. "Max's danger was coyness," maintained V. S. Pritchett in his assessment of *The Bodley Head Max Beerbohm* in the *New Statesman,* "a fault common to the minor writers of the period, where funny wordiness was apt to lead even the more rumbustous into a fit of the giggles. And one can complain," continued Pritchett, "now that we expect prose not to dwell too lovingly on its comforts, on the lengthiness of the conversational manner. Perhaps the decline of conversation is a barrier now between him and ourselves."

In 1898 Beerbohm succeeded Bernard Shaw as drama critic for London's *Saturday Review.* For the next twelve years he would share his impressions of dramatic interpretations of the works of Henrik Ibsen, J.M. Barrie, August Strindberg, Edmond Rostand,

Shaw, and Arthur Wing Pinero then appearing on that city's stages. While reflecting opinions that some might take issue with—Beerbohm found many of Shakespeare's plays tiresome, Shaw terribly overrated, and the experimental drama of the period pretentious and second rate—Hilary Spurling noted in her review of *More Theatres, 1893-1903* in the *Spectator:* "Playgoers in general will marvel at the stamina which enabled Max not simply to sit through so much arrant tat, but to report on it each week with such unfailing candour and good temper." Beerbohm's drama reviews were collected in three volumes: *Around Theatres, More Theatres, 1893-1903,* and *Last Theatres, 1904-1910,* collectively published between 1924 and 1970. While some critics viewed Beerbohm as "an elegant dilettante who used the theatre simply as a pretext for self-display," according to a *Times Literary Supplement* contributor in a review of *A Catalogue of the Caricatures of Max Beerbohm* and *A Peep into the Past and Other Prose Pieces,* "That view will not bear close inspection. . . . [W]hat he did consistently was to expose the huge tide of fanciful rubbish that came his way to the test of common sense: sometimes with logic, sometimes with mockery, and sometimes with anger."

Beerbohm left both the *Saturday Review* and England in 1910; apart from the years encompassing World Wars I and II he would make his home in Rapallo, on the Italian Riviera. Despite his retirement from the London literary scene, his writing continued, if sporadically: 1912's *A Christmas Garland* was deemed a classic parody with its portraits of such notables as H. G. Wells, Arnold Bennett, and Joseph Conrad. Novelist Henry James is reported as calling *A Christmas Garland* "the most intelligent thing that has been produced in England for many a long day." While refusing to write during the final two decades of his life, Beerbohm gave a series of radio talks during the war years that focused on his memories of an earlier time—his much loved and lost 1890s. Unlike other writers, he would also see his literary reputation grow during his lifetime; Beerbohm's death in Rapallo in 1956 was mourned by many in the literary world. His death came a few weeks after his second marriage; he was eighty-four years old.

In addition to essays, criticism, and reviews, Beerbohm also tried his hand at several fictional genres, with characteristic comedic success. While considered dated by modern standards, *The Happy Hypocrite: A Fairy Tale for Tired Men* was a lighter, more humorous version of Wilde's classic parable *The Portrait of Dorian Gray. Zuleika Dobson*—decorated by Beerbohm with eighty watercolor caricatures despite its author's dislike for illustrated novels—received critical accolades at the time of its initial publication in 1911. A parody of his years at Oxford, *Zuleika Dobson* recounts the devastation caused by the appearance of a beautiful young woman upon the grounds of Oxford during Eights Week; in a finale that a few reviewers considered to be of questionable taste, a mass suicide takes place after a multitude of Oxonian undergraduates succumb to the young woman's feminine charms.

The short story collection *Seven Men* was published in 1919 and revised as *Seven Men and Two Others* in 1950. Received to critical praise, this collection of profiles of fictitious versifiers includes a description of "Enoch Soames," a decadent poet of self-described brilliance who sells his soul to the devil for the chance to travel one hundred years into the future to look himself up in the British Museum's library card catalogue. "Max Beerbohm hardly knew failure," wrote John Mortimer in his review of *Letters of Max Beerbohm, 1892-1956* in the *New York Review of Books;* "time and again the nail is delicately but sharply fit on the head, the point firmly driven home. Beerbohm believed that good sense about trivialities is better than nonsense about things that matter, but in his best stories there is more than a whisper of magic realism—a murmur, however distant, of questions about the nature of reality."

Several volumes of Beerbohm's letters have been collected: *Letters of Max Beerbohm, 1892-1956,* and *Max and Will: Max Beerbohm and William Rothenstein, Their Friendship and Letters, 1893-1945* reveal a great deal about the writer's idiosyncratic lifestyle, which was guided almost totally by his love of the past. In addition, the first collection provides readers with an overview of Beerbohm's personal relationships: from his eventual wife, Florence Kahn, to literary giant Bernard Shaw: "How adroitly Beerbohm parries Shaw's criticisms!," noted Gross. "How nimbly, writing to him, he stops just short of open insult!—and yet he is careful to make clear his admiration too."

Caricatures of Twenty-Five Gentlemen, published in 1896, was the first work to showcase Beerbohm's other talent: visual satire. 1904's *The Poet's Corner* and later collections of caricatures are notable for the author/artist's depiction of persons he never met in real life; in fact, the portraits of Wilde and Swinburne, whom he did know, were based on a time previous to their acquaintance. This affection for re-

cent history would also be reflected in 1922's *Rossetti and His Circle,* which depicts friends and members of the Pre-Raphaelite Brotherhood from Dante Gabriel Rossetti and William Morris to Robert Browning and Alfred, Lord Tennyson, in twenty-three watercolor wash cartoons. "The fun that Beerbohm pokes at Rossetti, his colleagues and camp-followers, is of the gentlest sort, but unerringly on target. . . .," according to *Spectator* critic David Wright in his review of *Rossetti and His Circle.* "There is wit and barbed insight but no malice in these caricatures; as he himself remarked, Beerbohm mocked only what he loved."

In 1939 Beerbohm received Britain's greatest honor: he was knighted as "Sir Max." His personal fastidiousness was memorialized by Ezra Pound as "Brennbaum the Impeccable" in that writer's *Hugh Selwyn Mauberley;* he became almost a cult figure, such works as "Enoch Soames" and *A Christmas Garland* hailed as unsurpassable classics. "Many men, from time to time, have expressed a desire to live in the past," wrote a *Times Literary Supplement* reviewer in an assessment of *A Catalogue of the Caricatures of Max Beerbohm* and *A Peep into the Past and Other Prose Pieces;* "Max Beerbohm must be among the very few who have actually done so, and with complete success. . . . [H]e remained as detached from the realities of the age in which he lived . . . as he was oblivious of the Vespas and lorries charging past the terrace at Rapallo. That the decision to opt out, consciously arrived at and consistently maintained, was fully justified is proved by his art."

BIOGRAPHICAL/CRITICAL SOURCES:

BOOKS

Behrman, S. N., *Portrait of Max: An Intimate Memoir of Sir Max Beerbohm,* Random House (New York), 1960.

Cecil, David, *Max: A Biography,* Constable (London), 1964.

Danson, Lawrence, *Max Beerbohm and the Act of Writing,* Clarendon Press (Oxford), 1989.

Dictionary of Literary Biography, Gale (Detroit), Volume 34: *British Novelists: 1890-1929: Traditionalists,* 1985, Volume 100: *Modern British Essayists, Second Series,* 1990.

Felstiner, John, *The Lies of Art: Max Beerbohm's Parody and Caricature,* Knopf, 1972.

Grushow, Ira, *The Imaginary Reminiscences of Sir Max Beerbohm,* Ohio University Press, 1984.

Lynch, John Gilbert Bohun, *Max Beerbohm in Perspective,* Knopf, 1922.

McElderry, Bruce Robert, Jr, *Max Beerbohm,* Twayne (New York), 1972.

Riewald, J. G., editor, *The Surprise of Excellence: Modern Essays on Max Beerbohm,* Archon, 1974.

Twentieth-Century Literary Criticism, Gale, Volume 1, 1978, Volume 24, 1987.

Viscusi, Robert, *Max Beerbohm, or, The Dandy Dante: Rereading with Mirrors,* Johns Hopkins University Press (Baltimore), 1986.

PERIODICALS

Listener, September 3, 1970, p. 317.

London Review of Books, December 8, 1988, p. 22.

Los Angeles Times Book Review, October 10, 1985.

Nation, March 8, 1971, pp. 311-12.

New Republic, April 10, 1965, pp. 19-20.

New Statesman, August 28, 1970, pp. 244-45; August 25, 1972, p. 262; September 5, 1975, pp. 280-81; August 19, 1988, p. 39.

New York Review of Books, November 25, 1965, p. 31; January 25, 1973, pp. 16-19; November 5, 1987, p. 3; November 23, 1989, p 42; December 22, 1994, p. 10.

New York Times Book Review, April 11, 1965, pp. 1, 34; September 3, 1995, pp. 11-12.

Saturday Review, April 17, 1965, pp. 46-47; September 9, 1972, pp. 59-60.

Spectator, October 11, 1969, pp. 483-84; August 30, 1975, p. 284-85; July 27, 1985, p. 27; October 10, 1987, pp. 37-38; December 18-25, 1993, pp. 71-73.

Times Literary Supplement, October 16, 1969, p. 1183; December 12, 1970, p. 1411; September 15, 1972, p. 1043; August 29, 1975, pp. 962-63; August 30, 1985, p. 959; September 9, 1988, p. 980; December 17, 1993, p. 28.

Washington Post Book World, May 2, 1971, p. 4; June 18, 1989, pp. 3, 10.*

*   *   *

BEGELMAN, Mitchell (Craig) 1953-

PERSONAL: Born March 14, 1953, in New York, NY. *Education:* Harvard University, A.B. and A.M., both 1974; Cambridge University, Ph.D., 1978.

ADDRESSES: Office—Joint Institute for Laboratory Astrophysics, University of Colorado at Boulder, Campus Box 440, Boulder, CO 80309-0440; fax 303-492-5235. *E-mail*—mitch@jila.colorado.edu.

CAREER: University of Colorado at Boulder, assistant professor, 1982-87, associate professor, 1987-91, professor of astrophysical, planetary, and atmospheric sciences, 1991—, department head, 1995—, member of Joint Institute for Laboratory Astrophysics, 1982-84, fellow, 1984—, member of Center for Astrophysics and Space Astronomy, 1986—. Cambridge University, fellow of Institute of Astronomy, 1978-79, 1981-82; University of California, Berkeley, postgraduate research astronomer, 1979-82; N. Copernicus Astronomical Center, Warsaw, Poland, visiting scientist, 1980. National Research Council, Astronomy and Astrophysics Survey Committee, member of Interferometry Panel, 1989-90; National Aeronautics and Space Administration, member of review panel for Long-Term Space Astrophysics Program, 1992, 1994, Space Interferometry Science Working Group, 1992-94, Small Explorer Peer Review Panel, 1993, and Space Interferometry Mission Science Working Group, 1996—.

MEMBER: International Astronomical Union, American Astronomical Society, Royal Astronomical Society (fellow), Cambridge Philosophical Society (fellow), Phi Beta Kappa.

AWARDS, HONORS: Fellow in England, Science Research Council, 1978-79, 1981-82; Presidential Young Investigator Award, National Science Foundation, 1984; fellow, Alfred P. Sloan Foundation, 1987; Helen B. Warner Prize, American Astronomical Society, 1988; Science Writing Award, American Institute of Physics, 1996, for *Gravity's Fatal Attraction: Black Holes in the Universe.*

WRITINGS:

(With Martin Rees) *Gravity's Fatal Attraction: Black Holes in the Universe,* Scientific American Library (New York City), 1996.

Contributor to books, including *The Interstellar Medium in External Galaxies,* edited by J. M. Shull and H. A. Thronson, Jr., Kluwer Academic Publishers (Dordrecht, Netherlands), 1990; *Astrophysical Jets,* edited by D. Burgarella, M. Livio, and C. P. O'Dea, Cambridge University Press (Cambridge, England), 1993; and *The Environment and Evolution of Galaxies,* edited by Shull and Thronson, Kluwer Academic Publishers, 1993. Contributor of about eighty articles to scientific journals and popular magazines, including *Nature.*

BENDA, Julien   1867-1956

PERSONAL: Born in 1867, in France; died in 1956. *Education:* Attended the Lycee Condorcet; attended the University of Paris, Sorbonne. *Politics:* Communist.

CAREER: Writer and philosopher.

WRITINGS:

NONFICTION; EXCEPT AS NOTED

L'Ordination (novel), [France], 1912.
Le Bergsonisme, ou, Une philosophie de la mobilite, [France], 1912.
Belphegor, [France], 1919.
La Trahison des clercs, Grasset (Paris, France), 1927; translated by Richard Aldington as *The Treason of the Intellectuals,* Norton (New York), 1928; reprinted, 1969.
La France byzantine, [France], 1945.
La Jeunesse d'un clerc (volume one of autobiography), Gallimard (Paris, France), 1968.
Un Regulier dans le siecle (volume two of autobiography), Gallimard, 1968.
Exercice d'un enterre vif (volume three of autobiography), Gallimard, 1968.
La fin de l'eternel, Gallimard, 1977.
Le Rapport d'Uriel: Essai, Actes Sud (Arles, France), c. 1992.

Also contributor of articles to periodicals, including *Revue Blanche* and *Cahiers de la Quinzaine.*

SIDELIGHTS: French author and philosopher Julien Benda is best remembered for his 1927 attack on many of his fellow academicians, published in translation in 1928 as *The Treason of the Intellectuals.* He also wrote other philosophical essays, three volumes of autobiography, and a 1912 novel, *L'Ordination,* which would have won France's prestigious Goncourt literary prize except for what the *Biographical Dictionary of French Political Leaders Since 1870* labeled "anti-Semitic prejudice of certain jury members"— Benda came from a Jewish background.

Benda was born in 1867 and began his writing career during the 1890s—the years of the infamous Dreyfus affair in France. Alfred Dreyfus was a French Army officer, a Jew, who was wrongly accused and imprisoned for promising military secrets to the Germans. It was partially due to anti-Semitic feelings among many French people that the charges against Dreyfus

were upheld. Benda was one of several intellectuals of his day who came forth to defend Dreyfus; he began publishing articles in the *Revue Blanche,* a pro-Dreyfus journal. Benda's efforts in Dreyfus's cause also contributed to his losing the Goncourt prize for *L'Ordination.*

In the same year that *L'Ordination* saw print, Benda also published *Le Bergsonisme, ou, Une philosophie de la mobilite,* an attack on the philosophy of Henri Bergson, a Nobel Prize winning Frenchman who held the belief that the essential essence of reality must be understood by intuition rather than intellectual efforts. Bergson, interestingly, had attended the same *lycee,* or high school, as his rival philosopher, Benda. Benda continued to advocate the importance and responsibilities of intellectuals in *The Treason of the Intellectuals.* Though he asserted that intellectuals should remain true to the pursuit of classical knowledge and be unaffected by popular fads, he also urged that they step into political matters—such as the Dreyfus affair—on the side of pure justice. A *Times Literary Supplement* critic, reviewing a 1968 one-volume publication of Benda's autobiographical works, also gave the philosopher credit for predicting trends in academia: "He foresaw how dons and pundits would aspire to forgiveness and flattery from their students, how they would hope for acceptance in the fraternal sauna of the mob. There was little doubt in Benda's crystalline intelligence that teachers would sell out rather than be hissed."

During the 1930s, Benda became increasingly concerned about the rise of fascism in Europe. He eventually became convinced that the French Communist Party was the only viable resistance to fascism available in his own country, and so became a communist. When the Nazis occupied France, Benda went into hiding; then, after the war, he spoke out strongly against intellectuals who had collaborated with the Germans.

Benda recorded not only his years in hiding but his youth, formative development, and years of intellectual pursuit in the volumes *La Jeunesse d'un clerc, Un Regulier dans le siecle,* and *Exercice d'un enterre vif.* According to a *Times Literary Supplement* reviewer, in his autobiography Benda reveals his belief that the true intellectual "knows that classical antiquity and the seventeenth century in Europe have said almost all that needs saying about man; he knows that Congolese drum-calls are not Mozart and that Che Guevara is not Plato." The critic concluded: "it is good to have this book in hand."

BIOGRAPHICAL/CRITICAL SOURCES:

BOOKS

Benda, Julien, *La Jeunesse d'un clerc* (volume one of autobiography), Gallimard (Paris, France), 1968.

Benda, *Un Regulier dans le siecle* (volume two of autobiography), Gallimard, 1968.

Benda, *Exercice d'un enterre vif* (volume three of autobiography), Gallimard, 1968.

Biographical Dictionary of French Political Leaders Since 1870, edited by David S. Bell, Douglas Johnson, and Peter Morris, Simon & Schuster (New York), 1990.

Nichols, Ray L., *Treason, Tradition, and the Intellectual: Julien Benda and Political Discourse,* Regents Press of Kansas (Lawrence, KS), c. 1978.

PERIODICALS

Times Literary Supplement, October 10, 1968, p. 1148.

*   *   *

BENJAMIN, Denis R(ichard) 1945-

PERSONAL: Born February 8, 1945, in Johannesburg, South Africa; naturalized U.S. citizen, 1980; married Vivien Kotkin, 1968; children: Craig, Graham. *Ethnicity:* "Caucasian." *Education:* University of the Witwatersrand, B.Sc. (with first class honors), 1964, M.B., B.Ch. (cum laude), 1968. *Avocational interests:* Mycology, sailing, hiking, food and cooking, golf, ikebana.

ADDRESSES: Home—14295 Sheinwood Rd. N.W., Seattle, WA 98177. *Office*—Children's Hospital and Medical Center, 4800 Sandpoint Way N.E., Seattle, WA 98105; fax 200-527-3840. *E-mail*—dbenjam @u.washington.edu.

CAREER: Johannesburg General Hospital, Johannesburg, South Africa, intern in surgery, 1969; Non-European Hospital, Johannesburg, intern in medicine, 1969; Transvaal Memorial Hospital for Children, intern in pediatrics, 1970; University of Washington, Seattle, resident in anatomic pathology at University and Affiliated Hospitals, 1970-72, and clinical pathology, 1972-74, chief resident in laboratory medicine, 1973-74, assistant professor, 1975-80, associate professor, 1980-90, professor of laboratory medicine and

pathology, and adjunct professor of pediatrics, 1990—. Children's Orthopedic Hospital and Medical Center, assistant pathologist, 1974, head of Division of Laboratory Medicine, 1975, director of School of Medical Technology, 1975, associate director of Department of Laboratories, 1977-84, director of the laboratory, 1984—; Children's Hospital and Medical Center, member of medical executive committee, 1984—, and hospital steering committee, 1994—. Children's Cancer Study Group, pathologist for acute myeloid leukemia, 1980-90; consultant to Project Hope and Harvard Medical International.

MEMBER: International Pediatric Pathology Association, North American Mycological Association, Society for Pediatric Pathology (chair of research committee, 1988-91; member of council, 1988-94), College of American Pathologists, Academy of Clinical Laboratory Physicians and Scientists, American Association for the Advancement of Science, Council of Biology Editors, Washington State Society of Pathologists, King County Medical Society, Puget Sound Mycological Society.

WRITINGS:

Mushrooms: Poisons and Panaceas, W. H. Freeman (New York), 1995.

Contributor to medical books. Contributor of about a hundred articles to medical journals and popular magazines, including *Seattle's Child, Mushroom: Journal of Wild Mushrooming,* and *Journal of Irreproducible Results.* Editor in chief, *Pediatric Pathology and Laboratory Medicine,* 1994—; associate editor, *Pediatric Pathology,* 1986-92.

WORK IN PROGRESS: The Art of Mushroom Hunting.

*   *   *

BENJAMIN, Harold H. 1924-

PERSONAL: Born April 19, 1924, in Philadelphia, PA; son of Louis (in sales) and Anna (a store owner; maiden name, Hulnick) Benjamin; married Harriet Miller, June 29, 1947; children: Ann, Lauren. *Education:* Pennsylvania State University, B.A., 1947; Cornell University, J.D., 1950; International College, Ph.D., 1984. *Religion:* Jewish.

*ADDRESSES: Home—*1 Northstar, Marina del Rey, CA 90291. *Office—*Wellness Community, 2716 Ocean Park Blvd., No. 1040, Santa Monica, CA 90405.

CAREER: Attorney in New York City and Beverly Hills, CA, 1950-81; Wellness Community, Santa Monica, CA, founder and president, c. 1982—. *Military service:* U.S. Army Air Forces, 1943-46; became second lieutenant.

WRITINGS:

From Victim to Victor, Dell (New York), 1988.
The Wellness Community Guide to Fighting for Recovery from Cancer, Putnam (New York), 1994.

SIDELIGHTS: Harold H. Benjamin told *CA:* "My primary reason for writing is that I want cancer patients worldwide to realize that, when cancer is diagnosed, they don't have to be hopeless, helpless, and passive. They can participate in their fight for recovery, and such participation may have an effect on the course of the illness. It will certainly have an effect on their lives."

*   *   *

BENSON, Stella   1892-1933

PERSONAL: Born January 6, 1892, in Much Wenlock, Shropshire, England; died December 6, 1933; married John O'Gorman Anderson, 1921.

CAREER: Writer. Worked for Charity Organization Society, and ran a shop in Hoxton, London, 1913-17; involved in women's suffrage campaign from 1914; worked in Berkeley, California, 1918-20; travelled to China and India, 1920-21, and lived in China 1921-33.

AWARDS, HONORS: Royal Society of Literature Benson medal, 1932; Femina Vie Heureuse prize, 1932.

WRITINGS:

I Pose (novel), [London], 1915.
This Is the End (novel), [London], 1917.
Living Alone, (fantasy novel), Macmillan (London), 1919.

Also author of other novels, including *The Poor Man,* 1922; *Pipers and a Dancer,* 1924; *Goodbye, Stranger,* 1926; *The Far-Away Bride,* 1930, published as *Tobit Transplanted,* 1931; and *Mundos: An Unfinished Novel,* 1935.

SHORT STORIES

The Awakening: A Fantasy, Lantern Press (San Francisco), 1925.
The Man Who Missed the Bus, Elkin Matthews & Marrot (London), 1928.
Christmas Formula and Other Stories, Furnival Books (London), 1932.
Collected Short Stories, Macmillan, 1936.

Also author of *Hope Against Hope and Other Stories,* 1931.

OTHER

Also author of poetry, including *Twenty,* 1918, and *Poems,* 1935; the play *Kwan-Yin,* produced in 1922; and *The Little World,* 1925; *Worlds Within Worlds,* 1928; and *Some Letters 1928-1933,* edited by Cecil Clarabut, 1978. Also served as editor for books, including *Come to Eleuthera; or, New Lands for Old,* c. 1929, and *Pull Devil Pull Baker,* by Nicolas de Toulouse Lautrec de Savine. 1933.*

*   *   *

BERBERICK, Nancy Varian   1951-

PERSONAL: Born July 23, 1951; married Bruce A. Berberick, 1973. *Education:* Attended Bergen Community College, Paramus, NJ, 1969-72.

*ADDRESSES: Agent—*Maria Carvainis Agency, 235 West End Avenue, New York, NY 10024.

CAREER: Writer.

WRITINGS:

FANTASY NOVELS

Stormblade: Dragonlance Saga Heroes Volume Two, TSR (Lake Geneva, WI), 1988.
The Jewels of Elvish, TSR, 1989.
Shadow of the Seventh Moon (Garroc series), Ace (New York), 1991.

A Child of Elvish, Ace, 1992.
The Panther's Hoard (Garroc series), Ace, 1994.

* * *

BERGER, Elmer   1908-1996

OBITUARY NOTICE—See index for *CA* sketch: Born May 27, 1908, in Cleveland, OH; died October 5, 1996, in Longboat Key, FL. Theologian and author. A rabbi, Berger was an outspoken opponent of Zionism and of the creation of the nation of Israel. In support of these beliefs, he worked with the American Council for Judaism and the American Jewish Alternatives to Zionism groups. Ordained as a rabbi in 1932, he served at Temple Beth Jacob in Pontiac, Michigan, then at Temple Beth El in Flint, Michigan, in the 1930s and early 1940s. Beginning in 1943, he served the American Council for Judaism as its national executive director until becoming its executive vice president from 1955 until 1967. He was also director of American Friends of the Middle East and began serving as the president of American Jewish Alternatives to Zionism in 1968. He wrote several books, including *The Jewish Dilemma, Who Knows Better Must Say So, Peace in the Middle East: How to Achieve It?, Judaism or Jewish Nationalism,* and *Memoirs of an Anti-Zionist Jew.*

OBITUARIES AND OTHER SOURCES:

BOOKS

Who's Who in World Jewry, Olive Books of Israel (Tel-Aviv), 1978.

PERIODICALS

New York Times, October 9, 1996, p. D19.

* * *

BERGER, Meyer   1898-1959(?)

PERSONAL: Born September 1, 1898, in New York, NY; died following a stroke, February 8, 1959 (one source says 1960), in New York, NY; son of Ignace (a tailor) and Sarah (a candy store operator; maiden name, Waldman) Berger; married Mae Gamsu, August 27, 1926. *Politics:* Independent Democrat. *Religion:* Jewish. *Avocational interests:* Photography, sound equipment.

CAREER: Sold newspapers at the age of eight; became a night messenger at the *New York World* (newspaper) at the age of eleven, then became police reporter, 1919-28; *New York Times,* reporter, columnist, re-writer, 1928-37, 1938-59; *New Yorker,* staff writer, 1937-38. *Military service:* U.S. Army, 106th Infantry, 27th Division, served in World War I, attained rank of sergeant; awarded the Silver Star, the Purple Heart, and the Conspicuous Service Cross.

AWARDS, HONORS: Nominated for a Pulitzer Prize, c. 1932, for stories on Al Capone's tax evasion trial; Pulitzer Prize, 1950, for his 4,000 word story on the mass killings by Howard Unruh in Camden, NJ.

WRITINGS:

NONFICTION

The Eight Million: Journal of a New York Correspondent, Simon & Schuster (New York, NY), 1942.
(With James Keller) *The Men of Maryknoll,* Scribners (New York, NY), 1943.
Growth of an Ideal, 1850-1950: The Story of the Manhattan Savings Bank, Beck Engraving Co. (Philadelphia, PA), 1950.
The Story of the New York Times, 1851-1951, Simon & Schuster, 1951.
New York: City on Many Waters, Arts (New York, NY), 1956.
The Library, New York Public Library (New York, NY), 1956.
Meyer Berger's New York, Random House (New York, NY), 1960.

Also contributor to periodicals, including *New York World, New York Times, New Yorker, Saturday Evening Post, Reader's Digest, Holiday,* and *Nation's Business.*

SIDELIGHTS: Meyer Berger was a Pulitzer Prize-winning journalist who spent the bulk of his career on the staff of the *New York Times.* He covered stories such as Chicago gangster Al Capone's trial for tax evasion, which garnered him a nomination for the Pulitzer during the 1930s, as well as the fatal shooting rampage of Howard Unruh in Camden, New Jersey—the story which finally won him the prize itself in 1950. Though he reported on other crime news such as the tax trial of another underworld figure, Dutch Schultz, and on noteworthy events such as the first return of World War II American war dead, Berger will also be remembered for his columns, which discussed human and general interest features discovered in his beloved New York City. In addition to his newspaper work, Berger had several books to his credit, including *The Eight Million: Journal of a New York Correspondent,* a collaboration with Catholic priest James Keller about missionaries trained at the Maryknoll Seminary entitled *The Men of Maryknoll,* and *The Story of the New York Times, 1851-1951.* Many of his columns were collected in book form as well, including the posthumously published *Meyer Berger's New York.*

Berger was born to a poor family of Jewish immigrants in 1898 in New York City. His father was a tailor in Brooklyn, and Berger began working at the age of eight, selling newspapers. By the age of eleven, he had made the transition to performing messenger duty for the paper itself, the *New York World.* During his adolescence, he rose to chief office boy, and James S. Featherston in the *Dictionary of Literary Biography* quoted Berger's recollection of those times: "Here I absorbed all the legends of the craft, ancient and contemporary. I contracted newsprint fever in this way, by a kind of osmosis." Berger also offered the opinion that "here I learned, I think, a sounder journalism than is taught in graver halls of learning." Berger never finished high school, because he had to work to help support his family.

When World War I began, Berger enlisted in the U.S. Army. He wound up in the infantry and rose to the rank of sergeant, receiving the Silver Star for carrying some of his wounded fellow soldiers to safety in the face of heavy fire. When he returned home, Berger also returned to the *New York World,* but began serving as that paper's police reporter. He remained until 1928, when he was hired by the *New York Times.* Initially Berger was assigned to write the news that concerned the burroughs of Brooklyn and Queens, and, as Featherston put it, "his first stories to attract widespread attention were about a series of murders among Brooklyn waterfront gangsters." The reporter steadily rose in status until he was assigned to report on Capone's trial.

In 1937, Berger was hired away by the *New Yorker,* but he did not get along well with the publication's famed editor, Harold Ross, who wanted Berger's writings to take a higher tone. Featherston quoted one of Berger's colleagues at the *New Yorker,* A. J. Liebling, as saying, "Berger had once written a *New Yorker* profile of a man who fished for lost coins

through subway gratings, and Ross had been trying for months to disinfect the magazine by running pieces about the Supreme Court and the Persian Room of the Plaza." By 1938, Berger returned to his comfortable place at the *New York Times.*

Berger's first book, *The Eight Million,* saw print in 1942. In it, according to Stanley Walker in *New York Herald Tribune Book Review,* the journalist "succeeds in giving a fascinating picture of that part of New York which has always been his main interest—which is to say, the low-life, the criminal, the eccentric, and those important little people who somehow manage to have a touch of drama in their lives." Among the "eccentric," perhaps, is the wife of one of Berger's city editors, of whom he recalls that, being an overweight invalid confined to her bed, she would hold weekly concerts in her bedroom. At this time, Berger was still a copy-boy, and it was one of his duties to attend these concerts. He also provides more historical anecdotes in *The Eight Million,* including some stories about the corrupt guards in the city jail known as the Tombs, who used to sell death masks of criminals to circus entrepreneur P. T. Barnum. Edward Frank Allen in the *New York Times Book Review* predicted "there should be a lot of satisfied customers for the book" and declared it to be "the work of a really first-rate reporter, one of the best New York has seen for many years."

Though Berger was Jewish, he collaborated with the Rev. James Keller on a book about missionary priests who were educated for their service at Maryknoll-on-the-Hudson. The reporter got to know many of Maryknoll's staff, and continued to visit the place after the project was finished. *The Men of Maryknoll,* published in the middle of World War II, featured accounts of brave clergymen who went to the jungles from Indonesia to Bolivia, ministering to flocks ranging from persecuted Christians to lepers. Clare Godfrey in the *Weekly Book Review* hailed it as "a high-spirited, robust story of American courage, informed by faith and integrated by the love of God." *Catholic World* praised it as "a series of stories whose interest never flags." Berger was even personally thanked by Pope Pius XII for his work on *The Men of Maryknoll.*

Another of Berger's important books was 1951's *The Story of the New York Times.* Published for the occasion of the paper's one hundredth anniversary, it recounted various aspects of its subject's history. Included in its pages are anecdotes about the *Times'* first publisher, Henry J. Raymond, who guided the paper through its crusade against the corruption of nineteenth-century New York city politician Boss Tweed; the story of how later publisher Adolph Ochs gave the paper its slogan, "All the News That's Fit to Print," while restoring it to greatness; managing editor Carr Vattel Van Anda, who caught renowned scientist Albert Einstein in a mathematical error; and tales of the paper's many scoops, including information about the sinking of the *Titanic* in 1912. Harold Hutchings in *Chicago Tribune Books* lauded *The Story of the New York Times* as Berger's "most extensive contribution to the 'newspaper of record' he serves." Erwin D. Canham in the *New York Times Book Review* concluded that the book "will be of value now and for years to come to all who are interested in the preservation of a free press."

Berger died following a stroke in 1959. A collection of his columns about life in New York City, *Meyer Berger's New York,* was published the following year. The volume includes the story of a game warden at work on Manhattan Island, as well as that of a blind violinist who received eight offers of a free violin after Berger first reported his wish to again own one of the instruments. "Berger makes no attempt to conceal his insatiable romance with New York," noted Philip Hamburger in the *New York Times Book Review.* Walker, in yet another piece for the *New York Herald Tribune Book Review,* praised the book's "great value" and urged journalism students to "take Berger as a model for this particular type of writing."

In addition to receiving wonderful reviews for his writing, Berger was greatly admired by his colleagues as a human being. When he won the Pulitzer Prize for his article about Unruh, a veteran of World War II who suddenly went berserk and started shooting people in New Jersey, Berger sent the one thousand dollar honorarium which accompanied the prize to Unruh's mother.

BIOGRAPHICAL/CRITICAL SOURCES:

BOOKS

Dictionary of Literary Biography, Volume 29: *American Newspaper Journalists, 1926-1950,* Gale, 1984.

PERIODICALS

Catholic World, February, 1944, p. 508.
Chicago Tribune Books, September 30, 1951, p. 6.

New York Herald Tribune Book Review, June 14, 1942, p. 15; May 29, 1960, p. 12.
New York Times Book Review, June 14, 1942, p. 8; September 23, 1951, pp. 1, 29; March 20, 1960, p. 3.
Weekly Book Review, December 5, 1943, p. 42.*

—*Sketch by Elizabeth Wenning*

* * *

BERGER, Stefan 1964-

PERSONAL: Born September 26, 1964, in Langenfeld, Germany; son of Karl (an electrician) and Inge (an accountant; maiden name, Multaup) Berger; married Jutta Grub (a university lecturer), November 2, 1991; children: Kristina. *Ethnicity:* "German." *Education:* Attended Albertus Magnus University, 1985-87; Trinity College, Oxford, D.Phil., 1991. *Politics:* "Labour." *Religion:* Lutheran.

ADDRESSES: Home—1 Pentyrch St., Cathays, Cardiff CF2 4JW, Wales. *Office*—EUROS, University of Wales, P.O. Box 908, Cardiff CF1 3YQ, Wales.

CAREER: University of Plymouth, Plymouth, England, lecturer in British social history, 1990-91; University of Wales, Cardiff, lecturer in European studies, 1991—. *Military service:* Conscientious objector to military service.

MEMBER: German History Society, Labour History Society.

AWARDS, HONORS: Rhodes scholar, Oxford University, 1987-90.

WRITINGS:

The British Labour Party and the German SPD, Oxford University Press (Oxford, England), 1994.
The Force of Labour, Berg Publishers (London, England), 1995.
National Identity and Historical Consciousness in Germany, Berghahn Books, in press.
Social Democracy in Context, Longman, in press.
Labour and Nationalism, Manchester University Press (Manchester, England), in press.

Contributor to journals and newspapers, including *Past and Present, New Left Review,* and *Journal for Area Studies.*

WORK IN PROGRESS: Apologias for the Nation State, publication by Routledge expected in 1998.

SIDELIGHTS: Stefan Berger told *CA:* "Growing up in a Social Democratic working-class family in Langenfeld, Germany, I was the first member of the family to attend university. Selected first a scholar of the German National Scholarship Foundation in 1985, I became a German Rhodes Scholar at Trinity College in 1987. There I completed a doctorate on the British Labour Party and the German Social Democrats. In it, I compared the organizations, ideologies, and mentalities of the two parties between 1900 and 1931; I also investigated the relations between the two groups.

"I have always combined my intellectual interest in twentieth-century labor movements with a firm political commitment: first as an active member in the German Social Democratic Party and later in the British Labour Party. I was also active in the German peace movement in the late 1980s.

"My second book, *The Force of Labour,* was a study of the connection between labor and the working class in seven Western European countries; namely England, France, Germany, Italy, Spain, the Netherlands, and Sweden. My explicit aim was to bring out the similarities and differences between developments in these countries. My commitment to labor history is reflected in my current work on labor and nationalism, as well as in my preparation of a manuscript on the German SPD in the twentieth century in its international context. I am the coordinator of the Cardiff research group on Western European labor movements and am responsible for a master's degree program at the university on Western European labor studies, which approaches the topic in an explicitly comparative and interdisciplinary way.

"Ever since the reunification of Germany in 1990, I have keenly followed the re-emergence of a historiographic and political nationalism in that country. The changing political culture of Germany has been the subject of a number of journal articles, as well as my manuscript on national identity and historical consciousness. I also contribute occasionally to the German daily newspaper *Frankfurter Rundschau.*

"If I had to name the two historians whose work probably had the greatest influence on my own intellectual development, I would have to mention Eric Hobsbawm and George Iggers."

*   *   *

BIENVENU, Marcelle   1945-

PERSONAL: Born February 26, 1945, in St. Martinville, LA; daughter of Marcel M. (a newspaper editor and publisher) and Rhena (a homemaker; maiden name, Broussard) Bienvenu; married Rock H. Lasserre, Jr., October 6, 1990. *Education:* University of Southwestern Louisiana, B.A., 1967. *Religion:* Roman Catholic.

ADDRESSES: Home and office—1056 Mimosa Lane, St. Martinville, LA 70582.

CAREER: Times-Picayune, New Orleans, LA, feature writer, 1967-71; Time-Life Books, New York City, researcher and consultant, beginning in 1971; Chez Marcelle, near Lafayette, LA, owner and operator, 1981-84; *Times-Picayune,* author of the weekly column "Cooking Creole," 1984—. *Times of Acadiana,* food writer 1986—. Emeril's Restaurant, cookbook writer, 1993—; catering director and public relations consultant for restaurants, including Commander's Palace, K-Paul's Louisiana Kitchen, and Brennan's of Houston. Acadian Memorial Foundation, member, 1993—.

MEMBER: Les Dames d'Escoffier.

WRITINGS:

Who's Your Mama, Are You Catholic, and Can You Make a Roux? (cookbook), Times of Acadiana Publishing (Lafayette, LA), 1991.
Cajun Cooking for Beginners, Acadian House Publishing (Lafayette), 1994.
(With Emeril Lagasse) *Louisiana Real and Rustic,* Morrow (New York City), 1996.

Editor of *The Picayune's Creole Cook Book,* 1987. Contributor to books, including *Foods of the World, American Cooking: Creole and Acadian,* and *The American Wilderness: The Bayous,* all published by Time-Life. Contributor to magazines and newspapers.

SIDELIGHTS: Marcelle Bienvenu told *CA:* "I write because I enjoy it and because the subject of food and its history, and its influences on our lives, is very interesting to me. Coming from a small town in South Louisiana and having been raised in an area that is very unique in its history, culture, and cuisine, I want people to know about it.

"I write almost every day, in my office located in the back yard of my home on the bayou. My inspiration has come from my father, who was a newspaper publisher and editor. In fact, his family has been in the newspaper business since 1886. I have also been inspired by Ella Brennan of the famous New Orleans restaurant clan. She has always been a great mentor."

*   *   *

BIRDZELL, L(uther) E(arle), Jr. 1916-

PERSONAL: Born December 18, 1916, in Grand Forks, ND; son of Luther E. (a lawyer) and Bessie Leola (a housewife; maiden name, Perring) Birdzell; married Violet Joslyn Magowan (a housewife), May 8, 1943; children: Luther Earle, David Magowan. *Education:* University of Chicago, A.B., 1939; Harvard Law School, LL.D., 1942.

ADDRESSES: Home—51 Prairie Avenue, Newport, RI 02840.

CAREER: Debevoise, Plimpton & McLane, New York City, lawyer, 1944-47; McCutchen, Thomas, Matthews, San Francisco, CA, lawyer, 1947-52; General Electric Co., New York City, lawyer, 1952-77.

WRITINGS:

Competing: The Enterprise of Business, National Chamber Foundation, 1981.
Ethical Problems of Inside Counsel, Matthew Bender, 1984.
(With Nathan Rosenberg) *How the West Grew Rich,* Basic Books, 1986.

SIDELIGHTS: Explaining the nature of the historical argument of *How the West Grew Rich* (which he wrote with Nathan Rosenberg), L. E. Birdzell, Jr. told *CA:* "Growth in wealth is a form of social change, and societies do not generally allow social change unless they are too weakly organized to pre-

vent it. Beginning at the close of the Middle Ages, advances in trade and transportation knit the West into an economic society without supplying a strong political organization of corresponding geographic scope. Being an economic empire without a political *imperium,* the West escaped the social bond into some two or three centuries of rapid economic and intellectual advance and radical social change."

How the West Grew Rich received a great deal of critical attention and was the subject of some debate. British and Canadian reviewers questioned the significance of the book's analysis for those Western societies that have not seen the same levels of growth, and at least one U.S. reviewer took exception to the authors' celebration of capitalism. For many, however, *How the West Grew Rich* was the source for praise.

The *New York Review of Books* devoted nearly four pages to a David S. Landes article analyzing the authors' arguments. Despite ascribing, among other weaknesses, a derivative quality to the book's early chapters, Landes concluded: "These weaknesses, however, are more than compensated by the fundamental good sense of the authors, who recognize the difference between what probably was and what should have been. They keep their eye on the subject, do not let themselves get diverted by passion or moral indignation, do not feel an obligation to do penance and thereby prove their personal virtue and good feeling. One may not always agree with them, but that is to be expected: there is no big picture that can't use some emendation."

In the *New York Times Book Review,* Donald N. McCloskey called Birdzell's and Rosenberg's account "a sweet and lucid tale." Like Landes, McCloskey found favor with the book's representation of history as well as its analysis, pronouncing it "a lively and intelligent book." Eric J. Hobsbawn also had words of approbation for the execution of *How the West Grew Rich;* "It is written very lucidly, based on sound literature and," he acknowledged in the *Los Angeles Times Book Review,* ". . . it follows a conventional track, even as the authors shake their heads over the footprints of their predecessors, such as Karl Marx."

In Hobsbawn's opinion, however, the authors go awry with the book's editorial emphasis, "For to write a book praising the principles that are said to have made the West rich is not to give an adequate account of either the how or the why." McCloskey conceded that *How the West Grew Rich* "is an argument for capitalism," but concluded that the book had earned its thesis: ". . . this is no pamphlet. It is jammed with economic argument and historical fact. Scholarly, amusingly written, accurate, it is a good college course in 'What We Know about Economic History.' If what we know adds up to three cheers for capitalism that's just too bad."

Birdzell himself addressed the potential for voices critical of the analysis and arguments of *How the West Grew Rich*. "Trying to understand the phylogeny of Western society is no doubt deconstructively critical of those who think the point is to change it," he told *CA*. "But in the twentieth century we have seen perhaps a hundred million lives lost at the hands of those whose passion for changing the world outran their understanding of it, so that there is ample motivation for some deconstructive understanding."

A graduate of Harvard Law School who served as legal counsel for General Electric Company for 25 years, Birdzell is also the author of *Competing: The Enterprise of Business* (published in 1981) and *Ethical Problems of Inside Counsel*, published by Matthew Bender in 1984.

BIOGRAPHICAL/CRITICAL SOURCES:

PERIODICALS

Globe and Mail (Toronto), February 20, 1988.
Los Angeles Times Book Review, January 12, 1986, p. 1.
New York Review of Books, May 29, 1986, p. 46.
New York Times Book Review, February 9, 1986, p. 18.
Times Literary Supplement, September 12, 1986, p. 1000.*

*   *   *

BISHOP, James Jr. 1936-

PERSONAL: Born September 6, 1936, in New York, NY; son of James (a farmer) and Lucile (an artist; Brokaw) Bishop; married Caroline Mallory, March 21, 1960 (divorced); children: Anne, James, William. *Education:* Attended St. Paul's School, Concord, New Hampshire; Colby College, Waterville, Maine, B.A. *Politics:* Independent. *Religion:* Episcopal. *Avocational interests:* Studying and teaching music.

ADDRESSES: Home—113 Wilson, Sedona, AZ 86336. *Office*—Box 2917, Sedona, AZ 86339. *Agent*—Jonathan Matson, 276 Fifth Avenue, New York, NY 10001.

CAREER: Newsweek, New York City, researcher, 1958-1963, Los Angeles, correspondent, 1963-66, Washington, D.C., bureau chief, 1966-1977; U.S. Department of Energy, Deputy Assistant Secretary, 1978-79; Arts and Culture Commission, Sedona, AZ, 1990—.

AWARDS, HONORS: William Allen White Gold Medal, 1992.

WRITINGS:

(With Henry W. Hubbard) *Let the Seller Beware*, National Press (Washington, D.C.), 1969.
(Editor) *Creating Abundance: America's Least-Cost Energy Strategy*, McGraw Hill (New York), 1984.
(With Kate Ruland-Thorne) *Experience Jerome and the Verde Valley: Legends and Legacies*, Thorne Enterprises (Sedona, AZ), 1990.
Epitaph for a Desert Anarchist: The Life and Legacy of Edward Abbey, Atheneum (New York), 1994.

WORK IN PROGRESS: Essays on the new west; researching Native American tourism, water rights, and justice.

SIDELIGHTS: James Bishop, Jr., told *CA*: "After careers in journalism and government, I've turned to teaching at the university level—wonderful experience: Scott Momaday, Terry Tempest Williams, William Eastlake, Edward Abbey, D.H. Lawrence. Through their words—and through the reactions of my students—my abilities to capture the Southwest, its inhabitants, its triumphs and tragedies are sharper, deeper, ever reminding me of exactly how vital the Southwest is to the American Myth. The 'geography of hope,' as Wallace Stegner puts it. I am becoming part of the land, the rivers and the red rock canyons, and I will write until I drop."

*   *   *

BLISSETT, Luther
  See HOME, Stewart

BLUESTEIN, Barry (M.) 1950-

PERSONAL: Born May 15, 1950, in New York, NY. *Education:* Boston University, B.A., 1972.

ADDRESSES: Agent—Susan Ramer, Don Congdon Associates, 156 Fifth Ave., No. 625, New York, NY 10010.

CAREER: Season to Taste Books Ltd. (retail cookbook store), Chicago, IL, co-owner, 1988-93; writer, 1993—.

MEMBER: International Association of Cooking Professionals.

WRITINGS:

WITH KEVIN L. MORRISSEY

Dip It!, Contemporary Books (Chicago, IL), 1990.
Light Sauces, Contemporary Books, 1991.
Quick Breads, Contemporary Books, 1991.
The 99% Fat-Free Cookbook, Doubleday (New York), 1994.
Home Made in the Kitchen, Penguin (New York), 1994.
The 99% Fat-Free Book of Appetizers and Desserts, Doubleday, 1996.
The Complete Cookie, Doubleday, 1996.
The Home Made in the Kitchen Household Almanac, Penguin, in press.

WORK IN PROGRESS: Fat-Free Fast, with Morrissey, publication by Doubleday expected in 1998.

* * *

BOK, Hannes (Vajn) 1914-1964

PERSONAL: Original name, Wayne Woodard (adopted the name Hannes Vajn Bok); born July 2, 1914, in Kansas City, MO; died April 11, 1964. *Education:* Attended high school in Duluth, MN.

CAREER: Illustrator and writer.

AWARDS, HONORS: Hugo Award for cover art, 1953; Bokanalia Foundation established 1967.

WRITINGS:

FANTASY NOVELS; AND ILLUSTRATOR

The Sorcerer's Ship, originally published in *Unknown,* 1942, Ballantine (New York), 1969.
(With Abraham Merritt) *The Fox Woman and the Blue Pagoda,* New Collectors Group (New York), 1946.
(With Merritt) *The Black Wheel,* New Collectors Group, 1947.
Beyond the Golden Stair, Ballantine, 1970.
Spinner of Silver and Thistle, SISU (San Francisco, CA), 1972.
(With Merritt) *The Fox Woman and the Blue Pagoda, and The Black Wheel* (omnibus), Arno Press (New York), 1976.

OTHER

The Hannes Bok Memorial Showcase of Fantasy Art, edited by Emil Petaja, SISU, 1974.
A Hannes Bok Sketchbook, edited by Gerry de la Ree and Gene Nigra, de la Ree (Saddle River, NJ), 1976.
Beauty and the Beasts: The Art of Hannes Bok, edited by Gerry de la Ree, de la Ree, 1978.
A Hannes Bok Treasury, edited by Stephen D. Korshak, Underwood Miller (Lancaster, PA), 1993.
A Hannes Bok Showcase, edited by Korshak, Charles F. Miller (Lancaster, PA), 1995.

Contributor of stories and illustrations to periodicals, including *Weird Tales, Unknown, Cosmic Stories, Fantastic Universe, Future Fiction, Imagination, Planet Stories, Stirring Science Stories, Super Science Stories, Science Fiction Quarterly,* and *Famous Fantastic Mysteries.* Contributor of illustrations to specialty-press books. Illustrator of book jackets for publishers, including Arkham House, Fantast Press, Gnome Press, and Shasta Publishers.*

* * *

BONELLO, Frank J. 1939-

PERSONAL: Born May 11, 1939, in Detroit, MI; son of Anthony and Michelina (Cassar) Bonello; children: John, David. *Education:* University of Detroit, B.S., 1961, M.A., 1963; Michigan State University,

Ph.D., 1968. *Politics:* Independent. *Religion:* Roman Catholic.

ADDRESSES: Home—18280 Amberly Lane, South Bend, IN 46637. *Office*—Department of Economics, 408 Decio, University of Notre Dame, Notre Dame, IN 46556.

CAREER: University of Notre Dame, Notre Dame, IN, assistant professor, 1968-74, associate professor of economics, 1974—. Also worked for U.S. Agency for International Development, *World Book Encyclopedia,* and U.S. Chamber of Commerce.

WRITINGS:

The Formulation of Expected Interest Rate, Michigan State University Press (East Lansing, MI), 1970.

Computer Assisted Instruction in Economic Education, University of Notre Dame Press (Notre Dame, IN), 1974.

Supply Side Economics, Dushkin (Guilford, CT), 1985.

(With Thomas Swartz) *Taking Sides: Clashing Views of Alternative Economic Issues,* Dushkin, 1992, 7th edition, 1995.

(Editor) *Urban Finance Under Siege,* M. E. Sharpe (Armonk, NY), 1993.

*   *   *

BOROWSKI, Tadeusz 1922-1951

PERSONAL: Born November 12, 1922, in Zytomierz, Poland, U.S.S.R.; committed suicide, July, 1951, in Warsaw, Poland; son of a laborer and a seamstress. *Education:* Studied in Warsaw University underground, 1940. *Politics:* Communist.

CAREER: Writer. Worked as a night watchman, c. 1940; imprisoned in Auschwitz and Dachau concentration camps, 1943-45; political journalist and publicist, Munich, Germany, 1948-51.

WRITINGS:

(Published anonymously) *Gdziekolwiek ziemia* (poetry; title means "Wherever the Earth"), privately printed (Warsaw), 1942.

Imiona nurtu (poetry; title means "The Names of the Current"), [Warsaw], 1945.

(With K. Olszewski) *Poszukiwania* (poetry; title means "Tracing"), [Warsaw], 1945.

(With Olszewski and J. Nel Siedlecki) *Bylismy w Oswiecimiu* (title means "We Were in Auschwitz"), [Warsaw], 1946.

Pewien zolnierz, [Warsaw], 1947.

Kamienny swiat (title means "World of Stone"), [Warsaw], 1948; translation by Barbara Vedder published as *This Way for the Gas, Ladies and Gentlemen, and Other Stories,* Viking (New York), 1967.

Pozegnanie z Maria (short stories; title means "Farewell to Maria"), [Warsaw], 1949.

Czerwony maj, [Warsaw], 1953.

Utwory zebrane (title means "Collected Works"), five volumes, Zaklad Narodowy (Warsaw), 1954.

Proza z lat 1948-1952, [Warsaw], 1954.

Wspomnienia, wiersze, opowiadania (prose), Panstwowy Instytut (Warsaw), 1977.

Dzien na Harmenzach, Wydawn (Krakow), 1978.

Selected Poems, translated by Tadeusz Pioro, Hit & Run Press (Walnut Creek, CA), 1990.

ADAPTATIONS: The story "Bitwa pod Grunwaldem" ("The Battle of Grunwald") was filmed by Andrzej Wajda as *Landscape after a Battle.*

SIDELIGHTS: Considered by critics to be one of the finest literary talents to emerge from his native Poland after World War II, Tadeusz Borowski's works reflect the tragic circumstances of his youth. Arrested and imprisoned in the Auschwitz concentration camp in 1943 shortly after the underground publication of his first collection of poetry, Borowski witnessed the horrors both there and at Dachau, where he was sent prior to the Allied liberation in 1945. These experiences were reflected in his 1945 poetry collection *Imiona nurtu,* as well as several volumes of nihilistic stories which were translated by Barbara Vedder for English-speaking readers in 1967 as *This Way for the Gas, Ladies and Gentlemen, and Other Stories.* Together with other survivors of the death-camps of Eastern Europe, Borowski's works are part of what is referred to as the "literature of atrocity."

Born to an impoverished couple in 1922, Borowski was raised in the Soviet Ukraine. His childhood was marked by poverty and tragedy; by the time he was four years old his father had been accused of political dissidence and removed to a labor camp in the Arctic; his mother was sent to Siberia when Borowski was scarcely eight years old, and he was put in the care of an aunt. Borowski and his parents were reunited in the late 1930s; the outbreak of World War II found them living under German rule in Nazi-occupied Poland. Borowski and his family moved to Warsaw during the German occupation, and the young writer was forced to complete his education in a clandestine fashion because educating Poles was prohibited by Nazi decree. Determined to pursue college studies, Borowski attended underground lectures at Warsaw University, where he met other young poets and wrote and published his first book of poetry.

Gdziekolwiek ziemia, a collection of metaphoric verse that centered on the death of civilized man within the concentration camps, was printed by its author and distributed in secret in 1942; despite the fact that the volume was published anonymously, Borowski and his fiancee were arrested by the Gestapo shortly after its release. Accused of activism against the occupation, the couple was shuttled through several prison camps before reaching their final destination: Auschwitz. The ability to survive, which Borowski had learned during the extreme poverty of his childhood, helped him to survive the brutal conditions at Auschwitz. Quickly realizing that survival meant betraying other prisoners before they could betray him, he gained a job as a hospital orderly, working closely alongside his Nazi captors and, in some sense, serving as an accomplice in the continued brutality that was inflicted upon camp inmates. Moved to Dachau as liberation forces drove the Germans back behind their former borders, Borowski was eventually freed in 1945.

Borowski's stark and brutally realistic fiction was presented from the viewpoint of a moralist and a cynic. It was the short stories in *Pozegnanie z Maria* ("Farewell to Maria"), which feature the ruthless tactics necessary for human survival in Nazi death camps, that firmly established Borowski as an important new voice in Polish literature. 1948's *Kamienny swiat* contains twenty short stories depicting life after the occupation; selections from both were later translated as *This Way for the Gas, Ladies and Gentlemen.* The anthology's title story recounts the events of a single day in the life of the camp "labour Kommando," the man responsible for unloading the trainloads of incoming Jews destined for extermination. In one scene, the narrator dispassionately describes a Jewish woman's efforts to flee from the side of her frightened young child in order to save her own life. In "Kamienny swiat" ("The World of Stone") Borowski peopled his stories with antiheroes facing choices that could only result in injustice. He juxtaposes the horror of war, in which the regular "disappearance" of neighbors and horrible fate of

Jews and Poles were considered commonplace, with the mindless bustle of "normalcy" that returned immediately to Munich's city streets after the war: the reader must question what makes a human life or moral code "normal."

"In these stories," noted George Gomori in *Reference Guide to Short Fiction,* "Borowski stresses the banality of evil. His SS-men are not demonic, they are not even particularly sadistic; their main characteristic is cool indifference, although some of them show interest in the efficient realization of their 'job.'" While several reviewers have faulted this aspect of Borowski's writing, calling the cool indifference of his narration a sign of nihilism and amorality, others have applauded his approach, noting that such indifference intensifies the moral outrage of the reader not only to the moral degeneracy of the perpetrators of the violence, but also to that of the victims of Auschwitz and Dachau themselves. Borowski "showed Auschwitz as he had known it," according to A. Alvarez in the *New York Times Book Review,* "stripped of illusion, morality and fellow-feeling, where each man is remorselessly for himself and hates those who persecute him less than those he persecutes because the latter arouse guilt and guilt is debilitating."

In addition to his short stories, Borowski also composed a great deal of poetry; he considered himself to be more of a poet than a prose writer. Despite the quantity of his verse, it was not made available in English translation until 1990's *Selected Poems,* which includes poems from *Gdziekolwiek ziemia* and from later writings. "Certain elements of Borowski's poetic attitude, evident in his early poems—negativism, destructive catastrophism, an inability to accept and cope with reality—reveal a personality that is exceptionally vulnerable to outside pressure," noted *World Literature Today* reviewer Bogdana Carpenter, who described Borowski's later, post-war verses as "journalistic, simplistic, vociferous in the style of propaganda pamphlets."

Borowski's own adjustment to the normalcy of life after the dehumanizing horrors he witnessed during World War II—a result of his disillusionment and his own guilt at the means by which he survived the camps—was difficult. "The whole world is really like the concentration camp," he wrote in *This Way for the Gas;* "the weak work for the strong, and if they have no strength or will to work—then let them steal, or let them die." Haunted by the spectre of thousands of condemned faces from the death camps, he harnessed his personal guilt and hopes for a better life in supporting the Communist party. In 1949 he became a confirmed Stalinist and performed intelligence work for the secret police during the early years of the Cold War. Having returned to Poland in 1946, he worked in Warsaw as a journalist, composing brilliantly aggressive pro-communist propaganda for newspapers. Finally, at the age of twenty-nine, Borowski could no longer battle his inner torment; he committed suicide by suffocating himself with gas in his own oven and his body was found in his Warsaw apartment on July 3, 1951.

BIOGRAPHICAL/CRITICAL SOURCES:

BOOKS

Bosmajian, Hamida, *Metaphors of Evil: Contemporary German Literature and the Shadow of Nazism,* University of Iowa Press (Dubuque), 1979.

Langer, Lawrence L., *Versions of Survival: The Holocaust and the Human Spirit,* State University of New York Press, 1982.

Milosz, Czeslaw, *History of Polish Literature,* Macmillan (New York), 1969.

Reference Guide to Short Fiction, St. James Press (Detroit, MI), 1991, pp. 82-83.

Twentieth-Century Literary Criticism, Volume 9, Gale (Detroit), 1983, pp. 19-27.

PERIODICALS

Dissident, March-April, 1968, pp. 184-86.

Nation, June 19, 1976, pp. 760-62.

New Republic, April 10, 1976, pp. 31-32; October 27, 1986, pp. 34-35.

New Statesman, May 5, 1967, pp. 622-23.

New York Review of Books, May 27, 1976, pp. 14-15.

New York Times Book Review, February 29, 1976, p. 3.

Polish Review, summer, 1967, pp. 43-52.

Times Literary Supplement, September 21, 1967.

Washington Post Book World, March 7, 1976.

World Literature Today, spring, 1991, p. 326.*

*   *   *

BOURDAIN, Anthony 1957(?)-

PERSONAL: Born c. 1957. *Education:* Attended Vassar University, Culinary Institute of America.

ADDRESSES: Agent—c/o Villard Books, 201 East 50th St., New York, NY 10022.

CAREER: Writer. Chef at Supper Club, New York, NY, later at Vince & Linda at One Fifth, New York, NY.

WRITINGS:

Bone In the Throat: A Novel of Death and Digestion, Villard (New York, NY), 1995.

SIDELIGHTS: Writer Anthony Bourdain is a chef at a Manhattan restaurant called Vince & Linda at One Fifth. The author also casts the hero of *Bone In the Throat: A Novel of Death and Digestion,* his 1995 comic thriller, as a New York chef. The hero, Tommy Pagano, does not join the mob—much to the disappointment of certain members of his extended family—but instead trains as a chef. Nonetheless, Pagano becomes involved in brutal Cosa Nostra activities when he gets a job at a restaurant in Little Italy. He soon discovers that the FBI has created the restaurant as part of an operation to sting a mob loan shark.

Although a reviewer for *Entertainment Weekly* called the plot of *Bone in the Throat* "a dumbed-down version of *The Godfather,*" and a *Library Journal* contributor offered a similarly negative assessment. The *New York Times Book Review*'s Marilyn Stasio praised Bourdain's "clever narrative," and characterized his "comic vision" as "deliciously depraved." A *Publishers Weekly* contributor called the book, "A perfect sendup of macho mobsters and feebs alike."

BIOGRAPHICAL/CRITICAL SOURCES:

PERIODICALS

Entertainment Weekly, August 4, 1995, p. 53.
Library Journal, June 1, 1995, p. 158.
New York Times, April 12, 1995, p. B4.
New York Times Book Review, August 6, 1995, p. 23.
Publishers Weekly, May 15, 1995, p. 56.*

*   *   *

BOWN, Deni 1944-

PERSONAL: Surname rhymes with "town"; born January 28, 1944, in Doncaster, Yorkshire, England;

daughter of Frederick W. H. (an army officer) and Margaret (maiden name, Staples; present surname, Howard) Hobbs; married and divorced twice; married Peter J. A. A. Muir, November 20, 1993; children: Anna F. Green, William H. Y. Green, Robin Bown. *Ethnicity:* "Caucasian." *Education:* Victoria University of Manchester, B.A. (with first class honors), 1966. *Avocational interests:* Ethnobotany, ecology, travel, gardening, dance, yoga, ethnic food, frogs ("all aspects but culinary"), plants in art.

ADDRESSES: Office—Deni Bown Associates, Belvoir House, Tattam Close, Woolstone, Milton Keynes MK15 0HB, England; fax 01908-670368. *Agent*—Jane Martin, Deni Bown Associates, Belvoir House, Tattam Close, Woolstone, Milton Keynes MK15 0HB, England.

CAREER: Laurence Urdang Associates, Aylesbury, England, etymologist, 1972-77; Newbury College, Newbury, England, lecturer, 1982-84; Deni Bown Associates, Milton Keynes, England, writer and photographer.

MEMBER: Herb Society (member of council, 1993-96), British Herb Trade Association, Garden Writers Guild, Women in Enterprise.

AWARDS, HONORS: Wildlife Photographer of the Year Award, British Broadcasting Corp., 1986; award from Garden Writers Association of America, 1990, for *Alba: The Book of White Flowers.*

WRITINGS:

AUTHOR AND PHOTOGRAPHER

Aroids: Plants of the Arum Family, Timber Press (Portland, OR), 1988.
Fine Herbs, Unwin Hyman, 1988, published as *Ornamental Herbs for Your Garden,* HarperCollins (San Francisco, CA), 1993.
Alba: The Book of White Flowers, Timber Press, 1989.
Through the Seasons (juvenile), six volumes including *Pond, Stream, Wood, Park, Garden,* and *Field and Hedgerow,* Wayland, 1989.
Westonbirt Arboretum, Julian Holland Publishing, 1990.
Orchids, Heinemann, 1991.
Four Gardens in One: The Royal Botanic Garden, Edinburgh, H.M.S.O., 1992.

The Encyclopedia of Herbs and Their Uses, Dorling Kindersley (New York), 1995.
Growing Herbs, Dorling Kindersley, 1995.

Contributor to books, including *The Last Rainforests,* Mitchell Beazley, 1990; *The RHS Encyclopedia of Gardening,* Dorling Kindersley, 1992; and *The Complete Book of Plant Propagation,* Mitchell Beazley, 1996.

SIDELIGHTS: Deni Bown told *CA:* "I am a freelance writer and photographer, specializing in botany, gardening, herbs, and natural history. My interest in plants began with a childhood fascination for my grandfather's lilies and tulips and with a passion for spotting wildflowers. After university, I worked with Laurence Urdang Associates as the editor of place names for the *Collins English Dictionary.* I then pursued a varied career in horticulture, running an organic smallholding, growing orchids for Peter de Savary, and working with Judith and Simon Hopkinson for five years to establish Hollington Herbs.

"Joy is behind my writing and photography. All aspects of plant life inspire me, from details of biology, shapes, textures, colors, and scents to uses and meanings. My aim is to communicate the importance of plants—ecological, cultural, economic, and aesthetic—in ways that combine the practical and scientifically accurate with the inspirational in terms of words and images."

*   *   *

BOYETT, Steven R. 1960-

PERSONAL: Born in 1960, in Atlanta, GA.

ADDRESSES: Agent—c/o Ace Publishing, 200 Madison Ave., New York, NY 10016.

CAREER: Writer.

WRITINGS:

FANTASY NOVELS

Ariel: A Book of the Change, Ace (New York), 1983.
The Architect of Sleep, Ace, 1986.
(With Alan Aldridge) *The Gnole,* Heinemann (London), 1991.

BRAMAH, Ernest 1868-1942

PERSONAL: Full name, Ernest Bramah Smith; born March 20, 1868, near Manchester, Lancashire, England; died June 27, 1942; married Lucie Maisie Barker, 1897. *Education:* Attended Manchester Grammar School.

CAREER: Farmer for three years; worked on a provincial newspaper, then secretary to Jerome K. Jerome, and staff member on Jerome's magazine *Today;* editor, *The Minster,* London, 1895-96; writer.

WRITINGS:

FANTASY NOVELS; KAI LUNG SERIES

Kai Lung's Golden Hours, Grant Richards (London), 1922, Doran (New York), 1923.
Kai Lung Unrolls His Mat, Doubleday (New York), 1928.
The Moon of Much Gladness, Cassell (London), 1932, published as *The Return of Kai Lung,* Sheridan (New York), 1938.

NOVELS

What Might Have Been: The Story of a Social War, Murray (London), 1907, published as *The Secret of the League,* Nelson (London), 1909.
The Bravo of London, Cassell, 1934.

SHORT STORIES; KAI LUNG SERIES

The Wallet of Kai Lung, Page (Boston), 1900.
The Story of Wan and the Remarkable Shrub and The Story of Ching-Kwei and the Destinies, Doubleday, 1927, published in *Kai Lung Unrolls His Mat,* 1928.
Kai Lung Beneath the Mulberry Tree, Richards Press (London), 1940.
Kai Lung: Six, Non-Profit Press (Tacoma, WA), 1974.

SHORT STORIES

The Mirror of Kong Ho, Chapman and Hall (London), 1905, Doubleday, 1930.
Max Carrados, Methuen (London), 1914, Hyperion (Westport, CT), 1975.
The Eyes of Max Carrados, Grant Richards, 1923, Doran, 1924.
The Specimen Case, Hodder and Stoughton (London), 1924, Doran, 1925.

Max Carrados Mysteries, Hodder and Stoughton, 1927, Penguin (Baltimore, MD), 1964.
A Little Flutter, Cassell, 1930.
Best Max Carrados Detective Stories, edited by E. F. Bleiler, Dover (New York), 1972.

OTHER

English Farming and Why I Turned It Up, Leadenhall (London), 1894.
A Guide to the Varieties and Rarity of English Regal Copper Coins: Charles II-Victoria, 1671-1860, Methuen, 1929.

Manuscript Collections: Humanities Research Center, University of Texas, Austin; University of Illinois Library.*

* * *

BRANCA, Vittore (Felice Giovanni) 1913-

PERSONAL: Born July 9, 1913, in Savona, Italy; son of Giovanni and Lucia Branca; married Olga Montagner, July, 1938; children: Simona, Daniela, Donata, Lodovico. *Education:* University of Pisa, D.Litt, 1935. *Religion:* Catholic. *Avocational interests:* Swimming, climbing.

ADDRESSES: Home—San Marco 2885, Venice, Italy. *Office*—Fondazione Giorgio Cini, Venice, Italy.

CAREER: Accademia della Crusca, Florence, Italy, professor, 1937-48; Maria Assunta University, Rome, Italy, professor of Italian literature, 1948-50; University of Catania, Italy, professor of Italian literature, 1950-53; University of Padua, Padua, Italy, professor of Italian literature, 1953—; University of Bergamo, Italy, rector, 1968-72. *Military service:* Served in the Italian Resistance during World War II; awarded the Gold Medal of the Resistenza and the Commandeur de l'Ordre de la Pologne Liberee.

Head of the division of arts and letters for United Nations Educational Scientific and Cultural Organization (UNESCO), 1950-53, vice-president of the National Italian Commission, 1973—; vice-president and secretary general of the Fondazione Giorgio Cini in Venice; chair of the cultural committee of Italian RAI-TV, 1969-75; literary adviser to publishing houses; editor of the magazines *Lettere Italiane* and *Studi sul Boccaccio.*

MEMBER: International Federation of Modern Languages and Literatures (committee member), Instituto Veneto Scienze Lettere e Arti (president, 1979-85), Accademia dei Lincei, Accademia Arcadia, Accademia Polacca della Scienze, Academie du Monde Latin, Medieval Academy of America.

AWARDS, HONORS: Gold Medal from the Italian Ministry of Education, and Gold Medal from the Polish Ministry of Culture; honorary memberships in the Modern Language Association of America, the American Academy of Arts and Sciences, the British Academy, and the Moscow Union of Writers; honorary doctorates from the University of Budapest, University of New York, University of Bergamo, University of Paris—Sorbonne, and McGill University.

WRITINGS:

NONFICTION

Il Cantare trecentesco e il Boccaccio del "Filostrato" e del "Teseida", Sansoni (Florence, Italy), 1936.

Linee di una storia della critica al "Decameron," con bibliografia boccaccesca, Soc. Ed. Dante Alighieri (Rome, Italy), 1939.

(Editor) *Rime, Amorosa Visione, Caccia di Diana,* Laterza (Bari, Italy), 1939.

(Editor) *Rimatori del Dolce Stil Nuovo,* Soc. Ed. Dante Alighieri, 1941.

(Editor) *I mistici del Duecento e del Trecento,* Soc. Ed. Dante Alighieri, 1942, second edition, 1964.

(Editor) *Epistolae, Orationes, Carmina* (two volumes), Olschki (Florence, Italy), 1943.

(Editor) *Amorosa Visione,* Sansoni, 1944.

(Editor) *Il Varmo,* Le Monnier (Florence, Italy), 1945.

Emilio De Marchi, Morcelliana (Brescia, Italy), 1946.

Alfieri e la ricerca dello stile, Le Monnier, 1946, second edition, 1960, revised edition, Zanichelli (Bologna, Italy), 1981.

(Editor) *Il Conciliatore* (three volumes), [Italy], 1947-53, second edition, 1965.

Schemi letterari e schemi biografici nell'opera del Boccaccio, Olschki, 1947.

(Editor) *Il Decameron* (two volumes), Le Monnier, 1950-52, second edition, 1965.

Il Cantico di Frate Sole, Olschki, 1950, second edition, 1965.

(Editor) *Ricordi,* Le Monnier, 1956, third edition, 1970.

Boccaccio Medievale, Sansoni, 1956, third edition, 1970, new edition published by Accresciuta,

1976, expanded version translated by R. Clements as *Boccaccio: The Man and His Works,* New York University Press (New York, NY), 1976.

(Editor) *Rime—Caccia di Diana,* Liviana (Padova, Italy), 1957.

Tradizione delle opere di Giovanni Boccaccio, Storia e Letteratura (Rome, Italy), 1958.

L'Incompiuta seconda centuria dei "Miscellanea" di Angelo Poliziano, Olschki, 1961.

(With P. G. Ricci) *Un autografo del Decameron,* Cedam (Padova, Italy), 1962.

(Editor) *Tutte le opere di Giovanni Boccaccio,* Mondadori (Milan, Italy), 1964.

(Editor) *Opere,* Mursia (Milan, Italy), 1965.

(Editor) *De Coelibatu—De Officio Legati,* Olschki, 1968.

(Editor with E. Montale) *I cipressi di Bolgheri,* Le Monnier, 1969.

Momenti e protagonisti della letteratura italiana, Sansoni, 1969, fifth edition, 1972.

Sebastiano Ciampi, Accademia Polacca (Varsavia, Italy), 1969.

(Editor) *Tutte le opere,* La Scuola (Brescia, Italy), 1970.

(Editor with M. Pastore Stocchi) *Miscellaneorum Centuria Secunda,* Casa Ed. Alinari (Florence, Italy), 1972.

(Editor) *Decameron,* critical edition, Accademia della Crusca (Florence, Italy), and facsimile edition, Alinari, both 1976.

Filologia e critica letteraria, Rizzoli (Milan, Italy), 1977.

(Editor) *Profilo biografico,* Sansoni, 1977.

(Editor and author of introduction and notes) *Filippo, Saul, Mirra, Agamennone,* Rizzoli, 1981.

Vita: Vittorio Alfieri, Mursia (Milan, Italy), 1983.

(With Sante Graciotti) *Barocco in Italia e nei paesi slavi del Sud,* Olschki, 1983.

Boccaccio e dintorni, Olschki, 1983.

Poliziano e l'umanesimo della parola, G. Einaudi (Torino, Italy), 1983.

(With Stefano Rosso-Mazzinghi) *Angelo Giuseppe Roncalli: Dal Patriarcato di Venezia alla cattedra di San Pietro,* Olschki, 1984.

Ponte Santa Trinita: Per Amore di liberta, per amore di verita, Marsilio editori (Venice, Italy), 1987.

(Editor) *Mercanti scrittori: Ricordi nella Firenze tra medioevo e rinascimento,* Rusconi (Milan, Italy), c. 1987.

SIDELIGHTS: Italian author and editor Vittore Branca has had a long and distinguished career as a professor of Italian classical literature, teaching at institutions such as Maria Assunta University in Rome and the University of Padua. He has written several works of literary criticism, as well as edited several volumes of the writings of classical Italian authors. His titles include *Emilio De Marchi, Alfieri e la ricerca dello stile,* and *Vita: Vittorio Alfieri,* but Branca is known especially for his expertise on fourteenth-century Italian author Giovanni Boccaccio. Cecil Grayson in *Times Literary Supplement* hailed Branca as "the scholar who has done most in recent decades to advance our knowledge and understanding of this author." Branca has edited both critical and facsimile versions of Boccaccio's *Decameron,* and has had one of his books about the classical writer, *Boccaccio: The Man and His Works,* published in English. Branca has also served as the editor of the periodicals *Lettere Italiane* and *Studi sul Boccaccio.* The scholar has received some prestigious awards for his academic work, including gold medals from the Italian Ministry of Education and the Polish Ministry of Culture.

As Grayson reported, Branca produced most of his facsimile edition of *Decameron* on an ancient manuscript said to have been copied by Boccaccio himself. This manuscript passed through many hands, including Guiliano de Medici, Duke of Nemours, and the Duke of Hamilton. Branca fills in gaps by drawing upon other old manuscript copies of the work. Speaking of "the problems of punctuation" and "separation of words," Grayson affirmed that "the editor relies on his own exceptional knowledge of Boccaccio's habits," and concluded that "this edition is a remarkable achievement of patience, philological skill and literary expertise."

Branca's *Boccaccio* is a combination of translations of several Italian books about the subject—primarily *Boccaccio Medievale.* The work examines both Boccaccio's life and works. Grayson pointed out that it provides information not previously available to readers of English, because it debunks Boccaccio's own stories about his alleged love affair with Maria d'Aquino, purported to be the illegitimate daughter of the King of Naples. Branca places Boccaccio against what Grayson described as a "background . . . of mercantile affairs and a rapidly evolving bourgeois society." Grayson hailed *Boccaccio* as "a useful volume" in which its subject has been "precisely documented."

Another of Branca's later editorial efforts, *Mercanti scrittori: Ricordi nella Firenze tra medioevo e rinascimento,* gives interested readers a clearer pic-

ture of the background culture he explored in *Boccaccio.* The volume is a collection of the family diaries of medieval and renaissance Florence merchants. This was unique because the Italian business classes did not habitually record their personal and business affairs for future generations. David Abulafia, reviewing *Mercanti scrittori* in *Times Literary Supplement,* asserted that Branca's introduction to the work "is a model of limpid clarity," and further noted that the authors included in the collection demonstrate "a remarkable awareness of [then] current literary trends."

BIOGRAPHICAL/CRITICAL SOURCES:

PERIODICALS

Times Literary Supplement, November 26, 1976, p. 1497; June 5, 1987, p. 614.

*   *   *

BRAVE BIRD, Mary
   See CROW DOG, Mary (Ellen)

*   *   *

BRENNER, Mayer Alan 1956-
   (Rick North)

PERSONAL: Born May 3, 1956, in Los Angeles, CA; married Sandra Gail Daye, 1983; children: one daughter. *Education:* University of California, Los Angeles, B.S. (engineering; summa cum laude), 1978, M.D., 1982.

ADDRESSES: Home and office—1815 Westholme Avenue, #4, Los Angeles, CA 90025. *Agent*—Joshua Bilmes, Scott Meredith Literary Agency, 845 Third Avenue, New York, NY 10022.

CAREER: Designer of computer software and systems for health care; writer.

WRITINGS:

FANTASY NOVELS; DANCE OF THE GODS SERIES

Catastrophe's Spell, DAW (New York), 1989.
Spell of Intrigue, DAW, 1990.

Spell of Fate, DAW, 1992.
Spell of Apocalypse, DAW, 1994.

OTHER

(As Rick North) *Space Pioneers* (novel), Zebra (New York), 1991.

* * *

BROSS, Donald G. 1932-

PERSONAL: Born November 28, 1932, in Guthrie, OK; son of Eugene (a farmer) and Louise (maiden name, Tontz; present surname, Kelso) Bross; married Dixie Ross (a homemaker), April 12, 1950; children: Ted, Larry, Delmar, Patricia. *Education:* Attended University of Oklahoma. *Politics:* Independent. *Religion:* Disciples of Christ. *Avocational interests:* Travel, church work.

ADDRESSES: Home—5350 West Camp Rd., Guthrie, OK 73044.

CAREER: Southwestern Bell, Oklahoma City, OK, line worker, telephone installer, and supervisor, 1951-84.

WRITINGS:

Surrogate Son (novel), Book World (Sun Lakes, AZ), 1992.
Farewell, Ma Bell (humor), Dixidon Press, 1996.
(Coauthor) *Mountain Madness* (nonfiction), New Horizon Press (Far Hills, NJ), 1996.

WORK IN PROGRESS: A contemporary novel, *Hobo Heaven;* research on true crimes.

SIDELIGHTS: Donald G. Bross told *CA:* "Although I make a little money by writing and hope to make more, my primary motive for doing so is the love of telling a story, of seeing my characters grow and develop, and then leading them through life, often using the 'what if' method for plotting.

"Much of my work has been influenced by my being raised on a farm when times were hard, and by spending thirty-two years with the Bell System in various and challenging positions. Although I waited until I was sixty years of age to have a book pub-

lished, I was influenced by an English teacher I had in high school, as well as by a professor in college.

"Although I am a senior citizen and retired, my writing process begins early, often at 4:30 or 5:00 in the morning. Accompanied by a thermos of coffee, I usually work at my computer for some three hours before taking a break for breakfast. What I accomplish during the remainder of the day depends on how much time I have to spend caring for a handicapped wife and dependent mother.

"My life and background inspired me to write *Surrogate Son* and *Farewell, Ma Bell.* As for *Mountain Madness,* I happened onto the story by chance and thought of this as an opportunity to shift gears and do the necessary research before writing. Although I am working on a novel, I have a lead on another true crime story that might be worth pursuing."

* * *

BROWN, Louis M(orris) 1909-1996

OBITUARY NOTICE—See index for *CA* sketch: Born September 5, 1909, in Los Angeles, CA; died of heart failure, September 12, 1996, in Beverly Hills, CA. Attorney, businessman, educator, author. Brown, who was admitted to the California Bar and the U.S. Supreme Court Bar, later championed the idea of preventive law—consulting with a lawyer before the start of legal troubles. His legal career began in 1933 and continued throughout the remainder of his life at firms such as Irell and Manella. He also was in business, serving companies such as Dura Steel Products as vice president. In 1950, he joined the University of Southern California, Los Angeles, as a lecturer in law, becoming a full professor of law in 1974. He was named professor of law emeritus in 1980. In 1963, he founded the Emil Brown Fund for Preventive Law prize and served as the award's administrator until 1985. He also founded Client Counseling Competition, which was renamed in his honor in 1993 as the Louis M. Brown International Client Counseling Competition. Awards from the American Bar Association and the Los Angeles County Bar Association were also named in his honor. Throughout his career, he also taught at schools such as Southwestern University Law School and Whittier College Law School. Much of his work was devoted to preventive law. In 1978, he worked with the

Beverly Hills Bar Association to design attorney services for unmarried couples, mainly for those who were planning to live together. It was the first such practice in the nation and helped clients create a document similar to a prenuptial agreement. Writing was also part of his activities. He wrote the "Legal View" column for the *Los Angeles Times,* beginning in 1991. He also penned numerous books, including *Preventive Law, How to Negotiate a Successful Contract, Lawyering Through Life: The Origin of Preventive Law,* and *Legal Audit: International Corporate Investigations* (with Anne O. Kandel).

OBITUARIES AND OTHER SOURCES:

BOOKS

Who's Who in America, 52nd edition, Marquis, 1997.

PERIODICALS

Los Angeles Times, December 6, 1996, p. A32.
New York Times, December 7, 1996, p. 52.

*   *   *

BRUHNS, Karen Olsen   1941-

PERSONAL: Born April 19, 1941, in the United States. *Ethnicity:* "Mixed." *Education:* University of California, Berkeley, B.A. (cum laude), 1963, Ph.D., 1967. *Politics:* "Various." *Religion:* None.

ADDRESSES: Office—Department of Anthropology, San Francisco State University, 1600 Holloway, San Francisco, CA 94132; fax 415-338-0530. *E-mail*—kbruhns@sfsu.edu.

CAREER: University of California, Los Angeles, acting assistant professor of anthropology, 1967-68; University of Calgary, Calgary, Alberta, assistant professor of anthropology, 1968-70; San Jose State University, San Jose, CA, assistant professor of anthropology, 1970-72; San Francisco State University, San Francisco, CA, faculty member, 1972-80, professor of anthropology, 1980—. California Academy of Sciences, research associate in anthropology, 1984—; Museo del Banco Central de Ecuador, research associate in archaeology, 1986-94. Crew member for projects in northern California, 1959-63, and Mexico, 1964; director of field projects in Colombia, Ecuador, and Peru, 1969-70, at Zapatera Island, Nicaragua, 1974, Cihuatan Settlement, El

Salvador, 1975-79, 1994-95, Cuello Project, Belize, 1980, Paute Valley, Ecuador, 1980—, and Merced County, CA, 1987-88; field class instructor at sites in Santa Cruz County, CA, 1971, 1972.

MEMBER: Society for American Archaeology, Archaeological Institute of America, American Association for the Advancement of Science, Institute of Andean Studies (member of board of directors, 1977-91), Sigma Xi.

AWARDS, HONORS: Canada Council grants, 1969, 1970; grants from Center for Field Research and Earthwatch, 1977, 1978, and Programa de Antropologia para el Ecuador, 1985; George Lindsey Fund grants, California Academy of Sciences, 1985, 1987; grants from Museo del Banco Central del Ecuador, 1986, 1987, 1988.

WRITINGS:

(With T. W. Weller) *A Coloring Album of Ancient Mexico and Peru,* St. Hieronymous Press (Berkeley, CA), 1971, revised bilingual edition, 1974.
Ancient South America, Cambridge University Press (New York), 1994.
(With Karen E. Stothert) *Women in Ancient America,* University of Oklahoma Press (Norman), 1996.

Contributor to books, including *The Southeast Mesoamerican Periphery,* edited by Edward Schortman and Patricia Urban, University of Texas Press (Austin, TX), 1986; *The Role of Gender in Pre-Columbian Art and Architecture,* edited by Virginia Miller, University Presses of America (Lanhan, MD), 1988; and *Wealth and Hierarchy in the Intermediate Area,* edited by Frederick Lange, Dumbarton Oaks (Washington, DC), 1992. Contributor of more than fifty articles and reviews to periodicals, including *Mexicon, Antiquity, Textile Museum Journal, Journal of Field Archaeology, American Antiquity, Journal of Irreproducible Results,* and *Man.*

WORK IN PROGRESS: Naked Ladies and Horrid Rites, a catalog raisonne of pre-Columbian art works being reproduced in modern times; research on Cerro Narrio, Pirincay, and the Ecuadorian formative.

SIDELIGHTS: Karen Olsen Bruhns told *CA:* "It is the obligation of researchers to make their work available to the larger scientific community. My work is influenced by the guidelines of where I am going to publish it. I review my data, I think about them, then I spend a lot of time staring at the screen. I choose my subjects according to the need for a textbook in the areas I teach and research in."

*   *   *

BUCHANAN, Paul G. 1954-

PERSONAL: Born October 15, 1954, in Rockville Center, NY. *Education:* St. Michael's College, B.A., 1976; Georgetown University, M.A., 1978; University of Chicago, Ph.D., 1985.

ADDRESSES: Home—3835 Rilma Ave., Sarasota, FL 34234. *Office*—Department of Social Sciences, New College, Sarasota, FL 34243. *E-mail*—buchanan@ virtu.sor.vsf.edu.

CAREER: Naval Postgraduate School, Monterey, CA, assistant professor, 1985-87; University of Arizona, Tucson, assistant professor, 1987-95; New College, Sarasota, FL, assistant professor of social sciences, 1995—. U.S. Department of Defense, regional policy analyst, 1993-94.

MEMBER: American Political Science Association, Latin American Studies Association, Pi Sigma Alpha.

AWARDS, HONORS: Heinz fellow; Fulbright fellow; Kellogg fellow; Tucker fellow; fellow of Council on Foreign Relations.

WRITINGS:

State, Labor, Capital: Democratizing Class Relations in the Southern Cone, University of Pittsburgh Press (Pittsburgh, PA), 1995.

Contributor of more than twenty articles and reviews to periodicals.

WORK IN PROGRESS: Pluralism, Markets, and the Quest for Cooperative Security; research on political economy and interest mediation in post-authoritarian settings.

*   *   *

BUDAPEST, Zsuzsanna E(mese) 1940-

PERSONAL: Born in 1940, in Hungary; immigrated to the U.S., 1956; married; children: two sons. *Education:* Has studied improvisation. *Religion:* Wicca.

ADDRESSES: Office—c/o The Feminist WICCA, 442 Lincoln Boulevard, Venice, CA 90291.

CAREER: Writer and lecturer. Founder, Sisterhood of the Wicca. Organizer, International Goddess Festival.

MEMBER: Susan B. Anthony Coven No. 1 (high priestess).

WRITINGS:

Selene, the Most Famous Bull-Leaper on Earth, illustrated by Carol Clement, Diana Press (Baltimore), 1976.
The Holy Book of Women's Mysteries, privately published, 1979, Wingbow Press (Berkeley, CA), 1989.
The Grandmother of Time: A Woman's Book of Celebrations, HarperSanFrancisco (San Francisco), 1989.
Grandmother Moon: Lunar Magic in Our Lives, HarperSanFrancisco, 1991.
The Goddess in the Office: A Personal Energy Guide for the Spiritual Warrior at Work, HarperSanFrancisco, 1993.
The Goddess in the Bedroom: A Passionate Woman's Guide to Celebrating Sexuality Every Night of the Week, HarperSanFrancisco, 1995.

Also author of *Feminist Book of Light and Shadows.*

SIDELIGHTS: Active in the realm of feminist spirituality, Hungarian-born Zsuzsanna E. Budapest is the author of several books on modern-day witchcraft—or Wicca—and the New Age cult of the Goddess. Founder of California's Sisterhood of the Wicca and high-priestess of the Susan B. Anthony coven during the 1970s, Budapest continues to focus both her writing and her energies towards sharing her woman-centered spiritual consciousness with others. "I saw how naturally women pray to the moon, light candles, dance, make music, break bread, improvise," she told Jennifer Baumgardner in *Ms.* "I realized that this is our female religion, what we used to do for millennia."

Budapest's "Goddess" books are directed toward a broad female audience that includes those women not yet familiar with Wicca. 1993's *The Goddess in the Office: A Personal Energy Guide for the Spiritual Warrior at Work,* dedicated to Anita Hill, is described by Baumgardner as "a marriage of common sense and magic." Budapest offers the reader ancient runes to battle technological tie-ups, herbs and spells to aid one's chances of a promotion, and even potent hexes to use as a last resort when harassed by unruly coworkers (just be sure to keep a pig's tongue, a rusty nail, and a vial of urine handy). Although Budapest's books are light reading, they also serve as "crash courses in goddess history, ancient mythology, contemporary feminist history, herbal medicine, folklore, and magic" according to Baumgardner, "all presented in a nonintimidating, easily digestible form."

In addition to writing, Budapest also lectures and conducts seminars on various aspects of feminist spirituality, and is the impetus behind the International Goddess Festival, which draws women from all corners of the globe together in California for one weekend every year. Her other books include *Grandmother Moon: Lunar Magic in Our Lives,* published in 1991, and *The Holy Book of Women's Mysteries,* a manual detailing woman-centered celebrations of birth, conception, and menopause.

BIOGRAPHICAL/CRITICAL SOURCES:

BOOKS

Guiley, Rosemary Ellen, editor, *Encyclopedia of Witches and Witchcraft,* Facts on File (New York City), 1989.
Walker, Barbara, *The Woman's Encyclopedia of Myths and Secrets,* Harper (New York City), 1983.

PERIODICALS

Library Journal, March 1, 1993, p. 82.
Ms., March/April, 1995, p. 73.
New Republic, August 3, 1992, pp. 29-33.
Whole Earth Review, spring, 1992, pp. 39-40.

*   *   *

BUKIET, Melvin Jules

PERSONAL: Born August 21, in New York, NY; son of Joseph and Rose Bukiet; married Jill Goodman, 1983; children: Madelaine, Louisa, Miles. *Education:* Sarah Lawrence College, B.A., 1974; Columbia University, M.F.A., 1976. *Politics:* Libertarian. *Religion:* Jewish.

ADDRESSES: Home—529 West 113th St., New York, NY 10025. *Agent*—Jennifer Lyons, Joan Daves Agency, 21 West 26th St., New York, NY 10010.

CAREER: Mt. Vernon Public Library, writing teacher, 1983; The Writer's Voice, writing teacher, 1988-1993; *Tikkun,* New York City, fiction editor, 1992—; Sarah Lawrence College, Bronxville, NY, visiting professor, 1993—; Columbia University, New York City, visiting professor, 1996.

MEMBER: PEN, Authors Guild, Poets and Writers.

AWARDS, HONORS: Yaddo Fellow, 1982; Edward Lewis Wallant Award for best Jewish-American fiction, 1992; named a National Jewish Book Award Finalist, 1993; named to the National Book Critics' Circle Recommended Reading List, 1995.

WRITINGS:

Sandman's Dust, Arbor House (New York City), 1986.
Stories of an Imaginary Childhood, (short stories), Northwestern University Press (Evanston, IL), 1992.
While the Messiah Tarries, (short stories), Harcourt Brace (New York City), 1995.
After, St. Martin's (New York City), 1996.

Contributor of short stories to periodicals, including *Antaeus, Kenyon Review,* and *Story Quarterly.* Also contributor of essays, reviews, and editorials to various periodicals.

WORK IN PROGRESS: A novel, entitled *Strange Fire.*

SIDELIGHTS: Melvin Jules Bukiet's first book, a novel called *Sandman's Dust,* was published in 1986 and concerned the visit of a strange circus to a small town. Several years later, Bukiet published several works of fiction treating various aspects of Jewish life, including the 1992 volume *Stories of an Imaginary Childhood, While the Messiah Tarries,* a 1995 collection, and *After,* a novel published in 1996.

Sandman's Dust is set in 1941, in a small New Jersey town that is visited by an unusual circus. Throughout the narrative, fantastical events occur, characters transform in bizarre ways, and the real and unreal are combined. Critics noted that Bukiet's volume reflected the influence of Ray Bradbury's *Something Wicked This Way Comes.*

Bukiet's collection *Stories of an Imaginary Childhood* is a vision of life in a pre-Nazi Polish *shtetl,* or village, seen through the eyes of a Jewish boy. A *Publishers Weekly* contributor characterized the stories as "well-intentioned but overwritten," and noted the influence of writer Isaac Bashevis Singer. The reviewer declared that some of Bukiet's characters were quite lively, especially the character of the gravedigger, Zalman. *Times Literary Supplement* contributor Bryan Cheyette affirmed that at their best, "Bukiet's stories are deceptively simple and allude subtly to the inner turmoil of their protagonist."

In his 1995 story collection *While the Messiah Tarries,* Bukiet again deals with Jewish life, but this time sets most of his tales in his native New York City. A *Publishers Weekly* reviewer asserted that the collection contained "remarkable, offbeat stories" and praised Bukiet's comic timing. In his enthusiastic review of *While the Messiah Tarries, Washington Post Book World* contributor Michael Dirda declared: "The assurance of the prose, the entrancing voice of the storyteller, the allure of the title . . . and, above all, that feather's touch of humor—all these were quite irresistible. But what about the plot? That too, it turned out, couldn't be better." Dirda also asserted that in *While the Messiah Tarries* he found evidence of "the ease and self-confidence that comes with true mastery."

BIOGRAPHICAL/CRITICAL SOURCES:

PERIODICALS

Fantasy Review, January, 1986, p. 17.
Publishers Weekly, March 23, 1992; April 24, 1995.
Tikkun, November/December, 1994, pp. 75, 79.
Times Literary Supplement, June 26, 1992, p. 21.
Washington Post Book World, August 13, 1995, p. 2.

*   *   *

BURCIAGA, Jose Antonio   1940-1996

OBITUARY NOTICE—See index for *CA* sketch: Born August 23, 1940, in El Chuco, TX; died of cancer, October 7, 1996, in Carmel Highlands, CA. Artist, journalist, poet, author. Burciaga was a Chicano artist and writer who received critical praise for his poems and essays. His art often accompanied his prose, yet also was featured in solo shows. He received his artistic training at schools such as the University of Texas, Corcoran School of Art, and the San Francisco Art Institute. From 1964 until 1968 he worked as a freelance technical illustrator in El Paso, Texas, then served as an illustrator with the U.S. Army from 1968 until 1970. Stints followed as an illustrator with the Central Intelligence Agency, Interstate Commerce Commission, and the Freelance Illustrators of San Francisco, Bay Area, and Silicon Valley. In 1985 he began work as a resident fellow at Stanford University, a post he still held at the time of his death. Burciaga also established the Disenos Literarios Publishing Company and was a winner of the National Book Award. He was a project director of the San Mateo County Arts Council's Multicultural Task Force, and he wrote editorials for the *Los Angeles Times.* He was bestowed with other honors, including the Caracol Literary Magazine Poetry Prize, the San Jose GI Forum Freedom of the Press Award, and the World Affairs Council International Journalism Award. His books include *Love/Amor Undocumentado, Restless Serpents, Drink Cultura Refrescante, Weedee Peepo: A Collection of Essays, Versos Para Centro-america, Wachuseh,* and *Drink Cultura Chicanismo.* He also co-founded the comedy group Culture Clash.

OBITUARIES AND OTHER SOURCES:

BOOKS

Who's Who Among Hispanic Americans, 3rd edition, Gale (Detroit, MI), 1994.

PERIODICALS

Los Angeles Times, October 11, 1996, p. A22.

*   *   *

BUSHYAGER, Linda E(yster)   1947-

PERSONAL: Born in 1947.

ADDRESSES: Agent—c/o Dell Publishing Co., 1340 Broadway, New York, NY 10036.

CAREER: Writer.

WRITINGS:

FANTASY NOVELS

Master of Hawks, Dell (New York), 1979.
The Spellstone of Shaltus, Dell, 1980.

BUTLER, Judith P.

PERSONAL: Partner of Wendy Brown; children: Isaac Daniel Butler-Brown. *Education:* Yale University, B.A., 1978, M.Phil., Ph.D. (philosophy), 1984.

ADDRESSES: Office—Department of Rhetoric, University of California, Berkeley, 2125 Dwinelle Hall, Berkeley, CA 94720-0001.

CAREER: Educator and writer. University of California, Berkeley, currently professor of rhetoric and comparative literature.

WRITINGS:

Subjects of Desire: Hegelian Reflections in Twentieth-Century France, Columbia University Press (New York City), 1987.
Gender Trouble: Feminism and the Subversion of Identity, Routledge (New York City), 1990.
(Editor, with Joan Wallach Scott) *Feminists Theorize the Political,* Routledge, 1992.
Bodies That Matter: On the Discursive Limits of "Sex", Routledge, 1993.
(Editor, with Linda Singer and Maureen MacGrogan) *Erotic Welfare: Sexual Theory and Politics in the Age of Epidemic,* Routledge, 1993.
Subjection, Stanford University Press (Stanford, CA), 1996.

SIDELIGHTS: Feminist theoretician and educator Judith P. Butler is the author of several books that attempt to reevaluate the social relationships involving sex and gender. Her major contributions to the area of woman-centered philosophy include 1993's *Bodies That Matter: On the Discursive Limits of "Sex",* and *Gender Trouble: Feminism and the Subversion of Identity,* a 1990 work that has become a standard text in gender studies classes. In each of her works, Butler argues that the idea that men and women are in any way dissimilar is a cultural rather than a biological reality.

In *Gender Trouble* Butler goes against the work of such feminist theoreticians as Simone de Beauvoir by confronting "gender" not as a distinction of physical differences, but as an artificial construct created for the purposes of oppression within a patriarchal society. According to Butler, the classification of a person according to "sex" and/or "gender" is only valid within a society that adheres to the definitions attached to those terms. She maintains that homosexual culture is not immune to such oppression: it adopts similar sex/gender classifications as the heterosexual mainstream; consequently, terms like "butch" and "queen," when used between homosexuals, are symptoms of the same sex/gender prejudices.

Butler continues her exploration of gender in *Bodies That Matter.* In this volume she focuses on the way power effects human sexuality, using such cultural manifestations as contemporary films and literature to reflect upon the construction and enforcement of sexual hierarchies within society. Bryan S. Turner praises the book in a review for *Contemporary Sociology,* noting that "Butler's work will almost certainly become a major dimension of the current analysis of the body, particularly in feminist theory [in] the psychoanalytic tradition of Jacques Lacan."

BIOGRAPHICAL/CRITICAL SOURCES:

PERIODICALS

American Literature, December, 1995, p. 893.
Canadian Literature, winter, 1995, p. 159; spring, 1996, p. 189.
Choice, January, 1988, p. 780; October, 1990, p. 385.
Contemporary Sociology, May, 1995, p. 331.
Drama Review, fall, 1995, pp. 170-78.
Journal of Modern History, March, 1991, p. 124.
Philosophical Review, January, 1990, pp. 129-31.
Times Literary Supplement, June 1, 1990, p. 588.*

*   *   *

BUTLER, Rohan D'Olier 1917-1996

OBITUARY NOTICE—See index for *CA* sketch: Born January 21, 1917, in London, England; died October 30, 1996. Historian and author. Butler is remembered for his work as a historian, which included editing documents from the British Foreign Office. Early in his career, Butler became a fellow of All Souls College at Oxford University in 1938. It was a post he held until 1984, when he became fellow emeritus. While at Oxford University, he also worked stints as a senior research fellow and subwarden. During World War II, he served in the British Army as well as with the Special Operations Executive and the Ministry of Information. In 1944 he joined the Foreign Office, and later worked with E. L. Woodward to edit documents for publication. His contributions to this multi-volume work, titled *Documents on British*

Foreign Policy: 1919-1939, lasted from 1945 to 1965. In 1963 he began five years as historical adviser to Britain's Secretary of State for Foreign Affairs, assuming the same position for Foreign and Commonwealth Affairs from 1968 until 1982. He began another series called *Documents on British Policy Overseas,* focusing on the postwar years. He served as senior editor for the series from 1973 until 1982. He retired from the Foreign Office in 1982. During his career he also served as Leverhulme Research Fellow and governor for the Felsted School. Among Butler's other writings were *The Roots of National Socialism* and *Choiseul.* The latter work, about the Duc de Choiseul, earned him France's Prix Jean Debrousse and election to the position of laureate with the Institute of France. He was also honored as companion of the Order of St. Michael and St. George.

OBITUARIES AND OTHER SOURCES:

BOOKS

Who's Who, St. Martin's Press, 1996.

PERIODICALS

Times (London), November 14, 1996, p. 25.

*   *   *

BYALICK, Marcia 1947-

PERSONAL: Born April 9, 1947, in Brooklyn, NY; daughter of Al (a dry cleaner) and Mona (a homemaker; maiden name, Goldsmith) Finkelstein; married Robert Byalick (a psychologist), November 22, 1967; children: Jennifer, Carrie. *Ethnicity:* "Jewish." *Education:* Brooklyn College of the City University of New York, M.A., 1969. *Politics:* Liberal Democrat. *Religion:* Jewish. *Avocational interests:* Theater, exercise, "any excuse to get together with friends and family."

ADDRESSES: Home and office—22 Lydia Ct., Searingtown, NY 11507; fax 516-621-4919.

CAREER: Writer. Hofstra University, writing teacher, 1993—.

AWARDS, HONORS: Seven awards from Long Island Press Club, 1986-93, for work as a columnist; *It's a Matter of Trust* was selected as one of the best books for teenagers, New York Public Library, 1996.

WRITINGS:

(Co-author) *The Three Career Couple* (humorous self-help), Peterson's Press, 1993.
(Co-author) *How Come I Feel So Disconnected . . . If This Is Such a User Friendly World?,* Peterson's Press, 1995.
It's a Matter of Trust (young adult novel), Harcourt (Orlando, FL), 1995.
Whose Eyes Are These? (young adult novel), Harcourt, 1997.
(Co-author) *The Craving Brain: The Biobalance Approach to Controlling Addiction,* HarperCollins (San Francisco, CA), in press.

Author of the young adult novel, *You Don't Have to Be Perfect to Be Excellent,* 1993. Columnist, *Distinction,* 1996. Editor in chief, *Women's Record,* 1985-93.

C

CAHAN, Abraham 1860-1951

PERSONAL: Born July 7 (some sources say July 6), 1860 in Podberezy, Lithuania; immigrated to the United States, June 6, 1882; died August 31, 1951; son of Schachne (a teacher) and Sarah Goldarbeiter Cahan; married Anna Bronstein, December 11, 1886. *Education:* Vilna Teachers' Institute, 1877-81. *Politics:* Socialist. *Religion:* Jewish. *Avocational interests:* Bird-watching.

CAREER: Teacher in Velizh, Lithuania, 1881; laborer, teacher, freelance journalist, and labor organizer, New York City, 1882-97; coeditor, *Neie Tseit,* New York City, 1886; editor, *Arbeiter Zeitung,* New York City, 1891-94; editor, *Die Zukunft,* New York City, 1893-94; reporter, *New York Commercial Advertiser,* New York City, 1897-1901; cofounder of *Jewish Daily Forward,* New York City, 1897, editor-in-chief, 1903-46, editor, 1946-51.

WRITINGS:

Social Remedies, New York Labor News Co. (New York), 1889.
Yekl: A Tale of the New York Ghetto, Appleton (New York), 1896.
The Imported Bridegroom, and Other Stories of the New York Ghetto, Houghton Mifflin (New York), 1898.
The White Terror and the Red: A Novel of Revolutionary Russia, Barnes (New York), 1905.
Rafael Naarizokh: An Erzaylung Vegin a Stolyer Vos Iz Gekommen Zum Saykhl, Forward Press (New York), 1907.
Historia fun di Fareingte Shtaaten, 2 vols., Forward Publishing Co. (New York), 1910.

Neshoma Yesoroh; Fanny's Khasonim, Forward Association (New York), 1913.
The Rise of David Levinsky, Harper (New York), 1917.
Bleter fun Mein Leben, 5 vols., Forward Association, 1926-1931; also published as *The Education of Abraham Cahan,* 2 vols. [partial translation], translated by Leon Stein, Abraham P. Conan, and Lynn Davison, Jewish Publishing Society of America (Philadelphia), 1969.
Palestina, Forward Publishing Association, 1934.
Rashel: A Biografia, Forward Publishing Association, 1938.
Yekl and The Imported Bridegroom, and Other Stories of Yiddish New York, Dover (New York), 1970.
Grandma Never Lived in America: The New Journalism of Abraham Cahan, edited by Moses Rischin, Indiana University Press (Bloomington, IN), 1986.

Contributor to such periodicals as *McClure's, Workman's Advocate, Short Stories,* and *New York Sun.*

SIDELIGHTS: Abraham Cahan was a journalist and intellectual leader among the large Jewish immigrant population that inhabited Manhattan's Lower East Side during the late-nineteenth and early-twentieth centuries. He was the longtime editor of the *Jewish Daily Forward,* a Yiddish newspaper that reached a circulation of nearly 250,000 under Cahan's direction. He was also the author of such fictional works as *Yekl: A Tale of the New York Ghetto* (1896) and *The Rise of David Levinsky* (1917), which describe the experiences of Jewish immigrants adapting to life in the United States.

Cahan was born in a Lithuanian village in 1860. He attended Vilna Teachers' Institute, where instruction was conducted in Russian, and graduated in 1881. He accepted a teaching position in rural Velizh, where he became involved in socialist politics, particularly expressing anti-Czarist views. In the backlash that followed the assassination of Czar Alexander II in 1881, Cahan was the subject of surveillance, and his apartment was searched by law officers. He soon left the country and arrived in Philadelphia in 1882. Cahan settled in New York City among the Jewish community of Manhattan's Lower East Side and began working as a laborer in a cigar factory. His experiences as a factory worker combined with his radical political views led Cahan to participation in the growing labor movement, and—once he had learned to speak English—he gained a reputation as an imposing orator in behalf of union causes.

In 1886 Cahan began editing the radical newspaper *Neie Tseit,* and when that venture failed, he began contributing his writings to other political periodicals, notably the *Workman's Advocate,* which was sponsored by the Socialist Labor party. Over the next several years Cahan became an editor and contributor to such other Yiddish labor newspapers as *Arbeiter Zeitung,* which had published his earliest short stories, and *Die Zukunft,* a publication of the Socialist Workers party. In the mid 1890s he began to focus on fiction, and "A Providential Match," his first story translated into English was published in 1895. After reading this story, the novelist and critic William Dean Howells took an interest in Cahan and helped secure publication of his novel *Yekl: A Tale of the New York Ghetto* in 1896. Depicting the attempts of immigrant Jake Podgorny to shed his foreign values and adapt to American society, *Yekl* focuses on the unresolved conflicts that inhere in the immigrant experience. While the novel was not a notable popular success at the time of its publication, it later gained a wider audience when it served as the basis for the film *Hester Street* in the 1970s.

In 1897 Cahan and several of his associates in the labor movement collaborated on a new publication, *Jewish Daily Forward,* a Yiddish newspaper on which Cahan served as editor for the first four months. He subsequently accepted a position in New York *Commercial Advertiser,* an English-language newspaper where he was supervised by Lincoln Steffens. During his tenure at the *Commercial Advertiser,* Cahan also continued to pursue fiction writing. The collection *The Imported Bridegroom, and Other Stories of the New York Ghetto* was published in 1898 and focuses on homesickness, loneliness, disappointment, and the cultural conflicts faced by immigrants in New York's Jewish ghetto. Following Steffens's departure from the *Commercial Advertiser* in 1901 Cahan rejoined *Jewish Daily Forward,* and—after a brief dispute and resignation in 1902—retained control of the publication for the rest of his career.

Additional fiction works in both English and Yiddish complemented Cahan's journalistic endeavors. His novel *The White Terror and the Red: A Novel of Revolutionary Russia* was published in 1905, anticipating the first Revolution and its violent anti-Semitism. Cahan's influence in the Jewish community and in New York labor circles continued to rise during the 1900s and 1910s, and in 1913 he was invited to submit a nonfiction series on the commercial activities of Jewish immigrants to *McClure's* magazine. His fictional "Autobiography of an American Jew" was so successful that it later served as the basis for his novel *The Rise of David Levinsky.* Published in 1917, the novel offers a retrospective assessment of the career of a successful garment manufacturer who arrived in the United States an orphan, with only a few cents in his pocket. Considered by critics to be Cahan's most successful fictional work, *The Rise of David Levinsky* presents a broad scope of immigrant life and—through the reflections of the dissatisfied millionaire Levinsky—challenges shallow American standards of success.

Posthumous publications of Cahan's writings include two volumes of *The Education of Abraham Cahan* (1969), a translation of his Yiddish autobiography, and *Grandma Never Lived in America: The New Journalism of Abraham Cahan,* a collection of articles and short stories that was published in 1986. Covering the period of his early political life and his initial experiences in the United States, *The Education of Abraham Cahan* won praise from Thomas Lask in the *New York Times,* for a prose style that is "plain, rapid, without literary flourishes and extremely concrete." Commenting on *Grandma Never Lived in America* in *New York Times Book Review,* Alison Knopf found that the work "sensitively describes the immigrants' conflicts and hesitations about conforming to American life." In a retrospective sketch occasioned by the publication of *Grandma Never Lived in America, Voice* critic Paul Berman concluded that "[B]ecause Cahan always knew he was writing about exotic themes, he went out of his way to make his habitats and characters accessible, to explain strange customs and beliefs, and these explanations turn out to be as useful in our day as in his. . . . He has remained . . . what he always was: a serious, talented writer on immigrant themes."

BIOGRAPHICAL/CRITICAL SOURCES:

BOOKS

Dictionary of Literary Biography, Gale, Volume 9: *American Novelists, 1910-1945,* 1981, Volume 25: *American Newspaper Journalists, 1901-1925,* 1984, Volume 28: *Twentieth-Century American-Jewish Fiction Writers,* 1984.

PERIODICALS

New York Times, January 3, 1970, p. 23.
New York Times Book Review, May 11, 1986, p. 25.
Village Voice Literary Supplement, June 1986, pp. 16-17.*

*   *   *

CAMERON, Eleanor (Frances)   1912-1996

OBITUARY NOTICE—See index for *CA* sketch: Born March 23, 1912, in Winnipeg, Manitoba, Canada; died October 11, 1996, in Monterey, CA. Librarian, educator, author. Cameron was a prolific writer of children's fiction, having penned her first juvenile work, *The Wonderful Flight to the Mushroom Planet,* for her son in the 1950s. Cameron, however, began her career several decades earlier, working as a clerk for the Los Angeles Public Library and then for the Board of Education Library. Stints as a librarian followed at the Foote, Cone & Belding and the Honig, Cooper & Harrington advertising agencies and for the Dan B. Miner Company. She also served as the Gertrude Clarke Whittall Lecturer for the Library of Congress and was an advisory board member at the Center for the Study of Children's Literature. She rounded out her career as an editorial board member for *Cricket* magazine and for *Children's Literature in Education.* Her first book was actually an adult novel, entitled *The Unheard Music.* Her children's literature included stories in the futuristic series "Mushroom Planet," including *Mr. Bass's Planetoid.* She authored other books such as *A Spell Is Cast,* which won a Mystery Writers of America Award, *A Room Made of Windows,* winner of a *Boston Globe/ Horn Book* Award, and *The Court of the Stone Children,* recipient of a National Book Award. She was also praised for her "Julia Redfern" series, which

included *Julia's Magic* and *The Private Worlds of Julia Redfern.* In 1993 she published *The Seed and the Vision: On the Writing and Appreciation of Children's Books.* In 1985 she was honored with the Kerlan Award for her work.

OBITUARIES AND OTHER SOURCES:

BOOKS

Who's Who, 148th edition, St. Martin's, 1996.

PERIODICALS

Los Angeles Times, October 15, 1996, p. A22.
New York Times, October 15, 1996, p. B10.
Washington Post, October 14, 1996, p. B4.

*   *   *

CANNON, John (Darcy)   1918-

PERSONAL: Born May 10, 1918, in London, England; son of Charles Henry (a theatrical manager) and Minnieham (Clarke) Cannon; married Camilla Mary Nichol-Smith, January 19, 1949; children: David Alexander, Nicola Jane. *Education:* Attended schools in England. *Politics:* "Left of centre Conservative." *Religion:* Church of England.

ADDRESSES: Home—6 Dales Close, Windmill Hill, Near Herstmonceux, East Sussex BN27 4TJ, England.

CAREER: City and South London Press, reading assistant, 1933-34; Link House Publications Ltd., London, England, editorial assistant, 1934-35, assistant editor of *Amateur Cine World* and *Miniature Camera World,* 1935-37, assistant editor of *The Caravan,* 1937-39, associate editor, 1949-51; County Associations Ltd., London, general editor of "County Guide" series, 1951-54; British Institute of Management, London, assistant editor of *The Manager* and editor of *Work Study and Industrial Engineering,* 1954-57; Chemstrand Ltd., London, publicity manager, 1957-60; United Merchants & Manufacturers (UK) Ltd., London, publicity manager, 1960-63; British Enkalon Ltd., Leicester, England, publicity manager, 1963-81; publicity consultant, Brand-Rex Ltd., Glenrothes, Scotland, 1981-86; retired. *Military service:* British Army, 1939-48; became major; mentioned in dispatches, Italy, 1944.

WRITINGS:

The Car That Talked, Nuffield (London), 1951.
The Adventures of Jerry Parker, Nuffield, 1952.
The Further Adventures of Jerry Parker, Nuffield, 1953.

Also compiler of crossword puzzles for specialized magazines. Contributor to motoring and industrial magazines.

*   *   *

CANTSIN, Monty
  See HOME, Stewart

*   *   *

CARABELLI, Giancarlo 1939-

PERSONAL: Born August 26, 1939, in Novara, Italy; son of Giuseppe and Maria Mazzola; married Marcella Bassi (a translator), 1968; children: Ricardo Aladino. *Education:* Universita of Milan, Laurea, 1969.

ADDRESSES: Home—Via Lanzone da Corte 7, I-20123 Milan, Italy. *Office*—Istituto di discipline filosofiche, Via Savonarola 38, I-44100 Ferrara, Italy.

CAREER: University of Ferrara, Ferrara, Italy, lecturer, 1973-82, professor of the history of philosophy, 1983—.

WRITINGS:

Hume e la retorica dell'ideologia: Uno studio dei "Dialoghi sulla religione naturale," La Nuova Italia (Florence, Italy), 1972.
Tolandiana: Materiali bibliografici per lo studio dell'opera e della fortuna di John Toland, 1670-1722, La Nuova Italia, 1975.
Intorno a Hume, Il Saggiatore (Milan, Italy), 1992, translation by Krakover Hall published as *On Hume and Eighteenth-Century Aesthetics: The Philosopher on a Swing,* Peter Lang Publishing (New York), 1995.
In the Image of Priapus, Duckworth (London, England), 1996.

CARBY, Hazel V. 1948-

PERSONAL: Born January 15, 1948, in Oakhamton, Devon, England; daughter of Carlin Colin and Iris Muriel Carby; married Michael Denning, May 29, 1982; children: Nicholas Carby-Denning. *Education:* Birmingham University Center for Contemporary Cultural Studies, Ph.D., 1984.

ADDRESSES: Office—Department of African American Studies, Yale University, P.O. Box 2288, Yale Station, New Haven, CT 06520.

CAREER: Educator. Wesleyan University, Middletown, CT, associate professor, 1982-89; Yale University, New Haven, CT, professor of African American studies, 1989—.

WRITINGS:

Reconstructing Womanhood: The Emergence of the Afro-American Woman Novelist, Oxford University Press (New York City), 1987.

SIDELIGHTS: A professor of African American studies at Yale University, Hazel V. Carby is the author of *Reconstructing Womanhood: The Emergence of the Afro-American Woman Novelist.* Published in 1987, *Reconstructing Womanhood* has been hailed by both feminist scholars and literary critics for its role in casting a new light upon a wealth of written work that had previously been ignored, both because its creators were women and because they were black.

Focusing particularly on the work of African American woman novelists of the late nineteenth and early twentieth century, Carby's work "maps the intersection of sex, race, and class in black feminist literary expression," according to William L. Andrews in a review in *Callaloo.* In a close examination of the works of writers such as Frances E. W. Harper, Ida B. Wells, Anna Julia Cooper, and Pauline E. Hopkins, who courageously addressed issues of racial and sexual inequality while at the same time condemning the white, middle-class biases of the women's suffrage movement at the turn of the century, Carby uncovers the realities of these women's lives: the everyday activities, prejudices, and economic and political concerns that made their writing a powerful tool for enacting social change. "These writers," maintains Andrews, "also constructed alternative concepts of womanhood designed to liberate and empower their readers at a crucial era in American feminism, when racial and class consciousness was preventing a truly progressive women's movement from developing."

Praising Carby's treatment of the works of Harlem Renaissance writers Nella Larsen and Jessie Fauset, *American Literature* critic Angelo Costanzo notes that *Reconstructing Womanhood* "explains how these writers changed the romantic conventions to suit their thematic concerns and, in doing so, established a black woman's literary tradition that continues through the years in the works of Ann Petry, Gwendolyn Brooks, and Toni Morrison." Carby's ability to broaden her role from literary critic to include that of historian and political commentator as well is commended by *American Historical Review*'s Frances Richardson Keller, who notes that she "succeeds in bringing to life [these authors'] struggles toward their vision. She has skillfully conceived and artfully written an honest, searching book of enormous value."

BIOGRAPHICAL/CRITICAL SOURCES:

PERIODICALS

American Historical Review, June, 1989, p. 875.
American Literature, October, 1988, pp. 481-82.
Callaloo, spring, 1989, pp. 423-24.
Choice, July, 1988, p. 1692.
Nation, April 30, 1988, p. 615.
New York Times Book Review, July 3, 1988, p. 15.
Signs, summer, 1989, p. 934.
Times Literary Supplement, June 3, 1988, p. 623.
Village Voice Literary Supplement, October, 1992, p. 18.
Women's Review of Books, February, 1988, p. 15.

*   *   *

CARDOZO, Michael H(art, IV) 1910-1996

OBITUARY NOTICE—See index for *CA* sketch: Born September 15, 1910, in New York, NY; died from chronic lung disease, October 20, 1996, in Washington, DC. Attorney, educator, author. Cardozo, a cousin of U.S. Supreme Court Justice Benjamin N. Cardozo, also devoted his career to the law, serving more than sixty years as an attorney. He began work at the law firm of Parker & Duryee in New York, New York, in 1935. Stints with the U.S. Securities

and Exchange Commission, Office of Lend-Lease Administration, and the U.S. Department of State followed. Among his credits are work for the North Atlantic Treaty Organization (NATO) and contributions to the Marshall Plan. Cardozo later joined the faculty of Cornell University, serving at the school from 1952 until 1963. From 1958 until 1959 he was a Fulbright and Guggenheim fellow in Belgium; during his career he also founded a Fulbright scholar alumni association and served as its president for a time. In 1963, Cardozo began ten years as executive director of the Association of American Law Schools. In 1973 he took up private practice. Cardozo also served as a visiting law professor at schools such as the University of Pennsylvania and Northwestern University. He was also a consultant to groups such as the U.S. Senate, U.S. House of Representatives, and the Naval War College. Cardozo also dabbled in writing, founding the *Preview* law journal, working on the editorial board and later editing the *Journal of Supreme Court History,* and serving *The Practical Lawyer* magazine on its board of editors. He also authored several books, including *Exchange of Patent Rights and Technical Information under Mutual Aid Programs, Diplomats in International Cooperation: Stepchildren of the Foreign Service,* and the *History of the Association of American Law Schools, 1950-1963.*

OBITUARIES AND OTHER SOURCES:

BOOKS

Who's Who, 148th edition, St. Martin's, 1996.

PERIODICALS

New York Times, October 22, 1996, p. D27.
Washington Post, October 22, 1996, p. E4.

*   *   *

CARMICHAEL, Marie
  See STOPES, Marie (Charlotte)

*   *   *

CARSTENS, Catherine Mansell
  See MAYO, C(atherine) M(ansell)

CESPEDES, Frank V. 1950-

PERSONAL: Born August 19, 1950, in New York, NY; son of Edward and Rita (Dorio) Cespedes; married Bonnie Costello (a professor), 1977; children: Elizabeth, Helen. *Education:* City College of the City University of New York, B.A., 1972; Cornell University, Ph.D., 1977; Massachusetts Institute of Technology, M.S., 1983.

ADDRESSES: Home—97 Aldrich St., Roslindale, MA 02131. *Office*—Center for Executive Development, 124 Mount Auburn St., Cambridge, MA 02138. *E-mail*—fcespedes@cedinc.com.

CAREER: Harvard University, Harvard Business School, Boston, MA, professor of business administration and leader of Strategic Marketing Management Program, 1978-95; Center for Executive Development, Cambridge, MA, managing partner. Consultant to companies in North and South America, Europe, and Asia.

WRITINGS:

(With Linda Micheli, Donald Byker, and Thomas Raymond) *Managerial Communications,* Scott, Foresman (Glenwood, IL), 1984.
(With E. Raymond Corey and V. Kasturi Rangan) *Case Studies in Industrial Distribution,* Harvard Business School Press (Boston, MA), 1989.
(With Corey and Rangan) *Going to Market: Distribution Systems for Industrial Products,* Harvard Business School Press, 1989.
Organizing and Implementing the Marketing Effort: Text and Cases, Addison-Wesley (Reading, MA), 1991.
Concurrent Marketing: Integrating Product, Sales, and Service, Harvard Business School Press (Boston, MA), 1995.
Managing Marketing Linkages, Prentice-Hall (Englewood Cliffs, NJ), 1996.

Contributor of about twenty-five articles to periodicals, including *Harvard Business Review, Business Horizons, Industrial Marketing Management, Journal of Personal Selling and Sales Management, Organization Science,* and *Strategy and Business.*

WORK IN PROGRESS: Research on executive development.

CHAQUERI, Cosroe
See SHAKERI, Khosrow

*   *   *

CHORBAJIAN, Levon 1942-

PERSONAL: Born August 9, 1942, in East Orange, NJ; son of Vahinag and Antoinette (Chadarevian) Chorbajian; married Beverly Byrnes (a criminal defense attorney), 1978; children: Ruby, Garo, Seta, Von. *Education:* Temple University, B.A., 1964; University of Michigan, M.A., 1965; Brandeis University, Ph.D., 1974. *Religion:* Armenian Apostolic. *Avocational interests:* Gardening, landscaping, carpentry.

ADDRESSES: Home—79 Gray St., Billerica, MA 01821. *Office*—Department of Sociology, University of Massachusetts, Lowell, MA 01854; fax 508-934-3003. *E-mail*—chorbajil@woods.uml.edu.

CAREER: U.S. Peace Corps, Washington, DC, volunteer, 1966-68; University of Massachusetts, Lowell, professor of sociology, 1970—. Senior Fulbright lecturer in the U.S.S.R., 1986-87, and in the Republic of Armenia, 1996. Zoryan Institute for Contemporary Armenian Research and Documentation, chairperson of board of directors. Managing editor, *Journal of Sport and Social Issues* and *ARENA Review,* both 1982-86.

WRITINGS:

The Caucasian Knot: The History and Geopolitics of Nagorno-Karabagh, Zed Books (London, England), 1994.
(Translator from French) Pierre Verluise, *Armenia in Crisis: The 1988 Earthquake,* Wayne State University Press (Detroit, MI), 1995.

Editor of *Readings in Critical Sociology,* 1989, and *The Hand in Your Pocket May Not Be Your Own,* 1991.

*   *   *

CHRIST, Carol P(atrice) 1945-

PERSONAL: Born December 20, 1945, in Pasadena, CA; daughter of John Anthony and Janet Claire (Bergman) Christ; married Roger Robinson, 1979 (divorced, 1988); children: none. *Ethnicity:* "German, Swedish, Irish, Scotch, English." *Education:* Stanford University, B.A. with honors in Humanities, 1967; Yale University, Ph.D., in religious studies, 1974. *Politics:* "Seeking radical transformation, peace, and justice." *Religion:* "The ancient religion of the Goddess." *Avocational interests:* "Swimming in the grey-blue sea, watching the sun set rose gold into the ocean."

ADDRESSES: Home and office—Vatopediou 7, Athens 11523, Greece, and Molivos 81108, Lesbos, Greece. *Agent*—Kim Witherspoon, 157 West 57th St., Suite 700, New York, NY 10019.

CAREER: Assistant Professor of Religion, Columbia University, 1972-77; Director of Ariadne Institute for the Study of Myth and Ritual; tenured professor of religious studies and women's studies at San Jose State University, CA, 1977-88; Harvard Divinity School, Boston, MA, visiting lecturer and research associate, 1986-87; Stauffacher Distinguished Visiting Professor of Religion at Pomona College, 1988; Rockefeller Distinguished Professor at Californiaa Institute of Integral Studies, 1994. Contributing editor, Journal of Feminist Studies in Religion.

MEMBER: American Academy of Religion; on editorial boards of *Woman of Power, Feminist Studies, Anima, Metis, Religious Studies Review,* and others.

AWARDS, HONORS: Phi Beta Kappa; Danforth Graduate Fellow, 1967-74; Woodrow Wilson Fellow, 1967-68; National Endowment for the Humanities Awards, 1981-82.

WRITINGS:

(Editor with Judith Plaskow and contributor) *Womanspirit Rising: A Feminist Reader in Religion,* Harper (San Francisco, CA), 1979; reprinted with new preface, 1989.

Diving Deep and Surfacing: Women Writers on Spiritual Quest, Beacon Press (Boston, MA), 1980; reprinted with new introduction, 1986; reprinted with new afterword, 1995.

Laughter of Aphrodite: Reflections on a Journey to the Goddess, Harper, 1987.

(Editor with Plaskow) *Weaving the Visions: New Patterns in Feminist Spirituality,* Harper, 1989.

Odyssey with the Goddess: A Spiritual Quest in Crete, Continuum (New York, NY), 1995.

Rebirth of the Goddess: Finding Meaning in Feminist Spirituality, Addison Wesley, 1997.

SIDELIGHTS: Feminist theologian and historian of religion Carol P. Christ has written and edited six books that express a feminist view of religion and spirituality. Her first, *Womanspirit Rising: A Feminist Reader in Religion,* was edited with Judith Plaskow and published in 1979. *Womanspirit Rising* contains twenty-four essays, by various professors of theology and religion and members of the grassroots women's spirituality movement. The essays explore religious traditions, including Judaism, Christianity, and Goddess worship, searching for history, ritual, and innovations that name and celebrate women's experience. Writing in the *New York Times Book Review,* Dorothy Dinnerstein termed *Womanspirit Rising* an "interesting, well-edited collection" of essays that are "all literate and humane, many vividly moving, some dazzling." One of Christ's contributions, "Spiritual Quest and Women's Experience," was one of the essays Dinnerstein found "most rewarding" in the collection. A contributor to *Kirkus Reviews* concluded that *Womanspirit Rising* "looks like the best of the books on religion and feminism currently in print." Christ's other essay in the volume, "Why Women Need the Goddess," has been widely quoted and reprinted and is recognized as a classic essay on the reemergence of the symbol of the Goddess in feminist experience.

In her next book, *Diving Deep and Surfacing: Women Writers on Spiritual Quest,* Christ uses the writings of Kate Chopin, Margaret Atwood, Doris Lessing, Adrienne Rich, and Ntozake Shange as a backdrop for her exploration of women's spiritual quest, which she suggests is different than men's—more grounded in the body and nature. "Christ preaches a sensible, sometimes even moving sermon, using her poets and novelists as a vehicle," wrote a *Kirkus Reviews* critic.

Readers receive a more personal perspective on spirituality from Christ's next volume, *Laughter of Aphrodite: Reflections on a Journey to the Goddess,* which recounts her own transformation from mainstream Christian to Goddess worshipper. Published in 1987, *Laughter of Aphrodite* traces Christ's attempt to find room for feminism in Christianity, which she believes devalues women. Unsuccessful in this quest, Christ turns to the ancient tradition of Goddess worship, researching various societies with female-centered religions. Although *Los Angeles Times Book Review* contributor Dolly Patterson complained of Christ's "one-sided view of Christianity," other critics reacted more favorably to *Laughter of Aphrodite.* Writing in the *Women's Review of Books,* Robin

Herndobler called *Laughter of Aphrodite* "a moving and beautiful book, a journey to mature spirituality."

In her 1989 book, *Weaving the Visions: New Patterns in Feminist Spirituality,* Christ again collaborated with Plaskow to select theological essays with a feminist perspective. *Weaving the Visions,* which serves as a companion volume to *Womanspirit Rising,* includes writings by Alice Walker, Elisabeth Schussler Fiorenza, Starhawk, and Paula Gunn Allen. The essays explore women's spirituality in various cultures, addressing subjects as diverse as Mesoamerican Goddesses, female Native American spirits, lesbian religious communities in medieval Christian Europe, the Yoruba-Lucumi religion of West Africa, and women leaders in Haitian Vodou. Writing in the *New York Times Book Review,* Amy Edith Johnson praised *Weaving the Visions,* noting that "the scholarly rigor of some essays and the personal lyricism of others will each find their readers." According to a *Publishers Weekly* contributor, the book "demonstrat[es] the fecundity of current feminist theological scholarship."

Christ continues her exploration of female-centered spirituality in *Odyssey with the Goddess: A Spiritual Quest in Crete,* which was published in 1995. *Odyssey with the Goddess* tells of a pilgrimage Christ embarks upon in Crete, where she attempts to come to terms with a profound despair evoked by the death of her mother and the end of a love affair. Crete, which is believed to be the site of an ancient pre-patriarchal society, is sacred to contemporary Goddess worshippers. In *Odyssey with the Goddess* Christ interweaves descriptions and histories of sacred sites and rituals with an account of her own spiritual rebirth. This structure, according to *Booklist* contributor Patricia Monaghan, "allows her to movingly combine autobiography and scholarship."

Reviewing *Odyssey with the Goddess* in the *Women's Review of Books,* Carol LeMasters was less favorable in her assessment. The critic commented: "[w]hile some of her insights are valid, they would have been considered elementary in feminist circles twenty years ago: you don't need male approval to be worthwhile; relationships with women are valuable too." Yet LeMasters also commented that "Christ's descriptions of her solitary spiritual experiences can be quite moving." A *Library Journal* contributor called *Odyssey with the Goddess* "a welcome addition" to women's spirituality collections and praised Christ's "luminous prose." *Booklist* contributor Monaghan concluded that Christ is "a foremost figure in the academic reconsideration of the Goddess."

In *Rebirth of the Goddess: Finding Meaning in Feminist Spirituality* Christ creates a systematic "thealogy" (from *thea,* meaning Goddess, and *logos,* meaning words) of the Goddess. In this work, Christ articulates and explains the profound moral and intellectual challenge the rebirth of the ancient religion of the Goddess poses to deeply held habits of thought. In chapters that consider method, history, historiography, and the traditional topics of deity, humanity, nature, and ethics, Christ argues that the Goddess calls humans to overcome the classical dualisms that separate mind from body, humanity from nature, and divinity from the earth. Interpreting the Goddess as the ground of all being, the soul of the earth-body, Christ urges the reader toward moral and spiritual transformation to achieve a life of greater peace, harmony, and justice with each other and all beings in the web of life.

Christ told *CA:* "My work has been guided from the beginning by a deeply shattering recognition (while in graduate school) that women's voices, women's experience, women's knowledge, and women's wisdom have been excluded from the canons of the (so-called) 'great' religions of the world. My search to express women's religious experience (and my own) has led me to the study of women's writing, to a critique of traditional theologies, and to the study of the ancient religion of the Goddess and its reemergence in our culture. After I moved to Greece, my knowledge of the Goddess moved from my head to my feet, finding grounding in the earth and the body, providing a deeper and more sustaining knowledge. My work has also been shaped by my quest to find a way to integrate the knowledge of the mind with the knowledge of the body in what I have variously called 'embodied thinking' and 'narrative theo(a)logy'."

BIOGRAPHICAL/CRITICAL SOURCES:

BOOKS

Sands, Kathleen M. *Escape from Paradise: Evil and Tragedy in Feminist Theology,* Fortress Press (Minneapolis, MN), 1994.

PERIODICALS

Booklist, April 1, 1980, p. 1092; June 1, 1987, p. 1476; March 15, 1995, p. 1286.
Commonweal, November 20, 1987, p. 683.
Kirkus Reviews, December 15, 1978, pp. 1391-92; February 1, 1980, p. 174.

Library Journal, April 1, 1989, p. 94; March 1, 1995, p. 79.
Los Angeles Times, August 2, 1987, p. 13.
New York Times Book Review, July 29, 1979, pp. 10-11, 20; April 30, 1989, p. 33.
Publishers Weekly, March 17, 1989, p. 88.
Women's Review of Books, September, 1987, p. 16; December, 1995, pp. 23-24.

*   *   *

CIMENT, Jill 1953-

PERSONAL: Name is pronounced "sih-*ment*"; born March 19, 1953, in Canada; daughter of Gloria (Miller) and Mortimer Ciment; married Arnold Mesches; children: none. *Education:* California Institute of Arts, B.F.A.; University of California-Irvine, M.F.A.

ADDRESSES: Agent—Mary Evans, 242 East Fifth Ave., New York, NY 10003.

CAREER: Author, 1986—.

AWARDS, HONORS: Grants from National Endowment for the Arts, 1995, and New York State Foundation for the Arts, 1996.

WRITINGS:

Small Claims (short stories and novella), Weidenfeld & Nicolson (New York City), 1986.
The Law of Falling Bodies (novel), Poseidon Press (New York City), 1993.
Half a Life (autobiography), Crown (New York City), 1996.

Also contributor to periodicals, including *Mississippi Review, CQ,* and *South Carolina Review.*

SIDELIGHTS: When author Jill Ciment published her autobiography *Half a Life* in 1996, it wasn't a surprise to fans of her quirky writings, which feature young girls growing up in dysfunctional families. Ciment's outrageous characters and story lines do not seem so very improbable when compared to her own life, from which she draws her intimate knowledge of poverty, an unconventional mother-daughter relationship, and survival techniques that often run counter to the law. In a review of *Half a Life,* a reviewer in *Publishers Weekly* described its author as a former

"shoplifter, porno model, gang member, forger and seductress." Ciment's evolution from such beginnings to become a popular writer is revealed as a especially remarkable feat when readers of *Half a Life* learn that the author's delinquent behavior included poor attendance at school.

Prior to publishing her autobiography, Ciment published two books of fiction: 1986's *Small Claims,* a collection of short stories and a novella; and the 1993 novel *The Law of Falling Bodies.* Both works feature autobiographical elements that link them closely, the most important being the key figures of a young woman and her mother. *Small Claims* received critical notices that found flaws and promise in Ciment's stories; a *Publishers Weekly* reviewer, for example, credited the author with interesting characters and ideas but concluded that "these stories . . . seem to exist in a void, relating to little more than themselves." More optimistically, Lisa Zeidner wrote in the *New York Times Book Review* that the book "suggests what Ms. Ciment can accomplish with wit and precision, when she extends the range of her subjects."

Such promise was fulfilled by Ciment's next work, her first full-length work of fiction. *The Law of Falling Bodies* was heralded by critics as evidence that the author had developed her skills considerably in the intervening years. The mother and daughter of this story are a nomadic pair who travel throughout the Southwest as "Mom" attempts to make a living selling an aphrodisiac perfume from her Airstream trailer. Responding to the novel in the *New York Times,* reviewer Michiko Kakutani pronounced that Ciment had "an uncommon gift for language" and that, despite first-novel failings, *The Law of Falling Bodies* was a "keenly observed and beautifully written novel." Likewise, the *Village Voice Literary Supplement*'s Laurie Muchnick was charmed by the author's methods. "Ciment uncovers the bizarre undercurrent beneath the placid surface of everyday life," the reviewer remarked. "She takes the conventions of several genres—road novels, coming-of-age stories, romances—and blends them, with a twist of wit and sharp observation, into something fresh and original."

BIOGRAPHICAL/CRITICAL SOURCES:

PERIODICALS

Los Angeles Times Book Review, November 2, 1986, p. 2.

New York Times, August 16, 1993, p. C17.
New York Times Book Review, October 19, 1986, p. 30; May 23, 1993, p. 29.
Publishers Weekly, July 18, 1986, p. 81; January 4, 1993, p. 58; May 13, 1996, p. 63.
Village Voice Literary Supplement, April, 1993, p. 6.

*   *   *

CLEGG, Holly Berkowitz 1955-

PERSONAL: Born August 23, 1955, in Fort Worth, TX; daughter of Jerry (in investments) and Ruth (a tutor) Berkowitz; married Michael V. Clegg (an attorney), September 1, 1979; children: Todd, Courtney, Haley. *Education:* Tulane University, B.A., 1977; attended Cordon Bleu Cooking School, London, England; also studied cooking in Paris, France. *Religion:* Jewish. *Avocational interests:* Tennis, cooking.

ADDRESSES: Home—13431 Woodmont Ct., Baton Rouge, LA 70810-5334. *Agent*—Gene Winick, McIntosh & Otis, Inc., 510 Madison Ave., Suite 607, New York, NY 10017.

CAREER: Petroleum Club, Houston, TX, menu planner and coordinator of social functions; Sherwood Forest Country Club, Baton Rouge, LA, party planner; Bocage Racquet Club, Baton Rouge, food service manager; Mercantile (department store chain), Fairfield, OH, houseware spokesperson, 1995—. Guest on national television programs, including *NBC Weekend Today.*

AWARDS, HONORS: Woman of Achievement Award; named Entrepreneur of the Year.

WRITINGS:

A Trim and Terrific Louisiana Kitchen, privately printed, 1993.
Trim and Terrific American Favorites: Over 250 Fast and Easy Low-Fat Recipes, C. N. Potter (New York), 1996.
Trim and Terrific One-Dish Favorites, C. N. Potter, 1997.

CLOSE, Reginald Arthur 1909-1996

OBITUARY NOTICE—See index for *CA* sketch: Born February 3, 1909, in London, England; died November 4, 1996. Educator, civil servant, author. Close devoted much of his career to the British Council, an organization he helped establish. His work took him to various cities worldwide, including Prague, Tokyo, and Athens. In his early career, he taught English in Hong Kong, beginning in 1933. He joined the British Council in 1938, beginning a thirty-year association. His posts included lecturing at the Institute of English Studies in Athens, Greece, being headmaster of a school in Concepcion, Chile, working as a representative in Prague, Czechoslovakia, opening a British Council office in Tokyo, Japan, and establishing a committee in London, England, to assist overseas students. He received the honor of OBE when sent to Prague and CBE after he had returned to Greece in the 1960s. He was also named honorary research fellow at University College, London. During his career he wrote for the London *Times* and penned books such as *The English We Use, English as a Foreign Language, The New English Grammar: More Lessons in English as a Foreign Language, A Reference Grammar for Students of English, An English Grammar for Greek Students,* and *A Teachers' Grammar.*

OBITUARIES AND OTHER SOURCES:

BOOKS

International Author and Writers Who's Who, International Biographical Centre, 1989.
Writers Directory, St. James Press, 1995.

PERIODICALS

Times (London), November 15, 1996, p. 23.

*   *   *

CLUFF, Russell M. 1946-

PERSONAL: Born April 27, 1946, in Colonia Juarez, Chihuahua, Mexico; U.S. citizen; son of Halver J. (a schoolteacher and builder) and Margaret (a primary schoolteacher; maiden name, Brown) Cluff; married Connie Peterson (an academic administrator), April 2, 1969; children: Russell M., Jr., Randall H.,

Allison Cluff Johnson, Hollie, Karen. *Ethnicity:* "Caucasian." *Education:* Brigham Young University, B.A., 1972, M.A., 1974; University of Illinois at Urbana-Champaign, Ph.D., 1978. *Avocational interests:* Music (playing guitar, singing, collecting music).

ADDRESSES: Home—254 North 2250 W., Provo, UT 84601. *Office*—Department of Spanish and Portuguese, 4048 JKHB, Brigham Young University, Provo, UT 84602; fax 801-378-8932. *E-mail*—Russell_Cluff@byu.edu.

CAREER: Brigham Young University, Provo, UT, instructor in Spanish, 1968-70, 1971-72; University of Minnesota—Morris, assistant professor of Spanish, 1978-81; University of Notre Dame, Notre Dame, IN, assistant professor of Spanish, 1981-83; Brigham Young University, associate professor, 1983-90, professor of Spanish, 1990—, P. A. Christensen Lecturer, 1996, coordinator of Latin American studies, David M. Kennedy Center for International Studies, 1993-96, and director of study abroad programs in Mexico and the Dominican Republic. University of Kansas, lecturer, 1988.

MEMBER: Modern Language Association of America, Phi Kappa Phi, Sigma Delta Pi.

WRITINGS:

Siete acercamientos al relato mexicano actual, Universidad Nacional Autonoma de Mexico (Mexico City), 1987.

(Editor and translator, with L. Howard Quackenbush, and co-author of introduction) Gonzalo Rojas, *Schizotext and Other Poems/Esquizotexto y otros poemas,* Peter Lang Publishing (New York City), 1988.

(Editor) Josefina Lara Valdez, *Diccionario bio-bibliografico de escritores contemporaneos de Mexico,* Universidad Nacional Autonoma de Mexico, 1988.

(Editor) Magaly Martinez Gamba, *Restos y cenizas,* Universidad Nacional Autonoma de Mexico, 1988.

(Editor) Luis Arturo Ramos, *Melomanias: La ritualizacion del universo,* Universidad Nacional Autonoma de Mexico, 1990.

(Editor and translator, with Quackenbush, and co-author of introduction) Guillermo Samperio, *Beatle Dreams and Other Stories,* Latin American Literary Review Press (Pittsburgh, PA), 1994.

(With Valdez) *Diccionario bio-bibliografico de escritores de Mexico, 1920-1970,* Instituto Nacional de Bellas Artes (Mexico City), 1995.

Panorama critico-bibliografico del cuento mexicano a partir de 1950, Coordinacion de Difusion Cultural, Universidad Nacional Autonoma de Mexico, 1996.

(Editor and author of epilogue) Virgilio Diaz Grullon, *Cronicas de Altocerro* (stories), Universidad Nacional Autonoma de Mexico, 1996.

Contributor to books published primarily in Spanish. Contributor of articles, translations, and reviews to academic journals and literary magazines. Member of editorial board, *Chasqui,* 1979-94.

WORK IN PROGRESS: Translating Carlos Montemayor's *Finisterra and Other Poems,* with L. Howard Quackenbush; *Acercamientos al cuento mexicano actual,* an expanded edition of *Siete acercamientos al relato mexicano actual; Historia del cuento mexicano desde 1950,* a history of the Mexican short story since 1950; *La novela veracruzana, siglo XX* (tentative title), a book on twentieth-century novelists of Veracruz; a book-length study of the short story sequence in Mexico; translating a collection of poetry by Marco Antonio Campos; translating a collection of Mexican poetry since the 1940s, to be edited by Federico Patan; research on the twentieth-century Chihuahua novel, the Caribbean short story, and the Central American short story.

SIDELIGHTS: Russell M. Cluff told *CA:* "Writing is creating. I believe that creating, in just about any form, is one of the most fulfilling aspects of life. All types of writing stimulate me, and I engage primarily in the following areas: literary essays, biography, bibliography, and translation.

"Personal (as well as general) history is one of the most stimulating factors behind my writing. Indirectly, I am a product of the Mexican Revolution of 1910. My grandparents were living in Mexico when the revolution broke out. Three of the four were born in the United States, but my paternal grandmother (from a Danish family) was born in Colonia Diaz, a small town in Chihuahua that was destined to be wiped off the face of the map. Having been given the name of the dictator who allowed my people to settle in that country, his enemies delighted in seeing the town destroyed. My Danish great-grandfather was buried in that vicinity, and my family has no idea where his grave lies today. My grandparents all returned to Mexico sometime around 1917 with my mother and father in tow as small children. My seven siblings and I were born in Mexico and, at the age of eighteen, we were obliged to choose our citizenship. For educational reasons, as much as anything else, I chose U.S. citizenship. While I have never regretted that decision on the pragmatic level, I have never ceased to consider myself a true Mexican.

"It is in my professional life that I am allowed to choose activities that keep my Mexicanness alive. My primary research and writing activities concern Mexican writers and Mexican literature. My research also allows me to travel frequently to Mexico and to realize meaningful contacts with Mexican literati. I am especially fond of the short story in that country, which explains why the bulk of my literary essays treat this genre. I also enjoy interviewing the writers. Such interviews are often the first discursive information available on up-and-coming writers.

"I suppose that my most important work to date, in terms of 'service,' is the *Diccionario bio-bibliografico de escritores de Mexico.* One of the most artistically rewarding publications is *Beatle Dreams and Other Stories.* Guillermo Samperio is a truly exciting writer and personality, with a highly respectable production and a promising future. Being able to create the English text for some of his best stories has been a highlight in my career and in that of my co-translator. I am, however, equally fond of our edition and translation of *Schizotext and Other Poems* by the Chilean poet Gonzalo Rojas. In terms of future literary translations, I will be quite selective, given the great amount of time required and the difficulties of placing translations for publication in the English market.

"My greatest satisfaction is writing critical essays. My book *Siete acercamientos al relato mexicano actual* contains several essays that still interest me today. I am now working on a revised, augmented edition that I believe will be more representative of some of the best stories written in Mexico, and yet will still not represent the general treatment I plan to give the genre in the future.

"I am also working on a book concerning the short story sequence in Mexico. In the twentieth century, the story sequence is most commonly associated with the extraordinary success of Sherwood Anderson's book *Winesburg, Ohio,* often in conjunction with work by James Joyce and William Faulkner. Critical work on Spanish-American short story sequences amounts to no more than six essays at present and, in

each case, the critics (myself included) have followed the models of their counterparts from the English-speaking world. There are many parallels between the developments of this tradition in Mexico and those in the United States, which I shall explore in my new study.

"More recently, I have developed a burning interest in the narrative of the Dominican Republic. I will be spending several months there in the near future. I will take with me an edition of the short stories by the Dominican writer Virgilio Diaz Grullon, which I will be able to present to the author in person. I am now working on an extensive bibliography of the novel and short story in this country."

*   *   *

COBB, James H(arvey) 1953-

PERSONAL: Born February 18, 1953, in Tacoma, WA; married; wife's name, Kathryne (an international banker). *Ethnicity:* "White/Caucasian." *Education:* University of Puget Sound, B.A., 1976. *Politics:* Independent. *Avocational interests:* Wargaming on the Internet and elsewhere, military and western history, science fiction conventions, collecting firearms books.

ADDRESSES: Home—Tacoma, WA. *E-mail*—DDG79@aol.com (America Online). *Agent*—Henry Morrison, Inc., P.O. Box 235, Bedford Hills, NY 10507.

CAREER: Writer. Member of U.S. Naval Institute and Museum of the Rockies.

MEMBER: U.S. Navy League, Northwest Science Fiction Society, Fort Lewis Museum Association, Port Defiance Zoo Society.

WRITINGS:

Choosers of the Slain (suspense novel), Putnam (New York City), 1996.
Stormdragon, Putnam, in press.

WORK IN PROGRESS: Projects on science fiction set in the earth's future, a continuation of the "Amanda Garrett" series, and young adult literature.

SIDELIGHTS: James H. Cobb told *CA:* "I came into my interest in naval affairs early on, born out of my family's long and proud association with the navy. My grandfather served aboard the U.S.S. *Arizona* during World War I. My uncle did duty in the Aleutian islands and off Okinawa during World War II, and a close friend of our family accompanied Admiral Byrd on one of his expeditions to the South Pole. Then, there was my uncle Marshal.

"Marshal was a master chief petty officer of the U.S. Navy. He'd been everywhere and done everything: duty aboard the China River gunboats, military police patrol in the old Shanghai international district, Pearl Harbor, the Doolittle Raid, the Solomons and the Philippines, Korea. . . I could and did sit and listen to his yarns for hours.

"Much to my regret, when my time came, I was unable to follow a career in the services. Instead, I became a kind of cut-rate Rudyard Kipling, seeking to tell the stories of America's warriors as well as I could.

"My employment history might generously be described as 'varied.' I have worked as a ranch hand, a security guard, a disc jockey, and a truck dispatcher. I have sold soccer equipment, radio advertising, and photocopying machines, and I have managed book stores and a motion picture theater. I have also had the opportunity to travel extensively, not only in the United States, where I've spent a lot of time poking around in the wilderness country of the west, but overseas as well. To date, I have visited North Africa, Spain, Japan, South Korea, Hong Kong, and both Taiwan and Communist China.

"Through it all, I have maintained my interest in armed forces affairs. The city of Tacoma is an excellent place to live if you are a military buff. To the south is Fort Lewis and McChord Air Force Base, each with a superb military museum. To the east is the U.S. Army's Yakima Firing Range. To the north, on Puget Sound, is an entire complex of naval installations, including the Everett Fleet Base, the Bremerton Naval Shipyard, the Bangor Nuclear Submarine Facility, and Whidby Island Naval Air Station. I have visited all of them at one time or another.

"I have cultivated friendships with a number of service and ex-service personnel, all of whom have been most helpful in the development of my writing. I've also been able to collect a sizeable library of books and other publications on military history and related subjects. Through my membership in the Navy League and the U.S. Naval Institute, I have been able

to take part in numerous in-port visits and 'Tiger cruises' aboard active-service naval vessels, ranging from aircraft carriers and battleships to nuclear submarines. All of these experiences have come together to form what I hope is a reasonably solid background for my work.

"My other hobbies include an eclectic series of collections: firearms, western history, Japanese animated science fiction and classic children's literature.

"I have several writing projects in mind, above and beyond the Amanda Garret techno-thriller series. I would like to attempt a book or series set in the same near-future time frame, but focusing on a U.S. Army Light Armored Cavalry Squadron. I also have an experimental concept under development for a far-future 'pure' combat science fiction trilogy, using the style and structure of the current-day techno-thriller. In addition, I would like to attempt with the classic western what I have tried to do with the techno-thriller genre: the development of a dynamic and realistic heroine within a previously male-dominated action adventure format.

"Beyond that, we'll have to see."

* * *

COCKRELL, Thomas D(errell) 1949-

PERSONAL: Born August 26, 1949, in Mississippi; son of Bobby (a machinist) and Edna Earle (Chambers) Cockrell; married Rhonda Suzette Latch (a pharmacy technician), May 29, 1993. *Ethnicity:* "Caucasian/English heritage." *Education:* Mississippi State University, B.S., 1971, M.A., 1981, Ph.D., 1989. *Politics:* Independent. *Religion:* United Methodist. *Avocational interests:* Using a metal detector to search for historical relics.

ADDRESSES: Home—208 West Main St., Blue Mountain, MS 38610. *Office*—Department of History, Blue Mountain College, BMC Box 276, Blue Mountain, MS 38610; fax 601-685-4776.

CAREER: Louisville Police Department, Louisville, MS, police officer, 1971-74, 1975-76, 1977-78; high school social studies teacher in Mississippi, 1974-75; activities director at a Methodist church, Philadelphia, MS, 1976-77; Mississippi Farm Bureau Insurance Co., Winston County, salesperson, 1978-79;

Louisville Fire Department, firefighter, 1979-89; Louisiana State University in Shreveport, librarian, archivist and assistant professor of history and political science, 1989-90; Mississippi State University, lecturer in history, 1990-92; Blue Mountain College, Blue Mountain, MS, associate professor of history and head of social science, 1992—. East Mississippi Community College, instructor, 1983-87. Tippah County Historical Museum, member of steering committee, 1996—; guest on local television programs.

MEMBER: Southern Historical Association, Mississippi Historical Society, Tippah County Historical Society (member of executive board, 1996—), Phi Alpha Theta.

AWARDS, HONORS: Mississippi Press Association Award, 1984, for a series of stories; Working for Academic Excellence Award, Mississippi Legislature, 1994-95.

WRITINGS:

The Descendants of William Jasper Cockrell and Martha Ann Crowson, privately printed, 1982.
(Editor with Michael B. Ballard) *A Mississippi Rebel in the Army of Northern Virginia: The Civil War Memoirs of Private David Holt,* Louisiana State University Press (Baton Rouge, LA), 1995.

Contributor to books, including *Encyclopedia of African-American Civil Rights from Emancipation to the Present,* Greenwood Press (Westport, CT), 1992. Contributor of articles and reviews to journals, including *Journal of Mississippi History, Mountain Breeze,* and *Mississippi Outdoors.*

WORK IN PROGRESS: Editing the Civil War memoir of a Union soldier, with Michael B. Ballard.

SIDELIGHTS: Thomas D. Cockrell told *CA:* "My primary motivation for writing is sheer interest in the subject matter as it relates to my field of study. History fascinates me. As I attempt to relate life today with the lives of those who lived before us, it becomes apparent that we are not so different. We have the same basic problems and needs, and we are affected by acts both directly and indirectly related to us. By analyzing how others coped with life, we have a better understanding of how we may cope as well.

"Basically I am self-motivated; however, in the academic field one is challenged to publish. As a student of my mentor, Joseph F. Marszalek, Jr., I was chal-

lenged to do my very best in graduate school. His influence, along with that of other professors and scholars, encouraged me to go beyond teaching and explore the fascinating world of writing."

*   *   *

COE, Lewis 1911-

PERSONAL: Born September 14, 1911, in Kansas City, MO; son of Willard L. (an army officer) and Mary (a homemaker; maiden name, Acuff) Coe; married Alice Fisher, September 29, 1940. *Ethnicity:* "English." *Education:* Attended high school in Galva, IL. *Politics:* Republican. *Religion:* Protestant. *Avocational interests:* Photography, amateur radio, collecting telegraph memorabilia.

ADDRESSES: Home—115 East 113th Ave., Crown Point, IN 46307-9706.

CAREER: Worked as a telegraph operator for Postal Telegraph and a radio engineer for Mackay Radio, 1929-45; electrical worker, 1945-68; Purdue University, West Lafayette, IN, audiovisual specialist, 1968-72.

MEMBER: Veteran Wireless Operators, Antique Wireless Association, Morse Telegraph Club.

AWARDS, HONORS: Marconi Medal of Achievement, Veteran Wireless Operators, 1993, for writing about the history of radio.

WRITINGS:

Great Days of the Heliograph, privately printed, 1987.
The Telegraph: A History of Morse's Invention and Its Predecessors in the United States, McFarland and Co. (Jefferson, NC), 1993.
The Telephone and Its Several Inventors: A History, McFarland and Co., 1995.
Wireless Radio: A History, McFarland and Co., 1996.

WORK IN PROGRESS: Research on visual signaling.

SIDELIGHTS: Lewis Coe told *CA:* "My first book on the heliograph was written to provide some record of an almost forgotten subject. The telegraph book was inspired by the closing of Western Union, which marked the end of an era that began in 1844. The telephone book pays tribute to Elisha Gray, who is generally ignored in telephone history, along with many other inventors. *Wireless Radio* points out the many ways in which radio is used, aside from conventional entertainment broadcasting. I had hands-on experience in all of these fields and decided that the books would make a worthwhile contribution to history."

*　　*　　*

COLEMAN, William Oliver

PERSONAL: Born in Sydney, Australia; son of Peter and Verna (a biographer; maiden name, Scott) Coleman; married Anna Tatsun, December 10, 1994; children: Simon. *Education:* University of Sydney, B.Ec. (with honors), 1981; London School of Economics and Political Science, London, Ph.D., 1989.

ADDRESSES: Office—University of Tasmania, GPO Box 252C, Sandy Bay, Hobart, Tasmania 7001, Australia; fax 61-03-234570. *E-mail*—William.Coleman @econ.utas.edu.au.

CAREER: University of Exeter, Exeter, England, tutorial fellow, 1987-88; Victoria University of Wellington, Wellington, New Zealand, lecturer, 1988-91; University of Tasmania, Hobart, Australia, senior lecturer, 1991—.

WRITINGS:

Money and Finance in the Australian Economy, Irwin, 1994.
Rationalism and Anti-Rationalism in the Origins of Economics, Edward Elgar (Brookfield, VT), 1995.

*　　*　　*

COLLINS, Patricia Hill　1948-

PERSONAL: Born May 1, 1948, in Philadelphia, PA; married Roger L. Collins (an educator); children: Valerie Lisa. *Education:* Brandeis University, A.B., 1969, Ph.D., 1984; Harvard University, M.A.T., 1970.

ADDRESSES: Office—Department of African American Studies, University of Cincinnati, ML 370, Cincinnati, OH 45221.

CAREER: Educator and sociologist. Harvard U.T.T.T. program, teacher, 1970-73; St. Joseph Community School, curriculum specialist, 1973-76; African American Center, Tufts University, director, 1976-80; University of Cincinnati, Cincinnati, OH, assistant, then associate professor, 1987-93, professor of African American studies, 1993—, Charles Phelps Taft Professor of Sociology, 1996, chair, minority fellowship program committee, 1992—.

AWARDS, HONORS: C. Wright Mills Award, National Society of the Study of Social Problems, 1990, for *Black Feminist Thought: Knowledge, Consciousness, and the Politics of Empowerment.*

MEMBER: American Sociological Association.

WRITINGS:

Black Feminist Thought: Knowledge, Consciousness, and the Politics of Empowerment, Unwin Hyman (Boston), 1990.
(Contributor) Joan E. Hartman and Ellen Messer-Davidow, editors, *(En)Gendering Knowledge: Feminists in Academe,* University of Chicago Press (Chicago), 1991.
(Editor, with Margaret L. Andersen) *Race, Class, and Gender: An Anthology,* Wadsworth (Belmont, CA), 1992, second edition, 1994.
(Contributor) Donna Bassin, Margaret Honey, and Meryle Mahrer Kaplan, editors, *Representations of Motherhood,* Yale University Press (New Haven, CT), 1994.
(Contributor) Gail Dines and Jean M. Humez, editors, *Gender, Race, and Class in Media: A Text-Reader,* Sage (Thousand Oaks, CA), 1995.

Contributor to periodicals, including *Signs, Teaching Sociology,* and *Western Journal of Black Studies.*

SIDELIGHTS: A professor of African American studies and sociology at the University of Cincinnati since 1987, Patricia Hill Collins came to national critical attention as the author of *Black Feminist Thought: Knowledge, Consciousness, and the Politics of Empowerment.* Awarded the C. Wright Mills Award by the National Society of the Study of Social Problems in 1990, Collins's book provides a history and outline of contemporary black feminist thought through the use of source material that includes music, literature, oral history, and academic research.

Collins's work is built upon three main tenets: that oppressions are interconnected; that the need for self-definition has required women of color to create alternative world-views; and that externalities such as standards of beauty and success have been racialized in favor of white women. She then examines how race combines with gender to create, for African American women, narrow roles that define them within their families, on the job, and in a multitude of other social contexts.

In describing black feminist thought, Collins rejects traditional theories of knowing, such as relativism and positivism. Desiring to take into consideration the social, material, and political positions of the knower, she is also aware that race—and, to an increasing degree, gender—are highly subjective forms of categorization. In this and other areas of her study, Collins points up the problems inherent in the traditional Afrocentric and feminist viewpoint. "Indeed, an extraordinary number of conventional notions about black women are turned on their heads as a black woman's standpoint takes form," comments Rose M. Brewer in *Contemporary Sociology.* "Given the richness of her analysis," Brewer adds, "I have little doubt that [such 'truths' should be challenged]. . . . Collins speaks through powerful voices, and we all need to listen and respond."

Collins's work, which includes co-editorship of 1992's *Race, Class, and Gender: An Anthology,* has been groundbreaking in both reevaluating Afrocentric and feminist thought and placing it within the larger social context, moderating the accusations, by some, that African American intellectualism has been a threat to the economic and political gains of black men made in the past century. Through presenting the development of black feminist theory in a manner that calls much of its derivation into question, she forces a reconsideration of oppression, domination, and the politics of empowerment.

BIOGRAPHICAL/CRITICAL SOURCES:

PERIODICALS

Black Enterprise, July, 1992, p. 12.
Choice, February, 1996, p. 909.
Contemporary Sociology, January, 1992, p. 132.
Gender and Society, September, 1992, pp. 508-17.
Signs, winter, 1992, p. 467.

Village Voice Literary Supplement, November, 1995, p. 24.
Women's Review of Books, February, 1991, p. 13.*

*   *   *

COLLINS, Ronald K. L. 1949-

PERSONAL: Born July 31, 1949, in Santa Monica, CA; son of LeRoy (self-employed) and Yolanda (self-employed) Collins; married Susan A. Cohen (employed in the field of public interest), May 25, 1986; children: Dylan Lee. *Ethnicity:* "Italian-Irish." *Education:* University of California, Santa Barbara, B.A., 1971; Loyola Marymount University, J.D. *Politics:* "Progressive."

ADDRESSES: Home—61 Walnut Ave., Takoma Park, MD 20912. *Office*—School of Law, Seattle University, 950 Broadway Plaza, Tacoma, WA 98402. *E-mail*—collins@seattleu.edu.

CAREER: Temple University, Philadelphia, PA, professor of law, 1988-90; George Washington University, Washington, DC, professor of law, 1992-95; Seattle University, Tacoma, WA, professor of law, 1995—. Center for Science in the Public Interest, member.

MEMBER: Simone Weil Society, Legal Aid Society of Orange County.

WRITINGS:

(Editor) *Constitutional Government in America,* Carolina Academic Press (Durham, NC), 1981.
(Editor) Grant Gilmore, *The Death of Contract,* Ohio State University Press (Columbus, OH), 1995.
(With David M. Skover) *The Death of Discourse,* Westview (Boulder, CO), 1996.

Contributor to books, including *Simone Weil's Philosophy of Culture,* Cambridge University Press, 1993. Contributor to periodicals.

WORK IN PROGRESS: Seeds in the Soil, completion expected in 1997; *Shelley's Rule,* a novel about "life, law, and law school," with Skover, 1998; *Principles of Power,* with Skover.

SIDELIGHTS: Ronald K. L. Collins and David M. Skover told *CA:* "We have been writing together for a decade. Ron lives in the East, and Dave in the West, yet each word, line, paragraph, section, and chapter of our collaborative works is written together in the same room, with Dave manning the keys and Ron pacing. We thrive on the synergy generated by our different intellects, personalities, and interests.

"We refuse, in Marshall McLuhan's words, to drive into the future with eyes fixed on the rear-view mirror of the past. Thus, we enjoy probing relatively new and unsettled terrains, however uncertain or unruly these efforts may be. In the article 'The Future of Liberal Legal Scholarship,' for example, we urged liberals in 1988 to recognize that Earl Warren is dead and to break out of the mind cells of an era long gone. Similarly, in *The Death of Discourse,* we examined America's free speech as it is, rather than as it should be, and pointed to the pomp and hypocrisy surrounding the First Amendment. We believe in testing Niccolo Machiavelli's claim that it is 'more fitting to go directly to the effectual truth of the thing than to the imagination of it.' Like Antaeus, we need to touch the earth, if only better to appreciate the poetic imagination.

"May our collaboration continue as long as Fortuna smiles. Why? Perhaps it has something to do with the pair principle—the uncanny excitement that comes with mixing two minds in order to communicate with one 'voice.' It is a wondrous experience, this art of *re*creation."

Collins added: "I enjoy writing, more than most other things. For me, writing is an experiment, as life is. It is a way, both in form and substance, to test new waters, new ways, even new worlds. Part of this experiment is the attempt to make writing mean different things as the reader senses different patterns in the writer's quilt. Hence, style is nearly as important as substance. In the best of writing, the two are blended into one. That is why I have always enjoyed reading Plato's dialogues, Weil's notebooks, Wittgenstein's tracts, McLuhan's anti-books, and yes, Nietzsche's aphorisms, among others.

"Free speech! Free writing! Free thought! Three maxims in search of a mind.

"Over the years I have written with several souls, David M. Skover being the best."

COLUMBUS, Chris(topher) 1959-

PERSONAL: Born in 1959, in Spangler, PA; son of Alex (a miner and factory worker) and Irene (a factory worker) Columbus; married Monica Devereux (a dancer); children: Eleanor, Brandon, and a third child. *Education:* Graduated from New York University film school, 1980.

ADDRESSES: Agent—Jack Rapke, Creative Artists Agency, 9830 Wilshire Blvd., Beverly Hills, CA 90212.

CAREER: Screenwriter. Director of motion pictures, including *Adventures in Babysitting,* 1987; *Heartbreak Hotel,* 1988; *Home Alone,* 1990; *Only the Lonely,* 1991; *Home Alone 2: Lost in New York,* 1992; *Mrs. Doubtfire,* 1993; and *Nine Months,* 1995.

WRITINGS:

SCREENPLAYS

Reckless, Metro-Goldwyn-Mayer (MGM)/United Artists (UA), 1984.
Gremlins, Warner Bros., 1984.
Young Sherlock Holmes, Paramount, 1985.
The Goonies, Warner Bros., 1985.
Heartbreak Hotel, Buena Vista, 1988.
Only the Lonely, Twentieth Century-Fox, 1991.
(With Richard Outten) *Little Nemo: Adventures in Slumberland* (taken from a story by Jean Moebius Giraud and Yutaka Fujioka based on the comic strip Little Nemo in Slumberland by Winsor McKay), Hemdale, 1992.
Nine Months, Twentieth Century-Fox, 1995.
Jingle All the Way, Twentieth Century-Fox, 1996.

TELEPLAYS

(With others) *Galaxy High School* (television series), CBS-TV, 1986.

ADAPTATIONS: Gremlins was adapted by George Gipe as a novel for Avon, 1984; *Young Sherlock Holmes* was adapted by Peter Lerangis as *Steven Spielberg Presents Young Sherlock Holmes: The Storybook* for Simon & Schuster, 1985.

WORK IN PROGRESS: Writing an adaptation of *Theater of Blood,* a camp horror film from the early 1970s.

SIDELIGHTS: "Blessed with a golden touch and an apparently faceless style, [Chris] Columbus looks to be the Zelig of modern Hollywood directors," judged Ty Burr in *Entertainment Weekly.* Columbus is a Hollywood filmmaker who has particularly distinguished himself in the comedy genre. He began his show business career as the screenwriter for *Reckless,* the story of a beautiful high-school student who falls in love with a socially inferior biker. Columbus next supplied the script for *Gremlins,* a horror film in which hordes of small, malicious creatures undermine stability in smalltown America.

Columbus not only wrote but also directed *Only the Lonely,* a romantic comedy about a lonely, middle-aged police officer still suffering under his domineering mother. Columbus described *Only the Lonely* to Chris Willman in the *Los Angeles Times* as "the first film I wrote that was based on aspects of my life that really had no reference to other films I had seen." Willman praised *Only the Lonely* as a "low-key and leisurely paced adult comedy."

In 1993 Columbus wrote and directed *Mrs. Doubtfire,* a comedy about an enterprising actor who parts from his wife but maintains ties with his three children by posing as their domineering, English nanny. David Denby, a reviewer for *New York,* was among those critics who decried Columbus's achievement as one more of "engineering than inspiration." Denby conceded, however, that Williams's performance salvages the film. "He's a hell of an old lady," Denby concluded, "and . . . that's just barely enough." Burr judged: "*Mrs. Doubtfire* is a kiddie movie that's slick enough to flatter and amuse the kid in most adults."

Columbus followed *Mrs. Doubtfire* by writing and directing *Nine Months,* a comedy about a psychologist who undergoes considerable anxiety after learning of his girlfriend's pregnancy. Columbus "punches up all the photogenic elements he can to *woo-hoo* at the audience and skip over any real tension in the relationship," judged Steve Daly in *Entertainment Weekly.* A critic in *Rolling Stone* described *Nine Months* as a "knockabout romantic comedy."

Columbus is as well-known for his writing as his directing. He made his directorial debut in 1987 with *Adventures in Babysitting,* the story of a teenage woman's efforts to guard three children during a "comic-nightmare night in Chicago," according to Burr. In 1990, Columbus directed *Home Alone,* the fourth-highest grossing picture to date. Its sequel, *Home Alone 2: Lost in New York,* released in 1992,

earned over $172 million within two years. Starring Macaulay Culkin as Kevin McCallister, both movies focus on a young boy separated from his family. In the original picture, Culkin's character is left home in Chicago by mistake as the family leaves for a Christmas vacation in Europe. He must take on adult responsibilities, like cleaning and shopping, while waiting for his relatives to return. Two would-be burglars shake up McCallister's world even more as he saves his home from their assault. *Home Alone 2* moves the action to the streets of New York, as McCallister accidently follows the wrong adult and boards the wrong plane at the beginning of another family vacation.

Columbus temporarily put his writing on hold for another film, directing *Jingle All the Way,* which was released late in 1996. Again, a child is at the center of the story. A hard working father, played by Arnold Schwarzenegger, desperately tries to find a Turbo Man action figure for his son during the holiday shopping rush. Within its first two weeks at theaters, *Jingle All the Way* grossed over $30 million.

Columbus has enjoyed success as a screenwriter and as a director but he favors directing. "It doesn't really matter to me if I write my own script or if I direct someone else's script as long as I'm directing a film," he told Willman in the *Los Angeles Times.* He added that "writing was just a way to become a director as quickly as possible."

BIOGRAPHICAL/CRITICAL SOURCES:

BOOKS

Contemporary Theatre, Film and Television, Volume 10, Gale (Detroit, MI), 1993.

PERIODICALS

Chicago Tribune, May 25, 1990.
Entertainment Weekly, April 22, 1994, pp. 64-66; January 19, 1996, pp. 58-59; December 13, 1996.
Los Angeles Times, May 27, 1991; November 7, 1993.
Newsweek, November 23, 1992, pp. 76-77; November 29, 1993, p. 72.
New York, November 30, 1992, pp. 164-65; November 29, 1993, pp. 64-65.
Premiere, October, 1990, p. 74.
Rolling Stone, August 10, 1995, p. 62.*

CONATI, Marcello 1928-

PERSONAL: Born April 26, 1928, in Milan, Italy; son of Lorenzo (a lyricist) and Anita Grazia Conati; married Licia Vallon. *Education:* Conservatorio di Musica, Parma, 1953; Conservatorio di Musica, Milan, 1959.

ADDRESSES: Home—Borgo Riccio da Parma, 50, 43100 Parma, Italy. *Office*—CIRPM, via Conservatorio 31/B, 43100, Parma, Italy.

CAREER: Pianist, composer, music teacher, and author. Director of the Centro Internazionale di Ricerca sui Periodici Musicali, Parma-Colorno; music teacher at the Conservatorio "A. Boito," Parma; Comitato di Redazione "Rivista Italiana di Musicologia," Bologna; Commissione Artistica Orchestra Sinfonica "A Toscanini," Parma; Comitato Direttivo Instituto "Gramsci," Parma; Consiglio d'Amministrazione Conservatorio "A. Boito," Parma.

MEMBER: Societa Italiana di Musicologia, Societa Italiana di Etnomusicologia, Ordine dei Giornalisti.

WRITINGS:

Canti popolari della Val d'Enza e Val Cedra Palatina (Parma), 1976.
(Editor with Mario Medici) *Carteggio Verdi-Boito,* 1978, translated by William Weaver as *The Verdi-Boito Correspondence,* University of Chicago Press (Chicago, IL), 1994.
(Editor) *Interviste e incontri con Verdi,* Il Formichiere (Milan), 1980, translated by Richard Stokes as *Interviews and Encounters with Verdi,* Gollancz (London), 1984, also published as *Encounters with Verdi,* Cornell University Press (Ithaca, NY), 1984.
La bottega della musica, Il Saggiatore (Milan), 1983.
Verdi: "Rigoletto," Guida, Mondadori (Milan), 1983.
La Musica, 1855. La Musica, 1857-1859, UMI (Ann Arbor, MI), 1989.
La Musica, 1876-1878. La Musica, 1883-1885, UMI, 1989.
Strenna teatrale europea, 1838-1848, UMI, 1989.
L'Italia musicale, 1847-1859, UMI, 1992.
Rigoletto: Un'analisi drammatico-musicale (music criticism), Marsilio (Venice), 1992.
Simon Boccanegra di Giuseppe Verdi, Ricordi (Milan), 1993.

SIDELIGHTS: An Italian composer, musician, and music scholar, Marcello Conati has written and edited numerous works on nineteenth-century Italian composers, including several volumes devoted to Giuseppe Verdi, whose works include the operas *Rigoletto, La traviata,* and *Aida.* Conati's contributions to Verdi scholarship include the notable 1978 volume *Carteggio Verdi-Boito,* which was translated into English in 1994 as *The Verdi-Boito Correspondence,* and 1980's *Interviste e incontri con Verdi,* published in English as *Interviews and Encounters with Verdi* in 1984.

The Verdi-Boito Correspondence, which Conati edited with Mario Medici, draws together more than 300 letters exchanged over a period of twenty years between the composer and Arrigo Boito, the librettist with whom he produced the tragedy *Otello* in 1887 and the comedy *Falstaff* in 1893. *Opera News* called *The Verdi-Boito Correspondence* "indispensable," and in recommending the volume, Bonnie Jo Dopp in *Library Journal* characterized the collection as "important" for both its scope and its themes. She remarked on "the greatness possible (in art and friendship) when two talented men collaborate with mutual loving respect."

The anthology *Interviews and Encounters with Verdi* collects contemporary accounts of the reclusive Verdi, who was known as "the Bear of Busseto" for the fierceness with which he guarded his privacy at his country home near Parma. The reminiscences collected in the volume have been culled from journalistic accounts, diary entries, and books of the period, and most have not previously been available to twentieth-century readers. John Higgins in the London *Times* noted that "the editing is scrupulous, the annotations most scholarly and the presentation of each author admirable." Peter G. Davis in the *New York Times Book Review* called the volume "the most fascinating and revealing book ever compiled about this elusive figure who took infinite pains to hide his true personality from posterity." The critic further declared the collection "brilliantly researched, organized and edited."

BIOGRAPHICAL/CRITICAL SOURCES:

PERIODICALS

Choice, December, 1984, p. 567.
Library Journal, April 15, 1994, p. 80.
New York Times Book Review, June 17, 1984, p. 7.
Opera News, December 24, 1994, pp. 41-42.
Publishers Weekly, April 4, 1994, p. 67.
Times (London), May 17, 1984.*

CONSTANTINE, J. Robert 1924-

PERSONAL: Born January 28, 1924, in Jeffersonville, IN; son of Dennis (a machinist) and Gertrude (Kuehn) Constantine; married Velva Hoffman, September 6, 1946; children: Cassandra Constantine Brooks, Melissa Constantine Libal. *Ethnicity:* "German-Italian." *Education:* Indiana University—Bloomington, A.B., 1950, M.A., 1951, Ph.D., 1953. *Politics:* Democrat.

ADDRESSES: Home—1209 Calusa Dr., Barefoot Bay, FL 32976.

CAREER: Vincennes University, Vincennes, IN, instructor in history, 1953-57; Indiana University—South Bend, associate professor of history, 1957-59; Indiana State University, Terre Haute, professor of history, 1959-89. Eugene V. Debs Foundation, secretary, 1963-84. *Military service:* U.S. Army, 1943-46; served in European theater.

AWARDS, HONORS: Named Scholar of the Year, Indiana Commission on the Humanities, 1991.

WRITINGS:

(Editor) *The Letters of Eugene V. Debs, 1874-1926,* three volumes, 1990, published in one volume as *Gentle Rebel,* University of Illinois Press (Champaign, IL), 1995.

WORK IN PROGRESS: Research on Eugene V. Debs's interest in literature and writers.

*   *   *

CONWAY, D. J. 1939-

PERSONAL: Born May 3, 1939, in Hood River, OR; daughter of E. Gordon and Leota Lottie (Smith) Long; married Howard Carr, September, 1957 (marriage ended, November, 1973); married Charles D. Conway (a millwright), March 31, 1979; children: Sharon E. Carr (deceased), David H. Carr, Jeanne Carr McLarney. *Ethnicity:* "Irish/German/American Indian." *Education:* Attended high school. *Religion:* "Wiccan/Pagan." *Avocational interests:* Painting, herb gardening, playing musical instruments.

ADDRESSES: Home—Roseburg, OR. *E-mail*—DJCONWAY@juno.com.

CAREER: Writer, 1981—.

WRITINGS:

NONFICTION

Celtic Magic, Llewellyn Publications (St. Paul, MN), 1990.
Norse Magic, Llewellyn Publications, 1990.
Ancient and Shining Ones, Llewellyn Publications, 1993.
Maiden, Mother, Crone, Llewellyn Publications, 1994.
Dancing with Dragons, Llewellyn Publications, 1994.
By Oak, Ash, and Thorn, Llewellyn Publications, 1995.
Moon Magick, Llewellyn Publications, 1995.
Flying Without a Broom, Llewellyn Publications, 1995.
Falcon Feather and Valkyrie Sword, Llewellyn Publications, 1995.
Animal Magick, Llewellyn Publications, 1995.
Astral Love, Llewellyn Publications, 1996.
Magickal, Mythical, Mystical Beasts, Llewellyn, 1996.
Lord of Light and Shadow, Llewellyn, 1997.

FANTASIES

The Dream Warrior, Llewellyn Publications, 1996.
Soothslayer, Llewellyn Publications, 1997.

WORK IN PROGRESS: Warrior of Shadows, a fantasy, publication by Llewellyn Publications expected in 1998.

SIDELIGHTS: D. J. Conway told *CA:* "I started writing in the second grade but, through my first marriage and the raising of three children, my writing was sporadic. While I struggled to support the children on my own after the divorce, there was no time or energy for writing. After the second marriage, poor health made it imperative that I not work outside the home, so I turned my energy back to writing. Now I write full-time.

"For my nonfiction books, I was probably most influenced by the works of Joseph Campbell and Maritas Gimbutas. For the fiction, my favorite authors are Andre Norton, Barbara Hambley, Anne McCaffrey, Diana Paxton, Terry Pratchett, and Marion Zimmer Bradley.

"My nonfiction writing is sparked mainly by reading mythologies, history, and archaeology. My fiction bubbles up from deep inside, and I am never quite certain what sparked it.

"I write because I can't keep from writing, and I am intensely interested in the psychic experiences mentioned in my books. A fiction book generally starts with one scene and a main character. I may not know where this scene fits or what the rest of the book is about at first, but it catches my interest and I play the 'what if' game. I then rough out a plot to see if it will hold together. This plot is then expanded to a tentative chapter-by-chapter outline. I may or may not stick closely to the outline, depending upon what twists and turns come unexpectedly to the story line. I keep 'idea notebooks,' some of which go back to the 1960s."

*   *   *

CONWAY, Harry 1927-

PERSONAL: Born February 3, 1927, in Leipzig, Germany; immigrated to the United States; became a naturalized citizen; son of Hermann (in business) and Eugenie (Chwat) Calmanowitz; married Brigitte Wojciechowski, November 26, 1972; children: Carol Jane. *Ethnicity:* "German." *Education:* Received B.A. from Mackenzie College; received B.S. and M.E. at Mackenzie University; attended Harvard University; attended Yale University. *Religion:* Jewish.

ADDRESSES: Home—R.D. #2, Box 120, Middlebury, VT 05753.

CAREER: Co-inventor of wireless simultaneous interpretation technology; Round Hill IVC, Inc., Greenwich, CT, chief executive officer, 1954-87. Has served on the Council for Economic Development, Council on Latin America, and Council on International Relations in New York; and with the International Chamber of Commerce in Washington, DC. Has lectured at Harvard University.

MEMBER: Past member of the U.S.-Japan Society, and the Japan-California Society.

AWARDS, HONORS: Honorary member of the World Seapower Symposium of the Naval War College, Newport, RI.

WRITINGS:

NONFICTION

The Germans: When Lies Were Decreed as Truth . . . And a Nation Allowed Itself to Be Deceived!, Shengold (New York), 1996.

Also contributor of articles to periodicals.

WORK IN PROGRESS: Research on political science and social criticism.

SIDELIGHTS: Inventor, historian, and author Harry Conway spent much of his childhood under the Nazi regime of German dictator Adolf Hitler, during years that saw increasing restriction on and threat to his Jewish family. Finally, after the event known as *Kristallnacht*—in which Germans attacked and looted Jewish homes, businesses, and synagogues—Conway's family fled the country. Conway sojourned in several countries, including Italy and Switzerland, and received the majority of his college education in Brazil. Conway eventually immigrated to the United States and became a citizen.

As a young man in America, Conway let his interest in languages lead him to become the co-inventor of wireless simultaneous interpretation technology. This technology is similar to that in use at the United Nations building in New York City, except that it is portable and wireless, allowing fast and relatively easy installation. Conway became the chief executive officer of a business which implemented such interpretation systems at all manner of international forums and business meetings in 1954, and continued in this endeavor until his retirement in 1987.

Conway writes of his and his family's experiences, both in Nazi Germany and while fleeing their native land, in his 1996 book, *The Germans: When Lies Were Decreed as Truth . . . And a Nation Allowed Itself to Be Deceived!* As his subtitle implies, the author blends with his family's story his own analysis of what Germany went through as a nation during its experience of National Socialism (Nazism). Conway states in his preface to *The Germans* that after Nazism became popular because it promised a better economy for most of the country's citizens, "lies became the decrees that regulated life in Germany down to the minutest detail. In that most carefully orchestrated euphoria, very few noticed what was being done to them. In a relatively short time, the fabric of German society with its renowned culture was changed into [one of] total obedience to the state under penalty of death, accompanied by the relentless persecution of the Jewish minority." Conway continued to explain that "[t]he Germans themselves, and millions elsewhere, suppressed their innermost instincts of right and wrong, looked the other way while horrible deeds were carried out against their fellow man, often before their very eyes. A mere handful of Germans saw early on what was happening, conspired to terminate the evil, failed—and paid with their lives."

Conway declares his own motivations and intentions for writing *The Germans* in the book's introduction. "I have known for decades that someday, I would write this book. . . . [C]learly I wanted to communicate with mainly a new generation of readers. About the facts. To invent nothing. To make understandable, warts and all, what happened at an incisive moment in history.

"That which I wrote about my family is symptomatic of many others who went through similar experiences, seldom written about. Because they were able to leave in time, their story was not considered as important as that of the millions that failed to do so. Quite properly so. And yet, what they lived through is worth telling about."

BIOGRAPHICAL/CRITICAL SOURCES:

BOOKS

Conway, Harry, *The Germans: When Lies Were Decreed as Truth . . . And a Nation Allowed Itself to Be Deceived!,* Shengold, 1996.

*   *   *

COOK, Wesley
 See ABU-JAMAL, Mumia

*   *   *

COOLEY, Nicole (Ruth) 1966-

PERSONAL: Born October 1, 1966, in Iowa City, IA; daughter of Peter (a professor and poet) and Jacqueline (a homemaker) Cooley; married Alexander Hinton (an anthropologist), January 9, 1994. *Ethnicity:* "White." *Education:* Brown University, B.A. (magna cum laude), 1988; University of Iowa, M.F.A., 1990; Emory University, Ph.D. and Certificate in Women's Studies, 1996. *Politics:* Democrat.

ADDRESSES: Home—1431 Emory Rd., Atlanta, GA 30306. *Agent*—Sally Wofford-Girand, Elaine Markson Literary Agency, Inc., 44 Greenwich Ave., New York, NY 10011. *E-mail*—ahinton@emory.edu.

CAREER: Emory University, Atlanta, GA, instructor in English, 1992-95; writer, 1995—. Gives readings from her works.

MEMBER: Modern Language Association of America, Associated Writing Programs.

AWARDS, HONORS: Elias Lieberman Award, Poetry Society of America, 1984, for best poem by a high school student; resident, Yaddo Corp., 1992, 1995; Annual Fiction Prize, *Ambergris,* 1993; resident, Ragdale Foundation, 1993; Discovery/*Nation* Poetry Award, 1994; grant from Georgia Arts Council, 1995; Walt Whitman Award, Academy of American Poets, 1995, for *Resurrection;* grant from National Endowment for the Arts, 1996.

WRITINGS:

Resurrection (poems), Louisiana State University Press (Baton Rouge, LA), 1996.

Work represented in anthologies, including *Voices of the X-iled: A Generation Speaks for Itself,* Doubleday (New York City), 1994; *Something in Common: Louisiana Poems Today,* Louisiana State University Press, 1996; and *The 1995/1996 Anthology of Magazine Verse and Yearbook of American Poetry,* Monitor Book (Palm Springs), 1996. Contributor of about forty stories, poems, articles, and reviews to periodicals, including *Negative Capability, Iowa Review, New England Review, Ploughshares, Nation, See: A Journal of Visual Culture,* and *Icarus.* Fiction editor, *Iowa Review,* 1989-90.

WORK IN PROGRESS: A novel, *Judy Garland, Ginger Love;* a poetry collection, *The Afflicted Girls.*

SIDELIGHTS: Nicole Cooley told *CA:* "My book *Resurrection* is a collection of poems. The poems explore the connection between women and mental illness. I write about the women in my family, in particular my great-grandmother Rose, who came to the United States from Hungary. Rose floats through the whole book, appearing in many poems as a guide, a storyteller, and a voice of warning for the speaker. The title *Resurrection* derives from the notion that, as the writer of these poems, I am 'resurrecting' the women in my family—dead or otherwise silenced.

"In some of the poems, I employ other voices, such as the voices of the women artists Frida Kahlo and Diane Arbus. As well, the book contains poems about Harry Houdini and his wife Bess, Alice Liddell (the 'real' Alice in Wonderland) and Charles Dodgson (who is the writer Lewis Carroll), Victor Hugo's daughter Adele, and Patty Hearst. These poems resurrect the voices of historical figures. The poems take place in New Orleans, the city where I grew up. The landscape of the south is represented here. Furthermore, the poems bring up a variety of other cities, such as Chicago, Detroit, New York, and the country of Cambodia.

"Sisters are foregrounded in the book. An epigraph for the book is from Jean Genet's famous play about two sisters *The Maids.* Many of the poems play on the construction of sisters in fairy tales: the bad sister versus the good sister. Themes of the book include hunger and refusal, danger versus safety, and the rules and rituals of Catholicism (which also relates to the title of the book and the idea of Christ's resurrection)."

*   *   *

COOMARASWAMY, Ananda K(entish) 1877-1947

PERSONAL: Born in 1877; died September 9, 1947, in Needham, MA; son of a Ceylonese lawyer; married four times; fourth wife, Dona Luisa; children: Rama. *Education:* University of London, D.Sc.

CAREER: Author. Head of Mineralogical Survey of Ceylon, c. 1908; Museum of Fine Arts, Boston, MA, fellow for research in Indian, Persian and Muhammadan Art, c. 1917-47.

WRITINGS:

Voluspa, Essex House Press, 1909.
The Indian Craftsman, Probsthain (London), 1909.

(With Y. Daud) *Essays in National Idealism,* Columbo Apothecaries Co. (Colombo, Sri Lanka), 1909.

Selected Examples of Indian Art, Essex House Press, 1910.

(With Daud) *Art and Swadeshi,* Old Bourne Press (London), 1912.

(With Daud) *Burning and Melting,* Old Bourne Press, 1912.

(With Sister Nivedita) *Myths of the Hindus and Buddhists,* Harrap (London), 1913.

Arts and Crafts of India and Ceylon, Foulis (Somerset, England), 1913.

Visvakarma, Luzac (London), 1914.

(With A. Sen) *Vidyapati,* Old Bourne Press, 1914.

Vidyapati Bangiya Padabali: Songs of the Love of Radha and Krishna, Old Bourne Press, 1915.

Rajput Painting, Oxford University Press (London), 1916, reprinted, Hacker Art Books (New York, NY), 1975.

Buddha and the Gospel of Buddhism, Harrap (London), 1916.

(With K.G. Duggirala) *The Mirror of Gesture,* Harvard University Press (Cambridge, MA), 1917.

Introduction to Indian Art, Theosophical House (Wheaton, IL), 1923.

The Dance of Shiva: Essays on Indian Art and Culture, Sunwise Turn (New York, NY), 1924.

History of Indian and Indonesian Art, Hiersemann (Germany), 1927, reprinted, Dover Publications (New York, NY), 1965.

Yaksas, Smithsonian Institute (Washington, D.C.), 1928, Pt. II, 1931, revised and enlarged edition, edited by Paul Schroeder, Indira Gandhi National Centre for the Arts (New Delhi), 1993.

Buddha and the Gospel of Buddhism, Harrap, 1928.

A New Approach to the Bedas, Luzac, 1933.

Transformation of Nature in Art, Harvard University, 1933.

The Rg. Veda as Land-Nama-Bok, Luzac, 1935.

Spiritual Authority and Temporal Power in the Indian Theory of Government, American Oriental Society (New Haven, CT), 1942.

Why Exhibit Works of Art, Dover Publications, 1943, reprinted with the title *Christian and Oriental Philosophy of Art,* Dover Publications, 1956.

Hinduism and Buddhism, published, 1943, reprinted, Greenwood Press (Westport, CT), 1971.

Figures of Speech, or, Figures of Thought: Collected Essays on the Traditional, or, Normal, View of Art, Luzac, 1946.

Am I My Brother's Keeper?, introduction by Robert Allerton Parker, Books for Libraries Press (Freeport, NY), first edition, 1947, reprinted as

The Bugbear of Literacy, Perennial Books (Middlesex, England), 1979.

The Dance of Shiva: Fourteen Indian Essays, revised edition, Sagar Publications (New Delhi), 1968.

The Vedas: Essays in Translation and Exegesis, Prologos Books (Beckenham, England), 1976.

A University Course on Indian Art, edited by S. Durai Raja Singam, Petaling Jaya (Malaysia), 1978.

The Sacred and the Secular in India's Performing Arts, edited by V. Subramaniam, Ashish (New Delhi), 1980.

Sources of Wisdom, Ministry of Cultural Affairs (Colombo, Sri Lanka), 1981.

(With I.B. Horner) *The Living Thoughts of Gotama the Buddha,* Munshiram Manoharlal (New Delhi), 1982.

Symbolism of the Indian Architecture, introduction by Pramod Chandra, Historical Research Documentation Programme (Jaipur, India), 1983.

Paroksa: Coomaraswamy Centenary Seminar Papers, Lalit Kala Akademi (New Delhi), 1984.

Fundamentals of Indian Art, introduction by S. Durai Raja Singam, Historical Research Documentation Programme, 1985—.

Selected Letters of Ananda K. Coomaraswamy, edited by Alvin Moore, Jr. and Rama Poonambulam Coomaraswamy, Indira Gandhi National Centre for the Arts, 1988.

Time and Eternity, Select Books (Bangalore, India), 1989.

What Is Civilization: and Other Essays, Oxford University Press (Delhi, India), 1989.

Essays in Early Indian Architecture, edited and with an introduction by Michael W. Meister, Indira Gandhi National Centre for the Arts, 1992.

TRANSLATOR

(With Gopala Kristnayya Duggirala) *The Mirror of Gesture, Being the Abhinaya Darpana of Nandikesvara,* Munshiram Manoharlal, 1917.

Also author of *Medieval Sinhalese Art,* 1908; *Catalog of the Indian Collection, Museum of Fine Arts, Boston,* Volumes 1-6, 1923-30; *Catalog of the Golubew Collection,* 1929; and *Elements of Buddhist Symbolism,* 1933. Contributor of introductory essay to *The Wall-Paintings of India, Central Asia and Ceylon,* 1938.

SIDELIGHTS: Ananda K. Coomaraswamy was a scientist by training but soon after he left college, he switched his interest to art history. Son of a Ceylonese lawyer and a British mother, he was a man caught between two worlds. He became engaged in the debate over whether Indian artists had produced any works of note; many of his British friends insisted that the only worthwhile art came from Europe. He spent much of the rest of his life detailing and chronicling the art works of the Eastern world.

Coomaraswamy moved to the United States in 1917; his political views were not popular at the time because he believed that Indian and Ceylonese men should not participate in World War I. He became employed at the Boston Museum of Fine Arts, where he continued to write prodigiously until his death in 1947. There was a resurgence in interest in his work many years after his death. Indian scholars became more interested in his work, and North American readers enjoyed reissued volumes of his work. His life has also been extensively chronicled by biographers and many of his works contained in new collections.

BIOGRAPHICAL/CRITICAL SOURCES:

BOOKS

Bagchee, Moni, *Ananda Coomaraswamy: A Study,* Bharata Manisha (Varanasi), 1977.

Chandra, Jagdish, compiler, *Bibliography of Indian Art, History and Archaeology,* Delhi Printers Prakashan (Delhi), 1978.

Fernando, Ranjit, editor, *The Unanimous Tradition: Essays on the Essential Unity of All Religions,* Institute of Traditional Studies (Colombo, Sri Lanka), 1991.

Kamaliah, K.C., *Ananda Coomaraswamy, Wise Man from the East,* Kamaliah (Madras, India), 1977.

Kumar, Kalyan, editor, *Ananda Coomaraswamy: A Centenary Volume,* Centre of Advanced Study in Ancient Indian History & Culture (Calcutta, India), 1981.

Lipsey, Roger, *Daedalus: Lectures Commemorating the Birth Centenary of A.K. Coomaraswamy,* Institute of Indian Art History (Dharwad, India), 1980.

Lipsey, Roger, editor, *Coomaraswamy,* Princeton University Press (Princeton, NJ), 1977.

Mohan, Jag, *Ananda K. Coomaraswamy,* Govt. of India (Delhi), 1979.

Mukandilala, *Kalaguru Ananda Coomaraswamy,* Prakasana Vibhaga (Delhi), 1978.

Narasimhaiah, C.D., editor, *Ananda Coomaraswamy Centenary Essays,* University of Mysore (Mysore, India), 1982.

Naravane, Vishwanath S., *Ananda K. Coomaraswamy,* Twayne Publishers (Boston), 1978.

Rao, Ramachancra, C.V., *A.K. Coomaraswamy, an Inspirer of Indian Renaissance and Other Cultural Causerie,* Manasa Publications (Nellore), 1980.

Sastri, P.S., *Ananda K. Coomaraswamy,* Arnold-Heinemann Publishers (New Delhi), 1974.

Singam, Raja S.D., *Who Is This Coomaraswamy?,* Petaling Jaya, 1980.

Singam, S. Durai Raja, compiler, *Ananda Coomaraswamy: Remembering and Remembering Again and Again,* Petaling Jaya, 1974.

Sivaramamurti, C., "Ananda Kentish Coomaraswamy: His Immortal Thought and Vision" in his *The Painter in Ancient India,* Abhinav Publications (New Delhi), 1978.

PERIODICALS

National Review, August 1, 1986, p. 44.
New York Times Book Review, March 12, 1978, pp. 31-32.*

*   *   *

CORRAN, Mary 1953-

PERSONAL: Born Mary Waterhouse, August 18, 1953, in Birmingham, England; married Thomas H. Corran in 1977. *Education:* Attended Roedean School, Brighton, Sussex; Lady Margaret Hall, Oxford University, M.A. (in modern history), 1980.

ADDRESSES: Home and office—13 Sutton Place, Hackney, London E9 6EH, England. *Agent*—Michael Thomas, A. M. Heath, 79 St. Martin's Lane, London WC2N 4AA, England.

CAREER: Trainee system analyst, Reading, Berkshire, 1980-82; oil analyst, various stockbroking companies, banks and financial institutions, City of London, 1982-92; writer.

WRITINGS:

FANTASY NOVELS

Imperial Light, Millennium (London), 1994.
Fate, Millennium, 1995.
Darkfell, Millennium, 1996.

CROCE, Paul Jerome 1957-

PERSONAL: Born June 24, 1957, in Washington, DC; son of Andrew P. (a government worker) and Agnes (a school guidance counselor; maiden name, Wilson) Croce; married Ann Jerome (a college professor), December 28, 1985; children: Peter Sloane, Elizabeth Wilson. *Ethnicity:* "European (Irish and Italian)." *Education:* Georgetown University, B.A. (cum laude), 1979; Brown University, M.A., 1981, Ph.D., 1987. *Politics:* Democrat. *Religion:* "Catholic and Quaker."

ADDRESSES: Home—320 West Minnesota Ave., DeLand, FL 32720. *Office*—Dept. of American Studies, Stetson University, DeLand, FL 32720; fax: 904-822-7268. *E-mail*—pcroce@stetson.edu.

CAREER: Brown University, Providence, RI, tutor and teaching assistant, 1976-85; Georgetown University, Washington, DC, summer instructor, 1983-84, visiting assistant professor, 1985-87; Stetson University, DeLand, FL, instructor in social science, 1988, assistant professor, 1989-95, associate professor of American studies, 1995—. Visiting professor at Rollins College, 1987-89. Has served as an editorial consultant for Harcourt Brace Jovanovich, 1988-89; organized conference sessions for Florida Teachers of History, California American Studies Association, Cheiron, History of Science Society, Organization of American Historians, American Academy of Religion, and the American Studies Association, 1988-1996; served as a panelist for the National Endowment of Humanities Summer Stipends in American History, 1991; served on the dissertation prize committee of the Forum for the History of Human Science. Has presented papers at many conferences and lectured in several academic arenas; appeared on radio talk shows.

MEMBER: Cheiron (International Society for the History of the Behavioral and Social Sciences), American Academy of Religion, American Association of University Professors (local chapter representative), American Historical Association, Organization of American Historians, American Studies Association, Society for the Advancement of American Philosophy, History of Science Society, Charles Sanders Peirce Society, Society for Values in Higher Education, Southeastern Nineteenth Century Studies Association.

AWARDS, HONORS: Pi Sigma Alpha, 1979; Brown University teaching fellowship, 1981-83, and research grants, 1984 and 1985; Society for Values in Higher Education fellowship, 1983; National Endowment for the Humanities summer stipend, 1989, and fellowship, 1996; Phi Alpha Theta, 1990; Stetson University summer grants, 1990, 1991, 1992, 1994, and 1996.

WRITINGS:

Science and Religion in the Era of William James, Volume 1: Eclipse of Certainty, 1820-1880, University of North Carolina Press (Chapel Hill, NC), 1995.

Contributor to books, including *The Oxford Companion to United States History, The W.E.B. DuBois Encyclopedia, American National Biography, Swedenborg and His Influence, Religion and the Life of the Nation: American Resources,* and *The History of Science in the United States: An Encyclopedia.*

Contributor of articles and reviews to periodicals, including *American History Review, Journal of the History of the Behavioral Sciences, Journal of American Studies of Turkey, History of the Human Sciences, Transaction: Social Science and Society, Intellectual History Newsletter, Journal of Popular Culture, New York History, Chrysalis: Journal of the Swedenborg Foundation, Journal of American History, American Studies, Contemporary Psychology, Journal of the American Academy of Religion, American Literary Realism, Newsletter for the History and Sociology of Marginality in Science, International Journal for the Philosophy of Religion, Religious Studies Review, DeLand Beacon, Daytona Beach News-Journal, Atlanta Journal-Constitution, Public Perspectives,* and the *Orlando Sentinel.*

WORK IN PROGRESS: Research toward second volume of study of William James' early intellectual development, *Conciliating Truth and Change, 1860-1884.*

SIDELIGHTS: Author and scholar of American popular culture Paul Jerome Croce has many areas of interest within his field, and has written on subjects ranging from the breakdown of mass culture to the influence of animated film pioneer Walt Disney on popular culture. Croce has contributed to the books of others, including a volume on Swedish mystic Emanuel Swedenborg. His own first book, *Science and Religion in the Era of William James, Volume 1: Eclipse of Certainty, 1820-1880* traces the thought of

American philosopher William James from his early cultural and familial background. Croce's main assertion is that James was born into an era during which certainty in both religion and science was shaken by British scientist Charles Darwin's theory of evolution. He examines the role James' father, Henry James, Sr., a noted Swedenborgian, had upon his developing thought on religious matters, and also discusses the role of James' intellectual circle, which included the scientist Louis Agassiz and philosophers Chauncey Wright and Charles Saunders Peirce.

Science and Religion in the Era of William James "brings together a wealth of material and produces a masterful profile of James's intellectual milieu," judged Stephen G. Alter in *ISIS.* "The strength of Croce's work is in his ability to capture the innermost thoughts of a vanished era," commented Nicholas J. Cull in *American Studies.* L. B. McHenry, writing in *Choice,* hailed *Science and Religion in the Era of William James* as "a splendid account of the impact of the second scientific revolution." *Journal of American History* contributor Olaf Hansen concluded that Croce "has written a fascinating account of the conflicts and turmoil of the American nineteenth century, alerting the reader to seminal scenes of contradictions in the shaping of the overall image of this decisive phase in the making of American cultural history."

Croce told *CA:* "Writing is not my living. I love teaching, and I find that having my own writing projects helps me when evaluating my students' writing. The diverse range of teaching across different times and topics helps keep the knowledge base broad, and that is an important context for writing even specialized books.

"As a student, I first became attracted to William James when I read his essay, 'The Will to Believe,' which was first delivered as a lecture to students in 1895. I found it a persuasive explanation of a way to justify religious belief in the face of secular challenges. As a historian I felt compelled to understand how an intellectual develops a theory that offers answers to nagging cultural questions. Where did the William James of 'The Will to Believe' come from? This led me into an inquiry into his early intellectual development. I noticed that there was considerable work on the theoretical work of the mature James, and much scholarly discussion of psychological factors influencing the young James, but there was little evaluation of the intellectual factors that shaped his early career.

"When I began to research the intellectual circles around William James, I noticed that he was at the center of a broad shift in cultural attitudes toward science and religion. Early in the nineteenth century, professionals in these fields generally presented their statements about the natural and spiritual worlds with an air of certainty; but by the end of the century, leaders in both fields could not muster the same confidence, even if their followers often found their declarations of ambiguity and uncertainty highly distasteful.

"My investigations into the contexts around James' education surely intersected with the cultural history of professionalism, but with a twist: I found that beneath the brash social confidence of professional experts lay a core of theoretic uncertainty. Moreover, the gradual rise of secularism in the history of religions and the emergence of probabilistic thinking in the sciences were major factors in the development of a culture of uncertainty among intellectuals.

"I found that James was particularly well-suited to explaining this cultural shift. His early years coincided with some major religious and scientific developments leading toward theoretic uncertainty, including his learning from his unorthodox father and from secular teachers and friends. While he studied science at Harvard's Lawrence Scientific School and Medical School, he witnessed major American debates about the truth of Darwinism. The theory of natural selection not only encouraged secularism but also challenged scientific determinism because of its implicitly probabilistic explanation about the gradual emergence of new species. What's more, as he grew up, he stayed keenly interested in these issues and wrote essays, such as 'The Will to Believe,' in which he presented ways to cope with uncertainty. With an outlook that is at once spiritual and pragmatic, James offers a mediating vision which is a template for recognizing the virtues of conviction without being tied to the authority of certainty.

"At the deepest level, I wrote this book to find answers to two gnawing questions: first, how can one be religious in the modern world? and, is there a way around our cultural polarization between the acolytes of certainty and the advocates of pluralistic uncertainty? I think James' pragmatic spirituality offers answers to these questions and lessons for our times. As a scholar, however, I have focused in Volume One of my *Science and Religion in the Era of William James,* on three circles of influence on his emerging intellect: his family, his teachers, and his peers. In my projected second volume, *Conciliating Truth and Change, 1860-1884,* I will trace James' response to these influences as he began his career and shaped his influential theories.

"In other writings, including the essays 'The Erosion of Mass Culture' and 'Before We Can All Get Along: The Case for Intellectual Non-Violence,' I explore the implications of these outlooks for contemporary culture. These more popular writings, which explore deep issues in terms of their broadest implications, are a helpful and even vital part of a scholar's work. I also find that writing essays helps my teaching, because ideas that emerge in discussions with students are the seeds for many newspaper and magazine articles. And so, indeed, writing is a secondary but essential adjunct to my daily task in the classroom. I try to infuse my teaching of American culture with the same purpose I bring to writing books and articles. I hope to inspire my audiences with a vision that can spur both tolerance and conviction."

BIOGRAPHICAL/CRITICAL SOURCES:

PERIODICALS

American Studies, Volume 30, 1996.
Choice, October, 1995.
ISIS, Volume 87, number 2, 1996.
Journal of American History, September, 1996.

*   *   *

CROSSLEY, Pamela Kyle 1955-

PERSONAL: Born November 18, 1955, in Allen County, OH; daughter of Kenneth Charles August and Marilyn (a civil servant; maiden name, Detrick; present surname, Kaufman) Crossley. *Education:* Swarthmore College, B.A. (with high honors), 1977; Yale University, M.A., 1978, M.A., 1979, M.Phil., 1981, Ph.D., 1983.

ADDRESSES: Office—Department of History, Dartmouth College, Hanover, NH 03755; fax 603-535-3353.

CAREER: Dartmouth College, Hanover, NH, assistant professor, 1985-90, associate professor, 1990-93, professor of history, 1993—.

MEMBER: American Historical Association, Association for Asian Studies.

AWARDS, HONORS: Mellon fellow, American Council of Learned Societies, 1984-85; fellow, National Academy of Sciences, 1987; fellow of Wang Institute, 1987-88, and Marion and Jasper Whiting Foundation, 1989; Woodrow Wilson fellow, 1991-92; Guggenheim fellow, 1994-95.

WRITINGS:

Orphan Warriors: Three Manchu Generations and the End of the Qing World, Princeton University Press (Princeton, NJ), 1990.
The Manchus, Basil Blackwell, 1996.
(With Richard Bullier, Daniel Headrick, Steven Hirsch, and others) *The Earth and Its Peoples: A Global History,* Houghton (Boston, MA), 1996.
A Translucent Mirror: History and Identity in Qing Imperial Ideology, University of California Press (Los Angeles, CA), 1997.

Contributor to books, including *Education and Society in Late Imperial China,* edited by Alexander Woodside and Benjamin A. Elman, University of California Press, 1994; and *The Routledge Companion to Historiography,* edited by Michael Bentley, Routledge, 1996. Contributor of articles and reviews to journals and newspapers, including *Harvard Journal of Asiatic Studies, American Historical Review, Late Imperial China,* and *New Republic.*

WORK IN PROGRESS: A Cultural History of Eurasia Before 1500, a comparative history of ideologies of rule in the Ottoman, Romanov, and Qing empires; research on the relationship of the identification of precious objects and concepts of rulership in China.

SIDELIGHTS: Pamela Kyle Crossley told *CA:* "I am most influenced by historians who have tried to explain complexities in plain language. The reverse is more fashionable now, and unfortunately aggravates my own weakness for trying to crowd simultaneities of meaning into a single spot on a page. So, I am an unwilling member of the atonal school of historical writing, at times. This is deplorable. As time goes by, we all learn more and more, but have less and less space and time in which to say it. Time is not on the side of coherent thinking and writing about the past.

"As a historian, I am conscious of the fact that few people seem aware of the degree to which the transition from the great imperial structures of early modern times to the republican and self-described 'nationalist' is still incomplete. To the extent that we do not understand the full influence of imperial (which is not to say imperialist) ideas, we are still controlled by them. The will to construct a demonstrably false, but somehow important, threshold dividing the new age of 'identity,' 'position,' 'post-colonialism' from 'past' modes of thought has somehow led many people to imagine that the contemporary world has a strong and distinct historical dynamic for which little or no convincing evidence can be adduced. Some changes in weather have been mistaken, perhaps, for evolution of climate."

*   *   *

CROW DOG, Mary (Ellen)   195(?)- (Mary Brave Bird)

PERSONAL: Born in the 1950s; family name, Brave Bird; married Leonard Crow Dog (a medicine man), in the 1970s.

ADDRESSES: Office—c/o HarperPerennial, 10 East 53rd St., New York, NY 10022.

CAREER: Author.

WRITINGS:

(Under name Mary Brave Bird, with Richard Erdoes) *Ohitika Woman* (autobiography), Grove Press, 1990, reprinted under name Mary Crow Dog as *Lakota Woman,* HarperPerennial, 1991.

SIDELIGHTS: Mary Crow Dog is the author of an autobiography that chronicles a personal journey from her troubled early years to her work as an advocate for Native American rights. The 1990 volume *Ohitika Woman* was cowritten with fellow activist and writer Richard Erdoes. Originally authored with her family name of Brave Bird, Crow Dog reissued the book in 1991 under the title *Lakota Woman,* assuming the surname that she currently uses. The volume was well-received by critics who praised Crow Dog's forthright style. As her story relates, Crow Dog was born in the 1950s to Sioux parentage but was told little about her ancestral background. Her mother refused to speak their native tongue with her young daughter because she felt that learning anything about Sioux culture would only hinder the girl's assimilation into mainstream American society. Crow Dog was later sent to a Catholic boarding school and suffered physical abuse at the hands of the teachers. As a teenager she led a transient life, living in a number of places both on and off the reservation, and grappling with alcohol abuse. She took part in a 1972 cross-country march in Washington, DC, with a group of Native American activists that came from her generation; there they occupied the federal building housing the Bureau of Indian Affairs offices.

As *Lakota Woman* recounts, the turning point in Crow Dog's life came in South Dakota, the year following her participation in the occupation of Wounded Knee by American Indian Movement (AIM) activists. The 71-day siege of a museum, church, and trading post marked the beginning of a new era for this younger and radical group of Native American activists who had marshaled forces around AIM in 1968. In 1890 Wounded Knee had been the site of the last major conflict between Native Americans and United States government troops, and the casualty list of that battle was typical of previous debacles— twenty-nine soldiers killed, and two hundred Native Americans—including women and children—slain. Seventeen years old and pregnant during the occupation, Crow Dog went into labor during the action, but more significantly discovered a previously-unknown part of her heritage. She became acquainted with Leonard Crow Dog, a medicine man whom she later married, and began learning from him and others the intricate rituals of Native American spirituality. The remainder of *Lakota Woman* is engaged in retelling the story of her subsequent years as an activist, mother, and spouse. Crow Dog discusses the political events in which she and her husband have participated, and their day-to-day life together that is often complicated by his extreme idealism. Throughout the work she injects her own frank opinions regarding the long legacy of mistreatment of the Sioux and other Native Americans by the U.S. government. Comparing the AIM objectives with those of the civil-rights struggles by African Americans, Crow Dog remarked "They want in. We Indians want out!" She also reflects on the misogyny present in contemporary relations between Native American men and women.

Lakota Woman was favorably reviewed by critics. *Voice Literary Supplement* reviewer Elizabeth Devereaux described it as "a tale of impoverishment and enrichment." Writing for the *Washington Post Book World,* critic Gretchen M. Bataille lauded the autobiography for presenting the author's "growing awareness of who she is as a Sioux woman and as a

political force for change for her people." Penny Skillman of *Belles Lettres* observed that "Crow Dog tells such an entertaining story . . . that it is easy at times to overlook the fact that the tale is about the Native American struggle to stave off genocide."

BIOGRAPHICAL/CRITICAL SOURCES:

BOOKS

Crow Dog, Mary, and Richard Erdoes, *Lakota Woman,* HarperPerennial, 1991.

PERIODICALS

Atlantic Monthly, May, 1990, p. 133.
Belles Lettres, summer, 1991, p. 5.
New York Times Book Review, July 1, 1990, p. 15.
Voice Literary Supplement, November, 1991, p. 27.
Washington Post Book World, June 19, 1990.*

*   *   *

CSABA, Laszlo 1954-

PERSONAL: Born March 27, 1954, in Budapest, Hungary; son of Ede (an economist) and Marta (Biro) Csaba; married Gabriella Onody, March 22, 1980; children: Zoltan, Orsolya. *Ethnicity:* "Hungarian." *Education:* Budapest University of Economics, B.A., 1976, M.A., 1978; Hungarian Academy of Sciences, Ph.D., 1984, postdoctoral study, 1996. *Religion:* Roman Catholic. *Avocational interests:* Opera, travel, classical music, soccer.

ADDRESSES: Home—Dohany u. 94, 1074 Budapest, Hungary. *Office*—Kopint-Datorg Economic Research, Csokonai u. 3, 1081 Budapest, Hungary.

CAREER: Institute for World Economy, Budapest, Hungary, began as junior fellow, became senior fellow, 1976-87; Kopint-Datorg Economic Research, Budapest, senior economist, 1988—. College of Foreign Trade, professor of international economics; Hungarian Academy of Sciences, member of Committee on Economics, 1985—; Bocconi University, Milan, Italy, visiting professor, 1991; University of Helsinki, visiting professor, 1993. Advisor to the Hungarian minister of finance, 1991-93, 1994-95.

MEMBER: European Association for Comparative Economics (vice-president, 1990-94, 1996-98).

AWARDS, HONORS: Awards from Hungarian Academy of Sciences, 1984, for *Eastern Europe in the World Economy,* and from Ministry of Foreign Relations, 1994, for *The Capitalist Revolution in Eastern Europe.*

WRITINGS:

Eastern Europe in the World Economy, Cambridge University Press (New York), 1990.
Systemic Change and Stabilization in Eastern Europe, Dartmouth Publishing (England), 1993.
Privatization, Liberalization, and Destruction, Dartmouth Publishing, 1994.
The Capitalist Revolution in Eastern Europe, Edward Elgar (Brookfield, VT), 1995.

Contributor to books, including *East European Economic Thought,* edited by H. J. Wagener, Routledge, 1997.

WORK IN PROGRESS: Research on the second wave of systemic changes in Eastern Europe, on the enlargement of the European Union, and on economic theory and policy interactions.

*   *   *

CSOORI, Sandor   1930-

PERSONAL: Name pronounced "shan-door cho-ri,"; born February 3, 1930, in Zamoly, Transbanubia, Hungary. *Education:* Attended the Calvinist grammar school, Papa, c. 1943; attended Lenin Institute (Budapest), 1951.

ADDRESSES: Agent—c/o Magveto Konyvkiado, Vorosmarty ter 1, 1806 Budapest V, Hungary.

CAREER: Staff member of *Papai Neplap* (Papa Popular News), from 1949; *Veszprem Megyei Nepujsag* (Veszprem County Popular Newspaper), from 1949; *Szabad Ifjusag* (Free Youth), from 1952; and *Irodalmi Ujsag* (Literary News), 1953-54. *Uj Hang* [New Voice], head of poetry section, 1955-56; Hungarian Film Studio, dramaturge, from 1971. Joined opposition movement, 1980; Hungarian Democratic Forum, founding member, 1987.

MEMBER: Illyes Gyula Foundation (chair), World Federation of Hungarians (president).

AWARDS, HONORS: Attila Jozsef Prize, 1954, for *Felroppen a madar;* Cannes Film Festival Prize, 1964 and 1968; Herder Prize, Vienna University, Austria, 1981; Kossuth Prize, Office of the Prime Minister (Hungary), 1990.

WRITINGS:

POETRY

Felroppen a madar (title means "The Bird Takes Wing"), Szepirodalmi (Budapest), 1954.
Ordogpille (title means "Devil's Moth"), Magveto (Budapest), 1957.
Menekules a maganybol (title means "Flight from Solitude"), Magveto (Budapest), 1962.
(With Frigyes Hidas) *Szigoru korban elunk* (title means "We Live in Harsh Times"), NPI (Budapest), 1967.
Masodik szuletesem (title means "My Second Birth"), Magveto, 1967.
Lekvarcirkusz bohocai (title means "Clowns of a Jam Circus"), Mora (Budapest), 1969.
Parbeszed, sotetben (title means "Dialogue, in the Dark"), Magveto, 1973.
A latogato emlekei (title means "The Memories of a Visitor"), Magveto, 1977.
Joslas a te idodrol (title means "Predictions About Your Time"), Magveto, 1979.
A tizedik este (title means "The Tenth Evening"), Magveto, 1980.
Wings of Knives and Nails, edited and translated by I. L. Halasz de Beky, Vox Humana (Toronto), 1981.
Elmaradt lazalom (title means "Nightmare Postponed"), Magveto, 1982.
Varakozas a tavaszban (title means "Waiting in the Spring"), Magveto, 1983.
Memory of Snow, translated by Nicholas Kolumban, Penmaen Press (Great Barrington, MA), 1983.
Kezemben zold ag (title means "In My Hand a Green Branch"), Magveto, 1985.
Labon jaro verofeny (title means "Bright Sunshine on Foot"), Mora, 1987.
Csoori Sandor breviarium (includes prose; title means "Breviary"), Eotvos (Budapest), 1988.
A vilag emlekmuvei (title means "Monuments of the World"), Magveto, 1989.
Barbarian Prayer: Selected Poems, Corvina (Budapest), 1989.
Selected Poems of Sandor Csoori, translated by Len Roberts, Copper Canyon Press (Port Townsend, WA), 1992.

SCREENPLAYS

(With Ferenc Kosa) *Itelet* (title means "Sentence"), Mafilm (Budapest), 1967.

(With Kosa) *Nincs ido* (title means "There Is No Time"), Hunnia Filmstudio (Budapest), 1972.

(With Kosa) *Forradas* (with *Itelet* and *Nincs Ido;* title means "Scars"), Magveto (Budapest), 1972.

(With Sandor Sara) *80 huszar* (title means "Eighty Hussars"), Magveto, 1980.

(With Sara) *Tuske a korom alatt* (title means "Thorn Under the Fingernail"), Budapest Studio (Budapest), 1987.

FICTION

Faltol falig (title means "From Wall to Wall"), Magveto (Budapest), 1969.

Utazas, felalomban (title means "Journey While Half-Asleep"), Magveto, 1974.

Iszapeso (title means "Mud-Rain"), Magveto, 1981.

OTHER

Tudositas a toronybol (title means "Report from the Tower"), Magveto (Budapest), 1963.

Kubai naplo (title means "Cuban Diary"), Magveto, 1965.

A kolto es a majompofa (title means "The Poet and the Monkey Face"), Magveto, 1966.

Biztato (title means "Reassurance"), Kalaka (Lyndhurst, NJ), 1973.

Nomad naplo (title means "The Wanderer's Diary"), Magveto, 1979.

(Editor) *Szarny es piramis* (title means "Wing and Pyramid"), by Laszlo Nagy, Helikon (Budapest), 1980.

Tenger es diolevel (title means "The Sea and the Walnut Leaf"), Puski (New York), 1982.

(Editor) *Mert szemben ulsz velem* (title means "Because You Sit Opposite Me"), by Gyula Illyes, Helikon, 1982.

Keszulodes a szamadasra (title means "Preparation for the Day of Reckoning"), Magveto (Budapest), 1987.

Nappali hold (title means "Moon at Daylight"), Puski (New York), 1991.

Editor of *Hitel.*

SIDELIGHTS: Sandor Csoori ranks among the leading poets in twentieth-century Hungary. Recognized for his numerous collections of poems that frequently deal with the individual's struggle against a dehuman-

izing, technological society, he is also the author of many thought-provoking sociographic essays, as well as several screenplays, and is the editor of a premier cultural journal. "One of the eminent poets in Hungary, Sandor Csoori is an exceptionally strong talent," wrote Ervin C. Brody in his politico-literary assessment for the *Literary Review.* "His poems, dramas, and essays exhibit a never-ending concern over a threatened culture and national identity."

The son of Protestant peasants, Csoori was born and raised in western Hungary. His education would have ended with grade six had he not won free admission to a Calvinist high school in Papa, where he excelled in literary studies. Even before his graduation, he had already accepted a position with the *Papai Neplap,* a local newspaper, which published his first poem. After writing a column for another newspaper, Csoori moved to Budapest. There he studied at the Lenin Institute, but he soon came to hate the strict dogma taught at the school. He returned to his family farm and was distressed by the hardships caused by the socialist changes in agriculture.

The literary life of Budapest drew Csoori back to the city. During the early 1950s Csoori worked on the staffs of several newspapers, earning a Literary Foundation fellowship. In 1954 he issued *Felroppen a madar,* a collection of folk poetry composed over a five-year period. These laudatory poems about patriotism and community under the socialist Rakosi government won the renowned Attila Josef Prize and earned him a seat on the editorial board of *Szabad Ifjusag,* a literary magazine. Csoori's next collection, *Ordogpille,* which took a more intimate and imaginative turn, marked a change in the poet's vision.

To discuss subjects unmanageable in verse, Csoori wrote several screenplays and dozens of essays. *Tudositas a toronybol* focuses on the trials of the peasantry caused by cooperative farming. *A kolto es a majompofa* and *Faltol falig* present aspects of folk culture, while *Utazas, felalomban* and *Nomad naplo* treat human nature. Csoori took a hard look at Hungarian literature in *Keszulodes a szamadasra,* harshly criticizing the Hungarian intellectuals who caved in under socialist pressure instead of rebelling against the government and its failures. In *World Literature Today,* George Gomori remarked, "What makes some of [Csoori's] essays . . . memorable is not only his terse, expressive, and occasionally coded language, but also his unceasing effort to regain the ground lost by Hungarian literature during the last thirty years and to instill a new moral responsibility in his contemporaries." In the subsequent collection *Nappali hold,* Csoori illustrated the changes in Hungarian society since 1989. "Csoori's poetry is harmoniously complemented by his prose works, essays, sociography, and longer studies," remarked Brody. "His clear, sensitive, and poetic language made him one of the best Hungarian stylists."

Following the publication of *Ordogpille,* Csoori's verse demonstrated a new concern with individuality and employed greater breath of imagery. *Menekules a maganybol, Masodik szuletesem, Parbeszed, sotetben,* and *A latogato emlekei* show the more introspective side of the poet. In these lyrical works, Csoori treated such themes of love, fidelity, hope, defeat, and loneliness in a personal yet universal manner. In the 1982 collection, *Elmaradt lazalom,* he probed his feelings of grief over the tragic, lingering death of his lover.

Despite the popularity of Csoori's verse in Hungary, it was little known outside his homeland until the publication in 1989 of *Barbarian Prayer,* an English-language anthology that includes works from Csoori's entire career. Much of Csoori's oeuvre deals with "a search for answers to continuing turmoils of culture versus anarchy masquerading as authoritarian order," according to Eric Mottram in *New Hungarian Quarterly.* Other critics have commented on the poet's accessible style. "Csoori's style can be described as a mixture of the traditional and the modern," commented Gomori in another review for *World Literature Today.* "His imagery is sensuous and natural, but his technique is 'dislocated' and visionary. Behind his floating lines stands an elegiac attempt to capture the unfathomable richness of the world and the sadness of universal transience." Calling Csoori a "remarkably fine poet" and a "major European poet," Mottram asserted, "His techniques of imagery have an imaginative excitement that demonstrates a particular creativity at work against cultural destruction." He added, "Csoori transforms as he transmits so that you feel the force of language emerging from the emotional, political site, whether you have experienced the historical actuality of it, or not. . . . Above all, he invents a language for distress and lack, deprivation fought by human resistance."

Csoori has long believed in the role of poet as prophet. In the 1990s, as the editor of the cultural journal *Hitel,* he openly promoted the efforts of the Hungarian Democratic Forum, the populist-based majority party. Yet by 1993 his disappointment with politics was evident in his verse that appeared in *Hitel,* and he retired quietly from the political scene. Brody summed up Csoori's work with these words: "His work—especially his poetry—with its fierce emotional intensity, but also with an often disturbing complexity, spoke about the primary issues of the day and corresponded to the mood of a large part of the population. He knew that art speaks more powerfully than official propaganda in conveying the truth about the era. For him literature was the battle of independence of the man who aims at completeness."

BIOGRAPHICAL/CRITICAL SOURCES:

PERIODICALS

Literary Review, spring, 1995.
New Hungarian Quarterly, summer, 1990, pp. 112-16.
World Literature Today, summer, 1982, pp. 547-48; winter, 1982, p. 151; summer, 1988, p. 486; summer, 1990, p. 500; winter, 1993, p. 215.*

*   *   *

CURTIUS, Ernst Robert   1886-1956

PERSONAL: Born April 14, 1886, in Thann, Alsace, Germany (now France); died April 19, 1956, in Rome, Italy. *Ethnicity:* German. *Education:* Attended Protestant schools in Strasbourg, including the University of Strasbourg; studied in Berlin and Heidelberg.

CAREER: University of Bonn, Bonn, Germany, lecturer, beginning 1914, professor, 1929-51; University of Marburg, Marburg, Germany, professor, 1920-24; University of Heidelberg, Heidelberg, Germany, professor, 1924-28.

WRITINGS:

Die franzosiche Kulture, 1930, translation by Olive Wyon published as *The Civilization of France,* 1930, reprint, Books for Libraries Press, Freeport (New York), 1971.
Europaische Literatur und lateinisches Mittelalter, 1948, translation by Willard R. Trask published as *European Literature and the Latin Middle Ages,* Princeton University Press (Princeton, NJ), 1953, reprint, 1967.
Kritische Essays zur europaischen Literatur, 1954, translation of the second edition by Michael

Kowal published as *Essays on European Literature,* Princeton University Press, 1973.

Also author of *Die literarischen Wegbereiter des neuen Frankreich* (title means "The Literary Pioneers of the New France"), 1919; *Franzosischer Geist im neuen Europa* (title means "The French Mind in the New Europe"), 1925; *Deutscher Geist in Gefahr* (title means "The German Mind in Peril"), 1932; and *Marcel Proust,* 1952.

SIDELIGHTS: German scholar Ernst Robert Curtius is considered one of the leading literary historians of European literature in the twentieth century. He is well known for his ability to explain the works of modern writers, many of whom he knew personally, and for his theories of literary evolution. Curtius's numerous critical works are reprinted regularly and continue to bring him renown. "His intellect, combined with a clear sense of the legitimate argument, enabled him to achieve a critical authority of unusual dimensions," asserted J. E. Chamberlin in the *Hudson Review.*

Born in Alsace, a region that has been a part both of Germany and of France over the course of modern history, Curtius was throughout his career interested in bringing the literature of France to the appreciation of the German readership. Curtius's ability to read many languages enabled him to study works in their original language. He looked upon European literature as a family of related works, which he elucidated in a large body of critical work.

After focusing upon French literature in the early decades of the twentieth century, Curtius turned to the literature of his own Germany. In 1932 he published *Deutscher Geist in Gefahr* ("The German Mind in Peril"), a work in which he criticized German society and the paths it was treading socially and politically. With the rise of the Nazis, Curtius found it prudent to remove himself from protest against then current German culture and affairs. During World War II he buried himself in research on Latin literature of the Middle Ages. *European Literature and the Latin Middle Ages,* published in translation in 1953, was the result. This lengthy work of literary criticism and scholarship is considered to be Curtius's masterpiece. In it he discusses the relationship of modern European literature to its antecedents in classical Roman literature. Curtius put forth the theory of *topoi*—organizing patterns or ideas from classical antiquity—which he believed could be found in European literature of many eras. According to Curtius, these patterns link the literature of European countries in an intricate web of relationships.

Curtius assembled critical studies written over a thirty year period for *Essays on European Literature.* Here, he discussed the works of many authors, including such modern writers as Hugo von Hofmannsthal, Jose Ortega y Gasset, James Joyce, and T.S. Eliot, as well as classical writers, such as Virgil. Curtius attempted to "synthesize the ancient and the modern into a dynamic and vital culture that serves the living," related Gary T. Davenport in the *Sewanee Review.* "This impulse, surely one of the major coordinates in the determination of the modern mind, has rarely been studied so thoroughly and sympathetically as by Curtius." In Davenport's view, these essays "constitute an unbroken, sympathetic, and intelligent involvement with the problems of modern civilization." Likewise, Chamberlin praised Curtius for his critical method and the "intelligence and wit which give the essays a compelling charm." Declared Davenport, "His scholarship, erudition, energetic style, and passionate humanity make him a joy to read."

BIOGRAPHICAL/CRITICAL SOURCES:

BOOKS

On Four Modern Humanists: Hofmannsthal, Gundolf, Curtius, Kantorowicz, edited by Arthur R. Evans, Jr., Princeton University Press (Princeton, NJ), 1970.

Richards, Earl Jeffrey, *Modernism, Medievalism, and Humanism: A Research Bibliography on the Reception of the Works of Ernst Robert Curtius,* Niemeyer (Tubingen, Germany), 1983.

PERIODICALS

Hudson Review, autumn, 1974, pp. 451-59.
Sewanee Review, spring, 1974, pp. 23-25.
Times (London), April 21, 1956.
Virginia Quarterly, summer, 1991, p. 107.*

D

DALKEY, Kara (Mia) 1953-

PERSONAL: Born in 1953.

ADDRESSES: Agent—c/o Ace Publishing, 200 Madison Ave., New York, NY 10016.

CAREER: Writer.

WRITINGS:

FANTASY NOVELS

The Curse of Sagamore, Ace (New York), 1986.
The Nightingale, Ace, 1988.
Euryale, Ace, 1988.
The Sword of Sagamore, Ace, 1989.

*   *   *

DALTON, Annie 1948-

PERSONAL: Born December 5, 1948, in London, England; married Andrew F. Stimson (a zoologist), June 29, 1979; children: one son. *Education:* Attended Camberwell School of Arts and Crafts, and Hornsey School of Art.

ADDRESSES: Agent—Laura Cecil, 27 Alwyne Villas, London N1 2HG, England.

CAREER: Writer.

WRITINGS:

FANTASY NOVELS

Out of the Ordinary, Methuen (London), 1988.
Night Maze, Methuen, 1989.
The Afterdark Princess, Methuen, 1990.
The Witch Rose, Methuen, 1990.
The Alpha Box, Methuen, 1991.
Demon-Spawn, Blackie (London), 1991.
Naming the Dark, Methuen, 1992.
Swan Sister, Methuen, 1992.
The Real Tilly Beany, Methuen, 1993.
Tilly Beany and the Best Friend Machine, Methuen, 1993.

*   *   *

D'ANCONA, Matthew 1968-

PERSONAL: Born January 27, 1968, in London, England; son of John (a consultant) and Helen (a teacher) D'Ancona; married Katherine Bergen, May 13, 1995. *Education:* Magdalen College, Oxford, graduated (with first class honors), 1989.

ADDRESSES: Home—Garden Flat, 1 Westgate Terr., London SW10 9BT, England. *Office*—*Sunday Telegraph,* 1 Canada Sq., Canary Wharf, London E14 5AR, England; fax 0171-538-7872. *Agent*—Giles Gordon, Curtis Brown, 6 Ann St., Edinburgh EH4 1PJ, Scotland.

CAREER: Times, London, England, assistant editor, 1990-95; *Sunday Telegraph,* London, deputy editor and political columnist, 1996—. Oxford University, fellow of All Souls College, 1989-96. Civic Forum, member of board of trustees, 1996—.

MEMBER: Beefsteak Club.

AWARDS, HONORS: Charles Douglas-Home Trust Award, 1994.

WRITINGS:

(Coauthor) *Eyewitness to Jesus,* Doubleday (New York), 1996, also published as *The Jesus Papyrus.*
The Ties That Bind Us, Social Market Foundation, 1996.

WORK IN PROGRESS: A sequel to *Eyewitness to Jesus,* with Carsten Thiede.

*   *   *

DANOW, David K.   1944-

PERSONAL: Born August 30, 1944, in New York, NY. *Education:* University of Rochester, A.B., 1966; Brown University, Ph.D., 1977. *Avocational interests:* Travel.

ADDRESSES: Office—Department of Comparative Literature, University of California, Riverside, CA 92521.

CAREER: University of California, Riverside, professor of Russian and comparative literature.

AWARDS, HONORS: Fulbright scholar, St. Petersburg, U.S.S.R. (now Russia), 1975-76.

WRITINGS:

The Thought of Mikhail Bakhtin: From Word to Culture, St. Martin's (New York City), 1991.
The Dialogic Sign: Essays on the Major Novels of Dostoevsky, Peter Lang (New York City), 1991.
Models of Narrative: Theory and Practice, St. Martin's, 1992.
The Spirit of Carnival: Magical Realism and the Grotesque, University Press of Kentucky (Lexington, KY), 1995.

DASHWOOD, Edmee Elizabeth Monica de la Pasture   1890-1943
(E. M. Delafield)

PERSONAL: Born June 9, 1980, in Sussex, England; died after a short illness, December 2, 1943, in Cullompton, Devonshire, England; daughter of Count Henri de la Pasture and Elizabeth Lydia Rosabelle; married Paul Dashwood, 1919; children: one son, one daughter.

CAREER: Writer. Member of the voluntary aid detachment in World War I; worked for the southwestern region of the Ministry of National Service; magistrate. Director of *Time and Tide.*

WRITINGS:

Zella Sees Herself, Heinemann (London), 1917, Knopf (New York), 1917.
The War-Workers, Heinemann, 1918, Knopf, 1918.
The Pelicans, Heinemann, 1919, Knopf, 1919.
Consequences, Hodder & Stoughton (London), 1919, Knopf, 1919.
Tension, Hutchinson (London), 1919, Macmillan (New York), 1920.
The Heel of Achilles, Macmillan, 1921.
Humbug: A Study in Education, Hutchinson, 1921, Macmillan, 1922.
The Optimist, Hutchinson, 1922, Macmillan, 1922.
A Reversion to Type, Hutchinson, 1923, Macmillan, 1923.
Messalina of the Suburbs, Hutchinson, 1924.
Mrs. Harter, Hutchinson, 1924, Harper (New York), 1925.
The Chip and the Block, Hutchinson, 1925, Harper, 1926.
Jill, Hutchinson, 1926, Harper, 1927.
The Entertainment and Other Stories, Hutchinson, 1927, Harper, 1927.
The Way Things Are, Hutchinson, 1927, Harper, 1928.
The Suburban Young Man, Hutchinson, 1928.
What Is Love?, Macmillan (London), 1928, republished as *First Love,* Harper, 1929.
Turn Back the Leaves, Harper, 1930.
Diary of a Provincial Lady, Macmillan, 1930, Harper, 1931.
Women Are Like That, Harper (London), 1930.
Challenge to Clarissa, Macmillan, 1931, republished as *House Party,* Harper, 1931.
To See Ourselves: A Domestic Comedy in Three Acts, Gollancz (London), 1931.

Thank Heaven Fasting, Macmillan, 1932, republished as *A Good Man's Love,* Harper, 1932.

The Provincial Lady Goes Further, Macmillan, 1932, republished as *The Provincial Lady in London,* Harper, 1933.

The Time and Tide Album, Hamilton (London), 1932.

Gay Life, Macmillan, 1933, Harper, 1933.

General Impressions, Macmillan, 1933.

The Glass Wall. A Play in Three Acts, Gollancz, 1933.

The Provincial Lady in America, Macmillan, 1934, Harper, 1934.

(Author of introduction) *The Brontes, Their Lives Recorded by Their Contemporaries,* Hogarth Press (London), 1935.

Faster! Faster!, Macmillan, 1936, Harper, 1936.

Straw Without Bricks: I Visit Soviet Russian, Macmillan, 1937, republished as *I Visit the Soviets,* Harper, 1937.

Nothing Is Safe, Macmillan, 1937, Harper, 1937.

Ladies and Gentlemen in Victorian Fiction, Hogarth Press (London), 1937, Harper, 1937.

As Others Hear Us. A Miscellany, Macmillan, 1937.

When Women Love, Harper, 1938, republished as *Three Marriages,* Macmillan, 1939.

Love Has No Resurrection and Other Stories, Macmillan, 1939.

The Provincial Lady in Wartime, Macmillan, 1940, Harper, 1940.

No One Now Will Know, Macmillan, 1941, Harper, 1941.

Late and Soon, Macmillan, 1943, Harper, 1943.

SIDELIGHTS: Edmee Elizabeth Monica de la Pasture Dashwood, better known under the pseudonym E. M. Delafield, was an extremely prolific writer of fiction during the 1920s and 1930s. Best known for her semi-autobiographical series of novels that followed the character of the Provincial Lady, Delafield became well-known in both her native England and in the United States.

Delafield's mother, also a novelist, published from 1900 to 1918. With the publication of Delafield's first novel in 1917, she effectively took up where her mother left off, though her novels were less sentimental than her mother's. Margaret B. McDowell, writing in the *Dictionary of Literary Biography,* argues that Delafield's books "focus on the relationship between parents and children, theories of child-rearing, the educational system, the influence of heredity on children, differences in social class, and criminal cases."

One of her most famous books, *Messalina of the Suburbs,* is a fictionalized account of a famous murder case that occurred in London in 1922. In it Elsie Palmer marries a man she doesn't love, takes a lover, and is complicit in her lover murdering her husband, even though she never puts the connections together. Both Elsie and her lover are executed for their crime. McDowell claims that the charm of the book lies in Delafield focusing on "that which is common (and commonplace) in Elsie and in the other people in her life. The woman, dull in all respects, gradually intrigues the reader, because her ordinary characteristics suggest that murder can take place among people the reader might know."

"Convincing realistic background, explicit detail, and natural patterns of conversation mark the Provincial Lady volumes," comments McDowell. The character made its debut in a series of humorous vignettes run by *Time and Tide.* The character was so popular that Delafield decided to use her in a full-length novel. The Provincial Lady is a member of the nobility, but full of concerns that endear her to those who aren't. She is concerned with running her country home in a frugal way, in light of the depression, and her keen observations on the hypocrisies and vanities of the people around her are a constant source of amusement. *Diary of a Provincial Lady* debuted in 1930 and has been a well-loved classic since then.

The second book in the series, *The Provincial Lady Goes Further,* follows her adventures as she begins to take herself seriously as a writer. In this volume, she has the courage to leave her family and her small town to pursue her dreams. In *The Provincial Lady in America,* that character journeys to the United States, where she visits New York and Washington, and attends an American football game, which she finds a uniquely American and uniquely confusing sport. The Provincial Lady also travels to Soviet Russia in *Straw Without Bricks,* and tries to be a patriotic war worker in *The Provincial Lady in Wartime.* Although Delafield wrote dozens of books, her Provincial Lady series stands out in terms of reader popularity. Margaret Haig Thomas, Lady Rhondda wrote in *Time and Tide* that "E.M. Delafield has written. . .greater books than this. She has written none more likely to endure."

BIOGRAPHICAL/CRITICAL SOURCES:

BOOKS

Current Biography Yearbook, H.W. Wilson, 1944.

Johnson, Brimley R., *Some Contemporary Novelists (Women),* Leonard Parsons, 1920, pp. 177-84.

Mather, Rachel R., *The Heirs of Jane Austen: Twentieth-Century Writers of the Comedy of Manners,* Peter Lang (New York), 1996.

McCullen, Maurice L., *E.M. Delafield,* Twayne (Boston), 1985.

Powell, Violet Georgiana, Lady, *The Life of a Provincial Lady: A Study of E.M. Delafield and Her Works,* Heinemann (London), 1988.

Staley, Thomas F., editor, *Dictionary of Literary Biography,* Volume 34: *British Novelists, 1890-1929: Traditionalists,* Gale Research (Detroit), 1985, pp. 90-97.

Twentieth-Century Literary Criticism, Vol. 61, Gale Research (Detroit), 1996, pp. 123-138.

Wickham Legg, L.G., and E.T. Williams, *Dictionary of National Biography,* Oxford University Press (London), 1959.

PERIODICALS

Bookman, August, 1932, pp. 240-41.
Listener, September 1, 1988, p. 28.
Nation, December 20, 1922, pp. 694-95.
New York Times Book Review, August 1, 1982, p. 27; December 25, 1983, p. 19.
Saturday Review of Literature, January 14, 1933, p. 376.
Time and Tide, December 13, 1947, pp. 1346-48.
Times Literary Supplement, April 26, 1985, p. 479.
Washington Post Book World, July 11, 1982, p. 12; December 29, 1985, p. 12.*

*   *   *

DAY, J(ames) Edward 1914-1996

OBITUARY NOTICE—See index for *CA* sketch: Born October 11, 1914, in Jacksonville, IL; died of a heart attack, October 29, 1996, in Hunt Valley, MD. Attorney, executive, civil servant, author. Day, who began his legal career in 1939, gained national attention in the early 1960s when he was appointed as Postmaster General of the United States and instituted several successful improvements to the system. Day worked for the law firm Sidley, Austin, Burgess and Harper in Chicago before serving in the U.S. Naval Reserve during World War II. He returned to the firm after the war, then worked as legal assistant to Illinois Governor Adlai Stevenson. In 1950,

Stevenson appointed Day as Commissioner of Insurance for the state of Illinois. In 1953, he joined the Prudential Insurance Company of America and eventually became its senior vice president in charge of western operations. In 1960, President-elect John F. Kennedy appointed Day to his cabinet as Postmaster General. During Day's tenure, he decreased the service's deficit, improved morale, worked to decrease racism, and implemented the ZIP Code (Zone Improvement Code) system. Day resigned in 1963 to return to the private sector, where he could receive a higher salary; he was only making $25,000 annually as the Postmaster General. He joined Sidley and Austin in 1963 as a partner, then began work with Cox, Lanford, and Brown and also Squire, Sanders and Dempsey. He also found time to work with the Boy Scouts of America and the YMCA. In his later years, Day, known for his wit, took to farming, first raising yaks, then cows and llamas. He named one of his animals after Hillary Clinton. Day also wrote several books, including *Humor in Public Speaking, Descendants of Christopher Day of Bucks County, PA, Farming for Fun, My Appointed Round: 929 Days as Postmaster General, Carrol Shanks of Prudential, An Unlikely Sailor,* and *The Man from Palmyra (A Surgeon's Life).*

OBITUARIES AND OTHER SOURCES:

BOOKS

Biographical Directory of the United States Executive Branch, 1774-1989, Greenwood Press, 1990.
Who's Who in America, Marquis Who's Who, 1997.

PERIODICALS

Los Angeles Times, November 1, 1996, p. A34.
New York Times, November 1, 1996, p. B15.

*   *   *

DEAN (DYER-BENNETT), Pamela (Collins) 1953-

PERSONAL: Born in 1953.

ADDRESSES: Agent—c/o Tor Publications, 2775 Modugno, St. Laurent, PQ, Canada H4R 1Z8.

CAREER: Writer.

WRITINGS:

FANTASY NOVEL

The Secret Country, Ace (New York), 1985.
The Hidden Land, Ace, 1986.
The Whim of the Dragon, Ace, 1989.
Tam Lin, Tor, 1991.
The Dubious Hills, Tor (New York), 1994.

*   *   *

DEITZ, Tom 1952-

PERSONAL: Full name, Thomas Franklin Deitz; born in 1952; raised in Georgia. *Education:* Has earned B.A. and M.A. degrees.

ADDRESSES: Home—Georgia. *Agent*—c/o Avon Books, 1350 Avenue of the Americas, New York, NY 10019.

CAREER: Writer.

MEMBER: Society for Creative Anachronism.

WRITINGS:

FANTASY NOVELS; DAVID SULLIVAN SERIES

Windmaster's Bane, Avon (New York), 1986.
Fireshaper's Doom, Avon, 1987.
Darkthunder's Way, Avon, 1989.
Sunshaker's War, Avon, 1990.
Stoneskin's Revenge, Avon, 1991.
Ghostcountry's Wrath, AvoNova (New York), 1995.
Dreamseeker's Road, AvoNova, 1995.

FANTASY NOVELS; SOULSMITH SERIES

Soulsmith, AvoNova, 1991.
Dreambuilder, AvoNova, 1992.
Wordwright, AvoNova, 1993.

OTHER FANTASY NOVELS

The Gryphon King, Avon, 1989.
Above the Lower Sky, AvoNova, 1994.
The Demons in the Green, AvoNova, 1996.

DELAFIELD, E. M.
    see **DASHWOOD, Edmee Elizabeth Monica de la Pasture**

*   *   *

de la TEJA, Jesus F(rancisco)
    See **TEJA, Jesus F(rancisco) de la**

*   *   *

de ROUGEMONT, Denis (Louis) 1906-1985

PERSONAL: Born September 8, 1906, in Neuchatel, Switzerland; died after a long illness, December 6, 1985, in Geneva, Switzerland; son of Georges and Alice-Sophie (Bovet) de Rougement; married second wife Anahite Repond, February 2, 1952; children: (first marriage) Nicolas, Martine. *Education:* Studied at the University of Neuchatel, University of Vienna, and University of Geneva. *Avocational interests:* Drystone walling.

CAREER: Author, editor and publisher of reviews in Switzerland and Paris, France. University of Frankfort-on-the-Main, Germany, lecturer in French literature, 1935-36; Ecole Libre des Hautes Etudes, New York, NY, professor, 1941-42; Voice of America, New York, NY, senior French-language script writer, 1942-43; European Cultural Center, Geneva, Switzerland, founder and director, beginning 1950; European Cultural Foundation, founder and governor, beginning 1954; Institut Universitaire d'Etudes Europeennes, Geneva, professor, 1963-85. *Military service:* Served in Swiss Army.

MEMBER: Congress for Cultural Freedom (chair, executive committee, 1951-66); Round Table Council of Europe (chairman, 1953, 1955); European Association of Music Festivals (chairman, 1951-85); Academy of Moral Science and Politics (Paris; corresponding member); Academy of Athens.

AWARDS, HONORS: Prix Rambert, 1938; Prix Gottfried Keller, 1946; Prix Eve Delacroix, 1957; Grand Prix de la Foundation Schiller, 1962; Prix Litteraire du Prince de Monaco, 1963; Prix Litteraire de la Ville de Geneve, 1967; Paul Tillich award,

1969; Prix Robert Schuman, 1970; Biancamano prize, 1977. Recipient of honorary degrees from Zurich University and National University of Ireland.

WRITINGS:

Le Paysan du Danube (limited edition), Payot (Lausanne), 1932.

Politique de la personne, Je Sers (Paris), 1934, enlarged edition, 1946.

Penser avec les mains, Albin Michel (Paris), 1936.

Journal d'un intellectuel en chomage, Albin Michel, 1937.

(Translator from the Latin) Martin Luther, *Traite du serf-arbitre,* with introduction and notes, Je Sers, 1937.

Journal d'Allemagne, Gallimard (Paris), 1938.

L'Amour et l'Occident, Plon (Paris), 1939, enlarged edition, 1956, English translation by Montgomery Belgion published as *Love in the Western World,* Harcourt, Brace, 1940 (published in England as *Passion and Society,* 1940), translation of enlarged edition, Pantheon, 1956, reprinted, Schocken, 1990.

Nicholas de Flue (dramatic legend; music by Arthur Honegger), Institut Neuchatelois et Foetisch (Lausanne), 1939.

Mission ou demission de la suisse, la Baconniere (Neuchatel), 1940.

(With Charlotte Muret) *The Heart of Europe* (translation from the French), Duell, Sloane & Pierce (New York, NY), 1941.

La Part du Diable, Brentano (New York, NY), 1942, revised edition, 1944, translation by Haakon Chevalier published as *The Devil's Share,* 1945, translation by K. Raine published as *Talk of the Devil,* 1946.

Les personnes du drame (limited edition), Pantheon Books (New York, NY), 1944, translation by Richard Howard published as *Dramatic Personages,* Holt, 1964.

Lettres sur la bombe atomique, with illustrations by Matta, Brentano (New York, NY), 1946, translation by Parmenia Migel published as *The Last Trump,* Doubleday, 1946.

Journal des deux mondes, Guilde du Livre (Lausanne), 1946, expanded edition, Gallimard (Paris), 1948.

Vivre en Amerique, Stock (Paris), 1947.

Doctrine fabuleuse (limited deluxe edition), Ides et Calendes (Neuchatel), 1947, translation published as *The Growl of Deeper Waters: Essays,* University of Pittsburgh Press, 1976.

Suite neuchateloise (limited deluxe edition), Ides et Calendes, 1948.

L'Europe en jeu, la Baconniere, 1948.

La Confederation suisse, Rocher, 1953.

(Translator) Karl Barth, *Dogmatique* [Geneva], 1953.

L'Aventure occidentale de l'homme, Albin Michel, 1957, translation by Montgomery Belgion published as *Man's Western Quest: The Principles of Civilization,* Harper, 1957.

Comme toi-meme: Essais sur les mythes de l'amour, Albin Michel, 1961, translation by Richard Howard published as *Love Declared: Essays on the Myths of Love,* Pantheon, 1963, translation published in England as *Essays on the Myths of Love,* Faber, 1964.

Vingt-huit siecles d'Europe, Payot, 1961, reprinted with new introduction by Jacques Delors, 1990, translation by Nobert Guterman of original edition published as *The Idea of Europe,* Macmillan, 1966.

Les chances de l'Europe, Payot, 1962, translation by Alan Braley published as *The Meaning of Europe,* Stein & Day (New York, NY), 1965.

The Christian Opportunity (essays), translated by Donald Lehmkuhl, Holt, 1963.

La Suisse, ou l'histoire d'un peuple heureux, Hachette (Paris), 1965.

Journal d'une epoque (1926-1946), Gallimard, 1968.

L'Un et le divers, [France], 1970.

Lettre ouverte aux europeens, [France], 1970.

Le cheminement des esprits, [France], 1970.

Les Dirigeants et les finalites de la societe occidentale, [France], 1972.

L'Avenir est notre affaire, [France], 1977, translation published as *The Future in our Concern,* 1981.

(Editor) *Rapport au peuple europeen sur l'etat de l'union de l'Europe,* Stock, 1979, translation published as *The State of the Union of Europe: Report of the CADMOS Group to the European People,* Pergamon, 1979.

Inedits: Extraits de cours, edited by Jean Mantzouranis and Francois Saint-Ouen, la Baconniere, 1988.

Ecrits sur l'Europe, edited by Christophe Calame, Difference (Paris), 1994.

Editor of *Nouveaux cahiers,* Paris, 1936-41. Also author of numerous pamphlets and booklets, including *Les Mefaits de l'instruction publique,* 1929, and *L'Europe et sa culture,* 1949. Contributor to anthologies and author of prefaces to various works. Contributor to leading periodicals in Europe and North and South America.

SIDELIGHTS: Denis de Rougemont, a prolific Swiss author of more than thirty books translated into seventeen languages, began his literary career as publisher of a French literary review in the 1930s. Through the pages of the review he took part in the revival of interest in the existential teachings of Soeren Kierkegaard, popular with Parisian literary crowd at the time. In 1941, he came to the United States to teach at the Ecole Libre des Hautes Etudes in New York City. While de Rougemont ended up staying in the United States until the end of World War II, he contributed to the war effort as chief editor of the "Voice of America" French-language programs broadcast to Europe. After World War II, de Rougemont became an advocate of European unity, promoting a Europe divided much like his native Switzerland's confederation of states rather than separate sovereign nations. He promoted his ideas on this and other issues through his work at the European Cultural Center in Geneva which he founded in 1950 and with the executive committee of the Congress for Cultural Freedom which he chaired for sixteen years.

In 1939, de Rougement published *L'Amour et l'Occident,* later translated into English as *Love in the Western World* (or *Passion and Society,* in the British edition). The book proved to be his most important and enduring work, and was still being reprinted nearly sixty years after its original publication date. In *Love in the Western World* de Rougemont traced the development of the Western idea of love as shown in the literature of Europe. The author began his study with a commentary on the medieval legend of Tristan and Iseult, a tragic love story. According to George Woodcock, writing in the *Sewanee Review,* de Rougemont proposed that "the protagonists of the Tristan legend were not in love with each other but in love with love, and that this kind of passion that was fueled by the imagination and that did not conclude in marriage and a satisfactory sexual relationship was doomed to end in self-destruction." In the book, de Rougemont also looked at Richard Wagner's treatment of the same legend in his opera, *Tristan und Isolde.*

Reviewers found de Rougemont's philosophy set forth in the book challenging, but worthy of discussion. A *New York Times* critic called the volume "enormously provocative." A *Times Literary Supplement* reviewer similarly maintained, "This is a brilliant book with unusual qualities of penetrating vision and a lively style." The *New Yorker*'s Clifton Fadiman recommended the book "to serious students of the social an religious myths on which the mind structure of modern Europe still rests, though not too securely." While Woodcock berated the author for "attempting to write literary history so as to justify a highly orthodox view of "Christian love,'" in *Commonweal* G. N. Shuster declared de Rougemont's analysis, "a worthy essay in fundamental Christian moral apologetic."

De Rougemont's other books dealt with a variety of subjects, including Swiss history, which he wrote about in *The Heart of Europe* and the Devil and his influence in contemporary society in *The Devil's Share.* In 1961, he returned to the subject of *Love in the Western World* with *Love Declared: Essays on the Myths of Love,* published in English translation in 1963. In a series of essays de Rougemont discussed the idea of love as embodied in two mythic figures, Tristan and Don Juan. While a *Newsweek* reviewer called the book "brilliantly suggestive," in *Library Journal* Robert Perkins noted, "The use De Rougemont makes of the myths as a means of cultural comparison of East and West is fascinating." "Much of the best in the book," maintained Edmund Fuller in the *New York Times Book Review,* "is his tracing of the mythic types (his "myth-analysis') in the work of modern novelists—and, by metaphor, in the actual lives of two philosophers as images of their intellectual experiences."

BIOGRAPHICAL/CRITICAL SOURCES:

PERIODICALS

Commonweal, August 30, 1940, p. 392.
Library Journal, May 1, 1963, p. 1894.
Newsweek, May 20, 1963, p. 107.
New Yorker, August 17, 1940, p. 60.
New York Times, October 20, 1940, p. 34.
New York Times Book Review, July 7, 1963, p. 10.
Sewanee Review, spring, 1986, pp. 272-279.
Times Literary Supplement, April 27, 1940, p. 210.

OBITUARIES:

PERIODICALS

New York Times, December 7, 1985, p. 12.
Times (London), December 10, 1985.
Washington Post, December 16, 1985.*

de TOTH, Andre 1913-
(Endre Toth)

PERSONAL: Born Sasvrai Farkasfawi Tothfalusi Toth Endre Antai Mihaly, May 15, 1913, in Mako, Hungary; immigrated to the United States, 1943; son of an ex-Hussar officer; married Veronica Lake (an actor), 1944 (divorced, 1952); married seventh wife, Ann; children: nineteen. *Education:* University of Budapest, law degree (with honors).

ADDRESSES: Agent—c/o Faber & Faber, 53 Shore Rd., Winchester, MA 01890.

CAREER: Film director, scenarist, producer, sculptor, and painter. Joined Bavarisch Pictura Productions, Vienna, Austria, 1929; worked in Hungary as a scriptwriter, film editor, unit director, and actor, in the 1930s; joined London Film Productions, 1939; Alexander Korda productions, U.S. associate, 1940; associated professionally with David O. Selznick, 1943; associated professionally with Hunt Stromberg-United Artists, 1944-45; Enterprise, staff director, 1946-47; Twentieth Century-Fox, 1948-49; Columbia and Warner Bros., director, 1951; Warner Bros., contract director, 1952; associated with Sam Spiegel, Horizon Pictures, Columbia, 1962; associated with Harry Saltzman, Lowndes Productions, United Artists, 1966-68. Has also worked in Italy and the United States as a film director, producer, and occasional coauthor of scripts and stories for films.

Director of films, including *Passport of Suez,* 1943; codirector, *None Shall Escape, Dark Waters,* and *Guest in the House,* all 1944; *Ramrod* and *The Other Love,* both 1947; *Pitfall,* 1948; *Slattery's Hurricane,* 1949; *Man in the Saddle* (also known as *Outcast*), 1951; *Carson City, Springfield Rifle,* and *Last of the Comanches* (also known as *The Sabre and the Arrow*), all 1952; *Thunder over the Plains* and *The Stranger Wore a Gun,* both 1953; *House of Wax,* Warner Bros., 1953; *The Bounty Hunter, Tanganyika, Crime Wave* (also known as *The City Is Dark*), and *Riding Shotgun,* all 1954; *The Indian Fighter,* 1955; *Monkey on My Back,* 1957; *Hidden Fear,* United Artists, 1957; *The Two-Headed Spy* and *Day of the Outlaw,* both 1959; *Man on a String* (also known as *Confessions of a Counterspy*), 1960; (with Filippo Sanjust and Primo Zeglio) *Morgan the Pirate* (also known as *Morgan il pirata*), Metro-Goldwyn-Mayer (MGM), 1961; codirector, *The Mongols* (also known as *I Mongoli*), 1961; codirector, *Oro per i Cesari* (also known as *Gold of the Caesars*), 1962; also director of *The Dangerous Game.* Director of Hungarian films,

under the name Endre Toth, including *Oet ora 40* (also known as *At 5:30*), *Ket lany az utcan* (also known as *Two Girls of the Street*), *Semmelweiss, Hat het boldogsag* (also known as *Six Weeks of Happiness*), *Balalaika,* and *Toprini nasz* (also known as *Wedding in Toprin*), all 1939.

Has appeared on screen in *A Personal Journey with Martin Scorese through American Movies* (documentary), Miramax, 1995; and as Vandermeer, *Spontaneous Combustion,* 1989. Also appeared in an episode of *American Cinema,* PBS, 1995. Executive producer, *Billion Dollar Brain,* United Artists, 1967; and executive producer, *Play Dirty* (also known as *Written on the Sand*), United Artists, 1969; producer, *El Condor,* National General, 1970.

AWARDS, HONORS: Academy Award nomination, best original story, 1950, for *The Gunfighter;* Edinburgh International Film Festival, retrospective of de Toth's Hollywood movies, 1994.

WRITINGS:

Fragments: Portraits from the Inside (memoir), Faber & Faber (Winchester, MA), 1994.

Also author (with William Bowers) of the story "The Gunfighter."

SCREENPLAYS

(With John Ward Hawkins) *Hidden Fear,* United Artists, 1957.
(With Filippo Sanjust and Primo Zeglio) *Morgan the Pirate,* Metro-Goldwyn-Mayer, 1961.

Also coauthor of screenplays, including *The Life of Emile Zola* (uncredited), with Geza Herceg, 1937; *Lydia* (uncredited), co-scenarist, 1942; *None Shall Escape,* 1944; *Young Widow,* 1946; *Dishonored Lady,* 1947; and *Westward Ho the Wagons!,* 1956. Coauthor of Hungarian screenplays, under the name Endre Toth, including *Oet ora 40* (also known as *At 5:30*), *Ket lany az utcan* (also known as *Two Girls of the Street*), *Semmelweiss, Hat het boldogsag* (also known as *Six Weeks of Happiness*), *Balalaika,* and *Toprini nasz* (also known as *Wedding in Toprin*), all 1939.

ADAPTATIONS: The screenplay *The Gunfighter,* released by Twentieth Century-Fox in 1950, was based on a story by de Toth and William Bowers.

SIDELIGHTS: Described as an energetic man distinguished by the patch he wears over one eye, Andre de Toth directed more than twenty movies in Hollywood as well as others in such countries as his native Hungary, Italy, and England. Rejecting a traditional family career in the Hussars, de Toth worked in the Hungarian film industry and intermittently tried to break into Hollywood during the 1930s before leaving his homeland permanently in 1939. De Toth's memoirs, *Fragments: Portraits from the Inside,* published when the author was in his eighties, are considered refreshingly frank and humorous about certain overblown Hollywood personalities and the author's own numerous failures.

De Toth credits what success he had in school to his working for a county newspaper, and to writing, directing, and acting in school plays. "I have never felt more important in my life," de Toth told *World Film Directors.* After rejecting a career in the military, de Toth attended the University of Budapest, studying law and political science. During this time, he also worked on films in Budapest and elsewhere in Europe under the mentorship of Ferenc Molnar. De Toth spent the 1930s travelling between Hungary and Hollywood and England, gradually building his reputation and earning positions of greater and greater responsibility. In 1939, he returned to Budapest as a film director, but left again with the outbreak of World War II. He directed his first film for Hollywood, *Passport to Suez,* in 1943.

De Toth directed mainly action movies and westerns. He is best known as the director of *House of Wax,* actor Vincent Price's first horror film, and "the most popular and commercially successful film that ever used the three-dimensional process," according to Danny Peary in his book, *Cult Movies: The Classics, the Sleepers, the Weird, and the Wonderful.* Although a reviewer in the *New York Times* called *House of Wax* "a raw, distasteful fable fit only to frighten simple souls," other critics found that even in two-dimensional showings on television the film is fun to watch. Several present-day critics noted the irony in the fact that, having only one eye, de Toth is himself unable to perceive the illusion of three-dimensions. Nonetheless, it has been said that, as a contributor to *Motion Picture Guide* commented: "*House of Wax* was not the first 3-D picture released, but it made better use of the process than any of the others."

De Toth worked on stories and scripts for films as well. He helped write as well as direct *Hidden Fear* (1957), a crime film with a plot generally considered implausible and nonsensical, shot on location in Copenhagen, Denmark; and *Morgan the Pirate,* whose story is so slight that the *New York Times* praised de Toth's decision as director to keep the characters at the edge of the screen, leaving the large-scale actions of soldiers and sailors to carry the story. His most memorable writing credit, for which he was nominated, along with William Bowers, for an Academy Award, is for the 1950 western starring Gregory Peck, *The Gunfighter.* A critic in the *New York Times* observed: "good writing, good direction and good acting . . . provides some of the slickest, sharpest drama that you will get in this type of film."

De Toth's memoir, *Fragments: Portraits from the Inside,* recounts the numerous mishaps and failures that marked his long film career, including being shot, being accused of being a Nazi spy, and breaking his neck four times. "Life stepped on me with hobnailed boots," de Toth told a contributor in *The Scotsman.* Many of the stories of old Hollywood as de Toth remembers it are hardly flattering to the standard image of that era, a quality that convinced some reviewers of de Toth's sincerity. "His book doesn't exactly raise a hurray for Hollywood, but as a portrait of the industry's not-so-great-and-good it is happily indiscreet and highly engaging," judged London *Times* contributor Anthony Quinn. A reviewer in *Film Review* praised the "wealth of superbly told anecdotes." Geoff Brown, writing in the same issue of the London *Times* as Quinn, called *Fragments* a "vivid book." "Although *Fragments* seems to have been hastily put together, it has a sincerity which most film biographies lack. Its author is unfailingly self-deprecating, and often very funny," remarked William Cash in the *Times Literary Supplement.*

BIOGRAPHICAL/CRITICAL SOURCES:

BOOKS

Motion Picture Guide, Cinebooks, 1986.
Peary, Danny, *Cult Movies: The Classics, the Sleepers, the Weird, and the Wonderful,* Dell (New York), 1981.
World Film Directors, Volume 1, edited by John Wakeman, H. W. Wilson Co., pp. 237-41.

PERIODICALS

Filmfax, September/October, 1995, pp. 38-41, 80-81.
Film Review, December, 1994.
The Herald (England), August 13, 1994.

New York Times, June 24, 1950; April 11, 1953; July 21, 1961.

Times (London), September 11, 1994; September 15, 1994.

Times Literary Supplement, November 25, 1994, p. 17.

The Scotsman, August 16, 1994.

*   *   *

DIPPEL, John V(an) H(outen) 1946-

PERSONAL: Born September 5, 1946, in East Orange, NJ; son of Jonn Willard (an attorney) and Rosalie (a teacher, administrative assistant, and homemaker; maiden name, Peppler) Dippel; married Cecilia A. Lotse, September 30, 1978; children: Stephen, David. *Ethnicity:* "Caucasian." *Education:* Princeton University, B.A., 1968; Trinity College, Dublin, M.Litt., 1972; Columbia University, Ph.D., 1978. *Politics:* Democrat. *Avocational interests:* Tennis, sailing, music.

ADDRESSES: Home and office—333 Hudson Terr., Piermont, NY 10968; fax 914-365-0592. *E-mail*—JDippel333@aol.com.

CAREER: Stevens Institute of Technology, Hoboken, NJ, adjunct professor of humanities, 1978-80; Jan Krukowski and Associates, New York City, senior associate and promotional writer, 1981—. Rockland Council for Young Children, member of board of directors, 1988-96; Community Playgroup of Piermont, member of board of directors, 1984-89, president of board, 1988-89. *Military service:* U.S. Army, Military Intelligence, 1968-70.

MEMBER: American Historical Association, World War II Studies Association.

WRITINGS:

Two Against Hitler, Praeger (New York), 1992.

Bound upon a Wheel of Fire: Why So Many German Jews Made the Tragic Decision to Remain in Nazi Germany, Basic Books (New York), 1996.

Contributor to magazines and newspapers, including *New Republic, Atlantic Monthly, International Journal of Intelligence and Counterintelligence,* and *New Leader.*

WORK IN PROGRESS: Research on changes in the role and image of American men since World War II.

SIDELIGHTS: John V. H. Dippel told *CA:* "After many years of trying, unsuccessfully, to write and publish fiction, I returned in the early 1980s to an interest in twentieth-century Germany, an interest that dates back to my having worked there one summer during college, and later having taught in a university in Muenster after finishing a stint in the army. I have been intrigued by the myths we create to understand and deal with other countries and their past. Because of Germany's central role in shaping this century, it seems to me crucial that we come to terms with the kind of society it was and how it descended into madness under Hitler. My first book, *Two Against Hitler,* looked at a little-known espionage collaboration between a German professor of economics and an American diplomat in Berlin, partly to re-examine our view that all Germans were fervent Nazis; some had, in fact, risked their lives to undermine the regime. This same interest in revealing the complexities of the German situation led me to write my second book, *Bound Upon a Wheel of Fire: Why So Many German Jews Made the Tragic Decision to Remain in Nazi Germany,* which sought to depict the conflicting emotions and attitudes that kept many German Jews from leaving the Third Reich during the early 1930s.

"Most recently, my interest in more closely scrutinizing cultural assumptions has spurred research into the reasons for the changes in the self-image and roles of American men since World War II. My view is that the position of men changed dramatically, not as a reaction to the women's movement of the 1970s, but due to the different way Americans came to see their society after emerging victorious on the battlefield. Democratic values, greater tolerance, respect for other races, and a strong abhorrence of authoritarian systems were eventually transferred from the broad social arena to individuals coming of age in the 1950s and 1960s.

"As a writer who is deeply concerned with effective communication, I have attempted to combine a thorough, scholarly survey of a particular topic with a writing style that makes the material easily accessible (and enjoyable) for the lay reader as well as professional historians. Having completed a doctorate in English literature and worked for many years in the field of promotional writing, I have been able to bring this background to bear in my historical research and writing."

DIPPLE, Elizabeth (Dorothea) 1937-1996

OBITUARY NOTICE—See index for *CA* sketch: Born May 8, 1937, in Brodhagen, Ontario, Canada; died November 30, 1996, in Evanston, IL. Educator and author. Dipple established a reputation in English literature as a professor and author. She began her career, which spanned four decades, at the University of Washington in Seattle in 1963 as an assistant professor. She became an associate professor in 1969, then moved on to Northwestern University in the same capacity in 1971. While at Northwestern, she was honored with a distinguished teaching award. She wrote several books, including *Plot, Unsolvable Plot, The Fore Conceit of Sidney's Ecologues,* and *Iris Murdock: Work for the Spirit.*

OBITUARIES AND OTHER SOURCES:

BOOKS

Directory of American Scholars, Volume 2: *English, Speech, and Drama,* 8th edition, Bowker, 1982.

PERIODICALS

Chicago Tribune, December 13, 1996, section 2, p. 12.

*   *   *

DR. LOON
See MARTIEN, Jerry

*   *   *

DODGE, Tom 1939-

PERSONAL: Born February 12, 1939, in Houston, TX; son of Clarence Mann (a construction worker) and Juanita Basham (a church worker); married, June 16, 1960; wife's name, Brenda (a registered nurse); children: Lyndon, Lowell, Karen Dodge Hoover. *Ethnicity:* "German-English." *Education:* University of Texas at Arlington, B.A., 1964; North Texas State University, M.A., 1968. *Politics:* "None." *Religion:* "Jogging." *Avocational interests:* "Eating chocolate."

ADDRESSES: Home—302 Stiles Dr., Midlothian, TX 76065. *Agent*—Janet Manus, Janet Wilkens Manus Literary Agency, Inc., 417 East 57th St., Suite 5D, New York, NY 10022.

CAREER: High school English teacher in Mansfield, TX, 1965-68; Blinn College, Brenham, TX, instructor in English, 1968-70; Mountain View College, Dallas, TX, professor of English, 1970-94. KERA-Radio, commentator for the affiliate of National Public Radio, 1988—. *Military service:* U.S. Army, 1961-62.

WRITINGS:

(Translator) *A Generation of Leaves* (poems), Texas Portfolio Press, 1977.
A Literature of Sports (anthology), Heath (Lexington, MA), 1980.
Oedipus Road (nonfiction), Texas Christian University Press (Fort Worth, TX), 1996.

Contributing editor, *D,* 1990-93.

WORK IN PROGRESS: A biographical novel about O. Henry.

SIDELIGHTS: Tom Dodge told *CA:* "I wrote *Oedipus Road* for the same reason I write everything else: it was a good story. That I was a part of the story made it easier in most ways. Taking care of an elderly parent with Alzheimer's is an interesting story these days, but there was more. As my mother's immediate memory slipped away, she became compelled to talk about the past. In so doing, she (painfully) told me that the man I had believed for fifty-five years was my real father was only a stand-in for my birth father, a neighbor. My search for him became a book.

"Resulting from this search, I located a new family, including a brother and sister, nieces and nephews, cousins and uncles, all accepting me with enthusiasm and love. My father, Clarence Mann, had died in 1972. As for my mother, she lives still, even contentedly, in an assisted-living facility nearby. We have become closer than ever before.

"*Oedipus Road* appeals to readers on several levels and seems very popular, especially with those who have Alzheimer's in their families.

"My writing process is rather ordinary. Each morning I turn on my computer, sit down, and start. I must have planned the scenes or commentary before I sit down. I usually do this during my daily runs. If nothing comes, I don't try to force it. I wait until it is ready.

"My advice to beginning writers is: words are the tools of your craft. A screwdriver will do the work of a chisel, but the result won't be pretty."

*   *   *

DOLAN, Frederick Michael 1955-

PERSONAL: Born March 17, 1955, in Bakersfield, CA; son of Frederick Michael (in business) and Sylvia Cecelia (a homemaker; maiden name, Tonrich) Dolan; married Victoria Carey Elliott (a journalist), June 29, 1985; children: Caitlin Emily, Alethea Cecelia. *Education:* University of California, Irvine, B.A., 1977, M.F.A., 1979; Princeton University, Ph.D., 1987. *Politics:* "Skeptical." *Religion:* "Art." *Avocational interests:* Painting, music, fiction, cinema, hiking, cycling, city life.

ADDRESSES: Home—Berkeley, CA. *Office*—Department of Rhetoric, 2125 Dwinelle Hall, University of California, Berkeley, CA 94720-2670; fax 510-642-8881.

CAREER: University of California, Berkeley, assistant professor, 1988-94, associate professor of rhetoric, 1994—.

MEMBER: International Association for Philosophy and Literature, Modern Language Association of America, American Political Science Association, American Studies Association.

AWARDS, HONORS: Fellow, Doreen B. Townsend Center for the Humanities, 1989-90; American Cultures fellow, 1991; Humanities research fellowship, 1992-93; research fellow, Center for German and European Studies, 1993.

WRITINGS:

(Editor with Thomas L. Dumm) *Rhetorical Republic: Governing Representations in American Politics,* University of Massachusetts Press (Amherst, MA), 1993.
Allegories of America: Narratives, Metaphysics, Politics, Cornell University Press (Ithaca, NY), 1994.

Contributor of articles and reviews to academic journals, including *Political Theory, Contemporary Lit-* *erature, Massachusetts Review, Text and Performance Quarterly, Postmodern Culture, Diacritics,* and *Canadian Journal of Political and Social Theory.* Co-editor, *Foundations of Political Theory Newsletter.* Also co-editor of *Atopia: Political Theory, Philosophy, Aesthetics,* a book series published by Stanford University Press.

WORK IN PROGRESS: A book and essays on the location, actor, and content of the political in the wake of Nietzsche's and Heidegger's deconstruction of traditional metaphysics; research on love and the political, formulating Hannah Arendt's conception of "love of the world" through comparison with other theories of love, worldliness, and attachment (Nietzsche, Bataille, Lacan, Marcuse).

SIDELIGHTS: Frederick Michael Dolan told *CA:* "I was born in Bakersfield, California, where my father had been sent to open an office, but I grew up largely in Orange County, now considered trendy, but then very much a provincial backwater whose population was actively hostile to culture, the life of the mind, and any politics to the left of the John Birch Society. Escape was possible through the public library, that of the local campus of the University of California, and trips to the exotic art galleries, bookstores, theaters, newsstands, and shops of Los Angeles; and escape was everything. The memories of childhood and youth that I treasure now are moments such as my discovery of Beckett's *How It Is* in the local library; I hadn't known that such a book was *possible.* I was so excited that I couldn't wait to take it to the reading room but simply sat down in the stacks and started reading, happy and astonished.

"As my adolescence during the late sixties and seventies coincided with the worst atrocities of the Vietnam war, it was impossible not to develop a skeptical curiosity about the origins of the modern world, as well as a longing for something less destructive or a desire to pinpoint and save what is fine in modernity. Modern art, literature, philosophy, political and social thought, and, for a long moment, psychology, became my passions, though they were pursued largely in isolation until college, where my teachers introduced me to the work of the Frankfurt School and I began to glimpse the possibility of a relationship between art and politics in critical social and political theory. Though retired, Herbert Marcuse still gave the occasional lecture at the University of California at San Diego, and those who had studied with him or other members of the Frankfurt School were all over Irvine, so the tradition enjoyed a lively presence. Their approach to the tradition began to pale, however, when I read Derrida, Foucault, and Lacan, who led me to Nietzsche, Heidegger, and Gadamer, and these figures inspired most of my work during graduate school at Princeton.

"The desire to write about America, toward which I had such an ambivalent attitude, came upon me while I was living in Paris and working on my doctoral thesis. There I enjoyed the luxury of relating to America as a text, an icon, and the many occasions on which I was asked to explain our peculiar nation made me realize just how *constructed* America is, and it led me to think about the relationships among representations of America, American attempts to represent the world and itself, and the metaphysical desire for adequate representations that Nietzsche and Heidegger expose and criticize. I'm happy I wrote about America above all because it deepened my understanding of American literature, poetry, and philosophy, but I don't any longer find American ideology amusing. The Republic seems to be rushing toward catastrophe, and cool heads are unlikely to prevail in a nation that has always been actively hostile to intellectual life and now boasts the most illiterate and confused population in the industrialized world.

"Writing for me is above all a mode of self-education or self-cultivation. I write first of all to find out what I have to say about the authors, ideas, texts, or sentences that provoke me to think. One hopes, on good days one even expects, that it might play a small role in the education of others, but precisely what role is hard to say, and should be. The study of modern thought and the experience of modern art have taught me that being human, at this moment, means being unfinished, transitory, ephemeral, a perpetual newcomer in a world that is always something of a mystery, and also that the temptation to dissolve the mystery by reifying it into some brittle ideology is the most self-defeating of all those to which we might yield. Writing, which hazards assertions only by qualifying others, and which cannot qualify without risking a statement, is my way of embracing these aspects of human existence."

*　　*　　*

D'ORSO, Michael 1953-
(Mike D'Orso)

PERSONAL: Born October 12, 1953; in Portsmouth, VA; son of James and Claire D'Orso; divorced; children: Jamie (daughter, aged 12). *Education:* College of William and Mary, B.A. in Philosophy, 1975, M.A. in English, 1981. *Avocational interests:* basketball, pocket billiards, movies, music.

ADDRESSES: Home—515 Mayflower Rd., Norfolk, VA 23508. *Agent*—Black Literary Agency, 156 Fifth Ave., Suite 608, New York, NY 10010.

CAREER: Journalist. *Commonwealth Magazine,* Richmond, VA, staff writer, 1981-84; *Virginian-Pilot,* Norfolk, VA, features writer, 1984—;

AWARDS, HONORS: National Headliner Award; Penney-Missouri Prize; National Association of Black Journalists Award; Best Sports Stories, published by *The Sporting News* (three times); International Reading Association Award; American Association of Sunday and Feature Editors Award; American Academy of Family Physicians National Journalism Awards (two times); National Unity Awards in Media; Virginia Press Association awards (fifteen times); Virginia College Stores Association Book of the Year, 1988, for *Somerset Homecoming;* Gustavus Myers Center for the Study of Human Rights citation, 1992, for *The Cost of Courage; The Library Journal*'s Best Book of the Year list, 1992, for *For the Children;* Gold Medallion Book Award finalist, 1993, for *Rise and Walk;* Lillian Smith Book Award, 1996, for *Like Judgment Day.*

WRITINGS:

(With Dorothy Spruill Redford) *Somerset Homecoming: Recovering a Lost Heritage,* Doubleday (New York), 1988.

(As Mike D'Orso) *Fast Takes: Slices of Life through a Journalist's Eye,* Hampton Roads (Norfolk VA), 1990.

(With Carl Elliott) *The Cost of Courage: The Journey of an American Congressman,* Doubleday, 1992.

(With Madeline Cartwright) *For the Children: Lessons from a Visionary Principal—How We Can Save Our Public Schools,* Doubleday, 1993.

(With Dennis Byrd) *Rise and Walk: The Trial and Triumph of Dennis Byrd,* HarperCollins (New York), 1993.

(As Mike D'Orso) *Pumping Granite, and Other Portraits of People at Play,* Texas Tech University Press (Lubbock, TX), 1994.

(As Michael D'Orso) *Like Judgment Day: The Ruin and Redemption of a Town Called Rosewood,* Grosset/Putnam (New York), 1996.

(With Dee Hakala) *Thin Is Just a Four-Letter Word,* Little, Brown (New York) 1997.

Contributor of articles to periodicals, including *Sports Illustrated, The Oxford American, Studies in American Fiction, Oklahoma Today, Reader's Digest, Self,* and *People Weekly.*

WORK IN PROGRESS: Co-writing autobiography of U.S. Congressman and civil rights activist John Lewis, to be published by Simon & Schuster.

SIDELIGHTS: Journalist Michael D'Orso has coauthored several autobiographical works, as well as his *Like Judgment Day: The Ruin and Redemption of a Town Called Rosewood,* a 1996 account of the destruction of an African-American community in Florida in 1923. Among his collaborations are the 1993 volumes *Rise and Walk: The Trial and Triumph of Dennis Byrd,* which chronicles the recovery of an injured professional football player, and *For the Children: Lessons from a Visionary Principal—How We Can Save Our Public Schools,* comprising the case study of a dedicated educator who transforms a troubled school into a community haven.

Somerset Homecoming: Recovering a Lost Heritage was written by D'Orso with Dorothy Spruill Redford, a single mother and social worker in Portsmouth, VA, who, inspired by the 1977 telecast of Alex Haley's *Roots,* set out on a journey to discover her own ancestral heritage. That journey, which would last nine years, led her to the remains of a decrepit plantation in North Carolina, where she found the records of the first slaves brought to that estate in the eighteenth century to plant rice: her ancestors. Redford's subsequent efforts to locate living descendents of those slaves and of their owners and to bring them together for a reunion resulted in the 1986 event for which the book is named. Alex Haley, who wrote the book's foreword, called it "the best, most beautifully researched and most thoroughly presented black family history that I know of." Carl Senna, writing in the *New York Times Book Review,* called it "moving . . . as much about a remarkable woman as about an American people."

In *The Cost of Courage: The Journey of an American Congressman,* coauthored with Carl Elliott, Sr., the 1990 recipient of the John F. Kennedy Profiles in Courage Award, D'Orso recounts Elliott's career from tenant farmer to rural lawyer to the U.S. Congress, where he participated in passing the National Defense of Education Act and served on the House

Rules committee during the Kennedy administration. Ultimately unseated by advocates of racial segregation in the charged political atmosphere of the civil rights movement in Alabama during the 1960s, Elliott retired from public life after an unsuccessful bid for the governor's office. In a *Publishers Weekly* review of *The Cost of Courage,* praise of the work centered on the narrative as "rich in portrayals of political figures, including the 'fearsome magnetism' of a ruthless [George] Wallace." Alex Raksin of *The Los Angeles Times Book Review* called the book "refreshing . . . thanks to the richly evocative text shaped by co-writer Michael D'Orso."

For the Children, written by D'Orso and Madeline Cartwright, details Cartwright's experiences as an elementary school principal in Philadelphia's Strawberry Mansion district, an inner city neighborhood plagued by poverty and violence. Taking an active role in maintaining high standards of instruction, physical cleanliness, and parental involvement, Cartwright restored the school to a central position within the community. Reviewing *For the Children* in *Library Journal,* Arla Lindgren called it "a powerful book" which "should be required reading for politicians, sociologists, educators, and anyone interested in the future of this country."

Rise and Walk: The Trial and Triumph of Dennis Byrd, which John Maxymuk of *Library Journal* characterized as "very moving and inspirational" was also published in 1993. This nonfiction work treats the recovery of New York Jets defensive lineman Dennis Byrd, who was paralyzed after colliding with another player during a football game in November, 1992. Informed that he would never walk again, Byrd relied on a combination of medical treatment, physical therapy, Christian faith, and a supportive family to overcome his injuries. According to Andrea Cooper in *New York Times Book Review,* Byrd's story is "undeniably gripping." The Fox Television Network made *Rise and Walk* into a movie of the same name, which premiered on the Fox network in January 1994.

Like Judgment Day documents the destruction of the town of Rosewood, Florida, in January, 1923. Ignited by a white woman's accusation of rape, members of a white community murdered a number of black inhabitants of nearby Rosewood and drove others away from the area through repeated acts of arson and intimidation. With survivors scattered, the incident lay buried for six decades until the descendant of one of the victims began a personal investigation into the episode, a quest that would culminate in a successful damage suit against the State of Florida. Tracing both the perpetrators and the victims of the incident, D'Orso "vividly captures each figure and event, resisting the impulse to gloss over inconvenient material," according to reviewer Nell Irvin Painter in the *Washington Post Book World.* A *Publishers Weekly* contributor called the account "a significant contribution to American history." *The New Yorker* credited D'Orso for writing this book "with the insight of a serious novelist." The 1997 motion picture *Rosewood,* directed by John Singleton, relied on D'Orso's book as a reference; Singleton wrote an introduction to the paperback editon of the book, which was published as a tie-in to the Warner Brothers Film.

BIOGRAPHICAL/CRITICAL SOURCES:

PERIODICALS

Library Journal, June 15, 1993, pp. 79, 82; October 1, 1993, p. 100.
Los Angeles Times, January 26, 1992.
New Yorker, June 17, 1996.
New York Times Book Review, October 3, 1993, p. 25; November 14, 1993, p. 15.
Publishers Weekly, January 6, 1992, p. 60; January 1, 1996, p. 65.
Washington Post Book World, February 4, 1996, pp. 3, 6.

* * *

D'ORSO, Mike
    See D'ORSO, Michael

* * *

DREW, Wayland 1932-

PERSONAL: Born September 12, 1932, in Oshawa, Canada; married, 1957; wife's name, Gwendolyn; children: one son, three daughters. *Education:* Attended Oshawa Collegiate and Vocational Institute, and University of Toronto.

ADDRESSES: Agent—Amanda Urban, International Creative Management, 40 West 57th Street, New York, NY 10019.

CAREER: Writer.

WRITINGS:

NOVELS

The Wabeno Feast, Anasi (Toronto), 1973.
Dragonslayer (novelization of screenplay), Del Rey (New York), 1981.
The Memoirs of Alcheringia, Del Rey, 1984.
The Gaian Expedient, Del Rey, 1985.
The Master of Norriya, Del Rey, 1986.
The Erthring Cycle, Nelson Doubleday (New York), 1986.
Batteries Not Included (novelization of screenplay), Berkley (New York), 1987.
Willow (novelization of screenplay), Del Rey, 1988.
Halfway Man, Oberon Press (Ottawa, Ontario), 1989.

OTHER

(With Bruce Littlejohn) *Superior: The Haunted Shore,* Beaufort (New York), 1975.
(With wife, Gwendolyn Drew) *Browns Weir* (travel), Oberon Press, 1983.
(With Littlejohn) *A Sea Within: The Gulf of St. Lawrence* (travel), McClelland and Stewart (Toronto), 1984.

* * *

DRUM, Alice 1935-

PERSONAL: Born June 22, 1935, in Gettysburg, PA; daughter of David Wentz and Charlotte (Kinzey) McDonnell; married Donald Richard Guise (divorced, August, 1975); married Ray K. Drum, March 2, 1979; children: (first marriage) Gregory, Brent, Richard, Robert, Clay; (second marriage) Trevor. *Ethnicity:* "Caucasian." *Education:* Wilson College, B.A. (magna cum laude), 1957; American University, Ph.D., 1976; Harvard University, Certificate in Educational Management. *Politics:* Democrat. *Religion:* Episcopal. *Avocational interests:* Reading, hiking, travel.

ADDRESSES: Home—Lancaster, PA. *Office*—Office of the Vice President, Franklin and Marshall College, Lancaster, PA 17604-3003; fax 717-399-4455. *E-mail*—drum@admin.fandm.edu.

CAREER: American University, Washington, DC, instructor in English, 1976; Antioch University, Columbia, MD, adjunct professor of general studies, 1976-78; Gettysburg College, Gettysburg, PA, adjunct assistant professor of English, 1977-80; Georgetown University, Washington, DC, lecturer in general studies, 1980-81; Hood College, Frederick, MD, assistant professor of English, 1981-85, coordinator of writing program, 1981-83, assistant director of Learning Center, 1982-83, associate dean of academic affairs, 1983-85; Franklin and Marshall College, Lancaster, PA, adjunct associate professor of English, 1985—, dean of freshmen, 1985-88, vice president of the college, 1988—, dean of educational services, 1988-94. University of Maryland at College Park, lecturer, 1980-83. Lancaster County District Attorney Commission, chairperson, 1990; Lancaster County Commission on Youth Violence, member, 1991-93; Lancaster County Drug Task Force Review Commission, member, 1993-94; Mayor's Youth Leadership Conference, facilitator, 1990-93; active as member and officer of community organizations, including Community Concert, United Way, and local public library.

MEMBER: Modern Language Association of America, American Association of Higher Education, American Council on Education, Association of American Colleges, College English Association, National Association of Student Personnel Administrators, Eastern Association of College Deans (president, 1988-89), Northeast Modern Language Association, Phi Beta Kappa (president of Theta chapter, 1990-91), Phi Kappa Phi.

AWARDS, HONORS: Mellon grant, 1979.

WRITINGS:

(With Richard Kneedler) *Funding a College Education,* Harvard Business School Press (Boston, MA), 1996.

Contributor to books, including *Institutional Research: New Challenges to an Evolving Role,* Association for Institutional Research, 1987. Contributor of articles and poems to periodicals, including *College Composition and Communication, World Literature Written in English, Chronicle of Higher Education,* and *Virginia Country Quarterly.* Member of editorial board, *NASPA Journal,* 1992-95, 1996—.

WORK IN PROGRESS: Research on Jane Austen and on the history of higher education.

DUBY, Georges (Michel Claude) 1919-1996

OBITUARY NOTICE—See index for *CA* sketch: Born October 7, 1919, in Paris, France; died of cancer, December 3, 1996, in Aix-en-Provence, France. Educator, historian, author. Duby was highly acclaimed as a medieval scholar and impressed readers worldwide with books such as *The Age of the Cathedrals: Art and Society, 980-1420.* His interest in history also prompted him to reveal aspects of women's history through the five-volume *Histoire des Femmes* and books written with Michelle Perrot such as *Power and Beauty: Images of Women In Art.* Early in his career, Duby was an assistant in the faculty of letters at the Universite de Lyon beginning in 1944. After stints as professor of medieval history at Universite de Besancon and Universite d'Aix Marseille, he began twenty-two years at the College de France as a professor of the history of medieval societies in 1970. He also found time to lecture throughout the world and was a prolific author. Although he wrote in French, many of his works appeared in English translation. His other books included *The Legend of Bouvines, History Continues* (with Perrot), *William Marshal: The Flower of Chivalry,* and *The Knight, the Lady and the Priest: The Making of Modern Marriage in Medieval France.* He was honored with many awards, including Commander of the Legion of Honor, election to the Academie Francaise, and membership in the British Academy. He appeared frequently on radio and television.

OBITUARIES AND OTHER SOURCES:

BOOKS

International Who's Who, Europa Publications, 1993.

PERIODICALS

New York Times, December 8, 1996, section 1, p. 63.
Times (London), December 9, 1996, p. 23.

*   *   *

DuFRESNE, Jim 1955-

PERSONAL: Born August 14, 1955, in Farmingham, MA; son of Harris (an engineer) and Eleanor (a nurse; maiden name, Nicolas) DuFresne; married Peggy Zwers (a sales manager), October 10, 1981; children: Jessica, Michael. *Ethnicity:* "French-Canadian." *Education:* Michigan State University, B.A.

ADDRESSES: Home—P.O. Box 852, Clarkston, MI 48347; fax 810-969-2422. *E-mail*—kidven.aol.

CAREER: Booth Newspapers, Lansing, MI, outdoor writer, 1987—.

WRITINGS:

Isle Royale National Park: Foot Trails and Water Routes, Mountaineers Books (Seattle, WA), 1984, 2nd edition, 1991.

Voyageurs National Park: Water Routes, Foot Paths, and Ski Trails, Mountaineers Books, 1986.

(With Ken Leghorn) *Glacier Bay National Park: A Backcountry Guide to the Glaciers and Beyond,* Mountaineers Books, 1987.

Michigan: Off the Beaten Path, Globe Pequot (Chester, CT), 1988, 4th edition, 1996.

Michigan State Parks: A Complete Guide for Campers, Boaters, Anglers, Hikers, and Skiers, Mountaineers Books, 1989.

Michigan's Best Outdoor Adventures with Children, Mountaineers Books, 1990.

Fifty Hikes in Lower Michigan: The Best Walks, Hikes, and Backpacks from Sleeping Bear Dunes to the Hills of Oakland County, Backcountry Publications (Woodstock, VT), 1991.

Wild Michigan, Northword Press (Minocqua, WI), 1992.

Porcupine Mountains Wilderness State Park: A Backcountry Guide for Hikers, Campers, Backpackers, and Skiers, Pegg Legg Productions (Clarkston, MI), 1993.

Alaska: A Travel Survival Kit, 4th edition, Lonely Planet Publications (Oakland, CA), 1994.

Backpacking in Alaska: A Lonely Planet Walking Guide, Lonely Planet Publications, 1995.

Trekking in Alaska: A Walking Guide, Lonely Planet Publications, 1995.

(With Jeff Williams) *Tramping in New Zealand: A Walking Guide,* Lonely Planet Publications, 1995.

*   *   *

DULLES, Eleanor Lansing   1895-1996

OBITUARY NOTICE—See index for *CA* sketch: Born June 1, 1895, in Watertown, NY; died October 30, 1996, in Washington, DC. Educator, diplomat, author. Dulles worked for the U.S. State Department during an era that was ripe with chauvinism toward women. Despite the obstacles against her, she was an economic specialist whose efforts helped rebuild West Berlin after World War II, earning her the name "the Mother of Berlin." Dulles was part of a family that was highly involved in civil service. Under President Dwight D. Eisenhower's administration, her brother John Foster Dulles was secretary of state, while her brother Allen W. Dulles was director of the CIA. Dulles' interest in helping those impacted by war began early in her life. During World War I she went to France to assist refugees. She returned to the United States for work at the American Tube and Stamping Company. In 1924, she began teaching at Simmons College in Boston, with stints at Bryn Mawr College and the University of Pennsylvania to follow. In 1936, she began work with the U.S. Government's Social Security Board, leaving that position to join the U.S. State Department in 1942. Her work as a diplomat included being an economic officer, financial attache in Austria, and special assistant in the Office of German Affairs. It was through her work with the German office that she helped revitalize the German economy after World War II, bringing its unemployment levels down significantly from thirty-three percent. She also worked to secure funds for West Berlin's Congress Hall, hospitals, and educational facilities. After twenty years, she was fired from the State Department and went on to hold positions such as professor at Georgetown University, visiting professor at Duke University, consultant for the U.S. Department of State, and organizer of the John Foster Dulles Centennial Program at Princeton University. During her hundred-and-one-year life, she penned books such as *Eleanor Lansing Dulles—Chances of a Lifetime, The French Franc: 1914-1928, The Bank for International Settlements at Work, Depression and Reconstruction: A Study of Causes and Controls, John Foster Dulles: The Last Year,* and *Berlin: The Wall Is Not Forever.* She received the Grand Cross of Merit from the Federal Republic of Germany, Carl Schurz Plaque, an honorary professorship at the University of Berlin, and a Tribute of Appreciation from the U.S. State Department (1985).

OBITUARIES AND OTHER SOURCES:

BOOKS

Who's Who in America, 51st edition, Marquis, 1996.

PERIODICALS

New York Times, November 4, 1996, p. B10.
Times (London), November 5, 1996, p. 23.
Washington Post, November 2, 1996, p. B4.

DUPREE, Nathalie 1939-

PERSONAL: Born December 23, 1939; daughter of Walter G. (a military colonel) and Evelyn (Cook) Meyer; married Jack Bass, April 10, 1996. *Ethnicity:* "All American." *Education:* Attended the Cordon Bleu cooking school in London, England. *Politics:* Democrat. *Avocational interests:* Art, music, literature, hiking.

ADDRESSES: Home—148 Westminster Dr., NE, Atlanta, GA 30309. *Agent*—Angela Miller.

CAREER: Professional chef. Restaurant chef in Majorca, Spain; then opened a country restaurant in Georgia; founder, chef, and teacher of Rich's Cooking School, 1975-84.

Hosted more than 300 half-hour shows: 140 for PBS, 165 for TVFN, and 78 for the Learning Channel since 1986. Appeared on Cable News Network (CNN), *The Today Show,* National Broadcasting Company (NBC), *Good Morning America,* American Broadcasting Corporation (ABC), and *CBS This Morning,* Columbia Broadcasting System (CBS); appears in daily radio program, *Home Cooking* (syndicated on more than 1000 stations), has served as a columnist for the *Atlanta Journal-Constitution, Los Angeles Times,* and *Atlanta* magazine. Has served as consultant to Best Foods, Proctor & Gamble, Lea & Perrins, Borden, General Foods, White Lily Foods Company, Publix, and Campbell soups, Pam.

MEMBER: International Association of Culinary Professionals (past president), James Beard House, American Institute of Wine and Food, Les Dames d'Escoffier.

AWARDS, HONORS: Recipient of James Beard Award for Americans, 1994; TasteMaker's Award; National Magazine Writers Award.

WRITINGS:

COOKBOOKS

New Southern Cooking with Nathalie Dupree, Knopf (New York, NY), 1988.
Nathalie Dupree's Matters of Taste, Knopf, 1990.
Nathalie Dupree Cooks for Family and Friends, William Morrow (New York, NY), 1991.
Nathalie Dupree's Southern Memories, Clarkston Potter (New York, NY), 1993.

Nathalie Dupree Cooks Great Meals for Busy Days, Clarkston Potter, 1994.
Nathalie Dupree Cooks Everyday Meals from a Well-Stocked Pantry, Clarkson Potter, 1995.
Nathalie Dupree Cooks Quick Meals for Busy Days, Clarkson Potter, 1996.

Also contributor to periodicals, including *Traditional Home, New Woman, Home, Redbook, Bon Appetit, Family Circle, Ladies' Home Journal,* and *New York Times.*

WORK IN PROGRESS: Nathalie Dupree Entertains.

SIDELIGHTS: Chef, television personality, and author Nathalie Dupree initially gained her culinary skills at the prestigious Cordon Bleu cooking school in London, England. Her first position after leaving that institution was as a chef in a restaurant in Spain, but then she returned to the United States to open a country restaurant of her own in the state of Georgia. In 1975, Dupree founded the famed Rich's Cooking School, renowned not only in the South but throughout America and the world. She served there as teacher and director for almost ten years. She has also hosted her own television cooking show, which has run not only on the Public Broadcasting System (PBS), but on the cable stations the Learning Channel and the TV Food Network. In addition to her stint at the Cordon Bleu, Dupree has continued to learn about the culinary arts through study with some of the best chefs in Europe and the United States, including Louisiana's Cajun cuisine specialist, Chef Paul Prudhomme.

Dupree has written cooking columns for several publications. She began writing for the *Atlanta Journal-Constitution,* then prepared articles for the *Los Angeles Times* syndicate. Most recently, a Dupree column has appeared in *Atlanta* magazine. Dupree has penned cookbooks which have proved popular, including *Nathalie Dupree Cooks Quick Meals for Busy Days, Nathalie Dupree's Southern Memories,* and *Nathalie Dupree Cooks for Family and Friends.* She has sold more than a half million hardback books.

Dupree told *CA:* "When I write, I want to communicate the ways in which food plays a part in our lives—for we all need food, it is our primary, central issue—and as such it impacts our lives from birth to death. My books are for all those moments—I write about food for mothers-to-be and food for funerals—and my stories embrace food and relationships.

"Ideas will come to me at any time—walking, on the golf course, at a meal with friends. I try to respond to the needs of the majority—whether it's for quick meals or pantry foods, or to explain a region's food."

*   *   *

DURFEE, Mary 1951-

PERSONAL: Born September 2, 1951, at Rapid City Air Force Base, SD; married Donald A. Durfee, May 5, 1979. *Education:* University of Colorado, B.A., 1974; Cornell University, M.A., 1983, Ph.D., 1990. *Politics:* "Avid watcher, occasional participant." *Avocational interests:* Music, gardening, walking.

ADDRESSES: Home—Hancock, MI. *Office*—Department of Social Sciences, Michigan Technological University, 1400 Townsend Dr., Houghton, MI 49931-1295.

CAREER: Worked for NCR Corp., 1980-81; Colgate University, Hamilton, NY, lecturer, 1983-84; Canisius College, Buffalo, NY, assistant professor, 1985-86; Antioch College, Center for Adult Learning, Yellow Springs, OH, adjunct assistant professor, 1987-89; Wittenberg University, Springfield, OH, visiting assistant professor, 1990-91; University of Dayton, Dayton, OH, adjunct assistant professor, 1992; Michigan Technological University, Houghton, assistant professor of social sciences, 1992—. University of Dayton, adjunct assistant professor, 1987-90.

MEMBER: American Political Science Association, International Studies Association, American Society of International Law.

WRITINGS:

(With James N. Rosenau) *Thinking Theory Thoroughly: Coherent Approaches to an Incoherent World,* Westview (Boulder, CO), 1995.

Contributor to periodicals, including *Publius: The Journal of Federalism, Transboundary Resources Reports, College Teaching,* and *Administrative Science Quarterly.*

WORK IN PROGRESS: Bridging the Gap of Indecision: The Evolution of Great Lakes Institutions; research on bacteriology and diplomacy in the Great Lakes, 1912-1929; research on pollution prevention and industrial ecology.

SIDELIGHTS: Mary Durfee told *CA:* "When I started the Great Lakes book, I asked my friend and co-author Jim Rosenau whether he found deciding to write a book marriage-like or rational. He didn't answer directly, although he provided key advice: 'Don't procrastinate' just because I may not see the entire structure at the beginning. I have now concluded that it is marriage-like. All of a sudden, there is nothing else to do but get married (or launch a book). Once underway, the book seems to have a constancy that reminds me of being married—sometimes annoying, sometimes very exciting, but mostly just an everyday fact of life.

"I imagine that I will be writing about the Great Lakes for the rest of my life. While there is considerable intellectual fascination associated with the Lakes, I have to admit I write about them simply because they are so physically astonishing. I live near Lake Superior, and I never tire of looking at it. The external geography matches my internal geography."

*   *   *

DUTKINA, Galina (Borisovna) 1952-
(Galina Annikova)

PERSONAL: Born July 11, 1952, in Tambov, Russia; daughter of Boris Andreevich (an educator and academic administrator) and Victoria Georgievna (a high school English teacher; maiden name, Annikova) Lisitsyn; married Nikolay Alekseevich Dutkin, January 26, 1972 (divorced September 17, 1986); children: Darya. *Ethnicity:* "Russian." *Education:* Moscow State University, Institute of Asian and African Countries, diploma, 1979; Russian Academy of Sciences, Ph.D., 1992. *Religion:* Christian. *Avocational interests:* Painting, photography, travel.

ADDRESSES: Home—116 Leningradskoe shosse, Flat 90, Moscow 125445, Russia; fax 095-458-8078. *Agent*—Akiko Kurita, JFC, 27-18-804 Nakaochiai, 2-chome, Shinjuku-ku, Tokyo 161, Japan.

CAREER: Moscow Radio, Japanese Section, Moscow, U.S.S.R., editor and announcer, 1974-79; Progress Publishing House, Moscow, senior editor in Oriental department, 1980-83; Raduga Publishing House, Moscow, Russia, expert editor in foreign literature department, 1983-93; Center for Postgraduate Training of High School Professors, Moscow, professor, 1993-95; freelance journalist and translator, 1995—.

MEMBER: European Association for Japanese Studies, Russian Journalists Union, Russian Translators Union.

WRITINGS:

Misuteri Mosukuwa (in Japanese; title means "Mysterious Moscow: The Diary of Galya-san"), Shinchosha (Tokyo, Japan), 1993.
Moscow Days (essays), Kodansha International (New York), 1996.

Contributor to books, including *Japan: Culture and Society Under Scientific and Technological Revolution,* Nauka (Moscow, U.S.S.R.), 1985; and *Modulations in Tradition: Japan and Korea in a Changing World,* University of Tampere, 1993. Contributor to periodicals, including *Asia and Africa Today, Modern Foreign Literature Studies Journal,* and *New Time.* Some work appears under the name Galina Annikova. Translator into Russian from Japanese and English, including books by Vonda MackIntyre, Robert Asprin, Montague R. James, N. Hoakin, Fay Weldon, and Francis King.

WORK IN PROGRESS: Castles in the Air, an autobiographical novel.

SIDELIGHTS: Galina Dutkina told *CA:* "I am writing because I cannot live without it; this is my way of life. I have been writing since I was a kid, but it was mainly verses. With age I came to understand how to make a book; that is, my job as an editor gave me some experience and revealed some of the 'know-how' of writing prose. All that was bottled inside me then is now boiling, trying to get out.

"I have been greatly influenced by romantic American literature (especially Jack London) and by the refined Japanese classics. As for Russian literature, the decadent literature of the early twentieth century had a great impact on me.

"When I write, I try not to think but just listen to my heart, and the words come to me. I decided to write a book about modern Russia because I had a feeling that people in the world underestimate the importance of some processes going on in my country nowadays. I did my best to understand the situation myself and to express clearly my point of view."

DWYER, James Francis 1874-1952

PERSONAL: Born April 22, 1874, in Camden, New South Wales; died November 11, 1952.

CAREER: Traveller and writer.

WRITINGS:

FANTASY NOVELS

The White Waterfall, Doubleday (New York), 1912.
The Spotted Panther, Doubleday, 1913.
Evelyn: Something More Than a Story, Vanguard Press (New York), 1929.
The Lady with Feet of Gold (Spillane series), Jenkins (London), 1937.
The City of Cobras (Spillane series), Jenkins, 1938.

NOVELS

The Green Half-Moon, McClurg (Chicago, IL), 1915.
O Splendid Sorcery, Vanguard Press, 1930.
The Romantic Quest of Peter Lamonte, Sampson Low (London), 1932.
Cold-Eyes, Methuen (London), 1934.
Hespamora, Methuen, 1935.

SHORT STORIES

The Bust of Lincoln, Doubleday, 1912.
Breath of the Jungle, McClurg, 1915.

OTHER

Leg Iron on Wings, Georgian House (New York), 1949.*

* * *

DYSON, Michael Eric 1958-

PERSONAL: Born October 23, 1958, in Detroit, MI; son of Everett and Addie Dyson; married Marcia Louise Dyson, June 24, 1992; children: Michael II, Maisha. *Education:* Carson-Newman, B.A. (magna cum laude), 1982; Princeton University, M.A., 1991; Ph.D., 1993. *Politics:* Democratic Socialist of America. *Religion:* Baptist.

ADDRESSES: Office—University of North Carolina, 134 1/2 East Franklin St., Chapel Hill, NC 27599.

CAREER: Mathy College, Princeton University, Princeton, NJ, assistant master; Hartford Seminary, faculty member; Chicago Theological Seminary, instructor, later assistant professor; Brown University, Providence RI, assistant professor; University of North Carolina, Chapel Hill, professor of African and Afro-American studies.

AWARDS, HONORS: National Magazine Award from the National Association of Black Journalism, 1992.

WRITINGS:

Reflecting Black: African-American Cultural Criticism (essays), University of Minnesota Press (Minneapolis, MN), 1993.
Making Malcolm: The Myth and Meaning of Malcolm X, Oxford University Press (New York, NY), 1995.
Between God and Gangsta Rap: Bearing Witness to Black Culture (essays), Oxford University Press, 1996.

SIDELIGHTS: An educator and ordained Baptist minister, Michael Eric Dyson has published several collections of writings on a wide range of African American cultural issues. *Reflecting Black: African-American Cultural Criticism* collects Dyson's journalistic writings from 1989 to 1993 on such figures as Michael Jackson, Michael Jordan, and Spike Lee, and concerning such topics as racism, sexism, film, politics, and music. While critic George Packer complained in *Chicago Tribune Books* that jargon obscures the argument in several cases, he praised Dyson's analytical ability, particularly in his critique of religious issues. According to Patricia Hill Collins in *Contemporary Sociology,* "Dyson manages to merge sophisticated theoretical analysis with a comprehensible and plausible interpretation of contemporary black culture," and Jonathan Scott, writing in *Modern Fiction Studies* called the work "in a fundamental sense . . . an autobiographical account of a good man's intellectual formation and moral activity in the world."

In his 1995 work, *Making Malcolm: The Myth and Meaning of Malcolm X,* Dyson examines the appeal of the controversial political leader to the current generation of African American males and locates Malcolm's legacy in the development of alliances between African Americans and other racial and social minorities within the United States. *Nation* reviewer Lawrence Muhammad questioned Dyson's assessment of Malcolm's influence among black youth of the rap generation. According to Muhammad, "*Making Malcolm* carefully separates the legacy from any antisocial implications, but Dyson doesn't say if Malcolm's evolution to virtue has positively influenced today's troubled teens." A *Publishers Weekly* contributor declared that Dyson's work comprises a "thoughtful, scholarly essay."

Dyson's *Between God and Gangsta Rap: Bearing Witness to Black Culture,* published in 1995, offers a collection of essays on subjects ranging from his brother's imprisonment for murder to the music of singers Mariah Carey and Vanessa Williams and offers a consideration of racial issues in the O. J. Simpson murder trial. *Time* magazine reviewer Christopher John Farley called the work "provocative," and in *Booklist* Mike Tribby praised Dyson's critique of gangsta rap music, noting his "literate and compelling argument that cultural warfare over popular music . . . is just a convenient way for society to avoid dealing with larger issues of race and class."

BIOGRAPHICAL/CRITICAL SOURCES:

PERIODICALS

Booklist, December 15, 1995, p. 671.
Chicago Tribune Books, August 8, 1993, p. 6-7.
Contemporary Sociology, July, 1994, pp. 607-08.
Library Journal, January, 1996, p. 126.
Los Angeles Times Book Review, March 26, 1995.
Modern Fiction Studies, winter, 1994, pp. 923-25.
Nation, September 27, 1993, pp. 320-23; February 13, 1995, pp. 213-15.
New York Times Book Review, November 27, 1994, p. 13; December 10, 1995, p. 26.
Publishers Weekly, October 10, 1994, pp. 55-56; October 2, 1995, p. 59.
Time, December 18, 1995, p. 80.*

E

EATON, Edith Maude 1865-1914
(Sui Sin Far, a pseudonym)

PERSONAL: Born in 1865, in Macclesfield, England; immigrated to Canada, c. 1872; died in Montreal, Quebec, Canada, 1914; daughter of Edward Eaton and Lotus Blossom Trufusis. *Education:* Attended British and Canadian grade schools.

CAREER: Writer and journalist. Worked as a stenographer, Montreal, Quebec, Canada, c. 1884-90; canvassed newspaper subscriptions in San Francisco's Chinatown, c. 1898; freelance writer, 1898-1912.

WRITINGS:

(As Sui Sin Far) *Mrs. Spring Fragrance* (novel), A. C. McClurg & Co., 1912, expanded as *Mrs. Spring Fragrance and Other Writings,* edited by Amy Ling and Annette White-Parks, University of Illinois Press (Urbana), 1995.

Under pseudonym of Sui Sin Far, contributor of numerous short stories and essays to periodicals, including *Delineator, Good Housekeeping, Land of Sunshine, New England Magazine, Independent, Overland,* and *The Westerner.*

SIDELIGHTS: Edith Maude Eaton, who wrote under the pseudonym Sui Sin Far, was the first professional writer of Asian descent—her father was English and her mother Chinese—to have her works published in North America. Using her talents as a writer and journalist to illuminate the plight of Chinese immigrants and their mixed racial heritage, Eaton's articles and short fiction, printed in many of the most widely read periodicals of the early twentieth century, were an attempt to counterbalance the popular "yellow peril" narratives, designed to arouse racist, anti-Asian sentiments. Her work also resisted the traditional social confines of Asian women; her only book-length work, 1912's *Mrs. Spring Fragrance,* features a title character who is a sophisticated, energetic, and thoroughly Westernized upper middle-class woman.

Eaton's personal knowledge of poverty, sexism, and racism inspired the strong elements of social conscience that would run through all of her written work. Asserting her own mixed race by using the Chinese translation of "water lily" as a pseudonym, she published a series of articles and short stories illuminating the Chinese American experience, all the while battling the same social prejudices about which she wrote. While Eaton would slowly gain a following, her sister, Winifred Eaton, enjoyed instant and enormous publishing success under the pseudonym "Onoto Watanna," writing exotic stories featuring stereotypical oriental settings.

Despite her numerous written works focusing on changing the popular stereotype of Chinese immigrants, Eaton would be neglected for more than half a century following her death in 1914. It would not be until the 1980s that her contributions to improving the conditions of Asian Americans would finally be recognized.

BIOGRAPHICAL/CRITICAL SOURCES:

BOOKS

Ammons, Elizabeth, *Conflicting Stories: American Women Writers at the Turn into the Twentieth*

Century, Oxford University Press (New York City), 1991.

Lai, Him Mark, Ruthanne Lum McCunn, and Judy Yung, editors, *Chinese America: History and Perspectives,* Chinese Historical Society of America (San Francisco), 1987.

Ling, Amy, *Between Worlds: Women Writers of Chinese Ancestry,* Pergamon (New York City), 1990.

Tsutakasa, Mayumi, and Alan Chong Lou, editors, *Turning Shadows into Light: Art and Culture of the Northwest's Early Asian/Pacific Community,* Young Pine Press (Seattle), 1982.

White-Parks, Annette, *Sui Sin Far/Edith Maude Eaton: A Literary Biography,* University of Illinois Press (Urbana), 1995.

PERIODICALS

American Literary Realism, autumn, 1983.
American Literature, March, 1996, p. 284.
Arizona Quarterly, winter, 1991.
Choice, March, 1996, p. 1137.
MELUS, spring, 1981.
Women's Studies International Forum, Volume 9, 1986.*

*   *   *

EBERHART, Mignon G(ood)   1899-1996

OBITUARY NOTICE—See index for *CA* sketch: Born July 6, 1899, in Lincoln, NE; died October 8, 1996, in Greenwich, CT. Author. Eberhart was a popular writer in the mystery genre, noted especially for her depiction of female sleuths, such as Sarah Keate and Susan Dare. In a career that spanned some sixty years, she wrote nearly as many books. Before her marriage and a later career as an author, she attended Nebraska Wesleyan University from 1917 to 1920. Her first book was published in 1929, her last in 1988. Her second book, *While the Patient Slept,* was awarded the Scotland Yard Prize in 1930, and was adapted for film and released in 1935. Other books by Eberhart include *R.S.V.P. Murder, Winners at Large, Message from Hong Kong, El Rancho Rio, Family Fortune, Nine O'Clock Tide, Next of Kin, Alpine Condo Cross-Fire,* and *Three Days for Emerald.* Her work, noted for being set in exotic locations, was frequently adapted for film. Novels that saw treatment on the big screen included *The White Cockatoo, Murder by an Aristocrat,* and *Hasty Wedding,* which

was released as *Three's a Crowd.* She was also the author of the story for the 1939 film, *The Murder of Dr. Harrigan.* In 1970 she received the Grand Masters Edgar Award, an honor from the Mystery Writers of America. At one time, Eberhart served as president of that organization.

OBITUARIES AND OTHER SOURCES:

BOOKS

Writers Directory, St. James Press, 1996.

PERIODICALS

New York Times, October 9, 1996, p. D19.
Washington Post, October 11, 1996, p. B6.

*   *   *

EDDISON, E(ric) R(ucker)   1882-1945

PERSONAL: Born November 24, 1882, in Adel, Yorkshire; died August 18, 1945; married Winifred Grace Henderson, 1909; children: one daughter. *Education:* Attended Oxford University.

CAREER: Civil servant, Board of Trade, from 1906; deputy comptroller-general, Department of Overseas Trade, 1930-37.

AWARDS, HONORS: Knight Commander of the Order of St. Michael and St. George, 1924; Companion of the Order of the Bath, 1929.

WRITINGS:

FANTASY NOVELS

The Worm Ouroboros: A Romance, Clark (Edinburgh), 1922, Dutton (New York), 1926.
Mistress of Mistresses: A Vision of Zimiamvia, Dutton, 1935.
A Fish Dinner in Memison, Dutton, 1941, Pan Ballantine (London), 1972.
The Mezentian Gate, Curwen Press (London), 1958, Ballantine (New York), 1969.

OTHER

Editor, *Poems, Letters, and Memories of Philip Sydney Nairn,* privately printed, 1916.

Styrbiorn the Strong (novel), Boni (New York), 1926.
Editor and translator, *Egil's Saga,* by Snorri Sturlson, University Press (Cambridge), 1930, Greenwood Press (New York), 1968.*

*   *   *

EDGERTON, Teresa (Ann)   1949-

PERSONAL: Born in 1949.

ADDRESSES: Agent—c/o Ace Publishing, Berkeley Publishing Group, 200 Madison Ave., New York, NY 10016.

CAREER: Writer.

WRITINGS:

FANTASY NOVELS

Child of Saturn (Green Lion series), Ace (New York), 1989.
The Moon in Hiding (Green Lion series), Ace, 1989.
The Work of the Sun (Green Lion series), Ace, 1990.
Goblin Moon (Goblin series), Ace, 1991.
The Gnome's Engine (Goblin series), Ace, 1991.
The Castle of the Silver Wheel (Chronicles of Celydonn trilogy), Ace, 1993.
The Grail and the Ring (Chronicles of Celydonn trilogy), Ace, 1994.
The Moon and the Thorn (Chronicles of Celydonn trilogy), Ace, 1995.

*   *   *

EDWARDS, Claudia J(ane)   1943-

PERSONAL: Born July 13, 1943, in Monterey, CA. *Education:* University of Texas, B.A., 1965.

ADDRESSES: Route 1, Box 100C, Hereford, Arizona 85615.

CAREER: Peace Corps volunteer, Palau, Micronesia, 1966-68; Joseph City Public School, AZ, elementary school teacher, 1969-70; Sierra Vista Public Schools, elementary school teacher, 1970—; writer.

WRITINGS:

FANTASY NOVELS

Taming the Forest King, Popular Library (New York), 1986.
A Horsewoman in Godsland, Popular Library, 1987.
Bright and Shining Tiger, Popular Library, 1988.
Eldrie the Healer, Pageant (New York), 1989.

*   *   *

EDWARDS, Graham   1965-

PERSONAL: Born in 1965, in Shepton Mallett, Somerset, England; married; children: two. *Education:* Attended art school in London.

ADDRESSES: Agent—c/o HarperCollins, 77-85 Fulham Palace Road, London W6 8JB, England.

CAREER: Designer and writer.

WRITINGS:

FANTASY NOVEL

Dragoncharm, HarperCollins (London), 1995.

*   *   *

EGAN, Jennifer   1962-

PERSONAL: Born September 7, 1962, in Chicago, IL; daughter of Donald Egan (a lawyer) and Kay Kimpton (an art dealer; maiden name, Kernwein); married David Herskovits (a theater director), June 25, 1994. *Education:* University of Pennsylvania, B.A., 1985; St. John's College, Cambridge, M.A., 1987.

ADDRESSES: Home—131 West 28th St., #4D, New York, NY 10001. *Agent*—c/o Nan A. Talese/ Doubleday, 1540 Broadway, New York, NY 10036.

CAREER: Free-lance writer, 1991—.

AWARDS, HONORS: Cosmopolitan/Perrier Short Story Award, 1991; fellowships from the National

Endowment for the Arts, New York Foundation for the Arts, and Guggenheim Foundation, 1996.

WRITINGS:

The Invisible Circus (novel), Nan A. Talese/ Doubleday (New York), 1995.
Emerald City and Other Stories (short stories), Nan A. Talese/Doubleday, 1996.

Also contributor to periodicals and anthologies, including *New Yorker, Seventeen, GQ, Mademoiselle, Ploughshares, Prize Stories 1993: The O. Henry Awards,* and *New York Times* magazine.

WORK IN PROGRESS: "A novel, a second story collection (both as yet untitled); also a smattering of journalism and essays."

SIDELIGHTS: Fiction writer Jennifer Egan saw her stories in print in some very prestigious magazines, including the *New Yorker* and *GQ,* before her first novel, *The Invisible Circus,* was published by Doubleday in 1995. She quickly followed this well-reviewed book with a collection of short stories, *Emerald City and Other Stories.*

The protagonist of *The Invisible Circus* is Phoebe O'Connor, whose sister, Faith, eight years her senior, leapt from a cliff in Italy under shadowy circumstances after becoming immersed in the political and psychedelic counterculture of the late 1960s. Though Phoebe was only ten when her sister died, she grew up mesmerized by Faith's brief, chaotic life and crushed by a certainty that her own would never match its intensity. At eighteen, Phoebe bolts from her San Francisco home to Europe. There, armed with the postcards Faith sent home during the trip that ended in her death, Phoebe begins following her sister's itinerary, awaiting her own entry to the transcendent world she believes Faith has reached. What she learns about her sister's death is far more troubling and complex than Phoebe could have imagined, yet finally, unexpectedly, liberating.

Critics have offered much praise for *The Invisible Circus.* Dave Edelman, reviewing the volume in *Washington Post Book World,* felt Egan had overdone some of its 1960s atmosphere, but declared it to be "an auspicious first novel for a very promising writer." Alice Truax in the *New York Times Book Review* asserted that the story of Phoebe and Faith "is told with great assurance and power. Ms. Egan por-trays the sisters with a quiet, heartbreaking clarity—she understands perfectly that grieving children will gladly exchange their futures for the privilege of remaining faithful to the dead who have left them behind." *Times Literary Supplement* contributor Sarah Francis hailed the novel as "a powerful and often disturbing study of the profound reverberations of death within a family." Francis concluded: "Egan weaves a colourful web of repetitions and re-workings, further tangled by her creative use of metaphor and her eye for the smallest detail."

Emerald City and Other Stories includes "Sacred Heart," a tale of a Catholic schoolgirl, troubled by her parents' divorce, who becomes obsessed with a classmate prone to self-mutilation. In "Why China?" a businessman, dragging his family through China for reasons he himself is not sure of, encounters the man who swindled him out of $25,000 two years earlier. The title story concerns a photographer's assistant and his girlfriend, a failing fashion model who has been told her look isn't "ugly" enough to succeed in today's market. They live in New York, which Egan compares to the Emerald City in L. Frank Baum's *The Wizard of Oz,* a chaos of glittering surfaces that suggest great meaning and depth, but are finally empty. Like *The Invisible Circus, Emerald City and Other Stories* has garnered its share of appreciation from literary critics. In *New York Times Book Review,* Donna Seaman hailed the building blocks of this collection as "boldly modulated short stories, tales of displacement and blazing moments of truth." Claire Messud, holding forth in the *Times Literary Supplement,* called it "a privilege to be taken with Egan on the world tour of her characters' lives. . . . These stories are elegant, and full of insight." Sara Nelson in *Glamour* concluded: "*Emerald City* will take your breath away."

BIOGRAPHICAL/CRITICAL SOURCES:

PERIODICALS

Glamour, February, 1996, p. 122.
Los Angeles Times Book Review, March 5, 1995, pp. 2-3.
New York Times Book Review, May 7, 1995, p. 46; March 17, 1996, p. 16.
Time, January 15, 1996, p. 72.
Times Literary Supplement, May 14, 1993, p. 24; July 14, 1995, p. 22.
Washington Post Book World, March 26, 1995, p. 6.

EISENBERG, Ellen M. 1962-

PERSONAL: Born April 20, 1962, in Washington, DC; daughter of Meyer (a lawyer) and Carolyn (a teacher; maiden name, Schoen) Eisenberg; married Ami Korsunsky, September 14, 1985; children: Alexander Samuel, Benjamin Ze'ev. *Ethnicity:* "Jewish." *Education:* Carleton College, B.A. (magna cum laude), 1985; University of Pennsylvania, Ph.D., 1990. *Religion:* Jewish.

ADDRESSES: Home—2610 High St. S.E., Salem, OR 97302. *Office*—Department of History, Willamette University, 900 State St., Salem, OR 97301. *E-mail*—eeisenbe@willamette.edu.

CAREER: Social Science Research Council, research assistant with Persistent Poverty Project, 1988-89; Willamette University, Salem, OR, assistant professor, 1990-95, associate professor of history, 1995—. Oregon Women's Penitentiary, Holocaust educator, 1995-96.

MEMBER: Phi Beta Kappa.

WRITINGS:

Jewish Agricultural Colonies in New Jersey, 1882-1920, Syracuse University Press (Syracuse, NY), 1995.

Contributor to periodicals, including *American Jewish Archives, Communal Societies, Journal of American Ethnic History,* and *Rural Roots.*

WORK IN PROGRESS: Research on Jewish immigration to the United States and Argentina and on Jews in Oregon.

* * *

EKMAN, Kerstin 1933-

PERSONAL: Born August 27, 1933, in Risinge, Sweden; father, a manufacturer. *Education:* Uppsala University, M.A., 1957.

ADDRESSES: Home—Sweden. *Agent*—c/o Doubleday, 1540 Broadway, New York, NY 10036.

CAREER: Writer. Worked as a high school teacher of Swedish and Swedish literature; worked as a literary critic.

AWARDS, HONORS: Best Swedish Detective Story Prize, 1961, for *Tre sma maestare;* elected to Swedish Academy, 1978 (resigned in protest, 1989, due to Academy's insufficient support to Salman Rushdie); Selma Lagerloef Prize, 1989; Award for Best Crime Novel from the Swedish Crime Academy; August Prize; Literary Prize of the Nordic Council, for *Haendelser vid vatten,* translation published as *Blackwater.*

WRITINGS:

Moerker och blaebaersris (title means "Darkness and Blueberry Scrub"), [Sweden], 1972, Literaturfraemjandet (Stockholm), 1990.

Haexringarna (first novel in tetralogy; title means "The Witches' Circles"), Bonnier (Stockholm), 1974.

Springkaellan (second novel in tetralogy; title means "The Spring"), Bonnier, 1976.

Vykort fraan Katrineholm, Bonnier, 1977.

Aenglahuset (third novel in tetralogy; title means "House of Angels"), Bonnier, 1979.

Doedsklockan (detective novel; title means "The Death Knell"), Bonnier, 1979.

En stad av ljus (fourth novel in tetralogy; title means "A Town of Light"), Bonnier, 1983.

Hunden, Bonnier, 1986.

Roevarna i Skuleskogen (novel; title means "The Robbers in Skule Forest"), Bonnier, 1988.

Knivkastarens kvinna (verse epic; title means "The Knife Thrower's Woman"), MaenPocket (Stockholm), 1991.

Haendelser vid vatten, Bonnier, 1993, English translation by Joan Tate published as *Blackwater,* Doubleday, 1996.

Also author of *30 meter mord,* 1959; *Han roer paa sig,* 1960; *Kalla famnen,* 1960; *Tre sma maestare* (detective novel; title means "Three Little Masters"), 1961; *Den brinnnande ugnen,* 1962; *Pukehornet,* 1967; *Menedarna* (documentary historical novel; title means "The Perjurers"), 1970; and *Mine Herrar . . . ,* 1986.

SIDELIGHTS: Kerstin Ekman's first novel to be published in English—*Haendelser vid vatten,* translated by Joan Tate as *Blackwater*—"is being marketed as a thriller—but of the longer, denser and more erotic variety, the kind that comes along once every few years and usually attracts a big audience," according to Beverly Lowry in the *New York Times Book Review.* The novel traces how the murders of a man and woman affect the rural neighboring Swedish community of Blackwater and specific townspeople eighteen years later. Writing in *Publishers Weekly,* Sybil Steinberg praised the novel as "splendid fiction, dark and compelling . . . told smoothly through multiple points of view." Commenting on Ekman's descriptive prose, *Washington Post Book World* contributor Sven Birkerts observed: "Ekman's somber moods are most effective. Nature here is no picturesque backdrop, but an animated presence, the kind we might ourselves register if we were lost in the deep words at sunset." Similarly, Lowry remarked: "Throughout the novel, Ms. Ekman's descriptions of the countryside are lush and lovingly rendered. Landscape—what we've come to call the environment—becomes a character here, as fully developed and as important to the plot as human beings." As investigation of the murders—which had remained unsolved for nearly twenty years—resumes due to new evidence, Blackwater draws tightly in to protect its own citizens. Seemingly shocked by the crime but suspicious of any questions about the past, the residents reject implications that a Blackwater citizen could be the perpetrator. Birkerts praised Ekman's ability to create vivid characters. "It is a thrilling tangle, this cast of characters that seems to generate more and more darkness as we turn the pages." Describing *Blackwater* as a fascinating, gripping, and dutifully crafted narrative, Lowry concluded: "Ms. Ekman provides us with a rich adventure, the kind of long, lush page-turner many of us crave but rarely get our hands on."

BIOGRAPHICAL/CRITICAL SOURCES:

BOOKS

Schottenius, Maria, *Den kvinnliga hemligheten: En studie i Kerstin Ekmans beraettarkonst,* Bonnier, 1992.

PERIODICALS

Library Journal, January, 1996, p. 141.
New Statesman and Society, April 21, 1995, p. 37.
New York Times Book Review, March 17, 1996, p. 24.
Publishers Weekly, December 4, 1995, p. 51.
Washington Post Book World, March 3, 1996, p. 9.*

*   *   *

ELIOT, Karen
  See HOME, Stewart

ENGLISH, Lyn D.   1953-

PERSONAL: Born May 5, 1953, in Brisbane, Queensland, Australia; daughter of Brian Henry (a company manager) and Denise Dagmar (a homemaker; maiden name, Milliner) English; married Graeme Sydney Halford (a professor of psychology), December 12, 1991. *Ethnicity:* "Australian." *Education:* Queensland University of Technology, Dip.T., 1973, B.Ed., 1978, M.Ed., 1981; University of Queensland, Ph.D., 1988. *Religion:* Anglican. *Avocational interests:* Aerobics.

ADDRESSES: Home—11 Narnoo St., Chapel Hill, Brisbane, Queensland, Australia. *Office*—Queensland University of Technology, Locked Bag 2, Red Hill, Brisbane, Queensland 4059, Australia; fax 617-3864-3643. *E-mail*—L.English@qut.edu.au.

CAREER: Classroom teacher at state primary schools in Queensland, Australia, 1974-78; Open Access Unit, Brisbane, Australia, mathematics curriculum coordinator, 1979-85; Queensland University of Technology, Brisbane, lecturer, 1982-88, senior lecturer, 1988-92, associate professor of mathematics education, 1992—, assistant director, Centre for Mathematics and Science Education, 1993—.

MEMBER: International Council for Philosophical Inquiry with Children, International Group for the Psychology of Mathematics Education, Mathematics Education Research Group of Australasia, Australian Association of Mathematics Teachers, American Educational Research Association, American Psychological Association, National Council of Teachers of Mathematics (United States), Society for Research in Child Development (United States), Queensland Association of Mathematics Teachers, Queensland Association for Philosophy for Children.

AWARDS, HONORS: Grants for research in mathematics education.

WRITINGS:

(With A. R. Baturo) *Sunshine Maths,* Years 1-7, Longman Cheshire (Melbourne, Australia), 1983-85.
(With G. Booker, C. Irons, and T. Cooper) *Primary School Mathematics: Teaching Numeration,* Centre for Research and Learning in Mathematics, Brisbane College of Advanced Education (Carseldine, Australia), 1986.

Primary School Mathematics: Teaching the Operations, Centre for Research and Learning in Mathematics, Brisbane College of Advanced Education, 1986.

Using Calculators in Primary Mathematics, Centre for Research and Learning in Mathematics, Brisbane College of Advanced Education, 1986.

(With husband Graeme S. Halford) *Mathematics Education: Models and Processes,* Lawrence Erlbaum (Mahwah, NJ), 1995.

(Editor and contributor) *Mathematical Reasoning: Analogies, Metaphors, and Images,* Lawrence Erlbaum, 1996.

Contributor to books, including *Education of Gifted and Talented Children from Populations with Special Needs,* Commonwealth Schools Commission (Canberra, Australia), 1985; *Learning and Teaching Cognitive Skills,* edited by G. Evans, Australian Council for Educational Research (Melbourne), 1991; and *Research in Early Number Learning,* edited by J. Mulligan and M. Mitchelmore, Australian Association of Mathematics Teachers, 1996. Contributor of more than fifty articles to professional journals, including *Contemporary Educational Psychology, Thinking and Reasoning, Teaching Children Mathematics, Mathematics Teacher, Journal of Mathematical Behavior,* and *Educational Studies in Mathematics.* Editor of special issue, *Mathematical Cognition.*

WORK IN PROGRESS: A cross-cultural and longitudinal study of the mathematical and analogical reasoning patterns of young children, with colleagues at the University of Maryland at College Park.

SIDELIGHTS: Lyn D. English told *CA:* "Prior to joining my university, I used to write mathematics curriculum materials for children living in remote areas of outback Queensland, Australia. These children could not attend school because of their isolation and had to study by correspondence. I traveled extensively in these areas, advising parents and tutors about how to teach their children mathematics, using the instructional materials I wrote. I also wrote a series of mathematics textbooks based on my work with these children. From there, I progressed to writing academic books that address the psychological processes of mathematics learning. My experience with the children, together with my various research projects on children's mathematical learning, has provided me with the background and motivation to pursue an academic writing career."

ERSKINE, John   1879-1951

PERSONAL: Born October 5, 1879, in New York, NY; died June 2, 1951; married Pauline Ives, 1915 (divorced); married Helen Worden; children: two. *Education:* Columbia University, B.A., 1900, M.A., 1901, Ph.D., 1903.

CAREER: Amherst College, MA, lecturer, 1903-09; associated with Columbia University, 1909-23; New York Symphony Orchestra, pianist; Juilliard School of Music, New York City, president, 1928-37.

WRITINGS:

FANTASY NOVELS

The Private Life of Helen of Troy, Bobbs Merrill (Indianapolis), 1925.

Galahad: Enough of His Life to Explain His Reputation, Bobbs Merrill, 1926.

Adam and Eve: Though He Knew Better, Bobbs Merrill, 1927.

Penelope's Man: The Homing Instinct, Bobbs Merrill, 1928.

Tristan and Isolde: Restoring Palamede, Bobbs Merrill, 1932.

Venus, The Lonely Goddess, Morrow, 1949.

OTHER NOVELS

Sincerity: A Story of Our Time, Bobbs Merrill, 1929, published in England as *Experiment in Sincerity,* Putnam (London), 1930.

Uncle Sam in the Eyes of His Family, Bobbs Merrill, 1930.

Unfinished Business, Bobbs Merrill, 1931.

Bachelor-of-Arts, Bobbs Merrill, 1934.

Forget If You Can, Bobbs Merrill, 1935.

Solomon, My Son!, Bobbs Merrill, 1935.

The Brief Hour of Francois Villon, Bobbs Merrill, 1937.

The Start of the Road, Stokes (New York), 1938.

Give Me Liberty, Stokes, 1940.

Casanova's Women: Eleven Months of a Year, Stokes, 1941.

Mrs. Doratt, Stokes, 1941.

The Voyage of Captain Bart, Lippincott (Philadelphia, PA), 1943.

SHORT STORIES

Peter Kills the Bear, Mathews and Marrot (London), 1930.

Cinderella's Daughter and Other Sequels and Consequences, Bobbs Merrill, 1930.

Young Love: Variations on a Theme, Bobbs Merrill, 1936.

The Memory of Certain Persons, Lippincott (London), 1947.

PLAYS

A Pageant of the Thirteenth Century for the Seven Hundredth Anniversary of Roger Bacon, Columbia University (New York), 1914.

Hearts Enduring: A Play in One Scene, Duffield (New York), 1920.

Jack and the Beanstalk, music by Louis Gruenberg (produced in New York, 1931), Bobbs Merrill, 1931.

Helen Retires (opera libretto), Bobbs Merrill, 1934.

POETRY

Actaeon and Other Poems, Lane (New York), 1907.

The Shadowed Hour, Lyric (New York), 1917.

Collected Poems 1907-22, Duffield, 1922.

Sonata and Other Poems, Duffield, 1925.

EDITOR

Selections from Spenser's The Faerie Queen, Longman (New York), 1905.

Selections from Tennyson's Idylls of the King, Holt, 1912.

(With W. P. Trent) *Great Writers of America,* Holt, 1912.

Lafcadio Hearn, *Interpretations of Literature,* Dodd Mead (New York), 1915.

Lafcadio Hearn, *Appreciations of Poetry,* Dodd Mead, 1916.

Lafcadio Hearn, *Life and Literature,* Dodd Mead, 1917.

(With others) *The Cambridge History of American Literature,* 4 volumes, Putnam, 1917-21, published in England as *A History of American Literature,* 4 volumes, Cambridge University Press, 1918-21.

Lafcadio Hearn, *Talks with Writers,* Dodd Mead, 1920.

Lafcadio Hearn, *Books and Habits,* Dodd Mead, 1921.

Lafcadio Hearn, *Pre-Raphaelite and Other Poets,* Dodd Mead, 1922.

A Musical Companion: A Guide to the Understanding and Enjoyment of Music, Knopf, 1935.

OTHER

The Elizabethan Lyric, Macmillan (New York), 1903.

Leading American Novelists, Holt (New York), 1910.

(With Helen Erskine) *Written English: A Guide to the Rules of Composition,* Century (New York), 1910.

The Moral Obligation to Be Intelligent and Other Essays, Duffield, 1915, revised edition, Davies (London), 1921.

Democracy and Ideals, Doran (New York), 1920.

The Kinds of Poetry and Other Essays, Duffield, 1920.

The Literary Discipline, Duffield, 1923.

American Character and Other Essays, Chautauqua Press (New York), 1927.

Prohibition and Christianity, and Other Paradoxes of the American Spirit, Bobbs Merrill, 1927.

The Delight of Great Books, Bobbs Merrill, 1928.

The Influence of Women and Its Cure, Bobbs Merrill, 1936.

Song without Words: The Story of Felix Mendelssohn (biography), Messner (New York), 1941.

The Complete Life, Messner, 1943.

The Philharmonic Symphony Society of New York: Its First Hundred Years, Macmillan, 1943.

What Is Music?, Lippincott, 1944.

The Human Life of Jesus (biography), Morrow (New York), 1945.

My Life as a Teacher, Lippincott, 1948.

My Life in Music, Morrow, 1950.

* * *

ESPRIU, Salvador 1913-1985

PERSONAL: Born July 10, 1913, in Santa Coloma de Farners, Spain; died of heart failure, February 22, 1985; buried in Arenys, Spain; son of Francesc Espriu i Torres (a lawyer) and Escolastica Castello i Molas de Espriu. *Education:* Universitat Autonoma de Barcelona, earned law degree and licentiate, c. 1924.

CAREER: Writer. Worked as director of insurance firm, c. 1924; lawyer, 1940-60.

MEMBER: International Association for the Defense of Threatened Cultures and Languages (president).

AWARDS, HONORS: Nobel Prize for Literature nominations, 1970 and 1980; Montaigne Prize,

University of Tuebingen, 1970; Premi d'Honor de las Lletres Catalanes, 1971; Premi de la Critica, 1972; honorary doctorates, University of Barcelona and University of Toulouse, both 1980; Premi Ciutat de Barcelona, 1981; gold medals, Barcelona and Catalonia, both 1982.

WRITINGS:

Israel: Esbozos biblicos (Biblical sketches), Oliva de Vilanova (Barcelona), 1929.

El Dr. Rip (dramatic monologue), Llibreria Catalonia (Barcelona), 1931, enlarged edition published as *El Dr. Rip i altres relats,* Edicions 62 (Barcelona), 1979.

Laia, Llibreria Catalonia, 1932.

Aspectes (short stories), Llibreria Catalonia, 1934.

Miratge a Citerea (title means "Mirage at Citerea"), Quaderns Literaris (Barcelona), 1935.

Ariadna a laberint grotesc (title means "Ariadna in the Grotesque Labyrinth"), Quaderns Literaris, 1935.

Letizia i altres proses (title means "Letizia, and Other Stories"), Janes (Barcelona), 1937.

Cementiri de Sinera (poetry; title means "Sinera's Cemetery"), Palau-Fabre & Triadu (Barcelona), 1946.

Primera historia d'Esther, Ayma (Barcelona), 1948, translation by Philip Polack published as *Primera historia d'Esther,* Dolphin (Oxford), 1989.

Les cancons d'Ariadna (poetry; title means "The Songs of Ariadna"), Ossa Menor (Barcelona), 1949, enlarged edition, Proa, 1973.

Obra lirica (title means "Lyrical Work"; includes *Cementiri de Sinera* and "Mrs. Death"), Ossa Menor, 1952.

Anys d'aprenentatage (title means "Years of Apprenticeship"; includes *Laia, Aspectes, La pluja,* and *Miratge a Citerea*), Selecta (Barcelona), 1952.

El caminant i el mur (poetry; title means "The Wayfarer and the Wall"), Ossa Menor, 1954.

Final del laberint (poetry; title means "End of the Labyrinth"), Atzavara (Barcelona), 1955.

Antigona; Fedra (adapted from the plays *Antigone* by Sophocles and *Phaedra* by Llorenc Villalonga, respectively), Moll (Palma de Mallorca), 1955.

Evocacio de Rossello-Porcel i altres notes (essays; title means "Evocation of Rossello Porcel, and Other Notes"), Horta (Barcelona), 1957.

La pell de brau (poetry), Salve (Barcelona), 1960, translation by Burton Raffel published as *The Bull-Hide,* Writers' Workshop (Calcutta), 1977.

Obra poetica, Alberti (Barcelona), 1963.

Gent de Sinera (play; title means "People of Sinera"), produced in Spain, c. 1965.

Narracions, Edicions 62, 1965.

(With Ricard Salvat) *Ronda de Mort a Sinera* (play), Barrigotic (Barcelona), 1966, translation by Peter Cocozzella published as *Death around Sinera* in *Modern International Drama,* Volume 14, number 1, 1980.

(Editor) *Pla Narbona, dibuixos, dibujos, drawings,* Llibres de Sinera (Barcelona), 1968.

Obres completes (five volumes), Edicions 62, 1968-90.

Tarot per a algun titella del teatre d'Alfaranja, Tarot (Barcelona), 1969.

Setmana Santa (title means "Holy Week"), Poligrafa (Barcelona), 1971.

Formes i paraules: Aproximacio a l'art d'Apel-les Fenosa, en homenatge, Edicions 62, 1975, translation by J. L. Gili published as *Form and Words,* Dolphin, 1980.

Lord of the Shadow: Poems by Salvador Espriu, Dolphin, 1975.

(With Cesar Estrany) *Dibuixos (amb algun mot) sobre temes classics,* Estrany (Barcelona), 1976.

Una altra Fedra, si us plau (play; title means "Another Phaedra, If You Please"), Edicions 62, 1978.

D'una vella i encerclada terra, Excursionista de Catalunya, 1980.

Fem pinya!, Diafora (Barcelona), 1981.

Vox diccionari manual de sinonims amb antonims i exemples, Biblograf (Barcelona), 1981.

Les roques i el mar, el blau, Edicions del Mall (Barcelona), 1981.

Sobre Xavier Nogues i la seva circumstancia, Edicions 62, 1982.

Aproximacio a Santa Coloma de Farners, Edicions del Mall, 1983.

Llibre de Sinera, Edicions 62, 1983.

Poemes i dibuixos, Taller de Picasso (Barcelona), 1984.

Petites proses blanques, la pluja i altres relacions, Gaya Ciencia (Barcelona), 1984.

Per a la bona gent (poetry; title means "For the Good People"), Edicions del Mall, 1985.

Fragments; Versots; Intencions; Matisos (poetry; title means "Fragments; Versifications; Intentions; Shades of Meaning"), Edicions 62, 1987.

Selected Poems of Salvador Espriu, translation by Magda Bogin, Norton (New York), 1989.

Work represented in anthologies, including *Antologia de contistes catalans,* edited by Joan Triadu, Selecta, 1950.

SIDELIGHTS: According to many critics, Salvador Espriu ranks among twentieth-century Spain's greatest Catalan writers. Espriu was born in 1913 in Santa Coloma de Farners, a Catalan town north of Barcelona. When Espriu was still an infant his family moved to Barcelona, where his father had found work as an estate attorney. Espriu spent much of his childhood in Barcelona, which he later fictionalized as Lavinia. The Esprius often vacationed in Arenys, a coastal town, and Espriu became quite fond of Arenys and its inhabitants; he later wrote of the community as Sinera in various tales and verses.

Though he aspired to more scholarly pursuits, Espriu studied law in Barcelona, and it was in that profession that he eventually commenced working after his father's death in 1940. Espriu headed his late father's law practice for the next twenty years, and he also helped manage an insurance firm established by his physician brother, Josep. Espriu was a loner who held a particularly somber view of life. Accordingly, he soon turned to writing as a means of expressing himself on matters ranging from Biblical events to Catalan life. In 1929 he published *Israel: Esbozos biblicos,* a compilation of sketches derived from Espriu's Bible readings. Two years later he produced *El Dr. Rip,* a dramatic monologue in which a doctor considers his own inevitable demise from cancer. Espriu further demonstrated his versatility with *Laia,* the tale of a wicked seductress who dooms her exuberant lover.

Throughout the 1930s, Espriu produced an extensive range of writings. In 1934 he published *Aspectes,* a short-story collection notable for introducing Espriu's alter-ego, Salom de Sinera, a character who would reappear in later works, and in 1935 Espriu completed *Ariadna a laberint grotesc* (which means "Ariadna in the Grotesque Labyrinth"), a collection of literary sketches, ballads, and anecdotal accounts. Also in 1935, he published *Miratge a Citerea* (which means "Mirage at Citerea"), a novel presented as the diary of Carlota, a teenage girl. And in 1937 he produced the short story collection *Letizia i altres proses,* which means "Letizia, and Other Stories", and which includes a modernization of the Phaedra legend in which Carlota serves as a first-person narrator.

Espriu failed to publish anything during World War II, but two years after the war he completed his first verse collection, *Cementiri de Sinera,* which means

"Sinera's Cemetery." In this volume Espriu shows himself to be a rather minimalist poet holding a bleak, existentialist outlook. He also proves somewhat of a rebel, for he published the volume in Catalan at a time, following the nationalists' triumph, when Catalan discourse, at least in print, was widely considered offensive. Espriu followed *Cementiri de Sinera* with the dramatic *Primera historia d'Esther,* in which a Biblical play is enacted in Sinera. A *Times Literary Supplement* reviewer noted that in this tale Espriu managed to "superimpose the Old Testament story [of Esther] on the world of his own childhood."

Espriu's next notable verse collection, *Les cancons d'Ariadna* (which means "The Songs of Ariadna"), serves as further indication of his stature as a master of minimalist melancholia. *Dictionary of Literary Biography* contributor Peter Cocozzella noted that the poems in *Les cancons d'Ariadna* amply demonstrate Espriu's artistry as a poet of both "microcosmic concentration and . . . macrocosmic projection." In addition, Cocozzella observed that Espriu generates a "primordial tension which . . . determines the dialectic" between the two aforementioned elements of his poetry.

In 1952 Espriu published *Obra lirica* (which means "Lyrical Work"), a poetry collection addressing such subjects as death, the Spanish Civil War, and life in Sinera. Two years later he completed *El caminant i el mur* (which means "The Wayfarer and the Wall"), a three-part verse volume exemplifying the more metaphysical aspects of Espriu's art. In this volume Espriu writes of the minotaur, the river Styx, and Biblical demons. Less grandiose evocations of doom are evinced in *Final del laberint* (which means "End of the Labyrinth"), Espriu's 1955 volume, in which rural events and images are emphasized.

Among the most significant of Espriu's ensuing works is *The Bull-Hide,* a series of poems concerning Catalan life. A *Times Literary Supplement* reviewer described *The Bull-Hide* as "a sequence in which the collective situation of the peninsular peoples is focused through themes and images taken from the history of the Jews in exile." The same reviewer praised *The Bull-Hide* as "one of [Espriu's] finest collections of poems." In 1960 Espriu adapted *The Bull-Hide* for the stage, and during the 1960s he produced such stage works as *Gent de Sinera* (which means "People of Sinera") and, with Ricard Salvat, *Ronda de Mort a Sinera* (which means "Death around Sinera").

Espriu published significantly less during the 1970s, but produced several more volumes in the early 1980s. Notable among these publications is *Per a la bona gent* (which means "For the Good People"), which includes both poignant, personal poems and more humorous verses. Emilie L. Bergmann, writing in *World Literature Today,* reported that the volume serves as "a clear demonstration of the expressive power of Catalan as a poetic language."

Since his death in 1985, Espriu has remained, despite his prolific output, somewhat unknown to English-language readers. However, *Selected Poems of Salvador Espriu,* translated by Magda Bogin, was favorably received upon its publication in 1989. A *Voice Literary Supplement* reviewer acknowledged Espriu as "the foremost young Catalan writer of the prewar years" and declared that *Selected Poems* "brilliantly captured Espriu's taut energy, his bluntness and restraint."

BIOGRAPHICAL/CRITICAL SOURCES:

BOOKS

Contemporary Literary Criticism, Volume 9, Gale, 1978.
Dictionary of Literary Biography, Volume 134: *Twentieth-Century Spanish Poets, Second Series,* Gale, 1994.

PERIODICALS

Los Angeles Times, February 27, 1985, p. B2.
Modern Language Review, October, 1994, pp. 889-901.
Parnassus, fall/winter, 1979, pp. 64-83.
Times Literary Supplement, July 11, 1968, p. 727; February 6, 1976, p. 127.
Voice Literary Supplement, July, 1989, p. 6.
World Literature Today, spring, 1977, pp. 224-27; spring, 1979, p. 275; spring, 1982, p. 323; spring, 1985, pp. 77-78; winter, 1987, pp. 86-87; spring, 1989, p. 295.*

ESTOW, Clara 1945-

PERSONAL: Born April 20, 1945, in Cali, Colombia; U.S. citizen. *Education:* Southern Illinois University at Carbondale, B.A., 1965; Brandeis University, M.A., 1967, Ph.D., 1975.

ADDRESSES: Home—1546D Drift Rd., Westport, MA 02790. *Office*—Department of Hispanic Studies, University of Massachusetts, Boston, MA 02125.

CAREER: University of Massachusetts at Amherst, instructor, 1968-71, assistant professor, 1974-82, associate professor, 1982-94, professor of Hispanic studies, 1994—, department head, 1989-92, department head at Harbor Campus, Boston, 1995—, director of Latin American studies program, 1995-98, member of executive committee, Center for World Languages and Cultures. International Institute Foundation in Spain, director of executive committee, 1989-90; Colombia Consulate, Boston, liaison for international faculty exchange; Massachusetts Foundation for the Humanities, workshop leader, 1992-95. Camp Hemlock Hill, director, 1968.

MEMBER: American Academy of Research Historians of Medieval Spain, Society for Spanish and Portuguese Historical Studies, Association Villard de Honnecourt for the Interdisciplinary Study of Medieval Technology, Science, and Art.

WRITINGS:

Pedro the Cruel of Castile, 1350-1369, E. J. Brill (Kinderhook, NY), 1995.

Contributor to books, including *Upon My Husband's Death: Widows in the Literature and Histories of Medieval Europe,* edited by Louise Mirrer, University of Michigan Press (Ann Arbor, MI), 1992; and *Spain and the Mediterranean,* edited by Benjamin Taggie and others, Thomas Jefferson University Press, 1992. Contributor of articles and reviews to periodicals, including *Mediterranean Studies, Medieval Forum, Fifteenth Century Studies,* and *Speculum.*

F

FAIG, Kenneth W(alter), Jr. 1948-

PERSONAL: Born August 24, 1948, in Cincinnati, OH; son of Kenneth Walter (in laundry industry) and Edith Frances (a bank teller and medical secretary; maiden name, Kennedy) Faig; married Carol Ann Gaber (an office worker), May 19, 1979; children: Edith Mary, Walter Gerard. *Ethnicity:* "White." *Education:* Northwestern University, B.A., 1970, graduate study, 1970-72. *Religion:* Roman Catholic. *Avocational interests:* "Amateur journalism."

ADDRESSES: Home—2311 Swainwood Dr., Glenview, IL 60025-2741. *Office*—PolySystems, 30 North LaSalle St., No. 3600, Chicago, IL 60602.

CAREER: North American Company for Life and Health Insurance, Chicago, IL, actuary, 1973-87; All State Life Insurance Co., Northbrook, IL, actuary, 1987-89; PolySystems, Chicago, actuary, 1989—. Moshassuck Press, publisher, 1987—.

MEMBER: National Amateur Press Association, Society of Actuaries, Rhode Island Historical Society, Rhode Island Genealogical Society, Providence Preservation Society, Foster Preservation Society, The Fossils.

WRITINGS:

H. P. Lovecraft: His Life, His Work, Necronomicon Press (West Warwick, RI), 1979.
The Parents of H. P. Lovecraft, Necronomicon Press, 1990.
Some of the Descendants of Asaph Phillips and Esther Whipple, Moshassuck Press, 1993.

Tales of the Lovecraft Collectors (fiction), Necronomicon Press, 1995.

WORK IN PROGRESS: Two New England novels, completion expected in 2002; research on H. P. Lovecraft and Edith Miniter; research on tontines in Foster, RI; research on St. Dymphna.

SIDELIGHTS: Kenneth W. Faig, Jr. told *CA:* "As a writer, editor, publisher, and researcher, my principal aim is to pursue themes and subjects which would otherwise remain unexplored."

*   *   *

FAIRSTEIN, Linda A. 1947(?)-

PERSONAL: Born May 5, 1947 (one source says 1948), in Mt. Vernon, NY; daughter of Samuel Johnson (a physician) and Alice (a registered nurse; maiden name, Atwell) Fairstein; married Justin N. Feldman (a lawyer), May 2, 1987; children: three stepchildren. *Education:* Vassar College, A.B., 1969; University of Virginia School of Law, J.D., 1972. *Religion:* Jewish.

ADDRESSES: Office—Office of the District Attorney, Sex Crimes Prosecution Unit, 1 Hogan Place, New York, NY 10013. *Agent*—c/o Esther Newberg, International Creative Management, 40 West 57th St., New York, NY 10019.

CAREER: New York County District Attorney's Office, appointed to staff, 1972, chief of sex crimes prosecution unit, 1976—, deputy chief of trial division, 1981—. Member of the board of directors for several non-profit organizations, including Mount Sinai Hospital Friends of the Rape Crisis Intervention Program, 1990—, New York Women's Agenda, 1993—, and Phoenix House Foundation, 1994—. Member of Governor Cuomo's Task Force on Rape, 1989-92; co-chair of New York Women's Agenda Domestic Violence Committee, 1993—; member of President Clinton's Violence against Women Advisory Council, 1995; member of American Bar Association National Conference of Lawyers and Representatives of the Media, 1995—. National Lecturer on such topics as violence against women, domestic violence, and aspects of the criminal justice system to professional organizations, colleges and universities, health care professionals, and women's groups.

MEMBER: Women's Bar Association, American College of Trial Lawyers, Federal Bar Council (member of Board of Trustees, 1993—), Mystery Writers of America, Sisters in Crime, New York Women's Forum, Association of the Bar of the City of New York (Judiciary committee member, 1985-88; Legal Issues affecting Crime Victims committee member, 1993—).

AWARDS, HONORS: Emory Buckner Award, Federal Bar Council, 1991, for Distinguished Public Service; First Distinguished Alumna Award, University of Virginia Women's Center, 1991; "Life of the City Award," *New York Woman,* 1991; named one of twenty "Outstanding Young Lawyers" who make a difference, American Bar Association, 1991; "Woman of Achievement Award," American Association of University Women, 1992, for outstanding achievement in the legal profession; Proskauer Award, United Jewish Appeal-Federation of Jewish Philanthropies of New York, Lawyers Division, 1992, for distinguished public service; Woman of the Year Award, *Glamour,* 1993, for publication of *Sexual Violence: Our War against Rape;* Woman of the Year Award, *New Woman,* 1993; 1994 Achievement Award, National Women's Political Caucus; Woman of the Year Award, Women's Projects and Productions, 1994; Public Figure Leadership Award, Older Women's League, 1994; Distinguished Woman of the Year Award, Boy Scouts of America, 1994; Women's Focus Award, Central Synagogue, 1996; International Woman of Achievement Award, Soroptomists, 1996; *Sexual Violence* was named a *New York Times* notable book of the year; Humanitarian Award, National Conference of Christians and Jews, 1996.

WRITINGS:

Sexual Violence: Our War against Rape, Morrow (New York), 1993.
Final Jeopardy, Scribner (New York), 1996.
Likely to Die, Scribner, 1997.

SIDELIGHTS: In *Sexual Violence: Our War against Rape* New York attorney Linda A. Fairstein draws on her experience as head of the Sex Crimes Unit to write an account of actual crimes combined with descriptions of the horrors of rape and the progress of the law. While presenting actual cases, Fairstein describes the response of her co-workers as they defend victims and pursue the criminals. In addition, Fairstein portrays rape for the violent crime that it is, whether it is committed by a total stranger or a known acquaintance of the victim. *Washington Post Book World* contributor Elizabeth Fox-Genovese observes that "the finest quality of this book lies in the author's ability to sustain a balance between her feelings as a woman and her professional loyalty to co-workers whom she obviously respects." Susan Estrich declares in the *Los Angeles Times Book Review* that Fairstein "has written a smart, serious, interesting book." Ann Jones, writing in the *Women's Review of Books,* concludes that one of the "remarkable" things about *Sexual Violence* is that "we're in the presence here of a genuinely unassuming and dedicated public servant who will not be discouraged. In her spare time, Fairstein has written the kind of book that makes you want to shake her hand and then get to work."

Following the success of her first publication, Fairstein tried her hand at fiction. *Final Jeopardy* presents New York Assistant District Attorney Alexandra Cooper who, like Fairstein, is in charge of prosecuting sex crimes. When a friend staying at Alexandra's house on Martha's Vineyard is found dead, the young attorney finds herself questioning if she was really the target of the crime. Fairstein "brings to her exciting first novel the same passions and insights into the criminal and crime-busting minds that marked her memoir, *Sexual Violence,*" asserts a *Publishers Weekly* contributor. *Library Journal* contributor Charles Michaud similarly observes: "This thriller, which will keep readers asking questions and turning pages, has the potential to be one of the summer's big hits."

Fairstein told *CA:* "I have just started my twenty-fifth year as a prosecutor in New York City, which is an enormously satisfying and constantly interesting job.

I have now had the opportunity to write about it as both non-fiction and fiction. For me, the series of crime novels is an extraordinary opportunity to inform readers about the criminal justice system and to entertain them at the same time."

BIOGRAPHICAL/CRITICAL SOURCES:

PERIODICALS

Interview, June, 1989.
Kirkus Reviews, April 1, 1996.
Library Journal, April 15, 1996.
Los Angeles Times Book Review, December 19, 1993, pp. 1, 15.
Ms., September, 1987; June, 1988.
New York Times Book Review, September 19, 1993, p. 1; December 5, 1993, p. 68; July 16, 1995, p. 32; December 3, 1995, p. 88.
New York Times Sunday Magazine, February 25, 1990.
Publishers Weekly, April 1, 1996.
Tribune Books (Chicago), May 28, 1995, p. 8.
Washington Post Book World, January 16, 1994, p. 5.
Women's Review of Books, January, 1994, p. 14.

* * *

FAQIH, Ahmed 1942-

PERSONAL: Born December 28, 1942, in Mizda, Libya; son of Ibrahim (a shopkeeper) and Mabruka (a homemaker; maiden name, Abulqasim; present surname, ul-Tir) El Faqih; married Baya al-Ashter, 1966; children: Ibrahim, Hisham, Lamia, Aladdin, Najla. *Ethnicity:* "Arab." *Education:* University of Edinburgh, Ph.D.

ADDRESSES: Home and office—5 Porchester Square Mews, The Colonnades, London W2, England.

CAREER: Worked for twenty-five years as a journalist and literary editor for journals in Arab countries such as Libya; *Azure,* editor in chief.

WRITINGS:

Gardens of the Night (trilogy of novels), Quartet Books (London, England), c. 1995.

Author of *The Gazelles,* a play produced at Shaw Theatre; also author of another play in English, which was also produced. Author of novels, short stories, and essays in Arabic, some of which appear in English-language periodicals.

WORK IN PROGRESS: Fields of Ashes, a novel; two books of short stories; translations of his Arabic works into English.

SIDELIGHTS: Ahmed Faqih told *CA:* "I have published twenty books so far—novels, short stories, plays, and essays. They were published in Arabic, and some of them were translated into other languages. In the English language, two plays have been performed and short stories have been published in many journals.

"I write to satisfy a natural inclination to let go of the steam gathering beneath my ribs, also to communicate with my fellow human beings. The struggle between old values and new ones, as reflected in human behavior, is what inspires me most."

* * *

FAY, Erica
See STOPES, Marie (Charlotte)

* * *

FEIST, Raymond E(lias) 1945-

PERSONAL: Born in 1945, in California; married Kathlyn Starbuck (a novelist); children: one daughter. *Education:* Attended University of California, San Diego.

ADDRESSES: Agent—c/o Doubleday, 1540 Broadway, New York, NY 10036.

CAREER: Writer.

WRITINGS:

FANTASY NOVELS; RIFTWAR SERIES

Magician, Doubleday (New York), 1982, published in two volumes as *Magician: Apprentice* and *Magician: Master,* Bantam (New York), 1986, revised edition, Doubleday, 1992.
Silverthorn, Doubleday, 1985.

A Darkness at Sethanon, Doubleday, 1986.
Prince of the Blood, Doubleday, 1989.
The King's Buccaneer, Doubleday, 1992.

FANTASY NOVELS; EMPIRE SERIES

(With Janny Wurts) *Daughter of the Empire,* Doubleday, 1987.
(With Wurts) *Servant of the Empire,* Doubleday, 1990.
(With Wurts) *Mistress of the Empire,* Doubleday, 1992.

FANTASY NOVELS; THE SERPENTWAR SAGA

Shadow of a Dark Queen, Doubleday, 1994.
Rise of a Merchant Prince, Morrow, 1995.

OTHER NOVELS

Faerie Tale, Doubleday, 1988.

*   *   *

FERGUSSON, Bruce (Chandler)   1951-

PERSONAL: Born March 7, 1951, in Bridgeport, CT. *Education:* Attended Wesleyan University.

ADDRESSES: Agent—c/o William Morrow and Co., Inc., 1350 Avenue of the Americas, New York, NY 10019.

CAREER: Times, Hartford, CT, reporter and photographer; worked briefly in advertising; writer.

WRITINGS:

FANTASY NOVELS

The Shadow of His Wings, Arbor House (New York), 1987.
The Mace of Souls, Morrow (New York), 1989.

*   *   *

FERREE, Myra Marx   1949-

PERSONAL: Born October 10, 1949, in Morristown, NJ; daughter of Irwin F. (a factory worker) and

Marguerite (Sosnoski) Marx; married G. Donald Ferree, Jr., June 5, 1971. *Education:* Bryn Mawr College, A.B., 1971; Harvard University, Ph.D., 1976. *Religion:* Episcopalian.

ADDRESSES: Home—Storrs, CT. *Office*—Department of Sociology, U-68, University of Connecticut, Storrs, CT 06269-2068. *E-mail*—ferree@uconnvm.uconn.edu.

CAREER: University of Connecticut, Storrs, professor of sociology and women's studies, 1976—. Guest professor, University of Frankfurt, 1985, and Flinders University, 1993.

MEMBER: American Sociological Association (vice president, 1996), Eastern Sociological Society.

AWARDS, HONORS: Fellow, German Marshall Fund, 1990.

WRITINGS:

(With Beth Hess) *Controversy and Coalition,* Twayne (New York), 1985, 2nd edition, G. K. Hall (Thorndyke, ME), 1994.

Coeditor of the book *Feminist Organizations,* Temple University Press (Philadelphia, PA). Editor of the series "Perspectives on Gender," Routledge.

WORK IN PROGRESS: Gender in Germany: Comparative Feminist Politics; research on the abortion discourse in Germany and the United States; research on emergent feminism in Russia.

*   *   *

FICOWSKI, JERZY   1924-

PERSONAL: Born September 4, 1924, in Warsaw, Poland; son of Tadeusz (a lawyer and civil servant) and Halina Ficowski; married Wanda Komala (an artist), May 4, 1951 (divorced); married Elzbieta Bussold (a writer), November 21, 1968; children: (first marriage) Krystyna, Magdalena; (second marriage) Anna. *Education:* Attended the University of Warsaw, 1946-50. *Avocational interests:* The study of Gypsy folklore; history and cultural heritage of Polish Jews; the life and work of Polish-Jewish writer Bruno Schulz.

ADDRESSES: Home—Plac Inwalidow 4/6/8, m. 41, 01-553 Warsaw, Poland.

CAREER: Writer. Travelled with Gypsy caravans, 1948-50; worked with Mazowsze (Polish national song and dance ensemble), 1951. *Military service:* Served in the Polish underground Home Army during World War II; fought in Warsaw Uprising, 1944; imprisoned, 1944-45.

MEMBER: Stowarzyszenie Pisarzy Polskich (Polish Writers' Association), PEN Club, Polish Centre (board member), Gypsy Lore Society (England); honorary member of Gypsy Cultural Society (Poland), Polish Society of Righteous Among the Nations, and Polish Society of Children of the Holocaust.

AWARDS, HONORS: Polish PEN Club Award, 1977, for translation work; Poets' and Painters' Press Award, London, 1981; Alfred Jurzykowski Foundation Award, New York, 1984; K. Tzetnik Award in Holocaust Literature, Jerusalem, 1986; Jan Karski Award at the Yivo Institute, New York, 1994.

WRITINGS:

Cyganie polscy, Wydawn (Krakow), 1953, translated as *The Gypsies in Poland: History and Customs,* Interpress (Warsaw), 1989.

Galazka z drzewa slonca, Nasza Ksiegarnia (Warsaw), 1961, translated by Lucia M. Borski as *Sisters of the Bird and Other Gypsy Tales,* illustrated by Charles Mikolayczak, Abingdon (Nashville), 1976.

Odczytanie popiolow, Association of Jews of Polish Origin in Great Britain, 1979, translated by Keith Bosley with Krystyna Wandycz as *A Reading of Ashes: Poems,* foreword by Zbigniew Herbert, Menard Press (London), 1981.

(Editor) *Letters and Drawings of Bruno Schulz,* translated by Walter Arendt with Victoria Nelson, preface by Adam Zagajewski, Harper (New York City), 1988.

(Editor and author of introduction) Bruno Schulz, *Xiega balwochwalcza,* translated by Bogna Piotrowska as *The Book of Idolatry,* Interpress, 1988.

(Editor and author of introduction) Ewa Kuryluk, *The Drawings of Bruno Schulz,* Northwestern University Press (Evanston, IL), 1990.

Author of numerous collections of poetry published in Polish, including *Olowiana zolnierze* ("Tin Soldiers"), 1948, *Amulety i definicje* ("Amulets and Definitions"), 1960, and *Smierc jednorozca* ("Death of a Unicorn"), 1981. Author of short story collections, including *Czekanie na sen psa* ("Waiting for the Dog to Sleep"), 1970. Translator of works by: J. Katzenelson, *Piesn o zamordowanym zydowskim narodzie* ("Song of the Murdered Jewish Nation"), 1983, 1986; Gypsy poet Papuscha, 1956, 1973, 1990; translator of Yiddish, Romanian, and Spanish works into Polish, including Frederico Garcia Lorca's *Gypsy Romances* and poems from the classic *Book of One Thousand and One Nights.*

SIDELIGHTS: Jerzy Ficowski is a Polish poet, translator, and expert on Gypsy lore. Born into an educated Warsaw family in 1924, Ficowski served in the Polish underground Home Army during World War II and was imprisoned after the Warsaw Uprising of 1944. After the war's end, he studied sociology and philosophy at Warsaw University, but also embarked on a two-year-long journey with a group of Gypsies. Ficowski was fascinated by this nomadic population—historically treated as Eastern European society's outcasts—and later wrote several books based on his studies. These include *Cyganie polscy,* a 1953 look at Poland's Gypsy population, and *Galazka z drzewa slonca,* a collection of Gypsy tales narrated by Ficowski, published in 1961. The 1976 work *Sisters of the Bird and Other Gypsy Tales* is a selection from *Galazka z drzewa slonca* and, apart from "Gypsies in Poland," is Ficowski's only work in this area to be made available in English translation.

Ficowski's own poetry also achieved recognition; during the 1960s and 1970s numerous volumes of his verse appeared in print in Poland. However, the writer ran afoul of Communist authorities and his work was banned in his homeland after 1975. Only one of Ficowski's collections of poetry has been translated into English, 1981's *A Reading of Ashes: Poems,* undertaken by Keith Bosley with Krystyna Wandycz from the Polish version, originally published in English in London. The translation introduces English readers to Ficowski through twenty-five poems that share as their basis the Holocaust, providing a literary commentary on the systematic murder of Poland's Jewish population, then the largest in Europe. The collection was translated into several other languages, including Swedish, German, French, Hebrew, and Yiddish. A poem "List do Marc Chagalla" ("A Letter to Marc Chagall"), later included in *A Reading of Ashes,* was published in France with original illustrations by Marc Chagall.

Ficowski has also delved extensively into the life and work of Bruno Schulz, a Polish-Jewish writer and artist who was killed by the Nazis. The first of his two volumes on Schulz, *Letters and Drawings of Bruno Schulz,* was published in English translation in the late 1980s. Schulz, a high school art teacher in a small town in Poland, gained fame in the 1930s with two acclaimed collections of short stories, one of which he illustrated himself; his renderings recall the more sinister moments of German Expressionism. In *Letters and Drawings* editor Ficowski has assembled a scrapbook-like montage of drawings juxtaposed with Schulz's extensive correspondence; he has also tracked down and interviewed individuals who knew the late artist personally. Of his editorship, Stanislaw Baranczak of the *New Republic* asserted, "[i]t is largely thanks to him that we are left today not only with Schulz's self-portrayal as it is reflected obliquely on the pages of his two wondrous collections of short stories, but also with Schulz's image in a more literal sense: with his unforgettable face staring at us from the pages of this book." Ficowski also served as editor of 1990's *The Drawings of Bruno Schulz,* a comprehensive collection of other of Schulz's artistic endeavors; he also penned the book's introduction.

BIOGRAPHICAL/CRITICAL SOURCES:

PERIODICALS

New Republic, January 2, 1989, p. 29.
New York Times Book Review, August 25, 1991, p. 54.
Wilson Library Bulletin, March, 1991, p. 134.
World Literature Today, summer, 1982, p. 543.

*   *   *

FINLEY, Karen 1956-

PERSONAL: Born in 1956, in Evanston, IL; daughter of an appliance salesman and a civil rights activist; married Brian Routh (a performance artist; divorced); married Michael Overn (a theatrical manager); children: Violet Marie. *Education:* San Francisco Art Institute. *Religion:* Roman Catholic.

ADDRESSES: Home—Nyack, NY. *Agent*—c/o City Lights Books, Inc., 261 Columbus Ave., San Francisco, CA 94133.

CAREER: Performance artist in New York City and elsewhere since the 1980s. Visual artist; has exhibited paintings, sculptures, and other installations. Sound recordings have included *Jump in the River; Never Get Old* (with Sinead O'Connor), Chrysalis, 1988.

AWARDS, HONORS: New York Dance and Performance Award, 1987, for *The Constant State of Desire;* National Endowment for the Arts grant, 1991; Guggenheim fellowship, 1993.

WRITINGS:

(And illustrator) *Shock Treatment,* City Lights (San Francisco), 1990.
(And illustrator) *Enough Is Enough: Weekly Meditations for Living Dysfunctionally* (aphorisms), Poseidon Press (New York City), 1993.
A Certain Level of Denial, illustrated by husband, Michael Overn, in press.
Living It Up, Random House, in press.

Also author of performance pieces *The Constant State of Desire,* 1987; *We Keep Our Victims Ready,* 1990; and *A Certain Level of Denial,* 1992.

WORK IN PROGRESS: A performance piece, *The American Chestnut.*

SIDELIGHTS: Karen Finley is a painter, sculptor, performance artist, and writer who is best known as one of the "N.E.A. Four," a group of theatrical artists who were denied funding from the National Endowment for the Arts in 1990 after their works were criticized as pornographic by influential conservative media commentators. Finley herself was singled out by critics Rowland Evans and Robert Novak; reviewing her 1990 performance of *We Keep Our Victims Ready* in the *Washington Post,* Evans and Novak dubbed her "a nude, chocolate-smeared young woman." In the second act of her show, Finley did indeed coat her naked body with chocolate and cover herself with alfalfa sprouts and other items while delivering an emotionally charged diatribe on such topics as rape, poverty, suicide, incest, female exploitation, and homophobia.

Reaction to Finley's stage presentations has run the gamut between defending the artist's feminist stance and condemning her radical posturing as "obscene." Marcelle Clements, who interviewed Finley for the *New York Times* shortly after the artist's N.E.A. funding was denied, declared that "Finley does on stage and in public what many of the bravest performers practice only as exercises in the relative safety and privacy of acting classes. Her work is nearly always shocking and invariably . . . political. It is also sometimes humorous and often fearsome. Her beat is the intolerable." However, Laura Jacobs took exception to Finley's performance in the *New Leader,* noting the actress's "sledgehammer polemics" and stating that Finley "never moves beyond confrontational complaint. . . . *Victims* is not obscene. It is simply loud and dogmatic, with a striking, inflammatory gimmick."

In late 1990 Finley published *Shock Treatment,* which includes the texts of two of her performance pieces along with writings not intended for the stage. A reviewer in *Publishers Weekly* noted that the book "boldly crosses the border between the political and the profane at a time when that region is in hot dispute." Tom Hall, assessing *Shock Treatment* for the *San Francisco Review of Books,* declared, "There is a great ugly humor here that must be uplifting and life-affirming for victims of our male-oriented society."

Finley followed *Shock Treatment* with *Enough Is Enough: Weekly Meditations for Living Dysfunctionally,* a collection of humorous aphorisms that was published in 1993. In a favorable review, a *Publishers Weekly* critic called the book a "slyly hilarious lampoon of the self-help and daily meditations genres."

BIOGRAPHICAL/CRITICAL SOURCES:

PERIODICALS

Belles Lettres, summer, 1991, pp. 32-36.
Nation, December 10, 1990, pp. 737-39.
New Leader, October 29, 1990, p. 23.
New York Times, July 22, 1990, pp. 5, 7; June 5, 1994, sec. 2, pp. 1, 30.
Publishers Weekly, September 14, 1990, pp. 90, 92; October 5, 1990, p. 94; September 20, 1993, pp. 56-57.
San Francisco Review of Books, January, 1991, p. 56.
Washington Post, May 11, 1990.*

*   *   *

FIRESTONE, Shulamith 1945-

PERSONAL: Born in 1945, in Ottawa, Ontario, Canada; married. *Education:* Attended Yavneh of Telshe Yeshiva and Washington University, St. Louis; Art Institute, Chicago, B.F.A. (painting).

ADDRESSES: Office—c/o William Morrow Publishers, 1350 Avenue of the Americas, New York, NY 10019.

CAREER: Writer and activist; cofounder of feminist organizations, including Radical Women, 1967, Redstockings, 1969, and New York Radical Feminists, 1969.

WRITINGS:

(Editor) *Notes from the First Year: Women's Liberation,* NYRW (New York City), 1968.
(Editor) *Redstocking,* [New York City], 1969.
(Editor, with Anne Koedt) *Notes from the Second Year: Radical Feminism,* [New York City], 1970.
The Dialectic of Sex: The Case for Feminist Revolution, Morrow (New York City), 1970, revised edition, Bantam (New York City), 1971.

SIDELIGHTS: Noted for her role as co-founder of New York Radical Women, the Redstockings, and New York Radical Feminists, Shulamith Firestone played a leading role in the formation of an independent women's movement during the 1960s and 1970s. Rather than working solely in support of groups like the National Organization for Women (NOW), which operated within the status quo to achieve equal opportunity for women, Firestone's brand of feminism attempted to radically transform American social and political life, linking itself to such left-wing protest movements as those to end the Vietnam conflict and gain civil rights for African Americans.

Frustrated with the overall hostility toward a feminist ideology, Firestone joined several other women in establishing the Chicago Westside feminist group in 1967; this would be the first women's liberation group formed in the United States. She then moved to New York City and organized New York Radical Women (NYRW). Over the next two years Firestone would found two more women's liberation groups: Redstockings, which took its name from "Bluestocking," a nineteenth-century term derogatorily used to describe a female intellectual; and the even more leftist New York Radical Feminists (NYRF). Firestone's problem with each of these groups was that their platforms were not radical enough in believing that socialism alone would liberate women; she eventually disassociated herself with radical feminist group politics altogether.

Although Firestone had not thought of herself as a writer, her work with NYRW inspired 1968's *Notes from the First Year: Women's Liberation,* an analysis of female oppression and a description of that group's relationship to the mainstream women's liberation movement. Firestone edited and contributed to this volume, as well as to a subsequent volume, 1970's *Notes from the Second Year: Radical Feminism.* In both books her contributions focused on philosophical position papers, or "Manifestos," and controversies within the NYRW in which she had been personally involved.

By the time *The Dialectic of Sex: The Case for Feminist Revolution,* was published in 1970, Firestone's involvement with the organized women's liberation movement had ended. Instead, she used her book to put forth her own feminist version of the Marxist dialectic, in which sex and the circumstances of reproduction replace economic class and the means of production as the driving forces behind history. In Firestone's view the source of women's oppression is biology; just as the liberation of the proletariat required an economic upheaval, so the liberation of the female sex would require a biological revolution resulting in an androgynous culture brought about by technological reproduction: test-tube conception and the development of artificial wombs for fetal gestation.

Not surprisingly, *The Dialectic of Sex* created a great deal of controversy. Condemned by the majority of mainstream reviewers for its radical position, Firestone's book nonetheless became a national bestseller and was considered by many feminists as one of the most influential books of the era. "No survey of feminist theory can be considered complete unless it includes *The Dialectic of Sex* as one of the leading expressions of the radical feminist perspective," commented Eileen Bresnahan in *Feminist Writers;* "no history of second-wave feminism can be written without acknowledging Shulamith Firestone as one of the movement's major architects."

BIOGRAPHICAL/CRITICAL SOURCES:

BOOKS

Donovan, Josephine, *Feminist Theory: The Intellectual Traditions of American Feminism,* Ungar (New York City), 1994.
Echols, Alice, *Daring to Be Bad: Radical Feminism in America, 1967-1975,* University of Minnesota Press (Minneapolis), 1989.

Feminist Writers, St. James Press (Detroit), 1996.
Tong, Rosmarie, *Feminist Thought: A Comprehensive Introduction,* Westview Press (Boulder, CO), 1989.

PERIODICALS

Books & Bookmen, June, 1971, p. 64; December, 1972, p. 46; February, 1980, p. 61.
Choice, November, 1971, p. 1217.
Commentary, March, 1971, p. 64.
Commonweal, April 2, 1971, pp. 90-92.
Encounter, June, 1971, p. 39.
New Republic, November 28, 1970, p. 24.
New York Review of Books, November 1, 1970, p. 3799; September 1, 1971, p. 2593.
New York Times Book Review, July 30, 1972, p. 2.
Observer, April 25, 1971, p. 32.
Spectator, May 8, 1971, p. 634.
Time, March 20, 1972, p. 99.
Times Literary Supplement, April 23, 1971, p. 474.*

*   *   *

FITZGERALD, Astrid 1938-

PERSONAL: Born July 28, 1938, in Switzerland; immigrated to the United States, 1961; daughter of Ernst (an inventor) and Martha (a painter; maiden name, Greuter) Huerlimann; married Daniel Fitzgerald (died September 22, 1965); married Richard Geldard (a writer), October 15, 1983; children: (first marriage) Kent. *Ethnicity:* "Caucasian." *Education:* Attended College St. Agnes, Fribourg, Switzerland, 1955, a polytechnic school in London, England, 1958, Art Students League, New York City, 1962, Fashion Institute of Technology, 1968, and Pratt Graphics Center, 1972. *Politics:* "Idealist." *Avocational interests:* Travel to archaeological sites, hiking.

ADDRESSES: Home—650 West End Ave., New York, NY 10025. *Office*—118 Lower Granit Rd., Kerhoukson, NY 12446.

CAREER: Freelance fine artist, 1965—. Golden Mean, member of board of advisers. Work exhibited in group and solo shows, including Atlantic Gallery, Off-Broadway Gallery, and Pietrasanta Fine Arts, all New York City, and in Switzerland; represented in museums and corporate collections, including Aldrich Museum of Contemporary Art, Rockefeller Center

Collection, and Chemical Bank Collection; commissioned work for International Business Machines (IBM) Corp., Kindercare Corp., Hyatt Regency Hotel, Albuquerque, NM, and Union Bank of Switzerland, New York City.

AWARDS, HONORS: Michael M. Engel Memorial Award, National Arts Club, 1973; Charles Levitt Award, National Academy Galleries, 1978; Jurors Award, Annual Small Works Competition, New York University, 1980.

MEMBER: New York Kunsthalle, Swiss Institute (New York City).

WRITINGS:

(Illustrator and photographer) *Traveler's Key to Ancient Greece,* Knopf (New York), 1989.
An Artist's Book of Inspiration (quotations), Lindisfarne Press (Hudson, NY), 1996.

Contributor to *Parabola.*

SIDELIGHTS: Astrid Fitzgerald told *CA:* "I am a fine artist and designer and lover of ancient philosophy and the sacred sciences. My paintings are based on the Golden Mean proportions, and I also find inspiration in images from the far reaches of space and the concepts of quantum physics. I have exhibited my work widely, both here and in Europe.

"I am primarily a visual person whose early work was based on aesthetics. Over time, thought, idea, and content, however, became the points of departure. In 1994 I began to question my reasons for painting and the contemporary art scene in general. What is the mission of art? What is creativity? I reread my favorite passages by philosophers, artists, writers, and performing artists. I hit a golden vein: the perennial philosophy and its relationship to creativity and art. Each chapter of my book is prefaced by my own observations, and each quotation is preceded by a lead-in phrase which guides the reader."

*   *   *

FLANNERY, Tim(othy Fridtjof) 1956-

PERSONAL: Born January 28, 1956, in Melbourne, Australia. *Education:* LaTrobe University, B.A.,

1977; Monash University, M.Sc., 1981; University of New South Wales, Ph.D., 1985. *Politics:* "Policy-based." *Religion:* "Post-Christian." *Avocational interests:* Historical geology, history, paleontology, mammalogy, zoogeography, reading exploration history, music and plays of the Restoration, fishing, medieval literature.

ADDRESSES: Office—Australian Museum, 6 College St., Sydney South, New South Wales 2001, Australia.

CAREER: Australian Museum, Sydney, principal research scientist, 1985—.

AWARDS, HONORS: Edgeworth David Medal, Royal Society of New South Wales, 1990; Book of the Year, *The Age,* 1995; South Australian Arts Festival Award, 1996; Rudi Lemberg Travelling Fellowship, Australian Academy of Science, 1996; Eureka Pol Prize, 1996, for environmental research; South Australian Premier's Literary Award, 1996.

WRITINGS:

(With Michael Archer and Gordon Grigg) *The Kangaroo,* Kevin Weldon (Sydney), 1985.
(With Paula Kendall) *Australia's Vanishing Mammals,* Reader's Digest (Sydney), 1990.
The Future Eaters: An Ecological History of the Australasian Lands and People, Reed (Melbourne), 1994.
Possums of the World: A Monograph of the Phalangeroidea, GEO Productions (Sydney), 1994.
Mammals of New Guinea, Comstock Publishing (Ithaca, NY), 1995.
Mammals of the South-West Pacific and Moluccan Islands, Comstock Publishing, 1995.
(Editor) *1788 Watkin Tench,* Text Publishing (Melbourne), 1996.
Throwim 'Way Leg: Fifteen Years with Trap in Hand in the New Guinea Bush, Reed, 1997.

WORK IN PROGRESS: Research on the geological history of northern Australia.

SIDELIGHTS: Tim Flannery told *CA:* "I was named for the Norwegian polar explorer and humanitarian Fridtjof Nansen. In the tradition of nineteenth century endeavor, I would like to think I am a terror to my enemies and an ornament to my nation. Above all I should like to be considered a patriot."

FORD, G. M. 1945-

PERSONAL: Born July 9, 1945, in Everett, MA; son of Gerald Manson (a contractor) and Elizabeth Clara (a secretary) Ford; children: Jedediah Castiglione. *Education:* Hawthorne College, B.A.; Adelphi University, M.A. (English); University of Washington, Seattle, M.A. (political science). *Politics:* "Left of Ho Chi Minh." *Religion:* "Heathen." *Avocational interests:* Fishing, boating.

ADDRESSES: Home and office—433 13th Ave. East, No. 205, Seattle, WA 98102; fax 206-720-1522. *Agent*—Bernard Shie, Cliff, P.O. Box 1020, Merlin, OR 97532. *E-mail*—JXXF@eskimo.com.

CAREER: Rogue Community College, Grants Pass, OR, English teacher, 1972-85; City University, Bellevue, WA, communications teacher, 1986-92.

AWARDS, HONORS: Nominated for Anthony Award, Shamus Award, and Lefty Dilys Award.

WRITINGS:

MYSTERY NOVELS

Who in Hell Is Wanda Fuca?, Walker and Co. (New York City), 1995.
Cast in Stone, Walker and Co., 1996.
The Bum's Rush, Walker and Co., 1997.

WORK IN PROGRESS: A Steak in the Action, publication by Avon (New York City) expected in 1998.

SIDELIGHTS: G. M. Ford told *CA:* "I have read detective novels since childhood. I simply had to write one before I died. The rest, as they say, is history. I am most influenced by Rex Stout, John D. McDonald, Ross McDonald, and Robert B. Parker. I have, at one time or another, included little homages to each in my books. I write from six o'clock in the morning until two o'clock in the afternoon, five days a week. I do not outline. I make it up as I go along."

*   *   *

FORMISANO, Ronald P. 1939-

PERSONAL: Born March 31, 1939, in Providence, RI; son of Victor and Eva (Picerne) Formisano; children: two. *Education:* Brown University, B.A., 1960;

University of Wisconsin, M.A., 1962; Wayne State University, Ph.D., 1966.

ADDRESSES: Home—4921 North West 19th Place, Gainesville, FL 32605. *Office*—History Department, 4131 Turlington Hall, University of Florida, Gainesville, FL 32611.

CAREER: Wayne State University, Detroit, MI, instructor in history, 1965-67; University of Pittsburgh, Pittsburgh, PA, visiting assistant professor, 1967-68; University of Rochester, Rochester, NY, assistant professor, 1968-73; Clark University, Worcester, MA, associate professor of history, 1973-79, professor of history, 1979-89; University of Florida, Gainesville, professor of history, 1989—.

MEMBER: Organization of American Historians, American Historical Association, Southern Historical Association.

AWARDS, HONORS: Younger Humanists' Fellowship, National Endowment for the Humanities (NEH), 1972-73; fellowship from NEH/American Antiquarian Society, 1976-77; Charles Warren Fellow, 1980; Fulbright Chair of Political Science, University of Bologna, 1994.

WRITINGS:

The Birth of Mass Political Parties: Michigan, 1827-1861, Princeton University Press (Princeton, NJ), 1971.
The Transformation of Political Culture: Massachusetts Parties, 1790s-1840s, Oxford University Press (New York), 1983.
(Editor with Constance K. Burns) *Boston, 1700-1980: The Evolution of Urban Politics,* Greenwood Press (Westport, CT), 1984.
Boston against Busing: Race, Class, and Ethnicity in the 1960s and 1970s, University of North Carolina Press (Chapel Hill), 1991.
The Great Lobster War, University of Massachusetts Press (Amherst, MA), 1997.

Contributor to journals, including *American Political Science Review, American Historical Review, American Quarterly, Journal of American History, Journal of Interdisciplinary History, Michigan History,* and *Mid-America.*

SIDELIGHTS: Educator and author Ronald P. Formisano's studies on American political parties prior to the Civil War have yielded several volumes of cultural history. His first work, 1971's *The Birth of Mass Political Parties: Michigan, 1827-1861,* examines the roots of modern party politics, while *The Transformation of Political Culture: Massachusetts Parties, 1790s-1840s,* published in 1983, provides an in-depth discussion of the evolution of partisanship in earlier centuries. Expanding the time period of his previous books, the anthology entitled *Boston, 1700-1980: The Evolution of Urban Politics,* which Formisano edited with Constance K. Burns, contains ten essays that undertake a broader history of politics in one of the most historical, colorful, and most often studied cities in the United States.

Formisano's more recent work, 1991's *Boston against Busing: Race, Class, and Ethnicity in the 1960s and 1970s,* which been widely adopted for classroom use, examines one of the most controversial issues of the mid-to-late twentieth century: the desegregation of public schools. Inspired by a class on desegregation that he taught at Clark University in 1975, Formisano based this volume on research in primary and secondary sources, as well as oral interviews with participants in desegregation programs. "The book is both a study of white opposition to school desegregation," notes Richard J. Meister in a review of *Boston against Busing* for the *Journal of American History,* "and a commentary on the failure of American society to respond to 'the incongruity between the promise of American democracy and the grim reality of ghetto poverty.'"

BIOGRAPHICAL/CRITICAL SOURCES:

PERIODICALS

American Historical Review, February, 1975; June, 1987, p. 734; December, 1991, pp. 1638-39; February, 1992, p. 136.
Boston Globe, March 17, 1991, p. A17.
Journal of American History, March, 1992, pp. 1525-26.
Library Journal, March 15, 1991, p. 98.

* * *

FORSTENZER, Thomas R. 1944-
(Tom Forstenzer)

PERSONAL: Born March 18, 1944, in New York, NY; children: three. *Education:* Reed College, B.A., 1965; Stanford University, M.A., 1967, Ph.D., 1972.

ADDRESSES: Office—UNESCO, 7 place de Fontenoy, 75700 Paris, France; fax 331-45-68-19-90.

CAREER: Rutgers University, New Brunswick, NJ, professor of history, 1970-80; United Nations Educational, Scientific, and Cultural Organization (UNESCO), Paris, France, consultant, 1980-83, began as staff member, became executive officer, 1984—.

AWARDS, HONORS: Woodrow Wilson fellow.

WRITINGS:

Youth in the 1980's, UNESCO Press, 1979.
French Provincial Police and the Fall of the Second Republic: Social Fear and Counter Revolution, Princeton University Press (Princeton, NJ), 1981.
(Under name Tom Forstenzer; with Federico Mayor) *The New Page,* Dartmouth Publishing (Brookfield, VT), 1995.

* * *

FORSTENZER, Tom
See FORSTENZER, Thomas R.

* * *

FOSTER, Cecil (A.) 1954-

PERSONAL: Born September 26, 1954, in Bridgetown, Barbados, West Indies; son of Fred and Doris Goddard; married Glenys Cadogan; children: Munyonzwe, Michelio, Mensah. *Education:* Harrison College of Barbados, diploma in mass communications; York University, B.B.A., B.A. (with honors).

ADDRESSES: Home—125 Greenbush Cres., Thornhill, Ontario L4J 5M3, Canada.

CAREER: Caribbean News Agency, senior reporter and editor, 1975-77; *Barbados Advocate News,* reporter and columnist, 1977-79; *Toronto Star,* Toronto, Ontario, Canada, reporter, 1979-82; *Contrast,* Toronto, editor, 1979-82; *Transportation Business Management,* editor, 1982-83; *Globe and Mail,* Toronto, reporter, 1983-89; *Financial Post,* senior editor, 1989—.

MEMBER: PEN Canada (director, 1992—), Writer's Union of Canada, Glen Shield Soccer Club (executive member and fundraiser, 1991-93), Harambee Cultural Centres, Canadian Artist Network, Blacks in Action.

WRITINGS:

Distorted Mirror: Canada's Racist Face, Harper-Collins (Toronto), 1991.
No Man in the House (novel), Random House (Toronto), 1991, Ballantine (New York), 1992.
Sleep On, Beloved (novel), Ballantine (New York), 1995.

Also author of *A Place Called Heaven: The Meaning of Being Black in Canada,* HarperCollins (Toronto). Contributor of articles and reviews to periodicals, including *Chatelaine, Maclean's,* and *Canadian Business.*

SIDELIGHTS: A native of the West Indies, Cecil Foster is the author of several books, all of which describe both the hardships and achievements of blacks in the West Indies and Canada. He has garnered the most attention for his novels *No Man in the House* and *Sleep On, Beloved.*

Foster's native Barbados forms the backdrop for *No Man in the House,* the story of 10-year-old Howard Prescod and his family's struggle to survive their impoverished world in the early 1960s, during their country's fight for independence from Britain. Howard's parents have left him and his brothers to begin a new, and hopefully brighter, life in England. In the meantime, Howard's God-fearing grandmother and his aunts work to feed the family and hold it together. Howard's salvation from his desperate existence comes in the form of a man, Humphrey Bradshaw, the first black headmaster of Howard's school. From Bradshaw, Howard learns that education is his ticket out of poverty and oppression by others, and also realizes the importance of personal and political independence.

No Man in the House is loosely based on Foster's own life in Barbados. In an interview with Donna Nurse published in *Books in Canada,* Foster commented on the similarities between Howard Prescod and himself, responding: "I grew up in a very poor neighbourhood, Lodge Road, where I set the book. There was me and two brothers and as in *No Man in the House,* my parents had gone off to England to live. I was the last of the three, somewhat like Howard himself. By the time you get into the third

chapter or so, the resemblance to me has to some degree disappeared." Foster told Nurse of the influence of his family and grandmothers before adding: "I also got a strong sense of the importance of education—it was seen as a way out. When I was growing up the ambitious ones among us saw ourselves as emigrants in the making."

Critics applauded *No Man in the House,* which a *Publishers Weekly* reviewer deemed a "finely crafted, affecting debut novel of triumph over social and historical inequities." Michael Harris, writing in the *Los Angeles Times Book Review,* commented on Foster's depictions of women in *No Man in the House,* opining: "[T]he beleaguered grandmother, Howard's young aunts and the other village women are vividly drawn; their angry, loving voices are riches in an impoverished world." Further praise was issued by M. G. Vassanji, a contributor to *Canadian Forum:* "It is the major strength of Foster's novel, and the mark of its honesty that it celebrates the human spirit and acknowledges the humanity of its characters as it describes their weaknesses and struggles."

Foster followed *No Man in the House* with *Sleep On, Beloved,* a novel about a Jamaican woman who emigrates to Canada. Foster's protagonist, Ona Morgan, is a dancer with Kingston's National Dance Troupe, but must leave the company when she becomes pregnant with the troupe's married director's child. She later leaves her homeland and her infant daughter, Suzanne, to seek a new life in Canada. Ona obtains work in a garment factory, where she must yield to the sexual advances of her boss, who controls her with his threats of deportation. By the time Ona can send for Suzanne, the girl is nearly a teen, and the years of separation between mother and daughter, coupled with Suzanne's difficulty in assimilating to a new culture, prove troubling.

Foster told Nurse that he wrote *Sleep On, Beloved* to illustrate "that multiculturalism can work. That multiculturalism worked in the Caribbean where we had people from different places getting along and that the best form of multiculturalism is when you allow people to be natural." Some reviewers of *Sleep On, Beloved* maintained that Foster's lectures on the difficulties West Indians face in white culture diminish the success of his story. For example, reviewer Lynne Van Luven responded negatively to Foster's "extra lectures" and wrote in *Quill and Quire* that although Foster's novel "tells a sad and unsettling story of the bigotry faced by a struggling black family, . . . Foster should have trusted that his characters' lives would speak for themselves. They do, and eloquently." Donna Nurse, reviewing *Sleep On, Beloved* for *Maclean's,* found flaws existing in the story line, but applauded the novel as "a poignant and disturbing portrait of the formidable impediments that may constrain Caribbean immigrants, barriers that make the dream of a new family life in Canada so difficult to achieve." Uma Parameswaran in a review in *Books in Canada,* declared: "*Sleep On, Beloved* speaks from the inside of the community, and some details are disturbing. . . . The novel's merit lies in being a record of Caribbean experience in Canada."

BIOGRAPHICAL/CRITICAL SOURCES:

PERIODICALS

Books in Canada, May, 1995, pp. 36-37; September, 1995, pp. 18-21.
Boston Globe, October 19, 1992, p. 40.
Canadian Forum, August, 1991, pp. 28-29.
Library Journal, May 1, 1995, p. 65.
Los Angeles Times Book Review, November 8, 1992, p. 6.
Maclean's, May 22, 1995, p. 65.
Publishers Weekly, August 24, 1992, pp. 62-63.
Quill and Quire, March, 1995, p. 72.
School Library Journal, April, 1993, p. 149.*

*   *   *

FRANEY, Pierre   1921-1996

OBITUARY NOTICE—See index for *CA* sketch: Born January 13, 1921, in Tonnerre, France; came to the United States in 1939, naturalized citizen, 1942; died following a stroke, October 15, 1996, in Southampton, England. Chef, food critic, lecturer, author. Franey is best remembered for his talents in the culinary arts and is credited with making gourmet cuisine easier for the average person to create. Franey's love of cooking began in his early childhood and was later encouraged through an apprenticeship at a small restaurant on the Place de la Republique in Paris. Soon thereafter he secured work at the Drouant restaurant, but opted to work at the 1939 World's Fair in New York at a restaurant in France's pavilion. Franey was reluctant to return to France after the fair, since World War II had begun in Europe. He remained with the restaurant, which reopened as Le Pavillon in Manhattan. In 1942 Franey joined the U.S. Army and was recruited to serve as a personal chef to General Douglas MacArthur, a post he declined. Instead, he was assigned to culinary school in Alabama, but was later transferred to England for artillery duty. Franey had received his U.S. citizenship in 1942, and returned to his job at Le Pavillon after the war, becoming head chef. He also worked at La Cote Basque and the Hedges restaurants before becoming a vice president with the Howard Johnson's restaurant chain in 1960. Franey also served as president of the Vatel Club from 1955 until 1960. He began work as a culinary arts writer with his friend Craig Claiborne, who had been a food critic for the *New York Times.* The pair began by compiling a food newsletter and also teamed to produce books such as *Classic French Cooking, The Master Cooking Course,* and *Cooking with Craig Claiborne and Pierre Franey.* In 1976 the duo began writing a column for the *New York Times* called "The 60-Minute Gourmet," which instructed average people on how to assemble haute cuisine at home. Franey also coauthored books with fellow food writers such as Bryan Miller and Richard Flaste. Among Franey's other works are *Pierre Franey's Low Calorie Gourmet* and an autobiography, *A Chef's Tale.* In his later career, Franey appeared on programs for public television and he lectured and conducted cooking demonstrations for groups. While on board the ship the Queen Elizabeth II to present a demo for passengers, Franey suffered a stroke enroute to England, where he later died.

OBITUARIES AND OTHER SOURCES:

PERIODICALS

Chicago Tribune, October 16, 1996, sec. 3, p. 14.
New York Times, October 16, 1996, p. D24.
Washington Post, October 17, 1996, p. B6.

*   *   *

FRANKEL, Marvin E(arl)   1920-

PERSONAL: Born July 26, 1920, in New York, NY; son of Charles and Anne Frankel; married Betty Streich, June 20, 1945 (divorced, 1965); married Alice Kross (a physician), August 22, 1965; children: (first marriage) Eleanor, (second marriage) Mara, (stepchildren) David Schorr, Ellen Schorr. *Education:* Queens College, A.B., 1943; Columbia University, LL.B., 1948. *Politics:* Democrat. *Religion:* "None."

ADDRESSES: Office—919 Third Ave., New York, NY 10022. *Agent*—c/o Hill & Wang, 19 Union Sq. West, New York, NY 10003.

CAREER: Called to the bar in April, 1949; trial lawyer, 1949-52; assistant to U.S. Solicitor General, 1952-56; Proskauer Rose Goetz & Mendelsohn, attorney, 1956-62, 1978-83; Columbia University, professor of law, 1962-65; U.S. District Judge in New York City, 1965-78; Kramer, Levin, Nessen, Kamin & Frankel, trial attorney, 1983—; writer. Lawyers' Committee for Human Rights, Chair of the Board. *Military service:* United States Army, 1942-46.

MEMBER: New York State Bar Association, Bar Association for the City of New York.

WRITINGS:

Criminal Sentences: Law without Order, Hill & Wang (New York), 1973.
(With Gary P. Naftalis) *The Grand Jury: An Institution on Trial,* Hill & Wang, 1977.
Partisan Justice, Hill & Wang, 1980.
(With Ellen Saideman) *Out of the Shadows of Night: The Struggle for International Human Rights,* Delacorte (New York), 1989.
Faith and Freedom: Religious Liberty in America, Hill & Wang, 1994.

Contributor to periodicals, including *New Leader.*

SIDELIGHTS: Marvin E. Frankel is a former judge who has published various volumes on various judiciary issues. Frankel's first book, *Criminal Sentences: Law without Order,* questions the considerable authority accorded judges, especially with regard to the issuing of wide-ranging sentences for similar crimes. To promote more rational—and consistent—sentencing, Frankel calls for judges to be held more accountable for their decisions. Frankel's key observation here, as Lesley Oelsner noted in the *New York Times Book Review,* "is not so much that there is this range of discretion but that there are no guidelines for using it." A *New Republic* reviewer deemed *Criminal Sentences* "soundly argued and sensitively written" and expressed the hope that "this book may well one day prove to be extremely important, suggestive and helpful" to administrations inclined to modify the American judicial system.

In 1977 Frankel collaborated with former federal prosecutor Gary P. Naftalis on *The Grand Jury: An Institution on Trial,* a volume calling for reforms in the judicial process that was originally designed as a privately-convening body for collecting evidence and determining the viability of trial. In *The Grand Jury,* Frankel and Naftalis argue that too often grand juries are far from private investigations, leaking information to press and prosecutors. Frankel and Naftalis also argue that grand juries sometimes serve to taint the character of individuals being investigated. To improve the grand jury system, Frankel and Naftalis offer various proposals. They suggest, for instance, that grand jury prosecutors be disallowed from calling press briefings. Furthermore, they endeavor to protect the rights of witnesses by allowing them legal counsel in the jury room. Jon R. Waltz, writing in the *Washington Post Book World,* proclaimed *The Grand Jury* "a book of crystalline clarity and added that the book sets up a model . . . for anyone who hopes to write comprehensibly about other important and complicated subjects."

Among Frankel's other writings is *Partisan Justice,* which questions the exploitation of the legal system as a means of distorting and deviating from justice. In this volume Frankel calls for more limited use of trail by jury and suggests, instead, that the public turn more often to nonjudicial mediation. In his *Washington Post Book World* review of *Partisan Justice,* Jon R. Waltz wrote, "Frankel's prose is tight and elegant and he is nothing if not provocative," and he added that Frankel "writes from a rich experience and with a practiced eye."

Frankel told *CA:* "*Criminal Sentences* proposed a Sentencing Commission. The idea was adopted by Congress and in some fifteen states. It has been reviewed and works poorly in the federal courts, better in the states."

BIOGRAPHICAL/CRITICAL SOURCES:

PERIODICALS

Nation, December 20, 1980, pp. 682-83.
New Republic, May 15, 1973, p. 31.
New York Times, August 14, 1990, p. D1.
New York Times Book Review, May 13, 1973, pp. 4-5; July 24, 1977, p. 8.
Publishers Weekly, February 26, 1973, p. 117.
Washington Post Book World, June 26, 1977, p. 3; June 29, 1980, p. 7.

FRANKLIN, Kay 1933-1996

OBITUARY NOTICE—See index for CA sketch: Born July 30, 1933, in Newark, NJ; died October 15, 1996. Educator, librarian, activist, author. Franklin is remembered for her books concerning Indiana and Michigan regional history, particularly the Indiana Dunes. She began her career as a teacher, with stints in Utah and California from 1956 to 1958. In 1961 she became head teacher at the University of Chicago's nursery school. In 1978 she founded Dunes Enterprises, a publishing company, and began work as a freelance writer in 1979. In the late 1970s she began teaching at Purdue University on a part-time basis. Through Purdue she taught inmates at Indiana State Prison about writing. Her later career saw work at the Public Library in Michigan City, Indiana, as a programming and publicity director. She initiated numerous programs at the library, including a Writing Out Loud program and a class in memoir compilation. She was diligent in her efforts to raise public awareness of the Indiana Dunes area. She worked as an activist, testifying before Congress in an unsuccessful effort to have Beverly Shores, Indiana, became part of a national park. She wrote about the area as well, in books such as *Duel for the Dunes, The Indiana Dunes: A Selected Bibliography,* and *'Round and About the Dunes,* coauthored with Norma Schaeffer. Her book *Duel for the Dunes* was honored by groups such as the Great Lakes Regional Women in Communications and the Michiana Women in Communications. She also contributed to the anthology, *Where We Live: Essays about Indiana.*

OBITUARIES AND OTHER SOURCES:

PERIODICALS

Chicago Tribune, October 15, 1996, sec. 1, p. 11.

* * *

FRANKLYN, Ross
See HARDY, Francis Joseph

* * *

FREE, Lloyd A. 1908-1996

OBITUARY NOTICE—See index for CA sketch: Born September 29, 1908, in San Jose, CA; died November 11, 1996, in Bethesda, MD. Attorney, educator, pollster, author. Free was known for his expertise in polling techniques, both in the United States and abroad. He received particular attention for a study of Americans concerning the size of government. He learned that people said they wanted a smaller government with fewer taxes, but also advocated costly government programs. Free began his career as a lawyer in private practice in 1934, then joined the faculty at Princeton University in 1939. He served as editor of *Public Opinion Quarterly* and also took time out to serve in the U.S. Army during World War II. Among his wartime contributions were evaluating Nazi propaganda and predicting where the German Army might advance. He later was an adviser to the United Nations and worked with the U.S. State Department. In the mid-1950s, he founded (with Hadley Cantril) the Institute for International Social Research and served as its director. During his career, he also helped his father, Arthur, successfully run as a republican for Congress, although Lloyd, himself, was a democrat. He also taught political science in China and was a radio commentator for CBS and the BBC. He later helped Nelson Rockefeller run for governor and president. Among Free's books are *The Political Beliefs of Americans, State of the Nation, How Others See Us,* and *Attitudes of the Cuban People Toward the Castro Regime.*

OBITUARIES AND OTHER SOURCES:

PERIODICALS

Los Angeles Times, November 13, 1996, p. B10.
New York Times, November 14, 1996, p. B15.

* * *

FREEMAN, Anne Hobson 1934-

PERSONAL: Born March 19, 1934, in Richmond, VA; daughter of Joseph Reid Anderson (an electrical engineer) and Mary Douthat Marshall (a teacher) Hobson; married George Clemon Freeman, Jr. (a lawyer), December 6, 1958; children: Anne Colston McEvoy, George Clemon, Joseph Reid Anderson. *Education:* Bryn Mawr College, A.B., 1956; London University, postgraduate study, 1956-57; University of Virginia, M.A., 1973. *Politics:* Democrat. *Religion:* Episcopalian.

ADDRESSES: *Home*—P.O. Box 680, Callao, VA 22435. *Agent*--Virginia Barber, 101 Fifth Ave., New York, NY 10003.

CAREER: Writer, 1956—. International News Service, Eastern Europe, reporter, 1957; Virginia Museum of Fine Arts, Richmond, editor of members' bulletin, 1959-66; University of Virginia, Charlottesville, lecturer in English, 1973-88; Bryn Mawr *Bulletin,* chair of advisory committee, Bryn Mawr, PA, 1978-81; Hunton & Williams (law firm), Richmond, VA, firm historian, 1984-88.

MEMBER: Virginia Writers Club, Virginia Historical Society (board of directors, 1984-90), Ellen Glasgow Society, Country of Virginia Club, Richmond Area Democratic Women's Club, Museum of the Confederacy (Richmond, VA).

AWARDS, HONORS: Mademoiselle Fiction Contest prize, 1956; Fulbright fellow, 1956-57; Emily Clark Balch Prize for Fiction, 1985; M. Carey Thomas Essay Prize; Virginia Center for Creative Arts fellow.

WRITINGS:

The Style of a Law Firm: Eight Gentlemen from Virginia, Algonquin Books (Chapel Hill, NC), 1989.
A Hand Well Prayed: The Life of Jim Wheat, Jr., Cadmus (Philadelphia, PA), 1994.

Contributor of articles and stories to anthologies and periodicals.

WORK IN PROGRESS: A novel set in 19th century Virginia; research on the history of Virginia from 1865 to the present.

SIDELIGHTS: Anne Hobson Freeman's four years of work as a firm historian for the noted Virginia law firm Hunton and Williams led to publication of her first book, *The Style of a Law Firm: Eight Gentlemen from Virginia.* The volume examines what Dennis Drabelle in his *Washington Post Book World* review called "the lives and times of the men who shaped the firm in its formative decades." Now employing over 350 lawyers and maintaining offices in seven cities, Hunton and Williams began in Virginia's capital city of Richmond as a simple partnership between two young attorneys. Throughout the firm's long history it has been home-base for many distinctive men of law, including former U.S. Supreme Court Justice Lewis F. Powell, Jr., who was appointed by President Richard M. Nixon in 1971.

Focusing as it does on the lawyers who kept the firm operating for so many years, *The Style of a Law Firm*

contains many interesting vignettes of life among Richmond's monied class. In 1924, one of the originators of the firm, Eppa Hunton, met England's King George V when the American Bar Association held its yearly meeting in London. Another member of the firm abandoned plans to wed famous Virginian novelist Ellen Glasgow in order to pursue a relationship with Queen Marie of Romania. While made up of wealthy men and women, the firm often advised clients to take what might have been seen as a progressive stand on various issues. Freeman, for example, cites the firm's actions in support of compliance with court-ordered desegregation. With a wealth of interesting stories to tell, "Anne Hobson Freeman has made an intelligent and readable case," according to Drabelle, "for admiring eight Virginia gents and some of the values they advocated."

BIOGRAPHICAL/CRITICAL SOURCES:

PERIODICALS

Washington Post Book World, March 11, 1990, p. 6.*

*   *   *

FREEMAN, Harry M. 1943-

PERSONAL: Born September 17, 1943, in Meridian, MS; married Bebe Roberts, June 4, 1966; children: Ben. *Ethnicity:* "Caucasian." *Education:* Mississippi State University, B.S., 1966; Loyola University, New Orleans, LA, M.B.A., 1968; University of Cincinnati, M.S., 1974. *Politics:* Democrat. *Religion:* Unitarian-Universalist. *Avocational interests:* Juggling, biking, tennis, racquetball.

ADDRESSES: Home—1023 Chartres, No. 6, New Orleans, LA 70116. *Office*—804 Engineering Bldg., University of New Orleans, New Orleans, LA 70148; fax 504-280-5586. *E-mail*—hmfce@uno.edu.

CAREER: U.S. Environmental Protection Agency, Cincinnati, OH, staff member, 1968—. University of New Orleans, director of Louisiana Environmental Leadership Program. *Military service:* U.S. Public Health Service, 1968-70.

MEMBER: International Juggling Association, American Institute of Chemical Engineers.

WRITINGS:

Standard Handbook of Hazardous Waste Treatment and Disposal, McGraw (New York City), 1989.
Hazardous Waste Minimization, McGraw, 1990.
(Editor) *Industrial Pollution Prevention Handbook,* McGraw, 1995.

WORK IN PROGRESS: Revising *Standard Handbook of Hazardous Waste Treatment and Disposal;* research on voluntary environmental improvement programs.

SIDELIGHTS: Harry M. Freeman told *CA:* "I enjoy bringing a lot of things and people together to produce something of value. There is a lot of fulfillment in seeing a book produced that makes it look like we really did know what we were doing all of the time. That, and the fun of getting cards and letters from people I don't even know, complimenting the books, make it all worthwhile.

"I am an optimist when it comes to believing that, environmentally speaking, things have improved and will continue to improve in the future. Consequently, I like to highlight and emphasize technologies that support my belief. I particularly like Greg Easterbrook's style in *A Moment on Earth.*

"Since I am really more of an editor or compiler than an author, my process consists of soliciting ideas from colleagues all over the country and the world, encouraging them and others to participate in the preparation of my books, then keeping all of them on the Reservation long enough to produce the manuscripts that will allow me to do my thing, which will eventually lead to the books coming off the presses.

"I think we all should leave a little something for having been here. Part of my something is giving my colleagues (and myself) the opportunity to provide small contributions that will make the world even better than it is."

*   *   *

FREZZA, Robert (A.)   1956-

PERSONAL: Born August 5, 1956, in Washington, DC; son of Anthony J. (an engineer) and Ethel H. (Deba) Frezza. *Ethnicity:* "Italian/Czech American." *Education:* Loyola College, B.A. (cum laude), 1977; University of Maryland at College Park, J.D. (with

honors), 1980. *Politics:* Republican. *Religion:* Roman Catholic. *Avocational interests:* Theater, baseball, amphibians.

ADDRESSES: Home—8133 Turn Loop Rd., Glen Burnie, MD 21061. *E-mail*—rfrezza@juno.com.

CAREER: U.S. Army Claims Service, Fort Meade, MD, deputy chief of personnel in Claims and Recovery Division, 1985-93; writer, 1993—. *Military service:* U.S. Army, Judge Advocate General's Corps, 1980-84; became captain; received Army Commendation Medal.

AWARDS, HONORS: U.S. Army Achievement Award for Civilian Service; Commander's Award for Civilian Service.

WRITINGS:

A Small Colonial War (military science fiction), Del Rey Books (New York), 1989.
McLendon's Syndrome (humorous science fiction), Del Rey Books, 1993.
Fire in a Faraway Place (military science fiction), Del Rey Books, 1994.
Cain's Land (military science fiction), Del Rey Books, 1995.
The VMR Theory (humorous science fiction), Del Rey Books, 1996.

Contributor of short fiction to *Amazing.*

WORK IN PROGRESS: The Black Hats, a historical novel set during the Civil War, completion expected in 1998; research on the Civil War and World War II.

*   *   *

FRYE, Marilyn   1941-

PERSONAL: Born in 1941, in Tulsa, OK. *Education:* Stanford University, B.A., 1963; Cornell University, Ph.D., 1969.

ADDRESSES: Office—Department of Philosophy, 503 South Kedzie Hall, Michigan State University, East Lansing, MI 48824-1032.

CAREER: Michigan State University, Lansing, currently professor of philosophy.

WRITINGS:

The Politics of Reality: Essays in Feminist Theory, Crossing Press (Trumansburg, NY), 1983.
Willful Virgin: Essays in Feminism, 1976-1992, Crossing Press, 1992.

Contributor of essays to journals, anthologies, and periodicals, including *Signs: Journal of Women in Culture and Society.*

SIDELIGHTS: Marilyn Frye, professor of philosophy at Michigan State University, is the author of *The Politics of Reality: Essays in Feminist Theory.* Published in 1983, this collection of nine essays has been hailed by critics as a valuable study of radical lesbian feminist philosophy. Calling the work "the summer storm readers have been thirstily awaiting" in her review of the work for *Women's Review of Books,* Helene V. Wenzel notes that "it is to the credit of Frye's carefully wrought feminism and considerable thoughtful-ness (sic) that this book does not read either as polemic or apology for lesbianism. Rather, it presents a careful re-visioning of reality for us all."

In *The Politics of Reality* Frye discusses, among other things, feminist "separatism." In its most extreme form, this voluntary separation—political in impetus—translates into a total withdrawal from all manifestations of a patriarchal society, including engaging in heterosexual relationships with men. In Frye's view, choosing *not to* becomes empowering as an active form of resistance to female oppression. Also discussed are radical feminist theories and goals, which include the direct transformation of all political, social, and economic structures perceived as vehicles of oppression. With a writing style described by a *Choice* reviewer as "both scholarly and direct without being ponderous," Frye's straightforward

analysis of feminist terminology has made *The Politics of Reality* a required text in numerous women's studies courses.

Frye continues her radical feminist dissection of patriarchy in 1992's *Willful Virgin: Essays in Feminism, 1976-1992.* In addition to a collection of book reviews, *Willful Virgin* includes a study of the hidden patriarchal constraints upon feminists within the academic environment, a discussion on how to preserve one's integrity as a feminist within an oppressive culture, and the title essay, "Wilful Virgin, or, Do You Have to Be a Lesbian to Be a Feminist?" In the essay "White Women Feminist," Frye instructs readers in learning to view the world from a more tolerant, less culturally biased perspective. While noting that some of the essays had become dated in the years since their initial publication, a reviewer for *Ethics* writes that "Frye's honesty, integrity, and talent for making us see the world differently are also very much present."

Frye's work continues to be groundbreaking in the arena of women's studies. As Wenzel notes, "At a time when professional respectability and security . . . demand that lesbian feminists in academe keep one foot in the closet while women's studies goes about its projects of 'mainstreaming' and 'integration,' based in large part on 'gentlemen's agreements,' Frye's book is a bold and courageous tour de force."

BIOGRAPHICAL/CRITICAL SOURCES:

PERIODICALS

Choice, November, 1983, p. 472.
Ethics, April, 1995, pp. 695-96.
Signs, winter, 1995, p. 471.
Women's Review of Books, October, 1983, pp. 5-6.

G

GAIDUK, Ilya V(alerievich) 1961-

PERSONAL: Born July 9, 1961, in Turkmenistan, U.S.S.R.; son of Valerii P. (a construction engineer) and Lidiia G. (a medical doctor; maiden name, Lavrova) Gaiduk. *Ethnicity:* "Russian." *Education:* Attended Moscow Pedagogical Institute, 1980-84; Russian Academy of Sciences, Institute of World History, Ph.D., 1990. *Avocational interests:* Classical music.

ADDRESSES: Home—Yubileinyi Prospect 1, Apt. 262, Reutov, Moscow, Russia. *Office*—Institute of World History, Russian Academy of Sciences, 32a Leninskii Prospect, Moscow 117334, Russia; fax 095-938-2288. *E-mail*—ilya@igh1.msk.su.

CAREER: High school teacher in Moscow, Russia, 1984-87; Russian Academy of Sciences, Institute of World History, Moscow, junior research fellow, 1990-93, research fellow, 1993—.

MEMBER: Norwegian Nobel Institute (fellow).

WRITINGS:

The Soviet Union and the Vietnam War, Ivan R. Dee (Chicago, IL), 1996.

Contributor to books, including *The Vietnam War,* edited by Peter Lowe, Macmillan (London, England), and works published in Russian. Contributor to periodicals, including *History: Journal of the Historical Association.*

WORK IN PROGRESS: Research on Soviet policy toward the conflict in Indochina, 1954-63.

SIDELIGHTS: Ilya V. Gaiduk told *CA:* "Writing is an indispensable part of the profession of the historian. You can study any particular period of the past for a long time. After much work devoted to finding new archival documents, materials, evidence, after attempting to reconstruct the sequence of events and the roles of various people, after the effort to understand perceptions and think of the principal actors, you suddenly recognize that it is time to write. This recognition stems, not only from the pressure of obligations you have assumed and promises you have made, but also from the understanding that writing helps you to put everything you have learned into a system, to perceive fully the meaning of this or that events, to apprehend the importance of particular details in the overall picture.

"Although writing itself is easy for me (usually my ideas run far ahead of my capacity to type at the computer) the process of writing is very painful, sometimes agonizing. The process demands the tedious preliminary work of analyzing the material I have found, sorting out necessary documents, selecting the most important of them to serve as illustrations of the concepts I developed during research, and formulating arguments in support of the concepts. When I sit down at the computer or at the desk and start to write, everything I want to say is in my head and almost ready to materialize. The problem is not to forget something, not to omit an important detail. The greatest incentive for me in this process is the strong desire to tell a story about historical events that took place many years ago, events that could be no less fascinating for the reader than a spy novel or a love story invented by a fiction writer.

"Several years ago I had an opportunity to read documents on the Vietnam war in the Soviet archives. I was intrigued by the fact that everything I had known about this war and the Soviet involvement in it was absolutely wrong. I had a distorted picture of what happened there at that time. Later, when I read books on the Vietnam war that were written and published in the West, I discovered that they could not answer many of my questions, and their authors generally had a vague notion about the policy of the Soviet Union in Southeast Asia. Therefore, I decided to tell people about my discoveries in Soviet and American archives in the form of a story that could be interesting to read."

* * *

GALANTIN, I(gnatius) J(oseph) 1910-

PERSONAL: Born September 24, 1910, in New York, NY; son of Ignatius Peter and Mary Elizabeth (Binder) Galantin; married Virginia Elizabeth Jaeckel, June 14, 1935; children: Mary Joy Galantin Veazey, Vivien Elizabeth Galantin Creelman, Linda. *Education:* U.S. Naval Academy, B.S., 1933; National War College, graduated, 1955. *Ethnicity:* "Magyar." *Politics:* "Conservative." *Religion:* Protestant. *Avocational interests:* Reading history, travel, golf.

ADDRESSES: Home—Fleet Landing, 5606 Sirius Ct., Atlantic Beach, FL 32233.

CAREER: U.S. Navy, career officer, 1933-70, commissioned ensign, 1933, promoted to rear admiral, 1957, became admiral, 1967, retired, 1970; stationed on battleship *New York,* 1933-35; submarines *Argonaut, R-11* and *Halibut,* commander, World War II; Naval Group, China, submarine liaison officer, 1945; Submarine Division 51, commander, 1949; Submarine Squadron 7, commander, 1953-54; fleet oiler *Navasota,* commander, Korean War; assigned to Office of Chief of Naval Operations, 1955-57; member of North Atlantic Treaty Organization (NATO) staff of Commander-in-Chief of Allied Forces in Southern Europe, Naples, Italy, 1957-59; Cruiser Division 2 of 6th Fleet, commander task group, 1960; Navy Department, director of submarine and anti-submarine warfare, 1961, director of Special Projections Office in charge of development and production of *Polaris* weapon system, 1962-65; U.S. project officer for implementation of U.S.-U.K. *Polaris* Sales Agreement, 1963-65; Chief of Naval Material, 1965-1970.

AWARDS, HONORS: Military: Received Distinguished Service Medal, Navy Cross, Silver Star (3), Navy Unit Commendation Ribbon.

MEMBER: U.S. Naval Institute, Retired Officers Association, Naval Submarine League, American Defense Preparedness Association.

WRITINGS:

Take Her Deep: A Submarine against Japan in World War II, Algonquin Books (Chapel Hill, NC), 1987.
Submarine Admiral: From Battlewagons to Ballistic Missiles, University of Illinois Press (Urbana, IL), 1995.

SIDELIGHTS: Both of Admiral I. J. Galantin's books are autobiographical accounts of the challenges and adventures associated with his 41-year career in the U.S. Navy. *Take Her Deep: A Submarine against Japan in World War II* focuses on the 15-month period from August, 1943, to December, 1944, when Galantin served as the commander of the submarine, *Halibut,* on duty in the Pacific. Especially exciting, according to a reviewer in *Publishers Weekly,* is Galantin's "nail-biting narrative" of the *Halibut*'s last mission when Japanese depth charges badly damaged the submarine's hull, nearly sinking the vessel. Recalling the moment when he had to accept the fact that the damage to the submarine would prematurely retire her from active duty, in his book Galantin lists the boat's many contributions to the war effort. He writes: "Since her first arrival in Pearl [Harbor] in 1942 she had sailed on ten war patrols, steamed over 110,000 miles, endured countless depth charges, bombs, and even gunfire. . . . She had sunk twelve ships, damaged at least nine others, used her gun effectively. She earned seven battle stars, the Navy Unit Commendation, and the Philippine Republic Presidential Unit Citation." For his own contributions, Galantin was awarded the Navy Cross, three Silver Star medals, and the Navy Unit Commendation Ribbon.

For his 1995 title, *Submarine Admiral: From Battlewagons to Ballistic Missiles,* Galantin widened his focus from that of one submarine to the history of submarines in general. According to a *Publishers Weekly* reviewer, what Galantin produced was "an authoritative overview of the evolution of the sub and its role in the U.S. Navy." Galantin gives a quick look at the submarine's historic development, including the Navy's first acquisition of a submarine in 1900 and the construction of long-range combat submarines used in World War II. From this point on in the history of the underwater craft, Galantin is able to give an insider's account of improvements in the submarine due to his own work with the vessels. He had his World War II experiences on the *Halibut* as well as his subsequent positions as head of the submarine branch in the Navy Department, director of the submarine/anti-submarine warfare division, and director of the Special Projects Office of the Navy, developing the *Polaris* Missile system for submarines, from which to draw information.

Told largely in anecdotal fashion, *Submarine Admiral* includes Galantin's personal glimpses of important figures in the development of the U.S. Navy. In particular, he details his close association with Hyman G. Rickover, known as the developer of nuclear-powered submarines. In another vignette from his life, Galantin relates how he directed a demonstration of the newly perfected submarine-launched *Polaris* missile for President John F. Kennedy in November, 1963, just six days before the president was assassinated in Dallas. In the book's epilogue, Galantin ponders the role of the submarine in the post-Cold War world and concludes, "To maintain its primacy of power and leadership, the United States must control and use the inner space of the sea. . . . Our presence and authority there are required absolutely."

BIOGRAPHICAL/CRITICAL SOURCES:

BOOKS

Galantin, I. J., *Submarine Admiral: From Battlewagons to Ballistic Missiles,* University of Illinois Press (Urbana, IL), 1995.
Galantin, I. J., *Take Her Deep: A Submarine against Japan in World War II,* Algonquin Books (Chapel Hill, NC), 1987.

PERIODICALS

Booklist, October 1, 1987, p. 212; September 1, 1995, p. 9.
Library Journal, October 15, 1987, p. 79.
Publishers Weekly, August 7, 1987, p. 441; July 24, 1995, p. 56.
U.S. Naval Institute Proceedings, June 1959, p. 9; April 1985, p. 80.

GANS, Roma 1894-1996

OBITUARY NOTICE—See index for *CA* sketch: Born February 22, 1894, in St. Cloud, MN; died October 4, 1996, in Pittsfield, MA. Educator and author. Gans gained prominence as the author of several books on teaching children to read, as well as thrilling her younger audience with science books, covering topics such as caves, dinosaurs, birds, and rocks. She began her educational career in 1917 as a mathematics teacher in Minnesota. In 1925, she became the assistant superintendent of schools in Superior, Wisconsin, a post she held until 1929. In that year, she accepted an assistant professorship at Teachers College, Columbia University, in New York. While in New York, Gans wrote several books in the field of education, including *Guiding Children's Reading through Experiences: Practical Suggestions for Teaching,* which was published in 1941. She retired from Columbia in 1959, and devoted her time to writing books for children. Over the years, Gans received many honors for her prolific writing. Among them was the Delta Kappa Gamma Society's Educator Award. She also contributed hundreds of articles to journals. Her other works include *When Birds Change Their Feathers, Reading Is Fun, Rock Collecting,* and *Common Sense in Teaching Reading: A Practical Guide.*

OBITUARIES AND OTHER SOURCES:

PERIODICALS

New York Times, October 13, 1996, Section 1, p. 44.

*   *   *

GANZ, Lowell 1948-

PERSONAL: Born August 31, 1948, in New York, NY; son of Irving (an executive) and Jean (Farber) Ganz; married Jeanne Russo (a secretary), December 26, 1976; children: Scott, Allison, Simon. *Education:* Attended Queen's College.

ADDRESSES: Home—Los Angeles, CA. *Agent*—Creative Artists Agency, 9830 Wilshire Blvd., Beverly Hills, CA 90212; c/o Writers Guild of America West Inc., 8955 Beverly Blvd., West Hollywood, CA 90048.

CAREER: Director, producer, and writer. Adjunct professor of graduate film screening at University of Southern California. Director of episodes of television shows, including *Makin' It,* ABC, 1979; *Joanie Loves Chachi,* ABC, 1982-83; and for *Angie, The Bad News Bears,* and *Brothers and Sisters,* all 1979. Has appeared on screen in *Splash,* Buena Vista, 1984; *Parenthood,* Universal, 1989; and in the television documentary *Naked Hollywood,* Arts and Entertainment, 1991.

Producer of television shows, including (with others) *Laverne and Shirley,* ABC, 1976-83; and (with others) *Foul Play,* ABC, 1981. Executive producer of various television shows, including (with Brian Levant and Fred Fox, Jr.) *Happy Days,* ABC, 1974-84; (with Mark Rothman) *Busting Loose,* CBS, 1977; (with Rothman and Ned Shankman) *The Ted Knight Show,* CBS, 1978; (and creator with Garry Marshall) *Makin' It,* ABC, 1979; and (with others) *Joanie Loves Chachi,* ABC, 1982-83. Executive producer of pilots, including (with Rothman) *The Rita Moreno Show,* CBS, 1978; (with Rothman) *The Lovebirds,* CBS, 1979; (with Rothman; and director) *The Further Adventures of Wally Brown,* NBC, 1980; and (with Marshall and Ronny Hallin) *Herndon and Me,* ABC, 1983. Producer, with Arthur Silver, of the pilot *Flatfoots,* NBC, 1982. Executive producer, with Babaloo Mandel, of television programs, including *Gung Ho,* ABC, 1986; (and creator) *Channel 99,* CBS, 1988; *Knight and Daye,* NBC, 1989; and *Parenthood,* NBC, 1990. Creative consultant with Mandel for *Take Five* (also known as *Kooper with a "K"*), CBS, 1987.

AWARDS, HONORS: Academy Award nomination, best screenplay written directly for the screen, National Film Critics Screenplay of the Year award, and Writers Guild best screenplay nominee, all 1984, all for *Splash.*

WRITINGS:

SCREENPLAYS, WITH BABALOO MANDEL

Night Shift, Ladd Co./Warner Bros., 1982.
(With Bruce Jay Friedman) *Splash* (adapted from a story by Friedman and Dave Thomas), Buena Vista, 1984.
(With Dan Aykroyd) *Spies Like Us,* Warner Bros., 1985.
(With Deborah Blum) *Gung Ho,* Paramount, 1986.
Vibes (adapted from a story by Ganz, Mandel, and Blum), Columbia, 1988.

(With Ron Howard) *Parenthood* (adapted from a story by Ganz, Mandel, and Howard), Universal, 1989.
City Slickers (adapted from a story by Billy Crystal), Castle Rock/Columbia, 1991.
A League of Their Own, Columbia, 1992.
(With Billy Crystal) *Mr. Saturday Night,* Columbia, 1992.
(With Crystal) *City Slickers II: The Legend of Curly's Gold,* Columbia, 1994.
Greedy, Universal, 1994.
(With Crystal) *Forget Paris,* Columbia, 1995.

Also author, with Mandel, of *Over My Dead Body, Dance Skins,* and *Perfect Couple.*

SCREENPLAYS

Author of screenplays, including *The Greatest Show on Earth, Kiamesha, Happy Hour,* and (with Garry Marshall) *C. Dmias.*

TELEVISION SERIES, WITH MANDEL

(With others) *Laverne and Shirley,* ABC, 1976-83.
(With others) *Busting Loose,* CBS, 1977.
Take Five, CBS, 1987.

TELEVISION PILOTS, WITH MANDEL

Herndon and Me, ABC, 1983.
Channel 99, NBC, 1988.
(With others) *Knight and Daye,* NBC, 1989.
(With others) *Parenthood* (adapted from film), NBC, 1990.

TELEVISION SERIES

(With others) *The Ted Knight Show,* CBS, 1978.
Makin' It, ABC, 1979.
Here's Boomer, NBC, 1981.
(With others) *Joanie Loves Chachi,* ABC, 1982-83.
The New Odd Couple, ABC, 1982-83.
(With others) *Gung Ho,* ABC, 1986-87.

Also writer for episodes of (with others; and story editor) *The Odd Couple,* 1970; *Friends and Lovers,* 1974; and *Walkin' Walter,* 1977.

TELEVISION PILOTS

(With Mark Rothman) *The Rita Moreno Show,* CBS, 1978.
(With Rothman) *The Lovebirds,* CBS, 1979.
(With Arthur Silver) *Flatfoots,* NBC, 1982.

OTHER

(With Garry Marshall) *Wrong Turn at Lungfish* (play), produced off-Broadway, 1993.

SIDELIGHTS: Lowell Ganz and Babaloo Mandel are prominent Hollywood screenwriters best known for their various comedies. In 1982 the team's first script, *Night Shift,* was produced. It concerns a meek morgue attendant, Charles Lumley III, who allows his workplace to be converted—by a hyperactive co-worker—into a house of prostitution. *Night Shift* was directed by Ron Howard, and the film's central role is played by actor Henry Winkler. The dominant personality in *Night Shift,* however, is Michael Keaton, who plays Blaze, the scheming morgue employee capable of endless get-rich schemes and cock-eyed notions. Blaze is the catalyst for the action, including an escapade with hoodlums, that culminates in the timid Charles finally asserting himself and, in the process, winning the love of his neighbor, a particularly endearing prostitute named Belinda.

Upon release, *Night Shift* proved quite popular with critics. Among the film's supporters was *Los Angeles Times* reviewer Sheila Benson, who affirmed that this comedy is "so likeable, so inventive, so deftly performed and so very, very funny that enthusiasm for it blurs what should be critical functions." She proclaimed Ganz and Mandel "stunningly adept writers" and added that their team constitutes "a delightful, original and inventive partnership."

Ganz and Mandel next teamed with Bruce Jay Friedman and director Howard on *Splash,* a comedy about a likeable produce wholesaler who falls in love with a mermaid who has come ashore specifically to find him. Action ensues when the couple are united only to find themselves tracked by a monomaniacal biologist determined to capture the mermaid for his own purposes. *Newsweek* reviewer David Ansen deemed the film "an enchanting piece of fluff—a romantic comedy that is truly romantic and truly comic, a deft blend of hip satire and fairy-tale charm." *New Yorker* critic Pauline Kael observed that *Splash* "has a friendly, tantalizing magic. . . . The day after you've seen it, you may find yourself running the images over in your mind, and grinning."

After the success of both *Night Shift* and *Splash,* Ganz and Mandel found themselves increasingly popular in Hollywood. In 1985 they collaborated with comedian Dan Aykroyd on the script for *Spies Like Us,* a comedy in which a deranged American general plans to stage a Soviet offensive in order to bomb the United States with newly developed missiles. As part of the general's bizarre scheme, two bumbling agents are dispatched into the Soviet Union to serve as decoys. The escapades of these agents—played by Aykroyd and his former *Saturday Night Live* cohort Chevy Chase—become the focus of *Spies Like Us.* In his *Chicago Tribune* review, Larry Kart termed *Spies Like Us* "an uneasy blend of seriousness and farce." Among the film's more vehement detractors was *Washington Post* reviewer Paul Attanasio, who acknowledged Ganz and Mandel as "perhaps Hollywood's most talented comic writing team" but denounced *Spies Like Us* as "a comedy with exactly one laugh."

In 1986, *Gung Ho* reunited the Ganz-Mandel team with director Ron Howard. Here *Night Shift* performer Michael Keaton appears as an auto worker who becomes a liaison between his coworkers and the factory's team of dissatisfied Japanese managers. Vincent Canby, writing in the *New York Times,* thought *Gung Ho* was "a very mild, socially significant situation-comedy. It's more cheerful than funny."

Vibes continued the Ganz-Mandel team's comedic run. In this film, pop singer Cyndi Lauper and actor Jeff Goldblum play a pair of psychics unwittingly lured into a treasure hunt by a devious con artist. In the *New York Times,* Janet Maslin declared that the film "has all the ingredients of lighthearted adventure-comedy except the essential one: laughs." Rita Kempley, meanwhile, contended in the *Washington Post* that for "innocent movie-goers, the best recourse is extrasensory deprivation."

Parenthood, the next film from a script by Ganz and Mandel, concerns beleaguered family man Gil Buckman, played by comedian Steve Martin, who finds that in both his personal and professional capacities he is constantly overwhelmed. When obligations to Gil's immediate family threaten to become manageable, members of his extended family, including an emotionally withdrawn father and a profligate brother, exact their own demands on his time. Gil's marriage seems likely to become undone by the various domestic machinations, but ultimately he realizes a measure of stability and, with it, more substantial marital accord.

Reviewers generally acknowledged *Parenthood* as an ambitious, often entertaining film. Stephen Holden described the film in his *New York Times* review, as a "bittersweet adult comedy," noted that though it "presents more characters than a two-hour movie could hope to handle comfortably, the director and the screenwriters . . . have still concocted a rich evocation of the swirl of suburban family life." And *Washington Post* reviewer Rita Kempley called *Parenthood* a "feel-good family comedy . . . a veritable diaper bag of laughs."

In 1991 Ganz and Mandel provided the script for *City Slickers,* a comedy about a trio of friends who decide to leave New York City to vacation as cattle rustlers in the west. Brian D. Johnson, writing in *Maclean's,* called *City Slickers* "an inventive, sophisticated comedy that lassos the heart." In 1994 Ganz and Mandel teamed with Crystal in writing a sequel, *City Slickers II: The Legend of Curly's Gold,* wherein the three friends return west to search for hidden treasure. *Variety* critic Leonard Klady called *City Slickers II* "a welcome sequel" and proclaimed it "the yee-hah! film of the season."

In between the two *City Slickers* films, Ganz and Mandel wrote the scripts for a range of comedies. In 1992 they collaborated with Crystal on *Mr. Saturday Night,* which featured Crystal, as selfish, obnoxious comedian Buddy Young. The film charts Young's career over five decades worth of triumphs and failures, and it reveals the self-destructiveness inherent in Young's endless efforts to become the virtual king of comics.

Some reviewers of *Mr. Saturday Night* found the film an unlikely blend of humor and bathos, and some critics even complained that Crystal had undermined his film by so relentlessly revealing his character's appeal and his repulsiveness. Among those reviewers who found the film nonetheless successful despite some significant shortcomings was Michael Sragow, who, in his *New Yorker* review, described *Mr. Saturday Night* as "an out-of-control Jewish-show-biz dinosaur" but added that "its authenticity and entertainment value outweigh its bloat."

Ganz and Mandel also supplied the scripts for *A League of Their Own,* a comedy about a women's baseball league. *A League of Their Own* was regarded in some quarters as acceptably entertaining. Among those critics voicing such an opinion was *Newsweek*'s David Ansen, who deemed the film a "very likable pop historical comedy."

Ganz and Mandel continued their screenwriting collaboration with actor-director Crystal in *Forget Paris.* The movie features Crystal as Mickey, a professional basketball referee who falls in love with airline employee Ellen, played by Debra Winger. The pair meet initially in Paris, and after they return to America they marry. In the ensuing years, however, Ellen grows increasingly impatient with his long stints away from home while refereeing. In turn, the marriage grows weaker. Stanley Kauffmann noted that the film "is laboriously pumped along" by "plenty of laughs."

In addition to his work with Mandel, Ganz collaborated with Garry Marshall on *Wrong Turn at Lungfish,* a stage comedy about a dying old man and his relationship with a young woman who reads to him. Richard Christiansen, writing in the *Chicago Tribune,* noted that the play is "witty and derivative, wise and crass, poignant and gross," and he proclaimed *Wrong Turn at Lungfish* "a distinct mixed blessing."

BIOGRAPHICAL/CRITICAL SOURCES:

PERIODICALS

Chicago Tribune, December 11, 1985; August 5, 1988; August 1, 1989; August 2, 1989; June 18, 1990.

Commonweal, September 11, 1992, p. 41.

Globe and Mail (Toronto), August 6, 1988.

Los Angeles Times, July 29, 1982; August 5 ,1988; August 2, 1989; January 6, 1991, pp. 7, 25.

Maclean's, June 24, 1991, p. 48.

National Review, August 3, 1992, pp. 46-47.

New Republic, April 9, 1984, p. 24; April 21, 1986, pp. 24-25; August 3, 1992, p. 28; June 12, 1995, p. 32.

Newsweek, March 12, 1984, p. 89; December 6, 1985; July 6, 1992, p. 54; March 1, 1993, p. 64; March 14, 1994, p. 72; June 27, 1994, p. 54.

New York, October 5, 1992, pp. 101-02.

New Yorker, March 19, 1984, pp. 123-27; August 2, 1989; October 5, 1992, pp. 162-64.

New York Times, July 30, 1982, p. C8; December 6, 1985; March 14, 1986; August 5,1988.

People, October 19, 1992, pp. 163-66.

Rolling Stone, October 29, 1992, p. 78.

Time, March 31, 1986; October 5, 1992, pp. 84-86.

Variety, June 6-12, 1994, pp. 33, 44.

Washington Post, March 9, 1984; December 9, 1985; August 5, 1988; August 2, 1989; August 4, 1989.*

GARBER, Zev 1941-

PERSONAL: Born March 1, 1941, in New York, NY; son of Morris Benjamin (a pharmacist) and Pearl (a homemaker; maiden name, Borko) Garber; married Lois Koppelman, December 26, 1963 (divorced, November, 1975); married Susan Ehrlich (a writer), October 4, 1985; children: Asher, Dorit Garber. *Education:* Hunter College of the City University of New York, B.A., 1962; attended University of California, Los Angeles, 1962-65; University of Southern California, M.A., 1970. *Politics:* "Centralist-Right." *Religion:* Jewish. *Avocational interests:* Films, plays.

ADDRESSES: Home—4540 Stern Ave., Sherman Oaks, CA 91423. *Office*—Los Angeles Valley College, 5800 Fulton, Van Nuys, CA 91401.

CAREER: Los Angeles Valley College, Van Nuys, CA, professor of Jewish studies, 1970—; writer. Visiting professor of religious studies at University of California, Riverside, 1983—. Educational consultant to Philadelphia Center for the Holocaust. Member of conference committee of Annual Scholars' Conference on the Holocaust.

MEMBER: American Oriental Society, American Schools of Oriental Research, American Academy of Religion, Society of Biblical Literature, Association of Jewish Studies, National Association of Professors of Hebrew.

WRITINGS:

Shoah: The Paradigmatic Genocide: Essays in Exegesis and Eisegesis, University Press of America (Lanham, MD), 1994.

Contributor to periodicals, including *Shofar.*

EDITOR

Methodology in the Academic Teaching of Judaism, University Press of America, 1986.
(With A. Berger and R. Libowitz) *Methodology in the Academic Teaching of the Holocaust,* University Press of America, 1988.

Editor in chief of *Studies in the Shoah* series, University Press of America. Contributor to books, including *What Kind of God?: Essays in honor of Richard Rubenstein,* University Press of America, 1995.

Editor of *Iggeret;* editor of *Shofar* issues; contributing editor of *Israel Today* (became *Los Angeles Jewish News*). Member of editorial board of *Shofar.*

WORK IN PROGRESS: "Ongoing researching and writing on themes related to the Shoah."

SIDELIGHTS: Zev Garber is an educator specializing in the Holocaust, which he prefers to refer to as the Shoah. Garber explained to John Dart in the *Los Angeles Times* that the term *Holocaust* originally referred to religious sacrifices and thus bears a Biblical connotation that "makes the six million Jews an offering to God, and the priests are the Nazis." He told Dart that the Hebrew word *Shoah,* which means "destruction," is more appropriate. "Language determines how we think," Garber observed. "And because *Shoah* is a Hebrew term, we don't lose the Jewishness of the victims."

Garber wrote *Shoah: The Paradigmatic Genocide: Essays in Exegesis and Eisegesis,* and he has edited academic volumes. In addition, he serves as editor in chief of the University Press of America's *Studies in the Shoah* series.

Garber told *CA:* "My main research focuses on the central issues of human life, meaning, and consciousness in the post-Shoah (Holocaust) world. My writings and scholarly papers address historical, literary, pedagogical, philosophical, and theological concerns. What unites my approach to the Shoah is the quest for a meaningful agenda to learn and teach the Holocaust fifty years later, when the entire horrific enterprise is either forgotten, questioned, revised, or denied. For an age that ponders technologically administered mass death, global indifference, tribalism, and God forsakeness, my thinking is offered as a meditation in human responsibility and theological responsibility.

"The essence of Shoah thinking is 'dislike of the unlike.' It is the recognition of this force in our lives that must be at the core of any Holocaust presentation. I am concerned, therefore I am; I am appalled, therefore I write: Mankind is improvable. We must all be reminded of this, and writers and educators, above all, must believe it."

BIOGRAPHICAL/CRITICAL SOURCES:

PERIODICALS

Los Angeles Times, April 9, 1994, B1.

GARFUNKEL, Trudy 1944-

PERSONAL: Born July 12, 1944, in Brooklyn, New York; daughter of Hyman Garfunkel (a sculptor/in business) and Beatrice Garfunkel (an office manager; maiden name, Lipshitz). *Education:* Attended University of Buffalo, 1961-63; New York University, B.A., 1965. *Politics:* Independent. *Religion:* Jewish. *Avocational interests:* Gardening, painting, dance.

ADDRESSES: Home—70-03 Main St., Kew Gardens Hills, NY 11367. *Agent*—Richard Curtis, Curtis Associates, 171 East 74th St., New York, NY 10021.

CAREER: Dial Press, New York City, Publicity-Advertising Manager, 1967-82; Garfunkel Communications, New York City, Director, 1982—. Serves as chairperson of the Information Committee of the New York City Ballet.

MEMBER: Author's Guild.

AWARDS, HONORS: On Wings of Joy: The Story of Ballet from the 16th Century to Today selected for "Books for the Teen Age" by the New York Public Library; Orbus Pictus Award nomination, 1996, for *Letter to the World: The Life and Dances of Martha Graham.*

WRITINGS:

On Wings of Joy: The Story of Ballet from the 16th Century to Today, Little, Brown (Boston, MA), 1994.
Letter to the World: The Life and Dances of Martha Graham, Little, Brown, 1995.
Start Exploring: Ballet, Running Press (Philadelphia, PA), 1996.

WORK IN PROGRESS: Coppelia: Behind the Scenes at the Ballet; an illustrated history of American theatrical entertainments.

SIDELIGHTS: As a writer of children's books about dance, Trudy Garfunkel has satisfied two of her greatest and oldest passions: writing and ballet. A publicist/consultant by trade, Garfunkel has done many different kinds of writing on the job, from press releases to ghost writing magazine articles. She decided to write her first book when she was in her forties, after finally rejecting the excuse that she did not have enough time. An important motivation was the desire to give children something akin to her own childhood experience.

Garfunkel told *CA:* "For my love of books I thank my mother who early on instilled the idea that reading was something you did for fun and personal enjoyment and enlightenment; it was not just a chore to be gotten through for school homework assignments. Books were always treasured gifts in our house. Throughout my life I've tried to transmit this love of books and reading to the young people I've come in contact with. I've tried to write books that are not only educational but are fun to read."

Her first book, *On Wings of Joy: The Story of Ballet from the 16th Century to Today,* addresses the subject of ballet from the broadest perspective and relates the history of ballet from the Renaissance to modern day. *Booklist* critic Frances Bradburn praised Garfunkel for her ability to place the art of ballet and the lives of dancers, choreographers, and composers into a larger historical picture. Bradburn called *On Wings of Joy* a "a truly fascinating look at [ballet]." Striking a similar note, *School Library Journal* reviewer Kay McPherson commented that "Garfunkel covers an enormous amount of material in a readable and comprehensive manner without missing a beat."

Garfunkel narrowed her focus when she wrote her second book, *Letter to the World: The Life and Dances of Martha Graham.* This biography provides a detailed account of Graham's career as a dancer and choreographer and her contributions to early modern dance. A *Publisher's Weekly* reviewer deemed *Letter to the World* "a useful introduction to the dancer and the dance." A contributor to *Dance Magazine* called the book "well worth reading," continuing, "This biography has the forthright directness one associates with a thoroughly modern artist." Garfunkel hopes that such information will help young readers appreciate live dance performances and that her books will provide them with the means to learn about dance. She told *CA:* "It helps, I think, to know something about why [performances] are the way they are, how they got that way, who created them. Also, the lives of those who have left behind a lasting artistic legacy can provide inspiration to young people. Even though a knowledge of the past is necessary to explain the present, unfortunately, many kids today are not exposed to this cultural heritage. Fewer and fewer resources are given to arts education and appreciation in our schools. I hope that my books, in some small way, will help remedy this lack."

BIOGRAPHICAL/CRITICAL SOURCES:

PERIODICALS

Booklist, October 15, 1994, p. 409; June 1-15, 1995, p. 1766.
Dance Magazine, December 1995, p. 57.
Publishers Weekly, May 8, 1995, p. 298.
School Library Journal, November 1994, p. 124-25; July 1995, p. 85.

* * *

GATES, Bill 1955-

PERSONAL: Born William Henry Gates III, October 28, 1955, in Seattle, WA; son of William Henry, Jr. (an attorney) and Mary (a corporate director and university regent; maiden name, Maxwell) Gates; married Melinda French (a manager at Microsoft Corporation), January 1, 1994; children: one daughter. *Education:* Attended Harvard University, 1973-75. *Avocational interests:* Tennis, studying biotechnology.

ADDRESSES: Office—Microsoft Corporation, 1 Microsoft Way, Redmond, WA 98052.

CAREER: Began developing and marketing computer software while still in high school; computer programmer for TRW, 1973; MITS, Albuquerque, NM, computer programmer, 1975; Microsoft Corporation, Redmond, WA, 1975—, co-founder (with Paul Allen), currently chair and chief executive officer; author and public speaker.

AWARDS, HONORS: Howard Collum Award, Reed College (Portland, OR), 1984; National Medal of Technology, U.S. Department of Commerce Technical Administration, 1992; named CEO of the Year, *Chief Executive Magazine,* 1994; Lifetime Achievement Award for Technical Excellence, *PC Magazine,* 1995.

WRITINGS:

(With Nathan Myhrvold and Peter Rinearson) *The Road Ahead* (includes companion interactive CD-ROM), Viking (New York), 1995.

SIDELIGHTS: "We have met the future, and its name is Bill." Thus declared Boyd Tonkin in a *New Statesman and Society* review of *The Road Ahead,* software

guru and information visionary Bill Gates's long-awaited tome on the information superhighway and how it will figure in our lives in the decades to come. Released just before Christmas 1995, *The Road Ahead* marked the end of a particularly eventful year in the life of the cofounder, chair, and CEO of computer software giant Microsoft Corporation. As Philip Elmer-DeWitt explained in *Time,* "For more than a decade he has towered over the world of computing. . . . But this was the year that Bill Gates . . . rose above the confines of computer land and became a global celebrity. . . . His is the ultimate revenge of the nerd."

Gates has provided the business and technical leadership for Microsoft since 1975, when he and a high school friend established the company to develop and market software for the fledgling personal computer (PC) industry. Since then, Microsoft has come to dominate PCs the world over, both in the workplace and at home. As of the end of 1995, for example, eight out of ten PCs used Microsoft's operating-system software (MS-DOS, Windows, Windows 95, or Windows NT) and five out of ten ran various Microsoft application programs to handle word processing (Word), electronic spreadsheets (Excel), filing (Access), and scheduling (Project), either separately or as part of the all-in-one program "suite" known as Office. And on the home PC front, Microsoft's Flight Simulator game, Bookshelf reference collection, and Encarta encyclopedia are perennial bestsellers. All of this helps Microsoft claim nearly half the revenues in PC software worldwide.

Gates's goal in writing *The Road Ahead* when he began the project in the spring of 1994 was to share his thoughts on one aspect of computing that Microsoft had not yet tackled in any major way—the information superhighway. Later, when asked by Steven Levy and Mark Whitaker of *Newsweek* why he had decided to make that the subject of his first book, Gates said: "I think it's a period where people are hearing about information superhighways and the Internet, and they're wondering where this is going to go. . . . I wanted to write the book so that if you knew about PCs you wouldn't feel like I was talking down to you, but that you wouldn't have to know much at all to read it." In short, said Levy, Gates assumes "the role of a high-tech Disney, guiding us through the way we will live after this new revolution morphs us into wireheads."

In *The Road Ahead,* Gates begins with an overview of the computer industry, including the early days of the personal computer, his introduction to the field, and the beginnings of Microsoft. He then discusses some of the fascinating new technology just now coming into use, ideas that are on the horizon, and possibilities that are still a number of years away.

"To say he is bullish [on the future] is an understatement," observed Levy. "For those of us who suspect that this world presents exciting new opportunities, Gates tells us our hopes will be fulfilled and attempts to outline specifically how our chances for fortune will expand." He does so not only in terms of new gadgets we will be using, such as hand-held "wallet PCs," but also in terms of new services we can expect and even new ways of doing business via the Internet—what he calls "friction-free capitalism." (Under this scenario, distributive middlemen will become relics of the past, and consumers will deal directly with businesses large and small all over the world.) In addition, information of every type imaginable will be available at the touch of a fingertip, and accessing it can be customized to suit each individual's own pre-programmed needs, desires, and interests. And, says Gates, more and more people will "telecommute" to work in the future, thus easing some of the urban congestion that he feels is responsible for many of today's major social problems.

Describing *The Road Ahead* as "an amiable blend of business memoir and hi-tech manifesto," Tonkin nevertheless expressed some uneasiness about the isolation and self-centeredness such a future holds. Gates's "model of communication rules out all those encounters with the new, the strange, the different—with *otherness*—that go to make up a personality who can acquire tastes and exercise free choice," noted Tonkin. "The libertarian thinker Ivan Illich called his book about humane technology *Tools for Conviviality.* Microsoft's Utopia sounds much more like *Gizmos for Narcissism.*"

Commenting in the *Spectator,* Tobias Jones made a similar point about the vision of the future contained in *The Road Ahead.* "In the new dawn which Bill Gates describes the sun has no part to play," Jones declared. "His 'road ahead' has no scenery, and it promises to lead only to a facsimile life played out in the brave new world of technology. . . . Over this adolescent *Star Trek* fantasy, Gates spreads a thin veneer of idealism. . . . Like the hippies in the Sixties, Gates and his nerds in the Nineties promise to usher us all along the yellow-brick road to love and peace." Jones concluded his review with an observa-

tion shared by a few other critics—namely, that Gates ultimately reveals himself to be "an economist, not a prophet," whose interest in new technologies actually ranks second to his interest in how businesses (i.e., Microsoft) can best exploit those innovations.

As a result, declared Joseph Nocera in the *New York Times Book Review,* Gates's book "is perhaps best characterized as the latest product generated by the Microsoft Corporation. . . . [It is] bland and tepid. It reads as if it had been vetted by a committee of Microsoft executives. . . . Again and again, [Gates] pulls back from the supposed glories of future technologies to pose the questions that really engage him: how much these technologies will cost, how many people will buy them and how much money can be made from them." In the end, commented Nocera, the vision Gates serves up to his readers "is a narrow and constricted [one], amounting to little more than a recitation of the emerging conventional wisdom about the information superhighway. . . . If this book really represents the sum of his vision on the future, then his own road ahead is going to be a long, hard slog."

Geoff Lewis of *Business Week* was also disappointed in how little Gates actually reveals about how he and Microsoft see the future. Like Nocera, Lewis found *The Road Ahead* so "breezy, well-modulated, and almost completely humorless" that "it often reads like the product of a much larger committee [than the three credited authors]. . . . But the real disappointment . . . is the way it obscures what Gates is really thinking. Instead of learning what's going on behind those egghead glasses, we get a very conventional recitation of what is by now very conventional wisdom." Rather than picking up the book, concluded Lewis, "readers might do better to focus on the entertaining CD-ROM version of *The Road Ahead.* . . . It sticks pretty close to the book, but at least it shows some of Microsoft's promotional flair."

Writing in the *New York Review of Books,* James Fallows suggested that in light of Microsoft's domination of the computer culture, it might be best to regard *The Road Ahead* "as a preemptive effort to explain that Gates himself, the company he has built, and the industry he symbolizes are all benign forces to be trusted and believed in. Gates's presentation of himself in the book is consistent with the blandness of his formal speeches and most of the interviews he has given over the years. But it is also puzzling. . . . In his business life the author of *The Road Ahead* is an interesting and complex figure, as driven and as capable of driving others as Lyndon Johnson was in politics. . . . [That man] is missing from the book, replaced by someone determined to sound respectable in front of the grown-ups."

When asked in the *Newsweek* interview if he was trying to reassure people with his upbeat take on the future, Gates responded: "I wrote exactly what I think is going to unfold. My basic approach to computing from the beginning has been optimistic." Meanwhile, Gates is busy tackling the challenges of the present while contemplating the future. A latecomer to the Internet, Microsoft launched its own online service, the Microsoft Network (MSN), in August, 1995, at the same time it released Windows 95, its long-anticipated upgrade of the popular Windows program. With other services such as America Online and CompuServe already firmly established in the marketplace, however, MSN faces an uphill climb for subscribers. And others have beaten Microsoft to the punch in developing software to search the Internet; as of mid-1996, for example, Netscape Communication's popular Netscape Navigator program was used by about eighty percent of the people who browse the World Wide Web.

As someone who sees a variety of different technologies coalescing in one super-PC, Gates has not limited his efforts to the Internet. In 1995, he purchased the Bettmann Archives, one of the world's foremost collections of historical photographs, with plans to turn it into a vast digital library. The following year, he bought the electronic rights to Ansel Adams's works. Also in 1996, he teamed up with the NBC television network to create a 24-hour cable and online news service (known as MSNBC) to compete with CNN. In addition, Gates is involved in developing interactive entertainment products with Hollywood's DreamWorks SKG studio, in creating interactive television systems with cable giant Telecommunications Inc., and in building telecommunications satellites with Teledesic Corporation.

Yet as Levy observed about the man he described as "the richest man on the planet, and maybe the smartest," even though Gates may be seeking a higher public profile while taking on projects that seem somewhat removed from Microsoft's core business, "he has never presented himself as anything other than a software entrepreneur, passionately devoted to maintaining his company's continued leadership and profits. If submitting to interviews, or writing a book, will help matters, so be it. The road ahead is

important to Gates, but what keeps him going is his drive to get there first."

BIOGRAPHICAL/CRITICAL SOURCES:

BOOKS

Boyd, Aaron, *Smart Money: The Story of Bill Gates,* Morgan Reynolds, 1995.

Gates, Bill, Nathan Myhrvold, and Peter Rinearson, *The Road Ahead,* Viking, 1995.

Ichbiah, Daniel, and Susan L. Knepper, *The Making of Microsoft: How Bill Gates and His Team Created the World's Most Successful Software Company,* Prima, 1991.

Manes, Stephen, and Paul Andrews, *Gates: How Microsoft's Mogul Reinvented an Industry—and Made Himself the Richest Man in America,* Doubleday, 1993.

Wallace, James, and Jim Erickson, *Hard Drive: Bill Gates and the Making of the Microsoft Empire,* Wiley, 1992.

Zickgraf, Ralph, *William H. Gates: From Whiz Kid to Software King,* Garrett Educational Corp., 1991.

PERIODICALS

Business Week, June 27, 1994; November 28, 1994; December 4, 1995, pp. 13-16.

Forbes, July 17, 1995, p. 110.

Fortune, January 16, 1995; December 11, 1995, p. 38.

Nation, February 5, 1996, pp. 28-31.

New Statesman and Society, November 24, 1995, p. 48.

Newsweek, June 24, 1991; October 11, 1993; July 11, 1994; November 27, 1995, pp. 54-57, 73-74.

New York Review of Books, February 15, 1996, pp. 14-18.

New York Times, April 2, 1996, p. C13.

New York Times Book Review, December 24, 1995, p. 7.

New York Times Magazine, August 25, 1991; November 5, 1995.

PC Magazine, December 19, 1995, p. 135.

People, August 20, 1990, pp. 91-98.

Spectator, December 2, 1995, p. 43.

Time, June 14, 1993; January 30, 1995, p. 79; June 5, 1995, pp. 46-54; October 23, 1995, p. 107; December 25, 1995-January 1, 1996, p. 101.*

—Sketch by Deborah Gillan Straub

GATES, William Henry III
  See GATES, Bill

*   *   *

GAUBATZ, Kathlyn Taylor   1957-

PERSONAL: Born April 10, 1957, in Oakland, CA; daughter of John B. and Thelma K. Taylor; married Kurt Gaubatz (a professor), May 31, 1980; children: Jayne, Andrew. *Education:* University of California, Berkeley, A.B., 1979; Princeton University, M.A., 1984, Ph.D., 1989.

ADDRESSES: Office—Compass Community Services, 942 Market St., 6th Floor, San Francisco, CA 94102.

CAREER: Brandeis University, Waltham, MA, assistant director of National Institute for Sentencing Alternatives, 1980-81; New England Coalition Against Prisons, Boston, MA, coordinator, 1981-82; Compass Community Services, San Francisco, counselor, 1989-90, coordinator and case manager in Homeless Family Program, 1990-91, program director at CCR Family Center and Market Street Counseling Center, 1991-94, executive director, 1994—.

MEMBER: Phi Beta Kappa.

WRITINGS:

Crime in the Public Mind, University of Michigan Press (Ann Arbor, MI), 1995.

*   *   *

GEMMELL, David A(ndrew)   1948-
  (Ross Harding)

PERSONAL: Born August 1, 1948, in London, England; married; wife's name, Valerie; children: one son, one daughter. *Ethnicity:* British. *Education:* Attended Faraday Comprehensive School.

ADDRESSES: 180 Mill Lane, Hastings TN35 5EU, England.

CAREER: Worked for Pepsi Cola, London, 1965; *Westminster Press,* London, reporter and editor,

1966-72; *Hastings Observer,* editor, 1976; *Folkestone Herald,* editor, 1984; full-time writer, 1986—.

WRITINGS:

FANTASY NOVELS; DRENAI SERIES

Legend, Century (London), 1984, published in the United States as *Against the Horde,* New Infinities (Delavan, WI), 1988.
The King beyond the Gate, Century, 1985, New Infinities, 1988.
Waylander, Century, 1986, New Infinities, 1988.
Quest for Lost Heroes, Legend (London), 1990.
Drenai Tales (omnibus; includes *Waylander, Legend, The King beyond the Gate,* and an original short story), Legend, 1991.
Waylander II: In the Realm of the Wolf, Legend, 1992.

FANTASY NOVELS; SIPSTRASSI SERIES

Wolf in Shadow, Century, 1987, published in the United States as *The Jerusalem Man,* Baen (New York), 1988.
Ghost King, Century, 1988.
Last Sword of Power, Legend, 1988.
The Last Guardian, Legend, 1989.
Stones of Power (omnibus; includes *Wolf in Shadow, Ghost King, Last Sword of Power* and *The Last Guardian*), Legend, 1992.
Bloodstone, Legend, 1994.
The Complete Chronicles of the Jerusalem Man (omnibus; includes *Wolf in Shadow, The Last Guardian,* and *Bloodstone*), Legend, 1995.

FANTASY NOVELS; MACEDON SERIES

Lion of Macedon, Legend, 1990, Del Rey (New York), 1992.
The Dark Prince, Legend, 1991.

FANTASY NOVELS; THE HAWK QUEEN SERIES

Ironhand's Daughter, Legend, 1995.
The Hawk Eternal, Legend, 1996.

SHORT STORIES

The First Chronicles of Druss the Legend, Legend, 1993.
The Second Chronicles of Druss the Legend: Druss the Axeman, Legend, 1995.

OTHER

Knights of Dark Renown (novel), Legend, 1989.
The Lost Crown (for children), Hutchinson (London), 1989.
Morningstar (novel), Legend, 1992.
(As Ross Harding) *White Knight, Black Swan* (novel), Arrow (London), 1993.

ADAPTATIONS: Several of Gemmell's novels have been adapted by Stan Nicholls and released as graphic novels, including *Legend,* illustrated by Fangorn, Legend, 1993; and *Wolf in Shadow,* illustrated by Fangorn, Legend, 1994.

*   *   *

GIDAL, Nachum
See GIDAL, Tim Nachum

*   *   *

GIDAL, Tim Nachum   1909-1996
(Nachum Gidal, Nachum Gidalewitsch)

OBITUARY NOTICE—See index for *CA* sketch: Original name Nachum Ignaz Gidalewitsch; name legally changed in 1936; born May 18, 1909, in Munich, Germany; emigrated to the United States, 1948; naturalized citizen, 1953; died October 6, 1996, in Jerusalem, Israel. Educator, photojournalist, writer. Gidal gained recognition for his work *The Jews In Germany from Roman Times to the Weimar Republic.* While attending the University of Munich and the University of Berlin, Gidal began his career as a photojournalist. In Germany, he worked for several magazines, including *Berliner Illustrierte* and *Die Woche.* In 1936, Gidal began freelancing for American and British magazines in Palestine (now Israel) and in 1938 landed a position with London's *Picture Post.* During World War II, Gidal served with the British Army in the Middle East, Burma, China and North Africa as a photographer. After the war, he continued to work as a freelance photographer, lectured at the New School for Social Research in New York and the Hebrew University of Jerusalem, and had many exhibitions of his work. Throughout his lifetime, Gidal wrote and illustrated many books, some under the names of Nachum Gidal and Nachum Gidalewitsch. He and his wife, Sonia, wrote a series

of "My Village" books which included his photographs. His works include *My Village in Morocco* and *My Village in Thailand* (with Sonia Gidal), *Land of Promise: Photographs from 1850 to 1948* (as Nachum Gidal), and *Chroniclers of Life: The Modern Fotoreportage.*

OBITUARIES AND OTHER SOURCES:

BOOKS

Macmillan Biographical Encyclopedia of Photographic Artists and Innovators, Macmillan Publishing Co., 1983.

PERIODICALS

Times (London), November 13, 1996, p. 21.

*   *   *

GIDALEWITSCH, Nachum
See GIDAL, Tim Nachum

*   *   *

GILDEA, Robert   1952-

PERSONAL: Born December 9, 1952, in Egham, England; son of Denis (a civil servant) and Hazel (a counselor) Gildea; married Lucy-Jean Lloyd, March 21, 1987; children: Rachel, Georgia, William. *Education:* Merton College, Oxford, B.A., M.A., 1974; attended St. Antony's College, Oxford, 1974-76; St. John's College, Oxford, D.Phil., 1978. *Politics:* Labour.

ADDRESSES: Home—185 Divinity Rd., Oxford OX4 1LP, England. *Office*—Merton College, Oxford University, Oxford OX1 4JD, England.

CAREER: Oxford University, Oxford, England, fellow and tutor in modern history at Merton College, 1979—, reader in modern history, 1996—.

MEMBER: Royal Historical Society (fellow).

WRITINGS:

Education in Provincial France, 1800-1916, Oxford University Press (Oxford, England), 1983.

Barricades and Borders: Europe, 1800-1916, Oxford University Press, 1987, 2nd edition, 1996.

France, 1870-1914, Longman, 1988, 2nd edition, 1996.

The Past in French History, Yale University Press (New Haven, CT), 1994.

France since 1945, Oxford University Press, 1996.

WORK IN PROGRESS: Research on the French under German occupation in the Loire region, 1940-45.

*   *   *

GILLER, Robert M(aynard) 1942-1996

OBITUARY NOTICE—See index for *CA* sketch: Born September 14, 1942, in Chicago, IL; died in an automobile accident, October 18, 1996, in Manahawkin, NJ. Physician and author. Giller is remembered as the physician who authored several health-care books regarding stress and weight loss. Giller was a resident of internal medicine at Cornell University Hospital from 1968 to 1969. In 1969, Giller left Cornell to serve with the United States Army Medical Corps. In 1974, he set up private practice, and in 1975, joined the faculty of the New School for Social Research. Giller's theory that stress creates chemical changes in the body brought him into the spotlight. Through the use of vitamins, minerals, and diet restrictions, other than pure willpower, Giller treated athletes and performers in reducing their stress levels. His written works include *A Guide for Health* and *Maximum Metabolism: The Diet Breakthrough for Permanent Weight Loss.* He is also the co-author, with Kathy Matthews, of such volumes as *Natural Prescriptions: Dr. Giller's Natural Treatments and Vitamin Therapies for More Than 100 Common Ailments* and *Medical Makeover: The Revolutionary, No-Willpower Program for Lifetime Health.*

OBITUARIES AND OTHER SOURCES:

BOOKS

Who's Who, 148th edition, St. Martin's, 1996.

PERIODICALS

New York Times, October 22, 1996, p. D27.

GLASPELL, Susan 1882(?)-1948

PERSONAL: Born July 1, 1882 (some sources say 1876), in Davenport, IA; died July 27, 1948, in Provincetown, MA; daughter of Elmer S. and Alice (Keating) Glaspell.; married George Cram Cook (a writer), 1913 (died, 1924); married Norman Matson, 1925 (divorced, 1932). *Education:* Drake University, Ph.D., 1899; attended University of Chicago, 1902.

CAREER: Writer. Worked as reporter for *Des Moines Daily News* and *Des Moines Capital* in Des Moines, IA, 1899-1901; freelance writer in Davenport, IA, 1900-11; Provincetown Players, Provincetown, MA, co-founder and writer, 1915-22; Federal Theater Project's Midwest Play Bureau, 1936-38.

AWARDS, HONORS: Pulitzer Prize for drama from Columbia University, 1931, for *Alison's House.*

WRITINGS:

NOVELS

The Glory of the Conquered: The Story of a Great Love, Frederick A. Stokes Co., 1909.

The Visioning, Frederick A. Stokes Co., 1911.

Fidelity, Maynard & Co., 1915.

Brook Evans, Frederick A. Stokes Co., 1928, published as *The Right to Love,* 1930.

Fugitive's Return, Frederick A. Stokes Co., 1929.

Ambrose Holt and Family, Frederick A. Stokes Co., 1931.

The Morning Is Near Us, Frederick A. Stokes Co., 1939.

Cherished and Shared of Old, Julian Messner, 1940.

Norma Ashe, Lippincott, 1942.

Judd Rankin's Daughter, Lippincott, 1945, published as *Prodigal's Giver,* 1946.

PLAYS

(With husband, George Cram Cook) *Suppressed Desires* (one-act), produced in 1915.

Trifles (one-act), produced in 1916.

Close the Book (one-act), produced in 1917.

The Outside (one-act), produced in 1917.

The People (one-act), produced in 1917.

Woman's Honor (one-act), produced in 1918.

(With Cook) *Tickless Time* (one-act), produced in 1918.

Bernice (three-act), produced in 1919.

Plays (includes *Suppressed Desires, Trifles, Close the Book, The Outside, The People, Woman's Honor, Tickless Time,* and *Bernice*), Maynard & Co., 1920.

Inheritors, Small, Maynard & Co., 1921.

The Verge (produced in 1921), Small, Maynard & Co., 1922.

Chains of Dew, produced in 1922.

(With husband, Norman Matson) *The Comic Artist,* Frederick A. Stokes Co., 1927.

Alison's House, Samuel French, 1930.

Plays (includes *Trifles, The Outside, The Verge,* and *Inheritors*), edited by C. W. E. Bigsby, Cambridge University Press, 1987.

Plays represented in various anthologies.

OTHER

Editor, George Cram Cook, *Greek Coins,* George H. Doran Co., 1925.

The Road to the Temple (biography of first husband, George Cram Cook), Frederick A. Stokes Co., 1927.

Also author of *Lifted Masks: Stories,* 1912; and *A Jury of Her Peers* (short stories), 1927. Contributor to periodicals.

ADAPTATIONS: Brook Evans was filmed as *Right to Love* in 1930.

SIDELIGHTS: Susan Glaspell was a prominent American writer who won acclaim for her stage works and fiction that appeared during the first half of the twentieth century. Glaspell was born in 1876 in Davenport, Iowa. She earned a doctorate at Drake University in nearby Des Moines in 1899, after which she began working as a reporter for both the *Des Moines Daily News* and the *Des Moines Capital.* By 1901, Glaspell was also publishing regularly in various magazines aimed at female readers. Eight years later she produced her first novel, *The Glory of the Conquered: The Story of a Great Love.* In this melodrama, a young woman artist marries a scientist who soon dies, and the heroine devotes her art to expressing the love she enjoyed in marriage.

In 1910 Glaspell toured Europe. After returning to the United States, she entered into a romance with George Cram Cook, an idealistic writer who was supporting his wife and children by working as both a farmer and a writer. After a few years, Cook and

his wife divorced and Glaspell moved with him to New York City.

Glaspell's early fiction—both her magazine stories and *The Glory of the Conquered*—were rather simplistic melodramas in which heroines sought to realize both romance and riches. But after meeting Cook, whom she married in 1913, Glaspell began to incorporate his socialist ideals into her own writings. In 1911 she published *The Visioning,* a novel in which a self-absorbed young woman becomes a socialist. The heroine, Katherine Wayneworth Jones, is the daughter of a prestigious military officer. As such, she has enjoyed privileged status while growing up on various military bases. But after preventing a friend from committing suicide, Jones begins to understand what she perceives as the crushing nature of life in a capitalist, sexist society.

Jones learns that one of her own suitors had once exploited her suicidal friend. In addition, she discovers that the friend's own upbringing was harsh and restrictive. Later, Jones befriends Alan Mann, a charismatic repairman who exposes her to radical volumes on socialism and evolutionism. Jones, who has spent much of her life enjoying the favoritism incurred as a consequence of her father's military prominence, is initially offended to learn that Mann had been courtmartialed and dishonorably discharged from the army. By novel's end, however, she is in love with him.

In her next novel, 1915's *Fidelity,* Glaspell writes of a young woman whose predicament recalls Glaspell's early affair with Cook. As was Glaspell, the heroine of *Fidelity* is in love with a married man. Unlike Glaspell, though, *Fidelity*'s heroine rejects her lover's proposal of marriage and travels alone to New York City. In 1915 Glaspell and Cook founded the Provincetown Players, which was designed to produce the works of promising new American playwrights. Most prominent among the writers drawn to the Provincetown Players was Eugene O'Neill, who would later write such works as *The Iceman Cometh* and *Long Day's Journey into Night.*

Glaspell, however, also proved an accomplished playwright. Among her first plays produced by the Provincetown Players is the one-act *Trifles,* in which two women talk in a kitchen while their husbands conduct a murder investigation. The women, who are dismissed by the men as inconsequential, realize that the killer, a reclusive woman, had been driven to kill her husband by his abusive behavior.

Another of Glaspell's more noted plays is *The Outside,* a one-act drama about two elderly women, an optimist and a pessimist, who compare perspectives. Glaspell followed *The Outside* with two rather modest one-act plays: *Woman's Honor,* in which several women volunteer to provide alibis for a suspected killer, and *Tickless Time,* wherein a couple forsake the use of a clock.

In 1919 the Provincetown Players staged Glaspell's first three-act play, *Bernice.* In this play an unfaithful husband vows to become a better person after learning that his wife his killed herself in despair over his infidelity. Glaspell then wrote *Inheritors,* in which a carefree young woman learns of life's cruelties and determines to maintain humanitarian principles. More disturbing is Glaspell's next drama, *The Verge,* which concerns a rich, idealistic woman who longs for romantic experiences. She becomes increasingly involved with an aspiring ascetic who becomes, in turn, repelled by her longing for physical love. The relationship ends with a sudden, violent act.

Although Glaspell enjoyed a fair measure of success with the Provincetown Players, her husband longed for more personally fulfilling ventures. In 1922 the couple departed for Greece, where Cook—a long-time enthusiast of Greek classicism—established himself as a scholar. Two years later Cook contracted an illness and died. Glaspell later produced *The Road to the Temple,* a biography of Cook which incorporated his writings.

While touring Europe as a widow, Glaspell befriended Norman Matson, a writer. In 1925 the couple married, and in 1927 they collaborated on *The Comic Artist,* a stage comedy. The next year Glaspell completed another novel, *Brook Evans,* a melodrama in which a headstrong woman comes to understand her own mother's reckless ways. Glaspell followed *Brook Evans* with *Fugitive's Return,* wherein a suicidal woman moves to Greece and eventually comes to understand how her own insecurities undermined relationships with her various lovers, including the husband who had abandoned her. Unfortunately, by the time of *Fugitive's Return*'s publication, Glaspell's own marriage was deteriorating, and by 1931 she and Matson were divorced.

In 1930, even as her marriage was failing, Glaspell enjoyed her greatest career success with *Alison's House,* a play in which the relatives of a dead poet, Alison, confront their own feelings about love. Alison's brother is determined to sell the family home despite his living sister's objections. After this sister also dies, the brother discovers her collection of Alison's unpublished poems. The brother shares these poems with his prodigal daughter, who has returned after having an affair with a married man. Through the poems, the brother and his daughter realize a greater understanding of love and each other. For this play, Glaspell was awarded a Pulitzer Prize.

Despite the recognition accorded *Alison's House,* Glaspell completed no further plays but concentrated instead on fiction. In 1931 she published *Ambrose Holt and Family,* the story of a family man torn between his urge to write poetry and his desire for material gain. After the suicide of his father, the hero finds himself liberated from various anxieties, and he vows to renew himself as a poet.

Nine years passed before Glaspell produced her next novel, *The Morning Is Near Us.* In this work a woman returns to her family home after learning that she has inherited it from her late father, who had sent her away when she was a child. Curious as to why her presumably uncaring father had left her the home, the heroine begins an inquiry into her family's past. She learns that her father is not dead but is living in an asylum, where he had been imprisoned after killing a man for insulting the heroine's mother. The father eventually escapes from the asylum and manages to tell his daughter that she is actually the daughter of her mother's lover and that it was the mother who insisted that she be sent away.

In the 1940s Glaspell published only a few more works. In 1942 she produced *Norma Ashe,* a characteristically melodramatic tale which recalls a once promising student's decline into poverty and unhappiness. When the heroine, now aged and the mother of a grown son, returns to her old university, she discovers that a formerly inspirational instructor is now professing less humanitarian views. Nevertheless, the heroine manages to befriend a young student, to whom she imparts her ideals and hopes for a greater humankind.

Glaspell's last novel, *Judd Rankin's Daughter,* is the story of a woman divided by sympathies for her husband, a leftist, and respect for her father, a conservative. When the heroine's son returns from service in World War II, he joins with an outspoken opponent of his father. Family tensions increase when the heroine's father publishes a book which her son initially interprets as justification for his own misanthropy. But when the heroine pays a visit to her aging father, she realizes that his admittedly conservative values have some merit.

Glaspell died in Provincetown in 1948. In the ensuing years, recognition of her work has diminished somewhat. She is, however, remembered for her key role in the Provincetown Players and for her important contributions to American theatre.

BIOGRAPHICAL/CRITICAL SOURCES:

BOOKS

Dictionary of Literary Biography, Volume 9: *American Novelists, 1910-1945,* Gale, 1981; Volume 78: *American Short-Story Writers, 1880-1910,* Gale, 1989.
Waterman, Arthur E., *Susan Glaspell,* Twayne, 1966.

PERIODICALS

Belles Lettres, spring, 1994, p. 65.
Times Literary Supplement, February 5, 1988, p. 139.*

*   *   *

GOBBELL, John J.   1937-

PERSONAL: Born August 28, 1937, in San Diego, CA; son of Williard M. (a physician) and Dorothy P. (a homemaker) Gobbell; married July 15, 1960; wife's name Janine; children: Jennifer Gobbell Cheffer, John J., Jr. *Ethnicity:* "American." *Education:* University of Southern California, B.A., 1960. *Politics:* Republican. *Religion:* Episcopalian. *Avocational interests:* Yacht racing.

ADDRESSES: Home—659 Promontory Dr. E., Newport Beach, CA 92660. *Office*—Gobbell Co., 1001 Dove St., Suite 190, Newport Beach, CA 92660. *E-mail*—jgobbell@pacbell.net. *Agent*—Wallace Agency, 177 East 70th St., New York, NY 10021.

CAREER: KPMG Peat Marwick (certified public accountants), Los Angeles, CA, consultant, 1967-70; Angeles Corp. (investors), Los Angeles, director of personnel, 1970-73; Boyden Associates, Inc. (executive recruiters), New York City, vice-president of branch in Newport Beach, CA, 1973-83; Gobbell Co. (executive recruiters), Newport Beach, managing di-

rector, 1983—. USC Commerce Associates, president. Orange County Fictionaires (reading group), president, 1996. *Military service:* U.S. Navy, 1960-62, deck officer on a destroyer; became lieutenant.

WRITINGS:

The Brutus Lie (novel), Scribner (New York), 1991.
The Last Lieutenant (novel), St. Martin's (New York), 1995.

WORK IN PROGRESS: Traitor on the Bridge; a screenplay adaptation of *The Brutus Lie.*

SIDELIGHTS: John J. Gobbell told *CA:* "My primary motivation for writing is that I finally figured out a way to put my daydreams to work. I am influenced by top-of-the-line thriller and action-adventure authors. My writing process is helter-skelter, undisciplined, and totally unplanned. Scheduling helps, but I am soon distracted and in the process of shooting myself in the foot. I keep trying. I was inspired to write on the subjects I have chosen because I enjoy reading about man, machine, and overcoming enormous circumstances, using wit and intelligence in an extremely limited time."

*   *   *

GOINGBACK, Owl   1959-
(Jay Littlehawk)

PERSONAL: Born May 1, 1959, in St. Louis, MO; son of Quiet Starr (a book store manager); married Nancy Santos Bello (a professional cook), January 5, 1978; children: Jason, Michael. *Ethnicity:* "Native American." *Education:* Attended Embry Riddle Aeronautical University, Branch Office Torreson Air Force Base, Spain. *Avocational interests:* History, martial arts.

ADDRESSES: Home and office—P.O. Box 5080, Winter Park, FL 32793. *Agent*—Andrew Zack Literary Agency, P.O. Box 247, Westfield, NJ 07091-0247. *E-mail*—Genie: O.GOINGBACK.

CAREER: Restaurant owner, c. 1981-86; freelance writer, 1986—; lecturer on Native American folklore; speaker at science fiction conventions. *Military service*—U.S. Air Force, 1976-81; attained the rank of sergeant; good conduct medal and Air Force Longevity award.

MEMBER: Science Fiction and Fantasy Writers of America; Horror Writers Association.

AWARDS, HONORS: Nominated for a Nebula Award from the Science Fiction and Fantasy Writers of America, for best short story of 1995, for "Grass Dancer."

WRITINGS:

Crota (novel), D. I. Fine (New York), 1996.
The Gift (juvenile), Wright Group (Bothell, WA), 1997.
Eagle Feathers (juvenile), Wright Group, 1997.
Shaman Moon (novel), White Wolf Publishing (Clarkston, GA), 1997.

Also contributor of stories to anthologies and books, including *Grails: Quests, Visitations and Other Occurrences,* Unnameable Press (Atlanta, GA), 1992; *Confederacy of the Dead,* Roc (New York), 1993; *When Will You Rage?,* White Wolf Publishing (Clarkston, GA), 1994; (Under both name Owl Goingback and pseudonym Jay Littlehawk) *Tales from the Great Turtle,* Tor Books (New York), 1994; *South from Midnight,* Southern Fried Press, 1994; *Werewolf Storytellers Handbook,* White Wolf Publishing, 1994; *Grails: Visitations of the Night,* Roc, 1994; *Excalibur* (includes the Nebula nominee "Grass Dancer"), Warner Books (New York), 1995; *The Book of Kings,* Roc, 1995; *The Fragile Path,* White Wolf Publishing, 1995; *Once Upon a Midnight,* Unnameable Press, 1995; *Phantoms of the Night,* DAW Books (New York), 1996.

WORK IN PROGRESS: A fantasy novel.

SIDELIGHTS: Native American author Owl Goingback has penned many science fiction and fantasy stories, and contributed to several anthologies in those genres. Goingback's first novel, *Crota,* was published in 1996. *Crota* is a horror novel, and the horrifying creature of the title springs from Native American myth. The human characters include Sheriff Skip Harding, who investigates the field-dressed bodies of the Crota's victims as if they are the victims of a particularly vicious human serial killer until Native American game warden Jay Little Hawk persuades him otherwise. William Marden, reviewing *Crota* in the *Orlando Sentinel,* noted the novel's "giving a scientific explanation for the survival of a creature that has lived since the time of the dinosaurs." He concluded by hailing the work as a "compelling page turner" which "fulfills its initial promise with a

dynamic ending complete with an unexpected but heartwarming twist."

Goingback has also written two books for children, *The Gift* and *Eagle Feathers.* For adults, he followed *Crota* with another novel, *Shaman Moon,* a tale of a Native American werewolf.

Goingback told *CA:* "I was raised in a rural farming community in the Midwest. Having few neighbors, and even fewer friends, I turned to books for companionship. I started out by reading mostly mysteries, but soon developed a fondness for science fiction, fantasy, and horror. Many a lonely night was spent being happily entertained by such masters of the genre as Ray Bradbury, Edgar Rice Burroughs, and H. P. Lovecraft. It was during those early years that I made my first attempts at writing stories. Some were good. Others were mercifully disposed of.

"Since my family didn't have much money, I knew that going to college was out of the question; therefore, I dropped out of high school in my senior year—at the ripe old age of seventeen—and enlisted in the Air Force to take advantage of the G. I. Bill. I gave up rural life for travels and adventures in Europe and the Middle East, learning that all people have basically the same hopes, desires, and dreams.

"At the age of twenty-one, I left the military to open a small restaurant in central Georgia. It was there, during lulls in business, that I returned to my love of writing. I started out writing self-defense articles for martial arts magazines, but switched to fiction writing at the advice of a friend. Drawing on my Native American heritage, I was soon weaving stories that earned critical acclaim from my peers.

"In 1986, I gave up the restaurant business in order to devote more of my time to my literary endeavors. I consider myself a modern storyteller, intertwining tales of fiction with issues of importance. Like the legends and folklore told by the oral storytellers of my people, the fiction stories I write are teaching stories. They all contain a bit of knowledge that I am sharing with others, but that knowledge is often hidden and it is up to the reader to find it."

BIOGRAPHICAL/CRITICAL SOURCES:

PERIODICALS

Orlando Sentinel, April 7, 1996.
San Francisco Examiner, July 9, 1996.

GOLD, Jerome 1943-

PERSONAL: Born September 8, 1943, in Chicago, IL; son of Sidney Singman and Edith (Hoffman) Gold; married Clotilde Rita Litchfield, August 20, 1965 (divorced, April, 1977); children: Jack Michael, David Charles, Leah Molina Antonia. *Ethnicity:* "Jewish." *Education:* Fullerton College, A.A., 1968; University of Montana, B.A., 1970, M.A., 1976; University of Washington, Seattle, Ph.D., 1988. *Avocational interests:* Scuba diving, running.

ADDRESSES: Home—Seattle, WA. *Office*—c/o Black Heron Press, P.O. Box 95676, Seattle, WA 98145.

CAREER: Juvenile rehabilitation counselor at a prison for children in the Pacific Northwest, 1991—. *Military service:* U.S. Army, 1963-66, 1981-82; served in Vietnam; earned Combat Infantryman's Badge and Senior Parachutists Badge. Achieved the rank of Major.

MEMBER: Amnesty International.

AWARDS, HONORS: Bumbershoot Book Award, 1996, for *Publishing Lives.*

WRITINGS:

The Negligence of Death (novel), Black Heron Press (Seattle, WA), 1984.
(With Les Galloway) *Of Great Spaces* (stories), Black Heron Press, 1987.
War Stories (chapbook of stories), Wonder Publishing (Seattle), 1990.
The Inquisitor (novel), Black Heron Press, 1991.
Life at the End of Time (chapbook of stories and essays), Black Heron Press, 1992.
(Editor) *Hurricanes,* Black Heron Press, 1994.
Publishing Lives: Interviews With Independent Book Publishers in the Pacific Northwest and British Columbia, Black Heron Press, 1996.
The Prisoner's Son (novel), Black Heron Press, 1996.

Work represented in anthologies, including *clear-cut: anthology,* Sub Rosa Press (Seattle), 1996; and *Ear to the Ground,* Cune Press (Seattle), 1997. Contributor of articles, essays, stories, poems, and reviews to periodicals, including *Redneck Review of Literature, Fever, Writers Northwest, Village Idiot, Left Bank,* and *Chiron Review,* and *Hawaii Review.*

WORK IN PROGRESS: Conducting interviews for *Publishing Lives,* Volume II: *In the Shadow of the*

Giants (tentative title), publication by Black Heron Press expected no later than 1999; research on book publishing.

SIDELIGHTS: Jerome Gold told *CA:* "Early on, my work was influenced by the writing and moral courage of Ernest Hemingway, George Orwell and Andre Malraux, then by the intellectual rigor of Shakespeare, Tolstoy and Dostoevski, and by their desire to comprehend the world. More recently (fifteen years ago) I came to admire the work of Philip K. Dick, Joan Didion, and Ursula K. LeGuin. Stylistically, I am indebted to Hemingway, Isak Dineson, and James Joyce.

"In terms of life influences, I think I inherited a certain intolerance for social injustice from my father. Also, I was a soldier in Vietnam; there seems no escaping that experience, at least in the United States. More important, I think, was my involvement as a local-level organizer during the War Against Poverty in the early 1970s. What I learned then about America and Americans I have carried with me for a quarter century.

"I am currently conducting interviews for a follow-up book to *Publishing Lives.* Where the first volume is composed of interviews with publishers, the second will include interviews with publishers, wholesalers, and distributors. My idea is to track, through interviews, the route of a book from the publisher to the reader. I am interested in the interplay between the personality of the individual cultural gatekeeper and the decisions he or she makes concerning the progress of the book.

"I am researching book publishing, but I am also concerned with the moral consequences of violence. I have spent much of my adult life in this investigation and expect I will continue. Themes of trauma, betrayal, and violence figure largely in my fiction. Of course, I anticipate other stories will develop from this investigation."

*   *   *

GOLDBERG, Miriam Levin 1914(?)-1996

OBITUARY NOTICE—See index for *CA* sketch: Born July 18, 1914 (one source says 1916), in Baku (now Azerbaijan), Russia; immigrated to the United States, c. 1919; died of emphysema, November 21, 1996, in

New York, NY. Educator, author. Goldberg gained prominence for her work in the field of education, particularly with challenged and gifted children. Goldberg came to the United States at the age of five when her family emigrated from Russia. She first began working with emotionally challenged children in 1937, at the Grove School in Madison, Connecticut. She taught there for eight years before moving to New York City to accept a position in a nursery school in the Bronx. In 1950, she joined the faculty of Columbia University's Teachers College, where she remained for twenty-six years. In 1955, her first book, *Planning for Talented Youth,* which she wrote with A. Harry Passow and Abraham J. Tannenbaum, was published. She followed this with several others, including *Research on the Talented, A Comparison of Mathematics Programs for Able Junior High School Students,* and *Effects of Various Approaches to Beginning Reading for Disadvantaged Children.*

OBITUARIES AND OTHER SOURCES:

PERIODICALS

New York Times, December 2, 1996, p. B12.

* * *

GOLDBERG, Natalie

PERSONAL: Born in the United States.

ADDRESSES: Agent—c/o Bantam Books, 1540 Broadway, New York, NY 10036.

CAREER: Writer and teacher of writing.

WRITINGS:

Chicken and in Love (poems), Holy Cow Press (Minneapolis, MN), 1980.
Writing Down the Bones: Freeing the Writer Within (nonfiction), Shambhala (Boston) 1986, abridged version released on audio-cassette by Shambhala, 1990.
Wild Mind: Living the Writer's Life (nonfiction), Bantam (New York), 1990.
Long Quiet Highway: Waking Up in America (nonfiction), Bantam, 1993.
Banana Rose (novel), Bantam, 1995.

Contributor of articles to periodicals, including *Writer's Digest.*

SIDELIGHTS: Natalie Goldberg is a teacher of writing and conductor of numerous writing workshops who shares her love of writing and seeks to inspire and instruct aspiring writers in two of her books, *Writing Down the Bones: Freeing the Writer Within* and *Wild Mind: Living the Writer's Life.* Interwoven among Goldberg's instructions are autobiographical portions that reveal Goldberg's own methods and struggles as a writer, as well as other more spiritual aspects of her life, especially the effect that Goldberg's study of Zen Buddhism has had on her life.

Laced with quotations from Zen masters, *Writing Down the Bones,* Goldberg's 1986 writer's guide, encourages others to look within themselves to find their own creative voice. This volume met with mixed reviews from critics such as *Sewanee Review*'s George Garrett, who asserted: "Not much practical advice for dealing with publishers or the big bad world here; but there are some helpful thoughts about creative flexibility and process. Most of what she says has to do with poetry, but it is more or less transferable wisdom." Goldberg, however, received praise for her 1990 book, *Wild Mind: Living the Writer's Life,* in which she shares more personal, intimate glimpses of her own life than in *Writing Down the Bones,* and demonstrates to reluctant writers how she integrates writing into her busy life. *Bloomsbury Review* contributor Kay Marie Porterfield found *Wild Mind* a "cause for celebration," and opined that Goldberg "provides both novice and seasoned writers with inspiration and insight into the process of writing from the heart."

In her 1993 publication, *Long Quiet Highway: Waking Up in America,* Goldberg reveals more details of her life as a woman, writer, and teacher, with special emphasis on feminism and meditation. At the heart of *Long Quiet Highway,* in particular, is Goldberg's relationship with Zen master Katagiri Roshi, whose life and teachings changed Goldberg's view of life, and of writing. Although highly personal in nature, *Long Quiet Highway* is rife with insight for writers and other artists. Critically well-received, *Long Quiet Highway* elicited praise from Mark Gerson, writing in *Quill and Quire:* "From the classrooms of her suburban childhood to her painful acceptance of Roshi's death, Goldberg writes from the heart of her experience, with an honest simplicity that is compelling." *Bloomsbury Review* contributor Judith K. Mahrer also applauded *Long Quiet Highway,* proclaiming: "I was deeply touched by this book. I felt I had been privileged to share, in very special ways, in the life of someone who has worked diligently to make sense of her life and to give it meaning. . . . Unlike her two earlier books, this is not a book on writing technique, though writing is one of the major themes. This book is really about waking up and living a conscious life."

Goldberg issued *Banana Rose,* her first novel, in 1995. The novel is set in the 1960s and opens in Taos, New Mexico, where Goldberg lives. Nell Schwartz, a frustrated artist from Brooklyn, New York, has come to Taos, to live in a commune. She renames herself Banana Rose and soon falls in love with Gauguin, a Minnesotan musician whose real name is George Howard. The couple leaves the commune for an adobe hut with no indoor plumbing, where they spend time making love, preparing vegetarian meals, and smoking marijuana with their friends, who have names such as Happiness and Neon. But, as the magic of their lives meets reality, their friends return to the more conventional world one by one. Banana Rose and Gauguin, too, leave Taos for Minneapolis, and quickly assimilate into the average American lifestyle, marrying, taking jobs, and reclaiming their original names. Ultimately, they divorce. Older and wiser, Nell moves back to New Mexico, where her artistic creativity blossoms.

Goldberg's depiction of the New Mexico landscape impressed reviewer Georgia Jones-Davis, who remarked in the *Los Angeles Times* that the author "allows [New Mexico's] raw, panoramic splendor to function like a living, breathing character in the story. . . . The spiritual quality of the place, the colors of the earth and sky, the smell of rain, the forked lightning, the shadows on Taos Mountain—none of this is lost on her characters." Commenting on the novel as a whole, Jones-Davis added: "*Banana Rose* is a problematic yet touching novel, awkward in places, poetic and amazingly powerful in others."

BIOGRAPHICAL/CRITICAL SOURCES:

BOOKS

Long Quiet Highway: Waking Up in America, Bantam, 1993.
Wild Mind: Living the Writer's Life, Bantam (New York), 1990.
Writing Down the Bones: Freeing the Writer Within, Shambhala (Boston), 1986.

PERIODICALS

Bloomsbury Review, March, 1991, p. 16; March-April, 1993, pp. 12, 22.

Los Angeles Times, January 31, 1995, p. E5.
Los Angeles Times Book Review, February 21, 1993, p. 6.
New York Times Book Review, April 16, 1995, p. 16.
Publishers Weekly, December 28, 1992, p. 52; January 9, 1995, p. 54; January 23, 1995, p. 44.
Quill and Quire, July, 1993, p. 53.
Sewanee Review, Summer, 1988, pp. 516-525.
Women's Review of Books, July-August, 1987, pp. 11-12.

*   *   *

GOLDING, Alan 1952-

PERSONAL: Born October 4, 1952, in London, England; son of Charles and Dorothy Margaret (a homemaker; maiden name, Marshall) Golding; married Lisa Beth Shapiro (a psychiatric social worker), May 19, 1984; children: Chase, Jordan. *Ethnicity:* "White." *Education:* University of Exeter, B.A., 1974; University of Chicago, M.A. (with honors), 1975, Ph.D. (with honors), 1980. *Politics:* "Left liberal." *Religion:* None. *Avocational interests:* Soccer, camping, hiking.

ADDRESSES: Home—Louisville, KY. *Office*—Department of English, University of Louisville, Louisville, KY 40292; fax 502-852-4182. *E-mail*—acgold01@ulkyvm.louisville.edu.

CAREER: Kishwaukee College, Malta, IL, faculty member, 1976; Roosevelt University, Chicago, IL, faculty member, 1977-79; University of California, Los Angeles, visiting lecturer in composition, 1980-84; University of Mississippi, Oxford, assistant professor of American literature, 1984-87; University of Louisville, Louisville, KY, assistant professor, 1987-90, associate professor, 1990-96, professor of American literature, 1996—.

AWARDS, HONORS: Fulbright fellow, 1974-80; award for best paper, Society for Eighteenth Century Studies, 1985; President's Award, University of Louisville, 1989.

WRITINGS:

From Outlaw to Classic: Canons in American Poetry, University of Wisconsin Press (Madison, WI), 1995.

Contributor to books, including *World, Self, Poem,* edited by Leonard M. Trawick, Kent State University Press (Kent, OH), 1990; *The Objectivist Nexus,* edited by Peter Quartermain and Rachel Blau DuPlessis, University of California Press (Los Angeles, CA), 1997; and *The Recovery of the Public World: Essays in Honor of Robin Blaser, His Poetry and Poetics,* edited by Ted Byrne and Charles Watts, 1997. Contributor of about forty articles and reviews to periodicals, including *Aerial, Contemporary Literature, Sagetrieb, Cafe Review, American Literary History,* and *Arizona Quarterly.*

WORK IN PROGRESS: Research on "issues of mainstream and margin in recent American poetry;" research on the institutionalization of avant-gardes.

* * *

GOODWIN, Jan   1944-

PERSONAL: Born February 10, 1944, in London, England. *Education:* Educated in Switzerland and England.

ADDRESSES: Home—New York City. *Agent*—Connie Clausen Associates, 250 East Eighty-seventh St., New York, NY 10028.

CAREER: Journalist. *Women's Realm,* London, England, diary and features editor; London News Service, England, news editor; *Us,* New York City, executive editor; *Ladies' Home Journal,* New York City, executive editor, 1978-88; Save the Children Federation, Westport, CT, program manager, 1988-91; writer. Has worked as a foreign correspondent for various newspapers and as a reporter for British Broadcasting Corporation Radio in London. Participant in Public Broadcasting Service (PBS) documentary on Afghan war, *Witnesses;* guest on television shows, including *Good Morning America, Nightline,* and *The Today Show;* guest lecturer on human rights issues; participant in president's "Conflict Resolution Conference," 1991, and the "Religion and Human Rights Conference," 1994. Director, United States Friends of Afghanistan committee; member of National Cambodia Crisis committee, Human Rights Watch committee, and National Committee for the Prevention of Child Abuse.

AWARDS, HONORS: Front Page Award, 1985, and named Newswoman of the Year, both for series on Afghanistan and Cambodia; Emma Award, for political coverage; Clarion Award, for series on child pornography; nominated for Pulitzer Prize, for *Price of Honor: Muslim Women Lift the Veil of Silence on the Islamic World.*

WRITINGS:

Caught in the Crossfire (nonfiction), Dutton, 1987.
Price of Honor: Muslim Women Lift the Veil of Silence on the Islamic World, Little, Brown (New York), 1994.

Contributor to periodicals, including *Cosmopolitan, Ladies' Home Journal, Mirabella, New Woman,* and *Redbook.*

Author's works have been translated into German, Dutch, Japanese, French, and Hebrew.

SIDELIGHTS: Jan Goodwin is an acclaimed writer on current events and socio-cultural issues. A long-time journalist and magazine editor, Goodwin traveled to Afghanistan in 1985 to report on the invasion of Afghanistan by the Soviet Union. "As a reporter who has covered four wars, I was shocked by the brutality of this conflict and by the frequent atrocities carried out against the civilian population," Goodwin stated, as quoted in *Ladies' Home Journal.* Although journalists were banned from the region, Goodwin disguised herself as an Afghan and spent three months with the freedom fighters known as the Mujahideen. The resultant book, *Caught in the Crossfire,* published in 1987, provides a vivid account of a conflict in which the Soviets—despite their superior forces—resorted to such extreme measures as chemical warfare and genocide. J. Y. Smith, writing in the *Washington Post Book World,* affirmed that "Goodwin has an extraordinary story" and added, "she tells it with great verve and an engaging enthusiasm."

Goodwin's next book, *Price of Honor: Muslim Women Lift the Veil of Silence on the Islamic World,* concerns the repression of women in Islamic society. In researching *Price of Honor,* Goodwin amassed considerable material derived from hundreds of personal interviews, visits to ten Middle Eastern countries, and extensive research. Included in the volume are accounts of sexual abuse, a bartered child, and a death threat against an outspoken television commentator, all, according to the author, under the auspices of Islamic law. Reviewer Donna Seaman in *Booklist* asserted that "Goodwin takes pains to present balanced and well-documented information, making her revelations all the more alarming." Calling the book "chilling" and written with "disturbingly graphic detail," a *Kirkus Reviews* commentator deemed *Price of Honor* "a significant book that gives a voice to millions of silent and silenced Muslim women."

Goodwin told *CA:* "The topics of my books and many of my articles have grown out of my long-term human rights activism. When one has traveled as extensively as I have, and witnessed the horrors of wars and extreme poverty, it is impossible to ignore what is happening in 'hidden corners' of the world."

BIOGRAPHICAL/CRITICAL SOURCES:

PERIODICALS

Booklist, February 15, 1994, p. 1039.
Economist, July 16, 1994, pp. 81-82.
Kirkus Reviews, January 1, 1994, p. 36.
Ladies' Home Journal, April, 1987, pp. 22, 24, 158.
Listener, August 27, 1987, p. 18.
Los Angeles Times Book Review, March 8, 1987, p. 2.
New Yorker, July 11, 1994, p. 91.
Spectator, August 15, 1987, p. 28.
Washington Post Book World, March 22, 1987, p. 10.

* * *

GOTTFRIED, Robert R(ichard) 1948-

PERSONAL: Born June 11, 1948, in Mexico City, Mexico; U.S. citizen; married Yolande McCurdy. *Education:* Davidson College, A.B. (cum laude), 1970; University of North Carolina at Chapel Hill, Ph.D., 1980. *Religion:* Roman Catholic.

ADDRESSES: Office—Department of Economics, University of the South, 735 University Ave., Sewanee, TN 37375-1000; fax 615-598-1145. *E-mail*—rgottfri@seraph1.sewanee.edu.

CAREER: Universidad Rafael Landivar, Guatemala City, Guatemala, Fulbright lecturer in economics, 1979; University of the South, Sewanee, TN, MacArthur assistant professor, 1982-85, professor of economics, 1985—, head of Social Science Foreign Language Program, 1991-94, department head, 1994—. University of Puerto Rico, Center for Energy and Environment Research, Oak Ridge associated universities faculty research participant, 1983; Centro

Agronomico Tropical de Investigacion y Ensenanza (Costa Rica), member of Regional Watershed Management Project, 1988-89; U.S. Man and the Biosphere Directorate for Temperate Ecosystems, member, 1989-92; Universidad Nacional (Heredia, Costa Rica), researcher for Central American Commission on Forests and the Environment, 1995-96.

MEMBER: International Society for Ecological Economics, International Society of Tropical Foresters, Association of Environmental and Resource Economists, Phi Beta Kappa, Omicron Delta Epsilon, Sigma Delta Pi.

WRITINGS:

Economics, Ecology, and the Roots of Western Faith: Perspectives From the Garden, Rowman & Littlefield (Lanham, MD), 1995.

Contributor to books, including *Green National Product,* edited by Clifford Cobb, University Press of America (Lanham), 1994; and *Watershed Management: Balancing Sustainability With Environmental Change,* edited by R. J. Naiman, Springer-Verlag (New York), 1992. Contributor to professional journals, including *Social and Economic Studies, World Development, American Economist, Agriculture and Human Values,* and *Ecological Economics.*

WORK IN PROGRESS: Research on shrimp ponds and mangroves in the Guayas River Estuary of Ecuador.

* * *

GOW, Andrew Colin 1962-

PERSONAL: Born November 30, 1962, in Ottawa, Ontario, Canada; son of Harry William (a criminologist) and Martine Denise (a social worker and civil servant; maiden name, Baugniet; present surname, Cooper) Gow; married Heather Joan McAsh (a teacher), November 12, 1988; children: Ezekiel Hart, Elspeth Sommer. *Ethnicity:* "Mongrel." *Education:* Carleton University, Ottawa, Ontario, B.A. (with honors), 1984; University of Toronto, M.A., 1988; University of Arizona, Ph.D., 1993. *Politics:* "Canadian." *Religion:* "Yes!"

ADDRESSES: Office—Department of History and Classics, 2-28 Tory Bldg., University of Alberta,

Edmonton, Alberta, Canada T6G 2H4. *E-mail*—andrew.gow@ualberta.ca.

CAREER: University of Alberta, Edmonton, assistant professor of history, 1993—. Volunteer firefighter, 1994-96.

MEMBER: Sixteenth Century Studies Association, Renaissance Studies Association, Fruehe Neuzeit Interdisziplinaer (member of board of directors).

WRITINGS:

(Translator) Heiko A. Oberman, *The Reformation: Roots and Ramifications,* Eerdmans (Grand Rapids, MI), 1994.

The Red Jews: Anti-Semitism in an Apocalyptic Age, 1200-1600, E. J. Brill (Kinderhook, NY), 1995.

WORK IN PROGRESS: Research on Albrecht of Mainz and Justus Jonas, the Reformation at Halle and the politics of piety.

*   *   *

GOZZANO, Guido 1883-1916

PERSONAL: Born December 19, 1883, in Turin, Italy; died of tuberculosis, August 9, 1916, in Aglie, Italy; son of Fausto (an engineer) and Diodata (an actress; maiden name, Mautino) Gozzano. *Ethnicity:* Italian. *Education:* Graduated from the Liceo Cavour, at the Istituto Ricaldone and the Collegio Nazionale di Savigliano; attended the Facolta di Giurisprudenza, 1904.

CAREER: Poet.

WRITINGS:

La via del rifugio (poems; title means "Road of the Shelter"), Streglio (Turin), 1907.

I colloqui: Liriche di Guido Gozzano (poems; title means "Conversations"), Treves (Milan), 1911.

I tre talismani, La Scolastica editrice (Ostiglia, Italy), 1914.

La principessa si sposa: Fiabe, Treves, 1917.

L'altare del passato, Treves, 1918, revised and enlarged, 1930.

Verso la cuna del mondo: Lettere dall'India (1912-1913) (letters; title means "Towards the Cradle

of the World"), Treves, 1918, translation by David Marinelli published as *Journey toward the Cradle of Mankind,* Northwestern University/Marlboro Press (Evanston, IL), 1996.

L'ultima traccia, Treves, 1919.

Primavere romantiche, Arti Grafiche Canavesane (Appia-Rivarolo, Italy), 1924.

I primi e gli ultimi colloqui, Treves, 1925.

Opere, di Guido Gozzano, five volumes, edited by P. Schinetti, Treves, 1935-37.

Opere, edited by Carlo Calcaterra and Alberto De Marchi, Garzanti (Milan), 1948, revised, 1953, revised and enlarged, 1956.

La fiaccola dei desideri: Fiabe, Garzanti, 1951.

Lettere d'amore di Guido Gozzano e Amalia Guglielminetti, edited by Spartaco Asciamprener, Garzanti, 1951.

Le poesie, Garzanti, 1960.

Fiabe, Garzanti, 1961.

Poesie e prose, edited by Marchi, Garzanti, 1961.

La moneta seminata e altri scritti, edited by Franco Antonicelli, All'Insegna del Pesce d'Oro/Scheiwiller (Milan), 1968.

Lettere a Carlo Vallini; con altri inediti, edited by Giorgio De Rienzo, Centro Studi Piemontesi (Turin), 1972.

Poesie, edited by Edoardo Sanguineti, Einaudi (Turin), 1973.

I colloqui e prose, edited by Marziano Guglielminetti, Mondadori (Milan), 1974.

Cara Torino, Viglongo (Turin), 1975.

Poesie, edited by Giorgio Barberi Squarotti, Rizzoli (Milan), 1977.

Guido Gozzano: Tutte la poesie, edited by Andrea Rocca, Mondadori, 1980.

The Man I Pretend to Be: The Colloquies and Selected Poems of Guido Gozzano, translated and edited by Michael Palma, Princeton University Press (Princeton, NJ), 1981.

I sandali della diva: Tutte le novelle, edited by Giuliana Nuvoli, Serra & Riva (Milan), 1983.

Opere di Guido Gozzano, edited by Giusi Baldissone, UTET (Turin), 1983.

Un Natale a Ceylon e altri racconti indiani, edited by Piero Cudini, Garzanti, 1984.

Guido Gozzano: The Colloquies and Selected Letters, translated by J.G. Nichols, Carcanet (New York), 1987.

SIDELIGHTS: Guido Gozzano was one of the first Italian poets of the twentieth century to deviate from the course set by Gabriele D'Annunzio, whose highly sentimental poetry marked by high diction and a refined style then set the standard. For the musicality and often melancholy tone of his verse, Gozzano is often grouped with the Crepuscolari, or twilight poets. In addition to his verse, Gozzano also wrote tales, fables, and children's poetry.

Born to the Italian bourgeoisie, Gozzano lived well and was educated at national schools. After graduating from the Collegio Nazionale di Savigliano, Gozzano enrolled in law school; these career plans were changed, however, when Gozzano attended seminars lead by Arturo Graf. At this time he also suffered an initial and serious bout of tuberculosis. In 1907 Gozzano published his first volume of verse, *La via del rifugio,* poems of recollection in which he demonstrated his command of then traditional verse forms and dwelled on the nineteenth-century world. That same year, Gozzano entered into a close relationship with Amalia Guglielminetti and nearly died from a tuberculosis attack.

Gozzano's second collection of poetry, *I colloqui: Liriche di Guido Gozzano,* published a few years before the poet's death from tuberculosis, was a popular and critical success. Divided into three sections, the work deals with the sentimental and hedonistic pleasures of youth, encounters with death, the poet's inability to love, and his rejection of then contemporary literary styles. In these works, Gozzano adopted a colloquial style and ironic tone. In doing so, he stood the middle ground between formalism and what would later be called avant-garde experimentalism. In 1912 Gozzano, hoping to improve his health, traveled to India. During his voyage, he wrote poetic and descriptive letters, which were first published in the newspaper *La Stampa* and were posthumously collected.

Upon his death, Gozzano left many unfinished works. Portions have been made available for English-language readers in several translations: *The Man I Pretend to Be: The Colloquies and Selected Poems of Guido Gozzano, Guido Gozzano: The Colloquies and Selected Letters,* and *Journey toward the Cradle of Mankind.* "It is much easier for readers to enjoy Guido Gozzano's verse than it is for critics to define its nature and its genesis," asserted Thomas G. Bergin in a review of Gozzano's *The Man I Pretend to Be* for *World Literature Today.* Calling him a "very original poetic voice," Bergin added: "Whatever be his pigeonhole, Gozzano has notable gifts. He has a sensitive ear for musical rhythms and a nimble dexterity in weaving patterns of rhymes."

BIOGRAPHICAL/CRITICAL SOURCES:

BOOKS

Dictionary of Literary Biography, Volume 114: *Twentieth-Century Italian Poets,* Gale (Detroit), 1992.

PERIODICALS

Publishers Weekly, March 4, 1996, p. 60.
World Literature Today, winter, 1982, p. 96.*

*　　*　　*

GRANDIN, Temple 1947-

PERSONAL: Born August 29, 1947, in Boston, MA; daughter of Richard McCurdy (a real estate agent) and Eustacia (a writer, singer, and actress; maiden name, Purves) Grandin. *Education:* Franklin Pierce College, B.A. (with honors), 1970; Arizona State University, M.S., 1975; University of Illinois—Urbana, Ph.D., 1989. *Politics:* Republican. *Religion:* Episcopalian. *Avocational interests:* "Star Trek."

ADDRESSES: Home—2918 Silver Plume Dr., C-3, Fort Collins, CO 80526. *Office*—Animal Science Department, Colorado State University, Fort Collins, CO 80523. *Agent*—Patricia Breinin.

CAREER: Arizona Farmer Ranchman, Phoenix, livestock editor, 1973-78; Corral Industries, Phoenix, equipment designer, 1974-75; independent consultant, Grandin Livestock Systems in Tempe, AZ and Urbana, IL, 1975-90, and in Fort Collins, CO, 1990—; Colorado State University, Fort Collins, began as lecturer, became assistant professor of animal science, 1990—. Chair of the handling committee, Livestock Conservation Institute, Madison, WI, 1976-95. Animal Welfare Committee of the American Meat Institute, 1991—.

MEMBER: Autism Society of America (member of board of directors, 1988-92), American Society of Animal Science, American Society of Agricultural Consultants (member of board of directors, 1981-83), American Society of Agricultural Engineers, American Meat Institute (supplier member), American Registry of Professional Animal Scientists.

AWARDS, HONORS: Meritorious service award, Livestock Conservation Institute, 1986; distinguished alumni award, Franklin Pierce College, 1989; Trammel Crow Award, Autism Society of America, 1989; named One of Processing Stars, *National Provisioner*, 1990; Industry Innovator's Award, *Meat Marketing and Technology Magazine*, 1994; Industry Advancement Award, American Meat Institute, 1995; Animal Management Award, American Society of Animal Science, 1995; Harry Rowsell Award, Scientists' Center for Animal Welfare, 1995; Brownlee Award, Animal Welfare Foundation (Vancouver, Canada), 1995.

WRITINGS:

(With Margaret M. Scariano) *Emergence: Labeled Autistic* (autobiography), Arena Press (Novato, CA), 1986.

(Editor and contributor) *Livestock Handling and Transport*, CAB International (Wallingford, England), 1993.

Thinking in Pictures and Other Reports from My Life with Autism (autobiography), foreword by Oliver Sacks, Doubleday (New York, NY), 1995.

Also author of *Recommended Animal Handling Guidelines for Meat Packers;* contributor of articles to periodicals and professional journals, including the *Journal of Child and Adolescent Psychopharmacology* and *Meat and Poultry, Journal of Animal Science, Applied Animal Behavior Science, Journal of the American Veterinary Medical Association, Veterinary Medicine, Agri-Practice, Zoo Biology, Beef Magazine.*

WORK IN PROGRESS: Editor and contributing writer, *Genetics and the Behavior of Domestic Animals*, Academic Press (San Diego, CA), in press.

SIDELIGHTS: Highly-accomplished inventor and animal scientist Temple Grandin has designed numerous pieces of livestock-handling equipment that provide for the humane treatment of livestock on farms and in slaughterhouses. Her inventions are used worldwide by farmers and meat packers. Her autobiographies, *Emergence: Labeled Autistic*, which she wrote with Margaret M. Scariano, and *Thinking in Pictures: And Other Reports from My Life with Autism*, chronicle Grandin's life and shed light on the autistic mind.

Diagnosed as autistic at the age of two and a half, Grandin, like many autistic children, hated to be held, and she would stiffen her body to fend off her mother's hugs; she shunned others, preferring solitude, and was given to fits of rage; she also was limited in her verbal skills, and she was easily startled by noise and keenly aware of odors. Fortunately, however, she was surrounded by nurturing parents, aunts, and teachers, who devoted themselves to her instruction. Her mother enrolled her in private schools and coached her in reading, while encouraging the girl's creativity and imagination.

As she grew older, Grandin's verbal skills improved, but she exhibited the obsessive behavior often exhibited by autistics, behavior she found tormenting. She became easily fixated, for example, on rotating objects. When she heard a minister quote the biblical passage: "I am the door: by me if any man enter in, he shall be saved," the literal-minded Grandin, from then on, sought out special doors. Her penchant for doors brought her much-needed peace; when she found them, they led to places of comfort for her troubled mind.

One summer, while visiting her aunt's cattle ranch, Grandin experienced something that would change her world, and, perhaps, decide her life's work. Grandin was fascinated by the squeeze chute that was used to hold animals still while they were inoculated. Desiring hugs, but fearful of the pain caused her by human touch, she tried out the machine on herself, while her aunt manned the controls. Grandin found this mechanical hug exhilarating and relaxing. She subsequently designed a similar machine for herself, which she keeps in her home to provide stimulation and relaxation. Schools and institutes for autistic children have implemented Grandin's squeeze chute in their treatment programs. The machine has also proven beneficial to children with other anomalies, such as hyperactivity.

Grandin demonstrated her squeeze machine to neurologist Oliver Sacks, who wrote of her in *An Anthropologist from Mars*, portions of which first appeared in the *New Yorker*. "It was the most bizarre thing I had ever seen," Sacks wrote, "and yet, for all its oddness, it was moving and simple. Certainly there was no doubt of its effect. Temple's voice, often loud and hard, became softer and gentler as she lay in her machine. 'I concentrate on how gently I can do it,' she said, and then spoke of the necessity of 'totally giving in to it. . . . I'm getting real relaxed now,' she added quietly. 'I guess others get this through relation with other people.'" Remarking on Grandin's inability to feel for others as most people can, Sacks added: "As she lies in her machine, she says, her thoughts often turn to her mother, her favorite aunt, her teachers. She feels their love for her, and hers for them. She feels that the machine opens a door into an otherwise closed emotional world and allows her, almost teaches her, to feel empathy for others."

Grandin's experience in the squeeze machine has also given her insight into the way animals feel, for they, also, retreat from human touch. "The way I would pull away from being touched," Grandin told Sacks, "is the way a wild cow will pull away—getting me used to being touched is very similar to taming a wild cow." Such insights into the animals she has observed have caused her to feel most at home when with cattle, and to become one of the foremost developers of gentle livestock-handling equipment. All of her designs are intended to lessen fear in animals and minimize their pain, and Grandin has been instrumental in the development of improved, animal-friendly dip-vats, stockyards, research laboratories, ramps at slaughter plants, and slaughter techniques, as well as numerous other products or methods dealing with cattle. In 1995, one-third of the cattle in the United States and Canada were handled in facilities she designed at slaughter plants.

Grandin's accomplishments and autism are documented in her autobiographies. The first, *Emergence,* seeks to promote understanding of autism and its disturbing symptoms—especially the autistic's tendency to avoid touch—and describes Grandin's joy at her discovery of the squeeze machine. Commenting in *Psychology Today,* Paul Chance praised *Emergence,* writing: "[S]he does believe that for some autistic children, at least, tactile stimulation that they themselves control may have therapeutic value. . . . She has provided us with a fascinating look at autism from the inside."

Grandin's second life account is *Thinking in Pictures,* which, unlike her first book, she wrote without the assistance of a professional writer, thus giving readers greater insight into her thought patterns. As the title indicates, *Thinking in Pictures* focuses greatly on the author's ability to visualize, which has resulted in her success as a designer. In her interview with Sacks, Grandin commented about the benefits of visualization on her development of the chute that cows walk on their way to slaughter, telling him, "I visualize the animal entering the chute, from different angles, different distances, zooming in or wide-angle, even from a helicopter view—or I turn myself into an animal, and feel what it would feel entering the chute." Grandin's explanations of her visual techniques in *Thinking in Pictures* fascinated reviewer Stacey D'Erasmo, who wrote in *Voice Literary*

Supplement: "Grandin has replaced the teleology of autobiography with something much closer to her heart: a diagram, in this case a diagram of her own mind. Slowly and patiently she explains it, taking care to be thorough: this is how it works, this is what caused how it works, here is the research, there are the consequences. She is a sober and literal architect. . . . But Grandin's own metaphors for herself veer between the animal and the mechanical. She is a computer; she is a cow. . . . Her great gift, as the title of her book suggests, is her ability to visualize, to think in pictures."

BIOGRAPHICAL/CRITICAL SOURCES:

BOOKS

Grandin, Temple, *Emergence: Labeled Autistic,* Arena Press (Novato, CA), 1986.

Grandin, Temple, *Thinking in Pictures: And Other Reports from My Life with Autism,* Doubleday (New York), 1995.

PERIODICALS

Booklist, October 15, 1995, p. 374.
Canadian Veterinary Journal, August, 1995.
Journal of the American Veterinary Medical Association, vol. 205, no. 3, 1994, p. 463.
Library Journal, May 15, 1986, p.71.
Los Angeles Times Book Review, May 4, 1986, p. 4.
New Scientist, December 23-30, 1995, pp. 70-71.
New Yorker, December 27, 1993, pp. 106-125.
Psychology Today, November, 1986, p. 86.
Publishers Weekly, October 30, 1995, p. 55.
Voice Literary Supplement, November, 1995, p. 13.
Washington Times, November 26, 1995, p. 37.*

*   *   *

GRAY, Richard A. 1927-

PERSONAL: Born October 6, 1927, in St. Paul, MN; son of James (a critic, novelist, and playwright) and Sophie (a critic, journalist, and homemaker; maiden name, Stryker) Gray; married first wife, Donna S. (divorced, 1969); married Dorothy Anne Woelfl, May, 1969; children: Sonya, Karen Gray Berwin. *Ethnicity:* "WASP." *Education:* University of Minnesota—Twin Cities, B.A., 1950, B.S.L.S., 1952. *Politics:* "Hard-core liberal." *Religion:* Agnostic. *Avocational interests:* Music, reading, travel, theater, art.

ADDRESSES: Home and office—4307 Northwood Dr., Louisville, KY 40220-3622. *E-mail*—dagray01@ulkyvm.louisville.edu.

CAREER: Ohio State University, Columbus, senior reference librarian and associate professor, 1963-69; American Library Association, Chicago, IL, senior editor in Publishing Division, 1969-74; R. R. Bowker, New York City, acquisitions editor, 1974-75; Pierian Press, Ann Arbor, MI, senior editor, 1986—.

MEMBER: Survival International, Friends of the Earth, Greenpeace, Heart/Earth Task Force.

WRITINGS:

Guide to Book Review Citations: A Bibliography of Sources, Ohio State University Press (Columbus), 1968.

(Compiler with Dorothy Villmow) *Serial Bibliographies in the Humanities and Social Sciences,* Pierian Press (Ann Arbor, MI), 1969.

(With H. Robert Malinowski and wife Dorothy A. Gray) *Science and Engineering Literature,* 2nd edition, Libraries Unlimited (Littleton, CO), 1976.

(With Timothy C. Weiskel) *Environmental Decline and Public Policy: Pattern, Trend, and Prospect,* Pierian Press, 1992.

(With Cecilia M. Schmitz) *The Gift of Life—Organ and Tissue Transplantation: An Introduction to Issues and Information Sources,* Pierian Press, 1993.

(With Schmitz) *Smoking—The Health Consequences of Tobacco Use: An Annotated Bibliography With an Analytical Introduction,* Pierian Press, 1995.

Contributor to periodicals, including *Reference Services Review* and *Serials Review.*

WORK IN PROGRESS: A book on religion and the environment; various Shakespearean studies.

SIDELIGHTS: Richard A. Gray told *CA:* "When I was a senior reference librarian in the 1960s, I was fortunate to find myself surrounded by a group of colleagues who were, not only congenial, but talented as well. Flourishing in the intellectual atmosphere of Ohio State University's Reference Department as I did, I came to believe that I had a debt to pay. Having profited so much from the accumulated industry of many creative people, I felt that I had an obligation to add to the profession's total stock of

reference works. By 1969 I was the author of two such works.

"In 1969 I left Ohio State University to work for the American Library Association's Publishing Department as an acquisitions editor. Although I enjoyed my years in Chicago, I regret to say that I wrote nothing during those years except long, critical letters to authors who, I was convinced, urgently needed my editorial guidance.

"I did not have occasion to write anything but two other reference tools, long, nagging letters, and reference book reviews until the gods smiled on me in 1986 by sending me to work for C. Edward Wall at the Pierian Press. Among its many other publishing properties, Pierian Press has an important library periodical called *Reference Services Review,* in which Ed Wall gave me an opportunity to publish the best expository writing that I have ever done. These articles indicate quite clearly what my interests as an expository writer have been for the last decade and remain today. They fall into several categories.

"One of these is language and linguistics. I have written about euphemism, twentieth-century censorship of the *Merchant of Venice,* and a negative assessment of reference librarians as reviewers of reference books. There were also two essays on the ethics of the medical profession.

"As a polemicist I have two preoccupations that haunt me day and night. The first is the attack that all, yes all, modern nations have conducted, and continue to conduct, on the indigenous peoples who are unlucky enough to lie within their national territorial domains. Here I do not refer solely to such rankly barbaric countries as Indonesia, Bangladesh, Chile, and Peru. Valiantly countervailing this universal complicity in ethnocide and genocide are a few admirable international organizations that exist to defend and protect beleaguered and indigenous peoples. These include Survival International, the International Work Group on Indigenous Affairs, and Anti-Slavery International. Wanting to publicize the invaluable work of these and other organizations, I have written articles on indigenous rights organizations, genocide in Bangladesh, and Thomas Clarkson and the Anti-Slavery Society.

"The second issue that preoccupies me is the central issue of our time, the decline and degradation of the global environment. I am convinced that a reversal of this decline is necessary for our survival as a species.

Believing this as I do, I was delighted to collaborate with the environmental anthropologist Timothy C. Weiskel on the articles that were published as *Environmental Decline and Public Policy.* As an environmental writer, I was by no means satisfied with the little I had done to publicize the global ecological crisis. As I worked with Weiskel on this book, I came to believe devoutly that we as a species need a new ethic to guide our decisions in environmental policy. Since then I have written articles on ecology and ethics and on theological responses to environmental decline. In the future I want to write a series of articles on the broad subject of religion and the environment. I believe that, in order to stop befouling our global nest, we must make the environment an integral part of the sacred.

"Twice I have collaborated with Cecilia M. Schmitz. The central issue in the first book turned on such philosophic issues as the definitions of life and death. The second book was an effort to marshall systematically the scientific evidence relating to tobacco use as a major health hazard. A third collaboration on alcohol and alcoholism is also under consideration."

* * *

GREEN, Duncan 1958-

PERSONAL: Born May 12, 1958, in Portsmouth, England; son of John (a naval engineer) and Jean (a homemaker; maiden name, Urquhart) Green; married Catherine Matheson (an aid worker), August 17, 1988; children: Calum David, Finlay Paul. *Ethnicity:* "Caucasian." *Education:* studied at Oxford University,1976-79, and received a first-class degree in physics. *Politics:* Democratic Socialist. *Religion:* none. *Avocational interests:* Salsa dancing and cooking, running, swimming.

ADDRESSES: Home—73 Dalberg Rd., London, England SW2 1AL. *Office*—Latin America Bureau, 1 Amwell St., London, England EC1R 1UL; fax 00-44-171-278-0165. *E-mail*—lab@gn.apc.org.

CAREER: Greater London Council, London, England, policy researcher, 1985-86; freelance journalist on Latin America, 1986-88; Latin America Bureau, London, England, writer and editor, 1989—. Member of editorial board of NACLA's *Report on the Americas.*

WRITINGS:

NONFICTION

Faces of Latin America, Latin America Bureau (London, England), 1991; second edition, 1997.
Guatemala: Burden of Paradise, Latin America Bureau, 1992.
Silent Revolution: The Rise of Market Economics in Latin America, Cassell (London, England), 1995.
Children of Latin America, Cassell, 1997.

Also contributor of articles to periodicals, including the *Financial Times* and the *Guardian.*

WORK IN PROGRESS: Streetwise: Lives of Children in Latin America and the Caribbean, publication expected in 1997.

SIDELIGHTS: British journalist and author Duncan Green is an expert on the subject of Latin American affairs, especially on the ways in which economic issues affect Latin American peoples. His writings on this subject include *Faces of Latin America* and *Silent Revolution: The Rise of Market Economics in Latin America.* Green has also written articles for periodicals, including the *Financial Times* and the *Guardian.*

In *Faces of Latin America,* Green provides readers with information on the economy, land, environment, cities, cultures, and religions of the region. He also discusses the role of gender in Latin American society. As with many publications of the Latin America Bureau, Green accentuates his prose with many photographs, captions, charts, and boxed quotations. Antoni Kapcia, reviewing the volume in *Bulletin of Hispanic Studies,* felt that it was journalistic in style and declared that "[i]ts critical posture is refreshing and challenging, confronting as it does the realities of the continent beyond the familiar exotica." Kapcia went on to conclude that "it must rank as one of the best recent publications for its purpose on Latin America."

As its subtitle implies, *Silent Revolution: The Rise of Market Economics in Latin America* focuses in on Green's analysis on the effects of the introduction of market-driven economies into Latin American nations—an economic system also known as the neoliberal model. In the case of many of the countries examined in the book, Green advocates a switch from this practice to a more state-controlled effort, such as those practiced by countries like South Korea and

Taiwan. J. L. Dietz in *Choice* lauded *Silent Revolution*'s accessibility and labeled it a "wonderful introduction to the complexities of the economic crisis still facing the region" that "should attract a wide audience." Alan Angell, critiquing the volume in *International Affairs,* however, had his reservations about some of Green's arguments. He felt Green might have been premature in writing off Chile's economic policy as a role model for the rest of South America. In Angell's eyes, "the author places too much weight on structural adjustment policies as an explanation of what went wrong with the Latin American economies." Angell also expressed the wish that Green had presented a more detailed alternative plan to market-driven economics in the region. He did, however, conclude by praising *Silent Revolution* as "a book to argue with, one to learn from, one to be provoked by." He also hailed it as "one of the most sustained and intelligent . . . critiques of neoliberalism yet to have appeared."

When asked about his primary motivation for writing, Green told *CA* that it was "to bring Latin America to life for readers outside the region and show how global and national processes affect real people's lives." Discussing his influences as a writer, he said that these were "the Latin Americans I meet; Latin American writers such as Eduardo Galeano; some U.S. authors, including Susan George; and good British journalists of all kinds." On the subject of his writing process, Green noted these steps. First, he "goes to Latin America and talks to the people who form the subject of the book." Then he "decodes all the impenetrable academic tomes written on the issue." At last, he "combines the two into a colorful, human, and reliable text that non-Ph.D.s can understand." Green also told *CA* that he takes his inspiration from "ordinary Latin Americans struggling to improve their lives" and from "choosing subjects which are important, but where information outside Latin America is slanted (e.g., economics) or patchy (e.g., children)."

BIOGRAPHICAL/CRITICAL SOURCES:

PERIODICALS

Bulletin of Hispanic Studies, October, 1994, p. 517.
Choice, March, 1996.
International Affairs, April, 1996, p. 644.

GREENSPAN, Stanley I(ra) 1941-

PERSONAL: Born June 1, 1941, in New York, NY; son of Phil and Jean Greenspan; married Nancy Thorndike, 1975; children: Elizabeth, Jake, Sarah. *Education:* Harvard University, B.A. (cum laude), 1962; Yale University, M.D., 1966. *Religion:* Jewish. *Avocational interests:* Sports.

ADDRESSES: Office—7201 Glenbrook Rd., Bethesda, MD 20814.

CAREER: Clinical child/adult psychiatrist and psychoanalyst, 1970—. George Washington University Medical School, clinical professor of psychiatry, behavioral science, and pediatrics, 1982—. National Institutes of Mental Health, research psychiatrist, Laboratory of Psychology, 1970, research psychiatrist, 1972-74, assistant chief, 1974, acting chief, 1974-75, then chief, 1975-82, Mental Health Study Center, chief, Clinical Infant Development Research Unit, Laboratory of Psychology and Psychopathology, 1982-84, chief, Clinical Infant/Child Development Research Center, 1984-86; Center for Clinical Infant Programs, founder and president, 1975-84. On editorial boards of *Journal of American Psychoanalytic Association, Journal of Preventive Psychiatry, Journal of Psychoanalytic Inquiry, Infant Mental Health Journal,* and *Journal of Psychotherapy Practice and Research.*

MEMBER: American Psychoanalytic Association, American College of Psychiatry, American College of Psychoanalysis.

AWARDS, HONORS: Edward A. Strecker award for outstanding contributions to American psychiatry; Public Health Service Special Recognition award; Heintz Hartman prize for contributions to psychoanalysis; Ittleson prize, American Psychiatric Association, for outstanding contributions to child psychiatry research.

WRITINGS:

A Consideration of Some Learning Variables in the Context of Psychoanalytic Theory: Toward a Psychoanalytic Learning Perspective, International Universities Press (New York City), 1975.
Intelligence and Adaptation: An Integration of Psychoanalytic and Piagetian Developmental Psychology, International Universities Press, 1979.

(With wife, Nancy Thorndike Greenspan) *The Clinical Interview of the Child,* McGraw-Hill (New York City), 1981.

Psychopathology and Adaptation in Infancy and Early Childhood: Principles of Clinical Diagnosis and Preventive Intervention, International Universities Press, 1981.

(With N. Greenspan) *First Feelings: Milestones in the Emotional Development of Your Baby and Child,* Viking (New York City), 1985.

(Editor) *Infants in Multirisk Families: Case Studies in Preventive Intervention,* International Universities Press (Madison, CT), 1987.

The Development of the Ego: Implications for Personality Theory, Psychopathology, and the Psychotherapeutic Process, International Universities Press, 1989.

(With N. Greenspan) *The Essential Partnership: How Parents and Children Can Meet the Emotional Challenges of Infancy and Childhood,* Viking, 1989.

(Editor, with George H. Pollock) *The Course of Life,* 4 volumes, International Universities Press, 1989-91.

Infancy and Early Childhood: The Practice of Clinical Assessments and Intervention with Emotional and Developmental Challenges, International Universities Press, 1992.

(With Jacqueline Salmon) *Playground Politics: Understanding the Emotional Life of Your School-age Child,* Addison-Wesley (Reading, MA), 1993.

Developmentally Based Psychotherapy, International Universities Press, 1995.

(With Salmon) *The Challenging Child: Understanding, Raising, and Enjoying the Five Difficult Types of Children,* Addison-Wesley, 1995.

Developmentally Based Psychotherapy, International Universities Press, 1996.

(With Beryl Lieff Benderly) *The Growth of the Mind and the Endangered Origins of Intelligence,* Addison Wesley (Reading, MA), 1996.

Author of numerous articles in scientific journals and a frequent contributor to *Parents' Magazine.*

SIDELIGHTS: At the end of a quarter century of practicing psychiatry, Stanley I. Greenspan is in a coveted position. He is a clinical professor of psychiatry, behavioral sciences, and pediatrics, the author of over one hundred scholarly articles, and author or editor of more than twenty-five books, and the recipient of several major awards for psychiatric research. In *First Feelings: Milestones in the Emotional*

Development of Your Baby and Child, he and wife Nancy Thorndike Greenspan describe the various stages in the emotional development of an infant: birth to three months, three months to ten months, nine to 18 months, 18 to 36 months, and 30 to 40 months. At each stage the Greenspans explain the interactions between parents and child and the concomitant emotions of each. They provide guidelines for observing children and suggestions for creating a supportive environment.

Playground Politics: Understanding the Emotional Life of Your School-age Child picks up where *First Feelings* leaves off. In it Greenspan and *Washington Post* staff writer Jacqueline Salmon outline the emotional milestones of the grade school years. They treat such topics as aggression, competition, and rivalry, self-esteem and peer relations, the foundations of learning, learning challenges, and sexuality and puberty. They also provide five principles for healthy parenting, which include floor time, problem-solving time, empathizing with the child's point of view, breaking challenges into small pieces, and setting limits. Likewise, in *The Challenging Child: Understanding, Raising, and Enjoying the Five Difficult Types of Children* Greenspan and Salmon provide practical advice to parents. They encourage parents not to feel guilty for having a difficult child, describe the five child personality types, and suggest many parenting techniques mentioned in earlier works.

In one of his most recent books, *Developmentally Based Psychotherapy,* Greenspan describes to other professionals how his years of research into the developmental stages of infancy and early childhood can be applied to therapeutic situations for both children and adults. In another new book, *The Growth of the Mind and the Endangered Origins of Intelligence,* Greenspan, along with Beryl Lieff Benderly, offers a new view of the origins of our minds' highest capacities. Contrary to traditional notions, he finds that intelligence as such does not arise from cognitive stimulation, but along with morality, empathy, and self-reflection, has a common foundation in specific early emotional experiences.

BIOGRAPHICAL/CRITICAL SOURCES:

PERIODICALS

American Journal of Psychiatry, March, 1995, p. 466.
Booklist, September 1, 1993, p. 7.
Choice, October, 1990, p. 392; November, 1993.

Publishers Weekly, February 15, 1995, p. 91; July 3, 1995, p. 53.
Social Services Review, March, 1994, p. 158.

*   *   *

GREKOVA, I.
See VENTSEL, Elena Sergeevna

*   *   *

GREKOVA, Irina Nikolaevna
See VENTSEL, Elena Sergeevna

*   *   *

GRIFFITH, Nicola 1960-

PERSONAL: Born September 30, 1960, in Leeds, England; immigrated to the United States, c. 1989; daughter of Eric P. (an accountant) and Margot (in business; maiden name, Murphy) Griffith; companion of Kelley Eskridge since December, 1989, married, September, 1993. *Ethnicity:* "European."

ADDRESSES: Home—Seattle, WA. *Agent*—Shawna McCarthy, Scovil Chichak Galen, 381 Park Ave. South, Ste. 1020, New York, NY 10016. *E-mail*—nicolaz@aol.com.

CAREER: Singer and lyricist for music group Janes Plane, 1981-82; freelance writer, c. 1988—.

MEMBER: Science Fiction and Fantasy Writers of America.

AWARDS, HONORS: Individual artist grant from the Georgia Council for the Arts, 1993; Lambda Literary Award, 1993, for *Ammonite,* 1996, for *Slow River;* artist's grant from the Atlanta Bureau of Cultural Affairs, 1994; James Tiptree, Jr. Memorial Award for "the work of speculative fiction which best examines and expands gender roles," for *Ammonite,* 1994.

WRITINGS:

Ammonite (novel), Ballantine/Del Rey (New York), 1993.

Slow River (novel), Ballantine/Del Rey, 1995.
(Co-editor) *Bending the Landscape* (volume 1; anthology) White Wolf Press (Atlanta, GA), 1997.
Penny in My Mouth, Avon (New York), 1998.

Contributor of short fiction to books, including *Ignorant Armies,* GW Books (England), 1989; *Interzone: The Fourth Anthology,* Simon and Schuster (New York), 1989; *Iron Women,* Iron Press (England), 1990; *Red Thirst,* GW Books, 1990; *Little Deaths,* edited by Ellen Datlow, Orion (London), 1994; *Best Lesbian Erotica,* edited by Tristan Taormino and Heather Lewis, Cleis (San Francisco), 1996; *Nebula Awards 30,* Harcourt Brace (San Diego), 1996; *The New Interzone Anthology,* St. Martin's (New York), 1996. Also contributor to periodicals, including *Interzone, Network, Para*doxa: World Literary Genres, Century, Asimov's, SF Eye,* and *Aboriginal Science Fiction.*

WORK IN PROGRESS: Co-editing more volumes of *Bending the Landscape;* a collection of essays and short fiction to be titled *Women and Other Aliens;* an as yet untitled anthology of short fiction whose focus is gender; research on religious cults, parrots, and the fictional depiction of gender since the 1920s.

SIDELIGHTS: Author and editor Nicola Griffith was born in Leeds, England, but immigrated to the United States in the late 1980s to be with her partner, Kelley Eskridge; the two women were married in September, 1993. Griffith's work was just beginning to gain inclusion in British science fiction anthologies and magazines when she moved, and she quickly began publishing in America as well. Her short story, "Song of Bullfrogs, Cry of Geese," appeared in *Aboriginal Science Fiction* in 1991, and her first novel, *Ammonite,* saw print in 1993. This book garnered her both a Lambda Literary Award and the James Tiptree, Jr. Memorial Award. Her second novel, *Slow River,* also received a Lambda Literary Award.

Griffith did not always write for a living. Earlier in her life, she was the lyricist and lead singer for a musical group. She discussed the experience with an interviewer in *Not for Hire* magazine: "Ah. Marvelous. . . . It was a truly exalted feeling to stand up there and *move* people: make them scared or exhilarated, make them dance, make them cry. . . . But then the band folded, as bands always do sooner or later, and I gradually stopped singing. . . . I don't sing as much as I used to because I write now, and writing comes from the same place inside."

Though the protagonists of both *Ammonite* and *Slow River* are lesbians, and both novels are works of science fiction, Griffith resists categorization. She told *Not for Hire:* "I write fiction and non-fiction. I write science fiction. I write lesbian fiction. I write literary fiction. I write feminist fiction. . . . The bottom line is that I write. I write well. Genre labels are a convenience for sales reps and retailers, a marketing concept." The author went on to note: "I'm amused more than anything by the wrong-headed reviews that harp on and on about the fact that my protagonists . . . are dykes. So what? Given the way I write and what I write about, that's about as relevant as their hair colour. But it seems to be a big deal for most critics."

Critics responded favorably to *Ammonite,* which has as its protagonist an anthropologist named Marghe, who visits Jeep, a planet populated by women. The inhabitants are capable of reproducing with each another and communicating with each other and with their planet using a form of telepathy after surviving a deadly virus that has killed all the men on the planet. *New Statesman & Society*'s David V. Barrett called *Ammonite* "utterly believable," and asserted that the novel "makes Nicola Griffith a name to watch." Gerald Jonas, writing in the *New York Times Book Review,* maintained that because Griffith "takes care to create fully rounded characters, her polemical concerns never unbalance the story." *Women's Review of Books* critic Suzy McKee Charnas declared: "What makes *Ammonite* unusually interesting and attractive is its picture of women living without men but, due to the effects of the virus, in tune . . . with the nature of their world."

Slow River, Griffith's second novel, is set in Europe in the not-too-distant future. The novel's protagonist, Lore Van de Oest, escapes her kidnappers and certain death after she learns that her wealthy family has declined to pay her ransom. Following her escape Van de Oest is rescued by a woman computer hacker named Spanner, "with whom she forms an uneasy alliance to scam the rich and naive," according to a *Publisher's Weekly* reviewer. In the same *Publisher's Weekly* review, the critic concluded that while Griffith's combination of first- and third-person narration at times leads to confusion, *Slow River* is an "exceptionally well-written novel" and Griffith is a "talented author." In his *New York Times Book Review* assessment of *Slow River,* Gerald Jonas found fault with what he considered Griffith's excessive attention to detail and her use of flashbacks and other complex narrative devices. In contrast, *Women's Re-*

view of Books contributor Pat Murphy offered praise for Griffith's attention to detail, particularly in describing the sewage treatment plant run by Van de Oest's family. Murphy declared: "Griffith manages to make the intricacies of the plant fascinating and understandable—and an essential aspect of the overall story of intrigue and betrayal."

Griffith's third novel, *Penny in My Mouth,* departs from the realm of science fiction to enter that of the thriller. Griffith described the book for *Not for Hire* as "a sort of Norwegian-lesbian-Travis-McGee-drug-smuggling-art-fraud thriller kind of thing." She reports that her genre-switch caused friction with the publisher of her first books, Ballantine/Del Ray, so she went to Avon for her third effort.

Griffith has also coedited the first volume of *Bending the Landscape,* an anthology of gay and lesbian fantasy fiction. Further volumes, with gay and lesbian science fiction and horror, are planned. "They're going to be good books," she affirmed to *Not for Hire.* Griffith also told the interviewer that she had no plans to write sequels to any of her successful novels. "Sequels don't interest me as a writer. I have far too many ideas for other books circling my head like planes waiting to land at a busy airport. Besides, I think readers are almost always disappointed by a sequel."

BIOGRAPHICAL/CRITICAL SOURCES:

PERIODICALS

New Statesman & Society, April 30, 1993, p. 47.
New York Times Book Review, March 14, 1993, p. 14; August 13, 1995, p. 30.
Not for Hire, spring, 1996.
Publishers Weekly, June 26, 1995, p. 90.
Washington Post Book World, July 30, 1995, p. 11.
Women's Review of Books, July, 1993, p. 30; July, 1995, p. 40.

OTHER

Web Site: http://www.america.net/~daves/ng

*   *   *

GRUNDY, Stephan 1967-

PERSONAL: Born June 28, 1967, in New York, NY. *Education:* Southern Methodist University, B.A. (in

English and German studies); attended Cambridge University, England.

ADDRESSES: Agent—c/o Bantam Books, 1540 Broadway, New York, NY 10036.

CAREER: Writer.

WRITINGS:

FANTASY NOVEL

Rhinegold, Bantam (New York), 1994.
Attila's Treasure, Bantam, 1996.

*   *   *

GUILLAUMIN, Colette 1934-

PERSONAL: Born in 1934, in France. *Education:* University of Paris, Sorbonne, doctorate, 1969.

ADDRESSES: Office—Unite de Recherche Migrations et Societes, Centre National de la Recherche Scientifique, Universite de Paris VII Denis Diderot, 2, place Jussieu, Tour Centrale, 75251 Paris Cedex 05, France.

CAREER: Centre National de la Recherche Scientifique, University of Paris VII, Paris, researcher; lecturer on feminist social theory. Member of editorial board, *Questions Feministes,* until 1980, and *Le Genre Humain.*

MEMBER: International Association for the Study of Racism (The Netherlands), Association Nationale des Etudes Feministes.

WRITINGS:

L'ideologie raciste: Genese et langage actuel, Mouton (Paris), 1972.
Sexe, race et pratique du pouvior. L'idee de nature, Cote-femmes (Paris), 1992, translated as *Racism, Sexism, Power, and Ideology,* Routledge (London), 1995.

Contributor of essays to anthologies, including *Race as News,* UNESCO Press (Paris), 1974; *L'idee de race dans la pensee politique contemporaine,* edited by P. Guiral and E. Temime, CNRS (Paris), 1977;

Race, Discourse, and Power in France, edited by M. Silverman, Avebury (Aldershot, Surrey), 1991; *Racisme et modernite,* edited by M. Wieviorka, La Decouverte (Paris), 1993; *Reading the Social Body,* edited by Catharine Burroughs and Jeffrey Ehrenreich, University of Iowa Press (Iowa City), 1993; *Ethnicisation des rapports sociaux, racismes, nationalismes, ethnicismes, et culturalismes,* edited by M. Fourier and G. Vermes, L'Harmattan (Paris), 1994; and *L'extreme-droite et les femmes,* Universite des femmes (Brussels), 1996.

Contributor to journals, including *Feminist Issues* and *L'Homme et la Societe.*

SIDELIGHTS: Feminist Colette Guillaumin is one France's most significant writers on the issues of gender and race. While somewhat eclipsed by fellow French feminist writers like Monique Wittig, Julia Kristeva, and Luce Irigary on an international level, Guillaumin's works of materialist-feminist philosophy have recently become more familiar to U.S. and British readers through their inclusion in numerous English-language anthologies. The 1995 translation of her *Racism, Sexism, Power, and Ideology* has allowed Guillaumin's voice to be clearly recognized within the world-wide feminist discourse on the subject of sexual and racial difference.

Central to Guillaumin's work is her critique of the ideologies of both "Nature" and "difference." Her first book, 1972's *L'ideologie raciste: Genese et langage actuel,* traces the history of racism—"natural" differences between individuals—to its foundations in the value system in use in nineteenth-century European society. She also examines the language used to categorize individuals according to their so-called "Nature," language that would accentuate such differences as sex, racial characteristics, or socioeconomic class.

In addition to her numerous contributions to anthologies, Guillaumin has been involved in an editorial capacity in two of France's leading feminist journals, *Le Genre Humain* and the now defunct *Questions Feministes.* It was in the latter journal that her best-known essays on male domination of women—the two-part "Pratique du pouvoir et idee de Nature," "Le discours de la Nature," and "Question de difference"—would first appear between 1979 and 1980. These three essays would later be translated with several of her other works in *Racism, Sexism, Power, and Ideology.*

Guillaumin's work on racism has been hailed by her colleagues as groundbreaking. A researcher in the "migrations et Societes" unit of Paris's National Center for Scientific Research, she also lectures at the Universite de Paris VII, in Jussieu.

BIOGRAPHICAL/CRITICAL SOURCES:

BOOKS

Adkins, Lisa, and Diana Leonard, *Sex in Question: French Materialist Feminism,* Taylor & Francis (Philadelphia), 1996.
Feminist Writers, St. James Press (Detroit), 1996.*

*   *   *

GUNDY, Jeff(rey Gene) 1952-

PERSONAL: Born August 7, 1952, in Flanagan, IL; son of Roger (a farmer) and Arlene (a farmer; maiden name, Ringenberg) Gundy; married Marlyce Martens, November 27, 1973; children: Nathan, Benjamin, Joel. *Ethnicity:* "Swiss/German." *Education:* Goshen College, B.A., 1975; Indiana University—Bloomington, M.A., 1978, Ph.D., 1983. *Religion:* Mennonite. *Avocational interests:* Guitar, soccer.

ADDRESSES: Home—124 South Lawn, Bluffton, OH 45817. *Office*—Department of English, Bluffton College, Bluffton, OH 45817. *E-mail*—gundyj@bluffton.edu.

CAREER: Indiana University—Bloomington, associate instructor in English, 1977-80; Goshen College, Goshen, IN, assistant professor of English, 1980; Hesston College, Hesston, KS, instructor in English, 1980-84; Bluffton College, Bluffton, OH, associate professor, 1984-89, professor of English, 1989—, C. Henry Smith Peace Lecturer, 1989. Gives lectures, workshops, and readings from his works at colleges and universities, including Fresno Pacific College, Otterbein College, Illinois State University, Conrad Grebel College, and University of Findlay.

MEMBER: Modern Language Association of America, National Council of Teachers of English, Poets, and Writers.

AWARDS, HONORS: Pushcart Prize nominations, 1989, 1991, 1993, 1994, 1995; fellow, Ohio Arts Council, 1988-89, 1991-92; fellow, White River Writers' Workshop, 1995.

WRITINGS:

Inquiries (poems), Bottom Dog Press (Huron, OH), 1992.
Flatlands (poems), Poetry Center, Cleveland State University (Cleveland, OH), 1995.
A Community of Memory: My Days with George and Clara (nonfiction), University of Illinois Press (Urbana, IL), 1996.

Contributor of more than a hundred-eighty poems, articles, and reviews to periodicals, including *Mennonite Life, Georgia Review, Cottonwood Review, Crazyhorse, Negative Capability,* and *Spoon River Quarterly.*

WORK IN PROGRESS: Studying the landscape and history of Illinois.

SIDELIGHTS: Jeff Gundy told *CA:* "Where do poems come from? For a long time I thought my past was so boring that there wasn't much to write about in it. And my current life, more or less placid, ordinary, small-town, is not running over with 'material' in the old sense of traumas, divorces, madness, and so on, either, though it is filled, pressed down and running over, with things to do, with stuff both physical and otherwise. What's happening, right now, can lead in so many directions.

"I heard the poet Robert Hass say recently that the work of poetry is to keep alive our capacity to respond to experience. He's too smart to be wrong. I might add, however, that the job of poetry and other imaginative writing also include retrieving experience that is threatening to vanish, unrecorded, unacknowledged; re-imagining experience that is already lost; and recording unconventional, unordinary responses and reactions.

"We start and end in mystery, after all, and what's in between is mostly none too sensical. Poetry may be a stay against confusion, as Frost said, or a way of living in the confusions, a raft to carry us through them. My poems tend to come out of intersections, knots where two or three little pieces of the big world come together for me, and those pieces may come from the literary world, family life, politics, music, sports, whatever of the welter I'm most struck by at the moment. There are, for example, the ancestors of the Ropp family, who gave money for the building I'm sitting in now, who stood firmly with the Amish bishops who came to Illinois in 1873 to cast Joseph Stuckey from the fold for his refusal to excommunicate Joseph Joder for his universalist poem. It's a long story, but worth hearing.

"I like William Stafford's idea of the poem as exploration, as free travel into realms that we make even as we discover them, through the gift of language. The Word, big or small 'w.' Talk about 'Christian poetry' suggests pompous pieties of the sort we have in plenty already. On the other hand, I once found myself writing in a notebook, 'All I am really interested in is God.' The best poems, I think, have some of the qualities of the words of Jesus: a combination of humility and moral urgency, a weird sense of humor, an attraction to the kinky otherness of the truth, and an appreciation of the need to approach it slantwise, lest we all go blind.

"Poetry also allows for (relatively) nonviolent resistance to group-think and for claiming a certain distance from the crowd, which all of us need and some of us even deserve. The band campers practicing outside my window right now are paying good money for the right to make those thunderous sounds, but I am here, too, after all. Why does it seem to be only the girls I hear saying 'Gather up!' so obediently? Are the boys just muttering, sullen? In high school, and still today, I would have walked barefoot on hot rocks before I marched around in a goofy uniform with a trumpet. Mainly, instead, I sat alone in my room, playing Dylan and the Beatles on the guitar. I'm still not troubled that I never learned piano, either. Last year we inherited a beautiful, old guitar from my wife's grandparents. This spring I bought a book with the words and chords for twelve-hundred songs, old and new, sardonic and sacred. The tunes and the words keep changing, and so do the instruments, but the singing goes on."

H

HALE, Nathan G., Jr. 1922-

PERSONAL: Born September 5, 1922, in Sacramento, CA; son of Nathan G. (a surgeon) and Harriett (Gerber) Hale; married, June 22, 1973; wife's name, Ann W.; children: David, Elizabeth. *Ethnicity:* "White." *Education:* Princeton University, B.A. (summa cum laude), 1947; University of Paris, Certificat d'histoire moderne et contemporaine, 1948; University of California, Berkeley, M.A., 1957, Ph.D., 1964. *Politics:* Independent. *Religion:* Episcopalian. *Avocational interests:* Piano, classical music, horseback riding, swimming.

ADDRESSES: Home and office—309 Pala Ave., Piedmont, CA 94611-3742.

CAREER: University of California, Berkeley, lecturer in history, 1965-69; University of California, Riverside, professor of history, 1970-79, professor emeritus, 1979—. Stanford University, visiting professor, 1982-83. Lassen Volcanic National Park Foundation, member of board of directors. Member of board of directors, Clausen House and Towne House Creative Living Center. *Military service:* U.S. Army, Signal Intelligence Service, 1943-46; served in Australia, the Philippines, and Japan; became first lieutenant.

MEMBER: American Historical Association, Organization of American Historians, San Francisco Psychoanalytic Institute (interdisciplinary member).

AWARDS, HONORS: Woodrow Wilson fellow in France, 1947-48; Guggenheim fellow, 1972-73; fellow, National Institute of Mental Health, 1977-78.

WRITINGS:

(With Karl Beutner) *Emotional Illness: How Families Can Help,* Putnam (New York), 1957.
(Editor and author of introduction) *James Jackson Putnam and Psychoanalysis: Letters Between Putnam, Sigmund Freud, William James, Ernest Jones, Sandor Ferenczi, and Morton Prince,* Harvard University Press (Cambridge, MA), 1971.
Freud and the Americans, Oxford University Press (Oxford), Volume I: *The Beginnings of Psychoanalysis in the United States, 1876-1917,* 1971, Volume II: *The Rise and Crisis of Psychoanalysis in America, 1917-1985,* 1995.
(Editor and author of introduction) *Psychotherapy and Multiple Personality: Selected Papers of Morton Prince,* Harvard University Press, 1975.

Contributor to books, including *Themes of Love and Work in Adulthood,* edited by Neil Smelser and Erik Erikson, Harvard University Press, 1980; and *American Psychiatry Since World War II,* edited by Roy Menninger and John Nemiah, 1996.

WORK IN PROGRESS: The Freud Bashers: A Critical Review.

*   *   *

HALEVI, Yossi Klein 1953-

PERSONAL: Born June 9, 1953, in Brooklyn, NY; son of Zoltan and Bertha (Hiller) Klein; married

Sarah Rintoul Halevi, June 26, 1983; children: Moriah, Gavriel. *Ethnicity:* "Jewish." *Education:* Brooklyn College of the City University of New York, B.A.; Northwestern University, M.A. *Politics:* "Militant centrist." *Religion:* "Practicing Jew, with strong sympathy for other religious paths."

CAREER: Writer.

WRITINGS:

Memoirs of a Jewish Extremist: An American Story, Little, Brown (Boston, MA), 1995.

*   *   *

HALFORD, Graeme S(ydney) 1937-

PERSONAL: Born November 11, 1937, in Sydney, Australia. *Ethnicity:* "Caucasian." *Education:* University of New England, B.A. (with honors), 1961, M.A. (with honors), 1966; University of Newcastle, Ph.D., 1969. *Avocational interests:* Flying, gliding, skiing, photography, farming, yacht sailing.

ADDRESSES: Home—11 Narnoo St., Chapel Hill, Queensland 4069, Australia. *Office*—Department of Psychology, University of Queensland, Brisbane, Queensland 4072, Australia; fax 61-73-365-4466. *E-mail*—gsh@psy.uq.edu.au.

CAREER: University of Newcastle, Newcastle, Australia, lecturer, 1965-70, senior lecturer in psychology, 1971-72; Queen's University, Kingston, Ontario, associate professor of psychology, 1972-75; University of Queensland, Brisbane, Australia, senior lecturer, 1975-79, reader, 1980-89, professor of psychology, 1989—. International Geosphere-Biosphere Programme, member of national committee.

MEMBER: International Society for the Study of Behavioral Development, Australasian Cognitive Science Society (president, 1993-95), Australian Academy of Science (member of national committee for psychology), Academy of the Social Sciences of Australia (fellow; convenor of Queensland branch, 1996-98), Australian Psychological Society (fellow), American Psychological Association (fellow), Society for Research in Child Development, Psychonomic Society.

AWARDS, HONORS: Convocation Medal for Professional Excellence, University of Newcastle, 1995.

WRITINGS:

The Development of Thought, Lawrence Erlbaum (Hillsdale, NJ), 1982.
Children's Understanding: The Development of Mental Models, Lawrence Erlbaum, 1993.
Developing Cognitive Competence: New Approaches to Process Modelling, Lawrence Erlbaum, 1995.

Co-author of the book *Mathematics Education,* Lawrence Erlbaum.

WORK IN PROGRESS: Research on cognitive psychology, human processing capacity, and human reasoning processes.

SIDELIGHTS: Graeme S. Halford told *CA:* "My books have been written to integrate the results of research and scholarship conducted over a number of years. The field of cognitive development raises some fundamental issues about how children acquire and organize information about their world. My work has been designed to investigate some fundamental properties of this process. A major aspect has been to find ways of defining human capacity to process information. Another aspect has been concerned with how abstract (that is, relational) schemas can be induced from experience with sets of structurally similar situations. The formation of relational schemas depends jointly on experience and on processing capacity, and much of my work has been designed to integrate these two aspects. The work also has implications for general cognition, and a theory of processing capacity in children, adults, and other animals has been developed. The work has been applied to a number of areas, including mathematics education."

*   *   *

HALL, Joan Wylie 1947-

PERSONAL: Born September 2, 1947, in Port Allegany, PA; daughter of Arthur T. (a railroad agent) and Marjorie (a home economics teacher and nurse; maiden name, Saunders) Wylie; married J. R. Hall (a professor of English and medievalist), August 17, 1974; children: Jennifer, Justin. *Education:* Saint Mary-of-the-Woods College (Indiana), B.A., 1969; University of Notre Dame, M.A., 1970, Ph.D., 1976. *Religion:* Roman Catholic. *Avocational interests:* Reading, visiting art and history museums—including "living history" museums, and literacy education.

ADDRESSES: Home—1705 Johnson Ave., Oxford, MS 38655. *Office*—English Department, University of Mississippi, University, MS 38677.

CAREER: Franklin News-Herald, Franklin, PA, general reporter, summers, 1966-69; University of Notre Dame, teaching assistant, 1971-72, part-time instructor, 1973-74; Saint Mary-of-the-Woods College, instructor, 1974-78; Harvard University, preceptor for junior English tutorials, 1983-84; University of Mississippi, part-time instructor, 1979-83 and 1984—.

MEMBER: Society for the Study of Southern Literature, South Central Modern Language Association, South Atlantic Modern Language Association, Modern Language Association, Mississippi Philological Association.

AWARDS, HONORS: Dissertation fellowship, University of Notre Dame; Travel to Collections grant, National Endowment for the Humanities.

WRITINGS:

Shirley Jackson: A Study of the Short Fiction, Twayne (New York), 1993.

Contributor to reference works. Also author of articles in journals, including *Explicator, University of Dayton Review, Papers on Language and Literature, American Notes & Queries, Publications of the Mississippi Philological Association, College Language Association Journal, Colby Library Quarterly, Faulkner Journal, Mississippi Quarterly, Renascence, Studies in Short Fiction, Willa Cather Yearbook,* and *Legacy: A Journal of American Women Writers.* Also author of numerous book reviews.

WORK IN PROGRESS: Ruth McEnery Stuart for Twayne's "United States Authors" Series, expected manuscript completion 1997; also working on projects on Carolyn Wells and turn-of-the-century women's humor (1890s-early 1900s), and on Frances Newman and other twentieth-century Southern women writers.

SIDELIGHTS: With her first book, 1993's *Shirley Jackson: A Study of the Short Fiction,* Joan Wylie Hall has contributed what has been regarded as a stimulating work of criticism and research to the study of American fiction. She shows Jackson as an underrated, misrepresented author who deserves greater critical attention. Although Jackson's short story "The Lottery" is required reading for many American students, her work is most often marginalized by being classified as horror, humor, or women's writing. Hall provides a thorough argument to add Jackson to the mainstream American literary opus, substantiating her argument with careful readings of Jackson's stories, excerpts from Jackson's own lectures, letters, and unpublished writings, and selected critical comments from others. She also highlights the fact that Jackson's reputation may have originally been obscured by her publisher's sensational packaging of "The Lottery."

Critics responded favorably to both Hall's scholarship and her goal of focusing a spotlight on Shirley Jackson's work. In the *South Atlantic Review,* Tricia Lootens remarked on the import of Hall's attempt to revive interest in Jackson, saying that *Shirley Jackson* "promises to serve both as a sourcebook and a catalyst. Perhaps inevitably, Hall's work documents (and deplores) the limits of Jackson scholarship to this point. Yet it also offers critical readings, primary sources, and bibliographical groundwork of the kind that can inspire and support studies to come." In a review for *Choice,* J. Overmyer concurred, noting that Hall's work "should go far to rescue Jackson's reputation from the abyss into which it has inexplicably fallen." In the realm of "weird fiction," where Jackson's writings have traditionally found approval, Hall's work was also welcomed. *Necrophile: The Review of Horror Fiction* contributor S. T. Joshi remarked: "Hall's focus is not, of course, upon Jackson as a weird writer, but her careful examination of the short fiction makes it evident that Jackson was a titan in our field. . . . One of criticism's noblest functions is to drive the reader back to the primary text, and Hall's study should make everyone initiate or renew an acquaintance with the remarkable short fiction of Shirley Jackson."

Hall's work on Jackson is characteristic of her general interest in writing about authors she perceives as "neglected." As she told *CA:* "I have published articles on Francis Bacon, Faulkner, Tennessee Williams, and Willa Cather, but scholars have written many books on each of these authors. I feel greater satisfaction in bringing critically neglected writers to the attention of today's readers. Nina Baym's and Judith Fetterley's books on mid-nineteenth-century American women writers have stimulated my interest in underrated women of more recent generations, such as Ruth McEnery Stuart, Carolyn Wells, and Shirley Jackson. Nancy Walker's studies of women's humor have further encouraged me to explore the comedy of these three writers. Archival research is especially rewarding; on my trip to the Shirley Jackson Papers at the Library of Congress, I was excited to find not only the typescript of her most famous story, "The Lottery," but also the manuscripts of many unpublished stories. With the permission of her daughter, Sarah Stewart—herself a writer—, I was able to print some previously unpublished material from the Jackson Papers in my book for Twayne's 'Studies in Short Fiction Series.'"

BIOGRAPHICAL/CRITICAL SOURCES:

PERIODICALS

Choice, October, 1993, p. 289.
Necrophile: The Review of Horror Fiction, summer, 1993, pp. 22-23.
South Atlantic Review, January, 1994, pp. 160-62.

*   *   *

HALLWAS, John E.   1945-

PERSONAL: Born May 24, 1945, in Waukegan, IL; son of Emil F. (a building contractor) and Ruth E. (Wells) Hallwas; married Garnette V. Stockstad, January 3, 1966; children: John Darrin, Evan Bradley. *Ethnicity:* "Caucasian." *Education:* Western Illinois University, B.S., 1967, M.A., 1968; University of Florida, Ph.D., 1972. *Avocational interests:* Nature study, skiing, ballroom dancing.

ADDRESSES: Home—8 Hickory Bow, Macomb, IL 61455. *Office*—Department of English, Western Illinois University, Macomb, IL 61455; fax 309-298-2781. *E-mail*—JE-Hallwas@wiu.edu.

CAREER: University of Florida, Gainesville, member of English faculty, summer, 1970; Western Illinois University, Macomb, began as assistant professor, became associate professor, 1970-81, professor of American literature, 1981—, distinguished professor, 1992-93, director of Regional Collections at university library, 1979—. Visiting lecturer at Carl Sandburg College, 1976, Monmouth College, 1979, Black Hawk College, 1990, and University of Illinois at Urbana-Champaign, 1995.

MEMBER: Society for the Study of Midwestern Literature, Association for the Study of Literature and the Environment, Illinois State Historical Society, Phi Beta Kappa, Phi Kappa Phi.

AWARDS, HONORS: Grants from Illinois Humanities Council, 1975, 1978, 1979, 1980, 1981, 1982, 1985; Faculty Service Award, National University Continuing Education Association, 1981, for excellence in adult-education programming; Citizen of the Year Award, city of Macomb, IL, 1990, for civic contributions; John Whitmer Historical Association Award, best article category, 1990, for the article "Mormon Nauvoo from a Non-Mormon Perspective;" Superior Achievement Award, Illinois State Historical Society, 1992, for *Macomb: A Pictorial History;* MidAmerica Award, Society for the Study of Midwestern Literature, 1994, for distinguished contributions to the study of Midwestern literature; *Spoon River Anthology* was named an "Outstanding Academic Book" of the year, *Choice,* 1995; Mormon History Association Award, best documentary, 1996, for *Cultures in Conflict.*

WRITINGS:

The Western Illinois Poets (monograph), Western Illinois University (Macomb, IL), 1975.
(Editor with Dennis J. Reader) *The Vision of This Land: Studies of Vachel Lindsay, Edgar Lee Masters, and Carl Sandburg,* Western Illinois University, 1976.
(Editor) *Western Illinois University Libraries: A Handbook,* Western Illinois University, 1980.
(Editor with Jerrilee Cain-Tyson and Victor Hicken) *Tales from Two Rivers,* Western Illinois University, Volume I, 1981, Volume II, 1982, Volume III, 1984, Volume IV (with David R. Pichaske), 1987, and Two Rivers Arts Council (Macomb), Volume V (with Alfred J. Lindsey), 1990, Volume VI (with Lindsey), 1996.
The Poems of H.: The Lost Poet of Lincoln's Springfield, Ellis Press (Peoria, IL), 1982.
The Conflict (play), produced at Argyle Park Theatre, 1982.
Four on the Frontier (one-act plays; includes "Warrior at Sundown," "American Prophet," "Abolitionist in Congress," and "The Backwoods Preacher"), performed on a tour of western Illinois communities, 1982-83.
Western Illinois Heritage, Illinois Heritage Press (Macomb), 1983.
Thomas Gregg: Early Illinois Journalist and Author (monograph), Western Illinois University, 1983.
McDonough County Heritage, Illinois Heritage Press, 1984.
(Editor with Robert Graybill, Judy Hample, and others) *Teaching the Middle Ages,* Volume II, Studies in Medieval and Renaissance Teaching (Warrensburg, MO), 1985.

(With Gene Kozlowski) *The Paper Town* (play), produced at Argyle Park Theatre, 1985.

Illinois Literature: The Nineteenth Century, Illinois Heritage Press, 1986.

Studies in Illinois Poetry, Stormline Press (Champaign, IL), 1989.

Macomb: A Pictorial History, G. Bradley Publishing (St. Louis, MO), 1990.

(Editor) *Spoon River Anthology: An Annotated Edition,* University of Illinois Press (Urbana, IL), 1992.

The Legacy of the Mines: Memoirs of Coal Mining in Fulton County, Illinois, Spoon River College (Canton, IL), 1993.

(With Roger D. Launius) *Cultures in Conflict: A Documentary History of the Mormon War in Illinois,* Utah State University Press (Logan, UT), 1995.

(Editor with Launius) *Kingdom on the Mississippi Revisited: Nauvoo in Mormon History,* University of Illinois Press, 1996.

Co-editor of the series "Prairie State Books," University of Illinois Press, 1987—. Contributor to books, including *Exploring the Midwestern Literary Imagination: Essays in Honor of David D. Anderson,* edited by Marcia Noe, Whitston (Troy, NY), 1993. Author of *Prairie State Journal: Inventing Illinois,* a weekly program broadcast by public radio stations in Illinois, 1992-93. Author of "Our Regional Heritage," a weekly column, *Macomb Journal,* 1981-84, "Visions and Values," a weekly self-syndicated column, 1984-85, and "Passages," a weekly column, *Jacksonville Journal Courier,* 1987-88. Contributor of about ninety articles and reviews to periodicals, including *Prairie Journal, Old Northwest, Great Lakes Review, Journal of Mormon History, Illinois Magazine, Illinois Issues, MidAmerica,* and *Journal of the Illinois State Historical Society. Western Illinois Regional Studies,* co-founder, 1978, co-editor, 1978-92, editorial chairperson, 1980-92; founding editor, *Essays in Literature,* 1973-79, and *Western Illinois Reader,* 1987-89; editor, *McDonough County Historical Society Newsletter,* 1981-90.

WORK IN PROGRESS: The Bootlegger: A Story of Small-Town America, a biography of bootlegger Kelly Wagle and a history of Colchester, IL); editing *Tales From Two Rivers,* Volume VI.

SIDELIGHTS: John E. Hallwas told *CA:* "Most of my writing relates to and interprets the cultural heritage of western Illinois, where I have spent all of my adult life. Although I was raised more than two hundred

miles away, in northern Illinois, I have lived here for more than thirty years, and I know more about the landscape, towns, people, and history of western Illinois than I will ever know about any other place. This is my home territory, a corn-and-soybean empire of expanding farms and declining villages, small cities and unsophisticated people, and I am deeply engaged with it.

"Life is enriched if people live in a place where they can feel a part of a meaningful cultural tradition. As a historian, editor, essayist, and literary scholar, I have tried to promote that kind of consciousness— often called a sense of place—and to reflect the culture of my region clearly enough so that readers anywhere might find it compelling.

"In recent years I have been especially interested in community history, with its dramatic interplay of will and circumstance, its portrayal of cultural construction, and its reflection of national values in local experience. In a nation devoted to self-realization, and now obsessed with individualism and divided into factions, we need to understand our cultural environment far better than we do, and to value the common experience far more than we do. We need to build community. If writing promotes that, it will have cultural significance, whether or not it reaches a national audience.

"Although I do not write poetry, three poets from my region have had a significant influence on my work. Vachel Lindsay, Edgar Lee Masters, and Carl Sandburg were deeply rooted in this part of the country, and they too were engaged with the culture of Illinois and the Midwest and concerned with the renewal of meaning and community in America."

*   *   *

HAMILTON, Neil (W.) 1945-

PERSONAL: Born December 24, 1945, in Minneapolis, MN; son of Francis Glenn (a company president) and Ruth Gordon (a homemaker; maiden name, Sand) Hamilton; married Jana Uve Baltins (an elementary schoolteacher), May 3, 1969; children: Sheen, Maya, Kyra. *Ethnicity:* "Norwegian/Scottish." *Education:* Colorado College, B.A. (cum laude), 1967; University of Minnesota—Twin Cities, J.D. (magna cum laude), 1970; University of Michigan, M.A., 1979.

Politics: Independent. *Religion:* Congregational. *Avocational interests:* Reading, running.

ADDRESSES: *Home*—52 North Mississippi River Blvd., St. Paul, MN 55104. *Office*—William Mitchell College of Law, 875 Summit Ave., St. Paul, MN 55105; fax 612-290-6414. *E-mail*—nhamilton@ wmitchell.edu.

CAREER: Gray, Plant, Mooty, Mooty & Bennett, Minneapolis, MN, associate attorney, 1970-71; Krieg, Devault, Alexander & Capehart, Indianapolis, IN, associate attorney, 1971-72; Airlangga University, Surabaya, Indonesia, visiting professor of law and fellow at International Legal Center, 1972-74; Case Western Reserve University, Cleveland, OH, assistant professor of law, 1977-80; William Mitchell College of Law, St. Paul, MN, Trustees Professor of Regulatory Policy, 1980—. U.S. Army Finance School, instructor in accounting, 1971-72. Midwest Corporate Counsel Center, president and executive director, 1985-90.

MEMBER: American Law Institute, American Association of University Professors, National Academy of Sciences, American Civil Liberties Union, Phi Beta Kappa, Coif.

AWARDS, HONORS: Fulbright scholar, University of Singapore, 1987.

WRITINGS:

(With Peter Hamilton) *Governance of Public Enterprise: A Case Study of Urban Mass Transit,* Lexington Books (Lexington, MA), 1981.
Zealotry and Academic Freedom: A Legal and Historical Perspective, Transaction Books (New Brunswick, NJ), 1995.

Contributor to books, including *Law and Public Enterprises in Asia,* Praeger (New York), 1976. Contributor of about twenty-five articles to law journals, including *William Mitchell Law Review, Antitrust Bulletin, Canada-United States Law Journal,* and *Minnesota Law Review.*

*   *   *

HARDING, Ross
  See GEMMELL, David A(ndrew)

HARDY, Francis Joseph 1917-
  (Frank J. Hardy, Ross Franklyn)

PERSONAL: Born March 21, 1917, in Southern Cross, Victoria, Australia; married Rosslyn Couper, 1939; children: one son, two daughters. *Education:* Attended state schools.

ADDRESSES: *Home*—131 Warner Ave., North Tonawanda, NY 14120-1617. *Office*—c/o State Mutual, 521 5th Ave., 17th Fl., New York, NY 10175.

CAREER: Has worked variously as a cartoonist, seaman, journalist, trade union organizer, and farm laborer. Freelance writer, lecturer, songwriter, and television personality. Co-founder, Australian Society of Authors, 1968-74. *Military service:* Australian Army, 1941-46.

MEMBER: Australian Society of Authors, Realist Writers Group, Carringbush Writers (president, 1980-83), Realist Writers Group (president, 1945-74).

AWARDS, HONORS: Logic award, 1972, for a television script; Television Society award, 1973; three Literature Board grants; A.N.A. Literature award (with others), 1980, for *Who Shot George Kirkland?.*

WRITINGS:

NOVELS

(As Ross Franklyn) *Power without Glory,* Realist (Melbourne), 1950.
The Four-Legged Lottery, Laurie (London), 1958.
The Outcasts of Foolgarah, Allara (Melbourne), 1971.
But the Dead Are Many: A Novel in Fugue Form, Bodley Head (London), 1975.
Who Shot George Kirkland? A Novel about the Nature of Truth, Arnold (Melbourne), 1981.
The Obsession of Oscar Oswald [with] "Warrant of Distress" by Oscar Oswald, Pascoe (Carleton, Victoria), 1983.

Novels also published under the name variation Frank J. Hardy.

SHORT STORIES

The Man from Clinkapella and Other Prize-winning Stories, Realist, 1951.

Legends from Benson's Valley, Laurie, 1963, with
  "The Eviction of Erine Lyle" published as *It's
  Moments Like These,* Gold Star (Melbourne),
  1972.
The Yarns of Billy Borker, Reed (Sydney), 1965.
Billy Borker Yarns Again, Nelson (Melbourne), 1967.
The Great Australian Lover and Other Stories,
  Nelson, 1972.
(With Athol George Mulley) *The Needy and the
  Greedy: Humorous Stories of the Racetrack,* Li-
  bra (Canberra), 1975.
(With Fred Trueman) *You Nearly Had Him That Time
  and Other Cricket Stories,* S. Paul (London),
  1978.
A Frank Hardy Swag, edited by Clement Semmler,
  Harper (Sydney), 1982.
The Loser Now Will Be Later to Win, Pascoe, 1985.
Hardy's People: Stories of Truthful Jones, Pascoe,
  1986.

OTHER

Journey into the Future (travel), Australasian Book
  Society (Melbourne), 1952.
*The Hard Way: The Story behind "Power without
  Glory"* (nonfiction), Laurie, 1961.
The Unlucky Australians (nonfiction), Nelson, 1968,
  revised edition, Gold Star, 1972.
Great Australian Legends, Hutchinson (Surry Hills,
  New South Wales), 1985.
*Retreat Australian Fair, and Other Great Australian
  Legends,* Hutchinson, 1990.
Faces in the Street: An Epic Drama (play), Stained
  Wattle Press (Westgate, New South Wales),
  1990.
Mary Lives! (play), Currency Press, 1992.

Author's work has been translated into several languages. Also author of plays *Black Diamonds,* 1956;
The Ringbolter, 1964; and *Who Was Harry Larsen?,*
1985. Author of numerous television scripts. Author's
works are collected in the Australian National Library, Canberra.

ADAPTATIONS: *Power without Glory* was adapted as
an Australian television series, 1976.

SIDELIGHTS: Author Francis Joseph Hardy first
made a name for himself in his native Australia with
the novel, *Power without Glory,* which Hardy initially
published and distributed himself in 1950, after publishing houses shied from the book due to its controversial nature. Indeed, only months after reviews of
Power without Glory reached the Australian papers,

Hardy found himself involved in a libel suit. Citing
the novel as a thinly disguised attack on millionaire
John Wren, Wren's wife sued Hardy over his fiction-
alization of her as the adulterous character Nellie
West. Finally acquitted after the nine-month-long
trial, Hardy was transformed into an international
celebrity; *Power without Glory* has since been reprinted several times, was translated into several languages, and has been adapted into a television series
in the mid-1970s.

Born in 1917 and raised in the Victoria community of
Bacchus Marsh, which he would later fictionalize as
"Benson's Valley" in several short story collections,
Hardy left school as soon as he reached adolescence
and was employed variously as a farm worker, a road
construction crew worker, and as a seaman. The
sufferings of Australia's working class during the
Depression era prompted the idealistic young Hardy
to join the Communist Party in 1939; he would re-
peatedly reflect upon the inequities of society in his
short fiction, as well as in novels such as 1975's *But
the Dead Are Many: A Novel in Fugue Form,* which
while taken to task by Peter Ackroyd in the *Spectator*—"Here is a creature which had long been thought
extinct, but which has now been discovered in Australia: the solemn novel of the brow-beating species"—was hailed by Van Ikin in *Contemporary Novelists* as "one of the major works of Australian literature in the 1970s."

While Hardy's novels most often treat serious topics—*The Four-Legged Lottery* focuses on the corruption in the horseracing industry, *But the Dead Are
Many* confronts the suicide of a left-wing intellectual,
and *Who Shot George Kirkland?* traces the path of a
journalist investigating the veracity of his sources
after breaking a damning story—he is also known for
his short fiction. "The Load of Wood," included in
1982's *A Frank Hardy Swag,* is considered among the
classic Australian short stories, and the poignant depictions of rural life during the Depression collected
in *Legends from Benson's Valley* reflect his ear for
speech and respect for character. Reflecting a more
humorous side, Hardy's creation of the character
Billy Borker, an imaginative, good-timing Aussie
with a knack for story-telling, breathed life into a
traditional rural stereotype and the short stories in
The Yarns of Billy Borker and *Billy Borker Yarns
Again* have gained a large following.

In *The Hard Way,* published in 1981, Hardy reflects
upon his early fame as the author of *Power without
Glory,* describes gathering information for his novel

while working in Melbourne during the late 1940s, and depicts the turmoil of his months in court over the novel. In later years, Hardy again showed the strong social conscience reflected in his earlier works. The 1983 novel *The Obsession of Oscar Oswald* is a condemnation of the machinations of twentieth-century financiers, lawyers, and collection companies through casting a fresh perspective on the predictions of dystopian novelist George Orwell. Accompanying the novel is the booklet *Warrant of Distress,* a tract purported by Hardy to be written by the novel's protagonist. Well known as a lecturer, journalist, playwright, and television celebrity, Hardy has continued to entertain Australians with his far-reaching interests and to illuminate for readers what he perceives as the economic fallout that results from living in a capitalist society.

BIOGRAPHICAL/CRITICAL SOURCES:

BOOKS

Contemporary Novelists, fifth edition, St. James (Chicago, IL), 1991, pp. 442-44.

PERIODICALS

Spectator, August 9, 1975, p. 149.
Times Educational Supplement, June 14, 1985, p. 28.
Times Literary Supplement, August 1, 1975, p. 865.

* * *

HARDY, Frank J.
   See HARDY, Francis Joseph

* * *

HARDY, Lyndon (Maurice)   1941-

PERSONAL: Born April 16, 1941, in Los Angeles, CA; married Joan Taresh, 1966; children: two. *Education:* California Institute of Technology, B.S. (in physics), 1962; University of California, Ph.D. (in high-energy physics), 1966.

ADDRESSES: 19616 Redbeam Ave., Torrance, CA 90503.

CAREER: Engineer, TRW Systems, Redondo Beach, CA, beginning 1966; writer.

WRITINGS:

FANTASY NOVELS

Master of the Five Magics, Del Rey (New York), 1980.
Secret of the Sixth Magic, Del Rey, 1984.
Riddle of the Seven Realms, Del Rey, 1988.

* * *

HARRIS, Martyn   1952-1996

OBITUARY NOTICE—See index for *CA* sketch: Given name is pronounced "Martin"; born October 7, 1952, in Swansea, Wales; died of cancer, October 4, 1996. Journalist and author. Harris gained prominence in the field of journalism, most recently as the columnist who wrote about his ordeal with cancer. Harris began his thirteen-year stint with London's *Daily Telegraph* in 1983 as a columnist. Before that time, he was a lecturer at ICL in London and an editor of IPC's computer magazines, and a feature writer for *New Society.* His first novel, *Do It Again,* was published in 1989, and dealt with man's journey back to his left-wing beginnings. His other novel, titled *The Mother-in-Law Joke,* was published in 1992. In 1995, Harris was diagnosed with cancer. His columns about his struggle appeared in both the London *Daily Telegraph* and *The Spectator.*

OBITUARIES AND OTHER SOURCES:

BOOKS

Writers Directory, St. James Press, 1996.

PERIODICALS

Times (London), October 17, 1996, p. 25.

* * *

HART, Ellen   1949-

PERSONAL: Born August 10, 1949, in Minneapolis, MN; daughter of Herman C. and Marjory (Anderson) Boehnhardt; spouse: Kathleen Kruger; children: Shawna Kruger Gibson, Tom Gibson, Bethany Kruger. *Education:* Ambassador College, B.A., 1971.

ADDRESSES: Office—c/o Seal Press, 3131 Western Ave., Ste. 410, Seattle, WA 98121; or c/o Ballantine, 201 East 50th St., New York, NY 10022.

CAREER: Chef.

AWARDS, HONORS: Lambda nominee for Best Lesbian Mystery, 1992, for *A Killing Cure: A Jane Lawless Mystery;* Lambda Literary Award for Best Lesbian Mystery, for *A Small Sacrifice,* 1994; Minnesota Book Award for Best Crime Fiction, for *A Small Sacrifice,* 1995, and for *Faint Praise,* 1996.

WRITINGS:

MYSTERIES

Hallowed Murder, Seal Press (Seattle, WA), 1989.
Vital Lies, Seal Press, 1990.
Stage Fright, Seal Press, 1992.
A Killing Cure: A Jane Lawless Mystery, Seal Press, 1993.
A Small Sacrifice: A Jane Lawless Mystery, Seal Press, 1994.
This Little Piggy Went to Murder, Ballantine (New York), 1994.
For Every Evil, Ballantine, 1995.
Faint Praise, Seal Press, 1995.
Robber's Wine, Seal Press, 1996.
The Oldest Sin, Ballantine, 1996.
Murder in the Air, Ballantine, 1997.

SIDELIGHTS: Six of Ellen Hart's mystery novels feature the same heroine: the smart, savvy, restaurateur and lesbian amateur detective Jane Lawless. (*This Little Piggy Went to Murder* presents a new character, Sophie Greenway.) Another character who appears on the Lawless series is Cordelia Thorne, Jane's good friend and regular "deputy" on all her sleuthing experiences. A *Publishers Weekly* reviewer described *Hallowed Murder,* in which Lawless investigates the drowning death of a sorority sister and related events, as a "novel of ideas," adding that the "plot is deftly paced." About *Vital Lies,* in which the fictional Fothergill Inn and its associated Minnesota residents form the nucleus of the plot, a *Publishers Weekly* reviewer comments, "this compelling whodunit has the psychological maze of a Barbara Vine mystery and the feel of Agatha Christie."

A Killing Cure focuses on the members of the exclusive Amelia Gower Women's Club—two of whom meet mysterious deaths—and its philanthropic arm, the Gower Foundation. A *Publishers Weekly* reviewer

observed, "Jane and Cordelia make a successful duo as entertainers and investigators," while a *Library Journal* critic noted, "strong characters, setting, and investigation." Maria Kuda, writing in *Booklist,* labelled the book a "top-notch" mystery upholding "the venerable whodunit tradition of maximal suspense and character development but minimal gore." *A Small Sacrifice* examines a group of Cordelia's college friends who band together to help another member of their group, an alcoholic actress. The appearance of a male classmate causes tension among members of the group, and his subsequent mysterious demise prompts Cordelia to request Jane's presence. A *Publishers Weekly* reviewer described the "absorbing" action as "driven by romantic and competitive connections that convincingly cross genders." A *Library Journal* critic praised Hart"s deft handling of a "sexually diverse batch of characters, rural setting, and focused plot."

Faint Praise, Hart's sixth Lawless mystery, "is the best caper yet for the lesbian restaurateur and amateur sleuth," according to Whitney Scott in *Booklist.* The events revolve around the unexplained death of a television personality and an apparently coincidental series of security breaches, assaults, and murders at his apartment house. In *Publishers Weekly,* Sybil Steinberg described the residents of Linden Lofts as "an appealing hodge-podge of eccentrics, lost souls, closeted gays, homophobes, cross-dressers and yuppies brought convincingly to life." A *Library Journal* critic notes that the book contains "wit, charm, and fine writing."

Hart's *This Little Piggy Went to Murder* introduces amateur detective Sophie Greenway, a food critic, who, unlike Jane, is heterosexual. Sophie's old friend Amanda, faces a crisis when mysterious events, including murder, suddenly affect her and members of her family. Maria Simson comments in *Publishers Weekly* that "there are some good, nail-bitingly tense scenes and lots of red herrings."

Ellen Hart told *CA:* "I teach Mystery Writing through The Loft, the largest independent writing community in the nation."

BIOGRAPHICAL/CRITICAL SOURCES:

PERIODICALS

Booklist, September 15, 1993, p. 131; October 15, 1995, p. 388.
Chicago Tribune, June 21, 1995, p. 1.

Library Journal, October 1, 1989, p. 122; September
   1, 1993, p. 225; October 1, 1994, p. 118; October 1, 1995, p. 124.
New York Times Book Review, November 29, 1992,
   p. 21.
Publishers Weekly, August 25, 1989, p. 58; February
   22, 1991, p. 214; September 7, 1992, pp. 91-92;
   August 9, 1993, p. 468; August 1, 1994, p. 73;
   November 7, 1994, p. 70; October 16, 1995, p.
   45.*

*   *   *

HARVIE, Christopher (Thomas) 1944-

PERSONAL: Born September 21, 1944, in
Motherwell, Scotland; son of George Naismith (a
teacher) and Isobel Mary (a teacher; maiden name,
Russell) Harvie; married Virginia Mary Roundell (an
editor), April 26, 1980; children: Alison Margaret.
Education: Edinburgh University, M.A., 1966,
Ph.D., 1972. *Politics:* Socialist-Scottish Nationalist.
Religion: Church of Scotland.

*ADDRESSES: Office—*University of Tuebingen,
Wilhelmstrasse 50, 72074 Tuebingen, Germany.

CAREER: Open University, Milton Keynes, England,
lecturer in history, 1969-80; University of Tuebingen,
Tuebingen, Germany, professor of British studies,
1980—. Held various Labour Party posts, 1962-80;
vice-president of Scottish Centre for Social and Economic Research, 1990—.

WRITINGS:

(Editor with Graham Martin and Aaron Scharf)
   Industrialisation and Culture, 1830-1914,
   Macmillan (London), 1970.
War and Society in the Nineteenth Century, Open
   University Press (Milton Keynes, England),
   1973.
*The Lights of Liberalism: University Liberals and the
   Challenge of Democracy, 1860-1886,* Allen Lane
   (London), 1976.
*Scotland and Nationalism: Scottish Society and Poli-
   tics, 1707-1977,* Allen & Unwin (London), 1977;
   revised edition published as *Scotland and Nation-
   alism: Scottish Society and Politics, 1707-1994,*
   Routledge (London), 1994.
(Editor with Arthur Marwick, Charles Knightly, and
   Keith Wrightson) *The Illustrated Dictionary of*

British History, Thames & Hudson (London),
   1981.
*No Gods and Precious Few Heroes: Scotland, 1914-
   1980,* Arnold (London), 1981; revised edition
   published as *No Gods and Precious Few Heroes:
   Scotland Since 1914,* Edinburgh University Press
   (Edinburgh), 1993.
Against Metropolis, Fabian Society (London), 1982.
(Editor with Ian Donnachie and Ian S. Wood) *For-
   ward: Labour Politics in Scotland, 1888-1988,*
   Polygon (Edinburgh), 1989.
*The Centre of Things: Political Fiction in Britain
   from Disraeli to the Present,* Unwin Hyman
   (London), 1991.
*Cultural Weapons: Scotland and Survival in a New
   Europe,* Polygon (Edinburgh), 1992.
(Contributor) Kenneth O. Morgan, editor, *The Oxford
   History of Britain,* Volume 4: *The Eighteenth
   Century and the Age of Industry,* Oxford Univer-
   sity Press (Oxford), 1992.
(Editor and author of introduction) John Buchan, *The
   Thirty-Nine Steps,* Oxford University Press (Ox-
   ford), 1993.
Fool's Gold: The Story of North Sea Oil, Hamish
   Hamilton (London), 1994.
The Rise of Regional Europe, Routledge (London),
   1994.

*   *   *

HASSELBACH, Ingo 1967-

PERSONAL: Born in 1967, in Berlin, East Germany;
son of two journalists. *Education:* Left school at age
sixteen to become a bricklayer's apprentice.

*ADDRESSES: Office—*c/o Random House, 201 East
50th St., New York, NY 10022.

CAREER: Writer.

WRITINGS:

Die Abrechnung: ein Neonazi steigt aus (title means
   "The Reckoning: a neo-Nazi Drops Out"),
   Aufbau-Verlang (Berlin, Germany), 1994.
(With Tom Reiss) *Fuehrer-Ex: Memoirs of a Former
   neo-Nazi,* Random House (New York, NY),
   1996.

SIDELIGHTS: When former neo-Nazi Ingo Hasselbach published two books denouncing the fascist
movement during the mid-1990s, he took the world

by surprise. It had been predicted that the young man would unite the German neo-Nazi movement and emerge as its foremost leader. He had been addressed by young skinheads as "Fuehrer," had founded the German National Alternative neo-Nazi party, and had participated in planning a neo-Nazi takeover of Germany. Now, both the political left and right were shocked to find Hasselbach rigorously denouncing the neo-Nazi movement. First he produced *Die Abrechnung: ein Neonazi steigt aus* ("The Reckoning: a neo-Nazi Drops Out"), which, with the help of his American co-author Tom Reiss, was revised and expanded in English as *Fuehrer-Ex: Memoirs of a Former neo-Nazi.* This powerful and startling memoir takes a look at the German neo-Nazi movement; it offers important insight as to why young men and women joined the movement and provides detailed descriptions of how they promote violence and hate. Moreover, Hasselbach identifies people that he worked with in the movement, including the American neo-Nazi Gary Lauck, who was arrested and extradited to Germany for his participation in a network that supplied propaganda materials and terrorist equipment.

Fuehrer-Ex is also full of highly personal details. It describes Hasselbach's illegitimate birth in East Berlin and his troubled childhood. He knew his father only as "Uncle Hans" and was beaten by his stepfather. Hasselbach received some comfort from his grandparents; he would later write in the *New Yorker,* "I think my grandparents meant so much to me because at heart they were the least ideological people I knew. Just as they had never been Nazis in the Third Reich, they were never Communists in the G.D.R. [German Democratic Republic]. They were always just people. And in my life that has been a rare quality." He explains how he turned to various groups as he tried to escape his unhappy family life; he was first a hippie, then a punk, then an anarchist skinhead, and finally a neo-Nazi. He tells of how he came to know Winfried Bonengel, a left-wing film maker who challenged his beliefs, and how his growing disgust for the neo-Nazi movement was solidified by the 1992 firebombing that killed three Turkish women in Moelln, Germany.

While Hasselbach's books have been hailed as important sources of information about the neo-Nazi movement and its roots, Hasselbach's own story of transformation has often left reviewers cold. In the *New York Times Book Review,* Stephen Kinzer noted that "[Hasselbach] had evidently beaten and stomped enough people to satisfy the brutal urges within him,

and his contacts with a left-oriented film maker opened up the possibility of a new life." Similarly, *Time* critic R. Z. Sheppard said: "Hasselbach's conversion seems less a moral rebirth than simply the end of an unpleasant, unpromising stage of life." Mort Rosenblum commented in the *Washington Post* that "*Fuehrer-Ex* is not a great book. It is stiffly written and drawn out with gruesome repetition. After detailing his role in firebombings and vicious assaults, the author wonders why so few people love him now that he has come clean."

This is the dilemma that Hasselbach is faced with: having denounced neo-Nazism, he is now hated by his former enemies and by his former colleagues. He is forced to act a fugitive in his own country, where he and his family have received death threats; he and his sister have been physically attacked and his mother received a letter-bomb that did not explode. In his efforts to dismantle the neo-Nazi movement and to discourage young people from joining fascist groups, he strikes a curious figure. In *New Statesman & Society,* Christopher Springate remarked: "There should be something deeply incongruous about asking for advice on how best to combat neo-Nazism from someone who has rubbed shoulders with many of the world's leading neo-Nazis, has played a major role in spreading radical right-wing thinking in eastern Germany and has taken part in secret Paramilitary exercises to prepare for the 'takeover of power.'" And yet, commentators also saw Hasselbach's memoir as an important, fascinating book with wide-reaching implications. R. Z. Sheppard concluded, "[if this book] demonstrates anything, it is that Germany's small but venomous neo-Nazi movement, along with supporters in Austria and the U.S., can tap the same depths of irrationality that possessed Central Europe 60 years ago." Or as Mort Rosenblum stated: "As the old Nazis die off, their legacy presents a deadly serious if often subtle danger. New-Nazism polarizes people with deep pockets and deep reserves of frustrated energy who seek to forge intolerance into a transnational ideology. Instead of ranting in beer halls, they communicate by electronic infobahn. They are out there. *Fuehrer-Ex,* whatever one thinks of him, is a convincing witness."

BIOGRAPHICAL/CRITICAL SOURCES:

PERIODICALS

New Statesman & Society, January 21, 1994, p. 16-17.
New Yorker, January 8, 1996, p. 36-56.

New York Times, February 2, 1994, p. A4.
New York Times Book Review, February 4, 1996, p. 10.
Publishers Weekly, November 13, 1995, p. 52.
Time, February 5, 1996, p. 74-75.
Washington Post, February 6, 1996, p. E2.*

* * *

HATCHER, Robin Lee 1951-
(Robin Leigh)

PERSONAL: Born May 10, 1951, in Payette, ID; daughter of Ralph E. and Lucile (Johnson) Adams; first marriage ended; married Jerry W. Neu, 1989; children: Michaelyn J. Hatcher, Jennifer Lee Whitt. *Ethnicity:* "Caucasian." *Education:* Attended high school. *Religion:* Christian. *Avocational interests:* Travel, theater.

ADDRESSES: Home—Meridian, ID. *Office*—P.O. Box 4722, Boise, ID 83711-4722. *E-mail*—robinlee@micron.net. *Agent*—Natasha Kern Literary Agency, P.O. Box 2908, Portland, OR 97208-2908.

CAREER: Novelist. Public speaker.

MEMBER: Romance Writers of America (past president; past chairperson of National Literacy Committee), Authors Guild, Novelists, Inc., Colorado Romance Writers.

AWARDS, HONORS: Affaire de Coeur, Favorite Author Gold Pen Award, 1991, Gold Certificate, Best American Novel, 1991, for *Promise Me Spring,* and Gold Certificate for Outstanding Hero, 1991, for *Rugged Splendor; Romantic Times,* Kiss Awards, 1991, for *Rugged Splendor,* and 1993, for *The Magic,* as well as Career Achievement Award and Storyteller of the Year Award; Bookrak Awards, 1993, for *Where the Heart Is,* and 1994, for *Forever, Rose;* Writer of the Year Award, Idaho Writers League; Robin Award was established in her honor by Laubach Literacy International.

WRITINGS:

ROMANCE NOVELS, EXCEPT WHERE NOTED

Stormy Surrender, Leisure Books, 1984.
Heart's Landing, Leisure Books, 1984.
Thorn of Love, Leisure Books, 1985.

Heart Storm, Leisure Books, 1986.
Passion's Gamble, Leisure Books, 1986.
Pirate's Lady, Leisure Books, 1987.
Gemfire, Leisure Books, 1988.
The Wager, Leisure Books, 1989.
Dream Tide, Leisure Books, 1990.
Promised Sunrise, Leisure Books, 1990.
Rugged Splendor, Avon (New York City), 1991.
Promise Me Spring, Leisure Books, 1991.
The Hawk and the Heather, Avon, 1992.
Devlin's Promise, Leisure Books, 1992.
A Frontier Christmas (novella collection), Leisure Books, 1992.
Midnight Rose, Leisure Books, 1992.
The Magic, Leisure Books, 1993.
Where the Heart Is, Leisure Books, 1993.
Forever, Rose, Leisure Books, 1994.
Remember When, Leisure Books, 1994.
A Purrfect Romance (novella collection), Harper-Paperbacks (New York City), 1995.
Liberty Blue, HarperPaperbacks, 1995.
Chances Are, HarperPaperbacks, 1996.
Kiss Me, Katie! HarperPaperbacks, 1996.
Dear Lady, HarperPaperbacks, 1997.
Patterns of Love, HarperPaperbacks, in press.

Two books appear under the name Robin Leigh. Contributor to periodicals, including *Romance Writers Report, Affaire de Coeur,* and *Romantic Times.*

WORK IN PROGRESS: A romance novel, *In His Arms,* publication by HarperPaperbacks expected in 1998.

SIDELIGHTS: Robin Lee Hatcher told *CA:* "It is my fundamental belief that every good novel has a romance in it, whether it's the love story of a man and a woman or the passion of a person for the land or the affection shared between a boy and his dog. Love—both the giving and receiving of it—is as basic a human need as the air we breathe or the food we eat. It should come as no surprise, then, that romance novels account for nearly half of all paperback books sold (and that doesn't take into account the sale of used books). People want to read stories of love, stories in which men and women are brought together and persevere despite adversity, stories that end with a deep and lasting commitment between hero and heroine.

"For much of my adult life, I worked outside the home. I was a single mom, struggling to raise two children on a small salary and no child support from the ex. There were times when I wanted to answer a 'call to adventure,' but I couldn't because I'm the practical sort. I knew the bills had to be paid come the first of the month, and there were people counting on me. Ah, but the heroines in the books I love to read, they answer that call. When the marauders storm the castle, they take up a sword and help win the day. When the villain kidnaps their children, they saddle up and chase him across the vast western deserts.

"Of course, adventure is not limited to dangerous exploits. It's an adventure just to fall in love. Remember how wonderfully terrible that is? Would any of us really like to go through that process again and again and again? During the courtship period, emotions run at a break-neck speed. Highs are extremely high, and lows extremely low. For me, at least, it was a relief to say the words 'I do.' It brought a sense of peace to be able to relax in the comfort of simply loving my husband without all the other emotions inherent in the courtship phase of relationships.

"Romance fiction allows us vicariously to experience those emotions once again without any of the risk or any of the pain. We can cry and rejoice with our heroines. We can cheer them on. We can mentally shout at them for not doing what we know they should do.

"As both writer and reader, I am drawn to the 'gentle tamer' of yesterday who had to carve out her place—with courage and intelligence—in a man's world. The heroines of romantic fiction accept the challenges presented to them by the society in which they live (past or present) and they triumph despite them. Isn't that still true to some degree? Women today are still carving out their places—with courage and intelligence—in a man's world. It isn't easy. It never has been.

"Some naysayers like to insinuate that readers of romance can't tell truth from fiction, that romance books give them false expectations of life. I beg to differ. We *do* know the difference. Those who read romance know the realities of the world around them. We know that all men are not tall, dark, and handsome any more than all women are lithe and beautiful. We don't expect our heroes and heroines to be perfect any more than we expect ourselves to be perfect. We also know that reading a romance lifts our spirits and renews our faith in the power of love. Reading romance empowers us by the very nature of that renewed faith.

"If I may get on my soapbox for a moment, why does anyone deem it his or her right to criticize what other people choose to read? The United States ranks forty-ninth in literacy in the world. Ninety-million adults in the United States (nearly half the population) demonstrate low levels of literacy. An estimated fifteen-million adults holding jobs today are functionally illiterate. Readers of romance are in love with the written word. Isn't that the best way to keep someone reading—by providing interesting, enjoyable, satisfying stories?

"Those are a few of my reasons for choosing to read and write romance novels."

*   *   *

HAYNES, David 1955-

PERSONAL: Born August 30, 1955, in St. Louis, MO. *Education:* Macalester College, B.A., 1977; Hamline University, M.A., 1989.

ADDRESSES: Home—St. Paul, MN. *Agent*—c/o Milkweed Editions, 430 1st Ave. N., Suite 400, Minneapolis, MN 55401.

CAREER: C. V. Mosby Publishing Co., St. Louis, MO, associate editor, 1978-81; schoolteacher in St. Paul, MN, 1981-93; writer, 1993—. Morehead State University, visiting scholar, 1994; Mankato State University, visiting writer, 1994; teacher at Writer's Center, Bethesda, MD, 1994-95, and Hamline University, 1995; Warren Wilson College M.F.A. Program for Writers, faculty member, spring, 1996, and 1997. National Board for Professional Teaching Standards, member of adolescent generalist standards committee, 1990—, teacher in residence, 1994—; Minnesota Humanities Commission, member of advisory committee, Teacher Institute, 1993-94. The Loft, member of board of directors, Regional Writing Center, 1985-89; New Rivers Press, member of board of directors, 1993—.

AWARDS, HONORS: Fiction prize from *City Pages,* 1984, for the story "Taking Miss Kezee to the Polls"; winner of the Loft Mentor Series, 1985-86; fellowships from Cummington Community of the Arts, 1986-89, and Ragdale Foundation, 1988-96; winner of the Loft International Residency Series, 1989; winner of Regional Writers Contest, Lake Superior Contemporary Writers, 1989; awards from Virginia

Center for the Creative Arts, 1989-95; *Right by My Side* was named "one of the best books for young adults" by the American Library Association, 1994, and was a Minnesota Voices Project winner, New Rivers Press; Minnesota State Arts Board fellowship, 1995; Haynes was selected as one of *Granta* magazine's Best of the Young American Novelists, 1996; Loft Career Initiative grant, 1996; Friends of American Writers Adult Literary Award for *Somebody Else's Mama.*

WRITINGS:

Right by My Side (novel), New Rivers Press (Minneapolis, MN), 1993.

ADULT NOVELS

Somebody Else's Mama, Milkweed (Minneapolis, MN), 1995.
Heathens, New Rivers Press, 1996.
Live at Five, Milkweed, 1996.
All American Dream Dolls, Milkweed, 1997.

JUVENILE FICTION

Business as Usual (West 7th Wildcats 1), Milkweed, 1997.
The Gumma Wars (West 7th Wildcats 2), Milkweed, 1997.

Contributor to anthologies, including "Breckenridge Hills, 63114" (essay), *Imagining Home,* University of Minnesota Press (Minneapolis), 1995. Also contributor of short stories to periodicals, including *Other Voices, Glimmer Train,* and *Colors.*

ADAPTATIONS: Two short stories were chosen to be recorded for the "Selected Shorts" program on National Public Radio.

SIDELIGHTS: David Haynes is an African American novelist and short story writer whose works are noted for the rarity of their depictions of black middle-class life in the American Midwest. "I don't tell the popular narratives, the commercial narratives, that one is supposed to tell as an African American writer, and there is a price to be paid for that," Haynes told Nathalie Op De Beeck in an interview for *Publishers Weekly.* While the author's characters occasionally encounter racist people and situations, their biggest problems are common to all humankind, and Haynes

focuses on themes of love and relationships, right living and identity crises. Critics have singled out the vivacity of Haynes's characters, and his ability to draw readers into their lives. With the publication of Haynes's second novel, 1995's *Somebody Else's Mama,* the author garnered praise for his seasoned depiction of Miss Kezee, a feisty elderly woman, as well as for his women characters in general. In addition, critics note the humor with which Haynes spices his realistic tales of family life. "For melodrama, look elsewhere," instructed the reviewer for the *Los Angeles Times Book Review.* "[Haynes] belongs to the old realist tradition that believes that everyday life, if truly rendered, is more than exciting enough."

In *Right by My Side: A Novel,* fifteen-year-old Marshall Field Finney attempts to regain his bearings after his mother leaves home. Life is further complicated when an enthusiastic teacher convinces Marshall's best friend to become a community activist, and Marshall's father begins dating the mother of one of Marshall's friends. "Haynes offers engaging characters who tackle fundamental issues such as love, family and benevolence," praised the reviewer for *Publishers Weekly.* Although Haynes himself doesn't consider the book young adult fare—"I thought *Right by My Side* was an adult book," he told Op De Beeck in 1996, three years after the book was published, "and I still think it's an adult book"—the reviewer for *School Library Journal,* Virginia Ryder, like others, predicted that "Teens will adore this book." Indeed, *Right by My Side* was honored by the American Library Association as one of the Best Books for Young Adults of 1993.

Somebody Else's Mama, considered by some critics to be Haynes's first adult novel, concerns the evolving relations between members of a family when Al, the father, decides to run for mayor and his wife, Paula, mother of their twin eleven-year-olds, decides to take in her ailing mother-in-law. The viewpoint of each of these adult characters takes center stage at various times throughout Haynes's narrative, revealing Paula's ambivalent relationship with her own mother, her mother-in-law Miss Kezee's dread of returning to the home she had gladly escaped many years before, and the shifting dynamics between father and mother, husband and wife, from each side. "Mr. Haynes's skillful transitions from Paula's point of view to Miss Kezee's to Al's, and from past to present, provide the reader with vivid insights into their complex relationships and their feelings about one another," remarked

Jill McCorkle in the *New York Times Book Review*. While a reviewer for *Publishers Weekly* found some aspects of Al's depiction less than convincingly rendered, a *Los Angeles Times Book Review* contributor noted that "Haynes is especially good with his women characters." McCorkle also praised Haynes's female characters, paying special tribute to Miss Kezee— "This cantankerous old woman is the book's great strength," McCorkle concluded. And while, McCorkle added, this character threatens at times to dominate the book, "It is her voice, demonstrating Mr. Haynes's flawless ear, that makes his novel come to life."

Live at Five, a novel published a year after *Somebody Else's Mama,* was described by Op De Beeck as Haynes's "most commercial novel," because it takes on some of the race and class issues that many African American novelists are best known for addressing in their works. Unlike his earlier novels, which are set in Missouri, *Live at Five* takes place in St. Paul, Minnesota. The main character, an African American named Brandon Wilson, anchors the news for Channel 13. For the sake of better ratings, he moves to a poor neighborhood to report on life in the ghetto. There he meets Nita Sallis, a single mother of three children, part-time student and caretaker for the building where Brandon finds his new home. What Brandon learns during his stint among the poor contradicts his expectations and results in a novel both "touching" and "wickedly funny," according to a *Publishers Weekly* reviewer.

Heathens, published the same year as *Live at Five,* has been described as both a collection of interrelated stories and as a novel. Also set in St. Paul, *Heathens* centers on the Gabriel family—the struggling teacher father; his love for LaDonna, who has been put in jail for her part in a questionable real estate deal; his mother, who enlists the help of the neighbors in her efforts to break up the couple; and their twelve-year-old son, coping with peer pressure and bigoted school officials. Like Haynes's earlier efforts, this work was noted for its humorous yet realistic portrayal of black American family life. "These are the people, like a lot of people in this country, who live on the borders," Haynes told Op De Beeck. "They're not poor, but they're certainly not well off. They don't live in neat ideological boxes." And while a reviewer for *Publishers Weekly* found the novel a bit "choppy and episodic," the "wit and even wisdom" with which the author portrays his characters and their problems was praised.

BIOGRAPHICAL/CRITICAL SOURCES:

PERIODICALS

Los Angeles Times Book Review, September 24, 1995, p. 6.
New York Times Book Review, June 18, 1995, p. 21; May 5, 1996, p. 22.
Publishers Weekly, March 1, 1993, p. 53; April 10, 1995, p. 55; February 19, 1996, p. 205; March 18, 1996, p. 60; April 22, 1996, pp. 48-49.
School Library Journal, December, 1993, p. 149.

*   *   *

HAYS, Daniel 1960-

PERSONAL: Born January 22, 1960, in New York, NY; son of David Hays (a director) and Leonora (a dancer; maiden name, Landau). *Education:* Connecticut College, B.A., Antioch College, M.S. *Politics:* "No." *Religion:* "Yes." *Avocational interests:* Tae kwon do, scuba diving, sailing, wilderness survival, "duct tape, and anything I can do passionately."

ADDRESSES: Home and office—P.O. Box 3830, Hailey, ID, 83333.

CAREER: Wilderness guide and therapeutic supervisor, 1990-95; teacher at Silver Creek Alternative School, Hailey, ID, 1996—.

WRITINGS:

(With David Hays) *My Old Man and the Sea: A Father and Son Sail around Cape Horn,* Algonquin Books (Chapel Hill, NC), 1995.

SIDELIGHTS: Daniel Hays and his father, David, undertook a 17,000 mile, 317-day ocean voyage that passed around Cape Horn on the 25-foot sailboat *Sparrow* in 1985, becoming "the first Americans to do so in such a small vessel," according to *Booklist* reviewer Brad Hooper. Daniel departed from New London, Connecticut, and headed southward to Jamaica, where his father joined him. They passed through the Panama Canal and sailed over to the Galapagos Islands, down to Easter Island, and around Cape Horn to the Falkland Islands, where David disembarked and flew home. Daniel returned to New London, stopping at Montevideo, Rio de Janeiro, and Antigua along the way. *My Old Man and the Sea: A*

Father and Son Sail around Cape Horn recounts the Hays's nautical odyssey, but as Hooper remarked, "enjoying sailing is definitely not a prerequisite for enjoying *their* sailing." A *Publishers Weekly* reviewer called the book "an engaging adventure, and a remarkable story of a father-son relationship." Written in the form of a diary, the Hays's story is narrated alternately by father and son. "The Hayses concentrate on telling the story," observed *Library Journal* book reviewer John Kenny, "which is remarkably free of the heavy emphasis on equipment, technique, and terms that are usually present in this genre." *My Old Man and the Sea* "will make you cry and smile and exult, even. It is," concluded William F. Buckley, Jr., writing in *New York Times Book Review,* "an engrossingly beautiful tale of adventure of the spirit, aboard a little boat that dared great deeds."

Daniel Hays told *CA:* "I write so I am not alone. Passion influences me; that is, everything from madness to lust to love to obsession, etc. My favorite authors are Tom Robbins, Kurt Vonnegut, Friedrich Nietzsche, William Shakespeare, Ken Kesey, Gabriel Garcia Marquez, and Hermann Hesse. I lose myself in love, grief, or chemically induced passion and then get lost in trying to immortalize the moment." He adds, "Personal madness (i.e., 'It seemed appropriate at the time. . . .')" influenced him to write the work he has completed thus far.

BIOGRAPHICAL/CRITICAL SOURCES:

PERIODICALS

Booklist, June 1, 1995, pp. 1721-722.
Library Journal, April 15, 1995, p. 104.
New York Times Book Review, July 23, 1995, pp. 1, 21.
Publishers Weekly, May 15, 1995, pp. 64-65.
Yankee, August, 1995, p. 115.

*   *   *

HEELEY, D(avid) A. 1971-

PERSONAL: Born December 2, 1971, in Durham City, England; son of Thomas Edward (a site service engineer) and Janice (a community center manager; maiden name, Atkinson) Heeley. *Ethnicity:* "White." *Education:* Attending University of Warwick. *Avocational interests:* Teaching karate, badminton, fencing.

ADDRESSES: Home—Nuneaton, England. *E-mail*—D.A.Heeley@kether.demon.co.ak.

CAREER: Writer.

WRITINGS:

Lilith (occult fantasy novel), Llewellyn Publications, 1996.
Ronin (occult fantasy novel), Llewellyn Publications, 1997.
Magus, Llewellyn Publications, in press.

WORK IN PROGRESS: Dark Eden, with John Simpson.

SIDELIGHTS: D. A. Heeley told *CA:* "My writing is a tool that I use to explore the possibilities of the universe. Though focused on the fantasy genre, it contains important elements of western and eastern philosophy, mysticism, and the synthesis of various religions. My writing is thus a peculiar mix of fact, fantasy, and conjecture. I also have a very strong interest in occult phenomena and martial arts. Authors who have influenced me include Frank Herbert, Louise Cooper, and Ursula Le Guin."

*   *   *

HEISSENBUETTEL, Helmut 1921-1996

OBITUARY NOTICE—See index for *CA* sketch: Born June 21, 1921, in Ruestringen, Germany; died September 19, 1996. Radio dramatist, educator, critic, author. Heissenbuettel achieved acclaim as one of Germany's post-World War II writers of avant-garde literature. After serving in the German Army during the war, he sought to educate himself, attending classes at universities until 1955. In that year he began work as a reader at Claassen Verlag, only to leave the firm two years later for work at South West German Radio. He eventually rose through the ranks to head the company's Radio-Essay department. He remained with the radio service until 1981, when he retired. In 1963, he also found time to lecture at the University of Frankfurt. Heissenbuettel's writings were deemed both controversial and influential. Among his books were *Texts* (in English translation), *Kombinationen: Gedichte 1951-1954* (title means "Combinations: Poems 1951-1954"), *Gelegenheits-gedichte und Klappen-texte* (title means "Occasional Poems and Blurbs"), *Wenn Adolf Hitler den Krieg nicht gewonnen haette, Das Ende der Alternative,*

Oedipus Made in Germany, Von fliegenden Froeschen. . . , and *Neue Herbste.* The author of poems, novels, and criticism, Heissenbuettel won awards for his work, including the Lessing Prize, Buechner Prize, and Hugo Jacobi Prize.

OBITUARIES AND OTHER SOURCES:

BOOKS

The International Who's Who, 59th edition, Europa, 1995.

PERIODICALS

Times (London), October 19, 1996, p. 25.

* * *

HEISSENBUTTEL, Helmut
  See HEISSENBUETTEL, Helmut

* * *

HELLENGA, Robert 1941-

PERSONAL: Born August 5, 1941, in Milwaukee, WI; son of Ted (a produce broker) and Marjorie (a Latin teacher) Hellenga; married Virginia Killion (a Latin teacher), in August, 1963; children: Rachel Hellenga Farr, Heather, Caitrine. *Education:* University of Michigan, B.A. (with high honors), 1963; Princeton University, Ph.D., 1969; attended University of Belfast and University of North Carolina. *Avocational interests:* Blues guitar (acoustic), cooking.

ADDRESSES: Home—343 North Prairie St., Galesburg, IL 61401. *Office*—Knox College, English Dept., Galesburg, IL 61401. *Agent*—Henry Dunow, Harold Ober Associates, 425 Madison Ave., New York, NY 10017.

CAREER: Professor of English and writer. Knox College, Galesburg, IL, assistant professor, 1968-76, associate professor, 1976—; Newberry Library Seminar in Humanities, faculty fellow, 1973-74; Director, ACM Florence Programs, 1981-82.

AWARDS, HONORS: Phi Beta Kappa; six awards from the Illinois Arts Council; NEA Fellowship, 1989; Society of Midland Author Award for Fiction, 1995.

WRITINGS:

The Sixteen Pleasures, Soho (New York), 1994.

Contributor of scholarly articles and fiction to periodicals, including *College English, New Literary History, Iowa Review, Mississippi Valley Review, Chicago Review, California Quarterly, Columbia, Ascent, Crazyhorse, TriQuarterly, The New York Times Magazine, Chicago Tribune Magazine,* and *Forum for Modern Language Studies.*

WORK IN PROGRESS: A novel about a man whose daughter was killed in the bombing of the train station in Bologna in 1980.

SIDELIGHTS: In November 1966, the Arno flood descended on Florence, Italy, destroying or threatening to destroy the city's invaluable art works, historic buildings, and antiquities. The international community quickly rallied around the devastated region, and art and book restorers from all over the world arrived to help repair the damage. In Robert Hellenga's first novel, *The Sixteen Pleasures,* among the would-be rescuers is Margot Harrington, an intelligent yet naive young heroine. Anne Whitehouse, writing in *Tribune Books,* praised *The Sixteen Pleasures* as having "a sympathetic heroine, a suspenseful plot, a cast of colorful characters and illuminating meditations on life, art and love."

Margot leaves her job as a book restorer in Chicago in response to the call to help save Florence's rare books—and to save herself from the vaguely dissatisfying life she had led up to that time. Upon her arrival, she is shortly assigned to a convent, and given charge of "The Sixteen Pleasures," a sixteenth-century erotic manuscript bound into a book of prayers. The convent's abbess asks Margot to repair and then sell the manuscript in the hope that it will bring in sufficient funds to support the remaining collection, a gift from an aristocratic nun in the eighteenth century. Margot meets the abbess's cousin and begins to trust the middle-aged Italian, against the nun's advice, with her heart as well as the manuscript given into her care. The resulting novel is "part *Bildungsroman,* part mystery, part romance, part guidebook," wrote Mark Mitchell in the *New York Times Book Review.*

Like his protagonist, Hellenga has lived in Florence, and the intimate knowledge of the place he gained, in addition to his expertise as a humanities scholar, provides the book with a solid foundation in fact that some critics noted as a highlight of the novel. Indeed, Phoebe-Lou Adams, writing in *Atlantic Monthly,* praised Hellenga's ability to generate an "astounding" degree of suspense in a plot centered around the austere activity of antique book restoration. Others pinpointed the strength of the novel in the intrinsic interest of Margot Harrington. "Everything about the narrator and heroine of this novel is appealing right from the first paragraph," enthused the reviewer for the *New Yorker.* On the other hand, Susan Salter Reynolds of the *Los Angeles Times Book Review* found that "Margot in love has a very strange, detached equanimity, . . . which one sees now and then in female characters drawn by men."

In addition, several critics commented on Hellenga's skillful rendering of a coming of age story within the confines of a suspense plot. According to *Washington Post Book World* contributor Charlotte Innes, though *The Sixteen Pleasures* shares with the best nineteenth-century novels the characteristic of being "enjoyably wide-ranging," Hellenga's effort attempts too much in too little space, with the result that "the characters' musings, though intelligent, don't go very deep." Whitehouse, however, judged the opposite. "The Mother Abbess, who serves as a kind of fairy god-mother to Margot, tells her, 'We can't make any sense out of life until we give up our deepest hopes,'" Whitehouse noted in conclusion. "*The Sixteen Pleasures* is both a fascinating entertainment and a penetrating depiction of this philosophy."

BIOGRAPHICAL/CRITICAL SOURCES:

PERIODICALS

Atlantic Monthly, June, 1994, p. 137.
Los Angeles Times Book Review, June 12, 1994, p. 6.
New Yorker, August 1, 1994, p. 81.
New York Times Book Review, May 8, 1994, p. 18; June 25, 1995, p. 32.
Tribune Books, June 19, 1994, sec. 14, p. 7.
Washington Post Book World, July 31, 1994, p. 7.

*　*　*

HEN, Yitzhak 1963-

PERSONAL: Born November 5, 1963, in Jerusalem, Israel; son of Jacob and Margalith (Harouss) Hen; married Rachel Shalomi. *Ethnicity:* "Jewish." *Education:* Hebrew University of Jerusalem, B.A. (cum laude), 1988, M.A. (cum laude), 1991; Cambridge University, Ph.D., 1994. *Religion:* Jewish.

ADDRESSES: Home—28 Hahagana St., Jerusalem 97852, Israel. *Office*—Department of History, University of Haifa, Haifa 31905, Israel. *E-mail*—rhhg101@research.haifa.ac.il.

CAREER: Writer; University of Haifa, Haifa, Israel, Department of History, professor, 1994—.

WRITINGS:

Culture and Religion in Merovingian Gaul, A.D. 481-751, E. J. Brill (Leiden, NY), 1995.

WORK IN PROGRESS: Editing *The Sacramentary of Echternach,* for Boydell & Brewer; research on Carolingian hagiography.

*　*　*

HENDRICKS, Vicki (Due) 1951-

PERSONAL: Born November 28, 1951, in Covington, KY; daughter of Vincent (in sales) and Claire (Charles) Due; married William C. Hendricks, June, 1973 (divorced, June, 1986); children: Benjamin. *Education:* Ohio State University, B.S., 1973; Florida Atlantic University, M.A., 1979; Florida International University, M.F.A., 1992. *Avocational interests:* Dining, sailing, scuba diving, skydiving, traveling.

ADDRESSES: Home—P.O. Box 630183, Miami, FL 33163. *Office*—Broward Community College, 7200 Pines Blvd., Pembroke Pines, FL 33024. *Agent*—Sobel and Weber, 146 E. Nineteenth St., New York, NY 10003.

CAREER: Broward Community College, Pembroke Pines, FL, professor, 1981-96; writer.

MEMBER: National Writers Association, Florida Center for the Book.

WRITINGS:

Miami Purity (novel), Pantheon (New York), 1995.

Work represented in anthologies, including *Dick for a Day,* edited by Fiona Giles, Villard, 1996; and *Taken at Their Word,* edited by John Dufressne and Cynthia Chinelly, LeBow, 1996. Contributor to periodicals, including *Boca Raton, Florida's Gold Coast* and *Gold Coast Life.* Fiction editor of *Quixote Quarterly,* summer, 1994.

WORK IN PROGRESS: Iguana Love and *A Female Flasher in Key West.*

SIDELIGHTS: Vicki Hendricks has been characterized by critics as a promising new writer who has won acclaim with her debut novel, *Miami Purity,* published in 1995. The novel's heroine is Sherri Parlay, an alcoholic stripper who has inadvertently killed her abusive lover. After recovering from her wounds, Parlay re-enters society and determines to regulate her life. She finds seemingly innocuous work at a dry cleaner, but soon enters into a sexually-charged romance with her employer's son. Eventually Sherri discovers her new lover's unsavory relationship with his jealous mother, and once again she is compelled by blind rage into committing murder.

Miami Purity has been hailed as sordid, sexually provocative, and endearing. John Williams, in a review in *Gentleman's Quarterly* (UK), asserted that Hendricks's book is "unambiguously dirty and perversely sweet," while Carole Borges Rosen, in her *Key West* appraisal, proclaimed *Miami Purity* "heat-drenched." The *New York Times Book Review*'s Robert Polito noted the book's ties to James M. Cain's classic *The Postman Always Rings Twice,* declaring that in both tales "the currency of passion is homicide, and death is the tab for infidelity." Polito noted that Parlay "comes on like a succubus spawned from channel-surfing Oprah, Geraldo, Rolanda, Maury, Montel, and Ricki—with a final click of the remote at 'America's Most Wanted.'" And *solares hill* contributor June Keith, acknowledging *Miami Purity*'s compelling pace, called Hendricks's first book "a page-turner that just wouldn't quit."

A *Kirkus Reviews* contributor focused on the strong sexual content in *Miami Purity,* calling the novel "a guilty pleasure." *Booklist*'s Bill Ott offered praise, declaring: "This is no ordinary first novel," and, while a *Publishers Weekly* contributor faulted Hendricks's narrative as somewhat underdeveloped and one-dimensional, the critic ultimately concluded that "if what Hendricks finally offers us is a one-note novel, it's a piercing one that few will forget." Rhonda Johnson, in an *Entertainment Weekly* assessment, lauded Hendricks's characterization of Sherri

Parlay, to whom she referred as "a minor masterpiece." Hendricks defended *Miami Purity* against charges of exploitive violence and sex. "The book explores taboos," she told a *Key West* interviewer, adding: "As for promoting violence, I don't think so. Someone would have to have it in them in the first place. There's nothing glorious in these [characters'] lives. Sexual reality in America is pretty grim."

Hendricks told *CA:* "As an obsessive reader since childhood, I have naturally wanted to create something on the order of those books I loved. The necessary perseverance was a long time in coming, though, and I never seriously attempted fiction until age thirty seven, when I needed thirty pages to apply to Florida International University's writing program.

"*Miami Purity* was started for a class in novel writing in which we were each required to analyze a novel quantitatively in great detail and use it as a model. I had discovered James M. Cain and chose his *The Postman Always Rings Twice* as the book I most admired. I hoped to achieve something of the concise style and power of Cain. The result was *Miami Purity,* a contemporary noir novel with a woman as a protagonist. I could not, of course, produce something as flawless as *Postman,* but its structure helped me to create a fast pace and tough characters who act on impulse. Cain's representation of the instinctive, animal side of human nature is what continues to attract my interest and motivate my writing in my second novel, *Iguana Love.*

"I am certain I would never have been able to write fiction without guidance in the craft of writing which I received in graduate school."

BIOGRAPHICAL/CRITICAL SOURCES:

PERIODICALS

Booklist, June 1 & 15, 1995, p. 1733.
Entertainment Weekly, August 4, 1995, p. 53.
Gentleman's Quarterly (UK), January, 1996, p. 40.
Key West, July 6-19, 1995.
Kirkus Reviews, June 15, 1995.
Library Journal, July, 1995, p. 120.
Miami Herald Tropic, November 12, 1995.
New York Times Book Review, July 30, 1995, p. 8.
Publishers Weekly, May 22, 1995, p. 48.
solares hill (Key West, FL), September 14, 1995, p. 20.
XS, July 11, 1995.

HEY, Jeanne A. K. 1963-

PERSONAL: Born February 16, 1963, in Marina di Pisa, Italy; daughter of E. Berry, Jr. (a physician) and Jeanne (a professor; maiden name, Cooper) Hey; married Thomas C. H. Klak (a professor), September 1, 1990; children: Jackson K. *Ethnicity:* "White." *Education:* Bucknell University, B.A., 1985; Ohio State University, M.A., Ph.D., 1992.

ADDRESSES: Office—218 Harrison Hall, Miami University, Oxford, OH 45056. *E-mail*—jhey@ miamiu.muohio.edu.

CAREER: Miami University, Oxford, OH, assistant professor of political science and international studies, 1992-97.

WRITINGS:

Theories of Dependent Foreign Policy and the Case of Ecuador in the 1980s, Ohio University Press (Athens, OH), 1995.

*   *   *

HILLABY, John (D.) 1917-1996

OBITUARY NOTICE—See index for *CA* sketch: Born July 24, 1917, in Pontefract, England; died from pneumonia, October 19, 1996, in York, England. Naturalist and author. Hillaby is mostly noted for his travelogues as he journeyed across the globe on foot. Before serving in the British Royal Artillery during World War II, Hillaby worked for local newspapers in England. In 1944, he became a broadcaster and also wrote articles for magazines. During the 1950s, he served the *Manchester Guardian* as zoological correspondent, the *New York Times* as science writer, and as a consultant for *New Scientist.* Although his first book, *Holiday Parade for Your Pleasure,* was published in 1946, it wasn't until 1964 that Hillaby thrilled his readers with *Journey to the Jade Sea.* This best-seller chronicled Hillaby's caravan through Zaire, Rwanda, and Kenya, covering more than 1,100 miles on foot or by camel. In all, it is estimated that Hillaby hiked more than 74,000 miles, a distance roughly equivalent to three times around the globe. He followed with several other "journey" books as he traveled through Europe and the United States. His travels ended in 1993, when Hillaby began suffering from osteoarthritis. Other works include *Journey through Europe, Journey through Britain, Journey to the Gods, Hillaby's World,* and *John Hillaby's Yorkshire: The Moors and Dales.*

OBITUARIES AND OTHER SOURCES:

BOOKS

Who's Who, 147th edition, St. Martin's, 1995.

PERIODICALS

Los Angeles Times, October 22, 1996, p. A20.
New York Times, October 23, 1996, p. B20.
Times (London), October 21, 1996, p. 23.

*   *   *

HINES, Joanna 1949-

PERSONAL: Born March 1, 1949, in London, England; daughter of E. C. (a journalist) and Nancy (Myers; a sculptor) Hodgkin; married Derek B. Hines (a writer), 1971; children: Allison, Jessica, Peter. *Ethnicity:* "British." *Education:* Somerville College, Oxford, B.A., 1970; attended London School of Economics and Political Science, London, 1971.

ADDRESSES: Home—Cornwall, England. *Agent*— Jennifer Kavanagh, 44 Langham St., London, England.

CAREER: Writer.

WRITINGS:

NOVELS

Dora's Room, Hodder & Stoughton, 1993.
The Cornish Girl, Hodder & Stoughton, 1994.
The Fifth Secret, Carroll & Graf (New York), 1995.
The Puritan's Wife, Hodder & Stoughton, 1996.

WORK IN PROGRESS: A contemporary novel; a historical novel, completion expected in 1998.

SIDELIGHTS: Joanna Hines told *CA:* "My novels cover a wide range, from psychological thrillers to historical sagas. Despite their differences, however, I hope they have in common strong story lines and vivid characters.

"My first novel, *Dora's Room,* was one of seven books chosen by booksellers W.H. Smith for the first of their annual Fresh Talent promotions.

"*The Cornish Girl* is a romantic novel set in a remote area of Cornwall in the middle seventeenth century. *The Fifth Secret,* by contrast, is a fast-moving story exploring the impact of alliances formed in childhood on a group of adult friends. *The Puritan's Wife* marks a return to the seventeenth century. It tells of the experiences in love and war of one of the characters who first appeared in *The Cornish Girl.* In a third historical novel, due to be completed in 1998, I intend to complete the saga. It will be set in Cornwall at the time of the Restoration of Charles II.

"At present I am working on a contemporary novel. As the above account demonstrates, I enjoy the contrasting challenges provided by the different types of novel."

* * *

HIRSCH, Robin 1942-

PERSONAL: Born November 18, 1942, in London, England; son of Herbert Max (a manufacturer) and Kaethe (an artist and craftsperson; maiden name, Lewald) Hirsch; married Leona Jaglom (a psychologist), 1984; children: Alexander, Benjamin. *Education:* Oriel College, Oxford, B.A., 1964, M.A., 1968; Pennsylvania State University, Ph.D., 1973.

ADDRESSES: Home—102 Garfield Pl., Brooklyn, NY 11215.

CAREER: Cornelia Street Cafe, New York City, co-founder, 1977, co-owner, 1977—. New Works Project (experimental theater company), founder, 1977, artistic director, 1977—, and creator of his solo performance cycle *Mosaic: Fragments of a Jewish Life.* Co-producer of the album *Cornelia Street: The Songwriters Exchange,* released by Stash Records. Teacher of literature, theater, and humanities at universities in Europe and the United States.

MEMBER: NYSCA (vice chair of Literature Panel, 1984—), Writers Room (member of board of directors, 1987—).

AWARDS, HONORS: Fellow of English-Speaking Union, 1967-72; Fulbright scholar, 1967-72; fellow of New York Foundation for the Arts, 1992, 1995; Robert and Adele S. Blank Jewish Arts Award, 1996, for *Last Dance at the Hotel Kempinski.*

WRITINGS:

Last Dance at the Hotel Kempinski: Creating a Life in the Shadow of History (memoir), University Press of New England (Hanover, NH), 1995.

Contributor to periodicals in the United States and abroad, including *Western Humanities Review, Modern International Drama, Forward, Culturefront,* and *Jewish Quarterly.*

WORK IN PROGRESS: A novel, *Blau;* a screenplay, *Weiss;* research on German Jews in the twentieth century.

SIDELIGHTS: Robin Hirsch told *CA:* "I have always written, but I didn't find my voice until I started to write from life. My parents were born in Berlin around the turn of the century. My father fought (as a Jew) in World War I on the German side, and was decorated. My mother was a member of that extraordinary cultural, intellectual, and social world that flourished in the twenties and made Berlin in some respects the capital of the world. And then came Hitler.

"My parents fled very much at the last moment to England, married in London where, during the Blitz in middle age, they started a family. My sister and I grew up with an ambiguous heritage. My father was interned as an enemy alien, we were bombed by my parents' erstwhile countrymen, my best friend at school when I was six called me a Nazi.

"Out of these experiences came my book, subtitled *Creating a Life in the Shadow of History.* It speaks to the heart of what might be called the 'second generation' experience. There was an explosion in the thirties, in which members of what was one of the most civilized cultures the world has known were systematically exterminated. Surviving shards from that explosion were scattered across the globe. I began to write very simply from life, partly (in contrast to those of the first generation, who needed to bear witness) to indicate that, even after the explosion, life continues. In the process I discovered my real job, which is to gather up these fragments in the hope that, one day, however painfully, a new whole may be born."

HISS, Alger 1904-1996

OBITUARY NOTICE—See index for *CA* sketch: Born November 11, 1904, in Baltimore, MD; died November 15, 1996, in New York, NY. Lawyer, statesman, writer. Despite the fact that Hiss was a key organizer of the United Nations, he gained notoriety in the late 1940s when he was accused of espionage. He was later convicted of perjury when he denied that he gave government documents to the Soviets. After receiving his law degree, Hiss became a law clerk for Justice Oliver Wendell Holmes in 1929. In 1933, after a short stint in private practice, Hiss joined the counsel of the Agricultural Adjustment Administration, part of President Franklin Roosevelt's New Deal. From there, he held several other positions within Roosevelt's Administration, and in 1945, accompanied Roosevelt to the Yalta Conference to discuss the founding of the United Nations Charter. In 1947, Hiss left government work to head the Carnegie Endowment for International Peace. In 1948 he was accused of espionage by a *Time* magazine editor named Whittaker Chambers, who claimed to be an ex-spy for the Soviets. Chambers charged that Hiss delivered microfilm to him in a hollowed-out pumpkin. Hiss denied knowing Chambers, but later when they actually met face-to-face during the Congressional hearing, it was revealed that Hiss did know the man, but as George Crosley, not Whittaker Chambers. Hiss was not convicted of espionage as the statute of limitations had expired. He was, however, convicted of perjury, mostly because the evidence against him was overwhelming. He maintained his innocence throughout the trial. As a result of his conviction, Hiss spent four years in prison and the rest of his life trying to clear his name. In 1957 he wrote *In the Court of Public Opinion,* chronicling the events which led to his trial and conviction. In the 1970s he began lecturing on the Yalta Conference, the New Deal, and his trial. He also wrote an autobiography, titled *Recollections of a Life.* His other works include *The Myth of Yalta* and was the editor for Holmes-Laski Letters.

OBITUARIES AND OTHER SOURCES:

BOOKS

Who's Who, St. Martin's Press, 1996.

PERIODICALS

Los Angeles Times, November 16, 1996, p. A1.

New York Times, November 16, 1996, p. A1, A31; December 6, 1996, p. D17.
Times (London), November 18, 1996, p. 23.

* * *

HOCKE, Martin 1938-

PERSONAL: Born September 6, 1938, Cologne, Germany; married Luise Eilers, 1960 (divorced); married Pauline Sunley, 1975; children: (first marriage) one daughter. *Education:* Attended Magdalen College, Brackley, Northamptonshire, England, 1950-55, and Royal Academy of Dramatic Art, London, 1955-57.

ADDRESSES: Agent—Dialogue Business Services, 5 Hillcrest, Broadway Road, Evesham, Worcestershire CV32 5HR, England.

CAREER: English teacher, Berlitz School and others, in Germany, Italy and Britain; briefly location manager for Paramount Pictures; actor and broadcaster, Italian radio; translator from Italian into English; freelance writer, 1988—.

WRITINGS:

FANTASY NOVELS

The Ancient Solitary Reign, Grafton (London), 1989.
The Lost Domain, HarperCollins (London), 1993.

* * *

HOME, Stewart 1962-
(Luther Blissett, Monty Cantsin, Karen Eliot)

PERSONAL: Born March 24, 1962, in London, England; son of Julia Callan (a nurse). *Ethnicity:* "Irish." *Education:* Attended Kingston Polytechnic.

ADDRESSES: Home—BM Senior, London WC1N 3XX, England.

CAREER: Writer. Artist, with solo and group shows in London and France, 1984—; gives readings and performances in Germany, Finland, the United States, and England.

WRITINGS:

The Assault on Culture: Utopian Currents from Lettrisme to Class War, Aporia Press (London, England), 1988.

Pure Mania (novel), Polygon (Edinburgh, Scotland), 1989.

The Festival of Plagiarism (nonfiction), Sabotage Editions (London), 1989.

Defiant Pose (novel), Peter Owen (London), 1991.

Neoist Manifestos (nonfiction), AK Press (Edinburgh), 1991.

No Pity (stories), AK Press (London), 1993.

Red London (novel), AK Press, 1994.

Cunt Lickers Anonymous (stories), Imprint 93 (London), 1995.

Cranked Up Really High: Genre Theory and Punk Rock, Codex (Hove, England), 1995.

(Under pseudonym Luther Blissett) *The Green Apocalypse* (nonfiction), Unpopular Books (London), 1995.

Conspiracies, Cover-Ups, and Diversions: A Collection of Lies, Hoaxes, and Hidden Truths (nonfiction), Sabotage Editions, 1995.

Neoism, Plagiarism, and Praxis, AK Press (San Francisco, CA), 1995.

Slow Death (novel), Serpent's Tail (New York), 1996.

Analecta (nonfiction), Sabotage Editions, 1996.

(Editor) *What Is Situationism?: A Reader,* AK Press (San Francisco), 1996.

Come Before Christ and Murder Love (novel), Serpent's Tail, 1997.

(With Florian Cramer) *The House of Seven by Nine Squares: Letters on Neoism, Psychogeography, and Epistemological Trepidation,* Invisible Books (London), in press.

Work represented in anthologies, including *Mind Invaders: A Reader in Psychic Warfare, Cultural Sabotage, and Semiotic Terrorism,* Serpent's Tail, 1997; and *Suspect Device: Terminal Fictions,* Serpent's Tail, in press. Some work appears under the pseudonyms Monty Cantsin and Karen Eliot.

WORK IN PROGRESS: Blow Job, a novel, publication by Serpent's Tail expected in 1998; *Lexicon Devil,* a "novel/anti-novel/non-novel;" research on aesthetic iconoclasm, the critique of art as bourgeois discourse, and philistinism.

SIDELIGHTS: Stewart Home told *CA:* "My novels are all concerned with rhetoric, chiefly in the form of extremist political discourse, although I also quite commonly treat art as a form of ideology in my fiction. Another element of these books is the deconstruction of conventions used in various forms of genre writing, particularly 'youthsploitation,' pornography, and hardboiled crime. However, *Come Before Christ and Murder Love* marked a significant shift in my concerns, since it is principally concerned with the occult, both as an ideology and as a means of organizing knowledge. It is left up to the reader to decide whether the first-person narrator is schizophrenic or, as he claims, the victim of state-sponsored mind control experiments. While the principal character in the earlier novels could be considered to be London, in *Come Before Christ* the narrative shifts to the United States and Zurich, as well as the English counties of Essex, Kent, and Suffolk. The narrative is extremely fractured and, as the narrator's assumed personas fall apart and are revealed as fictions, the distinct geographical locations of Greenwich and Spitalfields, in south and east London respectively, merge to create the meta-fictional landscape of 'Greenfields.'

"If the slogan 'sex, violence, and anarcho-sadism' could be applied to my earlier novels, my recent fiction is more accurately summed up with the phrase 'eating, f**king, and occultism.' In as far as all narrative tends toward the fictional, the novel *Come Before Christ* is further removed from the realm of make-believe than my nonfiction books. While all my books are playful, I relish the fact that I cannot impose a single understanding of them upon their readership. It is not for me to say whether my fiction is just a divertissement; it is up to each and every reader to decide how he or she wants to treat these works.

"On a more general level, and avoiding specific reference to my fiction, I am concerned with the transformation of everyday life into an Afro-Celtic carnival, a party that never ends. To do this, it is necessary to dissolve the identities and organizing principles of Babylon. Two of my most immediate targets in this war against 'what is' are those twin phantoms known as the avant-garde and the occult. While occultists spend a great deal of time faking the antiquity of the activities in which they are engaged, the avant-garde's insistence on the element of innovation within its creations leads to a spurious denial of its historic roots. In this sense, the avant-garde and the occult are two sides of the same coin. They are the positive and negative poles which generate that multifarious enigma known as contemporary society. Thus, since the avant-garde makes itself visible through manifestos, it must be banished. Correspondingly, the occult as a collection of hidden doctrines must be realized (that is, manifested) if it is to be simultaneously suppressed. Since the avant-garde is undesirable, I will vanquish it by uniting it with its polar opposite. By bringing together the avant-garde and the occult (in its Celtic-Druidic form) under the rubric of the avant-bard, I will dissolve both these phenomena, and thereby 'transvalue value.'"

BIOGRAPHICAL/CRITICAL SOURCES:

BOOKS

Ford, Simon, *Rapid Eye 3,* Creation Books (London), 1995, p. 59.

PERIODICALS

London Review of Books, June 23, 1994, p. 21.
New Statesman and Society, April 26, 1996, p. 31.
Times Literary Supplement, August 30, 1996, p. 22.

*   *   *

HOPCKE, Robert H(enry)   1958-

PERSONAL: Surname is pronounced "*Hop*-key"; born March 15, 1958, in Jersey City, NJ; companion of Paul A. Schwartz (a professor of philosophy and religion). *Education:* Attended University of Florence; Georgetown University, B.S. (summa cum laude), 1980; Pacific Lutheran Theological Seminary, M.A.Th., 1983; California State University, Hayward, M.S., 1986. *Avocational interests:* Opera, music, performing, travel, food.

ADDRESSES: Office—1942 University Ave., Suite 208-B, Berkeley, CA 94704; fax 510-548-2069. *Agent*—Candice Fuhrman, 201 Morningsun, Mill Valley, CA 94941. *E-mail*—rhopcke@symbolics.org.

CAREER: Unitas Personal Counseling, Berkeley, CA, senior intern, 1981-86, staff clinical supervisor, 1986-89; Operation Concern, San Francisco, CA, coordinator of AIDS Prevention Program, 1989-95; private practice of psychotherapy and couples counseling, 1995—. Pastoral Psychotherapy Group of Berkeley, member, 1986-88; Center of Symbolic Studies, co-founder, director, 1990—.

MEMBER: California Association of Marriage and Family Therapists.

WRITINGS:

A Guided Tour of the "Collected Works" of C. G. Jung, Shambhala (Boston, MA), 1989.
Jung, Jungians, and Homosexuality, Shambhala, 1989.
Men's Dreams, Men's Healing, Shambhala, 1990.
(Translator with Paul A. Schwartz) Manlio Brusatin, *The History of Colors,* Shambhala, 1991.
(Editor with Karin Carrington and Scott Wirth, and contributor) *Same-Sex Love: A Path to Wholeness,* Shambhala, 1993.
The Persona: Where Sacred Meets Profane, Shambhala, 1995.
There Are No Accidents: Synchronicity and the Stories of Our Lives, Riverhead Books (New York), 1997.

Contributor to books, including *Liminality and Transitional Space in Analysis,* edited by Murray Stein, Chiron Publications (Chicago, IL), 1990; and *Leatherfolk,* edited by Mark Thompson, Alyson Publications (Boston), 1991. Contributor of articles and reviews to periodicals, including *Quadrant, Journal of Analytical Psychology, Jung Institute Library Journal, Journal of Mental Health Counseling,* and *Spring.*

SIDELIGHTS: Robert H. Hopcke told *CA:* "My writing grows out of my work as a psychotherapist and my belief that communication—oral or written—can be a medium of healing. As a gay man living in a culture that does not often recognize my experiences as valid or interesting, my writings have provided ways in which I have let myself develop an imagination of what potentials might exist for contemporary gay men and lesbians in the experience of loving others. In my books and articles, my hope has been that all people, of whatever orientation, might come to know themselves more deeply.

"Having started from this particular set of interests, I find with age and experience that my interests as a writer have been slowly broadening, in part because, for now, I feel I have said all I have to say on the psychology of sexuality and gender, in part because I feel other parts of my own experience, other values and insights, coming to the fore. My book on synchronicity, for example, with its idea that coincidental events take on a meaning because of the basic narrative structure we create from the disparate experiences of our lives, comes out of my great love for fiction, both as an avid reader of literature and a dedicated writer of novels and short stories.

"Linked with my love for stories is my experience of living abroad for a year at a crucial juncture in my youth. I am drawn increasingly toward translating nonfiction, such as *The History of Colors,* and fiction, especially contemporary Italian literature, much of which is unknown in the United States.

"Other loves of mine circle about me as a writer, inviting me to find a form in which I might express the depth of what they have meant to me—dogs, for example, opera and music, food and cooking. Particular experiences also need expression of some sort: my friendships, my decade in the AIDS epidemic, my search for identity as an adopted child.

"People who know me wonder how I have managed to get so much writing done, but in terms of my process, I have never found it difficult to write. It always comes out of a deep passion for whatever subject takes me. When I am seized by the idea for a book, story, or article, I cannot *not* make the time to write. At a time in my life when I had to balance my writing with the demands of other things (school, new relationships, jobs), such 'possessions' in service of my muse were sometimes quite destructive. Older and wiser, I have been fortunate to set up my life so that I can accommodate this near-compulsive process without neglecting other aspects of my life. When a project is finished, I have learned that a post-partum depression will almost always ensue, and the only remedy is a self-granted vacation, during which I watch television, obsessively work crossword puzzles, or travel, usually to Italy or to warm climates and beaches.

"No statement about myself as an author could fail to mention the great deal of gratitude I have for my circle of friends and family, the majority of whom, interestingly enough, have not read much of what I have written. I would have it no other way. Being an author is what I do; it is a calling, of sorts, my profession, but it does not sum up all of who I am. My friends and family love me for who I am and not what I do. Whatever success I have enjoyed thus far, whatever my future achievements, they provide the emotional and social ground upon which I stand, without which I would not be able to write."

HOWEY, John 1933-

PERSONAL: Born January 13, 1933, in New Haven, CT; son of Joseph (a physicist) and Dorothy (a teacher; maiden name, Good) Howey; married Maria Hatges (an interior designer), September 8, 1968; children: John McDermott, Dorothy Howey Bardin. *Ethnicity:* "White." *Education:* Attended College of Wooster, 1951-52; Georgia Institute of Technology, B.S., 1956, B.Arch., 1957. *Politics:* Independent. *Religion:* Episcopalian. *Avocational interests:* Painting, carpentry, photography.

ADDRESSES: Home—Tampa, FL. *Office*—John Howey and Associates, 101 South Franklin St., Tampa, FL 33602.

CAREER: Architect with firms in Atlanta, GA, San Francisco, CA, and Tampa, FL, 1958-65; architect in Tampa, 1965-73; John Howey and Associates, Tampa, architect, 1973—. Baypark, Inc., president. *Military service:* U.S. Army, Corps of Engineers, 1957-58, 1961-62.

MEMBER: American Institute of Architects (fellow), Sertoma (life member), Exchange Club.

AWARDS, HONORS: Medal of Honor, Florida/Caribbean chapter of American Institute of Architects, 1985; grant from Graham Foundation, 1992.

WRITINGS:

The Sarasota School of Architecture, 1941-1966, MIT Press (Cambridge, MA), 1995.

Contributor to periodicals.

WORK IN PROGRESS: Research on American urbanism and on urban architecture in Florida in the twenty-first century.

SIDELIGHTS: John Howey told *CA:* "After practicing architecture in the Tampa Bay region, North Carolina, and the Bahamas for twenty-five years, on a dare from a fellow architect I undertook the writing of *The Sarasota School of Architecture, 1941-66.* Because I had written shorter articles during my career, and with the encouragement of a grant, I was able to attract two publishers to consider this important book on post-World War II architecture in Florida.

"My love of architecture, particularly in the design area, prompted me to record the twentieth-century record of Paul Rudolph and Victor Lundy and others in Florida. You might say this book was a farewell to twentieth-century architecture."

*   *   *

HUDDLESTON, Mark W. 1950-

PERSONAL: Born December 31, 1950, in Syracuse, NY; son of Charles P. (an accountant) and Joan Elaine (a homemaker; maiden name, Veldran) Huddleston; married Dianna Loesch, 1971 (divorced, 1982); married Melanie K. Sharp, 1983 (divorced, 1987); married Emma Elizabeth Bricker, October 6, 1990; children: Andrew, Katherine, Giles. *Ethnicity:* "Caucasian." *Education:* State University of New York at Buffalo, B.A., 1972; University of Wisconsin—Madison, M.A., 1973, Ph.D., 1978. *Politics:* Republican. *Religion:* Presbyterian. *Avocational interests:* Flying, scuba diving, photography, golf, hunting, fishing.

ADDRESSES: Home—44 Covered Bridge Ln., Newark, DE 19711. *Office*—Department of Political Science, University of Delaware, Newark, DE 19716; fax 302-831-4452. *E-mail*—mwh@udel.edu.

CAREER: State University of New York at Buffalo, assistant professor of political science, 1977-80; University of Delaware, Newark, assistant professor, 1980-83, associate professor, 1983-94, professor of political science, 1994—. Consultant to U.S. Office of Personnel Management, U.S. General Accounting Office, and U.S. Agency for International Development.

MEMBER: American Society for Public Administration, Phi Beta Kappa.

WRITINGS:

Comparative Public Administration, Garland Publishing (New York), 1984.
The Government's Managers, Priority Press (New York), 1987.
The Public Administration Workbook, Longman (White Plains, NY), 1987, 3rd edition, 1996.

(With William W. Boyer) *The Higher Civil Service in the United States,* University of Pittsburgh Press (Pittsburgh, PA), 1996.

Contributor to journals, including *Annals of the American Academy of Political and Social Science, Policy Studies Journal, Political Science Quarterly, Public Budgeting and Finance, Public Personnel Management,* and *Urban Interest.*

WORK IN PROGRESS: Public Administration in America, for Longman, completion expected in 1998.

*   *   *

HUGHES, Richard T(homas) 1943-

PERSONAL: Born February 21, 1943, in Lubbock, TX; married Janice Ann Wright; children: Christopher Andrew. *Education:* Harding University, B.A., 1965; Abilene Christian University, M.A., 1967; University of Iowa, Ph.D., 1967.

ADDRESSES: Office—Religion Division, Pepperdine University, Malibu, CA 90263; fax 310-317-7271. *E-mail*—rhughes@pepperdine.edu.

CAREER: Pepperdine University, Malibu, CA, assistant professor of religion, 1971-76; Southwest Missouri State University, Springfield, began as associate professor, became professor of religious studies, 1977-82; Abilene Christian University, Abilene, TX, scholar in residence, 1982-84, 1986-88, professor of history, 1983-88, department head, 1984-86; Pepperdine University, professor of religion, 1988-94, Distinguished Professor, 1994—, William Green Lecturer, 1992, acting chairperson of division, 1992-93. University of Iowa, visiting associate professor, 1977; Institute for Christian Studies, Harrell Lecturer, 1982; lecturer at educational institutions, including Harding College and University of Mississippi, 1974, Bethany College, 1980, Christian Theological Seminary and Brigham Young University, 1986, Columbia Christian College, 1990, and Seattle Pacific University, 1993.

MEMBER: American Society of Church History, American Academy of Religion.

AWARDS, HONORS: Grants from National Endowment for the Humanities, 1975, 1981, 1982; Graves

Award, American Council of Learned Societies, 1976; grants from Pew Charitable Trusts, 1989-91, and Lilly Endowment, 1992-93, 1994-95.

WRITINGS:

(With Leonard Allen and Michael Weed) *The Worldly Church: A Call for Biblical Renewal*, Abilene Christian University Press (Abilene, TX), 1988.

(With Allen) *Discovering Our Roots: The Ancestry of Churches of Christ*, Abilene Christian University Press, 1988.

(Editor) *The American Quest for the Primitive Church*, University of Illinois Press (Champaign, IL), 1988.

(With Allen) *Illusions of Innocence: Protestant Primitivism in America, 1630-1875*, University of Chicago Press, 1988.

(Editor) *The Primitive Church in the Modern World*, University of Illinois Press, 1995.

Reviving the Ancient Faith: The Story of Churches of Christ in America, Eerdmans (Grand Rapids, MI), 1996.

(Editor with Theron F. Schlabach) *Proclaim Peace: Christian Pacifism from Unexpected Quarters*, University of Illinois Press, 1997.

(Editor with William B. Adrian) *Models for Christian Higher Education: Strategies for Survival and Success in the Twenty-First Century*, Eerdmans, in press.

Contributor to books, including *The Lively Experiment Continued: Essays in Honor of Sidney E. Mead*, edited by Jerald C. Brauer, Mercer University Press (Macon, GA), 1987; *Religion and the Life of the Nation: American Recoveries*, edited by Rowland A. Sherrill, University of Illinois Press, 1990; and *The Variety of American Evangelicalism*, edited by Donald Dayton and Robert Johnston, University of Tennessee Press (Knoxville, TN), 1991. Contributor of about thirty articles to periodicals, including *Journal of Mormon History*, *Evangelical Studies Bulletin*, and *Journal of Church and State*. *Restoration Quarterly*, member of corporation board, 1987—, assistant editor, 1990-93; editor, *Mission Journal*, 1979-82; member of board of editors, *Religion and American Culture: A Journal of Interpretation*, 1990-93, and *Discipliana*, 1992-95.

WORK IN PROGRESS: *The Churches of Christ*, for Greenwood Press (Westport, CT); *American Myth, American Creed: The Power of Religion in American Life*, University of Illinois Press.

HURLEY, Ann 1947-

PERSONAL: Born June 11, 1947, in Connecticut; married Rodger Hurley; children: Rodger Wells, Robert Daniel, Elizabeth EulSoon, Catherine Jean.

ADDRESSES: Home—Granville, NY. *Office*—c/o Bucknell University Press, 440 Forsgate Dr., Cranbury, NJ 08512.

CAREER: Writer.

WRITINGS:

(Editor with Kate Greenspan) *So Rich a Tapestry: The Sister Arts and Cultural Studies*, Bucknell University Press (Lewisburg, PA), 1995.

WORK IN PROGRESS: *Reading the Poetry of John Donne in the Context of Late Renaissance Visual Culture* (tentative title).

*   *   *

HUTCHINSON, Allan C. 1951-

PERSONAL: Born October 16, 1951, in Manchester, England; son of Charles and Marie (Beaumont) Hutchinson; married; wife's name, Jane (separated, 1989); companion of Pam Marshall; children: Katie, Emily, Rachel. *Ethnicity:* "WASP." *Education:* University of London, LL.B. (with honors), 1974; Victoria University of Manchester, LL.M., 1978. *Politics:* "Good." *Religion:* None. *Avocational interests:* Soccer, Van Morrison.

ADDRESSES: Home—315 Jedburgh Rd., Toronto, Ontario M5M 3K7, Canada; fax 416-486-4540. *Office*—Osgoode Hall Law School, York University, 4700 Keele St., North York, Ontario M3J 1P3, Canada; fax 416-736-5736. *E-mail*—hutch@yorku.ca.

CAREER: Called to the Bar at Gray's Inn, 1975; York University, North York, Ontario, sessional lecturer in law, 1978-80; University of Newcastle-upon-Tyne, Newcastle-upon-Tyne, England, lecturer in law, 1980-82; York University, assistant professor, 1982-84, associate professor, 1984-88, professor of law, 1988—, associate dean of Osgoode Hall Law

School, 1994-96. Cambridge University, Cambridge Lecturer at Queen's College, 1985, 1987; visiting professor at Monash University, 1986, University of Toronto, 1989-90, and University of Western Australia, 1991; University of Sydney, Parsons Professor, 1995; University of London, Inns of Court fellow at Institute of Advanced Legal Studies, 1997; guest lecturer at colleges and universities throughout the English-speaking world, including University of Michigan, Harvard University, Murdoch University, University of Keele, Georgetown University, and Boston University. BBC-Radio, series producer.

WRITINGS:

(Editor with Patrick Monahan) *The Rule of Law: Ideal or Ideology,* Carswell of Canada, 1986.

Dwelling on the Threshold: Critical Essays on Modern Legal Thought, Carswell of Canada, 1987.

(Editor with G. Watson, R. Sharpe, and W. Bogart) *Canadian Civil Procedure,* 3rd edition, Emond-Montgomery of Canada, 1988.

(Editor) *Critical Legal Studies,* Rowman & Allenheld, 1988.

(Editor with Leslie Green) *Law and Community: The End of Individualism?,* Carswell of Canada, 1989.

(Editor) *Access to Justice: Barriers and Bridges,* Carswell of Canada, 1990.

(Editor with Watson, Bogart, K. Roach, and J. Mosher) *Civil Litigation: Cases and Materials,* 4th edition, Emond-Montgomery of Canada, 1991.

Waiting for Coraf: A Critique of Law and Rights, University of Toronto Press (Toronto, Ontario), 1995.

The Law School Book: Succeeding at Law School, Publications for Professionals (Toronto), 1996.

(Editor with Klaus Peterson) *Censorship in Canada,* University of Toronto Press, 1997.

Professional Responsibilities, Publications for Professionals, 1997.

Contributor to books, including *Postmodernism and Law,* edited by P. Goodrich, 1992; *Reading Dworkin Critically,* edited by A. Hunt, 1992; and *Canadian Tort Theory,* edited by K. Cooper-Stepheson and E. Gibson, 1992. Contributor of articles and reviews to scholarly journals and newspapers, including *Law and Society Review, New England Law Review, Human Values, Literary Review of Canada, Constitutional Forum,* and *Harvard Law Review. Osgoode Hall Law Journal,* editor in chief, 1983-85, book review editor, 1985—.

WORK IN PROGRESS: It's All in the Game: A Non-Foundational Account of Law, Politics, and Adjudication.

*   *   *

HYDE, Eleanor (M.)

PERSONAL: Born in Ohio; married Arthur Hyde (marriage ended). *Ethnicity:* "White, Scottish." *Education:* Attended Sorbonne, University of Paris, and Universite Laval. *Politics:* Independent. *Religion:* "None." *Avocational interests:* Animals, crime, language, fashion.

ADDRESSES: Home and office—New York, NY; fax 212-861-2116. *Agent*—Agnes Birnbaum, Bleecker Street Associates, 88 Bleecker St., Suite 6-P, New York, NY 10012. *E-mail*—EHyde@msn.com.

CAREER: American Institute of Physics, New York City, copyeditor, 1960-65.

MEMBER: International Association of Crime Writers, Mystery Writers of America (member of New York board of directors), Sisters in Crime, Dramatists Guild.

AWARDS, HONORS: British short story prize, 1969; short story award, 1971.

WRITINGS:

Those Who Stayed Behind (novel), New American Library (New York City), 1981.

In Murder We Trust (mystery novel), Fawcett Books (New York City), 1995.

Animal Instincts (mystery novel), Fawcett Books, 1996.

Home Permanent (one-act play), produced in New York City, at Harold Clurman Theatre, 1996.

Contributor to periodicals, including *Cosmopolitan.*

WORK IN PROGRESS: A mystery novel, the third in a series; a suspense novel; research on the history of Bucks County, Pennsylvania; research on fashion magazines.

SIDELIGHTS: Eleanor Hyde told *CA:* "Writing is the only thing I know how to do, or want to do. Jean Rhys, Scott Fitzgerald, and Graham Greene are writers whose styles I admire and very often turn to if I feel a block coming on. I also like to read Auden's poems for the same reason.

"I write on different subjects, depending on my interests. I would love to write plays, but playwriting is a collaborative art, and everyone from dramaturg to director to the actors want to take over the script and rewrite it their way. I also like to write satire and to write from different viewpoints. For example, I was publishing short stories in *Cosmopolitan* and feminist magazines at the same time."

I-J

IRIGARAY, Luce 1930-

PERSONAL: Born in 1930, in Belgium; immigrated to France, c. 1962. *Education:* University of Louvain, M.A. (philosophy and literature), 1955; University of Paris, M.A. (psychology), 1961; Institut de Psychologie de Paris, diploma (psychopathology), 1962; University of Paris X at Nanterre, Ph.D. (linguistics), 1968; University of Paris VIII, Ph.D. (philosophy), 1974; Ecole Freudienne, Ph.D. (honors).

ADDRESSES: Home and office—Paris, France.

CAREER: Writer, educator, and philosopher. Worked as a high school teacher in Brussels, 1956-59; Fondation Nationale de la Recherce Scientifique, Belgium, assistant researcher, 1962-64; University of Paris VIII, Vincennes, instructor, 1970-74; Centre National de la Recherche Scientifique, Paris, assistant researcher, then director of research, 1986—. Named to Chaire International de Philosophie, Erasmus University, Rotterdam, 1982; teacher at Ecole des Hautes Etudes en Sciences Sociales, 1985-86, College International de Philosophie, Paris, 1988-90, and Centre Americain d'Etudes Critiques, 1989-90. Lecturer at women's groups and conferences throughout Europe and North America.

WRITINGS:

Le Langage des dements (thesis), Mouton (The Hague), 1973.

Speculum de l'autre femme (thesis), Minuit (Paris), 1974, translation by Gillian C. Gill published as *Speculum of the Other Woman,* Cornell University Press (Ithaca, NY), 1985.

Ce Sexe qui n'en est pas un, Minuit, 1975, translation by Catharine Porter published as *This Sex Which Is Not One,* Cornell University Press, 1985.

Le Corps-a-corps avec le mere, La Pleine Lune (Ottawa), 1981.

Passions elementaires, Minuit, 1982, translation by Joanne Collie and Judith Still published as *Elemental Passions,* Routledge (New York City), 1992.

Amante marine. De Friedrich Nietzsche, Minuit, 1983, translated as *Marine Lover of Friedrich Nietzsche,* Columbia University Press (New York City), 1991.

La Croyance meme, Galilee (Paris), 1983.

L'Oubli de l'air: Chez Martin Heidegger, Minuit, 1983.

Ethique de la difference sexuelle, Minuit, 1984, translation by Gill and Carolyn Burke published as *An Ethics of Sexual Difference,* Cornell University Press, 1993.

Parler n'est jamais neutre, Minuit, 1985.

Sexes et parentes, Minuit, 1987, translation by Gill published as *Sexes and Genealogies,* Columbia University Press, 1993.

Le Temps de la difference: pour une revolution pacifique, Livre de Poche (Paris), 1989, translation by Karin Montin published as *Thinking the Difference: For a Peaceful Revolution,* Athlone, 1994.

Sexes et genres a travers les langues, Grasset (Paris), 1990.

Je, tu, nous: pour une culture de la difference, Grasset, 1990, translation by Martin published as *Je, Tu, Nous: Toward a Culture of Difference,* Routledge, 1993.

The Irigaray Reader, edited by Margaret Whitford, Blackwell (Cambridge, MA), 1991.

J'aime a tois: esquisse d'une felicite dans l'histoire, Grasset, 1992, translation by Alison Martin published as *I Love to You: Sketch for a Happiness within History,* Routledge, published as *I Love to You: Sketch of a Possible Felicity in History,* Routledge (London), 1995.

Contributor to journals, including *Critique, Langages,* and *Signs: Journal of Women in Culture and Society.*

SIDELIGHTS: Within the realm of feminist philosophic study—and even beyond academic circles—the work of French theoretician Luce Irigaray serves as a frequent point of comparison for such feminist thinkers as Judith Butler, Toril Moi, and Gayatri Chakravorty Spivak. Holding the position of director of philosophic research at Paris's National Center for Scientific Research, Irigaray's published works in translation include *This Sex Which Is Not One,* a 1993 lecture collection entitled *Sexes and Genealogies,* and the essay collection *An Ethics of Sexual Difference.* "Psychoanalyst and philosopher by profession, feminist by choice, and radical by nature, Irigaray is one of the most important women writers of contemporary France," notes Anna Otten in *Antioch Review.*

Born in Belgium in 1930, Irigaray travelled to France in the early 1960s, where she completed advanced degrees in psychology, psychopathology, linguistics, and philosophy. In addition to her academic pursuits during the 1970s she became actively involved in the French women's movement and wrote in defense of a woman's right to sexual autonomy. Irigaray would defend her own right to intellectual freedom just as fervently after her presentation of her doctorate dissertation, a feminist re-evaluation of Freudian theories later published as *Speculum of the Other Woman,* caused an uproar in French academic circles. The brilliant but now notorious student soon found that she was not to be welcomed in her intended career as an educator within Paris universities; instead, she turned her full attention to developing and refining her theories on creating a more gender-equitable social order.

Since the 1973 publication of *Le Langage des dements,* a study of the linguistic collapse that sometimes accompanies old age, Irigaray has continued to produce groundbreaking work in the area of psycholinguistics. Of particular interest to her, the relationship between language and gender has served as the subject of numerous essays.

Irigaray's work is strenuous reading for most laymen. She demands of her readers a rudimentary understanding of her previous theories and makes numerous allusions to classical works of Western philosophy. Wordplay, allusion, metaphor, neologisms, analogies, and spontaneous interjections appear throughout her prose, mortared together by an assortment of punctuation marks, while compound words are frequently shattered by hyphens in order to bring to light their sometimes surprising origins. While Irigaray's complex style has often been criticized, such "deconstruction" of the written word is also central to her overall thesis: language is an artificial patriarchal construction that must be imbued with female "subjectivity" in order to be fully reflective of all who use it. Her goal in writing: to encourage a more equitable society by understanding and accepting the innate character of both sexes on many levels of intercourse, including language.

The essays in Irigaray's *This Sex Which Is Not One,* published in 1985, provides beginning students of her work with a relatively uncomplicated introduction to her ideas on feminine sexuality. In addition to her customary critique of the work of such theorists as Freud and Jacques Lacan, she also discusses the relationship between language and sexuality, putting forward the suggestion that women should create a new level of communication. While such themes are characteristic of her work as a whole—from *Speculum of the Other Woman* to 1993's *An Ethics of Sexual Difference*—they often remain obscured by Irigaray's dense abstractions. However, her influence among feminist colleagues in Germany and Italy in particular remains vigorous; as more of her works become available, English readers who are able will have the opportunity to follow the path of her enormous intellect, while others will continue to see her ideas energetically debated by other scholars.

BIOGRAPHICAL/CRITICAL SOURCES:

BOOKS

Burke, Carolyn L., Margaret Whitford, and Naomi Schor, *Engaging with Irigaray: Feminist Philosophy and Modern European Thought,* Columbia University Press, 1994.

Grosz, Elizabeth, *Sexual Subversions: Three French Feminists,* Allen & Unwin (Sydney), 1989.

Moi, Toril, *Sexual/Textual Politics: Feminist Literary Theory,* Methuen (New York City), 1985.

Nordquist, Joan, *French Feminist Theory: Luce Irigaray and Helene Cixous: A Bibliography,* Reference & Research Services, 1990.

Whitford, Margaret, *Luce Irigaray: Philosophy in the Feminine,* Routledge, 1991.

PERIODICALS

Antioch Review, winter, 1986, p. 114.

Contemporary Literature, Volume 29, 1988, pp. 606-23.

Diacritics, winter, 1975, pp. 2-20; fall, 1978, p. 2; summer, 1982, pp. 11-20.

Ethics, April, 1995, p. 696.

French Review, March, 1995, p. 722.

Literature and Psychology, Volume 32, number 1, 1986.

Signs, autumn, 1980, pp. 66-68; autumn, 1981, pp. 56-59.

Women's Review of Books, March, 1986, pp. 12-13.*

*   *   *

IRON, Ralph
    See SCHREINER, Olive (Emilie Albertina)

*   *   *

JEBB, (Hubert Miles) Gladwyn   1900-1996

OBITUARY NOTICE—See index for *CA* sketch: Born April 25, 1990, in Rotherham, Yorkshire, England; died October 24, 1996, in Halesworth, England. Diplomat, politician, author. Jebb distinguished himself as a British diplomat, counting among his credits work in creating the United Nations. After service in the British Army during World War I, he entered diplomatic service in 1924. During his thirty-six years as a diplomat he held posts such as assistant Under-Secretary in the Ministry of Economic Warfare, acting counsellor in the Foreign Office, and head of the Reconstruction Department, all during World War II. During the war he also attended the Dumbarton Oaks Conference as a British delegate. Work at the conference led to the later formation of the United Nations, and Jebb would eventually become acting Secretary-General of the United Nations briefly in 1946. Other diplomatic work included being a British representative to the United Nations from 1950 to 1954 and serving as British Ambassador to

France from 1954 to 1969. Later he presided over the North Atlantic Treaty Organization from 1963 to 1967. In the 1970s he worked as a member of the European Parliament. He also was the Liberal Party's Deputy leader in the House of Lords from 1965 to 1988. Despite the demands of his career, he found time to write books, such as *The European Idea, Half-Way to 1984, Europe after De Gaulle, Memoirs of Lord Gladwyn,* and *Is Tension Necessary?*

OBITUARIES AND OTHER SOURCES:

BOOKS

Historical Dictionary of the Korean War, Greenwood Press (New York), 1991.

PERIODICALS

New York Times, October 26, 1996, p. 13.

*   *   *

JEFFERIES, Matthew (Martin)   1962-

PERSONAL: Born July 4, 1962, in Wiltshire, England; son of Martin Christopher (an accreditation consultant) and Iris Kathleen (a housing association executive; maiden name, Martin) Jefferies. *Education:* University of Sussex, B.A. (with first class honors), 1985; St. Antony's College, Oxford, D.Phil., 1991. *Politics:* Labour. *Avocational interests:* Popular music, politics, sports, art.

ADDRESSES: Home—12 Range Rd., Manchester M16 8ES, England. *Office*—Department of German, Victoria University of Manchester, Manchester M13 9PL, England; fax 011-44-161-275-3031. *E-mail*—matt.jefferies@man.ac.uk.

CAREER: University of Warwick, Coventry, England, lecturer in history, 1990-91; Victoria University of Manchester, Manchester, England, lecturer in German history, 1991—. Sovereign Education, lecturer and consultant.

MEMBER: German History Society, Bath City Independent Supporters Association, Oxford Society.

WRITINGS:

Politics and Culture in Wilhelmine Germany, Berg Publishers (Washington, DC), 1995.

Contributor to books, including *Green Thought in German Culture,* edited by C. Riordan, University of Wales Press, 1987; and *German History since 1800,* edited by M. Fulbrook, Edward Arnold, 1987. Contributor to periodicals, including *Journal of Design History, German History,* and *History.*

WORK IN PROGRESS: Peter J. Weber: A German Architect in Chicago, an exhibition catalog, for Art Institute of Chicago, completion expected in 1998.

SIDELIGHTS: Matthew Jefferies told *CA:* "My first writing was for the burgeoning 'fanzine' scene in England in the late seventies and early eighties. I began to secure financial rewards for my writing when I began to write concert reviews for the *New Musical Express,* the world's biggest-selling folk weekly, in 1982. In 1984 I started to write on music and sport for *Venue.* As my academic career began to make more demands on my time, the music and sports writing took a back seat (to my great regret).

"My first book *Politics and Culture in Wilhelmine Germany* was a reworking of my doctoral dissertation. Most of my other publications have been on German history, although I am currently working on an exhibition catalog for the Art Institute of Chicago. I have always written about subjects that interest me, but I would broaden my range of topics if my academic career allowed it. I have made no serious attempt to write fiction, but that day may yet come."

* * *

JELINEK, Elfriede 1946-

PERSONAL: Born October 20, 1946, in Muerzzuschlag, Steiermark, Austria; married Gottfried Hungsberg. *Education:* Attended University of Vienna and Vienna Conservatory of Music.

ADDRESSES: Home—Munich, Germany; Vienna, Austria.

CAREER: Writer.

AWARDS, HONORS: Austrian Youth Culture award, 1969; Austrian State Scholarship for Literature, 1972; Roswitha Memorial award, City of Bad Gandersheim, 1978; Interior Ministry of West Germany award for best screenplay, 1979; honored by Austrian Minister for Education and Art, 1983;

Heinrich-Boell award, 1986; Honorary Award for Literature of Vienna, 1989.

MEMBER: Graz Writers Union.

WRITINGS:

NOVELS

Lisas Schatten, Relief Verlag Eilers (Munich), 1967.
Wir sind lockvoegel baby!, Rowohlt (Reinbek bei Hamburg), 1970, translation by Michael Hulse published as *Wonderful, Wonderful Times,* Serpent's Tail (London), 1990.
Michael. Ein Jugendbuch fuer de Infantilgesellschaft, Rowohlt, 1972.
Die Liebhaberinnen, Rowohlt, 1975, translation by Martin Chambers published as *Women as Lovers,* Serpent's Tail, 1994.
bukolit. hoerroman, Rhombus (Wien), 1979.
Die Ausgesperrten, Rowohlt, 1980.
Die Klavierspielerin, Rowohlt, 1983, translation by Joachim Neugroschel published as *The Piano Player,* Weidenfeld & Nicholson (New York City), 1988.
Oh Wildnis, oh Schutz vor ihr, Rowohlt, 1985.
Lust, Rowohlt, 1989, translation by Michael Hulse, Serpent's Tale, 1992.
Totenauberg, Rowohlt, 1991.
Die Kinder der Toten, Rowohlt, 1995.
(With Jutta Heinrich and Adolf-Ernst Meyer) *Sturm und Zwang. Schreiben als Geschlechterkamp,* Klein (Hamburg), 1995.

PLAYS

Was geschah, nachdem Nora ihren Mann verlassen hat, produced in Graz, 1979.
Theaterstuecke. Clara S. Was geschah, nachdem Nora ihren Mann verlassen hat. Burgtheater, edited by Ute Nyssen, Prometh (Koln), 1984.
Krankheit oder moderne Frauen, produced in Bonn, 1987.
Praesident Abendwind, in Anthropophagen im Abendwind, produced in Berlin, 1988.
Wolken; Heim, Steidl (Gottingen), 1993.

Also author of *Raststaette,* 1995, and *Stecken, Stab und Stangle—Eine Handarbeit,* 1996.

OTHER

Author of screenplays, including *Die Ausgesperrten,* 1982, *Was die Nacht verspricht,* 1987, and *Malina,* 1990.

SIDELIGHTS: Austrian novelist and playwright Elfriede Jelinek is considered one of her country's most talented—and most outspoken—writers. Building each of her fictions on a strong Marxist- feminist foundation, Jelinek has, since making her literary debut in 1967 with *Lisas Schatten,* become more controversial with each new work she publishes. In novels such as *Women as Lovers, The Piano Player,* and *Lust,* her central protagonists are usually women; commodities; victims of male-perpetrated crimes that include domestic violence, sexual exploitation, and human alienation. Accused by male critics for her coarse depiction of such acts, Jelinek has also received disapprobation from other feminists who condemn her depiction of female sexuality and masochistic behavior.

Jelinek is a unique stylist, combining verbal components culled from cartoons, comic strips, Beatles' songs, and science fiction films to shock readers out of their cultural complacency. Her language is sometimes profane, sometimes brutally graphic. *Wonderful, Wonderful Times,* for example finds mindless SS-style violence reborn in an Austrian street gang, where "the lurid lives of individuals full of bitterness, failure, weakness, and hatred are an obvious metaphor for bourgeois Austria's Nazi past," according to *New Statesman and Society* reviewer Carole Morin. And Jelinek's *Lust,* which was condemned as pornography by some critics after its publication in 1989, depicts the futility of female desire as a bourgeois woman is relegated to the status of mere property by her capitalist husband.

In addition to her characteristic graphic portrayal of brutality towards women, Jelinek is not hesitant about displaying her Marxist leanings. Her concern for the welfare of the proletariat within capitalist Europe is encoded within all her fiction. In her play *Krankheit oder moderne Frauen,* first produced in Germany in 1987, she links the lingering deaths that result from the vampirism of her female protagonist with "the institutions of cultural and sexual repression or colonization (nationalism, ethnicity, race, class, patriarchy, heterosexuality, the natural, Christianity, marriage)," according to Sigrid Berka in *German Quarterly.* And in her highly praised 1983 work, *The Piano Player,* which Charlotte Innes terms "a brilliant if grim exploration of fascism" in her *Nation* review, Jelinek's thirty-year-old protagonist finds that learning to endure her status as a victim of her mother's oppressive restrictions is the only path to personal control.

Many of Jelinek's novels take place in a fictitious location—a nondescript rural Austrian village—that is devoid of nationalistic fervor or geographical uniqueness. She places her characters within a void, allowing their inner character and their social conditioning to propel the story to its fatalistic end. In *Women as Lovers,* originally published in 1975, Jelinek depicts two women and their struggle for independence. While both seek an idealized "true love," one eventually settles for "good enough" in the person of a hardworking electrician. The other, far more idealistic and adventurous, marries a man who turns out to be an abusive alcoholic; now despised by her fellow townspeople, she is punished for her idealism. Throughout the relating of this story Jelinek remains dispassionate. All the trappings of culture "are placed on the Jelinek operating table and stripped of all our most treasured notions," explains Innes. "Her method . . . involves presenting each chapter as a different cross section of the same bundle of themes. . . ; this may be as artificial a technique as any, but Jelinek knows it and has fun with it. It can be said without qualification that after . . . Jelinek, Austria will never seem quite the same."

BIOGRAPHICAL/CRITICAL SOURCES:

BOOKS

Dictionary of Literary Biography, Volume 85: *Austrian Fiction Writers after 1914,* Gale (Detroit), 1989.
Fiddler, Allyson, *Rewriting Reality: An Introduction to Elfriede Jelinek,* Berg (Oxford), 1994.
Johns, Jorun B., and Katherine Adams, editors, *Elfriede Jelinek: Framed by Language,* Ariadne Press (Riverside, CA), 1994.
Levin, Tobe, *Political Ideology and Aesthetics in Neo-Feminist Fiction: Verena Stefan, Elfriede Jelinek, Margot Schroeder,* Cornell University Press (Ithaca, NY), 1979.
Vansant, Jacqueline, *Against the Horizon: Feminism and Postwar Austrian Women Writers,* Greenwood Press (New York City), 1988.

PERIODICALS

Antioch Review, spring, 1990, p. 258.
German Quarterly, fall, 1995, pp. 372-84.
Los Angeles Times Book Review, December 16, 1990, p. 3.
Modern Austrian Literature, Volume 20, 1987; Volume 23, 1990.
Nation, March 18, 1991, p. 346.

New Statesman and Society, August 31, 1990, p. 38.
New York Times Book Review, November 27, 1988, p. 22.
Publishers Weekly, August 12, 1988, p. 440; November 23, 1990, p. 58; January 4, 1991, p. 36; June 12, 1995, p. 57.
Times Literary Supplement, July 21, 1989, p. 802; November 2, 1990, p. 1183.

*   *   *

JOHNSON, Colin
See MUDROOROO (Nyoongah)

*   *   *

JOHNSON, Daniel M.   1940-

PERSONAL: Born June 10, 1940, in Springfield, OH; son of Everett M. and Hilda M. (Waters) Johnson; married Carolyn Elaine Clark; children: Brent, Darin. *Education:* Texas Christian University, B.A., 1963, M.A., 1965; University of Missouri—Columbia, Ph.D., 1973. *Politics:* Democrat. *Avocational interests:* Reading, the outdoors.

ADDRESSES: Home—1912 Highland Park Circle, Denton, TX 76205. *Office*—School of Community Service, University of North Texas, P.O. Box 5428, Denton, TX 76205; fax 817-565-4663. *E-mail*—djohnson@scs.cmm.unt.edu.

CAREER: Blackburn College, Carlinville, IL, instructor in sociology, 1965-67; Christian College, Columbia, MO, instructor in sociology, 1967-69; Wichita State University, Wichita, KS, assistant professor of sociology and director of sociology honors program, 1969-70; Blackburn College, department head and chairperson, Division of Social Sciences, 1970-73; Sangamon State University, Springfield, IL, associate professor, 1973-78, professor of sociology and public affairs, 1978-79, director of Center for the Study of Middle Size Cities, 1975-79; Virginia Commonwealth University, Richmond, associate professor, 1979-80, professor of sociology, 1980-91, chairperson of Department of Sociology and Anthropology, 1980-83, founder and director of Survey Research Laboratory, 1983-88, interim associate dean, College of Humanities and Sciences, 1987-88; University of North Texas, Denton, professor of sociol-

ogy and dean of School of Community Service, 1991—, executive director of Metropolitan Universities Conference, 1993. Lincoln University, visiting assistant professor, summers, 1968-70; Duke University, Howard E. Jensen Lecturer, 1973; University of Missouri—Columbia, postdoctoral fellow, 1974-75. Texas Commission for National and Community Service, member, 1994-96; North Texas Consortium for Graduate Medical Education, member of board of directors, 1995; City of Denton, member of Task Force on Homelessness, 1991—; consultant to Collateral Communications, Richmond Urban Institute, and Association of Electric Cooperatives. Member of local board of directors of HOPE, Inc., 1992-95, Salvation Army, 1993—, and SPAN, 1995.

MEMBER: Metropolitan Universities Coalition, Council for the Arts and Sciences in Urban Universities, American Sociological Association, Population Association of America, Phi Kappa Phi.

AWARDS, HONORS: Outstanding Service Award, Population Action Council, Population Institute, 1983; Service Award, United Way of Greater Richmond, 1987; Certificate of Appreciation, Illinois Sociological Association, 1993; Equal Opportunity Award, University of North Texas, 1994; grants from National Institute of Child Health and Human Development, Illinois Law Enforcement Commission and Crime Prevention Commission, Ford Foundation, Asian American Mental Health Research Center, Virginia Commission of Game and Inland Fisheries, Virginia Office of Emergency Services, Virginia Governor's Employment and Training Department, Virginia Department of Transportation, Richmond Urban Institute, Social Science Research Council, and Belz Corp.

WRITINGS:

(Editor with Burkett Milner and Norman Langhoff) *Criminal Justice in Illinois: An Information Resource of Local Governments,* Illinois Law Enforcement Commission, 1978.
(Editor with Rebecca Monroe Veach) *The Middle Size Cities of Illinois: Their People, Politics, and Quality of Life,* Sangamon State University (Springfield, IL), 1980.
(With Rex R. Campbell) *Black Migration in America: A Social Demographic History,* Duke University Press (Durham, NC), 1981.
(Editor with David A. Bell) *Metropolitan Universities: An Emerging Model in Higher Education,* University of North Texas Press (Denton, TX), 1995.

Contributor to books, including *Cities and Sickness: Health Care in Urban America,* edited by Ann Lennarson Greer and Scott Greer, Sage Publications (Beverly Hills, CA), 1983; and *Churches in Transitional Neighborhoods: Options for Local Congregations,* edited by Phillip Rodgerson, Home Mission Board, Southern Baptist Convention, 1992. Contributor of more than twenty articles and reviews to periodicals, including *Metropolitan Universities: An International Forum, Journal of Contemporary Criminal Justice, Sociological Analysis, Virginia Town and City,* and *Rural Living.*

WORK IN PROGRESS: Religion and Demography, a synthesis and critical assessment of the religious factor in demographic processes; *The Mission of Higher Education in America,* with Bell, a critical content analysis of four-hundred college and university mission statements.

*   *   *

JOHNSON, Ferd   1905-1996

OBITUARY NOTICE—See index for *CA* sketch: Born December 18, 1905, in Spring Creek, PA; died following a brief illness, October 14, 1996. Cartoonist. Johnson gained prominence for his nationally syndicated comic strip, *Moon Mullins.* In 1923, at the age of seventeen, Johnson attended the Chicago Academy of Fine Arts, where he enrolled in a cartooning class taught by Frank Willard. Willard, who was also employed at the *Chicago Tribune,* had originally created the *Moon Mullins* comic during Calvin Coolidge's presidency. Willard took Johnson under his wing; Johnson became his assistant at the *Chicago Tribune* for the next thirty-five years. In 1958, Willard died, leaving Johnson to carry-on the tradition until 1991. In addition to the *Moon Mullins* cartoons, Johnson also was a sports illustrator for the *Chicago Tribune,* and created the *Texas Slim* and *Lovey Dovey* comic strips. He was also an avid painter whose works have been exhibited in art galleries in California.

OBITUARIES AND OTHER SOURCES:

BOOKS

Who's Who, 148th edition, St. Martin's Press, 1996.

PERIODICALS

Los Angeles Times, October 20, 1996, p. B3.

*   *   *

JOYAUX, Julia
  See KRISTEVA, Julia

K

KADEL, Andrew 1954-

PERSONAL: Born June 8, 1954, in Nampa, ID; son of Donald M. and Bernice (Chaney) Kadel; married Deborah Kilmer, May 31, 1975 (divorced, March, 1989); children: Rachel M., Elisabeth Kilmer, Magdalen Anne. *Education:* Oberlin College, A.B., 1976; Church Divinity School of the Pacific, M.Div., 1981; Rutgers University, M.L.S., 1989.

ADDRESSES: Home—99 Douglas Ave., Yonkers, NY 10703. *Office*—Burke Library, Union Theological Seminary, 13041 Broadway, New York, NY 10027; fax 212-280-1456. *E-mail*—akadel@uts.columbia.edu.

CAREER: Ordained Episcopal priest, 1982; curate of Episcopal church in Lincoln, NE, 1981-83; vicar of Episcopal church in Kirksville, MO, 1983-85; Princeton University, Princeton, NJ, bibliographic specialist at university library, 1987-89; Mercy College, Dobbs Ferry, NY, reference librarian, 1989-90; Union Theological Seminary, New York City, reference and collection development librarian at Burke Library, 1990—.

MEMBER: American Theological Library Association (convenor, 1994-96), Princeton University Library Assistants (vice president, 1988-89), Beta Phi Mu.

WRITINGS:

Matrology: A Bibliographhby of Writings by Christian Women from the First to the Fifteenth Centuries, Continuum (New York), 1995.

Contributor to *Journal of Religious and Theological Information.*

KALBERG, Stephen

PERSONAL: Education: State University of New York at Stony Brook, Ph.D., 1978.

ADDRESSES: Office—Department of Sociology, Boston University, 96 Cummington St., Boston, MA 02215.

CAREER: Boston University, Boston, MA, assistant professor of sociology, 1991—.

WRITINGS:

Max Weber's Comparative-Historical Sociology: An Interpretation and Critique, University of Chicago Press (Chicago, IL), 1994.

* * *

KAPLAR, Richard T. 1951-

PERSONAL: Born June 20, 1951, in Cleveland, OH; son of John F. and Adeline S. Kaplar; married Susan Schneider, 1977 (divorced, 1988); children: Paul Thomas, John Richard. *Education:* John Carroll University, A.B. (magna cum laude), 1973; American University, M.P.A., 1977. *Religion:* Roman Catholic.

ADDRESSES: Home—2790 Melchester Dr., Herndon, VA 22071. *Office*—Media Institute, 1000 Potomac St. N.W., Suite 301, Washington, DC 20007; fax 202-337-7092. *E-mail*—tmi@clark.net.

CAREER: Media Institute (nonprofit communications policy research organization), Washington, DC, vice-president, 1981—. *Military service:* U.S. Army, 1973-75. U.S. Army Reserve, 1975-80; became captain.

MEMBER: National Press Club, Rotary Club of Tysons Corner (president, 1989-90).

AWARDS, HONORS: Paul Harris fellow, Rotary International, 1986.

WRITINGS:

The Financial Interest and Syndication Rules: Prime Time for Repeal, Media Institute (Washington, DC), 1990.

Advertising Rights, the Neglected Freedom: Toward a New Doctrine of Commercial Speech, Media Institute, 1991.

(Editor) *Beyond the Courtroom: Alternatives for Resolving Press Disputes,* Media Institute, 1991.

(Editor) *Bad Prescription for the First Amendment: FDA Censorship of Drug Advertising and Promotion,* Media Institute, 1993.

(With Patrick D. Maines) *The Government Factor: Undermining Journalistic Ethics in the Information Age,* Cato Institute (Washington, DC), 1995.

(Editor) *Speaking Freely: The Public Interest in Unfettered Speech,* Media Institute, 1995.

Contributor to periodicals, including *Journal of Mass Media Ethics.*

*   *   *

KAPOOR, L(achman) D(as)   1916-
(L. D. Kapur)

PERSONAL: Born September 27, 1916, in Muzaffarabad, India; son of Bhagwan Das (a medical practitioner) and Janki (a homemaker; maiden name, Devi) Kapoor; married Prakash Nagpal, February 23, 1943; children: Suman Kapoor Virmani (daughter), Anil (son), Ashish (son). *Education:* Punjab University, B.Sc., 1937; Banaras Hindu University, M.Sc., 1940; London School of Pharmacy, London, Ph.D., 1958. *Religion:* Hindu. *Avocational interests:* The culture of herbs, Urdu poetry.

ADDRESSES: Home—11 Harvest Dr., Neshanic Station, NJ 08853; fax 908-369-4121.

CAREER: Forest Department of Jammu and Kashmir, Baramulla, India, exploitation officer for the survey and collection of forest products, 1942-44; Drug Research Laboratory of Jammu and Kashmir, Jammu, India, botanist, 1944-55; CSIR, Regional Research Laboratory, Jammu, senior assistant director, 1958-64; CSIR, National Botanical Research Institute, Lucknow, India, deputy director, 1964-76; retired, 1976. Consulting scientist to Lupin Laboratories, Baidyanath Ayurved Pharmaceuticals, and Mehta Pharmaceuticals.

MEMBER: American Society of Pharmacognosy (fellow), Indian Association of Science (fellow; life member).

AWARDS, HONORS: Prize from the president of India, 1972, for the invention of a "new apparatus for attars and perfumed waters."

WRITINGS:

(With R. N. Chopra, I. C. Chopra, and K. L. Handa) *Chopra's Indigenous Drugs of India,* revised edition, U. N. Dhur and Sons (Calcutta, India), 1958.

(With Ramkrishnan) *Advances in the Essential Oil Industry,* Today and Tomorrow Printers and Publishers (New Delhi, India), 1977.

The CRC Handbook of Ayurvedic Medicinal Plants, CRC Press (Boca Raton, FL), 1990.

The Opium Poppy: Botany, Chemistry, and Pharmacology, Haworth Press (New York), 1995.

Contributor of more than two-hundred-fifty articles to scientific journals. Some work appears under the name L. D. Kapur. Editor in chief, *RRL Bulletin,* 1963-64.

WORK IN PROGRESS: A book on licorice, including historical use, botany, chemistry, pharmacology, medicinal preparations, and industrial profiles, publication by Harwood Academic (Amsterdam, Netherlands) expected in 1998.

SIDELIGHTS: L. D. Kapoor told *CA:* "I feel obligated to share my knowledge of medicinal plants with other avid botanists. Writing is a passion for me. It allows for the representation of my feelings with my readers. I want readers to know the salient features of medicinal plants, their distribution, histology, physiology, chemistry, and their therapeutic uses both in Allopathic and traditional medicine.

"The acute depletion of these plants from their natural habitat because of over-exploitation posed a problem of scarcity of genuine vegetable plants to the pharmaceutical industry and to the practitioners of traditional medicine; hence, the idea of cultivation to overcome the shortage. To popularize this idea, I presented the cultural practices, in black and white, in scientific journals. All of my subjects have been discussed from different angles. I take the most exhaustive path to highlight the other side of the topic.

"I grew up in the environment of herbal therapy. It is no wonder that my love of medicinal plants is an acquired characteristic."

*   *   *

KAPUR, L. D.
See KAPOOR, L(achman) D(as)

*   *   *

KARLEN, Neal (Stuart) 1959-

PERSONAL: Born June 25, 1959, in Minneapolis, MN; son of Markle and Charlotte Hope (Greenfield) Karlen. *Education:* Brown University, B.A. (magna cum laude), 1982. *Religion:* Jewish.

ADDRESSES: Office—c/o Times Books, 201 East 50th St., New York, NY 10022.

CAREER: Columnist and freelance writer. *Newsweek,* New York City, staff writer and reporter, 1982-86; *Rolling Stone,* New York City, contributing editor, 1986-91. *CBS News/America Tonight,* New York City, on-air essayist, 1990; *Minneapolis-St. Paul Magazine,* Minneapolis, MN, columnist, 1990—; *New York Times,* New York City, contributing writer, 1992—.

MEMBER: Phi Beta Kappa.

AWARDS, HONORS: American Historical Society prize, Brown University, 1982; Minnesota State Arts Board grant for nonfiction writing, 1991.

WRITINGS:

The Emperor's New Clothes (libretto), produced in 1990.

(With Henny Youngman) *Take My Life, Please,* William Morrow (New York), 1991.
Babes in Toyland: The Making and Selling of a Rock and Roll Band, Times Books (New York), 1994.

Contributor to periodicals, including *Washington Post, Esquire, GQ,* and *Spy.*

SIDELIGHTS: With *Babes in Toyland: The Making and Selling of a Rock and Roll Band,* former *Rolling Stone* editor Neal Karlen looks at the rise of Babes in Toyland, one of the few successful all-female "grunge" rock bands. "Digging beneath the hardcore surface of this alternative scene," explained *Rolling Stone* writer Matt Damsker, "he unearths the fragile egos of musicians who sleep together in single hotel rooms, play on borrowed equipment and scrape together cash and emotional capital—against all odds of making it." "Karlen is sometimes more interested in his subjects' reputation than in their talent," declared a *Kirkus Reviews* critic, "so the content of their music gets scant attention." He also documents the struggle of their agent Tim Carr, who made a place for them at Warner Music—a major recording label—and then set out to make them famous quickly. By the time they joined the 1993 Lollapalooza tour, explained Karlen in a *Mademoiselle* article, the three members of Babes in Toyland—Kat Bjelland, Lori Barbero, and Maureen Herman—"hadn't even yet processed that Beavis and Butt-Head, the animated nitwits of MTV's top-rated show, had just screened their video and given the band their highest on-air recommendation: 'They're *cool!* These girls *rock!*'"

However, some reviewers argued that Karlen's portrayal of the rise of the band Babes in Toyland at times appears to be the story of its fall as well. "Though Karlen is clearly a fan of the band," stated *New York* magazine reviewer Walter Kirn, "his account of the tedious, idiotic hoo-ha surrounding its rise to fame is depressing." Throughout the recording of their first album for Warner, *Fontanelle,* Damsker explained, "Babes in Toyland frittered away expensive studio time, weathering a brief breakup and near-constant emotional breakdowns." The band's original bassist, Michelle Leon, left the band after her boyfriend's death. Bjelland feuded with Courtney Love, a former friend and leader of the grunge band Hole, and she married (and later divorced) an Australian punk rocker named Stuart Spasm. "Karlen's hyper-rhetoric sometimes intrudes," concluded the *Kirkus Reviews* critic, "but he isn't oblivious to the ironies in Warner's effort to sell the Babes without sacrificing their street credibility."

BIOGRAPHICAL/CRITICAL SOURCES:

PERIODICALS

Kirkus Reviews, May 15, 1994, p. 686.
Mademoiselle, Volume 99, October, 1993, pp. 180-84, 221-22.
New York, August 22, 1994, p. 47.
New York Times, August 28, 1994, p. 26.
New York Times Book Review, December 22, 1991, p. 14.
Publishers Weekly, June 27, 1994, p. 63.
Rolling Stone, October 6, 1994, p. 37.*

* * *

KASISCHKE, Laura 1961-

PERSONAL: Born December 5, 1961, in Lake Charles, LA; daughter of Edward (a postal worker) and Suzanne (a teacher; maiden name, Sullivan) Kasischke; married William Abernethy, August, 1994; children: John Sullivan Abernethy. Education: University of Michigan, B.A. (with high honors), 1984, M.F.A., 1987; graduate study at Columbia University.

ADDRESSES: Home—2997 South Fletcher Rd., Chelsea, MI 48118. Agent—Lisa Bankoff, International Creative Management, 40 West 57th St., New York, NY 10019.

CAREER: Writer. South Plains College, Levelland, TX, writing instructor, 1987-88; Eastern Michigan University, visiting lecturer in creative writing and literature, 1989-90; Washtenaw Community College, Ann Arbor, MI, instructor of creative writing and literature, 1990—; University of Nevada, Las Vegas, associate professor, 1994-95.

AWARDS, HONORS: Hopwood Awards, for poetry, 1982, for fiction, 1982, for essay, 1984, and for drama; Cowden fellowships, 1982-83; Michael Gutterman Poetry Award, 1983; Arts Foundation of Michigan grants, 1983-84; Warner Communications fellowship, Columbia University, 1985; Marjorie Rapaport Poetry Award, 1986; Michigan Council for the Arts Individual Artist grant, 1990; Ragdale Foundation fellowships, 1990-92; Elmer Holmes Bobst Award for Emerging Writers, 1991, for Wild Brides; MacDowell Colony fellow, 1992; Bread Loaf fellow in poetry, 1992; Alice Fay DiCastagnola Award, 1993; Pushcart Prize, 1993; Creative Artists Award, Arts Foundation of Michigan, 1993; National Endowment for the Arts fellowship, 1994; Barbara Deming Memorial Award, 1994; Poets & Writers Exchange fellowship, 1994.

WRITINGS:

Brides, Wives, and Widows (poetry), American Studies Press (Tampa, FL), 1990.
Wild Brides (poetry), New York University Press (New York), 1992.
Housekeeping in a Dream (poetry), Carnegie Mellon University Press (Pittsburgh, PA), 1995.
Suspicious River (novel), Houghton Mifflin (Boston, MA), 1996.

Contributor of poems to periodicals, including Antioch Review, Beloit Poetry Journal, Chelsea, Epoch, Georgia Review, Graham House Review, Green Mountains Review, Indiana Review, Kenyon Review, Michigan Quarterly Review, Missouri Review, New England Review, Ploughshares, Plum Review, Poetry, Prairie Schooner, Seneca Review, and Witness.

SIDELIGHTS: Laura Kasischke is an award-winning poet and novelist whose verses have been widely published in literary journals and gathered in a trio of collections: Brides, Wives, and Widows, Wild Brides, and Housekeeping in a Dream. In addition, when her first novel, the dark and violent Suspicious River, was published in 1996, it introduced Kasischke to an even wider readership. Suspicious River, narrated in the first person, tells the lurid tale of Leila Murray, a twenty-year-old married woman who works behind the desk of the Swan Motel in the small town of Suspicious River in western Michigan. For some unstated reason, Leila decides to become a prostitute and offers her favors to the motel's clients whenever her husband is out of town on business. The night she provides her services to Gary Jensen, a charismatic stranger in town, marks the beginning of Leila's obsession with the brutal stranger and the spiral that could lead to her death. As the story unfolds, Leila suffers flashbacks from her childhood, when her mother, a prostitute, was stabbed to death by a client, who happened to be Leila's uncle. Leila appears to be reliving her mother's past, moving to embrace an identical fate in a reading experience that George Stade of the New York Times Book Review likened to "driving too fast on the Pacific Coast Highway."

Suspicious River elicited much praise from critics. Boston Globe reviewer Diane White called it "an extremely intelligent novel, intricately constructed, beautifully written," and Erika Taylor, writing for the *Los Angeles Times,* labeled it an "impressive first novel" and "a story that is profoundly disturbing but also resonant with hope and rebirth." Moreover, in a review for the *Seattle Times,* Johanna Stoberock declared that Kasischke has written "a work of such eerie beauty, such immediate and vibrant imagery, that it will haunt readers for years." In the words of Stade, *Suspicious River* "is written with the skill of an old hand, though not with skill only. The novel's past and present spiral around and condition each other like the strands of a double helix. Chains of imagery, visual, olfactory and tactile, link up scenes in unexpected ways. The peripheral characters, the physical setting, the claustrophobic horrors of American small-town life are evoked with austere precision." "Leila's case got to me," confessed Stade, "in spite of my resistance to all it reveals of what I don't want to face in human nature, for Ms. Kasischke's characters are all too convincing." He concluded, "I truly and immensely admire this novel, but I am not sure I like it."

As would be expected of a poet's work, Kasischke's use of language in *Suspicious River* attracted the attention of reviewers. The author's style is to follow a plain short statement with several poetic sentence fragments. According to Molly E. Rauch: "Luscious, disjointed images pile upon one another until the novel is teeming with phrases—looping, frenzied words, breathlessly pounding toward a frozen white winter and the story's inexorable conclusion." "Her fine sense of the nuance of language is obvious on just about every page," White added. "The images she chooses are original, unexpected, uncliche'd. In less skillful hands Leila's would be just a depressing story about a very troubled young woman. Kasischke's writing endows it with universality and elevates it to tragedy. It's an amazing first novel." Stoberock concluded: "*Suspicious River* tells a difficult story, one borne by painful images that give Leila's journey no easy ending. It is also a novel of depth, beauty and insight, hauntingly told by a powerful writer."

Kasischke told *CA:* "The narrative of *Suspicious River* grew out of the writing of a poem, and the image which suggested the novel to me simply mushroomed until it could no longer be contained by that poem—an image of a young woman buried in red raked leaves at the side of a road. As cars blew past, the leaves rose briefly around her nude body like bloody baby-hands, then settled over her again, a grave. That was everything I needed to know in the beginning about Leila—the public violence of her life, a glimpse of her naked shame, and the season that contained her.

"The first draft of the novel did come very quickly, and I attribute this to the season. I began writing in mid-September, and ended in October—a very dramatic time in Michigan. Color, death, fury. As I wrote, it seemed to me that Leila's voice was part of that frantic change. An end or a beginning was approaching for her almost too quickly to record, and the trees, the gardens, the sky, the air seemed to be taking part in—or were victims of—the same violation and disorder Leila was experiencing. Every morning before work and every night after, I felt I had to hurry to write about that experience, had to get the season into the novel before it was over, and had to reach the end of Leila's story before she did."

BIOGRAPHICAL/CRITICAL SOURCES:

PERIODICALS

American Book Review, June, 1993, pp. 24-25.
Ann Arbor Observer, March, 1996.
Antioch Review, spring, 1994, p. 370.
Boston Globe, July 4, 1996, p. 63.
Georgia Review, Volume 50, number 2, p. 418.
Los Angeles Times, August 4, 1996, p. 6.
Nation, April 22, 1996, p. 35.
New York Times Book Review, May 5, 1996, p. 11.
Seattle Times, July 14, 1996.

*   *   *

KATZ, Lawrence S(anford)   1947-

PERSONAL: Born March 26, 1947, in Detroit, MI; son of David (a pharmacist) and Ilene Doris (a homemaker; maiden name, Raskin) Katz; married Karen Ann Tintori (a novelist), October 15, 1972; children: Mitchel Jay, Steven Robert. *Ethnicity:* "Jewish." *Education:* Wayne State University, B.A., 1969, J.D., 1972. *Politics:* Independent. *Religion:* Jewish. *Avocational interests:* Travel, politics, the arts.

ADDRESSES: Home—4193 Southmoor Lane, West Bloomfield, MI 48323. *Office*—38700 Van Dyke Ave., Suite 201, Sterling Heights, MI 48312; fax 810-939-9563. *E-mail*—unklarry@aol.com. *Agent*—Karen Solen, Writer's House, 21 West 26th St., New York, NY 10010.

CAREER: Law clerk and associate of Gerald M. Lorence, Detroit, MI, 1971-73; Weingarden & Hauer, Berkley, MI, associate, 1973-74; Goldstein & Raznick, Warren, MI, associate, 1974-76; Goldstein, Raznick & Katz, Warren, MI, partner, 1977-78; private practice of law, Sterling Heights, MI, 1978—. State Bar of Michigan, member; Attorney Grievance Commission, special investigator, 1977-80; Attorney Discipline Board, chairperson of Hearing Panel, 1987—. Macomb County Circuit Court, domestic relations mediator, 1986—. Civic Searchlight, Inc., director, 1993-95. Performer in radio and television commercials.

MEMBER: Society for American Baseball Research, Macomb County Bar Association.

AWARDS, HONORS: Award of Appreciation, State Bar of Michigan, Family Law Section, 1990.

WRITINGS:

Baseball in 1939: The Watershed Season of the National Pastime, McFarland and Co. (Jefferson, NC), 1995.

Contributor to books, including *The Perfect Game,* edited by Mark Alvarez, Taylor Publishing (Dallas, TX), 1993, 2nd edition, Barnes & Noble (New York), 1995. Contributor to periodicals, including *Baseball Research Journal, Sports Collectors Digest,* and *National Pastime.*

WORK IN PROGRESS: Research on nineteenth-century American history.

SIDELIGHTS: Lawrence S. Katz told *CA:* "I grew up in the 1950s, playing ball in the streets of Detroit and going to baseball games at Briggs (Tiger) Stadium with my boyhood friends. The most enduring recollections of my college years derive from my experiences as a reporter for the student paper. It was during this period that I discovered the pain and pleasure of writing and began to discover myself. I wanted to write about people, and I loved the arduousness of the writing process. I constantly rewrote, however, and realized that I would be unhappy with the deadline demands made on a reporter. During law school, I contributed feature articles to various publications and wrote briefs for a criminal lawyer.

"I have found writing most fulfilling—even the wrenching part of it—for as long as I can recall. As an attorney, I understand the power of the spoken word. Written expression, however, sticks to the paper; its form and substance suffers repeated scrutiny by, and can have a lasting effect upon, both the reader and the writer.

"Now, most of my writing is for the courts. The law truly is a jealous mistress. Despite the number of best-selling authors with legal backgrounds, many Americans will be disappointed to learn that trial lawyers will not be resigning *en masse* to write books.

"For many years, I channeled as much energy as possible into brief-writing, taking large numbers of cases, including many high-profile criminal cases, into the state and federal courts. In 1983, I joined the Society for American Baseball Research, a group that promotes research and writing about baseball and its history. I was encouraged by the mission of the organization. I decided to see if I could go back to writing for an audience of more than three judges.

"My first article on baseball appeared in 1989, in commemoration of the fiftieth anniversary of the Baseball Hall of Fame. My next effort, 'When Immortals Returned to the Minors,' was published in the *Baseball Research Journal* in 1990. This piece was selected for inclusion in the book *The Perfect Game.*

"From 1990 to 1994, in quiet moments at home, in the evenings and on weekends, augmented by trips to Chicago, Baltimore, Boston, and Cooperstown, I studied the human aspects of one year of this country's history. The result was *Baseball in 1939,* featuring interviews with fourteen baseball personalities, including four Hall of Famers.

"This book is not about the pennant race or who won the batting title. It is the story of a transitional year in American history as seen through the eyes of a baseball fan. It was inspired by the desire of a baby-boomer to feel and experience American life and culture just before the flood of change brought about by World War II. The medium is baseball, but the message is about how the country has changed over the past three generations."

*   *   *

KATZ, Welwyn Wilton   1948-

PERSONAL: Born June 7, 1948, in London, Ontario, Canada; daughter of Robert and Anne (Taylor)

Wilton; married Albert N. Katz, 1973 (separated 1989); children: Meredith Allison. *Education:* University of Western Ontario, B.S., 1970. *Avocational interests:* Playing the flute, reading myths and legends, finding recipes that incorporate the herbs she grows, knitting.

ADDRESSES: Home and office—549 Ridout St., N., Unit 502, London, Ontario N6A 5N5, Canada.

CAREER: Writer; South Secondary School, London, Ontario, Canada, teacher, assistant head of mathematics, 1970-77. Past refugee coordinator, Amnesty International; treasurer and member of the steering committee, London Children's Literature Round Table; former researcher, Girls' Group Home of London.

MEMBER: Writers' Union of Canada, Canadian Society of Children's Authors, Illustrators and Performers.

AWARDS, HONORS: Book of the Year Runner-up from the Canadian Library Association, 1985, for *Witchery Hill,* 1987, for *Sun God, Moon Witch,* 1988, for *False Face,* and 1989, for *The Third Magic;* Ruth Schwartz Award Finalist, 1987, for *False Face,* and 1988, for *The Third Magic;* International Children's Fiction Prize, Governor-General's Award Finalist, Max and Greta Ebel Award, and Trillium Award Finalist, all 1987, and selected one of *School Library Journal*'s Best Books and a Pick of the List from the *American Bookseller,* both 1988, all for *False Face;* Governor-General's Award, 1988, for *The Third Magic;* Young Adult Honour Book Award from the Canadian Library Association, 1996, for *Out of the Dark.*

WRITINGS:

The Prophecy of Tau Ridoo (juvenile), illustrated by Michelle Desbarats, Tree Frog Press, 1982.
Witchery Hill (young adult novel), Atheneum, 1984.
Sun God, Moon Witch (young adult novel), Douglas & McIntyre, 1986.
False Face (Junior Literary Guild selection), Douglas & McIntyre, 1987, Macmillan, 1988.
The Third Magic, Douglas & McIntyre, 1988, Macmillan, 1989.
Whalesinger, Douglas & McIntyre, 1990, Macmillan, 1991.
Come Like Shadows, Viking, 1993.
Time Ghost, Simon & Schuster/Margaret K. McElderry, 1995.
Out of the Dark, Groundwood, 1996.

SIDELIGHTS: For Welwyn Wilton Katz, it was the books of J. R. R. Tolkien that changed everything. As she once stated in *Something about the Author* (*SATA*), "I found that it was possible, using words alone, to create a whole world, a marvelously complex and unreal world that other people could believe in." Katz has used her interest in myths, legends, and the supernatural to weave stories that incorporate both current problems most teenagers face—insecurity, parental divorce to name just two—and timeless mythological themes that play out the conflict between good and evil. Whether on their home turf or transported to another time or planet, her characters deal with evil outside themselves or within, when the protagonist becomes the unwitting prey of evil powers.

Katz, a fifth-generation Canadian, credits her Scottish and Cornish ancestors with her abiding interest in Celtic myths. Unlike many writers, Katz does not recall writing very much when she was young. One exception was a high school final exam in which she was asked to write for three hours on one of five topics. "I spent two hours trying to decide which of those awful topics I would choose," she told *SATA,* "and the remaining hour 'taking dictation' from some inspired part of my brain, the words simply flowing out of me. . . . It was one of the most exciting experiences I've ever had." But even with the excellent grade she earned and the thrill of this feeling, it took a long time for Katz to try her hand at writing again.

An honors student in mathematics, Katz became a high school teacher, a position she held until she was twenty-eight. She found it difficult to adjust to being in the classroom, though she liked her students and made a good salary. She tried several makeovers—pierced ears, contact lenses, new clothes—but still felt awkward in her chosen profession. Uninspired, Katz worried that her whole life would continue on this steady, dull course and, as she told *SATA,* "it gave me the creeps."

It was at this point that she read Tolkien; the immediate effect was that Katz decided to write an adult fantasy novel. Initially, she devoted evenings and summers to her writing, but found that part-time writing didn't suit her. A year's leave of absence was followed by another, and by then she had finished her first draft, a hefty 750 pages. The ambitious story took place in a different world and had a huge cast of characters, whose complex setting demanded long, detailed exposition. By 1979, she had resigned as a teacher and used another year to rewrite the manuscript.

Katz sent it out to several publishers but none expressed interest. "When there was no one left to send it to, I cried a little—okay, a lot!—and then put the book on my top shelf. There it sits to this day," she wrote in *SATA*. But Katz made a very important discovery: she wanted to write. Furthermore, she learned about writing itself from doing the work, honing her technique and style. Among her characters were several children, and Katz thought she might try a children's book next.

Her breakthrough came in 1982, when her first novel *The Prophecy of Tau Ridoo* appeared. In it, the five Aubrey siblings find themselves in the strange and threatening world of Tau Ridoo, controlled by the terrifying Red General. He sends his deputies after the children, who become separated from each other. Cooky, a sorceress, comes to their aid and together they manage to defeat the evil General and to be reunited.

Witchery Hill's protagonist is Mike, whose parents have recently divorced. Along with his journalist father, Mike travels to Guernsey (one of the English Channel Islands) for a summer visit with the St. Georges, who are family friends. Mike's friendship with the eldest daughter, Lisa, reveals surprising turmoil beneath the apparently calm surface of her family life. Diabetic and fiercely attached to her father, Lisa suspects her stepmother is not only a witch, but trying to gain control of the local coven. The job of vanquishing the evil powers set loose on the island and destroying the coven falls to Mike, who must also reconcile himself to a less-than-perfect relationship with his father. A contributor in *Publishers Weekly* lauded Katz for holding the reader in "thrall," concluding that *Witchery Hill* "is a knockout, with each character deftly delineated and a socko finish." John Lord, writing in *Voice of Youth Advocates,* echoed this view, praising Katz's use of the setting, with its Stonehenge-like standing stones and its invitation to adventure in a world of facts interwoven with fantasy. "For the reader who needs action and intrigue," Lord stated, "this book is definitely 'IT.'"

Witchery Hill sprang out of a series of coincidences connected to Katz's chance visit to Guernsey, whose ferry docked in the small town where she dropped off a rental car. A randomly chosen hotel happened to be staffed by a woman with an interest in the island's folklore. Katz found references to witchcraft on the island as late as 1967 and came upon a manual of witchcraft in a bookstore. She decided to set her story on the island and to use a very powerful book of sorcery as the source of the witches' strife.

Historical facts were the inspiration for *Sun God, Moon Witch* as well. Katz read widely on dowsers (also known as water-witchers), who often reported strong electrical shocks when they came into contact with standing stones like those in the stone circles in England. Katz also recalled a family story about a dowser who had discovered a spring on their farm, and she knitted the two together. In *Sun God, Moon Witch,* Thorny McCabe is underwhelmed by the idea of summering with her cousin Patrick in an English village. But she soon discovers that the village is engaged in a controversy over the ancient stone circle of Awen-Ur. Like *Witchery Hill, Sun God, Moon Witch* revolves around the protagonist's struggle to keep evil from taking over the world.

False Face tackles a different kind of ethical dilemma—the appropriate handling of cultural artifacts—as played out against a difficult family drama. Protagonist Laney McIntyre finds an Indian mask in a bog near her London, Ontario, home. The tensions in her house following her parents' recent divorce are symbolized by their different reactions to Laney's find: as a successful antiques dealer, her mother encourages her to profit by it, but her father, a professor, encourages her to donate it to a museum. Meanwhile, the mask itself appears to be emitting corrupting powers that only she and her Indian friend Tom seem able to stop. *Voice of Youth Advocates*'s Rosemary Moran pointed out that the novel is "steeped in Canadian lore" and that the characters embodied the difficulties of dealing with different cultures "with enough suspense to keep the reader involved until the climax." A *Publishers Weekly* reviewer found that Katz "welds the supernatural element onto the family's conflicts with grace and competence."

Katz describes *The Third Magic* as a kind of predecessor to the King Arthur legend. The novel took her about three years to complete, much of it spent constructing Nwm, an imaginary world, in as much detail as possible. Morgan LeFevre, a fifteen-year-old, has accompanied her father to Tintagel to assist with a television documentary on the King Arthur legend. Centuries before, Morrigan, a sister in the matriarchal society of Nwm, had been sent to Tintagel, fated to become Morgan Le Fay. Because of her resemblance to Morrigan, Morgan is transported to Nwm, confronted by two warring forces of magic. To Margaret Miles of *Voice of Youth Advocates,* Katz tried hard but failed to find a new twist to the Arthurian and Celtic-based fantasies and wrote that Arthurian fans "may be interested in some aspects . . . but are likely to find it rather less magical than the classics of the genre." Although Robert Strang, in reviewing the book for *Bulletin of the Center for Children's Books,* complained of a plot "convoluted even by genre standards," he found it to be a "unique recasting of a legend."

Katz changed direction a bit with *Whalesinger,* which looks at the relationships between humans, animals, and nature. Set in spectacular Point Reyes National Seashore in northern California, *Whalesinger* features two teenagers with problems, both of whom are involved in a summer marine conservation program. Nick is an angry young man eager to blame the team leader for Nick's older brother's death in a shipboard explosion, and Marty is a learning-disabled, lonely girl who has an empathic bond with a gray whale and her calf. Katz uses the coastline as emblematic of nature's power—the action climaxes in an earthquake—and history—there are references to an accident that occurred centuries before when Sir Francis Drake visited the area. A critic in *Publishers Weekly* chided Katz for a "veritable bouillabaisse of fishy plot developments," finally determining that she "has gone overboard." *School Library Journal*'s Patricia Manning, however, applauded Katz for her "complex pattern of science, personalities, a lost treasure, and a whale mother with an ailing baby" and pronounced the book "intriguing."

With her interest in the supernatural, it's no surprise that Katz would find herself drawn to *Macbeth*—and making full use of the play's reputation among theater people for being cursed. Teenaged Kinny O'Neill, the protagonist of *Come Like Shadows,* has a summer job with the director of the Stratford, Canada, Shakespeare festival. When she finds the perfect mirror prop, Kinny has no idea that it contains the spirits of the eleventh-century witches that destroyed the real Macbeth. The company travels to perform in Scotland, the witches by now in modern dress and using the apparently helpless Kinny to further their plot to renew their coven. Barbara L. Michasiw wrote of the book in *Quill and Quire* that "*Come Like Shadows* is difficult to reconcile with reality. . . . This is a challenging story that will probably not be comfortably accessible" to all readers. Lucinda Snyder Whitehurst of the *School Library Journal* also found the alternating points of view, from Kinny to Macbeth, a little difficult to follow, but felt that it

would be "appreciated by drama and Shakespeare enthusiasts." Reviewing the book for *Voice of Youth Advocates,* Mary Jane Santos declared it "an intriguing mystery-fantasy with well developed characters and realistic dialogue."

Again and again, reviewers point to Katz's ability to use landscape and location to great advantage in her work. She proved herself especially adept in her 1995 novel, *Time Ghost,* which is set in the polluted world fifty years hence. Along with their friends—brother and sister Josh and Dani—Sara and her brother Karl accompany their grandmother to the North Pole. An argument between Sara and her grandmother catapults Sara and Dani back in time, to the late twentieth century before nature was irrevocably ruined. In *Booklist,* Carolyn Phelan predicted that readers would be drawn to the "flow of action and emotion, the deft descriptions of the natural world, and the sympathetic characters." Susan L. Rogers of *School Library Journal* was impressed with Katz's "absorbing story" that delivers "a serious ecological message," sentiments echoed by a *Publishers Weekly* critic, who also noted the ecological message and found it "stifles neither characters nor the plot."

After a break from myths, Katz returned to the ancient Norse tales for *Out of the Dark,* which *Children's Reader* reviewer Janet Wynne-Edwards termed "satisfying." Thirteen-year-old Ben, his younger brother Keith and their father move from Ottawa to start a new life in Newfoundland, in the town of Ship Cove, where his father grew up. Before her death, Ben's mother told him many of the Viking stories, and in her honor he begins to carve a knarr (a Viking ship), the myths and historical details helping him to deal with his own problems. As Wynne-Edwards wrote, "The young reader is not subjected to an anthropological checklist of artifacts and so may well retain this history."

Despite plots that sometimes strike reviewers as too complex, Katz consistently provides her readers with strong writing, compelling characters, and believable dialogue. She manages to work in her environmental concerns and her own fascination with ancient tales without overloading the story, earning her many awards and an enthusiastic, loyal following.

BIOGRAPHICAL/CRITICAL SOURCES:

BOOKS

Something about the Author, Volume 62, Gale, 1990.

Twentieth-Century Children's Writers, edited by Laura Standley Berger, St. James Press, 1995, pp. 503-04.

PERIODICALS

Booklist, May 1, 1995, p. 1573.
Bulletin of the Center for Children's Books, February, 1989, p. 150.
Canadian Children's Literature, number 47, 1987.
Children's Reader, winter, 1995-96.
Kirkus Reviews, August 1, 1988, p. 1151.
Publishers Weekly, November 2, 1984, p. 77; July 29, 1988, p. 234; December 21, 1990, p. 57; July 15, 1996, pp. 74-75.
Quill and Quire, February, 1993, p. 36.
School Library Journal, May, 1991, p. 111; December, 1993, p. 134; May, 1995, p. 108.
Voice of Youth Advocates, April, 1985, p. 48; February, 1989, p. 286; June, 1989, p. 116; October, 1993, p. 228.*

—*Sketch by Megan Ratner*

*   *   *

KAY, David A(llen)   1940-

PERSONAL: Born June 8, 1940, in Houston, TX; married; wife's name, Anita. *Education:* University of Texas, B.B.A., 1962; Columbia University, M.A. (international affairs), 1964, Ph.D., 1967.

ADDRESSES: Home—Vienna, Austria. *Office*—International Atomic Energy Agency, Wagramer Str 5, P.O. Box 100, A-1400, Vienna, Austria.

CAREER: Writer and editor. University of Wisconsin, Madison, assistant professor of political science, 1966-70; United States mission to the United Nations, advisor in international organizational affairs, 1967-68; Barnard College of Columbia University, New York City, associate professor of political science, 1970-71; University of Wisconsin, Madison, began as associate professor of political science, became professor of political science, 1971-74; American Society of International Law, Washington, DC, director of an international research project, 1974; United Nations Educational, Cultural, and Scientific Organizations (UNESCO), Paris, France, senior evaluator of programs, 1974-83; International Atomic Energy Agency, Vienna, Austria, monitor of developing nuclear energy technologies, 1983—; head of United Nations inspection team sent to eliminate Iraq's nuclear, chemical, and biological weapons industries, 1991.

MEMBER: American Political Science Association.

AWARDS, HONORS: Scholar, Carnegie Endowment for International Peace, 1971-72.

WRITINGS:

(Editor) *The United Nations Political System,* Wiley (New York), 1967.
The New Nations in the United Nations, 1960-1967: A Study in the Exercise of Political Influence in the United Nations, Columbia University Press (New York), 1970.
(Editor with Eugene B. Skolnikoff) *World Eco-Crisis: International Organizations in Response,* with an introduction by Maurice F. Strong, University of Wisconsin Press (Madison, WI), 1972.
(Editor with Skolnikoff) *International Institutions and the Environmental Crisis,* University of Wisconsin Press, 1972.
(Editor with Leland M. Goodrich) *International Organization: Politics and Process,* University of Wisconsin Press, 1973.
The International Regulation of Pesticide Residues in Food: A Report to the National Science Foundation on the Application of International Regulatory Techniques to Scientific/Technical Problems, West Publishing (St. Paul, MN), 1976.
The International Regulation of Pharmaceutical Drugs: A Report to the National Science Foundation on the Application of International Regulatory Techniques to Scientific/Technical Problems, West Publishing, 1976.
(Editor) *The Changing United Nations: Options for the United States,* Academy of Political Science (New York), 1977.
(With Valerie Hood and Mary Kimball) *A Global Satellite Observation System for Earth Resources: Problems and Prospects: A Report to the National Science Foundation on the Application of International Regulatory Techniques to Scientific/Technical Problems,* West Publishing, 1977.
The Functioning and Effectiveness of Selected United Nations System Programs, West Publishing, 1980.
(Editor with Harold K. Jacobson) *Environmental Protection: The International Dimension,* Allanheld, Osmun & Co. (Totowa, NJ), 1983.

Editor, International Organization, 1972—; contributor to the *New Republic* and *Physics Today.*

SIDELIGHTS: David A. Kay is the author of numerous works on the evolving spectrum of international relations in the twentieth century. After earning both a master's degree and a doctorate from Columbia University, Kay obtained a post as advisor to the United States State Department's mission to the United Nations during the late 1960s. He served as editor of his first book, *The United Nations Political System,* in 1967. Kay's doctoral dissertation from Columbia was later expanded and published in 1970 as a full-length book, *The New Nations in the United Nations, 1960-1967: A Study in the Exercise of Political Influence in the United Nations.* He taught for a number of years at the University of Wisconsin and Barnard College, but left academia in 1974 to direct a project for the American Society for International Law. He later relocated to Europe to take a post with UNESCO, the United Nations' non-political division, but continued to publish numerous books, including several reports on international regulatory laws for the National Science Foundation. One such work, authored with Valerie Hood and Mary Kimball, was 1977's *A Global Satellite Observation System for Earth Resources: Problems and Prospects.*

In 1983 Kay left UNESCO and Paris to take a job with the International Atomic Energy Agency in Vienna. His responsibilities included traveling to countries that were developing nuclear technology in order to monitor their compliance with international standards. A few months after the end of the Persian Gulf War in 1991, Kay flew to Iraq to oversee the eradication of that country's nuclear, chemical, and biological weaponry industries. After uncovering and confiscating some documents related to Iraq's nuclear arms technology, Kay and his team were detained by Iraqi military in a parking lot, and the story made international headlines. Kay related his experiences in Iraq in an article for the *New Republic.*

BIOGRAPHICAL/CRITICAL SOURCES:

PERIODICALS

New York Times, September 26, 1991.*

*   *   *

KELLY, Chris   1940-

PERSONAL: Born April 24, 1940, in Addington, Cheshire, England; son of James (a publican) and Marjorie Kelly; married Vivien Ann Day (a jeweler), December 22, 1962; children: Nicholas, Rebecca.

Ethnicity: "Caucasian." *Education:* Clare College, Cambridge, M.A., 1962. *Politics:* "Left of center." *Religion:* Roman Catholic. *Avocational interests:* Books, art, theater, "collecting the unnecessary," food, wine.

ADDRESSES: Home—24 Harmood St., London NW1 8DJ, England. *Agent*—Anthony Harwood, Aitken, Stone, & Wylie, 29 Fernshaw Rd., London SW10 0TG, England.

CAREER: Granada Television, Manchester, England, producer, 1965-70; Central Television, London, England, producer, 1989-92; Carlton Productions, London, producer, 1992—. Midsummer House Ltd., chairperson; River Court Films Ltd., director.

AWARDS, HONORS: Gold Award, Charleston International Film Festival, for a drama series.

WRITINGS:

The War of Covent Garden (novel), Oxford University Press (Oxford, England), 1989.
The Forest of the Night (novel), Oxford University Press, 1991.
Taking Leave (novel), Hodder & Stoughton (Sevenoaks, England), 1995.

WORK IN PROGRESS: Pegasus Falling, publication by Hodder & Stoughton expected in 1998.

SIDELIGHTS: Chris Kelly told *CA:* "Writing is the hardest and most rewarding thing I know; utterly involving, never as good as it could be, a confirmation of one's existence. I write on a lap-top computer, usually starting at nine in the morning and I work until about four in the afternoon. If I'm producing at the same time, I get up early and write hours before the day job. That's a hellish way to do it."

*   *   *

KELLY, R. M.
   See KELLY, Ronald

*   *   *

KELLY, Ronald   1959-
   (R. W. Kelly; Andrew Nesbit, Ron Spicer, pseudonyms)

PERSONAL: Born November 20, 1959, in Nashville, TN; son of Robert (a shop foreman) and Katherine

Earline (a homemaker; maiden name, Spicer) Kelly; married Joyce Clemons (a secretary). *Ethnicity:* "Irish-American." *Education:* Attended high school. *Politics:* "Moderate Conservative." *Religion:* Baptist. *Avocational interests:* Reading, drawing, computers, Civil War and old west history, collecting toys and books.

ADDRESSES: Home—577 Upper Helton Rd., Alexandria, TN 37012. *Agent*—Joshua Bilmes, Jabberwocky Literary Agency, P.O. Box 4558, Sunnyside, NY 11104-4558.

CAREER: Writer.

WRITINGS:

NOVELS, EXCEPT WHERE NOTED

Hindsight, Zebra Books (New York), 1990.
Pitfall, Zebra Books, 1990.
Something Out There, Zebra Books, 1991.
Moon of the Werewolf, Zebra Books, 1991.
Dark Dixie: Tales of Southern Horror (stories; audiobook), Spine-Tingling Press, 1992.
Father's Little Helper, Zebra Books, 1992.
Slocum and the Nightriders, Berkley Publishing (New York), 1993.
The Possession, Zebra Books, 1993.
Fear, Zebra Books, 1994.
Slocum and the Gold Slaves, Berkley Publishing, 1994.
Blood Kin, Zebra Books, 1996.

Work represented in anthologies, including *Borderlands 3, Hot Blood 5, Cemetery Dance, Cold Blood, Shock Rock, Dark at Heart, Dark Seductions,* and *The Earth Strikes Back.* Contributor of more than eighty novellas and stories to magazines.

WORK IN PROGRESS: Hell Hollow, a novel; *Restless Shadows,* a sequel to *Hindsight; The China Doll,* a young adult novel set during the Great Depression; *Dirty Little Secrets,* a mystery novel; two mainstream novels.

SIDELIGHTS: Ronald Kelly told *CA:* "Born in Tennessee, I often employ rural settings of the American south in which to spin my tales of horror and suspense. During my childhood in the small town of Pegram, I developed an interest in horror, mystery, and monster movies. I originally had hopes of becoming an artist or cartoonist, but I set my sights on writing instead when I began to write feature articles

for my high school newspaper. I graduated from high school in 1977 and immediately entered the work force, developing my writing skills during my spare time. Between 1978 and 1989 I held several jobs, including warehouse worker, drugstore night manager, and welder. In 1986, after delving into several different genres, I decided to return to my interest in horror and the macabre and began to channel my efforts in that direction. I sold dozens of short stories to small-press magazines, and in 1989 I sold my first novel."

*   *   *

KEMP, Roger L.   1946-

PERSONAL: Born August 1, 1946, in St. Paul, MN; married, wife's name Jill; children: Jonathan D. *Education:* San Diego State University, B.S., 1972, M.P.A., 1974; Golden Gate University, Ph.D., 1979, M.B.A., 1984; Harvard University, Diploma in State and Local Government, 1982.

ADDRESSES: Home—421 Brownstone Ridge, Meriden, CT 06451. *Office*—142 East Main St., Meriden, CT 06450; fax 203-630-4274. *E-mail*—roger.kemp@juno.com.

CAREER: City of Oakland, CA, assistant to the city manager, 1978-79; City of Seaside, CA, city manager, 1979-83; City of Placentia, CA, city administrator, 1983-87; City of Clifton, NJ, city manager, 1987-93; City of Meriden, CT, city manager, 1993—. Lecturer at colleges and universities, including University of Connecticut, Rutgers University, Newark Campus, Fairleigh Dickinson University, University of California, Irvine, California State University, Long Beach and Fullerton, and Golden Gate University; consultant to Clifton Center for Strategic Planning. *Military service:* U.S. Coast Guard, 1966-70.

MEMBER: International City/County Management Association (member of task force on local government management education), International Society for Strategic Management and Planning, National Association of Schools of Public Affairs and Administration (member of site visit accreditation team), American Society for Public Administration (member of board of directors, Connecticut chapter; past president of Monterey Bay chapter), Government Finance Officers Association, National Civic League, World

Future Society, Connecticut City Management Association (member of board of directors), Pi Alpha Alpha.

WRITINGS:

Coping with Proposition 13, Lexington Books (Lexington, MA), 1980.
Strategies for Hard Times, Krieger Publishing (Melbourne, FL), 1988.

Contributor to books, including *The Hidden Wealth of Cities,* JAI Press (Greenwich, CT), 1989; *World Infrastructure,* Sterling Publications (London, England), 1994; and *European Urban Management,* Publishing Group International (Hong Kong, China), 1994. Contributor of more than five hundred articles to national and international journals.

EDITOR

America's Infrastructure: Problems and Prospects, Interstate Press, 1986.
America's Cities: Strategic Planning for the Future, Interstate Press, 1988.
Privatization: The Private Provision of Public Services, McFarland and Co. (Jefferson, NC), 1991.
Strategic Planning in Local Government: A Casebook, Planners Press (Chicago, IL), 1992.
Strategic Planning for Local Government: A Handbook for Public Officials and Citizens, McFarland and Co., 1993.
America's Cities: Problems and Prospects, Avebury Press (London, England), 1995.
Economic Development in Local Government: A Handbook for Public Officials and Citizens, McFarland and Co., 1995.
Urban Economic Development: Successful Case Studies from American Cities, Cummings & Hathaway (East Rockaway, NY), 1995.
Handbook of Strategic Planning, Cummings & Hathaway, 1995.

Member of editorial board and book review editor, *Western Governmental Researcher;* member of editorial board, *Encyclopedia of the Future* and *World Encyclopedia of Cities.*

WORK IN PROGRESS: Local Government Productivity; Overview of Municipal Election Systems; Forms of Local Government, completion expected in 1998; *Cities in the Twenty-First Century,* 1999; research on the future of cities, urban life, and local politics.

SIDELIGHTS: Roger L. Kemp told *CA:* "Sometime during the mid-1980s I came to realize that there were few practical books on major issues and challenges facing America's cities. To the extent that there were books in these fields, they were usually written by academics. Since this time, I have written on such timely topics as the public infrastructure, privatization, strategic planning, cutback management, and municipal productivity. All books have a practical focus, and they are written for practitioners and citizens who wish to learn more about these subjects. My writings appear to fill a void in the literary marketplace.

"I hope to educate professionals, students, and citizens about major issues facing local government. Current research and publishing interests include such practical topics as local election systems, forms of municipal governance, and what cities will be like in the next century. My current publisher specializes in library reference works. I feel that this type of publisher will reach the widest audience for my work. Many times I edit volumes to bring together some of the best thinkers in a field, with the goal to orient readers to the subject, bring it all together at the end, and offer a future prognosis on the subject.

"As a working municipal chief executive officer for nearly fifteen years, I have a good feel for emerging topics in my field—America's cities. Having selected a topic, I will then conduct a nation-wide search for other works on my topic. I will spend up to two years collecting materials, selecting only the best for my edited volumes. My most recent work, *America's Cities: A Handbook on Productivity,* involved collecting numerous professional journal articles on the various functions of municipal government. The research effort for this project took about two years; the actual writing took one year. Virtually every night and weekend was spent writing this volume. When published, it will be the most comprehensive piece ever published in the field of government productivity.

"Seasoned world travelers know that U.S. cities lag behind cities in other countries in a number of different ways. In the not-so-distant past, federal grants to communities served as a form of income redistribution. Federal dollars were taken from wealthy areas of the country and given to poor communities to improve their lot. Nowadays, the president and Congress are preoccupied with national issues, such as reducing the debt, and grant funds from the central government have diminished to the point that they have been all but eliminated. Local problems now require locally funded solutions. Elected officials, municipal professionals, and citizens in general need to know how to manage services better, and how to raise revenues without resorting to increased taxation. My books have helped many to achieve these goals."

* * *

KENWORTHY, Eldon (G.)   1935-

PERSONAL: Born May 27, 1935, in Pasadena, CA; son of L. Clifford (a business executive) and Evangeline (a homemaker; maiden name, Blohm) Kenworthy; married Cynthia Witman, August, 1989; children: Lauren. *Education:* Oberlin College, A.B., 1956; Yale University, Ph.D., 1970.

ADDRESSES: Home—Route 4, Box 275, Walla Walla, WA 99362. *Office*—Whitman College, Walla Walla, WA 99362. *E-mail*—Kenworthy@whitman .edu.

CAREER: History teacher at a Quaker school in Germantown, PA, 1958-61; Cornell University, Ithaca, NY, began as assistant professor, became associate professor of government, 1966-92, acting department head, 1990, member of board of directors, Center on Religion, Ethics, and Social Policy, 1979-84, chair of board, 1982-83; Whitman College, Walla Walla, WA, Arnold Professor, 1991, 1992-93, associate professor, 1993-95, professor of politics, 1995—. Visiting faculty member at University of California, Santa Cruz, 1975-76, and State University of New York at Binghamton, 1976; Texas Christian University, Green Professor, 1982; lecturer at educational institutions, including Clayton State College, Syracuse University, Harvard University, Michigan State University, Swarthmore College, Hamilton College, and University of Western Ontario. Leader of workshops for public secondary schoolteachers; member of study tours of Costa Rica, Nicaragua, and Cuba.

MEMBER: Latin American Studies Association.

AWARDS, HONORS: Woodrow Wilson fellow, 1961-62, 1981-82; Social Science Research Council fellow in Argentina, 1964-65; fellow, National Endowment for the Humanities, 1973-74.

WRITINGS:

America/Americas: Myth in the Making of U.S. Policy toward Latin America, Pennsylvania State University Press (University Park), 1995.

Contributor to books, including *Reagan versus the Sandinistas,* edited by Thomas W. Walker, Westview (Boulder, CO), 1987; *Latin America: Its Problems and Its Promise,* edited by Jan Black, Westview, 2nd edition, 1991, 3rd edition, 1997; and *Understanding the Central American Crisis,* edited by Kenneth Coleman and George Herring, Scholarly Resources (Wilmington, DE), 1991. Contributor of more than thirty articles and reviews to scholarly journals and newspapers, including *World Policy Journal, Current History, Journal of Community Psychology, Bulletin of the Atomic Scientists, In These Times,* and *Democracy.*

WORK IN PROGRESS: Research on environmental issues in Central America.

* * *

KERR, Joan P(aterson)   1921-1996

OBITUARY NOTICE—See index for *CA* sketch: Born November 8, 1921, in New Jersey; died of cancer, November 21, 1996, in New Haven, CT. Writer. Kerr is remembered for her work with *American Heritage* magazine. After graduating from Vassar College in 1942, Kerr took a research position for *Life* magazine. In 1954, she joined the staff of *American Heritage* as an assistant editor. During her long career with *American Heritage,* she moved up through the ranks. In 1968, American Heritage Publishing with Kerr as editor, along with Oliver Jensen and Murray Belsky, published *American Album.* In 1974, Kerr, with Scottie Fitzgerald Smith and Matthew J. Bruccoli, put together a picture book, *The Romantic Egoists,* chronicling the lives of F. Scott and Zelda Fitzgerald. She also served as picture editor for *The American Past,* a series offered by the Book-of-the-Month Club. In 1995, *A Bully Father: Theodore Roosevelt's Letters to His Children* was published; Kerr compiled the letters and wrote the accompanying text.

OBITUARIES AND OTHER SOURCES:

PERIODICALS

New York Times, November 22, 1996, p. D19.

*   *   *

KERR, Walter (Francis)   1913-1996

OBITUARY NOTICE—See index for *CA* sketch: Born July 18, 1913, in Evanston, IL; died from congestive heart failure, October 9, 1996, in Dobbs Ferry, NY. Drama critic and author. The New York theater world had much respect for Kerr, long hailed as the "supercritic" (a term coined by *Newsweek* magazine as quoted in the *New York Times*) of that medium. While Kerr had a reputation as having a distaste for experimental works, nobody could attack his expertise on theater, as he wrote several plays and was highly educated. But despite his Catholic lifestyle, he never attacked a play on moral grounds, always defended freedom of expression and fought against censorship. Kerr's career as a critic began when he was only 13 and wrote film reviews for his hometown paper, the *Evanston Review*. Kerr earned a bachelors and master's degree from Northwestern University and in 1938 joined the drama department at the Catholic University of America in Washington, DC. He taught, wrote and directed plays there until 1949. Kerr wrote several moderately successful plays in the 1940s, including *Stardust* and *Sing Out, Sweet Land: A Musical Biography of American Song,* which made it to Broadway. The 1942 musical comedy, *Count Me In,* which he co-wrote with Leo Brady and Nancy Hamilton, was performed at the Barrymore Theater in New York. But the 1958 play *Goldilocks,* co-written with his wife, Jean, and directed by Kerr, lost most of its investment money despite a five-month run. Kerr started reviewing plays in New York in 1950 for the Jesuit publication *Commonweal* and in 1951 joined the New York *Herald Tribune*. He became so respected that theater lovers considered his reviews and the *New York Times* critics to be industry standards. Even those who didn't agree with his opinions often confessed that they loved to read his writings. When the *Herald Tribune* folded in 1966, Kerr joined the *New York Times*. Despite being criticized by playwright Terrence McNally and drama professor Robert Brustein for being biased against experimental works, Kerr maintained a high level of integrity, resisting attempts by the theater crowd to influence

him. Kerr served on the Pulitzer committee and himself won the Pulitzer Prize for drama criticism in 1978. Kerr also wrote several books on theater and criticism, most notably *How Not to Write a Play, The Decline of Pleasure* and *The Silent Clowns,* a critically acclaimed and popular tome about silent film comedians. Kerr retired from the *New York Times* in 1983, but occasionally contributed articles. In 1990, the refurbished Ritz Theater was renamed the Walter Kerr Theater. When Kerr died, all Broadway theaters dimmed their lights that night as a tribute.

OBITUARIES AND OTHER SOURCES:

BOOKS

Who's Who, 148th edition, St. Martin's Press, 1996.

PERIODICALS

Chicago Tribune, October 10, 1996, Sec. 3, p. 11.
Los Angeles Times, October 11, 1996, p. A22.
New York Times, October 10, 1996, p. D22.
Times (London), October 18, 1996, p. 25.

*   *   *

KHAZANOV, Anatoly M.   1937-

PERSONAL: Born December 13, 1937, in Moscow, U.S.S.R. (now Russia); married, November 5, 1963; wife's name, Irina; children: Yaakov. *Education:* Moscow State University, M.A., 1960, Ph.D., 1966; Academy of Sciences of the U.S.S.R., D.Sci., 1976.

ADDRESSES: Office—Department of Anthropology, 5240 Social Science Bldg., University of Wisconsin—Madison, 1180 Observatory Dr., Madison, WI 53706.

CAREER: Academy of Sciences of the U.S.S.R., junior scholar at Institute of Ethnography, 1967-75, senior scholar, 1975-81, acting junior scholar, 1980-85; Hebrew University of Jerusalem, Jerusalem, Israel, visiting professor, 1985-86, professor of sociology and social anthropology, 1986-90; University of Wisconsin—Madison, professor of anthropology, 1990—, fellow of Institute for Research in the Humanities, 1992. Centre for the Study of Nationalism, Prague, co-director, 1996. Moscow State University, senior lecturer, 1974, 1975, visiting professor, 1978, 1979; Chernigov Pedagogical Institute, senior lecturer, 1975; Kiev State University, visiting professor, 1976, 1979; Leningrad State University, visiting professor, 1977; Trenton State College, distinguished visiting professor, 1988-89; Victoria University of Manchester, honorary Lord Simon visiting professor, 1990; guest lecturer at colleges and universities around the world, including Princeton University, University of Toronto, University of Copenhagen, Cambridge University, Harvard University, McGill University, University of Leiden, and Dartmouth College. Academy of Sciences of Azerbaijan, adviser, 1978; State Historical Museum, Moscow, member of scientific council, 1979; Israeli Ministry of Science and Technology, member of Committee for the Absorption of Scientists From the Soviet Union, 1990-91. Conducted anthropological field work throughout Eastern Europe and Asia.

MEMBER: International Union of Anthropology and Ethnological Sciences, World Union of Jewish Studies, Permanent International Altaistic Conference, Association for Central Asian Studies, Association for the Study of Nationalities, American Anthropological Association, Mongolia Society, Israeli Anthropological Association (member of executive board, 1987-88), Israeli Association of Slavic and East European Studies, Central Asian Studies Association (England), British Academy (fellow), Genghiz Khan Society (Mongolia; honorary member).

AWARDS, HONORS: Grants from Ministry of Absorption of Scientists From the Soviet Union, 1985-86, and Jerusalem Anthropological Circle, 1985; fellow of Woodrow Wilson Center for International Scholars, Smithsonian Institution, 1986; grants from Israel Academy of Sciences, 1986-87, Shaine Fund, 1988, and Wenner-Gren Foundation for Anthropological Research, 1989-90, 1992-93, 1993-95, 1995-96; Guggenheim fellow, 1993-94; grant from Centre for the Study of Nationalism, 1996; senior research fellow, Central European University, 1996.

WRITINGS:

Nomads and the Outside World, Cambridge University Press (Cambridge, England), 1984, revised edition, University of Wisconsin Press (Madison, WI), 1994.
Soviet Nationality Policy During Perestroika, Delphic (Falls Church, VA), 1991.
(Editor with Ofer Bar Iosef, and author of introduction) *Pastoralism in the Levant: Archaeological Materials in Anthropological Perspectives,* Prehistory Press (Madison, WI), 1992.

After the U.S.S.R.: Ethnicity, Nationalism, and Politics in the Commonwealth of Independent States, University of Wisconsin Press, 1995.

Contributor to books, including *The Curtain Rises: Rethinking Culture, Ideology, and the State in Eastern Europe,* edited by Hermine G. De Soto and David G. Anderson, Humanities (Atlantic Highlands, NJ), 1993; *Central Asia in Historical Perspective,* edited by Beatrice F. Manz, Westview (Boulder, CO), 1994; and *Pivot Politics: Changing Cultural Identities in Early State Formation Processes,* edited by M. van Bakel, R. van Kessel-Hagesteijn, and P. van de Velde, E. J. Brill (London, England), 1994. Contributor of nearly a hundred articles and reviews to anthropology journals in the United States and abroad, including *Anthropology Today, Environmental Policy Review, Asian and African Studies, Philosophy of the Social Sciences, Central Asian Survey, Comparative Studies in Society and History,* and *Current Anthropology.* Member of editorial board, *Academic Proceeding of Soviet Jewry,* 1986-89, *Nationalities Papers,* 1989—, *City and Society,* 1995, *Eurasian Herald,* 1995, *Acta Eurasica,* 1995, and *Journal of Central Asian Studies,* 1996.

IN RUSSIAN

Essay on the History of the Sarmatian Military Act, Nauka (Moscow, U.S.S.R.), 1971.
(With V. P. Alexeev and L. A. Fainberg) *Primitive Society: Main Problems of Evolution,* Nauka, 1975.
The Gold of the Scythians, Sovetskii Khudozhnik (Moscow, U.S.S.R.), 1975.
The Social History of the Scythians: Main Problems of Development of the Ancient Nomads of the Eurasian Steppes, Nauka, 1975.
(With A. I. Pershits, L. E. Koubel, and M. A. Chlenov) *The Primitive Periphery of Class Societies,* Nauka, 1978.

Contributor of more than a hundred articles to Russian and Ukrainian anthropology journals.

* * *

KIDD, David Lundy 1926-1996

OBITUARY NOTICE—See index for *CA* sketch: Born November 23, 1926, in Corbin, KY; died of cancer, November 21, 1996, in Honolulu, HI. Educator, art collector, writer. Kidd gained prominence as the American who studied and taught Asian traditional arts to Asians who had lost touch with their past after the Communist takeover during the late 1940s. He became fascinated with Chinese life while an exchange student in Peking in 1946. For the next several years, Kidd lectured at Yenching University and Tsinghua University in Peking. In 1950, Kidd returned to the United States to lecture at the Asia Institute in New York City. In 1954, Kidd joined the faculty at Kobe University in Japan, lecturing there until 1971. In 1976, Kidd founded the Oomoto School of Traditional Japanese Arts in Kyoto, Japan, and served as its director. He contributed articles to many journals and art magazines, including *New Yorker* and *Oriental Art.* His account of the Communist's rise to power, the events in Tiananamen Square, and the eventual fall of the traditional system in China are recounted in his *All the Emperor's Horses,* published in 1960, and revised and re-released in 1988 as *Peking Story.*

OBITUARIES AND OTHER SOURCES:

PERIODICALS

New York Times, November 27, 1996, p. B7.

* * *

KIMBALL, Meredith M.   1944-

PERSONAL: Born March 1, 1944, in Hastings, NE; daughter of Marvin M. (a college administrator) and Donna Jane (a schoolteacher; maiden name, Delzell) Fink. *Ethnicity:* "Scottish/German." *Education:* Macalester College, B.A. (summa cum laude), 1966; University of Michigan, Ph.D., 1970.

ADDRESSES: Home—3905 West 19th Ave., Vancouver, British Columbia, Canada V6S 1C9. *Office*—Department of Psychology, Simon Fraser University, Burnaby, British Columbia, Canada V5A 1S6; fax 604-291-3427. *E-mail*—meredith_kimball @sfu.ca.

CAREER: University of Minnesota—Twin Cities, St. Paul, research assistant, 1964-66; University of British Columbia, Vancouver, assistant professor of psychology, 1970-76; Simon Fraser University, Burnaby, British Columbia, assistant professor, 1976-82, asso-

ciate professor, 1982-96, professor of psychology and women's studies, 1996—, head of women's studies department, 1991-93. Public speaker on women's and children's issues and on the ethics of justice and care; presents workshops.

MEMBER: Canadian Psychological Association (fellow; distinguished member, Section on Women and Psychology, 1994), Canadian Research Institute for the Advancement of Women (member of board of directors, 1978-81), Canadian Women's Studies Association, Association for Women in Psychology, British Columbia Women's Studies Association (coordinator, 1976-77).

AWARDS, HONORS: Grants from Canada Council, 1972-73, 1974-75; fellow, Social Science and Humanities Research Council of Canada, 1980-81; Distinguished Publication Award from Association for Women in Psychology, 1996, for *Feminist Visions of Gender Similarities and Differences.*

WRITINGS:

(With E. Gee) *Women and Aging,* Butterworth (Toronto, Ontario), 1987.
Feminist Visions of Gender Similarities and Differences, Haworth Press (Binghamton, NY), 1995.

Contributor to books, including *Women in Canada,* edited by M. Stephenson, New Press (Toronto), 1973; *Women Look at Psychiatry,* edited by D. Smith and S. David, Press Gang (Vancouver, British Columbia), 1976; and *The Impact of Television: A Natural Experiment Involving Three Towns,* edited by T. M. Williams, Academic Press (New York City), 1986. Contributor of articles and reviews to professional journals, including *Psychological Bulletin, Sex Roles,* and *International Journal of Women's Studies.* Guest editor, *Atlantis,* spring, 1979; member of editorial board, *Canadian Psychology,* 1987-90.

WORK IN PROGRESS: Research on the history of women in psychology and psychoanalysis.

* * *

KINSTLER, Clysta (Joyce)   1931-

PERSONAL: Born September 31, 1931; raised in Montana; daughter of Thomas E. (a farmer and carpenter) and Ethel Loretta (Long) Henry; married William Henry Michel, 1949 (divorced, 1964); married John C. Kinstler, 1968; children: (first marriage) seven. *Education:* Attended community college; California State University at Sacramento, B.A. (art history), 1970, B.A. (philosophy), 1973; University of California at Davis, M.A. (philosophy), 1976. *Avocational interests:* Gardening.

ADDRESSES: Home—3861 Lake Knoll Court, Loomis, CA 95650.

CAREER: American River College, Sacramento, CA, instructor in philosophy, 1976-90; writer.

WRITINGS:

The Moon under Her Feet (novel), Harper (New York), 1989.

Also author of the unpublished manuscript *Sisters of the Spirit,* "a trilogy about Herod the Great seen through the lives of Salome, his sister, Mariamne, the most famed of his nine wives, and her Priestess-mother, Alexandra."

WORK IN PROGRESS: A Sacred Place, biographical, creative non-fiction: "Kinstler, who has taught Comparative Religion and Philosophy for years and is now more Buddhist than Christian, believes all religious faith has the same source. Kinstler has been blessed with four sisters, all several years younger than herself. Each has lived most of her adult life in a different state, in unique circumstances, with far different social and religious influences. The five sisters, now mature with nothing—and everything—in common, suddenly discover a treasure they hold in trust: the ability to see in one another's various selves and lives, a rich source of self-knowledge and healing. One of them will write it."

SIDELIGHTS: Clysta Kinstler is the author of *The Moon under Her Feet,* a novel which, as Robert Irwin noted in the *New York Times Book Review,* "supposes that the ancient fertility cult of the Mother Goddess and the Dying King lingered on in Palestine until the lifetime of Jesus Christ and coexisted uneasily with the Judaism of the Pharisees and Sadducees." The novel's chief character is Mari, who has been raised within the tradition of the ancient cult and has been trained to become a priestess. After various escapades, including a stint in a harem, Mari actually becomes a priestess. The notion of reincarnation is

then introduced, and Mari is revealed to be, among other famous females, Mary Magdalene and the goddesses Isis. Mari's lover, Seth, has a similarly complex background, for he is a reincarnation of such figures as Judas Iscariot—Jesus's twin brother in this alternate history—and an Egyptian deity. "Together," as Irwin observed, "Seth and Mari are able to banter away about eternal salvation and Gnostic mysteries." While conceding that the novel's themes make for some "preposterous plotting," Irwin concluded that *The Moon under Her Feet* "is somehow very enjoyable. . . . I only wish Clysta Kinstler's version of the New Testament could have been the true one."

Kinstler told *CA:* "In *The Moon under Her Feet,* I wanted to challenge the most basic and untouchable of all western myths. By this I mean not only the Christian mythos, but the whole Judeo-Christian mythology that begins with the first chapter of Genesis. Feminist scholars had already done the work for me by giving me the tools and research. I only needed to rewrite it as fiction in order to direct it to the wider audience that is reached by art.

"We know that real social transformation can never be a surface phenomenon. It happens from the inside, out. We cannot have an impact unless we challenge the very root assumptions, those ideas we have enshrined under the mantle of the sacred. Just so there is no doubt about what ideas I mean, let me, once again, state the obvious. They are: a) God as an all powerful male, the sole creator of everything; b) God's apparent need and demand for worship and absolute, unquestioning obedience; c) God's separateness and otherness from everything He has created; d) our necessity to do penance to Him for our inferiority to Him; e) the idea that all who do not agree to this idea of God are evil and as God's enemies must be destroyed; f) that God intends the world and its blessings for the use and exploitation of those who believe in Him; and g) that God's justice demands the sacrifice of an innocent victim to atone for our imperfection, i.e., His son.

"Goddess myths give the lie to all these ideas by presenting a deity who does not *create* the world, but one who brings it forth from herself, and paradoxically takes it back again into herself, so that she represents the eternal, cyclic renewal of life from life. She does not command or demand anything of us, but she challenges us to seek meaning and purpose through the spiritual path that leads to identification with her; i.e., with the total PROCESS, rather than with our own solitary individual self.

"It seems paradoxical, also, to learn that the original stories of the sacrifice of the god-king come originally from this old so-called 'pagan' religion of the mother goddess, so despised by the authors of the Old Testament. In this sense, and in many others, early Christianity can be seen as a return to the 'old' religion. What can be the meaning of so barbarous a rite? Of the myth it commemorates?

"[Writer and philosopher] Joseph Campbell says that the sacrifice at the heart of Christian myth symbolizes the *transcendence* of that holiest of all western icons, the ego, the independent, individual self; through its *integration* into the whole of creation. (To *transcend* does not mean to elevate or hold on high; it means to go beyond, to overcome. To *integrate* means to become one with another, to lose one's identity in the whole.) The ancient myth symbolizes this process as a return to the Mother, the Earth, the ground; a descent and return, a death and rebirth. This is the goal of all religion, spiritual discipline, and psychological healing.

"It's hard enough to *become* an ego, a self, an autonomous being. It's so hard that our culture has fixated on it as if it were the final goal. We have forgotten that it is only half of the heroic journey, that if we do succeed in 'finding ourselves,' attaining selfhood, we are only halfway there. Attaining selfhood is just a necessary prerequisite for true liberation, which comes about through transcending, overcoming, going beyond the self we have worked so hard to discover and develop.

"In *The Moon under Her Feet,* I wanted to do with the Christian mythos what [author] Marion Zimmer Bradley did with the male-dominant stories of King Arthur and the Trojan War. I wanted to show the direct descent of Christian myth from Goddess mythology. To show that the holistic, non-violent teachings of Jesus were in fact a return to an earlier ethic of unity with the divine, each other, and the earth. Like Bradley did with her stories, I told mine from the viewpoint of the 'evil' or outcast female of the traditional version, Mary Magdalene. Women are the heroes and doers, the movers and shakers. They think and act out of their own deepest knowledge and beliefs, and take full responsibility for the consequences of their own actions. The theme is in the return to unity, the overcoming of dualism, descent and return, death and rebirth."

BIOGRAPHICAL/CRITICAL SOURCES:

PERIODICALS

New York Times Book Review, July 9, 1989, p. 14.
Placer Neighbors, August 28, 1988, p. 3.
Union (Sacramento, CA), June 15, 1989, pp. 1-2.

*   *   *

KIRKWOOD, Annie   1937-

PERSONAL: Born January 20, 1937, in Fort Worth, TX; married Byron Kirkwood, January 1, 1995; children: Mark Ortega, David A. Ortega, James L. Ortega; (stepsons) Brian, Edward. *Avocational interests:* Painting landscapes and seascapes, reading fiction, playing the piano.

ADDRESSES: Home and office—B and A Products, Route 1, Box 100, Bunch, OK 74931-9705; fax 918-696-5999. *E-mail*—Byron@baproducts, com.

CAREER: Employed by B and A Products, Bunch, OK.

WRITINGS:

Mary's Message to the World, Blue Dolphin Publishing (Nevada City, CA), 1991.
Messages to Our Family, Blue Dolphin Publishing, 1994.
Mary's Message of Hope, Blue Dolphin Publishing, 1995.
Instructions for the Soul, Blue Dolphin Publishing, 1996.

SIDELIGHTS: Annie Kirkwood told *CA:* "In 1987 I began to experience visitations from Mary, Mother of Jesus. It was her request that I take the messages and record them or write them on the computer. The Blessed Mother directed us in compiling the messages into a book. The Blessed Mother is who influences my work, but I must give credit to authors Jean K. Foster and Marianne Williamson, who have also been an influence.

"I have described my writing process as cosmic dictation after I heard the term used by a friend. At an inner signal and the outer signal of the smell of roses or the sensation of a hug, I sit at my computer, say my prayers, and blank my mind. Immediately I begin to hear the Blessed Mother's words. Mary, Mother of Jesus chooses the subjects."

*   *   *

KNAPP, Caroline   1959-

PERSONAL: Born in 1959, in Cambridge, MA; father a psychiatrist, mother an artist. *Education:* Brown University, received degree (magna cum laude).

ADDRESSES: Home—Cambridge, MA. *Agent*—c/o Dial Press, 1540 Broadway, New York, NY 10036.

CAREER: Boston Phoenix, Boston, MA, editor and columnist; freelance writer.

WRITINGS:

Alice K.'s Guide to Life: One Woman's Quest for Survival, Sanity, and the Perfect New Shoes, Plume (New York), 1994.
Drinking: A Love Story (autobiography), Dial Press (New York), 1996.

SIDELIGHTS: As a magna cum laude graduate from Brown University and a respected journalist, Caroline Knapp appeared to many to be the epitome of success. An editor at the *Boston Phoenix,* she also penned a regular column for the paper as "Alice K.," providing a humorous look at the concerns of young, single women. The popularity of this column resulted in the 1994 book *Alice K.'s Guide to Life: One Woman's Quest for Survival, Sanity, and the Perfect New Shoes.* Two years later, however, Knapp's readers would learn about the darker side of the writer's life—her struggle with alcoholism. After having existed as a "high-functioning" alcoholic for years, Knapp was convinced by a drunken incident that nearly ended in the death of a friend's child to enter a rehabilitation facility and stop using alcohol. The decision brought to an end a twenty-year habit; Knapp had started abusing alcohol at the age of fourteen.

Fresh from these experiences and now a member of Alcoholics Anonymous, Knapp wrote her autobiography, *Drinking: A Love Story.* Published in 1996, the book deals with the early roots of her alcoholism, her own father's dependence on alcohol, and how she managed to maintain her career despite regular drunken evenings, hangovers, and blackouts. In a *Newsweek* review, Laura Shapiro called Knapp "a rare writer, with a sophisticated, beautifully controlled style," and concluded, "*Drinking* not only describes a triumph; it is one." On a similar note, a reviewer for *Publishers Weekly* deemed the book "devoid of self-pity, an extraordinarily lucid and very well-written personal account." Moreover, the critic praised the work for its comprehensive treatment of alcohol abuse and recovery. Meryl Gordon, writing in *New York Times Book Review,* judged that "while [Knapp] can be a talented stylist, she hasn't recognized one basic fact: other people's hangovers are boring. Her book rambles. . . ." Christopher Lehmann-Haupt of the *New York Times,* however, praised *Drinking* as "an eloquent account" and noted, "What makes Ms. Knapp's book worth reading is . . . her fluency in writing about her addiction."

BIOGRAPHICAL/CRITICAL SOURCES:

PERIODICALS

Newsweek, May 20, 1996, p. 72.
New York Times, June 13, 1996, p. C18.
New York Times Book Review, June 2, 1996, p. 34.
Publishers Weekly, September 12, 1994, p. 86; March 25, 1996, p. 68.*

*   *   *

KNIGHT, Frida   1910-1996

OBITUARY NOTICE—See index for *CA* sketch: Name originally Frideswide Frances Emma Stewart; born November 11, 1910, in Cambridge, England; died October 2, 1996. Musician, educator, author. Knight gained prominence for her written works in the field of music, and for her work campaigning for the Communist Party. While recuperating from an illness as a young woman, Knight spent time in Europe during the 1930s, witnessing the rise of Fascism. After recovering and graduating from the Royal College of Music, she began teaching music. During the Spanish Civil War, Knight joined the Communist Party in England, and in 1937 set off to provide relief to refugees in Spain. She was later taken to an internment camp in France. She eventually escaped and later chronicled her exploits in an autobiography, titled *Dawn Escape.* She has contributed to numerous journals, including *Cambridge Review, Daily Telegraph,* and the *Morning Star.* Her other major works include *The French Resistance, Beethoven and the Age of Revolution, University Rebel: The Life of William Frend,* and *Cambridge Music.*

OBITUARIES AND OTHER SOURCES:

BOOKS

International Authors and Writers Who's Who, International Biographical Centre, 1989.

PERIODICALS

Times (London), November 1, 1996, p. 23.

* * *

KOLKOWICZ, Roman   1929-

PERSONAL: Born November 15, 1929, in Poland; emigrated to the United States, 1949; became naturalized citizen, 1955; son of William and Edwarda (Goldberg) Kolkowicz; married Helene S. Can, February 13, 1955; children: Susan, Lisa, Gabriella. *Ethnicity:* "Polish American." *Education:* University of Buffalo, B.A., 1954; University of Chicago, M.A., 1958, Ph.D., 1965.

ADDRESSES: Home—21310 Bellini Dr., Topanga, CA 90290. *Office*—Department of Political Science, 4289 Bunche Hall, University of California at Los Angeles, 405 Hilgard Ave., Los Angeles, CA 90024.

CAREER: Rand Corporation, Santa Monica, CA, member of research staff on Soviet politics, 1961-66; Institute for Defense Analyses, Washington, DC, senior associate, 1966-70; University of California, Los Angeles, professor of political science, 1970—. United States Senate Subcommittee on National Security, consultant, 1972—; Center for International Strategic Affairs, director, 1974-82; chair of the foreign policy platform of the California Democratic Party, 1972, 1976; Project on Arms Control (chaired by Jimmy Carter and Gerald Ford), co-director, 1983-85; Project on Politics and War, director, 1985—; has held visiting professorships at the City University of New York, the University of Virginia, 1966-67, and George Washington University, 1967-68. *Military service:* U.S. Army, 1954-56.

MEMBER: International Political Science Association, International Sociology Association, American Political Science Association.

AWARDS, HONORS: Ford Foundation grant, 1975-83; Rockefeller Foundation grant, 1975-77.

WRITINGS:

The Use of Soviet Military Labor in the Civilian Economy: A Study of Military "Shefstvo," Rand Corporation (Santa Monica, CA), 1962.

Conflicts in Soviet Party-Military Relations, 1962-63, Rand Corporation, 1963.

The Impact of Modern Technology on the Soviet Military: A Challenge to Traditional Military Professionalism, Rand Corporation, 1964.

The Role of Disarmament in Soviet Policy: A Means or an End?, Rand Corporation, 1964.

Soviet Strategic Debate: An Important Recent Addendum, Rand Corporation, 1964.

The Red "Hawks" on the Rationality of Nuclear War, Rand Corporation, 1966.

Political Controls in the Red Army: Professional Autonomy versus Political Integration, Rand Corporation, 1966.

The Impact of Modern Technology on the Soviet Officer Corps, Rand Corporation, 1966.

A General and the Apparatchiks, Rand Corporation, 1966.

The Soviet Army and the Communist Party: Institutions in Conflict, Rand Corporation, 1966.

Soviet Party-Military Relations: Contained Conflict, Rand Corporation, 1966.

The Dilemma of Superpower: Soviet Policy and Strategy in Transition, Institute for Defense Analyses (Arlington, VA), 1967.

The Soviet Military and the Communist Party, Princeton University Press (Princeton, NJ), 1967.

War, Revolution, Army: Communist Theory and Reality, Institute for Defense Analyses (Washington, DC), 1968.

(With Matthew P. Gallagher, Benjamin S. Lambeth, and others) *The Soviet Union and Arms Control: A Superpower Dilemma,* Johns Hopkins Press, 1970.

(Editor with Andrzej Korbonski) *Soldiers, Peasants, and Bureaucrats: Civil-Military Relations in Communist and Modernizing Societies,* Allen & Unwin (Boston, MA), 1982.

(Editor with Bernard Brodie and Michael D. Intriligator) *National Security and International Stability,* Oelgeschlager, Gunn & Hain (Cambridge, MA), 1983.

(Editor with Neil Joeck) *Arms Control and International Security,* Westview Press (Boulder, CO), 1984.

Communism, Militarism, Imperialism: Soviet Military Politics after Stalin, Westview Press, 1985.

(Editor with Ellen Propper Mickiewicz) *International Security and Arms Control,* Praeger (New York, NY), 1986.

(Editor with Mickiewicz) *The Soviet Calculus of Nuclear War,* Lexington Books (Lexington, MA), 1986.

(Editor) *The Logic of Nuclear Terror,* Allen & Unwin, 1987.

(Editor) *Dilemmas of Nuclear Strategy,* F. Cass (London, UK), 1987.

(Editor) *The Roots of Soviet Power: Domestic Determinants of Foreign and Defense Policy,* Westview Press, 1989.

SIDELIGHTS: Roman Kolkowicz has had a distinguished career as a political scientist and advisor with some of the most influential think tanks in North America, and is also the author and editor of numerous books and monographs on international security. Born in Poland, Kolkowicz came to the Untied States a few years after World War II and earned graduate degrees from the University of Chicago. Following his graduation he was hired by California's Rand Corporation as a member of its research staff on Soviet politics during the early 1960s; he later took a similar post with the Washington, DC-based Institute for Defense Analyses. His first writings were published during this era under the Rand imprint and include 1963's *Conflicts in Soviet Party-Military Relations, 1962-63* and *The Impact of Modern Technology on the Soviet Officer Corps,* published in 1966.

In 1970 Kolkowicz became a professor at the University of California at Los Angeles, a post he held for several years. From 1974 to 1982 Kolkowicz served as director for the Center for International Strategic Affairs, and from then resumed his involvement in numerous books on international relations and arms control. One such work was 1984's *Arms Control and International Security,* which he edited with Neil Joeck. Its chapters were comprised primarily of papers collected from a symposium given at UCLA's Institute on Global Conflict and Cooperation. Contributors include international luminaries such as nuclear scientist Hans Bethe and postwar American policy-maker McGeorge Bundy.

Kolkowicz was also editor of the 1986 volume *The Soviet Calculus of Nuclear War* with Ellen Propper Mickiewicz. Written and published just as an era of increased hostility between the two superpowers was coming to an end, Kolkowicz and Mickiewicz describe its mission as an attempt "to take a hard look at the forces, institutions, and people that shape the Soviet calculations about war and peace." To do this they cull the writings of a dozen Sovietologists and international political analysts; yet the work was published around the same period in which it was becoming evident that the new Soviet premier, Mikhail Gorbachev, was leading the Soviet nation down a much different political course, especially in regard to nuclear arms agreements. Matthew Evangelista reviewed *The Soviet Calculus of Nuclear War* for the *Bulletin of the Atomic Scientists* and noted that "Although many of the chapters are out of date, others provide important insights into the direction that Gorbachev's policies might take and the constraints they must face."

BIOGRAPHICAL/CRITICAL SOURCES:

PERIODICALS

Bulletin of the Atomic Scientists, December, 1986, p. 47.

Perspective, March, 1985, pp. 34-35.*

*   *   *

KOLLONTAI, Aleksandra M(ikhailovna Domantovich) 1872-1952

PERSONAL: Born April 1, 1872, in St. Petersburg, Russia; died March 9, 1952, in the U.S.S.R.; daughter of a Czarist general; married Vladimir Kollontai (an engineer), 1893 (separated); children: one son. *Education:* Attended school in Switzerland until 1917.

CAREER: Social revolutionary, lecturer, and writer. Soviet Central Committee, elected Commissar for Public Welfare, 1917; joined Worker's Opposition party, 1920-21; appointed by Josef Stalin as Soviet Minister to Norway, 1923-25 and 1927-30, Mexico, 1925-27, and Sweden, 1930-35; negotiated peace agreement between Moscow and Helsinki, 1944; advisor to Ministry of Foreign Affairs until 1952.

AWARDS, HONORS: Order of Lenin, 1933; Order of the Red Banner, 1942.

WRITINGS:

NONFICTION

The Life of the Finnish Workers, [Russia], 1903.
On the Question of the Class Struggle, [Russia], 1905.
Sotsial'nyia osnovy zhenskago voprosa (title means "The Social Basis of the Woman Question"), Izd. t-va Znanie (St. Petersburg), 1909.
Society and Maternity, [Russia], 1916.
The New Morality and the Working Class, [U.S.S.R.], 1918.
Sem'ia i kommunisticheskoe gosudarstvo, Kn-vo Kommunist (Moscow), 1918, translation published as *Communism and the Family,* Worker's Socialist Federation (London), 1918.
Rabotnitsa i krest'ianka v Sovetskoi Rossii, Mezhdunarodnyi sekritariat po rabote sredi (Petrograd), c. 1922.
The Autobiography of a Sexually Emancipated Communist Woman, translation by Salvator Attanasio, [U.S.S.R.], 1926, Herder & Herder (New York City), 1971.
Women Workers Struggle for Their Rights, 3rd edition, Falling Water Press (Bristol, England), 1973.
Selected Writings of Alexandra Kollontai, Allen & Busby (London), 1977.
Selected Articles and Speeches, International Publishers (New York City), 1984.

Contributor to periodicals, including *Pravda.*

FICTION

Love of Worker Bees (short stories), [U.S.S.R.], 1923, translation by Cathy Porter, Virago (London), 1977.
A Great Love (novel), [U.S.S.R.], 1923, second edition, 1927, translation by Lily Lore, Vanguard Press (New York City), 1929, translation by Porter, Virago, 1981.
Red Love (short stories), Seven Arts (New York City), 1927.
Free Love (novel), [U.S.S.R.], 1932.

SIDELIGHTS: Raised in an ill-fated world of wealth and privilege in turn-of-the-century Czarist Russia, Aleksandra M. Kollontai went on to play a significant role in the revolution that would take place in her homeland after the revolution of 1917. Through her political work and her writing, she attempted to ad-

vance the cause of women's rights during the early years of Russian communism.

As a girl, Kollontai had wanted to become a writer; she was also concerned by the poverty she witnessed around her. In 1896, inspired by the crushing social and economic injustices she saw being borne by Russian peasants and the working class, she began to study the philosophy of Karl Marx and contributed an article to a Marxist journal. Because of her continuing interest in Marxism, Kollontai left her family—her husband and young son—in St. Petersburg and spent a year in Zurich in the study of economics. Upon her return to St. Petersburg she abandoned not only her traditional domestic role, but her role as wife and mother as well, by committing herself to a life of political activism. One of the main focuses of her written work would be the rights of women.

In 1909, a year after going into voluntary exiling in Germany due to political pressures, Kollontai's *Sotsial'nyia osnovy zhenskago voprosa* (title means "The Social Basis of the Woman Question") was published in Russia. A serious attempt to distinguish the term "free love" from its associations with promiscuity and depravity, the work was grouped with the large amount of sexually explicit material then being published and received scant critical attention.

During Kollontai's exile she also authored several articles in which she broke with Lenin's vision of feminism and began to advance her own viewpoint on the woman question. In an essay written in 1913 she encouraged other women to develop their own independent nature. Woman had lost "her identity. . . ," Kollontai would write in 1926, in her *The Autobiography of a Sexually Emancipated Communist Woman,* "for the sake of the beloved, for the protection of love's happiness." She encouraged a new dimension to "woman" that expanded the role to include full participation in society.

After the overthrow of the Czarist regime in 1917 Kollontai returned to Russia and travelled throughout the country, encouraging women to see the opportunities open to them through the Soviet revolution. She soon became aware that the revolutionary movement alone would not change the state of women who were mired in an age-old conservative mindset. As Kollontai grew more reactionary in her efforts to break the hold of the Russian traditions that promoted such conservatism, the still-unstable Soviet government grew increasingly wary of her activities. Commissioned to the post of trade delegate to Norway,

Mexico and Sweden beginning in 1923, she was effectively removed from the Russian countryside. However, Kollontai would continue her efforts through her writings.

She published *Love of Worker Bees,* a collection of two novellas and a short story that dealt with many issues of concern to the so-called "New Woman," in 1923. Her second book, *A Great Love,* would be more autobiographical in nature; it described her life in exile in Germany from 1908 to 1917. The novel's protagonist becomes romantically involved with a married man—a communist economist—but the two separate after she realizes that her work on behalf of her socialist comrades is more important than love.

A loyal party member despite her outspokenness on behalf of women's rights, Kollontai survived the Stalinist purges of the 1940s to die of old age in 1952. With an increase in cultural interchange between the U.S.S.R. and the United States during the 1970s, several of her works became available in English translation, illustrating for capitalist readers the underlying conflicts between feminism and supposedly egalitarian communism.

BIOGRAPHICAL/CRITICAL SOURCES:

BOOKS

Clements, Barbara Evans, *Bolshevik Feminist: The Life of Alexandra Kollontai,* Indiana University Press (Bloomington), 1979.
Farnsworth, Beatrice, *Aleksandra Kollontai: Socialism, Feminism, and the Bolshevik Revolution,* Stanford University Press (Stanford, CA), 1980.
Kollontai, Aleksandra M., *The Autobiography of a Sexually Emancipated Communist Woman,* translation by Salvator Attanasio, [U.S.S.R.], 1926, Herder & Herder (New York City), 1971.
Porter, Cathy, *Alexandra Kollontai: The Lonely Struggle of the Woman Who Defied Lenin,* Dial Press (New York City), 1980.*

*   *   *

KOPPESCHAAR, Carl (Egon)   1953-

PERSONAL: Born June 13, 1953, in Amsterdam, Netherlands; son of Willem Reinier and Hendrika Fransisca (present surname, Stottelaar) Koppeschaar; married Louise Elisabeth Timmerman (a nurse); chil-

dren: Ralf Ewald. *Ethnicity:* "Dutch." *Education:* Attended University of Amsterdam, 1972-79. *Avocational interests:* Playing field hockey, travel, collecting antique guns.

ADDRESSES: Home—Haarlem, Netherlands. *E-mail*—carlkop@xs4all.nl.

CAREER: Writer.

WRITINGS:

De Maan, Uitgeverij J. H. Gottmer (Haarlem, Netherlands), 1993, published as *Moon Handbook,* Moon Publications (Chico, CA).

IN DUTCH

Planeten- & Sterrengids, Uitgeverij Fidessa (Bussum, Netherlands), 1975, annual update, 1976.
Glasvezelkabels, STUD Communicatie (Amsterdam, Netherlands), 1983.
Optische Transmissie, PTT Telecom (The Hague, Netherlands), 1988.
Satellietcommunicatie, PTT Telecom, 1990.
(With Stuart Atkins) *Van oerknal tot ruimteschip* (juvenile), Uitgeverij J. H. Gottmer, 1991.

De wereld van telecommunicatie, PTT Telecom, 1993.

Contributor to periodicals, including *KIJK.*

WORK IN PROGRESS: Welcome to Mars!

SIDELIGHTS: Carl Koppeschaar told *CA:* "I studied astronomy and physics before dedicating myself to science writing. In my pursuit of the shadow of the moon during total solar eclipses, I traveled to the most exotic places on earth. The only place left to visit was the moon, where I (whimsically) researched and wrote the *Moon Handbook.*

"My main interests are astronomy, physics, mathematics, geophysics, geology, paleontology, oceanography, meteorology, history, anthropology, travel, and photography. I am nearsighted. When I undo my glasses, I can see things very clearly from an extreme close distance. This enables me to enjoy both a macroscopic and microscopic view of my surroundings. In this way I find beauty in very small things. So I often write about items like grains of sand, raindrops, icicles, snow crystals, and tiny life forms that you can find between street tiles or in dust.

"I am webmaster of ASTRONET, a Dutch/English news service on astronomy, space flight, space research, earth sciences, meteorology, and related subjects. URL: http://www.xs4a11.nl/~carlkop/astroeng .html."

*   *   *

KRISTEVA, Julia 1941-
   (Julia Joyaux, a pseudonym)

PERSONAL: Born June 24, 1941, in Silven, Bulgaria; married Phillippe Sollers (an editor and novelist; divorced); children: one son. *Education:* Attended French schools in Bulgaria; Universite de Sofia, Bulgaria, diplomee, 1963; studied at Academie des Sciences en Litterature comparee, Sofia, and l'Ecole practique des Hautes-Etudes, France; University of Paris VII, Ph.D., 1973.

ADDRESSES: Office—Universite de Paris VII—Denis Diderot, UFR de Sciences des Textes et Documents, 34-44, 2e etage, 2, place Jussieu, 75006 Paris, France.

CAREER: Writer, educator, linguist, psychoanalyst, and literary theorist. Worked as a journalist in Bulgaria; Laboratoire d'anthropologie sociale, research assistant to Claude Levi-Strauss, 1967-73; University of Paris VII—Denis Diderot, instructor, 1972, then professor of linguistics, 1973—; established private psychoanalytic practice, Paris, 1978. Visiting professor, Columbia University, 1974, and University of Toronto, 1992.

AWARDS, HONORS: Chevalier des Arts et des Lettres; Chevalier de l'Ordre du Merite.

MEMBER: Societe psychanalytique de Paris.

WRITINGS:

NONFICTION

Semeiotike, Recherce pour une semanalyse, Le Seuil (Paris), 1969, abridged and translation published in *Desire in Language: A Semiotic Approach to Literature and Art,* Columbia University Press (New York City), 1980.

(Editor, with Thomas Sebeok) *Approaches to Semiotics, Volume One,* Mouton (The Hague), 1969.

(As Julia Joyaux) *Le Langage, cet inconnu, Une initiation a la linguistique,* Le Seuil, 1969, as Julia Kristeva, 1981, translated as *Language: The Unknown: An Initiation into Linguistics,* Columbia University Press, 1989.

Le Texte du roman: approache semiologique d'une stucture discursive transformationnelle, Mouton, 1970.

(Editor, with Josette Rey Debove and Donna Jean Umiker) *Essays in Semiotics: Essais de Semiotique,* Mouton, 1971.

(Editor) *Epistemologie de la linguistique. Hommage a Emile Benveniste,* Didier (Paris), 1971.

Lapu Revolution du langage poetique, L'avant-garde a la fin du XIXe siecle, Lautreamont et Mallarme, Le Seuil, 1974, abridged translation published as *Revolution in Poetic Language,* Columbia University Press, 1984.

Des Chinoises, Editions des femmes (Paris), 1974, translated as *About Chinese Women,* Urizen (New York City), 1977.

(Editor, with Jean-Claude Milner and Nicolas Ruwet) *Langue, discours, societe: pour Emile Benveniste,* Le Seuil, 1975.

(With others) *La Traversee des signes,* Le Seuil, 1975.

Polylogue, Le Seuil, 1977, translation published in *Desire in Language: A Semiotic Approach to Literature and Art,* Columbia University Press, 1980.

(With Jean Michel Ribettes) *Folle Verite, verite et vraisemblance du texte psychotique,* Le Seuil, 1980.

Pouvoirs de l'horreur, Essai sur l'abjection, Le Seuil, 1980, translation published as *Powers of Horror: An Essay on Abjection,* Columbia University Press, 1982.

Histoires d'amour, Denoel (Paris), 1983, translation published as *Tales of Love,* Columbia University Press, 1987.

Au commencement etait l'amour, Psychanalyse et foi, Hachette (Paris), 1985, translation published as *In the Beginning Was Love: Psychoanalysis and Faith,* Columbia University Press, 1987.

A Kristeva Reader, edited by Toril Moi, Columbia University Press, 1986.

Soleil noir: depression et melancolie, Gallimard, 1987, translation published as *Black Sun: Depression and Melancholia,* Columbia University Press, 1989.

Etrangers a nous-memes, Fayard (Paris), 1988, translation published as *Strangers to Ourselves,* Columbia University Press, 1991.

Lettre ouverte a Harlem Desir, Rivages (Paris), 1990, translation published as *Nations without Nationalism,* Columbia University Press, 1993.

Les Nouvelles Maladies de l'ame, Fayard, 1993, translation published as *New Maladies of the Soul,* Columbia University Press, 1995.

Le Temps sensible, Proust et l'Experience litteraire, Gallimard, 1994, translation published as *Time and Sense: Proust and the Experience of Literature,* Columbia University Press, 1996.

Contributor to periodicals, including *Critique, Langages, Langues francaises, L'Infiniti, Partisan Review, Revue francais de psychanalyse,* and *Signs.* Member of editorial board, *Tel quel,* 1971—.

NOVELS

Les Samourais, Fayard, 1990, translation published as *The Samurai,* Columbia University Press, 1992.

Le Vieil Homme et les loups, Fayard, 1991, translation published as *The Old Man and the Wolves,* Columbia University Press, 1994.

SIDELIGHTS: Julia Kristeva is one of the most influential and prolific thinkers of modern France. Trained in linguistics, psychoanalysis, and literary criticism, her cross-disciplinary writings have been praised by colleagues from a wide variety of academic departments. While her commitment to social change has caused her to be embraced by many as a feminist writer, Kristeva's relationship to feminism has been one of ambivalence. She is most widely known for her contribution to literary theory, such as 1980's *Desire in Language: A Semiotic Approach to Literature and Art* and her 1974 examination of modernist poetry and prose entitled *Lapu Revolution du langage poetique, L'avant-garde a la fin du XIXe siecle, Lautreamont et Mallarme,* published in translation in 1984 as *Revolution in Poetic Language.* In addition to her theoretical works, Kristeva has also published several novels; 1990's *Les Samourais* (translation published as *The Samurai*) is a semi-autobiographical work that incorporates characters representative of several Parisian intellectuals of the mid-1960s.

Born in communist Bulgaria in 1941, Kristeva attended French-language Catholic schools before embarking on a career as a journalist in her early twenties. In 1966, after the death of Nikita Kruschev heralded a new wave of Soviet repression in her native country, twenty-five-year-old Kristeva moved to Paris to continue her academic career. While pursuing an advanced degree in linguistics at the University of Paris, she published several essays in linguistic philosophy and contributed to *Tel quel,* a Marxist journal edited by Phillippe Sollers, who would later become her husband. Meanwhile, her renown grew both as a writer and scholar and she became accepted as a part of the heady intellectual circle of the period; she would soon be attending lectures by Jacques Lacan while working as a laboratory assistant for anthropologist Claude Levi-Strauss. While, politically, they would shift to the right over the next three decades, Kristeva's later writings would continue to be imbued with much of the revolutionary fervor Paris exhibited during this era, as well as by the Freudian and Lacanian psychoanalytic theory that captured her interest. Indeed, *New Maladies of the Soul,* an essay collection published in translation in 1995, includes a defense of psychoanalysis written in answer to the rising tide of anti-Freudian scholarship since undertaken in the field.

Kristeva bases her theoretical work on two components of all linguistic operation: the semiotic—that which expresses objective meaning—and the symbolic—the rhythmic, illogical element. What she terms "poetic language" is the intertwining of the semiotic and symbolic, transforming and reshaping one another while providing multiple meanings to their spoken form. Both writers and readers participate in this dialogue between the semiotic and symbolic, making poetic language subjective, versatile, open to myriad interpretations. Though most feminist theorists have considered Kristeva's ideas regarding the semiotic component of language to be valuable in their own women-centered critique, some have also criticized what they perceive as her tendency to stress the written works of men in her studies while ignoring those of women.

Kristeva's area of involvement has shifted in the past decade from linguistics to psychoanalysis. Her recent psychoanalytic works include *Powers of Horror: An Essay on Abjection, Tales of Love* and *Black Sun: Depression and Melancholia,* the last being an examination of female depression. All have been marked by her attempt to expand and amplify the Freudian and Lacanian views of early childhood development. Many of Kristeva's critics have deemed her derivation of a maternally based ethics a move away from feminism, a stance that would seem justified after the mid-1980s when Kristeva took a marked stance in opposition to the aims of the women's movement.

BIOGRAPHICAL/CRITICAL SOURCES:

BOOKS

Benjamin, Andrew E., and John Fletcher, editors, *Abjection, Melancholia, and Love: The Works of Julia Kristeva,* Routledge (New York City), 1990.
Contemporary Literary Criticism, Volume 77, Gale (Detroit), 1992.
Grosz, Elizabeth, *Sexual Subversions: Three French Feminists,* Allen & Unwin (Sydney), 1989.
Lechte, John, *Julie Kristeva,* Routledge, 1990.
Miller, Nancy K., and Carolyn G. Heilbrun, editors, *The Poetics of Gender,* Columbia University Press, 1986.
Oliver, Kelly, editor, *Ethics, Politics, and Difference in Julia Kristeva's Writings,* Routledge, 1993.

PERIODICALS

Choice, October, 1995, p. 286.
Hypatia, Volume 3, number 3, 1989.
London Review of Books, January 26, 1995, p. 17.
New York Times Book Review, November 15, 1992, p. 9.
Observer, December 6, 1992, p. 57.
Romantic Review, January, 1982.
Spectator, November 19, 1994.
Times Literary Supplement, December 4, 1992, p. 20.
Women's Review of Books, January, 1996, p. 19.
Yale-French Studies, Volume 62, 1981.

*   *   *

KUBLER, George (Alexander)   1912-1996

OBITUARY NOTICE—See index for *CA* sketch: Born July 26, 1912, in Los Angeles (some sources say Hollywood), CA; died October 3, 1996, in Hamden, CT. Art historian, educator, author. Kubler gained prominence in the field of art history for his work on Pre-Columbian art. Shortly after beginning his more than forty-year teaching career at Yale University in 1938, his first book, *The Religious Architecture of New Mexico in the Colonial Period and Since the American Occupation,* was published. His studies of Pre-Columbian art and architecture led Kubler to serve as a visiting professor to the University of Chicago, the University of Mexico, and the University of San Marcos in Lima, Peru, among others. He was also the director of the Tikal Project for Philadelphia's University Museum. Kubler contributed articles to art journals and to several anthologies, including the Smithsonian's *Handbook of South American Indians.* His major works include *Cuzco: Reconstruction of the Town and Restoration of Its Monuments, The Art and Architecture of Ancient America: The Mexican, Maya and Andean Peoples, The Iconography of the Art of Teotihuacan, The Shape of Time: Remarks on the History of Things,* and *Building the Escorial.*

OBITUARIES AND OTHER SOURCES:

BOOKS

Who's Who in American Art, 21st edition, Bowker (New Providence, NJ), 1996.

PERIODICALS

Los Angeles Times, October 3, 1996, p. A20.
New York Times, October 3, 1996, p. 52.

*   *   *

KUHRE, W. Lee   1947-

PERSONAL: Born November 9, 1947, in Fort Collins, CO; son of Mason and Jane (Case) Kuhre; married Marjorie Allan (a real estate assistant), September 11, 1971. *Ethnicity:* "Caucasian." *Education:* Colorado State University, B.S., 1970; University of San Francisco, M.S., 1982. *Politics:* Republican. *Religion:* Presbyterian. *Avocational interests:* Astronomy.

ADDRESSES: Home—Scotts Valley, CA. *Office*—Seagate Technology, 920 Disc Dr., P.O. Box 66360, Scotts Valley, CA 95067-0360.

CAREER: Anschutz Corp. (mining company), Denver, CO, environmental and safety manager, 1971-77; Kaiser Engineers, Oakland, CA, environmental and safety project manager, 1978-83; Pacific Bell, San Ramon, CA, environmental and safety manager, 1984-90; Seagate Technology (computer hardware manufacturer), Scotts Valley, CA, executive director of environmental health and safety, 1991—. University of San Francisco, senior lecturer, 1988—. Certified Hazardous Materials Manager; certified by AHERA; registered Environmental Assessor and Environmental Professional. East Bay Animal Referral, foster home provider; National Federation for the Blind, volunteer. *Military service:* U.S. Army Reserve, 1968-74.

MEMBER: Bay Area Environmental Safety Group, ISO 14000 West Coast Working Group.

WRITINGS:

Practical Management of Chemicals and Hazardous Waste, Prentice-Hall, 1994.

ISO 14001 Certification/Environmental Management Systems, Prentice-Hall, 1995.

ISO 14010s Environmental Auditing, Prentice-Hall, 1996.

ISO 14020s Environmental Labelling/Marketing, Prentice-Hall, 1997.

WORK IN PROGRESS: ISO 14030s Environmental Performance Evaluation, publication by Prentice-Hall expected in 1998; *ISO 14040s Life-Cycle Analysis,* Prentice-Hall, 1999.

L

LABANYI, Jo 1946-

PERSONAL: Born March 28, 1946, in Sudbury, Suffolk, England. *Education:* Attended Lady Margaret Hall, Oxford, 1963-67. *Politics:* "Labour."

ADDRESSES: Home—6 Navy St., London SW4 6EZ, England. *Office*—Department of Spanish, Birkbeck College, University of London, 439 Gordon Sq., London WC1H 0PD, England; fax 01-71-383-3729. *E-mail*—j.labanyi@spanish.bbk.ac.uk.

CAREER: University of London, Birkbeck College, London, England, professor of modern Spanish literature and cultural studies, 1971—.

MEMBER: International Association of Hispanists, Asociacion Internacional de Galdosistas, Association of Hispanists, British Comparative Literature Association.

AWARDS, HONORS: Short story translation prize from Translators Association; Kercheville Prize from *Anales Galdosianos,* for an article.

WRITINGS:

Ironia e historia en "Tiempo de silencio," Taurus (Madrid, Spain), 1985.
Myth and History in the Contemporary Spanish Novel, Cambridge University Press, 1989.
(Editor) *Galdos,* Longman (London, England), 1993.
(Translator) Galdos, *Nazarin,* Oxford University Press (Oxford, England), 1993.
(Editor with Lou Charnon-Deutsch) *Culture and Gender in Nineteenth Century Spain,* Oxford University Press, 1995.

(Coeditor) *Introduction to Spanish Cultural Studies: The Struggle for Modernity,* Oxford University Press, 1995.
The Politics of the Family in the Spanish Realist Novel, Oxford University Press, 1997.

Translator of Latin American novels and short stories. Contributor of articles and translations to literature and cinema journals.

WORK IN PROGRESS: A book on Spanish cinema of the 1940s.

* * *

LACHENBRUCH, David 1921-1996

OBITUARY NOTICE—See index for *CA* sketch: Surname is pronounced "*Lock*-en-brook"; born February 11, 1921, in New Rochelle, NY; died of complications from asthma, November 3, 1996, in Manhattan, NY. Editor and writer. Lachenbruch gained prominence as the editorial director for *Television Digest.* After graduating from the University of Michigan, he went to Asia to serve in the U.S. Army, while acting as a correspondent for the *Detroit Times* during World War II. Afterward, Lachenbruch worked as a reporter for the *York Gazette and Daily* in York, Pennsylvania, before joining the staff of *Television Digest,* a division of Consumer Electronics. In addition to contributing articles to trade journals, he also wrote columns for *TV Guide,* among others. His major works include *Color Television: How It Works, Videocassette Recorders: The Complete Home Guide,* and *A Look Inside Television*. In 1993, Lachenbruch was honored by being inducted into the Video Hall of Fame.

OBITUARIES AND OTHER SOURCES:

BOOKS

Who's Who in America, 52nd edition, Marquis, 1997.

PERIODICALS

New York Times, November 11, 1996, p. B9.

*   *   *

LACHMAN, Seymour P.   1933-

PERSONAL: Born December 12, 1933, in New York, NY; son of Louis (a presser) and Sarah (a homemaker; maiden name, Koniarsky) Lachman; married Susan Altman (a sociology professor), December 24, 1961; children: Elliot, Sharon. *Education:* Brooklyn College, B.A., 1955, M.A. 1958; New York University, Ph.D., 1963. *Politics:* Democrat. *Religion:* Jewish.

ADDRESSES: Home—2156 79th St., Brooklyn, NY 11229. *Office*—City University of New York Graduate School and University Center, 33 West 42nd St., New York, NY 10036.

CAREER: City University of New York (CUNY) Kingsborough Community College, Brooklyn, NY, dean and professor of history, 1963-69; CUNY Graduate School and University Center, New York City, professor of education, 1974-80; CUNY Baruch College, New York City, dean of community development, 1980—. New York City Board of Education, president, 1969-74; Conference on Public and Non-Public Schools, New York City, chair, 1975—, procedures editor, 1980-90; National Collaborative Public and Non-Public Schools, chair, 1988—; New York State Senate, senator from 22nd district, 1996—. National Committee on Middle East Studies of Greater New York, Conference on Soviet Jewry, chair, 1980-83.

MEMBER: Politics of Education Association, American Friends of Everyman's University (vice president), American Friends of Israel's Open University (vice president), Council of Jewish Organizations, Interfaith Coalition of Concern on Cults, Phi Delta Kappa.

WRITINGS:

(With David Bresnick and Murray Polner) *Black, White, Green, Red: The Politics of Education in Ethnic America,* Longman (New York), 1978.
(With Barry A. Kosmin) *One Nation under God: Religion in Contemporary American Society,* Harmony (New York), 1993.

Also consulting editor, *The United States and the Middle East,* 1982. Chair of advisory board, *Present Tense* magazine.

SIDELIGHTS: Dean Seymour P. Lachman and researcher Barry A. Kosmin, both of the City University of New York Graduate Center, are the originators of the National Survey of Religious Identification. In 1989 and 1990 the ICR Survey Research Group randomly polled 113,000 Americans by telephone, asking them, "What is your religion?" In April, 1991, the results of this survey were published first in hundreds of newspapers and then two years later in *One Nation under God: Religion in Contemporary American Society.* Filled with graphs, charts, and maps, *One Nation under God* lays out the survey results, and the authors then discuss such topics as the status of certain religious denominations, ethnic solidarity, and religion and politics. Lachman and Kosmin concluded: "There is little evidence that Americans have abandoned religion during the course of the twentieth century."

The raw data in *One Nation under God* may prove to be of use to social scientists and researchers of many kinds. "The authors are good generalizers and move things along well enough," commented Martin E. Marty of the *Christian Century.* "They do slow down for a longish, probably unnecessary and certainly routine hop, skip and jump over American religious history, but they compensate quickly with a brilliant chapter on geography, the 'Who's Where?' of American religion." In a review for *Commonweal,* James R. Kelly called some of the authors' conclusions "old stuff," adding, "There's little additional freshness or energy beyond their survey findings." Kelly, however, noted that "[s]ome of the chapters are good summaries of available data." A *Publishers Weekly* contributor concluded that the survey results "provide rich material for interpretation of the uniquely American religious experience."

BIOGRAPHICAL/CRITICAL SOURCES:

BOOKS

Lachman, Seymour P., and Barry A. Kosmin, *One Nation under God: Religion in Contemporary American Society,* Harmony (New York), 1993.

PERIODICALS

Christian Century, April 13, 1994, pp. 388-89.
Commonweal, March 11, 1994, pp. 25-26.
Publishers Weekly, October 25, 1993, p. 54.

* * *

LADD, Louise 1943-

PERSONAL: Born July 4, 1943, in Montclair, NJ; daughter of Chester R. (an air force officer) and Marion Ladd; married Calvin Cordulack, 1965-77; married Doug Taylor (an actor, director, playwright, and teacher); children: (first marriage) Julianne McKeon, Christopher, Jeffrey. *Ethnicity:* "White Anglo-Saxon Protestant." *Education:* Wellesley College, B.A., 1965. *Politics:* Democrat. *Religion:* Society of Friends (Quakers). *Avocational interests:* Reading, ice skating, acting, gardening, traveling.

ADDRESSES: Home and office—27 Bloomfield Dr., Fairfield, CT 06432. *Agent*—Mary Jack Wald, Mary Jack Wald Associates, Inc., 111 East 14th St., Suite 113, New York, NY 10003.

CAREER: Writer. Fairfield University, organizer and manager of summer theater; teacher of the Writers' Workshop, Fairfield, IL; also taught a seminar at Manhattanville College. Producer at the Connecticut Center Acting Ensemble for 19 years; also worked in the children's room at local libraries.

MEMBER: Society of Children's Book Writers and Illustrators, National League of American Pen Women, Women Writing the West.

WRITINGS:

YOUNG ADULT, EXCEPT WHERE INDICATED

A Whole Summer of Weird Susan, Bantam (New York City), 1987.
The Double Fudge Dare, Bantam, 1989.

The Anywhere Ring 1: Miracle Island, Berkley Publishing (New York City), 1995.
The Anywhere Ring 2: Castle in Time, Berkley Publishing, 1995.
The Anywhere Ring 3: Lost Valley, Berkley Publishing, 1996.
The Anywhere Ring 4: Cherry Blossom Moon, Berkley Publishing, 1996.
(Editor with husband Doug Taylor) *Sandy Dennis: A Personal Memoir* (adult biography), Papier-Mache Press (Watsonville, CA), 1997.

THE DIAMOND DUDE RANCH SERIES:

Call Me Just Plain Chris, TOR Books (New York City), 1997.
The Wrangler's Secret, TOR Books, 1997.
Prize-Winning Horse—Maybe, TOR Books, 1997.
The Perfect Horse, TOR Books, 1997.
Me, My Mare, and the Movie, TOR Books, 1997.
Rodeo!, TOR Books, 1997.
Home for Christmas, TOR Books, 1997.
Belle's Foal, TOR Books, 1997.

WORK IN PROGRESS: Elizabeth/Lilibet, an adult historical novel; *Hush-a-Bye Baby,* an adult suspense novel.

SIDELIGHTS: Louise Ladd told *CA:* "I began to write in my early forties, mainly so I could go to work in my bathrobe if I wanted. My husband Doug, a playwright as well as an actor, director, and teacher, encouraged me in spite of my first pathetic attempts at truly awful short stories. One, 'The Magic Umbrella,' written as an assignment for the Institute of Children's Literature, wasn't quite so bad. Bolstered by praise from Doug and my son, I slowly turned it into a novel for middle-grade readers, *A Whole Summer of Weird Susan.* By the time it was sold to Bantam Books almost two years later, I was hooked on writing as a lifestyle, a passion, and a source of deep satisfaction.

"Great good fortune guided me to join a workshop led by Jean Mercier, former editor of children's books at *Publishers Weekly,* who praised and red-penciled me into decent prose. All the lucky stars were shining when Mary Jack Wald agreed to represent my work. She has stuck by me through thick and thin and has come up with numerous great ideas just when I need them most.

"As a person who cannot live without books, I try to write the sort of humorous, adventurous stories I would enjoy if I were a child, in the hope that the joy of reading will be passed on to the growing generation. My motivations are not entirely altruistic, however; my natural 'voice' appears to be that of an eleven-to-thirteen-year-old. Nevertheless, I am indulging myself at the moment by working on two adult novels, which I find far easier to write. Writing for young people requires using very specific and limiting do's and don'ts, while with adults, it is great fun to use any old word I choose, no matter how sophisticated, and to toss in a *soupcon* of sex once in a while.

"I studied acting for many years, and my writing methods are essentially a direct translation of what I learned on stage. Playing a role or writing a scene, I try to allow my characters to behave naturally under fictitious circumstances. Coming up with story ideas is identical to creating improvisations in class, never forgetting the central impelling force: a sense of urgency. The highest compliment of all is when I am told, 'I couldn't put your book down,' especially when adults say it about my novels for kids!

"I approach writing as a job. After all, if I didn't write, I'd have to put on high heels and sit in an office, taking orders from someone else. On days when I face the computer with dread, thinking of the alternative cures writer's block within seconds. Basically I write because I love to create. Who could ask for anything more?"

*   *   *

LAMBERT, Page 1952-

PERSONAL: Born June 24, 1952, in Denver, CO; daughter of Loren E. (an author) and Jane B. Dunton; married J. Mark Lambert (a rancher), August 26, 1978; children: Joseph Matthew, Sarah Marie. *Ethnicity:* "Anglo." *Education:* Attended University of Colorado and University of Arizona.

ADDRESSES: Home—P.O. Box 5, Sundance, WY 82729. *Agent*—Matthew Bialer, William Morris Agency, 1325 Avenue of the Americas, New York, NY 10019.

CAREER: Writer. Presents workshops; gives readings from her works.

MEMBER: Western Writers of America, Women Writing the West (founding member), Wyoming Writers (past member of board of directors).

AWARDS, HONORS: Neltje Blanchan Memorial Award, 1991; fellow of Wyoming Arts Council, 1993; Pulitzer Prize nomination and National Book Award nomination, 1997, for *In Search of Kinship.*

WRITINGS:

In Search of Kinship: Modern Pioneering on the Western Landscape, Fulcrum Publishing (Golden, CO), 1996.
Shifting Stars (novel), TOR Books (New York, NY), 1997.

Work represented in anthologies, including *The Stories That Shape Us: Contemporary Women Write about the West,* edited by Teresa Jordan and James Hepworth, Norton (New York, NY), 1995; *Tumbleweeds: Writers Reading the West,* edited by William Fox, University of Nevada Press (Reno, NV), 1995; and *Leaning into the Wind: Writing from the Heart of the West,* edited by Gaydell Collier, Linda Hasselstrom, and Nancy Curtis, Houghton (Boston, MA), 1997. Contributor to magazines and newspapers, including *Parabola, Magazine of Myth and Tradition,* and *Guideposts.*

WORK IN PROGRESS: Research on public lands in the west, ancestry tracing, and the historical west.

*   *   *

LANCASTER, Michael (L.) 1928-

PERSONAL: Born January 10, 1928, in Radlett, Hertfordshire, England; son of William (a railway clerical officer) and Edith (Stansfield) Lancaster; married Renate Elisabeth Seeliger (a designer), March 25, 1955; children: June Hannah, Stephen William, Mark Julian. *Education:* Attended Hammersmith School of Building and Arts and Crafts (now University of Greenwich), 1949-55, and University of London, 1955-57. *Politics:* "Liberal/democrat." *Religion:* "Church of England (lapsed)."

ADDRESSES: Home and office—297 Lonsdale Rd., London SW13 9QB, England. *Agent*—Shelley Power, Le Montaud, 24220 Berbiguieres, France.

CAREER: British Rail, assistant architect, 1948-57; architect in London, England, 1957-58; Fry, Drew, Blake & Lasdun, resident architect in Ibadan, Nigeria, 1958-61, architect in London, 1961-63; Derek Lovejoy and Partners, Colombo Plan adviser for the new capital city of Islamabad, Pakistan, 1963-65; Gloucestershire College of Art and Design, began as senior lecturer, became principal lecturer in landscape architecture, 1967-70; Thames Polytechnic (now University of Greenwich), principal lecturer in landscape architecture and head of the division, 1970-91. Michael Lancaster Associates, principal, 1970-81, 1983—; Flora & Lancaster, partner, 1981-83; Thames Landscape Group, principal, 1985—; London Borough of Richmond, member of Conservation Areas Advisory Committee, 1988—; lecturer in Europe, Russia, Japan, and the United States; consultant in Oman, Libya, Saudi Arabia, Majorca, and England. *Military service:* British Army, Royal Army Education Corps, 1945-47; served in Egypt.

MEMBER: Royal Institute of British Architects, Colour Group, Landscape Institute (associate; member of council, 1970-74, 1976-78), Institute of Landscape Architects (member of council, 1968-72).

AWARDS, HONORS: Gold Medal, International Union of Architects, 1986, for *The Oxford Companion to Gardens.*

WRITINGS:

Britain in View: Colour and the Landscape, Quiller Press (London), 1984.
(Editor with Patrick Goode) *The Oxford Companion to Gardens,* Oxford University Press (Oxford, England), 1986.
The New European Landscape, Butterworth (London), 1994.
Colourscape, Academy Editions, 1996.

Author and presenter of "Over the Rainbow," an episode of the television series *The Colour Eye,* BBC2-TV, 1991; and *The Earthdwellers Guide,* a script for Central TV, 1992. Contributor to books, including *Garden Styles,* edited by David Joyce, Pyramid Books, 1990; and *Colour and the City,* edited by Traverne and Wagenaar, V & K Publishers, 1992. Contributor to periodicals, including *Planner, Hortus, Garden, Architectural Review,* and *Landscape Design.*

WORK IN PROGRESS: Writing on color, perception, and aspects of the environment and design.

SIDELIGHTS: Michael Lancaster told *CA:* "My basically unplanned career was transformed by a number of experiences that can only be described as revelatory. The first was a period of six months in Egypt in the army; the second comprised two tours of eighteen months spent in Nigeria with my family; the third was the two years spent in Pakistan with my wife and children. Apart from the colonial overtones and undertones, these three periods can be seen as first-hand experience of three kinds of civilization: the ancient and modern Egyptian, the so-called primitive, but extraordinarily vital, traditional cultures of Nigeria, and the mixed cultures of the Indian subcontinent. My working experience in the last two was marked by a transformation of attitude from that of the building itself to the essential character and function of the building in its context, which subsequently became the foundation of my teaching career, beginning in the School of Architecture, Planning, and Landscape, at the Gloucestershire College of Art and Design.

"A further revelation occurred/began to occur when I undertook a research project on the role of color in the landscape, which became my first book, somewhat misleadingly called *Britain in View* (to link it with a similar book). My initial surprise at the general ignorance of the subject, of the inadequate teaching and inappropriate uses, has scarcely diminished since that time, and it has given rise to a number of lectures, some television work, and my most recent book *Colourscape.*"

*   *   *

LANDES, Richard   1949-

PERSONAL: Born June 24, 1949, in Neuilly-sur-Seine, France; United States citizen; son of David S. (a professor of economics) and Sonia T. (a writer and lecturer) Landes; married Paula Fredriksen (a professor of religion), June 15, 1980; children: Aliza, Noa, Hannah. *Ethnicity:* "Mediterranean." *Education:* Harvard University, B.A., 1971; attended Ecole Normale Superieure, 1972; Princeton University, M.A., 1979, Ph.D., 1984. *Politics:* "Democrat by default." *Religion:* "Jewish (observant)." *Avocational interests:* Squash, travel, e-mail.

ADDRESSES: Home—12 Abbottsford Rd., Brookline, MA 02146; fax 617-566-2781. *Office*—Department of History, Boston University, 226 Bay State Rd., Boston, MA 02215; fax 617-353-2556. *E-mail*—rlandes @bu.edu and rlandes@tiac.net. *Agent*—Sandra Dijkstra, 1115 Camino del Mar, Suite 515, Camino del Mar, CA 92014.

CAREER: Columbia University, New York City, postdoctoral fellow, 1984-86; University of Pittsburgh, Pittsburgh, PA, assistant professor of history, 1986-91; Boston University, Boston, MA, began as assistant professor, became associate professor of history, 1991—. Center for Millennial Studies, director; also director of a project to publish the *Opera Omnia* of Ademar of Chabannes.

WRITINGS:

Naissance d'Apotre: Les origines de la "Vita prolixior" de Saint Martial de Limoges au XIe siecle, Brepols (Turnhout, Belgium), 1991.

(Editor with Thomas Head) *The Peace of God: Social Violence and Religious Response in France Around the Year 1000,* Cornell University Press (Ithaca, NY), 1992.

Relics, Apocalypse, and the Deceits of History: Ademar of Chabannes, 989-1034, Harvard University Press (Cambridge, MA), 1995.

(Editor with D. Van Meter) *The Apocalyptic Year 1000: Studies in the Mutation of European Culture,* Oxford University Press, in press.

WORK IN PROGRESS: Millennial Passions: Faultline of Western Culture, Volume I: *Roosters, Owls, and Bats and the Making of the Year 1000 (Origins to 1000),* Volume II: *While God Tarried: Disappointed Millennialism and the Genealogy of the West (1000-2000),* for Houghton (Boston, MA); research for a multi-volume, fictional saga on the millennial generation of 1000-1033.

SIDELIGHTS: Richard Landes told *CA:* "I write history because I believe that arguments matter; that with good will and learning, we can come to see things we would rather ignore, understand things in ways we would prefer not to deal with. I write because I believe that the Western tradition arises from a most remarkable and contradictory discourse, in which other voices are at once prized and cannibalized, in which the stories we tell ourselves about ourselves are at once unusually honest and terribly misleading. I write to take advantage of this extraordinary, self-critical, self-contradictory moment in our culture when many voices can be heard. I write lest the ensuing cacophony (willed, it seems, by the cultural-terrorist wing of post-modernism) drown out

coherence. I write so that many voices can play, rather than kill. I write because I believe, with Blake, that in the four-fold world a man calls his enemy brother and fights with him in an all-out comic struggle for mutual life; because I believe, with the composers of the Talmud or with a really good squash partner, that the joy comes from the consuming effort to push every limit of our capacities. If I am wrong at the end of the day, fine. Whatever emerges from the battles engaged should be considerably more interesting than what passes for our history right now.

"The major influences on my intellectual career range from Freud and Jung as psychologists; Michelet, Weber, Fromm, and McLuhan as imaginative historians; the Hebrew Bible and Blake as visionary orientations amidst the minute particulars; my mother, who taught me how to read; my father, who taught me how to think historically and love argument. I have been influenced by Richard Alpert (also known as Baba Ram Dass, Buba Rum Cake, et cetera) who taught me to follow my own path and when there was egg on my beard, to admit it: indeed that whole generation of the sixties, including Suzuki, Watts, N. O. Brown, and Fritz Pearls, whose strengths and weaknesses showed me both the potentials and limits of this frail yet glorious flesh, and allowed me to understand Augustine's pessimism without falling prey to it.

"My wife (justifiably) describes my writing process as the accordion method: huge flows of prose, followed by (necessarily) drastic cuts, followed by (equally necessary) explanatory expansions. It took me ten years to pass from my thesis to my first book. None of this would be possible, of course, without the computer. My current solution to the cuts: after my editor and I cut my present book down to size, I will put all my previous little orphans and bastards on my web-site so that 'real' historians can consult the kind of detailed issues that a trade press believes a 'lay' audience will not find interesting.

"I work on the unintended consequences of failed apocalyptic expectations. This comes rather easily since I am one such product, and can therefore look deep into the heart of the phenomenon without too much physical displacement. I backed up into the Middle Ages from a more contemporary interest in the processes of 'modernization' around the world, suspecting that Rostow was wrong to equate the medieval period with 'traditional' society and finding that, indeed, European modernity starts in the eleventh century in a religious form, with a new phase (what I could call secular) in the sixteenth. All this reconfigures our understanding of both the dynamics of modern technologically driven society and the resistances that other cultures exhibit when 'offered' our benefits package.

"Tracking down the role of a mistake (all those who thought the End would happen in their day have been wrong. . .so far) in shaping culture has been difficult. These are beliefs which, like the doppler effect on sound, fade rapidly with their disproof, and the texts tend to preserve only trace elements of beliefs that could, and often did, move people to extraordinary thoughts and deeds. This leads me, often enough, to argue, if not from silence, then from the (rather ample) evidence of a repressed discourse which, before the failure of prophecy, loomed far larger than our retrospective narratives and hostile archivists would have us believe. Having already discovered that medievalists (with notable exceptions) are a fairly starchy lot, and that I will offend many of them anyway, I find that playfulness is an appropriate accompaniment to standing traditional scholarship on its ear. Thus I speak of roosters (who crow the dawn is imminent), owls (hushing that the night is still long, the foxes out, the master asleep), and bats (we blind historians whose radar can only pick up what bounces off the owl-dominated documentation). I myself strive to be a truffle-snuffling pig, digging up all those choice apocalyptic incidents buried just below the surface of the texts."

*   *   *

LANDESMAN, Peter 1965-

PERSONAL: Born January 3, 1965. *Education:* Edinburgh University, 1986; Brown University, 1987; Cornell University, 1991; attended the National Academy of Art and Design, New York, 1994-95.

ADDRESSES: Home—Brooklyn, NY. *Agent*—Matthew Bialer, William Morris Agency, 1325 Avenue of the Americas, New York, NY 10019.

CAREER: Author, painter, and journalist.

AWARDS, HONORS: Joe Kaufman Prize for Best First Fiction, American Academy of Arts and Letters, 1996, for *The Raven.*

WRITINGS:

The Raven (novel), Baskerville Publishers (Dallas, TX), 1995.

Contributor to periodicals, including *New York* and *Harper's.*

WORK IN PROGRESS: Blood Acre (a novel).

SIDELIGHTS: A writer as well as a painter, Peter Landesman is the author of *The Raven,* a novel that revolves around the mysterious disappearance of the real-life pleasure boat *Raven* that disappeared on June 29, 1941, off the coast of southern Maine. In Landesman's version of the tale, thirty six passengers are on board for the sightseeing cruise that ends in tragedy. Only the bodies of the women passengers are discovered, along with the corpse of the captain, who is naked and tied to a tuna keg. They are found near Baily Island by a lobsterman who hides the evidence that suggests that a crime may have been committed. No other passengers are ever seen or heard of again. Amidst their grief, the townspeople wonder what could have happened. Was the craft sunk by a German submarine, or scuttled by the greedy captain for insurance money, or perhaps accidentally run aground in the foggy weather? Landesman shows how the repercussions of this sad day last for decades at the lobstering village where the bodies had kept washing ashore, as well as in their town of origin. In the final chapter, the author returns to that fateful day to solve the mystery of *The Raven.* A reviewer in *Publishers Weekly* commented, "[Landesman] has written an intriguing, promising literary debut."

BIOGRAPHICAL/CRITICAL SOURCES:

BOOKS

Landesman, Peter, *The Raven,* Baskerville Publishers (Dallas, TX), 1995.

PERIODICALS

Booklist, October 1, 1995, p. 252.
Publishers Weekly, September 4, 1995, p. 49.

*   *   *

LANZA, Joseph 1955-

PERSONAL: Born December 12, 1955, in Rochester, NY. *Education:* State University of New York at

Albany, B.A., 1977; Georgetown University, M.A., 1978.

ADDRESSES: *Agent*—c/o St. Martin's Press, 175 Fifth Ave., New York, NY 10010.

CAREER: Writer.

WRITINGS:

Fragile Geometry: The Films, Philosophy, and Misadventures of Nicolas Roeg, PAJ Publications (New York), 1989.

Elevator Music: A Surreal History of Muzak, Easy-Listening, and Other Moodsong, St. Martin's Press (New York), 1994.

The Cocktail: The Influence of Spirits on the American Psyche, St. Martin's Press, 1995.

Gravity: Tilted Perspectives on Rocketships, Rollercoasters, Earthquakes, and Angel Food, Picador USA (New York), in press.

SIDELIGHTS: Joseph Lanza is best known for his criticism and history of rather off-beat subjects. In 1989 he published *Fragile Geometry: The Films, Philosophy, and Misadventures of Nicolas Roeg,* a study of the director of such complex and provocative motion pictures as *Walkabout, Don't Look Now, The Man Who Fell to Earth,* and *Eureka. Video Watchdog* contributor Stephen R. Bissette commented: "By refusing to oust himself from his reading of Roeg and his films, or the process of composing his book, Lanza engages us in a manner attempted by precious few tomes dedicated to the cinema."

Lanza followed *Fragile Geometry* with *Elevator Music: A Surreal History of Muzak, Easy-Listening, and Other Moodsong.* In this work Lanza provides a well-considered chronicle of background music from the eighteenth century, when it was, according to Lanza, written by such composers as Antonio Vivaldi, through to present times. Among the twentieth-century figures featured in *Elevator Music* are such avant-garde composers as Paul Hindemith and Erik Satie, mainstream entertainers ranging from the soft-spoken Lawrence Welk to the flamboyant Liberace, and the less famous but significantly innovative George Owen Squier, who established the company now known as Muzak. In addition to considering the contributions of these and other figures, Lanza notes the extent to which background music has pervaded our culture, and he reports on such music's impressive success within the recording business. David Browne, writing in *Entertainment Weekly,* called *El-*

evator Music "one of the few pop-history books that won't put you to sleep—not to mention the only one that dares to probe the very real connections between shopping-mall music and Devo." *New York Times Book Review* contributor Irwin Chusid noted, "In *Elevator Music,* Joseph Lanza argues convincingly that mood music should be seriously studied."

Lanza is also the author of *The Cocktail: The Influence of Spirits on the American Psyche.* Here he traces the history and social significance of the cocktail, appraising such hard-alcohol concoctions as the martini and the manhattan for their social relevance and their changing status in twentieth-century American culture. He contends that the appeal of mixed drinks rose during the Prohibition period and that the drinks grew further in popularity after World War II as a consequence of cultural changes, including the appearance of fashion-conscious individuals devoted to trends in music and clothes. "A fascinating study of the cocktail and its impact on politics, movies, popular songs and social interaction," judged Digby Diehl in *Playboy. New York Times* reviewer Christopher Lehmann-Haupt observed that the influence accorded mixed drinks in *The Cocktail* "is bound to be tantamount to sounding brass, or a tinkling cymbal."

Lanza told *CA:* "With real life growing more fantastic, the term 'fiction' is becoming redundant. There is a growing market for books that write about persons and events as if they are part of a dream, with the authors caught in the dream they are narrating. Essays and biographies are taking on all of the embellishments and exaggerations once accorded short-stories and novels. I like to call this approach 'speculative non-fiction,' so long as it does not resort to libel."

BIOGRAPHICAL/CRITICAL SOURCES:

PERIODICALS

Entertainment Weekly, March 11, 1994, pp. 52-53; November 24, 1995, pp. 97-98.
Lingua Franca, May/June, 1995.
London Review of Books, July 6, 1995, pp. 3-6.
Los Angeles Times Book Review, May 1, 1994, p. 6.
New York Times, November 23, 1995, p. C18.
New York Times Book Review, February 27, 1994, p. 26.
Orlando Sentinel, August 8, 1995.
Playboy, November, 1995, p. 35.
Request, September, 1994.
San Francisco Chronicle, September 10, 1995.

Times Literary Supplement, July 14, 1995, pp. 6-7.
U.S. News and World Report, February 28, 1994, p. 14.
Video Watchdog, March/April, 1991, p. 57-61.
Village Voice Literary Supplement, April, 1994, p. 5.
Wired, May, 1994, p. 121.

* * *

LAUNIUS, Roger D. 1954-

PERSONAL: Born May 15, 1954, in Galesburg, IL; son of J. Doyle (in business) and Ferne (McCormick) Launius; married, January 4, 1976; wife's name, Vianne Tiffany; children: Dana Kristine, Sarah Anne. *Ethnicity:* "Celt." *Education:* Graceland College, B.A., 1976; Louisiana State University, M.A., 1978, Ph.D., 1982. *Politics:* Independent. *Religion:* Reorganized Church of Jesus Christ of Latter Day Saints. *Avocational interests:* Baseball, chess, computer information.

ADDRESSES: Home—1638 Howard Chapel Court, Crofton, MD 21114. *Office*—History Office, Headquarters, National Aeronautics and Space Administration, Code Z, Washington, DC 20546; fax 202-358-2866. *E-mail*—rlaunius@hq.nasa.gov.

CAREER: Camp Moore State Commemorative Area, Tangipahoa, LA, museum manager, 1982; Military Airlift Command, Scott Air Force Base, IL, historian, 1982-84; Ogden Air Logistics Center, Hill Air Force Base, UT, chief of Office of History, 1984-86; Air Force Systems Command, Andrews Air Force Base, MD, deputy command historian, 1986-87; Military Airlift Command, command historian, 1987-90; National Aeronautics and Space Administration, Washington, DC, chief historian, 1990—. McKendree College, instructor, 1983-84; Weber State College, adjunct professor, 1985-86; Graceland College, adjunct professor, 1990-95; Florida Institute of Technology, Krieger Lecturer, 1993; University of Alabama, Huntsville, Honors Lecturer, 1994; Anne Arundel Community College, adjunct professor, 1995—; Loyola College, Baltimore, MD, History of Technology Lecturer, 1995.

MEMBER: Organization of American Historians, American Historical Association, American Astronautical Society (chairperson of History Committee, 1992—; vice-president for publications, 1995—; member of executive committee, 1995—), American Astronomical Society, Society for the History of Technology, Society for History in the Federal Government, Society for Military History, National Council for Public History, Mormon History Association (president, 1993-94), Western History Association, John Whitmer Historical Association (president, 1990-92).

AWARDS, HONORS: W. Darrell Overdyke Award, North Louisiana Historical Association, 1981, for the article "The Secession Crisis in Rapides Parish;" Best Book Award, John Whitmer Historical Association, 1984, for *Zion's Camp;* grants from National Endowment for the Humanities, 1986, 1990; Sustained Superior Performance Awards, Military Airlift Command, annually, 1987-90; Best Book Award, John Whitmer Historical Association, 1988, for *Invisible Saints;* Evans Biography Award, Mountain West Center for Regional Studies, Utah State University, and Best Book Award, John Whitmer Historical Association, both 1989, for *Joseph Smith III;* Theology and Philosophy Award, *Dialogue: Journal of Mormon Thought,* 1990, for the article "An Ambivalent Rejection: Baptism for the Dead and the Reorganized Church Experience;" Best Book Awards, Mormon History Association and John Whitmer Historical Association, both 1991, for *Father Figure;* Ira C. Eaker Essay Award, *Airpower Journal,* 1991, for the article "A Revolution in Air Transport: Acquiring the C-141 *Starlifter;*" T. Edgar Lyon Award, Mormon History Association, 1991, for the article "Whither Reorganization Historiography;" Sustained Superior Performance Awards, National Aeronautics and Space Administration, annually, 1991-93, and 1995; grants from American Heritage Center, University of Wyoming, 1992, Gerald R. Ford Foundation, 1992-93, Hoover Presidential Library Association, 1993-94, and Religious Studies Center, Brigham Young University, 1993-94; Best Edited Work Award, John Whitmer Historical Association, 1994, for *Differing Visions;* James Madison Prize, Society for History in the Federal Government, 1994, for the article "NASA and the Decision to Build the Space Shuttle, 1969-72;" Current Affairs Award, *Dialogue: Journal of Mormon Thought,* 1994, for the article "The 'New Social History' and the 'New Mormon History': Reflections on Recent Trends;" Steven F. Christensen Award, Mormon History Association, 1995, for *Cultures in Conflict;* General Jay A. Matthews Prize, *Military History of the West,* 1995, for the article "A New Way of War: The Development of Military Aviation in the American West, 1908-1945;" T. Edgar Lyon Award, 1995, for the article "The Murders in Carthage: Non-Mormon Reports of the Assassination of the Smith Brothers."

WRITINGS:

AEROSPACE HISTORY

(Editor) *History of Rocketry and Astronautics,* Univelt (San Diego, CA), 1994.

NASA: A History of the U.S. Civil Space Program, Krieger Publishing (Malabar, FL), 1994.

Apollo 11 at Twenty-Five (electronic picture book), Space Telescope Science Institute (Baltimore, MD), 1994.

(Editor) *Organizing for the Use of Space: Historical Perspectives on a Persistent Issue,* Univelt, 1995.

Editor, "New Series in NASA History," Johns Hopkins University Press (Baltimore), 1990—. Contributor to books, including *Exploring the Unknown: Selected Documents in the History of the U.S. Civil Space Program,* edited by John M. Logsdon, National Aeronautics and Space Administration (Washington, DC), 1995. Contributor to magazines, including *Journal of the British Interplanetary Society, Military History of the West, Physics Today, Air Power History, Historian,* and *Quest: History of Spaceflight Magazine.* Editor, *Space Times: Magazine of the American Astronautical Society,* 1995—; guest editor, *Journal of the West,* 1997.

MORMON HISTORY

(Editor with F. Mark McKiernan) *An Early Latter Day Saint History: The Book of John Whitmer,* Herald Publishing House (Independence, MO), 1980.

Zion's Camp: Expedition to Missouri, 1834, Herald Publishing House, 1984.

The Kirtland Temple: A Narrative History, Herald Publishing House, 1986, 2nd edition, 1990.

(With Lois E. Braby) *The Restoration: Themes of a Growing Faith,* Herald Publishing House, 1987.

Invisible Saints: A History of Black Americans in the Reorganized Church, Herald Publishing House, 1988.

Joseph Smith III: Pragmatic Prophet, University of Illinois Press (Urbana, IL), 1988.

(Editor with McKiernan, and contributor) *Missouri Folk Heroes of the Nineteenth Century,* Independence Press (Independence), 1989.

Father Figure: Joseph Smith III and the Creation of the Reorganized Church, Herald Publishing House, 1990.

(Editor with W. B. Spillman) *Let Contention Cease: The Dynamics of Dissent in the Reorganized Church of Jesus Christ of Latter Day Saints,* Graceland/Park Press (Independence), 1991, 2nd edition, 1993.

(Editor with Linda Thatcher) *Differing Visions: Dissenters in Mormon History,* University of Illinois Press, 1994.

(Editor with John E. Hallwas) *Cultures in Conflict: A Documentary History of the Mormon War in Illinois,* Utah State University Press (Logan, UT), 1995.

(Editor with Hallwas) *Kingdom on the Mississippi Revisited: Nauvoo in Mormon History,* University of Illinois Press, 1996.

Editor, "John Whitmer Historical Association Monograph Series," 1989—. Contributor to books, including *Restoration Studies IV,* edited by Wayne Ham and Joni Wilson, Herald Publishing House, 1995; *We Have Been Believers,* Routledge Publishing, 1996; and *No Man Knows My History Revisited: A Fifty Year Retrospective,* edited by Newell G. Bringhurst, Utah State University Press, 1996. Contributor to magazines, including *Dialogue: Journal of Mormon Thought, Utah Historical Review,* and *Journal of the Southwest.* Contributing editor, *Restoration Trail Forum,* 1976-78; associate editor, *Saints Heritage,* 1987-88; member of editorial board, *John Whitmer Historical Association Journal,* 1985—, and *Journal of Mormon History,* 1990—.

WORK IN PROGRESS: Alexander William Doniphan of Missouri: The Soul of Moderation, for University of Missouri Press (Columbia, MO); *The Race for Space: Cold War Rivalries and the Voyage to the Moon,* Johns Hopkins University Press; *The Spaceflight Imperative: NASA and the Exploration of the Universe,* Garland Publishing (New York); *NASA and the Search for a Reusable Spacecraft: The Space Shuttle and National Politics, 1964-1977,* Johns Hopkins University Press; co-author of *Trailblazing: The Development of Aviation in the American West, 1903-1945; The New Aviation History: Essays on the Development of Flight in America;* research for a biography of Connie Mack, former owner of the Philadelphia Athletics.

*   *   *

LAW, Jonathan 1961-

PERSONAL: Born April 24, 1961, in Westonzoyland, Somerset, England; son of Stanley James (a headmaster) and Dianne (Croome) Law; married Catherine

Hodgson, December 4, 1997. *Education:* Keble College, Oxford, B.A., 1983. *Religion:* Anglican. *Avocational interests:* Literature and arts, music, walking, the countryside.

ADDRESSES: Home—24-B Bierton Rd., Aylesbury, Buckinghamshire, England. *Office*—Market House Books Ltd., Market Sq., Aylesbury, Buckinghamshire, England.

CAREER: Editorial and research assistant to historian and biographer Jeremy Wilson, 1987-89; Market House Books Ltd., Aylesbury, England, editor and writer, 1989—.

WRITINGS:

(Editor) *European Culture: A Contemporary Companion,* Cassell (London, England), 1993.
(Principal editor) *Brewer's Theatre,* Cassell, 1994.
(Editor) *Brewer's Cinema,* Cassell, 1995.
(Editor) *One Thousand Great Lives,* Robinson, 1996.

Contributor to dictionaries, encyclopedias, and other reference books.

*   *   *

LAZARE, Daniel (Henry) 1950-

PERSONAL: Born May 22, 1950, in New York, NY; son of Leon (a chemist) and Edythe (a library assistant; maiden name, Wander) Lazare; married Andrea Simon (an attorney), June 6, 1972; children: Sophia. *Education:* University of Wisconsin, B.A., 1972; Columbia University, M.A., 1982 *Politics:* Socialist.

ADDRESSES: Home—130 West Eighty-Sixth St., Apt. 8A, New York, NY 10024. *Agent*—Tina Bennett, Janklow & Nesbit, 598 Madison Ave., New York, NY 10022.

CAREER: Freelance journalist and writer, New York City, 1988—.

MEMBER: National Writers Union.

WRITINGS:

The Frozen Republic: How the Constitution Is Paralyzing Democracy, Harcourt, Brace (New York), 1996.

Occasional contributor to periodicals, including *New York Times, Good Housekeeping, Village Voice, Tikkun, Art and Antiques,* and *Utne Reader.*

WORK IN PROGRESS: A book about the automobile.

SIDELIGHTS: Daniel Lazare in *Frozen Republic: How the Constitution Is Paralyzing Democracy* "manages within the space of a relatively brief polemic to assign the four pages of parchment to the realm of magical objects in which a museum of natural history might also place the totem poles and the bones of a departed saint," asserts Lewis Lapham in the *New York Times Book Review.* Lazare's premise addresses historical drawbacks that stifle the sovereign power of the national government, particularly focusing on an essentially unamendable clause in Article V, which guarantees each state, regardless of size or population, two votes in the Senate. In *Booklist,* Gilbert Taylor summarized Lazare's thesis: "the Constitution, as a product of its era, unfairly lords the past over the present."

Organized chronologically, the book analyzes historical factors from the Constitution's development in the eighteenth century, to its questionable benefits during the slavery issues of the Civil War, to its applications regarding the political and economic emergence of the United States following World War II, and finally "to the blind worship of the sacred text that has accompanied the last 50 years of the country's descent into bankruptcy and the wisdom of Rush Limbaugh," claimed Lapham. In *Publishers Weekly,* Genevieve Stuttaford called Lazare's approach an "almost academic recap of American history." While Edwin M. Yoder, Jr. of the *Washington Post Book World* praised the author's "impressive display of erudition in both English and U.S. history," he questioned the plausibility of Lazare's "solutions" and challenged his hypothetical outcomes of potential constitutional reform by "we the people." About the author's premises, Yoder explained, "Lazare, so far as I can make out, is a Rousseauist populist who seems to believe that 'the people' (as ultimate sovereigns) can do no wrong and in any case should not be constrained by parchment barriers." Nonetheless, Yoder admired Lazare's enthusiasm and reflection, maintaining that "[o]ne rarely encounters political theorizing of comparable literacy and seriousness."

Lazare told *CA:* "My goal in writing is to shatter complacency and change the way Americans view the world around them. U.S. politics are unexamined in the extreme. Pundits and politicians invoke things like the Constitution, the American Dream, or individualism without paying the slightest heed as to what they might mean. My aim is to show that such concepts are problematic and debatable—indeed that they *should* be examined if society is ever to bring its growing list of problems under control.

"Concerning contemporary writers or thinkers whose work has been influential, I can really only think of two: Michel Foucault, particularly his study *Discipline and Punish: The Birth of the Prison,* and Tom Nairn, whose 1988 book, *The Enchanted Glass: Britain and its Monarchy,* did much to illuminate the connection between Britain's antiquated constitution and its deepening sense of social paralysis. There is a good deal to disagree with in both works, but a good deal that is stimulating and provocative as well.

"Concerning my writing process, I'm very orderly and punctual. I get up at about 5:45 a.m. and work to about 5:15 p.m., at which point I leave to pick up my five-year-old at day-care. I also take an hour or so off during the day to go to the gym.

"I chose to write about the Constitution simply because it is the most gaping hole in what passes for American political thought. Everyone invokes the Constitution and bows his or her head reverently whenever it comes up in conversation. But very few people think about the document in its entirety, much less question why society should be governed by a set of immovable laws dating from the late eighteenth century. My modest contribution is to suggest that people should think and that democracy is doomed if they don't."

BIOGRAPHICAL/CRITICAL SOURCES:

PERIODICALS

Appelate Practice Journal, spring, 1996, pp. 38-39.
Booklist, December 15, 1995, p. 672.
Harper's, March, 1996, pp. 8-12.
Indianpolis Star, May 4, 1996.
Kirkus Reviews, October 15, 1995.
Library Journal, December, 1995, p. 132.
Nation, February 26, 1996, pp. 29-31.
New York Times Book Review, February 4, 1996, p. 11.
Omaha World Herald, July 7, 1996, p. 25.
Portland Oregonian, June 9, 1996.
Publishers Weekly, October 16, 1995, p. 48.
St. Petersburg Times (Florida), May 26, 1996.

Star-Ledger (Newark, NJ), November 17, 1996, section 10, p. 7.
Washington Monthly, April, 1996, pp. 52-53.
Washington Post Book World, February 4, 1996, p. 11.

*   *   *

LEARY, Denis   1958-

PERSONAL: Born in 1958, in Worcester, MA; father a mechanic and mother a maid; married Ann Lembeck (a freelance writer), c. 1990; children: Jack, Devin. *Education:* Emerson College, B.A. (English), 1979.

ADDRESSES: Office—Full Circle Management 929 North Larabee St., Suite 16, West Hollywood, CA 90069. *Agent*—c/o William Morris Agency, 151 South El Camino Dr., Beverly Hills, CA 90212-2704.

CAREER: Comedian and actor. Has performed as a stand-up comedian. Work includes off-Broadway performances: *No Cure for Cancer,* 1991-92; *Birth, School, Work, Death,* 1993; television appearances: *No Cure for Cancer,* 1990, *Denis Leary: No Cure for Cancer,* 1993, *MTV Unplugged,* 1993, *A-hole,* 1993, as Jake in "Lust," *National Lampoon's Favorite Deadly Sins,* 1995, and host of *Comics Come Home,* 1995; album: *No Cure for Cancer,* 1993. Films appearances include *National Lampoon's Loaded Weapon I, The Sandlot, Who's the Man?, Judgment Night,* and *Demolition Man,* all 1993; *Gunmen* and *The Ref,* both 1994; *The Neon Bible,* and *Operation Dumbo Drop,* both 1995; and *Two If by Sea,* 1996. Executive producer of *Denis Leary: No Cure for Cancer,* 1993, and director of "Lust," *National Lampoon's Favorite Deadly Sins,* 1995. Co-founder and director of Emerson College Comedy Workshop.

AWARDS, HONORS: Critics Award, Edinburgh International Arts Festival, for *No Cure for Cancer,* 1990.

WRITINGS:

No Cure for Cancer, Anchor Books (New York), 1992.
Denis Leary: No Cure for Cancer (television screenplay), Showtime, 1993.
(With Mike Armstrong) *Two If by Sea* (screenplay), Warner Brothers, 1996.

SIDELIGHTS: Denis Leary is known for his work as a comedian and actor, having appeared in numerous movies and television specials, including a production of *No Cure for Cancer* for the Showtime cable television channel. Leary's script for his one-man show, *No Cure for Cancer,* was published in 1992. A series of monologues on subjects such as drugs, drinking, cigarettes, life, and death, Leary penned and first performed the work in Great Britain, after his wife experienced complications with a pregnancy while he was taping a program for the BBC. The couple were required to stay in England for several months, which gave Leary the opportunity to perform the show at the Edinburgh International Arts Festival; subsequently, he was given the festival's Critics Award.

Described by an *Entertainment Weekly* critic as "[a] thinking man's Andrew Dice Clay," Leary's work is characterized by a no-holds-barred approach used to discuss subjects ranging from fatherhood to eating red meat. Often he ranges outside the boundaries of political correctness, to satirize what he finds ridiculous, pretentious, and infuriating about our culture. Critics noted that, despite the absence of Leary's sarcastic tone of voice, his chain smoking, and staccato delivery, *No Cure for Cancer* manages to survive the transition from stage to print. A review in *Publishers Weekly* included the comment that, "[t]he volume obviously suffers without Leary's intense, cigarette-puffing presence, but the stage directions and typography help the energy and wit shine through." Mary Carroll, writing for *Booklist,* perceived that some readers may find *No Cure for Cancer* offensive but that "more tolerant folk (and Leary's fans from MTV and Nike ads) will find his primal grumbling brutal, funny, and true."

BIOGRAPHICAL/CRITICAL SOURCES:

PERIODICALS

Booklist, November 15, 1992, p. 572.
Entertainment Weekly, November 27, 1992, p. 74; March 25, 1994, pp. 28-31.
Premiere, April, 1994, p. 50
Publishers Weekly, September 28, 1992, p. 71.
US, February, 1996, pp. 63-64.*

*   *   *

LEAVELL, Linda 1954-

PERSONAL: Born July 30, 1954, in Louisville, KY; daughter of Frank Hartwell (a professor) and Marjory (maiden name, McNeal; present surname, Cretien) Leavell; married Robert Brooks Garner, May 21, 1989. *Ethnicity:* "White." *Education:* Baylor University, B.A., 1976; Rice University, M.A., 1984, Ph.D., 1986.

ADDRESSES: Home—Stillwater, OK. *Office*—Department of English, Oklahoma State University, Stillwater, OK 74078; fax 405-744-6236. *E-mail*—leavell@osuunx.ucc.okstate.edu.

CAREER: Rhodes College, Memphis, TN, visiting assistant professor of English, 1985-86; Oklahoma State University, Stillwater, assistant professor, 1986-91, associate professor of English, 1991—.

MEMBER: Modern Language Association of America, American Association of University Professors (president of Oklahoma Conference, 1996-97), South Central Modern Language Association (member of executive committee, 1996-98).

AWARDS, HONORS: Book Award, South Central Modern Language Association, 1996, for *Marianne Moore and the Visual Arts.*

WRITINGS:

Marianne Moore and the Visual Arts: Prismatic Color, Louisiana State University Press (Baton Rouge, LA), 1995.

Contributor to periodicals, including *American Literary History, Southern Review, Twentieth-Century Literature,* and *South Central Review.*

WORK IN PROGRESS: Research on American women regionalists.

*   *   *

LEHANE, Dennis 1965-

PERSONAL: Born August 4, 1965, in Dorchester, MA; son of Michael (a foreman) and Ann (a school cafeteria worker) Lehane. *Ethnicity:* "Caucasian." *Education:* Eckerd College, B.A.S., 1988; Florida International University, M.F.A., 1993. *Politics:* "Relatively apolitical." *Avocational interests:* Directing films.

ADDRESSES: Home and office—Brighton, MA; fax 617-254-1982. *Agent*—Ann Rittenberg, Ann Rittenberg Literary Agency, Brooklyn, NY 11215.

CAREER: Therapeutic counselor for mentally handicapped, emotionally disturbed children, 1986-91; Florida International University, Miami, instructor in English, 1991-93; Ritz-Carlton Hotel, Boston, MA, chauffeur, 1993-95; novelist, Brighton, MA, 1995—.

AWARDS, HONORS: Shamus Award, best first novel, 1994, for *A Drink before the War.*

WRITINGS:

A Drink before the War (mystery novel), Harcourt (Orlando, FL), 1994.
Darkness, Take My Hand (mystery novel), Morrow (New York City), 1996.
Sacred (mystery novel), Morrow, 1997.

Writer, director, and producer of the film *Neighborhoods.*

SIDELIGHTS: Dennis Lehane told *CA:* "My primary motivation for writing is that I'm not much good at anything else. Plus, if you choose a career in the arts, it's socially acceptable to sleep 'til noon and not groom yourself until dinner.

"In all seriousness, I'm not sure I have a primary motivation. I write because I enjoy it. I would do it whether I was being paid or not. I like telling stories. I like the way words look and the way they sound; I love their rhythm when they are strung together with precision.

"It's hard for me to point to particular influences on my work. I have been compared to Raymond Chandler on occasion, which I find odd, if only because I haven't read Chandler's work since I was nine or ten, and I don't remember much of it.

"While I write mysteries, I very rarely read them anymore, so I'm not sure anyone in that genre affects my own writing in any significant way. The summer I turned fourteen, I read *The Wanderers* by Richard Price, saw Martin Scorsese's *Mean Streets,* and heard Springsteen's 'Born to Run' for the first time, and I remember it all had a strong effect on me. For the first time in my life, I was exposed to literature, film, and music about the kind of people I grew up with, the kind of people I was interested in writing about.

"Otherwise, in terms of literature in general, I have been deeply impressed by the writings of Walker Percy, Don Delillo, Graham Greene, William Kennedy, Gabriel Garcia Marquez, Pete Dexter, Toni Morrison, and Andre Dubus, to name a few. I guess you can see some of their influences in the thematic concerns of my novels, though not really in the execution of the plot or in the tone of my 'voice.'

"I barely have a writing process. I have tried to force myself to write every day, keep a journal, and so on, but all that seems to do is make me self-conscious. I tend to write best in big bursts after long periods of silence. During those bursts, I usually write sixteen hours a day, day in and day out, until the battery runs dry. I don't recommend this process, but it's the only one that's ever worked for me.

"I'm not entirely sure what inspired me to write on the subjects I've chosen. I never intended to be a mystery novelist. Before I wrote my first mystery novel, I was writing a lot of very dark, esoteric short stories, heavily influenced by Dostoevsky and Raymond Carver, Walker Percy, too, probably. I felt like I needed a break, and I decided to try something 'fun.' This turned out to be *A Drink before the War,* my first book. Because I set it in Boston, I tried to tackle the subject of race relations. If you are going to set books in Boston, sooner or later you have to deal with it; it's so intrinsic to the character of the city.

"For my second book *Darkness Take My Hand,* I took an everything-and-the-kitchen-sink approach to it. I wanted to pay homage to the sort of moral murkiness that exists in the writings of Conrad and Greene and Delillo, to create a world in which you're never sure where anyone stands, where all motives are questionable, where the hero himself is very much in danger of becoming what he beholds as he chases some very twisted, evil characters around.

"To a large extent that's what interests me most. What is the hero's culpability in the events in which he's involved? When does the evil from 'without' threaten to become the evil 'within'? There's a popular idea in a lot of mysteries I've read that the hero must be the white knight, the upstanding man in an amoral world. It's a continuation of the Hemingway idea that a man must live by his code, and that code will see him through.

"Maybe because I'm a post-Watergate, post-Vietnam Gen Xer or whatever the current label is for people my age, I just never bought that good-will-out theory.

It seems far more interesting to me to write about very flawed men and women in a very flawed world, trying to do the best they can to get along. Good doesn't always win out, but the *attempt* to do good matters a bit."

* * *

LEIGH, Robin
   See **HATCHER, Robin Lee**

* * *

Le SUEUR, Meridel   1900-1996

OBITUARY NOTICE—See index for *CA* sketch: Born February 22, 1900, in Murray, IA; died November 14, 1996, in Hudson, WI. Author. Le Sueur received acclaim as the author of many historical biographies for children and several books on the hardships of the Great Depression. When she was a young girl, her mother married Alfred Le Sueur, who later adopted Meridel. Alfred Le Sueur founded the Industrial Workers of the World (IWW), the Socialist's party commonly known as the Wobblies. She became acquainted with many artists and literary figures such as Eugene Debs, Emma Goldman, and John (Jack) Reed. Considered left-wing radicals at the time, they influenced Le Sueur's writings. In the 1920s, Le Sueur attended the American Academy of Dramatic Arts and made her acting debut in *The Perils of Pauline* and *The Last of the Mohicans*. She also dabbled in writing; her short story "Afternoon" was printed in *Dial* magazine in 1927. She followed this with several stories, but her writing career was halted in the 1940s. Because of her political leanings and her association with the Wobblies and Marxists, Le Sueur was targeted by Senator Joseph McCarthy's Congressional investigation on Un-American activities. Although she wrote several books during this time, they weren't published until the 1970s. Her literary works include *Little Brother of the Wilderness: The Story of Johnny Appleseed, The Mound Builders, Women on the Breadlines, Annunciation, The Dread Road,* and a biography chronicling the lives of her parents, titled *Crusaders: The Radical Legacy of Marian and Arthur Le Sueur.*

OBITUARIES AND OTHER SOURCES:

BOOKS

American Women Writers, Frederick Ungar Publishing Co., 1979-1982.

PERIODICALS

New York Times, November 24, 1996, section 1, p. 46.

* * *

LIFSON, David S.   1908-1996

OBITUARY NOTICE—See index for *CA* sketch: Born December 29, 1908, in New York, NY; died November 5, 1996, in Manhattan, NY. Educator, playwright, author. Lifson gained prominence as a playwright, producing plays for the Jewish theater audience. While spending twenty years operating his own paint manufacturing company in New York, Lifson decided to try his hand as a playwright. In 1943, his first play, *Familiar Pattern,* was produced Off-Broadway. After leaving the paint business in 1957, Lifson began a teaching career at Pratt Institute, then Jersey City State College, and later at Monmouth College. In 1965, his thesis was published as *The Yiddish Theatre in America.* He contributed articles to magazines such as *Jewish Currents* and *Jewish Quarterly* as well as contributing to *Encyclopaedia Judaica* and *Encyclopaedia Britannica.* He wrote many plays, including *Gift of the Magi, Mummers and Men, Buffoons,* and *Oh, Careless Love!* His books include *Headless Victory, Epic and Folk Plays from the Yiddish Theatre,* and *Sholem Aleichem's Wandering Star and Other Plays of Jewish Life.*

OBITUARIES AND OTHER SOURCES:

BOOKS

National Playwright's Directory, 2nd edition, Eugene O'Neill Theatre Center, 1981.

PERIODICALS

New York Times, November 11, 1996, p. B10.

LITTLEHAWK, Jay
   See GOINGBACK, Owl

*   *   *

LOORI, John Daido 1931-

PERSONAL: Born June 14, 1931, in New Jersey; son of John Peter and Anna (DeStephan) Loori; married; children: three sons. *Education:* Undergraduate studies at Mammouth College; graduate studies at Rutgers University and New Brunswick Polytechnical Institute of Brooklyn. *Politics:* "Active." *Religion:* Zen Buddhist. *Avocational interests:* Photography, videography.

ADDRESSES: Home—Zen Mountain Monastery, Mt. Tremper, NY. *Office*—c/o Shambhala Publications Inc., Horticultural Hall, 300 Massachusetts Ave., Boston, MA 02115. *E-mail*—dharmacom@mhv.net.

CAREER: Zen Mountain Monastery, Mt. Tremper, NY, abbot and teacher, 1980—. Photographer and director of Dharma Communications. Was formerly a physical chemist. *Military service:* United States Navy, 1947-82.

WRITINGS:

The Way of Everyday Life, Center Publications, 1979.
Mountain Record of Zen Talks, Shambhala (Boston), 1988.
The Eight Gates of Zen: Spiritual Training in an American Zen Monastery, Dharma Communications (Mt. Tremper), 1992.
Two Arrows Meeting in Mid-Air: The Zen Koan, Tuttle (Boston), 1994.
The Still Point: A Beginner's Guide to Zen Meditation, Dharma Communications, 1996.
The Heart of Being: Moral and Ethical Teaching of Zen Buddhism, Tuttle, 1996.

WORK IN PROGRESS: Working titles: *Dogen's Mountains and Rivers Sutra: Translation and Commentary, Daily Zen Liturgy Manual, Dogen's 300 Koan Shobogenzo: Translation and Commentary* (with Kazuaki Tanahashi); *Cave of Tigers* (Dharma combat), *Zen and the Environment.*

SIDELIGHTS: John Daido Loori is a teacher of Zen Buddhism who uses an impressive array of tools to communicate with students. In addition to personal contact with individual students, he uses photography, writing, and the information superhighway to reach an international Zen community. His publications have been received as authoritative sources of information about Zen training and the use of koans (paradoxical questions that provide a subject for meditation).

During the 1960s Loori was introduced to Zen by photographer Minor White, who treated photography as a sacred art. Later, as a teacher trained in koan Zen and the style of 13th-century Zen Master Dogen, Loori created photographs to illustrate his first book, *The Way of Everyday Life,* a presentation of Dogen's teachings. The Zen Mountain Monastery's own Dharma Communications, which is directed by Loori, published his 1992 book *The Eight Gates of Zen: Spiritual Training in an American Zen Monastery.* The Eight Gates of Zen is the monastery's own name for an eight-fold path that is taught by practically all Buddhist schools; it is a means of discovering the union of individual and the universe.

In 1994, Loori introduced *Two Arrows Meeting in Mid-Air: The Zen Koan.* This book looks at twenty-one koans in detail. Loori explained the significance of koans to interviewer R.K. Dickson in *Bloomsbury Review:* "Classical koans are specifically designed to short-circuit the intellectual process and open up that aspect of consciousness that's more direct and intuitive. This way of using our minds is not part of the Western educational system. Whether a student is working on a classical koan or a koan of their own in everyday life, there is nothing a teacher can do except point. All the work is done by the student." *Library Journal* critic Glenn Masuchika recommended *Two Arrows* to Zen practitioners as a "workbook" and praised its "conversational" style. A *Publishers Weekly* reviewer deemed the book a "masterful study" and noted its superior "authority" as compared with similar books.

While Loori's work has been most accessible in printed form, he is actively exploring new forms of electronic communication; monastic life does not preclude use of the latest technology. Abbot Loori has created over 30 videos, both instructional and dharma discourses, and over 100 audio tapes of dharma discourses, produced by Dharma Communications. He has produced and directed video documentaries such as: *Now I Know You,* a tribute to the late Hakuyu Taizan Maezumi Roshi, and *Sacred Wilderness,* teachings of the wilderness and the environment. Loori Roshi's latest work is *The Mountains and the*

Rivers Sutra, a video interpretation of Master Dogen's teachings, with original music score and poetry reading. This unique genre of communication combines poetry, visual elements and music in the tradition of the ancient Zen Masters who used artistic expression to communicate the Dharma. Under Loori's direction, Dharma Communications is creating its first interactive CD-ROM, an introduction to Buddhism and Zen meditation, and Zen Mountain Monastery is on the Internet, providing a service called "Cybermonk." Loori told R.K. Dickson, "This offering provides substantial support for practitioners who would otherwise have no contact with Zen communities, teachers, or other practitioners. I think there is indeed a future for the teaching of Zen on the information superhighway in forms that are unimaginable to us at this time."

BIOGRAPHICAL/CRITICAL SOURCES:

PERIODICALS

Bloomsbury Review, September/October 1995, p. 24-29.
Library Journal, June 15, 1994, p. 73.
Publishers Weekly, July 11, 1994, p. 37.

*   *   *

LOUV, Richard 1949-

PERSONAL: Born February 1949, in Brooklyn, NY; married Kathy (Frederick; a nurse practitioner); children: Jason, Matthew. *Education:* William Allen White School of Journalism, Kansas City.

ADDRESSES: Office—c/o San Diego Union, P.O. Box 191, San Diego, CA 92112. *Agent*—James Levine, 330 Summit Avenue, New York, NY 10001.

CAREER: San Diego Union-Tribune, San Diego, CA, columnist; contributing editor to Parents Magazine; commentator for the Monitor Radio Network; consultant to the Benton Foundation; senior editor of KidsCampaigns website (www.kidscampaigns.org). Served as director of Project Concern's OPTION program; participated in conferences including Family Re-Union II, 1993, Family Re-Union III, 1994, and California Focus on Fathers; delegate to Russia for People to People; has spoken before numerous organizations, including the Domestic Policy Council, American Planning Conference and the Urban Land

Institute, and appeared on television shows, including ABC-TV's *Good Morning America* and NBC-TV's *Today Show* and *Donahue,* and on programs for National Public Radio and other radio networks and stations.

MEMBER: National Civic League (Senior Associate).

AWARDS, HONORS: Has received awards from the International Reading Association, National Association of Social Workers, San Diego Academy of Psychologists, California Association for the Education of Young Children, and San Diego Teen Center; Presidential Citation, American Institute of Architects, San Diego Chapter, 1995.

WRITINGS:

America II, Penguin (New York), 1983.
Childhood's Future, Houghton Mifflin (New York), 1990.
FatherLove, Pocket Books (New York), 1994.
101 Things You Can Do for Our Children's Future, Anchor (New York), 1994.
The Web of Life: Weaving the Values that Sustain Us, Conari Press (Emeryville, CA), 1996.

Contributor to periodicals, including *Baltimore Sun, Charlotte Observer, Chicago Tribune, Christian Science Monitor, Cleveland Plain Dealer, Detroit News, New York Times Magazine, Parents' Magazine, Philadelphia Inquirer, Reader's Digest, San Francisco Chronicle, Sierra,* and others.

SIDELIGHTS: In his *America II,* journalist Richard Louv, drawing on interviews and statistics, examines demographic changes in the so-called postindustrial United States. He focuses on rural migration, particularly to the Sun Belt, but also to the Pacific Northwest, Great Plains, and less densely populated portions of New England. He documents the various kinds of American housing, in the process examining the dreams of the inhabitants. Among his subjects are professionals who have returned to small-town living, others who live in tightly secured condominiums, those who support high-tech businesses in rural locations from their backwoods subdivisions, and others who populate developments where residents are categorized by income, age, marital status, and family size, and are made to adhere to strict rules. Louv maintains in *America II* that these migrations are in response to increasingly dehumanizing and fear-laden lifestyles. Commenting on Louv's book, Hal Goodman noted in *New York Times Book Review* that the author "neither proselytizes nor condemns—his tone is hopeful but worried—and he handles a sprawling topic well." However, Goodman concluded that Louv's view of America is based on the untried assumption that the United States already has a postindustrial economy.

Louv followed *America II* with *Childhood's Future,* a volume containing the wealth of three years of interviewing 3,000 parents, children, and others who deal with family matters professionally or on a volunteer basis. In the interviews that form the core of the first half of the book, married couples express their isolation from each other and their children. Both parents and children alike suffer from a lack of connections made during shared family activities. According to Louv, this isolation from parents is in many cases severe, painful, and in the end numbing. Louv indicts not only relaxed standards of morality and fidelity, but an economy that in the workplace ignores such important family matters as daycare accessibility, flexible work schedules, and maternity/paternity leaves. In the second half of *Childhood's Future,* Louv makes ample suggestions for reform: family-oriented workplaces, stronger school-community ties, more family time, and parent networks, among others. While he does not show concretely how these reforms can be accomplished on a broad scale, he describes the successful efforts of some individuals, communities, and businesses. *Washington Post Book World*'s Paul Taylor called *Childhood's Future* "a rich contribution to the literature of family life."

BIOGRAPHICAL/CRITICAL SOURCES:

PERIODICALS

Los Angeles Times Book Review, January 15, 1984, p. 2.
New Republic, December 2, 1991, pp. 40-44.
New York Times Book Review, January 8, 1984, p. 19; January 6, 1991, p. 22.
Washington Post Book World, February 24, 1991, pp. 4, 10.

*   *   *

LOWENSTEIN, Michael W.   1942-

PERSONAL: Born October 15, 1942, in Harrisburg, PA; son of Alfred N. (an attorney) and Sylvia Y. (a laboratory manager) Lowenstein; married, April 6, 1968 (marriage ended, February, 1994); wife's name, Eleanor S.; children: Joanna, Shari. *Ethnicity:* "Caucasian." *Education:* Villanova University, B.S., 1964; University of Pittsburgh, M.B.A., 1965. *Religion:* Jewish. *Avocational interests:* Reading, martial arts, bonsai, music.

ADDRESSES: Home and office—6920 Marshall Rd., Upper Darby, PA 19082; fax 610-394-6450.

CAREER: Customer Retention Associates, Upper Darby, PA, managing director, 1995—. Consultant to ROI Systems.

MEMBER: Society of Consumer Affairs Professionals, American Management Association, American Society for Quality Control.

AWARDS, HONORS: Golden Quill Award, ASQC Quality Press; Management Achievement Award, American Society of Association Executives.

WRITINGS:

Customer Retention, ASQC Quality Press (Milwaukee, WI), 1995.
(Co-author) *Redefining Consumer Affairs,* Society of Consumer Affairs Professionals, 1996.
Customer Retention Blueprints, Greenwood Press (Westport, CT), in press.

Contributor to periodicals.

WORK IN PROGRESS: Research on customer recovery.

SIDELIGHTS: Michael W. Lowenstein told *CA:* "My interest in the subject of customer retention and customer loyalty goes back over twenty years, to when I was responsible for marketing research for a major, limited edition collectibles marketer and then for a fast food restaurant chain. It was apparent to me then, as it is now, that the attitudes of customers often had little to do with their intended and actual purchase behavior; that is, loyalty.

"The process of writing books and articles on the subject, and the research involved, is important in keeping my ideas fresh. My style is more of a synthesizer than an innovator, and I look for material that supports the core concept of customer loyalty and value creation within corporations."

LUNDQUIST, Leslie (Dwynn Heeler)

PERSONAL: Born in Marietta, GA; daughter of Charles W. and Irene (Barrott) Heeler; married Garth Christian Lundquist (marriage ended); children: Christopher Martin. *Education:* Stanford University, A.B., 1982. *Religion:* "Spiritual thinker." *Avocational interests:* Music, dance, theater, herbal lore, natural health.

ADDRESSES: Home—Houston, TX. *E-mail*—leslie @cre8tive.com. *Agent*—Waterside Productions, Cardiff-by-the-Sea, CA.

CAREER: SRI International, Menlo Park, CA, began as computer operator, became supervisor of DEC Computer Facility and programmer for Artificial Intelligence Laboratory, 1979-83; Symbolics, Inc., Cambridge, MA, member of technical staff, 1983-84; Xerox Office Systems Division, Palo Alto, CA, senior technical writer, 1984-85; Boeing Computer Services, Advanced Technology Center, Bellevue, WA, systems analyst, 1987-88; Atherton Technology, Sunnyvale, CA, senior technical writer, 1989-90; Apple Computer, Cupertino, CA, senior technical writer for object-based systems and Taligent, 1990-92; Kaleida Laboratories, Mountain View, CA, publications manager, 1992-94; Creative Professional, Inc. (information design consultant), owner, 1994—. Women's Wire (computer online service), forum host, 1995; consultant to MITRE Corp., Massachusetts Institute of Technology, and Atari.

WRITINGS:

(With Dan Lynch) *Digital Money: The New Era of Internet Commerce,* Wiley (New York), 1996.

WORK IN PROGRESS: Research on Internet business models.

SIDELIGHTS: Leslie Lundquist told *CA:* "I like to write because I like to simplify complicated things for people to understand. I hate to write because that process can be difficult! I think of writers as honeybees, taking in information and digesting it into something wonderful.

"I like writing as a profession because it lets me manage and schedule my own time. I call it 'my secret life as a writer' because I tend to have a 'housewife' sort of life during the day, and I write late at night when my son is asleep. My friends never really see me working, although we discuss a lot of ideas that end up in my work. Thus I end up with a lot of acknowledgements to them.

"I'm glad I finally got to write a book about the Internet. I dreamed for about five years of writing a book, and when the opportunity finally came my way, it was just as great as I had imagined. I had always heard 'write about what you know,' and by writing I discovered that I already knew more than I had thought. Writing was just a matter of research to get the data in order and sitting down to write every day."

*   *   *

LYNCH, Chris 1962-

PERSONAL: Born July 2, 1962, in Boston, MA; son of Edward (a bus driver) and Dorothy (a receptionist; maiden name, O'Brien) Lynch; married Tina Coviello (a technical support manager), August 5, 1989; children: Sophia, Walker. *Education:* Suffolk University, B.A. in journalism, 1983; Emerson University, M.A. in professional writing and publishing, 1991. *Politics:* "Decidedly no affiliation." *Religion:* "Decidedly no affiliation." *Avocational interests:* Running.

ADDRESSES: Agent—Fran Lebowitz, Writers House, 21 West 26th St., New York, NY 10010.

CAREER: Writer. Teacher of writing at Emerson University, 1995, and Vermont College, 1997—. Proofreader of financial reports, 1985-89. Conducted a writing workshop at the Boston Public Library, summer, 1994.

MEMBER: Authors Guild, Author's League of America.

AWARDS, HONORS: Best Books of the Year list, *School Library Journal,* 1993, for *Shadow Boxer;* American Library Association (ALA) Best Books for Young Adults and Quick Picks for Reluctant Young Adult Readers citations, 1993, for *Shadow Boxer,* 1994, for *Iceman* and *Gypsy Davey,* and 1996, for *Slot Machine;* Blue Ribbon Award, *Bulletin of the Center for Children's Books,* 1994, for *Iceman* and *Gypsy Davey;* Editors' Choice award, *Booklist,* 1994, for *Gypsy Davey;* finalist, Dorothy Canfield Fisher Award and Book of the Year award from *Hungry Mind Review,* for *Slot Machine.*

WRITINGS:

Shadow Boxer, HarperCollins (New York), 1993.
Iceman, HarperCollins, 1994.
Gypsy Davey, HarperCollins, 1994.
Slot Machine, HarperCollins, 1995.
Political Timber, HarperCollins, 1996.

"BLUE-EYED SON" SERIES

Mick, HarperCollins, 1996.
Blood Relations, HarperCollins, 1996.
Dog Eat Dog, HarperCollins, 1996.

"HE-MAN WOMAN-HATERS CLUB" SERIES; FOR YOUNG
     READERS

Johnny Chest Hair, HarperCollins, 1997.
Babes in the Woods, HarperCollins, 1997.

OTHER

Also a contributor of a short story, "The Hobbyist," to *Ultimate Sports,* edited by Donald Gallo, Delacorte, 1995, and another short story to *Night Terrors,* edited by Lois Duncan, Simon & Schuster, 1996. Contributor of stories and articles to periodicals, including *Signal, School Library Journal,* and *Boston Magazine.*

Lynch's books have also been published in Ireland, Taiwan, and Italy, the last two in translation.

WORK IN PROGRESS: Three other titles in the "He-Man Woman-Haters Club" series for HarperCollins.

SIDELIGHTS: Chris Lynch writes tough and edgy streetwise fiction. Episodic and fast-paced, his stories and novels question the male stereotypes of macho identity and inarticulate violence. His youthful characters are often athletes, or wanna-be athletes, or kids who have been churned up and spit out by the system. Outsiders, Lynch's protagonists desperately want to just be themselves. "You were not born into physical greatness and all the love and worship and happiness that are guaranteed with it," the narrator muses in the short story "The Hobbyist." "But fortunately you were born American. So you can buy into it."

Using irony and a searing honesty that cuts through adolescent facades, Lynch lays out a deck of impressionistic cards of what it means to be young and urban and male in America in the 1990s, warts and all. "I was speaking at a school for disturbed kids," Lynch once commented in an interview, "and this one kid came up and said to me that everybody I write about is weird. And I thought, 'Yes. I've done my job.' Because beneath it all, we're all weird. And it's okay. It's okay to be who you are. You don't have to be what others say you should be. It's my job as a novelist to celebrate the oddities, or at least make them less stigmatized."

In his ten novels for young adults and young readers, Lynch has used sports such as boxing and hockey as metaphors for male rites of passage, has portrayed lonely outsiders and troubled families struggling to make it, and has dealt with racism and exploitation. Violence plays a part in these books, "the hovering menace that is urban life," as Lynch once described it, but his violence is never gratuitous. Lynch is part of a new generation of YA writers who are not afraid to tackle formerly taboo subjects, who are reaching out to adolescent readers with topics relevant to them and written in an idiom they understand. In a *Horn Book* review of several hard-hitting young adult novels including Lynch's *Iceman,* Patty Campbell noted that "in the hands of skillful writers, material that could be repellent is transcended to make a larger statement about coming of age. . . . Perhaps we can hope that it is a mark of the growing maturity of the genre . . . that serious YA novels, like adult novels, are coming to be judged on the basis of the quality of the whole work."

If Lynch can speak so directly to young readers, it is because he has been there. "Growing up I listened way too much to the rules as they were handed down," he recalled. Though his youth was a much more stable one than those of many of his fictional characters, he was no stranger to the urban melange that is the backdrop for most of his work. Fifth of seven children, he grew up in the Jamaica Plains district of Boston, one that was once an Irish stronghold, but which had become largely Hispanic by the time of Lynch's youth. His father died when Lynch was five, and the family was then brought up by a single mother. "She did a good job of covering it up, but things were pretty lean back then," Lynch commented. "We were definitely a free cheese family, though I never felt deprived as a kid." A somewhat reclusive child, Lynch attended Catholic schools through primary and secondary levels. "I wasn't what you'd call bookish," Lynch noted, "though I do have a very clear memory of sparking to the Dr. Seuss book club. It made a difference that I got my own book in the mail. It wasn't so much the book itself, but the fact that it was mine. . . . In the fourth or fifth grade I was eating up military history books, then some sports bios, but not fiction. Not yet."

His grammar school experience was what he calls "nurturing," but high school was a different matter for Lynch. "I hated high school—every minute. It was rigid, kind of a factory. An all-boys' football factory. Nothing like the arts was encouraged in any way." Though Lynch had participated in street hockey, football, and baseball as a younger kid, by high school he had stopped playing. "When it was fun I played," Lynch recalled. But the football-factory ethic ruined it for him, a sentiment echoed by protagonists in many of his novels. "I'm not against all athletics," Lynch said in his interview. "Sports has a tremendous potential for channeling energy. But instead it mostly encourages the macho ethos and schools let athletes run wild. This carries through life, and results in Mike Tysons. People who were never told what they could not do."

High school was discouraging enough for Lynch that he dropped out in his junior year and entered Boston University where he studied political science. "And then I thought, 'Oh no, I'm going to get stuck with this thing that is only a beard.'" A news-writing course at Boston University provided a stimulus for change, for discovering what he really wanted to be doing. "I transferred to Suffolk where I took more writing classes, finally majoring in journalism. But I was still hiding from myself. At Suffolk I took a novel writing class which helped lead me closer to what I was really going for all the time. But I just wouldn't allow it. Wouldn't let myself say that I wanted to be an artist."

After graduation, Lynch spent about six years trying to let himself admit that simple fact. He took jobs as a house painter, a driver of a moving van, and for several years proofread financial reports. "That kind of work can really give a person a shove," Lynch commented. "I figured there had to be something more out there. I had enough optimism to think there was something for me to learn." In 1989 Lynch enrolled in a master's program at Boston's Emerson University in professional writing and publishing. "So I was still hiding, you know, having to think of myself as an editor or publisher. Not a creative writer. All this reflects my feeling that you've got to put up first; you've got to earn titles. I actually only told my mother what I was doing *after* I published my first book."

At Emerson University Lynch found a new direction. Taking a children's writing class from Jack Gantos, he began what became his first published novel, *Shadow Boxer,* as a class assignment. "We were supposed to write five pages on a childhood incident," Lynch commented. "I had a vague idea of writing about some things my brother and I had done in our youth, but as soon as I sat down with it, I was off to the races. The stuff just poured out. Before this all my adult fiction had been too stylized, what everybody else was doing. What I thought was expected of me. I had no emotional investment in my own work, and that makes all the difference. With this assignment, the very first words actually made it into the actual published book. I was fortunate to discover early on in my career that one bit of writing magic—matching yourself and your material."

This early assignment grew until Lynch had written about sixty percent of his novel in class. If he had stutter-stepped about getting into writing, there was no hesitation once he'd begun. With the help of Gantos, he first tried to place his manuscript with various editors, then found an agent who quickly found a willing publisher. By 1992, he was on his way, *Shadow Boxer* being readied for publication. According to Lynch, the book is about twenty percent autobiographical, a story of two brothers learning to deal with life after the death of their father, a journeyman boxer. Fourteen-year-old George is left as the man of the house after his father dies from all the years of battering he has taken in the ring. George's mother is bitter, hating the sport which cost her husband his life, but George's younger brother, Monty, wants to follow in his father's footsteps. He begins to train at the local gym with his uncle, and George sets about to discourage him from this path, exacerbating their sibling rivalry. Told in brief, episodic vignettes with urban slang, the novel reaches its climax when Monty is shown a video of one of the brutal beatings his father took in the ring. In the end, Monty is finally convinced, and George gets the final lines: "We left the gloves there on the ground, where they could rot in the coming rain."

Reviewing *Shadow Boxer* in *Horn Book,* Peter D. Sieruta was particularly struck with the cast of characters Lynch captures "with unflinching honesty" in the working-class Boston neighborhood where George and Monty live. While Sieruta found that, for him, the episodic style weakened the plot, he noted that individual chapters "read like polished short stories and are stunning in their impact." Gary Young in *Booklist* commented that "this is a guy's book. It is also a tidy study of sibling rivalry." Other reviewers also noted how the novel transcended the usual sports story tag. Tom S. Hurlburt, writing in *School Library Journal,* pointed to the passages describing the problems of a single-parent family in an urban setting and concluded that "Lynch has written a gritty, streetwise novel that is much more than a sports story. . . ." John R. Lord also commented upon Lynch's episodic style in *Voice of Youth Advocates,* calling the book "a series of character sketches," and noting that it could serve well with "reading for the at-risk students." Named to the American Library Association's Best Book for Young Adults and Recommended Book for Reluctant Readers lists, *Shadow Boxer* also found a place with its intended audience: young male readers who were not often drawn to books.

Regarding his episodic style, Lynch commented that it was a "critical leap" for him to start writing that way. "I don't see transitions in my life," Lynch noted. "I can see moments. So it was incredibly liberating for me to realize that I don't have to write 'and then . . . and then' in my books any more than I have that in my life. Reading [Sherwood Anderson's] *Winesburg Ohio* and [Joan] Didion's *Play It As It Lays* made me understand how scenes assemble and at the end you don't miss the transitions. You still get the sense of the whole without 'and then'. I guess I write a little less episodically now than when I first started, but I don't see myself ever *not* writing in that general way." Lynch's short, snappy paragraphs also result in books that seem to grow organically. "I don't really plot my books. I write characters; that's where it all starts. If you have real people, stuff is going to happen to them. I don't feel like I've got to maneuver them; they have their own DNA and act within a range that is themselves. If I start heavily plotting, then the writing is just like filling in the numbers. It's lifeless." More than one critic has also noted that such writing—brief, hard-hitting vignettes that reveal character—makes it easier for reluctant readers to get into the material.

While *Shadow Boxer* was being prepared for publication, Lynch was already hard at work on his second novel, *Iceman,* the story of a troubled youth for whom violence on the ice is his only release. "For me, *Iceman* is the book that is closest to being autobiographical in the whole inability to express yourself. Where does that go, the frustration. It's got to go someplace. Writing it, I tapped into something very adolescent American male where anger is cool and you've got to suck it up. Acting out the whole

male role thing." Lynch's protagonist is fourteen-year-old Eric, a great hockey player with a reputation as a fine shooter and a strong defensive player with a penchant for hitting. Known as the "Iceman" for his antics on the ice, Eric actually seems to enjoy hurting people. His only friends are his older brother Duane, whose act of trading his skates for a guitar impresses Eric, and the local embalmer, McLaughlin, who equally impresses Eric with his devotion to his work.

Lynch divides the novel into three sections, echoing the periods of a hockey game, and the novel follows Eric's conflict-laden life to a certain epiphany. The source of his rage comes from his own dysfunctional family—his mother, a former nun, who continually spouts from the Bible, and a father who only comes alive when Eric is doing damage on the ice. Slamming out his frustrations on the hockey rink, he is soon shunned by even his own teammates. McLaughlin at first gives him some comfort in his world of death, and Eric for a time thinks he might want to go into mortuary science until he comes upon the embalmer entwined with one of the female corpses. This startling scene helps Eric to face some of his own worst demons and begin to control his anger, to stop working out his father's vicarious rage—to in fact, join the living. Randy Brough, writing in *Voice of Youth Advocates,* noted that he found "this novel of disaffected adolescence to be as satisfying as a hard, clean hip check," and Jack Forman in *School Library Journal,* while commenting that the book would appeal to hockey enthusiasts, also pointed out that "this novel is clearly about much more and is no advertisement for the sport." Forman concluded that *Iceman* "will leave readers smiling and feeling good." Stephanie Zvirin summed up the effect of the novel in *Booklist:* "This totally unpredictable novel . . . is an unsettling, complicated portrayal of growing up in a dysfunctional family. . . . A thought-provoking book guaranteed to compel and touch a teenage audience."

"I don't have any answers," Lynch explained, commenting on messages inherent in his books. "I just want to let you go on to a new set of questions. The world should be a little broader when you're done reading. There should be more options, not necessarily more choices. I don't go in much for ah-ha's in my work. When I do readings in schools and someone says 'That's me, that kid is me,' I am happy. I'd rather hit *my* group hard than cast wider nets. . . . One of the great things we can do as novelists is to take a good close-up view of characters. To get beneath the surface. With my third book, I was trying to show the confusion of life, the cyclical nature of it rather than a linear portrayal. The victim is perpetrator is victim. To show that even crappy people have their sides to them. To depict hope in the midst of it all."

That third book was *Gypsy Davey,* the story of a brain-damaged youth and his family who doesn't care, and of the tenement neighborhood surrounding the boy—cheap bars and drug dealers. Out of this bleak atmosphere, Lynch weaves a tale of hope, of young Davey who tries body and soul to break the cycle of parental neglect initiated by his parents and seemingly perpetuated by his older sister, Jo. Another dysfunctional family forms the centerpiece of this novel, and it is Davey's attempts to bring love to Jo's son, his nephew, that is one of the few bright spots. Jo and her child ultimately drive off with a stranger—a new lover? a social worker?—and Davey tells himself, in stream-of-consciousness exposition, that the kid will be okay, that there is hope. "I'm gonna have my own find somebody who's gonna love me and we're gonna have some babies and I'm gonna love 'em to pieces like nobody ever loved babies before." W. Keith McCoy, writing in *Voice of Youth Advocates,* noted that in spite of the dreary atmosphere of the novel, "Lynch provokes empathy for this family and its situation, and perhaps that is the only positive outcome in the book." Also focusing on the bleakness of the theme, especially as perceived by adults, Elizabeth Bush in *Bulletin of the Center for Children's Books* concluded that "young adults will appreciate its honesty and fast pace. . . . Lynch . . . paints characters who . . . ring true every time."

"For me the ending worked out with hope," Lynch said in his interview. "Davey remains intact in his purity. Things have happened to him, but there's still a charming sweetness. Something's out there that he's going to love and he's going to find it. . . . I plan to get back to Davey sometime."

Lynch's fourth book was something of a departure: On the surface it is a boys-at-summer-camp comedy about an overweight youth who resists attempts at turning him into a jock. Thirteen-year-old Elvin Bishop is attending a Christian Brothers summer camp with a heavy emphasis on sports as preparation for high school—the coaches literally 'slot' young athletes for upcoming sports. Friends with Mike, who seems to fit in anywhere, and Frank, who sells his soul to fit in, Elvin steers a middle course and finally finds a niche for himself with the help of an arts

instructor. He finally lets himself be himself, and finally sees that it's okay to be a non-athlete. But before this happens, he suffers from all forms of physical torture in football, baseball, and wrestling. According to Stephanie Zvirin, writing in *Booklist, Slot Machine* is a "funny, poignant coming-of-age story." While noting Lynch's ability to write broad, physical comedy as well as dark humor, Zvirin concluded that "this wry, thoughtful book speaks with wisdom and heart to the victim and outsider in us all." Maeve Visser Knoth in *Horn Book* also noted the use of humor and sarcasm in this "biting, sometimes hilarious novel," as well as the serious purpose in back of it all: "Lynch writes a damning commentary on the costs of conformity and the power gained by standing up for oneself."

"I experienced something similar to this in my freshman year," Lynch recalled. "Except that my camp was only overnight, not three weeks. What makes this book funny is Elvin's filtering of events. The dark underbelly is still there, but delivered through somebody the reader feels better about. He's making jokes about what's happening to him, but the events of the book are as grim as in some of my other books. . . . Elvin's voice more closely represents the way I talk than the other narrators. . . . I'm going to do more with Elvin as a narrator."

With his "Blue-Eyed Son" trilogy, Lynch returned to the grittier mean streets of Boston to explore latent and sometimes very overt racism. "Boston is the inspiration for this one," Lynch said. "It's the city that never changes. There was this whole flap about gays not being allowed in a St. Patrick's Day parade, then they were allowed, then they weren't. I kept looking at that situation, but not using it, that situation that says we're integrated, but actually it's a separate reality. The myth of diversity while there are white streets, black streets, Spanish streets. We have reversed the clock on civil rights, but it hasn't just happened. It's been happening all along. I wanted to look at racism in a microcosm. . . . I wanted to put the spotlight on us. This is what we look like. Do we know we look like this? Do we even recognize what we do as racism?"

Lynch's microcosm involves fifteen-year-old Mick, who sees his once predominately Irish neighborhood changing into a racially-mixed one as blacks, Latinos and Asians move in. Mick unwittingly becomes a neighborhood hero when he throws an egg at a Cambodian woman during a St. Patrick's Day Parade. Though Mick hates that his friends and older brother

Terry have planned to disrupt the parade by harassing gay and Cambodian marchers, he is forced into throwing the egg, an action caught on television. A hero in the local bar, he becomes an outcast at school. Only Toy, a mysterious sort of character, remains his friend, and soon Mick begins to break off ties with his close-knit Irish family and neighborhood and hangs out with Latinos instead. His drunken, oafish older brother has Mick beaten for such treachery, ending the first book of the trilogy, *Mick*. The story is carried forward in *Blood Relations* where Mick struggles to find himself, forming a brief liaison with beautiful Evelyn, and finally ending up in the bed of Toy's mother. The series is concluded with *Dog Eat Dog* in which the brothers face off for a final showdown and Mick's friend Toy comes out of the closet. "With realistic street language and an in-your-face writing style . . . Lynch immerses readers in Mick's world," Kelly Diller noted in *School Library Journal*. According to Diller, Lynch has created a "noble anti-hero." Reviewing *Blood Relations* in *School Library Journal*, Kellie Flynn commented that "this story moves quickly, Mick's seriocomic edginess is endearing, and the racism theme is compelling." However, Flynn also noted that the series concept made the ending of the novel something of a let-down, a point Elizabeth Bush returned to in a *Bulletin of the Center for Children's Books* review of the three books: "When the finish finally arrives, the unrelenting brutalities of the earlier volumes will leave the audience virtually unshockable."

While Lynch's inspiration for his books usually comes from his own life or from life around him in Boston, *Political Timber* was inspired by newspaper accounts of a teenager who ran for mayor of his small town. "I saw the kid's picture in the paper," Lynch commented, "and he was a goof. It was all a lark for him. I loved that spirit and I went with it." What resulted is a novel about a high school senior, Gordon Foley, who runs for mayor at the insistence of his grandfather who is an old machine politician serving time for fraud. While young Gordon thinks it's all great fun, his grandfather is actually using him as his proxy. Less bleak than much of his fiction, *Political Timber* is also unique in that it is specifically written for high teens, "a woefully under-served constituency," according to Lynch. "I wanted to portray an eighteen-year-old, someone who is on the cusp between the adult and kid world."

"I see my books increasingly as a body of work," Lynch concluded in his interview. "They deal with the whole idea of identity and individuality. . . . My job is to make noise and be relevant and catch momentarily the attention of what seems to be a neglected reading group. We need to attract teenagers to the concept and let them know it is here. They've been driven away by the idea that [young adult literature] is baby food. I want to attract them again, and then deliver them to the next level of writing."

BIOGRAPHICAL/CRITICAL SOURCES:

BOOKS

Lynch, Chris, *Shadow Boxer*, HarperCollins, 1993.
Lynch, Chris, *Gypsy Davey*, HarperCollins, 1994.
Lynch, Chris, "The Hobbyist," *Ultimate Sports*, edited by Donald Gallo, Delacorte, 1995.

PERIODICALS

Booklist, December 15, 1993, p. 747; February 1, 1994, p. 1001; March 15, 1994, p. 1358; October 1, 1994, p. 318; January 15, 1995, p. 860; September 1, 1995, p. 74; November 15, 1995, p. 547.
Bulletin of the Center for Children's Books, November, 1994, p. 93; October, 1995, p. 61; April, 1996, p. 270.
English Journal, November, 1994, p. 101; November, 1995, p. 96.
Horn Book, May/June, 1994, pp. 358-62; November/December, 1995, pp. 745-47.
Kirkus Reviews, November 15, 1993, p. 1464; February 1, 1994, p. 146; October 1, 1995, p. 1433.
Publishers Weekly, August 23, 1993, p. 73; September 12, 1994, p. 127; March 11, 1996, p. 66.
School Library Journal, April, 1993, p. 150; September, 1993, p. 252; December, 1993, p. 26; March, 1994, p. 239; October, 1995, p. 156; March, 1996, pp. 220-21.
Voice of Youth Advocates, December, 1993, p. 295; April, 1994, p. 28; December, 1994, p. 277; August, 1996, pp. 157-58.
Wilson Library Bulletin, September, 1994, p. 127.

OTHER

Lynch, Chris, interview with J. Sydney Jones, conducted June 13, 1996.*

—Sketch by J. Sydney Jones

LYNCH, Peter S. 1944-

PERSONAL: Born in 1944, in Boston, MA; son of Thomas Lynch (a mathematics professor); married; wife's name, Carolyn; children: Mary, Annie, Beth. *Education:* Boston College, B.A., 1965; University of Pennsylvania, Wharton School of Business, M.B.A., 1968. *Religion:* Roman Catholic.

ADDRESSES: Office—27 State St., Boston, MA 02109-2706.

CAREER: Fidelity Investments, Boston, MA, research analyst, 1969-74, research director, 1974-77, manager of Fidelity Magellan Fund, 1977-90, trustee, Fidelity Investment, 1990—. Guest lecturer, Boston College. Financial advisor, Lynch Fund, Boston College, Boston Public Library, Third Century Foundation, and Order of Malta. Chair, Catholic Schools Foundation. Member of board of directors, Morrison Knudsen, W.R. Grace. *Military service:* U.S. Army, 1968-70.

AWARDS, HONORS: Named to National Business Hall of Fame.

WRITINGS:

(With John Rothchild) *On up on Wall Street: How to Use What You Already Know to Make Money in the Market,* Simon & Schuster (New York, NY), 1989.

(With Rothchild) *Beating the Street: How to Pick Winning Stocks and Develop a Strategy for Mutual Funds,* Simon & Schuster, 1993.

(With Rothchild) *Learn to Earn: A Beginner's Guide to the Basics of Investing and Business,* Fireside (New York, NY), 1996.

SIDELIGHTS: During his tenure as one of Wall Street's most respected and successful investment managers, Peter S. Lynch turned Fidelity Investments Inc.'s Magellan Fund into the world's most profitable and valued mutual fund. Lynch shares his investment techniques and ideas in his books, *One up on the Wall Street: How to Use What You Already Know to Make Money in the Market, Beating the Street: How to Pick Winning Stocks and Develop a Strategy for Mutual Funds,* and *Learn to Earn: A Beginner's Guide to the Basics of Investing and Business.*

Of Lynch's first book, *One up on Wall Street,* Andrew Evan Serwer wrote in *Fortune:* "*One up on Wall Street* is Lynch's endorsement and description of . . . common-sense, eyes-open style of investing." "Lynch's thesis is sound, practical, hardly revolutionary—and amazingly underused," noted Serwer, further remarking "The way to pick a stock, [Lynch] explains, is to find a thriving business at a cut-rate price. . . . Investors should think of buying . . . a piece of a business." A reviewer for *Publishers Weekly* said that Lynch's book "is written in a light, entertaining style."

David R. Francis stated in the *Christian Science Monitor* that *One up on Wall Street* "offers primarily uncommon common sense in investment—no magic tips or neat gimmicks "guaranteed' to make a fortune. Lynch's secret basically is hard research work and alertness in seeking out genuine value in stocks, plus sufficient skepticism to avoid the fads and fashions that so often prevail on Wall Street."

Christian Science Monitor reviewer Guy Halverson wrote about Lynch's second book detailing investment instruction and information, *Beating the Street:* "In addition to enjoying Lynch's sprightly and humorous writing, the experts praise Mr. Lynch for what they perceive to be his sound investment strategy—especially Lynch's contention that stock-pickers do best when they thoroughly research the equities they wish to buy, and think in terms of the long-haul. Lynch says that investors need not be dependent on mutual funds."

Lynch's next book, *Learn to Earn,* is also an instructional book, but this work is aimed at school-aged children. A critic for the *Christian Science Monitor* commented that *Learn to Earn* "is a particularly fun read, coming from an unabashed champion of the system. . . . The book also covers basics of investing and typical phases in the life of a company."

BIOGRAPHICAL/CRITICAL SOURCES:

PERIODICALS

Business Week, March 22, 1993, p. 14.
Christian Science Monitor, April 28, 1989, p. 13; April 12, 1993, p. 7; January 29, 1996, p. 9.
Fortune, February 27, 1989, pp. 129-30.
Kiplinger's Personal Finance, June, 1996, p. 106.
New York Times Book Review, March 21, 1993, p. 10.
Publishers Weekly, December 23, 1988, p. 74; February 8, 1993, p. 68.
U.S. News & World Report, March 20, 1989, p. 86-88.*

LYON, Peter 1915-1996

OBITUARY NOTICE—See index for *CA* sketch: Originally named Robert Crawford Lyon; born September 30, 1915, in Madison, WI; died October 14, 1996, in Kingston, NY. Author. Lyon is remembered as the author of the 1964 George Polk Memorial Award-winning *Success Story: The Life and Times of S. S. McClure,* a biography of his grandfather, the editor of *McClure* magazine. During the late 1930s and early 1940s, Lyon wrote radio scripts for "Cavalcade of America," "Eternal Life," and "March of Time." He also served with the Office of War Information during World War II. He came under attack from Senator Joseph McCarthy's Congressional Investigation on Un-American Activities while Lyon was president of the Radio Writers Guild, now known as the Writers Guild of America. In 1955, his *Alcoholism* was published, a book which Lyon authored with Ruth Fox. He contributed many articles to magazines, such as *Redbook* and *Reader's Digest*. His other major works are *The Wild, Wild West, To Hell in a Day Coach: An Exasperated Look at American Railroads,* and *Eisenhower: A Portrait of the Hero*.

OBITUARIES AND OTHER SOURCES:

PERIODICALS

New York Times, October 20, 1996, p. 39.

M

MacLEAN, Sorley 1911-

PERSONAL: Born in 1911, in Somhairle MacGhill-Eain, Osgaig, Raasay Island, Scotland; married Renee Cameron, 1946; children: three daughters. *Education:* University of Edinburgh, B.A. (honors; English); Moray House College of Education, Edinburgh, teaching diploma.

ADDRESSES: Agent—c/o Carcanet Press Ltd., 208-212 Corn Exchange Bldgs., Manchester M4 3BQ, England.

CAREER: Portree High School, English teacher, 1934-37; Tobermory Secondary School, English teacher, 1938; English teacher in Boroughmuir, Edinburgh, 1947-56; Plockton Secondary School, Wester Ross, headmaster, 1956-72; University of Edinburgh, writer-in-residence, 1973-74; Sabhal Mor Ostaig Gaelic college, Isle of Skye, writer-in-residence, 1975-76. *Military service:* Signal Corps, 1940-43.

AWARDS, HONORS: Scottish Arts Council award, 1990. D.Litt.: University of Dundee, 1972; National University of Ireland, 1979; University of Edinburgh, 1980.

WRITINGS:

POETRY

(With Robert Garioch) *17 Poems for Sixpence,* Chalmers Press (Edinburgh), 1940.
Dain do Eimhir agus Dain Eile, Maclellan (Glasgow), 1943, English translation by Iain Crichton Smith published as *Poems to Eimhir and*

Other Poems, Gollancz-Northern House (London and Newcastle upon Tyne), 1971.
(With George Campbell Hay, William Neill, and Stuart MacGregor) *Four Points of a Saltire,* Reprographia (Edinburgh), 1970.
Spring Tide and Neap Tide: Selected Poems, 1932-1972, Canongate (Edinburgh), 1977.
From Wood to Ridge: Collected Poems in Gaelic and English, translated by the author, Carcanet (Manchester), 1989.
O Choille Gu Bearradh, Carcanet, 1990.
Aisling Agus Toir, An Sagart (Maigh Nuad), 1992.

OTHER

Ris a'bhruthaich: Criticism and Prose Writings, edited by William Gillies, Acair (Stornoway, Isle of Lewis), 1985.

*   *   *

MAHER, Bill 1956-

PERSONAL: Surname is pronounced "mar"; born January 20, 1956, in New York, NY; son of Bill (a news editor) and Julie (a nurse) Maher. *Education:* Attended Cornell University.

ADDRESSES: Office—c/o *Politically Incorrect with Bill Maher,* 7800 Beverly Blvd., Los Angeles, CA 90036.

CAREER: Actor and comedian, c. 1983—; creator, co-producer, and host of the comedy talk show *Politically Incorrect with Bill Maher,* 1993—. Appeared in films, including *D. C. Cab,* Universal, 1983; *Ratboy,* Warner Bros., 1986; *House II: The Second Story,* New World, 1987; *Cannibal Women in the Avocado Jungle of Death,* Guacamole, 1989. *Pizza Man,* Jonathan F. Lawton, 1991. Appeared in television films, series, programs, and specials, including *Newhart,* CBS, 1982; *Sara,* NBC, 1985; *Club Med,* ABC, 1986; *Funny, You Don't Look 200,* ABC, 1987; *Hard Knocks,* Showtime, 1987; *Out of Time,* NBC, 1988; *The Midnight Hour,* CBS, 1990; *One Night Stand,* HBO, 1990; *The 11th Annual CableACE Awards,* 1990, *The 16th Annual CableACE Awards* (host), TNT, 1995, and *The 17th Annual CableACE Awards,* TNT, 1995; *London Underground,* Comedy Central, 1991; *Say What?,* CBS, 1992; "We're Mad as Hell Hosted by Dennis Miller," 1992, and "Bill Maher: Stuff That Struck Me Funny" (executive producer), 1995, *HBO Comedy Hour; The A-List,* Comedy Central, 1992; *Comic Relief VI,* HBO, 1994; *State of the Union Undressed '94,* Comedy Central, 1994; *But . . . Seriously,* Showtime, 1994; *Real Sports with Bryant Gumbel,* HBO, 1995; *State of the Union Undressed '96,* Comedy Central, 1996; *Bill Maher: The Golden Goose Special,* HBO, 1996; *The Tonight Show,* NBC.

AWARDS, HONORS: CableACE Awards for best cable talk show host, 1995, 1996, and Emmy Award nominations for outstanding variety, music, or comedy series, 1995, 1996, all for *Politically Incorrect with Bill Maher.*

WRITINGS:

True Story: A Comedy Novel, Random House (New York), 1994.
Does Anyone Have a Problem with That?: Politically Incorrect's Greatest Hits, Villard Books (New York), 1996.

Also writer for *Politically Incorrect* and for his own comedy specials; contributor of articles to periodicals, including *Playboy.*

SIDELIGHTS: Actor and comedian Bill Maher has appeared in films, including *Pizza Man* and *Cannibal Women in the Avocado Jungle of Death,* and has made hundreds of television appearances, including four HBO comedy specials. He is perhaps best known, however, as the creator, co-producer, and host of the comedy talk show, *Politically Incorrect with Bill Maher.* His efforts with this program have garnered him five CableACE Awards and four Emmy

nominations. In addition to all of his work in the entertainment field, Maher has also published two books, 1994's *True Story: A Comedy Novel* and 1996's *Does Anyone Have a Problem with That?: Politically Incorrect's Greatest Hits.*

On *Politically Incorrect with Bill Maher,* Maher hosts a panel which mixes celebrities such as comedian Jerry Seinfeld and gay playwright and actor Harvey Fierstein with political figures such as African-American activist Reverend Al Sharpton and consultant Ed Rollins. Together, Maher and his guests discuss issues of the day such as second-hand smoke and the image of minorities on television. Opinions are mixed about the result. James Wolcott complained in the *New Yorker* that the show's "iconoclasm . . . is a slick coat of flash over an inside attitude." He went on to lament that "[t]he only truly politically incorrect performer to turn up on *Politically Incorrect* is self-proclaimed comedy pig Andrew (Dice) Clay, who isn't afraid to take a drag on *his* cigarette . . . as he defends the good name of strippers." An *Entertainment Weekly* critic took the middle position by asserting that "the show succeeds solely on the strength of its panel." Discussing both Maher and fellow comic Dennis Miller in a *Time* article, Richard Zoglin had high praise for Maher's work on *Politically Incorrect.* In his words, Maher is "helping stand-up comedy escape from its contemporary cul-de-sac, where Jerry Seinfeld clones obsess about sex, TV and life's little annoyances. [Maher] . . . read[s] the *whole* newspaper—not just the funny clippings [his] writers collect."

Maher's novel, *True Story,* is about several stand-up comedians trying to make their mark on the New York comedy scene of the late 1970s. When asked by Erica Kornberg in *Entertainment Weekly* whether his characters were based on real people, Maher replied: "In those days, we were all in New York—Richard Belzer, Jerry Seinfeld, Paul Reiser, Roseanne, and I. Yeah, they're all in there. Of course, I'm not going to say where." Of his motivations for writing *True Story,* Maher declared to Kornberg: "There has never been an accurate depiction of what it's like to be a stand-up comedian. Somebody had to write about it. . . . I just tried to make it read like a real novel."

Critical response to *True Story* was mixed. Gary Amdahl's review of the novel in the *Washington Post Book World* was extremely satirical and ambiguous, but he did hail Maher as "a renaissance Man" and "no dummy." Kornberg defended Maher's effort in the literary field by lauding him as "a comic who thinks beyond the joke, a comic with perspective, a comic who is . . . a novelist."

BIOGRAPHICAL/CRITICAL SOURCES:

PERIODICALS

Entertainment Weekly, July 23, 1993, p. 50; August 12, 1994, p. 50.
New Yorker, September 13, 1993, pp. 124-126.
Publishers Weekly, June 20, 1994, p. 101.
Time, May 30, 1994, p. 67.
Washington Post Book World, September 4, 1994.

*   *   *

MAIDEN, Jennifer   1949-

PERSONAL: Born April 7, 1949, in Penrith, New South Wales; married David Toohey, 1984; children: one daughter. *Education:* Macquarie University, B.A., 1974.

ADDRESSES: Home—P.O. Box 4, Penrith, New South Wales 2750, Australia.

CAREER: Tutor in creative writing, Outreach, Evening College Movement, and Blacktown City Council, all New South Wales, Fellowship of Australian Writers, and University of Western Sydney, 1976-91. Writer-in-residence, Australian National University, Canberra, New South Wales, State Torture and Trauma Rehabilitation Unit, and University of Western Sydney, all 1989.

AWARDS, HONORS: Australia Council grant or fellowship, 1974, 1975, 1977, 1978, 1983, 1984, 1986; Harri Jones memorial prize; Butterly-Hooper award.

WRITINGS:

POETRY

Tactics, University of Queensland Press (St. Lucia), 1974.
The Occupying Forces, Makar Press (St. Lucia), 1975.
The Problem of Evil, Poetry Society of Australia (Sydney), 1975.
Birthstones, Angus and Robertson (Sydney), 1978.
The Border Loss, Angus and Robertson, 1979.
For the Left Hand, South Head Press (Sydney), 1981.

The Trust, Black Lightning Press (Wentworth Falls, New South Wales), 1988.
The Winter Baby, Angus and Robertson, 1990.
Bastille Day, National Library of Australia (Canberra), 1990.
Selected Poems of Jennifer Maiden, Penguin (Ringwood, Victoria, and New York), 1990.
Acoustic Shadow, Penguin, 1993.

NOVELS

The Terms, Hale and Iremonger (Sydney), 1982.
Play with Knives, Allen and Unwin (Sydney), 1990.

SHORT STORIES

Mortal Details, Rigmarole (Melbourne), 1977.

*   *   *

MALPASS, E(ric) L(awson)   1910-1996

OBITUARY NOTICE—See index for *CA* sketch: Born November 14, 1910, in Derby, England; died October 16, 1996. Banker and author. Malpass gained prominence as the author of *Morning's at Seven,* which was widely acclaimed and made Germany's Der Spiegel bestseller list. Although a banker by trade, Malpass had a penchant for writing. It wasn't until 1957, however, that his first story was published. *Beefy Jones* was a humorous account of a local idiot and received the Palma d'Oro award in Italy. *Morning's at Seven,* published in 1965, was made into a film which received the Goldene Leinwand award in Germany as the year's most popular film. Among his works was a fictionalized account of the life of William Shakespeare, titled *Sweet Will.* Several of his other books depicted English life as it was between the world wars, including *The Wind Brings Up the Rain, Summer Awakening, Of Human Frailty, The Lamplight and the Stars,* and *Wenn der Tiger schlafen geht.*

OBITUARIES AND OTHER SOURCES:

BOOKS

Writers Directory, St. James Press, 1996.

PERIODICALS

Times (London), November 9, 1996, p. 25.

MANDEL, (Mark) Babaloo 1949(?)-

PERSONAL: Born c. 1949, in New York, NY; son of a taxi driver) and a homemaker; married Denise Horn, 1974; children: Joshua, Jesse, Jason, Jake, Jamie, Julie. *Education:* Attended New York Institute of Technology.

ADDRESSES: Home—Los Angeles, CA. *Agent*—Creative Artists Agency, 9830 Wilshire Blvd., Beverly Hills, CA 90212.

CAREER: Screenwriter and television producer. Executive producer with Lowell Ganz of television programs, including *Gung Ho,* ABC, 1986; (and creator) *Channel 99,* CBS, 1988; *Knight and Daye,* NBC, 1989; and *Parenthood,* NBC, 1990. Creative consultant with Ganz for *Take Five* (also known as *Kooper with a "K"*), CBS, 1987. Has appeared on screen in *Splash,* Buena Vista, 1984, and in the television documentary *Naked Hollywood,* Arts and Entertainment, 1991.

AWARDS, HONORS: Academy Award nomination, best screenplay written directly for the screen, National Film Critics Screenplay of the Year Award, and Writers Guild, best screenplay nominee, all 1984, all for *Splash.*

WRITINGS:

SCREENPLAYS, WITH LOWELL GANZ

Night Shift, Ladd Co./Warner Bros., 1982.
(With Bruce Jay Friedman) *Splash* (adapted from a story by Friedman and Dave Thomas), Buena Vista, 1984.
(With Dan Aykroyd) *Spies Like Us,* Warner Bros., 1985.
(With Deborah Blum) *Gung Ho,* Paramount, 1986.
Vibes (adapted from a story by Ganz, Mandel, and Blum), Columbia, 1988.
(With Ron Howard) *Parenthood* (adapted from a story by Ganz, Mandel, and Howard), Universal, 1989.
City Slickers (adapted from a story by Billy Crystal), Castle Rock/Columbia, 1991.
A League of Their Own, Columbia, 1992.
(With Billy Crystal) *Mr. Saturday Night,* Columbia, 1992.
(With Crystal) *City Slickers II: The Legend of Curly's Gold,* Columbia, 1994.
Greedy, Universal, 1994.
(With Crystal) *Forget Paris,* Columbia, 1995.

Also author, with Ganz, of *Over My Dead Body, Dance Skins,* and *Perfect Couple.*

TELEVISION SERIES, WITH GANZ

(With others) *Laverne and Shirley,* ABC, 1976-83.
(With others) *Busting Loose,* CBS, 1977.
Take Five, CBS, 1987.

TELEVISION PILOTS, WITH GANZ

Herndon and Me, ABC, 1983.
Channel 99, NBC, 1988.
(With others) *Knight and Daye,* NBC, 1989.
(With others) *Parenthood* (adapted from film), NBC, 1990.

SIDELIGHTS: [See GANZ, Lowell]

BIOGRAPHICAL/CRITICAL SOURCES:

PERIODICALS

Chicago Tribune, December 11, 1985; August 5, 1988; August 1, 1989; August 2, 1989.
Commonweal, September 11, 1992, pp. 41-42.
Globe and Mail (Toronto), August 6, 1988.
Los Angeles Times, July 29, 1982; August 5 ,1988; August 2, 1989.
Maclean's, June 14, 1991, p. 48.
National Review, August 3, 1992, pp. 46-47.
New Republic, April 9, 1984, p. 24; April 21, 1986, pp. 24-25; August 3, 1992, p. 28; June 12, 1995, p. 32.
Newsweek, March 12, 1984, p. 89; December 16, 1985; July 6, 1992, p. 54; March 14, 1994, p. 72; June 27, 1994, p. 54.
New York, October 5, 1992, pp. 101-02.
New Yorker, March 19, 1984, pp. 123-27; August 2, 1989; October 5, 1992, pp. 162-64.
New York Times, July 30, 1982, p. C8; December 6, 1985; August 5, 1988.
People, October 19, 1992, pp. 163-66.
Rolling Stone, October 29, 1992, p. 78.
Time, March 31, 1986; October 5, 1992, pp. 84-86.
Washington Post, March 9, 1984; December 9, 1985; August 5, 1988; August 2, 1989; August 4, 1989.*

* * *

MARANTO, Gina (Lisa) 1955-

PERSONAL: Born June 23, 1955, in Houston, TX; daughter of Joseph Vincent (an industrial editor) and

Margarette (a library cataloger; maiden name, Stubblefield) Maranto; married Mark Derr (a writer), September 11, 1982. *Education:* Attended Swarthmore College, 1975-76; Pomona College, B.A. (cum laude), 1977; Johns Hopkins University, M.A., 1980.

ADDRESSES: Home and office—Miami Beach, FL. *Agent*—Barney Karpfinger, Karpfinger Agency, 357 West 20th St., New York, NY 10011. *E-mail*—gmaranto@worldnet.att.net.

CAREER: Alumni Magazine Consortium, Baltimore, MD, contributing editor, 1981-82; *PC Tech Journal,* Baltimore, copy editor, 1983; Time, Inc., New York City, staff writer for *Discover,* 1983-87; Time-Life Books, Alexandria, VA, special contributor, 1987-93; freelance writer, 1993—.

AWARDS, HONORS: Oscar in Agriculture, Dekalb Corp., 1986; Science in Society Award, National Association of Science Writers, 1986.

WRITINGS:

Quest for Perfection: The Drive to Breed Better Human Beings, Scribner (New York), 1996.

Contributor to books, including *Secrets of the Inner Mind,* Time-Life Books (Alexandria, VA), 1993; *The Enigma of Personality,* Time-Life Books, 1993; and *Emotions,* Time-Life Books, 1994. Contributor of more than seventy articles and reviews to magazines and newspapers, including *Atlantic Monthly, Amicus Journal, Sea Frontiers, Sports Illustrated, Thinking Families,* and *Scientific American.*

WORK IN PROGRESS: Research on the psychology of envy, the history of tourism, and a human genome diversity project.

*   *   *

MARCUSE, Gary 1949-

PERSONAL: Born November 7, 1949, in Ithaca, NY; Canadian citizen; son of Frederick (a professor of psychology) and Dorothy (an artist; maiden name, Powis) Marcuse; married Betsy Margolick Carson, 1980. *Education:* Cornell University, B.F.A., 1973, M.A., 1975.

ADDRESSES: Office—Face to Face Media Ltd., 1818 Grant St., Vancouver, British Columbia V5L 2Y8, Canada. *E-mail*—marcuse@smartt.com.

CAREER: Director, producer, and story editor of documentaries and educational programs for television and radio. Canadian Broadcasting Corp., writer and broadcaster, 1975—, producer of *Sounds of Science,* 1986, guest host of *Arts National,* 1990, 1991; community program director for a station in Burnaby, British Columbia, 1977-78; sound recordist for documentary film and television productions, 1987—. Associate producer of "Blockade," an episode of the series *Witness,* CBC; executive producer and co-director of the series *First Nations: The Circle Unbroken,* 1991-93; producer and director of the television documentary *The Mind of a Child,* 1995; producer of *Scanning Television,* a media education kit, 1996; other work includes the children's series *Songs and Stories of Canada,* 1979, and *Alive in the Nuclear Age Project,* 1988-90.

MEMBER: Writers Guild of Canada, Academy of Canadian Television and Radio Artists, PEN Canada, Canadian Independent Film Caucus (co-chair of West Coast branch), Cineworks, Amnesty International, Canadian Committee to Protect Journalists, Friends of Public Broadcasting.

AWARDS, HONORS: Bronze Apple Award, Oakland Film and Video Festival, for the television series *Alive in the Nuclear Age Project;* Canadian Academy Award nominations, best writer of a radio documentary, Academy of Canadian Television and Radio Artists, 1985, for *The Cold War in Canada,* and 1989, for *R. D. Laing;* Chris Award from Columbus International Film and Video Festival, Silver Award from Charleston International Film and Video Festival, Silver Apple from National Educational Media Network, Golden Sheaf Award from Yorkton Short Film and Video Festival, Leo Award from British Columbia Motion Picture Association, and award from American Indian Film Festival, all 1995, for *The Mind of a Child;* Gold Medal from New York Festivals and Bronze Plaque from Columbus International Film and Video Festival, both 1996, for *Scanning Television.*

WRITINGS:

(With Reg Whitaker) *Cold War Canada: The Making of a National Insecurity State, 1945-1957,* University of Toronto Press (Toronto, Ontario), 1995.

Contributor of articles and reviews to magazines and newspapers, including *Quill and Quire, Georgia Straight, Weekend,* and *Makara.*

RADIO PROGRAMS

Oil Tankers on the West Coast, broadcast by CBC-Radio, 1980.

Banff at Fifty, broadcast by Radio Canada International, 1984.

From War to Peace, broadcast by Radio Canada International, 1985.

The Cold War in Canada, broadcast by CBC-Radio, 1985.

Fifty Years of Music in Canada (series), broadcast by CBC-Radio, 1986.

The New Right in BC, broadcast by CBC-Radio, 1987.

Murray Adaskin, broadcast by CBC-Radio, 1989.

R. D. Laing, broadcast by CBC-Radio, 1989.

Inside the Philippine Revolution, broadcast by CBC-Radio, 1991.

*   *   *

MARJOLIN, Robert (Ernest)   1911-1986

PERSONAL: Born July 27, 1911, in Paris, France; died April 15, 1986, in Paris, France; son of Ernest Octave (an upholsterer) and Elise (Vacher) Marjolin; married Dorothy Thayer Smith, 1944 (died, 1971); children: Elise, Robert. *Education:* Attended Yale University, 1932-33; Sorbonne, Licence en Philosophie, 1933, Law School, Agregation in law, 1936, Ph.D. and Agregation in economics, 1945. *Avocational interests:* Music, theatre, cinema, reading.

CAREER: Scientific Institute of Social and Economic Research, Paris, France, assistant to the president, 1934-37, chief assistant, 1938-39; joined Charles de Gaulle's Free French forces, London, England, 1941; came to Washington, D.C., to head French Supply Mission, organizing flow of food and raw materials to France, 1944; Provisional French Government, Paris, Ministry of National Economy, Paris, director of foreign economic relations, 1945, Plan for Modernization and Equipment, deputy general commissioner, 1946-48; Organization for European Economic Cooperation (OEEC), Paris, secretary-general, 1948-55; University of Nancy, France, professor of economics, 1955-58; vice-president of French delegation for negotiations for European Common Market, 1956-57; Commission of the European Economic Community (Common Market), Brussels, vice-president, 1958-67; University of Paris, professor of economics, 1967-69. Commissioned to study consequences of enlarging Common Market, 1978. Director, Shell Francaise.

MEMBER: Academie des Sciences Morales et Politiques.

AWARDS, HONORS: Rockefeller Foundation fellowship, 1932-33; Medal of Freedom (USA), 1947; King's Medal, 1947; Grand-Croix de l'Ordre d'Orange-Nassau (Holland); Cavaliere di Gran Croce nell'Ordine al Merito della Repubblica (Italy); Grand-Croix du Merite de la Republique Federale d'Allemagne; Grand-Croix de l'Ordre Royal du Phoenix (Greece), 1955; Commandeur de l'Ordre du Drapeau (Yugoslavia), 1956; honorary Commander of the Order of the British Empire (Great Britain), 1957; Officier du Merite Agricole, 1958; Grand-Officier de l'Ordre de la Couronne (Belgium); Grand-Croix de l'Ordre du Dannebrog (Denmark), 1958; honorary member, American Academy of Arts and Sciences, 1963; honorary degrees from Yale, 1965, Harvard, 1967, and University of East Anglia, 1967; Grand Croix de l'Ordre de Leopold II (Belgium), 1967; Commandeur de la Legion d'Honneur, 1978.

WRITINGS:

L'Evolution du syndicalisme aux Etats Unis de Washington a Roosevelt (title means "The Evolution of Trade-Unionism in the United States from Washington to Roosevelt"), Alcan (Paris, France), 1936.

Prix, monnaie, productions: Essai sur les mouvements economiques de longue duree (title means "Price, Money, and Production—An Essay on Long-Term Economic Movements"), Alcan, 1945.

Europe and the United States in the World Economy, Duke University Press (Durham, NC), 1953.

Europe in Search of Its Identity, Council on Foreign Relations (New York, NY), 1981.

Le travail d'une vie: Memoires, 1911-1986, R. Laffont (Paris, France), 1986, English translation by William Hall published as *Architect of European Unity: Memoirs, 1911-1986,* Weidenfeld & Nicolson (London, England), 1989.

Contributor to *Le Populaire* (French journal).

SIDELIGHTS: French economist Robert Marjolin was a key figure in the economic development of Europe after World War II. His importance might surprise those who consider his humble origins. The son of a Parisian upholster, Marjolin dropped out of school at age 14 and at age 20 joined the ranks of those unemployed by the world-wide economic depression of the thirties. Fortunately, his unemployment gave him the time necessary to attend university classes where he demonstrated natural ability in economics. Encouraged by his professors, he applied for and was granted a Rockefeller Foundation fellowship. His first book, *L'Evolution du syndicalisme aux Etats Unis de Washington a Roosevelt* ("The Evolution of Trade-Unionism in the United States from Washington to Roosevelt"), published in Paris in 1936, was a result of his year spent studying at Yale University as a Rockefeller fellow. Once he returned to Paris, he continued to work in economics, serving as assistant to the president of the Institute of Social and Economic Research during the 1930s.

The German invasion of France in 1940 thrust Marjolin into a place of prominence among those leading the resistance to the foreign occupation. Fleeing France the following year, he went to London to join the Free French forces of General Charles de Gaulle. From there he was sent to the United States to organize the gathering and distribution of food and other supplies bound for France. As the war ended, Marjolin returned to his native land to help in the massive effort of revitalizing the French economy. In 1945, he was named director of foreign economic relations for the French Provisional Government's Ministry of National Economy. That same year, he published *Prix, monnaie, productions: Essai sur les mouvements economiques de longue duree* ("Price, Money, and Production—An Essay on Long-Term Economic Movements"). In 1946 he was named deputy general commissioner for the Plan for Modernization and Equipment, a four-year program for French economic recovery.

Marjolin, like many of those responsible for putting together the plan for French economic revitalization, was a proponent of the United States of Europe movement. His appointment, in 1948, as first secretary general of the Organization for European Economic Cooperation (later, the Organization for Economic Cooperation and Development), founded to implement the U.S. Marshall Plan for the economic assistance of Europe, was a first step in what he foresaw as the political unification of that continent.

During the seven years he held this position. His first book in English, *Europe and the United States in the World Economy,* was published in 1953. The volume was a compilation of a series of lectures Marjolin gave at Duke University in Durham, North Carolina, in September and October of 1951. A *Nation* reviewer called the book "a compact and valuable summary of Europe's post-war achievements and needs." Similarly, William Diebold in *Political Science Quarterly* found the work to be a "succinct and lucid exposition of some of the major problems of European recovery."

In 1955, Marjolin resigned his post with the OEEC to take a teaching position at the University of Nancy. Soon, however, he again became involved in an international economic initiative. He took part in negotiations that led to the formation of the European Economic Community (known as the Common Market) in 1957. Between 1958 and 1967, Marjolin served two terms as one of the organization's vice-presidents. Marjolin's memoirs, published posthumously in English translation as *The Architect of European Unity: Memoirs, 1911-1986,* focused on this highly productive period in the economist's life. Reporting in *Foreign Affairs,* reviewer William Diebold, Jr., called the French edition of the volume "a most attractive book," observing that Marjolin included both "telling detail" and "reflections on the large issues" in his reminiscences. When Fritz Stern reviewed the English edition of the same book in *Foreign Affairs,* he called it "vivid, absorbing, [and] deeply appealing." In an *Encounter* examination of the volume, Richard Mayne referred to it as a "modest, frank, dazzlingly intelligent, and charming book."

BIOGRAPHICAL/CRITICAL SOURCES:

BOOKS

Annual Obituary: 1986, St. James Press, 1989.

PERIODICALS

Economist, September 30, 1989, pp. 92, 95.
Encounter, September-October, 1989, p. 49.
Foreign Affairs, summer, 1987, pp. 1112-13; winter, 1989-90, pp. 215-16.
Nation, May 16, 1953, p. 420.
New York Times, April 19, 1986, p. 32.
Political Science Quarterly, December, 1953, p. 634.
Times (London), April 18, 1986.*

MARKEL, Howard 1960-

PERSONAL: Born April 23, 1960, in Detroit, MI; son of Samuel (a stockbroker and executive) and Bernice (Lumberg) Markel; married Marcia Deborah Gordin, September 20, 1987 (died October 16, 1988). *Ethnicity:* "East European Jewish-American." *Education:* University of Michigan, A.B. (summa cum laude), 1982, M.D. (cum laude), 1986; Johns Hopkins University of Medicine, Ph.D., 1994. *Politics:* "registered as a Democrat." *Religion:* Jewish. *Avocational interests:* Reading, ice skating, baseball, movies.

ADDRESSES: Home—Ann Arbor, MI. *Office*—Medical School, 1924 Taubman Center, University of Michigan, Ann Arbor, MI 48109; fax 313-936-6897. *E-mail*—Howard.Markel@umich.edu.

CAREER: Johns Hopkins Hospital, Baltimore, MD, intern and resident in pediatrics, 1986-89, attending physician and fellow in adolescent medicine and history of medicine, 1989-93; University of Michigan, Ann Arbor, assistant professor of pediatrics and attending physician at university hospitals, 1993—, director of History Center for the Health Sciences, 1996—.

MEMBER: American Academy of Pediatrics, American Historical Association, American Jewish Historical Society, YIVO Institute for Jewish Studies, American Association for the History of Medicine.

AWARDS, HONORS: Generalist Faculty Award, Robert Wood Johnson Foundation; History of Medicine Scholars Award, Burroughs-Wellcome Foundation; Shannon Director's Award and Research Service Award, National Institutes of Health; Harriet Lane Home Fellowship Award, Johns Hopkins University.

WRITINGS:

(With Frank A. Oski) *The H. L. Mencken Baby Book,* Hanley & Belfus (Philadelphia, PA), 1990.
The Portable Pediatrician: A Textbook for Medical Students and Physicians, Mosby (St. Louis, MO), 1992.
(With Oski) *The Practical Pediatrician: The A to Z Guide to Your Child's Health, Safety, and Behavior,* W. H. Freeman (New York), 1996.
Quarantine!: East European Jewish Immigrants and the New York City Epidemics of 1892, Johns Hopkins University Press (Baltimore, MD), 1997.

Contributor of articles to medical journals and newspapers.

WORK IN PROGRESS: Bedside Manners: Essays on the Patient-Doctor Relationship, for W. H. Freeman; research on the history of U.S. immigration and public health since 1900.

SIDELIGHTS: Howard Markel told *CA:* "As a practicing pediatrician, medical educator, and historian of medicine, I spend a great deal of time explaining illness, not only to patients at the hospital and clinic, but also on the written page as a working writer. I divide my time among all of these activities at the University of Michigan Medical School and add to them by writing books and essays on a variety of topics, including child care issues, the history of American pediatrics and child care, medical education issues, and American immigration and public health history. At Michigan, I teach clinical pediatrics, history of medicine, and literature and medicine to medical students and physicians in training.

"I began writing professionally while I was an intern and resident in pediatrics at the Johns Hopkins Hospital. I stayed up all night on a regular basis (every third or fourth night) and found I was much more alert if I did not retire to bed, for an hour or two of restless sleep, but instead stayed up on the ward writing. I began with essays and opinion pieces that were published in the *Washington Post* and the *Baltimore Sun.* Soon I was writing my first book, *The H. L. Mencken Baby Book,* which was based on a series of baby care articles penned by the famed Baltimore journalist as a ghostwriter in 1908, for a women's magazine edited by Theodore Dreiser. After finishing my residency, I enrolled in the Ph.D. program in the history of medicine at Johns Hopkins, while maintaining my practice in general pediatrics and adolescent medicine. I remain convinced that I am better able to explain medicine to my patients and readers because of my broad understanding of the history of the field, and that I am a better historian of medicine because I practice as a physician.

"My book *The Practical Pediatrician: The A to Z Guide to Your Child's Health, Safety, and Behavior* was based on my work as a general pediatrician who has dealt with children and their parents on a daily basis over the past decade. I designed the book to be a ready reference on child care and children's health issues for the busy parent of the 1990s. It is arranged alphabetically, much like a dictionary or encyclopedia, so a parent can look up the topic quickly—usually in the middle of the night when most pediatric problems tend to occur. I emphasize throughout the book that the person who knows the child best is the parent. It is important for parents to trust their instincts and, when in doubt, ask someone. The major message is that there are many *do's* to reading a child—such as *do* love your child; *do* be consistent with your child; and *do* spend time with your child—and relatively few *don'ts*. In short, despite a wide variety of parenting techniques across the ages, the overwhelming majority of children do grow up to be healthy, productive adults.

"My historical research is centered on the American immigration experience and its relation to issues of public health and disease. In my book *Quarantine!: East European Jewish Immigrants and the New York City Epidemics of 1892* I focus on two deadly epidemics (typhus fever and cholera) that were literally imported into the United States by East European Jewish immigrants in 1892. The central question that I ask in this work is what happens when a scapegoated social group—such as newly arrived immigrants—is associated (either in fact or perception) with a deadly, contagious disease. I was inspired to write about immigrants largely because I am the grandchild of Russian Jewish immigrants who came here just prior to World War I. I write about epidemics, quarantines, and social scapegoating because I spent several years during my training at Johns Hopkins as an AIDS physician and was frequently asked by my patients if I thought they might be quarantined because of their illness.

"I write my manuscripts with a fountain pen and go through several drafts before I commit them to my computer-word processor. I prefer the feel of a pen and its scratching on yellow legal pads to the clickety-clack of a computer keyboard. It is a slower process, and it gives me time to think my thoughts more clearly. I am also more inclined to rewrite something in my own handwriting several times more than I will in a typed version, so my editors appreciate this technique as well. I enjoy writing more than any other professional activity I engage in, and I gain great joy from the books I have written and am now composing. Like any author, I enjoy explaining topics to my readers and am gratified to have the opportunity to connect intellectually with them. Combining this work with teaching and medical practice is a wonderful way to make a living. My favorite writers include William Shakespeare, Charles Dickens, and H. L. Mencken, who each had an extraordinary command of the English language, albeit in markedly different ways. I was also influenced by a number of physician-writers, including Lewis Thomas, Anton Chekov, and William Carlos Williams. I write about topics that interest me and that I have a passion for, believing fully that my readers will sense if I am bored and will soon become bored themselves."

*　　*　　*

MARKHAM, E(dward) A(rchibald) 1939-
(Paul St. Vincent)

PERSONAL: Born October 1, 1939, in Montserrat, West Indies; emigrated to England in 1956. *Education:* Attended Kilburn Polytechnic, 1960-62; University of Wales, B.A. (philosophy and English); attended University of East Anglia, 1966-67; attended University of London, 1967.

ADDRESSES: Agent—c/o Bloodaxe Books Ltd., P.O. Box 1SN, Newcastle upon Tyne NE99 1SN, England.

CAREER: Kilburn Polytechnic, London, lecturer, 1968-70; Abraham Moss Centre, Manchester, lecturer, 1976-78; Caribbean Theatre Workshop, Eastern Caribbean, director, 1970-71; Hull College of Higher Education, Yorkshire, director, 1979-80; Enga Provincial Government, Wabag, Papua New Guinea, media coordinator, 1983-85; *Artrage* magazine, London, editor, 1985-87; University of Ulster, Coleraine, writer-in-residence, 1988-91. *Ambit* magazine, London, assistant editor, 1980—; Enga *Nius* magazine, Papua New Guinea, editor, 1983-85; *Writing Ulster,* editor.

MEMBER: Poetry Society (member of the general council), 1976-77; GLA New Writing and Distribution Committee (member), 1986-87; Minorities Arts Advisory Service, London (1987—); Poetry Book Society, London (member of the managing committee, 1987—).

AWARDS, HONORS: C. Day Lewis fellowship, 1980-81.

WRITINGS:

POETRY

Cross-Fire, Outposts (Walton-on-Thames, Surrey), 1972.

Mad and Other Poems, Phaeton Press (Solihull, Warwickshire), 1973.

(As Paul St. Vincent) *Lambchops,* Omens (Leicester), 1976.

(As Paul St. Vincent) *Philpot in the City,* Curlew (Yorkshire), 1976.

(As Paul St. Vincent) *Lambchops in Disguise,* Share (London), 1976.

Master Class, Curlew (Yorkshire), 1977.

The Lamp, Sceptre Press (Knotting, Bedfordshire), 1978.

Love Poems, Lobby Press (Cambridge), 1978.

Games and Penalties, Poet and Printer (Hatch End), 1980.

Love, Politics, and Food, Von Hallett (Cambridge, MA), 1982.

Family Matters, Sow's Ear (Stafford, Warwickshire), 1984.

Human Rites: Selected Poems 1970-1982, Anvil Press Poetry (London), 1984.

Lambchops in Papua New Guinea, IPNGS (Port Moresby, Papua New Guinea), 1985.

Living in Disguise, Anvil Press Poetry (London), 1986.

Towards the End of a Century, Anvil Press Poetry, 1989.

Maurice V.'s Dido, Hearing Eye (London), 1991.

Letter from Ulster & The Hugo Poems, Littlewood Arc (Todmorden, Lancashire), 1993.

PLAYS

The Masterpiece, produced in Lampeter, 1964.

The Private Life of the Public Man, produced in St. Vincent, West Indies, 1970.

Dropping Out Is Violence, produced in Montserrat, West Indies, 1971.

SHORT STORIES

Something Unusual, Ambit (London), 1986.

Ten Stories, Sheffield Hallam University, School of Cultural Studies, 1994.

OTHER

(Editor with Arnold Kingston) *Merely a Matter of Colour,* Q (London), 1973.

(Editor) *Hinterland: Caribbean Poetry from the West Indies and Britain,* Bloodaxe (Newcastle upon Tyne), 1989; Dufour (Chester Springs, PA), 1990.

(Editor with Howard Fergus) *Hugo Versus Montserrat,* Linda Lee (London), 1989.

MARKHAM, Ian Stephen 1962-

PERSONAL: Born September 19, 1962, in Crediton, Devon, England; son of Stephen Keith (a chemist) and Beryl Evelyn (Walker) Markham; married Lesley P. Dunn, July 4, 1987. *Education:* King's College, London, B.D., 1985; Queen's College, Cambridge, M.Litt., 1990; University of Exeter, Ph.D., 1994. *Politics:* Labour. *Religion:* Church of England.

ADDRESSES: Office—Liverpool Hope University College, Hope Park, Liverpool L16, England.

CAREER: University of Exeter, Exeter, England, lecturer in theology, 1989-96; Liverpool Hope University, Liverpool, England, professor of theology, 1996—. Advertising Standards Authority, director and member of council, 1993—.

MEMBER: American Academy of Religion, Society for the Study of Theology.

WRITINGS:

Plurality and Christian Ethics, Cambridge University Press (Cambridge, England), 1994.

(Editor) *A World Religions Reader,* Blackwell Scientific (Oxford, England), 1996.

Truth and the Reality of God: A Godparent's Handbook, S.P.C.K., 1996.

WORK IN PROGRESS: Research on interfaith ethics.

*   *   *

MARTIEN, Jerry 1939-
(Dr. Loon)

PERSONAL: Born November 29, 1939, in Fullerton, CA.

ADDRESSES: Office—P.O. Box 1051, Arcata, CA 95518.

CAREER: Carpenter in the Humboldt Bay region, 1978—. Humboldt State University, lecturer, 1992—.

WRITINGS:

Journey Work (poems), Tangram, 1989.

Shell Game: A True Account of Beads and Money in North America, Mercury House (San Francisco, CA), 1996.

Some writing appears under the pseudonym Dr. Loon.

WORK IN PROGRESS: A poetry collection on parental care-taking; research on the economic history of northern California.

*   *   *

MAXWELL, Glyn 1962-

PERSONAL: Born in 1962, in Welwyn Garden City, England. *Education:* Attended Oxford University; attended Boston University.

ADDRESSES: Agent—c/o Bloodaxe Books, P.O. 1SN, Newcastle upon Tyne NE99 1SN, England.

CAREER: Freelance writer and editor.

AWARDS, HONORS: Eric Gregory award, 1991; Poetry Book Society Choice for *Tale of the Mayor's Son,* and recommendation for *Out of the Rain;* Somerset Maugham award for *Out of the Rain.*

WRITINGS:

POETRY

Tale of the Mayor's Son, Bloodaxe (Newcastle upon Tyne), 1990.
Out of the Rain, Bloodaxe, 1992.
Rest for the Wicked, Bloodaxe, 1995.

PLAYS

Gnyss the Magnificent: Three Verse Plays, Chatto and Windus (London), 1993.

NOVEL

Blue Burneau, Chatto and Windus (London), 1994.

*   *   *

MAYO, C(atherine) M(ansell) 1961-
   (Catherine Mansell Carstens)

PERSONAL: Born March 22, 1961, in El Paso, TX; daughter of Roger (in business) and Carolyn (Mayo) Mansell; married Agustin Carstens (a banker), July 19, 1986. *Ethnicity:* "Scotch-Irish." *Education:* University of Chicago, B.A., 1982, M.A., 1985. *Politics:* "Skeptical." *Religion:* None. *Avocational interests:* Collecting travel memoirs written by foreigners in Mexico.

ADDRESSES: Home and office—Tameme, Callejon de Torresqui 12, Barrio Santa Catarina, Coyoacan, 04010 Mexico D.F., Mexico.

CAREER: Euro American Capital Corp. Ltd., Mexico City, Mexico, economist, 1988-90; Instituto Tecnologico Autonomo de Mexico, Mexico City, professor of economics, 1990-94; *Tameme* (bilingual literary magazine), Mexico City, founder, 1994, editor, 1994—.

AWARDS, HONORS: Flannery O'Connor Award for Short Fiction, University of Georgia Press, 1995, for *Sky Over El Nido;* Bread Loaf fellow, 1996; Walter E. Dakin fellow, Sewanee Writers Conference, 1996; MacDowell and Yaddo fellowships.

WRITINGS:

Sky Over El Nido (stories), University of Georgia Press (Athens, GA), 1995.

Work represented in anthologies, including *American Poets Say Goodbye to the Twentieth Century,* edited by Andrei Codrescu, Four Walls Eight Windows Press (New York), 1996. Contributor of stories and poems to periodicals, including *Pig Iron, Paris Review, Southwest Review, Quarterly, Northwest Review,* and *Rio Grande Review.*

UNDER NAME CATHERINE MANSELL CARSTENS

Las Nuevas Finanzas en Mexico, Editorial Milenio (Mexico City), 1992.
Las Finanzas Populares en Mexico, Editorial Milenio, 1995.
Liberalizacion e Innovacion Financiera en los Paises Desarrollados y en America Latina, Centro de Estudios Monetarios Latinoamericanos (Mexico City), 1996.

Contributor to periodicals, including *El Trimestre Economico, Informe mensual sobre la economia mexicana, El Inversionista, Business Mexico, Mexico Journal, Hemisfile,* and *El Economista.*

WORK IN PROGRESS: Baja California, a travel book; *Revillagigedo,* short stories; research on the history, politics, and popular culture of Baja California.

*   *   *

MAYOR, Federico 1934-

PERSONAL: Born January 27, 1934, in Barcelona, Spain; married; children: three. *Education:* Complutense University of Madrid, Graduate in Pharmacy, 1956, Ph.D., 1958.

ADDRESSES: Agent—c/o Librairie Ernest Flammarion, 26 rue Racine, F-75278, Paris cedex 06, France.

CAREER: University of Granada, Granada, Spain, professor of biochemistry, 1963-73, director of Department of Pharmacy, 1967-68, rector, 1968-72, honorary rector, 1972—; Autonomous University of Madrid, Madrid, Spain, professor of biochemistry, 1973, founder of Severo Ochoa Molecular Biology Center, director, 1974-78; UNESCO, member of advisory committee for scientific research and human needs, Moscow, U.S.S.R., 1976, and Paris, France, 1977, member of advisory committee, European Center for Higher Education, Bucharest, Romania, 1976-78, representative of the director-general on the board of United Nations University, Tokyo, Japan, 1980-81; Spanish minister for education and science, 1981-82; Institute of the Sciences of Man, Madrid, director, 1983-87; UNESCO, director-general, 1987—. Oxford University, visiting professor and senior fellow of Trinity College, 1966-67; Autonomous University of Madrid, scientific chairperson of Severo Ochoa Molecular Biology Center, 1983-87. Spanish Ministry for Education, under-secretary, 1974-75; Office of the Spanish Prime Minister, chairperson of Advisory Committee for Scientific and Technical Research, 1974-78; Royal Foundation of Spain for Special Education, member, 1976-78; Spanish Parliament, member of parliament and chairperson of Parliamentary Commission for Education and Science, 1977-78; European Parliament, member, 1987. Ramon Areces Foundation, vice chair of scientific committee, 1982—. Issyk-Kul Forum (Frunze, Kirghiz Republic), founding member, 1986—.

MEMBER: International Brain Research Organization, International Cell Research Organization, World Academy of Art and Science, World Science Institute, European Academy of Arts, Sciences, and Literature (founding member), Academia Europaea, Spanish Society of Biochemistry (chairperson, 1970-74), Spanish Royal Academy of Pharmacy, Royal Academy of Fine Arts of San Fernando, American Chemical Society, American Association for the Advancement of Science, American Academy of Microbiology, Biochemical Society (England), Royal Society of Chemistry (England), French Society of Biological Chemistry, French Academy of Pharmacy (corresponding member), Ateneo Veneto, Philippine Academy of Language, National Academy of Science of Bolivia, Argentinian Academy of Pharmacy and Biochemistry, Bulgarian Academy of Sciences, Chinese Academy of Sciences, Rumanian Academy, Club of Rome.

AWARDS, HONORS: Honorary doctorates.

WRITINGS:

(Translator) Strohecker and Henning, *Vitamin Assay,* Paz Montalvo, 1967.

(Editor with S. Grisolia and R. Baguena) *The Urea Cycle,* Wiley (New York), 1977.

(Editor) *Scientific Research and Goals: Towards a New Development Model,* Pergamon (Oxford, England), 1982.

(Editor) *La lucha contra la enfermedad,* Lilly (Madrid, Spain), 1986.

Manana siempre es tarde (essay), Espasa Calpe (Madrid), 1987, published as *Tomorrow Is Always Too Late,* Stamford Publishing (Singapore, China), 1992.

(Editor with Severo Ochoa and M. Barbacid) *Oncogenes y Patologia Molecular,* CEURA (Madrid), 1987.

Aguafuertes (poems), Litoral (Malaga, Spain), 1991, published as *Patterns,* Forest Books (London, England), 1994.

(Coauthor) *The New Page* (essay), Dartmouth Publishing (Brookfield, VT), 1994.

La memoire de l'avenir (essay), UNESCO Publishers (Paris, France), 1994, published as *Memory of the Future,* 1995.

La Paix, Demain? (essay), Flammarion (Paris), 1995.

Contributor to books, including *Reflections on Biochemistry,* edited by A. Kornberg, B. L. Horecker, and others, Pergamon, 1976. Contributor of more than eighty articles to scientific journals.

McCAFFERY, Steve 1947-

PERSONAL: Born January 24, 1947, in Sheffield, England; married Margaret McCaffery, 1968 (divorced 1983); companion of Karen MacCormack, since 1984. *Education:* Hull University, B.A. (honors) 1968; York University, M.A., 1969.

ADDRESSES: Home—1086 Bathurst St., 2nd Fl., Toronto, Ontario M5R 3G9, Canada.

CAREER: University of California, San Diego, lecturer, 1989; Queen's University, Kingston, Ontario, lecturer in English, 1993-95.

WRITINGS:

POETRY

Dr. Sadhu's Muffins, Press Porcepic (Victoria), 1974.
'Ow's Waif, Coach House Press (Toronto), 1975.
Intimate Distortions, Porcupine's Quill (Erin, Ontario), 1978.
Evoba, Coach House Press (Toronto), 1987.
The Black Debt, Nightwood Editions (London, Ontario), 1989.
Theory of Sediment, Talonbooks (Vancouver), 1991.

NOVEL

Panopticon, blewointment press (Toronto), 1984.

OTHER

North of Intention, Root Books (New York), 1986.

*   *   *

McCLARY, Susan 1946-

PERSONAL: Born October 2, 1946, in St. Louis, MO. *Education:* Southern Illinois University, B.Mus., 1968; Harvard University, A.M., 1971, Ph.D., 1976.

ADDRESSES: Office—Department of Music, University of Minnesota, Minneapolis, MN 55455.

CAREER: Educator, writer, and composer. Trinity University, Hartford, CT, lecturer, 1977; University of Minnesota, Minneapolis, associate professor, 1977-90, professor of musicology, 1990—, acting director, Center for Humanistic Studies, 1984-85, and director, Collegium Musicum. Creator of several musical compositions for music theatre.

WRITINGS:

(Editor, with Richard Leppert) *Music and Society: The Politics of Composition, Performance, and Reception,* Cambridge University Press (Cambridge), 1987.
Feminine Endings: Music, Gender, and Sexuality, University of Minnesota Press (Minneapolis), 1991.
Power and Desire in Seventeenth-Century Music, Princeton University Press (Princeton, NJ), 1991.
Georges Bizet, "Carmen," Cambridge University Press, 1992.

SIDELIGHTS: Feminist musicologist Susan McClary's *Feminine Endings: Music, Gender, and Sexuality* is considered groundbreaking in its attempt to uncover the "traditional woman's voice" embedded within the Western musical cannon. Offering a feminist critique of composers ranging from Mozart to Madonna, McClary's work was praised by *Nation* reviewer Edward W. Said as a "greatly needed social commentary" on the past three centuries of musical compositions. A professor at the University of Minnesota since 1977, McClary began her career by researching the construction of even earlier musical compositions; her findings, which she published in musical journals, cast new light on the commonly-held view of seventeenth-century music. According to McClary, music of this period incorporates a far more sophisticated tonality than previously assumed.

In the essays collected in 1991's *Feminine Endings,* McClary challenges both the traditional Western assumption that music is unreflective of cultural norms and the time-honored techniques of musical interpretation. She develops a new methodology which utilizes gender and sexuality to differentiate elements such as cadences, beats, and overall musical composition. Within this new, "radical feminist" methodology, she highlights the overall "effeminate" qualities of musical culture, remarking that while music has a strong power over the physical body of the listener—"mak[ing] us experience our bodies in accordance with its gestures and rhythms," she notes—patriarchal pressures have, over the centuries, forced musical compositions to be narrowly intellectualized in ways that utilize objective, "masculine" standards of analysis. "No one will read these essays without thinking about and hearing music in new and interesting ways," noted *Choice* reviewer J. P. Ambrose.

Other works by McClary include *Power and Desire in Seventeenth-Century Music* and *Georges Bizet, "Carmen,"* part of Cambridge University Press's "Opera Handbook" series. Containing a detailed discussion of the well-known opera's musical background, a synopsis of *Carmen*'s plot, and information regarding recent film adaptations of Bizet's classic work, McClary also includes a chapter that harkens back to her earlier work: "Images of Race, Class, and Gender in Nineteenth-Century French Culture."

BIOGRAPHICAL/CRITICAL SOURCES:

BOOKS

Feminine Endings: Music, Gender, and Sexuality, University of Minnesota Press (Minneapolis), 1991.

PERIODICALS

Belles Lettres, summer, 1991, p. 40.
Choice, June, 1991, p. 1650; May, 1993, p. 1477.
Nation, December 30, 1991, p. 60.
New Republic, February 3, 1992, p. 32.
Signs, autumn, 1992, pp. 171-72.
Times Literary Supplement, November 13, 1992.
Women's Review of Books, September, 1991, p. 11.

*   *   *

McCLURE, Sandy   1948-

PERSONAL: Born September 19, 1948, in Philadelphia, PA; daughter of G. R. (a research scientist) and Helen (a homemaker; maiden name, Wells) Moreland; married John Bensinger (a teacher), August 14, 1994; children: Eileen McClure, Barb McClure, Gretchen, Rachel, Mansell. *Education:* Temple University, B.A., 1981.

ADDRESSES: Home—Hill School, Pottstown, PA 19464. *Office*—*Intelligencer,* 408 West Broad St., Quakertown, PA 18951. *Agent*—Elizabeth Frost Knappman, New England Publishing, Box 5, Chester, CT 06412.

CAREER: Town and Country, Pennsburg, PA, part-time sports reporter, 1979-81; *Free Press,*

Quakertown, PA, borough and environmental reporter, 1982-85; *Globe-Times,* Bethlehem, PA, city hall reporter, 1985-87; *Mercury,* Pottstown, PA, borough, police, and courthouse reporter, 1987-89; *Trentonian,* Trenton, NJ, statehouse and investigative reporter, 1989-95; *Intelligencer,* Doylestown, PA, reporter, 1995—.

AWARDS, HONORS: Pennsylvania Newspaper Publishers Association, G. Richard Dew Award, 1984, for investigative reporting and a news series, first place awards, 1985-86, for investigative reporting, and first place award, 1989, for spot news; Journalism Award, Common Cause of New Jersey, 1990; first place award, New Jersey Press Association, 1994, for responsible journalism in the enterprise category.

WRITINGS:

Christie Whitman for the People, Prometheus Books (Amherst, NY), 1996.

*   *   *

MCCOY, Donald R(ichard)   1928-1996

OBITUARY NOTICE—See index for *CA* sketch: Born January 18, 1928, in Chicago, IL; died of lung cancer, November 12, 1996, in Lawrence, KS. Educator, historian, author. McCoy was distinguished in the field of history for his written works and as the editor of the American Presidency biographical series. After serving in the U.S. Army Signal Corps at the end of World War II, McCoy began his teaching career at American University in Washington, D.C. From 1951 to 1952, McCoy was an archivist for the National Archives before starting a five-year stint at Cortland State Teachers College (now the State University of New York College) in Cortland, New York. In 1957, McCoy joined the faculty of the University of Kansas, where he taught for the next thirty-eight years. His first book, *Angry Voices: Left-of-Center Movements in the New Deal Era,* was published in 1958. Over the years, he received several honors for his writings, including the Byron Caldwell Smith award and was twice nominated for a Pulitzer Prize. He wrote more than one hundred historical papers, many of which were published in trade journals. His books include *Calvin Coolidge: The Quiet President, The National Archives: America's Ministry of Documents, 1934-1968, Coming of Age: The*

United States During the 1920s and 1930s, and *The Presidency of Harry Truman.*

OBITUARIES AND OTHER SOURCES:

BOOKS

Who's Who in America, 52nd edition, Marquis, 1997.

PERIODICALS

Washington Post, November 17, 1996, p. B6.

*   *   *

McMASTER, Rhyll 1947-

PERSONAL: Born August 13, 1947, in Brisbane, Queensland, Australia; married Roger McDonald, 1967 (divorced, 1994); children: three daughters.

ADDRESSES: *Agent*—Rose Creswell, Cameron's Management, Suite 5, Edgecliff Ct., 2 New McLean St., Edgecliff, New South Wales 2027, Australia.

CAREER: University of Queensland, Brisbane, secretary, 1966-71; Canberra Hospital, nurse, 1976-78; Braidwood, New South Wales, farmer, 1980-91.

AWARDS, HONORS: Harri Jones Memorial prize, 1971; Victorian Premier's prize, 1986, for *Washing the Money;* Grace Leven prize, 1987.

WRITINGS:

POETRY

The Brineshrimp, University of Queensland Press (Brisbane), 1972.
Washing the Money, Angus and Robertson (Sydney), 1986.
On My Empty Feet, Heinemann (Melbourne), 1993.
Flying the Coop, Heinemann, 1994.

*   *   *

McNEIL, W. K. 1940-

PERSONAL: Born August 13, 1940, near Canton, NC; son of William McKinley (a sales manager) and

Margaret Winifred (an office worker; maiden name, Rigdon) McNeil; married Grace Joy Taucan Morandarte (a homemaker), July 25, 1994. *Ethnicity:* "Caucasian." *Education:* Carson-Newman College, B.A., 1962; Oklahoma State University, M.A., 1963; State University of New York College at Oneonta, M.A., 1967; Indiana University—Bloomington, Ph.D., 1980. *Politics:* Independent. *Religion:* None. *Avocational interests:* Collecting books, records, and sheet music.

ADDRESSES: *Home*—P.O. Box 1097, Mount View, AR 72560. *Office*—P.O. Box 500, Mount View, AR 92560.

CAREER: State Department of Education, Albany, NY, historian, 1967-70; Smithsonian Institution, Washington, DC, folklorist, 1975-76; Ozark Folk Center, Mountain View, AR, folklorist, 1976—. National Folk Festival, member of advisory board.

MEMBER: American Folklore Society (fellow), Mid-America Folklore Society (president, 1981), Pennsylvania Folklife Society, New York Folklore Society, Texas Folklore Society, Missouri Folklore Society, Phi Alpha Theta.

AWARDS, HONORS: Outstanding Academic Book Award, *Choice,* 1995.

WRITINGS:

American Proverb Literature, Folklore Forum, 1971.
The Charm Is Broken: Readings in Arkansas and Missouri Folklore, August House (Little Rock, AR), 1984.
Ghost Stories From the American South, August House, 1985.
On a Slow Train Through Arkansaw, University Press of Kentucky (Lexington, KY), 1985.
Southern Folk Ballads, August House, 1987-88.
The Life and Adventures of an Arkansaw Doctor, University of Arkansas Press (Fayetteville, AR), 1989.
Ozark Mountain Humor, August House, 1989.

Other writings include the book *Ozark Country,* University Press of Mississippi (Jackson, MS). Book review editor, *Journal of American Folklore,* 1977-80, and *Mid-America Folklore,* 1980-83.

WORK IN PROGRESS: *Notable Women in American Folklore; A History of American Folklore Scholarship; Folklore in American Literature;* a biography of

Elton Britt; research for *The Ozarks of the Mind* and *Biographical Dictionary of Traditional Country Music*.

SIDELIGHTS: W. K. O'Neil told *CA:* "My primary motivation for writing is a love for whatever it is I write about. Most often it has been folklore, but I also have a strong interest in the Ozarks, music, literature, and crafts. There are many influences on my work, but it is hard to pick out any one person or thing. It will have to suffice that I am influenced by many things I have read and, in some way or other, by nearly every teacher I have had, at least on the graduate level.

"I am a pretty good procrastinator, so I have to force myself to stick to a schedule to complete things in a timely manner. I do my best work late at night and my worst early in the morning. For that reason, I almost never try to put things off until the next morning. I know that if I don't finish something at night, I will most likely never get it done.

"Once I have a book-length project in mind, I begin with the first chapter and write consecutively until I reach the end. I always have a book in mind before starting. I never start out to write an article and later decide to expand it into a book. Like all writers, I guess, I go into something of a trance when I start writing. Generally, I have great trouble starting a book, but once I get going, I can move along pretty fast.

"I tend to write about things that I like and that I know a lot about. Sometimes, though, I write to solve a mystery or answer questions I have about the topic. This is particularly the case with biographical works. I prefer writing about people who are deceased, because then the life story is over, though their influence is not always dead."

*   *   *

McQUEEN, Cilla 1949-

PERSONAL: Born January 22, 1949, in Birmingham, England; married Ralph Hotere, 1974; children: one daughter. *Education:* Columba College; Otago University, M.A. (honors), 1970.

ADDRESSES: Office—P.O. Box 69, Portobello, Dunedin, New Zealand.

CAREER: Teacher. Artist: individual shows at Bosshard Galleries, Dunedin, 1982; Red Metro Gallery, Dunedin, 1983.

AWARDS, HONORS: New Zealand Book award, 1983, 1989; P.E.N./Jessie Mackay award, 1983; Air New Zealand/P.E.N. travel award, 1984; Robert Burns fellowship, 1985, 1986; Fulbright Visiting Writer's fellowship, 1985; Inaugural Australian-New Zealand Writers' exchange fellowship, 1987; Goethe Institute scholarship, 1988; New Zealand Book award, 1991, for *Berlin Diary*.

WRITINGS:

POETRY

Homing In, McIndoe (Dunedin), 1982.
Anti Gravity, McIndoe, 1984.
Wild Sweets, McIndoe, 1986.
Benzina, McIndoe, 1988.
Berlin Diary, McIndoe, 1990.
Crikey, McIndoe, 1994.

PLAYS

Harlequin and Columbine, produced in Dunedin, 1987.
Red Rose Cafe, produced in Dunedin, 1990.

Also author of a radio play, *Spacy Calcutta's Travelling Truth Show,* 1986.

*   *   *

MEAD, Philip (Stirling) 1953-

PERSONAL: Born August 31, 1953, in Brisbane, Queensland, Australia; married Jenna Mead, 1974; children: one daughter. *Education:* Australian National University, B.A., 1975; La Trobe University, M.A., 1981; Melbourne University, Ph.D., 1990.

ADDRESSES: Office—English Department, University of Tasmania, Hobart 7000, Australia.

CAREER: University of Melbourne, Lockie lecturer in Australian Writing, 1987-95; University of Tasmania, Hobart, senior lecturer in English, 1995—. Founder, with Alan Gould, David Brooks, and Mark O'Connor, *Canberra Poetry.*

WRITINGS:

POETRY

Songs from Another Country, Open Door Press (Canberra), 1975.
Be Faithful to Go: Poems, Angus & Robertson (London), 1980.
The Spring-Mire: Poems, Brindabella Press (Canberra), 1982.
The River Is in the South, University of Queensland Press (St. Lucia), 1984.

OTHER

(Editor with Gerald Murnane and Jenny Lee) *The Temperament of Generations: Fifty Years of Writing in Meanjin,* Melbourne University Press (Carlton, Victoria, Meanjin), 1990.
(Editor with John Tranter) *The Penguin Book of Modern Australian Poetry,* Penguin Books (Ringwood, Victoria), 1991.

*   *   *

MEE, Susie (B.)   1938-

PERSONAL: Born December 29, 1938, in Trion, GA; daughter of J. Leo (an undertaker) and Addie (a restaurant hostess; maiden name, McWilliams) Baker; married Charles Mee, Jr. (divorced, 1981); children: Erin B., Chaz. *Ethnicity:* "Caucasian." *Education:* University of Georgia, B.F.A.; attended Yale University; Hollins College, M.A., 1994. *Politics:* Democrat. *Religion:* Baptist. *Avocational interests:* Opera, reading gardening books, theater.

ADDRESSES: Home and office—349 West 22nd St., New York, NY 10011. *Agent*—Cullen Stanley, Janklow & Nesbit Associates, 598 Madison Ave., New York, NY 10022-1614.

CAREER: New York University, New York City, part-time assistant professor of creative writing, 1987—. Staten Island College, teacher of poetry workshop, 1995—. Consultant to Teachers and Writers Collaborative. West 22nd Street Block Association (past vice-president).

AWARDS, HONORS: Yaddo resident; resident at MacDowell Colony and Virginia Center for the Creative Arts; grant from NYSCA, 1979; Artists Award, New York Foundation, 1990-93.

WRITINGS:

Stories of the Poets (biographical essays), Scholastic (New York City), 1989.
The Undertaker's Daughter (poems), Junction Press (Grand Junction, TN), 1993.
The Girl Who Loved Elvis (novel), Peachtree Publishers (Atlanta, GA), 1994.
Down Home: An Anthology of Southern Women Writers, Harcourt (Orlando, FL), 1995.

WORK IN PROGRESS: A memoir about being the daughter of an undertaker.

SIDELIGHTS: Susie Mee told *CA:* "I love language and getting into the heads of other people. These are my primary motivations for writing. I can be influenced by anything: something I have read or heard or overheard, memories (a lot), and dreams. I love southern writers, especially Faulkner and Flannery O'Connor. Doesn't everyone? I like first-person stories or monologues, and I write a lot of them. Sometimes these develop into stories. Sometimes I perform them as part of a one-woman show. I am currently performing a piece called 'The Undertaker's Daughter' here in New York City."

*   *   *

MEEHAN, Paula   1955-

PERSONAL: Born June 25, 1955, in Dublin, Ireland. *Education:* Trinity College, B.A., 1977; Eastern Washington University, M.F.A., 1983.

ADDRESSES: Agent—Peter Fallon, Loughcrew, Oldcastle, County Meath, Ireland.

CAREER: Literacy organizer, South Inner City, Dublin, 1984-88. Conducts workshops in poetry for community groups, including North Centre City Community Action Project and the Fatima Mansions Development Group. Since 1985 Irish co-coordinator, poetry master classes, Summer Writing Workshop in Dublin, Eastern Washington University. Since 1986 teacher of writing workshops in prisons, Arts Council Writers in the Prison Scheme. Poet-in-residence, The Frost place, Franconia, New Hampshire, spring, 1987; writer-in-residence, Trinity College, Dublin, 1992; writer by association, University College, Dublin, 1992; outreach residency with Verbal Arts Centre, Derry and Antrim counties, 1993; writer-in-residence, TEAM Theatre in Education, Dublin, 1994.

AWARDS, HONORS: Irish Arts Council bursary in literature, 1987, 1990.

WRITINGS:

POETRY

Return and No Blame, Beaver Row Press (Dublin), 1984.
Reading the Sky, Beaver Row Press, 1988.
The Man Who Was Marked by Winter, Gallery Press (Oldcastle, County Meath), 1991, and Eastern Washington University Press (Cheney, WA), 1994.
Pillow Talk, Gallery Press, 1994.

PLAYS

Kirkle (produced in Dublin, 1995).

*　*　*

MEHROTRA, Arvind Krishna 1947-

PERSONAL: Born April 16, 1947, in Lahore, Pakistan; married Vandana Jain, 1969; children: one son. *Education:* University of Allahabad, B.A., 1966; University of Bombay, M.A., 1968.

ADDRESSES: Home—Jyoti Apartments, 1 N.K. Mukerji Rd., Allahabad 211001, India.

CAREER: University of Allahabad, lecturer in English, 1968-77, reader in English, 1978—; University of Iowa, Iowa City, visiting writer, 1971-73; University of Hyderabad, India, lecturer in English, 1977-78. Editor, *damn youla magazine of the arts,* Allahabad, 1965-68; founder, Ezra-Fakir Press, Bombay, 1966.

AWARDS, HONORS: Homi Bhabha fellowship, 1981; *Gettysburg Review* award, 1994.

WRITINGS:

POETRY

Bharatmata: A Prayer, Ezra Fakir Press (Bombay), 1966.

Woodcuts on Paper, Gallery Number Ten (London), 1967.
Pomes/Poemes/Poemas, Vrischik (Baroda, India), 1971.
Nine Enclosures, Clearing House (Bombay), 1976.
Distance in Statute Miles, Clearing House, 1982.
Middle Earth, Oxford University Press (New Delhi), 1984.

OTHER

(Translator) *Three Poems,* by Bogomil Gjuzel, Ezra Fakir Press (Allahabad and Iowa City), 1973.
(Translator) *The Absent Traveller: Prakrit Love Poetry from the Gathasaptasati of Satvahana Hala,* Ravi Dayal (New Delhi), 1990.
(Editor) *Twenty Indian Poems,* Oxford University Press (New Delhi), 1990.
(Editor) *The Oxford India Anthology of Twelve Modern Indian Poets,* Oxford University Press, 1992.
(Editor with Daniel Weissbort) *Periplus: Poetry in Translation,* Oxford University Press, 1993.

*　*　*

MELICH, Tanya 1936-

PERSONAL: Born April 23, 1936, in Moab, UT; daughter of Mitchell (an attorney) and Doris (a community leader; maiden name, Snyder) Melish; married Noel L. Silverman, December 28, 1962; children: Karla Noelle, Evan Mitchell. *Education:* University of Colorado, B.S. (cum laude), 1958; Columbia University, M.A., 1961, and doctoral study. *Politics:* Independent Republican. *Religion:* American Baptist. *Avocational interests:* Theater, gardening.

ADDRESSES: Office—Political Issues Management, 136 East 57th St., No. 1305, New York, NY 10022. *Agent*—Noel L. Silverman, Silverman & Schulman, 136 East 57th St., New York, NY 10022.

CAREER: Salt Lake Tribune, Salt Lake City, UT, reporter, 1957; Foreign Policy Association, researcher and writer, 1962; American Broadcasting Co., director of national election research for *ABC News,* 1963-64; Lindsay for Mayor Campaign, research director, 1965; Rockefeller for Governor Campaign, scheduler, 1966; editorial assistant to Thomas E. Dewey, 1967-68; Rockefeller for President Campaign, co-director of Delegate Unit, 1968; Allen-van Slyck Group, public affairs writer, 1969;

U.S. Senator Charles Goodell Election Committee, New York state chairperson for research, 1970; Philip van Slyck, Inc., public affairs writer, 1971-72; Commission on Critical Choices, policy analyst, 1973; Academy for Educational Development, writer and editor, 1973; consultant to Nelson A. Rockefeller, 1974; Columbia Broadcasting System, Inc., Corporate Affairs Division, editor of corporate information, 1975-76, associate director of Public Policy Unit, 1976-78, director of civic affairs, 1978-81; Political Issues Management, New York City, president and consultant in public policy analysis and strategy, 1983—. Harvard University, fellow of Kennedy School of Government, 1980. National Women's Political Caucus, co-founder of Manhattan Women's Political Caucus, 1971, and New York Women's Political Caucus, 1972; National Women's Education Fund, member of board of directors, 1974-86, president, 1980-83; New York City Commission on the Status of Women, member of advisory committee, 1982—, and reproductive health committee, 1986—; New York State Commission on Judicial Nomination, member, 1983—; New York County Republican Party, vice-president, 1983—; Child Care Action Campaign, member of leadership council, 1984-86; Carnegie Council on Ethics and International Affairs, member, 1985-88; New York State Republican Family Committee, executive director, 1985-94; New York State Family Planning Advocates, member of board of directors, 1990—; Republican Pro-Choice Political Action Committee, member of board of directors, 1990—.

MEMBER: Phi Beta Kappa, Pi Gamma Mu, Pi Sigma Alpha, Sigma Epsilon Sigma, Women's City Club.

AWARDS, HONORS: Susan B. Anthony Women of Achievement Award, National Organization for Women, 1980; Outstanding Woman Award, National Women's Political Caucus, 1986; Woodrow Wilson fellow, 1988—; Alfred E. Moran Public Advocacy Award, 1990.

WRITINGS:

The Republican War Against Women: An Insider's Report From Behind the Lines, Bantam (New York City), 1996.

Contributor to books, including *The Lessons of Victory,* Dial, 1969; and *Jaws of Victory,* Little, Brown (New York City), 1974. Contributor to periodicals, including *Newsday, Women's Political Times,* and *Ripon Forum.*

MENDELSOHN, Jane 1965-

PERSONAL: Born in 1965; daughter of Frederick (a psychiatrist) and Leatrice (an art historian) Mendelsohn; married Nick Davis (a filmmaker). *Education:* Yale University, B.A., graduate study.

ADDRESSES: Home—New York, NY. *Agent*—c/o Knopf, 201 East 50th St., New York, NY 10022.

CAREER: Writer.

WRITINGS:

I Was Amelia Earhart (novel), Knopf (New York), 1996.

SIDELIGHTS: Author Jane Mendelsohn has had a great deal of popular and critical success with her first novel, 1996's *I Was Amelia Earhart.* Within months of its release it had sold over 150,000 copies, a fact *People* magazine contributor Joanne Kaufman considered "exceptional for a literary first novel." Part of Mendelsohn's triumph is due to the fact that *I Was Amelia Earhart* first caught the attention of the wife of popular radio talk show host Don Imus, then Imus himself, who went on to praise the novel's merits on the air for three days in a row. Since then, as Kaufman phrased it, "reviewers other than the I-man have also been generous."

Mendelsohn grew up in Manhattan, New York. She recalled for Kaufman that her parents divorced during her childhood and that she "was a very bookish little kid." She started writing while young, and revealed: "I wrote these mock Agatha Christie murder mysteries where there were always characters bursting through French doors." After studying English at Yale University as an undergraduate, she began attending Yale law school before deciding to devote herself to writing full-time. Mendelsohn had difficulty, at first, finding an agent or a publisher to handle *I Was Amelia Earhart;* agents indicated to her that while they liked the book, they feared it was not commercial enough to succeed in publication.

I Was Amelia Earhart is related through both the first- and third-person narratives, and tells the story of the pioneering feminist aviator's life before her disappearance while attempting to circumnavigate the world—including her relationship with publisher husband G. P. Putnam, who reportedly pushed her to ignore safety precautions in order that her book about the trip might be ready for release during the holiday season. For the fact-based first portion of the book, Mendelsohn follows the standard biographies of Earhart and also the pilot's own writings; however, for the second part of the book she offers readers a fantasy of what might have happened afterward. In the novel, Earhart and her navigator Fred Noonan crash upon a deserted island in the Pacific Ocean. Though Noonan is a drinker, and the two bicker at first, they eventually discover a deep love for each other. They cherish their solitude, their oblivion. When it seems that their rescue is imminent, they take off in the plane again, to crash on yet another tropical isle. Earhart now begins to write the story of her life, even though she is no longer living.

"If you can suspend disbelief and accept Earhart's self-conscious posthumous account," asserted Frances Stead Sellers in the *New York Times Book Review,* "her story becomes curiously compelling." Michiko Kakutani of the *New York Times* applauded *I Was Amelia Earhart* as "lyrical," and judged that it "invokes the spirit of a mythic personage, while standing on its own as a powerfully imagined work of fiction." Though Molly E. Rauch in *Nation* wasn't entirely favorable in her remarks about the novel, she conceded that Mendelsohn's "melding of fantasy and reality make us feel as though we are witnessing someone else's dream." Daphne Merkin, opining in *New Yorker,* had high praise for *I Was Amelia Earhart,* observing that it is "drenched in visual effects—many of which continue to dance before the retina after one has read them, more like images on canvas than like words on the page," and concluding that "[i]ts quiet air of astonishment lends the shine of newness to everything it touches."

BIOGRAPHICAL/CRITICAL SOURCES:

PERIODICALS

Nation, April 22, 1996, pp. 35-36.
New Yorker, May 20, 1996, pp. 96-97.
New York Times, April 26, 1996, p. C31.
New York Times Book Review, May 12, 1996, p. 10.
People, June 17, 1996, p. 157.*

*   *   *

MERTVAGO, Peter   1946-

PERSONAL: Born June 22, 1946, in Athens, Greece; U.S. citizen; married Ludmila Zernovoy, January 7,

1976; children: Vladimir, Nicholas. *Ethnicity:* "Russian." *Education:* New York University, B.A., 1968, M.A., 1970; Queen's College, Oxford, B.A. (with honors), 1972. *Religion:* Russian Orthodox. *Avocational interests:* Art (painting, printmaking).

ADDRESSES: Home—Elmhurst, NY.

CAREER: University of California, Berkeley, instructor in Latin, 1972-75; United Nations, New York City, translator and interpreter in English booth, 1976-79, interpreter in Geneva, Switzerland, 1979-95, senior interpreter in English booth, 1995—. University of Geneva, instructor, 1986-93.

WRITINGS:

The Comparative Russian-English Dictionary of Russian Proverbs and Sayings, Hippocrene Books (New York City), 1995.
Dictionary of One-Thousand Spanish Proverbs, Hippocrene Books, 1995.
Dictionary of One-Thousand French Proverbs, Hippocrene Books, 1995.
Dictionary of One-Thousand Italian Proverbs, Hippocrene Books, 1996.
Dictionary of One-Thousand German Proverbs, Hippocrene Books, 1996.

WORK IN PROGRESS: Escape Through Tibet, a true account of a White Russian's trek to freedom, as told to the author by the man who made it; *Simultaneous Interpretation From Russian Into English: A Handbook for Interpreters; The Proverbial Minimum: Five-Hundred Equivalent Proverbs in Seven European Languages,* including English, French, Spanish, German, Italian, Russian, and Latin.

SIDELIGHTS: Peter Mertvago told *CA:* "The primary motivation that prompted me to write the dictionary of Russian proverbs was the frequent need for such a reference book that I myself experienced in my work as a simultaneous interpreter. Though several monolingual compilations of proverbs existed, there was no work available that would give accurate English equivalents to Russian proverbs, or in any other way seek to explain or situate them in an English-language perspective. Yet both spoken Russian and Russian literature make such regular use of proverbs and sayings (perhaps to an extent that is more customary than in English) that is impossible to have any dealings with native Russians in their language without constantly running across them. All this, coupled with the surge of interest in Russia after the cold war, convinced me that the time was more than ripe for such a work, one that could be useful at a variety of levels, from the academic and pedagogical to that of common interest.

"Researching and preparing the dictionary took a good seven years and brought me in touch with the works of many eminent paremiographers past and present, but I was particularly struck by what was being done by G. L. Permiakov in the former U.S.S.R. He had, over many years, given voice to and developed concepts that I had only vaguely and intuitively begun to appreciate in my everyday practical contact with proverbs. His work on devising a 'proverb minimum' for Russian inspired me to consider this approach in the context of a core of equivalent proverbs common to the European languages that are still in use or widely recognized today. This spawned my series of separate dictionaries. I plan to tie all this practical work and theory together in one concise English-based volume that covers seven languages."

*   *   *

MILLER, Jean Baker 1927-

PERSONAL: Born September 29, 1927, in New York, NY; married; children: two children. *Education:* Sarah Lawrence College, B.A., 1948; Columbia University, M.D., 1952; Montefiore Hospital (New York City), internship, 1952-53, residency in medicine, 1953-54; residency in psychiatry at Bellevue Medical Center, 1955-56, Albert Einstein College of Medicine, 1955-56, and Upstate Medical Center, Syracuse, 1962-63; New York Medical College, psychoanalytic training 1955-60.

ADDRESSES: Home—105 Salisbury Road, Brookline, MA 02146. *Office*—c/o Stone Center, Wellesley College, Wellesley, MA 02181-8268.

CAREER: Psychiatrist and educator. Upstate Medical Center, University of the State of New York, Syracuse, instructor in psychiatry, 1961-66; Albert Einstein College of Medicine, New York City, interdisciplinary research fellow, 1965-67, instructor, 1967-73; London School of Economics, visiting lecturer, 1972-73; Tavistock Institute and Clinic, London, visiting associate, 1972-73 and 1976-77, co-teacher, 1977; Boston University School of Medicine,

associate clinical professor, 1974-82, clinical professor of psychiatry, 1982—; Harvard Medical School, assistant clinical professor, 1974-81, lecturer in psychiatry, 1981—; Wellesley College, Wellesley, MA, professor of psychology, 1981-84, and director, 1981-84, scholar-in-residence, 1984-86, director of education, 1986—, currently associated with Stone Center for Developmental Services and Studies. Psychiatrist, in private practice, 1956—.

AWARDS, HONORS: Association for Women in Psychology Distinguished Career award, 1980; Rockefeller Foundation fellowship, 1981; Massachusetts Psychological Association Allied Professional Award, 1982; National Organization for Women (Massachusetts Chapter), Woman of the Year Award, 1982; D.H.L., Brandeis University, 1987; Unitarian-Universalist Association National Women's Federation Ministry to Women Award, 1987; American Orthopsychiatric Association Blanche F. Ittelson Memorial Award, 1995; D.H.C., Regis College, 1995.

MEMBER: American Psychiatric Association, American Academy of Psychoanalysis, American College of Psychiatrists, American Orthopsychiatric Association, Massachusetts Psychiatric Society, Society of Medical Psychoanalysts.

WRITINGS:

(Editor) *Psychoanalysis and Women: Contributions to New Theory and Therapy,* Brunner/Mazel (New York City), 1973.

(Editor) *Psychoanalysis and Women,* Penguin (Baltimore), 1974.

Towards a New Psychology of Women, Beacon Press (Boston), 1976, second edition, 1986.

(With others) *Women's Growth in Connection: Writings from the Stone Center,* Guilford Press (New York City), 1991.

(With others) *Connections, Disconnections, and Violations,* Basic Books (New York City), 1996.

Miller's manuscripts are collected at Stone Center, Wellesley College, Wellesley, MA.

SIDELIGHTS: With the 1976 publication of *Towards a New Psychology of Women,* psychiatrist and educator Jean Baker Miller helped to revolutionize her colleagues's understanding of women. Challenging the tradition-bound, male-centered perspective of mental health practitioners, Miller maintained that by judging women against male standards of behavior, the profession actually pathologized rather than helped to aid the psychological distress of their female patients. At the time it was revised in 1986, the highly readable *Towards a New Psychology of Women* was still dubbed "a pacesetter in the field" by a *Choice* reviewer.

During the mid-1970s, the work of Sigmund Freud, who held that women were less capable than men, still provided the foundation for treating the psychological problems experienced by women. In Freud's view, emotional maturity was reached when a patient was able to separate from one's family and become autonomous. Consequently, women, whose primary area of concern was with family members, were derogatorily assessed by Freud and his followers as "dependent" and less mature that men.

At the time Miller wrote *Toward a New Psychology of Women* she had amassed twenty years of clinical experience on which to ground her observations. In her book she suggests that this understanding is distorted by its basis on only half of the human population. She notes that Western culture socially mandates gender roles in a manner restrictive to both genders, placing women in the role of caregiver and men in the role of protector and bread-winner, forced to disassociate from their need for emotional connectedness. However, women's caregiving duties are devalued in social and economic terms, resulting in their pathologization by society—and, relatedly, by the mental health community—for the same behaviors that are socially mandated for them. Rather than viewing characteristics such as "female intuition" as a failing, Miller suggests that women's heightened sensitivity and inner sense of connection to others is central to their development as healthy adults.

Several years after the publication of her groundbreaking book Miller would help found Wellesley College's Stone Center for Developmental Services and Studies, an organization of woman-centered psychiatrists who work to provide a link between psychological theory and clinical practice, publishing their findings in a Work in Progress series. In 1991, Miller co-edited a selection of the Center's findings as *Women's Growth in Connection: Writings from the Stone Center.*

In addition to her work at the Stone Center, Miller's distinguished career has included time spent as an educator and practicing psychotherapist. Her contributions to feminist scholarship in the area of psychology have been essential to the reevaluation of clinical

prejudices that once dubbed women as psychologically impaired, but now could begin to open their eyes to a world of possibilities.

BIOGRAPHICAL/CRITICAL SOURCES:

PERIODICALS

Choice, February, 1977, p. 1664; July, 1987, p. 1759.
New Statesman and Society, November 15, 1974.
New York Review of Books, October 3, 1974.
New York Times Book Review, November 14, 1976, p. 4; December 11, 1977, p. 49; May 3, 1987, p. 42.
Publishers Weekly, July 12, 1976, p. 66.

* * *

MILLER, Philip L(ieson)   1906-1996

OBITUARY NOTICE—See index for *CA* sketch: Born April 23, 1906, in Woodland, NY; died November 23, 1996, in New York. Musicologist, librarian, writer. Miller gained notice as the head of the New York Public Library's music department, increasing its collections to rival that of the Library of Congress. Miller began nearly forty years with the library in 1927 as an assistant. He is credited with organizing concerts in Bryant Park and orchestrating the extensive collection's move to its present location at the Library and Museum of the Performing Arts at Lincoln Center. Miller contributed many articles to music journals, including *Musical Quarterly, High Fidelity,* and *Saturday Review.* He wrote the second volume of the *Guide to Long Playing Records* series, titled *Vocal Music.* He also compiled, translated, and wrote the accompanying text to *The Ring of Words: An Anthology of Song Texts.*

OBITUARIES AND OTHER SOURCES:

BOOKS

Baker's Biographical Dictionary of Musicians, Macmillan, Schirmer Books, 1984.

PERIODICALS

New York Times, November 29, 1996, p. B19.

MILNE, G(eorge) W. A. 1937-

PERSONAL: Born May 1, 1937, in Stockport, England; son of Ernest (in sales) and Jessie Winifred (Howard) Milne; married Adell Browning, July 29, 1967 (divorced, 1983); married Madlyn Kay Skilling, February 17, 1984; children: Robert W., Andrew K., Joanne L., Jennifer B. *Ethnicity:* "Caucasian." *Education:* Victoria University of Manchester, B.Sc. (with honors), 1957, M.Sc., 1958, Ph.D., 1960. *Politics:* Independent. *Religion:* Protestant. *Avocational interests:* Sailing, skiing, carpentry, reading.

ADDRESSES: Home—9520 Linden Ave., Bethesda, MD 20814. *Office*—National Institutes of Health, Building 37, Room 5B29, Bethesda, MD 20892; fax 301-897-3487. *E-mail*—gwa@cu.nih.gov and Bill @phm.com.

CAREER: University of Wisconsin—Madison, postdoctoral fellow, 1960-62; National Institutes of Health, Bethesda, MD, visiting fellow and visiting associate at Laboratory of Chemistry, National Institute of Arthritis and Metabolic Diseases, 1962-65, research chemist at National Heart, Lung, and Blood Institute, 1965-81, and National Cancer Institute, 1981—, chief of Information Technology Branch, Developmental Therapeutics Program, Division of Cancer Treatment, 1981-88, research chemist, Laboratory of Medicinal Chemistry, 1988—, president of Interassembly Council of Assemblies of Scientists, 1981-83. Georgetown University, adjunct professor, 1967—. American Chemical Society, editor, 1989—. Westinghouse Science Talent Search, national judge, 1965-76; Washington Mass Spectrometry Discussion Group, chairperson, 1969-71; NHLBI Assembly of Scientists, president, 1980-81; consultant to National Bureau of Standards.

MEMBER: American Chemical Society (chair, Division of Computers in Chemistry, 1990-92; member of council, 1992—), American Society for Mass Spectrometry, American Association for the Advancement of Science.

AWARDS, HONORS: Travel grant, Wellcome Foundation, 1960; grants for the Soviet Union, National Academy of Sciences, 1968, 1970.

WRITINGS:

(Editor) *The CRC Handbook of Pesticides,* CRC Press (Boca Raton, FL), 1995.

Contributor to books. Contributor of nearly two hundred articles to scientific journals, including *ChemTech, Journal of Molecular Biology,* and *Journal of Medical Chemistry.* Editor in chief, *Journal of Chemical Information and Computer Sciences,* 1989—; associate editor, *Handbook of Data on Organic Compounds,* 1992—; member of editorial board, *Chemico-Biological Interactions,* 1969-74, and *Organic Mass Spectrometry,* 1973-81.

SIDELIGHTS: G. W. A. Milne told *CA:* "I was born in England in 1937, obtained a doctorate in chemistry from the University of Manchester in 1960, and traveled immediately to the University of Wisconsin. After two years there, I moved to the National Institutes of Health, where I have been ever since. I conduct research in chemistry as applied to problems in medicine.

"Much of my writing has been of scientific papers, but I have written or edited several books which, in part, have represented an attempt to gather, synthesize, and record the knowledge I have acquired on a specific subject. The art of gathering knowledge is something I have learned and practiced for my whole career, as have most research scientists. Recording and passing on this knowledge is, in my opinion, an important responsibility to which insufficient attention is paid.

"Through two marriages I have helped raise four children who, now all adults, are a source of great pride to me. Two of them followed me into science, but the other two are making quite independent careers for themselves. Communication with them on so many subjects, great and small, has been enormously educational for me. I learned that even closely related people can have such different interests, skills, and abilities that efforts to communicate successfully with a large number of people are fraught with difficulty. I regard the ability to communicate to be just as important as one's scientific knowledge. The relationship between science and the public is, in fact, badly impeded by scientists' collective inability to speak for themselves. Science has far more to offer than the public appreciates, because scientists continually do a poor job of communication. A goal of mine is to try to improve upon this situation."

* * *

MINSKY, Hyman P(hilip) 1919-1996

OBITUARY NOTICE—See index for *CA* sketch: Born September 23, 1919, in Chicago, IL; died of pancreatic cancer, October 24, 1996, in Rhinebeck, NY. Economist, educator, writer. Minsky achieved recognition in the field of economics for his theories of financial swings during times of economic booms. Minsky began his academic career in 1949 as an assistant professor at Brown University in Rhode Island. In 1957, he accepted a post at the University of California in Berkeley, where he remained until 1965, when he left to fill the post of professor of economics at Washington University in St. Louis. He was a visiting lecturer at Carnegie Institute of Technology and Harvard, among others. Minsky also served on the board of governors for the Federal Reserve System and as director of Mark Twain Bankshares. He contributed articles to several anthologies and was the editor of *California Banking in a Growing Economy.* In 1975, Minsky's *John Maynard Keynes* was published, detailing the theories of the British economist. His other works include *Can It Happen Again?* and *Stabilizing an Unstable Economy.*

OBITUARIES AND OTHER SOURCES:

BOOKS

Who's Who, 148th edition, St. Martin's, 1996.

PERIODICALS

New York Times, October 26, 1996, p. 13.

*   *   *

MISHRA, Sudesh (Raj)   1962-

PERSONAL: Born November 21, 1962, in Suva, Fiji. *Education:* University of Wollongon, B.A. (honors), 1984; The Flinders University of South Australia, Ph.D., 1989.

ADDRESSES: Office—CRNLE, Flinders University, Bedford Park, South Australia 5042, Australia.

CAREER: University of the South Pacific, lecturer in English, 1989-93; Australian Research Council Postdoctoral Research Fellow, Flinders University of South Australia, 1993. Member, and president since 1991, Fiji Writers' Association.

AWARDS, HONORS: Flinders University Postgraduate Scholarship, 1985-89; Harri Jones Memorial prize

for poetry, 1988; Australian Research Council Postdoctoral fellowship, 1993-96.

WRITINGS:

POETRY

Rahu, Vision International Publishers (Suva, Fiji), 1987.
Tandava, Meanjin Press (Melbourne), 1991.
Memoirs of a Reluctant Traveller, CRNLE-Wakefield Press (Adelaide), 1994.

PLAYS

Ferringhi, produced in Suva, Fiji, 1993.

OTHER

(Editor with Seona Smiles) *Trapped: A Collection of Writing from Fiji,* Fiji Writers' Association (Suva, Fiji), 1992.
Preparing Faces: Modernism and Indian Poetry in English, CRNLE-University of the South Pacific Press (Adelaide), 1995.

*   *   *

MITCHELL, Susan   1944-

PERSONAL: Born in 1944, in New York, NY. *Education:* Attended Wellesley College.

ADDRESSES: Agent—c/o HarperCollins Publishers, 10 East 53rd St., New York, NY 10022-5299.

CAREER: Has held teaching positions at Middlebury College, Vermont, and Northeastern Illinois University. Holds the Mary Blossom Lee Endowed Chair in Creative Writing, Florida Atlantic University.

AWARDS, HONORS: National Endowment for the Arts fellowship; grants from the state arts councils of Massachusetts, Illinois, Vermont, and Florida; Claire Hagler fellow, Fine Arts Work Center, Provincetown; Hoyns fellow, University of Virginia.

WRITINGS:

POETRY

The Water Inside the Water, Wesleyan University Press (Middletown, CT), 1983.
Rapture, HarperPerennial (New York), 1992.

MOI, Toril 1953-

PERSONAL: Born in 1953, in Norway. *Education:* University of Bergen, D.Art, 1985.

ADDRESSES: Office—Literature Program, Duke University, Durham, NC 27708-0670.

CAREER: Writer and educator. Oxford University, Oxford, lecturer, 1983-85; University of Bergen, Norway, director of Centre for Feminist Research in the Humanities, then adjunct professor of comparative literature; Duke University, Durham, NC, currently professor of literature.

WRITINGS:

(Contributor) *In Dora's Case: Feminism—Psychoanalysis—Hysteria,* edited by Charles Bernheimer and Claire Kahane, Columbia University Press (New York City), 1985.

Sexual/Textual Politics: Feminist Literary Theory, Methuen (New York City), 1986.

(Editor) *The Kristeva Reader,* Columbia University Press, 1986.

(Editor) *French Feminist Thought: A Reader,* Basil Blackwell (Oxford), 1987.

(Contributor) *Gender and Theory: Dialogues on Feminist Criticism,* edited by Linda Kauffman, Basil Blackwell, 1989.

(Contributor) *Between Feminism and Psychoanalysis,* edited by Tresa Brennan, Routledge (New York City), 1989.

Feminist Literary Theory and Simone de Beauvoir, Basil Blackwell, 1990.

Simone de Beauvoir: The Making of an Intellectual Woman, Basil Blackwell, 1994.

(Editor, with Janice A. Radway) *Materialist Feminism,* Duke University Press (Durham), 1994.

Contributor as translator and reviewer to journals, including *Vinduet, Edda, Kontrast,* and *French Studies.*

SIDELIGHTS: Norwegian-born feminist theorist Toril Moi is the author of several books designed to introduce feminist literary pedagogy to interested readers in an accessible manner. Her 1985 work, *Sexual/Textual Politics: Feminist Literary Theory,* reviews the two most widely utilized approaches to feminist literary theory: Anglo-American empirical studies and French poststructuralist *ecriture.* Moi's ability to present complex theoretical discussions in a lucid and objective manner have won her praise from academics and critics alike. Unique in her approach is Moi's attempt to reveal the theoretical assumptions underlying both forms of criticism and compare and contrast these assumptions with the social and political feminist agenda.

In *Sexual/Textual Politics* Moi discusses the work of many of the major feminist critics of the twentieth century. She begins with Virginia Woolf, whom she hails as the founder of the discipline. Elaine Showalter, Mary Ellman, Kate Millet, Ellen Moers, Sandra Gilbert and Susan Gubar are each critiqued in the book's first section, as Moi "uncovers the 'gaps,' 'absences,' and fissures in their texts through which ideology can be glimpsed," according to *Women's Review of Books* reviewer Ellen Cronan Rose. While praising French theorists—which include Helene Cixous, Luce Irigaray, and Julia Kristeva—as the true heirs of Woolf because of their grounding in theoretical, as opposed to empirical, discourse, this "does not blind Moi to the shortcomings of their writings," judged to Pamela McCallum in *Signs*—"on the contrary, she aims at a critique and reevaluation of their texts in the light of a more committed sexual/textual politics." While noting that some would take issue with Moi's critical appraisal of certain literary theorists, Rose concluded that "*Sexual/Textual Politics* commands our respect, . . . because of its unflinching integrity. Intended as an 'introduction to feminist literary theory,' this book exemplifies feminist theory-making at its rigorous best."

In addition to *Sexual/Textual Politics,* Moi is the author of several other books introducing the work of renowned feminist literary theorists. 1990's *Feminist Theory and Simone de Beauvoir* and *Simone de Beauvoir: The Making of an Intellectual Woman,* published in 1994, cover the career of a woman who Moi considers "the most important feminist intellectual of the twentieth century." As with all of Moi's writing, these books are engaging narratives easily traversed by the novice reader. Her contributions to broadening the public's understanding of feminist literary theory also prompted Moi to edit several anthologies of criticism, including *The Kristeva Reader, French Feminist Thought: A Reader,* and *Materialist Feminism,* which she co-edited with fellow critic Janice A. Radway in 1994.

BIOGRAPHICAL/CRITICAL SOURCES:

PERIODICALS

Arizona Quarterly, winter, 1989.
Bloomsbury Review, November, 1989, p. 30.

English Journal, March, 1991, p. 89.
Modern Fiction Studies, Volume 34, number 3, 1988.
Prose Studies, September, 1987.
Signs, summer, 1987, p. 822.
Women's Review of Books, February, 1986, p. 17; January, 1996, p. 9.*

*   *   *

MOOD, Terry Ann   1945-

PERSONAL: Born May 5, 1945, in Beverly, MA; daughter of Winston A. (a certified public accountant) and Helen J. (a teacher; maiden name, Wittenhagen) Mood; married John P. Leopold (a trial judge), March 24, 1990. *Education:* Brown University, B.A., 1967; Simmons College, M.S.L.S., 1969; University of Reading, M.A., 1989. *Religion:* Unitarian-Universalist. *Avocational interests:* Travel, reading, needlework.

ADDRESSES: Home—Englewood, CO. *Office*—Auraria Library, Lawrence at 11th St., Denver, CO 80204; fax 303-556-3528. *E-mail*—tleopold@carbon.cudenver.edu.

CAREER: Denver Public Library, Denver, CO, librarian, 1969-70; Metropolitan State College, Denver, periodicals librarian, 1970-75; University of Colorado, Denver, periodicals librarian at Auraria Library, 1975-81, language and literature librarian, 1981-91, humanities bibliographer, 1991—, English teacher, 1978, 1979, and assistant professor. Southeast Metropolitan Board of Cooperative Services, teacher in Adult Education Program, 1977-79.

MEMBER: American Library Association, Colorado Library Association.

AWARDS, HONORS: LSCA grant, 1985.

WRITINGS:

Colorado Local History: A Directory, Colorado Centennial-Bicentennial Commission (Denver, CO), 1975, 2nd edition, Colorado State Historical Society (Denver, CO), 1986.
Distance Education: An Annotated Bibliography, Libraries Unlimited (Englewood, CO), 1995.

Contributor of articles and reviews to library journals. Editor, *Columbine,* 1975-76.

WORK IN PROGRESS: The Folklore of New England: An Annotated Bibliography.

*   *   *

MOODY, Bill   1941-

PERSONAL: Born September 27, 1941, in Webb City, MO; son of Hugh and Helen (Shaw) Moody; children: Sarah. *Ethnicity:* "Caucasian." *Education:* University of Nevada at Las Vegas, M.A. (English), 1987.

ADDRESSES: Home—Las Vegas, NV. *Agent*—Philip Spitzer, 50 Talmage Farm Lane, East Hampton, NY.

CAREER: Jazz drummer, 1963—; free-lance writer, 1968—; disc jockey, 1989—. *Military Service:* United States Air Force, 1959-62.

MEMBER: Mystery Writers of America, International Crime Writers Association.

WRITINGS:

The Jazz Exiles: American Musicians Abroad (nonfiction), foreword by Stanley Dance, University of Nevada Press (Reno, NV), 1993.
Solo Hand (novel), Walker & Co. (New York), 1994.
Death of a Tenor Man: An Evan Horne Mystery (novel), Walker & Co., 1995.
Sound of the Trumpet: An Evan Horne Mystery (novel), Walker & Co., 1997.

WORK IN PROGRESS: Bird Lives, an Evan Horne mystery.

SIDELIGHTS: Author Bill Moody is also a jazz drummer and a disc jockey. His first book, 1993's *The Jazz Exiles: American Musicians Abroad,* was a nonfiction work published by the University of Nevada Press. After this effort, however, Moody turned to mystery fiction with 1994's *Solo Hand* and 1995's *Death of a Tenor Man.*

In *Solo Hand* Moody introduced protagonist Evan Horne. Horne is a jazz pianist, but as the novel opens he is in Los Angeles recovering from an automobile accident that has injured his right hand—the hand he needs most for piano solos. He becomes involved in a mystery when someone tries to blackmail a singer, Lonnie Cole, whom Evan has accompanied. Cole has just done a duet album with a famous country singer, and the mail brings a package of photographs of him and the country artist caught in embarrassing circumstances at a party, along with a request that Horne deliver a million-dollar extortion fee. In order to convince Cole that he is not involved in the plot himself, Horne undertakes the investigation, intent on discovering who is behind the blackmail attempt. In the process, Horne winds up knocked unconscious in a marina but triumphs despite his novice status as a sleuth. A *Publishers Weekly* reviewer praised *Solo Hand* as "entertaining," and further noted that "Moody's portrayals of the backstabbing music industry and a royalties scam ring true."

Moody puts his knowledge of jazz history to use when Evan Horne reappears in *Death of a Tenor Man*. This time Horne is in Las Vegas assuaging boredom by assisting with a friend's research into the death of real-life jazz tenor saxophonist Wardell Gray in 1955—a death officially attributed to a drug overdose. He is also playing unobtrusive piano at a shopping mall in the gambler's paradise, trying to get his injured hand back into shape for more demanding performances. While helping look up the facts on Gray's demise, Horne is threatened with bodily harm by organized criminal henchmen if he doesn't give up his inquiry, but this only piques him to peer more closely at the available information. On the trail of answers, Horne also discovers much about the racial tension in Las Vegas's past—Gray's body was found in the desert surrounding the city the day after he wielded his saxophone at the brand-new Moulin Rouge, which was the first Las Vegas casino and hotel open to both whites and African-Americans. Moody ornaments *Death of a Tenor Man* with other real jazz stories and musicians besides the late Wardell Gray, according to another *Publishers Weekly* critic, who went on to assert that the author "exhibits perfect pitch when writing lovingly about music. . . ; these pages sing." Marilyn Stasio, holding forth in the *New York Times Book Review*, also applauded Moody's efforts in *Death of a Tenor Man*. She called Evan Horne an "immensely likable hero" and declared that in this "sad, bluesy story" many other characters "have life and soul."

Moody told *CA:* "Perseverance and believing in your work are probably the two most important factors in getting published. Don't give up one publisher too soon."

BIOGRAPHICAL/CRITICAL SOURCES:

PERIODICALS

New York Times Book Review, January 7, 1996, p. 24.
Publishers Weekly, December 20, 1993, p. 53; October 23, 1995, pp. 60-61.

*   *   *

MORIMOTO, Anri 1956-

PERSONAL: Born October 19, 1956, in Tokyo, Japan; son of Tone (a graphic artist) and Takeko Morimoto; married, wife's name Eriko, February 10, 1980; children: Shoko, Akiko. *Ethnicity:* "Japanese." *Education:* International Christian University, B.A., 1979; Tokyo Union Theological Seminary, Th.M., 1982; Princeton Theological Seminary, Ph.D., 1991. *Religion:* Presbyterian.

ADDRESSES: Home—3-10-5 Osawa, Mitaka, Tokyo 181, Japan. *Office*—3-10-2 Osawa, Mitaka, Tokyo 181, Japan; fax 81-422-33-3372. *E-mail*—morimoto @icu.ac.jp.

CAREER: International Christian University, Tokyo, Japan, university minister, 1991—, director of religious center, 1995—, associate professor, 1997—.

MEMBER: Japan Society of Christian Studies, American Academy of Religion.

AWARDS, HONORS: Fulbright scholar, 1986; American Studies in Japan Book Award, 1996.

WRITINGS:

Jonathan Edwards and the Catholic Vision of Salvation, Pennsylvania State University Press (University Park, PA), 1995.
Christian Ethics in Ecumenical Context: Theology, Culture, and Politics in Dialogue, Eerdmans (Grand Rapids, MI), 1995.

WORK IN PROGRESS: Translating into Japanese *Christian Uniqueness Reconsidered,* for Orbis Books (Maryknoll, NY); *Meiji Christians and the Japanese Reception of Darwinism,* Oozora-sha (Japan).

MORRIS, Mervyn 1937-

PERSONAL: Born in 1937, in Kingston, South Australia, Australia; married; children: two sons, one daughter. *Education:* Attended Munro College; University of the West Indies; St. Edmund Hall, Oxford University.

ADDRESSES: Office—Department of English, University of the West Indies, Mona, Kingston 7, Jamaica.

CAREER: Munro College, Formerly Senior English Master; Warden of Taylor Hall, assistant registrar, beginning in 1966, senior lecturer in English, beginning in 1970, and currently reader in West Indian literature, University of the West Indies; University of Kent, Canterbury, visiting lecturer, 1972-73.

AWARDS, HONORS: Institute of Jamaica Musgrave Medal, 1976.

WRITINGS:

POETRY

The Pond, New Beacon (London), 1973.
On Holy Week, Sangster (Kingston), 1976; as *On Holy Week: A Sequence of Poems for Radio,* Dangaroo Press (Sydney), 1993.
Shadowboxing, New Beacon, 1979.
Examination Centre: Poems, Beacon Books, 1992.

OTHER

(Editor) *Seven Jamaican Poets: An Anthology of Recent Poetry,* Bolivar Press (Kingston), 1971.
(Editor) *My Green Hills of Jamaica, and Five Jamaican Short Stories,* by Claude McKay, Heinemann (Kingston), 1979.
(Editor with Pamela Mordecai) *Jamaica Woman: An Anthology of Poems,* Heinemann, 1980.
(Editor) *Selected Poems,* by Louise Bennett, Sangster (Kingston), 1982.
(Editor) *Focus 1983: An Anthology of Contemporary Jamaican Writing,* Caribbean Authors, 1983.
(Editor) *Riddym Ravings and Other Poems* by Jean Binta Breeze, Race Today (London), 1988.
(Editor) *It a Come,* by Michael Smith, City Lights (San Francisco, CA), 1989.
(Editor with Stewart Brown and Gordon Rohlehr) *Voice Print: An Anthology of Oral and Related Poetry from the Caribbean,* Longman (London and Chicago), 1990.

(Editor) *The Faber Book of Contemporary Caribbean Short Stories,* Faber (London), 1990.
(Editor with Edward Baugh) *Progressions: West Indian Literature in the 1970s,* University of West Indies (Kingston), 1990.
Is English We Speaking: West Indian Literature, British Library, 1993.

*   *   *

MORRISROE, Patricia 1951-

PERSONAL: Born in 1951. *Religion:* "Raised Catholic."

ADDRESSES: Office—c/o Random House, Inc., 201 East 50th St., 11th FL, New York, NY 10022.

CAREER: Biographer, journalist, and feature writer.

WRITINGS:

Mapplethorpe: A Biography, Random House (New York), 1995.

SIDELIGHTS: Patricia Morrisroe is a journalist whose first book-length publication is a biography of Robert Mapplethorpe, an artist best known for his photographic images of homosexual sadomasochism. A figure of controversy in the art world, not least because of his unusually graphic depictions of painful or bizarre sexual practices, Mapplethorpe also partook in the kinds of activities he captured on film, and often used his lovers as subjects. When he died in 1989 of complications arising from Acquired Immune Deficiency Syndrome (AIDS), he had not quite reached the pinnacle of his career, a peak that was reached in the following year, when his most shocking works were singled out in a national debate on government funding for the National Endowment for the Arts. Morrisroe's book, *Mapplethorpe: A Biography,* which appeared six years after the photographer's death, follows its subject from his middle-class suburban upbringing through his youthful search for identity and self-propelled rise to fame and notoriety in the New York art world.

Morrisroe first met Robert Mapplethorpe when she wrote an article about him for a London magazine in 1983, noted Regina Weinreich, who interviewed the biographer for the *New York Times.* According to Morrisroe in the London article, as quoted by

Weinreich, "Mapplethorpe looked very much like Anne Rice's Vampire Lestat, a very charismatic, good-looking, deathly pale individual." When Mapplethorpe announced that he had AIDS in 1988, Morrisroe approached the photographer with the idea of writing his biography; after she received his approval, she conducted more than three hundred interviews with friends, acquaintances, and former lovers of the artist, in addition to sixteen interviews with Mapplethorpe himself. "He was a difficult interview," Morrisroe told Weinreich, "entirely visual, nonverbal, nonanalytic. He left no diaries, only six letters. He hated to talk about his family and Floral Park [the New York suburb where Mapplethorpe grew up]."

The artist Morrisroe presents in *Mapplethorpe: A Biography* is "on the whole selfish, indifferent, greedy, monumentally self-promoting, with no great insight and no intuitive powers outside those that seduction and photography brought into play," according to the *Nation* reviewer Arthur C. Danto. "This is a courageous book: Patricia Morrisroe went to the bottom of the box and she did not flinch at the things she found there," Danto commented. Others similarly found Morrisroe's Mapplethorpe unpleasant and, for some, this indicated a failure on the part of the biographer. Objecting to what he characterized as Morrisroe's "hostility" toward Mapplethorpe and his world, Andrew Solomon of the *Los Angeles Times Book Review* judged that "Morrisroe never achieves even a shred of empathy for the photographer." In his conclusion, however, Solomon called *Mapplethorpe: A Biography* "curiously moving."

Other critics found Morrisroe's portrait of the artist as death-seeking satyr fascinating, if horrifying. "Those who knew and loved Mapplethorpe may find fault with the biographer for having used a wide-angle lens . . . which overly distorts her subject into the image of a monster," wrote *Washington Post Book World* contributor Kunio Francis Tanabe. "Be that as it may, there is enough evidence in Morrisroe's book and Mapplethorpe's own photographs to be thankful for not ever crossing his path." Elizabeth Young, writing in *New Statesman and Society,* called *Mapplethorpe: A Biography* "a powerful, painful book that makes it very clear what an exceptionally notorious and influential figure [Mapplethorpe] was."

While critics disagreed about the effectiveness of the biographer's stance toward her subject, some, like *Los Angeles Times Book Review* critic Solomon, claimed that the book held the same sort of fascination as Mapplethorpe's work. "Mapplethorpe was the consummate seducer," Solomon remarked, "and Morrisroe's book is similarly enticing; it lures you in by rapid degrees, and once you have started it you have little choice but to follow through, even if your finer sensibilities resist the world she is narrating."

BIOGRAPHICAL/CRITICAL SOURCES:

PERIODICALS

Los Angeles Times Book Review, July 9, 1995, pp. 4, 9.
Nation, June 12, 1995, pp. 830-32.
New Statesman and Society, September 15, 1995, pp. 31-32.
New Yorker, June 5, 1995, pp. 85-89, 91.
New York Times, October 8, 1995, p. 10.
New York Times Book Review, June 25, 1995, p. 12.
Washington Post Book World, May 28, 1995, p. 39.*

* * *

MORRISSEY, Kevin L. 1952-

PERSONAL: Born March 31, 1952, in Chicago, IL. *Education:* Northwestern University, B.A., 1974.

ADDRESSES: Agent—Susan Ramer, Don Congdon Associates, 156 Fifth Ave., No. 625, New York, NY 10010.

CAREER: National League for Nursing, New York City, vice president for communications, 1980-87; Season to Taste Books Ltd. (retail cookbook store), Chicago, IL, co-owner, 1988-93; writer, 1993—.

WRITINGS:

WITH BARRY BLUESTEIN

Dip It!, Contemporary Books (Chicago, IL), 1990.
Light Sauces, Contemporary Books, 1991.
Quick Breads, Contemporary Books, 1991.
The 99% Fat-Free Cookbook, Doubleday (New York), 1994.
Home Made in the Kitchen, Penguin (New York), 1994.
The 99% Fat-Free Book of Appetizers and Desserts, Doubleday, 1996.

The Complete Cookie, Doubleday, 1996.
The Home Made in the Kitchen Household Almanac,
    Penguin, in press.

WORK IN PROGRESS: Fat-Free Fast, with
Bluestein, publication by Doubleday expected in
1998.

*   *   *

MORTLAKE, G. N.
    See STOPES, Marie (Charlotte)

*   *   *

MUDROOROO (Nyoongah)   1938-
    (Colin Johnson)

PERSONAL: Born Colin Thomas Johnson, August 21,
1938, in East Cuballing, Western Australia; companion of Janine Mary Little, beginning in 1993. *Education:* Attended Murdoch University; Melbourne University, B.A. (honors), 1987.

ADDRESSES: Agent—Janine Little, 393 Bulner St.,
West Perth 6005, Australia.

CAREER: University of Northern Territory, Darwin,
lecturer, 1987; University of Queensland, Brisbane,
lecturer, 1988; Aboriginal Studies, Murdoch University, Perth, chair, 1991—; co-founder, Aboriginal
Oral Literature and Dramatists Association.

MEMBER: Australian Society of Authors, Aboriginal
Oral Literature, and Dramatists Association.

AWARDS, HONORS: Western Australia Premier's
prize for poetry and most outstanding entry, 1992.

WRITINGS:

POETRY

The Song Circle of Jackie, Hyland House (Mel-
    bourne), 1986.
Dalwurra, University of Western Australia Press
    (Nedlands), 1988.
The Garden of Gethsemane, Hyland House, 1991.

PLAYS

The Mudrooroo/Mueller Project, New South Wales
    University Press (Sydney), 1993.

NOVELS

(As Colin Johnson) *Wildcat Falling,* Angus and
    Robertson (Sydney), 1965.
(As Colin Johnson) *Long Live Sandaware,* Hyland
    House, 1979.
Master of the Ghost Dreaming, Angus and Robertson,
    1991.
Wildcat Screaming, Angus and Robertson, 1992.
The Kwinkan, Angus and Robertson, 1993.

Also author of *Doin Wildcat,* Hyland House.

OTHER

*Writing from the Fringe: A Study of Modern Aborigi-
    nal Literature,* Hyland House, 1990.
Aboriginal Mythology, Aquarian/HarperCollins (Lon-
    don), 1994.

*   *   *

MURDOCH, Norman H.   1939-

PERSONAL: Born May 15, 1939, in Du Bois, PA;
son of Walter H. (a Salvation Army officer) and
Irene (a Salvation Army officer; maiden name,
Douge) Murdoch; married Grace M. A. Bell, September 17, 1966; children: W. Randall Murdoch
Nidalmia, Amy Ruth, D. Ryan. *Ethnicity:* "Caucasian." *Education:* Asbury College, B.A., 1961;
Asbury Theological Seminary, M.Div., 1965, M.Th.,
1972; University of Cincinnati, M.Ed., 1968, M.A.,
1975, Ph.D., 1985. *Politics:* Democrat. *Religion:*
Christian. *Avocational interests:* Travel.

ADDRESSES: Home—9412 Bluewing Terr., Cincinnati, OH 45241. *Office*—Department of Humanities
and Social Sciences, University of Cincinnati, Mail
Loc. 206, Cincinnati, OH 45221; fax 513-556-3007.

CAREER: University of Cincinnati, Cincinnati, OH,
professor of history, 1968—. Milford Area Bicenten-
nial Commission, chairperson, 1986-92.

MEMBER: Organization of American Historians,
Association of Third World Studies, Oral History

Association, American Society of Church History, American Association of University Professors, Milford Historical Society (president, 1990), Wesleyan Theological Society, Fides et Historia.

AWARDS, HONORS: Grant for Zimbabwe, Center on Philanthropy, Indiana University-Bloomington, 1991; grants from University of Cincinnati for Chile, 1993, and India, 1994; Dillwyn F. Ratcliff Award, American Association of University Professors, 1995, for service in the cause of academic freedom.

WRITINGS:

A Centennial History: The Salvation Army in Cincinnati, 1885-1985, Salvation Army (Cincinnati, OH), 1985.
Origins of the Salvation Army, University of Tennessee Press (Knoxville, TN), 1996.

Contributor to books, including *Popular Politics, Riot, and Labour: Essays in Liverpool History, 1790-1940,* edited by John Belchem, Liverpool University Press (Liverpool, England), 1992. Contributor of nearly fifty articles and reviews to scholarly journals and popular magazines, including *Utopian Studies, Church History, Communal Societies, Journal of Social History, Christian History,* and *Wesleyan Theological Journal.*

WORK IN PROGRESS: Zimbabwe: The Salvation Army and the World Council of Churches, 1975-1985; editing *American History in Global Perspective,* with Mark A. Lause; research for an international history of the Salvation Army.

SIDELIGHTS: Norman H. Murdoch told *CA:* "Since 1991 I have been working on research projects with a long-term goal: publication of an international history of the Salvation Army. My particular emphasis has been on the Salvation Army in the Third World, since that has been the area neglected by other scholars.

"As a result of my research in Zimbabwe in 1991, I have focused on the Salvation Army's role in the colonial era down to independence in 1980. My interest has been the relations between the Anglo-American Army and its missionaries and the African and settler populations of Rhodesia/Zimbabwe. A particular interest has been in their relations in terms of land ownership and two major demonstrations by Africans, aimed at British and American intrusions into the African system in 1893-96 and 1980-83, at the beginning and end of the colonial era."

MURPHY, Francis X(avier) 1914-
(Xavier Rynne)

PERSONAL: Born June 26, 1914, in Bronx, NY; son of Denis (a police officer) and Anne Elizabeth (a homemaker; maiden name, Rynne) Murphy. *Education:* Attended St. Mary's College, 1928-34; St. Alphonsus, A.B., 1937; Catholic University of America, M.A., 1942, Ph.D., 1944. *Politics:* Democrat. *Religion:* Roman Catholic. *Avocational interests:* "Politico-Religious journalism; Vatican affairs."

ADDRESSES: Home and office—St. Mary's Rectory, 109 Duke of Gloucester St., Annapolis, MD 21401. *Agent*—Robert Giroux, Farrar, Straus, and Giroux, Inc., 19 Union Sq. W., New York, NY 10003.

CAREER: Entered Congregation of the Most Holy Redeemer, 1935; ordained Roman Catholic priest, 1940; United States Naval Academy, Annapolis, MD, chaplain, 1944-47; Catholic War Relief Services, Germany and Italy, assisted refugees and conducted research and publicity work, 1948-49; writer, 1949-51; parish priest at a Bronx, NY, Roman Catholic church, 1949-51; St. John's University, NY, lecturer, 1957-58; parish priest at a Bronx, NY, Roman Catholic church, 1958-59; Lateran University, Rome, Italy, professor of moral theology at Academia Alfonsiana, 1959-76, and lecturer in moral theology at Jesu Magister Institute, 1961-63; Holy Redeemer College, Washington, DC, rector, 1977-81, lecturer, 1981—. Vatican Council II, Peritus (expert), 1962-65; Population Reference Bureau, trustee, 1975-81; Princeton University, visiting professor of politics and humanities, 1971-72; Johns Hopkins University, adjunct professor of history, 1972-74; American Universities Field Services, visiting lecturer in Vatican politics, 1971-76; Towson State College, visiting professor of philosophy, 1973-74; Seton Hall University, visiting professor of Vatican politics, 1983; United Nations Symposium on Population and Human Rights, delegate, 1973-74; consultant to U.S. State Department on Vatican Affairs, 1978—; Holy Redeemer College, writer in residence, 1981-85; television and radio commentator on news events concerning the Roman Catholic Church and the Vatican, 1958-82. *Military service:* U.S. Army, seventh infantry regiment, third division; served as chaplain in Korea, Germany, and France, 1951-58; became major; received Bronze Star.

MEMBER: Medieval Academy of America (member emeritus), Patristic Conference (member since 1955), Folger Shakespeare Library.

AWARDS, HONORS: Woodrow Wilson International Center for Scholars, Smithsonian Institution, fellow, 1972-73.

WRITINGS:

A Monument to St. Jerome; Essays on Some Aspects of His Life, Works, and Influence, Sheed & Ward, 1948.
Fighting Admiral: The Story of Dan Callaghan, Vantage Press (New York), 1952.
Peter Speaks through Leo: Chalcedon 451, Catholic University of America, 1952.
John XXIII Comes to the Vatican, McBride, 1959.
Politics and the Early Christian, Desclee, 1967.
(With Gary MacEoin) *Synod '67: New Sound in Rome,* Bruce, 1968.
Moral Theology of the Primitive Church, Paulist, 1968.
John Paul II: The Pilgrim Pope, Custom Book, 1978.
This Church: These Times, Follett, 1980.
The Papacy Today, McMillan, 1981.
Catholic Perspectives on Population Issues II, Population Reference Bureau, 1981.
Moral Doctrines of the Early Church Fathers, Glazier, 1983.
The Christian Way of Life: Message of the Church Fathers, Glazier, 1986.
Patristic Heritage in the Renaissance and Modern Age, Shepherd Press, 1990.

Also author of *Catholic Perspectives on Population Issues I,* 1975; and *Christianity and Survival: Population and the Bomb.*

UNDER PSEUDONYM XAVIER RYNNE

Letters from Vatican City: Vatican Council II (First Session): Background and Debates, Farrar, 1963.
The Second Session: The Debates and Decrees of the Vatican Council II, September 29 to December 4, 1963, Farrar, 1964.
The Third Session: The Debates and Decrees of the Vatican Council II, September 14 to November 21, 1964, Farrar, 1965.
The Fourth Session: Debates and Decrees of the Vatican Council II (through c. 1965), Farrar, 1966.
Vatican Council II, revised and combined into one volume, Farrar, 1968.
John Paul II's Extraordinary Synod, Glazier, 1986.

Staff editor for sections on early Christianity and Byzantine theology, *New Catholic Encyclopedia,* McGraw-Hill, 1962-67; contributor of articles to numerous periodicals, including *Atlantic Monthly, New York Times, Washington Post, America, Wilson Quarterly,* and *Commonweal.*

WORK IN PROGRESS: Politics and the Last Christian (autobiography).

SIDELIGHTS: Ordained a Redemptorist priest in 1940, Francis X. Murphy is a prolific writer on contemporary issues within the Roman Catholic Church. He spent several years as a parish priest in New York and later served as a chaplain for the United States Army. In the late 1950s Murphy was sent to the Vatican-affiliated Lateran University in Rome, where he taught moral theology for almost two decades. The period that Murphy spent in Rome witnessed some of the most profound changes within the Church since its inception two thousand years before. The Vatican Council II of 1962 to 1965 gave a more influential role to lay people within parishes, lifted certain restrictions governing priests and nuns, abolished the use of Latin as the sole language of the holy mass, and altered some sacramental rituals. Murphy has since become a leading Vatican observer, writing numerous volumes on contemporary Catholic theology and lending his expertise to television coverage of important Vatican events.

Murphy's 1967 work *Politics and the Early Christian* discusses the confluence of political and moral issues that formed an integral part of early Roman Catholicism. Roman emperors persecuted the first Christians but later embraced the creed's tenets, and the foundation of the Church grew out of the organizational structure of the Roman Empire. Murphy's study analyzes the transformations in thought that took place during this era as well as the incorporation of Judaic doctrines into Christianity. *Commonweal* writer Paul J. Weber faulted *Politics and the Early Christian* for some factual errors and omissions concerning early Church theology but granted that "Murphy has made a substantial contribution to the understanding of a fascinating and significant period of history."

Murphy next chronicled the historic inaugural synod of Roman Catholic bishops in 1967 that gave the diverse multinational elements of the faith a chance to meet and discuss contemporary issues. The 1968 volume *Synod '67: New Sound in Rome* was cowritten with Irish writer Gary MacEoin and traces the first of these policy-making assemblies. Murphy authored several subsequent volumes over the next few years before the appearance of his 1981 work *The Papacy*

Today, which examines Roman Catholicism in the twentieth century. In this work Murphy discusses the Lateran Treaty of 1929, which called for a more dynamic papacy; the role of the papacy in combating fascism in Europe during the 1930s and 1940s; the election of popes by the College of Cardinals; and the changes implemented by Vatican Council II, giving women religious more opportunities to serve their communities and allowing lay people to assist in the sacrament of the Eucharist. *The Papacy Today* concludes with a look at the early reign of John Paul II, who in 1978 was the first non-Italian pope to be elected in 456 years. The first year of his leadership injected a new spirit of enthusiasm into clerics and laity alike for its harbinger of positive change, and Murphy's book was written as those early hopes diminished in the face of John Paul's growing conservatism. *Commonweal* contributor John Deedy described Murphy as an "engaging, enlightened, and often provocative" author and called *The Papacy Today* "engrossing," a work "the reader will find . . . fascinating down to its most incidental item of gossip." Critiquing the volume for the *Washington Post Book World,* Paul Piazza observed that "in addition to having both solid scholarship and an intimate knowledge of ecclesiastical politics, Murphy's study is honest and direct."

Reviewers have suggested that Murphy is also the author of a series of pseudonymous articles providing a behind-the-scenes look at the Vatican Council II and the debates that took place there over modernizing the Catholic Church. Published in the *New Yorker* under the name "Xavier Rynne" (a combination of Murphy's middle name and his mother's maiden name), the articles were collected into book form and published in 1963 as *Letters from Vatican City: Vatican Council II (First Session): Background and Debates.* G. E. Carter of *America* termed the contents "a monument of indiscretion" but tempered the assertion by granting that the book "is an incredibly well-documented piece. Someone was certainly 'taking notes,' and with great skill and acumen." Another volume by Rynne appeared under the title *The Second Session: The Debates and Decrees of the Vatican Council II, September 29 to December 4, 1963,* and *New York Times Book Review* critic James Finn remarked that it "is likely to stand as the most orderly, informative and entertaining account of the second session we will get." In 1965 a third volume by "Xavier Rynne" was published, entitled *The Third Session: The Debates and Decrees of the Vatican Council II, September 14 to November 21, 1964.* Critiquing that work for the *New York Times Book*

Review, John Cogley described the volume as "a high-style, journalistic record of all that went on, in the aula of St. Peter's and in the coffee bars, pensioni, and muraled corridors where Council strategies were planned by progressives and conservatives alike. It is written in the sharp-tooled *New Yorker* manner with vast theological sophistication and an abundance of insider's information." Two other books on the same subject also appeared under the pseudonym, but Murphy has consistently denied that he is "Xavier Rynne." However, in 1982 the *Times Literary Supplement* writer Peter Hebblethwaite noted that *The Papacy Today* contains portions of text in common with Rynne's *Letter from Vatican City* and that in the work Murphy praises Rynne as one of the foremost scholars of contemporary theology. Hebblethwaite interpreted this tribute as an insider's joke and asserted that "one can only conclude that Father Murphy has either plagiarized Rynne or finally broken cover." Murphy told *CA:* "Actually in 1991 I admitted publicly that I was Xavier Rynne with John Chapin as my editor."

Murphy also told *CA:* "After obtaining a doctorate in medieval history, I served as Catholic chaplain to the midshipmen at the U.S. Naval Academy in Annapolis from 1944 to 1947, thus obtaining some knowledge of politics; I continued this interest with refugee work and research in Italy, Germany, and France in 1948 and 1949. Later I did parish work in the Bronx and then spent seven years with the U.S. Army, including front line duty in Korea, and later in Berlin and Paris. Meanwhile I had published books and articles dealing with early Christian church fathers and was called to Rome to teach moral thinking of the early church, which I did from 1959 to 1976 at Academia Alfonsiana in Latin and Italian. I had just completed a biography of Pope John XXIII (1959) and got involved in preparations for Vatican Council II doing articles for the Catholic and secular press such as the *Washington Post.* Earlier still, I had written the life of Admiral Dan Callaghan, killed on the U.S.S. San Francisco at Guadalcanal in 1942, as well as the first article to appear in English on 'The Tomb of St. Peter' for the London-based *Tablet* in 1949. I had also written a history of the Council of Chalcedon in A.D. 451 entitled *Peter Speaks through Leo,* which was published in 1952, and attended Symposia and Patristic Congress weeks in Christ Church, Oxford, England, every four years from 1955 until 1987. Hence the call to Rome. Appointed a *peritus* or expert at Vatican Council II as theologian to Bishop Aloysius Willinger, C.SS.R. of Fresno, California, I was involved principally in the debate concerning the

'Dogmatic Constitution on the Church' and the 'Pastoral Constitution on the Church in Today's World' while cooperating mainly with the international journalists in helping them to understand the issues under debate.

"I was also writing articles and descriptions for Catholic periodicals such *America, Catholic World, Month,* and the London *Tablet.* When the articles 'Letters from Vatican City' appeared in the *New Yorker,* I was accused of being the author since my mother's name was Rynne and my middle name was Xavier. I merely denied I was Xavier Rynne although I enjoyed the attempt by journalists, lawyers, clergymen and others to trap me into an admission. This included a comparative study of my writings as Francis X. Murphy and the style of Xavier Rynne by a professor at the Jesuit Biblical Institute in Rome as well as a summons to be interviewed by Archbishop Pietro Parente, the Assessor of the Sacred Congregation of the Holy Office. I survived that ordeal intact.

"In 1963, I was invited by Dr. Martin R. P. McGuire of Catholic University in Washington, DC, to join his staff as a senior editor for early Christianity and the Byzantine world in producing the *New Catholic Encyclopedia;* I worked on that project for four years, editing some two million words and producing 135 articles on the early Church's history, biography, and theology. This involved going back and forth to Rome every four months or so.

"I made a lecture tour through the U.S., Africa, and the Far East in 1968 to assist in implementing the effects of Vatican Council II. I had written a series of four articles in the same year for the *Tablet* suggesting the Church could change its teaching on artificial birth control. With the publication of Pope Paul VI's Encyclical *Humanae Vitae* in July of that year banning artificial contraceptives, I got involved in the controversy stirred up by Father Charles Curran of Catholic University, who had been one of my first graduate students in Rome. I had also published articles and two books on the early Church, *Moral Theology of the Primitive Church* and *Politics and the Early Christian.* The latter contained a preface by then-Vice-President Hubert Humphrey whom I got to know through Dr. Edgar Berman, the famous surgeon and male chauvinist writer, who served as Humphrey's physician and political advisor. Under Mr. Humphrey's auspices I was appointed a fellow at the Woodrow Wilson International Center for scholars in 1972, after completing a year as visiting professor at Princeton University. I later taught Vatican

politics, history of political theory from Augustine to Machiavelli, and the Age of Justinian for two years at Johns Hopkins University. I also lectured on philosophy at Towson State College.

"I meanwhile followed up my involvement with the birth control issue beginning with a television interview with David Suskind in 1964 that resulted in my being frequently consulted by Planned Parenthood Association of New York and the U.S. through Martha Stuart, the press officer. When *Humanae Vitae* appeared, I was asked to vet Planned Parenthood's letter of response to help make it a balanced and meaningful protest.

"In Rome I was involved in various circles, particularly among the journalists in helping organize the press information meetings after the Sessions of the Roman Synod of Bishops in 1967 though 1976 with Peter Hebblethwaite, then an English Jesuit and editor of the *Month.* I had also helped other clerics in organizing the liaison with the press. With Gary MacEoin, an Irish ex-Redemptorist (the congregation of priests to which I belong), I had written an account of the first bishops' synod entitled *Synod '67: New Sound in Rome,* which was published in 1968.

"I made a month-long trip to Russia with Sergeant Shriver and his family as guests of the Soviet government in 1976. Mr. Shriver had helped negotiate some billion dollars of contracts for large installations such as hydroelectric plants, and we had *carte blanche* in our itinerary and visiting people. We spent an afternoon with the archbishop of Kiev, as well as time with the heads of the Supreme Soviet in several republics. Mr. Shriver delivered a brilliant talk on biomedical ethics at the University of Science in Novosibirsk and at the Cultural Center in Leningrad. I returned to New York via Rome, where I set up interviews for Mr. Shriver with Vatican leaders including Pope Paul VI.

"Returning to the U.S. in 1976, I was appointed rector of the Holy Redeemer College (a hostel of the Redemptorists where priests in special assignments or attending the universities in the area dwell) in 1977, a post I held until 1981. I kept myself busy lecturing, writing, and making television and radio appearances. I covered both the deaths and funerals of Pope Paul VI and John Paul I for ABC News in August and September of 1978, and the elections and installments of John Paul I and John Paul II. I likewise covered John Paul's visit to Great Britain. Meanwhile, I served as a trustee of the Population Reference Bureau in Washington, DC, from 1976 to 1981, and wrote two pamphlets on *Catholic Perspectives on Population.* In 1980 I covered the Roman Synod of Bishops on Family life for a news syndicate and wrote an article 'Of Sex and the Catholic Church' (not my title!) for the *Atlantic Monthly.*

"I managed to continue my academic interest during this period, especially with the help of the Folger Shakespeare Library. I was involved in the Petrarch Congress on 'Petrarch and the Christian Philosophy.' I helped sponsor the symposium on Thomas More conducted by the Folger Library, Holy Redeemer College, and Georgetown University. I also taught a seminar at the Folger Institute on 'The Heritage of the Church Fathers in the Renaissance' and delivered a lecture on 'Erasmus on Jerome and Augustine' published in *Medievalia.*"

BIOGRAPHICAL/CRITICAL SOURCES:

PERIODICALS

America, June 29, 1963.
Atlantic Monthly, February, 1981, pp. 44-57.
Commonweal, April 26, 1968, pp. 188-189; May 17, 1968, p. 274; November 6, 1981, pp. 628-630.
New Republic, March 17, 1982, pp. 27-30.
New York Times Book Review, June 28, 1964, p. 1; June 20, 1965, p.7.
Patristic Heritage, 1993, pp. 229-36.
Times Literary Supplement, February 12, 1982, p. 154.
Washington Post Book World, January 3, 1982, pp. 5, 9.

—*Sketch by Carol Brennan*

*   *   *

MURRAY, Rona 1924-

PERSONAL: Born February 10, 1924, in London, England; married Ernest Haddon, 1944 (marriage ended); married Walter Dexter, 1972; children: (first marriage) two sons, one daughter. *Education:* Attended Mills College, 1941-44; Victoria College, B.A., 1961; University of British Columbia, M.A., 1965; University of Kent, Ph.D., 1972.

ADDRESSES: Agent—Joanna Kellock, 11017 80th Avenue, Edmonton, Alberta T6G OR2, Canada.

ADDRESSES: Home—3825 Duke Rd., R.R.1, Victoria, British Columbia V8X 3W9, Canada.

CAREER: Writer. University of Victoria, special instructor, 1961-62; Rockland School, Victoria, head of English Department, 1962-63; University of British Columbia, teaching assistant/lecturer, 1963-66; Selkirk College, Castlegar, British Columbia, associate lecturer, 1968-74; Douglas College, Surrey, British Columbia, instructor, 1974-76; University of Victoria, visiting lecturer in creative writing, 1977-79, visiting lecturer in English, 1981-83.

AWARDS, HONORS: British Columbia Centennial One-Act Play award, 1958; Macmillan of Canada award, 1964; Norma Epstein award, 1965; Canada Council grant, 1976, 1979; Pat Lowther award, 1982.

WRITINGS:

POETRY

The Enchanted Adder, Klanak Press (Vancouver), 1965.
The Power of the Dog and Other Poems, Morriss (Victoria, British Columbia), 1968.
Ootischenie, Fiddlehead (Fredericton, New Brunswick), 1974.
Selected Poems, Sono Nis Press (Victoria, British Columbia), 1974.
From an Autumn Journal, League of Canadian Poets (Toronto), 1980.
Journey, Sono Nis Press, 1981.
Adam and Eve in Middle Age, Sono Nis Press, 1984.
The Lost Garden, Hawthorne Society (Victoria, British Columbia), 1993.

PLAYS

Blue Ducks' Feather and Eagledown, produced in Vancouver, 1958.
One, Two, Three Alary, produced in Castlegar, British Columbia, 1970; produced in Seattle, WA, 1983.
Creatures (produced in Seattle, 1980), published in *Event 7* (New Westminister, British Columbia).

SHORT STORIES

The Indigo Dress and Other Stories, Sono Nis Press, 1986.

OTHER

(Editor with Walter Dexter) *The Art of Earth: An Anthology,* Sono Nis Press, 1979.
Journey Back to Peshawar, Sono Nis Press, 1993.

*   *   *

MYERS, Tamar 1948-

PERSONAL: Given name is accented on the second syllable; born September 21, 1948, in the Belgian Congo (now Zaire); U.S. citizen; daughter of Russell F. (a minister and missionary) and Helen (a missionary; maiden name, Yoder) Schnell; married Jeffrey Myers (an engineer), November 28, 1970; children: Sarah, David, Dafna. *Ethnicity:* "Swiss/Danish/German." *Education:* American College in Jerusalem, B.A., 1970; Eastern Kentucky University, M.A., 1973. *Politics:* Independent. *Religion:* Episcopalian. *Avocational interests:* Gardening, oil painting, teaching piano lessons.

ADDRESSES: Home—Rock Hill, SC. *Agent*—Nancy Yost, Lowenstein Associates, Inc., 121 West 27th St., Suite 601, New York, NY 10001.

CAREER: Writer.

MEMBER: Mystery Writers of America, Novelists, Inc., Sisters in Crime, Politeia, Southeastern Palm and Exotic Plant Society, Blue Stockings Literary Club.

WRITINGS:

MYSTERY NOVELS, EXCEPT WHERE INDICATED

Too Many Crooks Spoil the Broth, Doubleday (New York), 1994.

Parsley, Sage, Rosemary, and Crime, Doubleday, 1995.
Angels, Angels Everywhere (stories), Avon (New York), 1995.
No Use Dying Over Spilled Milk, Dutton (Bergenfield, NJ), 1996.
Larceny and Old Lace, Avon, 1996.
Gilt by Association, Avon, 1996.
Just Plain Pickled to Death, Dutton, 1997.
The Ming and I, Avon, 1997.
So Faux, So Good, Avon, 1997.

WORK IN PROGRESS: Between a Wok and a Hard Place, a mystery novel, publication by Dutton expected in 1998; *Eat, Drink, and Be Wary,* a mystery novel, Dutton, 1998-99.

SIDELIGHTS: Tamar Myers told *CA:* "I was born and raised in the Belgian Congo, where my parents were Mennonite missionaries to a tribe of headhunters. We lived in a very remote region, hundreds of miles away from the nearest English-language bookstore. We had no radio or television. I wrote my first book-length manuscript at age ten to amuse myself and my three sisters.

"I began writing fiction in earnest in college, but it took twenty-three years to make my first sale. During that time I accumulated a stack of unsold manuscripts. Then, fortunately, I attempted a mystery with a humorous bent, using my background as a Mennonite of Amish descent. The novel sold immediately. In three years I signed contracts for ten humorous mystery novels: six centering on my Amish-Mennonite sleuth, Magdalena Yoder, and four featuring Abigail Timberlake, the owner of an antique shop called The Den of Antiquity. Because I now write four books a year, writing is a full-time job."

N-O

NAURECKAS, Jim 1964-

PERSONAL: Born November 8, 1964, in Libertyville, IL; son of Edward M. (a mechanical engineer) and Kathleen (a journalist; maiden name, Kearney) Naureckas. *Ethnicity:* "Irish-Lithuanian." *Education:* Stanford University, B.A., 1985.

ADDRESSES: Office—Fair, 130 West 25th St., New York, NY 10001.

CAREER: In These Times, Chicago, IL, staff writer, 1987-88; *Washington Report on the Hemisphere,* Washington, DC, managing editor, 1989; *Extra!,* New York City, editor, 1990—.

WRITINGS:

(With Steve Rendall and Jeff Cohen) *The Way Things Aren't: Rush Limbaugh's Reign of Error,* New Press, 1995.
(Editor with Janine Jackson) *The Fair Reader: An Extra! Review of Press and Politics in the Nineties,* Westview (Boulder, CO), 1996.

* * *

NELSON, T. G. A. 1940-

PERSONAL: Born January 31, 1940, in Aylesbury, England; son of George (a naval officer) and Alice Marion (a homemaker) Nelson; married Helen Newland Head, December 14, 1962; children: Vanessa Louise Nelson Todd, Juliet Marguerite Nelson Greentree, Christopher William. *Education:* Oxford University, B.A. (with honors), 1961, M.A., 1968. *Politics:* Independent. *Religion:* Independent.

ADDRESSES: Office—Department of English, University of New England, Armidale, New South Wales 2351, Australia. *E-mail*—tnelson@metz.une.edu.au.

CAREER: University of New England, Armidale, New South Wales, Australia, associate professor of English.

MEMBER: Australasian Drama Studies Association, Australian and New Zealand Association for Medieval and Renaissance Studies, British Society for Eighteenth-Century Studies.

WRITINGS:

Comedy: An Introduction to Comedy in Literature, Drama, and Cinema, Oxford University Press (Oxford, England), 1990.
Children, Parents, and the Rise of the Novel, University of Delaware Press (Newark, DE), 1995.

WORK IN PROGRESS: Woman as Poisoned Gift in Literature, Drama, and Cinema; research on the semiotics of eighteenth-century writing in English.

SIDELIGHTS: T. G. A. Nelson told *CA:* "My life is not a long disease, as was Alexander Pope's, and, unlike him, I do have a wife (the best on the planet) to help me through it. But I was dipped in ink quite early, and I still can't shake off my interest in humanity, past and present, and its literature. I have been diverted into literary criticism, but hope to do some more truly creative writing before I die."

NESBIT, Andrew
  See KELLY, Ronald

*   *   *

NICHOLS, Grace 1950-

PERSONAL: Born January 18, 1950; companion of John Agard (a poet); children: two daughters (one from a previous marriage). *Education:* Attended University of Guyana, Georgetown, diploma in communications.

ADDRESSES: Agent—Anthea Morton-Saner, Curtis Brown, 162-68 Regent St., London W1R STB, England.

CAREER: Teacher in Georgetown, 1967-70; reporter with national newspaper, Georgetown, 1972-73; Government Information Services, information assistant, 1973-76; freelance journalist in Guyana, until 1977.

AWARDS, HONORS: Commonwealth poetry prize, 1983; British Arts Council bursary, 1988.

WRITINGS:

POETRY

I Is a Long-Memoried Woman, Caribbean Cultural International (London), 1983.
The Fat Black Woman's Poems, Virago Press (London), 1984.
Come On into My Tropical Garden (for children), A. and C. Black (London), 1988.
Lazy Thoughts of a Lazy Woman, and Other Poems, Virago Press, 1989.

NOVEL

Whole of a Morning Sky, Virago Press, 1989.

OTHER (FOR CHILDREN)

Trust You, Wriggly, Hodder and Stoughton (London), 1980.
Baby Fish and Other Stories, Privately printed, 1983.
Leslyn in London, Hodder and Stoughton, 1984.
The Discovery, Macmillan (London), 1986.
(Editor) *Black Poetry,* Blackie (London), 1988; published as *Poetry Jump Up,* Penguin (London), 1989.

(With John Agard) *No Hickory No Dickory No Dock* (nursery rhyme), Viking (London), 1990.
(Editor) *Can I Buy a Slice of Sky?,* Blackie, 1991.
(Editor with John Agard) *A Caribbean Dozen,* Walker Books, 1994.
Give Yourself a Hug (poems), A and C Black (London), 1994.

*   *   *

NIELSON, James 1958-

PERSONAL: Born April 23, 1958, in Bellingham, WA; citizen of the U.S. and Canada; son of Joseph Roberts and Shirley (maiden name, Bartell; present surname, Andrues) Nielson; married Nyla Jean Matuk, June 1, 1991. *Education:* University of Washington, Seattle, B.A. (magna cum laude), 1984; McGill University, M.A., 1986, Ph.D., 1991. *Politics:* "Left wing." *Religion:* "Christian atheist." *Avocational interests:* Music, computers, walking.

ADDRESSES: Home—111 Howland Ave., Apt. 1, Toronto, Ontario, Canada M5R 3B7. *Office*—MediaLinx Interactive, 20 Richmond St. E., Suite 600, Toronto, Ontario, Canada M5C 2B5. *E-mail*—nielson@io.org.

CAREER: McGill University, Montreal, Quebec, lecturer in English, 1989-92; University of British Columbia, Vancouver, lecturer in English, 1992-95; MediaLinx Interactive, Toronto, Ontario, web consultant and researcher, HTML author, and internet programmer, 1995—. University of Michigan Press, translator, 1994-95; Morris and Helen Belkin Art Gallery, proofreader, 1995.

WRITINGS:

Unread Herrings: Thomas Nashe and the Prosaics of the Real, Peter Lang (New York), 1993.
(Translator with Genevieve James) Michel Serres, *Genesis,* University of Michigan Press (Ann Arbor, MI), 1995.

Contributor to books, including *Dictionary of Literary Biography,* Volume 136: *Sixteenth-Century British Non-Dramatic Writers,* Second Series, Gale (Detroit, MI), 1994. Contributor to periodicals, including *Shakespeare Quarterly* and *SEL: Studies in English Literature, 1500-1900.* Member of editorial advisory group, *Early Modern Literary Studies* (online journal), 1995.

WORK IN PROGRESS: A novel and a nonfiction book about the early 1970s.

SIDELIGHTS: James Nielson told *CA:* "For a long time I was following my fortune in academia, most recently teaching technical writing, composition, and literature at the University of British Columbia in Vancouver. I published scholarly articles and a book, and also translated a book from French.

"In the last couple of years, I have developed my computer programming, internet, and online publishing skills, and at present I am providing a number of internet-related services for a major national service provider. I am always interested in hearing about opportunities to work as a journalist, technical writer, editor, translator, online 'information architect,' or World Wide Web technician."

*   *   *

NORTH, Rick
   See BRENNER, Mayer Alan

*   *   *

NOTLEY, Alice 1945-

PERSONAL: Born November 8, 1945, in Bisbee, AZ; married Ted Berrigan (a writer), 1972 (died 1983); married Douglas Oliver, 1988; children: (first marriage) two sons. *Education:* Barnard College, B.A., 1967; University of Iowa, M.F.A., 1969.

CAREER: Writer.

AWARDS, HONORS: National Endowment for the Arts grant, 1980; Poetry Center award, 1982; G.E. Foundation award, 1983, Fund for Poetry grant, 1987 1989.

WRITINGS:

POETRY

165 Meeting House Lane, "C" Press (New York), 1971.

Phoebe Light, Big Sky (Bolinas, CA), 1973.
Incidentals in the Day World, Angel Hair (New York), 1973.
For Frank O'Hara's Birthday, Street Editions (Cambridge), 1976.
Alice Ordered Me to Be Made: Poems 1975, Yellow Press (Chicago, IL), 1976.
A Diamond Necklace, Frontward (New York), 1977.
Songs for the Unborn Second Baby, United Artists (Lenox, MA), 1979.
When I Was Alive, Vehicle (New York), 1980.
Waltzing Matilda, Kulchur (New York), 1981.
How Spring Comes, Toothpaste Press (West Branch, IA), 1981.
(With Andrei Codrescu) *Three Zero, Turning Thirty,* edited by Keith and Jeff Wright, Hard Press (New York), 1982.
Sorrento, Sherwood Press (Los Angeles), 1984.
Margaret and Dusty, Coffee House Press (Minneapolis, MN), 1985.
Parts of a Wedding, Unimproved Editions Press (New York), 1986.
At Night the States, Yellow Press, 1988.
Selected Poems of Alice Notley, Talisman House (Hoboken, NJ), 1993.

PLAY

Anne's White Glove (produced in New York, 1985), published in *New American Writing,* 1987.

OTHER

Doctor Williams' Heiresses: A Lecture, Tuumba Press (Berkeley, CA), 1980.
Tell Me Again (autobiography), Am Here (Santa Barbara, CA), 1981.
Homer's "Art", Institute for Further Studies (Canton, NY), 1990.
(With Douglas Oliver) *The Scarlet Cabinet: A Compendium of Books,* Scarlet Editions (New York), 1992.

*   *   *

O'BRIEN, Sean 1952-

PERSONAL: Born December 19, 1952, in London, England. *Education:* Selwyn College, Cambridge, B.A. (English), 1974; Birmingham University, M.A., 1977; attended Hull University, 1976-79; Leeds University, Post-Graduate Certificate in Education, 1981.

ADDRESSES: Home—56 Mafeking Rd., Brighton BN2 4EL, East Sussex, England.

CAREER: Beacon School, Crowborough, East Sussex, teacher, 1981-89; University of Dundee, fellow in creative writing, 1989-90; *The Printer's Devil* literary magazine, Brighton, East Sussex, founding editor, with Stephen Plaice, 1990.

AWARDS, HONORS: Eric Gregory award, 1979; Somerset Maugham award, 1984; Cholmondeley award, 1988.

WRITINGS:

POETRY

The Indoor Park, Bloodaxe (Newcastle upon Tyne), 1983.
The Frighteners, Bloodaxe, 1987.
Boundary Beach, Ulsterman (Belfast), 1989.
HMS Glasshouse, Oxford University Press (Oxford and New York), 1991.
A Rarity, Carnivorous Arpeggio Press (Hull), 1993.
Ghost Train, Oxford University Press (New York), 1995.

OTHER

Bloody Ambassadors: The Gruesome Stories of Irish People Tried for Murder Abroad, Poolbeg (Dublin), 1993.

*   *   *

OFFUTT, Chris 1958-

PERSONAL: Born in 1958, in the United States; married; wife's name, Rita. *Education:* Attended the Iowa Writers Workshop.

ADDRESSES: Office—c/o Simon and Schuster, 1230 Avenue of the Americas, New York, NY 10020.

CAREER: Worked odd jobs from the age of nineteen, including house painter and circus performer; freelance writer, c. 1992—.

WRITINGS:

Kentucky Straight (short stories), Vintage Books (New York), 1992.

The Same River Twice: A Memoir, Simon & Schuster (New York), c. 1993.

Also contributor of stories and articles to periodicals, including *Parenting, Gentlemen's Quarterly,* and *Esquire.*

SIDELIGHTS: Author Chris Offutt spent his youth in Kentucky, where the Appalachian Mountains touch the eastern part of the state. At nineteen, however, he left home to wander across the United States for many years, always with the intention of becoming a writer, an artist, a poet, or all three. The reality, however, was that he worked odd jobs—once wearing a walrus costume in a circus—and occasionally delved into small-time crime. Charles Solomon, reviewing Offutt's autobiographical *The Same River Twice: A Memoir* in the *Los Angeles Times Book Review,* reported that marriage and the desire to write "saved him from prison or a homeless shelter."

Though 1993's *The Same River Twice* saw print only a few months afterward, Offutt's first book-length publication was his 1992 collection of short stories, *Kentucky Straight.* As the title implies, the volume takes its setting and its characters from the countryside in which Offutt grew up. The stories include tales such as one about a man who makes a bet about the size of his penis during a poker game; another about a boy who is skeptical when his long-lost grandfather shows up; and another about a young man who dreams of using his skills at playing pool as a means to escape the family hog farm. Sue Halpern, assessing both of Offutt's books in the *New York Times Book Review,* noted that the author "has a keen ear for the strangeness of dialect, which he renders without affectation." The critic went on to quote from one of Offutt's stories, in which an adolescent male narrator informs readers: "She held my hand like you do a frog when you're fixing to cut its legs off and eat them." A *Publishers Weekly* reviewer also praised the "taut" stories of *Kentucky Straight.*

In *The Same River Twice,* Offutt alternates tales of his misadventures as a wanderer with chapters about anticipating, with his wife, Rita, the birth of his first child. Before he settled, he painted houses for a former Vietnam veteran who eventually committed suicide; he also, after getting drunk with the resident tattooed lady of the circus, had to take off his fake walrus head to vomit in the middle of a performance. But Offutt finds nothing he encountered during his years on the road as frightening as impending fatherhood. Many reviewers applauded *The Same River*

Twice, though Tim McLaurin, holding forth in *Washington Post Book World,* observed: "I found it hard to like Offutt when he was a would-be-poet bum. . . . Offutt seemed to be too much the dreamer, the person you talk to at a party who is always going to write a great novel—someday." But McLaurin admitted that in *The Same River Twice* Offutt has produced a "memorable account," and that "he is a writer now, and I hope for us all he sticks with it." Halpern responded favorably to *The Same River Twice* as well, hailing it as "rich and fantastic and desperately honest." Christopher Lehmann-Haupt of the *New York Times* lauded Offutt's second book as an "unusual poetic memoir," concluding that "[s]ide by side, the two narratives powerfully convey his sense of being trapped."

BIOGRAPHICAL/CRITICAL SOURCES:

PERIODICALS

Los Angeles Times Book Review, February 13, 1994, p. 15.
New York Times, January 7, 1993, p. C17.
New York Times Book Review, January 31, 1993, p. 10.
Publishers Weekly, September 14, 1992, p. 115.
Washington Post Book World, March 7, 1993, p. 2.*

*   *   *

OGUNDIPE-LESLIE, 'Molara

PERSONAL: Born in Lagos, Nigeria; married; children: two daughters. *Education:* Graduated from University of Ibadan, Nigeria (first-class honors).

CAREER: Writer and educator. University of Ibadan, former faculty member; Ogun State University, Nigeria, Department of English, former chair; lecturer in English and African literature at universities in Africa, Canada, and the United States, including Columbia University, Harvard University, University of California—Berkeley, and Northwestern University. Contributing essayist and member of editorial board, *The Guardian* (newspaper), Nigeria. National director of Social Mobilization, Federal Government of Nigeria, 1987-89.

MEMBER: Women in Nigeria (founding member), Association of African Women for Research and Development (founding member).

WRITINGS:

(Contributor) *Sisterhood Is Global: The International Women's Movement Anthology,* edited by Robin Morgan, Doubleday (Garden City, NY), 1984.
Sew the Old Days and Other Poems, Evans Bros. (Nigeria), 1985.
(Contributor) *Theorizing Black Feminisms,* edited by Stanlie James and Abena Busia, Routledge (New York City), 1993.
Re-Creating Ourselves: African Women and Critical Transformations, Africa World Press (Trenton, NJ), 1994.
(Editor, with Carole Boyce Davis, and contributor) *Moving Beyond Boundaries,* Volume 1: *International Dimensions of Women's Writing,* New York University Press (New York City), 1995.

Also author of *Towards a Double-Gendered Cosmos: Essays on African Literature.*

SIDELIGHTS: An educator, poet, and activist for social change within her native Nigeria, 'Molara Ogundipe-Leslie is the author of numerous essays that analyze the way social and economic class differences prohibit women from uniting to form a global feminist consciousness. A contributor to Robin Morgan's groundbreaking *Sisterhood Is Global: The International Women's Movement Anthology,* and the author of the 1994 essay collection *Re-Creating Ourselves: African Women and Critical Transformations,* Ogundipe-Leslie remains an outspoken critic of the patriarchal traditions that are still revered throughout the African continent.

In an essay entitled "The Female Writer and Her Commitment," originally published in *The Guardian* in 1983 and reprinted in *Re-Creating Ourselves,* Ogundipe-Leslie asserts that, in her view, "female writers cannot usefully claim to be concerned with various social predicaments in their countries or in Africa without situating their awareness and solutions within the larger global context of imperialism and neo-colonialism." Indeed, the colonization of many African nations by the British put an end to women's economic power and, thus, their autonomy. Similar to Marxist feminists, Ogundipe-Leslie contends that women's true liberation is conditional upon the breakdown of both patriarchy and capitalism.

Re-Creating Ourselves includes other essays that address such wide-ranging topics as little-studied works of literature, the masculine dialogue of revolutionary politics, and the implications of modern capitalism's inequitable economic practices. The diversity of these issues reflects their author's broad area of social concern as well as the philosophical basis of her feminism. "[M]en are not the enemy," Ogundipe-Leslie writes in the essay "Not Spinning on the Axis of Maleness," published in *Sisterhood Is Global* in 1984. "The enemy is the total societal system. . . . But," she adds of the social transformation necessary in order to attain an equitable global society, "men do become enemies when they seek to retard or even block these necessary historical changes."

BIOGRAPHICAL/CRITICAL SOURCES:

BOOKS

Morgan, Robin, editor, *Sisterhood Is Global: The International Women's Movement Anthology,* Doubleday (Garden City, NY), 1984.

Ogundipe-Leslie, 'Molara, interview in *In Their Own Voices: African Women Writers Talk,* James Currey (London), 1990.

Ogundipe-Leslie, 'Molara, *Re-Creating Ourselves: African Women and Critical Transformations,* Africa World Press (Trenton, NJ), 1994.

Otukunefor, Henrietta, and Obiagele Nwodo, editors, *Nigerian Female Writers: A Critical Perspective,* Malthouse (Lagos, Nigeria), 1989.

*　*　*

OKAI, John 1967-

PERSONAL: Born in 1967. *Education:* Attended University of Ghana; University of London, M.A. (Litt.); Gorky Literary Institute, M.Phil.

ADDRESSES: Office—Department of Modern Languages, University of Ghana, P.O. Box 25, Legon, Ghana.

CAREER: Writer. University of Ghana, Legon, lecturer in Russian.

AWARDS, HONORS: Royal Society of Arts fellowship, 1968.

WRITINGS:

POETRY

Flowerfall, Writers Forum (London), 1969.

The Oath of Fontomirom and Other Poems, Simon and Schuster (New York), 1971.

Lorgorligi: Logarithms and Other Poems, Ghana Publishing (Tema), 1974.

*　*　*

OSLIN, George P(oer) 1899-1996

OBITUARY NOTICE—See index for *CA* sketch: Born August 5, 1899, in West Point, GA; died October 24, 1996, in Delray Beach, FL. Public relations director and author. Oslin is credited with inventing the concept of the "singing telegram." Before Oslin's thirty-five year stint as the director of public relations for Western Union, he was a reporter for several newspapers, including the *Newark Evening News*. In 1929, Oslin joined the staff at Western Union. In 1933, he had the idea of sending a "singing" telegram to popular singer Rudy Vallee for his birthday. Over the years, Western Union has made millions of dollars delivering these singing messages. Oslin went on to write three books about the history of the telecommunications industry, including *The Story of Telecommunications, The Telegraph Industry,* and *Talking Wires: The Way of Life in the Telegraph Industry.*

OBITUARIES AND OTHER SOURCES:

BOOKS

Who's Who, 148th edition, St. Martin's, 1996.

PERIODICALS

New York Times, October 29, 1996, p. B19.

*　*　*

OSMOND, John 1946-

PERSONAL: Born October 21, 1946, in Abergavenny, Wales. *Education:* University of Bristol, B.A. (with honors), 1968.

ADDRESSES: Home—25 Westbourne Rd., Penas 12, Vale of Glamorgan, Wales; fax 01-22-270-9318.

CAREER: Western Mail, Cardiff, Wales, political correspondent, 1972-80; *ARCADE: Wales Fort-*

nightly, Cardiff, editor, 1980-82; HTV Television, Cardiff, producer, 1982-88; *Wales on Sunday,* Cardiff, assistant editor, 1988-90; free-lance writer and television producer, Cardiff, 1990-96; Institute of Welsh Affairs, director, 1996—. Well Area of Writers, chairperson, 1988-94; Parliament for Wales Campaign, chairperson, 1991-96.

MEMBER: Welsh Academy (executive member).

WRITINGS:

The Centralist Enemy, Christopher Davies, 1974.
Creative Conflict, Gomer Press (Llandysul, Wales), 1978.
Alternatives, Thorson, 1982.
The National Question Again, Gomer Press, 1985.
Work in the Future, Thorson, 1986.
The Divided Kingdom, Constable, 1988.
The Democratic Challenge, Gomer Press, 1992.
The Reality of Dyslexia, Cassell, 1993.
A Parliament for Wales, Gomer Press, 1994.
Welsh Europeans, Seren, 1996.

*　　*　　*

OSTROWER, Gary B. 1939-

PERSONAL: Born October 11, 1939, in New York, NY; son of Joseph and Ann (Weinstein) Ostrower; married Judith E. Samber, January 1, 1979; children: Sarah, Peter. *Education:* Alfred University, B.A., 1961; University of Rochester, M.A., 1962, Ph.D., 1970. *Avocational interests:* Coaching Little League, jogging, tennis.

ADDRESSES: Home—Alfred, NY. *Office*—Division of Human Studies, Alfred University, Alfred, NY 14802; fax 607-871-2339. *E-mail*—ostrower@bigvax .alfred.edu.

CAREER: Vassar College, Poughkeepsie, NY, instructor, 1967-68; Alfred University, Alfred, NY, professor of history, 1969—, Hagar Professor of Humanities, 1996-99. University of Pennsylvania, visiting lecturer, 1979-80. Village of Alfred, member of village board of trustees, 1981—.

MEMBER: Society for the Study of Internationalism (president, 1988-94), Organization of American Historians, Society for Historians of American Foreign Relations.

WRITINGS:

Collective Insecurity: The United States and the League of Nations, Bucknell University Press (Lewisburg, PA), 1979.
The League of Nations From 1919 to 1929, Avery Publishing Group (Garden City Park, NY), 1996.
The United States and the United Nations: 1940 to the Present, Twayne (New York City), 1997.

SIDELIGHTS: Gary B. Ostrower told *CA:* "I formed my first distinct memories during World War II, and from such a childhood I have developed a lifelong interest in the subject of war, peace, and diplomacy. Two teachers especially influenced my decision to make a career as a historian and professor: Martha Morrow of Woodbridge High School, in New Jersey, and David M. Leach at Alfred University. Their realism moderated a much more idealistic approach to politics that I received at home, where the United Nations (for which I retain a skeptical respect today) was viewed in almost reverential terms.

"Teaching in a predominantly undergraduate institution, I find little time to write during the academic year. I therefore write frenetically during summers and occasional vacations, and I pray for sabbaticals. My approach to history is quite traditional. It presupposes that genuine objectivity is unattainable, yet leaves me committed to fairness and the belief that history is much more than the tricks Voltaire claimed we play on the dead. I am convinced that the test of a good historian is in how he or she deals with data that does not support one's point of view. I think that I treat such data honestly; I hope my critics agree."

*　　*　　*

OWEN, Jan 1940-

PERSONAL: Born August 18, 1940, in Adelaide, South Australia; married Balazs Bajka, 1964 (divorced 1972); married Anthony Brown, 1972; children: (first marriage) one son, one daughter; (second marriage) one son. *Education:* University of Adelaide, B.A., 1963.

ADDRESSES: Home—14 Fern Rd., Crafers, South Australia 5152, Australia. *Agent*—Margaret Connolly, 17 Ormond St., Paddington, New South Wales, Australia.

CAREER: Waite Institute, Adelaide, laboratory assistant, 1957-60; Barr Smith Library, Adelaide, library assistant, 1961, librarian, 1962-64, 1966; South Australian Institute of Technology Library, librarian, 1969-71; Salisbury College of Advanced Education Library, librarian, 1971-75; Technical and Further Education College, Gillies Plains, librarian, 1981-84; creative writing teacher at Australian schools, colleges, and universities, 1985—.

AWARDS, HONORS: Ian Mudie award, 1982; Jessie Litchfield prize, 1984, for *Boy with a Telescope;* Grenfell Henry Lawson prize, 1985; Harri Jones Memorial prize, 1986, for *Boy with a Telescope;* Anne Elder award, 1986, for *Boy with a Telescope;* Mary Gilmore prize, 1987, for *Boy with a Telescope;* Wesley Michel Wright Poetry prize, 1992.

WRITINGS:

POETRY

Boy with a Telescope, Angus and Robertson (Sydney), 1986.
Fingerprints on Light, Angus and Robertson, 1990.
Blackberry Season, Molongolo Press (Canberra), 1993.
Night Rainbows, Heinemann (Melbourne), 1994.

P-Q

PAGE, Carl 1957-

PERSONAL: Born March 14, 1957, in Auckland, New Zealand. *Ethnicity:* "Caucasian." *Education:* University of Auckland, B.A., 1980, M.A. (with first class honors), 1982; Pennsylvania State University, Ph.D., 1987.

ADDRESSES: Home—213 Prince George St., Annapolis, MD 21401. *Office*—St. John's College, Annapolis, MD 21404.

CAREER: University of Auckland, Auckland, New Zealand, assistant lecturer, 1982; Pennsylvania State University, University Park, part-time instructor, 1984-85; Emory University, Atlanta, GA, assistant professor of philosophy, 1987-94, fellow of Sears Writing Program, 1989-90; St. John's College, Annapolis, MD, tutor, 1994—. Lecturer at educational institutions, including Georgia State University, 1988, Ohio Northern University, 1989, Rochester Institute of Technology, 1990, University of Georgia, 1993, Boston University, 1995, and Brock University, 1996.

MEMBER: American Philosophical Association, Society for Ancient Greek Philosophy, Metaphysical Society of America, Hegel Society of America.

WRITINGS:

Philosophical Historicism and the Betrayal of First Philosophy, Pennsylvania State University Press (University Park, PA), 1995.

Contributor to books, including *The Philosophy of H.-G. Gadamer,* edited by Lewis Hahn, Open Court (LaSalle, IL). Contributor of more than twenty articles and reviews to scholarly journals, including *Ancient Philosophy, Journal of the History of Ideas, Journal of Speculative Philosophy, Interpretation: A Journal of Political Philosophy, Metaphilosophy,* and *International Philosophical Quarterly.*

*   *   *

PANOURGIA, Neni K(onstantinou) 1958-
(Nenny Panourgia)

PERSONAL: Born May 1, 1958, in Athens, Greece; daughter of Konstantinos (an engineer and industrialist) and Dimitra (Tsakalou) Panourgia; married Stathis Gourgouris; children: Petros Konstantinos. *Ethnicity:* "Greek." *Education:* American College of Greece, B.A., 1981; Indiana University—Bloomington, M.A., 1985, Ph.D., 1992; attended University of Utah, 1989-90.

ADDRESSES: Home—53 Maple, Princeton, NJ 08540. *Office*—Program in Hellenic Studies, Joseph Henry House, Princeton University, Princeton, NJ 08544. *E-mail*—stathis@phoenix.princeton.edu.

CAREER: Intercultural Action Learning Program, teacher of Greek and anthropology, 1981, 1982; Indiana University—Bloomington, lecturer in Greek and exhibit curator at William Hammond Mathers Museum, 1983-85, associate instructor in anthropology, 1989; Columbia University, New York City, lecturer in Greek, 1991; Museum of Children's Health, Athens, Greece, coordinator of operations, 1994-95; Princeton University, Princeton, NJ, visiting fellow in Hellenic studies, 1995-96, teacher of Greek language and literature, 1996-97. University of Colorado, exhibit coordinator, 1987; Pantion University of Social and Political Sciences, visiting research fellow, 1994-95; lecturer at colleges and universities, including De Paul University, 1987, Ohio State University, 1991, University of Lund, 1992, Harvard University, 1994, Selwyn College, Cambridge, 1994, and New York University, 1994. Conducted field work in Greece, beginning in 1982.

MEMBER: International Psycho-Oncology Organization, International Society for the Study of European Ideas, Modern Greek Studies Association, Society for the Anthropology of Europe, Society for Medical Anthropology, Society for Humanistic Anthropology, Society for Cultural Anthropology, American Anthropological Association, Anthropology and AIDS Research Group.

AWARDS, HONORS: Grant for excavations at Isthmia, Wenner-Gren Foundation for Anthropological Research, 1991; grant from Greek Ministry of National Health, 1992.

WRITINGS:

Fragments of Death, Fables of Identity: An Athenian Anthropology, University of Wisconsin Press (Madison, WI), 1995.

Contributor to books, including *The European Legacy: Toward New Paradigms.* Contributor to periodicals, including *American Anthropologist, Journal of Modern Greek Studies,* and *Anthropology and Humanism.* Some writings appear under the name Nenny Panourgia.

WORK IN PROGRESS: Oedipal Sightings: Anthropology, Ethnography, and the Deconstruction of the Site, on ethnographic practice and theory; *Deforming Bodies Forming Subjects,* a collection of essays on the understanding of the self in cases of radical somatic changes; *Greek-Americans: Workings of an Ethnic Presence,* with Alexandros Kyrou, a collection of essays on the encounter of Greek-Americans with the dominant American culture.

BIOGRAPHICAL/CRITICAL SOURCES:

PERIODICALS

Choice, September, 1996.
Times Literary Supplement, November 1, 1996.

PANOURGIA, Nenny
  See PANOURGIA, Neni K(onstantinou)

*   *   *

PARIS, David C.   1949-

PERSONAL: Born October 21, 1949, in Rochester, NY; son of Giacomo (a power company supervisor) and Catherine D. (a secretary; maiden name, Biase) Paris; married Candace May (a librarian); children: Celia, Natalie, Stephanie. *Ethnicity:* "Italian." *Education:* Hamilton College, B.A., 1971; Syracuse University, Ph.D., 1975. *Politics:* Independent. *Avocational interests:* Reading, sports.

ADDRESSES: Home—7137 College Hill Rd., Clinton, NY 13323. *Office*—Hamilton College, 198 College Hill Rd., Clinton, NY 13323; fax 315-859-4632. *E-mail*—dparis@hamilton.edu.

CAREER: Virginia Polytechnic Institute and State University, Blacksburg, faculty member, 1975-79; Hamilton College, Clinton, NY, faculty member, 1979—.

MEMBER: American Political Science Association.

WRITINGS:

Ideology and Educational Reform: Themes and Theories in Public Education, Westview (Boulder, CO), 1995.

WORK IN PROGRESS: A book on national standards and charter schools; research on postsecondary education.

SIDELIGHTS: David C. Paris told *CA:* "My main interest is the connection between our ideas about society and politics and our actual policies and practices. My main motivation in writing is a desire to learn about the interplay of theory and practice. I am always struck by how difficult it is to translate one into the other and how nearly ordered ideas crumble in the face of multiple values and practical realities. There is perhaps no better, or more important, example of these problems than education. The schools are where ideas and realities meet and often clash. My favorite authors and analysts, in this and other areas, are those who eschew (left or right) ideology in favor of a hopeful mix of skepticism and realism."

PARTHASARATHY, R(ajagopal) 1934-

PERSONAL: Born August 20, 1934, in Tirupparaiturai, near Tiruchchirappalli, Tamil Nadu, India; married Shobhan Koppikar, 1969; children: two sons. *Education:* Siddharth College, Bombay University, M.A. (English), 1959; Leeds University, Yorkshire (British Council scholar), postgraduate diploma in English studies 1964.

ADDRESSES: Office—Department of English and Program in Asian Studies, Skidmore College, Saratoga Springs, NY 12866.

CAREER: Ismail Yusuf College, Bombay, lecturer in English, 1959-62; Mithibai College, Bombay, lecturer in English, 1962-63, 1964-65; British Council, Bombay, lecturer in English language teaching, 1965-66; Presidency College, Madras, assistant professor of English, 1966-67; South Indian Education Society College, Bombay, lecturer in English, 1967-71. Oxford University Press, regional editor, Madras, 1971-78, editor, New Delhi, beginning in 1978; University of Iowa, Iowa City, member of the International Writing Program, 1978-79; University of Texas at Austin, assistant instructor in English, 1982-86; currently member of faculty, Skidmore College, Saratoga Springs, NY. National Academy of Letters, New Delhi, member of the advisory board for English, beginning in 1978.

AWARDS, HONORS: Ulka poetry prize *(Poetry India),* 1966.

WRITINGS:

POETRY

Rough Passage, Oxford University Press (New Delhi), 1977.

OTHER

(Editor with J.J. Healy) *Poetry from Leeds,* Writers Workshop (Calcutta), 1968.
(Editor) *Ten Twentieth-Century Indian Poets,* Oxford University Press (New Delhi), 1976.
(Translator) *The Cilappatikaram of Ilanko Atikal: An Epic of South India,* Columbia University Press (New York), 1992.

PATEL, Gieve 1940-

PERSONAL: Born August 18, 1940, in Bombay, India; married Toni Diniz, 1969; children: one daughter. *Education:* St. Xavier's College, B.Sc.; Grant Medical College, M.B.B.S.

ADDRESSES: Home—SE Malabar Apartments, Nepean Rd., Bombay 400 036, India.

CAREER: Primary Health Centre, Sanjan, Gujarat, medical officer, 1969-71. Currently runs a private general medical practice, Bombay Central hospital. Also a painter: individual shows—Jehangir Art Gallery, Bombay, 1966-1984; Sridharani Gallery, New Delhi, 1966; Pundole Art Gallery, Bombay, 1972; Chemould Gallery, Bombay, 1975; Art Heritage Gallery, New Delhi, 1979.

AWARDS, HONORS: Woodrow Wilson fellowship, 1984; Rockefeller fellowship, 1992.

WRITINGS:

POETRY

Poems, Ezekiel (Bombay), 1966.
How Do You Withstand, Body, Clearing House (Bombay), 1976.
Mirrored, Mirroring, Oxford University Press (New Delhi), 1991.

PLAYS

Princes, produced in Bombay, 1971.
Savaksa (produced in Bombay, 1982), published in *Bombay Literary Review,* 1989.
Mister Behram (produced in Bombay, 1987), published by Praxis (Bombay), 1988.

*   *   *

PATERSON, Don(ald) 1963-

PERSONAL: Born October 30, 1963, in Dundee, Scotland.

ADDRESSES: Agent—c/o Faber and Faber, 3 Queen Sq., London WC1N 3AU, England.

CAREER: Jazz musician, London, 1982—. Dundee University, writer-in-residence, 1993-95.

AWARDS, HONORS: Eric Gregory award, 1990; Forward Poetry prize for best first collection, Arvon/Observer International Poetry Competition, and Scottish Arts Council Book award, all 1993, for *Nil Nil*.

WRITINGS:

Nil Nil (poetry), Faber (London), 1993.

*   *   *

PATTERSON, Glenn 1961-

PERSONAL: Born August 9, 1961, in Belfast, Northern Ireland; son of Phares (a sheet metal worker) and Agnes (a clerk; maiden name, Murphy) Patterson; married Alison Fitzgibbon (a theater administrator), May 12, 1995. *Education:* University of East Anglia, B.A. (with honors), 1985, M.A., 1986. *Religion:* Atheist.

ADDRESSES: Agent—Antony Harwood, Aitken & Stone, 29 Fernshaw Rd., London SW10 0TG, England.

CAREER: Arts Council of Northern Ireland, writer in the community, 1989-91; University of East Anglia, Norwich, England, creative writing fellow, 1992; National University of Ireland, University College, Cork, writer in residence, 1993-94; Queen's University, Belfast, Northern Ireland, writer in residence, 1994-97. RTE (Irish television network), presenter of the arts review program *Black Box,* 1995-96. Tinderbox Theatre Company, director; Arts Council of Northern Ireland, member, 1996—.

MEMBER: Society of Authors.

AWARDS, HONORS: Rooney Prize for Irish Literature, 1988; Betty Trask Award, 1988, for *Burning Your Own.*

WRITINGS:

Burning Your Own (novel), Chatto & Windus (London, England), 1988.
Fat Lad (novel), Chatto & Windus, 1992.
Black Night at Big Thunder Mountain (novel), Chatto & Windus, 1995.

WORK IN PROGRESS: A novel, *The International.*

PATTON, Arch 1908-1996

OBITUARY NOTICE—See index for *CA* sketch: Born January 11, 1908, in New York, NY; died November 23, 1996, in Bronxville, NY. Management consultant, speaker and author. Patton was one of the more high-profile management consultants until his retirement in 1974. He is perhaps best known for his ground-breaking 1951 survey that looked at how executives in different industries were paid. He was also author of the 1961 book *Men, Money and Motivation* and wrote several articles for *Fortune, Financial Executive,* and *Business Week.* Patton later complained that his survey on executive compensation, which was published yearly in the *Harvard Business Review* for more than 10 years after its inception, was misinterpreted by corporations and helped contribute to bloated salaries. Educated at Colgate University and Harvard Business School, Patton was director of McKinsey and Company, a management consulting firm. He was also the most prolific single contributor to the *Harvard Business Review.*

OBITUARIES AND OTHER SOURCES:

PERIODICALS

New York Times, November 30, 1996, p. 16.

*   *   *

PAVLIK, John V.

PERSONAL: Born in the United States; married; wife's name, Jackie; children: Tristan, Orianna (daughters). *Education:* University of Wisconsin—Madison, B.A., 1978; University of Minnesota—Twin Cities, M.A., 1980, Ph.D., 1983.

ADDRESSES: Office—Center for New Media, 2950 Broadway, Columbia University, New York, NY 10027. *E-mail*—jp35@columbia.edu.

CAREER: American Family Insurance Group, Madison, WI, public relations officer, 1977-78; University of Minnesota—Twin Cities, Minneapolis, instructor in journalism, mass communication, and marketing, 1981-82; Pennsylvania State University, University Park, assistant professor of communications, 1982-88, graduate studies director for the School of Journalism, 1984-86; Columbia University, Freedom Forum Media Studies Center, New York City, associate director for research and technology studies, member of editorial board, and developer of computer software, 1988-94, director of library, 1988-93, co-director of research group, 1990-94; San Diego State University, professor of communication and director, School of Communication, both 1994-95; Center for New Media, Columbia University, executive director, 1995—; Columbia University, Graduate School of Journalism, professor, 1995—. City of the Future, co-chair of InfoSan Diego, 1994-95; San Diego-Baja Communications Council, member of board of directors, 1995, and member of executive council. New York Festivals International Interactive Multimedia Awards, founding member of Board of Distinguished Judges and Advisers, 1992—; judge of Emmy Awards in news and documentaries and sports categories, 1989-94; Oates Clearinghouse for Computer-Based Education in Journalism and Mass Communication, member of software review board, 1986-88. Public speaker.

MEMBER: International Communication Association (chairperson of Public Relations Interest Group, 1992-93), Association for Education in Journalism and Mass Communication (vice head of Public Relations Division, 1987-89, and member of standing committee for research, 1995—), Institute, Academy, and Foundation for High Definition Television Arts and Sciences, San Diego Digital Multimedia Association (member of board of directors, 1995).

AWARDS, HONORS: Grants from Honeywell, Inc., Los Angeles Foundation, 1995, and Institute for Public Relations Research and Education, 1995.

WRITINGS:

Public Relations: What Research Tells Us, Sage Publications (Beverly Hills, CA), 1987.
(Editor with Everette E. Dennis) *Media Technology: A Freedom Forum Center Reader,* Mayfield Publishing (Mountain View, CA), 1993.
(Editor with Fred Williams) *The People's Right to Know: Media, Democracy, and the Information Highway,* Lawrence Erlbaum (Hillsdale, NJ), 1994.
New Media Technology: Cultural and Commercial Perspectives, Allyn & Bacon (New York), 1996.

Contributor to books, including *Designing Health Communication Campaigns: What Works?,* edited by Thomas E. Backer, Everett M. Rogers, and Pradeep Sopory, Sage Publications, 1992. Contributor of articles and reviews to professional journals including,

Journal of Consumer Affairs, Marketing, Public Relations Review, and *Teaching Public Relations. Journal of Public Relations Research,* member of editorial board, 1989-93, associate editor, 1994—; *Communication Quarterly International,* book review editor and member of advisory board, 1986-90.

*   *   *

PAYNE, (William) David 1955-

PERSONAL: Born April 13, 1955, in Henderson, NC; married.

ADDRESSES: Agent—Ned Leavitt, The Ned Leavitt Agency, 70 Wooster St., Suite 4F, New York, NY 10012.

CAREER: Writer.

AWARDS, HONORS: Houghton Mifflin fellowship, 1984.

WRITINGS:

Confessions of a Taoist on Wall Street: A Chinese American Romance, Houghton Mifflin (Boston), 1984.
Early from the Dance, Doubleday (New York), 1989.
Ruin Creek, Doubleday, 1993.

WORK IN PROGRESS: Behold this Dreamer (a sequel to *Ruin Creek*).

SIDELIGHTS: David Payne made his literary debut in 1984 with the novel *Confessions of a Taoist on Wall Street,* for which he was awarded the Houghton Mifflin fellowship. The story of a Chinese-American Taoist priest who leaves a Chinese monastery to work on the Wall Street stock exchange, and in the process searches for his missing father, was received favorably by some critics, and negatively by others. While some critics, notably the *New York Times Book Review*'s Merlin Wexler, found fault with Payne's narrative organization, characterizations, and dialogue, many commentators offered praise for *Confessions,* such as a *Library Journal* reviewer who dubbed the novel "a grand literary romance" in his highly favorable assessment, and *Washington Post Book World* contributor Joseph McLellan, who declared: "This novel, with its glorious style and rich profusion of detail, should remind readers of the time, fading into memory, when the works of John

Barth began to burst on the literary horizon. It is, for all its length, a book to be read twice—first to be gulped down in great chunks during sleepless nights; later to be sipped slowly, savoring details, like a well-brewed cup of tea."

The *Chicago Tribune Book World*'s Jim Spencer concluded that *Confessions* "is a novel of obvious genius and immense ambition that never coalesces, one that's like a laboratory specimen dissected beyond recognition." McLellan closed his *Washington Post Book World* assessment of *Confessions* by declaring that "above all, it is a story rich in incidents and characters, sometimes self-indulgent in its wordplay and manipulation of symbols, perhaps a bit longer than it needs to be, but absorbing and deeply rewarding."

In 1989, Payne followed *Confessions* with his novel of youthful innocence shattered: *Early from the Dance.* The work is set in the late 1960s and early 1970s in the coastal region of North Carolina known as the Outer Banks, where Payne was raised. The plot revolves around two friends, Adam and Cary, who fall in love with the same woman, Jane, and each suffer dire consequences. While Cary commits suicide, Adam lives with unrelenting remorse. Years later, when Adam and Jane meet again, the reader is given glimpses into the former lovers' lives through chapters told in first person that alternate between the two characters. "*Early from the Dance* is a substantial achievement, a book capacious enough to include the dazzlingly good, the heartbreakingly true, the alert, the obtuse, the overwritten, the obvious and even the false," maintained Richard Dyer, reporter for the *Boston Globe.* While *People Weekly* book reviewer Susan Toepfer decried *Early from the Dance* as "annoyingly self-indulgent," she found "many things right in Payne's second novel." For example, "in creating Cleanth, a charismatic lunatic who will be eerily familiar to those who came of age in the '60s and early '70s," she remarked, "Payne is at his most convincing." Writing for the *Los Angeles Times Book Review,* Gary Marmorstein commented, "The sexually charged tango that Adam and Jane do with two older partners is choreographed with sinewy definition and split-second time. This, the bulk of the book, is David Payne in top form, and it's some of the strongest, most demanding writing to be found in American fiction today. The rest appears to be something he had to get out of his system." Dyer, who labeled the novel's climax predictable and the denouement rushed and implausible, nevertheless praised the work highly: "The best things about *Early*

from the Dance are astonishing. Payne is young enough to remember things that haven't made their way into fiction before, and the details are texture, not decor; the sense of place is no less convincing than the sense of life as it was lived in a certain recent but now-distant time." Like Toepfer, who called Payne's prose "purple," Brock Cole of the *New York Times Book Review* judged, "David Payne appears to write easily and volubly. Occasionally he writes well, but too frequently he seems satisfied simply by the sheer rate at which the words are tumbling out." In contrast, Dyer described Payne's prose as "of a prism-cut precision and the dance of all the colors is in it; detail does not delay momentum but instead hurtles it forward. . . . [R]eading stretches of *Early from the Dance* is like attending a play in which every line is a curtain line." "Best of all," concluded Dyer, "Payne has the deepest human sympathy for his characters and knowledge of the heart; everyone in the book comes alive."

Like *Early from the Dance,* Payne's enthusiastically received 1993 novel, *Ruin Creek,* treats the theme of loss. It is the chronicle of a dying marriage told from viewpoints that alternate between the husband, wife, and son. *Boston Globe* reviewer Richard Dyer, in his assessment of the novel, declared: "David Payne may not be the most publicized American novelist homing in on 40, but he is certainly the most gifted." Although Dyer noted a few weaknesses in the novel's plot, he remarked, "The strength of *Ruin Creek* lies in the voices, the interplay of voices, the people, the rootedness in time and place that alone can support a flowering into the universal. There is a shimmer of nostalgia over the whole novel, and the glare of human cruelty cuts rights through it, but neither cancels the other out; this is a rare achievement." According to Tim McLaurin of the *New York Times Book Review,* who called *Ruin Creek* a "fine new novel," "Payne knows the hopes, fears and habits of his characters, and weaves a powerful, lyrical story for them that is a joy to read." A *Dallas Morning News* contributor echoed Dyer's assessment of Payne's talent, declaring that "David Payne is the most gifted American novelist of his generation. Certainly no other young writer has published three more impressive books."

BIOGRAPHICAL/CRITICAL SOURCES:

PERIODICALS

Boston Globe, September 25, 1989, p. 61; October 12, 1993, p. 30.

Dallas Morning News, October 10, 1993.

Library Journal, November, 1984.

Los Angeles Times Book Review, October 22, 1989, p. 7.

New York Times Book Review, October 21, 1984, p. 30; November 26, 1989, p. 30; October 24, 1993, p. 18.

People Weekly, October 9, 1989, pp. 36-37.

Washington Post Book World, December 9, 1984, pp. 5, 6.

*   *   *

PEDDICORD, Jo (Anne) 1925-

PERSONAL: Born November 14, 1925, in Cleveland, OH; daughter of Leo P. (a library clerk and treasurer) and Eunice M. (a homemaker) Johnson; married William A. Peddicord (divorced); children: Mary Jane Peddicord Glassman, David A. *Education:* Attended Ohio University, 1941-42, Newspaper Institute of America, 1962, American Institute of Banking, and National Writers School, 1986. *Avocational interests:* Skiing, tennis, golf, family, reading.

ADDRESSES: Home—Denver, CO. *Office*—c/o Golden Aspen Publishing, P.O. Box 370333, Denver, CO 80237-0333.

CAREER: Makeup artist and teacher, 1984—; freelance writer, public speaker, and publisher. Worked variously as a secretary, administrative assistant, and in cosmetic sales. Volunteer at Porter Hospital, 1992—.

MEMBER: National Writers Association, Colorado Independent Publishers Association, Publishers Marketing Association.

AWARDS, HONORS: Nominated one of five extraordinary people by *Mature Outlook* magazine, 1992.

WRITINGS:

Look Like a Winner after 50 with Care, Color and Style, Golden Aspen Publishing (Denver, CO), 1992, revised edition, 1994.

Author of syndicated column, *Beauty Beyond 50,* 1988—. Contributor of articles to periodicals, including *Christian Science Monitor, Senior Times, Huntington Dispatch, Senior Edition USA,* and *Denver Post*'s *Active Times* magazine.

WORK IN PROGRESS: Further writing on "looking like a winner after 50."

SIDELIGHTS: After speaking with hundreds of women as a makeup consultant, Jo Peddicord found a common thread woven among them: they all wanted advice on how to look vibrant and attractive despite the inevitable physical changes that occur with age. As a result, Peddicord began writing her column, *Beauty Beyond 50,* which is syndicated in more than 30 newspapers and magazines and addresses readers' beauty concerns. She also subsequently published her book, *Look Like a Winner after 50 with Care, Color, and Style.*

In her book Peddicord offers "head-to-toe solutions" to the special fashion and cosmetic needs of women past fifty, noting that (according to the 1991 United States census) some 43 million women in the United States are over the age of forty-five. This same group of women controls a great deal of the nation's wealth and buying power; yet, Peddicord points out, clothing manufacturers and cosmetic companies have been slow to acknowledge the aging populous of American women, continuing to use much younger women in their advertisements and being reluctant to change cuts of clothes and makeup formulas to accommodate the changes women face. Where housecoats were once the garb of most older, usually sedentary women, today's mature woman is likely to require both career and activewear in styles that flatter her changing shape. Peddicord thus offers hundreds of suggestions on how women over fifty can use beauty treatments, color, and style to boost their self-esteem, project a winning image, and rediscover purpose in the latter years of life.

The revised edition of *Look Like a Winner* contains a chapter not included in the first. In this chapter Peddicord offers encouragement and image advice to women who must endure what Peddicord terms "defeminizing" surgery, particularly mastectomy and ileostomy.

Peddicord told *CA:* "In spite of traumatic physical and social changes, women can develop a winning look that attracts employment, adventure, and fulfillment at any age. They can boost self-esteem by using the turnaround power of color and style to turnaround their life. My message is: It's possible to take age out of image. We don't have to look old. The dull, dowdy image is out. The colorful, upbeat image is in."

BIOGRAPHICAL/CRITICAL SOURCES:

PERIODICALS

Daily Globe (Minnesota), November 10, 1993.
Mature Outlook, December, 1992.
Plain Dealer (Cleveland), January 6, 1994.

* * *

PEERADINA, Saleem 1944-

PERSONAL: Born October 5, 1944, in Bombay, India; married Mumtaz Peeradina, 1978; children: two daughters. *Education:* St. Xavier's College, B.A., 1967; Bombay University, M.A., 1969; Wake Forest University, M.A., 1973.

ADDRESSES: Home—343 Anthony Ct., Adrian, MI 49221.

CAREER: Kirti College, Bombay, lecturer, 1969-71; Forsyth Country Day School, Winston-Salem, NC, instructor, 1973-74; Indian Institute of Technology, Bombay, lecturer, 1974-75; St. Xavier's College, Bombay, lecturer, 1976-77; Sophia College, Bombay, lecturer, 1977-84; Hindustan Thompson Associates, Bombay, copywriter, 1984-87; Adrian College/Alma College, Adrian, MI, visiting international scholar and professor, 1988-89; Siena Heights College, Adrian, MI, associate professor, 1989—.

AWARDS, HONORS: Fulbright Travel grant, 1971; British Council Writer's grant, 1983.

WRITINGS:

POETRY

First Offence, Newground (Bombay), 1980.
Group Portrait, Oxford University Press (Oxford), 1992.

OTHER

(Editor) *Contemporary Indian Poetry in English,* Macmillan (Bombay), 1972.
(Editor) *Cultural Forces Shaping India,* Macmillan, 1988.

PELEVIN, Victor 1962-

PERSONAL: Born November 22, 1962; son of Oleg and Zina (Efremova) Pelevin. *Education:* Attended Moscow Institute of Power Engineering and Moscow Institute of Literature. *Politics:* "Left of right centrists." *Religion:* "Tantric agnosticism."

ADDRESSES: Home—Moscow, Russia. *Agent*—Nicole Aragi, Watkins & Loomis, 133 East 35th St., New York, NY 10016.

CAREER: Writer.

AWARDS, HONORS: Russian literary prizes, including Little Booker Prize.

WRITINGS:

The Yellow Arrow, New Directions (New York), 1996.
Omon Ra (novel), Farrar, Straus (New York), 1996.
The Life of Insects, Farrar, Straus, in press.

WORK IN PROGRESS: A collection of stories, for New Directions.

* * *

PENROSE, Edith Tilton 1914-1996

OBITUARY NOTICE—See index for *CA* sketch: Born November 29, 1914, in Los Angeles, CA; died October 11, 1996, in Waterbeach, England. Educator, economist, writer. After receiving her B.A. from the University of California, in Berkeley, she accepted a research associate position with the International Labour Organization in Geneva, Switzerland in 1939. In 1941, she left Switzerland to work for the U.S. Embassy in London, England, a post she held for the next five years. After a short stint as a research associate for the United Nations, Penrose fell under the scrutiny of Senator Joseph McCarthy's Congressional Investigation of Un-American activities. As a result of the investigation, she and her husband, Ernest F. Penrose of England, left for Australia's National University in Canberra and eventually taught at the University of Baghdad in Iraq. In 1951, Penrose's *Economics of the International Patent System* was published. In 1960, she began an eighteen-year teaching career with the University of London, School of Economics and Political Science and the School of Oriental and African Studies. Her other works include *The Large International Firm in Developing Countries: The International Petroleum Industry, The Growth of Firms, Middle East Oil and Other Essays,* and with her husband, *Iraq: International Relations and National Development.*

OBITUARIES AND OTHER SOURCES:

BOOK

Who's Who, 148th edition, St. Martin's, 1996.

PERIODICALS

New York Times, October 21, 1996, p. B9.

*   *   *

PERELMAN, Bob 1947-

PERSONAL: Born Robert Perelman, December 2, 1947, in Youngstown, OH; married Francie Shaw, 1975; children: two sons. *Education:* University of Michigan, M.A. (classics) 1969; University of Iowa, M.F.A. (poetry), 1970; University of California, Ph.D. (English), 1990.

ADDRESSES: Office—Department of English, University of Pennsylvania, Philadelphia, PA 19104.

CAREER: University of Pennsylvania, Philadelphia, assistant professor, 1990—. *Hills* magazine, Berkeley, CA, editor, 1973-80.

WRITINGS:

POETRY

Braille, Ithaca House Press (Ithaca, NY), 1975.
Seven Works, Figures (Berkeley, CA), 1978.
a.k.a, Tuumba Press (Berkeley, CA), 1979.
Primer, This Press (San Francisco), 1981.
To the Reader, Tuumba Press, 1984.
The First World, Figures (Great Barrington, MA), 1986.
Face Value, Roof Press (New York), 1988.
Captive Audience, Figures, 1988.
Virtual Reality, Roof Press, 1993.

PLAY

The Alps (produced in San Francisco, 1980), published in *Hills* (Berkeley, CA), 1980.

OTHER

(Editor) *Writing/Talks,* Southern Illinois University Press (Carbondale), 1985.
The Trouble with Genius: Reading Pound, Joyce, Stein, and Zukovsky, University of California Press (Berkeley), 1994.

*   *   *

PERTWEE, Michael (Henry Roland) 1916-1991

PERSONAL: Born April 24, 1916, in London, England; died in 1991; son of Roland (a dramatist) and Avice (Scholtz) Pertwee; married, December 31, 1959; wife's name, Maya. *Education:* Attended Sherborne School, France. *Religion:* Church of England.

CAREER: Writer. *Military service:* British Intelligence Corps, 1939-45; became major.

WRITINGS:

PLAYS; PRODUCED IN LONDON

Death on the Table (also produced in New York), 1938.
(With father, Roland Pertwee) *The Paragon* (produced, 1948), English Theatre Guild (London), 1949.
Night Was Our Friend (two-act), English Theatre Guild, 1950.
(With Roland Pertwee) *The Baby-Sitters* (one-act), Samuel French (London), 1955.
(With Roland Pertwee) *Meet the Grove Family,* [England], 1955.
(Co-author) *It's Different for Men,* [England], 1955.
(With Roland Pertwee) *Deadly Poison,* Samuel French, 1955.
(With Roland Pertwee) *Dramatic Licences: An Incident in the Life of the Grove Family,* Samuel French, 1955.
(With Roland Pertwee) *A Fair Cow: An Incident in the Life of the Grove Family,* Samuel French, 1955.
(With Roland Pertwee) *A Good Turn-out,* Samuel French, 1955.
(With Roland Pertwee) *Looking Her Best,* Samuel French, 1955.
(With Roland Pertwee) *Pardon My French* (one-act), Samuel French, 1955.

(With Roland Pertwee) *A Pound of Flesh* (one-act), Samuel French, 1955.

(With Roland Pertwee) *Royal Welcome,* Samuel French, 1955.

(With Roland Pertwee) *Don't Talk to Strangers,* Samuel French, 1955.

One Woman's Poison (one-act), English Theatre Guild, 1956.

Deadly Hat-Pin (one-act), English Theatre Guild, 1957.

Waiting Room (one-act), English Theatre Guild, 1958.

She's Done It Again (two-act; produced, 1969), English Theatre Guild, 1970.

Don't Just Lie There, Say Something!, (produced, 1971), Samuel French (New York), 1973.

(With Brian Rix) *A Bit Between the Teeth* (produced, 1973), Samuel French (New York), 1976.

Sextet, Samuel French (New York), 1979.

(With John Chapman) *Look No Hans!,* Samuel French (London), c. 1986.

(With Chapman) *Holiday Snap* (produced, 1987), Samuel French (London), c. 1989.

Also author of plays *Find the Lady,* 1980, and *You'll Do for Me,* with Brian Rix, 1989; adaptor of *Birds of Paradise,* 1974, and *King's Rhapsody,* 1988; author of screenplays, including *Laughter in Paradise, On Monday Next Top Secret, Happy Ever After, Now and Forever, Against the Wind, Interrupted Journey, The Naked Truth, Too Many Crooks, Bottoms Up, Make Mine Mink, It Started in Naples, In the Doghouse, Mouse on the Moon, Ladies Who Do, Finders Keepers, Strange Bedfellows, A Funny Thing Happened on the Way to the Forum, Salt and Pepper, One More Time, Don't Just Lie There, Say Something,* and *Digby the Biggest Dog in the World.* Also author of teleplays, including *The Paragon, Chain Male, Rainy Day, In the Bag, Strictly Personal, Grove Family, Man in a Moon, The Frightened Man, Yakity Yak, The Old Campaigner, Never a Cross Word,* and *Man of Affairs.*

OTHER

Name Dropping (autobiography), Frewin (London), 1974.

ADAPTATIONS: Two of Pertwee's teleplays about The Saint, the Leslie Charteris detective, were adapted by Fleming Lee for the book *Leslie Charteris' The Saint Abroad,* Doubleday, 1969.

SIDELIGHTS: The son of dramatist Roland Pertwee, Michael Pertwee was a playwright who, at the time of his death in 1991, had produced and published dozens of stage plays, as well as motion pictures and teleplays, many in collaboration with his father. Especially given to farce, Pertwee's plays often parody conventional mores, while characterizing the complexities of domestic dilemmas and relationships.

The playwright also penned a 1974 autobiography, *Name Dropping,* in which he shared a life's worth of insight, anecdotes, and gossip concerning the world of theatre in London and the colorful personalities that comprise it. Written in Pertwee's characteristically light and humorous style, *Name Dropping* was deemed an easy, enjoyable read by reviewers, among them a reviewer for *Books and Bookmen,* Duncan Fallowell, who described the book as "above all a testament to abstract, almost direction-less energy, for Michael Pertwee does more work than a log-rolling pachyderm. . . . He has covered so much ground that almost anyone who breathed in the British cinema or theatre since the war and a few more besides has at least a sentence from him." Hugh Leonard, also writing in *Books and Bookmen,* concurred: "Mr. Pertwee has been in 'show business' from the cradle and knows how never to be dull. His book is a souffle, bright and anecdotal; it can be devoured at one sitting without the slightest threat to the digestive organs. . . . *Name Dropping* is fun, with a salutary touch of acid, and it doesn't overstay its welcome."

BIOGRAPHICAL/CRITICAL SOURCES:

BOOKS

Pertwee, Michael, *Name Dropping,* Frewin (London), 1974.

PERIODICALS

Books and Bookmen, January, 1975, pp. 58, 71.

* * *

PESKETT, William 1952-

PERSONAL: Born May 12, 1952; married Naomi Peskett. *Education:* Christ's College, Cambridge, degree in zoology.

ADDRESSES: Agent—c/o Secker and Warburg, 81 Fulham Rd., London SW3 6RB, England.

CAREER: Has worked as a journalist and biology teacher.

AWARDS, HONORS: Eric Gregory award, 1976.

WRITINGS:

POETRY

Cleaning Stables, Ulsterman (Belfast), 1974.
The Nightowl's Dissection, Secker and Warburg (London), 1975.
A Killing in the Grove, Ulsterman, 1977.
A More Suitable Terrain, Ulsterman, 1978.
Survivors, Secker and Warburg, 1980.

*   *   *

PHILLIPS, Susan S. 1954-

PERSONAL: Born June 8, 1954, in Los Angeles, CA; daughter of David Lloyd (an insurance broker) and Elizabeth Manning (an occupational therapist; maiden name, Smith) Sanders; married Raborn Stephens Phillips, July 12, 1975; children: Andrew Stephens, Peter Sanders. *Ethnicity:* "Caucasian." *Education:* Willamette University, B.A. (magna cum laude), 1976; University of California, Berkeley, Ph.D., 1988. *Religion:* Christian. *Avocational interests:* Flying.

ADDRESSES: Home—615 Parkside Ct., Kensington, CA 94708. *Office*—New College Berkeley, 2606 Dwight Way, Berkeley, CA 94704; fax 510-841-9776. *E-mail*—suphillips@aol.com.

CAREER: New College Berkeley, Berkeley, CA, adjunct professor of sociology, 1985—, academic dean, 1992-94, executive director, 1994—. Adjunct professor at University of California, San Francisco, Fuller Theological Seminary, Regent College, and Ontario Theological Seminary.

MEMBER: American Sociological Association, American Academy of Religion, Society of Biblical Literature.

AWARDS, HONORS: Choice Award, American Association of University and Research Libraries, for *The Crisis of Care.*

WRITINGS:

The Crisis of Care: Affirming and Restoring Caring Practices in the Helping Professions, Georgetown University Press (Washington, DC), 1995.

WORK IN PROGRESS: Research on the crisis of care in mental health professions.

SIDELIGHTS: Susan S. Phillips told *CA:* "I write to gain understanding and to communicate with others about what I consider important. I am a sociologist, and I long to understand people. Most of my writing has been about relationships, with the hope of encouraging care and compassion in a society that grants little time or reward for such qualities and acts. Showing good relationships is far more compelling than describing them, so, though my writing is nonfiction, it is thick with narrative. I delight and indulge in reading fiction, which helps me understand people but, alas, my gifts, calling, and skills are not in that sort of writing.

"My writing has been influenced by a lifetime of reading fine literature, as well as by a commitment to what George Eliot called 'spreading the skirts of light in the world.' Who I am and what I like about myself have been shaped by reading the stories and thoughts of perceptive, thoughtful people who cared enough about what they considered important to do the hard work of writing it down for others. I am grateful for their labor and care, and try, in a very small way at this point, to join them.

"Writing strikes me as miraculous. For me, it is creation by way of unveiling. Like Michelangelo uncovering the forms within the marble, I experience myself as peeling away layers of distraction and discovering the knowledge or conviction that lurks within me. When I sit down to write, I don't know what will appear, and what does appear almost always teaches me something. After that experience of self-illumination comes the hard work of shaping the writing so it is clear and comprehensible to others. The reward of writing is twofold for me: it brings interior clarity and the opportunity to communicate with others about things that matter.

"The subjects I have chosen to address in writing are those that so grip me with a sense of their vital significance that my resistance to writing crumples, and I am propelled to write. The subjects about which I've written have had to do with care in relationships—practices of care in the helping professions, caring for children in our society, sustaining and valuing friendship in a society that privileges only work and family, and so on. Those are subjects that engage me personally and professionally, emotionally and intellectually. Only subjects that pierce my heart and intrigue my mind marshal the force necessary to make me seek the clarity and conversation that writing creates."

* * *

PHILP, Richard B(lain) 1934-

PERSONAL: Born January 19, 1934, in Guelph, Ontario, Canada; son of Norman Lewis (a musician) and Minnie (maiden name, Humphries; later surname, Carter) Philp; married, wife's name Moira Shirley, November, 1955 (marriage ended, May, 1987); married Joan Taylor Whiteford, November 14, 1987; children: Robert Bruce, Erica Margaret Philp Gatten, Michael John, Anne Louise. *Ethnicity:* "British." *Education:* Has earned the following degrees: B.S, D.V.M., and Ph.D. *Avocational interests:* Painting, music, boating, cycling.

ADDRESSES: Home—419 Central Ave., London, Ontario, Canada N6B 2E4. *Office*—Department of Pharmacology and Toxicology, Medical Sciences Building, University of Western Ontario, London, Ontario, Canada N6A 5C1; fax 519-661-4051. *E-mail*—rphilp@julian.uwo.ca.

CAREER: University of Western Ontario, London, professor of pharmacology and toxicology, 1965—. Also practiced veterinary medicine; consultant to the pharmaceutical industry.

MEMBER: International Society for the Study of Xenobiotics, Pharmacological Society of Canada, Canadian Toxicological Society, New York Academy of Sciences.

WRITINGS:

Environmental Hazards and Human Health, Lewis Publishers (Boca Raton, FL), 1995.

Also author of *Methods of Testing Proposed Antithrombotic Drugs,* 1981. Contributor to books, including *Integrated Medicine,* Van Nostrand (New York), 1981; *Atheroembolism,* CRC Press (Boca Raton), 1986; and *Basic and Applied High Pressure*

Biology, University of Rochester Press (Rochester, NY), 1994. Contributor of more than eighty articles to scientific journals.

WORK IN PROGRESS: Several scientific manuscripts; research on the mechanics of anesthesia; research on the effects of acid rain and oxidants on marine sponges.

SIDELIGHTS: Richard B. Philp told *CA:* "Writing is an intrinsic part of the scientific process. The effective communication of research data and conclusions legitimizes the research and contributes to the ongoing process of each scientist building on the work of others. After a few years in veterinary practice, I decided to further my education and opted for a research career. I enjoy writing, and my recent teaching text on toxicology allowed me greater latitude in writing style and an opportunity to address some social aspects that are not usually available in conventional scientific writing."

* * *

PIERCE, Arthur 1959-

PERSONAL: Born July 19, 1959, in Rome, NY; son of Clifford N. (a transportation technician) and Beverly (a legal secretary; maiden name, Cook) Pierce. *Ethnicity:* "Caucasian." *Education:* State University of New York College at Oswego, B.A., 1985. *Politics:* Republican. *Religion:* Methodist. *Avocational interests:* The history of American popular music prior to 1945.

ADDRESSES: Home—339 Nassau St., Rome, NY 13440. *Office*—Syracuse Opera Company, 120 East Washington St., Syracuse, NY 13220.

CAREER: Syracuse Opera Company, Syracuse, NY, telemarketing director, 1986—. Fair Pickings (suppliers of radio programs on audio cassettes), owner and manager.

MEMBER: Rome Historical Society.

WRITINGS:

(With Douglas Swarthout) *Jean Arthur: A Bio-Bibliography,* Greenwood Press (Westport, CT), 1991.
(With Connie J. Billips) *Lux Presents Hollywood,* McFarland and Co. (Jefferson, NC), 1995.

(Editor) D. E. Wager, *Our City and Its People,* Berry Hill Press (Deansboro, NY), 1996.

WORK IN PROGRESS: Dragnet, a history of the radio and television series.

*   *   *

POGUE, Forrest Carlisle   1912-1996

OBITUARY NOTICE—See index for *CA* sketch: Born September 17, 1912, in Eddyville, KY; died of a stroke October 6, 1996, in Murray, KY. Military historian and author. Pogue is renowned for his four-volume chronicle of World War II General George C. Marshall. Pogue, after beginning a teaching career in 1933 at Murray State Teachers College (now Murray State University), was drafted into the United States Army in 1942. He was assigned to a special unit and was later given the task of documenting the Normandy Invasion by interviewing the participants. For his efforts, he was awarded the U.S. Bronze Star and the Croix de Guerre from France. Pogue's first book, *The Supreme Command,* published in 1954, was commissioned by General Dwight D. Eisenhower (later U.S. president) as a history of his military command. In 1956, Pogue became the director of the George C. Marshall Research Foundation in Virginia. It was then that he started his thirty-year project of delving into the life of Marshall. After conducting more than 300 interviews and spending many hours with Marshall himself, Pogue's biography was published. The work, *George C. Marshall,* contains four subtitled volumes, including *Education of a General: 1880-1939, Ordeal of Hope: 1939-1942, Organizer of Victory: 1943-1945,* and *Statesman: 1945-1959.* He also contributed to many other texts, including *D-Day: The Normandy Invasion in Retrospect, The Meaning of Yalta,* and *The Marshall Plan in Germany.* In 1994, the Forrest C. Pogue Center for Research Publications, part of the Virginia Military Institute, was dedicated.

OBITUARIES AND OTHER SOURCES:

BOOKS

Who's Who, 148th edition, St. Martin's, 1996.

PERIODICALS

New York Times, October 8, 1996, p. D25.
Washington Post, October 8, 1996, p. C4.

POLONSKY, Michael Jay   1959-

PERSONAL: Born May 14, 1959, in Baltimore, MD; son of Norman H. N. (an accountant) and Annette Fern (a chemist; maiden name, Lakein) Polonsky; married Clair Novis (in banking), December, 1993. *Education:* Towson State University, B.S., 1982; Rutgers University, Newark Campus, M.A. (mathematical economics), 1983; Temple University, M.A. (economics of industrial organizations), 1988; doctoral study at La Trobe University, 1991-93, and Australian Catholic University, 1994—.

ADDRESSES: Home—24 Moani St., Eleebana, New South Wales 2282, Australia. *Office*—Department of Management, University of Newcastle, Newcastle, New South Wales 2308, Australia; fax 61-49-216-911. *E-mail*—mgmjp@cc.newcastle.edu.au.

CAREER: Temple University, Philadelphia, PA, instructor in economics, 1985-86; University of the Witwatersrand, Johannesburg, South Africa, lecturer in business economics, 1986-88; Massey University, Palmerston North, New Zealand, visiting lecturer in finance, 1988; Charles Sturt University, lecturer in marketing and economics, 1989-90; University of Newcastle, Newcastle, Australia, lecturer in management, 1990—, coordinator of Marketing Group, 1990-95. Lecturer at Australian Catholic University, 1991, Australian Graduate School of Management, 1991, 1992, University of Wollongong, 1992, and Middlesex University, 1994. State of New Jersey, Treasury Department, project specialist for Office of Budget and Management, 1985-86; Australian Chamber of Manufacturers, member of Hunter Region Industry and Environment Group, 1990-93; consultant to Hunter Water Corp. and Coopers & Lybrand.

MEMBER: Australian and New Zealand Academy of Management, Australian Marketing Institute (founding member of Hunter Valley chapter), American Marketing Association, Academy of Marketing Science, Academy of Management (Industry and the Natural Environment Group), Greening of Industry Network, University Marketing Society (founder and coordinator).

AWARDS, HONORS: Best Paper in Track Award, Australia and New Zealand Academy of Management Conference, 1996, for the paper "Handling Controversial Accounts: A Preliminary Study of Advertising Agency Executives' Attitudes Towards Political Clients."

WRITINGS:

(With Hazel T. Suchard) *Country Education Pro-files—South Africa: A Comparative Study,* Department of Education, Employment, and Training (Canberra, Australia), 1993.

(Editor with H. Lozada and A. Mintu) *Environmental Issues in the Curricula of International Business: The Green Imperative,* Haworth (Binghamton, NY), 1994.

(Editor with A. T. Mintu-Wimsatt, and contributor) *Environmental Marketing: New Developments in Practice, Theory, and Research,* Haworth, 1995.

Contributor to books, including *Contemporary Issues in Marketing Management,* edited by G. S. Batra, Anmol Publications (New Delhi, India), 1996; and *Marketing: Concepts and Strategies,* 3rd edition, edited by J. R. McColl-Kennedy and G. F. Kiel, Thomas Nelson Australia (South Melbourne, Australia), 1997. Contributor of more than forty articles and reviews to periodicals, including *Journal of Market Focused Management, Journal of Macromarketing, Journal of Business Ethics, Marketing Intelligence and Planning, Greener Management International, Journal of Promotions Management,* and *International Journal of Management.* Guest co-editor, *Journal of Teaching in International Business,* 1993; member of editorial review board, *Journal of Marketing Theory and Practice,* 1994—.

WORK IN PROGRESS: Research on stakeholder theory and marketing, green marketing, ethics, and cross-cultural studies of youth attitudes toward political advertising.

*   *   *

POPPEMA, Suzanne T.   1948-

PERSONAL: Born May 8, 1948, in Holland, MI; daughter of Donald (a surveyor) and Rachel (a homemaker; maiden name, Pomerleau) Poppema; married John F. Cramer III (a physician), 1978; children: Peter, Andrew. *Education:* University of New Hampshire, B.A., 1970; Harvard University, M.D., 1974. *Politics:* Democrat. *Avocational interests:* Horseback riding, cycling, gardening, wine tasting.

*ADDRESSES: Office—*Aurora Medical Services, 1207 North 200th, Suite 214, Seattle, WA 98133.

CAREER: Physician. Medical director of a feminist nonprofit health collective in Seattle, WA, during the mid-1970s; family physician in city and county health clinics in Denver, CO, 1978-79; family physician in private practice in suburban Seattle, 1980-88; Aurora Medical Services, Seattle, medical director, 1986—. Also served as medical director for a hospital-affiliated women's health center and alcohol-treatment program in the Seattle area during the 1980s.

MEMBER: National Abortion Federation (vice president).

WRITINGS:

(With Mike Henderson) *Why I Am an Abortion Doctor,* Prometheus Books (Amherst, NY), 1996.

SIDELIGHTS: "I honor and care for patients who want to end pregnancies," outspoken feminist and pro-choice physician Suzanne T. Poppema declares in the introduction to her memoir. "I'm an abortion doctor, and I refuse to mask my work in qualifications or apologies." In *Why I Am an Abortion Doctor,* Poppema looks to the past to discover the roots of her activism. As she recalls, she was always an "assertive" child, but nothing in particular hinted at the beliefs she would later embrace. Born in Michigan, she grew up in rural New Hampshire, where her father was in forestry management. Her French-Canadian mother saw to it that she received a Catholic school education. Poppema characterizes her experiences under the tutelage of the nuns—who seemed in retrospect to have been so many female Darth Vaders—as rigid and very structured. And since there was little mention of sex in class, there certainly was no thought whatsoever given to abortion.

After graduating from high school in 1966, Poppema went on to the University of New Hampshire. There she majored in political science while also fulfilling all of the pre-med requirements. (An excellent student who very much enjoyed her studies in chemistry and biology, she had been seriously considering a career in medicine since at least her mid-teens.) At the same time, her politics began to undergo a transformation as she shed the moderate Republicanism of her parents and adopted the liberal outlook typical of many college students in the late 1960s.

It was not until she entered Harvard Medical School, however, that Poppema truly developed a feminist sense of the place she and other women held in society. It was in that environment, she recalls, that she "finally got a prolonged, real-world taste of what the medical profession of that era thought of women physicians. . . . That was the first time I felt truly assailed by that pervasive attitude of: We're not going to expect you to be smart, we're not going to let you show you're smart, and we're not giving you any credit for the fact that you're here—which we don't like in the first place."

Furthermore, she discovered, not only were female medical students regarded as "second best," but the female patients (especially poor ones) they encountered were usually treated in the campus facilities that medical school officials rightly or wrongly regarded as second class. Meanwhile, the more elite centers at Harvard were reserved for wealthy patients. "I think more than any other experience during medical school this helped politicize me," noted Poppema. "It demonstrated in the real world subtle and not-so-subtle discrimination occurs in the damnedest places."

Poppema spent her residency in Seattle, Washington, where the more informal and open-minded atmosphere nurtured her growing political and social awareness. To the surprise of her Harvard classmates, most of whom were planning careers in one lucrative specialty or another, she had gravitated toward the far less prestigious practice of family medicine. Eventually, Poppema became medical director of a feminist nonprofit health collective that emphasized care provided *by* and *for* women. "I was ready to go out and empower women, to save the world, and make sure they have healthy kids if they want them or no kids if they don't," she recalls. "The potential of family medicine seemed limitless."

As a family practitioner, Poppema is devoted to the idea that a partnership exists between the doctor and his or her patient. This is in direct contrast to the old-fashioned, paternalistic approach to medicine in which doctors merely give orders to their patients rather than engage them in a conversation about their health. Instead, says Poppema, a doctor must respect a patient as an intelligent person who deserves an attentive hearing. He or she should evaluate that patient not just as a set of symptoms but as a total human being influenced by factors outside the examining room such as social or financial status. It is then the doctor's duty to share the appropriate professional information with his or her patient, encouraging questions and allowing the patient to reach a fully informed decision on treatment.

In 1977, Poppema took some time off from her regular responsibilities and spent nine months traveling in the Far East, India, and the Middle East studying how other cultures practiced family medicine. The following year, she married a fellow physician and settled temporarily in Denver, where she worked in both city and county health clinics that served a mainly poor Hispanic and Asian American clientele. In late 1979, Poppema gave birth to her first son and moved back to the Seattle area. Several months later, in January 1980, she went into private practice with two other family physicians, both men. She quickly attracted a large number of female patients who were delighted to have a woman they could turn to for their health needs.

Poppema spent most of the 1980s tending to her private practice and a growing list of other activities. Early in the decade, for example, she began taking on a more public role as a voice for women's health issues. She lectured lay audiences, addressed professional gatherings, and appeared on numerous radio and television programs. She also served as medical director of a hospital-affiliated women's health center and of an alcohol-treatment program. And in 1982, she gave birth to her second son.

But the longer Poppema remained in family medicine, the more she became aware of what she calls "the ugly social encroachments that attend poverty: child abuse by alcoholic parents, exploitation of kids for sexual purposes, emotional abuse, and abandonment." Gradually, she came to realize that "in virtually every society where a wanted child is greeted by a healthy, accommodating family, that child can expect incredible life advantages—physically, emotionally, socially, and economically—compared with an unwanted child."

Poppema had always performed abortions as part of the comprehensive care she offered her patients, and since 1985 she had also worked for several hours a month at a Seattle abortion clinic. To her, making abortions available to women who wanted them enabled her "to help alleviate misery at every level of society." Thus, when she was asked to take over as owner, operator, and medical director of the Seattle clinic in 1986, she saw it as an opportunity to "live my politics."

Besides helping women deal with unplanned and unwanted pregnancies, Poppema felt that providing abortion services "also would reassert, from my standpoint, the right of the individual to make decisions that affect the sovereign human body. This is a fundamental human right, and one utterly lost on most, if not all, of those who advocate anti-choice. Men who never would imagine consenting to government control of their sexual organs or their health in general are perfectly willing to legislate that control over women. This is done under the guise of 'protecting unborn children' and with the convenient disregard for the health, education and other human needs of the unwanted who are born."

After a two-year period during which she juggled a hectic workload and mounting responsibilities at home, Poppema decided to give up her family practice in 1988 to devote herself full time to her clinic, known as Aurora Medical Services. (In addition to abortions, the clinic offers about a dozen other services, including family planning assistance, annual exams, vasectomies, and pregnancy tests.) As an abortion provider in an increasingly hostile anti-choice environment, she has found that one of the most difficult parts of her job "is trying to dissuade public opinion about what doesn't happen at my clinic and what does." People are surprised, she says, to discover that the facility is clean, quiet, and attractive and that the staff is well-trained and very professional.

Poppema also wrestles with other forms of "disinformation" that she feels contribute greatly to the "controversy and mystique" surrounding abortion in the United States today. Near the top of her list are society's attitudes toward sex. "The United States has shown an ongoing, bewildering resistance to accepting—much less embracing—information having to do with birth control, sexually transmitted diseases, and sex in general," Poppema declares. ". . . There is an almost ridiculous secret consensus in this country that says: The less we know about sexual matters, the less likely we'll be to suffer any bad consequences from sex."

Yet at the same time, she points out, there is a double standard at work. "Americans will heap great viewer interest on all manner of sexual content: the titillation value of soap operas, for example, or the voyeuristic outlet of talk shows. But just try to slip in a subtle (much less a not so subtle) message about a condom that can save lives and protect against unwanted pregnancies. You'd think such messages amounted to some sinister conspiracy."

Poppema's clinic has been at the forefront of a number of new developments in the struggle to make as many options as possible available to women wishing

to end a pregnancy. She is, for example, a longtime champion of the so-called "morning-after pill" that can prevent a pregnancy if taken shortly after unprotected intercourse. It angers and frustrates her that many physicians either don't know or don't care that regular birth-control pills can be used for this purpose in an emergency situation. And in 1994, her clinic became one of only a dozen or so nationwide chosen to test the effectiveness of RU-486 (Mifepristone), a drug that induces abortion. Poppema thinks that it may eventually "prove to be the undoing of the anti-choice movement in America."

All in all, Poppema is fairly optimistic that safe, legal abortions will remain available in the future. "Too many women—and a lot of men—simply wouldn't stand for [making abortion illegal again]," she explains. "Too many women have discovered that their politics change when their situations change." However, she is still wary of the passion and violence that has often marked the debate on the issue; she herself has worn a bulletproof vest to work since 1993 in the wake of several attacks (some with deadly consequences) on clinics and doctors.

In the meantime, Poppema vows to continue providing what she regards as a "vital public and healthcare service." Yet as even she admits, "it would sound noble to assert that the fundamental reason for what I do is the alleviation of suffering among unwanted children. . . . That's only part of why my work means so much to me. The main reason is that I believe women shouldn't have to explain to governments, religious groups, those of another opinion, or the patriarchy at large that they've made a decision to deal with a condition of their own bodies. . . . What I do is right and good and important. Perhaps my story will appall some, but it also may inspire others, particularly the young women who need to know that the struggle between feminism and the patriarchy has not been in vain."

Suzanne T. Poppema told *CA:* "[In writing *Why I Am an Abortion Doctor*] I hoped to inspire young people to become abortion providers, provide information for men and women who might need abortion services, and attempt to provide a rational, honest account of what happens in an abortion clinic."

BIOGRAPHICAL/CRITICAL SOURCES:

BOOKS

Poppema, Suzanne T., and Mike Anderson, *Why I Am an Abortion Doctor,* Prometheus Books, 1996.

PERIODICALS

Publishers Weekly, February 5, 1996, p. 74.

*   *   *

POPPLEWELL, Jack   1911-1996

OBITUARY NOTICE—See index for *CA* sketch: Born March 22, 1911, in Leeds, Yorkshire, England; died November 16, 1996, in Bath, England. Composer, lyric writer and playwright. Popplewell's prolific career began with sheer luck. A friend secretly entered one of his songs, *If I Should Fall in Love Again,* in a contest. It ended up winning first prize and was performed by many pop music stars, including Gracie Fields. Popplewell's first play, *Blind Alley,* was also a success and became the 1958 film *Tread Softly, Stranger.* He wrote several other songs and plays throughout his life, including the tune *My Girl's an Irish Girl* (which was recorded by Bing Crosby), and the plays *Breakfast in Bed* (1957), *Mississippi* (1969) and *The Queen's Favorites* (1975). Popplewell also wrote the television plays *Along Came a Spider* (1963), and *Born Every Minute* (1972).

OBITUARIES AND OTHER SOURCES:

PERIODICALS

Chicago Tribune, November 28, 1996, sec. 3, p. 11.
New York Times, November 28, 1996, p. D19.

*   *   *

PORCEL, Baltasar   1937-

PERSONAL: Born March 14, 1937, in Andratx, Mallorca, Spain; son of Baltasar (a sailor and farmer) and Sebastiana (a homemaker; maiden name, Pujol) Porcel; married Maria-Angels Roque (an anthropologist), July, 1972; children: Baltasar, Violant. *Ethnicity:* "Catalan." *Politics:* Democrat. *Religion:* Roman Catholic.

ADDRESSES: Home—Rambla Jacint Verdaguer 97, 08190 Valldoreix, Barcelona, Spain. *Office*—Institut Catalia de la Mediterrania, Ave. Diagonal, 407 bis, 08008 Barcelona, Spain; fax 34-4-218-4513. *Agent*—Antonia Kerrigan, Agencia Literaria Kerrigan/Miro/ Calonje, Travessera de Gracia, 12 5e 2a, 08021 Barcelona, Spain.

CAREER: Institut Catalia de la Mediterrania, Barcelona, Spain.

AWARDS, HONORS: Caballos Hacia La Noche (*Horses into the Night*) listed among the best books of 1995 by *Publisher's Weekly* and *Critics Choice.*

WRITINGS:

Caballos Hacia La Noche, (novel), translated by John L. Getman as *Horses Into the Night,* University of Arkansas Press (Fayetteville, AR), 1995.
Dias Immortales (title means "Immortal Days"), Aims International Books, 1996.

Author of a daily opinion feature, *La Vanguardia.*

WORK IN PROGRESS: A novel, *Springs and Autumns.*

SIDELIGHTS: Baltasar Porcel told *CA:* "My primary motivation for writing is a desire to interpret the world through imagination, through the strength of words, and to communicate this to people. What particularly influences my work is the world that I know about, the Mediterranean, and man in its passions. My writing process is to absorb sensations, to glimpse ideas. It is a slow elaboration of mental and emotional atmosphere, a redaction as exigent as enthusiastic. Definitively, what inspires me to write on the subjects that I choose is my relation with reality.

"In 1996 I published, in Spanish, a long book that is a historical report, through all the countries that include the Mediterranean cultures and their great creative moments from prehistory until today, with frequent lyrical incidences."

*   *   *

PORTE, Joan   1955-

PERSONAL: Born October 26, 1955, in Paterson, NJ; daughter of John (a car dealer) and Jean (a homemaker; maiden name, Garofalo) Porte. *Ethnicity:* "American." *Education:* George Washington University, B.A.; attended George Mason University. *Politics:* "Lover of freedom." *Avocational interests:* Work as a citizen activist.

ADDRESSES: Office—Card Pal, Inc., 2029 North Glebe Rd., Arlington, VA 22207. *Agent*—Gerald Porter, Hanson & Schwam Public Relations, 2020 Avenue of the Stars, 4th Floor, Los Angeles, CA 90067.

CAREER: Legislative assistant to Democratic Representative Robert Roe, 1976-79; Consumer Action Now, assistant to Lola Redford, 1979-81; National Society of Professional Engineers, political director, 1981-84; Associated Builders and Contractors, political director, 1984-86; Blue Horizons Travel, Inc., president, 1986—. Card Pal, Inc., founder.

MEMBER: Association of Irritated Citizens (president, 1995—).

WRITINGS:

Fortyish: Lessons for the Ages From a Baby Boomer, Scorpio (Arlington, VA), 1996.

Author of the screenplay *The Sedona Switches,* 1996. Contributor to *Minorities and Women in Business.*

SIDELIGHTS: Joan Porte told *CA:* "I was born in a log cabin in northern New Jersey to parents who tilled the sweet soil and tended the bovine animals of the meadowlands. Oh, all right, but it sounded good, didn't it? Actually, my father tilled a car dealership and my mother tended five kids, but I *was* born in northern New Jersey.

"I may have a rich family history, but I will never know. My paternal grandfather started life abandoned on a doorstep in Palermo, Sicily. I try not to think of the genetic connections that may be gliding through my DNA.

"If one believes in karma, then it was my fate to be surrounded constantly by politics and politicians. It is better than spending eighty years in the Black Hole of Calcutta, but not much. While working toward a bachelor's degree in political science from the George Washington University, I worked as a legislative aide for the now retired Representative Robert Roe of New Jersey. Once armed with my degree, I set out to learn what life was like on 'the other side,' in the world of the lobbyist. As a lobbyist for Consumer Action Now, a group started by Lola Redford, I pleaded for energy conservation and the increased use of solar energy. Then I learned about infrastructure and building safety as I addressed Congress on the

issues of concern for the National Society of Professional Engineers (NSPE).

"While I was at NSPE, another political creature came to maturity. That is the political action committee (PAC), which raises money from the membership of the interest groups and distributes them to candidates. During the end of my stay with NSPE, I moved from lobbyist to political director. It was a job that I held for several years with another group, the Associated Builders and Contractors.

"During this time I attended the School of Law at George Mason University. In a decision that I sometimes regret and may someday remedy, I left after a year. I was itchy for a change. I never felt fully comfortable with being part of special interest, and I had my fill of politics.

"Perhaps because my father was a small businessman, I felt the call of private enterprise. I was going to be away from politics . . . or so I thought. I soon learned that politics—like dust—finds its way into everything. Rules, regulations, bureaucrats are everywhere, even around people who are trying to run four-employee businesses. It was then I realized I couldn't ignore it any longer: I had to confront the political beast.

"This time I would not be representing a member of Congress or a special interest. This time I would be working to assist the most important figure in the political world: the private citizen. I would help private citizens control big government and other bureaucracies. At the same time I discovered that I could do more with a pen and paper than doodle, and I began to spend long hours in front of a computer screen, trying to give birth to sentences someone hadn't already unleashed on mankind."

*   *   *

POWER, Eileen (Edna Le Poer) 1889-1940

PERSONAL: Born in 1889, in Altrincham, Cheshire, England; died of heart failure in 1940, in London, England; daughter of a stockbroker; married Michael M. Postan (a writer and educator), 1938; children: Rhoda. *Education:* Graduated from Girton College, Cambridge, 1910; studied in Paris and Chartres, France, and at London School of Economics, 1911-13.

CAREER: Educator and historian. Girton College, Cambridge, director of historical studies, 1913-21; London School of Economics, lecturer and reader, 1921-31, professor of economic history, 1931-40. Co-founder and editor, *Economic History Review,* 1927.

WRITINGS:

The Paycockes of Coggshall, Methuen (London), 1920.

Medieval English Nunneries c. 1275-1535, Cambridge University Press (Cambridge), 1922.

Medieval People, Methuen, 1924, tenth edition, 1963.

(Editor, with R. H. Tawney) *Tudor Economic Documents,* Longman Green (London), 1924.

(Contributor) *The Legacy of the Middle Ages,* edited by C. G. Crump and E. F. Jacob, Clarendon Press (Oxford), 1926.

(Editor) *Poems from the Irish,* Benn (London), 1927.

(Translator) *The Goodman of Paris (Le menagier de Paris),* Routledge (London), 1928.

(Contributor) *Cambridge Medieval History,* volume seven, edited by Tanner and others, Cambridge University Press, 1932.

(Editor, with husband, Michael M. Postan) *Studies in English Trade in the Fifteenth Century,* Routledge, 1933.

The Wool Trade in English Medieval History (Ford lectures, 1939), Oxford University Press (New York City), 1941.

(Editor, with others) *Cambridge Economic History of Europe from the Decline of the Roman Empire,* Volume 1, Cambridge University Press, 1941.

(With Rhoda D. Power) *Boys and Girls of History,* Dobson (London), 1967, Roy (New York City), 1970.

Medieval Women, edited by M. Postan, Cambridge University Press, 1975.

SIDELIGHTS: Noted for her academic work in the area of medieval history in the years after World War I, Eileen Power's informative books on women's history were considered pioneering in their day. While not the first woman to undertake the study of medieval social and economic history, she became the most widely known because of her ability to engage not only an academic audience but the general reader as well. Power believed that the broad study of history was crucial to reducing and eliminating nationalism and provincialism. To that end she contributed to popular magazines, gave radio talks on historical topics, and wrote books on history for young readers.

Like many of her colleagues, Power was attracted to the Middle Ages because of its contrasts with the industrial age; unlike others she did not harbor any illusions about what life was like during this period. Her style of historical writing was unique in that she used individuals to represent historic "types" as a means of making the distant past easier for the average reader to relate to. This technique can be seen in her *Medieval People,* published in 1924. Ignoring high-profile individuals, the work presents the era through the lives of six "average" individuals, including a peasant, a prioress, and two men engaged in the wool trade. In engaging sketches Power includes a great deal of background information gleaned from various documents of the period.

At her untimely death in 1940, Power would leave, among other works, an unfinished world history for young people. Several of her lectures would be edited by her husband, Michael M. Postan, in 1975 and published as *Medieval Women.*

BIOGRAPHICAL/CRITICAL SOURCES:

BOOKS

Blacker, Carmen, *A Woman in History: Eileen Power 1889-1940,* Cambridge University Press (Cambridge), 1996.

Cantor, Norman F., *Inventing the Middle Ages,* Morrow (New York City), 1991 Shils, Edward, and Carmen Blacker, editors, *Cambridge Women: Twelve Portraits,* Cambridge University Press, 1996.

PERIODICALS

American Historical Review, Volume 93, 1988.*

*　　*　　*

POWER, Nancy Goslee 1942-

PERSONAL: Born February 6, 1942, in Georgetown, DE; daughter of James E., Jr. (in insurance business) and Ellen (a homemaker; maiden name, Williams) Goslee; children: Oliver Power. *Education:* Attended Garland Junior College, 1961, and Villa Mercedes, Florence, Italy, 1962.

ADDRESSES: Home—1015 Pier Ave., Santa Monica, CA 90405. *Office*—Nancy Goslee Power and Associates, Inc., 1643 12th St., Studio 5, Santa Monica, CA 90404; fax 310-396-7135. *Agent*—Helen Pratt, 1165 5th Ave., New York, NY 10029.

CAREER: Nancy Goslee Power and Associates, Inc., Santa Monica, CA, owner, 1971—.

AWARDS, HONORS: Angie Award, *Angeles,* 1990, for landscape design; Wood Design Honor Award, American Wood Council, 1990, for a church in Glendale, CA; Honor Roll Design Award, American Institute of Architects, 1990, for Schnabel House in Los Angeles, CA; Design Award, *Progressive Architecture,* 1993, for Walt Disney Concert Hall, Los Angeles.

WRITINGS:

The Gardens of California, C. N. Potter (New York City), 1995.

*   *   *

PRENDERGAST, Curtis 1915-

PERSONAL: Born October 21, 1915, in Stockton, CA; son of Arthur Curtis (an editor) and Catherine (Walker) Prendergast; married Elizabeth Caldwell Calhoun Clarke (a lieutenant in the Women's Army Corps, then homemaker), April 8, 1944; children: Catherine, James, David, Sarah. *Education:* Stanford University, A.B. (philosophy), 1937; attended the University of Colorado, Boulder (U.S. Navy School of Oriental Languages), 1944-45; attended the University of California, Berkley (graduate studies in Asian languages), 1946, (Korean studies), 1948. *Politics:* Democrat. *Religion:* Episcopalian. *Avocational interests:* Reading in history and contemporary politics.

ADDRESSES: Home and office—30130 Buck Bryan Road, Bolingbroke Creek, Trappe, MD 21673.

CAREER: Reporter for newspapers, the *Bee,* Fresno, CA, 1937-40, and the *News-Sun,* Waukegan, IL, 1947; United States Foreign Service, Third Secretary and Vice-Consul, 1947-50; Time Inc., correspondent for *Time, Life,* and other Time, Inc., publications, 1950-77; news bureau chief in Tokyo, Johannesburg, Paris, and London. *Military Service:* U.S Naval Reserve, lieutenant, 1942-46.

MEMBER: World Press Freedom Committee (Reston, VA), Time-Life Alumni Society (co-founder and past president).

WRITINGS:

(With Donald Wyman) *Easy Gardens,* Time-Life (New York, NY), 1978.
Bix Beiderbecke ("Giants of Jazz" series), Time-Life (Alexandria, VA), 1979.
The First Aviators, Time-Life, 1980.
(With Geoffrey Colvin) *The World of Time Inc.: The Intimate History of a Changing Enterprise,* Volume 3: *1960-1980,* Atheneum (New York, NY), 1986.

SIDELIGHTS: With *Fortune* magazine editor Geoffrey Colvin, veteran *Time* correspondent Curtis Prendergast is the author of *The World of Time Inc.: The Intimate History of a Changing Enterprise,* the third volume in the official history of the news conglomerate Time Inc. "While not as strongly or wittily written as the first two volumes by Robert T. Elson (published in 1968 and 1973), this third volume . . . covers a more complex period of enterprise, expansion and danger," writes former Time employee Byron Dobell in the *New York Times Book Review.* This volume covers the 1960-1980 time period and such complex subject matter as the death of Time founder Henry Luce in 1967, problematic relations with employees, the collapse of the Washington *Star,* an ill-fated attempt to launch a national weekly cable television magazine, the languishing of Time-Life books, the merger with forest products company Temple Industries, the relaunching of *Life* magazine, the acquisitions of Little, Brown and the Book-of-the-Month Club, the fates of the magazines *Time, People, Money, Fortune, Discover,* and *Sports Illustrated,* and the creation of Home Box Office (HBO). "The book is candid about the rising discontents over salaries, working conditions and employment practices toward women and minorities that produced a divisive strike in 1976," remarks Charles Champlin in the *Los Angeles Times Book Review.* Yet according to Champlin, these events "somehow lose something of their sting in the soothing annual report prose." Dobell, however, remarks, "One of the fascinations of this book is its use of internal memos to reveal the reasoning and passion behind the scenes." Citing the disagreements between editors and reporters covering the Vietnam War, Dobell continues, "Whatever reservations one must have about authorized histories, it is unlikely that any other major corporation would so frankly reveal its internal strife." Concludes R.J.

Gwyn in *Choice,* "Official histories such as this have their place as reference points for future historians."

BIOGRAPHICAL/CRITICAL SOURCES:

PERIODICALS

Choice, July-August, 1986, p. 1668.
Los Angeles Times Book Review, December 7, 1980, p. 19; February 16, 1986, pp. 1, 10.
New York Times Book Review, January 19, 1986, p. 23.

* * *

PRETI, Luigi 1914-

PERSONAL: Born October 23, 1914, in Ferrara, Italy; married Anna Fabbri; children: Paolo, Maria, Antonio. *Education:* University of Bologna, B.A.; University of Ferrara, LL.D., 1936. *Politics:* Social Democrat.

ADDRESSES: Home—Via P. Costa 34, 40125 Bologna, Italy. *Office*—Partito Socialista Democratico Italiano, Piazza di Spagna 35, Rome, Italy.

CAREER: Italian politician, lawyer, and professor. Constituent Assembly, member, 1946-47; Chamber of Deputies, member, 1947—, Internal Affairs Committee, c. 1954, vice president, 1980-83; Under-Secretary of State to Treasury, War Pensions Department, 1954; Minister of Finance, 1958-59, 1966-68, and 1970-72, of Foreign Trade, 1962-63, for the Budget, 1968-69, of Transport and Civil Aviation, 1973-74, of the Merchant Navy, 1979, of Transport, 1979-80; National Council, Partito Socialista Democratico Italiano, chair. Also worked as a lawyer and a professor of philosophy and pedagogy.

AWARDS, HONORS: Premio Internazionale "Cortina-Ulisse," c. 1973, for *Le lotte agrarie nella Valle Padana.*

WRITINGS:

Il governo nella Costituzione italiana, Giuffre (Milan), 1954.
Diritto elettorale politico, Giuffre, 1957.
Giovinezza, Giovinezza, Mondadori (Milan), 1964, translated by Isabel Quigly as *Through the Fascist Fire,* Secker and Warburg (London), 1968.

I miti dell'impero e della razza nell'Italia degli anni '30, Opere nuove (Rome), 1965.
Impero fascista, U. Mursia (Milan), 1968.
Dialoghi della nuova frontiera, A. Mondadori (Milan), 1970.
Socialismo democratico e comunismo di fronte all'elettorato italiano. Discorsi tenuti al teatro Odeon di Milano il 1 febbraio 1970 e al teatro Metropol di Rimini il 19 aprile 1970, Rizzoli (Milan), 1970.
Interpretazione di Dubcek, Rizzoli, 1971.
Italia malata, 2nd edition, Mursia (Milan), 1972.
Le lotte agrarie nella Valle Padana, G. Einaudi (Torino), 1973.
Un ebreo nel fascismo (novel), Rusconi (Milan), 1974.
Il compromesso storico: un problema che divide gli italiani, Rusconi, 1975.
La sfida tra democrazia e autoritarismo: evoluzione dei regimi politici dalla fine della prima guerra mondiale agli anni Ottanta, A. Mondadori, 1980.
Mussolini giovane, Rusconi, 1982.
Giolitti, i riformisti e gli altri, 1900-1911, Sugarco edizioni (Milan), 1985.
Giovani di Mussolini (novel), Rusconi, 1990.
Extracomunitari in Italia e in Europa, T. Pironti (Naples), 1991.
Romanzo del 18 aprile, A. Mondadori, 1992.
L'Italia nella tempesta, T. Pironti, 1993.

ADAPTATIONS: Giovinezza, Giovinezza was adapted for film by Franco Rossi, 1969.

SIDELIGHTS: For more than a half century, Luigi Preti has been active in the socialist Italian government. Between 1946 and 1980 he served in such varied positions as a member of the Chamber of Deputies and as the Minister of Finance, of Transport, and of the Merchant Navy. From 1980 to 1983, he held the position of vice president of the Chamber of Deputies. Early in his career, Preti began to write, choosing subjects pertinent to his interests and activities. Since his first publications on law, Preti has written numerous works on the history, government, and political scene of Italy. Of these works, his autobiographical novel *Giovinezza, Giovinezza,* which appeared in 1964, became a best seller and was translated into English in 1968 as *Through the Fascist Fire.* The novel deals fictionally with the 1935-1945 decade. It begins when dictator Benito Mussolini was at the pinnacle of his power and ends with his death by execution. At the outset, the protagonist Giulio is a staunch Fascist. By the end of the work, however, he has evolved into a Partisan patriot and then a supporter of the British and Americans. "It is easy to understand why it sold so well," wrote a reviewer for the *Times Literary Supplement.* "Thousands of Italians obviously had no difficulty in identifying themselves with Giulio . . . whose patriotism justifies everything." A film version of *Through the Fascist Fire* was released in 1969, but Preti was not happy with it, maintaining that the adaptation did not do justice to his novel.

BIOGRAPHICAL/CRITICAL SOURCES:

PERIODICALS

Times Literary Supplement, July 24, 1969, p. 807.
Variety, September 3, 1969.*

* * *

PUGH, Sheenagh 1950-

PERSONAL: Born December 20, 1950, in Birmingham, England; married Michael J. H. Burns, 1977; children: one son, one daughter. *Education:* University of Bristol, B.A. (honors).

ADDRESSES: Home—4C Romilly Rd., Canton, Cardiff CF5 1FH, Wales.

CAREER: Welsh Office, Cardiff, higher executive officer, 1971-79; Society of Civil Servants, Cardiff, branch secretary, 1974-79; Glamorgan University, tutor in creative writing, 1993—.

AWARDS, HONORS: Babel translation prize, 1984; British Comparative Literature Association translation prize, 1985; Cardiff International Literature Festival prize, 1988, 1994.

WRITINGS:

POETRY

Crowded by Shadows, Poetry Wales Press (Bridgend, Glamorgan), 1977.
What a Place to Grow Flowers, Triskele (Swansea), 1979.
Earth Studies and Other Voyages, Poetry Wales Press (Bridgend, Glamorgan), 1982.
Beware Falling Tortoises, Poetry Wales Press (Bridgend, Glamorgan), 1987.

Selected Poems, Seren Books (Bridgend, Glamorgan), 1990.
Sing for the Taxman, Seren Books (Bridgend, Glamorgan), 1993.

OTHER

(Translator) *Prisoners of Transience,* Poetry Wales Press, 1985.

* * *

PUGSLEY, Alex

PERSONAL: Born in Halifax, Nova Scotia, Canada; son of R. N. (an appeals court judge) and J. A. Pugsley. *Education:* University of Toronto, M.A.

ADDRESSES: Home—273 Crawford St., No. 2, Toronto, Ontario, Canada M6J 2V7.

CAREER: Writer.

WRITINGS:

(Co-author) *Kay Darling* (novel), Coach House Press (Toronto, Ontario), 1994.
(Co-author) *Ghetto of Cool People* (short documentary film), produced by Second Best Bed Productions, 1995.
Fidelio (documentary film), produced by Cumberland Co., 1996.

WORK IN PROGRESS: A novel.

* * *

QUARLES, Benjamin (Arthur) 1904-1996

OBITUARY NOTICE—See index for *CA* sketch: Born January 23, 1904, in Boston, MA; died November 16, 1996, in Cheverly, MD. Historian and author. Quarles was a historian who focused on the role African Americans played in United States history, but several of his early books, especially 1953's *The Negro in the Civil War,* also gained popular readership. A 1931 graduate of Shaw University, Quarles went on to earn master's and doctorate degrees in history from the University of Wisconsin. His first book, *Frederick Douglass,* was published in 1948. He gained a national reputation with *The Negro in the Civil War,* which recounted the stories of African Americans who fought in the Union Army, worked the Underground Railroad, spied, and ran the abolitionist propaganda machine. Quarles also wrote *The Negro in the American Revolution* in 1961, *Lincoln and the Negro* in 1962 and *Allies for Freedom: Blacks and John Brown* in 1974, and was a regular contributor to the *Journal of Negro History.* He taught at Shaw University, Dillard University in New Orleans and later at Morgan State. Quarles received 16 honorary degrees from universities in the Unites States, was a Guggenheim fellow from 1958 to 1959, and was an honorary consultant in United States history for the Library of Congress from 1970 until 1971.

OBITUARIES AND OTHER SOURCES:

BOOKS

Who's Who among Black Americans, 9th edition, Gale, 1996.

PERIODICALS

Los Angeles Times, November 19, 1996, p. A32.
New York Times, November 20, 1996, p. D21.

QUIRK, William J.   1933-

PERSONAL: Born November 13, 1933. *Education:* Princeton University, A.B., 1956; University of Virginia, LL.B., 1959.

ADDRESSES: Home—1717 Devine St., Columbia, SC 29201. *Office*—School of Law, University of South Carolina at Columbia, Columbia, SC 29208.

CAREER: Department of Buildings of the City of New York, NY, general counsel and assistant corporation counsel for real estate, 1966-70; Private practice of law in New York, 1969-77; University of South Carolina at Columbia, professor of law, 1970—.

WRITINGS:

(With R. Randall Bridwell) *Abandoned: The Betrayal of the American Middle Class Since World War II,* University Press of America (Lanham, MD), 1992.
(With Bridwell) *Judicial Dictatorship,* Transaction Publishers (New Brunswick, NJ), 1995.

Contributor of about forty articles to law journals and popular magazines, including *New York, New Republic, Newsday, Business and Society Review, Harper's, Fortune,* and *South Carolina Law Review.*

R

RAAD, Virginia 1925-

PERSONAL: Born August 13, 1925, in Salem, WV; daughter of Joseph M. (an oil and gas producer and theater owner) and Martha (Joseph) Raad. *Education:* Wellesley College, B.A.; attended New England Conservatory; Ecole Normale de Musique, Paris, Franace, diploma; University of Paris, doctorate. *Politics:* Republican. *Religion:* Roman Catholic. *Avocational interests:* Gardening, birding.

ADDRESSES: Home—60 Terrace Ave., Salem, WV 26426-1116.

CAREER: Professional musician and music teacher. Amnesty International Urgent Action Network, volunteer.

MEMBER: International Musicological Society, American Musicological Society, College Music Society, American Society for Aesthetics, American College of Musicians, Music Teachers National Association, Societe Francaise de Musicologie, Alpha Delta Kappa.

AWARDS, HONORS: Two grants from the French government; travel grant for Paris, American Council of Learned Societies; award, Delta Kappa Gamma, for outstanding West Virginia woman educator.

WRITINGS:

The Piano Sonority of Claude Debussy, Edwin Mellen (Lewiston, NY), 1994.

Contributor to journals, including *Piano Guild Notes, American Music Teacher, Clavier,* and *Musical Courier.*

SIDELIGHTS: Virginia Raad told *CA:* "My role as a performer in the educational institutions I visit has been to enlarge each individual's vision in the arts. Using the piano, I demonstrate music in its many phases in concerts, lecture recitals, and master classes. The variety of occasions has been exciting: in colleges and universities throughout the country, I have demonstrated impressionism using art slides, poetry, and the music of Claude Debussy. Often I returned to the same schools and explained romanticism. I lectured in French, then played the music of Claude Debussy as a special summer artist at Middlebury College. Students at the Annie Wright School explored music and painting in nineteenth-century France and finished the week-long visit with a rousing session of folk singing. Third graders of Harrison County in West Virginia, sitting on the floor around the piano in a large historic mansion, listened to Schumann and Chopin, then asked the most imaginative questions. At the University of Florida, I was part of a classroom setting. At the Dixon Gallery and Gardens, I performed in a special series. Whether at Lincoln University, Portland State, Annie Wright, or the University of Scranton, I always think of myself as a kind of educator.

"There is a need for diversely trained musicians in our society. As a pianist and musicologist, I endeavor to encourage young people in the schools where I perform."

RAND, Paul 1914-1996

OBITUARY NOTICE—See index for *CA* sketch: Born August 15, 1914, in Brooklyn, NY; died of cancer, November 26, 1996, in Norwalk, CT. Designer, typographer, painter and teacher. The United Parcel Service (U.P.S.), I.B.M., the American Broadcasting Company, and Westinghouse, are among the companies that have Rand to thank for designing their corporate logos and, in some cases, their identity to the public. Forbidden to draw pictures as a child by the Orthodox Jewish laws of his household, Rand began drawing secretly at age three and later convinced his father to pay an entrance fee for him at the Pratt Institute. He also attended the Parsons School of Design and the Art Students League, but Rand was influenced more by European commercial art and studied trade magazines of that medium. He went into business for himself in 1935, designing layouts for *Apparel Arts* and *Esquire* magazine. At a time when most commercial art in the United States was written copy and realistic drawings, Rand brought an avant-garde influence to his work for corporate publications and logos, which was simple, yet clever and artistic. His logos for I.B.M., U.P.S., and Westinghouse are used to this day. Rand became a professor of graphic design at Yale University in 1956 and wrote the books *Thoughts on Design* (1946), *Education of Vision* (1965), *Paul Rand: A Designer's Art* (1985), *Design, Form and Chaos* (1994) and *From Lascaux to Brooklyn* (1996). He also contributed illustrations to several books and magazines and was inducted into the Art Directors Hall of Fame of the New York Art Director's Club. He worked on commercial art from his Connecticut studio until his death.

OBITUARIES AND OTHER SOURCES:

BOOKS

Who's Who in America, 52nd edition, Marquis, 1997.

PERIODICALS

New York Times, November 28, 1996, p. D19.

*   *   *

RAPOPORT, Robert Norman 1924-1996

OBITUARY NOTICE—See index for *CA* sketch: Born November 1, 1924, in Brockton, MA; died November 4, 1996. Anthropologist and author. Rapoport was best known for his sociological studies on the modern family and the effect a family's environment had on relationships between husbands, wives and children. The former U.S. Army lieutenant was educated at the University of Chicago and Harvard University, where he earned his doctorate in 1951. He taught at Cornell University, Belmont Hospital in Sutton, Surrey, England, Harvard University, Northeastern University and Boston College before settling in London, England, and working at the Tavistok Institute of Human Relations. Rapoport's first book was 1952's *Changing Navaho Religious Values,* but his later work centered on family issues and many were co-written with his wife, Rhoda. Together they produced *Dual Career Families* (1971), (and with Ziona Strelitz) *Leisure and the Family Life Cycle* (1975), and *Growing through Life* (1980). Rapoport co-founded the Institute of Family and Environmental Research in Great Britain and was a pioneer in the field. His latest works were *New Interventions for Children and Youths: Action Research Approaches* (1987) and *Families as Educators for Global Citizenship* (1995).

OBITUARIES AND OTHER SOURCES:

BOOKS

The Writers Directory: 1996-1998, St. James Press, 1995.

PERIODICALS

Times (London), November 15, 1996, p. 23.

*   *   *

REDGRAVE, Corin 1939-

PERSONAL: Born July 16, 1939, in London, England; son of Sir Michael (an actor) and Rachel (an actor; maiden name, Kempson) Redgrave; married Deirdre Hamilton-Hill (an author; marriage dissolved); Kika Markham (an actress), 1985; children: Jemma, Luke, Harvey, Arden. *Education:* Attended Westminster School and King's College, Cambridge University. *Politics:* Marxist. *Avocational interests:* Music.

ADDRESSES: Office—Moving Theatre, London W6, England. *Agent*—c/o Kate Feast Management, 10 Fitzroy Rd., London NW1, England.

CAREER: Actor, political activist, and director. Moving Theatre (a repertory company), founder (with Vanessa Redgrave) and producer (with Redgrave). Film appearances include *A Man for All Seasons,* Columbia, 1966; *A Deadly Affair,* Columbia, 1967; *The Charge of the Light Brigade,* United Artists, 1968; *Oh! What a Lovely War,* Paramount, 1969; *The Magus,* Twentieth Century-Fox, 1969; Hunslett, *When Eight Bells Toll,* Cinerama, 1971; Eric Sange, *Serail,* Paramount, 1980; Duke of Cornwall, *Excalibur,* Warner Bros., 1981; Robert Dixon, *In the Name of the Father,* Universal, 1993; Hamish, *Four Weddings and a Funeral,* Gramercy Pictures, 1994; and Sir Walter Elliot, *Persuasion,* Sony Picture Classics, 1995. Also appeared as Dr. Edward Trenbow, *Between Wars,* 1968; Hawker, *Von Richthofen and Brown,* 1971; Gig, *La Vacanza,* 1971; Worsley, *Eureka,* 1982; and Sir Thomas Neathouse, *The Fool,* 1990.

Television movie appearances include Steerforth, *David Copperfield,* NBC, 1970. Also appeared in *Hassan* and *The Governor,* both for New Zealand television, 1977. Television special appearances include Octavius Caesar, *Antony and Cleopatra,* 1975; and *The Gambler,* 1971.

Stage appearances include (Stage debut) Lysander, *A Midsummer Night's Dream,* English Stage Company, Royal Court Theatre, London, 1962; Sebastian, *Twelfth Night,* English Stage Company, Royal Court Theatre, 1962; Pilot officer, *Chips with Everything,* English Stage Company, Royal Court Theatre, then Vaudeville Theatre, London, 1962; (Broadway debut) Pilot officer, *Chips with Everything,* Plymouth Theatre, New York City, 1963; Mr. Bodley, *The Right Honourable Gentleman,* Her Majesty's Theatre, London, 1964; Mr. Cecil Graham, *Lady Windermere's Fan,* Phoenix Theatre, London, 1966; Abelard, *Abelard and Heloise,* Wyndham's Theatre, London, 1971; Antipholus of Ephesus, *The Comedy of Errors,* Royal Shakespeare Company (RSC), Memorial Theatre, Stratford-on-Avon, England, 1972; Octavius Caesar, *Julius Caesar,* and in *Antony and Cleopatra,* both RSC, Memorial Theatre, 1972, then Aldwych Theatre, London, 1973; Norman, *The Norman Conquests,* Forum Theatre, Wythenshaw, England, 1976; John Calvin, *The Flag,* Bridge Lane Theatre, London, 1994; and *Julius Caesar,* Alley Theater, Houston, TX, 1996. Also stage director for productions of *The Scarecrow,* English Stage Company, Royal Court Theatre, 1961; and (with Gillian Hambleton) *The Flag,* Bridge Lane Theatre, 1994.

WRITINGS:

Michael Redgrave: My Father, Richard Cohen Books (London), 1995.

SIDELIGHTS: Actor and political activist Corin Redgrave is a member a theatrical family; he, both of his parents, and his sisters Vanessa and Lynn dedicated their lives to careers on stage and screen. Corin Redgrave has enjoyed a long and successful career dating from the early 1960s. In the mid-1990s he appeared in several major motion pictures: as Hamish in the Academy Award-nominated *Four Weddings and a Funeral,* as Sir Walter Elliot in *Persuasion,* adapted from Jane Austen's posthumously published novel of the same title, and as Inspector Dixon, a dishonest English police inspector, in *In the Name of the Father,* about the infamous Guildford Four. During this time, he also published a book about his father, Michael Redgrave, who died in 1985. American audiences know Michael Redgrave largely for his role in the film *The Lady Vanishes,* an Alfred Hitchcock thriller. In *Michael Redgrave: My Father,* Corin Redgrave discusses his father as a father figure, an actor, and a writer, devoting chapters of this biography to each subject. The work draws on Michael Redgrave's own memoirs, *In My Mind's I: An Actor's Autobiography,* published in 1983, and brings together family stories, personal memories, and entries from Michael Redgrave's diary. Unlike the 1983 autobiography, *Michael Redgrave* deals with the actor's bisexuality and homosexual love affairs. It also includes a list of Redgrave's performances and productions, as well as a chronology of his life. "This memoir is relatively angst-free and full of well-expressed passages of critical appreciation," remarked Michael Coveney of the *Observer.* "God knows we don't need another 'showbiz' book on our shelves," declared Melissa Benn in a review for *New Statesman and Society.* "But families like the Redgraves . . . need texts that tell us who they think they are." Benn concluded, "Michael Redgrave remains a mystery to the end: charming, flamboyant, inexpressibly pained. His son emerges sweet-tempered, wry and immeasurably tender."

BIOGRAPHICAL/CRITICAL SOURCES:

BOOKS

Contemporary Theatre, Film and Television, Volume 14, Gale (Detroit, MI), 1996.
Redgrave, Deirdre, and Danae Brook, *To Be a Redgrave,* Linden Press/Simon & Schuster, 1982.

PERIODICALS

National Review, March 7, 1994, pp. 71-72.
New Republic, January 3, 1994, pp. 28-29.
New Statesman and Society, June 2, 1995, p. 39.
Newsweek, October 9, 1995, p. 78.
New York, January 17, 1994, pp. 54-55.
Observer (London), June 18, 1995, p. 15.
Publishers Weekly, May 13, 1996. p. 62.*

* * *

REDONNET, Marie 1948-

PERSONAL: Born October 19, 1948, in Paris, France; daughter of Andre and Marguerite (Jarlo) Redonnet; divorced. *Education:* Attended university; currently working towards a doctorate.

ADDRESSES: Home—10 rue les diguiers, 75004 Paris, France; fax 01 48 87 02 93. *Agent*—c/o University of Nebraska Press, 312 North 14th St., Lincoln, NE 68588-0484.

CAREER: Writer. Associated with Conseil National de Recherche Scientifique (CNRS) and the University of Paris III, Sorbonne-Nouvelle.

WRITINGS:

Le Mort & Cie (poems), P.O.L. (Paris), 1985.
Doublures (short stories), P.O.L., 1986.
Splendid Hotel (novel), Editions de Minuit (Paris), 1986, translation by Jordan Stump published as *Hotel Splendid,* University of Nebraska Press (Lincoln), 1995.
Forever Valley (novel), Editions de Minuit, 1986, translation by Stump published as *Forever Valley,* University of Nebraska Press, 1995.
Rose Melie Rose (novel), Editions de Minuit, 1987, translation by Stump published as *Rose Mellie Rose,* University of Nebraska Press, 1995.
Tir et Lir (play), Editions de Minuit, 1988.
Nosie Dip (play), Editions de Minuit, 1989.
Silsie, Gallimard (Paris), 1990.
Seaside (one-act play), Editions de Minuit, 1992.
Candy Story (novel), P.O.L., 1992, translation by Alexandra Quinn published by University of Nebraska Press, 1996.
Nevermore (novel), P.O.L., 1994.
Le Cirque Pandor (play), P.O.L., 1994.
Fort Gambo (play), P.O.L., 1994.
Ville Rosa (short story), Editions de Flohic, 1996.

WORK IN PROGRESS: Livret d'Opere: Puert de Oro.

SIDELIGHTS: Considered by many critics to be one of the most talented contemporary French authors, Marie Redonnet has gained prominence in North America with the publication of what she calls her "triptych," a loosely connected trilogy of novels consisting of *Hotel Splendid, Forever Valley* and *Rose Mellie Rose.* These novels, translated by Jordan Stump and published by the University of Nebraska Press, are dominated by female characters and share themes of life, death, despair, desolation, and decay.

The first of Redonnet's triptych was published in 1986 in French as *Splendid Hotel,* and published in the 1995 English translation as *Hotel Splendid.* The book portrays the futile efforts of a woman to keep an encroaching swamp from swallowing the hotel she and her elderly sisters have inherited from their grandmother. Although the woman rushes from room to room to try to unstop the toilets, her efforts are in vain; the building eventually falls victim to the swamp, and its residents are either driven away or killed from diseases carried by sewage and rats. Commenting on the theme of futility in a *World Literature Today* review of the novel in French, Maria Green wrote: "*Splendid Hotel* ends with the final defeat of the narrator: the toilets are permanently plugged; only one guest stays, locked in his room, because he does not dare tackle the wrecked staircase. There are many ways of displaying mankind's Sisyphean efforts. Isn't a plumbing system beyond repair a striking one?"

The next volume in the trilogy is *Forever Valley,* published in France in 1986, and in an English translation in 1995. *Forever Valley* concerns a teenage girl who is coerced into prostitution by the priest who raised her. When she is not hustling or tending to the care of the ailing priest, the girl enjoys digging in the rectory garden, where she hopes to find the remains of the dead she believes are buried there. As in *Hotel Splendid,* however, water threatens to destroy the girl's world, as the construction of a dam in a neighboring community will soon flood the valley forever.

Stump's 1995 English translation of Redonnet's *Rose Mellie Rose,* which was published in France in 1987 as *Rose Melie Rose,* contains an interview with the author and completes the triptych. The novel relates the tale of Mellie, who is abandoned at birth in a grotto, but is found and raised by an elderly woman named Rose, who dies as Mellie reaches puberty.

Mellie then sets off to explore the world, journeying from her town to discover she lives on an island seemingly forgotten by the rest of the civilized world. Abandoned again, this time by her fisherman husband the night after their wedding, the pregnant Mellie returns to the grotto when the time comes to deliver her daughter, whom she names Rose. Then Mellie goes to the beach to die, completing the cycle of her life. "As so often in Redonnet's work," wrote John Taylor in his *Times Literary Supplement* review of Redonnet's trilogy, "the passing of one cycle to the next suggests that story-telling, like life, somehow continues. These perturbing tales offer no other comforting moral."

Redonnet's three novels elicited praise for both the author and the translator. Mary Beth Loup, writing in *Belles Lettres,* opined: "The reader will certainly be left with a strong visual image of the three girl-women, their striving, and their hopes. In transmitting that image to a wider audience, Redonnet has a powerful ally in her translator, Jordan Stump. His sympathy and enthusiasm are apparent in both the accuracy and sensitivity of his translation, and in the insight he displays in his interview with the author." Similarly, *Review of Contemporary Fiction* contributor Susan Ireland commented: "Jordan Stump's excellent translation successfully captures the haunting, impressionistic nature of Redonnet's prose. Strangely moving in its simplicity, [Redonnet's] work is to be highly recommended to all those who appreciate the soothing effects of fairy tales and legends."

Another of Redonnet's novels, *Candy Story,* was published in an English translation by Alexandra Quinn in 1996. Containing elements included in the earlier novels, such as a menacing swamp and a decaying hotel, *Candy Story* is a tale of political corruption and murder. The book is narrated by a young writer, Mia, whose lovers tend to forget her name, and each calls her "Candy" during their lovemaking. "The multiple layers here," wrote a *Publishers Weekly* critic, "are more than this slim novel can support, making it a better bet for readers who have already developed a taste for Redonnet's dark, mazy style."

BIOGRAPHICAL/CRITICAL SOURCES:

PERIODICALS

Belles Lettres, spring, 1995, pp. 8-9.
Publishers Weekly, September 26, 1994, p. 61; October 2, 1995, p. 66.

Review of Contemporary Fiction, summer, 1995, pp. 206-07.
Times Literary Supplement, June 2, 1995, p. 22.
World Literature Today, spring, 1987, pp. 248-49; autumn, 1988, p. 626; winter, 1988, p. 94; autumn, 1991, p. 672; autumn, 1992, p. 689.

*   *   *

REED, Jeremy   1951-

PERSONAL: Born in 1951, in Jersey, Channel Islands. *Education:* University of Essex, Colchester, B.A. (honors).

AWARDS, HONORS: Eric Gregory award, 1982; Somerset Maugham award, 1985.

WRITINGS:

POETRY

Target, Andium Press (Jersey, Channel Islands), 1972.
Vicissitudes, Morgue at Zero (London), 1974.
Agate Paws, White Dog Press (Osterley, Middlesex), 1975.
Diseased Near Deceased, Caligula (London), 1975.
The Priapic Beatitudes: 13 Runic Epiphanies to a Jade Novella, Laundering Room Press (Newcastle upon Tyne), 1975.
Emerald Cat, White Dog Press (Osterley, Middlesex), 1975.
Ruby Onocentaur, Guillotine Press (Hounslow, Middlesex), 1975.
Blue Talaria, White Dog Press, 1976.
Count Bluebeard, Aquila/Phaeton Press (Breakish, Skye), 1976.
The Isthmus of Samuel Greenberg, Trigram Press (London), 1976.
Jack's in His Corset, Many Press (London), 1978.
Saints and Psychotics: Poems, 1973-1974, Enitharmon Press (London), 1979.
Walk on Through, Spectacular Diseases (Peterborough), 1980.
Bleecker Street, Carcanet (Manchester), 1980.
No Refuge Here, Leaman, 1981.
A Long Shot to Heaven, Menard Press (London), 1982.
A Man Afraid, Enitharmon Press, 1982.

The Secret Ones, Enitharmon Press, 1983.

By the Fisheries, Cape (London), 1984.

Elegy for Senta, Privately printed, 1985.

Nero, Cape, 1985.

Skies, Enitharmon Press, 1985.

Border Pass, Privately printed, 1986.

Selected Poems, Penguin (London), 1987.

Engaging Form, Cape (London), 1988.

The Escaped Image, Words (Child Okeford, Dorset), 1988.

Nineties, Cape, 1990.

Dicing for Pearls, Enitharmon Press (Petersfield, Hampshire), 1990.

Volcano Smoke at Diamond Beach, Cloud (Newcastle upon Tyne), 1992.

Black Sugar: Trisexual Poems, Owen (London), 1992.

Also author of *Night Attack,* Open Arteries Press (Osterley, Middlesex).

NOVELS

The Lipstick Boys, Enitharmon Press, 1984.

Blue Rock, Cape, 1987.

Red Eclipse, Cape, 1989.

Inhabiting Shadows, Owen, 1989.

Isidore, Owen, 1991.

Red-Haired Android, City Lights (San Francisco, CA), 1992.

When the Whip Comes Down: A Novel about de Sade, Owen, 1992.

Delirium: An Interpretation of Arthur Rimbaud, City Lights, 1994.

Diamond Nebula: A Novel, Owen, 1994.

Chasing Black Rainbows, Owen, 1994.

OTHER

Madness: The Price of Poetry, Owen, 1989.

(Translator) *Novalis Hymns to the Night,* by Georg Phillipp Friedrich von Hardenberg, Enitharmon Press (Petersfield, Hampshire), 1989.

(Translator) *The Coastguard's House* (verse), by Eugenio Montale, Bloodaxe (Newcastle upon Tyne), 1990.

Lipstick, Sex, and Poetry: An Autobiography, Owen, 1991.

Waiting for the Man, Picador (London), 1994.

Pop Stars, Enitharmon Press, 1994.

Kicks, Creation (London), 1994.

REESBY, Ralph (Harold) 1911-

PERSONAL: Born June 15, 1911, in Egham, Surrey, England; son of Frederick (a partner in a metal works) and Minnie (a homemaker; maiden name, Groves) Reesby; married Theresa Eva Edith Eeils, August 4, 1931 (died November 4, 1975); children: Heather Reesby Bamford and Hazel Reesby Neve (twins), John. *Ethnicity:* "Long English family tree." *Education:* Attended School of Surgical Chiropody, 1946. *Politics:* Conservative. *Religion:* Methodist. *Avocational interests:* Writing, painting, fishing, cricket, golf.

ADDRESSES: Home and office—108 High St., Hythe, Kent, England. *Agent*—Carol Biss, 25 High St., Lewes, East Sussex BN7 2LU, England.

CAREER: Worked for Pollock Shipbuilders, Kent, England; Hiltons, Leicester, England, traveling shoe salesperson, 1924-28; S. Wright and Sons, Leicester, controlled production of military gear and special footwear during World War II; private practice of chiropody, 1946—. State registered chiropodist; member of Chiropodist Board.

MEMBER: Institute of Chiropody, Society of Chiropodists, Guild of Chiropodists, Royal British Legion.

WRITINGS:

Lady Dalsworth's Dilemma (romance novel), Book Guild (Lewes, England), 1992.

Twenty Minutes Past the Hour (historical novel), Book Guild, 1995.

Contributor to periodicals, including *Kent Life.*

WORK IN PROGRESS: The Elusive Manipulator, a novel; research on "Nepenthes, Byblis, and Ceahaotus."

SIDELIGHTS: Ralph Reesby told *CA:* "My principal reason for writing was to leave the name Reesby in book form that would, hopefully, be available worldwide. There are only two-hundred-twenty-two persons now that carry the name. I have one son, but he has no children.

"I was away from my parents for eight years, staying a fortnight in each town while employed as a traveling footwear salesman. I visited many small towns, as well as the principal cities of England. My formative years lacked the influence of companionship, yet I had the freedom to make mental notes of the scenes and districts I visited. Having now retired, I am able to record these in my writing, and to build stories around them.

"My book *Lady Dalsworth's Dilemma* reflects my connection with the Cotswolds: Maidenhead on Thames and Cliveden Mansion on Thames. My short story 'Three Maids in a Motor Boat' was written there. I also felt the influence of buildings such as Belvoir Castle, Castle Howard, Chatsworth, and Ashby de la Zouch with its castle, the scene of the long-ago royal tournaments and an atmosphere that recalls stories of Queen Rowena and Ivanhoe.

"A modern approach to a story I am now writing refers to Grace Darling at the Farne Islands as a background to semtex explosive and the tracing of confederates over the country I know so well. The story moves to Canada, then Australia, and finally returns to England, finishing at Witham in Essex."

*   *   *

REINICKE, Wolfgang H. 1955-

PERSONAL: Born in 1955, in Mannheim, Germany; married; children: one. *Education:* Queen Mary College, London, B.Sc., 1981; Johns Hopkins School of Advanced International Studies, M.A. (with distinction), 1983; Yale University, M.Phil., 1986, Ph.D., 1991.

ADDRESSES: Office—Brookings Institution, 1775 Massachusetts Ave. N.W., Washington, DC 20036-2188; fax 202-797-6004.

CAREER: Dresdner Bank A.G., London, England, assistant manager of operations and foreign exchange departments; Johns Hopkins School of Advanced International Studies, Washington, DC, adjunct professor and member of European Studies Forum; Brookings Institution, Washington, DC, member of senior research staff. World Economic Forum, fellow; American Institute for Contemporary German Studies, member of academic council and Washington German Study Group; consultant to National Academy of Sciences, U.S. Agency for International Development, and Roland Berger and Partner.

MEMBER: European Community Studies Association, American Political Science Association, American Economic Association, German Studies Association, Deutsche Vereinigung fuer politische Wissenschaft, Forum on Conflict Prevention and International Organizations, Council on Foreign Relations Study Group on Sovereignty, Non-State Actors, and a New World Politics.

AWARDS, HONORS: Fellow at University of Krakow, 1982, and Salzburg Seminar, 1983; fellow of Andrew W. Mellon Foundation, 1986-87.

WRITINGS:

Building a New Europe: The Challenge of System Transformation and Systemic Reform, Brookings Institution (Washington, DC), 1992.

(With others) *Konsolidierungs und Wachstumserfordernisse: Fiskalperspektiven der Bundesrepublik in den neunziger Jahren,* RWI (Essen, Germany), 1994.

(With Ullrich Heilemann) *Welcome to Hard Times: The Fiscal Consequences of German Unity,* Brookings Institution, 1995.

Banking, Politics, and Global Finance: American Commercial Banks and Regulatory Change, 1980-1990, Edward Elgar (Aldershot, England), 1995.

Deepening the Atlantic: Toward a New Transatlantic Marketplace?, Bertelsmann Foundation Publishers (Guetersloh, Germany), 1996.

Tugging at the Sleeves of Politicians: Think Tanks—American Experiences and German Perspectives, Bertelsmann Foundation Publishers, 1996.

Global Public Policy: Governing without Government?, Brookings Institution, 1996.

(With Christoph Bail and Reinhardt Rummel) *Perspectives on Transatlantic Relations,* Nomos (Baden-Baden, Germany), 1996.

Contributor to books, including *Bridging the Non-Proliferation Divide: The United States and India,* edited by Francine Frankel, University Press of America (Lanham, MD), 1995; *Preventing Conflict in the Post-Communist World: Mobilizing International and Regional Organizations,* edited by Abram Chayes and Antonia Handlêr Chayes, Brookings Institution, 1996; and *Asia, Europe, and America in a New Global Environment: A Challenge to Liberal Visions for the Next Century,* Friedrich Naumann Foundation (Washington, DC), 1996. Contributor to periodicals, including *Challenge, Roll Call, Studies in Comparative International Development, Europe in Washington, Economic Times,* and *World Link.*

WORK IN PROGRESS: Research on the globalization of the world economy and challenges to public policy, international economic institutions, transatlantic economic relations, export controls and technology transfer, and European integration.

*   *   *

REMNICK, David J. 1958-

PERSONAL: Born October 29, 1958, in Hackensack, NJ; son of Edward C. and Barbara (Seigel) Remnick; married Esther B. Fein (a reporter); children: Alexander, Noah. *Education:* Princeton University, A.B., 1981.

ADDRESSES: Home—233 West 72nd St., New York, NY 10023. *Office*—*New Yorker,* 20 West 43rd St., New York NY 10036.

CAREER: Washington Post, reporter, 1982-91; *New Yorker,* New York City, staff writer, 1992—.

AWARDS, HONORS: Livingston award, 1991; Pulitzer Prize for general nonfiction, 1993, and George Polk award, 1994, both for *Lenin's Tomb: The Last Days of the Soviet Empire;* Helen Bernstein award, New York Public Library, 1994.

WRITINGS:

Lenin's Tomb: The Last Days of the Soviet Empire, Random House (New York), 1993.
The Devil Problem (And Other True Stories), Random House, 1996.
Resurrection: The Struggle for a New Russia, Random House, 1997.

SIDELIGHTS: As a foreign correspondent for the *Washington Post,* David J. Remnick spent four years in Moscow, where he witnessed events leading to the sudden, non-violent collapse of the Soviet Union from 1991 to 1993. *Lenin's Tomb: The Last Days of the Soviet Empire,* which won the Pulitzer Prize for general nonfiction, is Remnick's attempt to recover the lost history of the Soviet Union. Full of interviews with reformers, students, workers, peasants, and intelligentsia in locations that range over eleven time zones, *Lenin's Tomb* "gives us flesh and bone, the sounds, sights, and smells of the Russian people," according *America* contributor David S. Toolan.

Lenin's Tomb elicited much praise from critics. In the *New York Review of Books,* John Bayley described the work as "extraordinary," "wonderful," and "compulsively vivid." Many commentators remarked on Remnick's method of gathering and presenting information. "The great merit of David Remnick's book is to bring to life the agony of the Communist regime during the critical period of unsuccessful reform," enthused Richard Pipes in *Commentary.* "This Remnick accomplishes not by theorizing, not by seeing events in 'broad perspective,' but by depicting, in vivid portraits, the minds and souls of those whose actions determined the outcome: courageous dissidents as well as the regime's conservative defenders, alongside passive and generally bewildered ordinary citizens." Pipes continued: "The result is a highly informative as well as lively account of Communism's breakdown by an eyewitness who, without hiding his aversion for the Communist regime and its apologists, succeeds in maintaining throughout the attitude of a professional journalist." "Remnick's book reads like a documentary detective novel, almost like a work of fiction, in which the author himself plays an important role," remarked Tatyana Tolstaya in the *New Republic.* "At the end of this 500-page account readers are left with the grateful feeling that they have been led through the labyrinth of Russian names, events and cataclysms by a charming and witty guide." "Remnick is devoid of . . . cultural racism. He doesn't make idiotic generalizations, he doesn't attribute implausible intentions and motivations to his subjects, he doesn't lie, he doesn't confuse; nor does he assume the pose of an aristocrat, who, wearied by the people's foolishness, extends the local peasant two limp fingers from his lace cuffs. He doesn't try to rise above his characters or above his readers," added Tolstaya. Pipes concluded: "Remnick's excellent book suggests that, in addition to thoroughgoing knowledge, there is no better guide to the understanding of human affairs than trusting one's eyes and ears."

BIOGRAPHICAL/CRITICAL SOURCES:

PERIODICALS

America, July 2, 1994, pp. 19-21.
Commentary, December, 1993, pp. 53-54.
New Republic, April 11, 1994, pp. 29-35.
New York Review of Books, August 12, 1993, pp. 3-4.

RICE, Condoleezza 1954-

PERSONAL: Born November 14, 1954, in Birmingham, AL. *Ethnicity:* "African-American." *Education:* University of Denver, B.A. (cum laude), 1974, Ph.D., 1981; University of Notre Dame, M.A., 1975. *Politics:* Republican. *Religion:* Presbyterian.

ADDRESSES: Office—Building 10, Stanford University, Stanford, CA 94305-2061.

CAREER: U.S. Department of State, Washington, DC, intern, 1977; Rand Corp., Santa Monica, CA, intern, 1980; Stanford University, Stanford, CA, assistant professor, 1981-87, associate professor, 1987-93, professor of political science, 1993—, assistant director of Center for International Security and Arms Control, 1981-86, member of executive committee, Institute for International Studies, 1988-89, 1991-93, senior fellow of the institute, 1991-94, provost of the university, 1993—. University of Michigan, visiting lecturer, 1988; Howard University, Patricia Roberts Harris Distinguished Visitor, 1991. National Security Council, director of Soviet and East European Affairs, 1989-90, senior director for Soviet affairs, 1990-91; special assistant to the president for national security affairs, 1990-91. Bellagio New Faces Conference, delegate for Arms Control Association and International Institute for Strategic Studies, 1984; Aspen Strategy Group, member, 1991-95. Member of board of directors, Chevron, Transamerica Corp., Rand Corp., Social Science Research Council's Committee on Problems and Policy, 1986-88, and Carnegie Endowment for International Peace, 1989; member of board of trustees, National Council for Soviet and East European Studies, 1988, and Carnegie Corporation of New York; member of selection committee, MacArthur Fellowship in International Security, 1983-85; member of international advisory council to J. P. Morgan. Mid-Peninsula Urban Coalition, member of board of directors, 1984, 1987-88; Community School of Music and the Arts, member of advisory board, 1988-89; KQED-TV, member of board of directors, 1989; member of the governor's advisory panel on the redistricting of California, 1991; Center for a New Generation, member of founding board of directors. Consultant to the Joint Chiefs of Staff, 1986-88, and *ABC News.*

MEMBER: American Political Science Association, American Association for the Advancement of Slavic Studies, Council on Foreign Relations (life member), Lincoln Club of Northern California, Phi Beta Kappa.

AWARDS, HONORS: National fellow, Hoover Institution on War, Revolution, and Peace, 1985-86; international affairs fellow, Council on Foreign Relations, 1986-87; LL.D., Morehouse College, 1991; D.H.L., University of Alabama, 1994; honorary doctorate, University of Notre Dame, 1995; John P. McGovern Medal, Sigma Xi, 1996.

WRITINGS:

Uncertain Allegiance: The Soviet Union and the Czechoslovak Army, Princeton University Press (Princeton, NJ), 1984.

(Editor with Alexander Dallin) *The Gorbachev Era,* Stanford Alumni Press Service (Stanford, CA), 1986.

(With Philip Zelikow) *Germany Unified and Europe Transformed: A Study in Statecraft,* Harvard University Press (Cambridge, MA), 1995.

Contributor to books, including *Contemporary Soviet Military Affairs,* edited by Jonathan Adelman and Christann Gibson, Unwin, Hyman (Boston, MA), 1989; *Grand Strategy,* edited by Paul Kennedy, Yale University Press (New Haven, CT), 1991; and *History of the White House and the Kremlin,* edited by Michael Fry, 1991. Contributor to journals, including *Time, Journal of Democracy, Journal of International Affairs,* and *Current History.* Member of board of directors, *World Politics,* 1987-89.

*   *   *

RICHARDS, Eugene 1944-

PERSONAL: Born April 25, 1944, in Dorchester, MA; married Dorothy Lynch (a reporter; died, 1983). *Education:* Northeastern University, B.A., 1967; graduate study at Massachusetts Institute of Technology.

ADDRESSES: Agent—c/o Apertures Press, 3025 Ontario Rd., Ste. 206, Washington, DC 20009.

CAREER: Photographer and writer. Art Institute of Boston, Boston, MA, instructor of photography, 1974-76; Union College, Schenectady, NY, instructor of photography, 1977; Maine Photo Workshop, Rockport, ME, artist in residence, 1977-78; International Center of Photography, New York City, artist in residence, 1978-79. Work exhibited in various galleries and museums, including Museum of Modern

Art, Addison Gallery of American Art, and J. B. Speed Art Museum. Work included in various exhibitions, including *We the People,* 1975, and *Fourteen New England Photographers,* 1978.

AWARDS, HONORS: Grants from National Endowment for the Arts, 1974, 1980; grant from Massachusetts Artists Foundation, 1978; fellowship from Massachusetts Artists Foundation, 1979; Guggenheim fellowship in photography, 1980; Book of the Year Award, Nikon, 1986, for *Exploding into Life;* Infinity Award for outstanding accomplishment in photographic reporting, International Center of Photography, 1987, for *Below the Line: Living Poor in America;* Canon Photo Essay Award, National Press Photographers Association, 1989.

WRITINGS:

(AND PHOTOGRAPHER)

Few Comforts or Surprises: The Arkansas Delta, M.I.T. Press (Cambridge, MA), 1973.
Dorchester Days, Many Voices Press (Wollaston, MA), 1978.
(With Dorothea Lynch) *Exploding into Life,* Aperture (New York), 1986.
Below the Line: Living Poor in America, Consumer Reports Books (Mount Vernon, NY), 1988.
The Knife and Gun Club: Scenes from an Emergency Room, Atlantic Monthly Press (New York), 1989.
(With Edward Barnes and Danny J.) *Cocaine True, Cocaine Blue,* Aperture, 1994.
Americans We: Photographs and Notes, Aperture, 1994.

Contributor of photographs to periodicals, including *Geo, Life,* and *New York Times Magazine.* Contributor of photographs to books, including *Photographer's Choice,* Addison House (Reading, MA), 1976; *Family of Children,* Ridge Press, 1977; *Family of Women,* Ridge Press, 1978.

SIDELIGHTS: Eugene Richards is a respected photographer who seems himself in the tradition of such esteemed photorealists as Robert Frank and Gene Smith. "Sometimes I look at their photographs and wonder why I even bother to try," Richards told Joe Novak in a 1980 *Photographic* profile. "At other times I feel them riding along with me."

Richards began his photography career in the early 1970s, after studying under photographer Minor White at the Massachusetts Institute of Technology (MIT). After leaving MIT, Richards worked as a VISTA volunteer in Arkansas, where he often ran afoul of his community's authorities. After having suffered beatings, Richards finally left the Arkansas Delta in 1973 and returned to his hometown of Dorchester, Massachusetts. There, he produced *Few Comforts or Surprises: The Arkansas Delta,* which garnered positive reviews from critics. Among the book's enthusiasts was *Commonweal* reviewer Todd Gitlin, who wrote: "Without political pointers to the future, we are left with the raw present, the terror and the pity of it. Richards' photographs have that eloquence which insists on the present."

Following the publication of *Few Comforts or Surprises,* he decided to photograph Dorchester and its inhabitants. His efforts resulted in *Dorchester Days,* which earned Richards further praise for his ability to capture the grim and disturbing aspects of everyday life. Julia Scully, writing in *Modern Photography,* noted that Richards employs some unlikely, idiosyncratic techniques—including blurred focus and awkward framing—to more graphically render his subjects. Through such devices, noted Scully, Richards "emphasizes the sense of craziness, of danger, of a world falling apart."

In the ensuing years, Richards continued to focus on life's tragic aspects. In 1986, he completed *Exploding into Life,* a collection of photos detailing the course of his wife Dorothea Lynch's ultimately fatal bout with breast cancer. Included in this volume are pictures of Lynch's disfigured torso, as well as a shot of Lynch vomiting from the effects of chemotherapy. Despite the grim and despairing nature of these photos, Richards described the project as a positive experience. "I had a great time making those photos," Richards related to *American Photographer* in 1989, "They're awful pictures, but it was a strangely joyous collaboration."

Richards' next volume is *Below the Line: Living Poor in America,* which appeared in 1988. In this stark photo-essay, Richards includes interviews with some of the poor that he photographed. The following year, Richards published *The Knife and Gun Club: Scenes from an Emergency Room.* "This," cautioned *People* reviewer Ralph Nowak, "is no book for the squeamish." Likewise, Sandra G. Boodman affirmed in the *Washington Post* that *The Knife and Gun Club* "is not a coffee-table book." Boodman described Richards' work as a "kaleidoscope of stark, sometimes brutally graphic, images."

Richards' next book, *Cocaine True, Cocaine Blue,* documents the catastrophic impact of this highly addictive narcotic on America's urban northeast. Brent Staples, writing in *New York Times Book Review,* called Richards' book "a record of the carnage as it is carried out" in various urban areas, and deemed Richards "a master of the brutal image."

In 1994, Richards completed *Americans We: Photographs and Notes,* a photograph collection devoted to the more arduous aspects of life in the United States. The volume includes images of violence and suffering, and it details the hardships endured by the increasing numbers of Americans living in poverty. Accompanying Richards' photographs are his own comments and observations on the photographs.

In the *Photographic* interview of 1980, Richards acknowledged that his works as a photographer has exposed him to considerable risk. "Everyone wondered when I was going to get my head knocked off," he told Joe Novak. "I guess I've just been lucky."

BIOGRAPHICAL/CRITICAL SOURCES:

PERIODICALS

American Photographer, November, 1989, pp. 36-49, 71-72.
Commonweal, November 30, 1973, pp. 242-44.
Modern Photography, June 9, 1979, pp. 9, 15, 178, 196.
New York Times Book Review, February 6, 1994, pp. 11-12.
People, June 12, 1989, p. 33.
Photographic, August, 1980, p. 19.
Washington Post, February 27, 1990, p. Z17; April 10, 1994, G4.

*   *   *

RIDDELL, Elizabeth (Richmond) 1907-

PERSONAL: Born March 21, 1907, in Napier, New Zealand; married Edward Neville Greatorex, 1935 (died, 1964).

AWARDS, HONORS: Walkley award; New South Wales Poet of the Year, 1983; New South Wales Best Book of the Year, 1983; Emeritus Fellow, Australia Council, 1984.

WRITINGS:

POETRY

Forbears, Angus and Robertson (Sydney), 1961.
Occasions of Birds, Officina Brindabella (Canberra), 1987.
From the Midnight Courtyard, Angus and Robertson, 1989.
Selected Poems, Angus and Robertson, 1992.
The Difficult Island, Molonglo Press, 1994.

Also author of *Poems,* Ure Smith (Sydney).

*   *   *

RINGGOLD, Faith 1930-

PERSONAL: Born October 8, 1930, in New York, NY; daughter of Andrew Louis (a sanitation worker) and Willi (a dressmaker and designer; maiden name, Posey) Jones; married Robert Earl Wallace, 1950 (divorced, 1956); married Burdette Ringgold, 1962; children: (first marriage) Barbara, Michele. *Education:* City College of the City University of New York, B.S., 1955, M.S., 1959. *Religion:* Protestant.

ADDRESSES: Home—La Jolla, CA; and Englewood, NJ. *Agent*—Marie Brown Associates, 625 Broadway, Room 902, New York, NY 10012.

CAREER: Artist and writer. Teacher of art in public schools in New York City, 1955-73; University of California, San Diego, professor of art, 1984—. Art work represented in museums and galleries, including Guggenheim Museum, Metropolitan Museum of Art, Museum of Modern Art, Studio Museum of Harlem, and High Museum of Atlanta.

AWARDS, HONORS: Creative Arts Public Service Award from the New York State Council on the Arts, 1971; travel award from American Association of University Women, 1976; award from National Endowment for the Arts, 1978; honorary degrees from Moore College of Art, 1986, and College of Wooster, 1987; Guggenheim fellowship, 1987; award from New York Foundation for the Arts, 1988; award from National Endowment for the Arts, 1989; Henry Clews Foundation Award, 1990; honorary degrees from Massachusetts College of Art and City College of the City University of New York, both 1991, and Brockport State University, 1992; Coretta Scott King

Illustrator Award from the American Library Association Social Responsibilities Round Table and Caldecott Honor Book Award from the American Library Association, both 1992, both for *Tar Beach.*

WRITINGS:

CHILDREN'S BOOKS, AND ILLUSTRATOR

Tar Beach, Crown (New York), 1991.
Aunt Harriet's Underground Railroad in the Sky, Crown, 1992.
Dinner at Aunt Connie's House, Hyperion (New York), 1993.
My Dream of Martin Luther King, Crown, 1996.
Bonjour, Lonnie, Hyperion, 1996.

OTHER

(Contributor) Amiri Baraka and Amina Baraka, editors, *Confirmation: An Anthology of African American Women,* Morrow (New York), 1973.
(With Linda Freeman and Nancy Roucher) *Talking to Faith Ringgold,* Crown, 1995.
We Flew Over the Bridge: The Memoirs of Faith Ringgold, Little, Brown (Boston, MA), 1995.

Art work represented in catalogues, including *Faith Ringgold: Twenty Years of Painting, Sculpture, and Performance, 1963-1983,* Studio Museum in Harlem, 1984; *Faith Ringgold: Painting, Sculpture, Performance,* College of Wooster Art Museum, 1985; and *Faith Ringgold: A Twenty-Five-Year Survey,* Fine Arts Museum of Long Island, 1990.

Contributor to periodicals, including *Artpaper, Arts, Heresies: A Feminist Publication on Arts and Politics, Feminist Art Journal, Women's Art Journal,* and *Women's Artists News.*

SIDELIGHTS: Faith Ringgold is a prominent artist and author whose works reflect her African American heritage. She was born in New York City during the Depression. As a child, Ringgold suffered from asthma and often stayed home from school. During these periods of recuperation, she listened to jazz bands broadcast on the radio, and she indulged her interest in drawing. In addition, her mother regularly took Ringgold to museums. Her father, meanwhile, would entertain her with social outings and storytelling. Ringgold attributes her artistic leanings to her somewhat unique childhood. After graduating

from high school, Ringgold studied art at the City College of New York. There she was taught to copy the works of such artists as Paul Cezanne and Edgar Degas, but she desired greater contact with African American art and artists. She undertook her own studies of such art and developed a powerful appreciation of it.

Before she could begin her own career as an artist, however, Ringgold married a jazz pianist and bore two children. The marriage soon collapsed, and Ringgold continued with her studies, graduated in 1955, and began teaching in New York City's public schools. She taught there for several years, then took her family to Europe to finally see the great art works that she had studied and then taught. Upon returning to the United States, Ringgold began promoting her own work throughout the country. These works, mostly paintings on African American themes, derived from European techniques. But as the civil rights movement continued to develop, Ringgold began adopting African and African American styles. In addition, she devoted herself increasingly to African American causes.

Although she has worked in sculpture and in painting canvas, Ringgold has won her greatest acclaim as an artist with her painted story quilts on which she relates her experience as an African American woman. She began framing her paintings on fabric in the early 1970s after discovering that Tibetans had practiced such artwork since the fourteenth century. In 1980, Ringgold made her first quilt and added writing to the borders of these paintings, which became known as story quilts. Such works as *Flag Story Quilt, Slave Rape Story,* and *Street Story Quilt* brought Ringgold greater recognition as an important, innovative artist. Her work is now part of the permanent collections at such institutions as the Metropolitan Museum of Art, the Museum of Modern Art, the Guggenheim Museum, the Boston Museum of Fine Art, and the Philadelphia Museum of Art.

Among Ringgold's artworks is the *Women on the Bridge* series of story quilts. Included in this series is the 1988 quilt "Tar Beach," which features a child, Cassie, talking and fantasizing while lying on the tarpaper rooftop of a Harlem building in the 1930s. An editor at Crown Books saw a poster of "Tar Beach" and contracted with Ringgold for a children's book based on the quilt. Ringgold then created a series of paintings depicting such scenes as the heroine of *Tar Beach* flying over the George Washington Bridge. Upon publication in 1991, *Tar Beach* won praise as an impressive and inspiring children's book. Rosellen Brown, writing in the *New York Times Book Review,* described Ringgold's artwork as "richly colored, sophisticated versions of what a child herself might paint," and concluded: "There's an air of triumph . . . in Ms. Ringgold's vision."

Ringgold followed *Tar Beach* with 1992's *Aunt Harriet's Underground Railroad in the Sky,* which features Cassie, the heroine of *Tar Beach,* and her brother, Be Be, as they magically encounter Harriet Tubman and trace their ancestors' flight from slavery through the Underground Railroad. Enola G. Aird wrote in the *New York Times Book Review* that "Ringgold's illustrations here are rich with meaning."

In ensuing children's books, Ringgold has continued to focus on African American history. In *Dinner at Aunt Connie's House,* published in 1993, a young girl visits her aunt, an artist whose walls are lined with her paintings of important African American women. In Ringgold's typically vivid illustrations, these women recall their struggles and triumphs. And in her 1996 volume *My Dream of Martin Luther King,* the civil rights activist's life is related through her own dream.

Aside from children's books, Ringgold is the author of *We Flew Over the Bridge: The Memoirs of Faith Ringgold.* Her artwork is featured on such volumes as *Faith Ringgold: Twenty Years of Painting, Sculpture, and Performance, 1963-1983* and *Faith Ringgold: Painting, Sculpture, Performance.*

BIOGRAPHICAL/CRITICAL SOURCES:

BOOKS

Chadwick, Whitney, *Women, Art, and Society,* Thames & Hudson, 1990.

Children's Literature Review, Volume 30, Gale, 1993.

Contemporary American Women Artists, Cedco Publishing, 1991.

Davis, Marianna W., *Contributions of Black Women to America: The Arts,* Kenday, 1982.

Gouma-Peterson, Thalia, *Faith Ringgold Change: Painted Story Quilts,* Bernice Steinbaum Gallery, 1989; amended by Faith Ringgold.

Holze, Sally Holmes, *Seventh Book of Junior Authors and Illustrators,* H. W. Wilson, 1996.

Miller, Lynn, and Sally S. Swenson, *Lives and Works: Talks with Women Artists,* Simon & Schuster, 1981.

Munro, Eleanor, *Originals: American Women Artists,* Simon & Schuster, 1979, pp. 409-16.

Sills, Leslie, *Inspirations: Stories of Women Artists for Children,* A. Whitman, 1988, pp. 40-51.

Slatkin, Wendy, *Women Artists in History: From Antiquity to the Twentieth Century,* 2nd edition, Prentice-Hall, 1990, pp. 190-92.

Turner, Robyn Montana, *Faith Ringgold,* Little, Brown, 1993.

Twentieth-Century Children's Writers, 4th edition, St. James Press, 1995.

Witzling, Mara R., editor, *Writing in Voicing Our Visions: Writings by Women Artists,* Universe, 1991.

PERIODICALS

ARTS, April, 1992, p. 88.

Artweek, February 13, 1992, pp. 10-11.

Atlanta Constitution, July 30, 1990, pp. E1-E5.

Black American Literary Forum, spring, 1985, pp. 12-13.

Bulletin of the Center for Children's Books, December, 1992, p. 121.

Detroit Free Press, February 1, 1996, pp. 1C-2C.

Entertainment Weekly, February 8, 1991, pp. 68-69.

Essence, May, 1990, p. 78.

Gallerie Women's Art, Volume 6, 1989, pp. 40-43.

Horn Book, May/June, 1991, p. 322; May/June, 1996, p. 351.

Journal and Guide, June 12-18, 1991, p. 3.

Los Angeles Times Book Review, February 24, 1991, p. 8.

Newsweek, September 9, 1991, pp. 64-65.

New York, February 18, 1991, p. 56.

New York Times, July 29, 1984, pp. 24-25; February 14, 1992.

New York Times Book Review, February 24, 1991, p. 30; February 21, 1993, p. 22.

Publishers Weekly, February 15, 1991, pp. 61-62; August 16, 1993, p. 104; October 16, 1995, p. 51; January 1, 1996, p. 70.

Quilt World, February/March, 1991, pp. 22-24.

San Diego Magazine Online, November, 1995.

San Diego Union, February 16, 1991, pp. C1, C3.

School Arts, May, 1989, pp. 23-26.

School Library Journal, December, 1991, pp. 88, 90; October, 1993, p. 110.

Village Voice Literary Supplement, April 1, 1991, p. 25.

Virginian-Pilot (Norfolk), July 19, 1991, pp. B1, B4.*

RIOS, Julian 1941-

PERSONAL: Born March 11, 1941, in Vigo, Spain; son of Fernando (a surgeon) and Regina F. (Taboas) Rios. *Education:* Attended Madrid University, 1958-62.

ADDRESSES: Agent—S.A. Balcells, Diagonal 580, 08021 Barcelona, Spain.

CAREER: Editor and author since the 1970s; founder of the *Espiral* magazine and literary series for the publishing firm Editorial Fundamentos, 1974. Has served on the editorial boards of magazines, including *Formations, Culturas-Diario-16,* and *Syntaxis.*

AWARDS, HONORS: Columbia University Translation Award, 1990, for the English-language version of *Larva.*

WRITINGS:

(With Octavio Paz) *Solo a dos voces,* Lumen (Barcelona), 1973.
(With Paz) *Teatro de signos,* Fundamentos (Madrid), 1974.
Larva (novel), Del Mall (Barcelona), 1983, translated by Rios, Richard Alan Francis, and Suzanne Jill Levine as *Larva: Midsummer Night's Babel,* Dalkey Archive Press (Elmwood Park, IL), 1990.
Poundemonium (novel), Del Mall, 1986.
Impresiones de Kitaj: La Novela Pintada, Mondadori (Madrid), 1989.
La Vida Sexual de las Palabras, Mondadori, 1991.
Las Tentaciones de Antonio Saura, Mondadori, 1991.
Retrato de Antonio Saura, Circulo de lectores (Barcelona), 1991.
(With Eduardo Arroyo) *Ulises Ilustrado,* Circulo de lectores, 1991.
(With Arroyo) *Hats Off to Alice!,* [Spain], 1993.

Contributor to American and European periodicals in French, Spanish, and English.

WORK IN PROGRESS: The novels *Auto de fenix* and *Belles lettres,* and a book on the American painter Roy Lichtenstein.

SIDELIGHTS: Julian Rios is among the most important post-modern authors in the Spanish language. His best-known works are the novels *Larva: Midsummer Night's Babel* and *Poundemonium,* the first two of a proposed series of five. Rios is famous in the literary world for his extreme love of word play; his books are filled with puns in many languages. In the reference work *Interviews with Spanish Writers,* the author is described as "a polyglot who assimilates sounds and tongues. In each of his pages, he strips the conventional Spanish language to the core, conquers it, gives it multiple meanings and multidimensional readings through a multilingual interplay." Furthermore, the interviewer noted, "[Rios's] characters play along with him in this masquerade of words and guide the reader from the text on the right-hand page to commentary notes on the left-hand page." Rios has been compared to such international giants of literature as James Joyce, Miguel de Cervantes, and Laurence Sterne.

Rios was born in Vigo, Spain, in 1941. He began writing from an early age and enjoyed playing games, including ones that involved wordplay. Rios's first book was a collaboration with Mexican writer Octavio Paz, which saw print in 1973. The volume, *Solo a dos voces,* takes the form of a conversation between Rios and Paz. Another collaboration with Paz was published the following year.

Almost ten years passed before Rios's next and most famous creation, *Larva,* appeared. *Larva* has been viewed by most critics as a novel in many parts. There is the main text, which appears on the right-hand pages, and the main notes to the text, which appear on the left. There is also a separate section called "Pillow Notes," as well as an index of names. A collection of Rios's own photographs serve as both illustration and a kind of separate text. As Rios explained in *Interviews with Spanish Writers,* comparing these sections to floors in a building, "there are various levels or stories in any minimally complex work. . . . One can remain on the ground floor, go up to the second level, stay somewhere in the middle, or survey the view from the roof. The reader can glance over something quickly and in passing, like in a stroboscope, or he can stop and observe the details."

The main characters in *Larva* are two lovers who happen to be writers, Milalias and Babelle. Also central to the novel is the literary figure of Don Juan, the famous lover—the book as a whole carries a sexual tone. Michael Dirda in the *Washington Post Book World* noted *Larva*'s "vitality, sexiness, and sinuous side-winding movement," in his review. In addition to other secondary characters such as Mr. X. Reis, Albert Alter, and the German Herr Narrator, Rios even includes himself as a fictional personage. Rios explained in *Interviews with Spanish Writers:*

"At the end of *Larva,* there is a scene in Reis's room in the Maide Vale neighborhood of London in which he speaks to a bearded stranger with round-rimmed glasses. Milalias, who is on his way to visit his beloved mentor, X. Reis, overhears their conversation in Spanish. Reis and the bearded man, who are sitting having a drink together, comment that they have the same name, because the stranger says that his dentist's nurse mispronounces his name as 'Mr. Rayos.'"

But despite the sexual situations and bizarre characters, according to Dirda in *Washington Post Book World,* "where *Larva* cracks open and takes wing is in its language, a kaleidoscopic display of linguistic excess that, like [James Joyce's] *Finnegan's Wake,* starts with 'the abnihilisation of the etym' and then turns the King's English into a 'kinks English' of puns, palindromes, acronyms and unruly garrulity." The critic concluded that the novel "shows off the whirl within the word and reminds us that language can aim to be other than a transparent window, that one can sometimes have more gain with less pane." Although Paul Julian Smith in the *Times Literary Supplement* warned that "one reader's revolution in poetic language will be another's textual torture," he lauded *Larva* as "an extraordinary homage to its predecessors," among which the critic includes Cervantes's *Don Quixote* and Sterne's *Tristam Shandy* in addition to *Finnegan's Wake.*

In 1986, the sequel to *Larva, Poundemonium,* was published. Originally meant to be part of yet another book in the five-volume project begun with *Larva,* it grew into its own volume, albeit a shorter one compared with *Larva* and with Rios's projected third novel, *Auto de fenix.* The work is titled *Poundemonium* because the figure of poet Ezra Pound is central to it, despite the fact that the action of the story takes place on the day following Pound's death. Rios expounded on the poet's importance for *Interviews with Spanish Writers:* "I have always considered him an emblematic figure, and very generous in three ways: first, because he was a magnificent poet and he managed to recapture lost traditions while innovating new styles; second, because he was very generous intellectually and he stimulated his colleagues and young writers." The third way, Rios continued, was "because he was very important as a transmitter and translator of other cultures. He brought us closer to cultures distant from ours, such as those of China and Japan, and he helped us reclaim our own classical cultures and make them newly relevant, as well as bring dead languages back to life."

While Pound is central to *Poundemonium,* his essence is summoned in the novel through the help of Rios's familiar characters, Milalias and Babelle. Rios explained in *Interviews with Spanish Writers* that "the book gets its principal cue from the descent into hell at the beginning of Pound's *Cantos.* . . . Of course, *Poundemonium* is a play on words between Pound and pandemonium. Anyway, in my book, that descent into hell leads us on a pilgrimage through certain areas of London." Rios went on to declare: "The image of Ezra Pound is gradually evoked by visits to his old haunts—where he worked, lived, and socialized—before concluding with a special purifying bath when the main character returns home to his love, Babelle, at sunrise. It is a trip to the end of the night that aspires to daylight."

Since the publication of *Poundemonium,* Rios has written several other books while continuing to work on the series he began with *Larva.* Among these are nonfiction volumes on artists that Rios admires, such as painters Ronald B. Kitaj and Antonio Saura. He has also collaborated with illustrator Eduardo Arroyo on two works. One, a 1993 effort, is titled *Hats Off to Alice!,* and further explores the character Lewis Carroll created in *Alice in Wonderland.* Juan Goytisolo, critiquing *Hats Off to Alice!* in the *Times Literary Supplement,* lauded "Rios's rich sinuous land of textuality."

BIOGRAPHICAL/CRITICAL SOURCES:

BOOKS

Interviews with Spanish Writers, Dalkey Archive Press (Elmwood Park, IL), 1991, pp. 239-258.

PERIODICALS

Nation, March 11, 1991, pp. 312-14.
Times Literary Supplement, May 3, 1991, p. 18; December 3, 1993, p. 13.
Washington Post Book World, February 24, 1991.*

—*Sketch by Elizabeth Wenning*

*   *   *

ROBERTSON, Joel C. 1952-

PERSONAL: Born March 18, 1952; son of James C. (a realtor) and Evelyn L. (a homemaker) Robertson; married Vickie (a registered nurse), June 6, 1981;

children: Nicole, Heidi, Brooke. *Education:* Ferris State University, B.S., 1974; University of Michigan, Pharm.D., 1975. *Avocational interests:* Mountain climbing, biking, horseback riding, cross country skiing, camping, backpacking.

ADDRESSES: Home—Saginaw, MI. *Office*—Robertson Institute, P.O. Box 887, Grand Haven, MI 49417; and Robertson Institute, P.O. Box 615, North Sydney, New South Wales 2059, Australia. *E-mail*—73759.404@compuserve.com.

CAREER: Gladwin Hospital, Gladwin, MI, director of clinical services, later director of Regional Health Center; private practice, 1984-91; Robertson Institute, Grand Haven, MI, owner and president, 1991—. Producer of more than three hundred-fifty television programs dealing with compulsive disorders and lifestyle adjustment problems, including the series *Peak Performance Living,* 1996; guest on television and radio programs.

AWARDS, HONORS: Grants from U.S. Department of Health, Education and Welfare, 1978, and U.S. Department of Defense, 1989.

WRITINGS:

Help Yourself: A Revolutionary Alternative Recovery Program, Oliver-Nelson (Nashville, TN), 1992.
Kids Don't Want to Use Drugs, Oliver-Nelson, 1992.
Help Yourself: Love Yourself, Non-Diet Weight Loss Plan, Oliver-Nelson, 1993.
Crises Response Planning: Managing a Crisis in the School Family, Grief Recovery, Inc., 1995.
Aftercare: Dealing with Death, Grief Recovery, Inc., 1995.
Peak Performance Living, HarperCollins (New York City), 1996.
Natural Prozac, HarperCollins, 1997.

Creator of training videotapes and audiocassette programs on behavioral topics and family issues. Contributor to books, including *The Question Book,* edited by Bobb Biehl, Oliver-Nelson, 1993; and *Family Matters Handbook,* Janet Thoma Books (Nashville), 1994. Contributor to periodicals, including *Today's Better Life, Health Confidential, American Journal of Preventive Psychiatry and Neurology, Adolescent Counselor, Physician and Sports Medicine, Detroit,* and *Professional Counselor.*

WORK IN PROGRESS: Our Compulsive Society.

SIDELIGHTS: Joel C. Robertson told *CA:* "My primary motivation in writing is a desire to take my experience of twenty years and interviews with more than ten-thousand people to the general public. Brain chemistry technology is a fascinating, yet complicated subject. Providing readers with information, which I refer to as 'self-care,' enables them to know more about themselves. This knowledge base allows them the ability to make better choices.

"The major influence in my work is the research that is done by the pharmaceutical industry. Although their philosophy is to change behavior through changing brain chemistry using medication, mine is to optimize brain chemistry through tailoring diet, activity, behavior, and spiritual plans."

*   *   *

ROBINSON, Patrick   1940-

PERSONAL: Born in 1940.

ADDRESSES: Office—c/o HarperCollins, 10 East 53rd St., New York, NY 10022-5299.

CAREER: Writer.

WRITINGS:

(With Richard Stone Reeves) *Classic Lines: A Gallery of the Great Thoroughbreds,* Oxmoor House (Birmingham, AL), 1975.
(With Reeves) *Decade of Champions: The Greatest Years in the History of Thoroughbred Racing, 1970-1980,* Fine Arts Enterprises (New York, NY), 1980.
(With John Bertrand) *Born to Win: A Lifelong Struggle to Capture the America's Cup,* Hearst Marine Books (New York, NY), 1985.
(With Daniel Topolski) *True Blue: The Oxford Boat Race Mutiny,* Doubleday Canada, 1989.
(With Sandy Woodward) *One Hundred Days: The Memoirs of the Falklands Battle Group Commander,* foreword by Margaret Thatcher, Naval Institute Press (Annapolis, MD), 1992.

SIDELIGHTS: Patrick Robinson is the co-author of numerous works on rather traditional yet heroic pursuits, including thoroughbred horse racing, sailing, and the 1982 Falkland Islands war. His first published volume appeared in 1975 under the title *Classic*

Lines: A Gallery of the Great Thoroughbreds, written with Richard Stone Reeves. In 1985, Robinson wrote of another costly and prestigious pastime in *Born to Win: A Lifelong Struggle to Capture the America's Cup,* written with John Bertrand.

Robinson's next tome is an account of a scandal that rocked the world of British rowing in 1987. This grueling and patrician sport typically attracts the most disciplined and achievement-oriented athletes on college campuses in both the United Kingdom and North America. *True Blue: The Oxford Boat Race Mutiny* appeared in 1989 and was authored with Daniel Topolski, coach of the Oxford University rowing crew at the time of the crisis. The controversial "mutiny" of the title refers to the attempted takeover, by a small rebel faction of American rowers, of the university's prestigious boating club prior to the season's highlight match against its rival Cambridge University.

As a former Olympic rower and winning coach, Topolski relates the demands he placed on those who had signed on to the grueling sport for Oxford. In *True Blue* the authors detail the dramatic confrontations that arose among the close-knit rowing team. The five outspoken Americans clashed on numerous occasions with the coach over training regiments and traditions, finally culminating in their insistence that their usual oarsperson would not be replaced by the university boat club president, as precedent demanded. The matter caused a stir on campus and the Americans eventually withdrew from the race, leaving a demoralized team that had taken sides against one another in the debate. In an almost fairy-tale ending, Topolski and Robinson narrate the means by which the Oxford team achieved a stunning victory over their Cambridge rivals despite these handicaps. A reviewer for the *Economist* described it as "a notably artful and exciting book."

Robinson's next work, 1992's *One Hundred Days: The Memoirs of the Falklands Battle Group Commander,* was written with the esteemed leader of the British naval forces during the Falkland Islands crisis of 1982, Sandy Woodward. The small war between Argentina and the United Kingdom over the islands in the South Atlantic Ocean lasted just more than three months, with Britain emerging victorious. Woodward, with Robinson's assistance, relates in the volume his decades of service in the Royal Navy that culminated in his successful leadership of the naval campaign. In *One Hundred Days,* the admiral reflects upon the historical precedents and instinctual hunches

leading to several decisive actions in the conflict. London *Times* critic Tom Pocock lauded Robinson's deft handling of the subject matter and the work's strong evocation of the admiral's voice, noting that Robinson's "efforts only occasionally show an over-polished sentence." The reviewer further asserted that "this is a book that will fascinate all who wonder how they themselves would have faced such responsibility."

BIOGRAPHICAL/CRITICAL SOURCES:

PERIODICALS

Economist, March 25, 1989, p. 98.
New York Times Book Review, June 14, 1992, p. 22.
Times (London), January 30, 1992, p. 4.*

*   *   *

ROBINSON, Sharon 1950-

PERSONAL: Born January 13, 1950, in New York, NY; daughter of Jackie (a baseball player) and Rachel Isum Robinson; married twice (both marriages ended); children: Jesse Simms. *Ethnicity:* "African American." *Education:* Harvard University, B.S.; Columbia University, M.S. *Religion:* Baptist. *Avocational interests:* Sports, reading.

ADDRESSES: Home—Norwalk, CT. *Agent*—Marie Brown, Marie Brown Associates, 625 Broadway, New York, NY 10012.

CAREER: Nurse mid-wife, 1975—; writer.

MEMBER: American College of Nurse-midwives, Jackie Robinson Foundation (member of board of directors), American College of Nurse-Midwives (ACNM) Foundation (member of board of directors).

WRITINGS:

Stealing Home: An Intimate Family Portrait by the Daughter of Jackie Robinson (nonfiction), HarperCollins (New York), 1996.

Contributor of a chapter on adolescence to a women's health textbook; contributor of articles to *Essence* magazine and to various midwifery journals.

WORK IN PROGRESS: A novel.

SIDELIGHTS: Sharon Robinson was born in 1950 to a famous father—Jackie Robinson, the first African American man to play major league baseball. She recounts what it was like for her and her brothers to grow up in the public environment that came with their father's pioneering achievement in the world of sports in her 1996 book, *Stealing Home: An Intimate Family Portrait by the Daughter of Jackie Robinson.* She reveals that her father tried very hard to be a good family man, and to give time and attention to his children. Nevertheless, she and her brothers, Jackie, Jr. and David, felt the strain of having to share their father with his admiring fans.

Sharon became a nurse midwife, and survived two failed marriages. In addition to the details of her life and her family's life, Robinson includes a collection of family photographs in *Stealing Home.* A *Publishers Weekly* critic responded favorably to the volume, predicting that "this loving biography" of Jackie Robinson "will add to his stature."

BIOGRAPHICAL/CRITICAL SOURCES:

BOOKS

Robinson, Sharon, *Stealing Home: An Intimate Family Portrait by the Daughter of Jackie Robinson,* HarperCollins (New York), 1996.

PERIODICALS

Publishers Weekly, May 13, 1996, p. 66.*

*　　*　　*

ROLLINS, Henry 1961-

PERSONAL: Original name, Henry Garfield; born February 13, 1961, in Washington, DC; son of Iris Garfield. *Education:* Attended American University, c. 1979.

ADDRESSES: Office—2.13.61, P.O. Box 1910, Los Angeles, CA 90078. *Agent*—c/o Imago Recording Co., 152 West 57th St., New York, NY 10019.

CAREER: Musician, lyricist, and writer. Lead singer with State of Alert, until 1981, Black Flag, c. 1981-86, and Rollins Band, c. 1987—. 2.13.61 (publishing company), founder, 1984, publisher, 1984—; co-founded One Records and Infinite Zero. Actor in motion pictures, including *The Chase,* 1994, and *Johnny Mnemonic,* 1995.

AWARDS, HONORS: Grammy Award nomination, best metal performance, 1995, for "Liar."

WRITINGS:

20, 2.13.61, 1984.
2.13.61, 2.13.61, 1985.
End to End, 2.13.61, 1985.
Polio Flesh, 2.13.61, 1985.
Hallucination of Grandeur, 2.13.61, 1986.
You Can't Run from God, 2.13.61, 1986.
Pissing in the Gene Pool, 2.13.61, 1987.
Works, 2.13.61, 1988.
1000 Ways to Die, 2.13.61, 1989.
Art to Choke Hearts, 2.13.61, 1989.
Knife Street, 2.13.61, 1989.
High Adventure in the Great Outdoors (includes *2.13.61, End to End,* and *Polio Flesh*), 2.13.61, 1990.
Bang! (includes *1000 Ways to Die* and *Knife Street*), 2.13.61, 1990.
One from None, 2.13.61, 1991.
Black Coffee Blues, 2.13.61, 1992.
Make a Grown Man Cry, 2.13.61, 1992.
Now Watch Him Die, 2.13.61, 1993.
Get in the Van: On the Road with Black Flag, 2.13.61, 1994.

Contributor to periodicals, including *Details, Face, Interview, Melody Maker, Sounds, Spin,* and *Village Voice.*

MUSICAL RECORDINGS WITH BLACK FLAG

My War, SST Records, 1983.
Family Man, SST Records, 1984.
Live '84, SST Records, 1984.
Slip It In, SST Records, 1984.
Loose Nut, SST Records, 1985.
The Process of Weeding Out, SST Records, 1985.
In My Head, SST Records, 1985.
Who's Got the Ten, SST Records, 1986.

MUSICAL RECORDINGS WITH ROLLINS BAND

Hot Animal Machine, Texas Hotel, 1987.
Drive By Shooting, Texas Hotel, 1987.
Life Time, Texas Hotel, 1988.
Do It, Texas Hotel, 1989.
Hard Volume, Texas Hotel, 1989.

Turned On, QuarterStick, 1990.
The End of Silence, Imago, 1992.
Electro Convulsive Therapy, Imago, 1993.
The Weight, Imago, 1994.

Also performed the song "Liar," c. 1995.

SPOKEN-WORD RECORDINGS

Short Walk on a Long Pier, Texas Hotel/2.13.61,
    1987.
Big Ugly Mouth, Texas Hotel, 1987.
Sweatbox, Texas Hotel, 1989.
Live at McCabe's, QuarterStick, 1992.
Human Butt, QuarterStick/2.13.61, 1992.
Deep Throat, QuarterStick/2.13.61, 1992.
The Boxed Life, Imago, 1993.

SIDELIGHTS: Henry Rollins is a musician and writer
who has drawn particular attention as the lead singer
in such bands as Black Flag and the Rollins Band.
Rollins was born Henry Garfield in 1961 in Washington, DC. After his parents divorced, Rollins lived
with his music-loving mother. They moved regularly,
and music, notably jazz and popular soul, remained
one of the few constants in his early life.

His unsettled home life scarcely proved stabilizing to
the scrawny but nonetheless aggressive Rollins. "I
was very loud and obnoxious and hyperactive,"
Rollins later recalled for Alan Prendergast in the *Los
Angeles Times.* As a consequence of his radical behavior, Rollins was eventually enrolled at a military
academy. There he was branded a failure by his
teachers and was the subject of torment from cruel
classmates. "I was there," Rollins later told Pat
Blashill in an interview in *Details,* "to be antagonized."

Rollins eventually tired of being physically intimidated and took to lifting weights to gain strength. He
also began indulging his enthusiasm for music by
becoming an active figure in Washington, DC's punk-
rock subculture. The increasingly muscular Rollins
took to slamming, a particularly violent form of dancing in which dancers pound into one another. "I lived
for the shows," he told Prendergast in the *Los Angeles Times.* "Violence was my girl."

As a further means of self-expression, Rollins established his own punk band, State of Alert. But he
continued to patronize other bands, notably Black
Flag. Rollins was a staunch supporter of Black Flag,

and he eventually met the band members. A few
months later, he attended a Black Flag concert in
New York City and was invited onstage to sing
briefly. Following that appearance, Rollins was invited to join the band and replace its lead singer, who
had decided to occupy himself playing guitar. Rollins
readily accepted Black Flag's offer, and for the next
few years he toured and recorded regularly with the
band.

Black Flag was hardly among the more widely known
bands of the early 1980s, and recordings such as
Family Man, My War, Loose Nut, and *The Process of
Weeding Out* could scarcely be regarded as commercial product. "I know I'm not going to sell millions
of records," Rollins told Prendergast. "I don't write
for the Everyman. I write for one man—me. If other
people dig it, that's cool." The band's followers,
however, were intensely loyal, and they sustained the
group through an often exhausting multi-year stint of
touring and recording. In one two-year period, for
instance, Black Flag produced the recordings *Family
Man, Live '84, Slip It In, Loose Nut, The Process of
Weeding Out,* and *In My Head.* During this period,
the band's music evolved from simple punk tunes to
aggressive but more complex songs incorporating the
extended instrumental interludes prominent in jazz.
Rollins's lyrics, meanwhile, expressed his outrage at
social conventions and revealed his interest in the
work of writers such as Henry Miller and Charles
Bukowski. Blashill explained: "[Rollins] doesn't intend his music or his words to be a catharsis or a kind
of sonic obliteration. When Henry talks about his
life—that is, when he performs—he says it's all about
choices. You choose your path, then you steam down
it. . . . And that's inspirational stuff for [Rollins]'s
audience."

With Black Flag, Rollins developed a reputation as a
poet who employed music as one means of expressing
himself. Indeed, by the time that Black Flag broke up
in 1986, Rollins had established himself independently as a writer. Through his own publishing company, 2.13.61, Rollins published such works as *20,
End to End,* and *Polio Flesh.* The name of the company comes from Rollins's birth date. "In his self-
published books, he is obsessed with spilling his
guts," commented Blashill. "But writing like this
isn't a hostile conversation that [Rollins]'s having
with himself. . . . It's [Rollins] getting straight with
himself, securing his own perimeters," noted
Blashill. Rollins explained his writing to Prendergast:
"There's no method to the madness; I don't even
know if there's madness. It's just expression—random

and real. . . . I just want to get to it better, to get more concise, to pinpoint things in my head."

Get in the Van: On the Road with Black Flag, published in 1994, chronicles the band's touring experiences from 1981 to 1986 through journal entries kept by Rollins. Blashill described Black Flag as "an incendiary monster truck of a band that defined American hardcore punk rock. Black Flag was ugly: They fought with each other, lived in a filthy tour van, and more than occasionally took it all out on people who thought they understood punk." Rollins diary excerpts in *Get in the Van* reveal exactly how rough this lifestyle was, and how it influenced him. *Times Literary Supplement* contributor Alex Truscott commented on Rollins's "intensity," and noted that "Rollins is painfully honest about his insecurities."

Rollins continued to remain active as a musician after Black Flag. In 1987 he established the Rollins Band, another group that produced loud, aggressive music. The band provided adequate musical support for Rollins, who proved an imposing spectacle with his hardened physique, severe hairstyle, colorful tattoos, and screaming delivery. Among the band's recordings are *Hot Animal Machine, Drive By Shooting, Life Time, Do It, Turned On, The End of Silence, Electro Convulsive Therapy,* and *The Weight.*

In 1987, the same year that he founded the Rollins Band, Rollins began making spoken-word recordings. He now has several such works to his credit, including *Short Walk on a Long Pier, Big Ugly Mouth, Sweatbox, Human Butt,* and *The Boxed Life.* He has also remained active as a writer of volatile prose works such as *Black Coffee Blues, Make a Grown Man Cry,* and *Now Watch Him Die.* Rollins commented to Blashill in *Details* that his written work has changed slightly. "These days I can use less words and say what I need to quicker. Like a smart bomb."

Rollins has also promoted the music of other artists. With prominent record producer Rich Rubin, Rollins established Infinite Zero, a recording label for re-releasing work from artists such as Tom Verlaine, Devo, and Gang of Four. "The goal of this label is basically to seduce a bunch of people who have thirty ears," Rollins told a reviewer in the *Boston Globe.* He wants listeners to hear "good things besides the good things they're listening to now." A man of many talents, Rollins is a musician, lyricist, poet, publisher, and actor. "In his music, his books, and his spoken-word pieces, he is a fearsome man confronting his fears. And ours," commented Blashill.

BIOGRAPHICAL/CRITICAL SOURCES:

BOOKS

Contemporary Musicians, Volume 11, Gale (Detroit, MI), 1994.

PERIODICALS

Boston Globe, February 10, 1995.
Creem, May, 1992.
Details, January, 1993; January, 1994.
Detroit Free Press, April 17, 1992.
Detroit News, May 1, 1993.
Down Beat, December, 1994.
Entertainment Weekly, March 12, 1993; February 18, 1994, p. 72.
Los Angeles Daily News, May 31, 1993.
Los Angeles Times, June 14, 1987.
Melody Maker, February 13, 1993.
New York Times Magazine, November 6, 1994, p. 38.
Publishers Weekly, October 3, 1994, p. 63.
Rolling Stone, April 16, 1992; March 18, 1993; December 23, 1993, p. 111.
Spin, May, 1992.
Times Literary Supplement, May 19, 1995, p. 18.
TV Guide, September 26, 1992.
Whole Earth Review, spring, 1995, p. 90.*

*   *   *

ROSENFELD, Sybil (Marion)   1903-1996

OBITUARY NOTICE—See index for *CA* sketch: Born January 20, 1903, in London, England; died October 2, 1996. Theater historian and writer. One of Britain's leading authorities on theater history, Rosenfeld led a scholarly life right up until her death. Born to a wealthy Jewish family, she was able to study what interested her. She graduated from King's College in London at age nineteen and, while working on her master's degree, was influenced by drama historian Allardyce Nicoll, who oversaw Rosenfeld's essay. Her first publication after graduating, 1939's *Strolling Players and Drama in the Provinces, 1660-1765,* earned her the British Academy's Rose Mary Crawshay Prize. She also wrote *Theatre of London Fairs in the 18th Century* (1966), *A Short History of Scene Design in Great Britain* (1972) and *Georgian Scene Painters and Scene Painting* (1982). Rosenfeld was also a founding editor of *Theatre Notebook* and often contributed to the *New Grove Dictionary of Opera.* Besides her professional life, Rosenfeld devoted much of her energy to Jewish education and charity and served twenty-five years as an honorary manager of the Jews' Free School. A few weeks before her death, Rosenfeld attended the International Shakespeare Conference in Stratford-upon-Avon.

OBITUARIES AND OTHER SOURCES:

BOOKS

International Authors and Writers Who's Who, 11th edition, International Biographical Centre, 1989.

PERIODICALS

Times (London), October 21, 1996, p. 23.

* * *

ROZELL, Mark J. 1959-

PERSONAL: Born October 26, 1959, in Paterson, NJ. *Education:* Eisenhower College, B.A., 1982; University of Virginia, M.A., 1983, Ph.D., 1987.

ADDRESSES: Office—School of Public Affairs, American University, Washington, DC 20016-8083.

CAREER: Mary Washington College, Fredericksburg, VA, associate professor of political science, 1986-95; American University, Washington, DC, associate professor of political science, 1996—.

MEMBER: American Political Science Association, Academy of Political Science, Southern Political Science Association.

AWARDS, HONORS: Fellow of National Endowment for the Humanities and American Political Science Association; Dirksen Center grant, Gerald Ford Foundation.

WRITINGS:

(Co-editor) *God at the Grass Roots,* Rowman & Littlefield (Lanham, MD), 1995.
The Press and the Bush Presidency, Praeger (Westport, CT), 1996.
In Contempt of Congress, Praeger, 1996.
Second Coming: The New Christian Right in Virginia Politics, Johns Hopkins University Press (Baltimore, MD), 1996.

RUBIN, Barnett R(ichard) 1950-

PERSONAL: Born January 10, 1950, in Philadelphia, PA; son of Arthur A. (in sales) and Shirley (a clinical psychologist; maiden name, Cooperman) Rubin; married Susan Lee Blum (a writer), August 10, 1975. *Ethnicity:* "Jewish." *Education:* Yale University, B.A. (magna cum laude with honors in history), 1972; University of Chicago, M.A., 1976, Ph.D., 1982; Ecole des Hautes Etudes en Sciences Sociales, Paris, graduate study and research under Fulbright Fellowship, 1977-78. *Politics:* Democrat. *Religion:* Jewish. *Avocational interests:* Cooking, eating, travel.

ADDRESSES: Office—Center for Preventive Action, Council on Foreign Relations, 58 East 68th St., New York, NY 10021; fax 212-517-4967. *E-mail*—brubin @email.cfr.org.

CAREER: Yale University, assistant professor of political science, 1982-89; United States Institute of Peace, Peace fellow, 1989-90; Columbia University, associate professor of political science, 1990-1996, director of Center for the Study of Central Asia, 1992-1995, director of Project on Political Order and Conflict in the Former Soviet Union, 1994-96; Council on Foreign Relations, New York City, senior fellow and director of the Center for Preventive Action, 1994—. Has given testimony before U.S. Congressional committees on foreign affairs.

MEMBER: Carter Center (International Negotiation Network member), Fondation Medecins sans Frontiers (member of Conseil Scientifique), Amnesty International USA (South Asia Coordination Group chair, 1981-89), Human Rights Watch/Asia (member of Executive Board and participant in missions to Pakistan, Afghanistan, Sri Lanka, and Tajikistan), Human Rights Watch/Helsinki (member of Steering Committee), International League for Human Rights (board member and participant in missions to Afghanistan and Pakistan), Humanitarian Fund for Tajikistan (subsequently the Project on Central Eurasia Asia, the Open Society Institute, Soros Foundation; board member and participant in missions to Tajikistan, Afghanistan, Uzbekistan, and Iran), National Democratic Institute for International Affairs (election observer in Pakistan, 1990).

AWARDS, HONORS: Grant from the Carnegie Corporation (with John Ruggle and others).

WRITINGS:

The Search for Peace in Afghanistan: From Buffer State to Failed State, Yale University Press (New Haven, CT), 1995.

The Fragmentation of Afghanistan: State Formation and Collapse in the International System, Yale University Press, 1995.

(Editor) *Toward Comprehensive Peace in Southeast Europe: Conflict Prevention in the South Balkans,* Preventive Action Reports, Volume 1, Council on Foreign Relations and the Twentieth Century Fund (New York), 1996

Contributor of articles to numerous journals, including *Christian Science Monitor, Current History, Foreign Affairs, Nation, New Republic,* and *New York Times.* Contributor of essays to many anthologies.

*   *   *

RYAN, Gig (Elizabeth)   1956-

PERSONAL: Born November 5, 1956, in Leicester, England. *Education:* Attended LaTrobe University, 1974; attended Sydney University, 1983-87; University of Melbourne, degree in Latin and Ancient Greek, 1993.

ADDRESSES: Home—1189 Burke Rd., Kew, Melbourne 3101, Australia.

CAREER: Author, songwriter, and musician.

AWARDS, HONORS: Australia Council Literature Board Writers grant, 1979, 1982, 1988; co-winner, Anne Elder award, 1988.

WRITINGS:

POETRY

The Division of Anger, Transit Press (Sydney), 1981.

Manners of an Astronaut, Hale and Iremonger (Sydney), 1984.

The Last Interior, Scripsi (Melbourne), 1986.

Excavation, Picador (Sydney), 1990.

*   *   *

RYNNE, Xavier
   See Murphy, Francis X(avier)

S

SADLER, Catherine Edwards 1952-

PERSONAL: Born December 3, 1952, in Los Angeles, CA; daughter of Anne (Josephson) Edwards; married Alan Sadler (an executive producer), June 20, 1976; children: Maxwell, Casey. *Education:* Attended American College of Switzerland, 1969-70, and the United States International University, 1970-71; Windham College, B.A., 1974.

ADDRESSES: Home—New York, NY. *Agent*—Toni Mendez, Inc., 140 East 56th St., New York, NY 10022.

CAREER: G. P. Putnam's Sons, New York City, editorial assistant, 1974-75, editor, 1975-77; freelance writer and journalist, 1977-82; author of children's books, 1978—; Conran's Stores, Inc., New York City, vice president of marketing and creative director, 1982-89; Koala Blue, Inc., Van Nuys, CA, vice president of marketing, 1989—.

MEMBER: Author's Guild, Direct Marketing Association, Catalog Council.

AWARDS, HONORS: Outstanding Science and Trade Book for Children Award, National Science Teachers Association and the Children's Book Council, 1981, for *A Duckling Is Born;* Notable Children's Trade Book in the Field of Social Studies, National Council for Social Studies and the Children's Book Council, 1982, for *Two Chinese Families,* and 1985, for *Heaven's Reward: Fairy Tales from China;* American Catalog Silver Award, *Conran's Catalogue,* 1986, 1987, and 1989.

WRITINGS:

Two Chinese Families, Atheneum (New York), 1981.
Sasha: The Life of Alexandra Tolstoy, Putnam (New York), 1982.
(Reteller) *Treasure Mountain: Folktales from Southern China,* Atheneum, 1982.
(Reteller) *Heaven's Reward: Fairy Tales from China,* Atheneum, 1985.

TRANSLATOR

A Foal Is Born, by Hans-Heinrich Isenbart, Putnam (New York), 1976.
A Flamingo Is Born, by Max Alfred Zoll, Putnam, 1978.
A Duckling Is Born, by Isenbart, Putnam, 1981.

Also adapter of *Sir Arthur Conan Doyle's The Adventures of Sherlock Holmes,* several volumes, Avon/Camelot, 1981.

SIDELIGHTS: Catherine Edwards Sadler has been involved in children's publishing from several different angles over the course of her career. The daughter of a writer, Sadler spent many years in Europe as a child and later noted that such extensive travels made a lasting impression on her young mind. Later, she took a job with a New York City publishing house after college; this (and her language skills) led to her work as a translator of several books for young children depicting the birth process of animals. Illustrated with actual photographs, *A Foal Is Born, A Flamingo Is Born,* and *A Duckling Is Born* appeared in the late 1970s and early 1980s.

Sadler married in 1976 and three years later she and her husband traveled to China. Their experiences in the southern city of Guilin formed the basis for Sadler's first authored book, *Two Chinese Families,* published in 1981. Aimed at the upper elementary grades, the book provides an at-home glimpse into life inside a socialist state. The Chengs and the Heus each have a child who attends the same school, and Sadler and her husband show the respective families engaged in their daily routines both before and after the school day. A *School Library Journal* review praised the book's "laudatory, uncritical tone."

From Sadler's experiences in China sprung the literary resources for two subsequent works, each collections of Chinese fairy tales that Sadler retold and published as *Treasure Mountain: Folktales from Southern China,* which appeared in 1982, and 1985's *Heaven's Reward: Fairy Tales from China.* Both were illustrated by Cheng Mung Yun. The first book concentrates primarily on folk tales from several different ethnic Chinese groups in southern China, with an introduction written by Sadler that explained the longstanding tensions in the region. *Treasure Mountain's* six stories highlight traditional Chinese values, but, as a *Booklist* critic noted, the story entitled "The Magic Brush" was "altered to reflect a Communist viewpoint." *Heaven's Reward* presents a wider range of tales from China, each one set in a different historical period and representing various strains of Chinese philosophy, such as Confucianism and Taoism.

Sadler has also authored a biography for young adults on a little-known daughter of a famous writer. In 1982's *Sasha: The Life of Alexandra Tolstoy,* she chronicles the rather unhappy early life of the daughter of nineteenth-century Russian novelist Leo Tolstoy. Sasha received little affection or attention from either parent, but grew up to sympathize with many of her father's determined opinions; they later grew close. Sadler's recounts Sasha's experiences as a battlefield nurse during World War I, and the circumstances that led Soviet authorities to incarcerate her for a time after the Russian Revolution of 1917. Eventually she emigrated to New York City and established the Tolstoy Foundation, which provided aid to refugees. Myrna Feldman, reviewing *Sasha* for *Voice of Youth Advocates,* deemed Sadler's book worthy not just for its portrait of Tolstoy's daughter, but for its description of "life and the politics of Russia during and after the Revolution."

Sadler has also adapted Sir Arthur Conan Doyle's nineteenth-century British prose found in his Sherlock Holmes detective stories into more accessible text for young readers. In 1981 several of these stories were published in *Sir Arthur Conan Doyle's The Adventures of Sherlock Holmes,* before Sadler traded her career as a writer for one as a marketing executive.

BIOGRAPHICAL/CRITICAL SOURCES:

BOOKS

Something about the Author, Volume 60, Gale, 1990, pp. 141-42.

PERIODICALS

Booklist, February 1, 1982, p. 708; February 15, 1982, pp. 758-59; October 15, 1982, pp. 315-16; January 15, 1983, p. 679; September 15, 1985, p. 139.
Publishers Weekly, November 6, 1981.
School Library Journal, February, 1982, p. 75, p. 80; November, 1982, p. 90; January, 1983, p. 88.
Voice of Youth Advocates, December, 1982, p. 45.*

* * *

ST. VINCENT, Paul
    See MARKHAM, E(dward) A(rchibald)

* * *

SAKUTARO, Hagiwara 1886-1942

PERSONAL: Born 1886, in Maebashi, Japan; died in 1942; son of a physician; married Uedo Ineko, 1919 (divorced, 1929); married Oya Mitsuko (divorced, 1940); children: two daughters (first marriage). *Ethnicity:* Japanese.

CAREER: Poet and essayist. Co-founded the magazine *Kanjo* with Muro Saisei, 1916; University of Meiji, instructor, 1934-42.

WRITINGS:

Tsuki ni hoeru (poems), 1917, translation by Hiroaki Sato published as *Howling at the Moon,* University of Tokyo Press, 1978.

Aoneko (poems; title means "The Blue Cat"), [Japan], 1923.

Junjo Shokyoku Shu (poems; title means "Short Songs of Pure Feelings"), [Japan], 1925.

Hyoto (poems; title means "The Ice Land"), [Japan], 1934.

Nekomachi (poems, title means "The Cat Town"), [Japan], 1935.

Kyoshu no shijin Yosa Buson (criticism; title means "Yosa Buson: The Poet of Nostalgia"), [Japan], 1936.

Face at the Bottom of the World and Other Poems, translation by Graeme Wilson, C.E. Tuttle (Rutland, VT), 1969.

Rats' Nests: The Collected Poetry of Hagiwara Sakutaro (selections), translated by Robert Epp, Yakusha (Stanwood, WA), 1993.

SIDELIGHTS: Sakutaro Hagiwara is thought by many to be the father of modern Japanese poetry, the man who set the Japanese language free from the rigid forms of tanka and haiku. In addition, Hagiwara broke new ground with his use of colloquial Japanese speech, sustained lyricism, and the existential ponderings prevalent in his verse. By his compatriot, Miyoshi Tatsuji, Hagiwara was, according to Graeme Wilson in his introduction to Hagiwara's *Face at the Bottom of the Earth,* considered to be "the greatest poet on earth" to emerge in the twentieth century. "Such a poet could hardly be found in a hundred years," Tatsuji further declared.

The son of a well-to-do physician in a provincial town, Hagiwara early showed his talent for poetry, submitting traditional tanka poems to a literary magazine while he was in his teens. Hagiwara suffered from ill health, and while unable to complete a high school degree due to illness, he independently studied Japanese and European literature. By 1910 he contributed regularly to poetry magazines and in 1916 he co-founded a poetry magazine; yet he remained dependent on his family for financial support throughout his life. In the new magazine, *Kanjo,* Hagiwara published much of his experimental poetry, which was soon collected in *Tsuki ni hoeru (Howling at the Moon).* In his introduction to his verse, Hagiwara declared, "Before this collection not a single poem had been written in colloquial language of this style, and before this collection the animation in the poetry one senses today did not exist." Hagiwara's work earned him the reputation of an innovator, and during the course of his career he published several additional volumes of verse, as well as well-received essays on poetic theory. "Hagiwara exploited the rich resources of the colloquial right down to the darker levels of the vernacular," stated Wilson; "his claim that 'all new poetic styles issued from this book' *(Howling at the Moon)* is, I think, a fair one."

Only since the late 1960s have Hagiwara's poems been made available for English language readers, in such translations as *Face at the Bottom of the World and Other Poems, Howling at the Moon,* and *Rats' Nests: The Collected Poetry of Hagiwara Sakutaro.* In the introduction to his translation of Hagiwara's poems, Wilson summed up the reasons for the poet's lofty stature: "The reasons for Hagiwara's importance in the history of modern Japanese literature (and, indeed, in the whole history of Japanese literature) may be summarized under the following six headings: his use of novel forms, his use of novel language, his escape from the bonds of traditional metric rhythms, his entirely personal music, his astonishing personal vision, and his unprecedented achievement of sustained lyricism." In a review of *Face at the Bottom of the World,* a critic for the *Times Literary Supplement* described Hagiwara's work as "hypersensitive, introspective, and often deeply affecting," and F.D. Reeve in *Poetry* commented that Wilson's "English versions are so readable that they tease us into wanting to know Japanese." Wilson concluded, "More than for all his other innovations, Hagiwara's chief claim to greatness lies in his unparalleled sustention of lyric intensity. The peculiarly piercing quality of his poetry has been compared to that of a babe newborn into our terrible world. But Hagiwara cried for a lifetime, and in poems that will last as long as the Japanese language."

BIOGRAPHICAL/CRITICAL SOURCES:

BOOKS

Modern Japanese Poets and the Nature of Literature, Stanford University Press (Stanford, CA), 1983.

Twentieth-Century Literary Criticism, Volume 60, Gale (Detroit), 1995.

Wilson, Graeme, "Introduction," *Face at the Bottom of the World and Other Poems,* translation by Wilson, C.E. Tuttle (Rutland, VT), 1969.

PERIODICALS

Japan Quarterly, Volume 19, number 2, 1972, pp. 170-81.

Pacific Affairs, fall, 1970, pp. 481-82.

Poetry, July, 1971, pp. 234-38.

Times Literary Supplement, July 2, 1971, p. 755.*

SALOM, Philip 1950-

PERSONAL: Born August 8, 1950, in Bunbury, Western Australia; married Helena Salom, 1978 (divorced 1993); married Meredith Kidby, 1994; children: (first marriage) one son, (second marriage) one daughter. *Education:* Attended Muresk Agricultural College, 1967-68; Curtin University, B.A. (English), 1976, Dip.Ed., 1981.

ADDRESSES: Home—Lot 501, Mills Rd., Glen Forrest, Western Australia 6071, Australia.

CAREER: Agricultural technician, gardener, and house painter, 1969-73; freelance writer and illustrator; Adult Aboriginal Education, Perth, and Student Guild, Curtin University, writer and illustrator, 1977-78; Department of Agriculture, Perth, extension project officer, 1978-80; Curtin University, tutor and part-time lecturer, 1982-90; Western Australia Colleges of Advanced Education, writer-in-residence, 1988; Singapore National University, writer-in-residence, 1989; B.R. Whiting Library/Studio, Rome, writer-in-residence, 1992; Murdoch University, lecturer, 1994.

AWARDS, HONORS: Commonwealth Poetry prize, 1981, 1987; Western Australian Literary award, 1984, 1988; Australia Council fellowship, 1985, 1987, 1989, 1992; Western Australian Department for the Arts fellowship, 1990; Western Australian Premiers prize for fiction, 1991; Australia/New Zealand Literary Exchange fellowship, 1992.

WRITINGS:

POETRY

The Silent Piano, Fremantle Arts Centre Press (Fremantle, Western Australia), 1980.
The Projectionist: A Sequence, Fremantle Arts Centre Press, 1983.
Sky Poems, Fremantle Arts Centre Press, 1987.
Barbecue of the Primitives, University of Queensland Press (St. Lucia), 1989.
Tremors, National Library (Canberra), 1992.
Feeding the Ghost, Penguin (Melbourne), 1993.

OTHER

Playback, Fremantle Arts Centre Press, 1991.

Author of screenplays, including *The Box,* 1977; *The Giant,* 1978; and *Always Then and Now,* 1993.

SAMUELSON, Hyman 1919-

PERSONAL: Born April 11, 1919; son of Samuel J. and Rebecca (Babetch) Samuelson; married Dora Reiner, December 28, 1941 (died December 30, 1944); married Louise Anderson, September 19, 1945; children: Jerry, Rebecca Samuelson Newberry, Deborah Samuelson Pearson, Aric. *Ethnicity:* "Caucasian." *Education:* Louisiana State University, B.A.; Tulane University, graduate study. *Religion:* Jewish.

ADDRESSES: Home—4012 Sierra Dr., Austin, TX 78731. *Office*—Slax Menswear, 5224 Burnet Rd., Austin, TX 78756.

CAREER: Slax Menswear, Austin, TX, sole proprietor, 1946—. *Military service:* U.S. Army, Corps of Engineers, 1941-45.

WRITINGS:

Love, War, and the 96th Engineers (Colored): The World War II New Guinea Diaries of Captain Hyman Samuelson, University of Illinois Press (Champaign, IL), 1995.

Author of privately printed books based on his diaries.

SIDELIGHTS: Hyman Samuelson told *CA:* "I always have written. I have kept diaries for more than sixty years. They have been stored away in boxes and foot lockers. I write about the people I am with—customers, family members, students in my confirmation classes at the temple. I write personal views about politics, books I've read, organizations I work with. My diaries are spiced with poems, philosophy, just the thoughts of an ordinary guy. They contain nothing profound. The writing is simple. They contain a considerable amount of conversation, very often conversation (dialogue) with myself.

"Dr. Gwendolyn Hall, a history professor at Rutgers University, read my World War II diaries for historical information, became fascinated with the material in the diaries, and, with my permission, had them published. Some other of my diaries will be of historical interest, I believe, after my death."

*   *   *

SARTI, Ron 1947-

PERSONAL: Born February 26, 1947, in Detroit, MI; son of Remo Mario and Lucille Ann (Dering) Sarti;

married Odile T. Malvoisin (a college teacher), June 22, 1974; children: Mark, Erica. *Ethnicity:* "Caucasian." *Education:* Wayne State University, B.A., 1969; Indiana University—Bloomington, Ph.D., 1984. *Religion:* Roman Catholic.

ADDRESSES: Home and office—Dayton, OH. *E-mail*—ron7172@aol.com. *Agent*—Donald Maass, Donald Maass Literary Agency, 157 West 57th St., Suite 703, New York, NY 10019.

CAREER: Administrator in higher education; writer. *Military service:* U.S. Army, 1969-72; became first lieutenant.

WRITINGS:

The Chronicles of Scar (fantasy novel), Avon (New York City), 1996.
Legacy of the Ancients: Book Two of the Chronicles of Scar (fantasy novel), Avon, 1997.

WORK IN PROGRESS: Book Three of the Chronicles of Scar, publication by Avon expected in 1998.

*   *   *

SASSEN, Saskia   1949-

PERSONAL: Full name, Saskia Sassen van Elsloo; born January 5, 1949, in The Hague, Netherlands; daughter of W. (in international business) and M. (van de Voort) Sassen van Elsloo; married Daniel Koob (divorced, 1980); married Richard Sennett (a writer and professor), October, 1987; children: (first marriage) Hilary (son). *Education:* Universite de Poitiers, Maitrise, 1974; University of Notre Dame, Ph.D., 1974; postdoctoral study at Harvard University, 1974-75. *Avocational interests:* Music, art, politics.

ADDRESSES: Home—New York, NY. *Office*—Department of Urban Planning, Columbia University, New York, NY 10027.

CAREER: City University of New York, New York City, assistant professor, 1976-80, associate professor, 1980-85, professor, 1985—; Columbia University, New York City, professor of urban planning, 1985—, department head, 1987-91. Consultant to the United Nations and to private foundations and government agencies.

MEMBER: American Sociological Association, American Political Science Association, American Collegiate Schools of Planning.

AWARDS, HONORS: Fellow of World Economic Forum and member of Council on Foreign Relations, Center for Advanced Study in the Behavioral Sciences (CASBS); Ford Foundation fellow; Russell Sage Foundation fellow; Revson Foundation fellow.

WRITINGS:

The Mobility of Labor and Capital, Cambridge University Press (New York City), 1988.
The Global City: New York, London, Tokyo, Princeton University Press (Princeton, NJ), 1991.
Cities in a World Economy, Sage Publications (Beverly Hills, CA), 1994.
Losing Control? Sovereignty in an Age of Globalization, Columbia University Press (New York City), 1996.
Migranten, Siedler, Fluchtlinge in Europa, Fischer Verlag (Frankfurt), 1996.

Contributor to professional journals. Many of Sassen's works have been translated into other languages.

WORK IN PROGRESS: Immigration Policy in a World Economy: From National Crisis to Multilateral Management.

*   *   *

SCHLEGEL, John Henry   1942-

PERSONAL: Born January 12, 1942, in Terre Haute, IN; son of Henry A. (an accountant) and Emily M. (a homemaker) Schlegel; married Joanne M. Sturman (a musician), August 26, 1967; children: Elizabeth, Steven. *Ethnicity:* "German-American." *Education:* Northwestern University, B.A., 1964; University of Chicago, J.D., 1967. *Politics:* "Mixed."

ADDRESSES: Home—32 South Dr., Buffalo, NY 14226. *Office*—Law School, O'Brian Hall, State University of New York at Buffalo, Buffalo, NY 14260. *E-mail*—schlegel@acsu.buffalo.edu.

CAREER: Legal Aid Bureau, Chicago, IL, lawyer, 1968-73; State University of New York at Buffalo, professor of law, 1973—.

MEMBER: American Society for Legal History, Law and Society Association, Conference on Critical Legal Studies.

WRITINGS:

American Legal Realism and Empirical Social Science, University of North Carolina Press (Chapel Hill, NC), 1985.

Contributor to professional journals, including *Stanford Law Review, Journal of Legal Education,* and *Law and Social Inquiry.*

WORK IN PROGRESS: A history of the Walter E. Meyer Research Institute of Law; research on American legal realism and American legal education.

SIDELIGHTS: John Henry Schlegel told *CA:* "I write to help myself and (derivatively) others to understand. Most influences on my writing are negative: Braudel, Hurst, Gordon, Hollinger. I write and rewrite, then write and rewrite some more; last comes form. I write about American legal education in order to understand how it came to be so awful and stay that way. My writing on American legal realism is simply my entry into that topic."

* * *

SCHMITZ, Cecilia M. 1960-

PERSONAL: Born May 31, 1960, in Denver, CO; daughter of John P. (a teacher) and Barbara M. (a nurse anesthetist) Schmitz. *Ethnicity:* "White." *Education:* University of Arizona, B.A., 1984, M.L.S., 1986.

ADDRESSES: Office—Libraries, Auburn University, Auburn, AL 36849. *E-mail*—SCHMITZ@lib.auburn.edu.

CAREER: Texas A&M University, College Station, microforms cataloger, 1987-88; Auburn University, Auburn, AL, social science cataloger, 1988—.

MEMBER: American Library Association, Association of College and Research Libraries, Association for Library Collections and Technical Services, American Business Women's Association, Alabama Library Association, Auburn Civitan Club, Phi Beta Kappa, Phi Kappa Phi, Beta Phi Mu.

AWARDS, HONORS: UMI Award of Excellence, 1994, for the book chapter "Major Microform Sets: The Alabama Experience."

WRITINGS:

(With Richard A. Gray) *The Gift of Life—Organ and Tissue Transplantation: An Introduction to Issues and Information Sources,* Pierian Press (Ann Arbor, MI), 1993.
(With Gray) *Smoking—The Health Consequences of Tobacco Use: An Annotated Bibliography With an Analytical Introduction,* Pierian Press, 1995.

Contributor to books, including *Advances in Collection Development and Resource Management,* edited by Thomas W. Leonhardt, JAI Press (Greenwich, CT), 1995. Contributor to periodicals, including *Library Hi Tech Bibliography, Technical Services Quarterly,* and *Texas Library Journal.*

WORK IN PROGRESS: A monograph on alcohol use and alcoholism.

* * *

SCHOGT, Henry G(ilius) 1927-

PERSONAL: Born May 24, 1927, in Amsterdam, Netherlands; son of Johannes Herman (a high school mathematics teacher) and Ida Jacoba (a high school mathematics teacher; maiden name, van Rijn) Schogt; married Corrie Frenkel, April 2, 1955; children: Barbara Schogt Bloemendal, Philibert, Elida. *Education:* University of Amsterdam, B.A. and M.A. (Slavic languages), 1952, B.A. and M.A. (Romance languages), 1951; University of Utrecht, Ph.D., 1960. *Politics:* Socialist. *Religion:* None. *Avocational interests:* Gardening, hiking.

ADDRESSES: Home—47 Turner Rd., Toronto, Ontario, Canada M6G 3H7. *Office*—University College, University of Toronto, Toronto, Ontario, Canada M5S 1A1.

CAREER: University of Groningen, Groningen, Netherlands, lecturer in Russian, 1952-63; University of Paris, Paris, France, visiting lecturer at the Sorbonne, 1963-64; Princeton University, Princeton, NJ, visiting lecturer in French and Russian, 1964-66; University of Toronto, Toronto, Ontario, associate professor, 1966-69, professor of French, 1969-92, graduate department head, 1972-77; retired, 1992. University of Utrecht, senior assistant, 1953-63.

MEMBER: Royal Society of Canada (fellow), Canadian Linguistic Association, Societe de linguistique de Paris.

WRITINGS:

Les Causes de la double issue de e ferme tonique libre en francais, G. A. van Oorschot (Amsterdam, Netherlands), 1960.
(Translator from Russian and author of introduction) Vsevolod Garsjin, *De Palm die door het dak breekt* (short stories), G. A. van Oorschot, 1966.
Le Systeme verbal du francais contemporain, Mouton (The Hague, Netherlands), 1968.
Semantique synchronique, synomymie, homonymie, polysemie, University of Toronto Press (Toronto, Ontario), 1976.
(With Pierre Leon and Edward Burstynsky) *La Phonologie,* Klincksieck (Paris, France), 1977.
Linguistics, Literary Analysis, and Literary Translation, University of Toronto Press, 1988.

Translator of Sem Dresden's *Persecution, Extermination, Literature,* published by University of Toronto Press. Contributor of articles and translations to periodicals.

WORK IN PROGRESS: A book of war memories, to be published in English; research on the lasting effects of the theories of Ferdinand de Saussure.

*　　*　　*

SCHREINER, Olive (Emilie Albertina) 1855-1920 (Ralph Iron, a pseudonym)

PERSONAL: Born March 24, 1855, in Wittenbergen Mission Station, Cape of Good Hope, South Africa; died December 11, 1920, at Wynberg, Cape Colony; daughter of Gottlob (a missionary) and Rebecca Lyndall Schreiner; married Samuel Cron Cronwright (a cattle breeder), 1894; children: one daughter (died). *Education:* Self-educated.

CAREER: Writer. Worked as a governess to Boer family near Karoo desert, 1874; co-organizer, Men's & Women's Club, London; involved in pacifist work in England, 1912-19.

WRITINGS:

NOVELS

(Under pseudonym, Ralph Iron) *The Story of an African Farm,* Chapman & Hall (London), 1883, Roberts Bros. (Boston), 1888.
Trooper Peter Halket of Mashonaland, Roberts Bros., 1897.
From Man to Man; or Perhaps Only. . . ., Unwin (London), 1926, Harper (New York City), 1927.
Undine, Harper, 1928.

SHORT STORIES

Dreams, [London], 1890, Roberts Bros., 1891, as *So Here Then Are Dreams,* Roycroft Shop (East Aurora, NY), 1901, expanded as *The Lost Joy and Other Dreams,* T. B. Mosher (Portland, ME), 1909.
Dream Life and Real Life: A Little African Story, Roberts Bros., 1893.
Stories, Dreams and Allegories, F. Stokes (New York City), 1923.
The Woman's Rose: Stories and Allegories, edited by Cherry Clayton, Ad Donker (Johannesburg), 1986.

OTHER

(With husband, Samuel C. Cronwright) *The Political Situation [in Cape Colony],* T. F. Unwin, 1896.
The South African Question; by an English South African, C. H. Sergel (Chicago), 1899.
An English-South African's View of the Situation: Words in Season, Hodder & Stoughton (London), 1899.
Closer Union: A Letter on the South African Union and the Principles of Government, Constitutional Reform Association (Cape Town), 1908.
Women and Labour, F. Stokes, 1911, selections published as *Women and War,* 1914.
Thoughts on South Africa, T. F. Unwin, 1923.
The Letters of Olive Schreiner, 1876-1920, edited by Samuel Cronwright-Schreiner, Little, Brown (Boston), 1924.
The Silver Plume: A Selection from the Writings of Olive Schreiner, edited by Neville Nuttall, [Johannesburg], 1957.
Olive Schreiner: A Selection, edited by Uys Krige, Oxford University Press (London), 1968.
A Track to the Water's Edge: The Olive Schreiner Reader, edited by Howard Thurman, Harper, 1973.

An Olive Schreiner Reader: Writings on Women and South Africa, edited by Carol Barash, afterword by Nadine Gordimer, Pandora (London), 1987.

Olive Schreiner: Letters, edited by Richard M. Rive, Oxford University Press (New York City), 1988.

"My Other Self": The Letters of Olive Schreiner and Havelock Ellis, 1884-1920, edited by Yaffa Claire Draznin, P. Lang (New York City), 1992.

Author's manuscripts are housed at the Sheffield City Library; Department of Historical Papers, University of the Witwatersrand Library, Johannesburg; Humanities Research Center, University of Texas at Austin; Thomas Pringle Collection for English in Africa, Rhodes University Library, Grahamstown; and the J. W. Jagger Library, University of Cape Town.

ADAPTATIONS: The Story of an African Farm was adapted as a stage play by Merdon Hodge, 1939; *Schreiner: A One-Woman Play* was written by Stephen Gray, David Philip (London), 1983.

SIDELIGHTS: More than a mere novelist, Olive Schreiner attained the status of a celebrity shortly after her first novel was released. Schreiner's semi-autobiographical *The Story of an African Farm,* first published in 1883 under the pseudonym Ralph Iron, was hailed by contemporary critics as a sensitive expression of a thinking woman's perspective on religion, marriage, and other social topics. Schreiner's concern with social issues, the secondary status of women, and the racism of her native South Africa would continue to serve as the focus of her work, both in fiction and nonfiction. Her *Women and Labour,* published in 1911, was long considered one of the major feminist tracts written in English; today, Schreiner's works are read and studied by a new generation of feminists who ascribe to her a leadership role in the advancement of women's rights.

Raised in relative poverty in rural Basutoland, South Africa, Schreiner would later hold the Victorian "woman's world" of fashion, family, and home furnishing in little regard. Self-educated through reading, she accumulated enough knowledge to become a teacher, serving five Boer families as a tutor between 1875 and 1881. Meanwhile, Schreiner saved her wages, planning to escape South Africa for a trip abroad to visit her brother in England as soon as she was able.

She also began writing, hoping to find a British publisher who would pay her enough for her work to fund her further education. In 1881, at the age of twenty-six, Schreiner travelled to London armed with three manuscripts. One bore the working title "Thorn Kloof"; as *The Story of an African Farm,* it would be published by Chapman & Hall two years after her arrival in England. The other two, both novels, would not be published until after their author's death.

The Story of an African Farm juxtaposes the lives of two orphaned cousins. Em, a traditional young woman, desires only a husband and motherhood to make her happiness complete; Lyndall, a strongheaded and outspoken embodiment of the "New Woman," refuses to marry despite becoming pregnant by her lover. Although she and her child ultimately die, Lyndall and her hopes for the future remain undefeated: "in the future . . . perhaps," she says, "perhaps, to be born a woman will not to be born branded." It would be the character of Lyndall that would make *African Farm* so controversial once its author was found to be a female.

After *The Story of an African Farm,* Schreiner continued to pursue a writing career, putting her energies into nonfiction dealing with a variety of social concerns. In *Women and Labour* she used scientific observation to argue that gender roles are "neither universal nor innate." Rather, she believed, future eras would find men and women living side by side as "comrades and co-workers." In her *Olive Schreiner: Her Friends and Times,* D. L. Hobman called *Women and Labour* "one of the noblest books which have ever appeared in defense of feminism."

Schreiner published several other novels, including 1926's *From Man to Man; or Perhaps Only. . . .* and *Undine,* released two years later. Although containing feminist themes similar to *African Farm* and finding critical favor for their depiction of the exotic African landscape, these later novels were deemed, on the whole, inferior to Schreiner's first published work of fiction.

Travelling in literary circles that included such forward-thinking left-wing intellectuals as Havelock Ellis, Eleanor Marx, and Edward Carpenter, Schreiner combined her writing with work on behalf of women's suffrage. In 1889 she returned to South Africa, marrying Samuel C. Cronwright in 1894 but retaining her maiden name. In 1914 she returned to England, where she would stay remain until just prior to the time of her death six years later. Both acclaimed and condemned by her contemporaries for her strongly held views, Schreiner was buried at

Buffels Kop in the Karoo, next to her infant daughter, husband, and dog.

BIOGRAPHICAL/CRITICAL SOURCES:

BOOKS

Berkman, A., *The Healing Imagination of Olive Schreiner,* University of Massachusetts Press (Amherst), 1989.

Buchanan-Gould, Vera, *Not without Honor: The Life and Writings of Olive Schreiner,* Hutchinson (New York City), 1948.

Colby, Vineta, *The Singular Anomaly: Women Novelists of the Nineteenth Century,* New York University Press (New York City), 1970.

Cronwright-Schreiner, Samuel C., *The Life of Olive Schreiner,* Unwin, 1924.

Dictionary of Literary Biography, Volume 18: *Victorian Novelists after 1885,* Gale (Detroit), 1983, pp. 270-77.

First, Ruth, and Ann Scott, *Olive Schreiner: A Biography,* Deutsch (London), 1980.

Friedmann, Marianne V., *Olive Schreiner: A Study in Latent Meanings,* Witwatersrand University Press (Johannesburg), 1955.

Hobman, D. L., *Olive Schreiner: Her Friends and Times,* Watts, 1955.

Horton, Susan R., *Difficult Women, Artful Lives: Olive Schreiner and Isak Dinesen, in and out of Africa,* Johns Hopkins University Press (Baltimore), 1995.

Monsman, Gerald, *Olive Schreiner's Fiction: Landscape and Power,* Rutgers University Press (New Brunswick, NJ), 1991.

Schreiner, Olive, writing as Ralph Iron, *The Story of an African Farm,* Chapman & Hall (London), 1883, Roberts Bros. (Boston), 1888.

Verster, Evelyn, *Olive Emilie Albertina Schreiner, 1855-1920,* University of Cape Town Libraries (Cape Town), 1946.

PERIODICALS

Dalhousie Review, July, 1929, pp. 168-80.
Massachusetts Review, autumn, 1975, pp. 647-64.
Minnesota Review, spring, 1979, pp. 58-66.
New Republic, March 18, 1925, p. 103.
New Yorker, January 27, 1992, p. 69.

OBITUARIES:

New York Times, December 13, 1920, p. 15.*

SCHUBERT, Frank N. 1943-

PERSONAL: Born June 3, 1943, in Washington, DC; son of Max and Elizabeth (Redlich) Schubert; married Irene Kettunen, May 29, 1969; children: Max. *Ethnicity:* "American." *Education:* Howard University, B.A., 1965; University of Wyoming, M.A., 1970; University of Toledo, Ph.D., 1973. *Avocational interests:* Brewing beer, collecting stamps, bicycling.

ADDRESSES: Home—8505 Cherry Valley Lane, Alexandria, VA 22309.

CAREER: U.S. Department of Defense, Washington, DC, historian for U.S. Army Center of Military History, 1973-75, Army Corps of Engineers, 1977-90, U.S. Army Center of Military History, 1990-93, and Chairman of the Joint Chiefs of Staff, 1993—. *Military service:* U.S. Army, 1965-68; served in Vietnam; became captain; received Army Commendation Medal.

AWARDS, HONORS: Building Air Bases in the Negev was named an Outstanding Government Book for 1992 by *Library Journal; On the Trail of the Buffalo Soldier* was named an Outstanding Reference Book of 1995 by *Choice; The Whirlwind War* was selected an Outstanding Government Book for 1995, *Library Journal.*

WRITINGS:

Soldiers of the American Revolution: A Sketchbook, U.S. Government Printing Office (Washington, DC), 1976.

(Editor) *March to South Pass: Lieutenant William B. Franklin's Journal of the Kearny Expedition of 1845,* U.S. Government Printing Office, 1979.

Vanguard of Expansion: Army Engineers in the Trans-Mississippi West, 1819-1879, U.S. Government Printing Office, 1980.

(Editor) *Explorer on the Northern Plains: Lieutenant Governor K. Warren's Preliminary Report of Explorations in Nebraska and Dakota in the Years 1855-'56-'57,* U.S. Government Printing Office, 1981.

(Editor) *The Nation Builders: A Sesquicentennial History of the Corps of Topographical Engineers, 1838-1863,* U.S. Government Printing Office, 1988.

Building Air Bases in the Negev: The U.S. Army Corps of Engineers in Israel, 1979-1982, U.S.

Army Center of Military History and U.S. Army Corps of Engineers (Washington, DC), 1992.

Buffalo Soldiers, Braves, and the Brass: The Story of Fort Robinson, Nebraska, White Mane Publishing (Columbia, MD), 1993, published as *Outpost of the Sioux Wars,* University of Nebraska Press (Lincoln, NE), 1995.

Mobilization: The U.S. Army in World War II, U.S. Army Center of Military History, 1995.

(Compiler) *On the Trail of the Buffalo Soldier: Biographies of African-Americans in the U.S. Army, 1866-1917,* Scholarly Resources (Wilmington, DE), 1995.

(Editor with Theresa L. Kraus) *The Whirlwind War: The United States Army in Operations Desert Shield and Desert Storm,* U.S. Army Center of Military History, 1995.

Black Valor: Buffalo Soldiers and the Medal of Honor, 1866-1917, Scholarly Resources, 1997.

Contributor to books, including *Exploration and Mapping of the American West: Selected Essays,* edited by Donna P. Koepp, Speculum Orbis Press (Chicago, IL), 1986; and *Soldiers and Civilians: The U.S. Army and the American People,* edited by Garry D. Ryan and Timothy K. Nenninger, National Archives and Records Administration (Washington, DC), 1987. Contributor of articles and reviews to periodicals, including *Engineer Update, National Pastime: A Review of Baseball History, Nine: Journal of Baseball History and Social Policy Perspective, Journal of Construction Engineering and Management, American Philatelist, Old Maps of the Southwest,* and *Military Engineer.*

WORK IN PROGRESS: Research on the history of baseball spring training.

SIDELIGHTS: Frank N. Schubert told *CA:* "By day, I am a public historian, conducting research and managing programs in areas deemed important by my employer. When I can, I also work on subjects of my own choosing, mostly buffalo soldiers and, more recently, baseball history. Both kinds of historical work—client-oriented and personally driven—have their satisfactions."

*   *   *

SCHUELER, G(eorge) F(rederick) 1944-

PERSONAL: Born August 9, 1944, in Columbus, OH; son of George and Edith (Pursley) Schueler;

married Karen R. Spitler, June 16, 1966; children: Gregory W., Jason W. *Education:* Stanford University, A.B. (with honors), 1966; University of California, Berkeley, M.A., 1968, Ph.D., 1973.

ADDRESSES: Home—3504 Delamar N.E., Albuquerque, NM 87107. *Office*—Department of Philosophy, University of New Mexico, Albuquerque, NM 87131. *E-mail*—schueler@unm.edu.

CAREER: University of New Mexico, Albuquerque, assistant professor, 1971-79, associate professor, 1979-90, professor of philosophy, 1990—, department head, 1996—. Spent sabbatical year at Oxford University, 1977-78, 1984-85, 1991-92.

MEMBER: American Philosophical Association.

AWARDS, HONORS: Grants from Council for Philosophical Studies, for Williams College, 1977, American Philosophical Association, Williams College, 1981, and National Endowment for the Humanities, University of California, Santa Cruz, 1990.

WRITINGS:

(Assistant editor) *Guidebook to Publishing in Philosophy,* 2nd edition, American Philosophical Association, 1986.

The Idea of a Reason for Acting, Edwin Mellen Press (Lewiston, NY), 1989.

Desire: Its Role in Practical Reason and the Explanation of Action, MIT Press (Cambridge, MA), 1995.

Contributor to books, including *Professional Responsibility in the Law,* edited by S. Gorovitz and B. Miller, Council for Philosophical Studies, 1977. Contributor of articles and reviews to philosophy journals, including *Teaching Philosophy, Medical Ethics for the Physician, Personalist, Journal of Critical Analysis, Ethics,* and *Mind.*

*   *   *

SCHWARTZ, Cheryl (A.) 1965-

PERSONAL: Born September 14, 1965, in Denver, CO; daughter of Gerald (self-employed) and Verna (a schoolteacher; maiden name, Lind) Schwartz. *Ethnicity:* "Caucasian." *Education:* Metropolitan State College, Denver, CO, B.A. *Politics:* Democrat.

Religion: Jewish. *Avocational interests:* Hiking, biking, photography, movies.

ADDRESSES: Home and office—P.O. Box 300231, Denver, CO 80203.

CAREER: GLBCSCC, Denver, CO, director of youth services, 1987-94, executive director, 1994-95; Catalyst Retreats, Denver, owner. Consultant on lesbian, gay, and bisexual youth issues and on human service programming.

WRITINGS:

The Journey Out, Puffin Books (New York, NY), 1995.

SIDELIGHTS: Cheryl Schwartz told *CA:* "My primary motivation for writing is to educate, enlighten, and support the reader. The lesbian, gay, and bisexual youth I have worked with greatly influenced my work. If not for them, I would not have had the information, motivation, and courage to write *The Journey Out.* It was my own experience as a lesbian, however, that inspired me to write the book. I believe that we grow, personally and professionally, through adversity. It took me a long time to be okay with myself and feel comfortable enough to share my experiences with others."

*   *   *

SEARS, Barry   1947-

PERSONAL: Born June 6, 1947, in Long Beach, CA; father's name, Dale Sears (in business); married Lynn Magnuson (a newspaper editor), 1969; children: Kristin, Kelly. *Education:* Occidental College, A.B., 1968; Indiana University, Ph.D., 1971.

ADDRESSES: Office—Marblehead, MA. *Agent*—c/o Regan Books, HarperCollins, 1000 Keystone Park, Scranton, PA 18512.

CAREER: Boston University School of Medicine, instructor, 1975-78; Arthur D. Little Inc., consultant in biochemistry, 1978; Massachusetts Institute of Technology, staff member in molecular biophysics, beginning in 1978; owner of a biotech company. That's Entertainment (a youth theater company), co-manager with wife Lynn Sears.

MEMBER: Biophysics Society.

WRITINGS:

(With Bill Lawren) *The Zone: A Dietary Road Map,* Regan Books (New York), 1995.

WORK IN PROGRESS: A cookbook based on the diet plan outlined in *The Zone: A Dietary Road Map.*

SIDELIGHTS: A biochemist whose area of specialization had been research into the application of nuclear magnetic resonance to the field of biochemistry, Barry Sears set himself on the road to becoming the author of a controversial diet plan when his father died of heart disease at the age of fifty-three. Following his own hospitalization for arrhythmia in 1984, "It became very easy for me," Sears told *People Weekly* interviewers Alex Tresniowski and Stephen Sawicki, "to turn my research interest toward understanding the role of fat in heart disease." That research yielded *The Zone: A Dietary Road Map,* which details Sears's theory that the current regimen for healthy eating—low in fat, high in carbohydrates—actually builds fat by increasing the body's levels of insulin. While not everyone is convinced that the traditional food pyramid should be discarded, *The Zone* has proven immensely popular, particularly among professional athletes and celebrities.

Sears's "zone" diet, which recommends a daily intake of 40 percent carbohydrates, 30 percent fat, and 30 percent protein, is an attempt to modulate the hormones that control the body's metabolic rate, and thereby control the production and utilization of fat. *The Zone* includes charts and formulas with which the reader may calculate his or her own individual requirements for protein, certain carbohydrates, and mono-unsaturated fats. This diet, as noted by the reviewer for *Publishers Weekly,* may benefit those who are "insulin resistant" and for whom the traditional United States Department of Agriculture (USDA) food pyramid is unhealthy. "It looks scientific, but it wouldn't pass muster within the discipline of clinical nutrition," complained C. Wayne Callaway, an endocrinologist who contributed to the formulation of the USDA dietary guidelines, to *People Weekly*'s Tresniowski and Sawicki. The *People Weekly* interviewers, however, cite others who enthusiastically support the "zone" system, including Jenny Thompson, winner of a gold medal for swimming in the 1992 Olympics and a "Zoner."

The Zone is a controversial eating plan that promises increased energy, improved health, and weight loss through a diet that emphasizes protein over carbohydrates. It is also, according to Helene Siegel in the *Los Angeles Times Book Review,* a symptom of a certain amount of diet-book burnout among the American public. Publishers have decided that people will buy "diet books wrapped in healthy lifestyle packages," Siegel continued. The resulting complexity of the eating regimen outlined in Sears's *The Zone* is thus merely a means of marketing the book for some, while for others it lends substance to an approach some swear by. "I never had the progress with my clients that I've had since they've started doing the Zone," enthused celebrity fitness trainer and consultant Teresa Olsen in the *People Weekly* article. "They're less hungry, less fatigued and more productive." And Sears, who was as surprised as his publisher when *The Zone* went through thirty-two printings in its first year, humbly told Tresniowski and Sawicki, "I'm gratified that I get one call after another from people who say, 'You've changed my life.'"

BIOGRAPHICAL/CRITICAL SOURCES:

PERIODICALS

Los Angeles Times Book Review, September 10, 1995, p. 4.
People Weekly, June 17, 1996, pp. 171-72, 174.
Publishers Weekly, May 1, 1995, p. 54.*

*   *   *

SEDGWICK, Fred 1945-

PERSONAL: Born January 20, 1945, in Dublin, Ireland; married Dawn Anne Toft, 1980; children: one son. *Education:* St. Luke's College, Certificate in Education, 1968; Open University, B.A., 1974; University of East Anglia, M.A., 1984.

ADDRESSES: Home—52 Melbourne Rd., Ipswich, Suffolk IP4 5PP, England.

CAREER: Teacher in Stevenage and Berkhamsted, Hertfordshire; Swing Gate First School, Berkhamsted, head teacher, 1975-81; Bramford Primary School, Ipswich, head teacher, 1981-84; Downing Primary School, Ipswich, head teacher, 1984-90. Open University, tutor, 1986-87; In-service education lecturer for local authorities and other organizations; freelance lecturer and writer.

WRITINGS:

POETRY

Really in the Dark, Priapus (Berkhamsted, Hertfordshire), 1976.
The Garden, Dodman (Hitchin, Hertfordshire), 1977.
(With John Cotton and Freda Downie) *A Berkhamsted Three,* Priapus, 1978.
Details, Mid-Day (Oxford), 1980.
From Another Part of the Island, Priapus, 1981.
A Garland for William Cowper, Priapus, 1984.
The Living Daylights, Headland (West Kirby, Wirral), 1986.
Falernian, Priapus, 1987.
(With John Cotton) *Hey!* (for children), Mary Glasgow (London), 1990; published with *The Biggest Riddle in the World,* as *Two by Two,* 1990.
Lies, Headland (Merseyside), 1991.
Pizza, Curry, Fish and Chips (for children), Longman (London), 1994.
Fifty, James Daniel Daniel John Press (Ipswich), 1995.

OTHER

Here Comes the Assembly Man: A Year in the Life of a Primary School, Falmer (Basingstoke, Hampshire), 1989.
(Editor) *This Way That Way: A Collection of Poems for Schools,* McDougal Littel (New York), 1989.
Lighting Up Time: On Children's Writing, Triad (Stowmarket, Suffolk), 1990.
The Expressive Arts, David Fulton (London), 1993.
(With Dawn Sedgwick) *Drawing to Learn,* Hodder and Stoughton (London), 1993.
Personal, Social, and Moral Education, David Fulton (London), 1994.
(Editor) *Collins Primary Poetry,* HarperCollins (London), 1994.
(With Dawn Sedgwick) *Art across the Curriculum,* Hodder and Stoughton (London), 1995.

Contributor of articles on education and other subjects to periodicals, including *Guardian, Times Educational Supplement, Art and Craft, Curriculum,* and *Cambridge Journal of Education.*

SELLERBERG, Ann-Mari 1943-

PERSONAL: Born December 21, 1943, in Karlskrona, Sweden; daughter of Yngve and Signhild (a teacher) Sellerberg; married Rune Persson, November 11, 1969; children: Fabian, Stina, Tove, Felix, Samuel.

ADDRESSES: Home—Moellevangsvagan 7, S-22240 Lund, Sweden. *Office*—Department of Sociology, University of Lund, Box 114, S-22100 Lund, Sweden.

CAREER: University of Lund, Lund, Sweden, professor of sociology.

MEMBER: International Association of Research in Economic Psychology, Swedish Sociological Association.

WRITINGS:

Women in the Swedish Labour Market in the Twentieth Century, C. W. K. Gleerup, 1973.
Konsumtionenes Sociology (title means "Sociology of Consumption"), Esselte. Scand. Univ. Books, 1977.
Avstaand och Attraktion: Om modets vaexlingar (title means "Distance and Attraction: On the Changes of Fashion"), Carlsson (Stockholm, Sweden), 1987.
A Blend of Contradictions: Georg Simmel in Theory and Practice, Transaction Books (New Brunswick, NJ), 1993.

* * *

SELSAM, Millicent Ellis 1912-1996

OBITUARY NOTICE—See index for *CA* sketch: Born May 30, 1912, in Brooklyn, NY; died October 12, 1996, in New York, NY. Author and teacher. With more than 130 titles to her name, Selsam helped many children and teenagers understand how the physical world works. Born and raised in New York City, Selsam developed an interest in nature and science from school field trips. A graduate of Brooklyn College, she earned her master's degree from Columbia University and became a science teacher in New York City public schools. Her first book, *Egg to Chick,* was published in 1946. Though mostly known as a children's science book writer, Selsam also published some learning books for teenagers and adults.

She started the *I Can Read Books* series for Harper and in 1977 co-edited the *First Look* series of childrens' science books. Her other publications include *Microbes at Work, Plants that Heal, The Language of Animals, The Apple and Other Fruits, Animals of the Sea, Sea Monsters of Long Ago, Tyrannosaurus Rex,* and *Night Animals.* Selsam's 1965 book, *Biography of an Atom,* earned her a Thomas A. Edison Award for best juvenile science book.

OBITUARIES AND OTHER SOURCES:

BOOKS

Something about the Author Autobiography Series, Volume 19, Gale (Detroit, MI), 1995.

PERIODICALS

New York Times, October 15, 1996, p. B10.
Washington Post, October 19, 1996, p. D6.

* * *

SENIOR, Olive (Marjorie) 1941-

PERSONAL: Born December 23, 1941, in Jamaica. *Education:* Carleton University, B.S., 1967.

ADDRESSES: Agent—Nicole Aragi, Watkins/Loomis Agency, 133 East 35th St., Ste. 1, New York, NY 10016.

CAREER: Daily Gleaner newspaper, Jamaica, reporter and sub-editor; Jamaica Information Service, information officer, 1967-69; Jamaica Chamber of Commerce, public relations officer, 1969-71; *JCC Journal,* editor, 1969-71; Institute of Social and Economic Research, University of the West Indies, Jamaica, publications editor, 1972-77; *Social and Economic Studies,* editor, 1972-77; freelance writer and researcher, part-time teacher in communications, publishing consultant, and speech writer, Jamaica, 1977-82; Institute of Jamaica Publications, managing editor, 1982-89; *Jamaica Journal,* editor, 1982-89; freelance teacher, writer, lecturer, internationally, 1989-94; University of the West Indies, Cave Hill, Barbados, visiting lecturer/writer-in-residence, 1990; Caribbean Writers Summer Institute, University of Miami, Florida, director of fiction workshop, 1994, 1995; St. Lawrence University, Canton, NY, Dana Visiting Professor of creative writing, 1994-95.

AWARDS, HONORS: Commonwealth Writers' prize, 1967; Gold, Silver, and Bronze medals for poetry and fiction, Jamaica Festival Literary Competitions, 1968-70; Winner in two categories, Longman International Year of the Child Short Story Competition, 1978; Institute of Jamaica Centenary medal for creative writing, 1979; UNESCO award for study in the Philippines, 1987; Jamaica Press Association award for editorial excellence, 1987; United States Information Service, International Visitor award, 1988; Institute of Jamaica, Silver Musgrave medal for literature, 1989; F.G. Bressani Literary prize for poetry, 1994, for *Gardening in the Tropics*. Hawthornden fellow, Scotland, 1990; International Writer-in-Residence, Arts Council of England, 1991.

WRITINGS:

POETRY

Talking of Trees, Calabash (Kingston, Jamaica), 1986.
Gardening in the Tropics, McClelland and Stewart (Toronto), 1994.

SHORT STORIES

Summer Lightning, Longman (London), 1987.
Arrival of the Snake-Woman, Longman, 1989.
(With others) *Quartet,* Longman, 1994.
Discerner of Hearts, McClelland and Stewart, 1995.

OTHER

The Message Is Change, Kingston Publishers (Kingston), 1972.
Pop Story Gi Mi (four booklets on Jamaican heritage for schools), Ministry of Education (Kingston), 1973.
A-Z of Jamaican Heritage, Heinemann and Gleaner Company Ltd. (Kingston), 1984.
Working Miracles: Women's Lives in the English-Speaking Caribbean, Indiana University Press (Bloomington), 1991.

*   *   *

SEPAMLA, (Sydney) Sipho 1932-

PERSONAL: Born in 1932, in Johannesburg, South Africa.

ADDRESSES: Office—c/o Fuba Academy, P.O. Box 4202, Johannesburg 2000, South Africa.

CAREER: Writer. Teacher in secondary school; personnel officer for company in East Rand; editor, *New Classic* and *S'ketsh!* magazines.

WRITINGS:

POETRY

Hurry Up to It!, Donker (Johannesburg), 1975.
The Blues Is You in Me, Donker, 1976.
The Soweto I Love, Three Continents Press (Washington, DC), 1977.
Children of the Earth, Donker, 1983.
Selected Poems, edited by Mbulelo Vizikhungo Mzamane, Donker, 1984.
From Gore to Soweto, Skotaville Publishers (Johannesburg), 1988.

NOVELS

The Root Is One, Rex Collings (London), 1979.
A Ride on the Whirlwind, Donker, 1981, Heinemann (London), 1984.
Third Generation, Skotaville, 1986.
Scattered Survival, Skotaville, 1988.

*   *   *

SHAH, (Sayed) Idries 1924-1996

OBITUARY NOTICE—See index for *CA* sketch: Born June 16, 1924, in Simla, India; died November 23, 1996, in London, England. Author and leader of Sufi community. Shah was the author of more than 30 books, most of which focused on the Islamic mysticism known as Sufi. Shah traced his descent from the Prophet Mohammed and the Emperors of Persia. His father was leader of the Sufis, his mother was Scottish, and Shah assumed the Sufi leadership role upon his father's death in 1969. His writings, such as *The Sufis* (1964), *Special Problems in the Study of Sufi Ideas* (1968), *Neglected Aspects of Sufi Study* (1977), and *The Commanding Self* (1994), were meant to educate the world on Sufism and dispel Western myths about the practice. Shah studied at Oxford and moved to England in the 1950s but traveled extensively. He served as the director of studies for the Institute for Cultural Research in London from 1966 until his death. Shah was awarded six first prizes from the United Nations Educational, Scientific, and Cultural Organization (UNESCO) International Book of the Year competition in 1972 and a Gold Medal from the Cambridge University poetry festival in 1973.

OBITUARIES AND OTHER SOURCES:

BOOKS

International Authors and Writers Who's Who, 13th edition, International Biographical Centre, 1993.
Writers Directory: 1996-1998, St. James Press, 1995.

PERIODICALS

New York Times, December 2, 1996, p. B12.

           *   *   *

SHAKERI, Khosrow   1938-
   (Cosroe Chaqueri)

PERSONAL: Born October 28, 1938, in Tehran, Iran; son of Mostafa (in business) and Zina (a homemaker; maiden name, Djamshidi) Shakeri. *Education:* San Francisco State College (now University), B.A., 1961; Indiana University—Bloomington, M.A., 1964; Sorbonne Nouvelle, University of Paris III, Ph.D., 1980. *Politics:* "Human rights activist." *Avocational interests:* Music (classical).

ADDRESSES: Home—40 Grande Rue, 92310 Sevres, France; fax 011-331-453-48860. *Office*—Center for Middle Eastern Studies, Coolidge Hall, Harvard University, 1737 Cambridge St., Cambridge, MA 02138; fax 617-496-8584. *E-mail*—ks172@aol.com.

CAREER: Mazdak Publications, Florence, Italy, general editor, 1969-78; Tehran University, Tehran, Iran, assistant professor of economics, 1979-80; Ecole des Hautes Etudes en Sciences Sociales, Paris, France, lecturer and associate professor of history, 1982-85; Woodrow Wilson International Center for Scholars, Washington, DC, resident scholar at Kennan Institute for Advanced Russian Studies, 1986; University of California, Los Angeles, visiting scholar at Center for Near Eastern Studies, 1986, visiting associate professor of history, 1987; Woodrow Wilson International Center for Scholars, research scholar at Kennan Institute for Advanced Russian Studies, 1987-88; Harvard University, Cam-

bridge, MA, visiting scholar and research fellow at Center for Middle Eastern Studies, 1988-91; University of Chicago, Chicago, IL, visiting scholar at Center for Middle Eastern Studies, 1991; DePaul University, Chicago, visiting associate professor of history, 1991-92; Harvard University, senior research fellow at Center for Middle Eastern Studies, 1992-94; Columbia University, New York City, assistant editor at Center for Iranian Studies, 1994-96; Harvard University, senior research fellow at Center for Middle Eastern Studies, 1996—. University of Paris III, Sorbonne Nouvelle, lecturer in modern Iranian history, 1977-80. National Union of Iranian Students, national secretary for international affairs, 1965, and for publications, 1968.

AWARDS, HONORS: Grant from U.S. Institute of Peace, 1991-93.

WRITINGS:

Historical Documents: The Workers', Social Democracy, and Communist Movement in Iran (in Persian), twenty-three volumes, Mazdak Publications (Florence, Italy), 1969—.
Beginning Politics: The Reproductive Cycle of Iranian Children's Tales and Games, a Historical Inquiry, Edwin Mellen (Lewiston, NY), 1992, revised edition, 1996.
(Under name Cosroe Chaqueri) *The Soviet Socialist Republic of Iran, 1920-1921: Birth of the Trauma,* University of Pittsburgh Press (Pittsburgh, PA), 1995.
Social-Democracy in the Iranian Constitutional Revolution, 1905-1911: Backdrop and Origins of the Iranian Left, Bibliotheca Persica, Columbia University (New York City), 1997.
The Armenians of Iran: The Paradoxical Role of a Minority in a Dominant Culture, Harvard University Press (Cambridge, MA), 1997.

Editor, translator, and contributor to *Documentary History of the Workers', Social Democratic, and Communist Movement in Iran,* a ten-volume work published variously in English, French, and German, 1975-91. Assistant editor, *Encyclopaedia Iranica.* Contributor of articles and reviews to periodicals, including *Central Asian Survey, Armenian Review,* and *Iranian Studies.* Editor, *Nameh-ye Parsi,* 1968, and *Ketab-e Jom'eh,* 1979-80; general editor, *Ketab-e Jom'ehha,* 1984-87.

WORK IN PROGRESS: Refiguring Islam: The Rise and Decline of the Neo-Islamic Regime in Iran, 1879-

1997; Victims of Faith: Iranian Communists and the Soviet Union, 1917-1940; A Documentary History of the Left in the Near East, 1908-1958, three volumes; *Rights and Wrongs: Iranian Religious Minorities in the Islamic Republic of Iran (The Zoroastrians, Armenians, Nestorian Christians, Jews, Baha'is, and Sabeaens); What Did the Rose Do to the Cypress?* the Persian, English, and French texts of an ancient tale, with an analytic introduction on the behavior of men and women in Iranian society; *Women as Role-Models in Persian History; Persian Proverbs and Their Social Meaning.*

SIDELIGHTS: Khosrow Shakeri told *CA:* "By the time one gets to my age, it is difficult to determine why one writes, for it has become a habit. Yet, one should be able to state that one writes because one needs to express oneself, not only for self-clarification, but also to be exposed to the criticism of one's colleagues or to pass one's knowledge to readers in general who might have an interest in what one writes.

"It is difficult to determine who in particular might have influenced me. English historians such as E. H. Carr and E. G. Browne, as well as French authors such as Joseph de Gobineau, Maxime Rodinson, and Francois Furet, or the Hungarian thinker Georgi Lukacs must have influenced me in my historical writings. If I am gradually turning to cultural history with a view of eventually writing historical novels, I am indebted to those writers who have blended their historical visions, sense of society, and writing techniques to produce epoch-making tales for humanity. Some of those who have certainly left their impact on me are Victor Hugo, Ernest Hamingway, Persia's Nezami-Ganjavi, and Colombia's Garcia Marquez.

"My writing process is very complicated. Once I am attracted, by accident or research, to a subject, which is usually an issue or a person forgotten or ignored in history or by historians, I work on it for years. I write about it, do further research on it, and rewrite it until I think I have grasped the problem and can present it to readers. Nothing I have written over the years has been published before a long period of intellectual fermentation.

"My primary inspiration to write what I have written thus far has been the comprehension of issues others have neglected and the reasons why they have neglected them."

SHEININ, David (M. K.) 1960-

PERSONAL: Born January 26, 1960, in Toronto, Ontario, Canada; son of Joseph (a civil engineer) and Rose (a biochemist) Sheinin; married Lucia Bohorquez, July 6, 1986; children: Daniela, Gabriela. *Ethnicity:* "Jewish." *Education:* University of Connecticut, Ph.D., 1989.

ADDRESSES: Office—Department of History, Trent University, Peterborough, Ontario, Canada K9J 7B8.

CAREER: Trent University, associate professor of history and comparative development studies and faculty member at Frost Centre for Canadian Heritage and Development. University of Idaho, associate of Martin Institute for Peace Studies and Conflict Resolution; University of London, research fellow, Institute of Latin American Studies, 1990-91.

MEMBER: Latin American Jewish Studies Association (member of board of trustees, 1992-95).

AWARDS, HONORS: Grants from Social Sciences and Humanities Research Council of Canada, 1989—; fellow, Herbert Hoover Presidential Library, 1990; grant from Nettie Lee Benson Latin American Collection, University of Texas, 1992; Harold Eugene Davis Prize, best article, Middle Atlantic Council of Latin American Studies, 1992; J. Franklin Jameson fellow in American History, American Historical Association and Library of Congress, 1992-93.

WRITINGS:

The Organization of American States: An Annotated Bibliography, Transaction Books (New Brunswick, NJ), 1995.
(Editor with Lois Baer Barr, and contributor) *The Jewish Diaspora in Latin America,* Garland Publishing (New York), 1996.
(Editor with Carlos A. Mayo, and contributor) *"Es Igual Pero Distinto": Essays in the Histories of Canada and Argentina,* Trent University (Peterborough, Ontario), 1996.

Contributor to books, including *Discovering the Women in Slavery,* edited by Patricia Morton, University of Georgia Press (Athens, GA), 1996. Contributor of articles and reviews to periodicals, including *Latin American Essays, Canadian Journal of History, International Journal, Hispanic Journal,* and *Critical Sociology.* Review editor, *Canadian Journal of Latin American and Caribbean Studies,* 1993, 1996.

WORK IN PROGRESS: *The Search for Authority: United States-Argentine Relations, 1910-30;* research on the Pan American Union and United States-South American relations, 1900-1940.

*   *   *

SHERBLOM, Liz 1942-

PERSONAL: Full name, Elizabeth C. Sherblom; born June 16, 1942, in Greenfield, MA; daughter of Daniel (in sales) and Jean (a homemaker; maiden name, Barton) Cotton; married John Sherblom (a professor of communication and journalism), June 6, 1985; children: Bill Gause, John Gause, Rick Gause. *Ethnicity:* "WASP." *Education:* Smith College, B.A., 1964; University of Maine at Orono, M.B.A., 1984.

ADDRESSES: *Home*—P.O. Box 329, Stillwater, ME 04489.

CAREER: Social Science Research Institute, Orono, ME, research survey worker, 1983; Northeast Research, Orono, project manager, 1983-84; Eastern Maine Vocational Technical Institute, Bangor, acting dean of students, 1984; University of Maine at Orono, business manager at York Complex, 1985; Market Decisions, Inc., South Portland, ME, director of consumer research, 1985-87; Eastern Maine Development Corp./Penobscot Valley Council of Governments, Bangor, data center manager, 1987-91; artist, 1991—. Town of Winterport, ME, selectman and member of Penobscot Valley Regional Planning Commission Task Force on Solid Waste Management, 1980-84. Natural Resources Council of Maine, director at large and chairperson of Lobbying Network, 1982-83.

WRITINGS:

(Editor with husband John Sherblom) *Much More Than Sexuality: Seventy Gay People Talk about Their Lives,* Audenreed Press (Brunswick, ME), 1996.

SIDELIGHTS: Liz Sherblom told *CA:* "It's hard to say precisely when we were inspired to put our book together. It had probably been building throughout each of our lives from many different experiences. The final catalyst, however, is clear and memorable.

"I was taking part in an envelope-stuffing session at the Eastern Maine AIDS Network back in 1993. A few of us were sitting around the table, chatting about nothing in particular. One of the men, a sophisticated former superintendent of schools in Connecticut, started talking about some of the outrageous things he'd done as a youth growing up in a small town in Maine. Among other things, he and a few friends had a particular teacher in high school they couldn't stand, so they carried her Volkswagen bug up to the third floor of the school building and left it there. The way he described the incident had all of us laughing. He had also worked in the civil rights movement in the south in the 1960s, and he had spent time on the Pine Ridge Reservation in South Dakota during Wounded Knee II.

"Another man had grown up as the son of a mill worker and had lost his mother at a young age. He'd always wanted to be a dancer on Broadway. He had no self-pity in telling his story, but there was indescribable pathos and poignancy in the way he told of his life and experiences.

"Other than being gay and living with AIDS, these two men had almost nothing in common. In ordinary circumstances, you probably would never have met them in the same social context. Listening to these people talk about their everyday lives made me realize again that people are people. Inside ourselves, we all have the same basic feelings. We are all motivated by love and dreams, hope and fear, joy and sorrow. I thought that, if people were given a chance to know a few gay people, if they could really listen to them share their stories and talk about the things that matter most to them, they would be able to look beyond the superficial stereotypes our society imposes and see them for who they are—just plain people living their lives like any of the rest of us.

"My husband John and I started trying to find gay people who were interested in telling their stories. We started with the few people we knew in several locations throughout the northeast, and we asked them to mention our project to others. Seventy people contacted us, and I interviewed each of them. I transcribed the interviews verbatim, and John and I edited them for brevity and narrative coherence. We made every effort to keep peoples' own words and styles of speaking, as well as the overall contexts of their stories. Underlying each story in our book is a complex, multi-faceted human being. Although sexual orientation is clearly an influence, it does not define the whole of any of these peoples' lives.

"*Much More Than Sexuality* was written for people of all ages and sexual orientations. It is written for young people struggling with their own fear of a gay identity, who are looking for positive role models among people similar to themselves, for heterosexual adults and young people who want to understand the real people behind the myths and stereotypes of homosexuality, and for the families, friends, and colleagues of gay people."

*   *   *

SHETTY, Manohar 1953-

PERSONAL: Born 1953, in Bombay, India. *Education:* Attended the University of Bombay.

ADDRESSES: Agent—c/o Oxford University Press, Geoffrey Parker's Country Workshop Ltd., Wimbish Village, Saffron Walden, Essex CB10 2XJ, England.

CAREER: Journalist, 1974—; *Goa Today,* Goa, editor.

WRITINGS:

POETRY

A Guarded Space, Newground (Bombay), 1981.
Borrowed Time, Praxis (Bombay), 1988.
Domestic Creatures: Poems, Oxford University Press (Oxford), 1994.

*   *   *

SHOEMAKER, Bill
  See SHOEMAKER, William

*   *   *

SHOEMAKER, William 1931-
  (Bill Shoemaker)

PERSONAL: Born August 19, 1931, in Texas; son of Ruby Call; married; wife's name, Amanda.

ADDRESSES: Home—2545 Fairfield Pl., San Marino, CA 91108.

CAREER: Professional jockey until 1989; horse trainer in Arcadia, CA, 1990—.

WRITINGS:

UNDER NAME BILL SHOEMAKER

Stalking Horse, Fawcett (New York, NY), 1995.
Fire Horse, Fawcett, 1995.
Dark Horse, Fawcett, 1996.

*   *   *

SHUGHART, William F. (II) 1947-

PERSONAL: Born December 3, 1947, in Harrisburg, PA; son of William F. and Mary L. Shughart; married Hilary C. Kauffman, December 29, 1986; children: William F. III, Frank J. *Education:* Texas A & M University, B.A., 1969, M.S., 1970, Ph.D., 1978. *Politics:* Libertarian. *Religion:* None. *Avocational interests:* Reading.

ADDRESSES: Home—21 County Road 3024, Oxford, MS 38655. *Office*—Department of Economics and Finance, University of Mississippi, University, MS 38677; fax 601-232-5238. *E-mail*—SHUGHART@bus .olemiss.edu.

CAREER: Center for Naval Analyses, systems analyst, 1973-74; University of Arizona, Tucson, visiting lecturer in economics, 1978-79; Federal Trade Commission, Bureau of Economics, Washington, DC, economist, 1979-82, special assistant to the director, 1982-83; Clemson University, Clemson, SC, assistant professor, 1983-84, associate professor of economics, 1984-85; George Mason University, Fairfax, VA, associate professor of economics and research associate at Center for the Study of Public Choice, 1985-88; University of Mississippi, University, professor of economics and finance and holder of Self Free Enterprise Chair, 1988—. Office of the Mississippi State Auditor, member of task force on privatization and chairperson of subcommittee on privatization criteria, 1992; State of Mississippi, member of Job Training Coordinating Council, 1992-94. Independent Institute, research fellow, 1995—; African Research Center for Public Policy and Market Process, member of advisory board, 1995—. *Military service:* U.S. Navy, petty officer, 1971-74.

MEMBER: American Economic Association, Public Choice Society, Southern Economic Association (member of board of trustees, 1996-98), Western Economic Association, Omicron Delta Epsilon, Phi Kappa Phi.

WRITINGS:

The Organization of Industry, Irwin (Homewood, IL), 1990, 2nd edition, Dame Publications (Houston, TX), 1997.

Antitrust Policy and Interest-Group Politics, Quorum Books (New York, NY), 1990.

(With William F. Chappell and Rex L. Cottle) *Modern Managerial Economics: Economic Theory for Business Decisions,* with instructor's manual and study guide, South-Western Publishing (Cincinnati, OH), 1994.

(Editor with Fred S. McChesney, and contributor) *The Causes and Consequences of Antitrust: The Public-Choice Perspective,* University of Chicago Press (Chicago, IL), 1995.

(Editor and contributor) *Taxing Choice: The Predatory Politics of Fiscal Discrimination,* Transaction Publishers (New Brunswick, NJ), in press.

Contributor to books, including *Advances in the Economics of Sport,* Volume I, edited by Gerald W. Scully, JAI Press (Greenwood, CT), 1992; *Disorder and Harmony: Twentieth Century Perspectives on Accounting History,* CGA-Research Foundation (Vancouver), 1996; and *Stree-ike Four! What's Wrong With the Business of Baseball?* edited by Daniel R. Marburger, Greenwood Press (Westport, CT), 1997. Contributor of about eighty articles and reviews to economic journals and newspapers, including *Antitrust Bulletin, American Economic Review, Atlantic Economic Journal, Economic Inquiry, Applied Economics,* and *Journal of Economic Behavior and Organization.* Associate editor, *Southern Economic Journal,* 1996—; book review editor, *Public Choice,* 1991—, and *Managerial and Decision Economics,* 1994—.

WORK IN PROGRESS: New Deal, Old Pork: The Politics and Economics of Federal Emergency Relief Spending During the Great Depression, with Chappell and Jim F. Couch.

* * *

SHUMAKER, Peggy 1952-

PERSONAL: Born March 22, 1952, in La Mesa, CA. *Education:* University of Arizona, B.A., 1974, M.F.A., 1979.

ADDRESSES: Office—P.O. Box 304, Ester, AK 99725.

CAREER: University of Arizona, Tucson, graduate assistant instructor, 1976-79; Arizona Commission on the Arts, writer-in-residence, 1979-85; Arizona State University, faculty associate in creative writing, 1983-85; University of Alaska, Fairbanks, visiting assistant professor in creative writing, 1985-86; Old Dominion University, Norfolk, VA, director of creative writing, 1986-88; University of Alaska, Fairbanks, codirector of creative writing, 1988—, head of department of English, 1991-93, associate professor, 1991-93, professor, 1993—. Managing editor, Epoch Universal Publications, 1980-81; adviser, *Dominion Review,* 1986-88; director, Old Dominion University Literary Festival, 1987-88; featured poet, Writers at Work Conference, Park City, Utah, 1989, Port Townsend Writers Conference, Washington, 1993, Artspeak, Wyoming Arts Council, 1995, and Quartz Mountain Oklahoma Art Institute, 1995; coordinator, Midnight Sun Writers Conference, 1990, and Alaskan Poetry Festival, 1990; Western Literature Presenting Network, member, 1994—; literary judge, WESTAF Western States Book Awards, 1995, and *Nimrod*/Pablo Neruda Prize for Poetry, 1995; coordinator, Midnight Sun Writers Series. Associated Writing Programs, member of board of directors, 1990—, vice president, 1991-92, president, 1992-93, board adviser, 1993-94.

AWARDS, HONORS: National Endowment of the Arts fellowship, 1989.

WRITINGS:

POETRY

Esperanza's Hair, University of Alabama Press (Tuscaloosa), 1985.

The Circle of Totems, University of Pittsburgh Press (Pittsburgh, PA), 1988.

Braided River (chapbook), Limner Press (Anchorage, AK), 1993.

Wings Moist from the Other World, University of Pittsburgh Press, 1994.

* * *

SIMON, Louis M(ortimer) 1906-1996

OBITUARY NOTICE—See index for *CA* sketch: Born October 25, 1906, in Salt Lake City, UT; died October 28, 1996, in Manchester, NH. Theater executive. Simon was best known for his work as public relations director for the Actors Fund of America charity from 1965 to 1982 and for writing a book, 1972's *A History of the Actors Fund of America,* on the subject. Simon worked for German producer Max Reinhardt in the 1920s and subsequently went with him to Hollywood. Simon later managed the Theater Guild in New York City and went on to become New Jersey's director of the Works Progress Administration Federal Theater. He served in the Army Special Services in World War II and worked for the Veteran's Administration after the war; he was in charge of Veterans' Hospital camp shows in New York City. Simon was educated at the University of Pennsylvania, Harvard University and Yale University.

OBITUARIES AND OTHER SOURCES:

PERIODICALS

New York Times, November 11, 1996, p. B9.

* * *

SITTON, Claude (Fox) 1925-

PERSONAL: Born December 4, 1925, in Emory, GA; son of Claude B. (a railroad worker and farmer) and Pauline (a schoolteacher; maiden name, Fox) Sitton; married Eva McLaurin Whetstone, June 5, 1953; children: Lauren Lea Sitton, Clinton, Suzanna Sitton Greene, McLaurin. *Ethnicity:* "Scotch-Irish." *Education:* Emory University, A.B., 1949. *Politics:* Democrat. *Religion:* Presbyterian.

ADDRESSES: Home—P.O. Box 1326, Oxford, GA 30267-1326. *E-mail*—csitton@Mindspring.com.

CAREER/WRITINGS: Journalist. International News Service, reporter, 1949-50; United Press, reporter, 1950-55; United States Information Agency, information officer, 1955-57; *New York Times,* New York City, copy editor, 1957-58, chief Southern correspondent, 1958-64, national news director, 1964-68; associated with *Raleigh Times,* Raleigh, NC, 1968; The News and Observer Publishing Company, Raleigh, editorial director, 1968-90, director, 1969-90, editor and vice-president, 1970-90; Emory University, Atlanta, GA, senior lecturer in history, 1991-94; contributor to the *New York Times Book Review.* Lay member of Georgia State Supreme Court Commission on Evaluation of Disciplinary Enforcement, 1995; board member, Georgia American Civil Liberties Union (ACLU), 1996-97; board of counselors of Oxford College, Emory University. *Military service:* U.S. Navy, 1943-46.

MEMBER: American Society of Newspaper Editors (director, 1977-83), National Conference of Editorial Writers, Pulitzer Prize Board (chair, 1992-93).

AWARDS, HONORS: Pulitzer Prize for commentary, Columbia University School of Journalism, 1983; L.H.D., Emory University, 1984.

SIDELIGHTS: Retired journalist Claude Sitton served as a senior lecturer in history at Georgia's Emory University, but his ties to the institution go back much further. Sitton was born in 1925 at the University's hospital, and earned an Emory degree in 1949. Sitton began his career as a reporter for various news services, and joined the *New York Times* in 1957. The next year, he was made the paper's chief Southern correspondent. As the civil rights movement grew into a fiery, multi-state battle across the South, Sitton often placed himself in dangerous situations. "It was the greatest job in the world," Sitton recalled in a 1990 interview with *Atlanta Journal* contributor Gary Pomerantz. "So many great stories to choose from." It was a dangerous time for outspoken pro-integration whites like himself, but one that had its rewards. When Sitton filed a story that quoted a Georgia sheriff's racist statements at a black voter registration drive, both President John F. Kennedy and his brother, Attorney General Robert Kennedy, took notice in the next morning's *New York Times* and federal agents were dispatched to the county to investigate the obvious hindrance to constitutional rights. In *Parting the Waters: America in the King Years, 1954-63,* a history of the civil rights movement, writer Taylor Branch called that story "perhaps the most remarkable news dispatch of the entire civil rights generation."

From 1964 to 1968, Sitton served as national news director at the *New York Times.* In 1968, he accepted a post at the *Raleigh Times* and at the Raleigh, North Carolina, *News and Observer* as editorial director; he eventually became editor of the *News and Observer* and vice president and director of The News and Observer Publishing Company. He wrote a weekly column for the editorial page whose well-aimed attacks aroused the ire of the state's more conservative elements. One of those was North Carolina's longtime Republican senator Jesse Helms; Sitton also wrote incisive analyses on public education, the Environmental Protection Agency, and civil rights issues. His columns brought him the Pulitzer Prize for commentary in 1983. Sitton later served on the prize foundation's board for nine years and chaired it from 1992 to 1993.

BIOGRAPHICAL/CRITICAL SOURCES:

BOOKS

Branch, Taylor, *Parting the Waters: America in the King Years, 1954-63,* Simon and Schuster (New York City), 1988.

PERIODICALS

Atlanta Journal, December 2, 1990, p. M1.
New York Times, March 29, 1970; April 19, 1983.

*   *   *

SKOCPOL, Theda (Ruth) 1947-

PERSONAL: Surname pronounced "scotch-pole"; born May 4, 1947, in Detroit, MI; daughter of Allan Earnest (a high school teacher) and Jennie Mae (a homemaker and substitute teacher; maiden name, Becker) Barron; married William John Skocpol (a physicist), June 10, 1967; children: Michael Allan. *Education:* Michigan State University, B.A., 1969; Harvard University, M.A., 1972, Ph.D. (with distinction), 1975. *Politics:* Democrat.

ADDRESSES: Office—Department of Sociology, Harvard University, 470 William James, Cambridge, MA 02138; and Department of Government, Harvard University, 233 Littauer, Cambridge, MA 02138.

CAREER: Harvard University, Cambridge, MA, assistant professor, 1975-78, associate professor, 1978-81, professor of sociology, 1986—, professor of government and sociology, 1995—; University of Chicago, Chicago, IL, professor, 1981-84, director of Center for Study of Industrial Studies, 1982-85, professor of sociology and political science, 1984-86; writer. Member of School of Social Science Institute for Advanced Study, Princeton, NJ, 1981; senior visiting scholar at Russell Sage Foundation, 1984-85.

MEMBER: Organization of American Historians, American Political Science Association, American Sociological Association, Social Science History Association, National Academy of Social Insurance, Sociological Research Association.

AWARDS, HONORS: Named National Merit Scholar, 1965-69; fellowships from Woodrow Wilson Foundation, 1969-72, and Danforth Foundation, 1969-74; C. Wright Mills Award from the Society for the Study of Social Problems, 1979, and award from American Sociological Association, 1980, both for *States and Social Revolutions: A Comparative Analysis of France, Russia, and China;* grants from Russell Sage Foundation, 1983-84, and Ford Foundation, 1986-87 and 1990-92; Guggenheim fellowship, 1990; Woodrow Wilson Foundation Award from the American Political Science Association, J. David Greenstone Award from the Politics and History section of the American Political Science Association, Best Book Award from the Political Sociology section of the American Sociological Association, Allan Sharlin Memorial Award from Social Science History Association, and Ralph Waldo Emerson Award from Phi Beta Kapp, all 1993, all for *Protecting Soldiers and Mothers: The Political Origins of Social Policy in the United States.*

WRITINGS:

States and Social Revolutions: A Comparative Analysis of France, Russia, and China, Cambridge University Press (New York), 1979.
Protecting Soldiers and Mothers: The Political Origins of Social Policy in the United States, Belknap Press of Harvard University Press (Cambridge), 1992.
Social Revolutions in the Modern World, Cambridge University Press (New York), 1994.
(With Kenneth Finegold) *State and Party in America's New Deal,* University of Wisconsin Press (Madison), 1995.
Social Policy in the United States: Future Possibilities in Historical Perspective, Princeton University Press (Princeton), 1995.
Boomerang: Clinton's Health Security Effort and the Turn Against Government in U.S. Politics, Norton (New York), 1996.

Contributor to periodicals.

EDITOR

(With Michael Burawoy) *Marxist Inquiries: Studies of Labor, Class, and States,* University of Chicago Press, 1982.

Vision and Method in Historical Sociology, Cambridge University Press (New York), 1984.

(With Peter B. Evans and Dietrich Rueschemeyer) *Bringing the State Back In,* Cambridge University Press (New York), 1985.

(With Margaret Weir and Ann Shola Orloff) *The Politics of Social Policy in the United States,* Princeton University Press, 1988.

With John L. Campbell) *American Society and Politics: Institutional, Historical, and Theoretical Perspectives,* McGraw-Hill (New York), 1995.

(With Rueschemeyer) *States, Social Knowledge, and the Origins of Modern Social Policies,* Princeton University Press, 1996.

WORK IN PROGRESS: The Missing Middle: Working Families and the Future of U.S. Social Policy, under contract to Norton and the Twentieth Century Fund.

SIDELIGHTS: Theda Skocpol, a prominent sociologist and author, is also distinguished as Harvard University's first female tenured professor in sociology. In the late 1970s she showed herself as a formidable authority in her field when she published *States and Social Revolutions: A Comparative Analysis of France, Russia, and China,* which won the American Sociological Association's highest award. *States and Social Revolutions* is an analysis of the French Revolution of 1789, the Russian revolutions of 1905 and 1917, and the Chinese revolution of 1911 to 1949. Countering the conventional Marxist interpretation of revolutions, which stresses the inevitability of class conflict stemming from economic inequality, Skocpol considers the aforementioned revolutions as dramatic struggles over state power involving various political, economic, and social factions that were, in turn, effected by the class conflicts emphasized in Marxist theory. In addition, Skocpol observes, these power struggles can be influenced by social problems and international pressures.

When it appeared in 1979, *States and Social Revolutions* received recognition as an important, and provocative, study. Lewis A. Coser, writing in the *New York Times Book Review,* noted that Skocpol "provides a fine example of what neo-Marxist comparative sociology can contribute to an understanding of the sociology of revolutions," and he concluded that her book "will be considered a landmark in the study of the sources of revolution." Another reviewer, Richard Lowenthal, questioned Skocpol's emphasis of seemingly objective forces, and he argued for greater consideration of human choice. But he conceded, in his *New York Review of Books* assessment, that *States*

and Social Revolutions constituted an "important and original book." *New Republic* reviewer Reinhard Bendix likewise decried what he perceived as the diminished role accorded individuals and ideas in Skocpol's analysis. But Bendix also acknowledged *States and Social Revolutions* as "a major new interpretation of revolution in lieu of the Marxian stereotype." He added that "proper modification of the framework [Skocpol] has used will lend itself to the analysis of other revolutions."

Skocpol's other key study is *Protecting Soldiers and Mothers: The Political Origins of Social Policy in the United States,* a historical analysis of welfare policies in the United States since the Civil War. Here Skocpol notes the role that political forces came to bear on the shaping and establishing of social policies, and she reports on the historical difficulties of implementing such policies in America's decentralized governmental system. She also addresses the key influence of women in the advocacy of welfare programs and social policies, and she argues that the United States, to the extent that it has developed social programs, has managed to develop them without seeming to compromise individuals' rights or the capitalist economy.

Protecting Soldiers and Mothers, like *State and Social Revolutions,* is considered a major work. Rosalind Rosenberg, writing in the *New York Times Book Review,* called *Protecting Soldiers and Mothers* "a monumental study" and added that "it will likely become a classic in the history of the modern welfare state." Paula Baker, meanwhile, wrote in *American Historical Review* that Skocpol's book "is a clear advance over works that find simple patriarchal or business control over social policy, or that see welfare systems as the inevitable outcome of industrialization." Miriam Cohen, in her *Journal of Social History* review, lauded the provocative nature of *Protecting Soldiers and Mothers,* declaring that "Skocpol's important and thought-provoking study will help to focus the discussion for years to come." And *Nation* reviewer Alex Keyssar, while contending that *Protecting Soldiers and Mothers* "falls well short of its objectives," agreed that it is "a sufficiently powerful book that . . . will surely generate a great deal of new research and writing about the history and social provision in the United States." He proclaimed this "no mean achievement."

Since publishing *Protecting Soldiers and Mothers* in 1992, Skocpol has produced such works as *Social Revolutions in the Modern World, Social Policy in the*

United States: Future Possibilities in Historical Perspective, and *Boomerang: Clinton's Health Security Effort and the Turn Against Government in U.S. Politics.* In addition, she has served as co-editor of such volumes as *American Society and Politics: Institutional, Historical, and Theoretical Perspectives* and *States, Social Knowledge, and the Origins of Modern Social Policies.*

Skocpol also received a fair measure of media attention in 1980 when she claimed that her employer, Harvard University, had denied her tenure because she was a woman. The next year, a committee of the university determined that Skocpol was justified in making the charge. In 1985, while Skocpol was teaching at the University of Chicago, Harvard extended the offer of a tenured professorship. Skocpol accepted. "The first few years at Harvard will be delicate," she acknowledged in the *Boston Globe,* "but I am convinced that there will be a collegial relationship." In 1995, Skocpol was jointly appointed Professor of Government at Harvard, where she reports she "is now very happy and fully involved in collegial life." In the ensuing years she published *Protecting Soldiers and Mothers* and thus further established herself as a leader in her field.

Skocpol told *CA:* "I use a historical approach in the social sciences to cast light on social and political dilemmas in the present-day world. My books now are often for broad public audiences, as well as for scholars and students."

BIOGRAPHICAL/CRITICAL SOURCES:

PERIODICALS

American Historical Review, April, 1993, pp. 458-60.
Boston Globe, December 6, 198, p. 52.
Contemporary Sociology, November, 1993, pp. 775-81.
Journal of Social History, winter, 1994, pp. 441-44.
Los Angeles Times Book Review, September 26, 1993, p. 10.
Nation, April 26, 1993, pp. 566-70.
New Republic, January 26, 1980, pp. 36-38; January 4, 1993, pp. 28-35.
New York Review of Books, October 21, 1979, pp. 13, 44-45; February 5, 1981, pp. 43-45; May 26, 1994, pp. 40-43.
New York Times Book Review, January 31, 1993, p. 16.
Society, November/December, 1993, pp. 94-96.

SLADER, John M. 1924-

PERSONAL: Born January 1, 1924, in Spalding, U.K.; son of Rev. Herbert (a Methodist minister) and Gertrude (a housewife; maiden name, Petch) Slader; married Nellie Gwendoline Coombs (a housewife), July 27, 1946. *Education:* Attended Queens College, Taunton, Somerset, U.K., 1934-40. *Politics:* Socialist. *Religion:* Protestant.

*ADDRESSES: Home—*5 Station Rd., Govilon, Abergavenny NP7 9RG, Wales, U.K.

CAREER: Evans & Reid Co. Ltd., Cardiff, Wales, navigating officer of merchant shipping, 1940-48; Vantona Textiles Ltd., London, import/export manager, 1949-70; Vantona International Ltd., London, export director, 1971-76; Compton Webb Ltd., export director, 1977-81. *Military service:* Merchant Navy, Second Mate (served during World War II), 1940-45.

MEMBER: Exmoor Society (English National Park).

WRITINGS:

Dicky Slader: The Exmoor Pedlar Poet, David & Charles (Newton Abbot, England), 1963.
Days of Renown, West Country Publications, 1965.
Downalong the Exe, West Country Handbook, 1966.
The Churches of Devon, David & Charles, 1968.
The Red Duster at War: A History of the Merchant Navy During the Second World War, William Kimber, 1988.
The Fourth Service: Merchantmen at War, 1939-1945, Robert Hale (London, England), 1994.
British Merchant Ship Losses in World War II: Lifeline of the World, Shipping Books Press, (Market Drayton, England), 1997.

Contributor to regional newspapers and magazines, including *Western Mail, Western Morning News, North Devon Journal, Country Fair, Contemporary Review,* and *Exmoor Review.*

WORK IN PROGRESS: The Maritime Poets of the Second World War, an anthology; *Son of the Manse,* 1930s autobiography; *The Unquiet Ocean,* a novel based on the emigration from Western England to Prince Edward Island, Canada, during the 19th Century; researching Kamal Athon Chunchie, a champion Christian minister of London's dockland and its seamen.

SIDELIGHTS: John M. Slader's first writings, which include *Dicky Slader: The Exmoor Pedlar Poet* and *Downalong the Exe,* discuss the history of the western part of England, where the Slader family originated. Later in life, however, the author turned to different subjects. It was Slader's service at sea during World War II that led him to shift his focus from England's history to the history of the world-wide merchant marine, which is covered in both *The Red Duster at War* and *The Fourth Service: Merchantmen at War, 1939-1945.*

Published in 1994, *The Fourth Service* contends that the Allied forces would not have overcome Hitler without the achievements of their combined merchant marines. Using secondary sources as his base, Slader relates his wartime experiences and observations to describe the British Merchant Marine's contribution to the war effort. Bryan Ranft, discussing *The Fourth Service* in the *Times Literary Supplement,* remarked that Slader, who served in the war, "provides a significant example of his generation's reasoning and feelings." Noting the wealth of information about World War II naval operations in Slader's work, Ranft concluded the book "shows present generations how some of their predecessors dealt with some truly appalling experiences."

BIOGRAPHICAL/CRITICAL SOURCES:

PERIODICALS

Times Literary Supplement, August 26, 1994, p. 25.

* * *

SMEDLEY, Agnes   1892-1950

PERSONAL: Born in 1892, in Missouri; died May 6, 1950, in London, England; daughter of Charles and Sarah (Ralls) Smedley; married Ernest Brundin, 1912 (divorced). *Education:* Attended Tempe, AZ, Normal School.

CAREER: Writer and activist. Teacher in rural schools, 1908; worked as a journalist for socialist newspapers, c. 1917; imprisoned for promoting Indian Anticolonialism; imprisoned while campaigning for women's right to birth control with Margaret Sanger; worked as a journalist in China, 1928-41; lectured on China throughout the United States, 1942-49.

WRITINGS:

Daughter of Earth (autobiographical novel), Coward-McCann (New York City), 1929, revised edition, 1935, published with a foreword by Alice Walker, Feminist Press (New York City), 1987.
Chinese Destinies: Sketches of Present-Day China, Vanguard Press (New York City), 1933.
China's Red Army Marches, Vanguard Press, 1934.
China Fights Back: An American Woman with the Eighth Route Army, Vanguard Press, 1938.
Battle Hymn of China, Knopf (New York City), 1943.
The Great Road: The Life and Times of Chu Teh, Monthly Review Press (New York City), 1956.
Portraits of Chinese Women in Revolution, edited by Janice R. MacKinnon and Steven R. MacKinnon, Feminist Press, 1976.

Smedley's manuscripts are housed at the Hayden Library, Arizona State University, Tempe.

Smedley's books have been translated into German, Spanish, and Russian.

ADAPTATIONS: Daughter of Earth was adapted for the stage by Linda Sargent, *Playbook,* 1986.

SIDELIGHTS: From a childhood spent in poverty, Agnes Smedley used her talent as a writer to further the causes of both women and the proletariat. Born in rural Missouri, she spent a short childhood in the impoverished coal-mining area of southern Colorado. Parentless by the age of sixteen, Smedley would work as a teacher in a country school before becoming active in campaigns against injustice and discrimination around the world. Combining her writing with travel throughout the United States and Europe, she would become involved with Indian nationalists against the British, raise her voice alongside birth-control pioneer Margaret Sanger in advancing the rights of women, and publish countless articles in support of socialist revolutionary policies

In 1929 Smedley published her semi-autobiographical *Daughter of Earth.* A portrayal of the struggles of a proletariat woman whose socialist beliefs cause her to fight the barriers within a patriarchal society, the novel was praised for its authentic portrayal of working class life. The year prior to the publication of *Daughter of Earth,* Smedley had travelled to China; she had quickly become actively involved in that country's revolutionary activities. Five books, including 1943's *Battle Hymn of China* and *The Great*

Road: The Life and Times of Chu Teh, would occupy the greater portion of the remainder of her life. *China's Red Army Marches,* published in 1934, follows the Red Army's movement inland in an effort to secure more territory. *The Great Road,* published in 1956, tells the story of the author's friend Chu Teh, a Chinese peasant who rose to become the leader of the Red Army. *Battle Hymn of China,* considered by many critics to be Smedley's best book on revolutionary China, was intended to impress upon the U.S. public the wealth of experience she had gained in Asia; expecting to be treated as an expert on the situation in China upon her return to her native country at the time of the book's publication, Smedley instead found herself a persona non grata. Fast in the grip of McCarthyism, the F.B.I. leveled charges of espionage against the book's author, who left for China but died before reaching Asia. Smedley's books were removed from circulation until renewed academic interest was fostered following the 1976 publication of *Portraits of Chinese Women in Revolution.*

BIOGRAPHICAL/CRITICAL SOURCES:

BOOKS

Feminist Writers, St. James Press (Detroit), 1996.
MacKinnon, Janice R., and Stephen R. MacKinnon, *Agnes Smedley: The Life and Times of an American Radical,* University of California Press (Berkeley), 1988.

PERIODICALS

Nation, February 19, 1949.

OBITUARIES:

PERIODICALS

New Republic, May 29, 1950.
New Statesman and Society, May 20, 1950.
New York Times, May 9, 1950.*

*　　*　　*

SOBEL, Dava   1947-

PERSONAL: Born June 15, 1947, in New York, NY; daughter of Samuel H. (a physician) and Betty (a chemist; maiden name, Gruber) Sobel; married Arthur C. Klein (an author); divorced, December 14, 1995; children: Zoe Rachel, Issac. *Education:* State University of New York at Binghamton, Bx.H.S. of Science, 1969. *Politics:* Democrat. *Religion:* Jewish. *Avocational interests:* Ballroom dancing, amateur astronomy.

ADDRESSES: Home and office—23 Deep Six Dr., East Hampton, NY 11937. *Agent*—Michael Carlisle, William Morris Agency, 1325 Avenue of the Americas, New York, NY 10019-6011.

CAREER: Author. *New York Times,* New York, science reporter, 1979-82; astronomy columnist for *East Hampton Independent* (East Hampton, NY) 1994—, and for The Discovery Channel On-Line, 1996—.

MEMBER: The Planetary Society, National Association of Watch and Clock Collectors, American Association of University Women.

AWARDS, HONORS: American Psychological Foundation National Media Award, 1980; Lowell Thomas Award from Society of American Travel Writers, 1992; gold medal from the Council for the Advancement and Support of Education (CASE), 1994, for an article on longitude published in *Harvard Magazine.*

WRITINGS:

(With Frank D. Drake) *Is Anyone Out There?: The Scientific Search for Extraterrestrial Intelligence,* Delacorte (New York, NY), 1992.
Longitude: The True Story of a Lone Genius Who Solved the Greatest Scientific Problem of His Time, Walker & Co. (New York, NY), 1995.

WITH FORMER HUSBAND, ARTHUR C. KLEIN

Backache Relief: The Ultimate Second Opinion from Back-Pain Sufferers Nationwide Who Share Their Successful Healing Experiences, Times Books (New York, NY), 1985.
Arthritis: What Works, St. Martin's (New York, NY), 1989.
Arthritis: What Exercises Work, St. Martin's, 1993; published with foreward by John Bland as *Arthritis: What Works; Breakthrough Relief for the Rest of Your Life, Even after Drugs and Surgery Have Failed,* St. Martin's, 1995.
Backache: What Exercises Work, St. Martin's, 1994.

Contributor of articles to periodicals, including *Astronomy, Audubon, Discover, Harvard Magazine,*

Ladies Home Journal, Life, New York Times Magazine, New Yorker, New Woman, Omni, Redbook, Vogue, and *Working Woman.*

WORK IN PROGRESS: Galileo's Daughter, a book about seventeenth century science and society.

SIDELIGHTS: Former *New York Times* science reporter Dava Sobel has earned her greatest critical recognition for the book *Longitude: The True Story of a Lone Genius Who Solved the Greatest Scientific Problem of His Time.* Described as an "elegant history" by *New York Times* critic Christopher Lehmann-Haupt, *Longitude* is the story of an eighteenth-century clockmaker's persistence in developing a sea-worthy clock by which sailors might determine longitude, the distance east or west on the earth. Throughout history, without a tool or method of determining their positions, many sailors sailed off-course, which, at best, delayed their deliveries of goods. Tragically, however, thousands of sailors perished at sea, due to their inability to calculate the location of land.

In 1714, Sobel relates, England's parliament addressed the dire problem by promising a reward of 20,000 pounds (the equivalent of millions of dollars by modern standards) to anyone who could solve the problem of determining longitude. Scientists knew that every hour's time difference between a ship and its destination (or port of origin) equalled a change in longitude of fifteen degrees east or west; the solution, therefore, was to create an instrument that would withstand the erratic changes in climate and humidity aboard a ship so that sailors could determine their position by the time.

John Harrison, a self-educated clockmaker, accepted the challenge, devoting some 46 years of his life to the building of weather- and motion-proof clocks. His effort produced the chronometer and earned admiration and a monetary prize from King George III. His work, however, was not without obstacles, and Sobel shares many of those obstacles, along with often amusing stories of solutions offered by others to the longitude problem, in her book, which, according to John Ellsworth, writing in the *New York Times Book Review,* "captures John Harrison's extraordinary character: brilliant, persevering and heroic in the face of adversity. He is a man you won't forget."

Longitude elicited further praise from critics, including Lehmann-Haupt who lauded Sobel's "remarkable ability to tell a story with clarity and perfect pacing."

Touched by Sobel's account of being reduced to tears upon visiting the maritime museum that houses Harrison's clocks, Lehmann-Haupt wrote: "Such is the eloquence of this gem of a book that it makes you understand exactly how she felt." Bruno Maddox expressed similar sentiments in his *Washington Post Book World* review: "*Longitude* is a simple tale, brilliantly told," Maddox wrote. "Perhaps one of the most impressive things about the book—given its subject matter—is the sheer simplicity of the whole thing. . . . She offers us no attack on the modern assumption that time is solid and objective; she wholly refrains from rubbing readers' noses in the artificiality of meaning, etc.; she offers us nothing, in short, but measured, nearly perfect prose and a magnificent story, an extraordinary book." *Longitude* spent sixteen weeks on the *New York Times* bestseller list.

Sobel is also the co-author, with her former husband Arthur C. Klein, of several books on back pain and arthritis, including 1989's *Arthritis: What Works.* Based on the authors' interviews with more than 1000 arthritis sufferers, *Arthritis: What Works* discusses various methods of treatment that patients report have alleviated their pain, from traditional therapy offered by physicians and drugs, to less conventional treatments used by holistic healers. In addition, the authors share recipes and diet plans considered to be helpful in attacking arthritis through nutrition. A companion, of sorts, to *Arthritis: What Works* is *Arthritis: What Exercises Work,* in which Sobel and Klein describe and illustrate exercises that were reported by the arthritis sufferers they interviewed to relieve symptoms of arthritis. The authors issued a similar book, *Backache: What Exercises Work,* after speaking with some 500 sufferers of back injury about activities that eased their pain and hastened their return to normal activity.

BIOGRAPHICAL/CRITICAL SOURCES:

PERIODICALS

Los Angeles Times Book Review, November 22, 1992, p. 6.
New York Times, November 2, 1995, p. C 21.
New York Times Book Review, October 11, 1992, p. 18; November 26, 1995, p. 15.
Publishers Weekly, August 18, 1989, p. 60; September 7, 1992, p. 89; June 27, 1994, p. 74; September 18, 1995, p. 119.
Washington Post Book World, November 26, 1995, p. 2.*

SONG, Cathy 1955-

PERSONAL: Born in 1955, in Honolulu, Oahu, HA; married Douglas Davenport; children: two. *Education:* Wellesley College, B.A., 1977; Boston University, M.F.A., 1981.

ADDRESSES: Home—Honolulu, Hawaii.

CAREER: Poet and educator. Instructor of creative writing at various universities.

AWARDS, HONORS: Yale Younger Poets Award, 1983, for *Picture Bride;* Shelley Memorial Award; Hawaii Award for Literature.

WRITINGS:

POETRY

Picture Bride, Yale University Press (New Haven, CT), 1983.
Frameless Windows, Squares of Light, Norton (New York City), 1988.
School Figures, University of Pittsburgh Press (Pittsburgh), 1994.

OTHER

(Editor, with Juliet Kono) *Sister Stew: Fiction and Poetry by Women,* Bamboo Ridge Press (Honolulu), 1991.

Contributor to periodicals, including *Asian-Pacific Literature, Hawaii Review, Poetry,* and *Seneca Review.*

SIDELIGHTS: Poet Cathy Song draws on not only her rich Korean and Chinese ancestry but her experiences as a woman born and raised an American in verses that have been compared by critics to the muted tints of watercolor paintings. Song has consistently maintained that the rich world she creates within her narrative poetry transcends her own ethnic and regional background, and resists classification as an "Asian American" or "Hawaiian" writer. Her verses have been collected in three volumes—1983's *Picture Bride,* 1988's *Frameless Windows, Squares of Light,* and *School Figures,* published in 1994. *Picture Bride* not only earned Song the 1983 Yale Series of Younger Poets Award, it was also nominated for that year's National Book Critics Circle Award. The success of her first book carried the young poet to national recognition, and other awards followed.

Born in Honolulu and encouraged at her writing even during her childhood, Song left Hawaii to attend college in New England. She received her bachelor's degree at Wellesley College in 1977, and then entered the master's program in creative writing offered by nearby Boston University. After graduating in 1981, Song returned to Honolulu, where she now lives with her husband and children, combining her own writing with teaching creative writing to students at several universities.

Uniting Song's poetic oeuvre is her abiding focus on family. The moral ties that bind women to children and parents, to their community, to tradition, and to the land are continuously interwoven throughout her verse. In the title poem from *Picture Bride,* for example, Song recalls the story of her grandmother: at age twenty-three she had come to the United States from Korea in order to marry a man who knew her only from a photograph. Though her future husband was much older than she, it was Song's grandmother's nature to endure. Similarly, using Song's characteristically vivid descriptions, other poems posit women in situations where their individuality must defer to the needs of others.

Frameless Windows, Squares of Light continues the theme of family history and relationships; as *Booklist* reviewer Pat Monaghan notes, "Song explores the nuances of intimacy with admirable clarity and passion." "The Tower of Pisa" concerns the poet's airline pilot-father, whose life she terms "one of continual repair." "Humble Jar" is written in praise of her mother, a seamstress. Song again treats the theme of womanhood in "A Mehinaku Girl in Seclusion," where a girl, her coming of age signaled by her first menstruation, is removed from her tribe for three years and "married to the earth." In this poem, Song's approach is unique. "Song is at her best when she wrenches free of her responsibility to family history," reviewer Jessica Greenbaum opined in *Women's Review of Books,* explaining that "A Mehinaku Girl" draws the reader into the inner life of its main character far more vividly than do Song's second-person recitations of family history.

In *School Figures* Song again casts the stories of her family in verse. Both "A Conservative View" and "Journey" explore the challenges that faced her parents, while "Sunworshippers" recalls for the poet her mother's sage advice against self-gratification. The thoughts, feelings, and impressions couched within each of Song's poems—whether quietly coming to terms with the death of a father or sitting amid the clatter of serving dishes and the buoyant chatter of family during diner—are transformed by the poet into universal images, transcending labels of race, gender or culture.

BIOGRAPHICAL/CRITICAL SOURCES:

BOOKS

Song, Cathy, *Frameless Windows, Squares of Light,* Norton, 1988.

PERIODICALS

Booklist, October 1, 1994, p. 231.
International Examiner (Seattle), May 2, 1984.
Library Journal, May 1, 1983, p. 909; June 15, 1988, p. 61.
MELUS, Volume 15, number 1, 1988; Volume 18, number 3, 1993.
Poetry, April, 1984; August, 1989.
Publishers Weekly, April 1, 1983, p. 59.
Women's Review of Books, October, 1988, p 19.

*   *   *

SOULJAH, Sister 1964-

PERSONAL: Born Lisa Williamson, 1964, in the Bronx, NY; married; children: one son. *Education:* Attended Cornell University, Spain's University, and Rutgers University.

ADDRESSES: Agent—Mr. Vernon J. Brown, V. Brown and Company, Inc., Ten Bank Street, 8th Floor, White Plains, NY 10606.

CAREER: Community activist, singer, and writer. Affiliated with the Commission for Racial Justice, United Church of Christ; founded African Youth Survival Camp, Enfield, NC (a summer camp for homeless children); member of rap group Public Enemy; released solo album, *360 Degrees of Power,* on Epic Records, 1992.

WRITINGS:

No Disrespect (autobiography), Times Books (New York), 1994.

SIDELIGHTS: Community activist, rap singer, and outspoken public figure Sister Souljah wrote her autobiography, *No Disrespect,* to credit the people who

had influenced her life and career, and to provide guidance to other African Americans growing up in similarly disadvantaged circumstances. The book, published in 1994, also attempts to shed light on relationships between African American men and women, offering both critiques and suggestions for improvement.

Souljah, born Lisa Williamson, grew up in public housing projects witnessed first-hand the effects that economic hardship and subtle discrimination had on her urban community. In *No Disrespect,* she writes of the unstable family life she experienced, and of her own determination to escape those circumstances. Souljah's mother encouraged her to read as a child, and her studiousness as a teen earned her scholarships that led to a university education. In her book she discusses the environmental roadblocks that confront young African American women. "I am especially concerned with the African female in America," she says, "the ghetto girl who nobody ever tells the definition of womanhood. . . . She has been taught very little about what structure and family really means."

After beginning her college career at Cornell University, Souljah transferred to New Jersey's Rutgers University to study history. During these years, she became a student activist. As she related to Kim Neely in *Rolling Stone,* Souljah made an important discovery while marching with other students through the predominantly African American city of Newark as part of an anti-apartheid demonstration. Observing the poverty in the community around her, Souljah realized: "These people can't free South Africa—they haven't even freed themselves!"

As she recalls in *No Disrespect,* Souljah's activism soon became more focused on concerns closer to home. She founded the African Youth Survival Camp, a retreat for homeless youngsters in North Carolina. Proceeds from a series of rap concerts provided money for the camp. Souljah also worked for the United Church of Christ's Commission for Racial Justice, a civil-rights organization run by future NAACP leader Benjamin Chavis. Souljah's book chronicles how this community activism, combined with musical leanings, attracted the attention of the rap group Public Enemy, one of the most outspoken acts of the genre. She became an occasional member of the groundbreaking yet controversial group, of whom *The African American Almanac* said: "As spokesmen of racial pride, and proponents of militant public activism, Public Enemy have redefined the sound and the lyrical message of rap music."

Souljah's work with Public Enemy eventually led to her own recording contract and 1992's *360 Degrees of Power,* a solo effort whose message *Rolling Stone* writer Neely described as "a call for black unity and empowerment, stressing education and economic self-sufficiency." Although Souljah speaks little of the album in her book, much of the same message unites the themes of *No Disrespect.* By this time in the author's life her increasing public presence—and outspokenness—was drawing some criticism, especially in the aftermath of the 1992 Los Angeles riots. Riots that followed the acquittal of the white policemen who had beaten African American Rodney King. In the wake of these polarizing events, Souljah's sometimes inflammatory comments on race relations in the United States were often taken at face value and out of context by the media.

Souljah's pronouncements attracted the ire of then-President George Bush and Presidential hopeful Bill Clinton, who roundly denounced them. Though she speaks little of this controversy in *No Disrespect,* her autobiography does include frank views on the virulent interracial disunity in America, and she offers her opinion on why this situation has deteriorated in the 1990s. A reliance on welfare, as well as the long after-effects of slavery, are some of the themes of the activist's platform. Souljah concludes *No Disrespect* with a chapter entitled "Listen Up! (Straighten It Out)," in which she offers a series of guidelines for the betterment of the African American community. "Remember: No one will save us but ourselves," she writes.

Los Angeles Times Book Review writer Heidi Siegmund called Souljah's autobiography "a queer duck. The book isn't filled with the revolutionary musings one might have expected. . . . Rather, it aims to be a discourse on troubled relations between black men and women in America. Unfortunately, Souljah keeps getting sidetracked by ego-gratifying tangents." Sandy Coleman of the *Boston Globe* faulted Souljah's "do-as-I-say-and-not-as-I-did approach" in the areas where the author's relationships with others come into play, and stated that "reading her words, I became increasingly angry about her choices and rationalizations." Souljah's "generalizations about black people and white people" were also a target of criticism from Coleman, who concluded by remarking that the author "would have advanced her cause further by offering more solutions in *No Disrespect* instead of more racial hatred."

BIOGRAPHICAL/CRITICAL SOURCES:

BOOKS

African-American Almanac, 6th edition, Gale, 1994, p. 1143.
Contemporary Musicians, Volume 4, Gale, 1991, pp. 199-200.
Newsmakers, 1992, Gale, 1992, pp. 403-6.

PERIODICALS

Boston Globe, February 16, 1995.
Library Journal, November 1, 1994, p. 88.
Los Angeles Times Book Review, March 19, 1995, p. 10.
Publishers Weekly, December 5, 1994, p. 60.
Rolling Stone, August 6, 1992, p. 15.
Time, June 29, 1992, p. 88.
U.S. News & World Report, June 29, 1992, p. 80.*

*   *   *

SPENCE, Donald P(ond) 1926-

PERSONAL: Born February 8, 1926, in New York, NY; son of Ralph Beckett (a professor) and Rita (a schoolteacher; maiden name, Pond) Spence; married Mary Newbold Cross, June 2, 1951; children: Keith, Sarah, Laura, Katherine. *Education:* Harvard University, A.B., 1949; Columbia University, Ph.D., 1955. *Politics:* Democrat. *Avocational interests:* carpentry (Habitat for America), choral singing.

ADDRESSES: Home—9 Haslet Ave., Princeton, NJ 08540.

CAREER: Psychologist, psychoanalyst, and writer. New York University, New York City, research assistant, research associate 1954-56, research assistant professor, 1956-63, research associate professor, 1963-66, associate professor, 1966-70, professor of psychology, 1970-74; Robert Wood Johnson Medical School, University of Medicine and Dentistry of New Jersey, Piscataway, NJ, professor of psychiatry, 1974—. Visiting professor at Stanford University, 1971-72, Princeton University, 1975-94, Louvain-le-Neuve, 1980, and William Alanson White Institute, 1992. *Military service:* U.S. Army, 1944-46; received two battle stars.

MEMBER: American Psychology Association (fellow), American Psychoanalytic Association, New York Academy of Science, Sigma Xi.

AWARDS, HONORS: Research Career Development Award, Level II, National Institutes of Mental Health (NIMH), 1961-65, renewed 1966-68; Research Scientist Award, 1968-72; Exceptional Merit Award, University of Medicine and Dentistry of New Jersey, 1981-82; listed in *Who's Who in America,* 1996.

WRITINGS:

(Editor) *The Broad Scope of Psychoanalysis: Selected Papers of Leopold Bellak,* Grune & Stratton, 1967.

(Editor) *Psychoanalysis and Contemporary Science,* Volume 4, International Universities Press, 1976.

Narrative Truth and Historical Truth: Meaning and Interpretation in Psychoanalytic Theory, Norton, 1982.

The Freudian Metaphor: Toward Paradigm Change in Psychoanalysis, Norton, 1987.

The Rhetorical Voice of Psychoanalysis: Displacement of Evidence by Theory, Harvard University Press, 1994.

Contributor to periodicals, including *British Journal of Psychology, International Journal of Psycho-Analysis, Journal of Abnormal and Social Psychology,* and *Journal of Verbal Learning and Verbal Behavior.* Member of editorial boards of *Psychoanalysis and Contemporary Thought, Psychological Inquiry,* and *Theory and Psychology.*

SIDELIGHTS: Donald P. Spence is widely regarded as a distinguished psychologist and psychoanalyst. He began his academic career in 1954 as a research assistant at New York University. In 1974, when he had become professor of psychology, he departed from New York University to work as professor of psychiatry at Robert Wood Johnson Medical School. In addition to these posts, Spence was a visiting professor at Princeton University from 1975 to 1994. He retired in 1995.

In 1982, after having served as editor of the 1967 volume *The Broad Scope of Psychoanalysis: Selected Papers of Leopold Bellak* and 1976's *Psychoanalysis and Contemporary Science,* Spence published *Narrative Truth and Historical Truth: Meaning and Interpretation in Psychoanalytic Theory,* a radical appraisal of Freudian theory. In this work he addresses

Freudian analysts' emphasis on uncovering repressed or forgotten traumas, and he exposes such analysts' perseverance in conforming these traumas to what he sees as questionable Freudian models. Spence, while professing to be in favor of the psychoanalytic process, also questions analyst-patient relationships in which analysts provide what he perceives as counterproductive fueling of patients' creativity, particularly with regard to recollections. Janet Malcolm, in her *New Yorker* assessment of *Narrative Truth and Historical Truth,* found the book appealing but ultimately negative. She concluded: "At the core of Spence's likable, attractive, cultivated, and professedly pro-psychoanalytic book lies a profound antipathy to psychoanalytic thought."

Spence followed *Narrative Truth and Historical Truth* with 1987's *The Freudian Metaphor: Toward Paradigm Change in Psychoanalysis,* in which he returns to the perception of patients' recollections as narratives, and he argues that Sigmund Freud, in devising the psychoanalytic process, failed to consider the extent to which narrative itself might influence the aforementioned process. In 1994 Spence published *The Rhetorical Voice of Psychoanalysis: Displacement of Evidence by Theory,* in which he declares psychoanalysis to be unscientific and unsubstantiated. Here Spence considers the possibility that psychoanalytic theory is grounded too often in rhetoric and that Freudian theory is largely unproven. And he suggests a possible corrective measure: Psychoanalysts might share their case reports to effect greater quantification of various theories in the field. *Times Literary Supplement* reviewer Roy Porter found *The Rhetorical Voice of Psychoanalysis* "scrupulously impartial in argument and dispassionate in tone."

Spence told *CA:* "*Narrative Truth* has been my most popular book, and it still remains in print (paperback) after more than 14 years. I am pleased by the fact that it continues to be cited in current publications, and I will probably never forget the phone call from Norton telling me they had accepted the manuscript (it was unsolicited, going in 'over the transom'). Coming a close second was the excitement of seeing Janet Malcolm's book review in the New Yorker—an excitement quickly tempered by her critique. I composed the book while on sabbatical in San Francisco, and almost any page will reawaken in me the sense of that house, the view from my study, and the feeling of the city, especially on a foggy day when the noise carried well, and I could hear boat whistles in the Bay."

BIOGRAPHICAL/CRITICAL SOURCES:

PERIODICALS

New Yorker, January 24, 1983, pp. 96-106.
Poetics Today, summer, 1990, pp. 437-442.
Times Literary Supplement, March 24, 1995, p. 26.

*   *   *

SPENCER, Mark 1956-

PERSONAL: Born February 12, 1956, in Richmond, VA; son of Howard (a farmer) and Evelyn (an executive secretary; maiden name, Morris) Spencer; children: Krista, David. *Education:* University of Cincinnati, B.A., 1979; Bowling Green State University, M.F.A., 1981; attended Oklahoma State University, 1981-82.

ADDRESSES: Home—1328 NW Elm, Lawton, OK 73507. *Office*—English Department, Cameron University, Lawton, OK 73505-6377. *Agent*—Sam Hughes, The Dickens Group, 1428 Mockingbird Valley Green, Louisville, KY 40207.

CAREER: Southwest Missouri State University, Springfield, assistant professor of English, 1983-87; Cameron University, Lawton, OK, associate professor of English, 1987—.

AWARDS, HONORS: Patrick T.T. Bradshaw Book Award, 1988, for *Spying on Lovers;* four short stories received special mention in *Pushcart Prize: Best of the Small Presses.*

WRITINGS:

Spying on Lovers (short story collection), Amelia Press (Bakersfield, CA), 1988.
Wedlock (two novellas), Watermark Press (Owings Mills, MD), 1990.
Love and Reruns in Adams County, (novel) Random House (New York, NY), 1994.

WORK IN PROGRESS: Novels *Only Missing* and *The Masked Demon: A Love Story.*

SIDELIGHTS: Mark Spencer, who writes about the South, explores the world of trailer parks and fast food establishments, focusing on extraordinary stories told by ordinary people. In *Wedlock,* Pamela, heroine of the title novella, works at the local McDonald's to support her second husband. Pamela's seemingly balanced life is totally disrupted by the return of her ex-husband, a former baseball star. A *Publishers Weekly* reviewer found the two novellas in Spencer's *Wedlock* somewhat unbalanced as a whole, but praised the author's narrative voice as important, quirky, "endearing and immensely likable."

Spencer told *CA:* "I try to write fiction that is both literary and accessible and that is—like life—both funny and sad. I like it when an English professor appreciates my work, but I *love* it when a high-school girl who works at Taco Bell does. I always strive to write vividly and honestly enough so that virtually every reader will recognize in my work something universal and true."

BIOGRAPHICAL/CRITICAL SOURCES:

PERIODICALS

Publishers Weekly, June 8, 1990, p. 48.

*   *   *

SPICER, Ron
  See KELLY, Ronald

*   *   *

SPIVAK, Gayatri Chakravorty 1942-

PERSONAL: Born in 1942, in India. *Education:* University of Calcutta, B.A., 1959; Cornell University, M.A., 1962, Ph.D., 1967.

ADDRESSES: Office—Department of English, Columbia University, 2960 Broadway, New York, NY 10027-6902.

CAREER: Writer and educator. Has taught English and comparative literature at several universities, including University of Iowa and University of Texas; served as Longstreet Professor of English, Emory University; and Andrew K. Mellon Professor of English, University of Pittsburgh; Columbia University, New York City, Avalon Foundation Professor in the Humanities, 1991—.

WRITINGS:

NONFICTION

Myself Must I Remake: The Life and Poetry of W. B. Yeats (juvenile), Crowell (New York), 1974.

In Other Worlds: Essays in Cultural Politics, Methuen (New York), 1987.

(Editor, with Ranajit Guha) *Selected Subaltern Studies,* Oxford University Press (New York), 1988.

The Post-Colonial Critic: Interviews, Strategies, Dialogues, edited by Sarah Harasym, Routledge (New York), 1990.

Outside in the Teaching Machine, Routledge, 1993.

The Spivak Reader, edited by Donna Landry and George McLean, Routledge (London), 1995.

Contributor to anthologies, including *Displacement: Derrida and After,* Indiana University Press (Bloomington), 1983; *Philosophical Approaches to Literature: New Essays on Nineteenth- and Twentieth-Century Texts,* Bucknell University Press (Lewisburg), 1984; *For Alma Mater: Theory and Practice in Feminist Scholarship,* edited by Paula Treichler, Cheris Kramarae, and Beth Stafford, University of Illinois Press (Urbana), 1985; *Post-Structuralism and the Question of History,* edited by Derek Attridge, Robert Young, and Geoff Bennington, Cambridge University Press, 1987; *Marxism and the Interpretation of Culture,* edited by Cary Nelson and Lawrence Grossberg, Macmillan (London), 1988; *The New Historicism,* edited by H. Aram Vesser and Stanley Fish, Routledge, 1989; *Feminists Theorize the Political,* edited by Judith Butler and Joan Scott, Routledge, 1992; and *Colonial Discourse/Postcolonial Theory,* Manchester University Press, 1994.

Contributor to journals, including *boundary 2, Critical Inquiry, Diacritics, Differences, Harper's, Journal of South Asian Literature, Modern Language Notes, New Literary History, Oxford Literary Review,* and *Socialist Review.*

TRANSLATOR

Derrida, Jacques, *Of Grammatology,* Johns Hopkins University Press (Baltimore), 1976.

Devi, Mahasweta, *Imaginary Maps,* Routledge (New York), 1995.

SIDELIGHTS: Indian literary theorist and educator Gayatri Chakravorty Spivak is concerned with the work of postcolonial and third-world writers. A self-proclaimed feminist Marxist deconstructivist, she is one of the most outspoken proponents of a revision of postcolonial literary theory. In her books, which include 1987's *In Other Worlds: Essays in Cultural Politics* and *The Post-Colonial Critic: Interviews, Strategies, Dialogues,* published in 1990, Spivak addresses the importance of acknowledging a writer's "positionality"—the unique multiple cultural, economic, racial, and political influences that influence one's writing. Spivak is also known for her work in translating Jacques Derrida's *Of Grammatology* and the stories of Indian writer Mahasweta Devi.

The assumption held by many critics that, for every way of thinking, there is a single, unique voice is an integral aspect of Spivak's work. In her influential essay "Can the Subaltern Speak?," published in *Marxism and the Interpretation of Culture,* Spivak explores the ways in which the "subaltern"—members of the non-ruling class—express the oppression they encounter. In attempting to speak for the subaltern, members of the intellectual elite can only present an interpretation of the subalternal voice filtered through an intellectual/elitist viewpoint. The subaltern are relegated to the position of subjects rather than participants in a two-way dialogue. Spivak encourages academics to understand how their positions of intellectual and economic privilege limit their integrity in serving as a spokesperson for the subaltern. In other discussions, the critic posits women in the role of subaltern, questioning the male-constructed voice of women within a patriarchal society.

The Post-Colonial Critic contains twelve interviews with Spivak; she expresses her views on a variety of subjects and includes a cogent analysis of the works of both Derrida and Karl Marx. A collection of essays, *In Other Worlds* is organized into three areas: a criticism of major literary works, a discussion of literary theory, and a critique of the diverse theoretical representations of the subaltern in literature. Calling Spivak's critique of Marxist analysis "acute, unusual, and scholarly," Roger Fowler notes in *Modern Language Review* that *In Other Worlds* "is a challenging and highly intelligent volume." Several of Spivak's most well-known essays were collected as *The Spivak Reader* and published in 1995.

BIOGRAPHICAL/CRITICAL SOURCES:

BOOKS

Varadharajan, Asha, *Exotic Parodies: Subjectivity in Adorno, Said, and Spivak,* University of Minnesota Press (Minneapolis), 1995.

PERIODICALS

Arena, Volume 97, 1991.
Choice, March, 1995, p. 1059.
Modern Language Review, October, 1989, p. 897; January, 1993, p. 160.
Oxford Literary Review, Volume 12, numbers 1-2, 1991.

*   *   *

STAINER, Pauline   1941-

PERSONAL: Born March 5, 1941, in Burslem, England. *Education:* St. Anne's College, Oxford University, B.A., 1963; Southampton University, M.Phil., 1967.

CAREER: Writer.

AWARDS, HONORS: Hawthornden fellowship, 1987; winner of Skoob Index on Censorship Competition, 1992; National Poetry Competition prize winner, 1992.

WRITINGS:

POETRY

The Honeycomb, Bloodaxe (Newcastle upon Tyne), 1989.
Little Egypt, The Brotherhood of Ruralists, 1991.
Sighting the Slave-ship, Bloodaxe, 1992.
The Ice-Pilot Speaks, Bloodaxe, 1994.

OTHER

Translator with Ase-Marie Nesse of *The No-Man's Tree,* Making Waves (Guildford, Surrey).

*   *   *

STAMPFER, Judah (Leon)   1923-1996

OBITUARY NOTICE—See index for *CA* sketch: Born November 11, 1923, in Jerusalem, Israel; died of pancreatic cancer, October 4, 1996, in New York, NY. Educator, poet and novelist. Though Stampfer spent most of his time teaching, translating and writing scholarly material, he managed to publish several poems and novels. An ordained rabbi, Stampfer graduated from the University of Chicago, earned a master's degree in education from Columbia University, and later received his doctorate from Harvard University in 1959. He was ordained a rabbi at Yeshiva University in 1947. Stampfer was one of the original faculty members at the State University of New York at Stony Brook and, at the time of his death, taught Shakespeare and rabbinical studies there. *Jerusalem Has Many Faces* (1950), his most critically acclaimed poem, came early in his writing career. His first novel, 1962's *Saul Myers,* was noted for its passion and wit. Stampfer also wrote articles on American taste in *Nation* magazine and authored occasional radio plays. Some of his scholarly works include *The Tragic Engagement: A Study of Shakespeare's Classical Tragedies* (1969), and *Face and Shadow: Approaches to the Modern Revolutionary Impulse* (1972).

OBITUARIES AND OTHER SOURCES:

BOOKS

Directory of American Scholars, Volume 2: *English, Speech, and Drama,* 8th edition, Bowker, 1982.

PERIODICALS

New York Times, October 14, 1996, p. A15.

*   *   *

STANCYKOWNA
See SZYMBORSKA, Wislawa

*   *   *

STANDS IN TIMBER, John   1884-1967

PERSONAL: Born in 1884; died in 1967.

CAREER: Authority on Cheyenne culture and history; writer.

WRITINGS:

(With Margot Liberty) *Cheyenne Memories,* assisted by Robert M. Utley, Yale University Press, 1967.

Reminiscences of John Stands in Timber, Cheyenne Indian, were recorded by Margot Liberty and published in microform by the *New York Times* Oral History Program, 1979.

SIDELIGHTS: The autobiography of John Stands in Timber was published the same year the author passed away. The 1967 volume, *Cheyenne Memories,* was told to Margot Liberty, an anthropologist and former teacher at a Native American school who taped Stands in Timber's memories; she was assisted in the project by Robert M. Utley. Liberty then transcribed the recollections into written form and compiled them into the volume. Stands in Timber was born in 1884 and his life spanned the dramatic decades during which the Cheyenne and other Native American peoples were forced off their ancestral lands and onto a system of reservations. Some of his reminiscences about Cheyenne culture during the final years of the nineteenth century had been published previously in other works on Native American life, but *Cheyenne Memories* provides a detailed description of the Cheyenne existence prior to their removal to reservations. The book is particularly rich with Stands in Timber's account of Cheyenne spirituality. He relates several important aspects of the faith including its creation myths, and the Sacred Arrows and Sacred Hat; in another section he discusses the cultural significance of the Cheyenne hero Sweet Medicine. *Cheyenne Memories* also incorporates the tribal history of the nomadic group that Stands in Timber learned from the elders. This chronicle includes the nineteenth-century battles with United States soldiers over Cheyenne land and the Cheyenne's struggle to remain independent. In other areas, the volume gives an account of the social and political structure of the Cheyenne that existed for many generations prior to the resettlement, and narrates the changes wrought by the move onto the reservations. Stands in Timber's memoirs also provide details about the means of subsistence and day-to-day life in the early decades of the twentieth century among the Cheyenne. The recollections in *Cheyenne Memories* are accompanied by extensive footnotes and explanations by Liberty.

BIOGRAPHICAL/CRITICAL SOURCES:

PERIODICALS

Choice, June, 1968.
Library Journal, February 1, 1968.*

STAPLETON, Amy 1959-

PERSONAL: Born in 1959. *Education:* University of Wisconsin, Ph.D. (German).

ADDRESSES: Home—Heidelberg, Germany. *Office—* c/o Peter Lang Publishing, Inc., 275 7th Ave., 28th Fl., New York, NY 10001.

CAREER: Writer.

WRITINGS:

Utopias for a Dying World: Contemporary German Science Fiction's Plea for a New Ecological Awareness, Peter Lang (New York), 1993.

SIDELIGHTS: Amy Stapleton's 1993 volume, *Utopias for a Dying World: Contemporary German Science Fiction's Plea for a New Ecological Awareness,* is a comprehensive and comparative look at examples of German science-fiction literature that call for awareness of the world's ecological crisis. Stapleton organizes the fiction she has chosen to include in her discussion into four categories, beginning with "Negative Utopias I," which looks at four novels and a series of novels that Stapleton feels challenge readers to examine their thoughts on subjects such as the structures of military forces and world governments, as well as the effects of technological advances on the environment. Matthias Horx, H.W. Franke, and Wolfgang Hohlbein are among the authors Stapleton highlights in "Negative Utopias I." In "Negative Utopias II," Stapleton presents examples of ways in which short-story writers incorporate ecological awareness into their writings, while her chapter "Uncertain Utopias" includes the author's discussion of several books that she finds generate pessimistic feelings about the future and ecology in their readers.

Finally, Stapleton's chapter entitled "Positive Utopias" explores the works of authors who present true utopias in their literature, while stressing that the dangers of progress prohibit the creation of utopias as seen in literature of the past. Among the authors Stapleton deems suitable for inclusion in her "Positive Utopias" portion of *Utopias for a Dying World* are Franke, Bernd Ulbrich, Karlheinz and Angela Steinmueller, and Johanna and Guenter Braun.

Utopias for a Dying World received a mixed review from *Science Fiction Studies* contributor Franz Rottensteiner, who questioned the reality of ecology as a prevailing theme in German science fiction. "Publishers very rarely publish sf with a didactic purpose in mind," Rottensteiner wrote, "and readers as a rule rarely buy sf to be enlightened, so that a large part of sf in Germany and elsewhere is really escape literature, especially those works that Stapleton doesn't care to mention. . . . I doubt that a 'plea for a new ecological awareness' is a common or dominant concern of German sf, which rather offers, as does sf everywhere, a wide range of themes, motifs, and viewpoints, as well as many levels of literary excellence or indifference." *Locus* critic Gary K. Wolfe also found that Stapleton's "range of texts covered is pretty narrow, and includes a number of dystopian and post-catastrophe works that support her thesis only in the broadest sense. . . . As a critical work about SF, then," Wolfe concluded, "the value of *Utopias for a Dying World* is limited, but as an account of several interesting recent German works— representative of the larger field or not—it may generate interest in a vital SF tradition too seldom made available to English readers."

BIOGRAPHICAL/CRITICAL SOURCES:

PERIODICALS

Locus, September, 1994, pp. 23-25, 67-69.
Science Fiction Studies, Volume 21, 1994, pp. 249-251.*

* * *

STEBENNE, David 1960-

PERSONAL: Surname is pronounced "*steb*-bin"; born July 4, 1960, in Providence, RI; son of William J. (an accountant) and Regina M. (a homemaker) Stebenne. *Education:* Yale University, B.A. (magna cum laude), 1982; Columbia University, J.D. and M.A., both 1986, M.Phil., 1987, Ph.D. (with distinction), 1991.

ADDRESSES: Office—Department of History, 106 Dulles Hall, Ohio State University, 230 West 17th Ave., Columbus, OH 43210-1367. *E-mail*—Stebenne .1@osu.edu. *Agent*—Gerard McCauley, Gerard McCauley Agency, Inc., P.O. Box AE, Katonah, NY 10536.

CAREER: Patterson, Belknap, Webb & Tyler, Washington, DC, law clerk, 1983; Bell, Boyd & Lloyd,

Washington, DC, law clerk, 1984; Dow, Lohnes & Albertson, Washington, DC, law clerk, 1985; Columbia University, New York City, research assistant at Freedom Forum Media Studies Center, 1986-87, special assistant to the executive director, 1988-90, senior officer for research and planning, 1990-92; Yale University, New Haven, CT, lecturer in history, 1991-93; Ohio State University, Columbus, assistant professor of history, 1993—.

MEMBER: American Historical Association, Organization of American Historians, Business History Conference.

AWARDS, HONORS: Grants from John F. Kennedy Library Foundation and Henry J. Kaiser Family Foundation, both 1988; Littleton-Griswold grant, American Historical Association, 1988; grant from Harry S Truman Library Institute, 1989; Moody grant, Lyndon Baines Johnson Foundation, 1989; fellow, Whiting Foundation, 1989-90.

WRITINGS:

Arthur J. Goldberg: New Deal Liberal, Oxford University Press (Oxford, England), 1996.

Contributor to books, including *The Media at War: The Press and the Persian Gulf Conflict,* Gannett Foundation, 1991; and *The Media and Campaign '92: A Series of Special Election Reports,* Freedom Forum Media Studies Center (New York City), 1993. Contributor of articles and reviews to periodicals, including *International Labor and Working Class History.*

WORK IN PROGRESS: A biography of Arthur Larson, under-secretary of labor, executive assistant to the president, and director of U.S. Information Agency under Dwight D. Eisenhower.

* * *

STEFAN, Verena 1947-

PERSONAL: Born in 1947, in Bern, Switzerland. *Education:* Trained as a physical therapist.

ADDRESSES: Home—Munich, Germany.

CAREER: Worked as a physical therapist until 1977. Has taught women's studies; co-founder, Brot Rosen (women's health collective), Berlin, c. 1969.

AWARDS, HONORS: Ehrengabe des Kantons Bern, 1977.

WRITINGS:

(With others) *Frauenhandbuch Nr. 1,* Verlag Frauen im Gerhard Verlag (Berlin), 1972.

Hautungen. Autobiografische Aufzeichnungen, Gedichte, Traume, Analysen (novel) Frauenoffensive (Munich), 1975, translation published as *Shedding,* Daughters (New York), 1978, included in *Literally Dreaming: Herstories with Shedding, "Euphoria," and "Cacophony,"* Feminist Press (New York City), 1994.

mit Fuebhen mit Fluegeln (poetry; title means "With Feet with Wings"), Frauenoffensive, 1980.

(Translator, with Meixner) Adrienne Rich, *Der Traum einer gemeinsamen Sprache (Dream of a Common Language),* Frauenoffensive, 1982.

(Translator, with Gabriele Meixner and Lesbische Voelker) Monique Wittig and Sande Zweig, *Ein Woerterbuch (Brouillon pour un dictionnaire des amantes),* Frauenoffensive, 1983.

Wortgetreu ich traume (short stories), Arche (Zurich), 1985, selections translated and published in *Literally Dreaming: Herstories with Shedding, "Euphoria," and "Cacophony,"* Feminist Press, 1994.

Es ist reich gewesen (autobiography; title means "Times Have Been Good"), Fischer (Frankfurt am Main), 1993.

SIDELIGHTS: Swiss writer Verena Stefan is the author of *Shedding,* a novel considered to be one of the first works of German feminist literature. First published independently in 1975, *Shedding* has since sold more than 300,000 copies in Germany alone, and has been translated into eight languages. Popular with many European college-educated women who had witnessed but not benefitted from the student movement of the late 1960s, the novel is a complex work; following the designs of French literary critics Luce Irigaray and Helene Cixous it breaks with traditional rules of writing. Attempting to form a revisioned understanding of women's identity, Stefan constructed a "non-patriarchal" language around poetry, nature metaphors, and gender-neutral terms, utilizing non-traditional grammatical styling as well.

Shedding recounts a series of significant events in the life of its protagonist, Veruschka. A member of a women's health group with whom she publishes a women's health manual, Veruschka becomes dissatisfied with gender roles and the relationship between sexuality and power. She eventually accepts herself as a bisexual, rejecting the necessity of altering her physical appearance just to be accepted by men. Veruschka's eventual decision to become a lesbian is also, for her, a political decision: She concludes that "sexism runs deeper than racism than class struggle." Throughout the novel, Stefan incorporates her protagonist's outer struggle within her inner journey towards self-love; she embraces the loneliness resulting from her sexual non-dependence upon men as a learning process and, by novel's end, comes to terms with her feelings for Fenna, a female friend who is an artist.

Remaining active in the women's movement since the publication of *Shedding,* Stefan has continued to write and has translated works by other feminist writers, such as authors Adrienne Rich and Monique Wittig. Despite the publication of several other works, including the 1985 short story collection *Wortgetreu ich traume,* and a 1993 memoir of her mother entitled *Es ist reich gewesen,* Stefan's name continues to be associated with one of her first, and most successful works, *Shedding.*

BIOGRAPHICAL/CRITICAL SOURCES:

BOOKS

Abel, Elizabeth, and others, editors, *The Voyage In: Fictions of Female Development,* University Press of New England (Hanover, NH), 1983.

Cocalis, Susan L., and Kay Goodman, *Beyond the Feminine: Critical Essays on Women and German Literature,* Heinz (Stuttgart), 1982.

Stefan, Verena, *Shedding,* Daughters, 1978.

*   *   *

STERN, Kenneth S. 1953-

PERSONAL: Born February 3, 1953, in New York City; son of Seymour (a physician) and Gertrude (a physician; Steinberg) Stern; married Marjorie Slome (a rabbi), June 11, 1989; children: Daniel and Emily. *Education:* Bard College, A.B., 1975; Willamette University School of Law, J.D., 1979. *Avocational interests:* Fishing, tennis.

ADDRESSES: Office—165 East 56th Street, New York, NY 10022.

CAREER: American Jewish Committee, New York City, anti-Semitism specialist, 1989—; Attorney at Law, Portland, Oregon and New York City, 1979-1989. Member of the board of directors of Multnomah Defenders, Inc. during the early 1980s and International Association of Jewish Lawyers and Jurists, 1983-88.

MEMBER: Selection committee, Koblitz Human Rights Awards, Bard College; selection committee, Revlon Harmony Awards.

WRITINGS:

Holocaust Denial, American Jewish Committee (New York), 1993.
Loud Hawk, University of Oklahoma Press (Norman, Okla.), 1994.

Author of booklets published by the American Jewish Committee: *Politics and Bigotry,* 1992, *Farrakhan and the Jews in the 90s,* 1992, *Hate on Talk Radio,* 1991, *David Duke: A Nazi in Politics,* 1991, *Crown Heights: A Case Study,* 1991, *Anti-Zionism: The Sophisticated Anti-Semitism,* 1990, *Skinheads,* 1990, *Patrick Buchanan: A Backgrounder,* 1990, *Bigotry on Campus,* 1989. Has also contributed numerous letters, editorials, and articles to print media and appeared on nationally-broadcast television programs.

WORK IN PROGRESS: Research on extreme racist Afrocentrism on campus.

*   *   *

STEVENS, April 1963-

PERSONAL: Born February 6, 1963, in New Milford, CT; daughter of Leonard (a writer) and Carla (a writer; maiden name, McBride) Stevens; married Alexander Neubauer (a writer), October 1, 1988; children: Samuel. *Education:* New School for Social Research, B.A., 1984.

ADDRESSES: Home—Cornwall, CT; and New York, NY. *Agent*—c/o Viking, 375 Hudson St., New York, NY 10014.

CAREER: Novelist.

WRITINGS:

Angel Angel, Viking (New York), 1995.

WORK IN PROGRESS: A novel.

SIDELIGHTS: First-time novelist April Stevens charmed critics with her 1995 book, *Angel Angel.* The story of a highly dysfunctional family, it follows the Irises through a series of crises beginning when the father, Gordie Iris, runs off to England with his mistress. His wife, Augusta, responds by retreating to her darkened bedroom for months on end; youngest son Henry—who has just failed to graduate from high school—devotes himself to creating a sculpture in his father's studio. When older brother Matthew returns home to help his family, he fails to stir them from their seclusion; however, he is seduced by Henry's live-in girlfriend Bette Mack, a vivid personality who finally manages to revive the entire family.

Reviews of *Angel Angel* were marked by high expectations for Stevens's future books and comparisons to John Updike, Anne Tyler, and Laurie Colwin. The book was not deemed faultless, but as being essentially satisfying and full of stylistic promise. Writing in *New York Times Book Review,* Gary Krist concluded that Stevens is "a writer who can move us in unexpected ways . . . it's this gift that enables her to overcome the initial artificiality of her design, turning *Angel Angel* into a surprisingly potent study of emotional healing." *Los Angeles Times* contributor Karen Stabiner opined: "It's clear that [Stevens] has a commanding ability, that she can write stark, plain prose that rolls along, picking up power like a snowball heading downhill. But there is a difference between simplicity and restraint—and it's hard not to wish that next time out, she will take a few more emotional chances. She can handle a bigger inventory of experiences. I look forward to whatever comes next."

BIOGRAPHICAL/CRITICAL SOURCES:

PERIODICALS

Kirkus Reviews, November 1, 1994, p. 1442.
Library Journal, March 1, 1995, p. 104.
New York Times Book Review, January 29, 1995.
Publishers Weekly, November 21, 1994, p. 66.

*   *   *

STEWART, Wynn 1934-1985

PERSONAL: Born June 7, 1934, in Morrisville, MO; died July 17, 1985, in Hendersonville, TN; children: one son, two daughters.

CAREER: Singer and songwriter. First radio performances, KWTO, Springfield, MO, 1947; recording artist, 1949-85; performed in clubs throughout the United States; Nashville-Nevada Club, Las Vegas, NV, owner, c. 1962-65; KTOO (radio station), Las Vegas, program director and broadcaster, c. 1965; appeared on own television show; toured with his band, The Tourists, beginning 1965.

WRITINGS:

ALBUMS

Songs, Capitol, 1965.
In Love, Capitol, 1968.
Above and Beyond, Hilltop, 1968.
Let the Whole World Sing It with Me, Capitol, 1969.
Yours Forever, Capitol, 1970.
It's a Beautiful Day, Capitol, 1971.
After the Storm, Playboy, 1976.

Also author of songs, including the record chart-toppers "Wishful Thinking," Jat Music, 1959, "Above and Beyond," 1960, "It's Such a Pretty World Today," 1967, "'Cause I Have You," 1967, "Love's Gonna Happen to Me," 1967, "Something Pretty," 1968, "In Love," 1968, "World-Wide Travelin' Man," 1969, and "It's a Beautiful Day," 1970; also author of "Wait 'Til I Get My Hands on You," 1985. Author of songs for other artists, including "Above and Beyond," for Buck Owens, 1960; (with Skeets McDonald and Harlan Howard) "You Took Her off My Hands (Now Please Take Her off My Mind)," for Ray Price, 1956.

SIDELIGHTS: Country singer-songwriter Wynn Stewart made his mark on the music world in the sixties and seventies. With his honky-tonk style and melancholy ballads, he recorded for a number of labels and saw a string of songs reach the top of the country music charts. His many hits included "Wishful Thinking" (1959), "Above and Beyond" (1960), "Big Big Day" (1961), "Another Day, Another Dollar" (1962), "'Cause I Have You" (1967), "Love's Gonna Happen to Me" (1967), "Something Pretty" (1968), "In Love" (1968), "World-Wide Travelin' Man" (1969), "It's a Beautiful Day" (1970), and "After the Storm" (1976). "It's Such a Pretty World Today" rose to the number one spot on the country music chart in 1967.

Like many country music singers, Stewart learned to sing at church and taught himself how to play the guitar. At age thirteen, he performed on KWTO radio

in Springfield, Missouri. Shortly afterward Stewart and his family moved to California, where he formed his own band and performed on radio shows in Los Angeles and Hollywood. At age fifteen he made his first recording with this band. In 1953 Stewart formed a new band. It soon became known for what is called the "California sound," which featured a loud, supercharged, uptempo, and strident sound. After working the local nightclub circuit and recording for Capitol Records, he enjoyed popularity on the Las Vegas nightclub circuit. For a time he had his own Nashville-Nevada Club in Las Vegas, worked as a disc jockey and program director at KTOO radio, and appeared on a weekly television show. After selling the club in the mid-sixties, Stewart moved to California. There he formed a band called The Tourists, with which he toured nationwide. For Stewart throughout his career, recording and touring went hand in hand. After enjoying a string of hits in the sixties, Stewart moved from record label to label but never regained his early popularity. In 1985 he died from a heart attack shortly before he was scheduled to begin another tour.

BIOGRAPHICAL/CRITICAL SOURCES:

BOOKS

Biographical Dictionary of American Music, Parker Publishing, 1973.
Encyclopedia of Folk, Country, and Western Music, St. Martin's, 1969.

PERIODICALS

Chicago Tribune, July 21, 1985.*

*   *   *

STONOV (VLODAVSKY), Dmitry 1898-1962

PERSONAL: Born January 8, 1898, in Bezdezh, Byelorus; died December 29, 1962, in Russia; son of Miron Vlodavsky (a merchant and manager); married Anna Idlin-Stonov, 1928; children: Leonid. *Ethnicity:* "Jew." *Education:* Attended a commercial high school.

CAREER: Professional writer. *Military service:* Served as a decorated officer in World War II.

WRITINGS:

The Family of Raskins (novel), Russian Publishing House, 1929.

Esterka (novella), Russian Publishing House, 1938.
Teklya and Her Friends (novel), Sovetsky Pisatel, 1959.
In the Past Night: The Siberian Stories, Texas Tech University Press (Lubbock, TX), 1995.

Author of seventeen additional books, two of which remain unpublished.
[Date of death provided by son, Leonid Stonov.]

*   *   *

STONOV, Natasha 1932-

PERSONAL: Born March 23, 1932, in Moscow, U.S.S.R. (now Russia); daughter of Semyon (an economist) and Rakhil (an economist; maiden name, Khaimchik) Gnoensky; married Leonid Stonov (a biologist and politician), February 27, 1955; children: Alexander. *Ethnicity:* "Jewish." *Education:* Attended Moscow Medical Institute, 1949-55; Academy of Medical Science, Ph.D., 1968. *Religion:* Jewish. *Avocational interests:* Literature, science, medicine.

ADDRESSES: Home—8231 North Keeler Ave., Skokie, IL 60076. *Office*—555 Vine Ave., Suite 107, Highland Park, IL 60035; fax 847-433-5530.

CAREER: Scientific officer for several Soviet medical institutes, Moscow, U.S.S.R., 1955-79; Chicago Action for Soviet Jews, Chicago, IL, coordinator of information from the former U.S.S.R., 1991—.

WRITINGS:

(Co-translator) Dmitry Stonov, *In the Past Night: The Siberian Stories,* Texas Tech University Press (Lubbock, TX), 1995.

Author of books on molecular biology. Contributor to scientific periodicals.

WORK IN PROGRESS: A book on the lives of Anna and Dmitry Stonov, with K. Darrel Jain.

*   *   *

STOPES, Marie (Charlotte) 1880-1958
(Marie Carmichael, Erica Fay, G. N. Mortlake, pseudonyms)

PERSONAL: Born October 15, 1880, in Edinburgh, Scotland; died of cancer, October 2, 1958, in Norbury Park, Surrey, England; married R. R. Gates (a biologist), 1911 (marriage annulled, 1916); married Humphrey Vernon Roe (an aircraft manufacturer), 1918 (died, 1949); children: one son. *Education:* University College, London, B.S., 1902; University of Munich, Ph.D., 1904; University of London, D.Sc., 1905.

CAREER: Writer and birth control pioneer. Manchester University, lecturer in botany, then paleobotany, beginning 1904; founder, Society for Constructive Birth Control and Racial Progress, 1921; co-founder, with husband, H. V. Roe, Mothers' Clinic for Constructive Birth Control, Holloway, North London, 1921.

WRITINGS:

FICTION

(As G. N. Mortlake) *Love Letters of a Japanese* (novel), S. Paul (London), 1911.
(As Erica Fay) *The Road to Fairyland* (juvenile), Putnam (London), 1926, (New York City), 1927.
(As Marie Carmichael) *Love's Creation* (novel), Bale & Danielsson (London), 1928.

NONFICTION

Ancient Plants, Blackie (London), 1910.
Married Love, A. C. Fifield (London), 1918, Critic & Guide Co. (New York City), 1920.
Wise Parenthood, A. C. Fifield, 1918.
A Letter to Working Mothers, privately printed (Leatherhead, Surrey), 1919.
Radiant Motherhood, G. P. Putnam (London), 1920, (New York City), 1921.
A New Gospel to All Peoples, A. L. Humphreys (London), 1922.
Contraception: Its Theory, History, and Practice, Bale & Danielsson, 1923.
Sex and the Young, Gill (London), 1926.
Enduring Passion, Putnam (London), 1928, (New York City), 1931.
Roman Catholic Methods of Birth Control, P. Davies (London), 1933.
Birth Control Today, Heinemann (London), 1934.
Marriage in My Time, Rich & Cowan, 1935.
Change of Life in Men and Women, Putnam, 1936.
Your Baby's First Year, Putnam (London), 1939.
Sleep, Hogarth Press (London), 1956.
Dear Dr Stopes (letters), edited by Ruth Hall, Deutsche (London), 1978.

Married Love was translated into twelve languages.

POETRY

Man, Other Poems and a Preface, Heinemann, 1913.
Love Songs for Young Lovers, Heinemann, 1919.
(As Erica Fay) *Kings and Heroes,* Putnam (New York City), 1937.
Oriri, Heinemann, 1939.
Wartime Harvest, A. Moring (London), 1944.
The Bathe, A. Moring, 1946.
Instead of Tears, A. Moring, 1947.
We Burn, A. Moring, 1951.
Joy and Verity, Heinemann, 1952.

PLAYS

(With Professor J. Sakurai) *Plays of Old Japan: The No,* Heinemann, 1913.
Conquest, S. French (London), 1917.
Gold in the Wood [and] *The Race,* A. C. Fifield, 1918.
Our Ostriches, Putnam (London), 1923.
A Banned Play and a Preface on the Censorship, Bale & Danielsson, 1926.

OTHER

Author's manuscripts are housed at the British Library and the Wellcome Institute.

SIDELIGHTS: Best known for her work as a pioneer in popularizing the use of birth control in the United Kingdom, Marie Stopes was also a prolific writer. Publishing several landmark books in the area of marriage and contraception practices, she also wrote plays, poetry, and several novels for both children and adults, sometimes under a pseudonym. While attracting the condemnation of the Catholic Church for her staunch advocacy of contraception and her establishment of Great Britain's first birth control clinic, Stopes' work as a social reformer would also pave the way for an increasing public acceptance of books on the subject of human sexuality.

"In my first marriage I paid such a terrible price for sex-ignorance that I feel that knowledge gained at such a cost should be placed at the service of humanity, . . ." Stopes would write in *Married Love,* her most popular book. "I hope [this] will save some others years of heartache and blind questioning in the dark." Revolutionizing the formal union between men and women by challenging and redefining traditional Victorian marriage, Stopes took the battle for women's equality into the bedrooms of Great Britain. Written in basic medical language and based on substantial research, *Married Love* was the first manual on sexual technique intended for women. It was published during an era of great social upheaval—women had just received the vote and World War I was underway—as the vestiges of Victorian prudery were being swept away. Though it shocked many readers, two thousand copies of *Married Love* sold in the first weeks of its 1918 publication. Stopes became an instant celebrity.

Throughout her life Stopes worked to find new ways to advance the cause of women's sexual freedom. With her second husband, Humphrey Vernon Roe, she established the Mother's Clinic for Constructive Birth Control, which was staffed entirely by women, provided free counseling, and distributed birth control to the poor at minimal cost, as well as the Society for Constructive Birth Control and Racial Progress. Her later writings include 1918's *Wise Parenthood* and 1934's *Birth Control Today,* both of which provided contemporary readers with up-to-date information on birth control methods.

BIOGRAPHICAL/CRITICAL SOURCES:

BOOKS

Aylmer, Maude, *The Authorized Life of Marie Stopes,* Williams & Norgate (London), 1924, revised as *Marie Stopes: Her Work and Play,* Putnam (New York City), 1933.
Box, Muriel, *The Trial of Marie Stopes,* Femina (London), 1967.
Briant, Keith, *Marie Stopes,* Hogarth Press, 1962.
Carpenter, Edward, *Love's Coming of Age,* Allen & Unwin, 1930.
Coldrick, Jack, *Dr. Marie Stopes and Press Censorship of Birth Control,* Athol (Belfast), 1992.
Hall, Ruth, *Passionate Crusader: The Life of Marie Stopes,* Deutsch (London), 1977.
Mort, Frank, *Dangerous Sexualities,* Kegan Paul (New York City), 1987.
Rose, June, *Marie Stopes and the Sexual Revolution,* Faber & Faber (London), 1992.
Stopes, Marie, *Married Love,* A. C. Fifield, 1918.

OBITUARIES:

PERIODICALS

Times (London), October 3, 1958.*

STORES, Teresa (T.) 1958-

PERSONAL: Born November 20, 1958, in Jacksonville, FL; daughter of O. J. (a boring contractor) and Nancy (a school counselor; maiden name, Lovell) Stores; married Mike Goldsmith, 1978 (divorced, 1988); life partner of Susan Jarvis (an artist). *Education:* Attended the University of Florida, 1976-77; University of Colorado at Boulder, B.A., 1987; Emerson College, M.F.A., 1993. *Politics:* "Active observer/Activist when pressed." *Religion:* "Born and raised Fundamentalist Southern Baptist; razed at thirty and reborn a fundamentally Yankee lesbian." *Avocational interest:* "People, words, and other living things."

ADDRESSES: Home—R.R. 1, Box 55, River Rd., Putney, VT 05346. *E-mail*—greycat14@aol.com or tstorz@sover.net.

CAREER: Has worked as a waiter; Ridgewood High School, Newport Richey, FL, teacher of English, 1988-91; Emerson College, Boston, MA, adjunct professor of writing, 1992-93; Kean College, Union, NJ, adjunct professor of writing, 1993-94; Merrill Lynch, Princeton, NJ, editor, 1993-95; freelance writer, 1993—; Community College of Vermont, Brattleboro, VT, adjunct professor of English, 1996-97; Holyoke Community College, Holyoke, MA, adjunct professor of writing, 1996-97; Colby-Sawyer College, New London, NH, adjunct professor of writing, 1996-97.

MEMBER: Women's Action Coalition, Lesbian Avengers, ACT-UP, Associated Writing Programs, National Writers Union, National Organization of Women, Modern Language Association.

WRITINGS:

Getting to the Point (novel), Naiad Press (Tallahassee, FL), 1995.
Side Tracks (novel), Naiad Press, 1995.

Contributor of stories and articles to periodicals, including *Sinister Wisdom, Sojourner, A Woman's Forum,* and *Evergreen Chronicles.*

WORK IN PROGRESS: Death in the Family: An Obituary, a cross-genre semi-autobiographical book about a death, a coming out, disowning, and a dysfunctional family; screenplays for both *Getting to the Point* and *Side Tracks; Virg,* a coming-of-age novel about a fundamentalist Christian girl in the 1970s suburban South.

SIDELIGHTS: Teresa Stores's novel *Getting to the Point* is somewhat autobiographical, in that its protagonist, Dix, divorces her husband when she acknowledges her lesbianism. Stores uses six viewpoint characters, however, to tell her story. The novel takes its title from its setting, a small town in Georgia called Point Will. It is to this location that Dix returns to a family that has for the most part disowned her because of her sexuality. Her dying grandmother—the reason for Dix's return—has, however, been protected from this knowledge. The grandmother is also the most loving member of the family and the one who holds it together. Dix's father, though, is the most hardened to his daughter—he won't even speak to her. Her brother—and her brother's wife—defend Dix's role in the family, but her sister-in-law draws the line at Dix being open about her sexual preference in front of her children. While Dix is dealing with these family members, as well as with the predicted heartache the loss of her grandmother will bring, her lover Sarah descends upon the household, forcing Dix and all of the other characters to confront their feelings about each other. As Pam Keesey explained in the *Lambda Book Report,* "Sarah has come to the Point to find Dix—not only to find Dix herself, but to find Dix' past: the home and the childhood summers that mean so much to her; the family whose imprint on Dix' adulthood is clearly etched; the grandmother whose impending death is such a turning point in Dix' life."

Several critics had high praise for *Getting to the Point.* Whitney Scott in *Booklist* called Dix's family "one of the most irascible . . . in literature," and lauded the book's "gritty energy." A reviewer for the *Alabama Forum* hailed *Getting to the Point* as "wonderful" and "well-crafted," one which "most Southern lesbians will relate to and enjoy." Keesey assessed the book as "a masterful portrait of family relationships. The characters feel like real people, full of memories, hopes and dreams while also being rife with contradictions." Anne Chambers in *MGW: Mom Guess What Newspaper* enjoyed Stores' first full-length effort as well, predicting that it would "have readers flipping the pages to see what law of Southern behavior will be broken next." Deborah Peifer, holding forth in the *Bay Area Reporter,* praised *Getting to the Point* as "a novel . . . that is so powerful it makes me grateful that I can read."

Stores told *CA:* "I am a writer because I am a Southerner. Southerners raise their young on stories as lush and intricate as a live oak canopy dripping Spanish moss. As far back as I can remember, I heard tales told: on the front porch, where the wisteria hung like clumps of grapes and the rockers squeaked slow; under the pecan tree, as we all shelled peas and churned fresh peach ice cream; during long Sunday drives to find tumbled-down grave markers covered with vines and weeds in a maze of dirt roads. The words and the tales were simple, told to entertain (the great-great uncle, a cook in the Civil War, whose arm was shot off into the pot and left there for the stew because the troops were starving), and to challenge (the black man who brought mare's milk to cure the last child of the fever that had already killed the mama and the other three young'uns, because they were all poor back then, black and white, 'just folks'), and to remember (the time Grandpa and his three brothers drove the Model A from Georgia to Miami, camping along the side of the one-lane dirt road, thick green like a jungle on each side, and a'most no people, for days), and to try to understand.

"When I wrote my novel, *Getting to the Point,* I was trying to understand.

I try to do all those things with my own words. The storytelling on which I was raised made a pattern in my mind, my unconscious, so woven together that I can never hope to unravel the ways it happens, but I still think, *tell a story that entertains, a story that challenges, a story that remembers, a story that tries to understand.*

"Though I was raised on stories, I was also raised working-class, middle-class, Wonder-Bread suburban. People in that world grew up to be nurses and teachers and construction workers. If you worked really hard, you might go to college and be a lawyer or a doctor, enter a profession where you could earn a decent living, buy a nice suburban home and settle down. No one ever considered becoming a writer.

"In 1986, while working toward a teaching certificate, I took a class with writer Alix Kates Shulman. I wrote down a few of the stories woven into my mind. I will always remember the windy, wet Colorado spring day when, as we stood outside class, she said, 'Yes, you can be a writer. You *should* be a writer. You *are* a writer.' It was the most radical thing I'd ever considered. I never looked back.

"Now I struggle, just like emerging writers everywhere, from freelance job to housesitting job to waiting tables to teaching to business, to find time/money/time/money to meet this insatiable need to write the stories down. I have written novels from four until eight in the morning daily before heading off to a full-time corporate office job and I have written short stories on order pads between waiting on tables at midnight. Sometimes I don't write at all and work nonstop to save enough money that I might do nothing *but* write for a month or two. And then I have to struggle again. My family thinks I can't keep a job, but the truth is that jobs are superfluous to my career: writing down the stories. I suppose one day my descendants will tell stories about me, too. I hope those stories, too, will entertain, teach, remember, and finally, understand."

BIOGRAPHICAL/CRITICAL SOURCES:

PERIODICALS

Alabama Forum, March, 1995.
Bay Area Reporter, February 16, 1995, p. 53; August 22, 1996, p. 43.
Booklist, March 15, 1995.
Lambda Book Report, March/April, 1995, p. 22.
MGW: Mom Guess What Newspaper, May 1, 1995.

* * *

STOUT, Chris E. 1959-

PERSONAL: Born May 8, 1959, in Dallas, TX; son of Carlos L. (a farmer) and Helen E. (a bookkeeper; maiden name, Simmons) Stout; married Karen Beckstrand (a psychologist), October 20, 1985; children: Grayson B. *Ethnicity:* "Caucasian." *Education:* Purdue University, A.A.S., 1979, B.S. (with honors), 1981; Forest Institute, doctorate, 1985; Harvard Medical School Fellow, 1987; Newport University, M.B.A., 1996. *Politics:* Democrat. *Religion:* Protestant. *Avocational interests:* Climbing, adventure travel, running, photojournalism.

ADDRESSES: Home—154 Ironwood Ct., Buffalo Grove, IL 60089-6626. *Office*—Forest Hospital, 555 Wilson Lane, Des Plains, IL 60016-4794; fax 847-913-0344. *E-mail*—cstout@ix.netcom.com.

CAREER: Forest Hospital, Des Plaines, IL, chief of psychology and director of research, 1985—. Illinois School and Chicago Medical School, associate professor of clinical psychology, 1990—. Forest Health Systems, Inc., senior vice-president of clinical applications, policy, and development; Alliance Research Group, director; Stout Ventures, principal; private practice of psychology, 1985—; lecturer in the United

States and abroad; guest on television and radio programs. U.S. Department of Commerce, member of board of examiners, Baldridge National Quality Award. Lake County Board of Health, vice-chairperson of Advisory Board and Coordinating Council; Lake County Mental Health Advisory Group, past chairperson.

MEMBER: American Psychological Association, American College of Health Care Executives, Illinois Psychological Association, National Academy of Neuropsychology (NAN), Society for Personality Assessment (SPA), Association for the Advancement of Psychology (AAP).

AWARDS, HONORS: Recipient of more than twenty-five honors for his work.

WRITINGS:

Parents' Handbook, Copley Press, 1990.
(With John Levitt and Douglas Ruben) *Handbook of Assessing and Treating Addictive Disorders,* Greenwood Press (Westport, CT), 1993.
From the Other Side of the Couch: Candid Conversations with Psychiatrists and Psychologists, Greenwood Press, 1993.
(With Morris B. Squire and Ruben) *Current Advances in Inpatient Psychiatric Care,* Greenwood Press, 1993.
(With Ruben and Leonard Koziol) *Handbook of Childhood Impulse Disorders and ADHD,* C. C. Thomas (Springfield, IL), 1993.
(With Ruben) *Transitions,* Praeger, 1994.
(With Koziol) *Neuropsychology of Mental Disorders,* C. C. Thomas, 1994.
(With Jerry Theis and James Oher) *The Complete Guide to Managed Behavioral Health Care,* Wiley (New York City), 1996.
The Integration of Psychological Principles to Policy Development, Praeger, 1996.

National columnist, *Behavioral Treatment.* Contributor to psychology journals. Editor in chief, *Clinical Review;* contributing editor, *Behavioral Treatment.*

WORK IN PROGRESS: Psychological Testing and Managed Care, for Wiley.

BIOGRAPHICAL/CRITICAL SOURCES:

OTHER

Web Site: http://www.smartwealth.com

STRAUSS, Jennifer 1933-

PERSONAL: Born Jennifer Wallace, January 30, 1933, in Heywood, Victoria, Australia; married Werner Strauss, 1958; children: three sons. *Education:* University of Melbourne, B.A. (honors), 1954; attended University of Glasgow, 1957-58; Monash University, Ph.D., 1991.

ADDRESSES: Home—2/12 Tollington Ave., East Malvern, Victoria 3145, Australia.

CAREER: University of Melbourne, lecturer, 1961-63; Monash University, Melbourne, lecturer, 1964-71, senior lecturer, 1971-91, associate professor, 1991—. Visiting scholar, University of North Carolina, Chapel Hill, 1974, and Australian National University, Canberra, 1988; visiting professor, Centre for Medieval Studies, University of Toronto, Ontario, 1982; member of literature committee, Ministry for the Arts, Victoria, 1983-85. Chair, Premier's Literary Awards Committee, 1989-91.

AWARDS, HONORS: Westerly Sesquicentenary prize, 1979.

WRITINGS:

POETRY

Children and Other Strangers, Nelson (Melbourne), 1975.
Winter Driving, Sisters (Melbourne), 1981.
Labour Ward, Melbourne Pariah Press (Melbourne), 1988.

OTHER

(Editor with Bruce Moore and Jan Noble) *Middle English Verse: An Anthology,* Monash University (Melbourne), 1976; revised edition, with Charles A. Stevenson, 1985.
"Stop Laughing! I'm Being Serious:" Studies in Seriousness and Wit in Contemporary Australian Literature, Foundation for the Study of Australian Literature (Townsville), 1990.
Boundary Conditions: The Poetry of Gwen Harwood, University of Queensland Press (St. Lucia), 1992.
(Editor) *The Oxford Book of Australian Love Poems,* Oxford University Press (Melbourne), 1993.

SUCH, David G. 1954-

PERSONAL: Born June 29, 1954; son of John (a machinist) and Mary (a bookkeeper; maiden name, Trelak) Such. *Education:* California State University, Fullerton, B.A., 1978; University of California, Los Angeles, M.A., 1980, Ph.D., 1985. *Politics:* "Whatever makes sense." *Religion:* "Musician."

ADDRESSES: Home—P.O. Box 92, Claremont, CA 91711.

CAREER: Freelance soloist, recording artist, composer, and producer, 1978—; Theatre of the Ear, KPKF radio, music director and composer, 1981-82; *Key to Rebecca* (television mini-series), KCOP, performer on the soundtrack, 1985; AVAZ International Music and Dance Troupe, music director, 1986-87; performed on numerous artists' compact disc recordings, 1991-94; *Qala Al-Rawi—Bedouin Honor and Women's Poetic Traditions* (one-act play), Barnsdale Park Theatre, performed music, 1991; "World Music and Beyond" concert series, Alligator Lounge, Santa Monica, CA, producer, 1994; *Sound of Dreams* (compact disc), leader of recording and producer, Pleasure Center Productions (in association with Space Age Bachelor Pad Records), 1995; California Institute for Men, Chino, CA, producer for the educational concert series "Music for A Small Planet," 1996.

University of California, Los Angeles, visiting assistant professor of folklore and mythology and of music, 1986-87; California State University, Northridge, lecturer in music, 1987-88; University of California, Los Angeles, visiting assistant professor of ethnomusicology and systematic musicology, 1987-89; California Polytechnic University, Pomona, lecturer in music, 1989; California State University, San Diego, lecturer in anthropology, 1989-91; New College of California, Integrated Biology and Humanities Program, administrative director, 1991-92; Emperor's College of Traditional Oriental Medicine, Santa Monica, CA, Dean, 1992-93; Hope University, Anaheim, CA, music director, 1995—; Mount San Antonio College, Walnut, CA, lecturer in anthropology, 1996—.

AWARDS, HONORS: California State Graduate Scholarship, 1978-80; Graduate Travel and Research Grant, UCLA, 1980; Institute of American Cultures Research Grant, UCLA, 1983; Faculty Research and Travel Grant, UCLA, 1986.

WRITINGS:

Avant-Garde Jazz Musicians: Performing "Out There," University of Iowa Press, 1993.

Contributor to books, including *The New Grove Dictionary of Jazz,* Macmillan, 1988; also contributor of articles and reviews to periodicals, including *Social History of Jazz, Galpin Society Journal, Journal of Asian Culture, African-American Review, Journal of American Folklore,* and *Pacific Review of Ethnomusicology.*

WORK IN PROGRESS: "Writing on my reflections on music and musicians with whom I have worked." Music for a second compact disc.

SIDELIGHTS: David G. Such told *CA:* "My interest in avant-garde jazz is the result of a lifetime commitment and love for music, especially music that is personal and as individualistic as the human mind and range of emotions can allow. When I was a child, music played a prominent role in my family, and I quickly grew to love it. My mother played piano at church; my brother played Polish-American polkas on the accordion at family gatherings; and after drinking a little too much wine, my father reveled in improvising disjointed, imaginative songs on the organ, though he never took a music lesson in his life.

"I never abandoned myself to formal music training, instead choosing to nurture my own love for music more as a personal expression than a replication of an established style. To summarize in few words what music is I conclude simply it is whatever sounds good.

"My interests in travel and the quest for knowledge greatly influenced my views on music. While traveling extensively I absorbed and researched the music of other cultures, especially Middle Eastern, east European, African, Irish, Spanish gypsy, India, and of course jazz. Of all these experiences, avant-garde jazz musicians influenced me perhaps the most. Their dedication to improvising music that is highly individualistic and personal makes the act of performing an extension of life that remains purely responsive to the creative impulse. Commercial gain is not a primary motivation for the type of music they perform; instead they choose to fuse music with life and to view life as creatively as their music. Avant-garde jazz musicians' approach to music holds valuable lessons for our society. Because their music is relatively unknown to most people, I felt it especially compelling to tell a part of their story to a wider audience. Writing seemed the most suitable medium for this purpose."

In *Avant-Garde Jazz Musicians: Performing "Out There"* Such provides histories of contemporary avant-gardists like Billy Bang and Milford Graves while discussing what he terms "out jazz." Economical, societal, geographical, and historical aspects of the musical genre are explored along with the important avant-garde musicians. "Such broaches important questions," writes a *Cadence* reviewer, "like those hinted in his chapter on perceptions of out music and metaphorical thought." The reviewer goes on to conclude that *Avant-Garde Jazz Musicians* "could (and probably should) be used in teaching college-level jazz history classes and classes in African American aesthetics and/or American musical culture."

BIOGRAPHICAL/CRITICAL SOURCES:

PERIODICALS

Cadence, July, 1994, p. 26.

*   *   *

SUI SIN FAR
  See EATON, Edith Maude

*   *   *

SULLIVAN, Andrew 1963-

PERSONAL: Born August 20, 1963, in Godstone, Surrey, England. *Education:* Attended Magdalen College, Oxford; Harvard University, M.A. (public administration), Ph.D. (political science). *Religion:* Roman Catholic.

ADDRESSES: Home—Washington, DC. *Office—New Republic,* Suite 600, 1220 19th St. N.W., Washington, DC 20036.

CAREER: New Republic magazine, Washington, DC, member of staff, 1986-91, editor, 1991—.

WRITINGS:

(Editor with Jacob Weisberg) *Bushisms,* compiled by Jonathan Bines, Workman (New York), 1992.

Virtually Normal: An Argument about Homosexuality, Knopf (New York), 1995.

Contributor of articles, editorials, and reviews to periodicals, including the *Advocate.*

SIDELIGHTS: In his 1995 book, *Virtually Normal: An Argument about Homosexuality, New Republic* editor Andrew Sullivan analyzes public thought regarding homosexuality, basing his discussion on the premise that homosexuality is innate, rather than merely a chosen lifestyle. The book opens with the author's recollections of an emotional childhood spent in England, where he recalls, even as a toddler, having crushes on several male classmates. Sullivan then traces the events that led to his discovery in his early twenties of his homosexuality, sharing that his first kiss with a man was "like being in a black-and-white movie that suddenly converted to color."

After his autobiographical introduction, Sullivan devotes a chapter each to his analysis of four different views of homosexuality, which he labels "prohibitionist," "liberationist," "conservative," and "liberal." The first of these views, the prohibitionist, uses the Bible to refute homosexuality. The liberationist believes, however, that homosexuality is a choice or preference, neither an innate human trait nor a sin. Conservatives, according to Sullivan, believe in guaranteed rights granting personal freedoms, but feel a certain moral standard must prevail in politics and society, a standard that often excludes homosexuals. Finally, Sullivan explains, the liberals view homosexuals as an oppressed minority group that must ardently fight for equal rights.

Sullivan takes exception to various aspects of each of the four views he examines. He embraces none of these arguments fully, but instead focuses his attention on two major concerns of homosexuals in the United States: the ability for openly gay people to serve in the military, and the legalization of same-sex marriages. When gay men and women are granted these basic rights, Sullivan postulates, then society will recognize and benefit from the many positive influences that homosexuals have to offer.

Regarding the service of homosexuals in the military, Sullivan chastises the "don't ask, don't tell" policy that allows gays to serve in the armed forces, but only if they keep their sexuality a secret. Calling for the United States government to allow avowed homosexuals into service, Sullivan declares that military service is a basic right of citizenship that should be open to everyone, regardless of sexual orientation. Homosexual marriages, too, according to Sullivan, should be sanctioned by the government to provide homosexuals with the right to enter into the covenant of marriage and the security of family. Commenting on both the military service and marriage issues, Sullivan told Richard Coles in a *New Statesman and Society* interview: "I believe that the attitudes of those institutions—marriage and the military—toward homosexuals represent the heart and soul of society's hostility to homosexuality. If you change those institutions, it's a stake through the heart of homophobia. . . . Early on I thought to myself. What do we want? What do I want? Well, I want fundamental equality. And what are the two things from which we are fundamentally excluded? These two."

Sullivan closes *Virtually Normal* with his thoughts on the contributions that homosexuals can make to society. Although often childless, Sullivan points out, gay men and women can serve in "broader parental roles," as teachers, nurses and doctors, priests and nuns, or as adoptive parents. Because they are usually childless, Sullivan suggests, gay couples can work longer hours and have more time to devote to community service, thus contributing more than their heterosexual counterparts. Sullivan also opines that same-sex unions tend to be strengthened by friendship, and are frequently more stable than heterosexual marriages.

Virtually Normal received mixed reviews, although most critics agreed that Sullivan has made a valuable contribution with his book. *Commonweal* editor Margaret O'Brien Steinfels questioned Sullivan's comment that "there is more likely to be greater understanding of the need for extramarital outlets between two men than between a man and a woman; and, again, the lack of children gives gay couples greater freedom. Their failures entail fewer consequences for others." Steinfels responded: "But then, why call it marriage at all?" Nevertheless, Steinfels found merit in Sullivan's book: "The inconsistencies of these final chapters notwithstanding, *Virtually Normal* is a book to take seriously. It is most engaging at those moments when the agonistic stance of the debater shifts to reveal a man who like the rest of us is trying to understand 'how we a society deal with that small minority of us which is homosexual.'"

Washington Post Book World contributor Camille Paglia also issued qualified applause for *Virtually Normal:* "Although its historical and scientific claims are often carelessly overstated—homosexuality is hardly 'universal' or 'a constant throughout all cultures and times'—*Virtually Normal* is a brilliant and revolutionary book that will transform gay studies, a discipline that has never produced complex argument of this high quality. . . . In a single stroke, Sullivan establishes himself as one of the politically most sophisticated voices on the international gay scene, where predictable, one-dimensional ideology is too often the depressing rule." Richard Bernstein, writing in the *New York Times,* also indicated several weaknesses in Sullivan's discourse, but declared: "Whether one is persuaded by Mr. Sullivan or not, few people are likely to remain entirely unmoved by at least some of his arguments or to feel exactly the same about homosexuality after reading his book as they did before. . . . With so much noise on the fringes of this matter, a quiet, dignified explication like Mr. Sullivan's can only lead to good."

BIOGRAPHICAL/CRITICAL SOURCES:

PERIODICALS

Advocate, September 19, 1995, pp. 66-68.
Commonweal, September 22, 1995, pp. 24-26.
New Statesman and Society, October 13, 1995, pp. 26-27.
New Yorker, October 11, 1995, pp. 87-91.
New York Times, October 4, 1991, p. A18; September 6, 1995, p. C15.
New York Times Book Review, August 20, 1995, p. 3.
Village Voice, September 19, 1995, pp. 85-87.
Washington Post Book World, September 10, 1995, pp. 1, 8.*

*   *   *

SULLIVAN, Randall 1951-

PERSONAL: Born December 1, 1951, in San Pedro, CA; son of Howard W. (a longshoreman) and Elaine V. (a secretary; maiden name, White) Sullivan; married Karen Kuhlman, 1971 (divorced, 1981); married Tara Fields, 1985 (divorced, 1988); married Joy Candace Welp, September 13, 1995. *Education:* University of Oregon, B.A., 1974; Columbia University, M.F.A., 1980. *Politics:* Independent. *Religion:* "Catholic (come lately)." *Avocational interests:* Carpentry, woodworking, sculpture.

ADDRESSES: Home—Portland, OR. *Agent*—Kathy Robbins, Robbins Office, 405 Park Ave., New York, NY 10022.

CAREER: *New York Daily News*, New York City, reporter, 1978-79; *Los Angeles Herald Examiner*, Los Angeles, CA, columnist, 1979-83; *Rolling Stone*, New York City, contributing editor, 1983-91; freelance writer, 1991—. Screenwriter.

MEMBER: Writers Guild of America (West), Phi Beta Kappa.

AWARDS, HONORS: Los Angeles Press Club Award, best feature, 1979; Hearst Writing Award, best feature, 1980; second prize, R. F. Kennedy Journalism Awards, 1980.

WRITINGS:

The Price of Experience: Power, Money, Image, and Murder in Los Angeles, Atlantic Monthly Press (New York), 1996.

Contributor to books, including *Best of California Magazine*, 1987; and *Best of Rolling Stone*, Doubleday (New York), 1993. Contributor of articles and stories to magazines, including *Esquire*, *California*, *Redbook*, *Epoch*, and *BOPP*.

WORK IN PROGRESS: *The Grace Period* (tentative title), about a small village in Bosnia that has been the site of many reported miracles, for Atlantic Monthly Press.

SIDELIGHTS: Randall Sullivan told *CA:* "I went into journalism after finishing my Masters of Fine Arts at Columbia because it was a way to earn a living without resorting to academia, thinking that I would return to fiction after a few years of newspapering. Something happened along the way, though. Part of it was that, while living in Los Angeles, I began investing my imagination in movie scenarios. It is terribly painful now to think of all the time and energy I squandered on meetings with producers and vice-presidents for development. What little that ever got made hardly came out as I had hoped.

"There was a deeper (perhaps more insidious) process at work, though. Somehow, though writing and publishing nonfiction, I began to want the world—the events that really take place—to reveal a poetic logic, believing that if I could just see it clearly and tell it strongly, truth would take on meaning.

"I haven't recovered yet from this peculiar ambition, but at least my yearning has become more personal. Now it is about reconciling events in the world around me with my internal experience. As a result, my work seems to be mutating into a genre I think of as investigative autobiography. Perhaps I should have stuck with fiction, but at this point I feel I have to follow the path I am on until either it peters out or I arrive at some destination."

*   *   *

SUNSHINE, Linda 1948-

PERSONAL: Born March 29, 1948, in Brooklyn, NY; daughter of Harold King (an optometrist) and Norma (Deutsch) Sunshine. *Education:* Ithaca College, B.A., 1970; attended New York University, 1971-73.

ADDRESSES: *Home*—New York, NY. *Office*—Stewart, Tabori & Chang, 575 Broadway, New York, NY 10012. *Agent*—Sarah Lazin, Sarah Lazin Books, 137 Fifth Ave., 4th Floor, New York, NY 10010.

CAREER: Crown Publishers, New York City, executive editor of Harmony Books, 1970-78; Simon & Schuster, New York City, editor in chief of Fireside Books, 1978-80; freelance editor and writer, 1980-93; Stewart, Tabori & Chang, New York City, editorial director, 1993—. Wavertree Corp., member of board of directors, 1984-89. God's Love We Deliver, volunteer.

MEMBER: Authors Guild, Women's Media Group.

WRITINGS:

Constant Stranger, Simon & Schuster (New York), 1982.
Plain Jane Works Out, Bantam (New York City), 1983.
The Plain Jane 1984 Calendar: A Year of Twinkies and Diet Soda, Bantam, 1983.
Plain Jane's Thrill of Very Fattening Foods Cookbook, St. Martin's (New York), 1985.
The Memoirs of Bambi Goldbloom; or, Growing Up in New Jersey (novel), Simon & Schuster, 1987.
(With John Wright) *The Best Hospitals in America*, Henry Holt (New York), 1987, revised edition, Gale (Detroit, MI), 1995.
Women Who Date Too Much (And Those Who Should Be So Lucky) (humor), New American Library (New York), 1988.
(With Wright) *The One Hundred Best Treatment Centers for Alcoholism and Drug Abuse*, Avon (New York), 1988.

"Mom Loves Me Best" and Other Lies You Told Your Sister (humor), New American Library, 1989.

One-Hundred-One Uses for Silly Putty (humor), Andrews & McMeel (Kansas City, MO), 1990.

How NOT to Turn into Your Mother (humor), Dell (New York), 1991.

Lovers (nonfiction), Andrews & McMeel, 1992.

Dating Iron John (humor), Carol Publishing (New York), 1993.

(With Woody Allen) *The Illustrated Woody Allen Reader,* Knopf (New York), 1993.

It Could Happen to You (novelization), Newmarket Press (New York), 1994.

(With Mary Tiegreen) *A Passion for Shoes,* Andrews & McMeel, 1995.

Bogus (novelization), Stewart, Tabori & Chang (New York), 1996.

EDITOR

Victoria's Book of Days, Morrow (New York), 1989.

The HBO Guide to Videocassettes, Harper (New York), 1989.

Victoria's On Being a Mother, Morrow, 1990.

By Any Other Name: A Celebration of Roses, Doubleday (New York), 1990.

In the Company of Cats, Andrews & McMeel, 1991.

It's a Boy!, Macmillan (New York), 1992.

It's a Girl!, Macmillan, 1992.

A Vow of Love, Andrews & McMeel, 1992.

Victoria's No Friend Like a Sister, Morrow, 1992.

To Grandmother, With Love, Andrews & McMeel, 1992.

Victoria's A Love Is Born: A Keepsake Journal for Mothers, Morrow, 1993.

Newborn Joy, Andrews & McMeel, 1993.

Ntozake Shange, *i live in music* (poems), Stewart, Tabori & Chang, 1994.

In the Heart of a Friend, Andrews & McMeel, 1994.

A Teacher Affects Eternity, Andrews & McMeel, 1994.

Leonard Cohen, *Dance Me to the End of Love* (poems), Stewart, Tabori & Chang, 1995.

e.e. cummings, *may i feel said he* (poems), Stewart, Tabori & Chang, 1995.

Father of My Heart, Morrow, 1995.

Words of Comfort, Andrews & McMeel, 1996.

Contributor to books, including *MGM: When the Lion Roared,* Turner Publishing, 1991. Contributor to magazines, including *New York Woman, Omni, Harper's Bazaar, Cosmopolitan, Glamour, Woman, New Woman,* and *American Woman.*

SZYMBORSKA, Wislawa 1923-
(Stancykowna)

PERSONAL: Born July 2, 1923, in Prowent-Bnin, near Poznan, Poland. *Education:* Attended Jagellonian University, 1945-48.

ADDRESSES: Home—Ul. Krolewska 82/89, 30-079, Cracow, Poland.

CAREER: Poet and critic. Poetry editor and columnist, *Zycie literackie* (literary weekly magazine), 1953-81.

MEMBER: Polish Writers' Association (member of general board, 1978-83).

AWARDS, HONORS: Cracow literary prize, 1954; Gold Cross of Merit, 1955; Ministry of Culture prize, 1963; Knight's Cross, Order of Polonia Resituta, 1974; Goethe Prize, 1991; Herder Prize, 1995; Polish PEN Club prize, 1996; Nobel Prize for Literature, 1996.

WRITINGS:

POETRY

Dlatego zyjemy (title means "That's Why We Are Alive"), [Warsaw], 1952.

Pytania zadawane sobie (title means "Questions Put to Myself"), [Warsaw], 1954.

Wolanie do Yeti (title means "Calling Out to Yeti"), [Warsaw], 1957.

Sol (title means "Salt"), Panstwowy Instytut Wydawniczy (Warsaw), 1962.

Wiersze wybrane (collection), Panstwowy Instytut Wydawniczy, 1964.

Sto pociech (title means "A Hundred Joys"), Panstwowy Instytut Wydawniczy, 1967.

Poezje wybrane (title means "Selected Poems"), Ludowa Spoldzielnia Wydawnicza, 1967.

Poezje (title means "Poems"), Przedmowa Jerzego Kwiatkowskiego (Warsaw), 1970.

Wybor poezje (collection), Czytelnik, 1970.

Wszelki wypadek (title means "There But for the Grace"), Czytelnik, 1972.

Wybor wierszy (collection), Panstwowy Instytut Wydawniczy, 1973.

Tarsjusz i inne wiersze (title means "Tarsius and Other Poems"), Krajowa Agencja Wydawnicza (Warsaw), 1976.

Wielka liczba (title means "A Great Number"), Czytelnik, 1976.

Sounds, Feelings, Thoughts: Seventy Poems, translated by Magnus J. Krynski and Robert A. Maguire, Princeton University Press (Princeton, NJ), 1981.

Poezje wybrane (II), (title means "Selected Poems II"), Ludowa Spoldzielnia Wydawnicza (Warsaw), 1983.

Ludzie na moscie, Czytelnik, 1986, translation by Adam Czerniawski published as *People on a Bridge: Poems,* Forest (London and Boston, MA), 1990.

Poezje = Poems (bilingual edition), translated by Krynski and Maguire, Wydawnictwo Literackie (Cracow), 1989.

Wieczor autorski: wiersze (title means "Authors' Evening: Poems"), Anagram, 1992.

Koniec i poczatek (title means "The End and the Beginning"), Wydawnictwo Literackie, 1993.

View with a Grain of Sand: Selected Poems, translated by Stanislaw Baranczak and Clare Cavanagh, Harcourt (New York City), 1995.

Also author of *Lektury nadobowiazkowe* (collection of book reviews; title means "Non-Compulsory Reading"), Wydawnictwo Literackie, 1973, and translator of French poetry. Work represented in anthologies, including *Polish Writing Today,* Penguin (New York City), 1967; *The New Polish Poetry,* University of Pittsburgh Press, 1978; and *Anthologie de la poesie polonaise: 1400-1980,* revised edition, Age d'homme, 1981. Also contributor, under pseudonym Stancykowna, to *Arka* (underground publication) and *Kultura* (exile magazine; published in Paris).

Szymborska's works have been translated into Arabic, Hebrew, Japanese, Chinese, and other languages.

SIDELIGHTS: Wislawa Szymborska was thrust into the international spotlight in 1996 after receiving the Nobel Prize for Literature. The reclusive and private Szymborska was cited by the Swedish Academy for "poetry that with ironic precision allows the historical and biological context to come to light in fragments of human reality." Her poetry, described by *Los Angeles Times* critic Dean E. Murphy, is "seductively simple verse . . . [which has] captured the wit and wisdom of everyday life for the past half century."

Though not widely known outside her native Poland, Szymborska received critical acclaim for the first collection of her work to appear in English translation, *Sounds, Feelings, Thoughts: Seventy Poems.* "Of the poetic voices to come out of Poland after 1945 Wislawa Szymborska's is probably the most

elusive as well as the most distinctive," writes Jaroslaw Anders in the *New York Review of Books.* Anders comments: "*Sounds, Feelings, Thoughts* contains poems from [Szymborska's] five books written since 1957, comprising more or less half of what the poet herself considers her canon. Its publication is of interest not only because of Szymborska's importance as a poet, but also because her work demonstrates that the diversity of poetic modes in Poland is much greater than is usually perceived." Alice-Catherine Carls, in a review of *Sounds, Feelings, Thoughts* in *Library Journal,* calls the work "one of those rare books which put one in a state of 'grace.'" Robert Hudzik, also in *Library Journal,* claims: "This volume reveals a poet of startling originality and deep sympathy."

The 1995 collection *Views with a Grain of Sand: Selected Poems* was also praised by many critics who laud Szymborska's directness and distinctive voice. Stephen Dobyns in the *Washington Post Book World* praises both the humor of Szymborska's work as well as the translation by Stanislaw Baranczak and Clare Cavanagh. Edward Hirsch in a *New York Review of Books* review concurs, arguing that the volume reveals "the full force of [Szymborska's] fierce and unexpected wit." Louis McKee, in a *Library Journal* review also praises the "wonderfully wicked" wit of Szymborska. Dobyns concludes: "The poems are surprising, funny and deeply moving. Szymborska is a world-class poet, and this book will go far to make her known in the United States."

BIOGRAPHICAL/CRITICAL SOURCES:

BOOKS

Levine, Madeleine G., *Contemporary Polish Poetry, 1925-1975,* Twayne (New York City), 1981.

PERIODICALS

Humanities Review, spring, 1982, p. 141.
Library Journal, September 1, 1981; July, 1995.
Los Angeles Times, October 4, 1996.
New Republic, January 1, 1996, p. 36.
New Yorker, December 14, 1992; March 1, 1993.
New York Review of Books, October 21, 1982, p. 47; October 21, 1993, p. 42; April 18, 1996, p. 35.
New York Times, October 4, 1996.
Observer (London), August 18, 1991, p. 51.
Wall Street Journal, October 4, 1996.
Washington Post Book World, July 30, 1995, p. 8.
World Literature Today, spring, 1982, p. 368.*

T

TALALAY, Kathryn M(arguerite) 1949-

PERSONAL: Born October 29, 1949, in New Haven, CT; daughter of Anselm (an inventor) and Marjorie Ruth (an art dealer; maiden name, Freedman) Talalay; married Frank James Ponzio III (a jazz pianist and composer), September 16, 1989. *Education:* Attended Bennington College, 1967-69; New York University, B.A. (classics), 1971; Case Western Reserve University, M.A. (musicology), M.L.S., 1975. *Religion:* Jewish.

ADDRESSES: Office—W. W. Norton and Co., 500 Fifth Avenue, New York, NY 10110.

CAREER: Indiana University School of Music, Head Reference Librarian and Research Librarian, 1975-90; American Academy of Arts and Letters, New York City, assistant archivist, researcher, 1990-1996; W.W. Norton and Co., New York City, project editor, 1996—.

MEMBER: Music Library Association, American Musicological Society, Center for Black Music Research.

AWARDS, HONORS: Indiana University grant recipient, 1977, 1980, 1982-83; Rockefeller Foundation scholar, 1988-89.

WRITINGS:

(Translator) *A Literal Translation of Joseph Haydn's Cantata,* Applausus (Bloomington), Indiana University, 1977.
The Deserter (comic opera), Indiana University, 1980.

Scores by Women Composers, Indiana University, 1988.
(With others) Notable Black American Women, Gale, 1992.
Composition in Black and White: The Life of Philippa Schuyler (biography), Oxford University (New York), 1995.
(With others) *Encyclopedia of African-American Culture and History,* MacMillan (New York), 1996.

Contributor of articles to professional journals.

WORK IN PROGRESS: (co-author) *Forgotten Scripts.*

SIDELIGHTS: Musicologist and editor Kathryn Talalay has chronicled an amazing life in *Composition in Black and White: The Life of Philippa Schuyler.* In writing the biography Talalay drew heavily on the Schuyler family papers, which are housed at the Schomburg Center for Research in Black Culture in New York City. Talalay recounted how Philippa Schuyler was a child prodigy during the 1930s, known as the "Shirley Temple of American Negroes" and "Harlem's Mozart." Philippa was the daughter of noted black journalist George Schuyler and his caucasian wife Josephine Cogdell, whose father was a Texas rancher. Cogdell believed that only through interracial marriage could race relations in the United States be improved.

Talalay described how from the outset the Schuylers—especially Josephine—pressured Philippa to be the perfect example of interracial union. With an I.Q. of 180, three-year-old Philippa could read and write. After a year of piano lessons, she performed Mozart publicly—at age four. Schuyler was schooled at home and entered numerous musical competitions. She was highly visible as a pianist when only eight years old. At age fifteen she soloed with the New York Philharmonic Orchestra, and the orchestra also performed one of her compositions, a symphony she had written two years earlier. Though Schuyler showed promise of becoming a great artist, she was only moderately successful with white audiences, a fact that limited her ability to pursue a concertizing career. She often performed abroad, where she found greater acceptance, and for a while beginning in 1959 she tried to pass as white under a Latin stage name. Despite her talent, Schuyler's life as a pianist was a lonely, unfulfilling one. Her attempts at romance were equally unsuccessful.

In the early 1960s, Schuyler began a new career as a journalist. Serendipitously she was in the Belgian Congo when it gained its independence, and Schuyler reported from the scene for United Press International. She later wrote a book on Zaire entitled *Who Killed the Congo?* (1962) and another about missionaries of the Roman Catholic church called *Jungle Saints* (1963). In 1965, Schuyler joined the staff of the *Manchester Union Leader,* an ultraconservative newspaper, for which she covered the Vietnam War. While rescuing orphans of war in 1967, she died in a helicopter crash. Although her life was cut short, Philippa Schuyler was a role model of her era and influenced the culture of her time.

Reviewers praised *Composition in Black and White.* Paula Woods, writing in the *Dallas Morning News* called the work "as compelling as the best fiction." Shirlee Taylor Hazlip in the *San Francisco Chronicle* described it as "a story of our times not to be missed." Marilyn Richardson from the *Women's Review of Books* hailed it as "one of the most vivid and artfully constructyed biographies yet written about any African-American woman. Carolyn See, writing in the *Washington Post,* called the work a "sad and thoughtful biography," and Phyllis Rose in the *New York Times Book Review* described it as an "enthralling, heartbreaking book." See called Schuyler's "a bleak, extraordinarily weird American life," adding, "Kathryn Talalay has done a gorgeous job with this unique material." Rose enthused, "This tragic tale makes an exhilarating book. Thanks to Kathryn Talalay, . . . for focusing on the Schuylers' story, researching it so energetically and telling it so sensitively." She concluded, "*Composition in Black and White* is a stimulating addition to the record of race relations in America, as well as a monument to an extraordinary woman—perhaps two extraordinary women—who might have otherwise vanished."

BIOGRAPHICAL/CRITICAL SOURCES:

PERIODICALS

Baltimore Sun, March 10, 1996, pp. H1, H3.
Daily Telegraph (London), July 27, 1996, p. A7.
Dallas Morning News, December 10, 1995, pp. J1, J9.
High Plains Literary Review, Vol. XI, No. 1, Spring 1996, 91-93.
New York Times Book Review, December 10, 1995, section 7, p. 16.
Observer (London), September 1, 1996, Book Review Section, p. 16.
Plain Dealer (Cleveland, Ohio), December 21, 1995.
Providence Sunday Journal, February 11, 1996, p. E7.
San Francisco Sunday Examiner and Chronicle, February 18, 1996, pp. 5ff.
Sunday Telegraph (London), July 28, 1996, p. R15.
Sunday Times (London), August 4, 1996, p. B6.
Washington Post, November 24, 1995, p. D3.
Women's Review of Books, Vol. XIII, April 1996, p. 9.

*   *   *

TAYLOR, Daniel (William)   1948-

PERSONAL: Born March 1, 1948, in Escondido, CA; married Jayne Smith, September 5, 1971; children: Matthew, Julia, Nathaniel, Anne. *Education:* Westmont College, B.A., 1970; Emory University, M.A. and Ph.D., both 1974. *Religion:* Christian.

ADDRESSES: Office—Department of English, Bethel College, 3900 Bethel Dr., St. Paul, MN 55112.

CAREER: Northwestern College, St. Paul, MN, English teacher, 1974-76; Westmont College, Santa Barbara, CA, English teacher, 1976; Bethel College, St. Paul, professor of English, 1977—.

AWARDS, HONORS: Woodrow Wilson fellow, 1970; grants from National Endowment for the Humanities, 1978, and U.S. Department of Education, 1982-83; *The Myth of Certainty* was selected Inspirational Book of the Year, Logos Bookstores, 1987.

WRITINGS:

(Editor with Lorraine Eitel) *The Treasury of Christian Poetry,* Revell (Old Tappan, NJ), 1982.

The Myth of Certainty: The Reflective Christian and the Risk of Commitment, Word (Waco, TX), 1986.

Letters to My Children: A Father Passes on His Values, InterVarsity Press (Downers Grove, IL), 1989.

The Healing Power of Stories: Creating Yourself Through the Stories of Your Life, Doubleday (New York), 1996.

Author of *Chicken Man and Other Stories,* not yet published, and *Bookstore,* a play. Contributor to books. Contributor of articles, stories, and reviews to periodicals, including *Christianity Today, Focus, Moody Monthly, Minnesota English Journal, Books and Culture,* and *Mars Hill Review.* Co-founder and co-editor, *Literature of the Oppressed,* 1987-93.

WORK IN PROGRESS: Death Comes to the Deconstructionist, a novel; *Before Their Time: The Life and Death of Premature Infants and What They Have to Teach Us,* completion expected in 1998; working as a stylist on a long-term Bible translation project, for Tyndale House (Wheaton, IL).

SIDELIGHTS: Daniel Taylor told *CA:* "I believe that writing generally, and literature in particular, embody our best attempts to record and contemplate the human experience. Stories offer us the most helpful answers to all of life's big questions. We live in stories the way fish live in water, surrounded by them but often unaware of the medium that sustains us. My writing is primarily an attempt to sniff out the best and healthiest stories available and try to learn and live what they have to teach."

* * *

TAYLOR, Gary 1953-

PERSONAL: Born in 1953.

ADDRESSES: Office—English Department, Brandeis University, RABB 144, Waltham, MA 02254.

CAREER: Catholic University of America, Washington, DC, professor; Brandeis University, Waltham, MA, professor, 1989—.

WRITINGS:

Three Studies in the Text of Henry (bound with *Modernizing Shakespeare's Spelling,* by Stanley Wells), Oxford University Press, 1979.

(Editor) William Shakespeare, *Henry V,* Oxford University Press, 1983.

(Editor with Michael Warren) *The Division of the Kingdoms: Shakespeare's Two Versions of King Lear,* Oxford University Press, 1983.

To Analyze Delight: A Hedonist Criticism of Shakespeare, University of Delaware Press, 1984, published in England as *Moment by Moment by Shakespeare,* Macmillan, 1985.

(With Stanley Wells) *William Shakespeare: A Textual Companion,* Oxford University Press, 1987.

Reinventing Shakespeare: A Cultural History, from the Restoration to the Present, Weidenfeld & Nicolson, 1989.

General editor with Stanley Wells of *William Shakespeare: The Complete Works,* Oxford University Press, original and modernized spelling editions both published in 1986, compact edition published in 1988, published as *The Complete Works of William Shakespeare,* 1987.

SIDELIGHTS: A Shakespeare scholar and the joint general editor of Oxford University Press's recent editions of Shakespeare's works, Gary Taylor has made a name for himself in a crowded field by offering some new and sometimes controversial views of the Bard's works and their impact on our culture. In 1985, while poring over manuscripts in the Bodleian Library at Oxford University, Taylor discovered a love poem that the text attributed to Shakespeare. The find sparked an excited debate among scholars over whether or not Shakespeare's canon would be amended for the first time in three hundred years. In essays, Taylor has asserted a different origin for the two versions of *King Lear,* countering the long-held view that each was a different distortion made by the author's successors and that the true text was a combination of the two. His books attempt to offer a new perspective on Shakespeare, exploring how the Bard's works have impacted the societies that have read and performed them, as well as how these societies have envisioned Shakespeare and his art to serve their changing needs.

The Division of the Kingdoms: Shakespeare's Two Versions of King Lear, a book which Taylor co-edited and to which he contributed two essays, proposes that "Shakespeare, like a host of other dramatists, may have revised his own plays as they moved through rehearsal and into production, so that the existence of two versions of the same play may indicate authoritative revision," Philip Edwards explains in the *Times Literary Supplement.* With respect to *King Lear,* this would suggest that the play as it is performed for modern audiences, a conflation of the First Quarto and First Folio, is not an accurate reconstruction of Shakespeare's original. Instead, notes Edwards, "Gary Taylor and others have been arguing that there is no common original and that the two texts represent an early version and a later revision."

This collection of essays "is an extremely long book, very detailed, and taxing to read," comments Edwards, "requiring the constant presence of copies of the Quarto text, the Folio text, and the received text." The reviewer concludes that "the question of revision in Shakespeare is interesting and at times has important implications. But we don't want to make a major doctrinal issue of the sanctity and the authority of both the *Lear* texts."

Taylor's most recent study, *Reinventing Shakespeare: A Cultural History, from the Restoration to the Present,* deals with society's changing view of Shakespeare, according to a *Publishers Weekly* contributor, but "also examines developments in publishing, journalism, theater, censorship, morality, education, sex, economics, [and] politics." In his examination of the interaction of the artist and the cultures of succeeding historical periods, Taylor offers "a fascinating account of culture as market, a place of business as well as entertainment, the engine of those processes through which name or reputation are secured and manipulated," according to Peter Ackroyd in the *Times.*

"Since Mr. Taylor's subject embraces many zany, offbeat materials, the curious alleyways are actually the chief pleasure here," *New York Times Book Review* contributor Gary Schmidgall notes of *Reinventing Shakespeare.* "The author has an eye for the arresting or telling bit of arcana." Yet, Schmidgall finds that "in the end, 'Reinventing Shakespeare' leaves one with a bad case of what, in Shakespeare's day, was called 'the sullens.' For one who had hitherto written 'To Analyze Delight: A Hedonist Criticism of Shakespeare,' Mr. Taylor curiously lacks the knack for humor in a darkling situation." Ackroyd offers a different evaluation, concluding that "by convincingly demonstrating the instability and relativity of even the most ferociously espoused critical values, Gary Taylor presents a dramatist who has become not valueless, but valuefree."

BIOGRAPHICAL/CRITICAL SOURCES:

PERIODICALS

Chicago Tribune, February 1, 1987, sec. 14, p. 7.

Christian Science Monitor, November 29, 1985, p. 34.
Globe and Mail (Toronto), August 1, 1987.
Los Angeles Times, December 15, 1985, sec. I, p. 1.
New York Times, September 1, 1989, sec. C, p. 23.
New York Times Book Review, September 17, 1989, p. 28.
Publishers Weekly, July 7, 1989, p. 44.
Times (London), February 8, 1990.
Times Literary Supplement, March 9, 1984.
Washington Post Book World, August 27, 1989.*

*   *   *

TAYLOR, Kathy 1950-

PERSONAL: Born June 14, 1950, in Whittier, CA; daughter of Daniel (an administrator and philosopher) and Rosalie (a librarian and bookkeeper; maiden name, Roney) Wilson; married Peter Taylor (a professor), June 14, 1970; children: Jordan, Anika. *Education:* Attended Penn State University; attended the Centro Internacional de Documentacion in Cuernavaca, Mexico, 1969; University of Iowa, B.A., 1980, M.A., 1982, Ph.D., 1988; attended Phillips Universitaet, Marburg, Germany, 1982-84. *Politics:* "Progressive." *Religion:* Society of Friends (Quaker). *Avocational interests:* Classical guitar, Latin American music of all kinds.

ADDRESSES: Home-1017 Abington Pike, Richmond, IN 47374. *Office*—Department of Languages and Literatures, Earlham College, Richmond, IN 47374.

CAREER: Scattergood High School, West Branch, IA, instructor in Spanish, 1974-78; University of Iowa, Iowa City, teaching assistant, 1979-82, 1984-87, adjunct instructor in Spanish, 1987; Earlham College, Richmond, IN, assistant professor, 1988-94, associate professor of Spanish, 1994—. Official translator for the First International Quaker Women's Conference on Theology at Woodbrooke, England; has done extensive volunteer work as an interpreter and translator for Hispanics and Latin American refugees; past international student exchange coordinator for Iowa City, IA, for students from Spain. Has presented papers at conferences in the United States and Mexico. Treasurer and/or member of school board for alternative community school, 1991-94, 1996—.

AWARDS, HONORS: Tuition scholarships from Penn State University, 1968-70, and University of Iowa,

1970-71; Department of Spanish and Portuguese scholarship, University of Iowa, 1982; Ada Louisa Ballard Dissertation Year Fellowship, University of Iowa, 1987-88.

WRITINGS:

The New Narrative of Mexico: Sub-versions of History in Mexican Fiction, Bucknell University Press (Lewisburg, PA), 1994.

Also contributor of articles, translations, and reviews to periodicals, including *Siempre, Lideres de opinion, Earlhamite, Massachusetts Review, MMLA, Hispania, Cafe Bellas Artes, Quince Dias,* and *Textos.*

WORK IN PROGRESS: A bilingual novel based on ethnographic research with Mexican taxi drivers, titled *Por el retrovisor/Through the Rearview Mirror,* is being considered for publicatiion. Selections from the book have appeared in *Quince Dias* (Mexico), *Cafe Bellas Artes* (Houston), and will be published in *Textos* (South Carolina).

SIDELIGHTS: Educator, translator, and author Kathy Taylor has translated Spanish literature into English, has done simultaneous oral interpretation for Hispanic refugees in the U.S., especially Central American refugees, and has served as an interpreter at the First International Quaker Women's Conference on Theology in Woodbrooke, England. Taylor wrote about this last experience, and the task of translation in general, in an article for *Earlhamite,* a publication of Indiana's Earlham College.

Taylor's first book, 1994's *The New Narrative of Mexico: Sub-versions of History in Mexican Fiction,* is a volume-length examination of Mexican literature. *The New Narrative of Mexico* takes a look at four novels by four different authors: Elena Poniatowska's *La noche de Tlatelolco;* Elena Garro's *Testimonios sobre Mariana;* Jose Emilio Pacheco's *Moriras Lejos;* and Federico Campbell's *Pretexta.* As the subtitle implies, these works are discussed by Taylor in the context of how the narratives of each relate to the problematics of writing history and the relationship of history and fiction in telling the "real" stories of a culture. *Choice* critic I. Molina praised *The New Narrative of Mexico,* judging it "[h]ighly recommended to all interested in history and literature."

Taylor's article in the *Earlhamite,* "Double Vision in the 'I' of the Translator," relates not only some of her thoughts and feelings about interpreting at the bilingual First International Quaker Women's Conference but her own principles concerning the act and practice of translation. "The perfect translation," she asserts, "requires a certain ironic contradiction. The message or person must actually become part of the target language or culture being translated while still remaining true to the original." Taylor explains further that "[t]he form, and to a certain extent, the meaning must change while they remain the same. The goal of the translator is to find equivalencies—often through compromise—between the two languages and cultures." At the end of the piece she concludes that "barriers to communication that exist between languages, cultures, and individuals are not really great chasms or semantic voids that must be leapt across. They are more like fast-flowing rivers of changing meanings and cultures in transition that we must ford carefully when there are no easy bridges."

Taylor also told *CA:* "I have been a teacher for many years, a profession that has been exciting and rewarding for me. At the heart of my teaching is my own intense interest in the study of language and culture. I try to open students not only to the satisfaction of learning to communicate in another language, but also to begin to understand the importance of language in the human experience. Language is fundamental to human identity. Reflecting the cultural landscape of our experience, it not only expresses who we are, but it continually transforms that experience.

"The way we communicate with each other reveals much about how we see ourselves and our world, how we shape and are shaped by our cultural contexts, and even how we think. The stories people tell, read or write reach across the boundaries of individual and collective cultural experience, across time and distance, to some common ground of understanding. The study of these stories and what they can tell us about others and ourselves is a journey I never tire of taking with students.

"As long as I can remember, I have been fascinated with stories, the magical combination of words we call narrative that can bring alive another world beyond our experience. As a child, I loved to hear the stories my father would tell of growing up on the prairie of western Kansas. While growing up in a Quaker community and post-graduate study center (Pendle Hill, in Wallingford, Pennsylvania) with many international visitors, I was often drawn to listen to stories my foreign friends would tell of their worlds far away. I learned early that not only do people have their own stories about experiences very different than my own, but they even have other words (i.e., languages) in which to tell them. As a young child, I loved to share in that world of stories and I delighted in learning phrases in other languages, to savor the magic power they seemed to hold.

"When I was in high school, I had a chance to travel in Europe with my family and then spend a year in Ireland. That year, as well as time since then living in Mexico and Germany has instilled in me a great appreciation for other languages, experiences, and ways of understanding that experience. Writing is a way of processing our experience, of making it our own and of sharing it with others. It is a form of discovery and therapy for the individual and the collective culture. It is also a form of translation, in which one tries to interpret some experience so that others may be able to understand it."

BIOGRAPHICAL/CRITICAL SOURCES:

PERIODICALS

Choice, September, 1994, p. 120.

* * *

TE AWEKOTUKU, Ngahuia

PERSONAL: Born in Ohinemutu, Rotorua, New Zealand. *Education:* Auckland University, M.A. (with honors), 1974; attended East-West Centre, University of Hawaii, 1975, 1978-80; Waikato University, Ph.D.

ADDRESSES: Office—Maori Studies Department, Victoria University of Wellington, P.O. Box 600, Wellington, New Zealand.

CAREER: Writer and educator. Waikato Museum of Art and History, curator, 1985-87; Auckland University, lecturer in art history, 1987-96; Victoria University of Wellington, professor of Maori studies, 1997—. Member of Haerwea (Maori consultant committee to the Auckland City Art Gallery), and National Film Archive Trust Board (New Zealand).

MEMBER: New Zealand Qualification Authority Art, Craft, and Design Advisory Group, Auckland Museum Advisory Panel, Council of the National Art Gallery.

AWARDS, HONORS: Victoria University fellowship, 1984.

WRITINGS:

FICTION

Tahuri (short stories), New Women's Press (Auckland), 1989, Women's Press (Toronto), 1991.

Contributor to books, including *The Exploding Frangipani,* edited by Cathie Dunsford and Susan Hawthorne, New Women's Press, 1990; Marian Evans and Heather McPherson, *Spiral Seven,* Spiral Press, 1992; *Vital Writing 3: New Zealand Stories and Poems 1991-1992,* edited by Andrew Mason, Godwit Press (New Zealand), 1992; *Miscegenation Blues: Voices of Mixed Race Women,* edited by Carole Campter, Sister Vision Press (Toronto), 1994; and *Below the Surface: Words and Images in Protest at French Testing on Moruroa,* edited by Ambury Hall, Random House (Auckland), 1995.

Also contributor to periodicals, including *Landfall.*

NONFICTION

Mana Wahine Maori: Selected Writings on Maori Women's Art, Culture, and Politics, New Women's Press (Auckland), 1991.
He Tinkanga Whakaaro: Research Ethics in the Maori Community, Ministry of Maori Affairs (Wellington, NZ), 1991.

Contributor to nonfiction anthologies, including (with Marilyn Waring) Robin Morgan, *Sisterhood Is Powerful,* Anchor Press (New York City), 1984; and *Feminist Voices: Women's Studies Texts for Aotearoa, New Zealand,* edited by Rosemary Du Plessis and others, Oxford University Press (Oxford), 1992.

Contributor to Maori anthologies, including *Nga Nui o Te Ra: Teaching, Nurturing, Developments of Maori Women's Weaving,* 1993; *The Vote, the Pill, and the Demon Drink: A History of Feminist Writing,* 1993; and *Mana Wahine: Women Who Show the Way,* 1994.

SIDELIGHTS: Ngahuia Te Awekotuku, a professor of Maori studies at Victoria University of Wellington, is noted as both a writer and speaker on issues of concern to women and New Zealand's indigenous Maori peoples. While studying at Auckland University in the early '70s, she became active in the growing women's liberation movement. After a trip to the United States was prohibited due to her sexual orientation—Te Awekotuku is openly lesbian—she became more militant and helped to found New Zealand's first gay liberation group in 1972. She also became involved in Nga Tamatoa, a Maori Rights group. About this period of her life she would write in her 1991 work, *Mana Wahine Maori: Selected Writings on Maori Women's Art, Culture, and Politics:* "Years of study at University fashioned a cosmopolitan exterior, and the galloping madness of antipodean hippiedom and antiwar actions soon sharpened my political edge, making me aware and verbal in the white middle-class world. . . . Despite a lightish skin—my people's delight—and an educated accent, I was still visibly, boldly, Maori. Nothing could ever change that—it was/is as permanent, wonderful, and as inexorable as my femaleness."

In addition to *Mana Wahine Maori* and contributions to several anthologies, Te Awekotuku is also the author of the 1989 short story collection *Tahuri,* which focuses on the coming-of-age of a young Maori girl as she witnesses sexual abuse but finds safety in the company of other Maori women. Autobiographical in nature, the stories in *Tahuri* suggest that lesbianism has a strong history in Polynesian society.

BIOGRAPHICAL/CRITICAL SOURCES:

BOOKS

Te Awekotuku, Ngahuia, *Mana Wahine Maori: Selected Writings on Maori Women's Art, Culture, and Politics,* New Women's Press, 1991, pp. 18-19.
Tolerton, Jane, *Convent Girls: New Zealand Women Talk to Jane Tolerton,* Penguin (Auckland), 1994.

*   *   *

TEJA, Jesus F(rancisco) de la 1956-

PERSONAL: Born July 17, 1956, in Cienfuegos, Cuba; became U.S. citizen; son of Francisco and Julia Maria (maiden name, Irimia; present surname, Castellano) de la Teja; married Magdalena Hernandez (a college dean), August 6, 1983; children: Eduardo, Julia. *Ethnicity:* "Hispanic." *Education:* Seton Hall University, B.A., 1979, M.A., 1981; University of Texas at Austin, Ph.D., 1988. *Politics:* Independent. *Religion:* Roman Catholic. *Avocational interests:* Music appreciation, travel, light home remodeling.

ADDRESSES: Home—Austin, TX. *Office*—Department of History, Southwest Texas State University, San Marcos, TX 78666; fax 512-245-3043. *E-mail*—JD10@swt.edu.

CAREER: Texas General Land Office, Austin, assistant archivist, 1985-89, archivist, 1989-90, director of archives and records, 1990-91, managing editor of *The Land Commissioners of Texas: 150 Years of the General Land Office,* 1986, and *Guide to Spanish and Mexican Land Grants in South Texas,* 1988; Southwest Texas State University, San Marcos, assistant professor, 1991-96, associate professor of history, 1996—. Austin Community College, adjunct instructor, 1988-90; Institute of Texas Studies, instructor, 1992, 1994; guest speaker at University of Texas at Austin, 1985, 1989, Victoria College and Texas Southern University, 1992, St. Mary's University and University of California, San Diego, 1993; and University of Texas at Arlington, 1995. Appeared in the videotape documentary *The Texas Revolution: From Anahuac to San Jacinto,* produced by Forest Glen Television Productions, Inc., 1989, the television documentary *The Alamo,* broadcast by The History Channel, 1996, and *America's Hispanic Heritage: Deep Roots, Continuing Enrichment,* a radio series produced by Media Works, 1996; expert witness in Texas District Court on land tenure patterns and land grant history. Catholic Archives of Texas, member of advisory committee, 1989—; Texas Conservation Fund, member of board of directors, 1991—; City of Austin, member of Library Commission, 1994—; Castlewood-Oak Valley Neighborhood Association, president, 1994—. South Austin Optimists Little League, coach, 1993-94.

MEMBER: Conference on Latin American History, Western History Association, Southwest Council on Latin American Studies (life member), Society of Southwest Archivists, Texas State Historical Association (life member), Texas Catholic Historical Society.

AWARDS, HONORS: Grant from John D. and Catherine T. MacArthur Foundation, 1991-92; Sons of the Republic of Texas, Summerfield G. Roberts Award, 1991, for *A Revolution Remembered,* and Presidio La Bahia Award, 1995, for *San Antonio de Bexar;* Citation, San Antonio Conservation Society, 1995, for *San Antonio de Bexar.*

WRITINGS:

(Editor and contributor) *A Revolution Remembered: The Memoirs and Selected Correspondence of Juan N. Seguin,* State House Press (Austin, TX), 1991.

(Technical editor) *Society of Southwest Archivists Guide to Archival and Manuscript Repositories,* Society of Southwest Archivists, 1993.

San Antonio de Bexar: A Community on New Spain's Northern Frontier, University of New Mexico Press (Albuquerque, NM), 1995.

The Settlement of Texas, Part I: *The Native Americans,* Part II: *The Hispanics and the Americans* (documentary videotape series), W. S. Benson and Co., 1996.

Working Texas: From Ranchers and Roughnecks to Sodbusters and Spacemen (documentary videotape), W. S. Benson and Co., 1996.

Contributor to books, including *Hispanic Texas: A Historical Guide,* edited by Helen Simons and Cathryn Hoyt, University of Texas Press (Austin), 1992; *Tejano Journey, 1770-1860,* edited by Gerald E. Poyo, University of Texas Press, 1996; and *Myths, Misdeeds, and Misunderstandings: The Roots of Conflict in United States-Mexico Relations,* edited by Jaime E. Rodriguez O. and Kathryn Vincent, Scholarly Resources (Wilmington, DE), 1997. Contributor of articles, translations, and reviews to periodicals, including *Locus: An Historical Journal of Regional Perspectives, East Texas Historical Journal, Historia Mexicana,* and *Gulf Coast Historical Review.* Member of editorial advisory board, *Southwestern Historical Quarterly,* 1996—; advisory editor, *New Handbook of Texas,* 1989-96.

WORK IN PROGRESS: "Spanish Colonial Texas," to be included in a survey on the demographic, economic, and social history of the Spanish North American borderlands; research on the history of the annual trade fair held at Saltillo, Mexico, from the eighteenth through the nineteenth centuries.

*   *   *

THOMAS, Kurt   1956-

PERSONAL: Born on March 29, 1956, in Miami, FL; son of Robert Edward (a meat-company manager) and Ellie (a secretary) Thomas ; married Elizabeth Osting, December 31, 1977 (divorced, 1981); mar-

ried LeAnn Hartsgrove, August 31, 1982; children: (second marriage) Kurt Thomas, Jr. *Education:* Indiana State University, graduate.

CAREER: Gymnast, coach, and author. Arizona State University, assistant gymnastics coach; School of Kurt Thomas Gymnastics, Scottsdale, AZ, owner, teacher, and coach; American Broadcasting Co. (ABC) Sports, gymnastics commentator; producer and performer in Kurt Thomas Gymnastics America shows. Member of U.S. Olympic Gymnastics Team, Montreal, Canada, 1976. Has made numerous television appearances and acted in the motion picture, *Gymkata.*

AWARDS, HONORS: National Collegiate Athletic Association all-around championship, 1976, 1977; first place, Romanian International Invitational, 1977, 1978; first place, Barcelona Invitational, 1977; gold medal for floor exercise, world championships, 1978; six gold medals, 1978, all-around championship, 1979, Dial-American Cup championships; gold medals in floor exercise and horizontal bar, silver medals in pommel horse, all-around, and parallel bars, world championships, 1979; James A. Sullivan Memorial Award for outstanding US amateur athlete, 1979; named Columbia Broadcasting System's (CBS) Athlete of the Year, 1979; Tangueray Gin and Dunlop's Laurel Wreath and Amateur Athlete of the Year citation, 1979; American Library Association's Best Books for Young Adults citation, 1981, for *Kurt Thomas on Gymnastics.*

WRITINGS:

(With Kent Hannon) *Kurt Thomas on Gymnastics,* Simon & Schuster (New York), 1980.

SIDELIGHTS: At 5-feet-5-inches tall, world-class gymnast Kurt Thomas likes to explain his decision to become a gymnast by alluding to his small stature. Not only was it easier for a short person to move gracefully around the various apparatuses used in gymnastics, he would explain, but being a gymnast had other advantages as well. "When you're a shrimp of a kid growing up in a tough section of central Miami," observed Grace Lichtenstein in a *New York Times Magazine* cover story, "you either learn to run fast, get beat up a lot, or become very agile."

Despite Thomas's agility, several obstacles stood in the way of his athletic success, including the death of his father when he was seven which prevented him from taking any expensive classes, his start at gymnastics at the comparative late age of 14, and the virtual non-existence of a gymnastics program at his high-school. Thomas seemed to have a natural talent for the sport that nothing could stop. In *Kurt Thomas on Gymnastics,* Thomas and his co-author, Kent Hannon, quoted the gymnast's Indiana State University coach, Roger Counsil, as saying, "the most amazing thing about Kurt is how fast he learns. . . . He doesn't do too well when you try to teach a trick to him directly. He has to actually see another gymnast do it or watch it on videotape. Once he does, he usually has the move down in about fifteen minutes."

The perfection of Thomas's moves were what caused all the excitement in men's gymnastics in the late seventies. In the introduction to *Kurt Thomas on Gymnastics,* Hannon credits Thomas with making the crowds at men's gymnastics meets cheer whereas previously most such gatherings "were conducted in relative silence." "Because he is so much better than almost everyone in the world," noted Lichtenstein in *New York Times Magazine,* "he is redefining the sport of men's gymnastics, putting it on a par with the women's version as a crowd-pleasing act." Thomas's skill as a gymnast won him numerous gymnastics awards, including six gold medals at the 1978 Dial-America Cup with nearly 30 million television viewers watching. Possibly his most impressive feat was capturing the gold medal at the world championships that same year, the first time an American male had done so in forty-six years. In 1979, he became the first gymnast ever to win the James E. Sullivan Memorial Trophy as the outstanding U.S. amateur athlete of the year. When he introduced a special twirling movement—now called the "Thomas Flair"—on the pommel horse, he became only the second American to have a gymnastics maneuver named after him in the history of the sport. Thomas hoped to win an Olympic gold medal at the 1980 Games in Moscow, but was deprived of the chance when the United States boycott was called in retaliation against the Soviet invasion of Afghanistan. He retired from amateur competition that same year, going on to perform professionally and serve as a coach at his own gymnastics school and summer camps.

Ironically, *Kurt Thomas on Gymnastics* appeared in 1980, just as Thomas's Olympic hopes and amateur career were coming to an end. Reviewers found the book entertaining for the story it had to tell and informative for the wealth of data on gymnastics it contained. Numerous black-and-white photographs of Thomas and other leading gymnasts amplify the text. Both Bob Ottum in *Sports Illustrated* and Wes

Lukowsky in *Booklist* thought readers would be surprised at the high quality of Thomas's book. Ottum noted, for example, that the title of the over-size volume might make potential readers pass it up, thinking it was just another instruction manual. On the contrary, he wrote, "Thomas has a lot of interesting things to say about an exotic sport that many Americans are just beginning to fully appreciate. And he says them exceedingly well." Lukowsky called the book "a page-turner" and "an excellent overview of a rapidly growing sport." Using numerous pictures, and what Ottum called a "chatty" prose style, the authors cover various topics, including how to watch a gymnastics meet, how the routines are scored, and a personal glimpse at the life of an amateur U.S. athlete as contrasted with that of an athlete in Soviet Russia or Japan. It is, according to a *Kirkus Reviews* critic, "an intelligent, readable guide to a sport long ignored in this country."

In 1991, hoping for a position with the 1992 Olympic team, Thomas made a fruitless attempt at a comeback. That year, he competed in the U.S. championships at Cincinnati, Ohio, but came in 22nd out of 49 participants. Annoyed at criticism from younger competitors, Thomas told Richard O'Brien in *Sports Illustrated,* "I'm coming back because I *can.* . . . And of course I'm doing it for the glory. I've got nothing to lose and everything to gain." Whatever the outcome of this or any other attempts Thomas might make to re-gain the fame he once enjoyed, his position in the history of his sport is secure. A decade after his award-winning performance at the world championships, O'Brien still called Thomas "perhaps the best male gymnast the U.S. has ever produced." And, as David Anderson pointed out in the *New York Times,* "As the first gymnast to win the Sullivan Award, he is forever part of the sports history in America."

BIOGRAPHICAL/CRITICAL SOURCES:

BOOKS

Thomas, Kurt, and Kent Hannon, *Kurt Thomas on Gymnastics,* Simon & Schuster (New York), 1980.

PERIODICALS

Booklist, September 15, 1980, p. 92.
Kirkus Reviews, July 15, 1980, p. 918.
New York Times, July 31, 1978; March 3, 1980.
New York Times Magazine, April 29, 1979, pp. 95-106.

Sports Illustrated, October 13, 1980, p. 20; June 17, 1991, p. 24.

—*Sketch by Marian C. Gonsior*

* * *

THOMPSON, Emma 1959(?)-

PERSONAL: Born c. 1959, in England; daughter of Eric (a director) and Phyllida (an actress) Thompson; married Kenneth Branagh (an actor, producer, and director), 1989 (divorced, 1995). *Education:* Attended Cambridge University.

ADDRESSES: Agent—c/o 83 Berwick St., London W1V 3PJ, England; and c/o Newmarket Press, 18 East 48th St., New York, NY 10017.

CAREER: Actress for stage, television, and film. Began career as a performer with Cambridge University's Footlights revue. Stage appearances include *Me and My Girl,* 1985; *Look Back in Anger,* 1989; *A Midsummer Night's Dream,* 1990; and *King Lear,* 1990. Television appearances include *Fortunes of War,* 1988; "The Winslow Boy," 1990; *Cheers,* 1992; *Look Back in Anger,* 1993; and "The Blue Boy," 1994. Film appearances include *Henry V,* 1989; *The Tall Guy,* 1989; *Impromptu,* 1990; *Dead Again,* 1991; *Howard's End,* 1992; *Peter's Friends,* 1992; *Much Ado about Nothing,* 1993; *The Remains of the Day,* 1993; *In the Name of the Father,* 1994; *Junior,* 1995; *Carrington,* 1995; and *Sense and Sensibility,* 1995.

MEMBER: Screen Actors Guild.

AWARDS, HONORS: British Academy of Film and Television Arts Award for best actress, 1986, for *Fortunes of War;* New York Film Critics Circle Award for best actress, 1992, Academy Award for best actress, British Academy of Film and Television Award for best actress, and Golden Globe Award for best actress in a drama, all 1993, all for *Howard's End;* Academy Award for best screenplay adaptation, 1996, for *Sense and Sensibility.*

WRITINGS:

Sense and Sensibility (screenplay; adapted from the novel by Jane Austen), Columbia, 1995, pub-

lished in *The Sense and Sensibility Diaries and Screenplay: The Making of the Film Based on the Jane Austen Novel,* Newmarket Press (New York), 1995.

SIDELIGHTS: Emma Thompson, a critically acclaimed and award-winning actress for film, stage, and television, wrote her first screenplay for Ang Lee's 1995 film adaptation of Jane Austen's novel, *Sense and Sensibility,* in which she also played the role of Elinor Dashwood. The Academy Award-winning screenplay, along with the journal Thompson kept during the production of the film, was published in 1995 as *The Sense and Sensibility Diaries and Screenplay: The Making of the Film Based on the Jane Austen Novel.* Stanley Kauffmann in his *New Republic* review of the film noted that Thompson "spent five years working intermittently on the script while she acted in seven films." Remaining faithful to Austen's original story with only "very slight" alterations, Thompson's *Sense and Sensibility* screenplay "can easily be chided by maniacally zealous Austenites," observed Kauffmann, "but such folk probably should not go to films of Austen unless they want to sneer."

Richard Schickel, writing for *Time,* found Thompson's adaptation "impeccable" and comparable to the romantic comedies of Frank Capra and Leo McCarey, adding that "[you] don't expect to find [this kind of joyous catharsis] in adaptations of classic literature . . . [or] in modern movies." Dana Kennedy in *Entertainment Weekly* thought Thompson's *Sense and Sensibility* "so crisp, merry, and timeless that it might inspire those who think of Austen as high school syllabus material to read the book." In his *Newsweek* review of the film, Jack Kroll called the screenplay "vigorous, faithful," and related Thompson's attitude toward critics who label Austen films as period pieces: "You don't think people are still concerned with marriage, money, romance, finding a partner? Jane Austen is a genius who appeals to any generation." Commenting on the actress's "restrained" performance in the role of Elinor, *New Yorker* cinema reviewer Terrence Rafferty remarked, "Thanks to Thompson's exertions—both as actress and screenwriter—the heroine's goodness never seems implausible, and Austen's quiet but insistent polemical fervor is never permitted to overtax the story's delicate comic structure." Janet Maslin summarized in her *New York Times* review of the film: "Emma Thompson . . . proves as crisp and indispensably clever a screenwriter as she is a leading lady."

BIOGRAPHICAL/CRITICAL SOURCES:

BOOKS

Shuttleworth, Ian, *Ken & Em: A Biography of Kenneth Branagh and Emma Thompson,* St. Martin's Press (New York), 1995.

PERIODICALS

Entertainment Weekly, December 22, 1995, pp. 60-61.
New Republic, January 8, 1996, pp. 34-35.
Newsweek, December 18, 1995, pp. 66-68.
New Yorker, December 18, 1995, pp. 124-27.
New York Times, December 13, 1995, section C, pp. 15, 19.
People, February 12, 1996, pp. 38-39.
Time, December 18, 1995, pp. 72-74.*

*   *   *

THOMPSON, Gregory Lee   1946-

PERSONAL: Born June 14, 1946, in Huntington Park, CA; son of Karl W. (a pilot) and Virginia A. (a homemaker; maiden name, Hanna) Thompson. *Ethnicity:* "White." *Education:* University of California, Davis, A.B., 1968; University of California, Berkeley, M.C.P., 1970; University of California, Irvine, Ph.D., 1987. *Politics:* Democrat. *Religion:* None. *Avocational interests:* Hiking, swimming, photography.

ADDRESSES: Home—2635 Lucerne Dr., Tallahassee, FL 32303. *Office*—Department of Urban and Regional Planning, Florida State University, Tallahassee, FL 32306-2030; fax 904-644-6041. *E-mail*—gthompsn@coss.fsu.edu.

CAREER: City of Edmonton Transit System, Edmonton, Alberta, Canada, transit planner, 1970-72; Canadian Transport Commission, Ottawa, Ontario, Canada, transportation analyst, 1972-73; City of Berkeley Planning Department, Berkeley, CA, transportation planner, 1973-74; San Diego Metropolitan Transit Development Board, San Diego, CA, senior planner, 1974-80; Hagley Museum and Library, Wilmington, DE, advanced research fellow, 1987-88; Florida State University, Tallahassee, began as assistant professor, became associate professor of

urban and regional planning, 1988—. Lakebreeze Homeowners Association, director.

MEMBER: American Planning Association, American Institute of Certified Planners, Lexington Group (in transportation history).

WRITINGS:

The Passenger Train in the Motor Age: California's Rail and Bus Industries, 1910-1941, Ohio State University Press (Columbus, OH), 1993.

WORK IN PROGRESS: Research on the demand for transit in contemporary suburbs; research for another book on railways.

*   *   *

THOMPSON, John N.   1951-

PERSONAL: Born November 15, 1951, in Pittsburgh, PA; son of John C. and Cecelia (Kravich) Thompson; married Jill Fansmith, 1973. *Education:* Washington and Jefferson College, B.A. (magna cum laude), 1973; University of Illinois at Urbana-Champaign, Ph.D., 1977.

ADDRESSES: Office—Departments of Botany and Zoology, Washington State University, Pullman, WA 99164; fax 509-335-3517. *E-mail*—jnt@wsu.edu.

CAREER: University of Illinois at Urbana-Champaign, visiting assistant professor of entomology, 1977-78; Washington State University, Pullman, assistant professor, 1978-82, associate professor, 1982-87, professor of botany and zoology, 1987—, Meyer Distinguished Professor, 1994—. University of Minnesota, Itasca Field Station, visiting faculty member, summers, 1978-79; Imperial College, Silwood Park, England, visiting faculty member, 1985-86; University of Calgary, Darwin Lecturer, 1994; Florida International University, Glaser Distinguished Professor, 1996. Centre for Population Biology, Ascot, England, ecologist in residence, 1997.

MEMBER: American Association for the Advancement of Science (fellow, 1988), American Society of Naturalists (vice-president, 1998), Ecological Society of America (chairperson of publications committee, 1988-92), Society for the Study of Evolution (member of council, 1988-90), British Ecological Society,

Royal Entomological Society of London (fellow), Phi Beta Kappa, Sigma Xi, Phi Sigma.

AWARDS, HONORS: Grants from National Science Foundation, 1980—; senior Fulbright scholar in Australia, 1991-92.

WRITINGS:

Interaction and Coevolution, Wiley (New York), 1982.
The Coevolutionary Process, University of Chicago Press (Chicago, IL), 1994.

Editor of "Monograph Series on Interspecific Interactions," University of Chicago Press. Contributor to encyclopedias. Contributor of more than seventy articles and reviews to scientific journals, including *Nature.* Member of editorial board, *Ecology and Ecological Monographs,* 1986-89.

WORK IN PROGRESS: Research on coevolution as a process organizing the earth's biodiversity; research on the ongoing role of evolution in shaping biological communities.

*   *   *

THORNTON, Ian 1926-

PERSONAL: Born July 14, 1926, in Yorkshire, England; son of John and Alice Mary Thornton; married first wife, Jean Frances, August 5, 1948 (marriage ended); married Ann Juliana Patterson, December 24, 1980; children: Jane Alison Thornton Plummer, Angus John. *Education:* University of Leeds, B.Sc. (with honors), 1951, Ph.D., 1953, D.Sc., 1984.

ADDRESSES: Home—70 Park St., South Yarra, Victoria 314, Australia. *Office*—School of Zoology, La Trobe University, Bundoora, Victoria 3083, Australia; fax 61-03-9-479-1551. *E-mail*—zooit@zoo.latrobe.edu.au.

CAREER: Gordon Memorial College, Khartoum, Sudan, lecturer in zoology, 1953-56; University of Hong Kong, Hong Kong, senior lecturer, 1956-63, reader in zoology, 1963-67, dean of Faculty of Science, 1960-63; La Trobe University, Bundoora, Australia, professor of zoology, 1968-92, professor emeritus, 1992—, dean of School of Biological Sci-

ences, 1970-72, 1979-81, 1985-87. *Military service:* British Army, parachutist, 1944-47; became lieutenant.

MEMBER: Australian Academy of Sciences (fellow).

AWARDS, HONORS: John Lewis Gold Medal from Royal Geographical Society of Australasia, 1993.

WRITINGS:

Darwin's Islands: A Natural History of the Galapagos, Doubleday (New York), 1971.
Insects of Hong Kong, Hong Kong University Press (Hong Kong), 1982.
Krakatau: The Destruction and Reassembly of an Island Ecosystem, Harvard University Press (Cambridge, MA), 1996.

WORK IN PROGRESS: Books on Indonesian national parks and developmental ecology; research on the reassembly of the Krakatau ecosystem.

*   *   *

TINKER, Jack (Samuel) 1938-1996

OBITUARY NOTICE—See index for *CA* sketch: Born February 15, 1938, in Oldham, England; died of a heart attack, October 28, 1996. Tinker had been the drama critic for London's *Daily Mail* since 1972 and was known as much for being the life of the party as he was for his reviews. With his only formal education coming from the Hulme Grammar School for Boys in Oldham, England, Tinker began his career at the *Surrey Advertiser* in 1957, moving to the *Evening Argus* in Brighton as a theater critic in 1961. He came to the *Daily Mail* in 1971 and became the paper's theater critic in 1972. His reviews reflected his wit and his appreciation for moving performances. Tinker was a prominent figure in London's West End theater scene and often entertained the pub crowd with funny anecdotes and jokes. Tinker was named Critic of the Year in 1982, 1989 and 1991 and won the De Courcy Critics Circle Award in 1991. Tinker also wrote a few plays, *Merman—The Lady and Her Songs* in 1985 and, with Martin Tickner, *In Praise of Rattigan* in 1983. Tinker authored two books, *The Television Barons* (1980) and *Coronation Street—25 Years* (1985). When he died, theaters in London dimmed their lights, an honor usually reserved for well-known performers.

OBITUARIES AND OTHER SOURCES:

BOOKS

The Writers Directory: 1996-1998, St. James Press, 1995.

PERIODICALS

New York Times, October 31, 1996, p. D21.
Times (London), October 29, 1996, p. 19.

*   *   *

TOROK, Lou 1927-

PERSONAL: Born August 7, 1927, in Toledo, Lucas County, OH; children: Victor Mitchell (foster son). *Ethnicity:* "Hungarian." *Education:* Self-educated. *Politics:* Democrat. *Religion:* Roman Catholic. *Avocational interests:* Walking, debating, swimming, research.

ADDRESSES: Home—Eastern Kentucky Correctional Complex, P.O. Box 636/109237, West Liberty, KY 41472; fax 212-941-0614. *Agent*—Jeff Herman, Jeff Herman Agency, Inc., 500 Greenwich St., Suite 501-C, New York, NY 10013.

CAREER: Advertising and marketing manager throughout the United States, 1950-85; retired, 1986. Child Abuse Institute of Research, founder and director, 1984; Prison Pen Pals, founder, 1974; Love Day, founder, 1992. *Military service:* U.S. Naval Reserve, active duty, 1944-46; served in the South Pacific during World War II.

MEMBER: Kiwanis International; lifetime membership, Sertoma International.

AWARDS, HONORS: Papal Medal.

WRITINGS:

Straight Talk from Prison, Human Sciences Press (New York), 1973.
The Strange World of Prison, Bobbs-Merrill (New York), 1974.
Finding Hope When You Are in Prison, Abbey Press (St. Meinrad, IN), 1992.

Author of pamphlets. Contributor to magazines and newspapers, including *America, Popular Mechanics,* and *Saturday Review of Literature.*

Torok's published and unpublished works are archived at the Ohioana Library, 65 South Front St., Suite 1105, Columbus, OH 43215, telephone (614) 466-3831

WORK IN PROGRESS: Salem Apology, a screenplay about the witch trial hysteria; *A Dog Named Balto,* a screenplay about a heroic sled dog in Alaska; *The Politics of Crime,* essays on criminal justice.

SIDELIGHTS: Lou Torok told *CA:* "I write to help young people understand the risks they take when they experiment with deviant behavior, drugs, alcohol, or other illegal activities. Young people need honest and reliable information about the process and problems of growing up in a complex society. I feel that my own life (abandoned at birth, raised in orphans' homes, military service, personal struggles for self-value) might make a change, if only young people understood that their own struggles for identity are not unique, and that they can learn from my own mistakes. I maintain a large personal correspondence with people of all ages."

*   *   *

TOTH, Endre
  See de TOTH, Andre

*   *   *

TOWNE, Marian K(leinsasser) 1933-

PERSONAL: Born July 24, 1933, in Freeman, SD; daughter of John Pierpont and Katherine (Tieszen) Kleinsasser; married Maynard Kaufman, December 26, 1951 (divorced, 1961); married Edgar Arthur Towne, December 18, 1961; children: (first marriage) Karl; (second marriage) Stephen E. *Ethnicity:* "Caucasian (German)." *Education:* Bethel College, North Newton, KS, B.A., 1955; University of Chicago, M.A., 1958; Christian Theological Seminary, M.A., 1978. *Religion:* Presbyterian. *Avocational interests:* Gardening, cooking, reading, politics, theater.

ADDRESSES: Home—5129 North Illinois St., Indianapolis, IN 46208-2613.

CAREER: Findlay College (now University), Findlay, OH, assistant professor of English, 1966-68; Indiana University-Purdue University at Indianapolis, Indianapolis, IN, affiliate faculty in speech, 1982-92; part-time instructor at Butler University, Indianapolis, Roosevelt University, Chicago, IL, and Bluffton College, Bluffton, OH; teacher at high schools in Kansas and Indiana. Caring Community, Inc., founding director; Bread for the World, member of national board of directors; consultant to Gleaners Food Bank and to church and community ministries. Democratic National Committee, member.

MEMBER: National Association of University Women, League of Women Voters, Presbyterian Women, Church Women United (member of national board of directors), Indiana Theatre Association.

AWARDS, HONORS: Valiant Woman Award, Church Women United.

WRITINGS:

Bread of Life: Diaries and Memories of a Dakota Family, privately printed, 1994.
A Midwest Gardener's Cookbook, Indiana University Press (Bloomington, IN), 1996.
Dreaming the Impossible Dream: The First Thirty Years of the Edyvean Repertory Theatre, privately printed, 1996.

WORK IN PROGRESS: Three historical dramas, *Rock in a Weary Land, Militant Madonna,* and *Contrary Music; Hoosier Women Making a Difference;* assisting African-American women to write their autobiographies.

SIDELIGHTS: Marian K. Towne told *CA:* "I write from my diverse experience and interests. My first major work was *Bread of Life,* based on the diaries my father kept during the Great Depression in South Dakota and during World War II. In the process of working through his diaries and writing fictional accounts based on my own memories of those events, I realized the importance of food to our family. That realization was the inspiration for the cookbook, which is the product of more than fifty years of cooking according to seasonal principles and living in five midwestern states.

"I was asked by a church friend to interview a great-aunt who had survived the tragedy of Jonestown. The manuscript was made into the videotape *Onliest One Alive: Surviving Jonestown, Guyana,* with funding from the Indiana Council for the Humanities. Since its publication I have been asked by three other African-American women to help them write their stories and memoirs.

"*Dream the Impossible Dream* was a labor of love. It was first commissioned on the theater's twenty-fifth anniversary. I had studied with Edyvean and participated in many aspects of the theater itself, which is the only professionally managed theater in a theological seminary in the United States.

"I believe I write to make sense of my experience and to discover what I think and feel. My historical plays are about Hutterite martyrs, a feminist, and John Donne."

*   *   *

TOWNES, Charles H(ard) 1915-

PERSONAL: Born July 28, 1915, in Greenville, SC; son of Henry Keith and Ellen Sumter (Hard) Townes; married Frances H. Brown, May 4, 1941; children: Linda Townes Lewis, Ellen Townes Screven, Carla Townes Keith, Holly Townes Robinson. *Education:* Furman University, B.A. (modern languages) and B.S. (physics), both with highest honors, 1935; Duke University, M.A., 1937; California Institute of Technology, Ph.D., 1939.

ADDRESSES: Home—1988 San Antonio Ave., Berkeley, CA 94707-1620. *Office*—Department of Physics, University of California, Berkeley, CA 94720.

CAREER: Bell Telephone Laboratories, member of technical staff, 1939-47; Columbia University, New York City, associate professor, 1948-50, professor of physics, 1950-61, department head, 1952-55, executive director of Columbia Radiation Laboratory, 1950-52; Massachusetts Institute of Technology, Cambridge, professor of physics, 1961-67, provost of the university, 1961-66; University of California, Berkeley, professor of physics, 1967-86, 1994—, professor emeritus, 1986-94. Institute of Defense Analyses, vice president and director of research, 1959-61. University of Paris, Fulbright lecturer,

1955-56; University of Tokyo, Fulbright lecturer, 1956; Enrico Fermi International School of Physics, director, 1963; Cambridge University, Scott Lecturer, 1963; University of Toronto, Centennial Lecturer, 1967; served in various lecturer positions for various institutions, including Lincoln Lecturer, 1972-73, Halley Lecturer, 1976, Krishman Lecturer, 1992, and Nishina Lecturer, 1992; member of board of trustees of California Institute of Technology, Carnegie Institution of Washington, Graduate Theological Union, and California Academy of Sciences; Woods Hole Oceanographic Institution, member of corporation. General Motors Corp., member of board of directors, 1973-86. President's Scientific Advisory Committee, member, 1966-69, vice chairperson, 1967-69; National Aeronautics and Space Administration, chairperson of scientific and technical advisory committee for manned space flight, 1964-69; President's Committee on Science and Technology, member, 1976. Holder of patents related to masers and lasers.

MEMBER: Institute of Electrical and Electronic Engineers (life member), American Physical Society (Richtmeyer Lecturer, 1959; president, 1967), Optical Society of America (honorary member), National Academy of Sciences (council member, 1968-72, 1978-81; chairperson of space science board, 1970-73), American Philosophical Society, American Astronomical Society, American Academy of Arts and Sciences, Royal Society (foreign member), Indian National Science Academy, Russian Academy of Sciences (foreign member), Pontifical Academy of Sciences, Max-Planck Institute for Physics and Astrophysics (foreign member), California Academy of Sciences.

AWARDS, HONORS: Guggenheim fellow, 1955-56; Stuart Ballantine Medal, Franklin Institute, 1959, 1962; officier, French Legion of Honor; Comstock Award, National Academy of Sciences, 1959, and John J. Carty Medal; Thomas Young Medal and prize, Institute of Physics and Physical Society of England, 1963; Nobel Prize, physics, 1964, for work on masers and lasers; Medal of Honor, Institute of Electrical and Electronic Engineers, 1967; Optical Society of America, C. E. K. Mees Medal, 1968, Frederic Ives Medal, 1996; Distinguished Public Service Medal, National Aeronautics and Space Administration, 1969; Wilhelm Exner Award of Austria, 1970; inducted into National Inventors Hall of Fame, 1976; Plyler Prize, American Physical Society, 1977; Niels Bohr International Gold Medal, 1979; National Science Medal, 1983; inducted into Engineering and

Science Hall of Fame, 1983; Commonwealth Award, 1993; ADION Medal, Nice Observatory, 1995; Rumford Premium, American Academy of Arts and Sciences; more than twenty-five honorary degrees from colleges and universities; inducted into South Carolina Hall of Fame.

WRITINGS:

(With A. L. Schawlow) *Microwave Spectroscopy,* 1955, reprinted, Dover, 1975.
Making Waves, American Institute of Physics (Woodbury, NY), 1994.

Also coeditor and contributor to the volumes *Quantum Electronics,* 1960, and *Quantum Electronics and Coherent Light,* 1964. Contributor to scientific journals. Member of editorial board, *Review of Scientific Instruments,* 1950-52, *Physical Review,* 1951-53, *Journal of Molecular Spectroscopy,* 1957-60, and *Proceedings of the National Academy of Sciences,* 1978-84.

*   *   *

TOWNSEND, Lindsay 1960-

PERSONAL: Born February 24, 1960, in Huddersfield, England; daughter of Gordon (an electrical engineer) and Joan (a secretary; maiden name, Townsend) McNally; married Alan Quicke (a librarian and writer), May 19, 1984. *Education:* University of Wales, University College of North Wales, Bangor, B.A. (with first class honors), 1981. *Avocational interests:* Reading, music (especially singing), swimming, walking.

ADDRESSES: Home—20 Easingwood Dr., Kirkheaton, Huddersfield, West Yorkshire HD5 0JX, England. *Agent*—Teresa Chris, Teresa Chris Literary Agency, 43 Musard Rd., London W6 8NR, England.

CAREER: Writer, 1992—.

MEMBER: Society of Authors, Romantic Novelists Association.

WRITINGS:

Voices in the Dark (novel), Hodder & Stoughton, 1995.

Night of the Storm (novel), Hodder & Stoughton, 1996.

WORK IN PROGRESS: A novel, tentatively titled *Firestalker.*

SIDELIGHTS: Lindsay Townsend told *CA:* "I write above all to tell stories, as compellingly and vividly as I can. For me, women's suspense is an active, heroic genre, with a lot of scope. It allows me to involve realistic, fallible characters in situations where big issues are at stake.

"The first novel, *Voices in the Dark,* was partly inspired by a love of both Italy and opera, but also tries to explore the long-term effect of war crimes on their perpetrators and their families. *Night of the Storm* pits a young nature photographer against the wildlife trade, weaving everyday relationships (including romance) into a plot driven by an important issue, the illicit traffic in rare species.

"In all my writing, I try to build an intricate construction of taut plotting and natural behavior, with even very minor elements of story and character contributing to the thrust of the book. This leads to a lot of rewriting as threads are picked up and woven in, and I also have to be willing to cut passages to maintain pace. Using a computer leaves me no excuse to avoid either.

"I am an energetic filler of notebooks when researching locations. Usually I write surrounded with photographs, postcards, maps, anything that provides significant detail or nudges the memory. Research for *Voices in the Dark* also involved singing lessons."

*   *   *

TRABA, Marta 1930-1983

PERSONAL: Born January 25, 1930, in Buenos Aires, Argentina; died in a plane crash, November 27, 1983, near Madrid, Spain; daughter of a journalist; married Alberto Zalamea, 1950 (divorced, 1967); married Angel Rama (a literary critic), 1969 (died, 1983); children: (first marriage) Gustavo, Fernando. *Education:* National University of Buenos Aires, diplomate, 1950; studied art with Gulio Carlo Argan and Pierre Francastel, 1951-53.

CAREER: Art critic and writer. University of the Americas, professor of art history, 1954-55; University of the Andes, Colombia, professor of art history, 1956-66; National University of Colombia, professor and director of culture, 1966-67; University of Puerto Rico, Rio Piedras, professor of art, 1970-71; Caracas Teacher's College, Caracas, Venezuela, professor of Latin American art, 1977; Central University of Caracas Institute of Art, research professor, 1977-79; lecturer in art at Harvard University, University of Massachusetts, Smith College, Oberlin College, University of Maryland, and Middlebury College, 1979-81; visiting professor of art, Princeton University. *Prisma* (art criticism journal), Bogota, founder and editor, 1957; Museum of Modern Art, Bogota, founder, 1963, director, 1963-68. Taught television courses on art history, Latin American art, and modern art, Colombia National Television, 1955-66; organizer of numerous art exhibitions throughout North and South America.

AWARDS, HONORS: Casa de las Americas Prize (Cuba), 1966, for *Las ceremonias del verano;* Guggenheim fellowship, 1968.

WRITINGS:

NOVELS

Las ceremonias del verano (title means "Summer Rites"), Casa de las Americas (Cuba), 1966.
Los laberintos insolados (title means "Sunstroked Labyrinths"), Seix Barral (Madrid), 1967.
La jugada del sexto dia (title means "The Sixth-Day Gambit"), University Press of Santiago (Chile), 1969.
Homerica latina (title means "A Latin American Epic"), Valencia Editores (Bogota), 1979.
Conversacions al sur, Siglo XXI (Mexico), 1981, translation published as *Mothers and Shadows,* Readers International (New York), 1989.

Also author of *En cualquier lugar* (title means "In Any Place"), 1984; and *Casa sin fin* (title means "Endless House"), 1984.

ART CRITICISM

El museo vacio (title means "The Empty Museum"), Mito (Columbia), 1952.
Arte en America, Pan American Union (Washington, DC), 1959.
La pintura nueva en Latino Americo (title means "New Latin American Painting"), Libreria Central (Bogota), 1961.

Los cuatro monstruos cardinales (title means "The Four Capital Monsters"), Era (Mexico), 1965.

Dos decadas vulnerables en las arte plasticas latinoamericanas, 1950-1970 (title means "Two Vulnerable Decades of Latin American Art"), Siglo XXI (Mexico), 1973.

Guide to Twentieth-Century Latin American Art, (Organization of American States), 1982.

Also author of *El Arte Bizantino* (title means "Byzantine Art"), 1965; *La rebelion de los santos* (title means "The Rebellion of the Saints"), 1971; *Propuesta polemica sobre el arte puertorriqueno* (title means "Polemic Proposals on Puerto Rican Art"), 1971; *En el humbral del arte moderno* (title means "On the Threshold of Modern Art"), 1972; *Mirar en Caracas* (title means "Looking in Caracas"), 1974; *La Zona del silencio* (title means "The Silent Zone"), 1975; and *Hombre americano a todo color* (title means "American Man in Full Color"), 1975.

Contributor to periodicals.

OTHER

Paso asi (short stories; title means "So It Was"), Arca Press (Montevideo), 1969.

SIDELIGHTS: A ardent supporter of contemporary art, writer and educator Marta Traba devoted her life to promote the artistry of Latin Americans both throughout the Americas and around the world. Raised in Buenos Aires, Argentina, Traba earned a scholarship to study art history, first in Chile, and then in Paris. It was after moving to Bogota, Colombia, in 1954 that she founded *Prisma,* a journal of art criticism, and began appearing on television to discuss the new directions in Latin American art.

Traba would begin writing fiction after her reputation as an art critic had been firmly established. She submitted *Las ceremonias del verano,* a novel that recalls her early days as a new mother, to the Casa de las Americas prize committee, and was surprised to win that coveted prize in 1966. Encouraged by that success, she published a collection of short stories in 1969, following it with several more novels. Her best-known novel, 1981's *Conversacions al sur,* published in translation as *Mothers and Shadows,* is the story of two Argentine women whose conversations bring to life the horrors of the brutally repressive political regimes of both Argentina and Chile. By forcing themselves to express their experiences—forced miscarriage, imprisonment and torture—both

Irene and Dolores are able to move beyond the past and regain their sense of self. "The sensitive development of a sympathetic and symbiotic relationship between two female characters is a unique contribution to Latin American literature, . . ." noted Evelyn Picon Garfield in *Women's Voices from Latin America.* "Traba vividly captures the defiance of these women and the madness of a populace that collectively turns its back on them."

Lecturing at Harvard University, Middlebury College, and other schools throughout North America between 1979 and 1981, Traba lived in the United States until 1982, when, along with her husband, the Uruguayan literary critic Angel Rama, her request for permanent residency was denied. The couple then moved to Paris; they would be killed together in a plane crash near the outskirts of Madrid, Spain, the following year.

BIOGRAPHICAL/CRITICAL SOURCES:

BOOKS

Agosin, Marjorie, editor, *A Dream of Light and Shadow: Portraits of Latin American Women Writers,* University of New Mexico Press (Albuquerque), 1995.

Garfield, Evelyn Picon, *Women's Voices from Latin America,* Wayne State University Press (Detroit), 1985.

Pinto, Magdalena Garcia, *Women Writers of Latin America: Intimate Histories,* University of Texas Press (Austin), 1988.

PERIODICALS

Chasqui: Revista de la literatura latinoamericana, May, 1992.

Modern Language Review, January, 1992.*

*   *   *

TRIBLE, Phyllis 1932-

PERSONAL: Born October 25, 1932, in Richmond, VA. *Education:* Meredith College, B.A. (magna cum laude), 1954; attended Union Theological Seminary, 1954-56; Columbia University, Ph.D., 1963.

ADDRESSES: Office—Union Theological Seminary, 3041 Broadway, New York, NY 10027-5710.

CAREER: Theologian and educator. Masters School, Dobbs Ferry, NY, teacher, 1960-63; Wake Forest University, Winston-Salem, NC, assistant, then associate professor of religion, 1963-71; Andover Newton Theological School, Newton Centre, MA, associate professor, then professor of Old Testament, 1975-79; Union Theological Seminary, New York City, professor of Old Testament, 1979-81, then Baldwin Professor of Sacred Literature, 1981—. Lecturer at numerous colleges and universities worldwide; visiting professor at Seinan Gakuin University, Fukuoka, Japan; University of Virginia; Boston University; Vancouver School of Theology; Brown University; Saint John's University; University of Notre Dame; and Iliff School of Theology, Denver, Colorado.

AWARDS, HONORS: National Endowment for the Humanities Younger Humanist fellowship, 1974-75; Meredith College Alumna Award, 1977; honorary degrees from Franklin College, 1985, and Lehigh University, 1994. National Endowment for the Humanities Younger Humanist fellowship, 1974-75; Meredith College Alumna Award, 1977; honorary degrees from Franklin College, 1985, and Lehigh University, 1994.

MEMBER: American Academy of Religion, Society of Biblical Literature (president, 1994).

WRITINGS:

God and the Rhetoric of Sexuality, Fortress Press (Philadelphia), 1978.
Texts of Terror: Literary-Feminist Readings of Biblical Narratives, Fortress Press, 1984.
Rhetorical Criticism: Context, Method, and the Book of Jonah, Fortress Press (Minneapolis), 1994.

Contributor to periodicals, including *Andover Newton Quarterly, Auburn News, Bible Review, Christian Century, Journal of the American Academy of Religion, Journal of Biblical Literature, Religion in Life, Soundings,* and *Theological Studies.*

SIDELIGHTS: Theologian Phyllis Trible is renowned for her work in feminist scholarship. "Ask graduate students in their twenties or established scholars in their thirties and forties how an interest was awakened in women's issues and biblical studies," contends Cullen Murphy in the *Atlantic Review,* "and the answer will often turn out to involve and article or a book by Trible." Central to Trible's scholarship is storytelling; how bible tales reveal humanity's past,

and how they ultimately expose the rationale used to justify women's reduced status within society. In works such as *God and the Rhetoric of Sexuality* and *Texts of Terror: Literary-Feminist Readings of Biblical Narratives,* she examines Hebrew tales culled from biblical sources. With her strong grounding in literary theory, Trible studies the parameters and metaphor of biblical language, providing cogent interpretations of sections that cast new light on the tradition of women's lives.

In both *God and the Rhetoric of Sexuality* and *Texts of Terror* Trible draws on examples from bible stories to reveal the complex lives of women in ancient times. Reworking stories using a variety of scholarly methods, she shows how successive translations have created meanings contrary to what the original written versions may have intended. For example, in a detailed examination of the creation stories of Eve and Adam she finds that they can be interpreted in a manner that shows Eve and Adam living together as equal creatures, with equal responsibility for their collective downfall. Trible goes on to illustrate that woman's creation from the rib of man was based on simple utility rather than the female's lesser status; when compared to man's creation from dust neither birth is more or less esteemed. Commenting on *God and the Rhetoric of Sexuality* in *Christian Century,* reviewer Marianne H. Micks terms the work "a superb example of a biblical scholar's use of 'rhetorical criticism.'"

Trible's *Rhetorical Criticism: Context, Method, and the Book of Jonah,* published in 1994, was written as an aid to students trying to understand how rhetorical criticism functions in analyzing works dating back to ancient Greece. This approach loses none of its power when employed in the interpretation of richly embroidered historic stories, contends Trible, who views the fundamental goal of the critic as discerning the underlying intentions of the storyteller. She encourages understanding words within their Hebrew contexts, while also recognizing how those words have been used in other contexts; recognizing instances when titles and proper names have been reversed; and gaining an awareness of the use of metaphor to reference earlier written sources.

Throughout her career, Trible has retained a flexible approach to scholarship, acknowledging this as a necessity given the requirements of dealing with original source material that dates thousands of years into the past. Praised for that flexibility, as well as for her critical analyses that seek to find a more equitable view of women, her works are foundational within the canon of feminist biblical scholarship.

BIOGRAPHICAL/CRITICAL SOURCES:

PERIODICALS

America, December 1, 1979, p. 350; December 1, 1984, p. 371.
Atlantic Monthly, August, 1993, pp. 29-64.
Choice, March, 1979, p. 96.
Christian Century, January 17, 1979, p. 57; January 20, 1982, p. 57.
Commonweal, February 22, 1985, p. 199.

* * *

TRILLING, Diana (Rubin) 1905-1996

OBITUARY NOTICE—See index for *CA* sketch: Born July 21, 1905, in New York, NY; died October 23, 1996, in New York, NY. Critic and author. A member of the group of writers and thinkers in the 1930 to the 1950s known as the "New York intellectuals," Trilling was known for her uncompromising views on culture, art and literature. The wife of famed literary critic Lionel Trilling, she often joked about working in his shadow. The two met in a speak-easy in 1927 and Trilling credited her husband with opening her horizons beyond her Radcliffe degree in fine arts. In 1941, she began a job at the *Nation* magazine where she worked as a literary critic until 1949, when she left that position to become a freelance writer. Her reviews and essays appeared in the *New Yorker, Atlantic, Saturday Review, Commentary,* and *Partisan Review.* She was able to write about the greatest authors of the day, like Evelyn Waugh and Jean-Paul Sartre. Those who disagreed with her views, however, also respected them. Trilling was known for well-reasoned and researched essays and not hasty opinions. She also edited two volumes on D. H. Lawrence and a twelve-volume collection of her husband's work. She wrote few books, but one of them, 1981's *Mrs. Harris: The Death of the Scarsdale Diet Doctor,* earned her wide recognition and a Pulitzer Prize nomination. Trilling continued to write until her death, dictating to a tape recorder when her eyes failed. She wrote her memoir, *The Beginning of the Journey: The Marriage of Diana and Lionel Trilling,* in 1993, and in early 1996 finished her last book, *A Visit to Camelot,* an account of her visit to the John F. Kennedy White House.

OBITUARIES AND OTHER SOURCES:

BOOKS

Who's Who, 148th edition, St. Martin's Press, 1996.

PERIODICALS

Chicago Tribune, October 25, 1996, Sec. 2, p. 11.
Los Angeles Times, October 26, 1996, p. A24.
New York Times, October 25, 1996, p. A33.
Washington Post, October 26, 1996, p. B5.

* * *

TRINH, T. Min-Ha 1952-

PERSONAL: Born in 1952, in Vietnam; immigrated to United States, 1970. *Education:* Attended schools in Vietnam, the Philippines, France, and the United States.

ADDRESSES: Office—Department of Women's Studies, University of California, Berkeley, Berkeley, CA 94720-0001.

CAREER: Writer and educator. University of California, Berkeley, Chancellor's Distinguished Professor of Women's Studies; San Francisco State University, associate professor of cinema.

WRITINGS:

(Editor, with Russell Ferguson, Martha Gever, and Cornel West) *Out There: Marginalization in Contemporary Culture,* [United States], 1990.
When the Moon Waxes Red: Representation, Gender, and Cultural Politics, Routledge (London), 1991.
Framer Framed: Film Scripts and Interviews, Routledge (New York), 1992.

Also author of *Un Art sans oeuvre,* 1981; *African Spaces: Designs for Living in Upper Volta* (with Jean-Paul Bourdier), 1985; *En miniscules* (poetry collection), 1987; and *Women, Native, Other: Writing Postcoloniality and Feminism,* 1989. Author of screenplays, including *Reassemblage,* 1982, *Naked Spaces—Living Is Round,* 1985, *Surname Viet, Given Name Nam,* 1989, and *Shoot for the Contents,* 1991.

Contributor of articles to periodicals, including *Aperture, City Lights Review,* and *Motion Picture.* Guest editor of *Discourse: Journal for Theoretical Studies in Media and Culture.*

SIDELIGHTS: Educator, writer, and filmmaker Trinh T. Minh-ha, a teacher both at the University of California, Berkeley, and San Francisco State University, is the author of several books, including 1989's *Woman, Native, Other: Writing Postcoloniality and Feminism* and *When the Moon Waxes Red: Representation, Gender, and Cultural Politics,* a collection of fourteen essays published in 1991. Well known as a feminist scholar and creative artist, her work has ranged from musical composition to filmmaking and essays on social theory. Trinh is the author of the poetry collection *En miniscules;* her films include *Reassemblage* (Senegal, 1982), *Naked Spaces—Living Is Round* (West Africa, 1985) and *Surname Viet, Given Name Nam* (1989). *Framer Framed: Film Scripts and Interviews,* published in 1992, includes the scripts for three of Trinh's films.

Trinh was born in Vietnam, immigrating to the United States in 1970 at the age of seventeen. Within her commitment to postcolonial theory and feminism Trinh's work has been called experimental, poetic, and revolutionary in nature. In the interviews collected in *Framer Framed,* she expresses her views on her art, on the feminist movement, and on her position as a postcolonial writer. As Trinh comments, "I . . . feel that a critical space of differentiation needs to be maintained since issues specifically raised by Third World women have less to do with questions of cultural difference than with a different notion of feminism itself—how it is lived and how it is practiced."

Trinh's work is notable for stretching boundaries, questioning the relationship between objects and their creative counterparts, and for its critical view of anthropology. In her films she disrupts the traditional distance between subject and filmmaker, interjecting a montage of external images into her range of view. In *Woman, Native, Other,* Trinh questions the validity of any notion of authenticity. Casting doubt upon the existence of a "true self," she suggests instead that one's identity is composed of countless layers representing socially derived labels that constantly flow into one another. She advocates not only reevaluating one's "self" but also recognizing the possibility of multiple selves that may be inconsistent with certain aspects of one's self-image. "I am always working at the borderlines of several shifting categories," Trinh says in an interview with Judith Mayne published in

Framer Framed, "stretching out to the limits of things, learning about my own limits and how to modify them."

BIOGRAPHICAL/CRITICAL SOURCES:

BOOKS

Trinh, T. Min-Ha, *Framer Framed: Film Scripts and Interviews,* Routledge (New York), 1992.

PERIODICALS

American Book Review, January, 1991, p. 11.
Diacritics, summer, 1995.
Heresies, Volume 6, number 2, 1987.

*   *   *

TROPMAN, John E. 1939-

PERSONAL: Born September 14, 1939, in Syracuse, NY; son of Elmer J. (a charity executive) and Elizabeth (a homemaker) Tropman; married, June 20, 1964; wife's name, Penelope; children: Sarah, Jessica, Matthew. *Education:* Oberlin College, A.B., 1961; University of Chicago, A.B., 1963; University of Michigan, Ph.D., 1967. *Politics:* Liberal. *Religion:* Roman Catholic. *Avocational interests:* Fishing, reading, classical music (baroque and pre-baroque), wine, food, travel.

ADDRESSES: *Home*—3568 River Pines Dr., Ann Arbor, MI 48103. *Office*—School of Social Work, University of Michigan, 1065 Frieze, Ann Arbor, MI 48109; fax 313-936-1961. *E-mail*—tropman@umich .edu and hgdecision@aol.com.

CAREER: University of Michigan, Ann Arbor, began as instructor, then assistant professor, later associate professor, currently professor of social work, member of Non Profit Management Program and Organizational Behavior Program. Carnegie-Mellon University, member of Executive Education Program; Fulbright lecturer in Japan, 1981. Special advisor to local charities.

MEMBER: American Sociological Association, Council on Social Work Education, Society for Judgment and Decision Making, Trout Unlimited, Nature Conservancy.

AWARDS, HONORS: Zell-Luri Prize, 1986; Wilbur J. Cohen Award, 1986; Monsignor O'Grady Award, 1987.

WRITINGS:

(Editor, with others) *Strategic Perspectives on Social Policy,* Franklin, 1976.

Effective Meetings: Improving Group Decision-Making, Sage Publications (Beverly Hills, CA), 1980, 2nd edition, 1995.

(With Roger M. Lind) *New Strategic Perspectives on Social Policy,* Elsevier (London, England), 1981.

Conflict in Culture: Permissions Versus Controls and Alcohol Use in American Society, University Press of America (Lanham, MD), 1986.

American Values on Social Welfare, Prentice-Hall (Englewood Cliffs, NJ), 1986.

(With Gersh Morningstar) *Entrepreneurial Systems for the 1990s: Their Creation, Structure, and Management,* Quorum (Westport, CT), 1986.

Public Policy Opinion and the Elderly, 1952-1978: A Kaleidoscope of Culture, Greenwood Press (Westport, CT), 1987.

(With Charles D. Garvin) *Social Work in Contemporary Society,* Prentice-Hall, 1992.

(With others) *Committee Management in Human Services,* 2nd edition, Nelson-Hall (Chicago, IL), 1992.

(Editor, with others) *Tactics and Techniques of Community Intervention,* 3rd edition, Peacock Publications (Itasca, IL), 1995.

Making Meetings Work: Achieving High Quality Group Decisions, Sage Publications, 1995.

The Catholic Ethic in American Society: An Exploration of Values, Jossey-Bass (San Francisco, CA), in press.

Also author of *Encyclopedia of Business,* Gale (Detroit, MI).

WORK IN PROGRESS: Non Profit Boards: What to Do and How to Do It; Why America Hates the Poor: An Analysis of Attitudes Toward the Poor; The Maestro Manager: Tips for CEOs; The Leadership Guide: Aids for Community Leaders.

SIDELIGHTS: John E. Tropman told *CA:* "I am a sociologist with a central interest in ideas values (ideas to which feeling is attached): the way values are structured, the way values (paradigms) change (evolution, revolution), and the way ideas/values emerge into policy (the policy process, the implemen-

tation process). I write for two reasons: to help myself understand the variety of processes (social, psychological), their connections and interpretations; and to provide people doing things (practitioners) with guides to help them and their organizations achieve high performance."

*   *   *

TSALOUMAS, Dimitris 1921-

PERSONAL: Born October 13, 1921, in Leros, Greece; married Ilse Wulff, 1958; children: two daughters, two sons. *Education:* University of Melbourne, B.A., Dip.Ed.

ADDRESSES: Home—72 Glenhuntly Rd., Elwood, Victoria 3184, Australia.

CAREER: Teacher with the Victoria Education Department and in secondary schools, 1958-82. Writer-in-residence, Oxford University, 1989.

AWARDS, HONORS: Australia Council grant, 1982, fellowship, 1984; National Book Council award, 1983; Patrick White award, 1994; Wesley M. Wright prize, 1994.

WRITINGS:

POETRY

Resurrection 1967, and Triptych for a Second Coming (in Greek), Arion (Melbourne), 1974.

Observations of a Hypochondriac (in Greek), Privately printed, 1974.

The House with the Eucalypts (in Greek), AKE Press (Athens and Melbourne), 1975.

The Sick Barber and Other Characters (in Greek), Ikaros (Athens), 1979.

The Son of Sir Sakis: A Roman Tale for Advanced Children (in Greek), Privately printed, 1979.

The Book of Epigrams (in Greek), Nea Poreia (Thessaloniki), 1981; enlarged edition, 1982; (in Greek and English) translated by Philip Grundy, University of Queensland Press (St. Lucia), 1985.

The Observatory: Selected Poems (in Greek and English), translated by Philip Grundy, University of Queensland Press, 1983.

Falcon Drinking: The English Poems, University of
Queensland Press, 1988.
Portrait of a Dog, University of Queensland Press
(Ringwood, Victoria), 1991.
The Barge, University of Queensland Press, 1993.

OTHER

(Editor and Translator) *Contemporary Australian Po-
etry* (in English and Greek), Nea Poreia, 1985,
University of Queensland Press, 1986.
(Editor) *Selected Poems 1972-1986,* by Manfred
Jurgensen, Albion Press (Newstead, Queensland),
1987.

*   *   *

TSUJI, Kunio   1925-

PERSONAL: Born September 24, 1925, in Tokyo,
Japan; son of Seigo (a journalist and musician) and
Kimi (a doll maker; maiden name, Yuda) Tsuji;
married Sahoko Goto (an art historian), June 6, 1953.
Education: Tokyo University, M.A., 1952, post-
graduate studies, 1952-54; attended the Sorbonne,
Paris, 1957-61.

ADDRESSES: Home—Takanawa 3-1-10-605, Mi-
natoku, Tokyo, Japan. *Agent*—c/o Kodansha International, 2-12-21 Otowa, Bunkyo-ku, Tokyo 112-01,
Japan.

CAREER: Gakushuin University, Tokyo, part-time
lecturer, 1956, 1961, professor of French literature,
1975-90; St. Paul's University, Tokyo, assistant professor of literature, 1966-72; Tokyo Agricultural
College, professor of literature, 1972-75; University
of Paris X, lecturer in cultural anthropology, 1980-
81; University of Paris III, lecturer in Japanese literature, 1983-84.

MEMBER: Japan Writers Association, Academy of
Japan.

AWARDS, HONORS: Modern Literature prize (Japan), 1963; New Writer's Prize, Japanese Educational Ministry, 1968, for *Azuchi Okanki;* The
Mainich, 1972, for *Julianus the Apostate;* Tanizaki
Prize, 1995, for *Life of Saigyo.*

WRITINGS:

FICTION

On the Corridor, Shincho-sha, 1963.
The Fort of Summer, Kawade-shobo-shinsha, 1965.
Azuchi Okanki, Chikuma-shobo, 1968, translation by
Steven Snyder published as *The Signore: Shogun
of the Warring States,* Kodansha International
(Tokyo), 1990.
The Canticle of Amakusa, Shincho-sha, 1971.
Sagano Moonlight Journal, Shincho-sha, 1971.
Julia and the Magic City (nursery story), Chikuma-
shobo, 1971.
Julianus the Apostate, Chuokoron-sha, 1972.
Poseidons Mask Festival, Chuokoron-sha, 1973.
A Journey toward a Midday Sea, Shuei-sha, 1975.
The Crowning of Spring, Shincho-sha, 1977.
Time's Door, Mainichi Newspapers, 1977.
Twelve Stories According to Twelve Portraits,
Bungeishunju-sha, 1981.
Angels Pass the Streets, Chuokoron-sha, 1985.
Seven Sceneries in a Person's Life, Chuokoron-sha,
1988.
Revolutionary the Chronicle of Fouche, Bungeishunju-
sha, 1989.

Also author of *Life of Saigyo* (historical novel), 1995.

OTHER

*Prolegomena for Novels—A Study of Narrativity and
Aesthetical Grounds of Novels,* Kawade-shobo,
1968.
Memoranda at Paris (5 volumes), Kawade-shobo,
1973-74.
A Journey toward Poesy, a Journey from Poesy
(travel), Chikuma-shobo, 1974.
Collected Essays of Kunio Tsuji (5 volumes),
Shincho-sha, 1974-81.
An Olive-Twig (essays), Chuokoron-sha, 1980.
Arimasa Mori (criticism), Chikuma-shobo, 1988.

Also contributor of articles to journals.

WORK IN PROGRESS: A series of short stories with
the theme of interviewing dead novelists; researching
the problem of contradiction between ethics and aestheticism.

SIDELIGHTS: The first work of novelist and literature professor Kunio Tsuji to be translated from Japanese to English is *The Signore: Shogun of the War-*

ring States. Written in 1968, the book showcases Tsuji's skill as both a scholar and fiction writer in its treatment of a complex historical figure, the sixteenth-century Japanese warlord Oda Nobunaga. In the novel, Tsuji attempts to humanize Nobunaga; a familiar figure to the Japanese reading audience, he has been universally portrayed as a cold and cruel killer who calmly supervised the annihilation of his enemies. Tsuji frames Nobunaga's story through the eyes of an Italian adventurer who comes to know the warlord on fairly friendly terms and who has sympathy for his rational if violent approach to unifying Japan. This seemingly unlikely relationship between Nobunaga and the Italian is precipitated by the ruler's interest in western firearms and his acceptance of the presence of Jesuit missionaries (in opposition to the Buddhists, who are one of his great enemies).

Tsuji's method of depicting the famous warlord has drawn the commendation of critics who value *Signore* for both its historical value and its thematic resonance for the twentieth century. Anthony J. Bryant, writing for the *Tokyo Journal,* marveled at Tsuji's ability to understand Oda and his peers: "[The novelist] provides motives and explanations for their relationships and actions, thereby outguessing a whole pack of rabid historians who psychoanalyze dead people. He does all this with such skill and aplomb and in such an understated way that the last page is turned before we realize that what we have read is more history than novel." When John Updike reviewed the novel for the *New Yorker,* he was reminded of the Japanese experience in World War II; he pondered that Tsuji was "a Japanese with memories of modern war and Japan's subsequent indoctrination in the virtues of peace, [who] worries at the riddle of martial morality." Updike further concluded, "the reader, and presumably the author, can hardly not think of the two atomic bombs that in a few blinding moments killed more Japanese than Nobunaga's thirty years of systematic mayhem, but did open the way to recovery." Also of note is Stephen Snyder's translation of the novel, which was credited as skillful and accurate.

BIOGRAPHICAL/CRITICAL SOURCES:

PERIODICALS

Booklist, April 15, 1990, p. 1609.
New Yorker, March 18, 1991, pp. 103-04.
Publishers Weekly, January 26, 1990, p. 404.
Tokyo Journal, May, 1990, p. 17.
World Literature Today, winter, 1991, pp. 190-91.

TSUSHIMA, Satoko 1947-
(Yuko Tsushima, a pseudonym)

PERSONAL: Born March 30, 1947, in Tokyo, Japan; daughter of Osamu Dazai (a writer); married in 1970 (divorced, 1976); children: one daughter, one son. *Education:* Shirayuri Women's University, B.A., 1969; attended Meiji University Graduate School, 1969-71.

ADDRESSES: Home—6-15-16-602, Honkomagome, Bunkyo-ku, Tokyo, Japan, 113. *Agent*—Tatemi Sakai, Orion Press, 1-58, Kanda-Jimboco, Chiyoda-ku, Tokyo, Japan.

CAREER: Writer. Institute of Occidental Languages, University of Paris, lecturer in Japanese literature, 1991-92.

AWARDS, HONORS: Kawabata Yasunari Prize, 1974, for *Danmari Ichi;* Tamura Toshiko Prize, 1975, for *Mugura no Haha;* Izumi Kyoka Prize, 1977, for *Kusa no Fushido;* Women's Literature Prize, 1978, for *Choji;* Noma Bungei New Writer Prize, 1979, for *Hikari no Ryobun;* Yomiuri Prize, 1986, for *Yoru no Hikari ni Owarete;* Hirabahashi Taiko Prize, 1989, for *Mahiru e;* Ito Sei Prize, 1995, for *Kaze yo, Sora Kakeru Kaze yo.*

MEMBER: Nihon Bungei Kyokai (Japanese literary association).

WRITINGS:

NOVELS

Doji no Kage (title means "The Shadow of a Child"), Kawaide Shobo (Tokyo), 1973.
Ikimono no Atsumaru Ie (title means "House Appointed to All Living"), Shinchosha (Tokyo), 1973.
Choji, Kawaide Shobo, 1978, translation by Geraldine Harcourt published as *Child of Fortune,* Kodansha International (New York), 1983.
Hikari no Ryobun (title means "Realm of Light"), Kodansha (Tokyo), 1979.
Moeru Kaze (title means "Burning Wind"), Chuokoronsha (Tokyo), 1980.
Yama o Hashiru Onna (title means "Woman Running in the Mountains"), Kodansha, 1980.
Hi no Kawa no Hotori de (title means "By the River of Fire"), Kodansha, 1983.
Yoru no Hikari ni Owarete (title means "The Light of Night Runs after Me"), Kodansha, 1986.

Mahiru e (title means "To High Noon"), Shinchosha, 1988.

Kaze yo, Sora Kakeru Kaze yo (title means "Wind, Wind That Runs through the Sky"), [Tokyo], 1995.

SHORT STORIES

Shanikusai (title means "Carnival"), Kawaide Shobo, 1971.

Danmari Ichi (title means "Silent Traders"), Kodansha, 1974.

Waga Chichitachi (title means "My Fathers"), Kodansha, 1975.

Mugura no Haha, Kawaide Shobo, 1975, title story published in translation as "The Mother in the House of Grass," in *Literary Review,* Volume 30, winter 1987.

Kusa no Fushido, Kodansha, 1977, title story published in translation as "A Bed of Grass," in *This Kind of Woman: Ten Stories by Japanese Women, 1960-1976,* edited by Yukiko Tanaka and Elizabeth Hanson, Stanford University Press (Stanford), 1982.

Yorokobi no Shima (title means "Island of Joy"), Chuokoronsha, 1978.

Saigo no Shuryo (title means "The Last Hunting"), Sakuhinsha (Tokyo), 1979.

Hyogen (title means "Ice Fields"), Sakuhinsha, 1979.

Suifu (title means "Water City"), Kawaide Shobo, 1982.

Oma Monogatari (title means "Phantom Stories"), Kodansha, 1984.

The Shooting Gallery, Women's Press (London), 1986, Pantheon (New York City), 1988.

Yume no Kiroku (title means "Records of Dreams"), Bungeishunju (Tokyo), 1988.

(Contributor) Yukiko Tanaka, editor, *Unmapped Territories: New Women's Fiction from Japan,* Women in Translation, 1991.

Contributor to anthologies, including *Mita Bungaku,* 1969.

OTHER

Tomei Kukan ga Mieru Toki (title means "When One Can See the Transparent Space"), Seidosha (Tokyo), 1977.

Yoru no Tii Paati (title means "The Evening Tea Party"), Jinbunshoin (Kyoto), 1979.

Nani ga Seikaku o Tsukuruka (title means "What Makes Personality"), Asahi Shuppan (Tokyo), 1979.

Yoru to Asa no Tegami (title means "Letters from Night and Morning"), Kairyusha, 1980.

Watashi no Jikan (title means "My Time"), Jinbunshoin, 1982.

Shosetsu no Naka no Fukei (title means "Landscape in the Novel"), Chuokoronsha, 1982.

Osanaki Hibi e (title means "To the Childhood Day"), Kodansha, 1986.

Hon no Naka no Shojotachi (title means "Girls in Books"), Chuokoronsha, 1989.

Contributor of short stories and essays to periodicals, including *boundary 2, Mita Bungaku, Bungei, Gunzo, Umi,* and *Bungakukai.* Some of Tsushima's writings have appeared under the name Yuko Tsushima.

SIDELIGHTS: Satoko Tsushima is one of the most significant feminist writers of contemporary Japan. Her award-winning novels and short stories, several of which have been translated into English, are noted for challenging prevailing social customs, especially those that diminish the freedom of women. In addition, through her fiction she examines such taboos as illegitimacy, incest, and other violent sexual behavior. Tsushima's characteristic descriptions of small but telling details and her references to dream images and mythology heightens the reader's understanding of each of her fictional characters.

Born in the city of Tokyo shortly after the end of World War II, Tsushima attended a Catholic girls' boarding school throughout her childhood and teenage years. It wasn't until 1969 that she left this structured academic environment and enrolled at Meiji University. Interested more in the wide variety of outside activities now open to her than her coursework, Tsushima attended class only occasionally, ultimately abandoning school for a career as professional writer with the story "Requiem—For Dog and Adult," published in the anthology *Mita Bungaku* in 1969.

Tsushima's third novel, translated as *Child of Fortune* in 1983, was published in 1978, when she was thirty-one. In it, the protagonist, an independent-minded young woman named Koko, is haunted by the memory of the dead brother who had once protected her fiercely. In contrast, Koko's living sister is an untiring critic of Koko's supposedly "immoral" behavior, a rejection of the liberated woman's lack of acceptance within Japanese society. In some of her more recent semi-autobiographical novels—called *shishosetsu*—Tsushima reflects upon the traditions of marriage and motherhood; unmarried motherhood and illegitimacy also inform several of her works, which openly break with social norms. The cycle of pregnancy, childbirth, and child-rearing dominates much of Tsushima's writing, providing a natural continuity for her female characters and allowing them to discard artificially social and moral strictures.

By enabling her female protagonists to live outside the mainstream of Japanese society, Tsushima "successfully points out the deficiencies of rigid social strictures that cripple people's ability to connect to each other and to live true to themselves," according to Tomoko Kuribayashi in *Feminist Writers.* "At the same time, she draws attention to women's energy and powers that are deeply rooted in their sexual and physical existence, while never neglecting the sense of desolation and loneliness that inevitably accompanies the life of a woman who elects to lead a life of her own."

BIOGRAPHICAL/CRITICAL SOURCES:

BOOKS

Feminist Writers, St. James Press (Detroit), 1996.

PERIODICALS

Japan Quarterly, Volume 35, number 4, 1988; Volume 39, number 1, 1992.

*   *   *

TSUSHIMA, Yuko
  See TSUSHIMA, Satoko

*   *   *

TUDGE, Colin   1943-

PERSONAL: Born April 22, 1943, in London, England; son of Cyril (a musician) and Maisie (a homemaker) Tudge; married September 9, 1966 (separated); children: two daughters, one son. *Ethnicity:* "British." *Education:* Peterhouse, Cambridge, B.A., 1965, M.A., 1966.

ADDRESSES: Home—59 Holmdene Ave., Herne Hill, London SE24 9LD, England. *Office*—fax 01-71-274-2257. *E-mail*—c.tudge@lse.ac.uk. *Agent*—John

Brockman Associates, 5 East 59th St., New York, NY 10022.

CAREER: Magazine journalist, 1965-80; *New Scientist,* features editor, 1980-84; BBC-Radio, presenter for Science Unit, 1985-90, including the series *Science on Three* and *Spectrum;* freelance writer, 1990—. University of London, visiting research fellow, Centre for Philosophy, London School of Economics and Political Science. Television presenter, including an episode of *Horizon,* BBC2-TV. London Zoo Reform Group, co-founder, 1991, member of council, 1992-94; London Zoo Board, member of council; Jersey Zoo, member of summer school.

MEMBER: Linnean Society (fellow).

AWARDS, HONORS: Named Glaxo/ABSW Science Writer of the Year, 1972, 1984, 1990; shortlisted for COPUS/Rhone-Poulenc Science Book of the Year Award, 1992, for *Last Animals at the Zoo,* and 1994, for *Engineer in the Garden;* BP Conservation Book of the Year Award, 1996, for *The Day Before Yesterday.*

WRITINGS:

The Famine Business, Faber (London), 1977.
(With Michael Allaby) *Home Farm,* Macmillan (London), 1977.
Future Cook, Mitchell Beazley (London), 1980.
The Food Connection, BBC Publications (London), 1985.
Food Crops for the Future, Basil Blackwell (Oxford), 1988.
Global Ecology, Natural History Museum, 1991.
Last Animals at the Zoo, Hutchinson Radius, 1991.
The Engineer in the Garden, J. Cape (London), 1993.
The Day Before Yesterday: Five Million Years of Human History, Simon & Schuster (New York), 1995.

Editor of the book *The Environment of Life,* Oxford University Press (Oxford). Author of "Scavenger," a column in *World Medicine* and *New Scientist's Forum,* 1984-90; food columnist, *Kew,* 1990-92. General editor, "New Scientist Guides," Basil Blackwell, 1984—. Contributor to magazines and newspapers.

SIDELIGHTS: Colin Tudge told *CA:* "I write largely because I enjoy the process of writing. I like to take a word processor on holiday, and I miss it if it is not there. Then I write a great deal that I never seriously expect to get published. I would like the world to be a better place, and I like to think that, by writing, I can change things. If I had not been a writer, I would have become a schoolteacher (and at times have regretted not doing so).

"Overall I suppose that writing is actually a very self-indulgent (perhaps ultimately self-indulgent) way to make a living. This does not mean it is not hard or serious. Writing provides a way of becoming involved in ideas and causes, without being exposed to reality; for example, to the tedium of most laboratory science, the politics of professional academe, or the very considerable burdens of modern schoolteaching.

"I am influenced by people I think do things better than I do (or perhaps possibly could). I am aware of the influence of Anthony Burgess, who writes extraordinarily well; of Charles Darwin, who had such a marvelous way of life (and managed to change the world more profoundly than anyone); of people like my friend and fellow scribbler Bernard Dixon, who gets such a lot done; or Helena Cronin, co-director of the Centre for Philosophy at the London School of Economics and the author of *The Ant and the Peacock,* who is so scholarly; and John Steinbeck, who I have not read for years, but who introduced me to Mack and the boys (in *Cannery Row* and *Sweet Thursday*) and implanted in my mind the notion that nine-to-five timetables were equivalent to death.

"Now that I have a word processor, I write paragraphs and passages as they come to me, until the whole thing becomes too messy and I start all over again. Diversion is vital. Good ideas and structures sort themselves out in your head, provided you plant the problems carefully and do not worry at them too much while the brain is working them out.

"Biology has always been my first love; the whole business of writing runs it a close second. I remember writing a long story about cats at the age of six, and essentially nothing much has changed since then. On the one hand, I have a penchant for practicalities (such as farming and conservation) and, on the other, a penchant for philosophy, particularly moral philosophy and the philosophy of science."

* * *

TURNER, Brian (Lindsay) 1944-

PERSONAL: Born in 1944, in Dunedin, New Zealand; divorced; children: one son.

ADDRESSES: Home—2 Upper Junction Rd., Sawyers Bay, Dunedin, New Zealand.

CAREER: Customs Department, Dunedin, customs officer, 1962-64, and Christchurch, 1964-66; Oxford University Press, Wellington, trade and university sales representative, and editor, 1968-74; Radio Otago, Dunedin, radio journalist, 1974; John McIndoe Ltd., Dunedin, managing editor, 1975-83, 1985-86.

AWARDS, HONORS: Commonwealth poetry prize, 1978; Robert Burns fellowship (University of Otago), 1984; John Cowie Reid Memorial prize, 1985; New Zealand Book award for poetry, 1993.

WRITINGS:

POETRY

Ladders of Rain, McIndoe (Dunedin), 1978.
Ancestors, McIndoe, 1981.
Listening to the River, McIndoe, 1983.
Bones, McIndoe, 1985.
All That Blue Can Be, McIndoe, 1989.
Beyond, McIndoe, 1992.

OTHER

Images of Coastal Otago, photographs by Michael de Hamel, McIndoe, 1982.
New Zealand High Country: Four Seasons, photographs by Gordon Roberts, Millwood Press (Wellington), 1983.
(With Glenn Turner) *Opening Up,* Hodder and Stoughton (Auckland), 1987.
The Last River's Song, photographs by Lloyd Godman, McIndoe, 1989.
The Guide to Trout Fishing in Otago, Otago Acclimatisation Society (Dunedin), 1994.

* * *

TYLER, Sandra 1963-

PERSONAL: Born February 5, 1963, in Staten Island, NY; daughter of David B. (a historian) and Elizabeth (an artist; maiden name, Sloan) Tyler. *Education:* Amherst College, B.A., 1985; Columbia University, M.F.A., 1990 (creative writing). *Politics:* Democrat. *Religion:* Episcopalian. *Avocational interests:* Visual arts—particularly pen and ink drawing, hiking, lake and ocean swimming.

ADDRESSES: Agent—Mary Evans, Mary Evans Inc., 242 East 5th St., New York, NY 10003.

CAREER: Montauk Light (newspaper), Bridge-hampton, NY, feature writer and reporter, 1985-86; *Ploughshares* (magazine), New York City assistant editor, 1986-88; *Columbia: A Magazine of Poetry and Prose,* New York City, editorial assistant, 1988; *Seventeen* (magazine), New York City, book reviewer, 1989-90; *Paris Review,* New York City, editorial assistant, 1989-1990; Manhattanville College, Purchase, NY, adjunct professor of creative writing, 1994-95; Columbia University, New York City, adjunct professor of creative writing, 1994-95; Wesleyan University, Middletown, CT, adjunct professor of creative writing, 1994—; Southampton College of LIU, Southampton, NY adjunct professor of creative writing, 1994—.

MEMBER: Author's Guild.

AWARDS, HONORS: Four graduate writing fellowships from Columbia University; grant from the New York Public Library; Notable Book of the Year, *New York Times,* 1992, for *Blue Glass;* Peter Burnett Howe Prize for fiction, Amherst College; First Prize for Fiction, National League of American Pen Women; MacDowell Colony fellowship for *Blue Glass,* 1994.

WRITINGS:

NOVELS

Blue Glass, Harcourt Brace (New York), 1992.
After Lydia, Harcourt Brace, 1995.

SIDELIGHTS: Author Sandra Tyler worked on the editorial staff of several magazines before she completed her master of fine arts degree in creative writing and published her first novel, 1992's *Blue Glass.* Tyler contributed book reviews to *Seventeen* magazine and has assisted in the manuscript selection process for *Ploughshares.* After *Blue Glass* received predominantly positive critical attention, Tyler followed it with her 1995 novel, *After Lydia.*

Tyler credits her artist mother for encouraging her artistic endeavors. "I never had a coloring book," Tyler recalled for Denise Mourges in the *New York Times.* "My mother would give me these big rolls of butcher paper and a bunch of paints." After Tyler graduated from Amherst College, her mother "also suggested" that she "go on to graduate school."

Blue Glass is told from the point of view of Leslie, a young girl, and flows from her somewhat idyllic childhood—a time when she worshipped her mother—through the disintegration of her parents' marriage during her late adolescence. During the course of the novel, Leslie's mother, Marion, is seen to have gradually lost her individuality in trying to provide the perfect home for her husband and daughter. Though Jean Hanff Korelitz in *Washington Post Book World* responded negatively to *Blue Glass,* asserting that it "fails to achieve any kind of momentum or narrative interest," other critics offered praise for the novel. Noted writer Jane Smiley, in an assessment in the *New York Times Book Review,* pointed out in particular Tyler's "evenhanded" balance of sympathy between the characters of mother and daughter, and hailed *Blue Glass* as a "lovely and unusual first novel." A *Kirkus Reviews* notice lauded the novel as well, calling it "one of those quietly compelling stories that touches the heart. A promising beginning."

After Lydia also explores the mother-daughter relationship, but from a much different perspective. Lydia, the mother in this novel, has been dead for a year. Everyone in her family believes that her death was an accident—except for Vickie, who, home for the occasion of her grandmother's eightieth birthday party, has begun to wonder if her mother committed suicide. Complicating her search for the answers are her encounters with Kyle, her first love, mysterious hints from Lydia's neighbor Gail, and her troubled relationship with her older sister Meryl. *After Lydia* never concludes whether Lydia's death was accidental or purposeful, but follows Vickie into the knowledge of how little we actually know about even our closest loved ones.

Opinion varied about Tyler's achievement in *After Lydia. Library Journal* contributor Nancy Pearl lamented that Tyler's second novel was "unfocused and predictable." A *Publishers Weekly* critic, however, praised *After Lydia* as "emotionally acute," while Scott Veale in the *New York Times Book Review* concluded that "Tyler is best at revealing the habitual role playing and fault lines beneath the everyday banter."

Tyler told *CA:* "I don't know whether I've ever been able to view life without some kind of fictional world overlapping the real one—I've been telling myself stories ever since I was a child, when I'd draw elaborate neighborhoods across large scrolls of paper, imagining entire peopled rooms behind the curtained windows.

"The act of writing absorbs me now in much the same way drawing did back when I'd spend my afternoons kneeling on the floor where I'd spread the paper, bearing down with felt tip pens. As well, my reliance on the visual has been carried over to my writing—most likely a scene will work if I can clearly picture the setting, the arrangement of furniture, the intensity of window light. I still draw, although mostly pen and ink sketches of solitary houses rather than whole neighborhoods, and still primarily as a form of self-entertainment. But it is only through writing that I was able to discover what it really means to persevere at a craft, a discovery I first made in high school when I'd come home and write and *rewrite* stories about old men on park benches and jazz musicians.

"It is that revision process that I have come to respect most in the long process toward completion, a respect I try to pass on to my writing students. And the act of reworking a short story I have always found to be the most satisfying, able to reap those rewards of a finished product more quickly than in the writing of a novel.

"So it was some time before I was willing to accept that *Blue Glass,* what originally I begun as a collection of interconnected stories, was actually a novel. *Blue Glass* began with a simple short story about what happens when a daughter visits her father for the first time after he has moved out of the house. From that story, I became interested in the mother who only figures as a silhouette in the upstairs bed-room window, watching as her daughter is picked up and driven away by the husband who left her. I hadn't realized how much the novel would evolve into one as much depicting the evolution of a mother/daughter relationship as the slow dissolution of a family.

"My second novel, *After Lydia,* is quite different in that it is much less linear and more layered, perhaps because it was written more consciously as a novel. But I found myself returning to that familiar but fertile terrain, the emotional dynamics between women: here again is the mother/daughter relationship but considered now from the perspective of two sisters as they try to come to terms with their mother's sudden death. With each new exploration into these dynamics, I seem to uncover new complexities, and the less I can imagine ever exhausting that terrain, so various and vital are the degrees of intimacies between women."

BIOGRAPHICAL/CRITICAL SOURCES:

PERIODICALS

Kirkus Reviews, March 15, 1992, pp. 351-52; October 15, 1994, p. 1370.
Library Journal, November 1, 1994, p. 112.
New York Times, May 14, 1995, p. 28.
New York Times Book Review, April 19, 1992, p. 9; April 23, 1995, p. 20.
Publishers Weekly, February 6, 1995, p. 76.
Washington Post Book World, May 3, 1992, p. 11.

U-V

UNO, Chiyo 1897-1996

PERSONAL: Born in 1897, near Hiroshima, Japan; died June 10, 1996, in Tokyo, Japan; married a banker (divorced); married second husband, Ozaki Shiro (a novelist; divorced); companion of Togo Seiji (a painter) for five years; married and divorced two additional times. *Ethnicity:* Japanese.

CAREER: Writer. Worked variously as an elementary school teacher's assistant, a waiter, and a kimono designer. Founder of *Sutairu* (Style), a Japanese fashion magazine, in 1936.

AWARDS, HONORS: First prize, for a short story, 1921; bestowed with the Third Order of the Sacred Treasure by the emperor of Japan; named a "person of cultural merit," 1989; has also been awarded the Joryu Bungaku Sho (Women's Literature Prize) twice, the Noma Hiroshi Prize, and the Art Academy Prize.

WRITINGS:

Iro zange, [Japan], 1935, published in the United States as *Confessions of Love,* translation by Phyllis Birnbaum, University of Hawaii Press (Honolulu), 1989.
Kimono tokuhon, [Japan], 1957.
Onna no nikki, [Japan], 1960.
Kaze no oto, [Japan], 1969.
Shitashii naka (essays), [Japan], 1970.
Teiketsu (short stories), [Japan], 1970.
Kofuku (short stories), [Japan], 1972.
Watakushi no bungakuteki kaisoki (reminiscences), [Japan], 1972.

Aru hitori no onna no hanashi, [Japan], 1972, published with another story as *Aru hitori no onna no hanashi; Ame no oto,* Bungei Shunju (Tokyo), 1983; published in the United States as *The Story of a Single Woman,* translation by Rebecca L. Copeland, P. Owen (London), 1992.
Koi wa tanoshii ka (essays), [Japan], 1974.
Am no oto, [Japan], 1974, published with another story as *Aru hitori no onna no hanashi; Ame no oto,* Bungei Shunju, 1983.
Yaeyama no yuki (short stories), [Japan], 1975.
Usuzumi no sakura, [Japan], 1975.
Mama no hanashi, [Japan], 1976.
(With Tsuneko Nakazato) *Ofuku shokan,* [Japan], 1976.
Mizunishi shoin no musume (short stories), [Japan], 1977.
Ikite yuku watakushi (autobiography; title means "I Will Go On Living"), Mainichi Shinbunsha (Tokyo), 1983.
Aru otoko no danmen (short stories), Kodansha, 1984.
The Sound of the Wind: The Life and Works of Uno Chiyo (includes the novellas, *The Puppet Maker, The Sound of the Wind,* and *This Powder Box*), translation by Copeland, University of Hawaii Press, 1992.

The original version of *The Puppet Maker* was published in 1942, *This Powder Box* first appeared in 1967, and *The Sound of the Wind* saw print in 1969. Also author of stories and novellas, including *Ohan.* Contributor to periodicals.

ADAPTATIONS: A program for Japanese television was created and aired based on Uno's autobiography, *Ikite yuku watakushi* (title means "I Will Go On Living").

SIDELIGHTS: Uno Chiyo was an influential fiction writer whose novels, short stories, and novellas often took her own romantic adventures as their subject matter. In *Confessions of Love,* a novel first published in 1935, Uno fictionalized the character of her real-life lover, the painter Togo Seiji, whose failed co-suicide with his former lover had scandalized the nation, and formed the basis of Uno's plot. In *The Story of a Single Woman,* Uno retells her own life story, from her childhood in a village near Hiroshima to the moment in 1930 when she decides to move in with the painter whose failed suicide reminds the protagonist of her own father's death. "Part of the fascination of Uno's writing is founded on just such an interplay of autobiographical/biographical fact with the contrary demands of fiction and art," observed Marilyn Jeanne Miller in a *World Literature Today* review of the English translation of *Confessions of Love.*

Uno's childhood, the subject of her novellas *The Sound of the Wind* and *The Story of a Single Woman,* was dominated by her father, who assured her that men did not like women with complexions as dark as hers, and whose too great love for mistresses and gambling was overlooked by his forgiving wife. The dramatic death of her father, depicted in *The Story of a Single Woman* with him crawling across the snow, fending off would-be helpers, and coughing up blood, combined with "her teenage discovery of the dramatic changes to be wrought with white face powder," set her free from her past, according to Ruth Pavey of *New Statesman and Society.* "Emboldened by her mask and the elegant clothes she was good at contriving, she embarked on her dual, entwined career as *femme fatale* and writer," Pavey continued.

Uno's early career as an elementary school assistant teacher was cut short when an affair she openly conducted with another teacher was used as an excuse to dismiss her. She left provincial Hiroshima for Tokyo, then in the throes of "*ero-guro-nansensu* (eroticism, grotesquerie and nonsense)," the wild era of the 1920s, according to Julian Loose in the *Times Literary Supplement.* There she waited tables in a cafe frequented by the literati, and began writing her own stories, featuring daring women whose mask-like makeup, passion for love affairs, and freedom to come and go as they please matched her own. "No one is as fortunate as a woman writer," Uno wrote after the demise of her second marriage, according to Loose. "No sooner does she break up with a man than she can write about it all without the slightest sense of shame."

In 1936, Uno started *Sutairu* (title means "Style") with one of her husbands, and the publication has been described as Japan's first fashion magazine. With time out for World War II, Uno devoted a large part of her energies to the world of magazine publishing over the next two decades. During her long career, she also published numerous serialized stories in newspapers, and a column offering romantic advice to lovelorn women. "However breezily she may have started as a writer," Pavey remarked, referring to the author's claim that she became a writer in an effort to earn more money than earlier careers had allowed, "the fine, fleeting lightness of her mature style, with its appearance of guileless candour, is as much suggestive of painstaking craft, skillfully disguised, as of naivety." Although critics disagree about the lasting importance of Uno's writings, the author is commonly regarded as one of the founders of modern Japanese literature. Loose asserted: "Indomitable and unapologetic, her song of herself helped make possible the bold, independent voices of a new generation of Japanese women writers."

"I never forced myself to do anything I didn't want to do," claimed Uno in a 1987 interview as quoted in the *New York Times* obituary. "I've lived my life just the way I wanted to." Indeed, remarked critic Loose in the *Times Literary Supplement,* "She not only lived a life of reckless freedom, she wrote about it, bringing a new zest and fresh perspective to the Japanese genre of autobiographical fiction." With the centrality in some of her most famous works of romantic liaisons among the bohemian set in the roaring twenties, Uno has garnered comparisons to Colette, while her flat, naive prose style recalls Marguerite Duras for others. Although critics disagree about the ultimate merit of her essentially autobiographical, intensely personal, often romantic works of fiction, Uno's standing among influential twentieth-century Japanese writers is unquestioned.

BIOGRAPHICAL/CRITICAL SOURCES:

PERIODICALS

Belles Lettres, spring, 1990, p. 20.
New Statesman and Society, November 27, 1992, p. 43.
Times Literary Supplement, March 16, 1990, p. 293; December 4, 1994, p. 20.
World Literature Today, Volume 63, number 4, pp. 743-44.

OBITUARIES:

PERIODICALS

New York Times, June 12, 1996, p. D23.*

*   *   *

Van HYNING, Thomas E.   1954-

PERSONAL: Born June 20, 1954, in Washington, DC; son of Sam J., Jr. (an economist) and Paula S. (an economist) Van Hyning. *Education:* University of Georgia, B.B.A., 1977; International Institute of the Americas, San Juan, PR, M.B.A., 1983; Southern Illinois University, Carbondale, M.S.Ed., 1987. *Avocational interests:* Sports, visiting historic sites.

ADDRESSES: Home—904 Lakeland Dr., Apt. A-3, Jackson, MS 39216. *Office*—Mississippi Department of Economic and Community Development, P.O. Box 849, Jackson, MS 39205; fax 601-359-5757.

CAREER: Southern Illinois University, Carbondale, researcher in Office of Leisure Research, 1985-88; Keystone College, La Plume, PA, assistant professor of travel and tourism, sports information director and assistant women's softball coach, 1988-93; Mississippi Department of Economic and Community Development, Jackson, research manager for Division of Tourism, 1994—. Hennig Associates, associate; San Juan Area Agency on Aging, planner; Municipality of Carolina, PR, budget analyst and planner; Municipal Services Administration, Hato Rey, PR, economist; consultant to University of Scranton, Caribbean Hotel Association, and Health Management Associates. Endless Mountains Visitors Bureau, member of board of directors, 1992-93; Habitat for Humanity, volunteer, 1995.

MEMBER: Travel and Tourism Research Association.

WRITINGS:

Puerto Rico's Winter League: A History of Major League Baseball's Launching Pad, McFarland and Co. (Jefferson, NC), 1995.

Contributor of about forty articles to magazines and newspapers, including *National Pastime, Travel and Tourism Executive Report, Baseball Research Jour-*

nal, Rotarian, Pennsylvania Business Journal, and *Therapeutic Recreation Journal.*

SIDELIGHTS: Thomas E. Van Hyning told *CA:* "My primary motivations are to make a contribution to society and bring out the best in my subjects. I am influenced by historic events in the Caribbean and by developments in tourism. I am inspired by my formative years in Puerto Rico, which helped to create my interest in tourism, winter baseball, and military history."

*   *   *

van ONSELEN, Charles   1944-

PERSONAL: Born in 1944; son of a police detective (father). *Education:* Attended Rhodes University; attended University of Witwatersrand; St. Antony's College, Oxford, Ph.D., 1974.

ADDRESSES: Agent—c/o Hill & Wang, 19 Union Sq. W., New York, NY 10003.

CAREER: Institute of Commonwealth Studies, London, junior research fellow; International Labour Office, Geneva, Switzerland, research officer; Centre for International and Area Studies, University of London, Ford Foundation research fellow, 1976-78; Yale University, New Haven, CT, visiting fellow, fall, 1978; University of the Witwatersrand, South Africa, Institute for Advanced Social Research, and African Studies Institute, director, 1979—. Has worked as an ore-setter in the Free State gold fields.

AWARDS, HONORS: Trevor Reese Memorial Prize, c. 1982, for *Studies in the Social and Economic History of the Witwatersrand.*

WRITINGS:

Chibaro: African Mine Labour in Southern Rhodesia, 1900-1933, Pluto Press (London), 1976.
(With I. R. Phimister) *Studies in the History of African Mine Labour in Colonial Zimbabwe,* Mambo Press (Gwelo, Zimbabwe), 1978.
Studies in the Social and Economic History of the Witwatersrand, 1886-1914, Volume 1: *New Babylon,* Volume 2: *New Nineveh,* Ravan Press (Johannesburg), 1982.
The Seed Is Mine: The Life of Kas Maine, a South African Sharecropper, 1894-1985, Hill & Wang (New York), 1996.

SIDELIGHTS: Charles van Onselen is a highly respected social historian whose area of expertise is the South African working class. As director of the African Studies Institute at the University of Witwatersrand since 1979, van Onselen has been part of a team "devoted not only to their teaching and writing," according to George Rude of the *London Review of Books,* "but to political activity in support of social justice and equality between the races." Van Onselen's most important contribution to the history of South Africa is widely considered to be documenting the lives of ordinary people, an outgrowth of his dedication to writing history from the bottom up rather than from the top down. *Chibaro: African Mine Labour in Southern Rhodesia, 1900-1933,* one of his first books, is an example of this dedication. A "caustic study," according to Andrew Roberts of the *New Statesman,* of black miners in Southern Rhodesia during the first third of the twentieth century, *Chibaro* describes not only how the miners were treated like slaves, but the ways they found to fight back. *Studies in the Social and Economic History of the Witwatersrand, 1886-1914,* van Onselen's two-volume collection of essays, contains "work of extraordinary insight and sensitivity," according to Richard Rathbone in the *Times Educational Supplement,* and sets the standard for the social history for the region. Van Onselen is also the author of *The Seed Is Mine: The Life of Kas Maine, a South African Sharecropper, 1894-1985,* a biography of a black South African sharecropper whose nearly century-long life coincided with the industrialization of South African society.

In the late nineteenth century, the mining potential of southern Africa began to be exploited, mainly by land owners from Europe. The mines in southern Rhodesia were poorer than those in South Africa, and the owners attempted to keep costs to the bare minimum by starving their workers, by housing them in crowded huts that bred disease, and by exploiting the system of *chibaro,* a long-term labor contract under which the miners differed little from slaves. "Most mine compounds were, in effect, prisons, and van Onselen aptly compares them to Soviet labour camps," Andrew Roberts wrote in the *New Statesman.* From this premise van Onselen proceeds to investigate in *Chibaro* the ways in which these workers exploited the system for their own benefit, either by joining together in unions, by occasionally striking, or by "loafing," that is, stealing back their labor from the owners. Published in the 1970s, "*Chibaro* is the first scholarly study of central Africa to discard the blinkers of liberal historiography," according to

Roberts, by concentrating on the miners as workers rather than as members of a racial group, that is, by portraying them as victims of industrialization rather than of racism. "As the economic history of southern Africa comes to be written we must hope that those who do it share van Onselen's ability to write terse and lucid prose, . . . and his humane insight into the economic microcosm of the individual worker," Roberts concluded.

Van Onselen's two-volume *Studies in the Social and Economic History of the Witwatersrand, 1886-1914,* traces the development of South Africa from a pastoral backwater to a booming industrialized country in the space of three decades, from the discovery of gold to the onset of World War I. "Van Onselen's great gift is his feel for the rich diversity of group experiences," according to George M. Fredrickson in the *New Republic,* and this work collects the author's short monographs on the area's workers, grouped by occupation. Beginning with a brief, conventional history of the period, focusing on the mining industry and the changes it brought to the area, "the chapters that follow are mainly concerned with the non-capitalist human elements within or on the fringes of the world the mine-owners made," according to Rude. Thus, van Onselen focuses on cabbies and brick-makers, washermen, and domestic servants, prostitutes and alcohol dealers, and the black outlaws who fled the city's prisons and mines for the hills, and whose story provides the author's "last, and perhaps most exciting, chapter," according to Rude.

Studies in the Social and Economic History of the Witwatersrand was widely lauded for its historiography, and for the light it sheds on the everyday lives of the ordinary people who made their living in Johannesburg during the turbulent years between 1886 and 1914. While Fredrickson faulted the author for failing to pay sufficient attention to the issue of race—"Because he fails to analyze the nature and function of racism, van Onselen deals only inferentially with a major issue of South African social history," Fredrickson noted—he nonetheless calls this work "social history of an exceptionally high quality." "It deserves to be widely read, even by people who have never felt much interest in South African history," Fredrickson concluded. "These two volumes cannot be recommended too highly," enthused Richard Rathbone in the *Times Educational Supplement.* "They are on the one hand remarkably professional. . . . On the other hand they share with the best of the new social history an intense humanity."

Van Onselen's 1996 publication, *The Seed Is Mine,* a biography of Kas Maine, a sharecropper, patriarch, healer, and memory-man for a family for which no official documentation exists. Maine was a remarkably successful farmer, at one time owning numerous livestock, expensive machinery, and having the ability to loan money to poorer, white sharecroppers. But the gradual institutionalization of racism, culminating in the apartheid laws of 1948, eventually deprived him of even the marginal prosperity he had earned. "Given the opportunity, he would have made a great venture capitalist," wrote Vincent Crapanzano in the *New York Times Book Review,* "but as a black man he never had the opportunity." Critics found *The Seed Is Mine* richly detailed, and took particular interest in the sections of the book which demonstrate the fluidity of race lines before the enactment of apartheid, when the tradition of Africaner paternalism painted a more generous face on racism. While critics felt that the amount of detail might overwhelm some readers, "for those studying South African history, [*The Seed Is Mine*] is a vital contribution," the reviewer for *Publishers Weekly* concluded.

BIOGRAPHICAL/CRITICAL SOURCES:

PERIODICALS

London Review of Books, July 7, 1983, pp. 14-15.
New Republic, February 27, 1984, pp. 37-39.
New Statesman, August 6, 1976, pp. 182-83.
New York Times Book Review, March 17, 1996, p. 7.
Publishers Weekly, January 29, 1996, p. 94.
Times Educational Supplement, January 21, 1983, p. 48.*

* * *

VAZQUEZ, Carmen Inoa   1942-

PERSONAL: Born July 16, 1942, in Bonao, Dominican Republic; naturalized U.S. citizen; daughter of Laureano (a landowner) and Victoria (a homemaker; maiden name, Vargas) Inoa; married Hector Vazquez (an economist), December 18, 1965 (deceased); children: Jaime Alberto, Miguel Anson. *Education:* Queens College of the City University of New York, B.A. (cum laude), 1976; City University of New York, Ph.D., 1981. *Religion:* Roman Catholic. *Avocational interests:* Playing tennis, reading, gardening.

ADDRESSES: Home—147-23 84th Dr., Briarwood, NY 11435. *Office*—104 East 40th St., Suite 406, New York, NY; fax 212-263-7947. *E-mail*—Carmen.Vazquez@hotmail.com.

CAREER: City College of the City University of New York, New York City, proctor supervisor, 1976-77; Morrisania Neighborhood Clinic, intern and consultant, 1979-80; Nassau County Medical Center, psychology intern, 1980-81; South Bronx Mental Health Council Alcoholism Clinic, clinical supervisor, 1981-82; Bellevue Psychiatric Hospital, New York City, staff psychologist, 1982-84, senior psychologist, 1984-90, director of Clinical Psychology Internship Training Program at New York University-Bellevue Hospital Center, 1984—. American Board of Professional Psychology, diplomate; Bilingual Treatment Program Clinic, New York City, founding director, 1988-96, supervisor, 1996; Kirby Forensic Psychiatric Hospital, member of board of visitors, 1988-93; psychotherapist in private practice. Hostos Community College of the City University of New York, adjunct professor, 1977-79; Empire State College of the State University of New York, adjunct instructor, 1978-84; New York University, clinical instructor, 1982-84, clinical assistant professor, 1984-92, clinical associate professor of psychiatry, 1992—; St. John's University, Jamaica, NY, affiliate clinical professor, 1983-87. National Council of Women—United Nations, member of board of the executive committee, 1986-87; New York State Board of Examiners for Psychology, member, 1988-93; New York City Department of Mental Health, Mental Retardation, and Alcoholism Services, member of Community Services Board, 1995—; New York City Depression Coalition, member. Guest on television and radio programs.

MEMBER: World Association for Psychosocial Rehabilitation, American Psychological Association, Association of Hispanic Mental Health Professionals (member of board of directors, 1985-87; president, 1993-95), American Psychiatric Association, Academy of Clinical Psychology (fellow), New York State Psychological Association (Division of Women's Issues in Clinical Psychology), Mental Health Association of New York and Bronx Counties, Community Association of Progressive Dominicans (member of board of directors, 1994—).

AWARDS, HONORS: Grants from National Institute of Mental Health, 1985-92, and New York State Regional Office of Mental Health Grants, 1991; Achievement Award for Teaching and Training,

American Psychological Association, 1990; Certificate of Recognition, Nassau County Medical Center, 1990; Clinical Excellence Award, Bellevue Hospital Center, 1993; Citation of Honor, Borough of Queens/Hispanic Heritage Celebration of Queens, 1996.

WRITINGS:

(With R. Gil) *The Maria Paradox: How Latinas Can Merge Old World Traditions with New World Self-Esteem,* Putnam (New York City), 1996.

Author of "Consejos," a quarterly advice column in *Latina,* 1996. Contributor to books, including *Ethnic Minority Perspectives on Clinical Training and Services in Psychology,* edited by H. F. Myers, P. Wohlford, and others, American Psychological Association (Washington, DC), 1991. Contributor to magazines, including *Hospital and Community Psychiatry, American Journal of Psychoanalysis, Hispanic Journal of Behavioral Sciences,* and *Focus Elders.* Newsletter editor for Mental Health Section, American Public Health Association, 1985-86.

SIDELIGHTS: Carmen Inoa Vazquez told *CA:* "I write to share my professional experiences with others, particularly with the intent of helping the reader to understand that she is not alone in her feelings. I am influenced by my own experiences as a person who immigrated to a new society. I am inspired when I see how much confusion and pain is produced by so many Latinas."

*   *   *

VENTSEL, Elena Sergeevna 1907- (Irina Nikolaevna Grekova, I. Grekova)

PERSONAL: Born March 21, 1907, in Reval, Tallinn. *Education:* Moscow University, degree in mathematics, 1929, Ph.D. (mathematics), 1954.

ADDRESSES: Home—Leningradskii Propsekt 44, Apt. 29, 125167 Moscow, Russia.

CAREER: Author, 1957—. Moscow Air Force Academy, Moscow, Russia, professor of cybernetics, 1955-67; Zhukovskii Military Academy, professor, 1967-70.

MEMBER: Union of Soviet Writers.

WRITINGS:

FICTION; UNDER PSEUDONYM I. GREKOVA

Pod fonarem (title means "Under the Streetlight"), Sovetskii pisatel' (Moscow), 1966.

Serezhka un okna (title means "Serezhka by the Window"), Detskaia literatura (Moscow), 1976.

Ania i Mania, Detskaia literatura, 1978.

Kafedra (title means "The Department"; originally published in *Novyi mir,* number 5, 1978), Sovetskii pisatel', 1980.

Vdovii parokhod (originally published in *Novyi mir,* volume 5, 1981), Institut d'Etudes Slaves (Paris), 1983, translation published as *The Ship of Widows,* Virago (London), 1985, translation by Cathy Porter published under same title, Northwestern University Press (Evanston, IL), 1994.

Russian Women: Two Stories (includes *Ladies' Hairdresser* and *The Hotel Manager*), Harcourt (New York, NY), 1983.

Porogi (title means "The Rapids"; originally published in *Oktiabr',* numbers 10-11, 1984), Sovetskii pisatel', 1986.

Vdovynyi paroplav: povisti, Vyd-vo khudozh litry "Dnipro" (Kiev), 1987.

Svezho predanie: roman, Hermitage Publishers (Tenafly, NJ), 1995.

Also author of *A Legendary Figure,* 1987, and *The Break,* 1987. Contributor and author of introduction, *Soviet Women Writing: 15 Short Stories,* Abbeville Press (New York, NY), 1990. Author of stories published in periodicals, including *Za prokhodnoi,* published in *Novyi mir,* number 7, 1962, translated as *Beyond the Gates* and published in *The Young Russians,* Macmillan (New York, NY), 1972; *Damskii master,* published in *Novyi mir,* number 11, 1963, translated as *Ladies' Hairdresser* and published in *Russian Literature Triquarterly,* Volume 5, 1973 and in *Russian Women: Two Stories,* Harcourt, 1983; *Letom v gorode* (title means "In Summer in Town"), published in *Novyi mir,* number 4, 1965; *Na ispytaniakh* (title means "At the Testing Ground"), published in *Novyi mir,* number 7, 1967; *Malen'kii Garusov* (title means "Little Garusov"), published in *Zvezda,* number 9, 1970; *Khoziaika gostinitsy,* published in *Zvezda,* number 9, 1976, translated as *The Hotel Manager* and published in *Russian Women: Two Stories,* Harcourt, 1983. Some works have appeared under the name Irina Nikolaevna Grekova.

UNDER NAME ELENA SERGEEVNA VENTSEL

Teoriia veroiatnostei, Gosudarstvennoe izdatel'stvo Fiziko-Matematicheskoi literatury (Moscow), 1958.

Elementy teorii igr, translations published variously as *Lectures on Game Theory,* Hindustan (New Delhi), 1961, *An Introduction to the Theory of Games,* Heath (Boston, MA), 1963, and *Elements of Game Theory,* Mir (Moscow), 1980.

Issledovanie operatsii, translation published as *Operations Research,* Mir, 1983.

Prikladnye zadechi teorii veroiatnostei, Radio i Dviaz (Moscow), 1983, translation published as *Applied Problems in Probability Theory,* Mir, 1986.

Also author of *Granulometricheskii sostav zagriaznenii kak odin iz Faktorov, opredeliaiushchikh protivoiznosnye svoistva masel* (title means "The Granulometric Structure of Pollution as One of the Factors Showing the Anti-Erosive Features of Oils," published in *Trenie i iznos,* Volume 13, number 4, 1992.

SIDELIGHTS: Elena Sergeevna Ventsel combined a career as a professor of mathematics and a writer of fiction in the former Soviet Union. Under her own name she published important studies of game theory and probability; under the pseudonym I. Grekova (derived from the French for the letter Y, *i grec,* meaning something like "Mrs. X"), she produces and continues to publish stories and novels that comment on women's life in Communist Russia. "Her protagonists are often middle-aged professional women struggling to balance the pressures of their careers with their personal lives," writes Barry P. Scherr in *Contemporary World Writers.* "Perhaps more successfully than any writer of her time, she has managed to capture the plight of women old enough to remember the purges and World War II and whose careers span the period from the end of the war through the Brezhnev years."

Ventsel's first work of published fiction appeared when the author was 50 years old and a full professor at the Moscow Air Force Academy. "Scientific training is far from uncommon among Soviet creative writers," explained *New Yorker* contributor John Updike: "Solzhenitsyn was a teacher of physics and mathematics; Voznesensky was educated as an architect; and a number of prose artists from Chekhov to Vassily Aksyonov have been accredited doctors."

Like many other writers in Soviet Russia, Ventsel offended the authorities with her works, some of which were critical of the Communists. In her case, the work was *Na ispytaniakh,* a critique of Stalinism published in the prestigious literary journal *Novy mir.* The story caused such an outcry among senior officials that Ventsel was forced to resign her professorial post. She continues to publish in post-Communist Russia.

Little of Ventsel's fiction has been translated into English. Two works that have seen print are *The Ship of Widows* and *Russian Women: Two Stories.* Both depict the lives of women under Soviet-style collectivism. *The Ship of Widows* takes place in the period following World War II and looks at the lives of five different women bereft by the war and forced by housing shortages into living together under a single roof. "The women are a microcosm of Soviet society," explained *New York Times Book Review* contributor Priscilla Meyer. Meyer concluded: "Readers will be shaken by [Grekova's] depiction of how social conditions can make liberal ideals almost impossible to hold." A reviewer in *Publishers Weekly* judged *The Ship of Widows,* "moving, even haunting at times."

Russian Women: Two Stories takes another look at women under the Soviet government. "Ladies' Hairdresser," Updike explained, "tells of a middle-aged female mathematician's rather maternal relationship with a twenty-year-old male hairdresser called Vitaly." The second story, "The Hotel Manager," is the story of Vera Platonovna Butova, who marries a military man and ends up as the successful manager of a small hotel. The tale covers Vera's marriage, but its main focus is on her relationship with the women in her life: her mother, her sister, her best friend, her adopted daughter, and her roommate. They are connected by a common dedication to work. "For I. Grekova's women, love comes and goes, but work is always there," noted Updike, praising Grekova's "candid, matter-of-fact glimpses into the Soviet system's imperfect workings." The reviewer continued: Grekova "also seems to see where the system cannot reach and perennial human happiness and misery take their course. Her window into this remote world is as transparent and sparkling as a woman's hand can make it." "One can understand the author's popularity in the rather bleak world of Soviet literature," *Times Literary Supplement* contributor Elizabeth Winter declared; "at least she tells it like it is."

BIOGRAPHICAL/CRITICAL SOURCES:

BOOKS

Contemporary World Writers, 2nd edition, St. James (Detroit, MI), 1993.
Menke, Elisabeth, *Die Kultur der Weiblichkeit in der Prosa Irina Grekovas,* O. Sagner (Munich), 1988.
Rancour-Laferriere, Daniel, *Russian Literature and Psychoanalysis,* John Benjamins (Amsterdam), 1989.

PERIODICALS

New Republic, October 2, 1989, p. 40.
New Yorker, April 15, 1985, pp. 110-26.
New York Times Book Review, February 8, 1987.
Publishers Weekly, April 4, 1994, p. 71.
Slavic Review, Volume 4, 1989.
Soviet Literature, Volume 4, 1986.
Times (London), April 13, 1985.
Times Literary Supplement, July 5, 1985, p. 756.
Village Voice, May 15, 1984, pp. 47-48.

* * *

VERLUISE, Pierre   1961-

PERSONAL: Born May 19, 1961, in Saint Maude, France; son of Francois (an architect and town planner) and Jeannie (a nurse; maiden name, Dehame) Verluise; married Sylvie Blanchet (a history-geography teacher), January 25, 1986; children: Roman (deceased), Tanguy, Cyrie, Ervan. *Education:* University of Paris, Sorbonne, degree in history and international relations, 1994. *Religion:* Catholic. *Avocational interests:* Sports (climbing, canoeing, kickboxing), reading.

ADDRESSES: Home—1 Ave. Lamartine, 94300 Vincennes, France. *Office*—73 rue de la Mare, 75020 Paris, France.

CAREER: Radio France Internationale, journalist, 1985-91; *Le Quotidien de Paris,* journalist, 1989-94; Sainte-Louise College, history teacher, 1992—. *Military service:* Mountain infantryman.

WRITINGS:

Armenie, la fracture (history), Stock (Paris), 1989, translation published as *Armenia in Crisis,* Wayne State University Press (Detroit), 1995.

Le nouvel emprunt russe (history; title means "The New Russian Loan"), Odilon Media (Paris), 1996.

WORK IN PROGRESS: A work on East/West relations from 1985 to the present.

SIDELIGHTS: French journalist Pierre Verluise accused the former Soviet Union of parasitism and blackmail in his as yet untranslated work *Le nouvel emprunt russe* (*The New Russian Loan*), which deals primarily with the 1985-1994 period. Verluise, who has long been interested in neglected and controversial topics, argued that the purpose of perestroika was to gain aid for the Soviet Union from the West and that in borrowing heavily from the West—particularly from European financial institutions—the Soviets gained both subsidies and political leverage from the West. Basing his assertions on over one hundred sources, Verluise maintained that the Soviet Union purposefully inflated its debt from 1985 onwards, while at the same time it deliberately allowed massive outflows of capital, which continued into the late 1990s. According to Verluise, 75 percent of Russian debt is held by Western European entities and in refusing to pay its debts the Soviets are forcing the West to subsidize Russia and its military actions. The work was praised highly by several prominent French officials, and *Wall Street Journal* reporter John Laughland was impressed by Verluise's ability to compute the complicated financial figures with which he supported his thesis. Laughland added that Verluise's "assertion that Russia is engaged in determined parasitism is as compelling as it is prophetic."

Verluise told *CA:* "From 17 to 25 years old, I read the main part of Edgar Morin's work, [including] *La Methode* and his book *La nature de L'URSS.* My second book, *Le nouvel emprunt russe,* presents in the fourth chapter extracts of authors who have, for the most part, influenced since my twenty-fifth birthday my way of understanding the Soviet and post-Soviet world: A. Zinoviev, M. Heller, N. Buhks, and E. Thom. On a more literary side, I have appreciated a lot of the work of Vasili Gossman and Alexander Solzhenitsyn."

Verluise added, "My first book, *Armenie, la fracture,* like my second book, *Le nouvel emprunt russe,* are the fruit of long inquiries close to first-hand sources: witnesses, actors, diplomats, bankers, strategists. In general, no information is put forward if it can't be supported by three different sources. Moreover, my style is probably pronounced by ten years of radio journalism, notably on Radio France International. The radio requires one to give only one idea [in a] sentence of 15 to 20 words. It may be the reason why the readers of my second book, dedicated to East-West financial questions, said they didn't [find it] difficult to understand. It is true that I try to take the reader into account.

"I try to publish, as far as possible, reference works, focused on unknown subjects or revealing upstreamed analysis that I suppose important [in the] long term."

BIOGRAPHICAL/CRITICAL SOURCES:

PERIODICALS

Wall Street Journal (European edition), April 26, 1996, p. 8.

*   *   *

VERONA, Stephen (Frederic) 1940-

PERSONAL: Born September 11, 1940, in Springfield, IL; son of Michael and Florence (Rosen) Verona; married Wendy Klein, June 20, 1965 (divorced, 1969). *Education:* Attended the School of Visual Arts, 1958-62. *Politics:* Republican. *Avocational interests:* Biking, bullfighting, hiking.

ADDRESSES: Home and office—1251 Stone Canyon Rd., Bel Air, CA 90077. *Contact*—Attorney Eric Weissmann, Weissmann Wolf, 9665 Wilshire Boulevard, Suite 900, Beverly Hills, CA 90212, (310) 858-7888.

CAREER: Writer, producer, director, artist. Director of more than 300 television commercials (50 of which have won awards), then began making short subject films, television specials, music features, and music videos. *Military service:* Served in the U.S. Army.

MEMBER: Academy of Motion Picture Arts and Sciences, Directors Guild, Writers Guild of America.

AWARDS, HONORS: Academy Award nomination for Best Short Subject—Live Action, 1972, for *The Rehearsal;* five San Francisco Film Festival Awards; five Chicago Film Festival Awards; three Atlanta Film Festival Awards; five CINE Golden Eagle Awards; Robert Flaherty Documentary Seminar Awards; Edward Steichen Photography Award, Museum of Modern Art; some of Verona's films have

also been added to the permanent collection of New York City's Museum of Modern Art.

WRITINGS:

ALL SCREENPLAYS UNLESS OTHERWISE NOTED

Lapis Lazuli, independently produced, 1967.
Forever a Festival, Alliance, 1969.
Wednesday's Child, Alliance, 1969.
The Mabinogian, independently produced, 1970.
(Co-author) *The Lords of Flatbush,* Columbia Pictures, 1974.
Pipe Dreams, Avco Embassy Pictures, 1976.
(Co-author) *Boardwalk,* Atlantic Releasing, 1979.
Primary Colors, Koch-Kirkwood, 1981.
Deception, independently produced, 1983.
Dear Diary, independently produced, 1985.
The Children of the Lords, United Artists, 1985.
The Lords of Flatbush 22 Years Later, Cannon, 1987.
Talking Walls, Drummond Productions, 1987.
Best in Show, independently produced, 1995.
The Family Man, independently produced, 1995.

Also author of *Gangsters,* 1991. Has written, produced, and directed numerous short-subject films, television specials, and commercials.

SIDELIGHTS: Stephen Verona told *CA:* "I am now spending much of [my] time PAINTING."

BIOGRAPHICAL/CRITICAL SOURCES:

BOOKS

Contemporary Theatre, Film, and Television, Volume 4, Gale, 1987, p. 462.

PERIODICALS

Atlanta Constitution, April 12, 1989, p. E3.

*   *   *

VICKREY, William (Spencer) 1914-1996

OBITUARY NOTICE—See index for *CA* sketch: Born June 21, 1914, in Victoria, British Columbia, Canada; died of a heart attack, October 11, 1996, in Harrison, NY. Economist and educator. After years of teaching at Columbia University, Vickrey finally got a break in October, 1996, when he won the Nobel Memorial Prize in Economic Science. It wasn't the fame or money he desired, but the chance to convey his views on "moral" economics. But he died of a heart attack just three days after receiving the award. Janny Scott, writing in the *New York Times,* described Vickrey as the "ultimate absent-minded professor, a brilliant eccentric using abstract economic theory to find solutions to every day problems." Vickrey began his scholarship at Yale University, where he graduated with a degree in mathematics. He then went on to begin a long career at Columbia University, receiving his master's degree in 1937 and his doctorate in 1947. Vickrey's economic theories concentrated on improving day-to-day life, including the problem of under-used trains, road funds, parking meters, and improving the quality of auctions. Some of Vickrey's theories were laughed at when presented, but later went into practice, like his idea that different types of vehicles should pay different bridge tolls. His current economic view, a controversial one, was that unemployment was a greater problem than running a deficit and recommended increasing the national deficit, if necessary, to combat unemployment. Most of his writings were academic tomes such as *Agenda for Progressive Taxation* (1949), *Microstatics* (1964), *Metastatics and Macroeconomics* (1964) and *The Tax System of Liberia: Report of the Tax Mission* (1970). Vickrey also contributed to books, including *Goals of Economic Life* (1950), *Post-Keynesian Economics* (1954), *Public Expenditure Decisions in the Urban Community* (1963), *Readings in Welfare Economics* (1969), *Public Finance* (1970), *Altruism Morality and Economic Theory* (1973), and *The Economics of Public Services* (1977).

OBITUARIES AND OTHER SOURCES:

BOOKS

Who's Who, 148th edition, St. Martin's Press, 1996.

PERIODICALS

Los Angeles Times, October 12, 1996, p. A1.
New York Times, October 12, 1996, Sec. 1, p. 52; October 25, 1996, p. 32.
Times (London), October 14, 1996, p. 25.

*   *   *

VIGHI, Marco   1945-

PERSONAL: Born July 30, 1945, in Naples, Italy; son of Luciano (a geologist) and Loredana (Mocellin)

Vighi; married Daniela Pezzoni, March 7, 1968; children: Veronica, Valentina, Virginia. *Education:* University of Milan, degree in biology, 1969.

ADDRESSES: Home—Via Umbria 99, 20134 Milan, Italy. *Office*—Institute of Entomology, University of Milan, Via Celoria 2, 20133 Milan, Italy; fax +39-22-668-0320. *E-mail*—entom@imiucca.csi.unimi.it.

CAREER: National Council of Research, Milan, Italy, scientist at Water Research Institute, 1970-83; University of Milan, Milan, associate professor of agricultural ecotoxicology, 1983—. European Union, member of scientific advisory committee to examine the toxicity and ecotoxicity of chemical compounds, 1991—.

WRITINGS:

Ecotossicologia, Edizioni Giuridico Scientifiche (Milan, Italy), 1989.
(Editor with E. Funari, and contributor) *Pesticide Risk in Groundwater,* Lewis Publishers (New York City), 1995.
(Editor with T. Swanson) *The Regulation of Persistent Chemicals: Economics and Environmental Toxicology,* Cambridge University Press, 1996.

Contributor to books, including *Pesticide Effects on Terrestrial Wildlife,* edited by L. Sommerville and C. H. Walker, Taylor & Francis (London, England), 1990; *Methods to Assess Adverse Effects of Pesticides on Non-Target Organisms,* edited by R. J. Tardiff, Wiley (New York City), 1992; and *Environmental Toxicology, Economics, and Institutions: The Atrazine Case Study,* edited by L. Bergman and D. M. Pugh, Kluver Academic (Dordrecht, Netherlands), 1994. Contributor of more than a hundred-twenty articles to scientific journals. Member of editorial board, *Ecotoxicology and Environmental Safety, Reviews in Environmental Pollution,* and *Ingegneria ambientale.*

*   *   *

vos SAVANT, Marilyn   1946-

PERSONAL: Born August 11, 1946, in St. Louis, MO; daughter of Joseph (a merchant and son of a coal miner) and Marina (daughter of a coal miner; maiden name, vos Savant) Mach; married third husband, Robert Jarvik (a physician and inventor), August 23, 1987; children: (first marriage) Mary,

Denny. *Ethnicity:* "German-Italian." *Education:* Attended college "briefly; formal schooling had become unbearable to me." *Politics:* "Independent." *Religion:* "None." *Avocational interests:* "Politics, quality education, and medical research."

ADDRESSES: Home—New York, NY. *Office—The Thinking American,* Inc., P.O. Box 967, Ansonia Station, New York, NY 10023.

CAREER: Parade magazine, contributing editor, 1986—; Jarvik Research, Inc., vice president, 1988—; *The Thinking American,* Inc., editor and publisher, 1996—. National Council on Economic Education, member of board of directors; National Association for Gifted Children, member of national advisory board.

MEMBER: The Metropolitan Club, Mensa.

AWARDS, HONORS: Listed in *The Guinness Book of World Records* under "highest I.Q." in both child and adult categories, 1985-89; inducted into the Guinness Hall of Fame, 1989.

WRITINGS:

(With Leonore Fleischer) *Brain Building: Exercising Yourself Smarter* (nonfiction), Bantam Books (New York), 1990.

Ask Marilyn: Answers to America's Most Frequently Asked Questions (nonfiction), St. Martin's Press (New York), 1992.

The World's Most Famous Math Problem: The Proof of Fermat's Last Theorem and Other Mathematical Mysteries (nonfiction), St. Martin's Press, 1993.

"I've Forgotten Everything I Learned in School!": A Refresher Course to Help You Reclaim Your Education (nonfiction), St. Martin's Press, 1994.

More Marilyn: Some Like It Bright! (nonfiction), St. Martin's Press, 1994.

The Power of Logical Thinking: Easy Lessons in the Art of Reasoning—and Hard Facts about Its Absence in Our Lives (nonfiction), St. Martin's Press, 1996.

Of Course I'm for Monogamy; I'm also for Everlasting Peace and an End to Taxes (nonfiction), St. Martin's Press, 1996.

Also author of *It Was Poppa's Will* (play), 1988. Contributed "Ask Marilyn" column to *Parade,* 1986—.

SIDELIGHTS: Marilyn vos Savant, who holds the distinction of having the highest recorded I.Q. scores in the world, has written widely on logical thinking. Among her publications are books of excerpts from her national column, "Ask Marilyn," and practical books on improving reasoning ability. In an interview with *Newsmakers,* vos Savant divulged that she chose a writing career because writing is "probably the field where people with higher I.Q.s can make the greatest contribution."

Vos Savant grew up as Marilyn Mach in a blue-collar downtown neighborhood in St. Louis. When she took the Stanford-Binet I.Q. (intelligence quotient) test at age ten after "ceiling" scores on other tests, vos Savant scored 228, 88 points higher than the genius level and the highest recorded score in the world. Numerous additional tests soon followed. Her parents "were unaware of the significance" of her scores, vos Savant told *CA,* and they thought her two older brothers "were far more worthy of serious family attention, which was perfectly normal for the '50s," she added. Though vos Savant attended classes for gifted students, she was "discouraged, frustrated, and downright blue much of the time," she told *CA.* Finishing in two-and-a-half years, she graduated in the middle of her high school class.

Vos Savant married her high-school sweetheart shortly afterward and had two children by the time she was nineteen. In addition to raising her children, she worked at the family businesses—then a growing collection of small shops—and attended a local community college part time, but she soon dropped out. "I detested academic environments," vos Savant told *CA.* "Besides, my children came first, and they were a joy to me. So I put my intellectual life on hold." After ten years, vos Savant divorced; she later remarried and divorced again after another ten years. "These were good years," vos Savant told *CA.* "The relationships were with two very fine gentlemen, and they ended amicably—like the passing of a friendship." She continued to work at the family business, which was growing prosperous, with both parents and her two brothers, but late at night, she developed her writing skills, sleeping very little and filling file cabinet drawers with essays and short stories and political satire, some of which was published under a pseudonym.

Vos Savant also began to join a number of high-I.Q. societies, and her name rapidly became well-known among them. In time, news of her scores, sent by half a dozen sources, reached *The Guinness Book of*

World Records. When vos Savant's name was published in the next volume, her identity became common knowledge, and she began to publish under her own name. (Her mother's maiden name was "vos Savant," and her grandmother's maiden name was "Savant," so the name appears twice in the family.)

In 1986, vos Savant first published her "Ask Marilyn" column for *Parade* magazine, the Sunday magazine for 340 newspapers, in which she answered letters from readers. Since then, she has received tens of thousands of letters asking questions on a wide range of topics: philosophy, politics, science, the arts, math problems, and brain teasers. Her column currently receives 35,000 letters annually and has even landed her on the front page of the *New York Times*.

The media exposure had an unexpected effect on vos Savant's life and ended her ties with the family business as it brought her to the attention of people worldwide, among them Dr. Robert Jarvik, the inventor of the artificial human heart, who called for a date after reading an article about her. In 1987, vos Savant and Jarvik were married in a ceremony at New York's Plaza Hotel. Science fiction writer Isaac Asimov, who gave vos Savant away, called the marriage "a meeting of the minds." Vos Savant told *CA:* "This was my first real marriage, and I adore him—Rob is brilliant, passionate, and handsome. And professionally, I am now in my real element. I have a national voice, a national ear to the country, and I am blissfully happy." She added, "The last time I took an I.Q. test was about ten years ago, and that'll be the last time for good. I think I've taken every test known to mankind, and I'm heartily sick of them!" In addition to writing, vos Savant participates in her husband's heart research. She also is preparing to launch her own publication, called *The Thinking American*. "Intelligence isn't what you know; it's what you understand," vos Savant told *CA*. "My publication shows us all *how* to think, not *what* to think."

In 1994, *The World's Most Famous Math Problem: The Proof of Fermat's Last Theorem and Other Mathematical Mysteries* elicited mixed reviews. "At times you may feel you're drowning," wrote Clarence Petersen in his review for *Tribune Books*. "Try to float; it's worth it." John Allen Paulos, writing in the *New York Times Book Review,* commended vos Savant for her stimulating approach to the subject of

math for a general audience, but commented that "her book is less satisfying than her columns."

Many of vos Savant's "Ask Marilyn" columns were compiled into collections and published as books, such as *Ask Marilyn: Answers to America's Most Frequently Asked Questions* and *More Marilyn: Some Like It Bright!* In reviewing her collection of columns, a reviewer in *Publishers Weekly* commented, "Hardly the pedantic intellectual one might expect, vos Savant is both earthy and glamorous, and more reminiscent of a Marilyn named Monroe than Einstein or Hawking." She is "an original thinker." A *Kirkus Reviews* contributor called vos Savant, "succinct yet eloquent" and "a quicksilver mind at work."

In 1996, *The Power of Logical Thinking: Easy Lessons in the Art of Reasoning—and Hard Facts about Its Absence in Our Lives* fared well among reviewers. "This book is a riveting, entertaining, wide-ranging survey of logical and mathematical booby traps that are sure to sharpen your understanding of probability and statistics," commented Martin Gardner, a *Scientific American* columnist for twenty-five years. Patricia Hassler, writing in *Booklist,* called *The Power of Logical Thinking* "a tour de force to delight the number-impaired . . . vos Savant's clear, logical approach to convoluted problems is a tonic."

BIOGRAPHICAL/CRITICAL SOURCES:

BOOKS

Newsmakers, Gale, 1988, pp. 450-57.

PERIODICALS

Booklist, March 1, 1996.
Boston Globe, March 14, 1990, Living section, p. 25.
Kirkus Reviews, September 15, 1992.
New York Times, July 21, 1991, p. 1.
New York Times Book Review, January 16, 1994, p. 22.
Publishers Weekly, January 4, 1992; August 1, 1994.
Tribune Books (Chicago), November 7, 1993, section 14, p. 10.

OTHER

Vos Savant, Marilyn, interview with Martin Gardner, conducted for *Scientific American*.

W

WADDELL, Thomas F. 1937-1987

PERSONAL: Born in 1937, in Paterson, NJ; died in 1987 from complications related to acquired immune deficiency syndrome (AIDS); married Sara Lewinstein (an athlete); children: Jessica. *Education:* Earned medical degree, 1965.

CAREER: Physician specializing in infectious diseases. Chief physician at Central Emergency facility in San Francisco until 1986. *Military service:* Served in the U.S. Army.

AWARDS, HONORS: Placed sixth in the decathlon at the Olympic Games in 1968.

WRITINGS:

(With Dick Schaap) *Gay Olympian: The Life and Death of Dr. Thomas Waddell,* Knopf (New York), 1996.

SIDELIGHTS: Dr. Thomas F. Waddell is remembered as a physician who specialized in infectious diseases, as a decathlete who competed in the Olympic Games in Mexico City in 1968, and as a homosexual who founded the Gay Games. Shortly before his death in 1987 from complications related to AIDS (acquired immune deficiency syndrome), Waddell began writing his memoir with the help of veteran sportswriter Dick Schaap, the author of several dozen books. *Gay Olympian: The Life and Death of Dr. Thomas Waddell* incorporates interviews with people who knew Dr. Waddell, letters from admirers, and letters that Waddell wrote to his daughter Jessica, who was four years old when her father died. Since his high school days, Waddell had been an avid ath-

lete, earning track and field records and a scholarship to Springfield College, where he excelled in football and gymnastics as well. Waddell joined the U.S. Army after completing his medical internship and tried out for the U.S. Olympic team. At the games he broke five personal records for the decathlon, but he only managed to place sixth in the all-around standings. While Waddell had hidden his sexual preference early in his life, during the 1970s he came out of the closet, and in 1981 he founded the Gay Games. After testing positive in 1986 for HIV, the virus that causes AIDS, Waddell relinquished his position as chief physician at the Central Emergency facility in San Francisco. He died a year later.

BIOGRAPHICAL/CRITICAL SOURCES:

BOOKS

Newsmakers, Gale (Detroit), 1988.

PERIODICALS

New York Times Biographical Service, July, 1987, p. 687.*

*   *   *

WALKER, Rebecca 1970-

PERSONAL: Born November 11, 1970, in Jackson, MS; daughter of Alice Walker (a writer); companion of Angel Williams. *Education:* Yale University, B.A. (cum laude), 1992.

ADDRESSES: Home and office—Brooklyn, NY. *E-mail*—minnie@nyo.com.

CAREER: Writer and activist. *Ms.* magazine, New York City, contributing editor, 1989—. Co-founder, Third Wave Direct Action Corporation, New York City, 1992; owner, Kokobar, Brooklyn, NY, 1996.

AWARDS, HONORS: Yale University Pickens Prize, 1992, for excellence in African American scholarship; Feminist of the Year award, Fund for Feminist Majority, 1992; Paz y Justicia award, Vanguard Foundation; California Abortion Rights Action League Champion of Choice award; Kingsborough Community College Woman of Distinction award.

WRITINGS:

(Editor) *To Be Real: Telling the Truth and Changing the Face of Feminism,* Anchor (New York City), 1995.
(Contributor) Barbara Findlen, editor, *Listen Up: Voices from the Next Feminist Generation,* Seal Press (Seattle), 1995.

Contributor to periodicals, including *Ms., New York Daily News, SPIN, Harper's, Sassy,* and *Black Scholar.*

WORK IN PROGRESS: Editing an anthology on bisexuality.

SIDELIGHTS: Through both her activism and her writing, Rebecca Walker has become a role model for a new generation of feminists attempting to reinterpret the legacy of the women's movement as we approach the twenty-first century. The daughter of acclaimed novelist Alice Walker, Rebecca Walker is the editor of *To Be Real: Telling the Truth and Changing the Face of Feminism,* published in 1995.

Born in 1970 in Jackson, Mississippi, Walker was raised in the cities of New York and San Francisco. Graduating from Yale University 1992, she decided to devote her talents to social activism on behalf of women. To that end she co-founded, with friend Shannon Liss, Third Wave Direct Action Corporation, an organization designed to inspire social activism among young women. Third Wave has been instrumental in registering young women voters in urban districts, an effort for which Walker was awarded the Feminist of the Year award from the Fund for Feminist Majority in 1992.

In addition to directing the activities of Third Wave, Walker recruited young writers from around the country as contributors to *To Be Real.* With each individual response to the question "Is there more than one way to be a feminist?", *To Be Real* illustrates the movement of younger women away from traditional mainstream feminism. In an essay entitled "Brideland," Naomi Wolf, author of the groundbreaking *The Beauty Myth,* writes about her attempts to incorporate her ardent feminist beliefs within a wedding ceremony. The bell hooks-authored "Beauty Laid Bare" concerns the materialism of African American culture, while in another essay, supermodel Veronica Webb discusses the conflicts between feminism and having a career as a model, noting that modeling allowed her a measure of economic power that she might not otherwise have had.

Walker frames *To Be Real* with an examination of the necessity for a "third generation" feminist movement. She cites alienation by a media focused on the older, baby boom generation, the perpetuation of traditional negative stereotypes, and the sometimes hidden resentment of older generations of feminists. Noting that a lack of understanding has caused many younger women not to recognize their debt to the women's movements of past decades, she encourages readers of *To Be Real* to become more informed before disavowing feminism altogether. While noting that *To Be Real* is hardly the definitive voice of younger North American feminists, a *Publishers Weekly* reviewer noted that "both its virtues and its flaws attest to the strength of our feminist inheritance—and its promise for the future."

A journalist, Walker has served as a contributing editor to *Ms.* magazine since 1989. She has also published articles in periodicals such as *Black Scholar, Harper's, New York Daily News, Sassy,* and *SPIN.* In 1994 *Time* magazine named her to its list of the fifty future leaders in the United States, an acknowledgement of her energetic efforts to aid in providing young women direction as feminism reaches a new incarnation.

BIOGRAPHICAL/CRITICAL SOURCES:

PERIODICALS

Girlfriends, May/June, 1996.
Harper's Bazaar, November, 1992.
Library Journal, November 15, 1995, p. 91.
New York, September 11, 1995, p. 87.
Publishers Weekly, October 2, 1995, p. 67.

WARD, Diane (Lee) 1956-

PERSONAL: Born November 9, 1956, in Washington, DC; married Chris Hauty, 1988; children: two sons. *Education:* Attended Corcoran School of Art, 1975-77.

CAREER: Writer.

AWARDS, HONORS: National Endowment for the Arts fellowship, 1980; San Francisco State Poetry Center's Book of the Year award, 1984; California Arts Council fellowship in literature, 1988-89.

WRITINGS:

POETRY

On Duke Ellington's Birthday, Privately published, 1977.
Trop-i-dom, Jawbone (Washington, DC), 1977.
The Light American, Jawbone, 1978.
Theory of Emotion, Segue/O Press (New York), 1978.
Never Without One, Roof Books (New York), 1984.
Relation, Roof Books, 1989.
Imaginary Movie, Potes and Poets Press (Elmwood, CT), 1992.
Exhibition, Potes and Poets Press, 1995.

*   *   *

WARLICK, Ashley 1972-

PERSONAL: Born April 14, 1972, in Salt Lake City, UT; daughter of Frank and Katherine Jane (Stephens) Warlick; married, August 6, 1994. *Education:* Attended Dickinson College, 1990-94.

ADDRESSES: Agent—Amanda Urban, International Creative Management, 40 West 57th St., New York, NY 10019.

CAREER: Novelist. Has also worked as a waitress, stocker, lifeguard, and nursery employee.

AWARDS, HONORS: Houghton Mifflin Literary Fellowship, 1995.

WRITINGS:

The Distance from the Heart of Things (novel), Houghton Mifflin (Boston, MA), 1996.

WORK IN PROGRESS: A novel, completion expected in 1997.

SIDELIGHTS: Publisher Houghton Mifflin launched Ashley Warlick's career in 1995 by making her the youngest writer to receive its Literary Fellowship. The then 23-year-old author produced *The Distance from the Heart of Things,* a novel about Mavis Black, a young woman who has just begun working as an accountant for the family vineyard in South Carolina. The action centers around a wedding and the gathering of various eccentrics who are family and friends; in this setting, Mavis tries to come to terms with her relationships with her relatives and with the college boyfriend she has left behind. With this book, Warlick not only succeeded in publishing what had begun as college project, she also joined the elite ranks of such writers as Robert Penn Warren, Elizabeth Bishop, and Philip Roth as a Houghton Mifflin fellowship recipient. This enviable status won her notices in the widely-read pages of *Entertainment Weekly* and *Publishers Weekly.* Erica K. Cardozo noted in *Entertainment Weekly* that her initial skepticism about the book was disarmed by its portrayal of Mavis, whom she called "a refreshing—almost shocking—anomaly in Generation X noveldom." A reviewer for *Publishers Weekly* credited Warlick with "a gift for fluent, lilting language" and a sure hand at painting the novel's Southern atmosphere.

BIOGRAPHICAL/CRITICAL SOURCES:

PERIODICALS

Entertainment Weekly, April 12, 1996, p. 62.
Publishers Weekly, January 15, 1996, p. 440-41.

*   *   *

WATT, Donley 1940-

PERSONAL: Born May 24, 1940, in Shawnee, Oklahoma; son of D. E. Watt (a landman in the oil business) and Georgianne (Baxter) Watt; married Lynn McFadden, an artist, May 2, 1978. *Education:* University of Texas at Austin, B.A. and M.A. in History, 1968 and 1970; completed all work toward Ph.D. in educational administration except dissertation; University of Arizona, M.F.A. in creative writing, 1990.

ADDRESSES: Home—6782 North Los Arboles, Tucson AZ, 85704.

CAREER: Austin Community College, Austin, TX, dean, 1973-77; Pelican Square Gallery, owner and operator, 1977; real estate investor and herb farmer, 1978-85; Shearer Publishing Co., Fredericksburg, TX, editor and writer, 1986; full-time writer since 1990; Northern Arizona University at Flagstaff, instructor, 1994.

AWARDS, HONORS: Johnnie Ray Harper Teaching Excellence Award, University of Arizona, 1989; Roberts Writing Award, 1990; Betty Greene Prize.

WRITINGS:

(With Lynn Watt) *Fredericksburg, Texas: Living with the Past,* Shearer Publishing (Bryan, TX), 1987.
The Journey of Hector Rabinal (novel), Texas Christian University Press (College Station, TX), 1994, translation in Spanish published as *La travesia de Hector Rabinal,* Universidad de las Americas (Puebla, Mexico), 1995.
Can You Get There from Here? (short stories), Southern Methodist University Press (Dallas, TX), 1994.

Has published short stories and book reviews in magazines and newspapers.

SIDELIGHTS: Donley Watt dabbled in several different lines of work before becoming a full-time writer. With degrees in history and graduate work in educational administration, Watt has worked in academia, oil, real estate, and agriculture. When he was in his mid-40s, he realized that he had always expected to be a writer; subsequently, he earned an M.F.A. in creative writing and, at age 54, published his first novel.

The novel, *The Journey of Hector Rabinal* (1994), was quickly picked up by a publisher, and was immediately followed by a collection of short stories, *Can You Get There from Here?* These books are based on Watt's own life and on the experiences of his friends, family, and neighbors. *Hector Rabinal* was inspired by Watt's discussions with a Mexican worker on his herb farm and by visits to a Guatemalan refugee camp in Mexico. The resulting story is about a Guatemalan man who is trying escape an oppressive political regime; after seeking refuge in Mexico and Texas, he is forced to return to Guatemala to search for his missing wife. Watt's short stories are about life in small Texas towns during the economic hard times of the 1980s. Watt is confident that he has plenty of material for future works—which is why he does not lament having become a writer late in life. He told the *Austin American-Statesman,* "The advantage of waiting before you start writing is that you accumulate a lot of stories. . . . I never have had writer's block."

BIOGRAPHICAL/CRITICAL SOURCES:

PERIODICALS

Austin American-Statesman, June 10, 1994, pp. E1, E4.

*   *   *

WAXMAN, Ruth B(ilgray)   1916-1996

OBITUARY NOTICE—See index for *CA* sketch: Born February 22, 1916, in Jaffa, Palestine (now Israel); died October 28, 1996, in Manhasset, Long Island, NY. Lecturer. Waxman argued for the rights of women in Conservative Judaism and helped improve the status women in the synagogue. Educated at the University of Chicago, where she received a doctorate in comparative literature, she went on to teach literature at several colleges and universities, including Wilson College, Adelphi University, and Long Island University. Moving to journalism in 1970, Waxman edited *Judaism: A Quarterly Journal of Jewish Life and Thought* from 1972 to 1994. In 1973, she co-edited with Robert Gordis the book *Faith and Reason.* Waxman lectured throughout her career on the role of women in the Jewish faith, literature and American society. She also taught at the State University of New York at Stony Brook and at Queens College.

OBITUARIES AND OTHER SOURCES:

BOOKS

Directory of American Scholars, Volume 4: *Philosophy, Religion, and Law,* 8th edition, Bowker, 1982.

PERIODICALS

New York Times, October 28, 1996, p. D11.

WEGEN, Ronald   1946-1985

PERSONAL: Born September 22, 1946, in New Jersey; died in 1985. *Education:* Pratt Institute, B.F.A., 1968. *Avocational interests:* Reading ancient history, cooking, hot bubble baths, opera, ballet, museums, and farming.

ADDRESSES: Home—New York, NY, and Bogota, Columbia.

CAREER: Author and illustrator of children's books. Previously worked in interior design for an architectural firm and as a jewelry and fabric designer for companies including Givenchy and Anne Klein; worked as a sculptor; exhibited artwork including paintings, drawings, and collage in Bogota, Columbia.

AWARDS, HONORS: American Library Association Honor book for *Where Can the Animals Go?;* New Jersey Authors Award for *The Halloween Costume Party.*

WRITINGS:

Sand Castle, Greenwillow (New York, NY), 1977.
Where Can the Animals Go?, Greenwillow, 1978.
Balloon Trip, Clarion, (New York, NY), 1981.
Sky Dragon, Greenwillow, 1982.
Billy Gorilla, Lothrop, Lee & Shepard (New York, NY), 1983.
The Halloween Costume Party, Clarion, 1983.
What's Wrong Ralph?, Lothrop, Lee & Shepard, 1984.
The Gingerbread Boy, Crown (New York, NY), 1990.

Also illustrator of Richard Bach's *There's No Such Place as Far Away* and Susan Fromberg Schaeffer's *The Rhymes and Runes of the Toad.*

SIDELIGHTS: Children's author Ronald Wegen described his own childhood as "great" and explained how his parents, who owned a bakery, always encouraged him to become an artist. After graduating from New York City's Pratt Institute, Wegen worked as an interior architect, jewelry designer, fabric designer, and sculptor. His work took him around the world; he lived in New York, London, Rome, Amsterdam, Bogota, and Rio, and traveled to Germany, Spain, Morocco, and the Caribbean. Wegen credited this nomadic lifestyle as the reason he never married or had children of his own. However, his five nieces and nephews supplied him with companionship and acted as a sounding board for his books.

Prior to his death in 1985, Wegen wrote and illustrated eight children's books and provided the illustrations for two others. Reviews reveal that it was his artwork that distinguished his books, which were often wordless or included sparse text. He garnered his best reviews for *Balloon Trip* and *Sky Dragon.* The first book, which pictures a balloon voyage taken by a father and his two children, was described by *Kirkus Reviews* as "quite glorious," and by *Publishers Weekly* as "a crackerjack performance." The second work features illustrations that show youthful readers how clouds can be seen as objects such as the title's "Sky Dragon"; *Booklist* described Wegen's artistic performance thus: "He twirls the clouds into shapes that are wispy yet imaginative renderings." As revealed in his books, Wegen's vivid imagination has also elicited comments such as "wacky," "surreal," and "spacey." One such story is the prize-winning *The Halloween Costume Party,* in which the central character is a little girl who goes to a party that—as she discovers at the end—is otherwise solely attended by little green beings from another planet.

BIOGRAPHICAL/CRITICAL SOURCES:

PERIODICALS

Kirkus Reviews, March 15, 1977, p. 282; June 1, 1978, p. 593; December 1, 1981, p. 1464; March 1, 1983, p. 243.
Publishers Weekly, September 18, 1981, p. 154; August 26, 1983, p. 386.
School Library Journal, December 1981, p. 58; October 1982, p. 144; August 1983, p. 59; October 1984, p. 153.

OTHER

Additional material for this sketch was provided by Lothrop, Lee & Shepard Books.*

*   *   *

WEISGALL, Jonathan M.   1949-

PERSONAL: Born March 17, 1949, in Baltimore, MD; son of Hugo D. (an opera composer) and

Nathalie (a homemaker; maiden name, Shulman) Weisgall; married Ruth Elizabeth Macdonald (an attorney), June 3, 1979; children: Alison, Andrew, Benjamin. *Education:* Columbia College (now University), B.A. (magna cum laude), 1970; Stanford University, J.D., 1973. *Politics:* Independent. *Religion:* Jewish. *Avocational interests:* Screenwiting.

ADDRESSES: Home—5309 Edgemoor Ln., Bethesda, MD 20814. *Office*—2101 L Street, N.W., Washington, DC 20037.

CAREER: Admitted to the Bars of New York State, District of Columbia, U.S. Supreme Court, U.S. Claims Court, and Supreme Court of the Republic of the Marshall Islands; Paul, Weiss, Rifkind, Wharton & Garrison, New York, NY, summer associate, 1972; United States Court of Appeals for the Ninth Circuit, San Francisco, CA, law clerk to the Hon. Ben C. Duniway, 1973-74; Covington and Burling, Washington, DC, associate, 1975-79; Ginsburg, Feldman, Weil and Bress, Washington, associate, 1980-81, partner, 1982-83; Jonathan M. Weisgall, Chartered, Washington, attorney, 1983—.

Adjunct professor of law at Georgetown University Law Center; executive producer of documentary film *Radio Bikini,* 1988; member of editorial board of, *Stanford Law Review.*

MEMBER: Phi Beta Kappa; Geothermal Energy Association, president, 1986—; Center for Energy Efficiency and Renewable Technologies, chairman of board of directors, 1986—; Arena Stage (regional theater company), member, board of trustees, 1989—.

AWARDS, HONORS: Hilmer Oehlmann, Jr. Memorial Prize for Legal Research and Writing, 1971; Academy Award nomination, Academy of Motion Picture Arts and Sciences, 1988, for *Radio Bikini.*

WRITINGS:

Operation Crossroads: The Atomic Tests at Bikini Atoll (nonfiction), Naval Institute Press (Annapolis, MD), 1994.

Also contributor to periodicals, including *Wisconsin Law Review, University of San Francisco Law Review, Foreign Policy, Los Angeles Times, SAIS Review, New York Times, Legal Times, U.S. Naval Institute Proceedings,* and *Bulletin of the Atomic Scientists.*

WORK IN PROGRESS: Research on the 1954 hydrogen bomb shot code-named Bravo.

Weisgall told *CA:* "I am also developing five or six screenplays that tie into issues of nuclear testing, human radiation experiments, fighting the government, etc."

SIDELIGHTS: Jonathan M. Weisgall became involved in the legal struggles of the Bikini Islanders displaced by the United State's 1946 atomic bomb test while in the late 1970; when he was an associate with the Washington, DC, law firm of Covington and Burling. He recounts the story in the preface to his 1994 book, *Operation Crossroads: The Atomic Tests at Bikini Atoll.* One of the partners at the firm was late for a lunch meeting, and asked him to take one of the calls. "It was from the Legal Aid Society of Hawaii, which had been asked by a sister organization, the Micronesian Legal Services Corporation, to help the people of Bikini Atoll in the Marshall Islands," Weisgall explained. Thus began his struggle to a win financial settlement for his clients. "An essential element to one of the lawsuits was proving that the United States had entered into a contract with the Bikinians, that the Bikinians had offered to leave their atoll in 1946 in return for America's promise to care for them. It was also important to show that the United States intended to remove the Bikinians only temporarily." Weisgall also represented U.S. military personnel exposed to the atomic blasts in the Pacific. As commentators have pointed out, *Operation Crossroads* is a well researched book, and it includes many revelations, such as the fact that the U.S. Army and the U.S. Navy competed with each other in nuclear weapons research, and that they went ahead and tested atomic bombs under conditions scientists had warned were unsafe.

Writing in the *Baltimore Sun,* Linnell Smith noted that the volume "examines public, congressional and scientific concerns and attitudes about the [atomic bomb] tests. And it joins the growing library of books about the long-term effects of nuclear testing and the secrecy surrounding it." In addition to penning *Operation Crossroads,* Weisgall has also served as the executive producer for the 1988 documentary film, *Radio Bikini,* which was nominated for an Academy Award. He has written about the Bikinians and other subjects in law journals and other periodicals, and plans research on the 1954 hydrogen bomb test. He explained to Smith: "I've found you can't write about nuclear issues without getting radicalized. There tends to be no middle ground."

BIOGRAPHICAL/CRITICAL SOURCES:

BOOKS

Weisgall, Jonathan M., *Operation Crossroads: The Atomic Tests at Bikini Atoll,* Naval Institute Press, 1994.

PERIODICALS

Baltimore Sun, June 12, 1994, pp. K1, K7.

* * *

WEISS, Andrea 1956-

PERSONAL: Born in 1956, in Bristol, PA; daughter of Martin and Ina (Zelman) Weiss; companion of Greta Schiller (a filmmaker), since 1981. *Education:* State University of New York at Binghamton, earned degree, 1976; Rutgers University, Ph.D., 1991. *Religion:* Jewish.

ADDRESSES: Office—Jezebel Productions, P.O. Box 1348, New York, NY 10011. *Agent*—Faith Evans Associates, 45 Clerkenwell Green, London EC1R OEB, England.

CAREER: Writer, film researcher and director. Has researched, directed, or co-produced documentary films, including *Before Stonewall: The Making of a Gay and Lesbian Community,* Public Broadcasting System (PBS), c. 1984; *International Sweethearts of Rhythm,* 1986; *Tiny & Ruby: Hell Divin' Women,* 1988; *Paris Was a Woman,* 1995; and *A Bit of Scarlet,* 1996.

AWARDS, HONORS: Emmy Award, 1987, for *Before Stonewall* (film version); fellowships from the New York Foundation for the Arts and the New York State Council on the Arts, both 1991; Artist-in-Residence in Berlin D.A.A.D. (German Academic Exchange Service, Artist Program), 1992; National Endowment for the Arts fellowship, 1993; Lambda Literary Award, 1996, for *Paris Was a Woman: Portraits from the Left Bank* (book version).

WRITINGS:

NONFICTION

(With Greta Schiller) *Before Stonewall: The Making of a Gay and Lesbian Community,* Naiad Press (Tallahassee, FL), 1988.

Vampires and Violets: Lesbians in Film, Penguin Books (New York), 1993.
Paris Was a Woman: Portraits from the Left Bank, HarperSanFrancisco (San Francisco, CA), 1995.

WORK IN PROGRESS: A work of fiction entitled *One Toe in the River Styx.*

SIDELIGHTS: Filmmaker and author Andrea Weiss is perhaps best known for her collaborations with Greta Schiller on such documentaries as *Before Stonewall: The Making of a Gay and Lesbian Community, International Sweethearts of Rhythm, Tiny & Ruby: Hell Divin' Women,* and *Paris Was a Woman. Before Stonewall*—which, as the title implies, chronicles the lives of gays and lesbians before the 1969 Stonewall riots became the turning point of the modern gay rights movement—won an Emmy after it was shown on public television. *International Sweethearts of Rhythm* informs viewers about the first all-female, racially integrated jazz band which capitalized on the greater freedom afforded women during World War II. *Tiny & Ruby* follows one of the members of the band through her life and long-term lesbian relationship with another musician. The latter two films have been popular attractions at gay and lesbian film festivals throughout the United States; according to Vicki L. Eaklor in the *American Historical Review,* they both "serve as powerful testaments to survival and affirmation in the face of prejudice and oppression."

Weiss has penned books in addition to her film work. Her first, also a collaboration with Schiller, was a written version of the *Before Stonewall* documentary. It argued that gay and lesbian subculture began to flourish in the United States in the early 1900s, as the country's urbanization increased. It continued to bloom during Prohibition and World War II, but was squelched during the 1950s. After the examples of the black civil rights and the women's liberation movements, however, the gay rights movement came into its own. A *Booklist* reviewer praised the volume as a "concise, personable essay" containing "excellent popular history."

The author's *Vampires and Violets: Lesbians in Film* saw print in 1993. Though acknowledging the comparative dearth of outright lesbian images in film, the book is deeply concerned with interpretation of film imagery over the decades by lesbians in film audiences. Weiss also asserts in *Vampires and Violets* that the lesbian vampire is "the most persistent lesbian image in the history of the cinema." Claire Monk, reviewing the tome in *Sight and Sound,* judged that Weiss "produces persuasive readings of films from Pabst's *Pandora's Box* to Su Friedrich's *Damned If You Don't."* *Publishers Weekly* lauded *Vampires and Violets* as an "accessible, worthy addition to gay and lesbian cinema studies," while *Booklist* concluded it to be a "must for women's studies, lesbian and gay studies, and extensive film collections."

Weiss examined the lesbian community in Paris during the years prior to World War II in her 1995 book, *Paris Was a Woman: Portraits from the Left Bank.* Though she discusses well-known figures of this world, such as poet Gertrude Stein and her lover Alice B. Toklas, Weiss also provides readers with the experiences of lesser-known members of their literary circle. In the pages of *Paris Was a Woman* are women such as Sylvia Beach, who published editions of the then-forbidden James Joyce novel *Ulysses* disguised as the works of English playwright William Shakespeare; and Winifred Ellerman Bryher, lover of the poet Hilda Doolittle (H.D.), who used much of her inherited money to help Jewish refugees fleeing the Nazi regime in Germany. Bernice Kert, critiquing *Paris Was a Woman* in the *Washington Post Book World,* confirmed that "Weiss's book is a good take on the era and its cast of characters." Weiss and Schiller collaborated to film the 1995 documentary *Paris Was a Woman,* which is, as its title indicates, based upon Weiss's book of the same name. *Village Voice* contributor Mark Huisman reviewed the documentary, and hailed it as "a delectably shimmering, finely crafted film."

BIOGRAPHICAL/CRITICAL SOURCES:

BOOKS

Weiss, Andrea, *Vampires and Violets: Lesbians in Film,* Penguin Books (New York), 1993.

PERIODICALS

American Historical Review, October, 1990, pp. 1146-47.
Booklist, June 15, 1988, p. 1696; November 15, 1993, p. 594.
New Statesman and Society, November 27, 1992, p. 44.
New York Times, June 16, 1991, p. LI 13.
Publishers Weekly, September 27, 1993, p. 57.
Sight and Sound, June, 1994, pp. 38-39.
Village Voice, November 6-12, 1996.
Washington Post Book World, March 3, 1996, p. 5.

WELCH, William   1917-1981(?)

PERSONAL: Born September 11, 1917, in New Haven, CT; died c. 1981; married in 1946; children: three. *Education:* Harvard University, B.A., 1938; Yale University, M.A., 1947; Columbia University, Ph.D., 1951.

CAREER: Hamilton College, began as instructor, became assistant professor of political science, 1948-52; U.S. Government, research analyst, 1952-60; University of California, visiting lecturer, 1960-61; University of Colorado, Boulder, associate professor of political science, 1961-68, assistant director of the honors program, 1962-67, faculty fellow, 1967-68, professor of political science, 1968-c.81. Washington Center for Foreign Policy Research, research associate, 1957-58.

WRITINGS:

American Images of Soviet Foreign Policy; an Inquiry into Recent Appraisals from the Academic Community, Yale University Press, 1970.
The Art of Political Thinking: Government and Common Sense, edited by Katharine S. Welch, foreword by Kenneth Boulding, Rowman and Littlefield, 1981.

Also author of *The Nature of Kruschevian Threats against the West,* 1965.

SIDELIGHTS: William Welch wrote *American Images of Soviet Foreign Policy; an Inquiry into Recent Appraisals from the Academic Community* in 1971. In it, he critiqued the twenty-two most important books on American-Soviet foreign policy. A *Choice* reviewer called the book "unique in its depth of analysis" and asserted that Welch's moderate political stance contributed to the balance of the ambitious volume, concluding that the book has value for both experts and students. D.F. Fleming, in a review of *American Images of Soviet Foreign Policy* in the *Nation,* declared that "no student of the cold war can afford to be without this book. It is a bibliographical mine, containing . . . excellent tables and figures, and valuable chapters." Fleming continued with his praise of the book, calling it "a brave and successful undertaking."

Welch's 1981 book, *The Art of Political Thinking: Government and Common Sense,* explored three controversial political topics: abortion, gay rights with regard to employment discrimination, and the

Vietnam War. Roger W. Smith maintained in *Perspective* that "this is an engaging book, beautifully written, and old-fashioned; a Jeffersonian kind of book that offers much good sense to the contemporary American citizen at whom it is aimed." An *Ethics* reviewer, however, faulted Welch for his excessive use of graphs, claiming that "there is neither art, nor thought, nor common sense in this."

BIOGRAPHICAL/CRITICAL SOURCES:

PERIODICALS

Choice, March, 1971, p. 142.
Ethics, July, 1982, p. 793.
Library Journal, March 1, 1971, p. 842.
Nation, May 10, 1971, pp. 603-4.
Perspective, March, 1982, pp. 35-36.

*   *   *

WESTON, Michael   1931-

PERSONAL: Born October 21, 1931, in Modbury, England.

CAREER: Writer, 1959—.

AWARDS, HONORS: Georgette Heyer Prize for Historical Fiction, 1986, for *The Cage: A Parable.*

WRITINGS:

The Princess Royal (play), broadcast by British Broadcasting Corporation, 1959.
Wine from Where the Mistral Blows (nonfiction), Wine and Shint Publications, 1981.
Grace Pensilva (novel), Bodley Head, 1985.
The Cage: A Parable (novel), Bodley Head, 1986.

WORK IN PROGRESS: The Kingdoms and the Kings, a novel.

SIDELIGHTS: British author Michael Weston's second novel, *The Cage: A Parable,* is perhaps the best known of his works. It earned him the Georgette Heyer Prize for Historical Fiction in 1986, and won him comparisons with illustrious authors such as Thomas Hardy and John Fowles. *The Cage* is set in the village of Windfall in Cornwall during the nineteenth century and is the story of Welland Halt, a stranger who arrives with his daughter Ruth to work in the tin mines. Halt achieves success of a sort, but his unwillingness to speak of his past earns him an enemy who plots his downfall. The *Publishers Weekly* critic who reviewed *The Cage* lauded it as "lyrical" and "powerfully characterized," citing incidents in an evangelical tent gathering and a "memorable conclusion that will haunt the reader for a long time." Philippa Toomey, writing in the London *Times* called the novel "grim and powerful."

BIOGRAPHICAL/CRITICAL SOURCES:

PERIODICALS

British Book News, February, 1986, p. 75; July, 1986, p. 389.
Publishers Weekly, October 31, 1986, p. 57.
Times (London), May 15, 1986.

*   *   *

WEXLER, Norman   1926-

PERSONAL: Born August 6, 1926, in New Bedford, MA; son of Harry and Sophia (Brisson) Wexler; children: Erica, Merin. *Education:* Attended Harvard University, 1948.

ADDRESSES: Home—Greenwich, CT. *Office*—c/o Writers Guild, 8955 Beverly Blvd., Los Angeles, CA 90048.

CAREER: Playwright and screenwriter. Playwright in residence, Cleveland Playhouse, Cleveland, OH, 1970.

MEMBER: Dramatists Guild, Writers Guild of America West, Academy of Motion Picture Arts and Sciences.

AWARDS, HONORS: National Endowment for the Arts grant, 1970; Academy Award nomination, best original story or screenplay, 1970, for *Joe;* (with Waldo Salt) Academy Award nomination, best adapted story or screenplay, and Writers Guild of America Award, both 1973, for *Serpico;* National Association for the Advancement of Colored People Image Award, c. 1975, for screenplay for *Mandingo;* National Science Foundation Grant.

WRITINGS:

PLAYS

The Rope (one-act), produced at Theatre De Lys, New York City, 1965.

A Week from Today (one-act), produced at Theatre De Lys, 1965.

Red's My Color, What's Yours? A Play without Love, produced at Drury Theatre, Cleveland Playhouse, 1970.

The Huff and the Puff (one-act), produced at Brooks Theater, Cleveland Playhouse, 1970.

What Ever Happened to Hugging and Kissing? (one-act comedy), produced at Brooks Theater, 1970.

SCREENPLAYS

Joe, Cannon Films, 1970, published as a book with an introductory review of the film by Judith Crist, Avon (New York), 1970.

(With Waldo Salt) *Serpico* (based on a novel by Peter Maas), Paramount, 1973.

Mandingo, Paramount, 1975.

Drum, United Artists, 1976.

Saturday Night Fever (based on a story idea by Nik Cohn), Paramount, 1977.

(With Sylvester Stallone) *Staying Alive,* Paramount, 1983.

(With Gary DeVore) *Raw Deal,* DeLaurentiis, 1986.

ADAPTATIONS: Saturday Night Fever was adapted into novel form by H.B. Gilmour and published by Bantam Books (New York), 1977.

WORK IN PROGRESS: Several works for the stage.

SIDELIGHTS: During the 1970s Norman Wexler established himself as one of the most acclaimed screenwriters working in the American film industry. He penned the screenplay for *Saturday Night Fever* as well as that of several other noted motion pictures, but eventually left Hollywood and returned to writing for the stage. Wexler, born in Massachusetts but raised in Detroit, was an up-and-coming playwright in New York City in the late 1960s who had once worked in the advertising industry with John Avildsen, an aspiring director. Avildsen convinced his playwright friend to try his hand at crafting a screenplay, and in just under two weeks Wexler produced a controversial story about class and political differences in contemporary America. A bit of luck helped the duo win a production deal with Cannon

Films, and the film *Joe* was the result. It was released in the summer of 1970 and went on to win an Academy Award nomination for best screenplay. The film's title character is a working-class bigot from Queens, New York, who is vociferous in his contempt of hippies, intellectuals, and minority groups. In a bar, Joe meets a Madison Avenue advertising executive who admits he has just killed his teenage hippie daughter's drug-pusher boyfriend. The two strike up an unlikely friendship that later turns into a rescue mission when the daughter, played by Susan Sarandon, vanishes into the hippie underground. Critics responded enthusiastically to *Joe*. A critic for *Variety* asserted that "Wexler has fleshed his serious skeleton with both melodrama plotting that sustains interest and the grittiest, most obscene dialog yet to boom from the silver screen. It works." *New York* critic Judith Crist described the storyline as "a ripsnorter, a New York City chronicle that gets to the heart of a number of our contemporary traumas."

Wexler's next project was the completion of a screenplay for the 1973 film *Serpico*. The script was an adaptation of a book by Peter Maas recounting the real-life story of two New York City police officers who went to the *New York Times* with tales of corruption and crime within the city's law enforcement community. The finished version was directed by Sidney Lumet and starred Al Pacino; Wexler shared screenwriting credits with Waldo Salt. *New York Times* critic Vincent Canby termed the movie "provocative, a remarkable record of one man's rebellion against the sort of sleaziness and second-rateness that has affected so much American life, from the ingredients of its hamburgers to the ethics of its civil servants and politicians." Next, Wexler became involved with a project that evolved into the 1975 film *Mandingo*, crafting its screenplay from a story that had been both a novel and a stage play. "What I tried to do was dispel all the racist myths," Wexler told *Variety* writer Andy Marx in 1994, but the movie suffered criticism for what some considered its heavy-handed treatment of interracial relationships in the antebellum South.

Wexler's most dramatic success, however, came with the 1977 release of the Paramount Pictures' film *Saturday Night Fever*. Wexler adapted this screenplay from a magazine story by Nik Cohn about a humdrum, working-class Brooklyn teenager who becomes a star at the local discotheque. Both the film and its soundtrack have been credited with launching the disco culture into mainstream America, each achieving enormous commercial success and becoming virtual icons of an era. Though critics generally disparaged the scripted caricatures of its protagonist, played by John Travolta, and his on-screen pals, *Saturday Night Fever* was an overwhelming commercial triumph. Nevertheless, its 1983 sequel, *Staying Alive,* fared less well. Directed by Sylvester Stallone and reviving Travolta's Tony Manero character, the film's title became virtually synonymous with the failure of formulaic sequels. Wexler was listed as co-screenwriter with Stallone, but apparently the two did not work together. "I was irate when they got Stallone and he re-wrote it and it turned into a bomb," Wexler said of the *Staying Alive* screenplay to Marx in *Variety*. Many critics described it as a simplistic reprisal of Stallone's successful "Rocky" formula. "What went wrong with *Staying Alive* is not difficult to figure out," noted the *New York Times'* Canby. "For starters there is the screenplay that . . . Stallone completely rewrote. . . . The only thing completely clear is that this screenplay totally misses the point of the appeal of *Saturday Night Fever.*"

Wexler co-wrote a screenplay for a 1986 Arnold Schwarzenegger vehicle called *Raw Deal,* but grew increasingly dissatisfied with the scriptwriting projects offered him. He also grew disillusioned with Hollywood, and eventually moved to Connecticut to begin writing for the stage again. "Making a movie is such a collaborative effort," he told Marx in the *Variety* interview. "You have to be promoter to get them made. I've always thought that writers should produce the work and it would settle into production. But it doesn't happen that way."

BIOGRAPHICAL/CRITICAL SOURCES:

PERIODICALS

Chicago Tribune, July 15, 1983; June 11, 1986.
Los Angeles Times, July 15, 1983; June 6, 1986.
New York, July 20, 1970, p. 54.
New York Times, July 16, 1970, p. 40; August 2, 1970, section 2, p. 7; December 6, 1973, p. 61; December 16, 1973, section 2, p. 3; May 8, 1975, p. 49; May 18, 1975, section 2, p. 19; December 16, 1977, p. C10; February 12, 1978, section 2, p. 15; July 15, 1983; July 24, 1983.
Publishers Weekly, September 14, 1970, p. 71.
Time, March 24, 1975.
Variety, February 25, 1970; July 15, 1970; February 24, 1971; April 11, 1994, p. 11.*

WHISLER, Thomas L(ee) 1920-

PERSONAL: Born February 12, 1920, in Dayton, OH; son of Rolland Foster and Thelma (Wildasin) Whisler; married Ann Elizabeth Wohlen, February 14, 1946; children: John, Barbara. *Education:* Attended University of Cincinnati, 1940; Miami University, B.S., 1941; University of Chicago, M.B.A., 1947, Ph.D., 1953.

ADDRESSES: Home—9 Wilson Ct., Park Forest, IL 60466. *Office*—Graduate School of Business, University of Chicago, 5801 Ellis Ave., Chicago, IL 60637.

CAREER: University of Missouri, Columbia, instructor, then assistant professor of business management, 1947-53; University of Chicago, Chicago, IL, faculty member of Graduate School of Business, beginning 1953, professor of industrial relations, beginning 1963, professor of business policy, 1975—. Visiting professor at Stanford University, 1959; instructor at Management Development Institute, Cairo, Egypt, 1963; Ford Foundation consultant to National Institute of Management Development, Cairo, Egypt, 1963, and to Center for Productivity, Study, and Research, State University of Ghent, 1968-69. *Military service:* United States Naval Reserves, 1942-46.

WRITINGS:

(Editor, with George P. Shultz) *Management Organization and the Computer,* Free Press (Glencoe, IL), 1960.
(Editor, with Shirley F. Harper) *Performance Appraisal: Research and Practice,* Holt (New York City), 1962.
(With Harald Meyer) *The Impact of EDP on Life Company Organization,* Life Office Management Association (New York City), 1967.
The Impact of Computers on Organizations, Praeger (New York City), 1970.
Information Technology and Organizational Change, Wadsworth Publishing (Belmont, CA), 1970.
Rules of the Game: Inside the Corporate Boardroom, Dow Jones-Irwin (Homewood, IL), 1983.

SIDELIGHTS: Writer and educator Thomas L. Whisler has been associated with the University of Chicago's Graduate School of Business since 1953, when he returned to his alma mater after teaching business management at the University of Missouri. Active as a consultant and visiting professor in the areas of industrial relations and management, he is the author of several books in the field of business, including 1970's *The Impact of Computers on Organizations,* and *Rules of the Game: Inside the Corporate Boardroom,* published in 1983.

BIOGRAPHICAL/CRITICAL SOURCES:

PERIODICALS

Library Journal, February 1, 1970, p. 491.
Times Literary Supplement, May 21, 1971, p. 587.*

* * *

WHITAKER, James   1931-

PERSONAL: Born in 1931.

ADDRESSES: Office—Daily Mirror, 1 Canada Square, Canary Wharf, London E14 5AP, England.

CAREER: Daily Mirror, London, England, royal court reporter; writer.

WRITINGS:

Pie on Earth, Outposts (London), 1966.
Skating through the Cemetery (poetry), Bream Press (Stanford-le-Hope, England), 1972.
Joseph Conrad at Stanford-le-Hope (biography), Bream Press, 1978.
Settling Down (biography), Quartet Publications (London), 1981.
Diana vs. Charles: Royal Blood Feud (biography), Dutton (New York), 1993.

SIDELIGHTS: James Whitaker is a British journalist who is probably best known to American readers as the author of *Diana vs. Charles: Royal Blood Feud,* which charts the decline of the marriage of England's Prince and Princess of Wales. Whitaker, who reports on the royal court for the London *Daily Mirror,* provides many controversial episodes in *Diana vs. Charles,* including some concerning Charles's alleged extramarital activities. Whitaker told the *Washington Post,* "When a big royal story comes, there is only one person who's called on our major, number one TV station to comment—and that's me." An *Economist* critic, comparing *Diana vs. Charles* with other books on the same subject, deemed Whitaker's book "the most gripping."

Among Whitaker's earlier writings is *Settling Down,* an account of the wedding between the Prince of Wales and the woman now known popularly as Princess Diana. *Listener* reviewer Russell Davies, assessing *Settling Down* and several other works devoted to the royal wedding, noted that "Whitaker does perhaps score his biographer rivals . . . in his willingness to be constructively brutal" about the Prince of Wales himself.

BIOGRAPHICAL/CRITICAL SOURCES:

PERIODICALS

Economist, June 19, 1993, pp. 94-95.
Listener, July 30, 1981, pp. 83-84.
Washington Post, May 27, 1993, pp. D1-D2.*

* * *

WILCOX, (William) Clyde   1953-

PERSONAL: Born April 9, 1953, in Fairmont, WV; son of William (a newspaper executive) and Sarah (a cook; maiden name, Tatterson) Wilcox; married Elizabeth Adell Cook; children: Elaine, Neil. *Ethnicity:* "White." *Education:* West Virginia University, B.A., 1975; Ohio State University, M.A., 1980, Ph.D., 1984.

ADDRESSES: Home—Wilcox-Cook Consulting, 1653 Trap Rd., Vienna, VA 22182-2065. *Office*—Department of Government, Georgetown University, Washington, DC 20057; fax 202-687-5858. *E-mail*—wilcoxc@gunet.georgetown.edu.

CAREER: Federal Election Commission, statistician, 1984-86; Union College, visiting assistant professor, 1986-87; Georgetown University, Washington, DC, assistant professor, 1987-91, associate professor, 1991-95, professor of government, 1996—.

WRITINGS:

Setups: Financing Congressional Campaigns (monograph), American Political Science Association (Washington, DC), 1988.
God's Warriors: The Christian Right in Twentieth Century America, Johns Hopkins University Press (Baltimore, MD), 1992.
(With Ted G. Jelen and wife Elizabeth Adell Cook) *Between Two Absolutes: Public Opinion and the*

Politics of Abortion, Westview (Boulder, CO), 1992.

(Editor with Stephen Wayne, and contributor) *The Quest for Office: National Electoral Politics,* St. Martin's (New York City), 1992.

(Editor with Cook and Sue Thomas, and contributor) *The Year of the Woman: Myths and Realities,* Westview, 1994.

(Editor with Paul Herrnson and Robert Biersack) *Risky Business? PAC Decisionmaking in Congressional Elections,* M. E. Sharpe (Armonk, NY), 1994.

The Latest American Revolution? (monograph), St. Martin's, 1995.

(Editor with Mark Rozell, and contributor) *God at the Grass Roots: The Christian Right in the 1994 Elections,* Rowman & Littlefield (Lanham, MD), 1995.

(With Clifford Brown, Jr. and Lynda Powell) *Serious Money: Fundraising and Contributing in Presidential Nomination Campaigns,* Cambridge University Press (Cambridge, England), 1996.

(With Jelen) *Public Attitudes on Church and State,* M. E. Sharpe, 1996.

(With Rozell) *Second Coming: The New Christian Right in Virginia Politics,* Johns Hopkins University Press, 1996.

Onward Christian Soldiers: The Christian Right in American Politics, Westview, 1996.

(Editor with Barbara Norrander, and contributor) *Understanding Public Opinion,* CQ Press (Washington, DC), 1996.

(Editor with Donald M. Hassler, and contributor) *Political Science Fiction,* University of South Carolina Press (Charleston, SC), 1996.

(Editor with Herrnson and Ronald Shaiko, and contributor) *The Interest Group Connection: Electioneering, Lobbying, and Policymaking in Washington,* Chatham House (Chatham, NJ), 1996.

(Editor with Thomas, and contributor) *Women in Elected Office: Past, Present, and Future,* Oxford University Press (New York City), 1996.

(Editor with John Bruce) *The Changing Politics of Gun Control,* Rowman & Littlefield, in press.

(Editor with Rozell) *God at the Grassroots, 1996,* Rowman & Littlefield, in press.

(Editor with Biersack and Herrnson) *Interest Groups and Lobbying in the New Republican Congress,* Allyn & Bacon (New York City), in press.

Contributor to books, including *Science Fiction and Market Realities,* edited by Gary Westfahl, George Slusser, and Eric S. Rabkin, University of Georgia Press (Athens, GA), 1996; *Gay Rights, Military Wrongs: Political Perspectives on Lesbians and Gays in the Military,* edited by Craig Rimmerman, Garland Publishing (New York City), 1996; and *The Other Elites: Women, Politics, and Power in the Executive Branch,* Lynne Reinner (Boulder), 1996. Contributor of more than a hundred articles and reviews to a wide variety of academic journals and newspapers, including *Women and Politics, Congress and the Presidency, Journal of Social Psychology, Social Science Quarterly, Journal for the Scientific Study of Religion, Review of Religious Research, Extrapolation, Journal of Popular Culture,* and *Journal of Irreproducible Results.*

* * *

WILEY, James (Milton) 1920-

PERSONAL: Born January 31, 1920, in Shreveport, LA; son of James Milton (in sales) and Lucille (Fitzpatrick) Wiley; married Rita Joel, June 19, 1973 (died June 23, 1985); married Margaret Wagner (a homemaker). *Ethnicity:* "White Anglo-Saxon." *Education:* Attended high school. *Politics:* Democrat. *Religion:* Christian. *Avocational interests:* Aerobic exercises, teaching twelve-step seminars.

ADDRESSES: Home—San Antonio, TX.

CAREER: Good Housekeeping, New York, NY, editorial assistant; *American Home,* co-editor, later vice-president and editorial director; Burlington Industries, New York, NY, director of home fashions; *San Antonio Homes and Gardens,* San Antonio, TX, founding editor; has worked in advertising as a manager of products publicity and creative director; free-lance writer and editor.

WRITINGS:

Power Recovery: The Twelve Steps for a New Generation, Paulist Press (Mahwah, NJ), 1995.

Contributor of more than a hundred articles to national and regional magazines. Contributing editor, *Seniors.*

WORK IN PROGRESS: The Phoenix Generation.

SIDELIGHTS: James Wiley told *CA:* "At the age of fourteen I entered and won second prize in an advertising copywriting contest sponsored by a local brewery. The assignment: to create a full-page newspaper ad promoting the merits of Velvet Beer. My winning headline: 'Living on Velvet.' My prize: six cases of Velvet Beer, which I watched my father drink.

"Since then, my primary motive for writing has always been to earn my living by doing something I dearly love: writing about any subject that seizes my interest. Now a septuagenarian, I have been legally blind for ten years. I wrote my first book with the aid of a software program called Zoomtext, which enlarges text on a computer monitor. My reading, editing, and page-proofing are done with the help of a closed-circuit television reading machine, which enlarges the text on a television screen.

"My first book *Power Recovery* was inspired by a young woman's remark in a meeting of Alcoholics Anonymous, a fellowship to which I have belonged for more than two decades. 'The first time I read the Big Book *Alcoholics Anonymous,* I thought it was quaint,' said the woman. 'It was written in 1939, twenty-six years before I was born. The language, the people, and the customs of the 1930s seemed archaic, like something from another time warp.' The Big Book is the standard work on the twelve-step program of recovery from alcoholism. I knew, as that woman did, that for more than half a century, since its publication, the basic text of the book has remained unchanged, never updated through three editions and twenty-six printings.

"Could there really be, I wondered later, a three-generation communications gap between young alcoholics and addicts of today and the 1939 prose of the Big Book? Are their experiences today really so different? 'Check it out,' I said to myself. So, for two years I sat on a metal chair with a small notebook and chronicled the confusion, the fear and pain, as well as the insights, the breakthroughs, and the humor shared by young recovering alcoholics and addicts in more than four-hundred Alcoholics Anonymous meetings. I enjoy working with young people and have sponsored more than thirty persons in Alcoholics Anonymous. I found that, to a generation which grew up on television, video games, and computer monitors, the Big Book often does represent a challenge.

"*Power Recovery,* the result, is both a how-to book and a peer group counseling guide. The text is a continuing dialogue between the author, explaining traditional twelve-step therapy, and nearly one hundred and fifty young people who interject their own comments on how it was with them as they came

unglued, hit bottom, came into recovery, and learned how to turn their lives around. The book takes up where *Alcoholics Anonymous* left off three generations ago.

"My writing process is centered in my bedroom. An L-shaped work station adjacent to my bed includes a computer/word processor and closed-circuit television reading machine, at angles to a traditional sixty-inch Louis XV walnut writing table. Normally, when I am working on a book, I write for three mid-week days, from ten in the morning until nearly midnight, behind drawn blackout draperies that maximize the contrast of white characters on a black screen. Often I roll out of bed around three o'clock in the morning, switch on the computer, write for an hour, then climb back into bed. I keep a portable tape-recorder on a shelf in my bathroom to 'jot down' ideas that come in the mornings while I am shaving."

*   *   *

WILLIAMS, (Elisabeth) Ann   1937-

PERSONAL: Born January 13, 1937, in Hampstead, London, England; daughter of Trevor Matthew (a mining engineer) and Evelyn Constance (a secretary; maiden name, Faulkner) Williams. *Ethnicity:* "English." *Education:* Birkbeck College, London, B.A. (with honors), 1960, Ph.D., 1964. *Politics:* None. *Religion:* Church of England. *Avocational interests:* History, ecclesiastical architecture, science fiction, "whodunnits."

ADDRESSES: Home—London, England.

CAREER: Polytechnic (now University) of North London, London, England, began as lecturer, became senior lecturer in medieval history, 1966-88; retired, 1988.

MEMBER: Royal Historical Society (fellow), Society of Antiquaries (fellow).

WRITINGS:

Victoria History of the County of Dorset, Volume III, Oxford University Press (Oxford, England), 1969.
(Editor with R. W. H. Erksine and Geoffrey Martin, and contributor) *Domesday Book,* 31 volumes, Alecto Historical Editions (London, England), 1986-92.

(With Alfred P. Smyth and David Kirby) *A Biographical Dictionary of Dark-Age Britain,* B. A. Seaby (London), 1991.

The English and the Norman Conquest, Boydell & Brewer (Woodbridge, England), 1995.

Contributor to books, including *Domesday 900,* Millbank Publications (London), 1986; *Studies in Medieval History Presented to R. Allen Brown,* edited by Christopher Harper-Bill and others, Boydell & Brewer, 1989; and *St. Wulfstan, Bishop of Worcester, 1062-1095,* edited by Julia Barrow and N. P. Brooks, Scolar Press, 1996. Contributor of articles and reviews to periodicals, including *Exeter History and Archaeology, Medieval History, Medieval Knighthood,* and *Anglo-Norman Studies.*

WORK IN PROGRESS: Kingship and Government in Pre-Conquest England, for Macmillan (London), completion expected before the year 2000; *The Twelfth-Century Surveys of Shaftesbury Abbey,* with J. S. Moore, British Academy (London); research on social and political history in tenth- and eleventh-century England.

SIDELIGHTS: Ann Williams told *CA:* "I am a research historian, now retired and able to devote myself to research. I taught for twenty-two years at the Polytechnic (now University) of North London, and this experience has been extremely useful in helping me to clarify my thoughts and (I hope) powers of exposition. All researchers should teach; students are great ones for ferreting out inconsistencies of argument and conclusions based on wishful thinking. History as a discipline has been under attack (in England at least) for some time, and medieval history in particular has been singled out for denigration. My chief purpose in writing and lecturing is to demonstrate the interest and utility of knowing the past. I believe with the twelfth-century historian Henry of Huntingdon that 'only brutes, whether they be men or beasts, neither know nor wish to know whence they come, nor their own origin, nor the events and deeds of their own country.'"

*   *   *

WILLIAMS, Patricia J(oyce) 1951-

PERSONAL: Born in 1951, in Boston, MA. *Education:* Wellesley College, B.A., 1972; Harvard University Law School, J.D., 1975.

ADDRESSES: Office—c/o School of Law, Columbia University, 435 West 116th St., New York, NY 10027-7201.

CAREER: Educator and writer. Golden Gate University, associate professor of law, 1980-84; City University of New York, Queens, associate professor, 1984-88; University of Wisconsin, associate professor, 1988-91; Columbia University, New York City, professor of law, 1991—.

WRITINGS:

The Alchemy of Race and Rights, Harvard University Press (Cambridge, MA), 1991.

The Rooster's Egg: On the Persistence of Prejudice, Harvard University Press, 1995.

Contributor to books, including *Malcolm X: In Our Own Image,* edited by Joe Woods, St. Martin's Press (New York City), 1992; *Constitutional Law,* edited by Mark V. Tushnet, New York University Press (New York City), 1992; *Race-ing Justice, Engendering Power: Essays on Anita Hill, Clarence Thomas, and the Construction of Social Reality,* edited by Toni Morrison, Pantheon (New York City), 1992; *Reading Rodney King: Reading Urban Uprising,* edited by Robert Gooding-Williams, Routledge (New York City), 1993; *Feminism and Community,* edited by Penny A. Weiss and Marilyn Friedman, Temple University Press (Philadelphia), 1995; *Constructing Masculinity,* edited by Maurice Berger, Brian Wallis, and Simon Watson, Routledge, 1995; and *Beacon Book of Essays by Contemporary American Women,* edited by Wendy Martin, Beacon Press (Boston), 1996.

Also contributor to newspapers and periodicals, including *Boston Globe, Christian Science Monitor, Harvard Law Review, Ms., Nation, New Yorker, Village Voice,* and *Washington Post.*

SIDELIGHTS: In her numerous articles in mainstream newspapers and periodicals, Patricia J. Williams, professor of law at Columbia University, has been an outspoken critic of U.S. race relations. Her *The Alchemy of Race and Rights,* published in 1991, and 1995's *The Rooster's Egg: On the Persistence of Prejudice,* both speak eloquently to the continuing tensions that exist between whites and African Americans.

Born in the highly segregated city of Boston in 1951, Williams was raised in the turbulent first years after public schools were forcibly integrated in Little Rock, Arkansas. Earning her B.A. from prestigious Wellesley College in 1972, she went on to Harvard University Law School, earning her J.D. in 1975. Williams's experiences at Harvard were shadowed by her sense of being an outsider: "My abiding recollection of being a student at Harvard Law School is the sense of being invisible," she writes in *The Alchemy of Race and Rights*. In this book, Williams goes on to discuss how race and class combine to affect the law, and thereby, personal rights. "[Personal] rights are islands of empowerment," she contends, explaining that "To be unrighted is to be disempowered, and the line between rights and no-rights is most often the line between dominators and oppressors." Individuals in positions of power are therefore assured of retaining their rights, Williams observes; for those disempowered by race, class, or gender, personal rights are not guaranteed.

The Rooster's Egg finds Williams examining newsworthy topics of the early 1990s. Supreme Court Justice Clarence Thomas's nomination hearings, 1992's Republican National Convention, first lady Hillary Rodham Clinton, and the wave of talk-show fever then sweeping the United States all come under discussion. In the midst of the decade's continued controversy surrounding the decision whether to continue or abandon welfare and affirmative action programs, Williams sees irony in the burgeoning popularity of figures like Rush Limbaugh and Howard Stern, "Radio Hoods" who, she contends, hide their racism and sexism behind the banner of the First Amendment. "What does it mean," she asks, "that a manic, penis-obsessed adolescent named Howard Stern is number one among radio listeners, that Rush Limbaugh's wittily smooth sadism has gone the way of prime-time television, and that these men's books tie for the number one slot on all the best seller lists?"

In both *The Rooster's Egg* and *The Alchemy of Race and Rights*, Williams's candid discussion of controversial issues has earned her a reputation as a radical. Some critics have also noted that her autobiographical writing style and her use of personal experience to support her contentions violate traditional academic practices. However, other critics have found much in her work to commend. "In luminous, supple prose, Williams helps us imagine the alternatives we need," notes Henry Louis Gates Jr. in his review of *The Alchemy of Race and Rights* for *Nation*. "And what some will condemn as her personalism—which I would describe, rather, as her refusal of impersonalism—proves an indispensable element of her own alchemy."

Williams continues to be a prolific commentator on U.S. society. In addition to *The Alchemy of Race and Rights* and *The Rooster's Egg*, she has contributed articles to numerous periodicals, including the *Boston Globe*, *Harvard Law Review*, *Nation*, *Village Voice*, and the *Washington Post*.

BIOGRAPHICAL/CRITICAL SOURCES:

BOOKS

Perrealut, Jeanne, *Writing Selves: Contemporary Feminist Autobiography*, University of Minnesota Press (Minneapolis), 1995.
Williams, Patricia J., *The Alchemy of Race and Rights*, Harvard University Press, 1991.
Williams, *The Rooster's Egg: On the Persistence of Prejudice*, Harvard University Press, 1995.

PERIODICALS

Choice, February, 1996, p. 903.
Ms., January, 1996, p. 90.
Nation, June 10, 1991, pp. 766-70.
New Republic, October 21, 1991, p. 39.
New Statesman and Society, August 9, 1991, p. 36.
New York Times Book Review, May 26, 1991, p. 10; October 29, 1995, p. 43.
Publishers Weekly, September 4, 1995, p. 59.

*   *   *

WILLIAMS, Trevor Illtyd   1921-1996

OBITUARY NOTICE—See index for *CA* sketch: Born July 16, 1921; died October 12, 1996. Chemist, writer, and science historian. From 1945 to 1995, Williams was at the helm of the British scientific quarterly *Endeavor*, and through the years contributed more than 1,500 articles and 4,000 book reviews to the periodical. Educated at Queen's College, Oxford, Williams first served as a research scholar at the School of Pathology before becoming deputy editor of *Endeavor* in 1945. Williams also wrote many books on the history of chemistry, science and technology including *The Twentieth Century* (1978), *Alfred Bernhard Nobel: Pioneer of High Explosives* (1973), *A Short History of Technology* (1960), and just a few days before his death his final work, *Our Scientific*

Heritage, was published. He also wrote biographies on English explorer Captain James Cook, Nobel Prize-winning pathologist Howard Florey, and chemist Robert Robinson. Williams also served on the council of the University College, Swansea, for 20 years and was a member of the British Science Museum's advisory council.

OBITUARIES AND OTHER SOURCES:

BOOKS

Who's Who, 145th edition, St. Martin's Press, 1993.

PERIODICALS

Times (London), October 23, 1996, p. 21.

*   *   *

WILLIAMS, Walter E(dward)   1936-

PERSONAL: Born March 31, 1936, in Philadelphia, PA; son of Catherine (a domestic worker) Williams; married Conchetta Taylor, 1960; children: one. *Ethnicity:* African American. *Education:* California State University, B.A., 1965; University of California at Los Angeles, M.A., 1967, Ph.D., 1972.

ADDRESSES: Office—Department of Economics, George Mason University, 4400 University Dr., Fairfax, VA 22030.

CAREER: Has worked as a taxi driver; Los Angeles City College, Los Angeles, instructor in economics, 1967-68; California State University, Los Angeles, assistant professor, 1967-71; Urban Institute, member of research staff, 1971-73; Temple University, Philadelphia, PA, associate professor of economics, 1973-80; George Mason University, Fairfax, VA, John M. Olin Distinguished Professor of Economics, 1980—. *Military service:* Served in the U.S. Army.

MEMBER: American Economics Association.

AWARDS, HONORS: Ford Foundation fellowship, 1970; Hoover Institute, national fellow, 1976; Faculty Member of the Year, George Mason University Alumni Association, 1985; named one of America's ten best college professors by Insight magazine, 1987.

WRITINGS:

(With James H. Reed) *Fundamentals of Business Mathematics,* W.C. Brown (Dubuque, IA), 1977.

(With Loren A. Smith and Wendell W. Gunn) *Black America and Organized Labor: A Fair Deal?,* Lincoln Institute for Research and Education (Washington, DC), 1979.

(With James T. Bennett) *Strategic Minerals: The Economic Impact of Supply Disruptions,* Heritage Foundation (Washington, DC), 1981.

America: A Minority Viewpoint, Hoover Institution Press (Stanford, CA), 1982.

The State Against Blacks, McGraw-Hill, (New York), 1982.

All It Takes Is Guts: A Minority View, Regnery Books (Washington, DC), 1987.

South Africa's War Against Capitalism, Praeger, 1989.

Do the Right Thing: The People's Economist Speaks, Hoover Institution Press, 1995.

Author of column for the *Philadelphia Tribune,* beginning in 1978; contributor to periodicals, including the *Saturday Evening Post, National Review,* and *American Economic Review.*

SIDELIGHTS: Walter E. Williams is a professor of economics at George Mason University and a nationally syndicated columnist. During the 1980s he gained a reputation as one of America's most conservative black voices. Williams, who earned advanced degrees from the University of California at Los Angeles, co-authored a business math textbook as well as two other joint efforts before the 1982 publication of his controversial book, *The State Against Blacks.* He is also the author of a nationally syndicated column.

In *The State Against Blacks,* Williams posits that African Americans are economically disadvantaged not because they live in a racist society, but rather because a host of government regulations combines with class bias to oppress them economically. This is an area into which Williams had already undertaken extensive scholarly investigations, beginning with his 1972 doctoral dissertation, *The Low Income Market Place.* In *The State Against Blacks,* Williams offers up statistical evidence—from minimum-wage laws to state and local licensing requirements for trade occupations—to support his theory that overregulation by the government has effectively kept those on the lowest rung of the economic ladder from even considering the possibility of upward mobility.

The *State Against Blacks* also tackles the standard concept of racial discrimination and attempts to debunk it. Williams points out how other minority groups have succeeded economically in America throughout the ages despite sometimes vicious discrimination, but the book's detractors mentioned that all other ethnic groups did not arrive in chains on American shores. Sherman W. Smith of the *West Coast Review of Books* pointed out that the author "would have us assume that before the laws and regulations of recent years, which he now contends to be a thorn in the path of their unemployment, the blacks stood on equal footing with the whites." Conversely, Chilton Williamson Jr., reviewing *The State Against Blacks* for the *National Review,* called it "a powerful assault against hoary myth and steadfast reaction, against complacency and ratiocination by rote."

All It Takes Is Guts: A Minority View is a collection of Williams's newspaper columns that he has written since 1978. Published in 1987, the book showcases Williams's no-nonsense approach to the problems that plague America's urban communities. In one essay, he recounts how his single mother, raising two children in an impoverished part of Philadelphia, would give him his lunch money in advance. Once, he spent it all by midweek and she refused to lend him more. Handouts do not work, he argues, and asserts that minorities in America do not participate in the free-market economy to their fullest advantage.

Williams also expanded his opinions on a controversial issue of the 1980s in the 1989 work *South Africa's War Against Capitalism.* Mass demonstrations took place in many American cities and on college campuses during the decade as liberals urged American businesses and universities not to invest or do business in South Africa because of its policy of apartheid. Williams often asserted that such political protests and boycotts were posturing. "They just want to take a cheap moral stand," he told the *Christian Science Monitor* in 1986. "It is moral posturing." In his book, Williams maintains that apartheid was not just a system of racial discrimination, but one that sought to limit free-market capitalism. He shows how sanctions—such as a two-decade United Nations ban on arms sales to the country—strengthened the system; when foreign companies left South Africa because of international pressure, white South Africans profited and were free to run their enterprises in any discriminatory way they chose.

BIOGRAPHICAL/CRITICAL SOURCES:

BOOKS

Contemporary Black Biography, Volume 4, Gale, 1993.

PERIODICALS

Book World, February 27, 1983, p. 3.
Choice, March, 1983, p. 1062; April, 1990, p. 1366.
Christian Science Monitor, September 16, 1986, p. 19.
Insight, May 11, 1987, p. 15.
Nation, April 2, 1983, p. 408.
National Review, November 26, 1982, p. 1499; January 22, 1990, p. 52; May 16, 1994, pp. 34-40.
Society, May/June, 1990, pp. 4-7.
USA Today, March 2, 1992, p. 9A.
Wall Street Journal, May 6, 1992, p. A1.
West Coast Review of Books, March/April, 1983, p. 46.

*   *   *

WILLIAMSON, Greg 1964-

PERSONAL: Born June 26, 1964, in Columbus, OH; son of John W. (a professor) and Margaret (Mathews) Williamson. *Education:* Vanderbilt University, B.A., 1986; University of Wisconsin—Madison, M.A., 1987; Johns Hopkins University, M.A., 1989.

ADDRESSES: Home—5704 Lofthill Ct., Alexandria, VA 22303. *Office*—Writing Seminars, 135 Gilman Hall, Johns Hopkins University, Baltimore, MD 21218.

CAREER: Johns Hopkins University, Baltimore, MD, lecturer in writing, 1989—.

AWARDS, HONORS: Nicholas Roerich Poetry Prize, 1995, for *The Silent Partner.*

WRITINGS:

The Silent Partner (poems), Story Line Press (Brownsville, OR), 1995.

Contributor of poems to journals, including *Poetry, Yale Review, Partisan Review, Paris Review, New Republic,* and *Southwest Review.*

WITZEL, Michael Karl 1960-

PERSONAL: Born January 22, 1960, in New Jersey; son of Karl D. and Gabriele (an illustrator) Witzel; married Gyvel Young. *Education:* Attended University of Texas at Arlington. *Avocational interests:* Photography, digital art.

ADDRESSES: Home—Wichita, KS. *Office*—c/o Motorbooks International, Box 1, 729 Prospect Ave., Osceola, WI 54020.

CAREER: Freelance writer.

MEMBER: International Petroliana Collectors Association, Society for Commercial Archeology.

AWARDS, HONORS: Thomas McKean Memorial Cup, Antique Automobile Club of America, 1992, and Nicholas-Joseph Cugnot Award of Distinction, Society of Automotive Historians, 1993, both for *The American Gas Station.*

WRITINGS:

The American Gas Station: History and Folklore of the Gas Station in American Car Culture, Motorbooks International (Osceola, WI), 1992.
The American Drive-In: History and Folklore of the Drive-In Restaurant, Motorbooks International, 1994.
Gas Station Memories, Motorbooks International, 1994.
Route 66 Remembered, Motorbooks International, 1996.

Columns include "Roadside America," in *Mobilia.* Contributor of photographs and articles to magazines, including *American Heritage of Invention and Technology, Rider, Route 66, Motorhome,* and *Volkswagen World.*

*   *   *

WOLFERMAN, Kristie C(arlson) 1948-

PERSONAL: Born November 9, 1948, in Kansas City, MO; daughter of Jack (in business) and Joann Elizabeth (a homemaker; maiden name, Plasterer) Carlson; married Frederick Ross Wolferman (a money manager), June 13, 1970; children: Stuart

Ross, Ethan Philip. *Education:* Middlebury College, B.A. (cum laude), 1970; University of Missouri, Kansas City, M.A., 1986. *Religion:* Presbyterian. *Avocational interests:* Tennis, hiking, reading, writing.

ADDRESSES: Home—1005 Brentwood Cir., Kansas City, MO 64112.

CAREER: Petit Appetit Cooking School for Young Cooks, founder and co-director, 1980-86; Pembroke Hill School, Kansas City, MO, elementary teacher, 1986—, teacher of seventh and eighth-grade writing workshops, 1994-96, also sponsor of several school activities and chairman of the language arts committee. Interviewed on public television; also appeared on public television doing cooking demonstrations. Has served as a docent at the Nelson-Atkins Museum of Art, beginning c. 1973; has done volunteer work with the March of Dimes.

MEMBER: International Reading Association; Friends of Art; Pi Beta Phi Alumnae Club; Historic Kansas City Foundation, Native Sons of Kansas City.

AWARDS, HONORS: Graybar American History Prize for outstanding senior thesis, 1970; honorary certificates of service, Nelson-Atkins Museum of Art, 1983, 1988; distinguished volunteer leadership grant, the March of Dimes, 1984; Alumni Faculty Grant from Crow Canyon Archaeology Center in Colorado, 1989, and from Bread Loaf Writers' Conference, 1991; recipient of the Green Chair for distinguished younger teachers, 1991-92; citizen ambassador and presenter, People-to-People Conference, Barcelona, Spain, 1995.

WRITINGS:

(With Mary Don Beachy) *When Peanut Butter Is Not Enough,* Petit Apetit (Kansas City, MO), 1986.
The Nelson-Atkins Museum of Art: Culture Comes to Kansas City, University of Missouri Press (Columbia, MO), 1993.

WORK IN PROGRESS: The Osage in Missouri, part of the "Missouri Heritage" series, expected publication in spring of 1997 by University of Missouri Press.

SIDELIGHTS: Kristie C. Wolferman has served professionally and as a volunteer in a variety of capacities. She founded a cooking school for young people, and helped to direct the institution for approximately six years. In the same vein, she did cooking demonstrations for public television, and co-authored her first book, *When Peanut Butter Is Not Enough,* with Mary Don Beachy.

Wolferman traces the history of the Nelson-Atkins Museum of Art in her 1993 work, *The Nelson-Atkins Museum of Art: Culture Comes to Kansas City.* A *Middlebury College Magazine* critic reviewing *Culture Comes to Kansas City* asserted that it was "one of the country's great art museums." She gives readers the life stories of the museum's two namesakes, Mary Atkins and William Rockhill Nelson, whose financial bequests formed the bulk of the financing used to establish the museum. The former was a reclusive widow and a relative unknown; the latter one of the better-known figures in Kansas City history as the editor and owner of the *Kansas City Star* newspaper. The estates of both, though Nelson's was much larger, eventually came together for the same purpose. Other benefactors, including J. C. Nichols, William Volker, and H. V. Jones, appear in the pages of *Culture Comes to Kansas City.*

In her book, Wolferman also discusses the museum itself, which was opened during the Great Depression of the 1930s. As Charles Coulter pointed out in the *Kansas City Star,* Wolferman's service as a docent at the Nelson-Atkins gave her easy access to the Nelson Gallery Archives; according to Coulter, "she has put them to good use, describing the museum from conception to the present." In that present, Coulter reported, the Nelson-Atkins contains not only a "stunning" collection of "European masterworks," respectable among galleries in the United States, but an Oriental art collection which is "one of the finest in the world." Also, as the subtitle of *Culture Comes to Kansas City* implies, Wolferman explains in the book the phenomenon that Coulter summed up thus: "How can a city like Kansas City, with its carefully nurtured inferiority complex, obtain and maintain a world-class facility such as the Nelson-Atkins Museum of Art?" Coulter felt that some of the author's detailing of the museum and its collection was "excessive," but concluded that for "her glowing tribute to the museum, she should be congratulated."

Wolferman told *CA:* "Even though I've had two books published, attended and taught many writing workshops, and write every day with my students, I don't really think of myself as a writer. I'm a wife, mother, teacher, organizer, friend, gardener, reader, tennis player, runner of errands, and a writer in my spare time. Being a writer is what I really want to be when I grow up, when I can afford myself the luxury of the time writing takes. Perhaps I'm getting close."

BIOGRAPHICAL/CRITICAL SOURCES:

PERIODICALS

Kansas City Star, December 19, 1993, p. J9.
Middlebury College Magazine, spring, 1994, p. 7.

* * *

WOLKEN, Jerome J(ay) 1917-

PERSONAL: Born March 28, 1917, in Pittsburgh, PA; son of Abraham I. and Dina (Lando) Wolken; married Dorothy O. Mallinger, June 19, 1945 (died, 1954); married Tobey J. Holstein, January 26, 1956; children: (first marriage) Ann Alex, A. Jonathan; (second marriage) H. Johanna, Erik Andrew. *Education:* Attended Pennsylvania State University, 1935-36, and Duquesne University, 1937-39; University of Pittsburgh, B.S., 1946, M.S., 1948, Ph.D., 1949.

ADDRESSES: Home—5817 Elmer St., Pittsburgh, PA 15232. *Office*—Department of Biological Sciences, Mellon Institute, Carnegie-Mellon University, 4400 Fifth Ave., Pittsburgh, PA 15213.

CAREER: Carnegie Institute of Technology (now Carnegie-Mellon University), Pittsburgh, PA, research fellow at Mellon Institute, 1943-47; Rockefeller University, research fellow, 1950-52; University of Pittsburgh, Pittsburgh, PA, research associate, 1953-54, assistant professor, 1954-57, associate professor, 1957-61, professor of ophthalmology and biophysics, 1961-64, research professor of physiology and ophthalmology, 1961-67, head of Eye Research Laboratory, Eye and Ear Hospital, 1954-57, director of Biophysical Research Laboratory, Eye and Ear Hospital, 1957-61; Carnegie-Mellon University, professor of biophysics and biological sciences, 1964—, department head, 1964-67, head of Biophysical Research Laboratory, 1964-76, research fellow at Carnegie Museum of Natural History, 1976—. Guest professor at universities and colleges, including Pennsylvania State University, 1963, University of Paris, 1967-68, 1971-72, University of Miami, Coral Gables, FL, 1967, University of London, 1971-72, and Pasteur Institute, Paris, 1972; Princeton University, research professor, 1978; Tohoku University, exchange professor, 1988. Inventor of an optical device lens for the visually handicapped, which can also be used for solar energy collection. *Military service:* U.S. Naval Reserve, active duty, 1941-43.

MEMBER: American Association for the Advancement of Science (fellow), Optical Society of America (fellow; president, 1964-65), American Institute of Chemists (fellow), American Chemical Society, American Society of Plant Physiologists, American Institute of Biological Sciences, Biophysical Society, Society of Gen. Physiologists, American Society of Cell Biology, Society for Neuroscience, Japanese Society for the Promotion of Science in Japan (fellow), Pennsylvania Academy of Sciences, New York Academy of Sciences (fellow), Sigma Xi, Phi Sigma, Explorers Club (fellow), Chemists Club of New York.

AWARDS, HONORS: Fellow of Atomic Energy Commission, 1949-50, and (in France), 1967-68, American Cancer Society, 1950, National Research Council, 1950, 1951-52, National Council to Combat Blindness (in Europe), 1957, and American Philosophical Society (in South America and the Galapagos Islands), 1970; Career Award, U.S. Public Health Service, 1962-65; grants from National Institutes of Health, National Science Foundation, and National Aeronautics and Space Administration.

WRITINGS:

Euglena: An Experimental Organism for Biochemical and Biophysical Studies, Rutgers University Press (New Brunswick, NJ), 1961, revised edition, Appleton (New York City), 1967.

Vision: Biochemistry and Biophysics of the Retina, C.C Thomas (Springfield, IL), 1966.

Photobiology, Reinhold Publishing (New York City), 1967.

Invertebrate Photoreceptors, Academic Press (New York City), 1971.

Photoprocesses, Photoreceptors, and Evolution, Academic Press (New York City), 1975.

(With Glenn Brown) *Liquid Crystals and Biological Structures,* Academic Press, 1979.

Light and Life Processes, Van Nostrand (New York City), 1986.

Light Detectors, Photoreceptors, and Imaging Systems in Nature, Oxford University Press (Oxford, England), 1995.

Editor of two scientific books. Contributor of more than a hundred-twenty articles to scholarly journals.

WRISTON, Walter B(igelow) 1919-

PERSONAL: Born August 3, 1919, in Middletown, CT; son of Henry Merritt (a history professor) and Ruth Colton (a chemistry teacher; maiden name, Bigelow) Wriston; married Barbara Brengle, October 24, 1942 (died, 1966); married Kathryn Ann Dineen (a lawyer), March 14, 1968; children: (first marriage) Catherine. *Education:* Wesleyan University, B.A. (with distinction), 1941; attended Ecole Francaise Middlebury, 1941; Tufts University, M.A., 1942; attended American Institute of Banking, 1946. *Avocational interests:* Reading, tennis.

ADDRESSES: Home—New York, NY. *Office*—Citicorp Bldg., Lexington Ave., New York, NY. *Agent*—c/o Scribner Educational Publishers, 866 3rd Ave., New York, NY 10022.

CAREER: U.S. Department of State, Washington, DC, junior foreign service officer, 1942; First National City Bank (became First National City Corporation), New York City, inspector in controller's division, 1946-50, assistant cashier, 1950-52, assistant vice president, 1952-54, vice president, 1954-58, senior vice president, 1958-60, executive vice president, 1960-67, president, 1968-70, chair and chief executive officer, 1970-84; writer. Director of various companies, including J. C. Penney Co., General Electric Co., and Chubb Corporation. Member of various commissions, including National Commission on Productivity and Labor-Management Advisory Committee, both 1970-74. *Military service:* U.S. Army, 1942-46.

MEMBER: Council of Foreign Relations, Business Council.

WRITINGS:

Risk and Other Four-Letter Words (essays), Harper (New York), 1986.

The Twilight of Sovereignty: How the Information Revolution Is Transforming Our World, Scribner (New York), 1992.

SIDELIGHTS: Walter B. Wriston is a notable banking executive who enjoyed considerable authority during his fourteen-year tenure as head of First National City Corporation (Citicorp). Wriston entered the banking profession in 1946 after having served briefly in the U.S. State Department and having completed three years of military service. Wriston first joined First National City Bank (Citibank) as a junior inspector in 1946; he held that position until 1949, when he became assistant cashier. By the early 1950s he had risen to vice president, and in the middle of the decade he assumed control of the bank's overseas divisions.

During his years in various vice presidential positions, Wriston proved an innovative and ambitious executive. In 1961, for instance, he helped create certificates of deposit (CD's), that offered substantially improved interest rates to companies interested in investing significant amounts ($100,000 or more) of surplus funds. At the same time, Wriston expanded the company's foreign divisions, thus making Citibank America's most prominent bank overseas.

In 1967 Wriston assumed the presidency of Citibank, and within a year of his leadership the bank became the nation's second largest bank with regard to total assets. Two years later he supervised the division of Citibank into five departments handling various aspects of financial operations. In addition, he helped develop the First National City Corporation (Citicorp), a holding company that assumed ownership of Citibank. As a corporation, Citicorp was able to participate in financial dealings unlawful to banks. Wriston's influence ultimately generated significantly greater profits, which were, in turn, passed on to Citibank customers through expanded services.

In 1970 Wriston was named chair and chief executive officer of both Citibank and Citicorp. He devoted himself to increasing Citicorp's profits, and by 1976 he had succeeded in doubling the corporation's asset growth. In addition, he implemented a then-revolutionary electronic banking system that enabled Citibank customers throughout the United States to enact transactions by machine.

During his chairmanship of Citibank and Citicorp Wriston occasionally courted controversy. He maintained a staunch advocacy of free-market economics and decried government interference in business, suggesting that federal intervention would scarcely be tolerated if directed towards academia or the press. He was also critical of the press, declaring that many writers inflated the importance of various events and thus were guilty of abusing the right of free press. Wriston asserted himself during New York City's economic crisis of the late 1970s, during which he called for more rigid budgetary guidelines from the city in return for further monetary aid from banks and investors.

In 1984 then sixty-five-year-old Wriston resigned from Citibank and Citicorp. Maintaining an office at the Citicorp Center, he is still interested in banking and business. Wriston has written two books on the subject, including 1986's *Risk and Other Four-Letter Words,* a collection of essays—derived from Wriston's speeches—on business-related subjects such as federal intervention and corporate taxation. Martin Mayer, writing in the *New York Times Book Review,* noted that Wriston's essays are "polemical in intent and execution," and added that "these pieces deal not so much with the issues of the day as with the philosophical underpinnings that enable true believers in the magic of the market to know instantly where they stand when an issue comes to their attention."

Wriston is also the author of *The Twilight of Sovereignty: How the Information Revolution Is Transforming Our World,* in which he explores the ways in which technology has changed business and communication. In particular, he argues that the stability of countries and companies may be undermined by the ready availability of information. As Peter Coy observed in *Business Week:* "Wriston writes that the information revolution is undermining the sovereignty of nations and corporations by giving the power of knowledge to anyone with a brain, a [personal computer], and an electrical outlet." Among the supporters of *The Twilight of Sovereignty* is Gerard A. Elfstrom, who wrote in *National Forum* that Wriston's volume "is significant for its wealth of concrete examples and his perspective as a central participant in the events he seeks to understand."

BIOGRAPHICAL/CRITICAL SOURCES:

BOOKS

Zweig, Phillip L., *The Man Who Owned the World: Walter Wriston, Citibank, and the Rise and Fall of American Financial Supremacy,* Crown (New York), 1995.

PERIODICALS

Boston Globe, November 17, 1992.
Business Week, October 12, 1992, pp. 14-16.
Christian Science Monitor, October 16, 1992, p. 8.
Far Eastern Economic Review, May 13, 1993, p. 46.
Fortune, November 30, 1992, p. 150.
New York Times, February 16, 1986, p. 21; April 25, 1993, p. C8.
New York Times Book Review, December 13, 1992.
Wall Street Journal, September 10, 1992, p. A12.*

WU, Edna
  See WU, Qingyun

*   *   *

WU, Qingyun 1950-
  (Edna Wu)

PERSONAL: Born August 28, 1950, in Hebei, China; immigrated to the United States, 1985; daughter of Ming and Xuejin (Zhao) Wu; married Yulong Jin, 1979 (marriage ended, 1996); children: Lin. *Ethnicity:* "Chinese." *Education:* Henan University, B.A.; Southern Illinois University, Carbondale, M.A., Pennsylvania State University, Ph.D. *Politics:* None. *Religion:* None. *Avocational interests:* Dance, theater, travel, movies.

ADDRESSES: Home—1233 North Hartview Ave., Valinda, CA 91744. *Office*—Chinese Studies Center, California State University, 5151 State University Dr., Los Angeles, CA 90032; fax 213-343-4234. *E-mail*—qwu@calstatela.edu.

CAREER: Zhengzhou University, Zhengzhou, China, lecturer in English, 1978-85; Pennsylvania State University, University Park, lecturer in Chinese, 1987-90; University of Texas at Austin, lecturer in Chinese, 1990-91; California State University, Los Angeles, assistant professor of Chinese, 1991—, director of Chinese Studies Center, and coordinator of Chinese Program.

MEMBER: Modern Language Association of America, Association of Asian Studies, Society for Utopian Studies, American Association of Comparative Literature.

AWARDS, HONORS: Academic Merit Prize for Translation, 1986, for *Liushu Fengsheng;* Outstanding Academic Book citation, *Choice,* 1996, for *Female Rule in Chinese and English Literary Utopias.*

WRITINGS:

(Translator with Shi Tianting) Kenneth Graham, *Liushu Fengsheng* (title means "The Wind in the Willows"), Henan Children's Press (Henan, China), 1985.
(Translator) *Nuowei Tonghua Xuan* (title means "Norwegian Fairy Tales"), Haiyan (Petrel) Press (China), 1986.

(Translator) Edgar Rice Burroughs, *Renyuan Taishan* (title means "Tarzan of the Apes"), Huanghe Literature and Arts Press (China), 1987.
(Translator with Thomas Beebee) Bai Hua, *The Remote Country of Women* (novel), University of Hawaii Press (Honolulu, HI), 1994.
Clouds and Rain: A China-to-America Memoir (novel), Evanston Publishing (Evanston, IL), 1994.
Female Rule in Chinese and English Literary Utopias, Syracuse University Press (Syracuse, NY), 1995.

Contributor of articles and translations to periodicals, including *Cowrie: Chinese Journal of Comparative Literature.* Some writings appear under the name Edna Wu.

WORK IN PROGRESS: Lesbian Literature by Chinese Women: A Critical Anthology; An Annotated Bibliography of Chinese Women's Literature, Feminist Criticism, and Translations, from the classical period to the present; *Discovering the Lost Tanci by Chinese Women,* about the poetic fiction form popular in China from the eighteenth to the early twentieth centuries; *A Male Mother,* a novel; *Two Eves in the Garden of Eden,* a screenplay.

SIDELIGHTS: Qingyun Wu told *CA:* "I came to the United States in 1985 and was very impressed by western feminist theories in general. When I started my doctoral study at Penn State in 1987, I had a strong desire to re-examine Chinese literature through a feminist critical eye. After some preliminary research, I decided to focus on the theme of female rule and the problem of women in Chinese and British and American literatures. I chose this comparative perspective for two major reasons: the issue of Chinese feminism in utopian literature had not yet been studied, and feminist utopian studies were largely Eurocentric. My desire to fill a blank in Chinese literary research and break ground in East-West comparative studies sustained my efforts in the following years until the work was completed in the form of a book in 1994. Although I benefited from the work of many authors in both the east and the west, I disliked trendy theoretical jargons. I preferred solid contextual research and honest analysis of the original texts. To me, writing can be very easy, if you are clear about what you want to say.

"Recently, I have been doing research on Chinese lesbian literature and Chinese women's *tanci* novels. I chose these subjects, again, because there is a lack or a blank. Moreover, I like to make marginal voices heard in the din of mainstream cultures. I will adhere to my East-West comparative strategy, because I do not wish this marginal voice to be heard only by China specialists.

"Apart from academic work, I do occasional creative writing. I like to write in a form that suits the mood at the moment I am writing. My novel *Clouds and Rain* is a typical example. I do not care what publishers, readers, and critics think of my writing, but I am sure there must be somebody who can appreciate it; that is, share the music of my soul."

*   *   *

WUERZBACH, Natascha 1933-

PERSONAL: Surname also transliterated as Wurzbach; born December 1, 1933, in Munich, Germany; daughter of Friedrich (an author) and Baroness Dolly (a modern dancer; maiden name, Massenbach) Wuerzbach. *Education:* University of Munich, doctorate, 1964. *Avocational interests:* writing fiction, music, gardening.

ADDRESSES: Home—Asbergplatz 13, 50937 Cologne, 41 Federal Republic of Germany. *Office*— Department of English, University of Cologne, Albertus-Magnus Platz, D 50923 Cologne, 41 Federal Republic of Germany.

CAREER: University of Munich, Federal Republic of Germany, junior lecturer, 1963-74; University of Cologne, Federal Republic of Germany, professor of English, 1975—.

MEMBER: Hochschulverband, Kommission fuer Volksdichtung der Societe Internationale d'Ethnologie et de Folklore, Anglistentag Verband Deutscher Anglisten.

WRITINGS:

Die Struktur des Briefromans und seine Entstehung in England, [Munich], 1964.
(Editor) *The Novel in Letters, Epistolary Fiction in the Early English Novel, 1678-1740,* [London], 1969.
(Editor) *British Theatre: Eighteenth Century English Drama,* [Frankfurt], 1969.
Anfaenge und gattungstypische Ausformung der englischen Strassenballade, 1550-1650, [Munich],

1981, English translation by Gayna Walls published as *The Rise of the English Street Ballad, 1550-1650,* Cambridge University Press, 1990.
(Editor with Marion Kannen) *Herzdame: Freundschaft und Liebe zwischen Frauen* (title means "Queen of Hearts: Friendship and Love between Women"), Kiepenheuer & Witsch (Cologne), 1993.
(With Simone M. Salz) *Motif Index of the Child Corpus: The English and Scottish Ballads,* translated from the original German manuscript by Gayna Walls, de Gruyter (Berlin), 1995.

Contributor of articles and reviews to professional journals, including *Poetics,* and to collections of essays.

WORK IN PROGRESS: Female development in the modern English novel.

SIDELIGHTS: In her 1990 book, *The Rise of the English Street Ballad, 1550-1650,* Natascha Wuerzbach provides an "exhaustive study" of that ancient type of verse according to Michael D. Bristol in *Renaissance Quarterly.* Originally published in German in 1981, the work focuses on traditional British rhymes of approximately one hundred lines that were sung or recited by street singers at sixteenth- and seventeenth-century markets and fairs. Besides being enjoyed in their oral presentation, the ballads were printed on single sheets of paper and sold to listeners. While many scholars have disregarded the street ballad as minor literature, Wuerzbach offers detailed analyses of more than two hundred ballad fragments and divides them into narrative, dramatic, and discursive in content. She also includes what Louis James in *Reviews of English Studies* called an "excellent account of early opposition to the street ballad."

In her *Modern Philology* review, Rochelle Smith asserted that *The Rise of the English Street Ballad, 1550-1650* is a welcome addition to literature on the British street ballads, noting that only one other book-length study on the topic has been published. London *Times* reviewer Michael Grosvenor Myer and Bristol responded favorably to Wuerzbach's exploration of the various devices used in the ballads by street singers eager to sell their "wares." According to Myer, the book contains "a cogent and fascinating exposition of the street ballad's relationship to the early journalistic press, and of the differences between 17th and 20th century journalism." Bristol maintained that "Wurzbach's book is an important contribution . . .

for its ground-clearing investigation of the social and communicative aspects of the street ballad." Smith concluded: "Perhaps the work's greatest impact will be to stir new interest in this fascinating but much neglected genre."

BIOGRAPHICAL/CRITICAL SOURCES:

PERIODICALS

Modern Philology, May, 1992, pp. 545-47.
Renaissance Quarterly, autumn, 1991, pp. 617-19.

Reviews of English Studies, February, 1993, pp. 93-94.
Times (London), September 22, 1990.
Times Literary Supplement, August 23, 1991, p. 5.

*   *   *

WURZBACH, Natascha
  See WUERZBACH, Natascha

Y-Z

YAP, Arthur   1943-

PERSONAL: Born January 11, 1943, in Singapore. *Education:* University of Singapore, B.A. (honors), 1965; University of Leeds, M.A., 1975; National University of Singapore, Ph.D., 1984.

ADDRESSES: Office—Department of English Language and Literature, National University of Singapore, Kent Ridge, Singapore 0511.

CAREER: Ministry of Education, Singapore, education officer, 1965-78; National University of Singapore, senior lecturer, 1979—.

AWARDS, HONORS: National Book Development Council of Singapore's Poetry award, 1976, 1982, 1988; Southeast Asia Writers award, 1983; Singapore's Cultural Medallion for poetry, 1983.

WRITINGS:

POETRY

Only Lines, Federal Publications (Singapore), 1971.
Five Takes, University of Singapore Press (Singapore), 1974.
Commonplace, Heinemann (Singapore), 1978.
Down the Line, Heinemann, 1980.
Man Snake Apple, Heinemann, 1986.

OTHER

A Brief Critical Survey of Prose Writings in Singapore and Malaysia, Educational Publications Bureau (Singapore), 1971.

Singapore Short Stories, Heinemann, 1978.
(Editor) *Language Education in Multilingual Societies,* RELC (Singapore), 1978.
English Grammar and Usage, Federal Publications, 1981.
Thematic Structure in Poetic Discourse, Copinter (Singapore), 1987.

*   *   *

YAU, John   1950-

PERSONAL: Born in 1950.

ADDRESSES: Office—P.O. Box 1910, Canal Street Station, New York, NY 10013.

CAREER: Art critic and independent curator. Distinguished visiting critic, Pratt Institute (Graduate School of Art), 1985-90, Maryland Institute, College of Art, spring, 1986, and School of Visual Arts, 1988-90; visiting poet, Brown University, spring, 1992: visiting scholar, Getty Center, winter, 1993; visiting professor, University of California, Berkeley, spring, 1994, and spring, 1995. Ahmanson Curatorial Fellow, Museum of Contemporary Art, Los Angeles, 1993-96.

AWARDS, HONORS: National Endowment for the Arts fellowship, 1977-78; Ingram Merrill Foundation fellowship, 1979-80, 1985-86; New York Foundation for the Arts award, 1988; Lavan award, 1988; General Electric Foundation award, 1988; Brendan Gill award, 1992; Jerome Shestack prize, 1993.

WRITINGS:

POETRY

Crossing Canal Street, Bellevue Press (Binghamton, NY), 1976.

The Reading of an Ever-Changing Tale, Nobodaddy Press (Clinton, NY), 1977.

Sometimes, Sheep Meadow Press (New York), 1979.

The Sleepless Night of Eugene Delacroix, Release Press (New York), 1980.

Notarikon, Jordan Davies (New York), 1981.

Broken Off by the Music, Burning Deck (Providence, RI), 1981.

Corpse and Mirror, Holt Rinehart (New York), 1983.

Radiant Silhouette: New and Selected Work 1974-1988, Black Sparrow Press (Santa Rosa, CA), 1989.

Dragon's Blood, Collectif Generacion (Colombes, France), 1989.

Big City Primer: Reading New York at the End of the Twentieth Century, Timken (New York), 1991.

Edificio Sayonara, Black Sparrow Press, 1992.

Postcards from Trakl, ULAE (New York), 1994.

Berlin Diptychon, Timken, 1995.

OTHER

(Editor with David Kermani) *Fairfield Porter: The Collected Poems with Selected Drawings,* Tibor de Nagy (New York), 1985.

In the Realm of Appearances: The Art of Andy Warhol, Ecco Press (Hopewell, NJ), 1993.

A.R. Penck, Abrams (New York), 1993.

Hawaiian Cowboys (novel), Black Sparrow Press, 1994.

*   *   *

YEAGER, Chuck 1923-

PERSONAL: Full name, Charles Elwood Yeager; born February 13, 1923, in Myra, WV; son of Albert Hal (a natural gas driller) and Susie May (a homemaker; maiden name, Sizemore) Yeager; married Glennis Faye Dickhouse (a homemaker), February 26, 1945; children: Sharon Yeager Flick, Susan F., Donald C., Michael D. *Ethnicity:* "Caucasian." *Education:* Air Command and Staff School, graduated 1952; Air War College, graduated 1961. *Politics:* Republican. *Religion:* Methodist. *Avocational interests:* Hunting, fishing, flying.

ADDRESSES: Home—P.O. Box 128, Cedar Ridge, CA 95924-0128.

CAREER: Enlisted in the U.S. Air Force, 1941, flew missions in Europe during World War II (shot down thirteen enemy aircraft), 1943-46, experimental flight test pilot, 1945-54, various command assignments in the United States, Germany, Spain, and France, 1954-62, commander of the 405th Fighter Wing, Seymour Johnson Air Force Base, NC, 1968-69, became brigadier general, 1969, vice commander of 17th Air Force, Ramstein Air Base, Germany, 1969-71, flew missions in the Vietnam War, U.S. defense representative to Pakistan, 1971-73, special assistant to commander of Air Force Inspection and Safety Center, Norton Air Force Base, CA, 1973, director of aerospace safety, 1973-75, retired, 1975; founded Yeager Consulting, 1975—. Has appeared on television, in film, and in commercials.

AWARDS, HONORS: Received the Distinguished Service Medal with oak leaf cluster, Silver Star with oak leaf cluster, Legion of Merit with oak leaf cluster, Distinguished Flying Cross with two oak leaf clusters, Bronze star with V device, Air Medal with 10 oak leaf clusters, Air Force Commendation medal, and Purple Heart during his years of military service; Mackay Trophy and Robert J. Collier Trophy from the National Aeronautic Association of the U.S.A., 1947, for the first supersonic flight in the XS-1; FAI Gold Air Medal from the International Aeronautical Federation (France), 1948; named one of Ten Outstanding Young Americans by the United States Jaycees, 1954; inducted into the International Space Hall of Fame, 1981; Theodore Roosevelt Distinguished Service Medal from the Theodore Roosevelt Association, 1985; Presidential Medal of Freedom, from the United States Executive Office of the President, 1985; Bradford Washburn Award from the Boston Museum of Science, 1985; Horatio Alger Award from the Horatio Alger Association of Distinguished Americans. Honorary degrees: D.Sc. from West Virginia University, 1948; D.Sc. from Marshall University, 1969; D.Aero.Sci from Salem College, 1975.

WRITINGS:

(With Leo Janos) *Yeager: An Autobiography,* Bantam (Toronto, Ontario), c. 1985.

(With Charles Leerhsen) *Press On! Further Adventures in the Good Life* (autobiography), Bantam (New York), 1988.

SIDELIGHTS: Brigadier General Chuck Yeager has had a distinguished and newsworthy career in the U.S. Air Force. During World War II he served as a fighter pilot, downing 13 German planes and once having his plane shot down. He earned several medals in the course of the war, including a Purple Heart. After the war's end, he became a test pilot for experimental aircraft, and it is in this capacity that he is best known to the world. In 1947, piloting an aircraft known as the XS-1, Yeager became the first man to fly faster than the speed of sound. As aircraft became increasingly sophisticated, Yeager continued to break flight records. During the 1960s and 1970s, he flew missions in the Vietnam War, achieving the rank of brigadier general in 1969. He retired from the Air Force in 1975, and formed his own consulting firm, Yeager, Inc. His activities included advising aircraft manufacturers, then public speaking and commercial spots after journalist Tom Wolfe recounted Yeager's achievements and his influence on the U.S. space program in the 1979 book, *The Right Stuff,* which was made into a motion picture in 1983. In collaboration with writer Leo Janos, Yeager wrote an account of his life, and the resulting book, *Yeager: An Autobiography,* became an immediate best-seller and topped the *New York Times* nonfiction list upon publication in 1985. Yeager explained to Esther B. Fein in the *New York Times:* "Nothing was wrong with Mr. Wolfe's book, although he did take a lot of liberties in describing how we felt and what we thought, and I wanted people to understand, from me, that sense of dedication and loyalty. A lot's been written before about the X-1 and the X-1A, but none told it exactly the way it was because none were written by me." Yeager followed the success of *Yeager* with another book, co-written with Charles Leerhsen, 1988's *Press On! Further Adventures in the Good Life.* Discussing the famous pilot and his first book in the *Detroit News,* writer Steve Thorpe declared that "Yeager is a true American hero, a symbol of the intrepid, curious, enterprising American spirit."

Yeager was born in 1923 in West Virginia, into a large, working-class family. He inherited his father's mechanical abilities and entered the U.S. Air Force as an airplane mechanic before World War II. As the war progressed, the Air Force became increasingly interested in finding pilots to fly missions against the Germans and the Japanese, and Yeager jumped at the chance to learn to fly. He relates in *Yeager,* however, that he was airsick during his first few flights. He overcame this initial weakness to fly several successful missions against the Germans—on one occasion,

he shot down five German planes in one day. On another day, however, Yeager himself was shot down by the Germans. When he landed he was picked up by members of the French Resistance, who helped him escape to Spain; once he reached Spain, however, he was captured and imprisoned by local authorities. He escaped his cell by cutting its bars with a small saw that he had hidden in his uniform.

One of Yeager's first assignments following World War II was as an Air Force flight instructor. But he soon transferred to the experimental test pilot program, flying high-speed rocket planes. He had attained the rank of captain by the time he broke the sound barrier—an achievement several other men died trying to accomplish. He described the experience in *Yeager:* "The faster I got, the smoother the ride was. Suddenly . . . [I was] flying supersonic! It was so smooth that Grandma would be sitting up there sipping lemonade. . . . The guys in the . . . tracking van interrupted to report they heard what sounded like a distant rumble of thunder: my sonic boom! The first one by an airplane ever heard on earth."

Yeager himself nearly died on at least one of his subsequent test flights—one that set a speed record for that time (1953) of 1650 miles an hour. He attained an altitude of seventy thousand feet, then his plane went out of control. He dropped fifty thousand feet before he managed to regain control and land the plane. Yeager attributes his longevity through such a risky career not only to luck, but to his careful preparation and knowledge of his equipment. Speaking of the death of a fellow fighter pilot, Richard Bong, to *Detroit Free Press* book editor Bob McKelvey, Yeager explained: "Dick wasn't interested in doing his homework." Bong died because he hadn't read in his flight manual how to activate an auxiliary fuel pump.

When Yeager retired from the Air Force in 1975, he taped for their archives much of the material that later went into *Yeager.* The book, which the Bantam publishing firm persuaded him to write, also features stories about Yeager from his friends and his wife, Glennis. Most reviewers of *Yeager* were quite positive; a negative note, however, was sounded by Christopher Lehmann-Haupt of the *New York Times.* He mentioned a "sense of mechanical banality" in the autobiography, and while he acknowledged the value of Yeager's story, felt that "its telling has largely leached it of its earthiness and vitality." Yet he conceded that within the pages of *Yeager* "you do glimpse the features of an authentic American hero—

a good old country boy who wanted nothing out of life but to fish and hunt and fly, yet who was cool in the face of death." Other critics gushed outright, such as Stanley L. Colbert in the Toronto *Globe and Mail*, who asserted of Yeager: "His stories of combat are fascinating and his account of his days as a test pilot, both before his singular feat and afterward as a world celebrity, are awesome." While Thorpe observed that Yeager's "descriptions of the grueling flight-testing and the wild carousing afterwards . . . are more interesting than Wolfe's," he attested that "Yeager is at his best in the book when writing about personal things."

Yeager's second book, *Press On! Further Adventures in the Good Life,* focuses primarily on his adventures after Wolfe helped return him to the public eye. It recounts both wilderness expeditions engaging in his hobbies of fishing and hunting, and interesting occurrences on book tours and as a commercial spokesperson. *Chicago Tribune* contributor Wes Smith reported that "in its brighter passages, this follow-up to the 1985 best-selling autobiography" relates the leisure activities of Yeager and long-time friend and fellow aviator Clarence Anderson—which Smith went on to describe as "Butch Cassidy and the Sundance Kid go airborne, if you will. Tom and Huck get rank. *Mano a mano* stuff. More fun than aerial combat, even." Burt Hochberg in the *New York Times Book Review* hailed *Press On!* as a "very entertaining mix of reminiscences."

BIOGRAPHICAL/CRITICAL SOURCES:

BOOKS

Ayres, Carter M., *Chuck Yeager: Fighter Pilot,* Lerner, 1988.
Contemporary Heroes and Heroines, Book I, Gale, 1990.
Cox, Donald W., *America's Explorers of Space,* Hammond, 1967.
Levinson, Nancy S., *Chuck Yeager: The Man Who Broke the Sound Barrier: A Science Biography,* Walker & Co., 1988.
Lundgren, William R., *Across the High Frontier: The Story of a Test Pilot, Major Charles E. Yeager, USAF,* Morrow, 1955.
Wolfe, Tom, *The Right Stuff,* Farrar, Straus, 1979.
Yeager, Chuck, and Leo Janos, *Yeager: An Autobiography,* Bantam, 1985.
Yeager, Chuck, and Charles Leerhsen, *Press On! Further Adventures in the Good Life,* Bantam, 1988.

PERIODICALS

Chicago Tribune, September 14, 1988.
Detroit Free Press, August 3, 1985.
Detroit News, June 30, 1985.
Globe and Mail (Toronto), July 27, 1985.
New York Times, June 26, 1985; July 1, 1985; December 2, 1985.
New York Times Book Review, November 6, 1988, p. 23.
Time, July 29, 1985, p. 69.

—*Sketch by Elizabeth Wenning*

* * *

YOUNG, Rosamond M. 1912-

PERSONAL: Born October 4, 1912, in Dayton, OH; daughter of Harry (a commercial artist) and Isabel (a homemaker; maiden name, Gilbert) McPherson; married William Adam Young (a camp director), November 17, 1953. *Ethnicity:* "White." *Education:* Oberlin College, A.B., 1930, A.M., 1936. *Politics:* Republican. *Religion:* Episcopalian. *Avocational interests:* Gardening, painting, travel, music.

ADDRESSES: Home—6441 Far Hills Ave., Dayton, OH 45459; fax 937-436-7721. *Agent*—Jane Jordan Browne, Multimedia Product Development, Inc., 410 South Michigan Blvd., Suite 724, Chicago, IL 60605.

CAREER: Teacher of Latin, German, English, and journalism at public schools in Dayton, OH, 1939-70; *Dayton Daily News,* Dayton, columnist, 1970-82, weekly columnist, 1982—.

MEMBER: Authors League of America, Society of Children's Book Writers and Illustrators.

AWARDS, HONORS: Aviation Space Writing Award, Space Writers of America, 1979, for *Twelve Seconds to the Moon;* Flying Colonel Award, Delta Airlines; Women in Communications Award, 1984; Distinguished Daytonian Award, Miami Jacobs Junior College, 1985; Thanks for the Memories Award, Alzheimer's Society, 1988; Humane Society of Greater Dayton, Cat's Meow Award, 1989, Caring and Sharing Award, 1991; fifteen Tops in Ohio Awards, Ohio Newspaper Women's Association, for columns; Litt.D., University of Dayton, 1994.

WRITINGS:

(Coauthor) *English I,* American Book Co. (New York), 1947.

(Coauthor) *English II,* American Book Co., 1947.

(Coauthor) *Our English Language,* Books 9-12, American Book Co., 1952.

Boss Ket (biography), Longmans, Green (New York), 1961.

Made of Aluminum (biography), McKay (New York), 1965.

The Spy with Two Hats (biography), McKay, 1966.

Queen of the North Parlor (collected columns), Landfall Press (Dayton, OH), 1976.

Twelve Seconds to the Moon, Journal Herald (Dayton), 1978, revised edition, U.S. Air Force Museum Foundation (Dayton), 1983.

Cat, Thy Name Is Edith (essays), Orange Frazer Press (Wilmington, OH), 1991.

Two Perfectly Marvellous Cats, J. N. Townsend Publishing (Exeter, NH), 1996.

WORK IN PROGRESS: A second book on Edith, for J. N. Townsend Publishing.

SIDELIGHTS: Rosamond M. Young told *CA:* "When I was twelve, *Winnie the Pooh* was published. My father gave me a copy for my birthday. It is a first edition, and I have it still. I fell in love with the book because it was more than the story of Christopher Robin and his friends in the hundred-acre wood. I loved it for its subtleties.

"I saved money from my allowance to buy the other Pooh books and learned them by heart. I told my parents I was going to write books when I grew up. My father bought me a little Remington portable typewriter, and I sat right down and wrote a book titled *The Life and Times of Napoleon Bonami,* typed on half-sheets of paper. I made a cover for it out of cardboard and adhesive tape, illustrated it, and gave it to my father. He paid me five dollars for it.

"At school, whenever the principal came into the room, the teacher asked me to read my latest composition aloud for him, and I found that it is fun to show off. My interest in writing made friends for me in college, including the love of my life, an English professor.

"The first week I taught school, all the teachers received a copy of *Ohio Schools,* the magazine of the Ohio Education Association. I noticed that teachers wrote articles for it. The second week of teaching, I wrote an article and sent it in. The article was printed, and ink flowed through my veins.

"A few years later, I was invited by the president of the American Book Company to come to New York and discuss being a textbook author. That was in 1944, and when the first books bearing my name were printed, I took copies to my mother and said, 'See, I told you I was going to write books.' She laughed and answered, 'I thought all little girls told their mothers that.'

"I have written texts and biographies and hundreds of newspaper columns and two books about cats. I like the cats books best, and I am going to write some more of them.

"All that I have written I owe to Winnie the Pooh."

* * *

ZAMIR, Israel 1929-

PERSONAL: Born June 28, 1929, in Warsaw, Poland; citizen of Israel; son of Isaac Bashevis (a writer) and Rachel (a teacher) Singer; married, August 17, 1960; wife's name, Aviva (a teacher); children: Meirav, Noam, Ilan, Yuval. *Education:* Attended Oranim College, 1959; Tel-Aviv University, B.A., 1983. *Politics:* Labor Party. *Religion:* Jewish.

ADDRESSES: Home—Kibbutz Beit-Alfa, 19140, Israel. *Agent*—Orly Peker, Namir RD 21, Tel-Aviv.

CAREER: Journalist. *Hotam* (weekly magazine), editor; *Al-Hamishmar* (daily newspaper), began as journalist, became editor, 1973-95; *Daf-Yarok* (kibbutz weekly magazine), editor; *Kar-Lamoshav* (agricultural magazine), editor, 1989—. University of Tel-Aviv, instructor of journalism, 1985-95. *Military service:* Soldier in the war of independence.

MEMBER: Israeli Press Association, Kibbutz Author Association.

WRITINGS:

Journey to My Father, Isaac Bashevis Singer, translated by Barbara Harshav, Arcade Publications (New York), 1995.

Also author of *Horshoe* (short story collection), 1980. Author of articles, short stories, and a play.

WORK IN PROGRESS: A work of fiction, *Sand in Eyes,* that "deals with the kibbutz during 'Yom-Kippur' War," a "second book, [which] is a collection of short stories," and *The Lovers,* a play.

SIDELIGHTS: An Israeli journalist, editor, translator, and teacher, Israel Zamir is also the only son of celebrated Yiddish novelist Isaac Bashevis Singer, a man with whom he forged a bond only in adulthood. Zamir's memoir of his father, *Journey to My Father, Isaac Bashevis Singer,* exposes the great man's flaws—his inability to be faithful to his wives, his neglect of his children—while it explains how the son grew to love and understand the father, even when he failed to agree with him. Critics praised the author's candor regarding his ambivalent feelings toward his father, as well as his well-composed portrait of an important twentieth-century author. "Clearly Isaac Bashevis Singer poured most of his life and love into his work," Rodger Kamenetz concluded his review in the *New York Times Book Review.* "For readers this has been a great gift, but in this bittersweet memoir we learn the cost to his family."

When Zamir was five years old, his father immigrated to the United States, leaving his son and his wife in Warsaw, promising to send for them but eventually divorcing Zamir's mother and remarrying. Zamir next saw his father twenty years later, after having emigrated to Israel with his strongly Zionist mother. At age twenty-five, Zamir went to New York to meet his father. He fought in the war for Israel's independence, and worked as a fisherman in Kibbutz Beit-Alfa. Critics noted that *Journey to My Father* emphasizes Zamir's low expectations of his first meeting with his estranged father. The man he discovered as they formed a relationship over the next thirty-five years was entirely devoted to his writing, and unpredictable and unfaithful to everyone else. "The traces of bitterness in Mr. Zamir's account are understandable," remarked Kamenetz in the *New York Times Book Review.*

Despite differences in religious and political convictions, Zamir came to understand and accept his father, and to cherish the relationship they developed. He eventually translated most of his father's works into Hebrew and accompanied him to Stockholm in 1978 when Singer won the Nobel Prize for literature. Zamir's memoir was widely praised for its acute portrayal of Singer: "[Zamir] provides quick, charming glimpses of his father in action," remarked Kamenetz. Others emphasized the universality of Zamir's focus on the relationship between a father

and a son: "Zamir's memoir is a testimony to the sweeping power of forgiveness and repentance," wrote Denise Sticha, reviewer for *Library Journal.*

Zamir told *CA:* "I worked as a journalist from 1973 to 1996. I covered most of the jobs in journalism: politics, army, agriculture, etc. I was the editor of three magazines: *Hotam,* a weekly magazine, of *Al-Hamishmar* for five years, and of *Daf-Yarok,* a kibbutz weekly magazine. Since 1989 I have been editor of *Kar-Lamoshav. Al-Hamishmar* was closed in 1995, so most of my years—1973 to 1995—I worked there."

BIOGRAPHICAL/CRITICAL SOURCES:

PERIODICALS

Booklist, November 1, 1995, p. 450.
Library Journal, December, 1995, p. 120.
New York Times Book Review, December 10, 1995, p. 35.
Publishers Weekly, September 25, 1995, p. 34.

*   *   *

ZETKIN, Clara   1857-1933

PERSONAL: Born in 1857, in Wiederau, Germany; died in 1933, in Moscow, U.S.S.R.; married Osip Zetkin, 1882 (died, c. 1890); children: two. *Education:* Studied at Leipzig Teacher's College for Women.

CAREER: Writer and socialist activist. *Die Gleicheit* (newspaper), Berlin, Germany, editor, 1892-1916; with Rosa Luxemburg, co-organizer of peace conference, Berne, Switzerland, 1915. Member of German Reichstag, 1920-32; member of executive committee and head of International Women's Secretariat, Communist International, 1921. Founder, International Socialist Women's Congress, 1907; co-founder, Spartacus League, 1916, Independent Social Democratic Party, 1917, and German Communist Party, 1918.

WRITINGS:

Erinnerungen an Lenin, [Berlin], 1929, translation published as *My Recollections of Lenin,* International Publishers (New York City), 1966.
Clara Zetkin, Selected Writings, edited by Philip Foner, International Publishers, 1984.

SIDELIGHTS: A German communist who made Russia her adopted country after the Bolshevik uprising of 1917, journalist and activist Clara Zetkin is remembered more for her advocacy of women's issues than for her writing. While, for many Marxists, the future of the revolutionary movement was of prime importance, Zetkin believed that women's social and economic equality should be championed despite the constraints of the international Marxist movement. Her views on women, many of which are recorded in *Clara Zetkin, Selected Writings,* were derived from the writings of Frederich Engels and August Bebel, both of whom proclaimed women's equality as a means to motivate women to support their brand of socialism. Modern-day revolutionary Angela Davis would hail Zetkin as one of the pioneering theorists of women's status within a capitalist society.

The editor of a socialist women's newspaper, *Die Gleicheit* [Equality] from 1892 until 1916, Zetkin maintained a high profile as an advocate for proletariat women, writing over thirty articles on women-centered issues during her tenure there. Her style was direct and persuasive, and it is conjectured that her views on women, which were often more radical than those of the leadership in the German Socialist Party, as well as her staunch opposition to World War I, may have contributed to her loss of the editorship. Equally direct in style, Zetkin's *My Recollections of Lenin,* published five years after Lenin's death, provides an account of her highly emotional relationship with that Soviet leader.

After the Bolshevik Revolution, Zetkin would work for the Communist International (Comitern), while also aiding in the organization of the highly radical Spartacus League and the German Communist Party. Her rejection of the policies of Adolf Hitler finally prompted Zetkin to abandon Germany in 1932; she died in Moscow a year later. In non-communist circles she is perhaps best remembered for her role in the establishment of an international women's day. Initially celebrated only by socialists and communists, March 8th would later be adopted by the international women's movement as a day to recognize women worldwide.

BIOGRAPHICAL/CRITICAL SOURCES:

BOOKS

Modern Encyclopedia of Russian and Soviet History, Volume 46, University of Florida, 1987.

Slaughter, J., and R. Kern, editors, *European Women on the Left,* International Publishers, 1981.*

* * *

ZIMMERMAN, Cynthia (Diane) 1943-

PERSONAL: Born January 8, 1943, in Toronto, Ontario, Canada; daughter of Louis (a social worker) and Ann (a homemaker; maiden name, Rosen) Zimmerman; married Robert Fothergill, June 8, 1969 (divorced); children: Liora Lyn. *Ethnicity:* "Jewish." *Education:* Attended University of British Columbia; University of Toronto, B.A., 1965, M.A., 1967, Ph.D., 1977.

ADDRESSES: Office—Department of English, Glendon College, York University, 2275 Bayview Ave., Toronto, Ontario M4N 3M6, Canada. *E-mail*—czimmerman@venus.yorku.ca.

CAREER: York University, Toronto, Ontario, lecturer, 1967-74, assistant professor, 1974-81, associate professor of English, 1981—.

WRITINGS:

(With R. Wallace) *The Work: Conversations with English Canadian Playwrights,* Coach House Press, 1982.
(Editor with H. Zeifman) *Contemporary British Drama, 1970-90,* Macmillan (New York), 1993.
(Editor) *Taking the Stage: Selections from Plays by Canadian Women,* Playwrights Canada Press (Toronto, Ontario), 1994.
Playwriting Women: Female Voices in English Canada, Simon & Pierre (Toronto), 1994.

Member of editorial advisory board, *Modern Drama,* 1990—.

WORK IN PROGRESS: Women Writing for the Canadian Stage, publication by Garland Publishing (New York) expected in 1998; research on current Canadian women playwrights.

SIDELIGHTS: Cynthia Zimmerman told *CA:* "Toronto, Canada, is now the third largest English-speaking theater center, second only to New York City and London. I have been teaching the writing of Canadian dramatists for years and continue to be struck by how little-known their work is outside our country. My commitment is to profile those who have become strong theatrical presences here in the hope that their plays will reach a wider audience."

*   *   *

ZWICKY, (Julia) Fay   1933-

PERSONAL: Born Julia Fay Rosefield, July 4, 1933, in Melbourne, Australia; married Karl Zwicky, 1957 (marriage ended); married James Mackie, 1990; children: (first marriage) one son, one daughter. *Education:* University of Melbourne, B.A. (honors), 1954.

ADDRESSES: Home—30 Goldsmith Rd., Claremont, Western Australia 6010, Australia. *Agent*—Australian Literary Management, 2A Armstrong St., Middle Park, Victoria 3206.

CAREER: Concert pianist, 1950-65; University of Western Australia, Perth, senior lecturer in English, 1972-87. Member of literature board, Australia Council, Sydney, 1978-81; poetry editor, *Westerly,* Perth, and *Patterns,* Fremantle, 1974-83; *Overland,* Melbourne, associate editor, 1988—; *Southerly,* Sydney, associate editor, 1989—.

AWARDS, HONORS: New South Wales Premier's award, 1982; Western Australian Literary award, for non-fiction, 1987; Western Australian Premier's award for poetry, 1991.

WRITINGS:

POETRY

Isaac Babel's Fiddle, Maximus (Adelaide), 1975.
Kaddish and Other Poems, University of Queensland Press (St. Lucia), 1982.
Ask Me, University of Queensland Press, 1990.
(With Dennis Haskell) *A Touch of Ginger,* Folio (Applecross), 1991.
Poems 1970-1992, University of Queensland Press, 1993.

OTHER

(Editor) *Quarry: A Selection of Western Australian Poetry,* Fremantle Arts Centre Press (Fremantle, Western Australia), 1981.
(Editor) *Journeys: Judith Wright, Rosemary Dobson, Gwen Harwood, Dorothy Hewett,* Sisters (Melbourne), 1982.
Hostages (short stories), Fremantle Arts Centre Press, 1983.
The Lyre in the Pawnshop: Essays on Literature and Survival 1974-1984, University of Western Australia Press (Nedlands), 1986.
(Editor) *Procession: Youngstreet Poets Three,* Hale and Iremonger (Sydney), 1987.